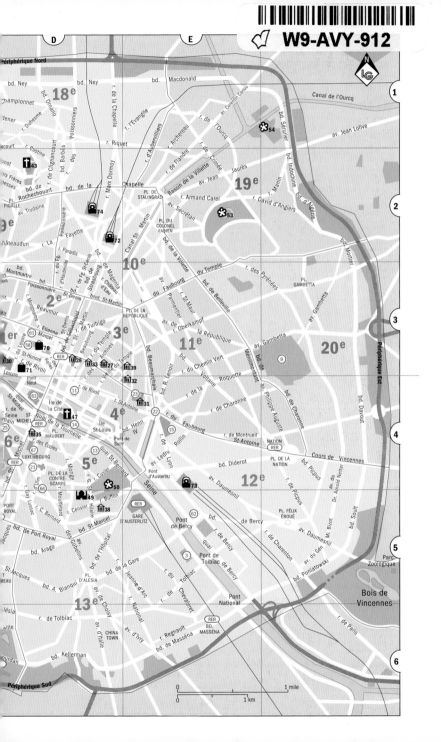

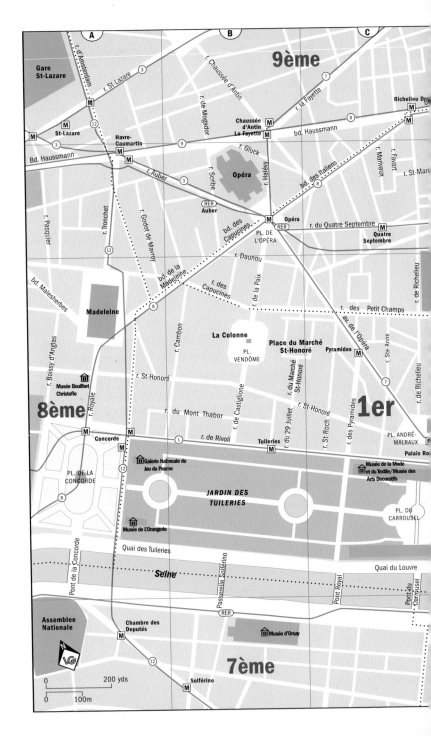

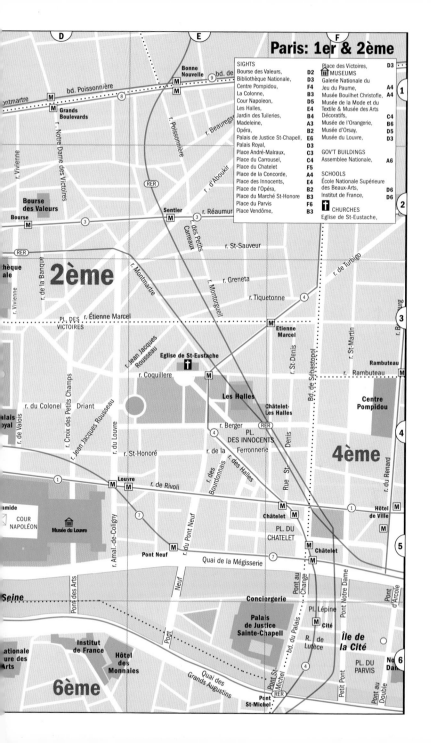

Paris: 1er & 2ème

SIGHTS
Bourse des Valeurs,	D2
Bibliothèque Nationale,	D3
Centre Pompidou,	F4
La Colonne,	B3
Cour Napoleon,	D5
Les Halles,	E4
Jardin des Tuileries,	B4
Madeleine,	A3
Opéra,	B2
Palais de Justice St-Chapell,	E6
Palais Royal,	D3
Place André-Malraux,	C3
Place du Carrousel,	C4
Place du Chatelet,	F5
Place de la Concorde,	A4
Place des Innocents,	E4
Place de l'Opéra,	B2
Place du Marché St-Honore	B3
Place du Parvis	F6
Place Vendôme,	B3

Place des Victoires,	D3
MUSEUMS	
Galerie Nationale du	
Jeu du Paume,	A4
Musée Bouilhet Christofle,	A4
Musée de la Mode et du	
Textile & Musée des Arts	
Décoratifs,	C4
Musée de l'Orangerie,	B6
Musée d'Orsay,	D5
Musée du Louvre,	D3
GOV'T BUILDINGS	
Assemblee Nationale,	A6
SCHOOLS	
École Nationale Supérieure	
des Beaux-Arts,	D6
Institut de France,	D6
CHURCHES	
Eglise de St-Eustache,	

Bonne Nouvelle
bd. Poissonnière
Grands Boulevards

Bourse des Valeurs
Bourse

2ème

r. St-Sauveur

r. Greneta

r. Tiquetonne

Etienne Marcel

PL. DES VICTOIRES
r. Étienne Marcel

r. de Turbigo

Rambuteau

Eglise de St-Eustache
r. Coquillere

r. du Colonel Driant

Les Halles
Châtelet-Les Halles

Centre Pompidou

4ème

r. St-Honoré
r. Berger
PL. DES INNOCENTS
Ferronnerie

Louvre
r. de Rivoli

COUR NAPOLÉON
Musée du Louvre

Châtelet
PL. DU CHATELET
Châtelet

Pont Neuf
Quai de la Mégisserie

Hôtel de Ville

Seine

Conciergerie
Pl. Lépine
Cité

Palais de Justice Sainte-Chapell

Île de la Cité

Institut de France
Hôtel des Monnaies

Quai des Grands Augustins

6ème

PL. DU PARVIS

Pont St-Michel

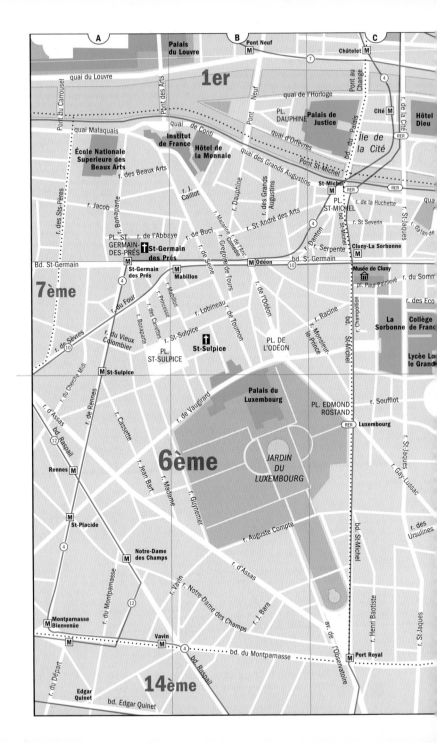

Paris: 5ème & 6ème

4ème

Hôtel de Ville

Pont Marie
quai des Célestins
quai de Bourbon
quai d'Anjou
Sully Morland
r. de l'Ave Maria
r. St-Paul
bd. Henri IV
bd. Bourdon

r. Chanoinesse
r. du Notre Dame
Île St-Louis
quai d'Orléans
quai de Béthune
r. St-Louis-en-l'Île
Pont St-Louis
Pont Louis Philippe
Pont Marie
Pont des Deux Ponts

Notre Dame

Montebello
Bucherie
Grange
PL. MAUBERT
quai de la Tournelle
Pont de la Tournelle
Pont de Sully
quai de Béthune
Musée de la Sculpture en Plein Air
Seine
Quai de la Rapée

Maubert-Mutualité
Musée de l'Assistance Publique
bd. St-Germain
Institut du Monde Arabe
quai St-Bernard

r. des Carmes
r. Montagne Ste Geneviève
r. F. Sauton
r. de Bièvre
r. des Bernadins
r. de Pontoise
r. de Poissy
r. du Cardinal Lemoine
r. des Fossés St-Bernard
r. Monge
r. Jussieu
JARDIN DES SCULPTURES EN PLEIN AIR

Cardinal Lemoine
Jussieu
r. des Boulangers
Arènes de Lutèce
r. Linné
r. Cuvier
JARDIN DES PLANTES
PL. VALHUBERT
Gare d'Austerlitz

Panthéon
r. Clovis
r. Descartes
r. Rollin
r. Lacépède
5ème
PL. DE LA CONTRESCARPE
r. Geoffroy St-Hilaire
Musée d'Histoire Naturelle
bd. de l'Hôpital

r. de l'Estrapade
r. Mouffetard
PL. MONGE
Monge
r. Buffon
r. Monge

r. L'homond
r. Erasme Brossolette
École Normale Supérieure
r. d'Ulm
Censier Daubenton
r. Poliveau
St-Marce

r. Claude Bernard
r. du Fer à Moulin
Val de Grâce
r. Berthollet
Gobelins

bd. de Port Royal

13ème

SIGHTS		MUSEUMS	
Arènes de Lutece,	E3	Musee de l'Assistance	
Hôtel Dieu,	C1	Publique,	D2
Hôtel de la Monnaie,	B2	Musée de Cluny,	C3
Hôtel de Ville,	D1	Musée d'Histoire Naturelle,	F4
Institut du Monde Arabe,	E2	Musée de la Sculpture en	
Jardin du Luxembourg,	B4	Plein Air,	F2
Jardin des Plantes,	F3		
Panthéon,	D4	SCHOOLS	
Palais de Justice,	C1	College de France,	C3
Palais du Louvre,	B1	École Nationale Supérieure	
Palais du Luxembourg,	B4	des Beaux-Arts,	A2
Place de la Contrescarpe,	D4	École Normale Supérieure,	D5
Place de l'Odéon,	B3	Institut de France,	1
Place Maubert,	D2	Lycée Louis le Grand,	C3
Place St-Germain des Prés,	A2	La Sorbonne,	C3
Place St-Sulpice,	A3		
Place Valhubert,	F3	CHURCHES	
Val de Grâce,	D6	Notre Dame,	D2
		St-Germain des Prés,	A2
		St-Sulpice,	B3

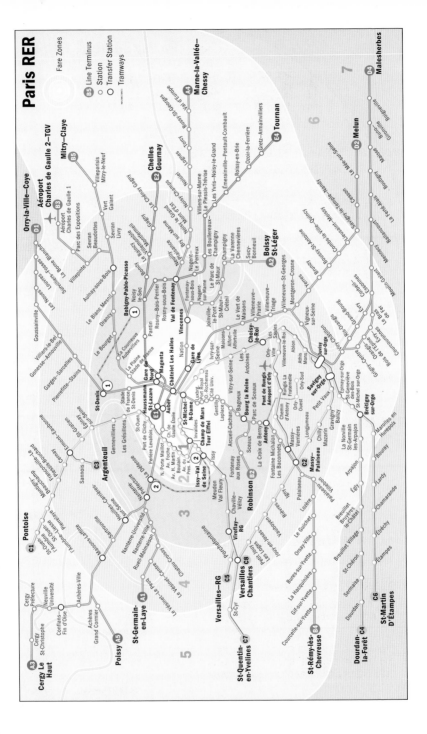

LET'S GO

PAGES PACKED WITH ESSENTIAL INFORMATION

"Value-packed, unbeatable, accurate, and comprehensive."

—*The Los Angeles Times*

"The guides are aimed not only at young budget travelers but at the independent traveler; a sort of streetwise cookbook for traveling alone."

—*The New York Times*

"Unbeatable; good sight-seeing advice; up-to-date info on restaurants, hotels, and inns; a commitment to money-saving travel; and a wry style that brightens nearly every page."

—*The Washington Post*

THE BEST TRAVEL BARGAINS IN YOUR BUDGET

"All the dirt, dirt cheap."

—*People*

"Let's Go follows the creed that you don't have to toss your life's savings to the wind to travel—unless you want to."

—*The Salt Lake Tribune*

REAL ADVICE FOR REAL EXPERIENCES

"The writers seem to have experienced every rooster-packed bus and lunar-surfaced mattress about which they write."

—*The New York Times*

"[Let's Go's] devoted updaters really walk the walk (and thumb the ride, and trek the trail). Learn how to fish, haggle, find work—anywhere."

—*Food & Wine*

"A world-wise traveling companion—always ready with friendly advice and helpful hints, all sprinkled with a bit of wit."

—*The Philadelphia Inquirer*

A GUIDE WITH A SPIRIT AND A SOCIAL CONSCIENCE

"Lighthearted and sophisticated, informative and fun to read. [Let's Go] helps the novice traveler navigate like a knowledgeable old hand."

—*Atlanta Journal-Constitution*

"The serious mission at the book's core reveals itself in exhortations to respect the culture and the environment—and, if possible, to visit as a volunteer, a student, or a teacher rather than a tourist."

—*San Francisco Chronicle*

LET'S GO PUBLICATIONS

TRAVEL GUIDES
Australia
Austria & Switzerland
Brazil
Britain
California
Central America
Chile
China
Costa Rica
Eastern Europe
Ecuador
Egypt
Europe
France
Germany
Greece
Hawaii
India & Nepal
Ireland
Israel
Italy
Japan
Mexico
New Zealand
Peru
Puerto Rico
Southeast Asia
Spain & Portugal with Morocco
Thailand
USA
Vietnam
Western Europe

ROADTRIP GUIDE
Roadtripping USA

ADVENTURE GUIDES
Alaska
Pacific Northwest
Southwest USA

CITY GUIDES
Amsterdam
Barcelona
Boston
Buenos Aires
London
New York City
Paris
Rome
San Francisco
Washington, DC

POCKET CITY GUIDES
Amsterdam
Berlin
Boston
Chicago
London
New York City
Paris
San Francisco
Venice
Washington, DC

LET'S GO

FRANCE

2009

COLLEEN O'BRIEN EDITOR
IYA MEGRE ASSOCIATE EDITOR
MARY POTTER ASSOCIATE EDITOR

RESEARCHER-WRITERS

SARAH ASHBURN	**EDWARD-MICHAEL DUSSOM**
CICELY CHEN	**VANDA GYURIS**
ABIGAIL CRUTCHFIELD	**JOE MOLIMOCK**

ELISSA C. REIDY MAP EDITOR
NATHANIEL RAKICH MANAGING EDITOR

ST. MARTIN'S PRESS ❧ NEW YORK

Maps by Let's Go copyright © 2009 by Let's Go, Inc.
Maps by David Lindroth copyright © 2009 by St. Martin's Press.

Distributed outside the USA and Canada by Macmillan.

ISBN-13: 978-0-312-38571-2
ISBN-10: 0-312-38571-4
First edition
10 9 8 7 6 5 4 3 2 1

Let's Go: France is written by Let's Go Publications, 67 Mount Auburn St., Cambridge, MA 02138, USA.

Let's Go® and the LG logo are trademarks of Let's Go, Inc.

HOW TO USE THIS BOOK

The French have been reveling in their cultural superiority for millennia—just take a look at the Cro-Magnon graffiti in Lascaux—though discussing it over *cafés au lait* is a more recent development. That said, France isn't all intimidating masterpieces and 12-course meals—and, even when it is, we're here to help. *Let's Go* is your own personal Virgil, guiding you through the seven layers of that pastry you can't pronounce and the 20 arrondissements of that city you can't bear to leave. The French may know *crêpes*, but we've mastered the art of budget travel—and we'd love to share it with you. Our dedicated Researcher-Writers have descended to the depths of Bordeaux's best wine *caves*, scaled the mountains of the Alps, scouted the French Riviera in various states of undress, and meticulously explored everything in between to bring you the freshest, most comprehensive budget travel guide possible. Here's how to use it:

COVERING THE BASICS. The first chapter, **Discover** (p. 1), outlines the best of France—just in case we haven't convinced you to go. Check out the **Suggested Itineraries** for routes that span the whole country and highlight some favorite hobbies (eating, *par example*). The **Essentials** (p. 8) section gets down to the nitty gritty, detailing the info you'll need to get around and stay safe on your journey. Peruse the **Life and Times** (p. 57) chapter to catch up on your French history and avoid some *faux pas*. For those who travel with a deeper purpose, the **Beyond Tourism** (p. 81) section has info on work, study-abroad, and volunteering opportunities all around France. Then comes the meat of the book: 17 **regional chapters** jam-packed with detailed coverage and the occasional hilarious tangent. Wrap it all up with the **Appendix** (p. 798), complete with a weather chart for major cities—so you don't bring a sweater to St-Tropez in June—and a phrasebook to help you smooth-talk your way through any situation.

RANKINGS, TIP BOXES, AND FEATURES. Our researchers list establishments in order of value from best to worst, with absolute favorites denoted by the *Let's Go* thumbpick (⬛). Since the lowest price does not always mean the best value, we've incorporated a system of price ranges (❶-❺) for food and accommodations. Tip boxes come in a variety of flavors: warnings (⬛), helpful hints and resources (⬛), inside scoops (⬛), and a smattering of stuff you should know (⬛, ⬛, ⬛). When you want a break from transportation info and listings, check out our features—which range in subjects from condiments to the end of the world—for unique opportunities, surprising insights, and fascinating stories.

VOULEZ-VOUS VOYAGER AVEC NOUS PARTOUT? From ⬛dragons to Dijon, from wineries to wakeboarding, and from mountains to Marie Antoinette, France has something for you. Start in Paris, in Perpignan, in Poitiers—breathtaking landscapes are all over. Finally, while we hope this guide helps you make the most of your journey, we also hope you'll leave it in the hotel room occasionally and venture out to unmapped territory. France is waiting—*allons-y!*

A NOTE TO OUR READERS. The information for this book was gathered by Let's Go researchers from May through August of 2008. Each listing is based on one researcher's opinion, formed during his or her visit at a particular time. Those traveling at other times may have different experiences since prices, dates, hours, and conditions are always subject to change. You are urged to check the facts presented in this book beforehand to avoid inconvenience and surprises.

CONTENTS

RESEARCHER-WRITERS

Sarah Ashburn   *Alsace, Lorraine, and Franche-Comté;*
Burgundy; Champagne; The North

After spending a semester in Botswana, Sarah still hadn't quenched her thirst for being abroad and jetted to France to indulge her love for Nutella sandwiches. She laced up her Nikes to remedy her off-kilter internal compass, running around the cities along her route to get a feel for the streets. Sarah trekked through it all: from the bike trails of the Côte d'Or to the stage at Les Eurockéens. An avid people-watcher, she spent much of her time camped out at cafes, sharpening her eye for all things romantic.

Cicely Chen   *Brittany, Normandy*

A Celtic harpist with a reverence for medieval architecture, Cicely investigated Brittany's Celtic heritage with seasoned knowledge and a zealous spirit. On her quest for local flavor, she delved into Normandy's regional dishes, even when an order of *moules* consisted of more *fruits de mer* than she expected. Her unfailing ambition was always triumphant, even when a lost laptop charger and elusive Wi-Fi threatened her pace. Cicely will attend the University of Pennsylvania School of Medicine this fall.

Abigail Crutchfield   *Dordogne and Limousin,*
Massif Central, Rhône-Alpes

After a harrowing daytrip on a *"vélo route"* fit for the Tour de France, this New York City native didn't think that outdoor activities were for her. Dozens of medieval villages and excessive amounts of goat cheese later, Abigail conquered her fear of heights to discover a love for hiking at La Grande Cascade. With passions for art and dining out, it's no wonder that Abigail felt at home in Lyon, but only the peaks of Val d'Isère were enough to distract her from craving a grande skim no-water extra hot chai.

Edward-Michael Dussom   *Aquitaine and Pays Basque,*
Languedoc-Roussilon, Provence

Despite eyebrow spasms, an encounter with Beelzebub, and a laptop death, the incomparable EM charmed his way through southern France while staying true to his hipster roots. This New Orleans native found cheap gourmet food everywhere he went—even if he had to cook it. Somewhere between trendy cafes in Paris's 6ème and frightening bridge experiences in Avignon, Edward-Michael took a break from barhopping and writing scathing copy to fall in love—with the mountain views in Cauterets.

RESEARCHER-WRITERS

Vanda Gyuris   *Loire Valley, Poitou-Charentes*

This multi-talented varsity swimmer biked from one château to the next, soaking up every bit of youth culture along the way. A standout Let's Go veteran, Vanda befriended many a senile local in her quest to point readers toward the freshest oyster. She embraced the student culture in Rennes, hitting the bohemian cafes with a trail of new *amis*. From the chaos of ferry schedules to overbooked-hostel mix-ups, Vanda made the job look easy, revamping the Loire route with unmistakable panache.

Joe Molimock   *Côte d'Azur, Corsica*

When Joe wasn't devouring whole chickens from the local Monoprix, he was scouting out the hottest nightlife and befriending the occasional lady restaurateur. Armed with a scooter, a child-size tent from Wal-Mart, and tragically inadequate shoes, this sweet-talking English major conquered Corsica's rocky terrain before finding the best of the Côte's glitz—though he never made it onto Beyoncé's yacht. Joe returned from his first time backpacking with a tan and more than 800 pages' worth of crazy stories.

CONTRIBUTING WRITERS

Samantha Gelfand   *Managing Editor, Let's Go: Paris 2009*

Brianna Goodale   *Paris*

Though Bri got her share of etiquette lessons from the count and countess she stayed with, she never hesitated to get down and dirty with her research. Between psychology classes at Nanterre, she even found time to explain to befuddled Parisians that yes, her name is Bri, but *non*, she is not *fromage*.

Sara O'Rourke   *Paris*

Sara is a Let's Go all-star and an expert in all things French. After editing *Let's Go: France* in 2008, this Social Studies major hit the road for a semester abroad in Paris. Scoping out the best nightlife, cafes, and running paths, Sara even accomplished the impossible—making friends with Parisian waiters.

Samuel Ronsin earned a Bachelor of Science in pure mathematics and a master's in theoretical economics at the École Normale Superieure. After an exchange program at Harvard, his interests—including fine art and electronic music— brought him to Berlin to pursue creative writing and video projects.

Laurent Deflandre is a student at the École Normale Supérieure and Sciences Po. A Derek Bok Center Award recipient, he taught French at Harvard University and studied public management at the Harvard Kennedy School. Deflandre holds master's degrees in History and Communication.

ACKNOWLEDGMENTS

LET'S GO

TEAM FRANCE THANKS: Sam, Bri, and Sara, for the City of Lights. Elissa, for navigation. Nathaniel, for making us write this. FRITA, for laughs and the couch. Lingbo, for reppin'. Prod & proofers for perfection. LG for everything. France for champagne and chocolate mousse. Lizzy's for our addiction. Pandora for the same songs. Hipster boys for ... you know.

COLLEEN THANKS: Iya and Mary for friendship and long hours. Nathaniel for motivation and personifying the Format Manual. Sarah, Cicely, and Abigail for hard work and fun stories. Mom for daytrips and the comforts of home. Bren for Passims. LG for a great summer. Woburn for support. Cambridge for making me grow up. Daniella for tea. DeWolfe for my bed. Friends.

IYA THANKS: Lone Rebel Icon, for ice cream. Martyr Poet, for slang. Nathaniel, for disagreeing. EM and Joe, for sparkle and sunshine. LGHQ, for bagels and late nights. Taosky, for all of the kitties. Friends, for (in)sanity. Mom, for making me call. Dad, for not making me call. George, for calling.

MARY THANKS: *merci mille fois* Mommer'n em & ⬛Thomas Aquinas; Rennie & Sharon; Char, Dee Dee & marycat; VaNdA; Iya; col & FRITA; the studs at LGHQ; the blocktopus+⬛popkins; the Bro-tel; Bolt Bus; and all members of the little bookgroup that couldn't.

ELISSA THANKS: To Colleen for awesomely awkward icebreakers; Iya for hilarious RW updates; Mary for her patience; EM, Joe, Vanda, Sarah, Cicely, and Abigail for allowing me to adventure vicariously; Gretch for her Illustrator expertise; Becca for watching LOTR; Illiana for hamster tales; Derek for appreciating Disney music; Nathaniel for the crossword; and the 4th floor for dance parties: bump that.

Editor
Colleen O'Brien
Associate Editors
Iya Megre, Mary Potter
Managing Editor
Nathaniel Rakich
Map Editor
Elissa C. Reidy
Typesetter
Jansen A. S. Thurmer

Publishing Director
Inés C. Pacheco
Editor-in-Chief
Samantha Gelfand
Production Manager
Jansen A. S. Thurmer
Cartography Manager
R. Derek Wetzel
Editorial Managers
Dwight Livingstone Curtis,
Vanessa J. Dube, Nathaniel Rakich
Financial Manager
Lauren Caruso
Publicity and Marketing Manager
Patrick McKiernan
Personnel Manager
Laura M. Gordon
Production Associate
C. Alexander Tremblay
Director of IT & E-Commerce
Lukáš Tóth
Website Manager
Ian Malott
Office Coordinators
Vinnie Chiappini, Jenny Wong
Director of Advertising Sales
Nicole J. Bass
Senior Advertising Associates
Kipyegon Kitur, Jeremy Siegfried,
John B. Ulrich
Junior Advertising Associate
Edward C. Robinson Jr.

President
Timothy J. J. Creamer
General Manager
Jim McKellar

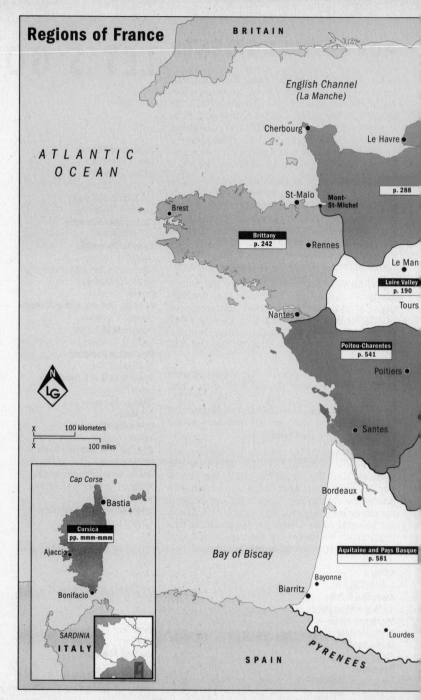

Regions of France

BRITAIN

English Channel
(La Manche)

ATLANTIC
OCEAN

Cherbourg

Le Havre

p. 288

St-Malo
Mont-
St-Michel

Brest

Brittany
p. 242

Rennes

Le Man

Loire Valley
p. 190

Tours

Nantes

Poitou-Charentes
p. 541

Poitiers

100 kilometers

100 miles

Santes

Cap Corse

Bastia

Bordeaux

Corsica
pp. mmm-mmm

Ajaccio

Bay of Biscay

Aquitaine and Pays Basque
p. 581

Bonifacio

Bayonne

Biarritz

SARDINIA

ITALY

Lourdes

SPAIN

PYRENEES

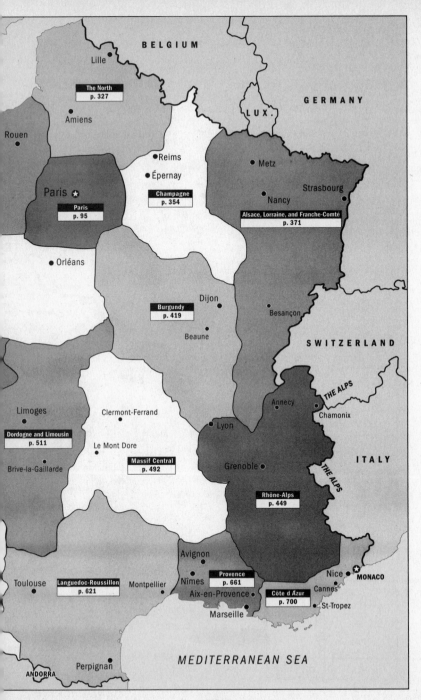

BELGIUM

Lille

The North
p. 327

GERMANY

LUX.

Amiens

Rouen

Reims

Metz

Strasbourg

Épernay

Nancy

Paris ☆

Champagne
p. 354

Paris
p. 95

Alsace, Lorraine, and Franche-Comté
p. 371

Orléans

Dijon

Burgundy
p. 419

Besançon

Beaune

SWITZERLAND

Limoges

Clermont-Ferrand

Annecy

THE ALPS

Chamonix

Dordogne and Limousin
p. 511

Lyon

Brive-la-Gaillarde

Le Mont Dore

Massif Central
p. 492

ITALY

Grenoble

THE ALPS

Rhône-Alps
p. 449

Avignon

Toulouse

Languedoc-Roussillon
p. 621

Montpellier

Nîmes

Provence
p. 661

Nice

Cannes

MONACO

Aix-en-Provence

Côte d'Azur
p. 700

St-Tropez

Marseille

Perpignan

MEDITERRANEAN SEA

ANDORRA

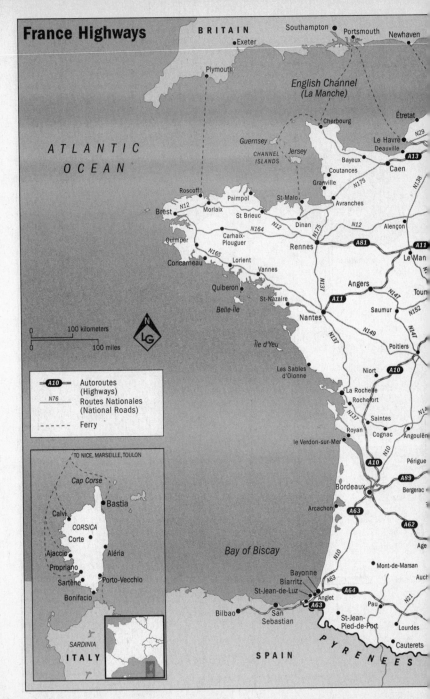

France Highways

BRITAIN

Southampton • Portsmouth • Newhaven

• Exeter

English Channel
(La Manche)

Étretat

• Plymouth

Cherbourg

Le Havre N29

ATLANTIC
OCEAN

Guernsey

Jersey

CHANNEL
ISLANDS

Deauville A13

Bayeux

Caen N138

Coutances

Roscoff

N175

Granville

Paimpol

St-Malo

Avranches

Alençon A11

Brest N12

Morlaix

St Brieuc

Dinan N175 N12

Quimper

Carhaix-
Plouguer

N164

Rennes

A81

Le Man

Concarneau N165

Lorient

Angers

N147 Tours

Vannes

N137

A11

N152

Quiberon

St-Nazaire

Saumur N147

Belle-Île

Nantes

N149

Poitiers

Île d'Yeu

N137

| 0 | 100 kilometers |
| 0 | 100 miles |

Les Sables
d'Olonne

Niort A10

La Rochelle
Rochefort

Saintes N14

N137

A10	Autoroutes (Highways)
N76	Routes Nationales (National Roads)
-----	Ferry

Royan Cognac Angoulên

le Verdon-sur-Mer

N10

A10

Périgue

TO NICE, MARSEILLE, TOULON

A89

Cap Corse

Bordeaux Bergerac

Calvi

Bastia

Arcachon A63

A62

CORSICA

Corte

Age

Ajaccio

Aléria

Propriano

Bay of Biscay

N10

Mont-de-Marsan Auch

Sartène

Porto-Vecchio

Bayonne

Biarritz

A63

Bonifacio

St-Jean-de-Luz

Anglet

Pau N21

Bilbao

San
Sebastian

A63

St-Jean-
Pied-de-Port

Lourdes

SARDINIA

ITALY

SPAIN

P Y R E N E E S

Cauterets

XIV

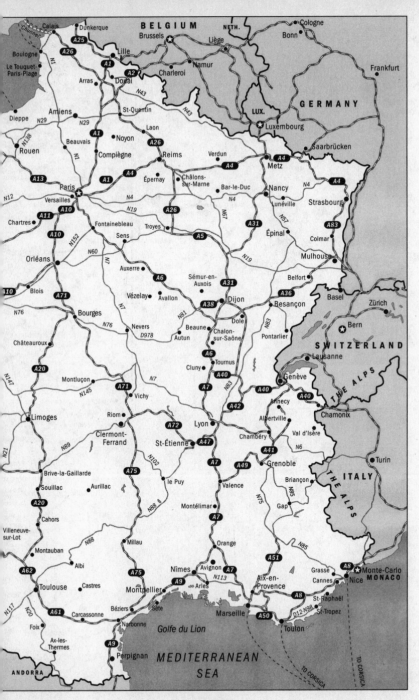

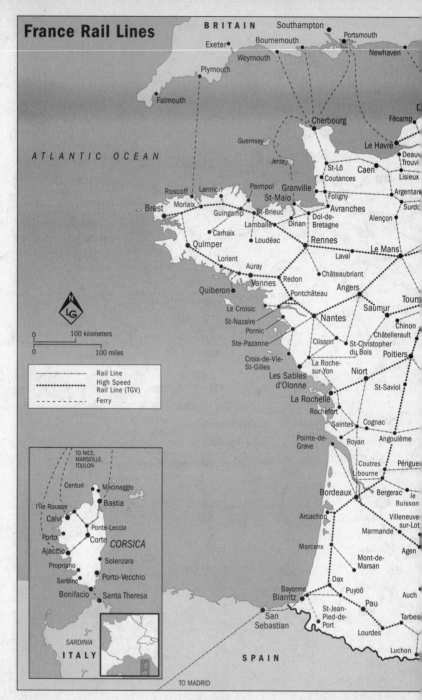

France Rail Lines

BRITAIN

Southampton
Portsmouth
Exeter
Bournemouth
Newhaven
Weymouth
Plymouth

Falmouth

ATLANTIC OCEAN

Cherbourg
Fécamp
Le Havre
Deauv
Guernsey
Trouvi
Jersey
St-Lô
Caen
Lisieux
Roscoff
Lannion
Paimpol
Granville
Coutances
Argentan
Brest
Morlaix
St-Malo
Foligny
Surdo
Guingamp
St-Brieuc
Avranches
Alençon
Dol-de-
Bretagne
Carhaix
Lamballe
Dinan
Quimper
Loudéac
Rennes
Le Mans
Lorient
Laval
Auray
Châteaubriant
Quiberon
Vannes
Redon
Angers
Tours
Pontchâteau
Saùmur
Le Croisic
Chinon
St-Nazaire
Nantes
Châtellerault
Pornic
Clisson
St-Christopher
Poitiers
Ste-Pazanne
du Bois
Croix-de-Vie-
La Roche-
St-Gilles
sur-Yon
Niort
Les Sables
d'Olonne
St-Saviol
La Rochelle
Rochefort
Saintes
Cognac
Pointe-de-
Royan
Angoulême
Grave
Coutres
Périgue
Libourne
Bordeaux
Bergerac
le
Buisson
Arcachon
Villeneuve-
sur-Lot
Marmande
Morcenx
Agen
Mont-de-
Marsan
Dax
Auch
Bayonne
Puyoô
Biarritz
Pau
Tarbes
San
St-Jean-
Sebastian
Pied-de-
Lourdes
Port
Luchon

SPAIN

TO MADRID

Corsica inset

TO NICE,
MARSEILLE,
TOULON
Centuri
Macinaggio
l'Île Rousse
Bastia
Calvi
Ponte-Leccia
Porto
Corte
CORSICA
Ajaccio
Propriano
Solenzara
Sartène
Porto-Vecchio
Bonifacio
Santa Theresa

SARDINIA
ITALY

Legend

0 ___ 100 kilometers
0 ___ 100 miles

——— Rail Line
••••••• High Speed
Rail Line (TGV)
- - - - - Ferry

PRICE RANGES
FRANCE

1 2 3 4 5

Our researchers list establishments in order of value from best to worst, honoring our favorites with the *Let's Go* thumbs-up (🖒). Because the best *value* is not always the cheapest *price*, we have created a system of price ranges based on a rough expectation of what you will spend. For **accommodations**, we base our range on the cheapest price for which a single traveler can stay for one night. For **restaurants** and other dining establishments, we estimate the average amount one traveler will spend in one sitting. The table below describes what you'll *typically* find in France at the corresponding price range, but keep in mind that no system can allow for the quirks of individual establishments.

ACCOMMODATIONS	RANGE	WHAT YOU'RE *LIKELY* TO FIND
❶	under €22	Campgrounds and dorm rooms, both in hostels and universities. Expect bunk beds and a communal bath. You may have to provide or rent towels and sheets.
❷	€22-34	Upper-end hostels, lower-end hotels, *chambres d'hôtes*, and *gîtes*. You may have a private bathroom, or there may be a sink in your room and a communal shower in the hall.
❸	€35-44	A small room with a private bath. Should have decent amenities, such as phone and TV. Breakfast may be included in the price.
❹	€45-62	Should have bigger rooms than a ❸, with more amenities or in a more convenient location. Breakfast probably included.
❺	over €62	Large hotels or upscale chains. If it's a ❺ and it doesn't have the perks you want, you've paid too much.

FOOD	RANGE	WHAT YOU'RE *LIKELY* TO FIND
❶	under €5	Probably street food or a fast-food joint, but also *pâtisseries* (yum) or a meal assembled from *marché* groceries. Often takeout, but you may have the option of sitting down.
❷	€5-10	Sweet and savory *crêpes* or sandwiches, salads, and appetizers at a cafe. Most ethnic eateries also fall into this price range. Either take-out or a sit-down meal, but only slightly more fashionable decor.
❸	€11-20	*Formules* (appetizer and *plat*) at a decent restaurant. More upscale ethnic eateries. Since you'll have the luxury of a waiter, tip will set you back a little extra.
❹	€21-30	A somewhat fancy restaurant. Serves hearty *menus*, but you're really paying for ambience and decor. Few restaurants in this range have a dress code, but some may look down on T-shirts and sandals.
❺	over €30	Your meal might cost more than your room, but there's a reason—it's something fabulous, famous, or both. Slacks and dress shirts may be expected. Offers foreign-sounding food and a decent wine list. Don't order a PB&J!

DISCOVER FRANCE

France is often distilled down to a pretty picture: the Eiffel Tower illuminated against the night sky, a field of lavender in Provence, or an extravagant château reflected in the still waters of the Loire. While these postcard images may be beautiful, to truly appreciate France you have to go beyond tourist icons and explore the diversity of people, cultures, and foods that make up this ever-changing nation. France's long and storied past fills textbook pages with tales of revolutions, conquests, intrigues, and, well, more revolutions, but it is present-day France that brings people back again and again. Cities bustling with expats, immigrants, businessmen, and students are surrounded by tiny towns that don't bustle at all. While tourist hordes can be overwhelming, it's not impossible to find a slice of solitude. A serene lake in Poitou-Charentes or the humbling WWI monuments in Pas de Calais are only a train ride and a world apart from Paris's crowded—though beautiful—attractions.

France lives up to its stereotypes, providing the best in fine wine, strong cheese, and that certain romantic *je ne sais quoi*, but it also goes beyond the clichés. Maybe you'll first experience the French spirit as you watch a fierce game of *pétanque* in a Provençal village. Maybe you'll taste it in a warm, buttery croissant at dawn after a night of clubbing in Lille or hear it at an open-air concert on the Breton coast. France does not fit within the confines of this page; it offers something for everyone. Whether it's a nine-course meal in Lyon, a hike to a hidden waterfall in the Pyrenees, or a stroll through one of Paris's less frequented parks, something in France will leave you breathless. Look beyond the postcard images, and France will never fail to surprise you.

FACTS AND FIGURES

OFFICIAL NAME: *République française.*

POPULATION: 64,057,790.

CAPITAL: Paris.

GDP PER CAPITA: US$33,200.

PRESIDENT: Nicolas Sarkozy.

MAJOR RELIGIONS: 85% Catholic, 6% Muslim, 4% unaffiliated, 3% Protestant, 1% Jewish.

AVERAGE LIFE EXPECTANCY: 80.87 years.

WINE PRODUCED PER YEAR: Approximately 9 billion bottles.

FROGS CONSUMED PER YEAR: 60-80 million frogs, or 120-160 million legs.

ESTIMATED NUMBER OF ROMANTIC ENCOUNTERS PER DAY: 4,959,476 in Paris alone. Ah, *l'amour!*

WHEN TO GO

In July, Paris's population starts to thin out; by August, residents have positively vanished, leaving only tourists and pickpockets. During this month of national vacation, the French hop over to the Norman coast, storm the beaches of the western Atlantic from La Rochelle down to Biarritz, and hike the rocky Corsican shores. From June to September, the Côte d'Azur becomes one long tangle of halter-topped, khaki-shorted Anglophones—a constant, exhausting party. Late spring and autumn are the best times to visit Paris and the south; winter in Paris can be grim, presided over by a terrible *grisaille*—chilly "grayness"—and the south gets hot and sticky in the summer. The rest of the country is relatively untouristed and easy to visit year-round. In terms of weather, the north and west of France are best in summer, while the center and east of the country, generally the least touristed areas of France, are ideal in spring and autumn. During the winter, the Alps provide some of the world's best skiing, while the Pyrenees offer a calmer, if less climatically dependable, alternative.

The farther south you travel in the summer, the more crucial hotel reservations become. Reserve a month ahead for the Côte d'Azur, Corsica, Languedoc, Provence, and the Pays Basque. Paris requires reservations year-round.

WHAT TO DO

BRIGHT LIGHTS, BIG CITY

While **Paris** (p. 95) is one of the world's best-known cities—for good reason— you'll also find plenty to do in France's regional centers. **Lyon** (p. 449) once had a reputation for being boringly bourgeois, but today it provides nonstop action and some of the nation's best cuisine. Throughout its 2600-year history, **Marseille** (p. 661) has been an action-filled melting pot. **Nice** (p. 700), on the Côte d'Azur, is a glamorous party town of beautiful beaches. With a hybrid Franco-German culture and world-class museums, **Strasbourg** (p. 387) was the obvious choice to house the European Parliament. Students are the heart of northern **Lille** (p. 327) and Breton **Rennes** (p. 242), cities that mix medieval *vieille villes* and major museums with a frenzied club scene. In the southwest, **Bordeaux** (p. 581) has great architecture and better wine, sophisticated **Montpellier** (p. 653) is the gay capital of France, and rosy **Toulouse** (p. 621) livens up the Languedoc with student-fueled nightlife and modern art.

YOUR CHÂTEAU OR MINE?

French châteaux range from imposing feudal ruins to the country homes of 19th-century industrialists. The greatest concentration is found in the **Loire Valley** (p. 190), where the hilltop fortresses of **Chinon** (p. 217) and **Saumur** (p. 219) contrast with the Renaissance grace of **Chambord** (p. 204), **Chenonceau** (p. 215), and **Cheverny** (p. 204). But the Loire has no monopoly on châteaux. At **Versailles** (p. 176), you'll discover an estate as big as the great Sun King Louis XIV's ego. In Provence, you'll be hard-pressed to decide whether the Palais des Papes in **Avignon** (p. 677) is a castle or a palace. Perhaps the most impressive château is the fortress of **Carcassonne** (p. 633)—a medieval citadel which still stands guard over the Languedoc. If you prefer more intimate, less touristed castles, head to the **Route Jacques Coeur** (p. 238) near **Bourges** (p. 233).

Religion has also played its part, giving rise to a wealth of architectural gems. Paris's **Notre Dame** (p. 138) is the most famous cathedral in France, but a more exquisite Gothic jewel is the nearby **Sainte-Chapelle** (p. 137). The Gothic style of architecture first reached maturity in the majestic cathedral at **Chartres** (p. 179), though several other medieval masterpieces await in **Strasbourg** (p. 387) and **Reims** (p. 354). A more modern sensibility animates Le Corbusier's postwar masterpiece chapel at **Ronchamp** (p. 409).

INTO THE WILD

The Alps deserve their fame, offering thrilling ski slopes at **Val d'Isère** (p. 486) and **Chamonix** (p. 479), but they are just one of France's four mountain ranges. To the north, you'll find the rolling **Jura Mountains** (p. 415) in Franche-Comté, while **Le Mont-Dore** (p. 498), in the Massif Central, provides spectacular hiking near extinct volcanoes. To the southwest, you can climb through the **Pyrenees** (p. 613) into Spain. If snow-capped peaks aren't your thing, discover lowland pleasures in the flamingo-filled plains of the **Camargue** (p. 688). Advanced hikers can trek the length of **Corsica's** interior (p. 758), but anyone can find great day and overnight hikes on the island, especially on the **Cap Corse** (p. 790).

LET THEM EAT CAKE

Paris (p. 95) has its share of Michelin-starred restaurants, but **Lyon** (p. 449) is the true capital of French cuisine, brimming with inventive—and pricey—culinary gems. Though the French hate to admit it, much of their cuisine bears the influence of other nations—tapas sneak onto menus in **Biarritz** (p. 590), Swiss *tartiflette* dominates in the Alps resort of **Chamonix** (p. 479), beer and sausages prove **Strasbourg's** (p. 387) German influence, and couscous and kebabs in most major metropolises suggest a North African influx. France's cuisine is also infused with hints of the ocean, thanks to over 3000km of seaside real estate. Whether it's Atlantic mussels in the port towns of **Normandy** (p. 288), bouillabaisse in **Marseille** (p. 661), or oysters in **Bordeaux** (p. 581), the bounty of the sea never fails to disappoint. Finally, don't forget France's most famous exports: mustard from **Dijon** (p. 419) or olive oil from **Provence** (p. 661) are excellent ways to bring a piece of France home with you.

LA VIE EN ROSÉ

France produces—and consumes—some of the world's finest inebriants. To get a taste, start with a champagne *apéritif* from **Reims's** *caves* (wine cellars; p. 359). Try the red wines in **Bordeaux** (p. 581) and **Burgundy** (p. 419) and the whites of Alsace's **Route du Vin** (p. 394) and the **Loire Valley** (p. 190). Top it all off with an after-dinner drink—either **cognac**, crafted in its namesake town (p. 554), or *calvados*, an apple brandy made in **Normandy** (p. 288).

TOP TEN LIST

MUSIC MAKES THE PEOPLE COME TOGETHER

Film festivals are one of France's claims to fame, but art appreciation isn't limited to movie screenings. Cities throughout France host annual music festivals, many of which take place during the summer in open-air settings.

1. Angoulême's **Festival Musiques Métisses** (p. 553), in June, features live *chaud* hits—music from south of the equator.

2. International folk musicians jam at Dinan's **Festival des Folklores du Monde** (p. 255) in July.

3. Belfort's **Les Eurockéennes** (p. 408)—France's largest open-air rock festival—heats up in July.

4. Aix-en-Provence's **Zik Zac Estival** (p. 677) in July is a celebration of hip hop and reggae.

5. Don your fedora at the **Nice Jazz Festival** (p. 713) in mid-July.

6. Quimper's **Semaines Musicales** (p. 275) brings orchestras and choirs to town in August.

7. Renowned pianists tickle the ivories at Toulouse's **Festival International de Piano aux Jacobins** (p. 628) in September.

8. Paimpol's **Fête du Chant de Marin** (p. 260) is a festival of sailors' songs held in early August.

9. Expect legendary, face-melting guitar riffs at **Flâneries Musicales d'Été** (p. 361) in Reims during six weeks in the summer.

10. Hear all the hottest mixes at Mulhouse's **Bêtes de Scène** (p. 405)—a mid-July concert series featuring underground DJs.

HERE COMES THE SUN

The Côte d'Azur attracts two types of people—the stars who create its glamor and the masses who come looking for it. Party among Europe's suntanned youth in **Nice** (p. 700) and **Juan-les-Pins** (p. 734) or head straight for the surf in the Atlantic waves in **Anglet** (p. 599). If sun and sand are your only desires, try Île Rousse (p. 778) in Corsica. Some of France's most beautiful beaches await in rugged Brittany, at **Belle-Île-En-Mer** (p. 278) and **Saint-Malo** (p. 250). Find solitude on the pristine *plages* of **Île d' Yeu** (p. 578) and **Île d'Aix** (p. 573).

◾LET'S GO PICKS: FRANCE

BEST PLACE TO KISS: On the steps leading to **Montmartre** (p. 116), the longest and most panoramic climb in Paris, especially at dusk.

BEST PREHISTORIC DECOR: The awesome cave paintings at **Lascaux** (p. 530) and **Les-Eyzles-de-Tayac** (p. 528).

BEST EXCUSE FOR DRINKING: The free *dégustations* don't stop as you stumble merrily along the av. de Champagne in **Épernay** (p. 361).

BEST PLACES TO LOSE YOUR TAN LINES: The delightfully debaucherous city of **Saint-Tropez** (p. 750) and clothing-optional beaches in **Corsica** (p. 758).

LONGEST SHOTS: The still-loaded German artillery in **Longues-sur-Mer** (p. 317); your chances at the famous **Monte Carlo Casino** (p. 721).

MOST UNUSUAL FOODS: Blood sausage in **Alsace** (p. 387) and bone marrow in **Paris** (p. 95). Eat up!

BEST LIVING CANVASES: The gorgeous orchards and harbor of **Collioure** (p. 648), which inspired Matisse, Dalí, and Picasso; **Arles** (p. 683), home of Van Gogh's cafes and lost ear; the fruit that Cézanne made famous in **Aix-en-Provence** (p. 672).

BEST REASONS TO GASP FOR AIR: Hiking **Mont Blanc** (p. 486); crossing the border into Spain through the **Pyrenees** (p. 613); biking to the **Loire Valley's** (p. 190) famous châteaux.

BEST REASONS TO WISH FOR WORLD PEACE: Normandy's WWII **D-Day Beaches** (p. 313); tiny **Oradour-sur-Glane** (p. 517), untouched since Nazis massacred its entire population; the bones of 130,000 unknown soldiers at the Ossuaire outside **Verdun** (p. 383).

BIGGEST EGOS: Louis XIV, responsible for **Versailles** (p. 176); Napoleon, who still haunts his hometown of **Ajaccio** (p. 761); François I, creator of France's biggest party house, **Chambord** (p. 204).

SUGGESTED ITINERARIES

The following itineraries are designed to lead you to the highlights of France's distinct regions, from cosmopolitan hubs to sleepy villages. While these itineraries are intended for those who haven't traveled around France very much, even seasoned Francophiles can use them as a template for additional daytrips and excursions. Still, there are many ways to explore the country, not all of which we can cover. For more ideas, especially on less touristy spots that you might otherwise skip over, see the regional chapter introductions.

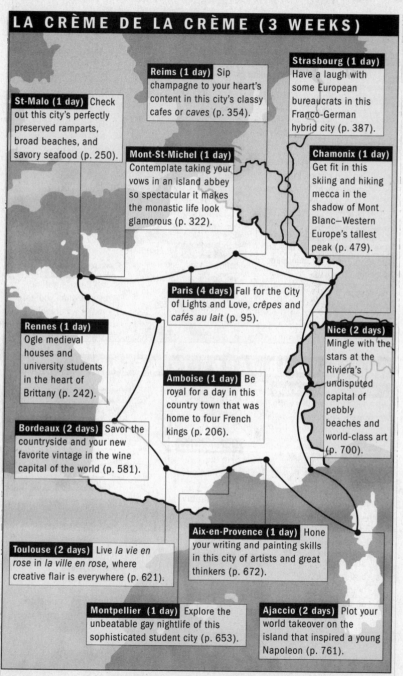

LA CRÈME DE LA CRÈME (3 WEEKS)

Reims (1 day) Sip champagne to your heart's content in this city's classy cafes or *caves* (p. 354).

Strasbourg (1 day) Have a laugh with some European bureaucrats in this Franco-German hybrid city (p. 387).

St-Malo (1 day) Check out this city's perfectly preserved ramparts, broad beaches, and savory seafood (p. 250).

Mont-St-Michel (1 day) Contemplate taking your vows in an island abbey so spectacular it makes the monastic life look glamorous (p. 322).

Chamonix (1 day) Get fit in this skiing and hiking mecca in the shadow of Mont Blanc—Western Europe's tallest peak (p. 479).

Paris (4 days) Fall for the City of Lights and Love, *crêpes* and *cafés au lait* (p. 95).

Rennes (1 day) Ogle medieval houses and university students in the heart of Brittany (p. 242).

Nice (2 days) Mingle with the stars at the Riviera's undisputed capital of pebbly beaches and world-class art (p. 700).

Amboise (1 day) Be royal for a day in this country town that was home to four French kings (p. 206).

Bordeaux (2 days) Savor the countryside and your new favorite vintage in the wine capital of the world (p. 581).

Aix-en-Provence (1 day) Hone your writing and painting skills in this city of artists and great thinkers (p. 672).

Toulouse (2 days) Live *la vie en rose* in *la ville en rose*, where creative flair is everywhere (p. 621).

Montpellier (1 day) Explore the unbeatable gay nightlife of this sophisticated student city (p. 653).

Ajaccio (2 days) Plot your world takeover on the island that inspired a young Napoleon (p. 761).

DISCOVER

LIFE'S A BEACH (10 DAYS)

Cannes (1 day) Work on your tan and your film repertoire in this surprisingly budget-friendly resort city (p. 736).

Antibes (1 day) Lounge on hot beaches with hot partygoers in this slice of paradise (p. 727).

Monaco (1 day) Make someone else buy you a drink in the wealthiest spot on the Riviera (p. 718).

START

Nice (2 days) Undress to impress on the beaches of this gorgeous locale (p. 700).

The Corniches (1 day) Relax after a long week of parties in these beautiful seaside villages (p. 714).

END

Marseille (2 days) Sunbathe on the Mediterranean by day and party in this spicy immigrant city by night (p. 661).

Calvi (1 day) Windsurfing, scuba diving, and kayaking are sources of bottomless fun for those too shy to join the topless (p. 772).

Bastia (1 day) Hike Cap Corse's natural reserve when you get tired of worshipping the sun (p. 785).

ROUTE GOURMANDE (2 WEEKS)

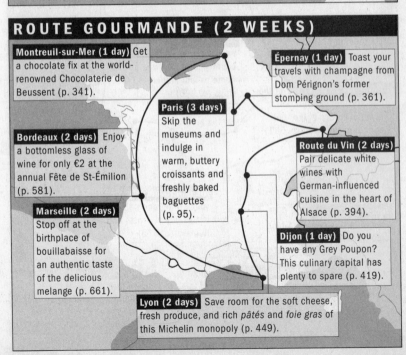

Montreuil-sur-Mer (1 day) Get a chocolate fix at the world-renowned Chocolaterie de Beussent (p. 341).

Épernay (1 day) Toast your travels with champagne from Dom Pérignon's former stomping ground (p. 361).

Paris (3 days) Skip the museums and indulge in warm, buttery croissants and freshly baked baguettes (p. 95).

Bordeaux (2 days) Enjoy a bottomless glass of wine for only €2 at the annual Fête de St-Émilion (p. 581).

Route du Vin (2 days) Pair delicate white wines with German-influenced cuisine in the heart of Alsace (p. 394).

Marseille (2 days) Stop off at the birthplace of bouillabaisse for an authentic taste of the delicious melange (p. 661).

Dijon (1 day) Do you have any Grey Poupon? This culinary capital has plenty to spare (p. 419).

Lyon (2 days) Save room for the soft cheese, fresh produce, and rich *pâtés* and *foie gras* of this Michelin monopoly (p. 449).

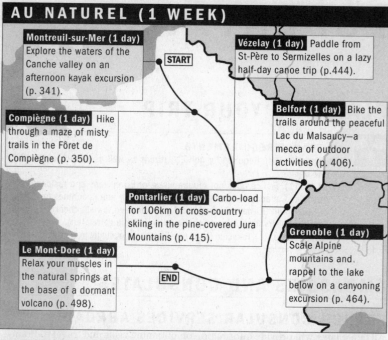

AU NATUREL (1 WEEK)

Montreuil-sur-Mer (1 day) Explore the waters of the Canche valley on an afternoon kayak excursion (p. 341).

Vézelay (1 day) Paddle from St-Père to Sermizelles on a lazy half-day canoe trip (p.444).

START

Compiègne (1 day) Hike through a maze of misty trails in the Fôret de Compiègne (p. 350).

Belfort (1 day) Bike the trails around the peaceful Lac du Malsaucy—a mecca of outdoor activities (p. 406).

Pontarlier (1 day) Carbo-load for 106km of cross-country skiing in the pine-covered Jura Mountains (p. 415).

Grenoble (1 day) Scale Alpine mountains and rappel to the lake below on a canyoning excursion (p. 464).

Le Mont-Dore (1 day) Relax your muscles in the natural springs at the base of a dormant volcano (p. 498).

END

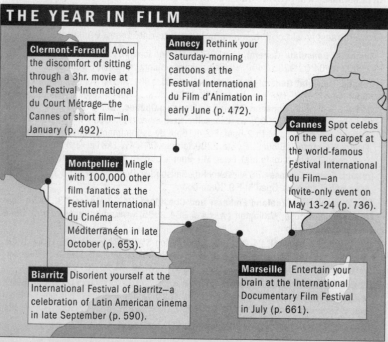

THE YEAR IN FILM

Clermont-Ferrand Avoid the discomfort of sitting through a 3hr. movie at the Festival International du Court Métrage—the Cannes of short film—in January (p. 492).

Annecy Rethink your Saturday-morning cartoons at the Festival International du Film d'Animation in early June (p. 472).

Cannes Spot celebs on the red carpet at the world-famous Festival International du Film—an invite-only event on May 13-24 (p. 736).

Montpellier Mingle with 100,000 other film fanatics at the Festival International du Cinéma Méditerranéen in late October (p. 653).

Biarritz Disorient yourself at the International Festival of Biarritz—a celebration of Latin American cinema in late September (p. 590).

Marseille Entertain your brain at the International Documentary Film Festival in July (p. 661).

ESSENTIALS

PLANNING YOUR TRIP

ENTRANCE REQUIREMENTS
Passport (p. 10). Required for non-EU citizens as well as citizens of the UK and Ireland.
Visa (p. 11). France does not require visas for EU citizens and residents of Australia, Canada, New Zealand, the US, and many more countries for visits of fewer than 90 days. To find out if you will need a visa, check with the French Ministry for Foreign Affairs (www.diplomatie.gouv.fr/en).
Work Permit (p. 11). Required for all non-EU citizens planning to work in France.

EMBASSIES AND CONSULATES

FRENCH CONSULAR SERVICES ABROAD

All consulates will provide information on obtaining visas and travel to France in general. The hours listed below are for visa concerns unless otherwise stated. Most consulates will receive inquiries by appointment. The website www.embassyworld.com has a complete up-to-date list of consulates.

Australia: Consulate General, Level 26, St-Martins Tower, 31 Market St., Sydney NSW 2000 (☎+64 02 9268 2400; www.ambafrance-au.org). Open M-F 9am-1pm.

Canada: Consulat Général de France à Montréal, 1501, McGill College, Bureau 1000, Montréal, QC H3A 3M8 (☎+1-514-878-4385; www.consulfrance-montreal.org). Open M-F 8:30am-noon. **Consulat Général de France à Québec,** 25 rue Saint-Louis, QC G1R 3Y8 (☎+1-418-266-2500; www.consulfrance-quebec.org). Open M-F 8:30am-noon without appointment; M-Th 2-5pm, F 2-4:15pm by appointment. **Consulat Général de France à Toronto,** 2 Bloor St. E., Ste. 2200, Toronto, ON M4W 1A8 (☎+1-416-847-1900; www.consulfrance-toronto.org). Open M-F 9am-12:30pm. By appointment only.

Ireland: French Embassy, 36 Ailesbury Rd., Ballsbridge, Dublin 4 (☎+353 1 277 5000; www.ambafrance.ie). Open M-F 9:30am-noon.

New Zealand: New Zealand Embassy and Consulate, 34-42 Manners St., 12th floor of Sovereign House, Wellington (☎+64 4 384 2555; www.ambafrance-nz.org). Open M-F 9:15am-1:15pm.

UK: Consulate General, 21 Cromwell Rd., London SW7 2EN (☎+44 20 7073 1200; www.consulfrance-londres.org). Open M-Th 8:45am-noon, F 8:45-11:30am. Visa service: P.O. Box 57, 6A Cromwell Pl., London SW7 2EW (☎+44 20 7073 1250).

US: Consulate General, 4101 Reservoir Rd. NW, Washington, D.C. 20007 (☎+1-202-944-6000; www.consulfrance-washington.org). Open M-F 8:45am-12:45pm; operator 8:45am-12:45pm and 2-5pm. Visa service ☎+1-202-944-6200. Open M-F 8:45am-12:30pm. Consulates also in Atlanta, Boston, Chicago, Houston, Los Angeles, Miami, New Orleans, New York City, and San Francisco. Check out www.ambafrance-us.org for more information.

CONSULAR SERVICES IN FRANCE

Travelers visit these embassies only when they encounter trouble abroad and need assistance. The most common concern that embassies address is the loss of a passport or a question about potentially dangerous local conditions. If you encounter serious trouble, your home country's embassy or consulate can usually provide legal advice and may even be able to advance you money in emergency situations. But don't expect them to get you out of every scrape; you must always follow French law while in France. In the case of arrest, know that your consulate has limited legal authority, and can do little more than suggest a lawyer. **Dual citizens** of France cannot call on the consular services of their second nationality for assistance. Hours vary; call before visiting. Visa services tend to be available only in the morning. Consulates are listed under **Practical Information** in pertinent cities throughout the book.

Australia: 4 rue Jean Rey, 75724 Paris (☎01 40 59 33 00; www.france.embassy.gov. au). Open M-F 9am-5pm.

Canada: 35 av. Montaigne, 75008 Paris (☎01 44 43 29 00; www.international.gc.ca/ canada-europa/france). Open daily 9am-noon and 2-5pm.

Ireland: 12 av. Foch, 75116 Paris (☎01 44 17 67 00; www.embassyofirelandparis. com). Open M-F 9:30am-noon. Other offices in Antibes, Cherbourg, and Lyon.

New Zealand: 7 ter, rue Léonard de Vinci, 75116 Paris (☎01 45 01 43 43; www.nzembassy.com/france). Open July-Aug. M-Th 9am-1pm and 2-4:30pm, F 9am-2pm; Sept.-June M-Th 9am-1pm and 2-5:30pm, F 9am-1pm and 2-4pm.

UK: 18 bis rue d'Anjou, 75008 Paris (☎01 44 51 31 02; www.amb-grandebretagne. fr). Open M-F 9:30am-12:30pm and 2:30- 4:30pm. Other offices in Bordeaux, Lille, Lyon, and Marseille.

US: 2 av. Gabriel, 75008 Paris Cedex 08 (☎01 43 12 22 22; http://france.usembassy. gov). 24hr. emergency assistance by phone. Open M-F 9am-noon. Tell the guard you want American citizen services. Other offices in Bordeaux, Lille, Lyon, Marseille, Nice, Rennes, Strasbourg, and Toulouse.

TOURIST OFFICES

The **French Government Tourist Office (FGTO),** also known as "Maison de la France," runs tourist offices in French cities and offers tourist services to travelers visiting France. The FGTO runs the useful website www.franceguide.com. *Let's Go* lists the tourist office in every town where one exists.

Australia and New Zealand: Level 13, 25 Bligh St., Sydney, NSW 2000 (☎+61 02 9231 5244; http://au.franceguide.com).

Canada: 1800 av. McGill College, Ste. 1010, Montréal, QC H3A 3J6 (☎+1-514-288-2026; http://ca-en.franceguide.com).

Ireland: See **UK** (http://ie.franceguide.com).

UK: Lincoln House, 300 High Holborn, London WC1V 7JH (☎+44 9068 244 123, 60p per min.; http://uk.franceguide.com).

US: 825 3rd Ave., New York City, NY 10022 (☎+1-514-288-1904; http://us.franceguide. com). 9454 Wilshire Blvd., Ste. 210, Beverly Hills, CA 30212 (☎+1-310-271-6665).

ESSENTIALS

DOCUMENTS AND FORMALITIES

PASSPORTS

REQUIREMENTS
Citizens of Australia, Canada, Ireland, New Zealand, the UK, and the US need valid passports to enter France and to re-enter their home countries. France does not allow entrance if the holder's passport expires in under six months; returning home with an expired passport is illegal and may result in a fine.

NEW PASSPORTS
Citizens of Australia, Canada, Ireland, New Zealand, the UK, and the US can apply for a passport at any passport office or at selected post offices and courts of law. Citizens of these countries may download passport applications from the official website of their country's government or passport office. Any new passport or renewal applications must be filed well in advance of the departure date, though most passport offices offer rush services for a very steep fee. Note, however, that "rushed" passports still take up to two weeks to arrive.

ONE EUROPE. European unity has come a long way since 1958, when the European Economic Community (EEC) was created to promote European solidarity and cooperation. Since then, the EEC has become the European Union (EU), a mighty political, legal, and economic institution. On May 1, 2004, 10 South, Central, and Eastern European countries—Cyprus, the Czech Republic, Estonia, Hungary, Latvia, Lithuania, Malta, Poland, Slovakia, and Slovenia—were admitted into the EU, joining 15 other member states: Austria, Belgium, Denmark, Finland, France, Germany, Greece, Ireland, Italy, Luxembourg, the Netherlands, Portugal, Spain, Sweden, and the UK. On January 1, 2007, two others, Bulgaria and Romania, came into the fold, bringing the tally of member states to 27.

What does this have to do with the average non-EU tourist? The EU's policy of **freedom of movement** means that most border controls have been abolished and visa policies harmonized. Under this treaty, formally known as the **Schengen Agreement,** you're still required to carry a passport (or government-issued ID card for EU citizens) when crossing an internal border, but, once you've been admitted into one country, you're free to travel to other participating states. Most EU states are already members of Schengen (minus Bulgaria, Cyprus, Ireland, Romania, and the UK), as are Iceland and Norway. In 2009, Cyprus, Liechtenstein, and Switzerland will bring the number of Schengen countries to 27. Britain and Ireland have also formed a **common travel area,** abolishing passport controls between the UK and the Republic of Ireland.

For more important consequences of the EU for travelers, see **The Euro** (p. 14) and **Customs in the EU** (p. 12).

PASSPORT MAINTENANCE
Photocopy the page of your passport with your photo as well as your visas, traveler's check serial numbers, and any other important documents. Carry one set of copies in a safe place, apart from the originals, and leave another set at home. Consulates also recommend that you carry an expired

passport or an official copy of your birth certificate in a part of your baggage separate from other documents.

If you lose your passport, immediately notify the local police and your home country's nearest embassy or consulate. To expedite its replacement, you must show ID and proof of citizenship; it also helps to know all information previously recorded in the passport. In some cases, a replacement may take weeks to process, and it may be valid only for a limited time. Any visas stamped in your old passport will be lost forever. In an emergency, ask for immediate temporary traveling papers that will permit you to re-enter your home country.

VISAS AND WORK PERMITS

VISAS

Citizens of Australia, Canada, Ireland, New Zealand, the UK, and the US do not need a visa for stays of up to 90 days for entrance into France, though this three-month period begins upon entry into any of the countries that belong to the EU's **freedom of movement** zone. For more information, see **One Europe** (p. 10). Those staying longer than 90 days may purchase a *long séjour* (long-stay visa) at their local French consulate; all forms and fees must be presented in person. A visa costs US$155 and allows the holder to spend one year in France. All foreigners (including EU citizens) who plan to stay in France between 90 days and one year must apply for a *carte de séjour temporaire* (temporary residence permit) at the prefecture in their town of residence within eight days of their arrival in France.

Double-check entrance requirements at the nearest embassy or consulate of France (listed under **French Consular Services Abroad,** p. 8) for up-to-date info before departure. US citizens can also consult http://travel.state.gov.

Entering France to study requires a special visa. For more information, see the **Beyond Tourism** chapter (p. 81).

WORK PERMITS

Admittance to a country as a traveler does not include the right to work, which is authorized only by a work permit. For more information about work permit requirements, see the **Beyond Tourism** chapter (p. 81).

IDENTIFICATION

When you travel, always carry at least two forms of identification on your person, including a photo ID. A passport and a driver's license or birth certificate will usually suffice. Never carry all of your IDs together; split them up in case of theft or loss and keep photocopies in your luggage and at home.

STUDENT, TEACHER, AND YOUTH IDENTIFICATION

The **International Student Identity Card (ISIC),** the most widely accepted form of student ID, provides discounts on some sights, accommodations, food, and transportation; access to a 24hr. emergency help line; and insurance benefits for US cardholders. In France, cardholders can receive discounts on plane and train tickets, on tours and excursions, or at museums. Applicants must be full-time secondary- or post-secondary-school students at least 12 years old. Because of the proliferation of fake ISICs, some services (particularly airlines) require additional proof of student identity.

The **International Teacher Identity Card (ITIC)** offers teachers the same insurance coverage as the ISIC and similar but limited discounts. To qualify for the card, teachers must be currently employed and have worked a minimum of 18hr. per week for at least one school year. For travelers who are under 26 years old but are not students, the **International Youth Travel Card (IYTC)** also offers many of the same benefits as the ISIC.

Each of these identity cards costs US$22. ISICs, ITICs, and IYTCs are valid for one year from the date of issue. To learn more about ISICs, ITICs, and IYTCs, try www.myisic.com. Many student travel agencies (p. 26) issue the cards; for a list of issuing agencies or more information, see the **International Student Travel Confederation (ISTC)** website (www.istc.org).

The **International Student Exchange Card (ISE Card)** is a similar identification card available to students, faculty, and children aged 12 to 26. The card provides discounts, medical benefits, access to a 24hr. emergency help line, and the ability to purchase student airfares. An ISE Card costs US$25; call ☎+1-800-255-8000 (in North America) or ☎+1-480-951-1177 (from all other continents) for more info or visit www.isecard.com.

CUSTOMS

Upon entering France, you must declare certain items from abroad and pay a duty on the value of those articles if they exceed the allowance established by France's customs service. Goods and gifts purchased at duty-free shops abroad are not exempt from duty or sales tax; "duty-free" means that you won't pay tax in the country of purchase. Fooled you too, huh? Duty-free allowances were abolished for travel between EU member states on June 30, 1999, but still exist for travelers arriving from outside the EU. Upon returning home, you must likewise declare all articles acquired abroad and pay a duty on the value of articles in excess of your home country's allowance. In order to expedite your return, make a list of any valuables brought from home and register them with customs before traveling abroad. It's a good idea to keep receipts for all goods acquired abroad. The movement of particular articles across country borders—including some foods—may be restricted or prohibited.

 CUSTOMS IN THE EU. As well as freedom of movement of people, travelers in the European Union can also take advantage of the freedom of movement of goods. This means that there are no customs controls at internal EU borders (i.e., you can take the blue customs channel at the airport), and travelers are free to transport whatever legal substances they like as long as it is for their own personal (non-commercial) use—up to 800 cigarettes, 10L of spirits, 90L of wine (including up to 60L of sparkling wine), and 110L of beer. Duty-free allowances were abolished on June 30, 1999, for travel between the original 15 EU member states; this now also applies to Cyprus and Malta. However, travelers between the EU and the rest of the world still get a duty-free allowance when passing through customs.

France requires a **value added tax (VAT)** of up to 19.6% (see **Taxes,** p. 17). Non-European Economic Community tourists bringing purchased goods home with them can usually be refunded this tax for purchases of over €175 (including VAT) per store. Ask for VAT forms at the time of purchase and present them at the *détaxe* booth at the airport. You must carry these goods with you at all times—at the airport and on the airplane. You must claim your refund within six months; it generally takes one month to process.

MONEY

CURRENCY AND EXCHANGE

The currency chart below is based on August 2008 exchange rates between European Union euro (EUR€) and Australian dollars (AUS$), Canadian dollars (CDN$), New Zealand dollars (NZ$), British pounds (UK£), and US dollars (US$). Check the currency converter on websites like www.xe.com or www. bloomberg.com for the latest exchange rates.

EURO (€)		
AUS$ = €0.59	€1 = AUS$1.70
CDN$ = €0.62	€1 = CDN$1.62
NZ$ = €0.47	€1 = NZ$2.15
UK£ = €1.26	€1 = UK£0.79
US$ = €0.65	€1 = US$1.54

As a general rule, it's cheaper to convert money in France than at home. While currency exchange will probably be available in your arrival airport, it's wise to bring enough foreign currency to last for at least 24-72hr.

When changing money abroad, try to go only to banks or *bureaux de change* that have at most a 5% margin between their buy and sell prices. Since you lose money with every transaction, it makes sense to convert large sums at one time (unless the currency is depreciating rapidly).

If you use traveler's checks or bills, carry some in small denominations (the equivalent of US$50 or fewer) for times when you are forced to exchange money at poor rates, but bring a range of denominations since charges may be applied per check cashed. Store your money in a variety of forms; ideally, at any given time you will be carrying some cash, some traveler's checks, and an ATM and/or credit card.

THE EURO. As of January 1, 2009, the official currency of 16 members of the European Union—Austria, Belgium, Cyprus, Finland, France, Germany, Greece, Ireland, Italy, Luxembourg, Malta, the Netherlands, Portugal, Slovenia, and Spain—will be the euro. The currency has some important—and positive—consequences for travelers hitting more than one euro-zone country. For one thing, money-changers across the euro-zone are obliged to exchange money at the official, fixed rate (below) and at no commission (though they may still charge a small service fee). Second, euro-denominated traveler's checks allow you to pay for goods and services across the euro-zone, again at the official rate and commission-free. At the time of printing, €1 = AUS$1.70 = CDN$1.62 = NZ$2.15 = UK£0.79 = US$1.54. For more info, check a currency converter (such as www.xe.com) or www.europa.eu.int.

TRAVELER'S CHECKS

Traveler's checks are one of the safest and most convenient means of carrying funds. American Express and Visa are the best-recognized brands. Many banks and agencies sell them for a small commission. Check issuers provide refunds if the checks are lost or stolen, and many provide additional services, such as toll-free refund hotlines abroad, emergency message services, and assistance with lost and stolen credit cards or passports. Traveler's checks are readily accepted in regions of France with high tourist traffic, but credit and ATM cards are more typical. Ask about toll-free refund hotlines and the location of refund centers when purchasing checks and always carry emergency cash.

American Express: Checks available with commission at select banks, at all AmEx offices, and online (www.americanexpress.com; US residents only). AmEx cardholders can also purchase checks by phone (☎+1-800-528-4800). Checks available in Australian, British, Canadian, European, and Japanese currencies, among others. AmEx also offers the Travelers Cheque Card, a prepaid reloadable card. Cheques for Two can be signed by either of 2 people traveling together. For purchase locations or more information, contact AmEx's service centers: in Australia ☎+61 2 9271 8666, in New Zealand +64 9 367 4567, in the UK +44 1273 696 933, in the US and Canada +1-800-221-7282; elsewhere, call the US collect at +1-336-393-1111. In France, call ☎01 47 77 70 00.

Travelex: Visa TravelMoney prepaid cash card and Visa traveler's checks available. For information about Thomas Cook MasterCard in Canada and the US, call ☎+1-800-223-7373, in the UK +44 800 622 101; elsewhere, call the UK collect at +44 1733 318 950. For information about Interpayment Visa in the US and Canada, call ☎+1-800-732-1322, in the UK +44 800 515 884; elsewhere, call the UK collect at +44 1733 318 949. For more information, visit www.travelex.com.

Visa: Checks available (generally with commission) at banks worldwide. For the location of the nearest office, call the Visa Travelers Cheque Global Refund and Assistance Center: in the UK ☎+44 800 895 078, in the US +1-800-227-6811; elsewhere, call the UK collect at +44 2079 378 091. Checks available in American, British, Canadian, European, and Japanese currencies, among others. Visa also offers TravelMoney, a prepaid debit card that can be reloaded online or by phone. For more information on Visa travel services, see http://usa.visa.com/personal/using_visa/travel_with_visa.html.

CREDIT, DEBIT, AND ATM CARDS

Where they are accepted, credit cards often offer superior exchange rates—up to 5% better than the retail rate used by banks and other currency-exchange establishments. Credit cards may also offer services such as insurance or emergency help and are sometimes required to reserve hotel rooms or rental cars. **MasterCard** (a.k.a. **EuroCard** in Europe) and **Visa** (e.g., **Carte Bleue** in France) are the most frequently accepted; **American Express** cards work at some ATMs and at AmEx offices and major airports.

The use of ATM cards is widespread in France. Depending on the system that your home bank uses, you can most likely access your personal bank account from abroad. ATMs get the same wholesale exchange rate as credit cards, but there is often a limit on the amount you can withdraw per day (usually around US$500). There is also typically a surcharge of US$1-5 per withdrawal.

Debit cards are as convenient as credit cards but withdraw money directly from the holder's checking account. A debit card can be used wherever its associated credit-card company (usually MasterCard or Visa) is accepted. Debit cards often also function as ATM cards and can be used to withdraw cash from associated banks and ATMs throughout France.

The two major international money networks are **MasterCard/Maestro/Cirrus** (for ATM locations ☎+1-800-424-7787 or www.mastercard.com) and **Visa/PLUS** (for ATM locations ☎+1-800-847-2911 or www.visa.com). **American Express** cards are not as prevalent in France as elsewhere, but they may be accepted in more upscale restaurants or in heavily touristed areas. Most ATMs charge a transaction fee that is paid to the bank that owns the ATM, although Bank of America cardholders can use **BNP/Paribas** ATMs without charge.

PINS AND ATMS. To use a cash or credit card to withdraw money from a cash machine (ATM) in Europe, you must have a four-digit Personal Identification Number (PIN). If your PIN is longer than four digits, ask your bank whether you can just use the first four or whether you'll need a new one. Credit cards don't usually come with PINs, so, if you intend to hit up ATMs in Europe with a credit card to get cash advances, call your credit-card company before leaving to request one. Travelers with alphabetic, rather than numerical, PINs may also be thrown off by the lack of letters on European cash machines. The following are the corresponding numbers to use: 1 = QZ; 2 = ABC; 3 = DEF; 4 = GHI; 5 = JKL; 6 = MNO; 7 = PRS; 8 = TUV; and 9 = WXY. Note that if you mistakenly punch the wrong code into the machine three times, it will swallow your card for good.

GETTING MONEY FROM HOME

If you run out of money while traveling, the easiest and cheapest solution is to have someone back home make a deposit to your bank account. Otherwise, consider one of the following options.

WIRING MONEY

It is possible to arrange a **bank money transfer,** which means asking a bank back home to wire money to a bank in France. This is the cheapest way to transfer cash, but it's also the slowest, usually taking several days or more. Note that some banks may only release your funds in local currency, potentially sticking you with a poor exchange rate; inquire about this in advance. If your home bank has a relationship with a bank in France, make sure to use that bank, as the rate will be better. Money transfer services like **Western Union** are faster and more convenient than bank transfers—but also much pricier. Western Union has many locations worldwide. To find one, visit www.westernunion.com or call in Australia ☎1800 173 833, in Canada and the US 800-325-6000, in the UK 0800 833 833, or in France 08 00 90 32 75. To wire money using a credit card, call in Canada and the US ☎800-CALL-CASH, in the UK 0800 833 833. Money transfer services are also available to **American Express** cardholders and at selected **Thomas Cook** offices.

US STATE DEPARTMENT (US CITIZENS ONLY)

In serious emergencies only, the US State Department will forward money within hours to the nearest consular office, which will then disburse it according to instructions for a US$30 fee. If you wish to use this service, you must contact the Overseas Citizens Services division of the US State Department (☎+1-202-501-4444, from US ☎888-407-4747).

COSTS

The cost of your trip will vary considerably, depending on where you go, how you travel, and where you stay. The most significant expenses will probably be your round-trip (return) airfare to France (see **Getting to France: By Plane,** p. 26) and a railpass or bus pass (see **Getting Around France,** p. 31). Before you go, spend some time calculating a reasonable daily budget.

STAYING ON A BUDGET

To give you a general idea, a bare-bones day in France (camping or sleeping in hostels/guesthouses, buying food at supermarkets) would cost about US$37 (€24); a slightly more comfortable day (sleeping in hostels/guesthouses and the occasional budget hotel, eating one meal per day at a restaurant, going out at night) would cost US$70 (€45); and, for a luxurious day, the sky's the limit. Don't forget to factor in emergency reserve funds (at least US$200) when planning how much money you'll need.

TIPS FOR SAVING MONEY

Some simpler ways include searching out opportunities for free entertainment, splitting accommodation and food costs with trustworthy fellow travelers, and buying food in supermarkets rather than eating out. Bring a **sleepsack** (p. 18) to save on sheet charges in hostels and do your **laundry** in the sink (unless you're explicitly prohibited from doing so). Museums often have certain days once a month or once a week when admission is free; plan accordingly. If you are eligible, consider getting an ISIC or an IYTC (p. 11); many sights and museums offer reduced admission to students and youths. For getting around quickly, bikes are the most economical option. Renting a bike is cheaper than renting a moped or scooter. Don't forget about walking, though; you can learn a lot about a city by seeing it on foot. Drinking at bars and clubs quickly becomes expensive. It's cheaper to buy alcohol at a supermarket and imbibe before going out. That said, don't go overboard. Though staying within your budget is important, don't do so at the expense of your health or a great travel experience.

TIPPING AND BARGAINING

By French law, service must be included at all restaurants, bars, and cafes. Look for *service compris* on the menu. If service isn't included, tip 15-20%. Even when it's included, it is polite to leave a *pourboire* (tip; from €0.50 to 5% of the bill) at a cafe, restaurant, or bar. Tip your hairdresser 20%; tip taxi drivers 10-15%. Concierges and other hotel staff may expect to be tipped for extra services (never less than €1.50).

You should inquire about discounts and less pricey options, but don't try to bargain at established places like hotels, hostels, restaurants, cafes, museums, and nightclubs. Bargaining is acceptable—and usually expected—at markets.

TAXES

The **value added tax (VAT)** is a general tax on doing business in France; it applies to a wide range of services and goods (e.g., entertainment, food, and accommodations). The tax can be up to 19.6% of the price of the good, although there is a reduced 5.5% tax on food. Some of the VAT can be recovered (p. 12).

PACKING

Pack lightly: lay out only what you absolutely need, then take half the clothes and twice the money. The **Travelite FAQ** (www.travelite.org) is a good resource for tips on traveling light. The online **Universal Packing List** (http://upl.codeq.info) will generate a customized list of suggested items based on your trip length, the expected climate, your planned activities, and other factors. If you plan to do a lot of hiking, also consult **The Great Outdoors**, p. 47. Some frequent travelers keep a bag packed with all the essentials: passport, money belt, hat, socks, etc. Then, when they decide to leave, they know they haven't forgotten anything.

ESSENTIALS

Luggage: If you plan to cover most of your trip on foot, a sturdy **internal frame backpack** is unbeatable. (For the basics on buying a pack, see p. 49) Unless you are staying in 1 place for a large chunk of time, a suitcase or trunk will be unwieldy. In addition to your main piece of luggage, a **daypack** (a small backpack or courier bag) is useful.

Clothing: No matter when you're traveling, it's a good idea to bring a warm jacket or wool sweater, a rain jacket (Gore-Tex® is both waterproof and breathable), sturdy shoes or hiking boots, and thick socks. Flip-flops or waterproof sandals are must-haves for grubby hostel showers, and extra socks are always a good idea. You may also want 1 outfit for going out and maybe a nicer pair of shoes. If you plan to visit religious or cultural sites, remember that you will need modest and respectful dress. See **Customs and Etiquette** (p. 68) for more info on fitting in. To get an idea of the climate, see the **Appendix** (p. 798); in general, France tends to be fairly temperate, but the August 2003 heat wave killed an estimated 14,802 people as it reached temperatures of up to 104°F, reminding all to come prepared for any weather.

Sleepsack: Some hostels require that you either provide your own linen or rent sheets from them. Save cash by making your own sleepsack: fold a full-size sheet in half the long way, then sew it closed along the long side and one of the short sides.

Converters and Adapters: In France, electricity is 230 volts AC, enough to fry any 120V North American appliance. 220/240V electrical appliances won't work with a 120V current, either. Americans and Canadians should buy an adapter (which changes the shape of the plug; US$5) and a converter (which changes the voltage; US$10-30). Don't make the mistake of using only an adapter (unless appliance instructions explicitly state otherwise). Australians, Brits, and New Zealanders (who use 230V at home) won't need a converter but will need a set of adapters to use anything electrical. For more on all things adaptable, check out http://kropla.com/electric.htm.

Toiletries: Condoms, deodorant, razors, tampons, and toothbrushes are generally available, but it may be difficult to find your preferred brand; bring extras. Contact lenses are likely to be expensive and difficult to find, so bring enough extra pairs and solution for your entire trip. Also bring your glasses and a copy of your prescription in case you need emergency replacements.

First-Aid Kit: For a basic first-aid kit, pack bandages, a pain reliever, antibiotic cream, a thermometer, a multifunction pocketknife, tweezers, moleskin, decongestant, motion-sickness remedy, diarrhea or upset-stomach medication (Pepto Bismol® or Imodium®), an antihistamine, sunscreen, insect repellent, and burn ointment.

Film: If you don't want to bother with film, consider using a **digital camera.** Although it requires a steep initial investment, a digital camera means you never have to buy film again. Just be sure to bring along a large enough memory card and extra (or rechargeable) batteries. Less serious photographers may want to bring a few disposable cameras. Despite disclaimers, airport security X-rays can fog film, so buy a lead-lined pouch at a camera store or ask security to hand-inspect it. Always pack film in your carry-on luggage, since higher-intensity X-rays are used on checked luggage.

Other Useful Items: For safety purposes, you should bring a **money belt** and a small **padlock.** Basic **outdoors equipment** (plastic water bottle, compass, waterproof matches, pocketknife, sunglasses, sunscreen, hat) may also be handy. Quick repairs of torn garments can be done on the road with a needle and thread; also consider bringing electrical tape for patching tears. Other things you're liable to forget include an umbrella, sealable **plastic bags** (for damp clothes, soap, food, shampoo, and other spillables), an **alarm clock,** safety pins, rubber bands, a flashlight, earplugs, garbage bags, and a small calculator. A **cell phone** can be a lifesaver (literally) on the road; see p. 42 for information on acquiring one that will work in France.

Important Documents: Don't forget your passport, traveler's checks, ATM and/or credit cards, adequate ID, and photocopies of all of the aforementioned in case these documents are lost or stolen (p. 10). Also check that you have any of the following that might apply to you: a hosteling membership card (p. 44); driver's license (p. 11); travel insurance forms; ISIC (p. 11); and/or railpass (p. 33) or bus pass (p. 35).

SAFETY AND HEALTH

GENERAL ADVICE

In any type of crisis, the most important thing to do is **stay calm.** Your country's embassy abroad (p. 8) is usually your best resource in an emergency; registering with that embassy upon arrival in the country is a good idea. The government offices listed in the **Travel Advisories** box (p. 20) can provide information on the services they offer their citizens in case of emergencies abroad.

LOCAL LAWS AND POLICE

La police in France are generally very responsive to requests for help. The emergency call number is ☎**17.** The legal blood-alcohol level for driving is 0.05%, 0.03% less than in New Zealand, Ireland, the UK, and the US—so exercise caution when getting behind the wheel.

DRUGS AND ALCOHOL

Possession of illegal drugs (including marijuana) in France can result in a substantial jail sentence or fine. Police may arbitrarily stop and search anyone on the street. Prescription drugs—particularly insulin, syringes, or narcotics—should be left in their original, labeled containers and accompanied by their prescriptions and a doctor's statement. In case of arrest, your home country's consulate can suggest attorneys and inform your family and friends but can't get you out of jail. For more info, US citizens can contact the **Office of Overseas Citizens Services** (☎+1-202-501-4444; http://travel.state.gov).

The French love alcohol, but they drink carefully. Though there is no law prohibiting open containers, drinking on the street is considered uncouth. Restaurants may serve alcohol to anyone 16 years old or older. Though mention of France often conjures images of black-clad smokers in berets, France no longer allows smoking in public places as of 2008. The government has no official policy on berets.

SPECIFIC CONCERNS

DEMONSTRATIONS AND POLITICAL GATHERINGS

In France, past demonstrations by students, labor groups, and other routine protesters have grown into more violent confrontations with the police. In 2006, opponents of a controversial labor deregulation bill sparked protests throughout France in February, March, and April. Millions of young protesters converged on France's urban centers to show their dissatisfaction in demonstrations. Although tensions have calmed somewhat, protests are a common threat in France. The most common form of violence when demonstrations get out of hand is property damage, and tourists typically are not targets, but travelers are still advised to avoid demonstrations. In general, use common sense in conversation and, as in dealing with any sensitive cultural issue, be respectful of other political and religious perspectives.

ESSENTIALS

ESSENTIALS

TERRORISM

Terrorism has not been as serious a problem in France as in other European countries, but after September 11, 2001, the French government heightened security in public places. For example, most train stations no longer permit luggage storage. Still, Al Qaeda cells, as well as other terrorist groups, have been identified in France. In addition, France has had tense relationships with Algeria since its colonial period, a situation that has been a source of sporadic violent outbursts. Domestic anti-Semites have firebombed several Jewish synagogues in the past few years. The box below lists offices to contact and webpages to visit to get the most updated list of your home country's government's advisories about travel.

TRAVEL ADVISORIES. The following government offices provide travel information and advisories by telephone, by fax, or via the web:

Australian Department of Foreign Affairs and Trade: ☎+61 2 6261 1111; www.dfat.gov.au.

Canadian Department of Foreign Affairs and International Trade (DFAIT): ☎+1-800-267-8376; www.dfait-maeci.gc.ca. Call for their free booklet, *Bon Voyage...But.*

New Zealand Ministry of Foreign Affairs: ☎+64 4 439 8000; www.mfat.govt.nz.

United Kingdom Foreign and Commonwealth Office: ☎+44 20 7008 1500; www.fco.gov.uk.

US Department of State: ☎+1-888-407-4747; http://travel.state.gov. Visit the website for the booklet, *A Safe Trip Abroad.*

PERSONAL SAFETY

EXPLORING AND TRAVELING

To avoid unwanted attention, try to blend in as much as possible. Respecting local customs (in many cases, dressing more conservatively than you would at home) may ward off would-be hecklers. Familiarize yourself with your surroundings before setting out and carry yourself with confidence. Check maps in shops and restaurants rather than on the street. If you are traveling alone, be sure someone at home knows your itinerary and never tell anyone you meet that you're by yourself. When walking at night, stick to busy, well-lit streets and avoid dark alleyways. If you ever feel uncomfortable, leave the area as quickly and directly as you can.

There is no surefire way to avoid all the threatening situations that you might encounter while traveling, but a good **self-defense course** will give you concrete ways to react to unwanted advances. **Impact, Prepare,** and **Model Mugging** can refer you to local self-defense courses in Australia, Canada, Switzerland, and the US. Visit www.modelmugging.org for a list of nearby chapters.

If you are using a **car,** learn local driving signals and wear a seat belt. Children under 40 lb. should ride only in specially designed car seats, available for a small fee from most car-rental agencies. Study route maps before you hit the road and, if you plan on spending a lot of time driving, consider bringing spare parts. For long drives in desolate areas, invest in a cell phone and a roadside assistance program (p. 38). Park your vehicle in a garage or well-traveled area and use a steering-wheel locking device in larger cities. Sleeping in your car is the most dangerous way to get your rest, and it's also illegal in many countries. For info on the perils of **hitchhiking,** see p. 39.

POSSESSIONS AND VALUABLES

Never leave your belongings unattended; crime can occur in even the most safe-looking hostel or hotel. Bring your own padlock for hostel lockers and don't ever store valuables in a locker. Be particularly careful on **buses** and **trains;** horror stories abound about thieves who wait for travelers to fall asleep. Carry your bag or purse in front of you where you can see it. When traveling with others, sleep in alternate shifts. When alone, use good judgment in selecting a train compartment: never stay in an empty one and use a lock to secure your pack to the luggage rack. Use extra caution if traveling at night or on overnight trains. Try to sleep on top bunks with your luggage stored above you (if not in bed with you) and keep important documents and valuables on you at all times.

There are a few steps you can take to minimize the financial risk associated with traveling. First, **bring as little with you as possible.** Second, buy a few combination **padlocks** to secure your belongings either in your pack or in a hostel or train-station locker. Third, **carry as little cash as possible.** Keep your traveler's checks and ATM/credit cards in a **money belt**—not a "fanny pack"—along with your passport and ID cards. Fourth, **keep a small cash reserve separate from your primary stash.** This should be about €30 sewn into or stored in the depths of your pack, along with your traveler's check numbers, photocopies of your passport, your birth certificate, and other important documents.

In large cities, **con artists** often work in groups and may involve children. Beware of certain classics: sob stories that require money, rolls of bills "found" on the street, mustard spilled (or saliva spit) onto your shoulder to distract you while they snatch your bag. **Never let your passport and your bags out of your sight.** Hostel workers will sometimes stand at bus and train-station arrival points to recruit tired and disoriented travelers to their hostel; never believe strangers who tell you that theirs is the only hostel open. Beware of **pickpockets** in city crowds, especially on public transportation. Also, be alert in public telephone booths: if you must say your calling-card number, do so very quietly; if you punch it in, make sure no one can look over your shoulder.

If you will be traveling with electronic devices, such as a laptop computer or a PDA, check whether your homeowner's insurance covers loss, theft, or damage when you travel. If not, you might consider purchasing a low-cost separate insurance policy. **Safeware** (☎+1-800-800-1492; www.safeware.com) specializes in covering computers and charges US$90 for 90-day comprehensive international travel coverage up to US$4000.

PRE-DEPARTURE HEALTH

In your passport, write the names of any people you wish to be contacted in case of a **medical emergency** and list any allergies or medical conditions. Matching a prescription to a foreign equivalent is not always easy, safe, or possible, so, if you take **prescription drugs,** consider carrying up-to-date prescriptions or a statement from your doctor stating the medication's trade name, manufacturer, chemical name, and dosage. While traveling, be sure to keep all medication with you in your carry-on luggage. For tips on packing a **first-aid kit** and other health essentials, see p. 18.

The French names for common drugs include *aspirine* (aspirin), *pénicilline* (penicillin), *antihistaminique* (antihistamines), and *ibuprofène* (ibuprofen).

IMMUNIZATIONS AND PRECAUTIONS

Travelers over two years old should make sure that these vaccines are up to date: MMR (for measles, mumps, and rubella); DTaP or Td (for diphtheria, tetanus, and pertussis); IPV (for polio); Hib (for *haemophilus influenzae* B); and HepB (for Hepatitis B). For recommendations on immunizations and prophylaxis, ask the Centers for Disease Control and Prevention (CDC; below) in the US or the equivalent in your country and check with a doctor for guidance.

USEFUL ORGANIZATIONS AND PUBLICATIONS

The American **Centers for Disease Control and Prevention** (**CDC;** ☎+1-877-FYI-TRIP; www.cdc.gov/travel) maintains an international travelers' hotline and an informative website. Consult the appropriate government agency of your home country for consular information sheets on health, entry requirements, and other issues for various countries (see the listings in the box on **Travel Advisories,** p. 20). For quick information on health and other travel warnings, call the **Overseas Citizens Services** (M-F 8am-8pm from overseas ☎+1-202-501-4444, from US ☎888-407-4747; line open M-F 8am-8pm EST) or contact a passport agency, embassy, or consulate abroad. For information on medical evacuation services and travel insurance firms, see the US government's website at http://travel.state.gov/travel/abroad_health.html or the **British Foreign and Commonwealth Office** (www.fco.gov.uk). For general health information, contact the **American Red Cross** (☎+1-202-303-4498; www.redcross.org).

STAYING HEALTHY

Common sense is the simplest prescription for good health while you travel. Drink lots of fluids to prevent dehydration and constipation and wear sturdy, broken-in shoes and clean socks.

ONCE IN FRANCE

ENVIRONMENTAL HAZARDS

Heat exhaustion and dehydration: Heat exhaustion leads to nausea, excessive thirst, headaches, and dizziness. In 2003, heat exhaustion killed nearly 15,000 people in France, so exercise caution to prevent it. Drink plenty of fluids, eat salty foods (e.g., crackers), abstain from dehydrating beverages (e.g., alcohol and caffeinated beverages), and wear sunscreen. Continuous heat stress may eventually lead to heat stroke, which is characterized by rising temperature, severe headache, delirium, and cessation of sweating. Victims should be cooled off with wet towels and taken to a doctor immediately.

High altitude: Allow your body a couple of days to adjust to less oxygen before exerting yourself. Note that alcohol is more potent and UV rays are stronger at high elevations.

Hypothermia and frostbite: A rapid drop in body temperature is the clearest sign of overexposure to cold. Victims may also shiver, feel exhausted, have poor coordination or slurred speech, hallucinate, or suffer amnesia. Do not let hypothermia victims fall asleep. To avoid hypothermia, keep dry, wear layers, and stay out of the wind. When the temperature is below freezing, watch out for frostbite. If skin turns white or blue, waxy, and cold, do not rub the area. Drink warm beverages, stay dry, and slowly warm the area with dry fabric or steady body contact until a doctor can be found.

Sunburn: Always wear sunscreen (SPF 30 or higher) when spending significant amounts of time outdoors. If you get sunburned, drink more fluids than usual and apply an aloe-

based lotion. Severe sunburns can lead to sun poisoning, a condition that can cause fever, chills, nausea, and vomiting. Sun poisoning should always be treated by a doctor.

INSECT-BORNE DISEASES

Many diseases are transmitted by insects—mainly mosquitoes, fleas, ticks, and lice. Be aware of insects in wet or forested areas, especially while hiking and camping. Wear long pants and long sleeves, tuck your pants into your socks, and use a mosquito net. Use insect repellents such as DEET and soak or spray your gear with permethrin. **Mosquitoes**—responsible for malaria, dengue fever, and yellow fever—can be particularly abundant in wet, swampy, or wooded areas, including the humid south of France. **Ticks**—which can carry Lyme and other diseases—can be particularly dangerous in rural and forested regions.

Lyme disease: A bacterial infection carried by ticks and marked by a circular bull's-eye rash of 2 in. or more. Later symptoms include fever, headache, fatigue, and aches and pains. Antibiotics are effective if administered early. Left untreated, Lyme can cause problems in joints, the heart, and the nervous system. If you find a tick attached to your skin, grasp the head with tweezers as close to your skin as possible and apply slow, steady traction. Removing a tick within 24hr. greatly reduces the risk of infection. Do not try to remove ticks with petroleum jelly, nail polish remover, or a hot match. Ticks usually inhabit moist, shaded environments and heavily wooded areas. If you are going to be hiking in these areas, wear long clothes and DEET.

Tick-borne encephalitis: A viral infection of the central nervous system transmitted during the summer by tick bites (primarily in wooded areas) or by consumption of unpasteurized dairy products. The risk of contracting the disease is relatively low, especially if precautions are taken against tick bites.

FOOD- AND WATER-BORNE DISEASES

Prevention is the best cure: be sure that your food is properly cooked and the water you drink is clean. Watch out for food from markets or street vendors that may have been cooked in unhygienic conditions. Other culprits are raw shellfish, unpasteurized milk, and sauces containing raw eggs. Buy bottled water or purify your own water by bringing it to a rolling boil or treating it with **iodine tablets;** note, however, that boiling is more reliable.

Giardiasis: Transmitted through parasites and acquired by drinking untreated water from streams or lakes. Symptoms include diarrhea, cramps, bloating, fatigue, weight loss, and nausea. If untreated, it can lead to severe dehydration. Giardiasis occurs worldwide.

Traveler's diarrhea: Results from drinking fecally contaminated water or eating uncooked and contaminated foods. Symptoms include nausea, bloating, and urgency. Try quick-energy, non-sugary foods with protein and carbohydrates to keep your strength up. Over-the-counter anti-diarrheals (e.g., Imodium®) may counteract the problem. The most dangerous side effect is dehydration; drink 8 oz. of water with ½ tsp. of sugar or honey and a pinch of salt, try uncaffeinated soft drinks, or eat salted crackers. If you develop a fever or your symptoms don't go away after 4-5 days, consult a doctor. Consult a doctor immediately for treatment of diarrhea in children.

OTHER INFECTIOUS DISEASES

The following diseases exist all over the world. Travelers should know how to recognize them and what to do if they suspect they have been infected.

AIDS and HIV: For detailed information on Acquired Immune Deficiency Syndrome (AIDS) in France, call the 24hr. National AIDS Hotline at ☎+1-800-342-2437.

Hepatitis B: A viral infection of the liver transmitted via blood or other bodily fluids. Symptoms, which may not surface until years after infection, include jaundice, appetite loss, fever, and joint pain. It is transmitted through unprotected sex and unclean needles. A 3-shot vaccination sequence is recommended for sexually active travelers and anyone planning to seek medical treatment abroad; begin it 6 months before traveling.

Hepatitis C: Like Hepatitis B, but the mode of transmission differs. IV drug users, those with occupational exposure to blood, hemodialysis patients, and recipients of blood transfusions are at the highest risk, but the disease can also be spread through sexual contact or sharing items like razors and toothbrushes that may have traces of blood on them. No symptoms are usually exhibited. If untreated, Hep C can lead to liver failure.

Sexually transmitted infections (STIs): Gonorrhea, chlamydia, genital warts, syphilis, herpes, HPV, and other STIs are easier to catch than HIV and can be just as serious. Though condoms may protect you from some STIs, oral or even tactile contact can lead to transmission. If you think you may have contracted an STI, see a doctor immediately.

OTHER HEALTH CONCERNS

MEDICAL CARE ON THE ROAD

Medical care in France is as good—and as expensive—as anywhere in the world. All but the smallest towns have a hospital, generally with English-speaking staff, which *Let's Go* lists under the Practical Information in each city listing. Every town has a **pharmacie de garde** (24hr. pharmacy). Pharmacies assume this duty on rotation; check with police or on pharmacy doors for location.

If you are concerned about obtaining medical assistance while traveling, you may wish to employ special support services. The **MedPass** from **GlobalCare, Inc.,** 6875 Shiloh Rd. E., Alpharetta, GA 30005, USA (☎+1-800-860-1111; www. globalcare.net), provides 24hr. international medical assistance, support, and medical evacuation resources. The **International Association for Medical Assistance to Travelers (IAMAT;** US ☎+1-716-754-4883, Canada 519-836-0102; www.iamat.org) has free membership, lists English-speaking doctors worldwide, and offers info on immunization requirements and sanitation. If your regular insurance policy does not cover travel abroad, you may wish to purchase additional coverage.

Those with medical conditions (such as diabetes, allergies to antibiotics, epilepsy, or heart conditions) may want to obtain a **MedicAlert** membership (US$40 per year), which includes among other things a stainless-steel ID tag and a 24hr. collect-call number. Contact the MedicAlert Foundation International, 2323 Colorado Ave., Turlock, CA 95382, USA (☎+1-888-633-4298, outside US 209-668-3333; www.medicalert.org).

WOMEN'S HEALTH

Women traveling in unsanitary conditions are vulnerable to **urinary tract (including bladder and kidney) infections.** Bring supplies from home if you are prone to infection, as they may be difficult to find on the road. **Tampons, pads,** and **contraceptive devices** are widely available, though your favorite brand may not be stocked—bring extras of anything you can't live without. **Abortion** is legal in France. Recent changes have relaxed restrictions on surgical and pharmaceutical abortions, permitting them up to 12 weeks into pregnancy. The *pillule du lendemain* (morning-after pill) is legal and available at pharmacies.

GETTING TO FRANCE

BY PLANE

When it comes to airfare, a little effort can save you a bundle. Courier fares are the cheapest for those whose plans are flexible enough to deal with the restrictions. Tickets sold by consolidators and standby seating are also good deals, but last-minute specials, airfare wars, and charter flights often beat these fares. The key is to hunt around, be flexible, and ask about discounts. Students, seniors, and those under 26 should never pay full price for a ticket.

AIRFARES

Airfares to France peak between June and September; holidays are also expensive. The cheapest times to travel are between November and April. Midweek (M-Th morning) round-trip flights run US$40-50 cheaper than weekend flights, but they are generally more crowded and less likely to permit frequent-flier upgrades. Not fixing a return date ("open return") or arriving in and departing from different cities ("open-jaw") can be pricier than round-trip flights. Patching one-way flights together is the most expensive way to travel. Flights between France's capitals or regional hubs—Bordeaux, Lyon, Marseille, Nice, Paris, Strasbourg, and Toulouse—will tend to be cheaper.

If France is only one stop on a more extensive globe-hop, consider a round-the-world (RTW) ticket. Tickets usually include at least five stops and are valid for about a year; prices range US$1200-5000. Try **Northwest Airlines/KLM** (☎+1-800-225-2525; www.nwa.com) or **Star Alliance,** a consortium of 16 airlines including United Airlines (www.staralliance.com).

Fares for round-trip flights to Paris from the US or Canadian east coast cost US$600-2000, US$400-1000 in low season (Nov.-Mar.); from the US or Canadian west coast US$1100-2400/900-2200; from the UK, UK£100-200/50-150; from Australia AUS$2500-5000/1900-2500; from New Zealand NZ$3000-6000/2500-3500.

BUDGET AND STUDENT TRAVEL AGENCIES

While knowledgeable agents specializing in flights to France can make your life easy, they may not spend the time to find you the lowest possible fare—they get paid on commission. Travelers holding ISICs and IYTCs (p. 11) qualify for big discounts from student travel agencies. Most flights from budget agencies are on major airlines, but in peak season some may sell seats on less reliable chartered aircraft.

The Adventure Travel Company, 124 MacDougal St., New York City, NY 10021, USA (☎+1-800-467-4595; www.theadventuretravelcompany.com.) Offices across Canada and the US including New York City, San Diego, San Francisco, and Seattle.

STA Travel, 5900 Wilshire Blvd., Ste. 900, Los Angeles, CA 90036, USA (24hr. reservations and info ☎+1-800-781-4040; www.statravel.com). A student and youth travel organization with over 150 offices worldwide (check their website for a listing of all their offices), including US offices in Boston, Chicago, Los Angeles, New York City, Seattle, San Francisco, and Washington, DC. Ticket booking, travel insurance, railpasses, and more. Walk-in offices are located throughout Australia (☎+61 3 9207 5900), New Zealand (☎+64 9 309 9723), and the UK (☎+44 8701 630 026).

USIT, 19-21 Aston Quay, Dublin 2, Ireland (☎+353 1 602 1904; www.usit.ie). Ireland's leading student/budget travel agency has 20 offices throughout Northern Ireland and the Republic of Ireland. Offers programs to work, study, and volunteer worldwide.

FLIGHT PLANNING ON THE INTERNET. The Internet may be the budget traveler's dream when it comes to finding and booking bargain fares, but the array of options can be overwhelming. Many airline sites offer special last-minute deals on the web.

STA (www.statravel.com) and **StudentUniverse** (www.studentuniverse.com) provide quotes on student tickets, while **Orbitz** (www.orbitz.com), **Expedia** (www.expedia.com), and **Travelocity** (www.travelocity.com) offer full travel services. **Priceline** (www.priceline.com) lets you specify a price and obligates you to buy any ticket that meets or beats it; **Hotwire** (www.hotwire.com) offers bargain fares but won't reveal the airline or flight times until you buy. Other sites that compile deals include www.bestfares.com, www.flights.com, www.lowestfare.com, www.onetravel.com, and www.travelzoo.com.

SideStep (www.sidestep.com) and **Booking Buddy** (www.bookingbuddy.com) are online tools that can help sift through multiple offers; these two let you enter your trip information once and search multiple sites. French websites like **FranceGuide** (www.franceguide.com) and **All Travel France** (www.alltravelfrance.com) sometimes have better deals than their American equivalents.

Air Traveler's Handbook (www.faqs.org/faqs/travel/air/handbook) is an indispensable resource on the Internet; it has a comprehensive listing of links to everything you need to know before you board a plane.

COMMERCIAL AIRLINES

The commercial airlines' lowest regular offer is the **APEX (Advance Purchase Excursion)** fare, which provides confirmed reservations and allows "open-jaw" tickets. Generally, reservations must be made seven to 21 days ahead of departure, with seven- to 14-day minimum-stay and up to 90-day maximum-stay restrictions. These fares carry hefty cancellation and change penalties (fees rise in summer). Book peak-season APEX fares early. Use **Expedia** (www.expedia.com) or **Travelocity** (www.travelocity.com) to get an idea of the lowest published fares, then use the resources outlined here to try to beat those fares. Low-season fares should be appreciably cheaper than the high-season (mid-June to Aug.) ones listed here. *Let's Go* treats ▓**budget airlines** (p. 32) separately from commercial airlines. For travelers who don't place a premium on convenience, we recommend these no-frills airlines as the best way to jet around Europe. Even if you live outside the continent, you can save a lot of money by hopping the absolute cheapest flight to Europe you can find and then using budget airlines to reach your final destination.

TRAVELING FROM NORTH AMERICA

The most common ways to cross the pond are those you've probably heard of. Standard commercial carriers like **American** (☎+1-800-433-7300; www.aa.com), **United** (☎+1-800-538-2929; www.ual.com), and **Northwest** (☎+1-800-447-4747; www.nwa.com) will probably offer the most convenient flights, but they may not be the cheapest. Check **Lufthansa** (☎+1-800-399-5838; www.lufthansa.com), **British Airways** (☎+1-800-247-9297; www.britishairways.com), **Air France** (☎+1-800-237-2747; www.airfrance.us), and **Alitalia** (☎+1-800-223-5730; www.alitaliausa.com) for cheap tickets from destinations throughout the US to all over Europe. You might find an even better deal on one of the following airlines, if any of their limited departure points is convenient for you.

Icelandair: ☎+1-800-223-5500; www.icelandair.com. Stopovers in Iceland for no extra cost on most transatlantic flights. For last-minute offers, subscribe to Lucky Fares.

Finnair: ☎+1-800-950-5000; www.finnair.com. Cheap round-trips from San Francisco, New York City, and Toronto to Paris; connections throughout Europe.

TRAVELING FROM THE UK AND IRELAND

Cheapflights (www.cheapflights.co.uk) publishes bargains on airfare from the British Isles. Below is a list of carriers with special deals, but there really is no reason for British and Irish globetrotters not to fly on budget airlines (p. 28).

Aer Lingus: Ireland ☎+353 818 365 000; www.aerlingus.ie. Return tickets from Dublin, Cork, Galway, Kerry, and Shannon to Paris, Rennes, and Nice (US$400-700).

KLM: UK ☎+44 8705 074 074; www.klmuk.com. Cheap return tickets from London and elsewhere to Paris, Marseille, Nice, and more.

TRAVELING FROM AUSTRALIA AND NEW ZEALAND

Qantas Air: Australia ☎+61 13 13 13, New Zealand +64 800 808 767; www.qantas.com.au. Flights from Australia and New Zealand to Paris for around AUS$2500.

Singapore Air: Australia ☎+61 13 10 11, New Zealand +64 800 808 909; www.singaporeair.com. Flies from Auckland, Christchurch, Melbourne, Perth, and Sydney to Western Europe.

Thai Airways: Australia ☎+61 1300 65 19 60, New Zealand +64 9 377 38 86; www.thaiair.com. Flights to international destinations including Paris.

BUDGET AIRLINES

Low-cost carriers are the latest big thing in Europe. With their help, travelers can often snag tickets for illogically low prices (i.e., less than the price of a meal in the airport food court), but you get what you pay for: namely, minimalist service and no frills. In addition, many budget airlines fly out of smaller regional airports several kilometers out of town. You'll have to buy shuttle tickets to reach the airports of many of these airlines, so plan on adding an hour or so to your travel time. After round-trip shuttle tickets and fees for services that might come standard on other airlines, that €1 sale fare can suddenly jump to €20-100. Prices vary dramatically; shop around, book months ahead, pack light, and stay flexible to nab the best fares. For a more detailed list of these airlines by country, check out www.whichbudget.com.

bmibaby: UK ☎0871 224 0224, elsewhere +44 870 126 6726; www.bmibaby.com. Departures from multiple cities in the UK to Paris, Nice, and other cities in France.

easyJet: ☎+44 871 244 2366, 10p per min.; www.easyjet.com. London to Bordeaux and other cities in France (UK£50-150).

Ryanair: Ireland ☎0818 30 30 30, UK 0871 246 0000; www.ryanair.com. From Dublin, Glasgow, Liverpool, London, and Shannon to destinations in France.

SkyEurope: UK ☎0905 722 2747, elsewhere +421 2 3301 7301; www.skyeurope.com. 40 destinations in 19 countries around Europe.

Sterling: Denmark ☎70 10 84 84, UK 0870 787 8038; www.sterling.dk. The 1st Scandinavian-based budget airline. Connects Denmark, Norway, and Sweden to 47 European destinations, including Montpellier, Nice, and Paris.

Transavia: UK ☎020 7365 4997; www.transavia.com. Short hops from Cracow to Paris from €49 one-way.

Wizz Air: UK ☎0904 475 9500, 65p per min.; www.wizzair.com. Paris from Budapest, Cracow, and Warsaw.

AIR COURIER FLIGHTS

Those who travel light should consider courier flights. Couriers help transport cargo on international flights by using their checked luggage space for freight. Generally, couriers are limited to carry-ons and must deal with complex flight restrictions. Most flights are round-trip only, with short fixed-length stays (usually 1 week) and a limit of one ticket per issue. Most of these flights also operate only out of major gateway cities, mostly in North America. Generally, you must be over 18 (in some cases 21). In summer, the most popular destinations usually require an advance reservation of about two weeks (you can usually book up to two months ahead). Super-discounted fares are common for "last-minute" flights (three to 14 days ahead).

FROM NORTH AMERICA

Round-trip courier fares from the US to France run about US$350. Most flights leave from Los Angeles, Miami, New York City, or San Francisco in the US; and from Montréal, Toronto, or Vancouver in Canada. The organizations below provide members with lists of opportunities and courier brokers for an annual fee. Prices quoted below are round-trip.

Courier Travel (www.couriertravel.org). Searchable online database. Multiple departure points in the US to various European destinations, including Nice and Paris.

International Association of Air Travel Couriers (IAATC; www.courier.org). From 7 North American cities to European cities, including Paris. 1-year membership US$45.

FROM THE UK, AUSTRALIA, AND NEW ZEALAND

The minimum age for couriers from the UK is usually 18. The **International Association of Air Travel Couriers** (www.courier.org; above) often offers courier flights from London to Tokyo, Sydney, and Bangkok and from Auckland to Frankfurt and London. **Courier Travel** (above) also offers flights from London and Sydney.

STANDBY FLIGHTS

Traveling standby requires considerable flexibility in arrival and departure dates. Companies dealing in standby flights sell vouchers rather than tickets, along with the promise to get you to your destination (or near your destination) within a certain window of time (typically 1-5 days). You call in before your specific window of time to hear your flight options and the probability that you will be able to board each flight. You can then decide which flights you want to try to catch, show up at the appropriate airport at the appropriate time, present your voucher, and board if space is available. Vouchers can usually be bought for both one-way and round-trip travel. You may receive a monetary refund only if every available flight within your date range is full; if you opt not to take an available (but perhaps less convenient) flight, you can only get credit toward future travel. To check on a company's service record in the US, contact the **Better Business Bureau** (☎+1-703-276-0100; www. bbb.org). It is difficult to receive refunds, and clients' vouchers will not be honored when an airline fails to receive payment in time.

TICKET CONSOLIDATORS

Ticket consolidators, or **"bucket shops,"** buy unsold tickets in bulk from commercial airlines and sell them at discounted rates. The best place to look is in the Sunday travel section of any major newspaper (such as *The New York Times*), where many bucket shops place tiny ads. Call quickly, as availability is extremely limited. Not all bucket shops are reliable, so insist on a receipt that gives full details of restrictions, refunds, and tickets and pay by credit card (in spite of the 2-5% fee) so you can stop payment if you never receive your tickets. For more info, see www.travel-library.com/air-travel/consolidators.html.

TRAVELING FROM CANADA AND THE US

Some consolidators worth trying are **Rebel** (☎+1-800-732-3588; www.rebel-tours.com), **Cheap Tickets** (www.cheaptickets.com), **Flights.com** (www.flights.com), and **TravelHUB** (www.travelhub.com). *Let's Go* does not endorse any of these agencies. As always, be cautious and research companies before you hand over your credit-card number.

CHARTER FLIGHTS

Tour operators contract charter flights with airlines in order to fly extra loads of passengers during peak season. These flights are far from hassle-free. They occur less frequently than major airlines, make refunds particularly difficult, and are almost always fully booked. Their scheduled times may change, and they may be canceled at the last moment (as late as 48hr. before the trip, and without a full refund). In addition, check-in, boarding, and baggage claim for them are often much slower. They can, however, be much cheaper.

Discount clubs and fare brokers offer members savings on last-minute charter and tour deals. Study contracts closely; you don't want to end up with an unwanted overnight layover. **Travelers Advantage** (☎+1-800-835-8747; www.travelersadvantage.com; US$90 annual fee includes discounts and cheap flight directories) specializes in **European travel** and tour packages.

BY CHUNNEL FROM THE UK

Traversing 31 mi. under the sea, the Chunnel is undoubtedly the fastest, most convenient, and least scenic route from Britain to France.

Trains: Eurostar, Eurostar House, Waterloo Station, London SE1 8SE, UK (UK ☎08705 186 186, elsewhere +44 1233 617 575; www.eurostar.com). Frequent trains between London and the continent. Destinations include Paris, Disneyland Paris, Lille, Avignon, and Calais. Book online, at major rail stations in the UK, or at the office above.

Buses: Eurolines (www.eurolines.com) provides bus-ferry combinations to France (p. 35). Service to major cities in France, including Paris, Lyon, and Marseille.

Cars: Eurotunnel, Ashford Rd., Folkestone, Kent CT18 8XX, UK (☎+44 8705 35 35 35; www.eurotunnel.co.uk). Shuttles cars and passengers between Kent and Nord-Pas-de-Calais. Return fares range UK£50-200 for a car, depending on length of stay. Travelers with cars can also look into sea crossings by ferry (below).

BY BOAT FROM THE UK AND IRELAND

The fares below are one-way for adult foot passengers unless otherwise noted. Though standard return fares are usually just twice the one-way fare, fixed-period returns (usually within 5 days) are almost invariably cheaper. Ferries run year-round unless otherwise noted. Bikes are usually free, although you may have to pay up to UK£10 in high season. For a camper/trailer supplement, you will have to add UK£20-140 to the "with car" fare. If more than one price is quoted, the quote in pounds is valid for departures from the UK, etc. A directory of ferries in this region can be found at www.seaview.co.uk/ferries.html.

Brittany Ferries: France ☎08 25 82 88 28; UK 0871 244 0744, www.brittany-ferries. com. Plymouth to Roscoff (6hr.; in summer 1-3 per day, less frequent in low-season; UK£42-66). Portsmouth to St-Malo (10¾hr., 1 per day, UK£47-51) and Caen (5¾hr., 2-4 per day, UK£46-55). Poole to Cherbourg (4½hr., 2-3 per day, UK£42-66).

Irish Ferries: France ☎01 56 93 43 40, Ireland +353 818 300 400, UK +44 8705 17 17 17; www.irishferries.ie. Rosslare to Cherbourg and Roscoff (18½hr., €56-69).

P&O Ferries: France ☎08 25 12 01 56, UK +44 871 664 5645; www.posl.com. Dover to Calais (1½hr., 25 per day, from UK£14).

SeaFrance: France ☎08 25 04 40 45; UK +44 871 423 7119; www.seafrance.com. Dover to Calais (2¼hr., 15 per day, UK£12).

ESSENTIALS

GETTING AROUND FRANCE

Traveling by car, though more expensive, offers greater freedom to explore the countryside. In fact, many of the country's most popular monuments are inconvenient or expensive to reach by public transportation. France is blessed with a well-maintained and exceptionally complete network of roads. Nevertheless, traveling by train is probably the most comfortable—and often the most economical—way to get where you're going. France's system of high-speed and local trains connects all but the most minor towns. For those places unreachable by train, there is usually a bus system, though sometimes they can be unreliable. Fares are either *aller simple* (one-way) or *aller-retour* (round-trip). "Period returns" require you to return within a specific number of days; "day return" means you must return on the same day. Unless stated otherwise, *Let's Go* always lists single one-way fares. Round-trip fares on trains and buses in France are simply double the one-way fare.

BY PLANE

COMMERCIAL AIRLINES

For small-scale travel on the continent, *Let's Go* suggests ✈budget airlines (p. 28) for budget travelers, but more traditional carriers have made efforts to keep up with the revolution. The **Star Alliance Europe Airpass** offers economy-class fares as low as US$65 for travel within Europe to 216 destinations in 44 countries. The pass is available to non-European passengers on Star Alliance carriers, including **Air France** and **AirCorsica**. See www.staralliance. com for more information. In addition, a number of European airlines offer discount coupon packets. Most are only available as tack-ons for transatlantic passengers, but some are stand-alone offers. Most must be purchased before departure, so research in advance.

EuropeByAir: ☎+1-888-321-4737; www.europebyair.com. FlightPass allows you to hop between 500 cities in Europe and North Africa. Most flights US$99.

Iberia: ☎+1-800-772-4642; www.iberia.com. EuroPass allows Iberia passengers flying from the US to France to tack on a minimum of 2 additional destinations in Europe. US$125-155 each.

BUDGET AIRLINES

The emergence of no-frills airlines has made hopscotching around Europe by air increasingly affordable. Though these flights often feature inconvenient hours or serve less popular regional airports, with ticket prices often dipping into single digits, it's never been faster or easier to jet across the continent. The following resources will be useful not only for crisscrossing France but also for those ever-popular weekend trips to nearby international destinations.

easyJet: ☎+44 871 244 2366, 10p per min.; www.easyjet.com. From Bordeaux to Lyon and between other cities in France.

Ryanair: Ireland ☎0818 30 30 30, UK 0871 246 0000; www.ryanair.com. From Paris to Porto and other destinations in France.

BY TRAIN

> **TRANSPORTATION LISTINGS: CENTER-OUT.** *Let's Go* employs the "center-out" principle for transportation listings: for each town, we describe only how to reach towns of similar or greater importance. If you're in a big city, information on reaching neighboring small towns will be in the small town listings themselves rather than in the big city.

Trains in France are generally comfortable, convenient, and reasonably swift. Second-class compartments, which seat from four to six people, are great places to meet fellow travelers. Trains, however, are not always safe; for safety tips, see **Personal Safety**, p. 20. For long trips, make sure you are on the correct car, as trains sometimes split at crossroads. Towns listed in parentheses on European train schedules require a train switch at the town listed immediately before the parentheses.

You can either buy a **railpass,** which allows unlimited travel within a region for a given period of time, or rely on buying individual **point-to-point** tickets as you go. Almost all countries give students or youths (usually defined as anyone under 26) direct discounts on regular domestic rail tickets, and many also sell a student or youth card that provides 20-50% off all fares for up to a year.

> **EVERYONE NEEDS VALIDATION.** In France, you must *composter* (validate) your ticket. Orange and yellow validation boxes can be found in every station, usually in front of the doors leading to the tracks, and you must have your ticket stamped with date and time by the machine before boarding the train.

RESERVATIONS. While seat reservations are required only for selected trains (usually on major lines), you are not guaranteed a seat without one (usually €3-20). You should strongly consider reserving in advance during peak holiday and tourist seasons (at the very latest, a few hours ahead). You will also have to purchase a **supplement** (€5-15) or special fare for high-speed or high-quality trains, including certain French TGVs. InterRail holders must also purchase supplements (€2-10) for many TGVs; supplements are often unnecessary for Eurail Pass and Europass holders.

OVERNIGHT TRAINS. On night trains, you won't waste valuable daylight hours traveling and you can avoid the hassle and expense of staying at a hotel. However, drawbacks include discomfort, sleepless nights, the lack of scenery, and, most importantly, safety concerns. **Sleeping accommodations** on trains differ from country to country, but typically you can either sleep upright in your seat (supplement about €4-6, if not free) or pay for a separate space. **Couchettes** (berths) typically have four to six seats per compartment (supplement about €10-20 per person); **sleepers** (beds) in private sleeping cars offer more privacy and comfort but are considerably more expensive (supplement €40-150). If you are using a railpass valid only for a restricted number of days, inspect train schedules to maximize the use of your pass: an overnight train or boat journey often uses up only one of your travel days if it departs after 7pm.

SHOULD YOU BUY A RAILPASS? Railpasses were conceived to allow you to jump on any train in Europe, go wherever you want whenever you want, and change your plans at will. In practice, it's not so simple. You still must stand in line to validate your pass, pay for supplements, and fork over cash for seat and couchette reservations. More importantly, railpasses don't always pay off. If you plan to spend extensive time on trains hopping between big cities, a railpass will probably be worth it. But in many cases, especially if you are under 26, point-to-point tickets may prove a cheaper option.

You may find it tough to make your railpass pay for itself in France, where train fares are reasonable and distances between destinations are relatively short. If, however, the total cost of your trips nears the price of the pass, the convenience of avoiding ticket lines may be worth the difference.

MULTINATIONAL RAILPASSES

EURAIL PASSES. Eurail is **valid** in France, as well as most of Western Europe, but **not valid** in the UK. **Eurail Global Passes,** valid for a consecutive given number of days, are best for those planning to spend extensive time on trains every few days. Global passes valid for any 10 or 15 (not necessarily consecutive) days within a two-month period are more cost-effective for those traveling longer distances less frequently. **Eurail Pass Saver** provides first-class travel for travelers in groups of two to five (prices are per person). **Eurail Pass Youth** provides parallel second-class perks for those under 26.

EURAIL GLOBAL PASSES	15 DAYS	21 DAYS	1 MONTH	2 MONTHS	3 MONTHS
Eurail Pass Adult	€503	€653	€810	€1145	€1413
Eurail Pass Saver	€426	€554	€688	€973	€1205
Eurail Pass Youth	€327	€423	€527	€745	€920

OTHER GLOBAL PASSES	10 DAYS IN 2 MONTHS	15 DAYS IN 2 MONTHS
Eurail Pass Adult	€594	€781
Eurail Pass Saver	€505	€665
Eurail Pass Youth	€387	€508

Passholders receive a timetable for major routes and a map with details on possible car-rental, hotel, and museum discounts. Passholders often also receive reduced fares or free passage on many bus and private railroad lines.

The **Eurail Select Pass** is a slimmed-down version of the Eurail Pass: it allows five, six, eight, 10, or 15 days of unlimited travel in any two-month period within three, four, or five bordering countries of 23 European nations. **Eurail Select Passes** (for individuals) and **Eurail Select Pass Saver** (for people traveling in groups of two to five) range from €319/270 per person (5 days, 3 countries) to €706/600 (15 days, 5 countries). The **Eurail Select Pass Youth** (2nd class) costs €207-459. You are entitled to the same freebies afforded by the Eurail Pass, but only when they are within or between countries that you have purchased.

SHOPPING AROUND FOR A EURAIL. Eurail Passes are designed by the EU itself and can be bought only by non-Europeans almost exclusively from non-European distributors. These passes must be sold at uniform prices determined by the EU. However, some travel agents tack on a handling fee, and others offer certain bonuses with purchase, so shop around. Also, keep in mind that pass prices usually go up each year, so, if you're planning to travel early in the year, you can save cash by purchasing before January 1 (you have 6 months from the purchase date to validate your pass in Europe).

It is best to buy your pass before leaving; only a few places in major European cities sell them, and at a marked-up price. You can get a replacement for a lost pass only if you have purchased insurance on it under the Pass Security Plan (€10). Eurail Passes are available through travel agents, student travel agencies like STA (p. 26), and **Rail Europe** (Canada ☎800-361-7245, US 888-382-7245; www.raileurope.com) or **Flight Centre** (US ☎866-967-5351; www.flightcentre.com). It is also possible to buy directly from Eurail's website, www.eurail.com. Shipping is free to North America, Australia, and New Zealand.

OTHER MULTINATIONAL PASSES. If your travels will be limited to one area, regional passes are often good values. Eurail offers regional passes to France and Germany, France and Italy, France and Spain, and France and Switzerland. Rail Europe offers all of the above in addition to a France and Benelux pass.

For those who have lived for at least six months in one of the European countries where **InterRail Passes** are valid, they prove an economical option. The InterRail Pass allows travel within 30 European countries (excluding the passholder's country of residence). The **Global Pass** is valid for a given number of days (not necessarily consecutive) within a 10-day to one-month period. (5 days within 10 days adult 1st class €329, adult 2nd class €249, youth 2nd class €159; 10 days within 22 days €489/359/239; 22 days continuous €629/469/309; 1 month continuous €809/599/399.) The **One Country Pass** limits travel within one European country. Passholders receive free admission to many museums as well as **discounts** on accommodations, food, and some ferries. Passes are available at www.interrailnet.com as well as from travel agents, at major train stations throughout Europe, and through online vendors (such as www.railpassdirect.co.uk).

DOMESTIC RAILPASSES

Although Eurail and its brethren are great if you're spending some time out of France, a railpass on a smaller scale may be what you need for purely domestic travel. A national pass—valid on all rail lines of a country's rail company—is sometimes more cost-effective than a multinational pass. However, many national passes are limited and don't provide the free or discounted travel on private railways and ferries that Eurail does. Some of these passes can be bought only in Europe, some only outside of Europe; check with a railpass agent or with national tourist offices.

NATIONAL RAILPASSES. The domestic analogs of the Eurail Pass, national railpasses are valid either for a number of consecutive days or for a specific number of days within a given time period. Usually, they must be purchased before you leave. The basic **France Railpass** (US$278-328) provides travelers with three days of unlimited train travel in one month. The **France Saverpass** (US$240-279) offers the same perks for people traveling with groups of two or more. Finally, the **France Day Railpass** (US$115-165) provides travelers with the opportunity to venture from Paris on daytrips to big cities like Lyon or Marseille. Senior and youth passes are also available. For more information on national railpasses, check out www.raileurope.com/us/rail/passes/france_index.htm.

RAIL-AND-DRIVE PASSES. In addition to simple railpasses, France (as well as Eurail) offers rail-and-drive passes, which combine car rental with rail travel— a good option for travelers who wish both to visit cities accessible by rail and to make side trips into the surrounding areas. Prices range US$348-784, depending on the type of pass, type of car, and number of people included. Additional days cost US$58-142 each (see **By Car**, p. 35).

> **FURTHER READING AND RESOURCES ON TRAIN TRAVEL**
> **Info on rail travel and railpasses:** www.raileurope.com.
> **Point-to-point fares and schedules:** www.raileurope.com/us/rail/fares_schedules/index.htm. Allows you to calculate whether buying a railpass would save you money.
> **Railsaver:** www.railpass.com/new. Uses your itinerary to calculate the best railpass for your trip.
> **European Railway Server:** www.railfaneurope.net. Links to rail servers throughout Europe.
> **Thomas Cook European Timetable,** updated monthly, covers all major and most minor train routes in Europe. Buy directly from Thomas Cook (www.thomascooktimetables.com).

BY BUS

European trains and railpasses are extremely popular, but in some cases buses prove to be the only option. Traveling by bus is generally inconvenient in France and typically only useful for short trips between destinations that are not served by train lines. However, **international bus passes** are often cheaper than railpasses and allow unlimited travel on a hop-on, hop-off basis between major European cities. The prices below are based on high-season travel.

Busabout, 258 Vauxhall Bridge Rd., London SW1V 1BS, UK (☎+44 20 7950 1661; www.busabout.com). Offers 3 interconnecting bus circuits covering 29 of Europe's best bus hubs. 1 circuit US$639, 2 circuits US$1069, 3 circuits US$1319.

Eurolines, 28 av. du Général de Gaulle, Paris (☎08 92 89 90 91; www.eurolines.com). The largest operator of Europe-wide coach services. Unlimited 15-day (high season €289, under 26 €238; mid-season €200/175; low season €178/150) and 30-day (high season €277/314; mid-season €276/226; low season €264/201) travel passes to 40 major European cities.

Ze Bus: ☎05 59 85 26 60; www.ze-bus.com. A hop-on, hop-off bus service that runs through western France. Stops include Paris, Cherbourg, Quiberon, La Rochelle, Biarritz, and smaller cities in between.

BY CAR

Cars offer speed, freedom, access to the countryside, and an escape from the town-to-town mentality of trains. Many places in France—especially many of the most popular tourist attractions, like the Loire châteaux or the D-Day beaches—are best reached by car. Other attractions can be reached in no other way. Although a single traveler won't save by renting a car, four usually will. If you can't decide between train and car travel, you may benefit from a combination of the two; Rail Europe and other railpass vendors offer rail-and-drive packages (p. 35). Fly-and-drive packages are also often available from travel agents or airline/rental agency partnerships.

Before setting off, know the laws of the countries in which you'll be driving (e.g., motorcycle drivers and passengers must wear helmets in France). For an informal primer on European road signs and conventions, check out www. travlang.com/signs. The **Association for Safe International Road Travel (ASIRT)**, 11769 Gainsborough Rd., Potomac, MD 20854, USA (☎+1-301-983-5252; www.asirt. org), can provide more specific information about road conditions. ASIRT considers road travel (by car or bus) to be relatively safe in France. French drivers, along with other Western Europeans, use unleaded gas almost exclusively.

DRIVING PERMITS AND CAR INSURANCE

INTERNATIONAL DRIVING PERMIT (IDP)

If you plan to drive a car while in France, you must be over 18 and have a recognized driver's license. French law allows travelers to drive with a valid American or Canadian license for a year, but an **International Driving Permit (IDP)** is also sufficient. It is helpful to have an IDP in case you're in a situation (e.g., an accident or stranded in a small town) where the police do not speak English; information on the IDP is printed in 11 languages, including French.

Your IDP, valid for one year, must be issued in your own country before you depart. An application for an IDP usually requires one or two photos, a current local license, an additional form of identification, and a fee. To apply, contact your home country's automobile association. Be vigilant when purchasing an IDP online or anywhere other than your home automobile association. Many vendors sell permits of questionable legitimacy for higher prices.

CAR INSURANCE

Most credit cards cover standard insurance. If you rent, lease, or borrow a car, you will need a **green card,** or **International Insurance Certificate,** to certify that you have liability insurance and that it applies abroad. Green cards can be obtained at car-rental agencies, car dealers (for those leasing cars), some travel agents, and some border crossings. Rental agencies may require you to purchase theft insurance in countries that they consider to have a high risk of auto theft.

RENTING A CAR

You can rent a car from a US-based firm (Alamo, Avis, Budget, or Hertz) with European offices, from a European-based company with local representatives (Europcar), or from a tour operator (Auto Europe, Europe By Car, and Kemwel Holiday Autos) that will arrange a rental for you from a European company at its own rates. Multinationals offer greater flexibility, but tour operators often strike better deals. It is always significantly less expensive to reserve a car from the US than from Europe. Ask airlines about special fly-and-drive packages; you may get up to a week of free or discounted rental. Expect to pay €120-350 per week, plus tax (about 20%), for a tiny car. Reserve ahead and pay in advance if at all possible. Always check if prices quoted include tax and collision insurance; some credit-card companies provide insurance, allowing their customers to decline the collision damage waiver. Ask about discounts and check the terms of insurance, particularly the size of the deductible. The minimum rental age in France is usually 21, and drivers under 25 may have to pay a young-driver insurance fee. At most agencies, all that's needed to rent a car is an International Driving Permit or recognized license and proof that you've had it for a year. A credit card, or additional personal identification, is sometimes also necessary.

Remember that, if you are driving a conventional rental vehicle on an unpaved road in a rental car, you are almost never covered by insurance; ask about this before leaving the rental agency. Be aware that cars rented on an **American Express** or **Visa/MasterCard Gold** or **Platinum** credit card in France might not carry the automatic insurance that they would in some other countries; check with your credit-card company. Insurance plans from rental companies almost always come with an **excess** of around US$5-15 per day for conventional vehicles. This means that the insurance bought from the rental company only applies to damages over the excess; damages up to that amount must be covered by your existing insurance. Many rental companies in France require you to buy a **Collision Damage Waiver (CDW)**, which will waive the excess in case of collision. **Loss Damage Waivers (LDWs)** do the same in case of theft or vandalism.

National chains often allow one-way rentals (picking up in one city and dropping off in another). There is usually a minimum hire period and sometimes an extra dropoff charge of several hundred dollars. Car rental in France is available through the following agencies:

Alamo (US ☎800-462-5266; www.alamo.com).

Auto Europe (☎+1-888-223-5555 or 207-842-2000; www.autoeurope.com).

Avis (France ☎08 20 05 05 05; www.avis.com).

Budget (US ☎800-472-3325, UK ☎0870 156 5656; www.budgetrentacar.com).

Europe by Car (☎+1-800-223-1516 or 212-581-3040; www.europebycar.com).

Europcar International, 3 av. du Centre, 78881 Saint Quentin en Yvelines Cedex (France ☎01 30 43 82 82, UK ☎0870 607 5000; US 877-940-6900; www.europcar.com).

Hertz (☎+1-800-654-3001; www.hertz.com).

Kemwel (☎+1-877-820-0668 or 800-678-0678; www.kemwel.com).

LEASING A CAR

For longer than 17 days, leasing can be cheaper than renting; it is often the only option for those aged 18 to 21. The cheapest leases are agreements to buy the car and then sell it back to the manufacturer at a prearranged price. As far as you're concerned, though, it's a lease and doesn't entail enormous financial transactions. Leases generally include insurance coverage and are not taxed. Expect to pay around US$1900-2200 (depending on size of car) for 60 days. Contact Auto Europe, Europe by Car, or Kemwel (above) before you go.

BUYING A CAR

It is illegal for a person who does not reside in France to register, or therefore insure, an automobile in the country. However, if you do have a permanent residence in France, buying a car is an option. Check with consulates for import-export laws concerning used vehicles, registration information, and safety and emission standards.

ON THE ROAD

Seat-belt use is mandatory in cars, and motorcycle drivers and passengers must wear helmets. Children under 10 years old are not permitted to sit in the front passenger seat. French police can fine anyone who does not comply with these laws. Always carry your driver's license, a vehicle registration document, and proof of auto insurance on the road.

To receive directions, estimates of driving time, and toll and gas costs, check out www.iti.fr or www.prix-carburants.gouv.fr. *L'essence* (gasoline) prices vary, but they average about €1.60 per liter in cities and around €1.40 per liter in outlying areas. *L'essence* tends to be cheaper than *l'essence sans plomb* (unleaded fuel). Ask at a French Government Tourist Office for *la carte de l'essence moins chère*—a map of supermarkets close to highway exits, where gas is cheaper.

The Autoroute, or French highway system, has Paris as its hub. But the open road isn't necessarily free; blue signs reading *"péage"* indicate an approaching toll, so be sure to bring your wallet. Speed limits range from 110-130kph (68-81 mph) on the Autoroute.

DRIVING PRECAUTIONS. When traveling in the summer, bring substantial amounts of water (a suggested 5L of water per person per day) for drinking and for the radiator. You should always carry a spare tire and jack, jumper cables, extra oil, flares, a flashlight, and heavy blankets (in case your car breaks down at night or in the winter). If you don't know how to change a tire, learn before heading out, especially if you are planning on traveling in deserted areas. If your car breaks down, stay in your vehicle.

DANGERS

In France, the most dangerous aspects of driving include narrow streets, careless drivers, and high speed limits. Generally, the speed limits are 90-130kph (56-81 mph) on open roads and *autoroutes* and 50kph (30 mph) in towns. The French are known to make last-minute maneuvers and fail to yield the right of way, so beware. The legal blood-alcohol content limit is .05%, and driving under the influence remains a problem in France.

Exercise caution in mountainous regions, where roads can be narrow and unpaved as well as icy in winter. Almost all roads in Corsica are mountainous and narrow, so be extra vigilant about following the rules of the road. Most accidents occur during the tourist season, when streets are crowded with unfamiliar drivers. For more info on the driving conditions in France, see the website of **Bison Futé** (www.bison-fute.equipement.gouv.fr.), an organization geared toward reducing road congestion.

CAR ASSISTANCE

Many car rentals include 24hr. roadside assistance. If you find yourself in trouble on the Autoroute without such service, go to a nearby orange SOS phone. Dial ☎15 for an ambulance and ☎17 for the police.

BY BOAT

Most European ferries are comfortable; the cheapest ticket typically still includes a reclining chair or couchette. Fares jump sharply in July and August. Ask for discounts; ISIC holders can often get student fares, and Eurail Pass holders get many reductions and free trips. Ferries are an economical alternative to pricey flights to Corsica. **Corsica Ferries** (Toulon ☎04 92 00 42 93, Nice 04 94 41 11 89; www.corsica-ferries.co.uk) offers service to the island from Nice and Toulon. The 6hr. crossing costs €40-50. Sleepers are available for overnight traveling. Reservations are recommended, especially in July and August.

BY BICYCLE

With a mountain bike, you can do some serious natural sightseeing. Some airlines will count your bike as your second free piece of luggage; others charge extra (around US$80-160 one-way). Rules vary by airline, but usually bikes must be packed in a cardboard box with the pedals and front wheel detached; many airlines sell bike boxes at the airport (at least US$15). Most ferries let you take your bike for free or for a nominal fee, and you can always ship your bike on trains. Renting a bike beats bringing your own if you plan to stay in one or two regions. Some youth hostels rent bicycles for low prices. In addition to **panniers** (US$40-150) to hold your luggage, you'll need a good **helmet** (US$10-40) and a sturdy **lock** (from US$30). For more information on biking in France, try **Mountaineers Books,** 1001 SW Klickitat Way, Ste. 201, Seattle, WA 98134, USA (☎+1-206-223-6303; www.mountaineersbooks.org).

For those nervous about striking out on their own, **Blue Marble Travel** (Canada ☎519-624-2494, UK 0871 733 3148, US 215-923-3788; www.bluemarble. org) offers bike tours for small groups throughout Europe, including trips like "Burgundy Biking" in France. **CBT Tours** (☎+1-800-736-2453; www.cbttours.com) organizes full-package culinary, biking, and sightseeing tours (US$2200-3400) throughout France. It is also possible to create a custom-designed tour. Contact CBT Tours for more information.

HEADS UP! While avid cyclists, the French aren't always as keen on cycling safety. When renting a bike, you may have to insist on being given *un casque* (a helmet) and *un anti-vol* (a lock). Don't be afraid to stand your ground; even if helmets aren't legally required, most bike shops have a few in their back room waiting for "crazy" customers like you.

BY MOPED AND MOTORCYCLE

Mopeds and motorized bikes don't use much gas, can be put on trains and ferries, and are a good compromise between costly car travel and the limited range of bicycles. However, they're uncomfortable for long distances, dangerous in the rain, and unpredictable on rough roads. Always wear a helmet and never ride with a backpack. If you've never ridden a moped before, a twisting alpine road is not the place to start. Expect to pay about US$20-35 per day; try auto repair shops and remember to bargain. Motorcycles are more expensive and normally require a license, but they are better for long distances. Before renting, ask if the price includes tax and insurance, or else you may be hit with an unexpected fee. Avoid handing your passport over as a deposit; if you have an accident or mechanical failure, you may not get it back until you cover all repairs. Pay ahead of time instead.

BY THUMB

LET'S NOT GO. We strongly urge you to consider the risks before you choose to hitchhike. We do not recommend hitchhiking as a safe means of transportation, and none of the info presented here is intended to do so.

No one should hitch without careful consideration of the risks involved. Hitching means entrusting your life to a random person who happens to stop beside you on the road, and hitchers always risk theft, assault, sexual harassment, and unsafe driving. Some travelers report that hitchhiking allows them to meet local people and travel in areas where public transportation is sketchy. The choice, however, remains yours.

Hitchhiking at night can be particularly dangerous; experienced hitchers stand in well-lit places. For women traveling alone, hitching is just too dangerous. A man and a woman are a safer combination, two men will have a harder time, and three will go nowhere. Experienced hitchers pick a spot outside of built-up areas where drivers can stop, return to the road without causing an accident, and have time to look over potential passengers as they approach. Hitching (or even standing) on *autoroutes* is usually illegal: one may only thumb at rest stops or at highway entrance ramps. Finally, success will depend on appearance. Drivers prefer hitchers who are neat and wholesome-looking. It's fairly difficult to *faire de l'autostop* (hitchhike) in France, but the method of travel is mildly popular in Corsica—particularly along hiking routes.

Most Western European countries offer a ride service that pairs drivers with riders; the fee varies according to destination. **Eurostop** (www.taxistop.be/index_ils.htm), Taxistop's ride service, is one of the largest in Europe. **Allostop** (www.allostop.net) is another sizable ride service. Not all organization screen drivers and riders; ask in advance.

KEEPING IN TOUCH

BY EMAIL AND INTERNET

Internet access is readily available throughout France, and only the smallest towns lack Internet cafes. In larger towns, Internet cafes are widespread and well equipped—if expensive.

Although in some places it's possible to forge a remote link with your home server, in most cases this is a much slower (and thus more expensive) option than taking advantage of free **web-based email accounts** (e.g., 🖳www.gmail.com and www.hotmail.com). **Internet cafes** and the occasional free Internet terminal at a public library or university are listed in the **Practical Information** sections of major cities. For lists of additional cybercafes in France, check out www.cyber-captive.com, www.netcafeguide.com, or www.world66.com/netcafeguide.

Increasingly, travelers find that taking their **laptop computers** on the road with them can be a convenient option for staying connected. Laptop users can call an Internet service provider via a modem using long-distance phone cards specifically intended for such calls. They may also find Internet cafes that allow them to connect their laptops to the Internet. Lucky travelers with wireless-enabled computers may be able to take advantage of an increasing number of Internet "hot spots," where they can get online for free or for a small fee. Newer computers can detect these hot spots automatically; otherwise, websites like www.jiwire.com, www.wififreespot.com, and www.wi-fihotspotlist.com can help you find them.

WARY WI-FI. Wireless hot spots make Internet access possible in public and remote places. Unfortunately, they also pose **security risks.** Hot spots are public, open networks that use unencrypted, unsecured connections. They are susceptible to hacks and "packet sniffing"—ways of stealing passwords and other private information. To prevent problems, disable ad hoc mode, turn off file sharing and network discovery, encrypt your email, turn on your firewall, beware of phony networks, and watch for over-the-shoulder creeps.

ESSENTIALS

BY TELEPHONE

CALLING HOME FROM FRANCE

Télécartes (prepaid phone cards) are a common and relatively inexpensive means of calling abroad. Each one comes with a Personal Identification Number (PIN) and a toll-free access number. You call the access number and then follow the directions for dialing your PIN. To purchase prepaid phone cards, check online for the best rates; www.callingcards.com is a good place to start. Online providers generally send your access number and PIN via email, with no actual "card" involved. You can also call home with prepaid phone cards purchased in France (see **Calling Within France**, p. 42).

PLACING INTERNATIONAL CALLS. To call France from home or to call home from France, dial:

1. The **international dialing prefix.** To call from **Australia,** dial 0011; **Canada** or the **US,** 011; **Ireland, New Zealand,** the **UK,** or **France,** 00.
2. The **country code** of the country you want to call. To call **Australia,** dial 61; **Canada** or the **US,** 1; **Ireland,** 353; **New Zealand,** 64; the **UK,** 44; **France,** 33.
3. The **city/area code.** *Let's Go* lists the city/area codes for cities and towns in France opposite the city or town name, next to a ☎, as well as in every phone number. If the first digit is a zero (e.g., 01 for Paris), omit the zero when calling from abroad (e.g., dial 1 from Canada to reach Paris).
4. The **local number.**

Another option is to purchase a **calling card,** linked to a major national telecommunications service in your home country. Calls are billed collect or to your account. To call home with a calling card, contact the operator for your service provider in France by dialing the appropriate toll-free access number (listed below in the third column).

COMPANY	TO OBTAIN A CARD:	TO CALL ABROAD:
AT&T (US)	☎+1-800-364-9292 or www.att.com	☎0800 99 00 11
Canada Direct	☎+1-800-561-8868 or www.infocanadadirect.com	☎0800 99 00 16 or 0800 99 02 16
MCI (US)	☎+1-800-777-5000 or www.minutepass.com	☎0800 99 00 19
Telecom New Zealand Direct	www.telecom.co.nz	☎0800 99 00 64
Telstra Australia	☎+1-800 676 638 or www.telstra.com	☎0800 99 00 61

Placing a collect call through an international operator can be expensive but may be necessary in case of an emergency. You can frequently call collect without even possessing a company's calling card just by calling its access number and following the instructions.

CALLING WITHIN FRANCE

A simple way to make domestic or international calls is to use a card-operated pay phone. *Télécartes* carry a certain amount of phone time depending on the card's denomination. These cards are usually the only way to pay at public phones, as coin-operated phones have largely been phased out. *Télécartes* are available in denominations of units; 120-unit cards cost about €24, and one minute of a local call uses about one unit. Emergency numbers, directory information (☎118 218), and *numéros verts* (toll-free numbers) beginning with ☎0800 can be dialed without a card. A bank card can often be used instead of a calling card at many public phones.

If the phone you use does not provide English commands, proceed with caution; French pay phones are notoriously unforgiving. *Décrochez* means pick up; *patientez* means wait. Do not dial until you hear *numérotez* or *composez*. *Raccrochez* means "hang up." To make another call, press the green button instead of hanging up. Phone rates tend to be highest in the morning, lower in the evening, and lowest on Sunday and late at night.

CABINE CALLBACK. Making international calls from France is easy— but getting the best deal on the dizzying array of phone cards offered at *tabacs* and post offices is anything but. While the spiffy *cabines* (public phone booths) that sit on most major streets have slots in which to insert a *télécarte* with a microchip, this is the most expensive way to call internationally. Savvy travelers ask for a *carte téléphonique internationale* at a *tabac*. These cards have a hidden trick that gets you more minutes: *cabine* callback. When using a non-*télécarte* phone card, don't dial the large, obvious four-digit number marked "free" on the instructions. Instead, when using a *cabine*, dial the smaller, less obvious 0800 number labelled "cabine callback" or just "callback." An automated voice will tell you, in French, to hang up. Do so, and in a minute or so the phone will ring. Pick up and dial your PIN and the number you're calling. It's a bit tedious, but this method will save you precious phone-card minutes otherwise wasted entering your PIN and dialing.

CELLULAR PHONES

If you plan to stay in France for several months, buying a French cell phone is worth the cost. Incoming calls to cell phones are often free (even from abroad), and local calls are usually charged the local rate. The cheapest phones are relatively inexpensive (from €60, but as low as €1 with certain plans), and French phones do not require a long-term plans. **Orange** and **SFR** generally provide the best deals and reception. Cell-phone calls can be paid for without signing a contract if you purchase a **Mobicarte** prepaid card.

The international standard for cell phones is **Global System for Mobile Communication** (GSM). To make and receive calls in France, you will need a GSM-compatible phone and a **SIM (Subscriber Identity Module) card,** a country-specific, thumbnail-size chip that gives you a local phone number and plugs you into the local network. Many SIM cards are prepaid, and incoming calls are frequently free. You can buy additional cards or vouchers (usually available at convenience stores) to "top up" your phone. For more information on GSM phones, check out www.telestial.com, www.orange.fr, www.roadpost.com, or www.planetomni.com. Companies like **Cellular Abroad** (www.cellularabroad. com) rent cell phones that work in a variety of destinations around the world.

> **TIP**
>
> **GSM PHONES.** Just having a GSM phone doesn't mean you're necessarily good to go when you travel abroad. The majority of GSM phones sold in the US operate on a different frequency (1900) than international phones (900/1800) and will not work abroad. Tri-band phones work on all three frequencies (900/1800/1900) and will operate through most of the world. Additionally, some GSM phones are SIM-locked and will only accept SIM cards from a single carrier. You'll need a SIM-unlocked phone to use a SIM card from a local carrier when you travel.

Check with your service provider to see if your phone's band can be switched to 900/1800, which will register your phone with one of the three French servers: **Bouyges** (www.bouygtel.com), **Itineris** (www.ifrance.com/binto/itineris. htm), or **France Télécom** (www.agence.francetelecom.com).

TIME DIFFERENCES

France is usually 1hr. ahead of Greenwich Mean Time (GMT) and observes Daylight Saving Time (when it is 2hr. ahead) from March to October.

3AM	4AM	5AM	6AM	11AM	NOON	9PM*
Vancouver Seattle San Francisco Los Angeles	Denver	Chicago	Lima New York Toronto	London	**PARIS**	Sydney Canberra Melbourne

*Note that Australia observes Daylight Saving Time from October to March, the Northern Hemisphere's opposite. Thus, it is 8hr. ahead of Paris from March to October and 10hr. ahead from october to March, for an average of 9hr.

BY MAIL

SENDING MAIL HOME FROM FRANCE

Airmail is the best way to send mail home from France. **Aerogrammes,** printed sheets that fold into envelopes and travel via airmail, are available at post offices. Write "airmail" or *"par avion"* on the front. Most post offices will charge exorbitant fees or simply refuse to send aerogrammes with enclosures. Surface mail is by far the cheapest and slowest way to send mail. It takes one to two months to cross the Atlantic and one to three to cross the Pacific—good for heavy items you won't need for a while, such as souvenirs that you've acquired along the way.

SENDING MAIL TO FRANCE

To ensure timely delivery, mark envelopes "airmail" or *"par avion."* In addition to the standard postage system, **Federal Express** (Australia ☎ +61 13 26 10, Canada and the US +1-800-463-3339, Ireland +353 800 535 800, New Zealand +64 800 733 339, the UK +44 8456 070 809; www.fedex.com) handles express mail services from most countries to France. Sending a postcard within France costs €0.20, while sending letters (up to 20g) domestically requires €0.54.

There are several ways to arrange pickup of letters sent to you while you are abroad. Mail can be sent via **Poste Restante** (General Delivery) to almost any city or town in France with a post office, but it is not very reliable. Address Poste Restante letters like so:

Napoleon BONAPARTE
Poste Restante
20000, Ajaccio
FRANCE

The mail will go to a special desk in the central post office, unless you specify a post office by street address or postal code. It's best to use the largest post office, since mail may be sent there regardless. It is usually safer and quicker, though more expensive, to send mail express or registered. Bring your passport (or other photo ID) for pickup; there may be a small fee. If the clerks insist that there is nothing for you, ask them to check under your first name as well. *Let's Go* lists post offices in the **Practical Information** section for each city.

American Express's travel offices throughout the world offer a free **Client Letter Service** (mail held up to 30 days and forwarded upon request) for cardholders who contact them in advance. Some offices provide these services to non-cardholders (especially AmEx Travelers Cheque holders), but call ahead to make sure. For a complete list of AmEx locations, call ☎ +1-800-528-4800 or visit www.americanexpress.com/travel.

 PARIS POST. Parisian *codes postales* (postal codes) start with 750 and end with the arrondissement number. That is, 75001 is the code for the 1er, 75002 is the code for the 2ème, and so on.

ACCOMMODATIONS

HOSTELS

Many hostels are laid out dorm-style, often with large single-sex rooms and bunk beds, although private rooms that sleep two to four are becoming more common. They sometimes have kitchens and utensils for your use, bike or moped rentals, storage areas, transportation to airports, breakfast and other meals, laundry facilities, and Internet. However, there can be drawbacks: some hostels close during certain daytime "lockout" hours, have a curfew, don't accept reservations, impose a maximum stay, or, less frequently, require that you do chores. In France, a dorm bed in a hostel will average around €10-25 and a private room around €20-80.

 A HOSTELER'S BILL OF RIGHTS. There are certain standard features that we do not include in our hostel listings. Unless we state otherwise, you can expect that every hostel has no lockout, no curfew, free hot showers, some system of secure luggage storage, and no key deposit.

HOSTELLING INTERNATIONAL

Joining the youth hostel association in your own country (listed below) automatically grants you membership privileges in **Hostelling International (HI)**, a federation of national hosteling associations. Non-HI members may be allowed to stay in some hostels, but they will have to pay extra to do so. HI hostels are scattered throughout France and are typically less expensive than private hostels. HI's umbrella organization's website (www.hihostels.com), which lists the web addresses and phone numbers of all national associations, can be a great place to begin researching hosteling in a specific region. Other comprehensive hosteling websites include www.hostels.com and www.hostelplanet.com.

Most HI hostels also honor **guest memberships**—you'll get a blank card with space for six validation stamps. Each night you'll pay a nonmember supplement (one-sixth the membership fee) and earn one guest stamp; six stamps make you a member. This system works well in most of France, but sometimes you may need to remind the hostel reception. A new membership benefit is the FreeNites program, which allows hostelers to gain points toward free rooms. Most student travel agencies (p. 26) sell HI cards, as do all of the national hosteling organizations listed below. All prices listed below are valid for one-year memberships unless otherwise noted.

Australian Youth Hostels Association (AYHA), 422 Kent St., Sydney, NSW 2000 (☎+61 2 9261 1111; www.yha.com.au). AUS$52, under 18 AUS$19.

Hostelling International-Canada (HI-C), 205 Catherine St., Ste. 400, Ottawa, ON K2P 1C3 (☎+1-613-237-7884; www.hihostels.ca). CDN$35, under 18 free.

Hostelling International Northern Ireland (HINI), 22-32 Donegall Rd., Belfast BT12 5JN (☎+44 28 9032 4733; www.hini.org.uk). UK£15, under 25 UK£10.

Youth Hostels Association of New Zealand Inc. (YHANZ), Level 1, 166 Moorhouse Ave., P.O. Box 436, Christchurch (☎+64 3 379 9970, in NZ 0800 278 299; www.yha.org.nz). NZ$40, under 18 free.

Youth Hostels Association (England and Wales), Trevelyan House, Dimple Rd., Matlock, Derbyshire DE4 3YH (☎+44 8707 708 868; www.yha.org.uk). UK£16, under 26 UK£10.

Hostelling International-USA, 8401 Colesville Rd., Ste. 600, Silver Spring, MD 20910 (☎+1-301-495-1240; www.hiayh.org). US$28, under 18 free.

HOTELS, GUESTHOUSES, AND PENSIONS

Hotel singles in France cost about €30 per night, doubles €45. All accredited hotels are ranked on a four-star system by the French government according to factors such as room size, facilities, and plumbing. You'll typically share a hall bathroom; a private bathroom or a shower with hot water may cost extra. If you want a double with two twin beds instead of one double, ask for *une chambre avec deux lits.* Some hotels offer *pension complet* (all meals) and *demi pension* (no lunch). Smaller guesthouses and pensions are often cheaper than hotels. If you make **reservations** in writing, indicate your night of arrival and the number of nights you plan to stay. The hotel will send you a confirmation and may request payment for the first night. It is most often easiest to make reservations over the phone or online with a credit card.

Hotels listed in the **Accommodations** section for each town or city in *Let's Go* are generally small, family-run establishments close to sights of interest. *Let's Go* doesn't list budget chains like Hôtels Formule 1, Etaps Hôtel, and Hôtels Première Classe, which can usually be found on the outskirts of town. They typically charge about €30-40 for one- to three-person rooms with sink, TV, hall showers, toilets, and telephones and are sometimes the cheapest—though least charming—option.

OTHER TYPES OF ACCOMMODATIONS

BED AND BREAKFASTS (B&BS)

For a cozy alternative to impersonal hotel rooms, B&Bs (private homes with rooms available to travelers) range from acceptable to sublime. Rooms in B&Bs generally cost €30-35 for a single and €40-45 for a double in France. Many websites provide listings for B&Bs; check out **InnFinder** (www.inncrawler. com), **InnSite** (www.innsite.com), **BedandBreakfast.com** (www.bedandbreakfast. com), **Pamela Lanier's Bed & Breakfast Guide Online** (www.lanierbb.com), or **BNB-Finder.com** (www.bnbfinder.com).

CHAMBRES D'HÔTE. France's *chambres d'hôte* (bed and breakfasts) give you the chance to stay with local families. Organized through the **Gîtes de France,** *chambres d'hôte,* or *fermes auberges* (if they are located on a working farm), provide an unparalleled glimpse into French culture. Many offer *tables d'hôte,* where guests are served a full French-style dinner with the hosts. Check tourist offices for listings of *chambres d'hôte* in the region.

UNIVERSITY DORMS

Many **colleges** and **universities** open their residence halls to travelers when school is not in session; some do so even during term time. Getting a room may take a couple of phone calls and require advanced planning, but rates tend to be low, and many offer free local calls and Internet access. For information on universities in France, consult the following source:

Centre National des Oeuvres Universitaires et Scolaires (CNOUS), 69 quai d'Orsay, 75007 Paris (☎01 44 18 53 00; www.cnous.fr). A regional guide of universities and lodgings throughout France available on the website, under "La Vie Etudiante: Logement." Click on "Carte des Cités U" at the bottom.

YMCAS AND YWCAS

Young Men's Christian Association (YMCA) and **Young Women's Christian Association (YWCA)** lodgings are usually cheaper than a hotel but more expensive than a hostel. Not all 30 French locations offer lodging; those that do are often located in urban areas. Many YMCAs accept women and families; some will not lodge those under 18 without parental permission.

World Alliance of YMCAs, 12 Clos Belmont, 1208 Geneva, Switzerland (☎+41 22 849 5100; www.ymca.int). Search "France" to get info on locations and programming.

HOME EXCHANGES AND HOSPITALITY CLUBS

Home exchange offers the traveler various types of homes (houses, apartments, condominiums, villas, even castles in some cases), plus the opportunity to live like a native and to cut down on accommodation fees. For more info, contact **HomeExchange.com Inc.,** P.O. Box 787, Hermosa Beach, CA 90254, USA (☎+1-310-798-3864 or toll-free 800-877-8723; www.homeexchange.com) or **Intervac International Home Exchange** (☎08 20 88 83 42; www.intervac.com).

Hospitality clubs link their members with individuals or families abroad who are willing to host travelers for free or for a small fee to promote cultural exchange and general good karma. In exchange, members usually must be willing to host travelers in their own homes; a small fee may also be required. **The Hospitality Club** (www.hospitalityclub.org) is a good place to start. **Servas** (www.servas.org) is an established, more formal, peace-based organization and requires a fee and an interview to join. An Internet search will find many similar organizations, some of which cater to special interests (e.g., women, GLBT travelers, or members of certain professions). As always, use common sense when planning to stay with or host someone you do not know.

LONG-TERM ACCOMMODATIONS

Travelers planning to stay in France for extended periods of time may find it most cost-effective to rent an **apartment.** A basic one-bedroom (or studio) apartment in Paris will range €500-1500 per month. Besides the rent itself, prospective tenants are usually required to front a security deposit (frequently 1 month's rent). Apartment hunters should be aware that landlords will often demand proof of income and a cosigner before agreeing to rent a space.

A good place to check for apartments is **craigslist** (www.craigslist.org), a forum for renters and rentees where you can see others' listings. You may have more success if you post your own housing needs and allow renters to contact you. For apartments and houses to buy or rent throughout France, try **Go-To-France** (www.go-to-france.co.uk). The site also offers practical advice for prospective renters.

CAMPING

The French are avid campers but approach the outdoors in a civilized way. After 3000 years of settled history, there is little wilderness in France. Even if you find any, forget those romantic dreams of roughing it, unless your definition of "roughing it" involves a stint in jail—it is illegal to camp in public spaces or to light your own fires. Organized *campings* (campgrounds) are ranked on a four-star system and often include amenities such as bars, supermarkets, playgrounds, and swimming pools. Campgrounds generally charge separately for the use of their sites (€1.50-7 per site or tent) and for the number of people staying in them (€3-6 per person, less for children). Most campsites have toilets, showers, and electrical outlets, though often at extra expense (€2-5). Where relevant, campgrounds are listed at the end of the **Accommodations** section of towns in *Let's Go*. A comprehensive search by region or criteria of over 10,000 campgrounds in France can be found at www.campingfrance.com. Some campgrounds rent tents or RVs. For more information on outdoor activities in France, consult the following resources or see **The Great Outdoors,** below.

> **Sites & Paysages de France**, av. des Côteaux, 66140 Canet en Roussillon (☎08 20 20 46 46). Publishes a brochure featuring regional campsites and outdoor activities. *Camping and Caravaning Guide France* (Michelin Travel Publications, US$14).

THE GREAT OUTDOORS

The **Great Outdoor Recreation Page** (www.gorp.com) provides excellent general information for travelers planning on camping or enjoying the outdoors.

LEAVE NO TRACE. *Let's Go* encourages travelers to embrace the "Leave No Trace" ethic, minimizing their impact on natural environments and protecting them for future generations. Trekkers and wilderness enthusiasts should set up camp on durable surfaces, use cookstoves instead of campfires, bury human waste away from water supplies, bag trash and carry it out with them, and respect wildlife and natural objects. For more detailed information, contact the **Leave No Trace Center for Outdoor Ethics,** P.O. Box 997, Boulder, CO 80306, USA (☎+1-800-332-4100 or 303-442-8222; www.lnt.org).

USEFUL RESOURCES

A variety of publishing companies offer guidebooks to meet the educational needs of novice or expert hikers. For information about camping, hiking, and biking, write or call the publishers listed below to receive a free catalog. Campers heading to Europe should consider buying an **International Camping Carnet.** Similar to a hostel membership card, it's required at a few campgrounds and sometimes provides discounts. It is available in North America from the **Family Campers and RVers Association** and in the UK from **The Caravan Club** (below).

Automobile Association, Contact Centre, Lambert House, Stockport Rd., Cheadle SK8 2DY, UK (☎+44 8706 000 371; www.theaa.com). Publishes *Caravan and Camping Europe* (UK£10) as well as road atlases for Europe, Britain, France, Germany, Ireland, Italy, Spain, and the US.

Cool Camping, Punk Publishing Ltd. 3 The Yard, Pegasus Place, London SE11 5SD (☎+44 20 7820 9333; www.coolcamping.co.uk/). Publishes *Cool Camping: France* (UK£13.45).

The Caravan Club, East Grinstead House, East Grinstead, West Sussex, RH19 1UA, UK (☎+44 1342 326 944; www.caravanclub.co.uk). For UK£34, members receive access to sites, insurance services, equipment discounts, maps, and a monthly magazine.

The Mountaineers Books, 1001 SW Klickitat Way, Ste. 201, Seattle, WA 98134, USA (☎+1-206-223-6303; www.mountaineersbooks.org). Over 600 titles on hiking, biking, mountaineering, natural history, and conservation.

Sierra Club Books, 85 2nd St., 2nd fl., San Francisco, CA 94105, USA (☎+1-415-977-5500; www.sierraclub.org). Publishes general resource books on hiking and camping.

NATIONAL PARKS

France has a system of nine national parks, five of which are on the French mainland (Les Cévennes, Les Ecrins, Le Mercantour, Les Pyrénées, and La Vanoise), three in French territories (La Guadeloupe, Réunion, and Parc Amazonien en Guyane), and one off France's southern coast (Port-Cros). National parks make up 0.7% of France's overall area and draw over seven million visitors each year. Check out the extensive **www.parcsnationaux-fr.com** for helpful information in multiple languages. All national parks have visitors centers with knowledgeable staff; be sure to stop at them before setting out on strenuous hikes. Most parks have camping areas and many have *gîtes*, for those who prefer not to rough it. France also has numerous locally run *parcs naturels régionaux* (regional parks) and *réserves naturelles* (natural reserves). For more info on France's parks and reserves, check out www.parcs-naturels-regionaux.fr, www.reserves-naturelles.org, and www.espaces-naturels.fr.

WILDERNESS SAFETY

Staying **warm, dry,** and **well hydrated** is key to a happy and safe wilderness experience. For any hike, prepare yourself for an emergency by packing a first-aid kit, a reflector, a whistle, high-energy food, extra water, raingear, a hat, mittens, and extra socks. For warmth, wear wool or insulating synthetic materials designed for the outdoors.

Check weather forecasts often and pay attention to the skies when hiking, as weather patterns can change suddenly. Always let someone—a friend, your hostel, or a park ranger—know when and where you are going. See **Safety and Health,** p. 19, for information on outdoor medical concerns.

See **Safety and Health,** p. 19,

CAMPING AND HIKING EQUIPMENT

WHAT TO BUY

Good camping equipment is both sturdy and light. North American suppliers tend to offer the most competitive prices.

Sleeping Bags: Most sleeping bags are rated by season; "summer" means 30-40°F (around 0°C) at night; "4-season" or "winter" often means below 0°F (-17°C). Bags are made of **down** (warm and light, but expensive, and miserable when wet) or of **synthetic** material (heavy, durable, and warm when wet). Prices range from US$50-250 for a summer synthetic to US$200-300 for a good down winter bag. **Sleeping bag pads** include foam pads (US$10-30), air mattresses (US$15-50), and self-inflating mats (US$30-120). Bring a **stuff sack** to store your bag and keep it dry.

Tents: The best tents are freestanding (with their own frames and suspension systems), set up quickly, and only require staking in high winds. Low-profile dome tents are the best all around. Worthy 2-person tents start at US$100, 4-person tents at US$160. Make sure yours has a rain fly and seal its seams with waterproofer. Other useful accessories include a **battery-operated lantern,** a plastic **ground cloth,** and a nylon **tarp.**

Backpacks: Internal-frame packs mold well to your back, keep a lower center of gravity, and flex adequately to allow you to hike difficult trails, while **external-frame** packs are more comfortable for long hikes over even terrain, as they carry weight higher and distribute it more evenly. Make sure your pack has a strong, padded hip belt to transfer weight to your legs. There are models designed specifically for women. Any serious backpacking requires a pack of at least 4000 cu. in. (16,000cc), plus 500 cu. in. for sleeping bags in internal-frame packs. Sturdy backpacks cost anywhere from US$125 to US$420—your pack is an area where it doesn't pay to economize. On your hunt for the perfect pack, fill up prospective models with something heavy, strap it on correctly, and walk around the store to get a sense of how the model distributes weight. Either buy a rain cover (US$10-20) or store all of your belongings in plastic bags inside your pack.

Boots: Be sure to wear hiking boots with good **ankle support.** They should fit snugly and comfortably over 1-2 pairs of **wool socks** and a pair of thin **liner socks.** Break in boots over several weeks before you go to spare yourself blisters.

Other Necessities: Synthetic layers, like those made of polypropylene or polyester, and a pile jacket will keep you warm even when wet. A **space blanket** (US$5-15) will help you to retain body heat and doubles as a **ground cloth.** Plastic **water bottles** are vital; look for shatter- and leak-resistant models. Carry **water-purification tablets** for when you can't boil water. Although most campgrounds provide campfire sites, you may want to bring a small **metal grate** or **grill.** For those places (including virtually every organized campground in France) that forbid fires or the gathering of firewood, you'll need a **camp stove** (starts at US$50) and a propane-filled fuel bottle to operate it. Also bring a **first-aid kit, pocketknife, insect repellent,** and **waterproof matches** or a **lighter.**

WHERE TO BUY IT

The online and mail-order companies listed below offer lower prices than many retail stores. A visit to a local camping or outdoors store will give you a good sense of the look and weight of certain items before you buy.

Campmor, 400 Corporate Dr., P.O. Box 680, Mahwah, NJ 07430, USA (☎+1-800-525-4784; www.campmor.com).

Cotswold Outdoor, Unit 11 Kemble Business Park, Crudwell, Malmesbury Wiltshire SN16 9SH, UK (☎+44 8704 427 755; www.cotswoldoutdoor.com).

Eastern Mountain Sports (EMS), 1 Vose Farm Rd., Peterborough, NH 03458, USA (☎+1-888-463-6367; www.ems.com).

L.L.Bean, Freeport, ME 04033, USA (US and Canada ☎800-441-5713, UK 0800 891 297; www.llbean.com).

Mountain Designs, 443A Nudgee Rd., Hendra, Queensland 4011, Australia (☎+61 7 3114 4300; www.mountaindesigns.com).

Recreational Equipment, Inc. (REI), Sumner, WA 98352, USA (US and Canada ☎800-426-4840, elsewhere +1-253-891-2500; www.rei.com).

CAMPERS AND RVS

Renting an RV costs more than tenting or hosteling but less than staying in hotels while renting a car (see **Rental Cars,** p. 36). The convenience of bringing along your own bedroom, bathroom, and kitchen makes RVing an attractive option, especially for older travelers and families with children.

Rates vary widely by region, season, and type of RV. Rental prices for a standard RV are around €1500 for 10 days, €2500 in high season (June-Aug.). See www.motorhomesworldwide.com for up-to-date quotes.

Auto Europe, 39 Commercial St., P.O. Box 7006, Portland, ME 04112, USA (☎+1-888-223-5555; www.autoeurope.com). Rents RVs in Marseille, Nice, and Paris.

ORGANIZED ADVENTURE TRIPS

Organized adventure tours offer another way of exploring the wild. Activities include hiking, biking, skiing, canoeing, kayaking, rafting, climbing, photo safaris, and archaeological digs. Tourism bureaus often can suggest parks, trails, and outfitters. Organizations that specialize in camping and outdoor equipment like REI and EMS (above) also are good sources for info.

Specialty Travel Index, P.O. Box 458, San Anselmo, CA 94979, USA (US ☎1-888-624-4030, elsewhere +1-415-455-1643; www.specialtytravel.com).

SPECIFIC CONCERNS

SUSTAINABLE TRAVEL

As the number of travelers on the road rises, the detrimental effect they can have on natural environments is an increasing concern. *Let's Go* promotes the philosophy of sustainable travel with this in mind. Through a sensitivity to issues of ecology and sustainability, today's travelers can be a powerful force in preserving and restoring the places they visit.

Ecotourism, a rising trend in sustainable travel, focuses on the conservation of natural habitats—mainly, on how to use them to build up the economy without exploitation or overdevelopment. Travelers can make a difference by doing advance research, by supporting organizations and establishments that pay attention to their carbon "footprint," and by patronizing establishments that strive to be environmentally friendly.

ECOTOURISM RESOURCES. For more information on environmentally responsible tourism, contact one of the organizations below:

Conservation International, 2011 Crystal Dr., Ste. 500, Arlington, VA 22202, USA (☎+1-800-406-2306 or 703-341-2400; www.conservation.org).

Green Globe 21, Green Globe vof, Verbenalaan 1, 2111 ZL Aerdenhout, the Netherlands (☎+31 23 544 0306; www.greenglobe.com).

International Ecotourism Society, 1333 H St. NW, Ste. 300E, Washington, DC 20005, USA (☎+1-202-347-9203; www.ecotourism.org).

United Nations Environment Program (UNEP), 39-43 Quai André Citroën, 75739 Paris Cedex 15 (☎01 44 37 14 50; www.uneptie.org/pc/tourism).

France has a wealth of resources for travelers interested in ecotourism that includes a growing number of green accommodations. National parks and the island of Corsica provide myriad opportunities for ecotourism. Sites like www.ecoclub.com and www.ecotourdirectory.com list up-to-date information on environmentally responsible travel, both in France and worldwide. For more France-specific information on ecotourism, check out the listings below or flip to **Beyond Tourism: Volunteering,** p. 82.

L'Association Française d'Ecotourisme (AFE), 31 rue des Filatiers, 31000 Toulouse (☎06 76 26 93 55; www.ecotourisme.info). Advice on ecotourism in France includes list of green accommodations and special environmentally friendly tours.

UNAT Tourisme Solidaire, 8 rue César Franck, 75015 Paris (☎01 47 83 21 73; www.unat.asso.fr) Helps travelers plan environmentally responsible trips to France.

Voyages Pour la Planète (☎05 61 23 22 59; www.voyagespourlaplanete.com). Lists eco-friendly accommodations and info for the environmentally conscious traveler.

RESPONSIBLE TRAVEL

Your tourist euros can make a big impact on the destinations you visit. The choices you make during your trip can have powerful effects on local communities—for better or for worse. Travelers who care about the destinations and environments they explore should make themselves aware of the social and cultural implications of the choices they make when they travel. Simple decisions such as buying local products, paying fair prices

ESSENTIALS

for products or services, and attempting to say a few words in the local language can have a strong, positive effect on the community.

Community-based tourism aims to channel tourist euro into the local economy by emphasizing tours and cultural programs that are run by members of the host community and that often benefit disadvantaged groups. This type of tourism also benefits the tourists themselves, as it often takes them beyond the traditional tours of the region. **Fugues en France,** 8 pl. de l'Hôtel de Ville, 21190 Mersault (☎03 80 21 71 18; www.bonappetit-france.com) provides extensive information on multilingual tours of vineyards and culinary centers in Bordeaux, Burgundy, and Provence. For more on French environmental concerns, see the French Institute for the Environment website (www.ifen.fr). The *Ethical Travel Guide* (UK£13), a project of **Tourism Concern** (☎+44 20 7133 3330; www.tourismconcern.org.uk), is an excellent resource for information on community-based travel, with a directory of 300 establishments in 60 countries.

TRAVELING ALONE

Traveling alone can be extremely beneficial, providing a sense of independence and a greater opportunity to connect with locals. On the other hand, solo travelers are more vulnerable targets of harassment and street theft. If you are traveling alone, look confident, try not to stand out as a tourist, and be especially careful in deserted or very crowded areas. Stay away from areas that are not well lit. If questioned, never admit that you are traveling alone. Maintain regular contact with someone at home who knows your itinerary and always research your destination before traveling. For more tips, pick up *Traveling Solo* by Eleanor Berman (Globe Pequot Press, US$18), visit www.travelaloneandloveit.com, or subscribe to **Connecting: Solo Travel Network,** 689 Park Rd., Unit 6, Gibsons, BC V0N 1V7, Canada (☎+1-604-886-9099; www.cstn.org; membership US$30-48).

WOMEN TRAVELERS

Women exploring on their own inevitably face some additional safety concerns. Single women can consider staying in hostels that offer single rooms that lock from the inside or in religious organizations with single-sex rooms. It's a good idea to stick to centrally located accommodations and to avoid solitary late-night treks or Métro rides.

Always carry extra cash for a phone call, bus, or taxi. **Hitchhiking** is never safe for lone women, or even for two women traveling together. Look as if you know where you're going and approach older women or couples for directions if you're lost or feeling uncomfortable in your surroundings. Generally, the less you look like a tourist, the better off you'll be. Dress conservatively, especially in rural areas. Wearing a conspicuous **wedding band** sometimes helps to prevent unwanted advances.

Young women in France will frequently face verbal harassment; while most of it is harmless, it can be very uncomfortable. Your best answer to verbal harassment is no answer at all; feigning deafness, sitting motionless, and staring straight ahead at nothing in particular will usually do the trick. The extremely persistent can sometimes be dissuaded by a firm, loud, and very public "Va-t-en!" (vah-ton; "Go away!" in French). Don't hesitate to seek out a police officer or a passerby—particularly an older woman—if you are being harassed. Memorize the emergency numbers in places you visit (police ☎17) and consider carrying a whistle on your keychain. A self-defense course will both prepare you for a potential attack and raise your level of awareness of your surroundings (see **Personal Safety,** p. 20). Also be sure you are aware of the health concerns that women face when traveling (p. 52).

GLBT TRAVELERS

France is fairly liberal toward gay, lesbian, bisexual, and transgendered travelers, and there are prominent gay and lesbian communities in Paris, Marseille, and other southern towns. In most larger cities, GLBT travelers are welcome and in good company. However, overt displays of sexual identity can evoke an unfriendly response in more remote regions of the country. To avoid hassles at airports and border crossings, transgendered travelers should make sure that all of their travel documents consistently report the same gender. Listed below are contact organizations, mail-order catalogs, and publishers that offer materials addressing some specific concerns. **Out and About** (www.planetout. com) offers a comprehensive website and a weekly newsletter addressing gay travel concerns. The online newspaper **365gay.com** also has a travel section (www.365gay.com/travel/travelchannel.htm).

Gay's the Word, 66 Marchmont St., London WC1N 1AB, UK (☎+44 20 7278 7654; http://freespace.virgin.net/gays.theword). The largest gay and lesbian bookshop in the UK, with both fiction and non-fiction titles. Mail-order service available.

Giovanni's Room, 345 S. 12th St., Philadelphia, PA 19107, USA (☎+1-215-923-2960; www.queerbooks.com). An international lesbian and gay bookstore with mail-order service (carries many of the publications listed below).

International Lesbian and Gay Association (ILGA), Avenue des Villas 34, 1060 Brussels, Belgium (☎+32 2 502 2471; www.ilga.org). Provides political information, such as homosexuality laws of individual countries.

ADDITIONAL RESOURCES: GLBT

Spartacus: International Gay Guide 2008. Bruno Gmunder Verlag (US$33).

Damron Men's Travel Guide, Damron Road Atlas, Damron Accommodations Guide, Damron City Guide, and *Damron Women's Traveller.* Damron Travel Guides (US$18-24). For info, call ☎+1-800-462-6654 or visit www.damron.com.

The Gay Vacation Guide: The Best Trips and How to Plan Them, by Mark Chesnut. Kensington Books (US$15).

Gayellow Pages USA/Canada, by Frances Green. Gayellow Pages (US$20). They also publish regional editions. Visit Gayellow pages online at http://gayellowpages.com.

TRAVELERS WITH DISABILITIES

The French Ministry of Tourism includes a branch called **Tourisme et Handicap,** 43 rue Marx Dormoy, 75018 Paris (☎01 44 11 10 41; www.tourisme-handicaps.com), which is devoted to providing information about access for disabled travelers at tourist sights and amenities in Paris and its suburbs. Disabled travelers can stay in France on a budget but may need to pay more than the average backpacker.

Those with disabilities should inform airlines and hotels of their disabilities when making reservations; some time may be needed to prepare special accommodations. Airports in France have published a guide for passengers with *mobilité réduite* (restricted mobility) that can be found at www.aeroportsdeparis.fr under the heading *"Départ."* Call ahead to restaurants, museums, and other facilities to find out if they are *accessible en chaise roulante* (wheelchair-accessible). Guide-dog owners should inquire as to the quarantine policies of each destination country.

Rail is probably the most convenient form of transport for disabled travelers in Europe: many stations have ramps, and some trains have wheelchair lifts, special seating areas, and specially equipped toilets. The French national railroad offers wheelchair compartments on all TGV (high-speed) and Conrail trains. All Eurostar, some InterCity (IC), and some EuroCity (EC) trains are wheelchair-accessible, and CityNightLine trains, French TGV, and Conrail trains feature special compartments. For those who wish to rent cars, some major **car-rental** agencies (e.g., Hertz) offer hand-controlled vehicles.

USEFUL ORGANIZATIONS

Accessible Journeys, 35 W. Sellers Ave., Ridley Park, PA 19078, USA (☎+1-800-846-4537; www.disabilitytravel.com). Designs tours for wheelchair users and slow walkers. The site has tips and forums for all travelers.

Flying Wheels Travel, 143 W. Bridge St., Owatonna, MN 55060, USA (☎+1-507-451-5005; www.flyingwheelstravel.com). Specializes in escorted trips to Europe for people with physical disabilities; plans custom trips worldwide.

Mobility International USA (MIUSA), P.O. Box 10767, Eugene, OR 97440, USA (☎+1-541-343-1284; www.miusa.org). Provides a variety of books and other publications containing information for travelers with disabilities.

Society for Accessible Travel and Hospitality (SATH), 347 5th Ave., Ste. 610, New York City, NY 10016, USA (☎+1-212-447-7284; www.sath.org). An advocacy group that publishes free online travel information. Annual membership (US$49, students and seniors US$29) buys access to members-only section of website as well as discounts with companies facilitating travel with disabilities.

MINORITY TRAVELERS

Like much of Europe, France has experienced a wave of immigration from former colonies in the past few decades. The Maghreb—an ethnic group composed of North Africans and Arabs—make up the greatest percentage of the immigrants, at over a million, followed by West Africans and Vietnamese. Many immigrants are uneducated and face discrimination, which leads to poverty and crime in the predominantly immigrant *banlieues* (suburbs). In the fall of 2005, riots swept France in retaliation for the deaths of two Parisian immigrant teenagers following an altercation with the police. In turn, there has been a surge of support for the far-right National Front party and its cry, *"La France pour les français."* Anyone who might be taken for a North African or a Muslim may encounter verbal abuse and is likelier than other travelers to be stopped and questioned by the police. Racism is especially prevalent in the southeast. The following organizations can give you advice and help in the event of an encounter with racism.

SOS Racisme, 51 av. de Flandre, 75019 Paris (☎01 40 35 36 55; www.sos-racisme.org). Provides legal services and helps negotiate with police.

Mouvement Contre le Racisme et Pour l'Amitié Entre les Peuples (MRAP), 43 bd. Magenta, 75010 Paris (☎01 53 38 99 99; www.mrap.asso.fr). Handles immigration issues; monitors publications and propaganda for racism.

DIETARY CONCERNS

While France is renowned for its food, this culinary empire is rather exclusive when it comes to those with special dietary requirements. Vegetarians will find few options when dining out, and vegans will find even fewer, while kosher diners will struggle outside large cities. Supermarkets are a savior, and the resources listed here can help lead you to restaurants that will be more accommodating to dietary restrictions.

The travel section of **The Vegetarian Resource Group's** website, at www.vrg.org/travel, has a comprehensive list of organizations and websites that are geared toward helping vegetarians and vegans traveling abroad. They also publish *Vegetarian France*, which can be purchased at www.vegetarian-guides.co.uk. For more information, visit your local bookstore or health-food store and consult *The Vegetarian Traveler: Where to Stay if You're Vegetarian, Vegan, Environmentally Sensitive,* by Jed and Susan Civic (Larson Publications; US$16). Vegetarians will also find numerous resources on the web; try www.vegelist.online.fr, which lists vegetarian restaurants and *chambres d'hôtes* in France, www.vegdining.com, www.happycow.net, and www.vegetariansabroad.com, for starters.

Lactose intolerance also does not have to be an obstacle to eating well in France. Though it may seem like everybody in France but you is devouring buttery croissants and *crèmes brulées*, there are ways for even the lactose intolerant to indulge in local cuisine. In restaurants, ask for items *sans lait* (milk), *fromage* (cheese), *beurre* (butter), or *crème* (cream).

Travelers who keep **kosher** should contact synagogues in larger cities for information on kosher restaurants. Your own synagogue or college Hillel should have access to lists of Jewish institutions across the nation. A useful worldwide kosher restaurant database with numerous listings in France is www.shamash.org/kosher. If you are strict in your observance, you may have to prepare your own food on the road. A good resource is the *Jewish Travel Guide*, edited by Michael Zaidner (Vallentine Mitchell; US$18). Travelers looking for **halal** restaurants may find www.zabihah.com a useful resource. Most large cities have a significant Muslim population and thus provide numerous halal dining opportunities.

OTHER RESOURCES

We try to cover all aspects of budget travel, but we can't put everything in our guides. Listed below are books and websites that can serve as jumping-off points for your own research.

USEFUL PUBLICATIONS

Au Contraire! Figuring Out the French, by Gilles Asselin. Intercultural Press, 2001 (US$28). Provides a look into subtle cultural patterns.

Culture Shock! France, by Sally Adamson Taylor. Marshall Cavendish, 2008 (US$16). Tips and warnings about France's cultural faux pas for travelers and expats.

WORLD WIDE WEB

Almost every aspect of budget travel is accessible via the web. In 10min. at the keyboard, you can make a hostel reservation, get advice on hot spots from other travelers, or find out how much a train from Marseille to Paris costs. Listed here are some regional and travel-related sites to start off your surfing; other websites are listed throughout the book. Because website turnover is high, use search engines (e.g., www.google.com) to strike out on your own.

LET'S GO ONLINE. Plan your next trip on our newly redesigned website, **www.letsgo.com.** It features the latest travel info on your favorite destinations as well as tons of interactive features: make your own itinerary, read blogs from our trusty researcher-writers, browse our photo library, watch exclusive videos, check out our newsletter, find travel deals, and buy new guides. We're always updating and adding new features, so check back often!

THE ART OF TRAVEL

Backpacker's Ultimate Guide: www.bugeurope.com. Tips on packing, transportation, and where to go. Also tons of country-specific travel information.

BootsnAll.com: www.bootsnall.com. Numerous resources for independent travelers, from planning your trip to reporting on it when you get back.

How to See the World: www.artoftravel.com. A compendium of great travel tips, from cheap flights to self-defense to interacting with local culture.

Travel Intelligence: www.travelintelligence.net. A large collection of travel writing by distinguished travel writers.

Travel Library: www.travel-library.com. A fantastic set of links for general information and personal travelogues.

World Hum: www.worldhum.com. An independently produced collection of "travel dispatches from a shrinking planet."

INFORMATION ON FRANCE

CIA World Factbook: www.odci.gov/cia/publications/factbook/index.html. Tons of vital statistics on France's geography, government, economy, and people.

Geographia: www.geographia.com. Highlights, culture, and people of France.

PlanetRider: www.planetrider.com. A subjective list of links to the "best" websites covering the culture and tourist attractions of France.

TravelPage: www.travelpage.com. Links to official tourist office sites in France.

World Travel Guide: www.travel-guides.com. Helpful practical info.

LIFE AND TIMES

LAND

France's geography is as varied as its wine and cheese selections. A roughly hexagonal territory about 80% the size of Texas, France's 547,030 sq. km are marked by breathtaking coastlines, idyllic islands, gently rolling hills and majestic mountains. Laden with waterfalls, the **Pyrenees** mountains form France's southwestern border with Spain, while the snow-capped peaks of the **Alps** and **Jura** separate France from Italy and Switzerland to the east. North of the Jura, the history-steeped waters of the **Rhine River** divide France and Germany. France shares its only artificial boundary with Belgium in the northeast.

The English Channel (known in France as *La Manche*, meaning "the sleeve") separates France's chalky northwestern cliffs from England's stony shoreline. The Atlantic Ocean meets the fine sand beaches in the west, while the sparkling Mediterranean laps onto the shores of the south. Seemingly boundless plains and river valleys comprise most of France's interior with the exception of the rugged **Massif Central**—an expansive plateau of mountains, crater lakes, caves, deep gorges, hot springs, and extinct volcanoes—in the country's center. **Corsica**, France's Mediterranean island, sits 170km off the French coast—the **Côte d'Azur**. Corsica's geography mirrors the topographic diversity of the mainland; white sand beaches neighbor granite bluffs on its coast, while rushing streams and pine forests dot the mountainous interior.

For information about French national parks, check out www.parcsnationaux-fr.com, and for more on French environmental concerns see the French Institute for the Environment's website, www.ifen.fr.

DEMOGRAPHICS

Basically, the French are all peasants.
—Pablo Picasso

ETHNIC MINORITIES

The influx of immigrants from France's former colonies in North Africa and the Caribbean has undeniably diversified its cuisine, music, and art. Unfortunately, such cultural exchange is not always embraced. As a political storm brews over the issue of immigration in France, ethnic minorities face hostility at times, and foreigners are often blamed for France's social ills. President **Nicolas Sarkozy** has developed a contentious relationship with ethnic minorities, particularly France's **African** and **Arab** populations. As ethnic minorities are concentrated in *banlieues* (low-income suburbs) surrounding major cities, Sarkozy's 2005 promise to clean out young troublemakers from a Paris suburb with a Kärcher (a brand-name, high-powered hose) is telling of the nation's heated ethnic tensions. Hostilities climaxed in the fall of 2005 when

NO WORK, ALL PLAY

GAY OLD TIME

Boasting a substantial GLBT population and the first openly gay mayor of a major European city, Paris is a queer-friendly city bursting at the seams with entertainment and resources. Most notably, the City of Lights participates in a campaign of marches across France to celebrate and raise awareness of queer communities. The highlight is the annual Gay Pride Festival, held on the last Saturday of June.

Nearly all of Paris's queer community turns out for this exuberant parade. The festive din can be heard from several Métro stops away. A fabulous Carnaval scene greets visitors as they reach the festival. Drag queens in feathered costumes pose daintily next to scantily clad dancers shimmying, pumping, and grinding on floats.

This might be the only time the Communist Party, the Socialist Party, and the right-wing UMP root for the same cause. A sense of organized chaos ensues as the crowds and floats wiggle and bob from Montparnasse to the Bastille, dancing, chanting, and waving banners. While there is a hint of political consciousness, it hardly distracts from the parade's glittery, celebratory mood.

Gay Pride Paris takes place during the last weekend in June (www.gaypride.fr).

unemployment among the primarily African and Arabic working class exploded into a series of violent riots throughout France. While the problems behind the riots persist, tensions appear to have cooled, at least for the moment.

RELIGIOUS MINORITIES

A **secular** nation, France adheres to the concept of *laïcité*—the separation of religious affairs from government matters and the absence of a state religion. This secularism was enacted in 2004 with a ban on conspicuous religious symbols in schools, including the Muslim headscarf. Despite measures to establish a state free of religious influence, France still bears the stamp of centuries dominated by the **Catholic** church. For example, the Feast of the Assumption remains a national holiday. Furthermore, secularism was forgotten in the 2007 presidential election, as the media asked candidates to state their religious affiliations, and both candidates referred to their Roman Catholic faith.

Meanwhile, religious intolerance of Muslim and Jewish communities has recently increased. French sympathies with Palestinian concerns have sparked anti-Semitic rhetoric and violence among extremists. Muslims have fallen victim to similar hate crimes, including grave desecrations.

GLBT

Major French cities are generally tolerant of homosexuality, and many have vibrant GLBT communities. **Paris** (p. 95) and **Montpellier** (p. 653) take the lead, both boasting gay pride events and dynamic GLBT nightlife. Paris reaffirmed its openness toward homosexuality in 2008 when openly gay **Bertrand Delanoë** of the Green Party was elected to a second term as mayor of the city. In 1999, France became the first traditionally Catholic country to recognize homosexual civil unions with the **Pacte Civil de Solidarité (PACS).** These unions do not secure the same state benefits as marriage, and gay couples continue to struggle to attain the same rights to adoption and reproductive technologies that married couples enjoy. In addition to such unfavorable legal statutes, homophobia remains prevalent in many small French towns.

WOMEN

National legislation passed in 2006 ensures paid maternity leave and subsidized childcare for new moms. While this law was hailed as a victory for women, it underscores the domestic societal roles that females are expected to assume. In fact, women in France remain severely underrepresented in high-paying careers and top government positions. However, the interests of women are recognized as a concern in the country. The late 20th century witnessed a rise in the popularity of women and gender studies in French university curricula, legitimizing women's struggles and achievements as a significant field. Furthermore, a government committee monitors and promotes **gender equality.**

HISTORY

France has more need of me than I have need of France.
—Napoleon Bonaparte

FROM GAULS TO GOTHS

Human life first appeared in France over two million years ago, but recognizable humans didn't show up until 25,000 BC, when Cro-Magnons (cavemen and cavewomen) began roaming the **Dordogne Valley** (p. 523). One man considerably left his skull for railroad workers to dig up in 1868, while the rest of the Cro-Magnon race handed down the vast and elaborate graffiti-filled caves of **Périgord** (p. 530). Unwilling to be overlooked, Neolithic peoples carved their own marks in the stone menhirs (monoliths) at **Carnac** (p. 279) in Brittany by 4500 BC. Peace continued through 500 BC, when the Celtic **Gauls** came from the east to join the Greek colonists who were settled at Massalia—modern day **Marseille** (p. 661)—during the seventh century BC. The tranquility didn't last: Roman forces hit town, making a province of **Provence** in 121 BC and quickly conquering the rest of southern France. Fierce resistance from France's northern Gauls under the leadership of ▨**Vercingetorix**—undeniably heroic even in Roman writings—kept the Romans out of their territory until he surrendered himself to **Julius Caesar** at Alesia and was beheaded in 54 BC. After suffering centuries of Germanic invasions, Gaul fell to the domination of the Franks in AD 481. Frankish king **Clovis I** began the Merovingian dynasty, converting himself and his kingdom to Christianity in AD 496. Clovis, having established **Paris** (p. 95) as his capital, dropped his name's "c" and changed the "v" to a "u" to become the first in a long line of French kings called "Louis." **Charlemagne**—whose condensed "magnus" sneakily deems him "Charles the Great"—became Holy Roman Emperor in AD 800 and inaugurated the more expansive Carolingian dynasty.

NEXT TIME, SIGN A PRENUP

The Carolingian dynasty soon gave way to the Capetian, when **Hugh Capet** consolidated power in AD 987. The line

25,000 BC
The first "Frenchmen" (Cro-Magnons) appear, creating cave paintings that foreshadow France's rich cultural legacy.

4500 BC
Neolithic peoples make their mark—or play a large-scale version of prehistoric chess at Carna—with strategically placed stone menhirs.

500 BC
Gauls settle in with Greece, and the two communities play nicely together.

121 BC
Romans, doing as they do, colonize the south.

52 BC
Caesar conquers Vercingetorix's band of northern rebels and names present-day Paris "Lutetia Parisorum."

AD 486
Clovis I founds the Frankish Empire. Deciding to become one of the cool kids, he changes his name to "Louis."

AD 768
Charlemagne becomes king of the Franks and founds the Carolingian Dynasty.

AD 885-86
Vikings lay siege to Paris during the reign of Charles the Fat.

1146
Capetian king Louis VII and wife Eleanor of Aquitaine set out to join the Crusades together.

1309
Pope Clement V moves the Vatican to Avignon.

1337
The Hundred Years' War against England begins and continues for the next 116 years—but who's counting?

1378
Despite the papacy's return to Rome, an anti-pope is established at Avignon, beginning the "Western Schism."

1431
Joan of Arc is burned at the stake by the English, who are not amused by her claims of divine conversation.

started strong until Louis the Fat—more properly **Louis VI**—came to power. Oddly enough, his gluttony was not the deadliest of the dynasty's sins. Instead, it was the carelessness of his successor, **Louis VII**, who inadvertently triggered 500 years of fighting between France and England by failing to gain legal rights to the estate of his first wife, **Eleanor of Aquitaine**. When this ex-queen ran off with England's Henry II in 1152, she took a broad swath of French land stretching from the Channel to the Pyrenees with her. The plot thickened when England's **Edward III** tried to claim the throne of France in 1337. He landed his troops in Normandy, setting off the **Hundred Years' War**, which lasted 16 years longer than the name implies. The English crowned their own **Henry VI** king of France 90 years later, but France's salvation arrived in the form of a 17-year-old peasant girl. **Joan of Arc**, allegedly inspired by the voice of God, won several victories, turning the tide against England. Joan, captured and sold to the English, was then burned at the stake for heresy in 1431. She has since been found innocent and was even canonized in 1920.

POPES VERSUS PROTESTANTS

Back during the Middle Ages, **Pope Urban II** had called for the **First Crusade** at the **Council of Clermont** in his quest to wrest Jerusalem from the Saracens. The ensuing wave of religious furor left an incredible legacy of cathedrals, convents, and monasteries, including the isolated isle of **Mont-Saint-Michel** (p. 322), in its wake. Dismayed by the church's growing power, King **Philip IV** had **Pope Boniface VIII** arrested—and all but killed—in 1303. Boniface died soon after, and his French successor, **Pope Clement V**, moved the pope's court from Rome to **Avignon** (p. 677), where it remained until 1378. The **"Western Schism"** of the next 40 years split the Catholic Church in two, as rival popes competed for influence from their respective thrones in Avignon and Rome. Toward the end of the conflict, the church came up with a brilliant solution: declaring a third pope. By 1414, divine rule was once again consolidated under one man, now **Pope Martin V**.

In the 16th century, religious conflict between **Huguenots** (French Protestants) and Catholics sparked the **Wars of Religion**. Queen **Catherine de Medici**, though fervently Catholic, played the typical meddling mother and orchestrated a marriage between her daughter and the Protestant **Henri de Navarre** in 1572. The Medicis trapped celebratory Huguenots in Paris on August 24, arranging a string of assassinations that triggered the 24 hours of nationwide carnage known as the **Saint-Bartholomew's Day Massacre**. Henri, who saved himself with a speedy conversion to Catholicism, ascended to the French throne as the first **Bourbon** monarch. In 1598, he eased tensions with the **Edict of Nantes**, which made Catholicism the official state religion but conceded tolerance to Huguenots.

BOURBON ON THE ROCKS

In the 17th century, a series of dynamic cardinal-king teams brought the Bourbon monarchy to the height of its power. **Louis XIII** and his capable and ruthless minister, **Cardinal Richelieu,** centralized power in the hands of the monarchy. The 1643 death of Louis XIII passed the scepter to **Cardinal Mazarin** and the four-year-old **Louis XIV.** Mazarin's death in 1661 left control to the youngster, and Louis went on to become the most self-indulgent king France had ever known. Always one for modesty, he declared himself the Sun King and adopted the motto *"l'état, c'est moi"* ("I am the state"). He began renovations on the magnificent palace of **Versailles** (p. 176) around 1668, moving political power out of Paris and into his personal *appartements*, where 3000 courtiers vied for his favor. For all its impressive ambition, the king's astounding extravagance nearly bankrupted his treasury and aggravated growing resentment among the lower classes.

YOU SAY YOU WANT A REVOLUTION

By the time **Louis XVI** inherited the throne in 1774, peasants had come to blame the monarchy for their terrible poverty, and with good reason. To quell the unrest, Louis called a last-resort meeting of delegates from the three classes, or "estates," of society—clergy, nobility, and everyone else—in 1789. The proceedings were predictably dominated by the First Estate, an outcome that was nonetheless upsetting to the bourgeois-dominated and widely ignored Third Estate. Thus, the nobodies who made up the majority soon broke away and proclaimed themselves a somebody—or, rather, the **National Assembly.** On June 17, the assembly arrived at the proceedings only to find that the other estates—in a demonstration of great maturity—had locked them out of their chamber. The assembly responded by congregating on the tennis courts of Versailles, where they signed the aptly named **Tennis Court Oath,** pledging not to disband until a new constitution had been drafted. News of these radical political moves spurred Paris bourgeoisie, who stormed the **Bastille** prison on July 14, 1789, and overtook the powerful symbol of the monarchy. The rioters liberated the political prisoners within and seized the arms for themselves, sparking a national revolt aimed at the overturn of the **Old Regime.** Despite the assembly's utopian principles—*liberté, égalité, and fraternité* (liberty, equality, fraternity)—and its enlightened **Declaration of the Rights of Man,** the revolution soon turned ugly. In 1793, after the people overthrew the monarchy and officially replaced it with the **First Republic,** the radical **Jacobins** seized power. This faction, led by **Maximilien Robespierre,** seized power and guillotined **Louis XV,** his queen **Marie Antoinette,** and anyone else suspected of royalism. This period of arbitrary mass slaughter, known as the **Reign of Terror,** finally expired when Robe-

LIFE AND TIMES

1562-98
The feud between Catholics and Protestants escalates into massacre during the Wars of Religion.

1638-48
In the last decade of the Thirty Years' War, the Catholic French begrudgingly side with the Protestant Dutch and Swedes to challenge the Hapsburg dynasty.

1682
Louis XIV, lover of things bright and shiny, officially establishes his court at the Château de Versailles.

1744
The famous quote *"Qu'ils mangent de la brioche"* ("Let them eat cake") is misattributed to Marie Antoinette, making her perhaps the most hated woman in French history.

1778
France comes to the rescue of rebellious colonists in the American Revolution.

June 1789
The French Revolution begins with the Tennis Court Oath and the storming of the Bastille.

August 1789
The National Assembly signs the Declaration of the Rights of Man.

LIFE AND TIMES

1792
Women of the Revolution sport figurines of the newly invented guillotine as earrings.

1793
Louis XVI and Marie Antoinette are executed by guillotine.

1794
Maximilien Robespierre heads to the guillotine, officially ending the Reign of Terror.

1801
Jacques-Louis David reinvents history, depicting Napoleon crossing the Alps on a white stallion instead of his actual vehicle of choice—a mule.

1812
Napoleon's troops occupying Moscow freeze in the Russian winter, and the few who survive ignobly withdraw.

1822
Louis Pasteur, darling of milk-drinkers, is born.

1829
Louis Braille brings dots into a whole new dimension.

1830
Louis-Philippe, king of the French but not of France, forms a constitutional monarchy.

1853-70
Baron Haussman reconstructs Paris, paving the way for its *haute couture* status.

spierre himself met the guillotine in 1794. Afterward, power was entrusted to a five-man **Directory**.

LITTLE DICTATOR, BIG AMBITION

The Directory governed France for four years, during which self-service and corruption became the political agenda. This vice plagued the country until 1799, when **Napoleon Bonaparte** and a handful of supporters staged a coup d'etat and established the **Consulate**. Time revealed this new government to be a dictatorship, as Napoleon obtained the title **"First Consul for Life"** in 1802 and went on to crown himself **emperor** two years later. As Emperor, he instituted the **Napoleonic Code**—a civil code that established property rights, emphasized accessible law, and streamlined the French legal system.

But France did not quench Napoleon's thirst for empire. His powerful army went on to crush the Austrians, Prussians, and Russians, but Britain was able to withstand his attack at the 1805 **Battle of Trafalgar.** Mother Nature proved to be yet another unbeatable force for Napoleon. In 1812, his Grande Armée of 500,000 captured Moscow only to find the city destroyed by fire. Lacking provisions in the middle of a devastating winter, the army began its retreat.

As Europe united against the little dictator, a war-weary French army refused to support his struggle. Napoleon abdicated in 1814 and was exiled to—and given—the Mediterranean island of **Elba**. The Bourbon **Louis XVIII** restored the monarchy, but Napoleon abandoned Elba and landed with a small party of followers at Cannes in 1815. He marched north, once again rallying French support as the king fled to Ghent. Napoleon's ensuing rule of the **Hundred Days** ended at the battle of **Waterloo**. Defeated, Napoleon abdicated once again and was exiled to the Atlantic island of St-Helena, where he died in 1821.

TAKE TWO (OR THREE)

Though quick to fill Napoleon's power vacuum, the Bourbon dynasty never fully regained its former glory. **Charles X,** the last Bourbon king of France, was a figure of passing popularity. His laws abolishing censorship and granting amnesty to political prisoners were acclaimed, but later legislation was less widely accepted. Charles X infuriated the working class with extensive compensation for aristocratic *émigrés* who had lost land in the Revolution and a decree that increased the power of the clergy. These rulings, in addition to a suspension of constitutional liberties, resulted in the **July Revolution** of 1830. Reflecting on the fate that befell the previous monarch, Charles X quickly abdicated. **Louis-Philippe** ascended the throne, beginning the **July Monarchy**. However, the king's favoritism for the bourgeoisie ultimately triggered the **Revolution of 1848**. The revolt culminated in the declaration of the **Second Republic**—a state of universal male suffrage. The people elected **Louis Napoleon,** nephew of Napoleon Bonaparte, to serve as president. Following in his uncle's footsteps, Napoleon staged a coup d'etat in 1851 and declared himself Emperor Napoleon III. Surprise, surprise.

Across the Rhine, **Otto von Bismarck,** a crafty nation-builder, goaded the French into the 1870-71 **Franco-Prussian War.** The Prussian and German armies boasted superior forces and emerged victorious over the French. Upon defeat, the French ceded **Alsace** (p. 387), a large part of **Lorraine** (p. 371) and ₣5 billion to the Germans. Just days later, the **Third Republic** was established in Paris. Dissatisfied with what they perceived to be a government of appeasement, Parisian radicals revolted by establishing the **Commune of 1871.** But the commune's utopian ideals were no match for the government's weapons, and over 20,000 *communards* perished in what came to be known as **Bloody Week.** In the wake of the conflict, the Third Republic gave rise to an era of renewed cultural modernization in France, symbolized by such feats as the construction of the **Eiffel Tower** (p. 145) for the 1889 Universal Exposition and the first Métro line's opening in 1900. However, the period of renewed prosperity was periodically rocked by outbreaks of political unrest. Most notably, the **Dreyfus Affair,** a controversy in which a Jewish army officer was wrongly convicted of treason, sparked widespread demonstration and disillusionment with Third Republic governance.

A PAIR OF GUERRES

Germany's 1871 unification rocked the balance of power in Europe. In 1907, France formed the **Triple Entente** with Britain and tsarist Russia, while Germany, Italy, and the Austro-Hungarian Empire formed the **Triple Alliance.** When **World War I** erupted in 1914, German armies advanced into France, but a stalemate developed as both armies dug trenches, and "victories" were based on mere meter-length advances. France and her allies triumphed in 1918 after US troops arrived. Devastated by four years of combat and the loss of 1.3 million men, France demanded crippling reparations from Germany.

During the depression of the 1930s, internal tensions between **Fascists** and **Socialists** left France ill equipped to confront the massive **World War II** mobilization of **Adolf Hitler's** Germany. Helpless in the face of the 1940 German invasion, the French government was forced to surrender in June— a defeat made more humiliating by the sight of Nazi troops marching through the Arc de Triomphe. The Germans occupied the north and directed a French puppet state based in **Vichy** (p. 506). While a small percentage of France's population joined the heroic Résistance to combat Nazi rule, many Frenchmen stood by idly or even aided German effort. General **Charles de Gaulle** led the government-in-exile from London and spearheaded the 1944 liberation campaign.

1862
Victor Hugo publishes *Les Misérables* while exiled in Britain.

1888
Van Gogh goes half-deaf in Arles.

1898
The Dreyfus Affair exposes French anti-Semitism.

1903
Maurice Garin wins the first Tour de France.

1914
The assassination of Archduke Franz Ferdinand sets off a chain reaction that marks the beginning of WWI.

1919
The Treaty of Versailles officially ends WWI, but France's excessive demands of Germany sow the seeds for WWII.

1940-44
The Nazi occupation of Paris leads to the establishment of a puppet regime in Vichy.

1940
Charles de Gaulle encourages the French Résistance in his June 18 radio address.

1943
Jacques Cousteau and Émile Gagnan invent the Aqualung, the first modern scuba system.

LIFE AND TIMES

1944
De Gaulle declares the Fourth Republic after the liberation of Paris; French women attain the right to vote.

1954
The Algerian National Liberation Front (FLN) launches the colony's war of independence.

1968
Student protesters cripple France with massive strikes.

1974
Simone de Beauvoir becomes chair of the Women's Rights League.

1981
Socialist François Mitterrand ascends the presidency.

1995
Center-rightist Jacques Chirac succeeds Mitterrand.

1998
France wins the World Cup.

1999
The euro is introduced as the official currency. RIP, franc.

2004
France outlaws religious symbols in public schools.

May 2005
France rejects the European constitution.

Fall 2005
A storm of racial tension erupts as riots sweep France.

GET UP, STAND UP

De Gaulle proclaimed the **Fourth Republic** in 1944, christening an era of female suffrage and a post-war economic boom. After assuming the premier-presidential role in 1945, the general stepped down in 1946, dissatisfied with his limited power. He left behind a weak parliamentary government unable to control rising turmoil in the disintegrating French colonial empire. After a violent struggle, the town of **Dien Bien Phu** in Vietnam achieved independence from France in 1954, helping to mobilize the native inhabitants of France's other protectorates and colonies. Morocco and Tunisia gained independence in 1956; Mali, Senegal, and the Côte d'Ivoire followed suit in 1960. But decolonization was not a peaceable process. When France refused to grant Algeria independence in 1954, bloody conflict erupted. Even a non-violent 1961 demonstration against curfew restrictions for Algerians in Paris provoked police to open fire on the largely North African crowd, killing hundreds. The French turned to their favorite general to deal with the crisis; in 1958 de Gaulle was called back as president. Promising a stronger presidency, the **Fifth Republic** was born. In 1962, a referendum from the new government granted independence to Algeria—the last existing colony—ending eight years of brutal conflict.

Meanwhile, the young and working-class populations became disillusioned with the de Gaulle administration. In May 1968, demonstrations shook France. Students battled police on the narrow streets of Paris's Latin Quarter, a majority of the French workforce went on strike, and intellectuals championed the revolutionary concept of free love and political and artistic freedom. De Gaulle responded by mobilizing military units and dissolving the National Assembly. The crisis had ceased by June, but the ideals of **mai '68** remain predominant in French national consciousness to this day.

TALKIN' BOUT MY GENERATION

In 1981, **Socialism** became a national trend as the party gained a majority in the National Assembly and Socialist **François Mitterrand** won the presidential election. Despite party achievements that included an increased minimum wage, the French economy did not fare well in the global marketplace of the late 20th century. Meanwhile, the far right began to flourish under the leadership of **Jean-Marie Le Pen**, who established the Front National (FN) party on an anti-immigration platform with racist overtones. Mitterrand did not seek re-election in 1995, and the center-right **Jacques Chirac** was elected president and served two terms.

The question of European integration has haunted France in recent decades (see **One Europe**, p. 10). Led by Charles de Gaulle, who famously declared, "It is the whole of Europe that will decide the destiny of the world," France was an early advocate of a unified Europe. Nevertheless, in June 2005 the

French electorate dashed Europe's hopes for a constitution. France's Euroskepticism suggested underlying discontent with its own stagnant economy and unresponsive government. After the political failure of the constitution's defeat, Prime Minister **Jean-Pierre Raffarin** resigned, making way for poet-philosopher **Dominique de Villepin.** The job was almost up for grabs again in 2006 when Villepin falsely accused **Nicolas Sarkozy**, then serving as interior minister, of corruption. Sarkozy escaped the cloud of charges in time to win the 2007 presidential election, defeating female Socialist candidate **Ségolène Royal.** His election cemented the power of the center-right, but "Sarko"—as he is known to the French—has more on his plate than a serving of brie; his administration is up against an economy beset by debt, racial conflict, high unemployment rates, and the threat of globalization.

July 2006
Zinedine Zidane headbutts an Italian opponent during the World Cup Final, which France later loses in penalty kicks.

May 2007
Conservative Nicolas Sarkozy is elected president of France.

KNOW YOUR REPUBLICS. The French have seen a few governments in their day—so many, in fact, that it's tough to keep them straight. Here's a short tutorial so you can keep up with at least the basic political discussion:

Valois Dynasty (1329-1589): Rulers included the Fortunate, the Wise, the Well-Beloved (later the Mad), the Victorious, the Universal Spider, and the Affable as well as bigwigs like François I and Catherine de Medici.

Bourbon Dynasty (1589-1792): Protestant Henry IV defeated the Medicis to launch this dynasty, converting to Catholicism in the process but making peace with Protestants in the Edict of Nantes. It took a revolution to finish these guys off—at least for the time being.

First Republic (1792-1804): This government had its own jumble of sub-governments. They included the National Convention (during which France adopted universal male suffrage), the Directory (when five men shared power—a.k.a. four too many), and the Consulate (Napoleon's debut).

First Empire (1804-14): Napoleon became—or rather, named himself—emperor. The Napoleonic Code he established still dominates French law.

House of Bourbon (1814-30): France just couldn't shake those Bourbons.

House of Orléans (1830-48): Also known as the tumultuous July Monarchy—a constitutional monarchy in which the bourgeoisie held power.

Second Republic (1848-52): Began with a—comparatively—mini-revolution and ended with a—comparatively—mini-coup d'état.

Second Empire (1852-70): Another Napoleonic coup began this empire—this time, it was Napoleon III, Napoleon I's nephew.

Third Republic (1870-1940): Adolph Thiers said a republic was "the form of government that divides France least." At this point, it just wasn't enough. The army clashes with protesters in the 1871 conflict of the Paris Commune.

Vichy France (1940-44): Named for the southern French town, this Nazi puppet government was led by Pétain and opposed by de Gaulle.

Provisional Government of the French Republic (GPRF; 1944-46): The Allies got their act together post-victory.

Fourth Republic (1946-58): Revival of the Third, meaning the same problems still existed. After the Algiers Crisis, de Gaulle took over—under the precondition that there would be a Fifth Republic.

Fifth Republic (1958-any day now): De Gaulle made the presidency stronger. A half-century later, it's still alive. At least for now.

CULTURE

America is like your mother—you go there for comfort. France is like your mistress—
you go there for pleasure.
    —Jean-Paul Jannot

THE ART OF DINING

De Gaulle complained that no nation with 400 types of cheese could ever be united. France's wide variety of provincial specialties definitely speaks to its unique cultural diversity, but the country is united on at least one front: a commitment to great food. Street-side markets provide fresh ingredients every day, and many people continue to forgo supermarket chains for their local *boulangeries* (bakeries) and *charcuteries* (delicatessens). Restaurants expect customers to spend hours savoring their meal, and even the cheapest bistros may serve three courses or more. When traveling through France, make sure to try region-specific dishes and drinks—from seafood and hot chocolate in the **Pays Basque** (p. 590) to apple tarts and *calvados* in **Normandy** (p. 288), these carefully prepared meals are often the best—and most flavorful—way to experience the French *joie de vivre*.

BON APPÉTIT. The French ease into their day with *le petit déjeuner* (breakfast), which typically consists of *le petit pain* (little bread) or sometimes croissants and *café au lait* (espresso with hot milk) or *le chocolat chaud* (hot chocolate). The largest meal is *le déjeuner* (lunch), served between noon and 2pm—though in larger cities the traditional leisurely lunch is disappearing, chased away by the stressful demands of a global economy. *Le dîner* (dinner) begins late, around 8pm, and is characterized by less cooking and ultimately a less elaborate meal, sometimes consisting of no more than cheese, *pâté*, and bread. A complete French meal includes *un apéritif* (a before-dinner drink), *une entrée* (an appetizer), *un plat principal* (a main course), salad, cheese, dessert, coffee, and *un digestif* (an after-dinner drink). While a home-cooked meal may skip most of these courses, restaurants tend to offer the full experience—but for a price, *bien sûr*.

FAST FOOD. Can't finish those last bites of your *plat principal?* The waitstaff will cast looks of confusion or downright scorn if you ask for a doggie bag—or dare to say you're in a hurry. The French take food quite seriously and resent those who wish to alter the complete dining experience. If you're in a rush or trying to save money, look for cafes advertising meals *à emporter* (to go), grab a ready-made sandwich at a *boulangerie* (bakery), or buy bread and produce from a market and make your own *déjeuner sur l'herbe* (picnic).

MENUS. Most restaurants offer a *menu à prix fixe* (fixed-price meal) that costs less than ordering *à la carte*. *Menus* vary, but may include an appetizer, *plat principal*, *fromage* (cheese), and dessert. The *formule* is a cheaper, two-course version. *L'eau gazeuse* (sparkling water) or *l'eau plate* (flat mineral water) are always offered first; for a free pitcher of tap water, ask for *une carafe d'eau*. If the stubborn waitstaff still brings you water you have to pay for, adding a "*du robinet*" (from the tap) should do the trick. When "*boisson comprise*" is written on the menu, you are entitled to a free drink (usually wine) with the meal. Be sure to polish off your dining experience with *un café* (coffee). Vegetarians will have the best luck at *crêperies*, ethnic restaurants, and establishments catering to a younger crowd. Beware: an aversion to meat will sometimes be taken as culinary sacrilege.

DO-IT-YOURSELF DINING. For a €15 spree you can eat a marvelous restaurant meal, but it's easy to assemble inexpensive meals yourself with a ration of cheese, *pâté*, bread, and wine. Start with bread from the *boulangerie*, and then proceed to the *charcuterie* (delicatessen) for *pâté*, *saucisson* (hard salami), or *jambon* (ham), or buy a freshly roasted chicken from the *boucherie* (butcher shop). *Charcuteries* also tend to offer a surprising selection of side dishes, both vegetarian and not; *tabouli*, a North African couscous dish, is a popular option. If you want someone else to do the work, *boulangeries* often sell fresh sandwiches. *Pâtisseries* (cake shops) will satisfy nearly any sweet tooth with treats ranging from the decadent, layered *mille-feuille* (or Napoleon) to the did-I-just-eat-a-whole-loaf-of-that *pain chocolat*.

THE BEST BAKERS. France is packed with *boulangeries* and *pâtisseries*—so many, in fact, that it's hard to tell the good from the bad. Look for a bakery with a blue sticker featuring a chef's hat, which declares the house a *pâtisserie artisanale*, where master bakers prepare breads on the premises.

CAFES. Cafes on a major boulevard can be more expensive than smaller establishments down a side street. Prices in cafes are two-tiered: cheaper *au comptoir* (at the counter) than *en salle* (in the seating area). Seating *à la terrasse* (outside, on the terrace) may cost even more. Beer and *pastis* are the staple café drinks, while coffee, *citron pressé* (lemonade), and *diabolo menthe* (peppermint soda) are popular non-alcoholic choices. If you order *café*, you'll get espresso; for coffee with milk, order *café au lait*. Coffee with cream is *café crème*. *Bière à la pression*, or draft beer, is 660mL of either *blonde* (pale) or *brune* (dark) lager; for something smaller, ask for *un demi* (330mL). Beware of fresh-squeezed juices, such as *citron pressé*, which contain nothing but fruit juice and water; add your own sugar or practice your best pucker face.

WINE: IT DOES A BODY GOOD

> Other countries drink to get drunk, and this is accepted by everyone; in France, drunkenness is a consequence, never an intention.
> —Roland Barthes

Le vin (wine) is an integral component of French culture. Though consumption is slowing as the French keep pace with the sobriety of modern life, this national treasure continues to play a major role in social occasions. France produces an astoundingly diverse array of reds, whites, and rosés; each varies according to the grape, region, and method of production. French vintners place great importance on the concept of *terroir*, the combination of soil composition, sunlight, and rain unique to each hectare of carefully cultivated land. The **Bordeaux** (p. 581) region, along the Dordogne and Garonne rivers of the southwest, is famous for its bold, full-bodied reds and sweet white **Sauternes**. Connoisseurs prize the reds and whites of **Burgundy** (p. 419), the region centered on Dijon and Beaune, for their subtle refinement. Farther south, the region of **Côtes du Rhône** turns out richly flavored reds, while the even warmer **Côtes de Provence** region is known for its rosés. The whites of the **Loire Valley** (p.

190) tend to be delicate and aromatic, while those of **Alsace** (p. 387), along the border with Germany, are fruitier. The sparkling whites of **Champagne** (p. 354) are synonymous with celebration worldwide. By law, only wines produced in this region may bear its illustrious name.

Though French wines are expensive in the US, quality wine is much more affordable in France. Budget travelers can pick up decent bottles in supermarkets for as little as €3-4. Those looking to splurge should head to the shops of *cavistes* (wine merchants), where knowledgeable staff can point out quality bottles in the €10-15 range. Visiting the vineyards where wine is produced makes for an educational experience and a bargain; tours typically end with free tastings, after which travelers can buy homegrown wines.

While wine is king in France, it is not the nation's only claim to alcoholic fame. Regional specialties such as **Provence's** potent licorice-flavored *liqueur* and anise-flavored *pastis*, **Normandy's** *bénédictine liqueur* and *calvados* (hard cider), and **Cognac's** self-titled drink are all worth a stop on the traveler's tour of France and its bacchanalian delights.

CUSTOMS AND ETIQUETTE

I like Frenchmen very much, because even when they insult you they do it so nicely.
 —Josephine Baker

PROJECT RUNWAY. Style and fashion are important in France, and dressing well is never taken lightly. The more of an effort you make to blend in, the more authentic your experience in France will be. For dress, what may look perfectly innocuous in Miami will stick out like a bad pair of acid-wash jeans in Marseille. The French are known for their conservative stylishness: go for dressy sandals or closed-toe shoes, dark jeans or khakis, and stylish shirts rather than Tevas and baggy pants. The French rarely wear shorts; if you choose to sport them, leave those daisy dukes at home and opt for Bermudas instead. For women, skirts or dresses (knee-length or longer) are generally most appropriate. Sneakers, athletic T-shirts, baseball caps, or any kind of sloppy clothing will mark you as a tourist immediately. Conservative and respectful clothing (including covered shoulders for women) is mandatory when visiting places of worship. Rule of ☝thumb: Keep it classy.

POOCHES. The French adore their dogs. Don't be surprised to find a pampered pet in your hotel, on your train, or even sitting under the table next to you in a restaurant. Perhaps because they are so well traveled, most French pooches are also generally well behaved. However, this civility has not yet translated to toilet training, so watch your step.

NO SMOKING (IN) JOINTS. A ban on smoking in public establishments went into full effect in January 2008, prohibiting the habit—or lifestyle, for most of the French population—in locations from nightclubs to cafes. Ignoring the ban will land you a fine of up to €450—a great incentive to go cold turkey.

ÉTAGES. The French call the ground floor the *rez-de-chaussée* and start numbering with the first floor above it (*le premier étage*). The button labeled "R" (not "1") is typically the ground floor. The *sous-sol* is the basement.

HOURS. Most restaurants open for lunch at noon and close in the afternoon before re-opening for dinner. For those craving a light meal at 3pm, some bistros and cafes remain open all day. Small businesses, banks, and post offices close daily noon-2pm. Many establishments shut down on Sundays and take half-days on Wednesdays, while most museums are closed on Mondays.

PAPER OR PLASTIC? Shopping in France is a joy and an art form. Fashion is serious business among the French. Stores nationwide have *soldes* (sales) in January and July, when you can get the best bargains. France uses the continental European sizing system, which differs from American and British sizes.

TYPE OF CLOTHING	FRENCH SIZES	AMERICAN SIZES	BRITISH SIZES
Women's Clothing	32	2	4
	34	4	6
	36	6	8
	38	8	10
	40	10	12
	42	12	14
	44	14	16
	46	16	18
Women's Shoes	36	5	4
	37	6	5
	38	7	6
	39	8	7
	40	9	8
	41	10	9
Men's Suits	44	34	34
	46	36	36
	48	38	38
	50	40	40
	52	42	42
	54	44	44
	56	46	46
	58	48	48
Men's Shoes	39.5	7	6
	41	8	7
	42	9	8
	43	10	9
	44.5	11	10
	46	12	11
	47	13	12

VERLAN: A USER'S GUIDE. French youngsters have developed a very particular form of slang, called *verlan*, which is genuinely decipherable once the basic concept is grasped. *Verlan* is based on the idea of reversing the order of syllables: the word *verlan* itself is a reversed form of *l'envers*, which means backward. One-syllable words such as *femme* (woman) or *mère* (mother) are simply reversed to form what is pronounced as "mef" or "rem." Two-syllable words such as *crayon* are broken up according to syllable, and the order is changed, to make words like *yoncré*. So when you hear an unfamiliar word, don't assume it's brand-new to your vocabulary; try deciphering it first—it might be *verlan*. Try this: *cainri*—it comes from *ricain*, an abbreviated form of "American."

LA LANGUE. The French are extremely proud of their language. When English words began sneaking in—*le jogging, par exemple*—the government took action, creating a law for the protection of the French language in 1994. Even as English has become the international language of business, English speakers are still often met with scorn. If your French is anything but fluent, waiters and salespeople who detect the slightest accent will often immediately respond in English. But, if you continue to speak in French, more often than not, the waiter or salesperson will respond in French. Those without knowledge of the most beautiful language in the world—according to the French— will fare well with English in most parts of the country; in rural and less touristed areas, such as the **Massif Central** (p. 492) or **Flanders** (p. 327), working knowledge of French is an asset. Believe it or not, French is not France's only language; while regional dialects such as **Basque, Corsican,** and **Breton** are in steep decline, they're hanging on, infusing their regions with a proud linguistic tradition and culture.

POLITESSE. The French put a premium on polite pleasantries. Smiling is very American, so put on your best brooding artist face. Always say *"bonjour Madame/Monsieur"* (*salut* is so 70s) when entering a business, restaurant, or hotel and *"au revoir"* or *"bonne journée"* ("good day") when leaving. If you bump into someone, drop him or her a quick *"pardon."* When meeting someone for the first time, a handshake is appropriate. However, friends and acquaintances—except two men, who often stick to a handshake—greet each other with *bisoux*, an airy kiss on each cheek. Feel the love in the South of France, where three kisses are the norm.

TABLE MANNERS. Bread is served with every meal; it is perfectly polite to use a piece to wipe your plate. Etiquette dictates keeping one's hands above the table, not in one's lap, and forearms, not elbows, should rest on the table. In restaurants, waiters will not bring the check until you ask. When you are ready to pay, say, *"L'addition, s'il vous plaît."* It is extremely impolite to address your waiter as *"garçon"* (boy); call him *"Monsieur"* instead.

PILLOW TALK. The French often mock English-speakers for unwittingly making sexual references in French. Here are a couple of commonly used expressions you should know about:

Je suis excité(e) might be an attempt to express excitement at a new museum or a film, but it actually means "I am sexually aroused."

Je suis plein(e) may seem to translate to "I am full (of food)," but, for a girl, this means "I have been sexually satisfied" or "I'm pregnant."

Oh my God! This English expression may seem harmless, but in French, *godde* means "vibrator."

PRETTY, PRICEY POTTIES. French public toilets are worth the €0.30 they require, as the newer models of these machines magically self-clean after each use. Older public toilets are often dirty or broken. Toilets in train stations and public gardens are tended by *gardiens* and generally cost €0.40-0.60, often in exact change. Public toilets can sometimes prove elusive, but private establishments do not look kindly on being used solely for their facilities; in an urgent situation, you may have to buy a drink or snack first. In rural areas, public toilets often consist of a very basic shack *sans* toilet paper; consider packing an extra roll of TP and a bottle of hand sanitizer.

SERVICE. There is no assumption in France that "the customer is always right"—complaining to managers about poor service is rarely worthwhile. When you're engaged in any official process like opening a bank account or purchasing insurance, don't fret if you get shuffled from one desk to another. Hold your ground, patiently explain the situation, and (maybe) you'll prevail.

TIPPING. In restaurants and cafes, the tip is almost always included in the tab, as indicated by the words *"service compris"* on the check. To acknowledge particularly good service, the French leave a euro or two in change on the table. Cab drivers should be tipped 15% of their fare. It's considerate to tip museum tour guides €1 after a free tour and guides for official tour companies 20%.

THE ARTS

ARCHITECTURE

ANCIENT BEGINNINGS. The prehistoric French proved their artistic and engineering finesse even before the "civilizing" effect of the Romans with the murals at **Lascaux** (p. 530) and menhirs (enormous upright stones) in **Carnac** (p. 279). The Roman Empire left its mark as well, especially in Provence, with the theater at **Orange** (p. 697) and the ruins of the amphitheater at **Nîmes** (p. 692). Nearby, the Roman arches of the **Pont du Gard** aqueduct (p. 697) brought some 10 million gallons of water per day to Nîmes's thirsty citizens.

CATHEDRAL CRAZE. Although ruins of the empire may be scarce, lasting evidence of Roman influence can be seen in the arches, thick walls, and barrel vaults of **Romanesque** churches built in the 11th to 12th centuries. Their quiet and simple—relatively speaking—beauty is epitomized by churches like the **Basilique Saint-Sernin** in Toulouse (p. 626) and the **Basilique Sainte-Madeleine** at Vézelay (p. 446). The 12th century also saw the emergence of **Gothic** architecture, whose name has nothing to do with the historic Goths, except that it, like the tribe, was perceived as vulgar. Flying buttresses distributed weight outward to the walls, enabling the vaults of Gothic cathedrals to soar to dramatic heights and allowing for thinner walls that showcase intricate stained glass. The cathedrals at **Amiens** (p. 346), **Chartres** (p. 179), and **Reims** (p. 354) exemplify the intricate sculptural details that define the Gothic style.

BRING IT ON. During the Renaissance, Italian influence produced buildings such as François I's elaborate **Château de Chambord** (p. 204). Châteaux sprang up in the Loire Valley as aristocrats scrambled to keep up with the royal example. Meanwhile, in response to his finance minister's 17th-century Baroque **Château de Vaux-le-Vicomte** (p. 187) outside Paris, Louis XIV converted his father's hunting lodge at **Versailles** (p. 176) into the world's largest and most flamboyant royal residence. The mid-18th century welcomed the columns and clean lines of **Neoclassicism**, exemplified by the grand **Église Sainte-Geneviève** in Paris, known since the revolution by its secular name, the **Panthéon** (p. 143).

POLISHING PARIS. "Capital of the World" may not be one of Paris's many nicknames, but the city does owe its current structure to Napoleon III's vision to make it just that. From 1852 to 1870, **Baron Georges-Eugène Haussmann** plowed long, straight boulevards through the tangled clutter and narrow alleys of medieval Paris. The wide avenues not only supported the city's famous cafe culture but also impeded insurrection by giving the French army the room to march down the boulevards and quell revolts. In the late 19th century, engineering entered the architectural scene when **Gustave Eiffel** created the star entry of the International Exhibition of 1889. The **Eiffel Tower** (p. 145) was first decried by Parisians as hideous and unstable—novelist **Guy de Maupassant** famously claimed to eat in the tower's restaurant daily because it was the one place in Paris without a view of the 986-foot eyesore—but it has since become the symbol of French culture. At the same time, **Art Nouveau** emerged as a leading decorative style, seen today in the swirling lines of Paris Métro stations where **Hector Guimard's** vine-like signs sprout from the ground.

MODERN MISERY. In contrast to the decorative whimsy of Art Nouveau, the prolific Swiss architect, painter, and writer known as **Le Corbusier** brought **Modernism** to France with his geometric use of concrete in individual homes, housing projects, commercial buildings, and even a mushroom-like chapel commemorating WWII at **Ronchamp** (p. 409). In the post-war years, **HLMs** (*habitations à loyer modéré;* housing projects) were originally intended as affordable housing but are now associated with unemployment, racism, and the plight of poor immigrants. In the 1980s, President **François Mitterrand's** F15 billion endeavor known as the Grands Projets heralded the construction of such icons as the **Parc de la Villette** (p. 152), the **Opéra** at the Bastille (p. 148), and **IM Pel's** glass pyramid at the **Louvre** (p. 154). Parisian skyscrapers built in the 1980s and 1990s are confined to the business suburb of **La Défense.**

FINE ARTS

LET THERE BE ART. Religion ruled the arts during the Middle Ages, as cathedrals, reliquaries, and religious texts were the dominant creative outlets. Brilliant stained glass and expertly chiseled stone at **Chartres** (p. 179), at **Reims** (p. 354), and in Paris's **Sainte-Chapelle** (p. 137) bridged the gap between God—or king—and a largely illiterate parish by illustrating a royally selected program of Bible stories. Monks created beautiful **illuminated manuscripts** by painstakingly adding gold and silver illustrations to sacred texts. The Middle Ages also saw the creation of Normandy's 11th-century **Bayeux tapestry,** a 70m long narrative of the **Battle of Hastings** (p. 312). The Burgundian noble, **Jean, Duc de Berry,** became a great patron of the arts toward the end of the Middle Ages. In the early 1400s, he commissioned the **Limbourg Brothers** to create the famous *Très Riches Heures du Duc de Berry,* a sumptuously decorated prayer book with illustrated scenes of daily life to mark each month of the year.

A TASTE OF ITALY. The art of 16th-century France drew its inspiration from the painting, sculpture, and architecture of the Italian Renaissance. At the invitation of François I, **Leonardo da Vinci** trekked from Florence, bearing the enigmatic **Mona Lisa** (p. 155), but ended up producing very little in France. Visitors can visit the town where Leonardo spent his final days in **Amboise** (p. 206).

I'D LIKE TO THANK THE ACADÉMIE. Italian influence persisted into the 17th century, as painters **Nicholas Poussin** and **Claude Lorrain**—whose serene landscapes would become the academic standard in French painting for two centuries—lived and painted next door in Italy. The French Baroque reached its height with the exorbitant spectacle of Louis XIV's renovated **Versailles** (p. 176). Realist painters **Georges de La Tour** and the **Le Nain Brothers** kept the lid on with their faithful renderings of daily life.

The 17th century also brought the rise of one of the earliest national art schools in Europe, the Académie Royale (founded in 1648), whose elitism and narrow definition of the "acceptable" in French art would become the bane of many a Realist painter's existence in the 19th century. Artists such as Louis XIV's court favorite, **Charles Le Brun,** dominated the Académie's salons—France's "official" art exhibitions—with Grand Manner history paintings, conservative portraiture, and large-scale scenes from classical mythology.

The early 18th century brought the opulent **Rococo** style in painting and interior decorating. Catering to the tastes of the nobility, **Antoine Watteau** painted their fantastic fêtes and secret rendez vous, while **François Boucher** depicted pastoral landscapes and naughty, rosy-cheeked shepherdesses.

WE'RE BRINGING ROME BACK. Neoclassicism witnessed—as the name would suggest—a revival of classical order and symmetry in the visual arts in France. In works like **Jacques-Louis David's** *Oath of the Horatii* (1784-85), artists idealized those Ancient Roman virtues that their ruling class patrons considered most necessary to contemporary society. The French Revolution inspired an update to the genre of history painting whereby scenes from front-page news stories—history in the making—took center stage in works like David's *The Oath of the Tennis Court* (1791) and *The Death of Marat* (1793). The **Louvre** (p. 154), which opened as a museum in 1792, grew in importance during this era.

Romanticism took hold in French painting in the works of **Théodore Géricault** and **Eugène Delacroix.** Géricault's epic *Raft of the Medusa* (1818-19) exposed the horrific aftermath of the scandalous shipwreck of the Medusa, offering a subtle commentary on the slave trade by heroicizing the black sailor who appears at the climax of the composition. Delacroix's paintings shocked salons of the 1820s and 1830s with their Romantic and colorful melodrama. Both Delacroix and his bitter rival, **Jean-Auguste-Dominique Ingres,** pursued Asian-inspired subjects with the advent of Orientalism, as in the latter's seductive masterpiece, *La Grande Odalisque* (*The Tall Concubine*; 1814), now on display in the Louvre.

KEEPIN' IT REAL (AND REAL FUZZY). After the Revolution of 1848, Realists like **Gustave Courbet** shifted their focus to a depiction of humble peasant life that was, well, more realistic than the idealized aristocratic view of country-dwellers favored by earlier members of the Académie. His *Burial at Ornans* provoked a scandal at its 1851 salon debut because the huge canvas depicted an ordinary, working-class village scene with stunning realism instead of an idealized historical drama. The salon rejected **Édouard Manet's** *Déjeuner Sur L'Herbe* (see **Musée d'Orsay,** p. 159) for its frank inclusion of female nudes in a commonplace setting, but the painting found a home among other rejected works at the Salon des Refusés in 1863.

By the late 1860s, Manet's new aesthetic had set the stage for **Impressionists Claude Monet, Camille Pissarro,** and **Pierre-Auguste Renoir,** whose careful use of light and color earned them posthumous fame even beyond the art historical community. Monet's garden at **Giverny** (p. 186), the source of his monumental 1890s **Water Lilies** series, is almost synonymous with Impressionism. This famous movement in turn encouraged **Edgar Degas's** Japanese print-inspired ballerinas, **Gustave Caillebotte's** rainy Paris streets, and **Berthe Morisot's** tranquil studies of women, as well as sculptor **Pierre-Auguste Rodin's** *The Kiss* (1886) and his lover **Camille Claudel's** *The Waltz* (1891-93).

IMPRESSIONISM II: REVENGE OF THE IMPRESSIONISTS. Paul Cézanne, whom many consider the "Father of Modern Art," kicked off the ambiguously labeled in-between period of "Post-Impressionism." His geometric still lifes, portraits, and obsessive deconstruction of the **Aix-en-Provence** landscape upset traditional spatial relationships and had a powerful influence on his Cubist followers. **Georges Seurat** developed **Pointillism,** painting thousands of tiny dots that from far away read as a single image. **Paul Gauguin** escaped to Arles, Brittany, Martinique, and Tahiti seeking refuge from the pressures of modern life in what he considered the "primitive." His large, flat blocks of typically garish color, bold outlines, and simplified human forms depicted a world where men roamed in a more natural state and women in a state of semi-nudity. Also in **Arles** (p. 683), Gaugin's Dutch associate, **Vincent van Gogh,** became famous for his thickly layered brush strokes, for his intense, expressive colors, and for cutting off part of his ear after the dispute that ended his friendship with his roommate. **Henri Matisse** became the forerunner of colorful **Fauvism** (from *fauves*, wild animals) with earlier oils like *The Dance* (1909) and the brightly colored paper cut outs of his old age, such as his 1940s *Jazz Series.*

HIP TO BE SQUARE. In the 1910s, former Fauvist **Georges Braque** and Matisse's Spanish-born rival, **Pablo Picasso,** developed **Cubism,** shifting their focus from what objects looked like to a distinctly modern concern with the process of visual perception. Using shaded planes and a limited palette, Braque and Picasso reassembled familiar images and objects in abstract form, later adding ready-mades and collage into the mix. The constant stylistic innovation throughout Picasso's oeuvre set the tone of modern art for decades. The **Musées Picasso** in Paris (p. 156) and **Antibes** (p. 727) pay tribute to his prolific career.

CECI N'EST PAS UNE MOUVEMENT. Prompted by their sense of loss after WWI, a group of artists sought to expose the artificial nature of modern consumerism and to question the very institutions that make up our visual culture. **Marcel Duchamp** unleashed the subversive **Dada** movement with works like *The Fountain* (1917), a factory-made urinal that he turned sideways and then signed.

Surrealism, on the other hand, created an unnerving mix of fantasy and the everyday, creating what the movement's leader, **André Breton,** called "an absolute reality, a surreality." Surrealism's exemplary works—**René Magritte's** apples and pipes, **Joan Miró's** dreamscapes, **Max Ernst's** birds, and **Salvador Dalí's** melting timepieces—arose out of the 1920s art scene. More recent 20th-century experiments in photography, installation art, and sculpture are on view at the **Centre Pompidou** (p. 141) and the **Fondation Cartier pour l'Art Contemporain** (p. 161).

LITERATURE AND PHILOSOPHY

In America only the successful writer is important; in France all writers are important.
—Geoffrey Cottrell

SATIRE AND SONG. Medieval aristocrats enjoyed tales of chivalry and courtly love penned by **Marie de France** and **Chrétien de Troyes** in the 12th century in addition to the famous **Roman de la Rose,** an elaborate allegory of *l'amour.* The medieval masses, on the other hand, indulged their common tastes when listening to *chansons de gestes,* or epic accounts of eighth- and ninth-century crusades and conquests. **John Calvin** helped ignite the **Protestant Reformation** in his 1536 criticism of the Catholic Church, *Institutes of the Christian Religion.* Around the same time, **François Rabelais** satirized French society in *Life of Gargantua and Pantagruel* (1532-64), a series of novels told from the perspective of two comical giants. In 1588, **Michel de Montaigne's** *Essais* ensured him eternal enemies, as students everywhere continue struggling to master his brainchild.

ENLIGHTEN ME. Although the French Enlightenment did not technically begin until the 1700s, its seeds were sewn a century earlier when **Cardinal Richelieu,** perhaps suffering a bout with obsessive compulsive disorder, founded the **Académie Française** in 1635 to codify and regulate French literature and language. Shortly thereafter, **René Descartes** used the Enlightenment ideal of rationalism to prove his own existence in the famously catchy—and logical—deduction, "I think, therefore I am." In the 18th century, **Denis Diderot** ambitiously set out to accumulate and record everything in his *Encylopédie.* Meanwhile, **Voltaire** critiqued social norms in his sharp satire *Candide,* as **Molière** had done in the previous century with comedic plays *Tartuffe, L'École des Femmes, Le Bourgeois Gentilhomme,* and others. **Jean-Jacques Rousseau,** whose 1762 *Social Contract* laid the foundation for modern democracy, promoted the Enlightenment ideals of tolerance and equality in his argument for sovereign rule by common popular agreement. In the same year, Rousseau, who left his own five children in an orphange, also tackled the evidently difficult problem of rearing children in *Émile.* Mathematician and philosopher **Blaise Pascal**—known to some for his triangle—demonstrated his true brilliance in contemplating everything from the abyss to the Bible in the 924 "thoughts" of his *Pensées* (1670).

HUNCHBACKS AND HOUSEWIVES. During the 19th century, French literature adopted the expressive ideals of **Romanticism,** which had already gained prominence in Britain and Germany. Great writers such as **Henri Stendhal** helped to establish the novel as the preeminent literary medium, but the novels of **Victor Hugo,** most famously *Les Misérables* (1862) and *The Hunchback of Notre Dame* (1831), dominated the Romantic movement long before they made inspiring musicals and Disney movies. During the same period, the young Aurore Dupin left her husband, took the pen name **George Sand,** and published passionate novels condemning sexist conventions. Novelists **Honoré de Balzac, Émile Zola, Guy de Maupassant, Alexandre Dumas,** and **Gustave Flaubert** contributed to the movement of **Realism** in literature, creating detailed characters and settings that endeavored to be true to life. Nevertheless, Flaubert's characters may have become a little too real—he narrowly escaped charges of immorality for *Madame Bovary* (1856), whose middle-class heroine spurns provincial life in favor of adulterous daydreams. A supposedly racy description of a woman's breasts and legs earned poet **Charles Baudelaire** a F300 fine from the same tribunal. Despite this notoriety in his own time, Baudelaire is now highly praised, especially for his 1857 poetry collection, *Les Fleurs du Mal.*

HIGHLIGHTS OF EXPATRIATE LITERATURE

JULIAN BARNES. *Flaubert's Parrot.* An elderly English doctor journeys to France to research Flaubert's life and find inspiration for his short story, "Un Coeur Simple."

F. SCOTT FITZGERALD. *Tender is the Night.* No one captures the 1920s flapper set quite like Fitzgerald. His story of scandal and intrigue on the Riviera is a classic.

ADAM GOPNIK. *Paris to the Moon.* A New York journalist settles down in Paris with his family. Observations on Parisian life are lyrically woven into larger cultural themes.

ERNEST HEMINGWAY. *A Moveable Feast.* The quintessential tale of a young expat in Paris. F. Scott Fitzgerald and Gertrude Stein make colorful cameo appearances.

W. SOMERSET MAUGHAM. *The Moon and Sixpence.* A dull London businessman leaves his family to paint in Paris and Tahiti. Loosely based on the life of Paul Gauguin.

GEORGE ORWELL. *Down and Out in London and Paris.* A writer takes grimy jobs in the dark underbelly of Paris. Beautifully descriptive and funny.

DAVID SEDARIS. *Me Talk Pretty One Day.* The wickedly irreverent expat delights in exposing the idiosyncrasies of life in France.

ÉTRANGER THINGS HAVE HAPPENED. Toward the end of the 19th century, the dream reality of **Symbolism** replaced the daily reality of Realism. Poets such as **Stéphane Mallarmé, Paul Verlaine,** and the precocious **Arthur Rimbaud** rejected mere description. **Marcel Proust's** investigation of the nature of time and love in the seven volumes of *Remembrance of Things Past* exemplifies the progressive efforts of **Modernism,** which began to take hold in the early 20th century. After WWII, **Existentialism** expressed **Jean-Paul Sartre's** belief that man is condemned to be free, and life gains meaning only through individual choice and action. Nobel laureate **Albert Camus,** an Algerian-born novelist best-known for *L'Étranger (The Stranger)*, shared Sartre's theoretical beliefs. The two were friends and allies until political conflicts—killer of many great working relationships—divided them in 1952. At the same time, Irishman **Samuel Beckett** took Sartre's ideas on the absurd to the extreme in the infamous *Waiting for Godot* (1948-49), which he first wrote in French.

(S)EX LIBRIS. Simone de Beauvoir, attached to Sartre both romantically and philosophically, attacked the mistreatment of women and the stereotypes of femininity in *The Second Sex*, inspiring a generation of second-wave feminists starting in the 1950s. In turn, works like **Marguerite Duras's** *The Lover,* **Hélène Cixous's** *Laugh of the Medusa*, and **Luce Irigaray's** *This Sex Which Is Not One* sparked feminist movements in France and abroad.

FIGHT FOR YOUR WRITE. Throughout the 20th century, writers from the French colonies of **Haiti, Québec, the Antilles, Maghreb** (Algeria, Morocco, Tunisia), and **West Africa** condemned France's rampant racism and colonial exploitation. These ideas were channeled into the **Négritude** movement in the 1930s by intellectuals **Aimé Césaire** of Martinique and **Léopold Sédar Senghor,** who would become president of Senegal. Similarly, Maghreb **Mehdi Charef** wrote provocative novels about *beur*—slang for Arab-French—culture and the continuing difficulties of cultural assimilation.

THE POST- MEN. France boasts prominent **postmodernist** figures who still influence literary, political, and intellectual thought. Despite its universality, the movement stubbornly resists definition and is best described as a rejection of stable meaning and identity—or else a pretentious response to the pretentiousness of Modernism. Its roots can be traced to the **Structuralist** ideas of 20th-century anthropologist **Claude Lévi-Strauss,** who believed that society determines behavior. **Post-Structuralist** theorists, influenced by the revolutionary moment of May 1968, claimed that language itself is inherently controlled. **Jacques Derrida's** theory of **deconstruction,** a way of reading texts by seeking to uncover the internal tensions they suppress, transformed philosophy, literary theory, and cultural criticism across the globe. Influential historian and philosopher **Michel Foucault,** author of *Madness and Civilization* (1961) and *The History of Sexuality* (1984), argued that society, including institutions like hospitals and schools, can only be understood in terms of the power dynamics it enforces.

FILM

AN INVENTION WITHOUT A FUTURE? After inventing the cinématographe—a device that was able to record, develop, and project motion pictures—the aptly named **Lumière brothers,** Louis and Auguste, screened the world's first film, *La Sortie des Usines Lumière (Quitting Time at the Lumière Factory)* in a Parisian cafe in 1895. Soon thereafter, Auguste declared, "The cinema is an invention without a future." Luckily, he was better at inventing than predicting the future, and Paris became the hub of early cinema, dominating production and distribution worldwide. Although WWI stunted economic growth, the inter-war period yielded diverse and influential films. Envisioned by **Fernand Léger** and **Dudley Murphy,** the 1924 experimental film *Ballet Mécanique* mesmerized viewers with its disorienting, fast-paced use of montage. The work of **Jean Renoir,** son of the Impressionist painter, routinely tops critics' lists of the greatest films ever made, particularly his powerful anti-war protest, *La Grande Illusion* (1938), and his biting social satire, *La Règle du Jeu* (*The Rules of the Game;* 1939).

THE INVENTION'S FUTURE. The 50s were a pivotal decade in French cinema. In 1956, a star was born when director **Roger Vadim** sent **Brigitte Bardot** shimmying naked across the screen in *And God Created Woman (Et Dieu... Créa la femme)*. The French **New Wave** movement—or La Nouvelle Vague—of the 50s and 60s was an iconoclastic rejection of traditional cinematic form that did away with the linear narrative and blurred the distinction between fiction and reality with its highly mobile, documentary-like filming techniques and amateur actors. The year 1959 was a watershed for the movement, releasing such heavyweights as **François Truffaut's** semi-autobiographical coming-of-age story

Les 400 Coups (The 400 Blows), **Jean-Luc Godard's** comedic, jump-cut-happy gangster flick *A Bout de Souffle (Breathless)*, and **Alain Resnais's** *Hiroshima, Mon Amour (Hiroshima, My Love)*. Famed critic **André Bazin**, mentor to Truffaut and Godard, was not only an invaluable supporter of the Nouvelle Vague; his seemingly endless body of film criticism and his co-founding of the influential *Cahiers du Cinéma* are what helped propel film studies to its position as a legitimate discipline of scholarship.

RIDING THE WAVE. French talent enjoyed international recognition in the 60s, producing mega-stars **Anna Karina, Jean-Paul Belmondo, Catherine Deneuve, Alain Delon, Jeanne Moreau,** and **Yves Montand.** Released in 1966, Italian director **Gillo Pontevorco's** *La Bataille D'Alger (The Battle of Algiers)* ruffled a few feathers with its eerily relevant portrayal of the violent French occupation of the African city. The French comedy tradition lived on in *La Cage aux Folles (The Birdcage)*, **Édouard Molinaro's** 1978 film about a gay couple who try to conceal their lifestyle and their transvestite club from their son and his recent fiancée.

The 80s gave rise to the **heritage film,** big-money costume dramas that painstakingly recreated historical ages in such popular works as **Claude Berri's** *Jean de Florette* (1986) and **Yves Robert's** *La Gloire de Mon Père (My Father's Glory;* 1990) and *Le Château de Ma Mère (My Mother's Castle;* 1990), both adaptations from Marcel Pagnol novels. It was also the decade of **Gerard Depardieu** —he appeared in no fewer than 30 films in the 80s alone. **Jean-Jacques Beineix's** cult classic, *Diva* (1981), established the so-called *cinéma du look*, the stylish-punk rock trend that brought US audiences *The Fifth Element* in 1997. The 90s ignited a new wave of political consciousness that included the at times confrontational *beur* cinema, films dealing with issues of immigration and racism affecting North African populations within France. **Mehdi Charef's** *Le Thé au Harem d'Archimède (Tea in the Harem;* 1985) and **Matthieu Kassovitz's** *La Haine (Hate,* 1995) exemplified the genre. In recent years, several more mainstream French hits—including **Jean-Pierre Jeunet's** *Le Fabuleux Destin d'Amélie Poulain (Amélie;* 2001), **Cédric Klapisch's** *L'Auberge Espagnole (The Spanish Apartment;* 2002) and **Michel Gondry's** *Les Sciences des Rêves (The Science of Sleep;* 2006)—have exploded onto the international scene, becoming instant blockbusters. At home, films like **Arnaud Desplechin's** *Comment Je Me Suis Disputé...Ma Vie Sexuelle (My Sex Life... Or How I Got Into an Argument;* 1996), **Claire Denis's** *Chocolat* (1988) and *L'intrus (The Intruder;* 2005), and **Bruno Dumont's** *La Vie de Jésus (The Life of Jesus;* 1997) continue to challenge audiences, carrying on the progressive legacy of French cinema.

MUSIC

Music expresses that which cannot be said and on which it is impossible to be silent.
—Victor Hugo

BALLADS AND BALLETS. Gregorian chants echoed in monasteries and troubadours crooned narrative ballads in the south of France in the 12th century. The religious trend continued through the 15th century, when Renaissance composer **Josquin des Prez** created reverent masses for the court of **Louis XII.** Things grew considerably more scandalous by the Baroque period and the court of Louis XIV, as notorious libertine **Jean-Baptiste Lully** received acclaim for his ballets and lavish operas. At the end of the 18th century, Robespierre's reign of terror rallied the *citoyens* and **Rouget de Lisle** provided an appropriately revolutionary soundtrack. Volunteers from Marseille claimed his 1792

War Song of the Army of the Rhine for their own, dubbing it **La Marseillaise** and designating it the national anthem in 1795.

ROMANCE AND RIOTS. Paris, having regained its position as the hub of European music in the 19th century, welcomed influential foreign composers, including notables like **Frédéric Chopin, Franz Liszt,** and **Felix Mendelssohn. Grand opera** merged with the simpler **opéra comique** to produce the **Romantic lyric opera,** an exotic amalgam of soaring arias and tragic death best exemplified by **Georges Bizet's** *Carmen* in 1875. The 20th century began a new period of intense, abstract, and at times bizarre invention, heralding the impressionistic **Claude Débussy** and avant-garde **Erik Satie,** whose works include the 1912 *Chilled Pieces* and *Dribbling Prelude (for a Dog)*. **Maurice Ravel's** Basque origins surfaced in the Spanish rhythms of his famed *Boléro* (1928), and the violently dissonant sounds of **Igor Stravinsky's** *Rite of Spring* provoked a monstrous riot at its 1913 premiere at the Théâtre des Champs-Élysées.

CLUBS AND CROONERS. Though a thoroughly American musical form, **jazz** found a welcoming second home in France during its formative years. Jazz crooner **Josephine Baker** left the US for Paris in 1925 and found France more accepting than her segregated home. She showed her appreciation by joining the resistance movement during WWII. In the years following the war, a stream of American jazz musicians—including a young **Miles Davis**—flowed onto the Paris music scene. The hundreds of jazz clubs in France today are a testament to the enduring popularity of this American tradition. **Cabaret,** which came to prominence around the same time as jazz, brought song, dance, comedy, and theater to smoky nightclubs across the country. **Édith Piaf's** iconic voice popularized cabaret music with such sultry ballads as "La Vie en Rose" in 1946 and the unforgettable "Je Ne Regrette Rien" in 1960.

YÉ-YÉ AND NON-NON. In the second half of the 20th century, French music was dominated by two opposing ambitions: to emulate the sound of American pop and to maintain a distinctly French musical tradition. The French love for rock and roll inspired **yé-yé,** a genre whose sound was borrowed from American styles. Parisian Jean-Phillips Smet Americanized his name to **Johnny Hallyday** before bursting into the pop scene as a teen idol in the 1960s, gyrating his hips to Elvis-inspired tunes. Meanwhile, 16-year-old **France Gall** cultivated a Lolita-esque appeal with hits like "Laisse Tomber Les Filles" (1964). The same decade also produced the guitar-strumming **Georges Brassens,** who sang lyrically complex and often subversive ballads, but gained more notice for his bristly moustache and ever-present pipe. Songwriter **Jacques Brel** performed songs of love and despair that have since been covered in more than a dozen languages. The era's undisputed bad boy, **Serge Gainsbourg,** shocked and delighted audiences with his crass lyrics and pleasure-seeking nihilism. The simulated orgasm at the climax of Gainsbourg's biggest hit, "Je T'Aime... Moi Non Plus" ("I Love You... Me Neither"), even got the pope's attention—the Vatican condemned the song for obscenity in 1969. Throughout it all, **Charles Aznavour**—much like another diminutive Frenchman—made up for his stature with his presence and endurance. The singer's career surged in the 50s and has yet to wane, despite a 2006 farewell tour. Aznavour celebrated his 84th birthday in 2008.

HIP-HOP ON POP. The French contemporary music scene offers sounds drawn from diverse ethnic roots. Full of catchy beats and sugary choruses, French pop has a lot of style, but many complain that it lacks substance. **Vanessa Paradis,** known best to non-Francophiles as the mother of Johnny Depp's child, recently won female performer of the year for the second time in the French equivalent of the Grammy Awards. American pop is also wildly popular on the sound waves, though a national law mandates that at least 40% of primetime programming be in French. Hip-hop and rap have entered the scene, led by the poetic **MC Solaar** and the often violent sounds of **NTM**. France also welcomes musicians from across the globe, such as Africans **Cheb Khaled** and **Abd al Malik,** Middle Eastern **Natacha Atlas,** Spanish **Manu Chao,** and Malian blind couple **Amadou and Mariam.** French pop icons like **Jean-Jacques Goldman, Gérald de Palmas,** and the band **Noir Désir** bring the sounds of 80s and 90s rock to the French language. French electronica duo **Air** has worked with pioneer artists like **Françoise Hardy** and **Jean-Jacques Perrey,** while Lebanese-born **Mika** brings his opera training to light-hearted beats like the 2007 "Big Girl (You Are Beautiful)." At the same time, the creative contributions of young singer-songwriters like **Bénabar, Thomas Fersen, Keren Ann, Christophe Maé,** and supermodel **Carla Bruni,** wife of President Sarkozy, infuse the French music scene with talent and sophistication.

SPORTS AND RECREATION

Our sport allows people to fight on a pitch the wars they cannot fight anymore on battlefields.
—Jo Maso

FOOTBALL

Along with food and fashion, *le football* is a seriously cherished aspect of French culture. Their national team, Les Bleus, emerged from a half-century of mediocrity to capture the 1998 World Cup as the host team, igniting an explosion of celebration from Paris to the Pyrenees. The charismatic star of the team, **Zinedine Zidane,** or "Zizou," has become a national hero, dominating billboards nationwide. After a devastating, goal-less elimination in the 2002 World Cup, Zizou led the French squad to the 2006 World Cup Finals, where it was defeated only by Italy's dominance in penalty kicks. Now that Zidane has retired—going out with a headbutting bang in his final match—France is looking to its next star, cool-headed **Thierry Henri,** to lead the team to international glory.

CYCLING

Cycling is more than a national obsession—it's an addiction. France gets its annual dose of pedal-pushing during the grueling three-week, 3500km **Tour de France.** Unfortunately, France's love for the sport hasn't translated to significant victory: American **Lance Armstrong** survived testicular cancer to capture a record-setting seven consecutive championships before retiring in 2005. The 2006 race was a hotbed of controversy as the first-place finisher, American **Floyd Landis,** was stripped of his title for confirmed doping charges. A year later, the tour was still plagued by doping drama, but the victor, Spaniard **Alberto Contador,** denied steroid usage. Contador did not get a chance to defend his title in 2008, as his new team, Astana, was excluded from the race because of—you guessed it—a doping scandal.

RECREATIONAL SPORTS

As much a French staple as wine or cheese, **pétanque,** once dominated by old Provençal men, has been gaining popularity among those with fewer wrinkles. The basic premise of the game, like Italian bocce or British lawn bowls, is to throw a number of large metal balls as close as possible—or, more importantly, closer than your opponent's—to a small wooden target ball.

LIFE AND TIMES

Thanks to the country's several mountainous regions and sufficient snowfall rates, Alpine and cross-country **skiing** are also extremely popular. Despite objections by French traditionalists, other non-indigenous sports, particularly **rugby** and **golf,** continue to grow in popularity.

HOLIDAYS AND FESTIVALS

Weddings, christenings, duels, burials, swindlings, diplomatic affairs—everything is a pretext for a good dinner.
 —Jean Anouilh

As their countless holidays attest the French love to celebrate. French festivals are a wonderful way to experience a region's best-loved traditions, and the inevitable inconveniences of trying to travel during a parade are offset by, well, the parade. **Bastille Day,** the most important national holiday, celebrates the anniversary of the storming of the Bastille on July 14, 1789. In Paris, this celebration begins with a solemn military march up the Champs-Élysées followed by dancing, drinking, and fireworks in the capital and throughout the country. When Bastille Day falls on a Tuesday or Thursday, the French often also take off Monday or Friday, a crafty practice known as *faire le pont* (making the bridge). In addition to the following national holidays, French law guarantees citizens 30 vacation days per year—compared to the average American's 12—which most locals use to travel during July and August; expect businesses to close and transportation outlets to clog. The holiday dates listed below are the annual dates, unless specified for 2009. For more information on specific or regional events, check out Festival listings for individual cities in the guide or visit www.franceguide.com.

DATE	NATIONAL HOLIDAY
January 1	*Le Jour de l'An,* or *La St-Sylvestre* (New Year's Day)
April 13 (2009)	*Le Lundi de Pâques* (Easter Monday)
May 1	*La Fête du Travail* (Labor Day)
May 8	*Fête de la Victoire 1945* (celebrates the end of WWII in Europe)
May 21 (2009)	*L'Ascension* (Ascension Day)
June 1 (2009)	*Le Lundi de Pentecôte* (Whit Monday)
July 14	*La Fête Nationale* (Bastille Day)
August 15	*L'Assomption* (Feast of the Assumption)
November 1	*La Toussaint* (All Saints' Day)
November 11	*L'Armistice 1918* (Armistice Day)
December 25	*Noël* (Christmas)

BEYOND TOURISM

A PHILOSOPHY FOR TRAVELERS

HIGHLIGHTS OF BEYOND TOURISM IN FRANCE

TEACH French inmates how to dance, act, and paint (p. 84).

STUDY in the historic halls of the Sorbonne, France's oldest university (p. 87).

CELEBRATE the harvest and pick grapes on a vineyard (p. 92).

FLIP to our "Giving Back" sidebar features for even more regional Beyond Tourism opportunities (p. 83, p. 152, p. 159, p. 392, and p. 612).

As a tourist, you are always a foreigner. Sure, hostel-hopping and sightseeing can be great fun, but connecting with a foreign country through studying, volunteering, or working can extend your travels beyond tourist traps. Instead of feeling like a stranger in a strange land, you can understand France like a local. Instead of being that tourist asking for directions, you can be the one who gives them (and correctly!). All the while, you get the satisfaction of leaving France in better shape than you found it (after all, it's being nice enough to let you stay here). It's not wishful thinking—it's Beyond Tourism.

As a **volunteer** in France, you can unleash your inner superhero with projects from saving endangered species to combating AIDS. This chapter is chock-full of ideas to get involved, whether you're looking to pitch in for a day or run away from home for a whole new life in French activism.

The powers of **studying** abroad are beyond comprehension: it actually makes you feel sorry for those poor tourists who don't get to do any homework while they're here. France is home to some of the world's oldest universities—including the Sorbonne, founded in 1257—that are renowned for their programs in philosophy and literature. If existentialism isn't your *tasse de thé*, France's distinguished culinary schools—including the Cordon Bleu in Paris—will refine your broiling abilities and your palate. Or why not try your hand at Impressionism in one of France's many fine arts schools? The study abroad opportunities in France are limitless and the perfect way to indulge in French culture.

Working abroad immerses you in a new culture and can bring some of the most meaningful relationships and experiences of your life. Yes, we know you're on vacation, but these aren't your normal desk jobs. (Plus, it doesn't hurt that it helps pay for more globetrotting.) Many travelers structure their trips around the work available to them along the way, and employment opportunities range from odd jobs on the go to full-time, long-term work. While such long-term work is tough to find for non-EU citizens without professional expertise, English and especially English-French bilingual skills are desirable and can facilitate the job search. Short-term work is more readily available and can range from grape-picking in a vineyard to busing tables at a street-side cafe. Both long-term and short-term jobs require a work permit, which is discussed in detail in the upcoming sections.

SHARE YOUR EXPERIENCE. Have you had a particularly enjoyable volunteer, study, or work experience that you'd like to share with other travelers? Post it to our website, www.letsgo.com!

VOLUNTEERING

Feel like saving the world this week? Volunteering can be a powerful and fulfilling experience, especially when combined with the thrill of traveling in a new place. Though France is considered wealthy by Western standards, there is no shortage of aid organizations that address the social issues the country faces, and short-term volunteering positions can be found in nearly every city. France offers something to fit your every volunteering preference, whether it is to work with the elderly, to advocate for the environment and work for wildlife conservation, or to help restore Provence's crumbling ruins.

Most people who volunteer in France do so on a short-term basis at organizations that make use of drop-in or once-a-week volunteers. The best way to find opportunities that match your interests and schedule may be to check with local or national volunteer centers listed below. The most common short-term volunteer activities include community groups that work with the disadvantaged in France's cities, environmental protection efforts, and work camps that help restore historical monuments. As always, read up before heading out.

Those looking for longer, more intensive volunteer opportunities usually choose to go through a parent organization that takes care of logistical details and often provides a group environment and support system—for a fee. There are two main types of organizations—religious and secular—although there are rarely restrictions on participation for either. Websites like **www.volunteerabroad.com, www.servenet.org,** and **www.idealist.org** allow you to search for volunteer openings both in your country and abroad.

I HAVE TO PAY TO VOLUNTEER? Many volunteers are surprised to learn that some organizations require large fees or "donations," but don't go calling them scams just yet. While such fees may seem ridiculous at first, they often keep the organization afloat, covering airfare, room, board, and administrative expenses for the volunteers. (Other organizations must rely on private donations and government subsidies.) If you're concerned about how a program spends its fees, request an annual report or finance account. A reputable organization won't refuse to inform you of how volunteer money is spent. Pay-to-volunteer programs might be a good idea for young travelers who are looking for more support and structure (such as pre-arranged transportation and housing) or anyone who would rather not deal with the uncertainty of creating a volunteer experience from scratch.

GENERAL VOLUNTEER ORGANIZATIONS

Care France, CAP 19, 13 rue de Georges Auric, 75019 Paris (☎01 53 19 89 89; www. carefrance.org). An international organization providing volunteer opportunities that range from combating AIDS to promoting human rights to improving urban development. Over 130,000 supporting offices throughout France.

France Bénévolat, 127 rue Falguière Hall B1, 75015 Paris (☎01 40 61 01 61; www.francebenevolat.org). 70 offices in France place volunteers.

International Volunteer Program, 678 13th St., Ste. 100, Oakland, CA 94612, USA (☎+1-866-614-3438; www.ivpsf.org). 4- to 12-week programs in arts and culture, humanitarian relief, environmental conservation, and community development. The program fee of US$1450-3050 includes in-country transportation and room and board. Application fee US$100. Intermediate knowledge of French required. 18+.

International Volunteer Programs Association (IVPA), 1 Brattle Sq., Ste. 552, Cambridge, MA 02138, USA (☎+1-914-380-8322; www.volunteerinternational.org). Web resource with an international search engine for volunteer and internship opportunities that also provides general information about volunteering abroad.

Volunteers for Peace (VFP), 1034 Tiffany Rd., Belmont, VT 05730, USA (☎+1-802-259-2759; www.vfp.org). 2- to 3-week work camps provide international volunteers the opportunity to live and work together in host communities while contributing to one of several projects, ranging from archaeological restoration to AIDS education. US$300 fee covers food, lodging, and supplies. Membership fee US$30.

YOUTH AND THE COMMUNITY

Community-based projects involve close work with disadvantaged populations in France, including at-risk youth and the poor, elderly, and disabled. A high unemployment rate has left many communities reliant on social programs, which range from elderly care to prison reform. These programs can be the most rewarding of all volunteer experiences, but due to their one-on-one nature, knowledge of French is often necessary.

L'Arche les Sapins, 39 rue Olivier de Serres, 75015 Paris (☎01 45 32 23 74; www.arche-france.org). Branch of an international Christian organization that places volunteers in a community home for the mentally challenged or learning disabled. Volunteers expected to make at least a 6-month commitment. Regular work hours, room, board, medical insurance, and monthly allowance provided. Ages 18-28.

Fondation Claude Pompidou, 42 rue du Louvre, 75001 Paris (☎01 40 13 75 00; www.fondation-

GIVING BACK

RESTORING THE REMPARTS

REMPART is the umbrella organization for over 200 projects throughout France. Opportunities within REMPART are available in projects that range from restoration of the historic Loire Valley châteaux to the beautification of smaller farms and barns. REMPART's foundational philosophy is "re-use and revive": the organization believes in not only restoring sites but also rejuvenating them to serve a recyclable purpose. To this end, volunteers assist in projects that transform crumbling medieval ruins to open-air theaters and abandoned, decrepit laundromats into museums.

Volunteer positions are available for people 18 years old and over and typically last a little under one month. All volunteers are given a training session tailored to their assigned project in which they are equipped with specialty tools and techniques. All participants are guaranteed housing for their project's duration. Registration fees vary from organization to organization but typically hover under €10 per day.

Visit www.rempart.org for a searchable database of projects based on region and type of work or to request a catalogue that lists the year's projects. To contact REMPART via snail mail, write to REMPART, 1 rue des Guillemites, 75004 Paris.

claudepompidou.asso.fr). Aids the sick, elderly, and disabled through home care and companionship.

Groupement Étudiant National d'Enseignement aux Personnes Incarcerées (GENEPI), 12 rue Charles Fourier, 75013 Paris (☎01 45 88 37 00; www.genepi.fr). Students work with inmates in French prisons to promote social rehabilitation. Offices throughout France. In operation for over 30 years.

Marseille Volontariat, 14 rue Paul Casimir, 13010 Marseille (☎04 91 79 70 72; www. marseille-volontariat.com). Helps volunteers find opportunities by field of civic interest. Areas include elderly care, insurance disputes, and prison education. All programs take place in Marseille. Contact the **Marseille Centre Regional Information Jeunesse** (☎04 91 24 33 50; www.crijpa.com) for housing assistance.

Secours Catholique: Delegation de Paris, 13 rue St-Ambroise, 75011 Paris (☎01 48 07 58 21; www.quiaccueillequi.org). Catholic organization that works to support unemployed adults, children with social problems, immigrants, and other marginalized groups in Paris. Local branches throughout France.

Secours Populaire Français, 9/11 rue Froissart, 75140 Paris (☎01 44 78 21 00; www. secourspopulaire.asso.fr). National organization that provides food and clothing to poor children and families and arranges sporting and cultural activities. Aims to improve the quality of life of disadvantaged communities.

ENVIRONMENTAL CONSERVATION

After oil spills occured in France in 1999 and 2002 and similar disasters took place elsewhere in Europe, both France and the EU enacted strict pollution controls to protect coastal areas. Yet France's natural resources still face challenges, and individual volunteers continue to supplement government funds and efforts to preserve the environment.

Canadian Alliance for Development Initiatives and Projects (CADIP), 129-1271 Howe St., Vancouver, BC V6Z 1R3, Canada (☎+1-604-628-7400; www.cadip.org). Specializes in programs for environmental activism and historical renovation throughout France. Most projects last 2-3 weeks. Program fee US$300; includes room and board.

Centres Permanents d'Initiatives pour l'Environnement (CPIE), 26 rue Beaubourg, 75003 Paris (☎01 44 61 75 35; www.cpie.fr). Organizes environmentally centered volunteer programs in mainland France, Corsica, and some Francophone countries.

Organisation Mondiale de Protection de l'Environnement, 1 Carrefour de Longchamp, 75116 Paris (☎01 55 25 84 84; www.wwf.fr). Offers various opportunities for environmental activism regarding issues like climate change, endangered species, and sustainable living. Part of the World Wildlife Fund. Sites around France and the EU.

Worldwide Opportunities on Organic Farms (WWOOF), WWOOF France, 2 pl. Diderot, 94300 Vincennes (www.wwoof.fr). Provides volunteers the opportunity to learn firsthand organic farming techniques, such as biodynamic, permaculture, and micro-agriculture. Volunteers receive room and board in exchange for work on organic farms. Must purchase book with a list of 300+ host farms (€25, €15 for electronic version).

HISTORICAL RESTORATION

The preservation and reconstruction of French landmarks is an ongoing concern. Volunteers looking for a more labor-intensive experience and an opportunity to learn about France's architectural history can assist in this process.

Association Chantiers Histoire et Architecture Médiévales (CHAM), 5-7 rue Guilleminot, 75014 Paris (☎01 43 35 15 51; www.cham.asso.fr). Groups restore heritage sites in France and Francophone countries. Costs vary by age, program, and length of stay.

Association Pour la Participation et l'Action Régionale (APARE), 25 bd. Paul Pons, 84800 L'Isle-sur-la-Sorgue (☎04 90 85 51 15; www.apare-gec.org). Arranges short-term historical restoration projects in Avignon with an emphasis on the close relationship between local communities and teams of volunteers. Projects typically 2-3 weeks. Camps for both teens (16-18; €305) and adults (18-25; €95-165). Registration price includes room, board, camp activities, and internal travel.

Club du Vieux Manoir, Ancienne Abbaye du Moncel, 60700 Pontpoint (☎03 44 72 33 98; www.cvmclubduvieuxmanoir.free.fr). Projects of varying lengths to restore castles and churches. Membership and insurance fee €15 per year. Program fee €14 per day. Most programs ages 14 and up.

REMPART, 1 rue des Guillemites, 75004 Paris (☎01 42 71 96 55; www.rempart.com). Union of 170 nonprofit French organizations that offers 2- to 3-week work camps in monument restoration. Daily costs for room and board vary by camp. Registration fee covers accident insurance. Ages 18+.

La Sabranenque, rue de la Tour de l'Oume, 30290 St-Victor la Coste (www.sabranenque. com). Discover Provence while restoring its ancient architecture. 2-week sessions June-Sept. 1-week hiking and volunteer programs in Mar. and Oct. 18+.

STUDYING

It's hard to dread the first day of school when Paris is your campus and exotic restaurants are your meal plan. A growing number of students report that studying abroad is the highlight of their learning careers. If you've never studied abroad, you don't know what you're missing—and if you have studied abroad, you do know what you're missing. Either way, don't miss it.

VISA INFORMATION. Non-EU citizens hoping to study abroad in France must apply for a special student visa from the French consulate. There is a short-stay visa for stays up to 90 days as well as two long-stay visas: one for three to six months and one for six months to a year. Prospective students must fill out two to four applications—depending on the consulate—for the appropriate visa and provide a passport valid for at least three months after the student's last day in France, plus two extra passport photos. (When in doubt, bring extra copies of everything.) Additionally, students must give proof of enrollment in or admission to a French learning institute, a letter from the home university or institution certifying current registration as a student, a financial guarantee with a monthly allowance of US$600 per month during the intended stay, and proof of medical insurance. Finally, there is a visa application fee of €60 for short-stay visas and €99 for long-stay. When in France, students with long-stay visas for more than six months must obtain a *carte de séjour* (residency permit) from the local *Préfecture de Police;* students should file to obtain the card as soon as possible upon arrival. They will be required to undergo a medical checkup in addition to providing much of the same information needed for a visa. **EU citizens** do not need a visa or a *carte de séjour,* provided they have backup identification, including proof of address. See www.diplomatie.gouv.fr/en for more information.

Study-abroad programs range from basic language and culture courses to university-level classes, often for college credit (it's legit, Mom and Dad). In order to choose a program that best fits your needs, research as much as you can before making your decision—determine costs and duration, as well as what kind of students participate in the program and what sorts of accommodations are provided. France has a wide range of study options that offer different experiences, from direct enrollment in French universities to American programs with American professors and French resources.

In programs that have large groups of students who speak the same language, there is a trade-off. You may feel more comfortable in the community, but you will not have the same opportunity to practice a foreign language or to befriend other international students. For accommodations, dorm life provides a better opportunity to mingle with fellow students, but there is less of a chance to experience the local scene. If you live with a family, you could potentially build lifelong friendships with natives and experience day-to-day life in more depth, but you might also get stuck sharing a room with their pet iguana. Conditions can vary greatly from family to family.

BEYOND TOURISM

UNIVERSITIES

Most university-level study-abroad programs are conducted in French, although many programs offer classes in English as well as lower-level language courses. Savvy linguists may find it cheaper to enroll directly in a university abroad, although getting college credit may be more difficult. As a student at a French university, you will receive a *carte d'étudiant* (student card) upon presentation of a *carte de séjour* (residency permit). The **Centre Régional des Oeuvres Universitaires et Scolaires** (**CROUS**; www.crous-paris.fr/index.asp) offers benefits and discounts to students, including cheap meals and housing assistance. You can search **www.studyabroad.com** for various semester-abroad programs that meet your criteria, including your desired location and focus of study. If you're a college student, your friendly neighborhood study-abroad office is often the best place to start. The following is a list of organizations that can help place students in university programs abroad or that have their own branch in France.

AMERICAN PROGRAMS

American Institute for Foreign Study (AIFS), College Division, River Plaza, 9 W. Broad St., Stamford, CT 06902, USA (☎+1-866-906-2437; www.aifsabroad.com). Organizes programs for high-school and college study in universities in Cannes, Grenoble, and Paris. Program fees are around US$6000 for the summer and US$16,000 per semester. Also holds offices in Paris, 19 rue de Babylone (☎01 44 39 04 24).

Council on International Educational Exchange (CIEE), 300 Fore St., Portland, ME 04101, USA (☎+1-207-553-4000 or 800-40-STUDY/407-8839; www.ciee.org). One of the most comprehensive resources for work, academic, and internship programs around the world, including in Paris and Rennes. Summer course geared toward students with little or no background in French; semester-long programs require at least 2 years of college French. Program fees are US$3000 for the summer, US$11,600-14,250 per semester, and US$21,500-23,800 per academic year.

Cultural Experiences Abroad (CEA), France, 2005 W. 14th St., Ste. 113, Tempe, AZ 85281, USA (☎+1-800-266-4441; www.gowithcea.com). Students can take classes in both English and French in Aix-en-Provence, Grenoble, the Riviera, and Paris. US$5000 for the summer, US$10,000-17,000 per semester.

European Institute for International Education, The Eur-Am Center, 32500 Telegraph Rd., Ste. 209, Bingham Farms, MI 48025, USA (☎+1-248-988-9341; www.euram-center.com). Provides both educational and private-sector opportunities for people of all ages. Run by the University of Southern Mississippi. Tuition US$3800-4000 for the summer and US$9400 for a semester.

Institute for American Universities, 1830 Sherman Ave., Ste. 402, Evanston, IL 60201, USA (☎+1-800-221-2051; www.iaufrance.org). University-affiliated summer and school-year programs in Aix-en-Provence and Avignon. Tuition around US$5500 for the summer and US$13,000-$16,000 for a semester.

School for International Training (SIT) Study Abroad, 1 Kipling Rd., P.O. Box 676, Brattleboro, VT 05302, USA (☎+1-888-272-7881 or 802-258-3212; www.sit.edu/studyabroad). Semester-long programs in France run approximately US$23,000. Also runs **The Experiment in International Living** (☎+1-800-345-2929; www.usexperiment.org). 3- to 5-week summer programs for high-school students. Homestays, community service, ecological adventure, and language training in France (US$5300-6800).

FRENCH PROGRAMS

French universities are far cheaper than their American equivalents. However, it can be hard to receive academic credit at home for a non-approved program. Expect to pay at least €900 per month (€1200 in Paris) in living expenses. EU citizens studying in France can take advantage of the three- to 12-month **Socrates-Erasmus** program (www.europe-education-formation.fr), which offers grants to support inter-European educational exchanges.

French universities are segmented into three degree levels: the first level involves a basic university degree, the second is the equivalent of a master's degree, and the third is a *doctorat*, or PhD. Programs at the first level—except the Grandes Écoles, described below—are two or three years long and generally focus on science, medicine, and the liberal arts. They must admit anyone holding a *baccalauréat* (French graduation certificate) or recognized equivalent to their first year of courses (British A-levels or two years of college in the US). The more selective and demanding Grandes Écoles cover specializations from physics to photography to veterinary medicine. These have notoriously difficult entrance examinations that require a year of preparatory schooling.

Foreign students can study throughout France at the many regional schools, although Paris is the hub of France's best-known universities and Grandes Écoles. Many French universities offer French language and cultural programs as well as general university classes, particularly during the summer.

Agence EduFrance (www.edufrance.fr). A 1-stop resource for North Americans considering studying for a degree in France. Info on courses, costs, and grant opportunities. Housing options available in universities or with French families.

American University of Paris, 6 rue du Colonel Combes, 75007 Paris (☎01 40 62 07 20; www.aup.fr). US admissions office at 950 S. Cherry St., Ste. 210, Denver, CO 80246 (☎+1-303-757-6333). Offers US-accredited degrees and summer programs in English on its Paris campus. Intensive French language courses offered. Tuition €12,587 per semester and €24,689 per year, not including living expenses.

Université Paris-Sorbonne, 1 rue Victor Cousin, 75230 Paris (☎01 40 46 22 11; www.paris-sorbonne.fr/en). The grandfather of French universities, the Sorbonne has been going strong since 1257. Offers 3- to 9-month programs for American students. Tuition €530-2750 for summer- and semester-long French culture courses.

LANGUAGE SCHOOLS

Enrolling at a language school has two major perks: a slightly less rigorous course load and the ability to teach you exactly what those kids in Toulouse are calling you under their breath. There can be great variety in language schools—some are independently run, while others are affiliated with a larger university, local, international—but one thing is guaranteed: rarely do they offer college credit. Language school programs are ideal for younger high-school students who might not feel comfortable with older students in a university program. Some worthwhile organizations include:

Alliance Française, École Internationale de Langue et de Civilisation Française, 101 bd. Raspail, 75270 Paris Cedex 06 (☎01 42 84 90 00; www.alliancefr.org). Instruction at all levels, with courses in legal, medical, and business French. Courses last 1-12 weeks and cost approximately €50 per week for daily 2hr. sessions. Also offers private lessons starting at €60 per hour. Enrollment fee €55.

Eurocentres, 56 Eccleston Sq., London SW1V 1PH, UK (☎+44 20 7963 8450; www.eurocentres.com). Language programs for beginning to advanced students with homestays in Amboise, La Rochelle, and Paris.

Institut de Langue Française (ILF), 3 av. Bertie-Albrecht, 75008 Paris (☎01 45 63 24 00; www.ilf-paris.fr). Language, civilization, and literature courses beginning at €75 for 4 weeks of instruction. Also offers au pair courses beginning at €360.

Language Immersion Institute, State University of New York at New Paltz, 1 Hawk Dr., New Paltz, NY 12561, USA (☎+1-845-257-3500; www.newpaltz.edu/lii). Short, intensive summer language courses and some overseas courses in French. Program fees are around US$1000 for a 2-week course, not including accommodations.

World Link Education: Study in France, 1904 3rd Ave., Ste. 633, Seattle, WA 98101, USA (☎800-621-3085 or 206-264-0941; www.wle-france.com). French language and culture classes in Annecy, Bordeaux, Chambery, Nice, and Paris. Tuition varies.

CULINARY SCHOOLS

Those truly devoted to the art of French cuisine should be prepared to shell out extra cash for semester- or year-long programs in the world's culinary capital. For more intimate courses based on farms and in homes—often instructed by well-known chefs or food critics—see out www.cookingschools.com.

Cordon Bleu Paris Culinary Arts Institute, 8 rue Léon Delhomme, 75015 Paris (☎01 53 68 22 50; www.cordonbleu.edu). The *crème de la crème* of French cooking schools. Programs range from the decadent Grand Diplôme (€35,955) to 2 hr. demonstrations on specific culinary themes (€33-50).

Eurolingua Institute, 5 rue Henri Guinier, 34000 Montpellier (☎04 67 15 04 73; www.eurolingua.com/Work_Experience(France).htm). Language school that offers internships in hotel work and culinary arts in Montpellier, Nice, and Martinique. Intermediate French level required. Tuition ranges from €750 for 3 months to €1350 for 1 year; full-time work pays €200 per month.

Gastronomicom: French Language and Gastronomy School, Résidence St-Loup, 1 av. des Soldats, 34300 Cap d'Agde (☎06 71 72 28 13; www.gastronomicom.fr). Located in a seaside resort on the Mediterranean coast, this school offers programs of study for students age 18-60, including short programs in chocolate and sugar decoration. 1-,

3-, and 7-month courses (€2100/4900/5500) in cooking, wine appreciation, pastry decoration, and intensive French. All plans of study include lectures and free tastings. 7-month course includes 4-month internship. €150 enrollment fee.

Grande École des Arts Culinaires et de l'Hôtellerie de Lyon (Lyon Culinary Arts and Hotel Management School), Château du Vivier, BP 25, 69131 Ecully Cedex, Lyon (☎04 72 18 02 20; www.each-lyon.com). Premier school affiliated with world-famous chef Paul Bocuse, located in France's capital city of haute cuisine. 6- and 12-week summer courses in English and French for amateurs (€3700-6700).

The International Kitchen, 330 N. Wabash Av., Ste. 2613, Chicago, IL 60611, USA (☎+1-800-945-8606 or 312-467-0560; www.theinternationalkitchen.com). Offers 2- to 8-night "cooking vacations" with famous chefs in Burgundy, Champagne, the Loire Valley, Paris, Provence, the Côte d'Azur, and the southwest (US$695-3275). Also offers a 1-day course in the Rhône-Alpes, Paris, Provence, and the Côte d'Azur (US$170-300), as well as wine- and chocolate-tastings (US$95-160).

ART SCHOOLS

One final—and, again, pricey—study-abroad option will let even the amateur finger painters discover their inner Rodins.

Centre de Sculpture, Fonderie de la Dure, Montolieu 11170, Toulouse (☎04 68 24 81 81; louise. sculpture@wanadoo.fr). Residency program for visual artists in nonprofit rural art center.

Lacoste School of Art, York Hall, 115 E. York St., Savannah, GA 31401, USA (☎+1-912-525-4786; www.scad.edu/lacoste). French location at rue du Four, 84480 Lacoste. Administered by the Savannah College of Art and Design. Summer and fall courses in architecture and painting preservation. Tuition €2885 per course. €4900 program fee includes room, board, weekend excursions, and museum admissions.

The Marchutz School, 1830 Sherman Ave., Ste. 402, Evanston, IL 60201, USA (☎+1-800-221-2051; www.iaufrance.org/marchutz). Run by the Institute for American Universities. Interdisciplinary programs in various media on the outskirts of Aix-en-Provence. Classes, seminars, private instruction, painting supplies, and excursions included. In English. Summer courses US$5615; semester courses US$15,555.

Painting School of Montmiral, rue de la Porte Neuve, 81140 Castelnau de Montmiral (☎05 63 33 13 11; www.painting-school.com). 2-week classes at student or professional levels in English or French. €1304, including accommodations and half board. €500 deposit required.

Pont Aven School of Art, 269 S. Main St., Providence, RI 02903, USA (☎+1-401-272-5445; www.pontavon.org). French location at 5 pl. Paul Gaugin, 29930 Pont-Aven (☎02 98 09 10 45). English-speaking school in Brittany offers courses in art history and studio art. 4- and 5-week summer sessions €6200-7780.

WORKING

Nowhere does money grow on trees (though *Let's Go*'s researchers aren't done looking), but there are still some pretty good opportunities to earn a living and travel at the same time. As with volunteering, work opportunities tend to fall into two categories. Some travelers want long-term jobs that allow them to integrate into a community, while others seek out short-term jobs to finance the next leg of their travels. With France's 7.2% unemployment rate, long-term jobs are hard to come by. Travelers without EU citizenship face a particular challenge when searching for a job in France: only employers who cannot find qualified workers in the EU may petition to bring in a long-term worker who is not an EU citizen. If you're undeterred by the less-than-welcoming attitude toward foreign workers, you may want to try a job that requires English-language skills, as bilingual candidates have a better chance of finding work. Working as an au pair or teaching English are both popular long-term employment options. If you're in the market for a short-term stint, be on the lookout for a service or agricultural job. **Transitions Abroad** (www.transitionsabroad.com) also offers updated online listings for work over any time span.

Many jobs in France are secured through alumni networks or personal contacts, but classified advertisements in newspapers and online are also great resources for job-hunters. **Agence Nationale pour l'Emploi** (www.anpe.fr) has listings for many skilled and unskilled jobs alike, while **Agence pour l'Emploi de Cadres** (www.apec.fr) catalogues professional job listings. **Michael Page** (www.michaelpage.fr) is another job recruiting agency with offices in major French cities as well as international locations. Note that working abroad often requires a special work visa.

MORE VISA INFORMATION. EU citizens have the right to work in France without a visa and can easily obtain a *carte de séjour* (residency permit) by presenting a passport, proof of employment, and other personal identification documents. Visit www.infomobil.org for a complete list of requirements. Non-EU citizens hoping to work in France for less than 90 days must apply for an **Autorisation Provisoire de Travail** at a local branch of **Direction Départementale du Travail, de l'Emploi, et de la Formation Professionnelle (DDTEFP)**. A passport and proof of short-term employment are necessary to secure authorization; a short-term Schengen visa (US$62) is also sometimes required. Non-EU citizens wishing to work in France for more than 90 days must have an offer of employment authorized by the French Ministry of Labor (www.travail.gouv.fr) before applying for a long-stay visa (US$131) through their local French consulate. Within eight days of arrival in France, holders of long-stay visas must apply for a *carte de séjour*. International students hoping to secure a job must possess a *carte de séjour d'étudiant* (student residency card) and apply for an Autorisation Provisoire de Travail at a DDTEFP office. Students in France, depending on the region, are permitted to work up to 17½-20hr. per week during the academic year and full-time (35-40hr. per week) during summer and holidays. Special rules apply for au pairs and teaching assistants; see www.consulfrance-washington.org for more information.

LONG-TERM WORK

If you're planning on spending a substantial amount of time (more than 3 months) working in France, search for a job well in advance. International placement agencies are often the easiest way to find employment abroad, especially for those interested in teaching. Although they are often only available to college students, **internships** are a good way to ease into working abroad. Many say the interning experience is well worth it, despite low pay (if you're lucky enough to be paid at all). Be wary of advertisements for companies claiming to be able get you a job abroad for a fee—often the same listings are available online or in newspapers. Some reputable organizations include:

American Chamber of Commerce in France, 156 bd. Haussmann, 75008 Paris (☎01 56 43 45 67; www.amchamfrance.org). Supports Franco-American business relations and is currently generating an online job and internship directory.

Association for International Practical Training (AIPT), 10400 Little Patuxent Pkwy., Ste. 250, Columbia, MD 21044, USA (☎+1-410-997-2200; www.aipt.org). Offers information on professional and academic exchange experiences.

Centre d'Information et de Documentation Jeunesse, 101 quai Branly, 75015 Paris (☎01 44 49 12 00; www.cidj.com). Provides information on preparing for a career in France. Open M-W and F 10am-6pm, Th 1-6pm, Sa 9:30am-1pm.

Council on International Educational Exchange (CIEE), 300 Fore St., Portland, ME 04101, USA (☎+1-207-553-4000 or 800-40-STUDY/407-8839; www.ciee.org). Tucked into their study-abroad listings is a resource for international internships.

French-American Chamber of Commerce (FACC), 122 E. 42nd St., New York City, NY 10168, USA (☎+1-212-867-0123; www.faccnyc.org). Information on international career development programs.

International Association for the Exchange of Students for Technical Experience (IAESTE), 20 Av. Albert Einstein, Bâtiment 705, 69621 Villeurbanne Cedex (☎04 72 43 83 91; www.iaeste.org). Chances are that your home country has a local office, too; contact it to apply for hands-on technical internships in France. You must be a college student studying science, technology, or engineering. "Cost of living allowance" covers most non-travel expenses. Most programs last 8-12 weeks.

TEACHING ENGLISH

While some elite private American schools offer competitive salaries, let's just say that teaching jobs abroad pay more in personal satisfaction and emotional fulfillment than in actual cash. Perhaps this is why volunteering as a teacher instead of getting paid is a popular option. Even then, teachers often receive some sort of a daily stipend to help with living expenses. In almost all cases, you must have at least a bachelor's degree to be a full-fledged teacher, although college undergraduates can often get summer positions teaching or tutoring. Because many bosses require that employees take English classes, demand for teachers is fairly high, despite France's resilient pride in its language.

Many schools require teachers to have a **Teaching English as a Foreign Language (TEFL)** certificate. You may still be able to find a teaching job without one, but certified teachers often find higher-paying jobs. The French-impaired don't have to give up their dream of teaching, either. Private schools usually hire native English speakers for English-immersion classrooms where no French is spoken. (Teachers in public schools will more likely work in both English and French.) Placement agencies or university fellowship programs are the best resources for finding teaching jobs. The alternative is to contact schools directly or to try your luck once you arrive in France. In the latter case, the best time to look is several weeks before the start of the school year. The following organizations are extremely helpful in placing teachers in France.

French Ministry of Education Teaching Assistantship in France, French Embassy, 4101 Reservoir Rd., Washington, DC 20007, USA (☎+1-202-944-6294; www.ambafrance-us. org). Program for US citizens sends up to 1700 grads and undergrads to teach English in France on a €900 monthly stipend.

International Schools Services (ISS), 15 Roszel Rd., P.O. Box 5910, Princeton, NJ 08543, USA (☎+1-609-452-0990; www.iss.edu). Hires teachers for more than 200 schools around the world. Candidates should have teaching experience and a bachelor's degree. 2-year commitment is the norm.

AU PAIR WORK

Au pairs are typically women (although sometimes men) aged 18-27 who work as live-in nannies, caring for children and doing light housework in foreign countries in exchange for room, board, and a small spending allowance or stipend. One job perk is that it allows you to get to know France without the expense of traveling. Drawbacks, however, can include mediocre pay and long hours. In France, au pairs are paid between €50 and €75 per week. Much of the au pair experience depends on the family with which you are placed. The agencies below are a good starting point for looking for employment. There is also a database for au pair agencies at www.europa-pages.com/au_pair/france.html.

Accueil International Services, rue Ducastel, 78100 St-Germain en Laye (☎01 39 73 04 98; www.accueil-international.com). Organization that promotes cultural exchange by placing international au pairs in French households.

Agence Au Pair Fly, 16 rue Madeleine Fourcade, 69007 Lyon (☎04 37 65 70 83; www.aupairfly.com). Opportunities range in length from 3 months to 1 year. 2 month min.

Childcare International, Trafalgar House, Grenville Pl., London NW7 3SA, UK (☎+44 20 8906 3116; www.childint.co.uk). Over 20 years of experience placing au pairs.

InterExchange, 161 6th Ave., New York City, NY 10013, USA (☎+1-212-924-0446 or 800-AU-PAIRS/287-2477; www.interexchange.org).

SHORT-TERM WORK

Believe it or not, traveling for long periods of time can be hard on the wallet. Many travelers try their hand at odd jobs for a few weeks at a time to help pay for another month or two of touring around. Seasonal work can be found in the hotel and restaurant businesses, in markets, and in agriculture. Another popular option is to work several hours a day at a hostel in exchange for free or discounted room and/or board. Most often, these short-term jobs are found by word of mouth or by expressing interest to the owner of a hostel or restaurant. Due to high turnover in the tourism industry, many places are eager for help, even if it is only temporary. Look in the "Positions Vacants" section of papers such as the "Guide du Job Trotter" or try www.jobs-ete.com for a summer job search engine. *Let's Go* lists temporary jobs of this nature whenever possible; look in the Practical Information sections of larger cities or see below.

Appellation Contrôlée, Neutronstraat 10, 9743 AM Groningen, the Netherlands (☎+31 50 549 2434; www.apcon.nl). Places EU citizens in grape-picking jobs during the harvest season for €50 per day.

Centre Régional Information Jeunesse (CRIJ) de Côte d'Azur, 19 rue Gioffredo, 06000 Nice (☎04 93 80 93 93; www.crijca.fr). Seasonal and long-term job opportunities in the region are posted online. CRIJ locations throughout France offer job search resources.

Fédération Unie des Auberges de Jeunesse, 27 rue Pajol, 75018 Paris (☎01 44 89 87 27; www.fuaj.org). Offers short-term work in member youth hostels, from catering to reception. Submit application to individual hostel.

FURTHER READING ON BEYOND TOURISM

Alternatives to the Peace Corps: A Guide of Global Volunteer Opportunities, edited by Paul Backhurst. Food First, 2005 (US$12).

The Back Door Guide to Short-Term Job Adventures: Internships, Summer Jobs, Seasonal Work, Volunteer Vacations, and Transitions Abroad, by Michael Landes. Ten Speed Press, 2005 (US$22).

Green Volunteers: The World Guide to Voluntary Work in Nature Conservation, by Fabio Ausenda. Universe, 2007 (US$15).

How to Get a Job in Europe, by Cheryl Matherly and Robert Sanborn. Planning Communications, 2003 (US$23).

How to Live Your Dream of Volunteering Overseas, by Joseph Collins, Stefano DeZerega, and Zahara Heckscher. Penguin Books, 2001 (US$20).

International Job Finder: Where the Jobs Are Worldwide, by Daniel Lauber and Kraig Rice. Planning Communications, 2002 (US$20).

Live and Work Abroad: A Guide for Modern Nomads, by Huw Francis and Michelyne Callan. Vacation Work Publications, 2001 (US$20).

Volunteer Vacations: Short-Term Adventures That Will Benefit You and Others, by Doug Cutchins, Anne Geissinger, and Bill McMillon. Chicago Review Press, 2006 (US$18).

Work Abroad: The Complete Guide to Finding a Job Overseas, edited by Clayton A. Hubbs. Transitions Abroad, 2002 (US$16).

Work Your Way Around the World, by Susan Griffith. Vacation Work Publications, 2007 (US$22).

BEYOND TOURISM

Higher Education in Another Nation

Have you ever dreamed of mastering your French kissing by practicing with locals? Have you considered taking classes in Paris, Lyon, or Lille as an excuse? Living the student life can

"Picture yourself pondering Sartre's philosophy while sipping wine in Bordeaux."

be even better abroad, and enrolling in a French university is an excellent alternative for those who want the French academic experience and the opportunity to explore other aspects of local culture. Everyone has heard of the Sorbonne—the elite school in the heart of Paris's Latin Quarter—but France is home to more than 50 universities throughout its diverse regions. Just picture yourself pondering the nuances of Sartre's philosophy while sipping wine in Bordeaux or considering Napoleon's military stratagems on a white sand beach in his Corsican hometown.

While there are some small-scale college workshops, the majority of French students head to university after *lycée* (high school), and classes can get pretty large—you may have up to 200 classmates. Forget about your teacher knowing your name; consider yourself lucky if he or she ever responds to your emails. Academics aside, you'll have plenty of classmates to charm, and—since the social scene happens primarily outside of the university, especially in big cities like Paris—you can look forward to having the whole city as your playground.

But university is not the only option; the country in which the essay was invented naturally has its share of challenging academic alternatives. Whereas most French universities are required to accept anyone with a *baccalauréat* (French high school graduation certificate) or recognized

equivalent (British A-levels or two years of US college), the specialized Grandes Écoles are notoriously selective. In fact, Grandes Écoles hopefuls must endure two years of *classes preparatoires* (often called *prepas*) before earning consideration from admissions boards; even then, only 5-10% of students are accepted. Though there are foreign students in the *prepas*, they are typically bilingual. If a Grande École is your ultimate goal, consider taking a vow of French.

Graduate school is yet another option for those craving a study-abroad experience. Among the most prestigious graduate schools are the École Normale Supérieure (ENS; www.ens.fr) for humanities, the Institut d'Études Politiques (www.sciences-po.fr) for government studies, the Hautes Études Commerciales (HEC; www.hec.fr) for business, and the École Polytechnique (www.polytechnique.fr) for engineering and math. You can enroll after passing an admission exam or through an exchange with your own university—check the websites for more info.

"Studying abroad entails more than enrollment in Cafes and Croissants 101."

Be aware that studying abroad in France entails more than enrollment in Cafes and Croissants 101. In addition to a diligent work ethic, the experience requires a lot of pre-departure preparation (see **Beyond Tourism: Studying**, p. 85). Furthermore, try to remain level-headed in dealings with the difficult academic administration; after all, the French did invent the guillotine.

A DIFFERENT PATH

Laurent Deflandre is a student at the École Normale Supérieure and Sciences Po. A Derek Bok Center Award recipient, he taught French at Harvard University and studied public management at the Harvard Kennedy School. Deflandre holds master's degrees in History and Communication.

PARIS

From students who obsess over Derrida's *Of Grammatology* to tourists who wonder why the French don't pronounce half of each word, everyone enjoys Paris (PAH-ree; pop. 2,159,000), where the law forbids buildings to exceed six stories—*pour que tout le monde ait du soleil* (so that all have sunshine). Parisians may English you—that is, respond in English when you try to speak in French—and your feet may feel like petrified stubs *de bois* by the end of each day, but Paris pulls through for those who look beyond the tourist magnets to the sensory magic around every corner. The aroma of a *boulangerie*, the gleam of bronze balconies, and the buzz of a good €2 bottle of red are worth dealing with the famed snobbery—and yes, the waiters are judging you. Paris is open to those willing to wander. It will charm and disdain you with equal gusto, but don't get too *le tired;* by your third or fourth sincere attempt at *s'il vous plait*, even the waiters soften up. Stick around long enough, and you'll be able to tell the *foux* from the *foux de fa fa*, the Lavazza from the Illy, and the meta hipster yuppie bars from the wannabe meta hipster yuppie bars. For more in-depth coverage on what's what in the City of Love, check out █Let's Go: Paris.

HIGHLIGHTS OF PARIS

SHARE the view with Quasimodo atop Notre Dame (p. 138), trendsetters on the 56th floor of Tour Montparnasse (p. 150), and lovebirds atop the Tour Eiffel (p. 145).

WANDER halls full of world-famous art at the Louvre (p. 154), Musée d'Orsay (p. 159), Musée de Cluny (p. 157), Musée Rodin (p. 158), and Musée Picasso (p. 156).

STORM the Bastille district (p. 115) and the Quartier Latin (p. 113)—both rad nightlife spots known better for their radical roles in history.

✈ INTERCITY TRANSPORTATION

BY PLANE

ROISSY-CHARLES DE GAULLE (ROISSY-CDG)

Flights: Most transatlantic flights use Charles de Gaulle (www.adp.fr).

Trains: RER to **Paris** from Roissy-CDG leaves from the Roissy train station in Terminal 2. RER B (a Parisian commuter rail line) runs to central Paris. To transfer to the Métro, get off at Gare du Nord, Châtelet-Les Halles, or St-Michel. To get to Roissy-CDG from Paris, take the RER B3 to its end (35min., every 15min. 5am-12:30am, €13).

Buses: █**Roissybus** (☎01 49 25 61 87) runs between rue Scribe at pl. de l'Opéra and Terminals 1, 2, and 3 (45min; every 15min. 6am-7pm, every 20min. 7-11pm; €8.90, under 5 free). **Air France Buses** (recorded info available in English ☎08 92 35 08 20) run to 2 areas of the city. Stops at or between Terminals 2A-D and F and at Terminal 1 on airport's departures level. Line 2 runs to the **Arc de Triomphe** (ⓂCharles de Gaulle-Etoile) at 1 av. Carnot and to **place de la Porte de Maillot/Palais des Congrès** (ⓂPorte Maillot) on bd. Gouvion St-Cyr (both 35min.; every 15min. 5:45am-11pm; €10,

Île-de-France

round-trip €17, 15% group discount). Line 4 runs to **rue du Commandant Mouchette** (ⓂMontparnasse-Bienvenüe) and to **Gare de Lyon** at 20 bis bd. Diderot (every 30min. 7am-9pm; €12, round-trip €20, 15% group discount).

ORLY

Flights: Charters and many continental flights use Orly (☎01 49 75 15 15).

Trains: RER. From Orly Sud: Gate G or I: Platform 1 or Orly Ouest Level G: Gate F, take the **Orly-Rail** shuttle (every 15min. 6am-11pm, €5.15) to the **Pont de Rungis/Aéroport d'Orly** stop, where you can board the RER C2 for destinations in Paris (35min.; every 15min. 6am-11pm; €5.40, children €3.80). **Jetbus** (every 15min. 6:20am-10:50pm, €5.20) provides a quick connection between Orly Sud: Gate H: Platform 2 or Orly Ouest Level 0: Gate C and ⓂVillejuif-Louis Aragon on Métro line 7.

Buses: RATP ▩Orlybus (☎08 36 68 77 14) runs between ⓂDenfert-Rochereau in the 14ème and Orly's south terminal (25min.; every 15-20min. 6am-11:30pm from Orly, 5:35am-11pm from Denfert-Rochereau; €6.30). You can also board at **Dareau-St-Jacques, Glacière-Tolbiac,** and **Porte de Gentilly. Air France Buses** run to Gare Montparnasse, near 6ème (ⓂMontparnasse-Bienvenüe), and the **Invalides** Air France agency, pl. des Invalides (30min.; every 15min. 6am-11:30pm; €14, round-trip €22). Stops at departure levels of Orly Ouest and Orly Sud.

Orlyval: ☎01 69 93 53 00. Run by **RATP.** Combination of Métro, RER, and VAL rail shuttle—probably your fastest option. **VAL** shuttle goes from **Antony** (RER line B stop) to Orly Ouest and Sud. VAL ticket €7.40; combination VAL-RER tickets €9.60. **To Orly:** Be careful when taking the RER B, because it splits into 2 lines right before the Antony stop. Get on the train that says St-Rémy-Les-Chevreuse or just look for the track that has a lit-up sign saying Antony-Orly. 35min. from Châtelet; every 10min. M-Sa 6am-10:30pm, Su and holidays 7am-11pm. **From Orly:** Trains arrive at Orly Ouest 2min. after reaching Orly Sud. 32min. to Châtelet; every 10min. M-Sa 6am-10:30pm, Su 7am-11pm.

BEAUVAIS

Flights: Ryanair, easyJet, and other intercontinental airlines use Aéroport Beauvais.

Buses: ☎03 44 11 46 86; www.aeroportbeauvais.com. Run between the airport and **boulevard Pershing** in the 17ème (Ⓜ Porte Maillot). Tickets €13.

BY TRAIN

If you're traveling to Paris from another European city, trains can be a scenic and inexpensive option. Prices and number of trips per day vary according to the day of the week, season, and other criteria.

SOYEZ PRUDENT. Exercise caution in train stations at night; Gare du Nord and Gare d'Austerlitz, in particular, are home to after-hours sketchiness. Also, buy tickets only at official counters; SNCF doesn't have any outfits in refrigerator boxes, no matter what you're told.

Gare d'Austerlitz: To the Loire Valley, southwestern France (Bordeaux, Pyrenees), Spain, and Portugal. To **Barcelona** (12hr.) and **Madrid** (12-13hr.).

Gare de l'Est: To eastern France (Champagne, Alsace, Lorraine, Strasbourg), Luxembourg, parts of Switzerland (Basel, Zürich, Lucerne), southern Germany (Frankfurt, Munich), Austria, Hungary, and Prague. To: **Luxembourg** (4-5hr.); **Munich** (9hr.); **Prague** (15hr.); **Strasbourg** (4hr.); **Vienna** (15hr.); **Zürich** (7hr.).

Gare du Nord: To northern France, Britain, Belgium, the Netherlands, Scandinavia, Eastern Europe, and northern Germany (Cologne, Hamburg). To **Amsterdam** (4-5hr.), **Brussels** (1hr.), and **London** (by Chunnel; 3hr.).

Gare de Lyon: To southern and southeastern France (Lyon, Provence, Riviera), parts of Switzerland (Geneva, Lausanne, Bern), Italy, and Greece. To: **Lyon** (2hr.); **Marseille** (3-4hr.); **Nice** (6hr.); **Florence** (13hr.); **Geneva** (4hr.); **Rome** (15hr.).

Gare Montparnasse: To Brittany and southwestern France on the TGV. To **Rennes** (2hr.).

Gare St-Lazare: To Normandy. To **Caen** (2hr.) and **Rouen** (1-2hr.).

BY BUS

International buses arrive at **Gare Routière Internationale du Paris-Gallieni** (Ⓜ Gallieni), just outside Paris at 28 av. du Général de Gaulle, Bagnolet 93170. **Eurolines** (☎08 92 89 90 91, €0.40 per min.; www.eurolines.com) sells tickets to most destinations in France and neighboring countries.

◆ ORIENTATION

The Seine (sehn) River flows from east to west through the heart of Paris, splitting the city into Rive Gauche (Left Bank) to the south and Rive Droite (Right Bank) to the north. Two islands in the Seine, **Île de la Cité** and neighboring

PARIS

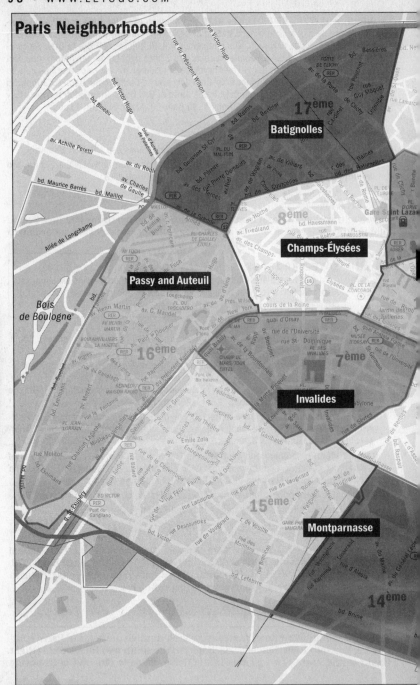

Paris Neighborhoods

Batignolles

17ème

8ème

Champs-Élysées

Passy and Auteuil

Bois de Boulogne

16ème

7ème

Invalides

15ème

Montparnasse

14ème

PARIS

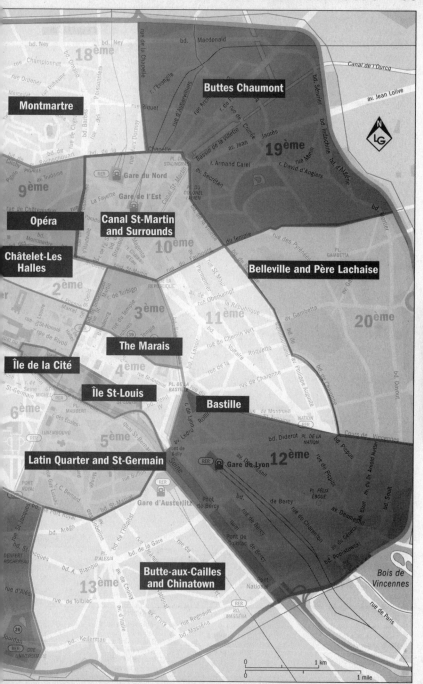

Montmartre

Buttes Chaumont

Opéra

Canal St-Martin and Surrounds

Châtelet-Les Halles

Belleville and Père Lachaise

The Marais

Île de la Cité

Île St-Louis

Bastille

Latin Quarter and St-Germain

Butte-aux-Cailles and Chinatown

PARIS

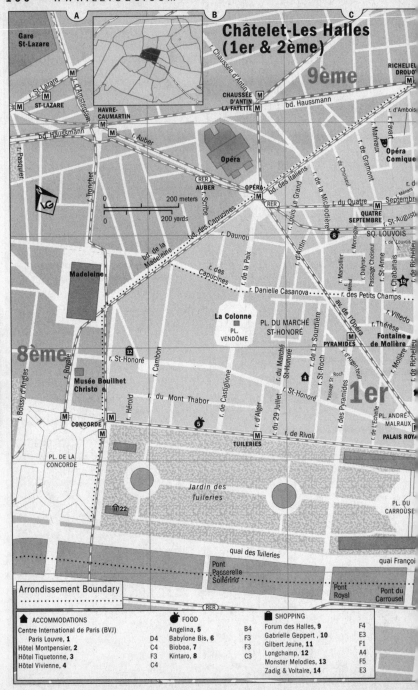

**Châtelet-Les Halles
(1er & 2ème)**

Gare
St-Lazare

9ème

RICHELIEU
DROUO

ST-LAZARE

CHAUSSÉE
D'ANTIN
LA FAYETTE

HAVRE-
CAUMARTIN

bd. Haussmann

r. d'Ambois

bd. Haussmann

r. Auber

Opéra

Opéra
Comique

AUBER
RER

OPÉRA

bd. des Italiens

QUATRE
SEPTEMBRE

SQ. LOUVOIS

r. des Capucines

r. Daunou

r. des
Capucines

r. de la Paix

r. Danielle Casanova

r. des Petits Champs

Madeleine

La Colonne

PL. DU MARCHÉ
ST-HONORÉ

Fontaine
de Molière

PL.
VENDÔME

PYRAMIDES

8ème

r. St-Honoré

PL. DU MARCHÉ
ST-HONORÉ

1er

Musée Bouilhet
Christo

r. du Mont Thabor

PL. ANDRÉ-
MALRAUX

PALAIS ROYA

CONCORDE

TUILERIES

r. de Rivoli

PL. DE LA
CONCORDE

Jardin des
Tuileries

PL. DU
CARROUSE

quai des Tuileries

quai Françoi

Pont
Passerelle
Solférino

Pont
Royal

Pont
du Carrousel

Arrondissement Boundary

ACCOMMODATIONS		FOOD		SHOPPING	
Centre International de Paris (BVJ)		Angelina, **5**	B4	Forum des Halles, **9**	F4
Paris Louvre, **1**	D4	Babylone Bis, **6**	F3	Gabrielle Geppert , **10**	E3
Hôtel Montpensier, **2**	C4	Bioboa, **7**	F3	Gilbert Jeune, **11**	F1
Hôtel Tiquetonne, **3**	F3	Kintaro, **8**	C3	Longchamp, **12**	A4
Hôtel Vivienne, **4**	C4			Monster Melodies, **13**	F5
				Zadig & Voltaire, **14**	E3

PARIS

★ NIGHTLIFE		
Le 18 Club, **15**		D3
Le Baiser Salé, **16**		F4
Banana Café, **17**		F4
Café Oz, **18**		F5
Le Champmeslé, **19**		C3
Au Duc des Lombards, **20**		F4
🏛 MUSEUMS		
Musée du Louvre, **21**		D5
Musée de l'Orangerie, **22**		A5

PARIS

The Marais (3ème & 4ème)

ACCOMMODATIONS
Le Fauconnier, 1 — D5
Le Fourcy, 2 — D5
Grand Hôtel Jeanne d'Arc, 3 — E4
Hôtel du Marais, 4 — C2
Hôtel Picard, 5 — D2
Maubuisson, 6 — C5

FOOD
404, 7 — A2
L'Apparement Café, 8 — D3
L'As du Falafel, 9 — D4
Briezh Café, 10 — D3
Bubbles, 11 — D4
Chez Janou, 12 — C2
Chez Marianne, 13 — C4
Chez Omar, 14 — F4
Georges, 15 — A4
Little Italy Trattoria, 16 — B3
Mariage Frères, 17 — C4
myberry, 18 — C4
Palais des Thés, 19 — C3
Piccolo Teatro, 20 — C4
La Victoire, 21 — C4

MUSEUMS
Fait & Cause, 22 — A4
Galerie Emmanuel Perrotin, 23 — D3
Galerie Thuillier, 24 — D3
Musée National d'Art Moderne, 25 — A4
Mémorial de la Shoah, 26 — C5
Musée Carnavalet, 27 — D4
Musée Picasso, 28 — D3

Arrondissement Boundary ·········

■ SHOPPING
Abou d'abi Bazar, 29 — E4
BHV, 30 — E4
Brontibay, 31 — D4
Culotte, 32 — D4
Factory's Paris, 33 — C4
Free "P" Star, 34 — C4
I Heart Ethel, 35 — E3
Loft Design By, 36 — D4
Monic, 37 — B4
Vertiges, 38 — A4

★ NIGHTLIFE
Amnésia Café, 39 — C4
Andy Wahloo, 40 — A2
La Belle Hortense, 41 — C4
Le Connétable, 42 — C3
Le Dépôt, 43 — A3
L'Estaminet, 44 — C2
Open Café, 45 — B4
Raidd Bar, 46 — B4
Le Yono, 47 — C4

PARIS

4ème

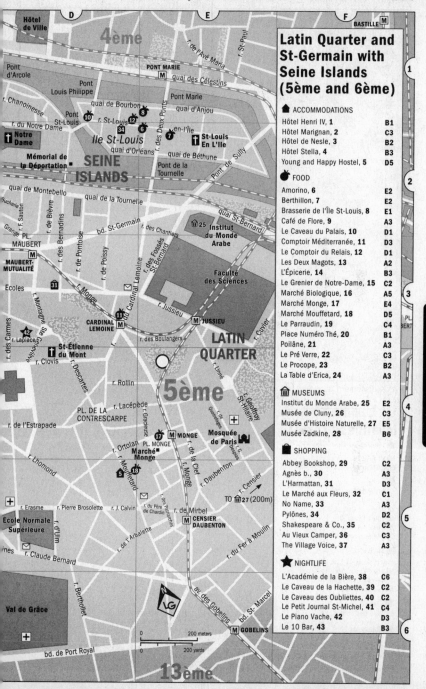

Latin Quarter and St-Germain with Seine Islands (5ème and 6ème)

🏠 ACCOMMODATIONS

Hôtel Henri IV, 1	B1
Hôtel Marignan, 2	C3
Hôtel de Nesle, 3	B2
Hôtel Stella, 4	B3
Young and Happy Hostel, 5	D5

🍴 FOOD

Amorino, 6	E2
Berthillon, 7	E2
Brasserie de l'Île St-Louis, 8	E1
Café de Flore, 9	A3
Le Caveau du Palais, 10	D1
Comptoir Méditerranée, 11	D3
Le Comptoir du Relais, 12	D1
Les Deux Magots, 13	A2
L'Épicerie, 14	B3
Le Grenier de Notre-Dame, 15	C2
Marché Biologique, 16	A5
Marché Monge, 17	E4
Marché Mouffetard, 18	D5
Le Parraudin, 19	C4
Place Numéro Thé, 20	B1
Poilâne, 21	A3
Le Pré Verre, 22	C3
Le Procope, 23	B2
La Table d'Erica, 24	A3

🏛 MUSEUMS

Institut du Monde Arabe, 25	E2
Musée de Cluny, 26	C3
Musée d'Histoire Naturelle, 27	E5
Musée Zadkine, 28	B6

🛍 SHOPPING

Abbey Bookshop, 29	C2
Agnès b., 30	A3
L'Harmattan, 31	D3
Le Marché aux Fleurs, 32	C1
No Name, 33	A3
Pylônes, 34	D2
Shakespeare & Co., 35	C2
Au Vieux Camper, 36	C3
The Village Voice, 37	A3

⭐ NIGHTLIFE

L'Académie de la Bière, 38	C6
Le Caveau de la Hachette, 39	C2
Le Caveau des Oubliettes, 40	C2
Le Petit Journal St-Michel, 41	C4
Le Piano Vache, 42	D3
Le 10 Bar, 43	B3

PARIS

PARIS

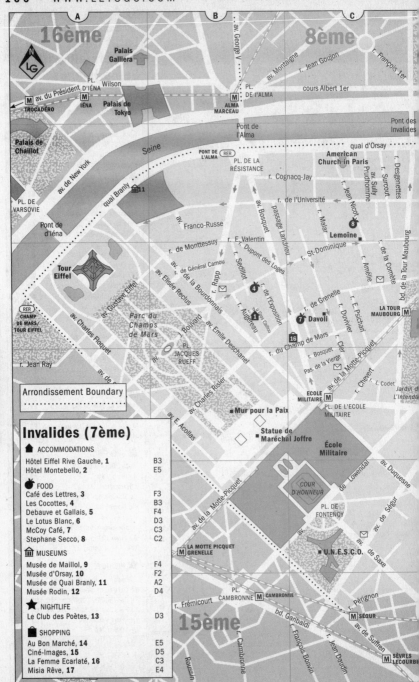

16ème

8ème

Palais
Galliera

av. George V

av. Montaigne

r. Jean Goujon

r. François 1er

PL. Wilson
D'IÉNA

av. du Président D'IÉNA

IÉNA

TROCADÉRO

Palais de
Tokyo

PL.
DE l'ALMA

ALMA
MARCEAU

cours Albert 1er

Pont des
Invalides

Palais de
Chaillot

Seine

Pont de
l'Alma

quai d'Orsay

PL. DE
VARSOVIE

quai Branly

PONT DE
L'ALMA (RER)

PL. DE LA
RÉSISTANCE

American
Church in Paris

r. Desgenettes

av. Sully Prudhomme

r. Surcouf

Pont de
d'Iéna

av. de New York

11

r. Cognacq-Jay

r. de l'Université

r. Jean Nicot

av. de la Tour Maubourg

av. Franco-Russe

r. de Monttessuy

r. E. Valentin

av. Bosquet

passage Landrieu

Malar

Lemoine

8

r. St-Dominique

r. de la Comète

Tour
Eiffel

av. de Général Camou

av. Élisée Reclus

av. de la Bourdonnais

r. Rapp

r. Sedillot

Dupont des Loges

r. de l'Exposition

r. Amélie

RER
CHAMP
DE MARS/
TOUR EIFFEL

av. Gustave Eiffel

Parc du
Champs
de Mars

J. Boulvard

av. Émile Deschanel

r. Augereau

1

4

r. Cler

r. de Grenelle

Davoli

7

16

r. E. Psichad

r. Duvivier

LA TOUR
MAUBOURG

M

av. Charles Floquet

PL.
JACQUES
RUEFF

r. du Champ de Mars

r. Bosquet

Pas. de la Vierge

r. Chevert

r. Cler

L. Codet

Jardin d
L'Intendo

r. Jean Ray

av. de

av. Charles Risler

av. de la Motte-Picquet

ECOLE
MILITAIRE

M

PL. DE L'ECOLE
MILITAIRE

Arrondissement Boundary

av. E. Acollas

Mur pour la Paix

Statue de
Maréchal Joffre

École
Militaire

COUR
D'HONNEUR

de Lowendal

av. Duquesne

av. de Ségur

Invalides (7ème)

🏠 ACCOMMODATIONS

Hôtel Eiffel Rive Gauche, 1   B3
Hôtel Montebello, 2   E5

🍎 FOOD

Café des Lettres, 3   F3
Les Cocottes, 4   B3
Debauve et Gallais, 5   F4
Le Lotus Blanc, 6   D3
McCoy Café, 7   C3
Stephane Secco, 8   C2

🏛 MUSEUMS

Musée de Maillol, 9   F4
Musée d'Orsay, 10   F2
Musée de Quai Branly, 11   A2
Musée Rodin, 12   D4

⭐ NIGHTLIFE

Le Club des Poètes, 13   D3

🛍 SHOPPING

Au Bon Marché, 14   E5
Ciné-Images, 15   D5
La Femme Ecarlaté, 16   C3
Misia Rêve, 17   E4

av. de la Motte-Picquet

LA MOTTE PICQUET
GRENELLE

M

PL. DE
FONTENOY

av. de Saxe

U.N.E.S.C.O.

r. Frémicourt

r. Cambronne

PL.
CAMBRONNE

CAMBRONNE

M

CAMBRONNE

bd. Garibaldi

r. Jean Daudin

r. François Bonvin

r. Roussin

15ème

r. Pérignon

SÉGUR

M

av. de Suffren

SÈVRES
LECOURBE

M

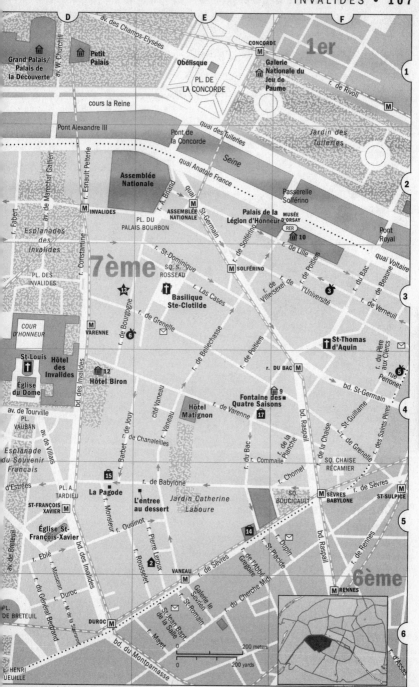

1er

av. des Champs-Elysées

CONCORDE
M

Grand Palais/
Palais de
la Découverte

Petit
Palais

Obélisque

PL. DE
LA CONCORDE

Galerie
Nationale du
Jeu de
Paume

r. de Rivoli

M

cours la Reine

Pont Alexandre III

Pont de
la Concorde

quai des Tuileries

Jardin des
Tuileries

Seine

quai Anatole France

Assemblée
Nationale

Passerelle
Solférino

r. A. Briand

INVALIDES

ASSEMBLÉE
NATIONALE

M

St-Germain

Palais de la
Légion d'Honneur

MUSÉE
D'ORSAY

Pont
Royal

Esplanade
des
Invalides

PL. DU
PALAIS BOURBON

RER
10

r. de Lille

quai Voltaire

PL. DES
INVALIDES

r. St-Dominique

SQ. S.
ROSSEAU

r. de Solférino

M SOLFÉRINO

r. de Poitiers

r. du Bac

r. de Beaune

7ème

13

r. de Grenelle

r. Las Cases

Basilique
Ste-Clotilde

r. de Villersexel

r. de
l'Université

3

r. de Verneuil

COUR
D'HONNEUR

M
VARENNE

r. de Bourgogne

6

r. de Bellechasse

r. de Poitiers

St-Thomas
d'Aquin

r. du Père
aux Clercs

rue
Perronet

St-Louis

Hôtel
des
Invalides

12
Hôtel Biron

bd. St-Germain

Église
du Dome

av. de Tourville

PL.
VAUBAN

cité Vaneau

r. Vaneau

Hôtel
Matignon

Fontaine des
Quatre Saisons

9

17

r. de Varenne

r. DU BAC M

r. St-Guillaume

r. des Saints Pères

av. de Villars

Esplanade
du Souvenir
Francais

r. de Jouy

r. de Chanaleilles

r. du Bac

r. de la
Planche

bd. Raspail

de la Chaise

SQ. CHAISE
RÉCAMIER

d'Estrées

15

r. de Babylone

r. Commaille

r. Chomel

PL. A.
TARDIEU

La Pagode

L'entree
au dessert

Jardin Catherine
Laboure

SQ.
BOUCICAULT

M SÈVRES
BABYLONE

r. de Sèvres

M

ST-SULPICE

ST-FRANÇOIS
XAVIER M

Église St-
François-Xavier

r. Monsieur

r. Ouginot

r. de Sèvres

14

r. St-Placide

r. Dupin

de l'Abbé
Grégoire

bd. Raspail

r. de Rennes

av. de Breteuil

r. Eblé

bd. des Invalides

r. Pierre Leroux

r. Rousselet

2

VANEAU

M

r. du Cherche Midi

6ème

r. du Général Bertrand

r. Masseran

r. Duroc

DUROC M

St-Jean Bapt.
de la Salle

St-Romain

Galerie le
Savien

M RENNES

PL.
DE BRETEUIL

r. Meyer

bd. du Montparnasse

0   200 meters

0   200 yards

L'HENRI
UEUILLE

d'Assas

PARIS

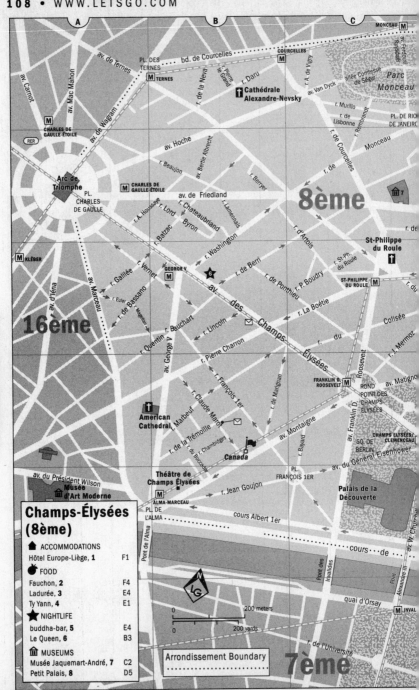

PARIS

Champs-Élysées (8ème)

🏠 ACCOMMODATIONS
Hôtel Europe-Liège, 1   F1

🍎 FOOD
Fauchon, 2   F4
Ladurée, 3   E4
Ty Yann, 4   E1

⭐ NIGHTLIFE
buddha-bar, 5   E4
Le Queen, 6   B3

🏛 MUSEUMS
Musée Jaquemart-André, 7   C2
Petit Palais, 8   D5

Arrondissement Boundary

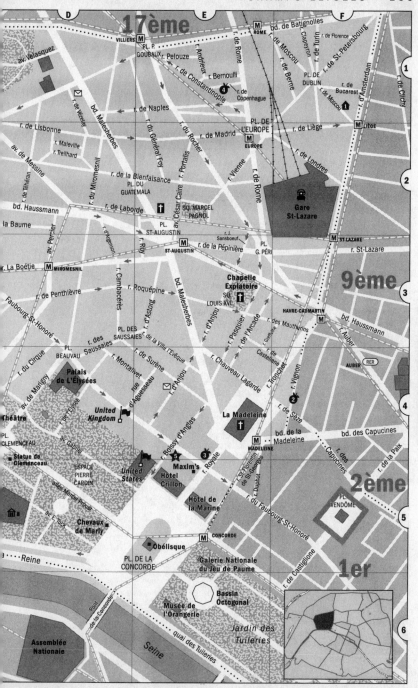

PARIS

PARIS

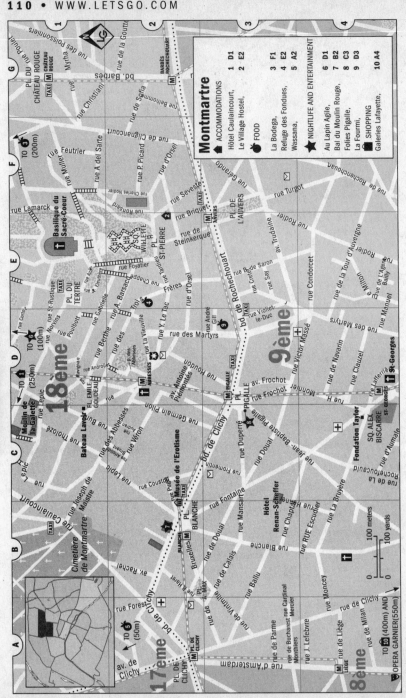

Montmartre

ACCOMMODATIONS
Hôtel Caulaincourt, 1 D1
Le Village Hostel, 2 E2

FOOD
La Bodega, 3 F1
Refuge des Fondues, 4 E2
Wassana, 5 A2

NIGHTLIFE AND ENTERTAINMENT
Au Lapin Agile, 6 D1
Bal du Moulin Rouge, 7 B2
Folies Pigalle, 8 C3
La Fourmi, 9 D3

SHOPPING
Galeries Lafayette, 10 A4

Île Saint-Louis, are in the center of the city. Central Paris is divided into **20 arrondissements** (districts) that spiral clockwise outward from the *centre-ville*—a bit like the shell of an *escargot*. Each arrondissement is referred to by its number (e.g. the 3rd, the 16th). In French, "third" is said *troisième* (trwaz-yem) and abbreviated "3ème"; "sixteenth" is *seizième* (sez-yem) and abbreviated "16ème." The same goes for every arrondissement except the first, which is said premier (prem-yay) and abbreviated "1er."

Sometimes it's helpful to orient yourself around central Paris's major monuments: on Rive Gauche, the Jardin du Luxembourg lies in the southeast, and the Eiffel Tower stands in the southwest; as you move clockwise and cross the Seine to Rive Droite, the Champs-Élysées and Arc de Triomphe occupy the northwest, and the Sacré-Coeur stands high in the northeast. Below, *Let's Go* splits Paris into neighborhoods according to divisions used by most Parisians. These divisions are not the official arrondissement boundaries, so each neighborhood introduction indicates the corresponding arrondissements.

ÎLE DE LA CITÉ AND ÎLE SAINT-LOUIS

Île de la Cité is situated in the center of the Île de France, the region surrounding Paris. From the sixth to 14th centuries, the island was the seat of the monarchy. Construction of the **Notre Dame** cathedral began here in 1163; the presence of the cathedral, as well as the **Sainte-Chapelle** (p. 137), ensured that the island would remain a center of Parisian life. All distances in France are measured from **kilomètre zéro,** a circular sundial in front of Notre Dame

Île St-Louis was originally two small islands—the **Île aux Vâches** (Cow Island) and the **Île de Notre Dame**—and was considered suitable for duels, cows, and little else throughout the Middle Ages. In 1267, the area was renamed for Louis IX after he departed for the Crusades. The two islands merged in the 17th century and Île St-Louis became a residential district. The island's *hôtels particuliers* (mansions) attracted an elite citizenry including Voltaire, Mme. de Châtelet, Daumier, Ingres, Baudelaire, Balzac, Courbet, George Sand, Delacroix, and Cézanne. In the 1930s, the idiosyncratic inhabitants declared the island an independent republic. The island still retains a certain remoteness from the rest of Paris. All in all, the island looks remarkably similar to its 17th-century self, retaining its history and genteel tranquility. St-Louis is a haven of boutiques, specialty shops, and art galleries that make for a pleasant wander.

CHÂTELET-LES HALLES (1ER, 2ÈME)

Châtelet-Les Halles (chat-a-lay lay zal) is home to much of Paris's royal history. Its most famous sight, the **Louvre,** housed French kings for four centuries. Today, the bedchambers and dining rooms of the palace house the world's finest art. The surrounding **Jardin des Tuileries** was redesigned in 1660 by Louis XIV's favored architect, André Le Nôtre. The Sun King's prized grounds now play host to strolling tourists and two more reputable art museums: the **Orangerie** and **Jeu de Paume.** Meanwhile, a different kind of royalty dominates Châtelet-Les Halles; Chanel, Cartier, and the Ritz hold court in the imposing **place Vendôme.** Souvenir shops crowd **rue du Rivoli** and **Les Halles,** while boutiques line **rue Saint-Honoré,** also home to the **Comédie Française,** where a talented troupe preserves Molière's tradition. Farther west, jazz clubs rule the night on **rue des Lombards.**

LET'S NOT GO. Although the 1er is one of Paris's safest regions aboveground, its Métro stops (Châtelet and Les Halles) are best avoided at night.

START: Ⓜ St-Paul.

FINISH: Ⓜ Rambuteau.

DISTANCE: 2.1km/1¼ mi.

DURATION: 4hr.

MEANDER THROUGH THE MARAIS

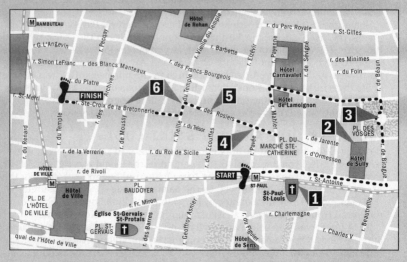

1. ÉGLISE SAINT-PAUL-SAINT-LOUIS. Exit the Métro station and walk east toward the large dark church. Inside are paintings of the kings Clovis, Charlemagne, Robert the Pious, and St-Louis. The site once held the embalmed hearts of Louis XIII and Louis XIV.

2. HÔTEL DE SULLY. Walk down rue St-Antoine toward pl. de la Bastille, where you'll find the *place*'s Colonne de Juillet, the site of the famous prison. A great example of how aristocratic wealth transformed this swampy area, Hôtel de Sully boasts a private *orangerie* (p. 141).

3. PLACE DES VOSGES. Continue in the direction of pl. de la Bastille and turn left onto rue de Birague, which leads directly onto pl. des Vosges. Built by Henri IV in 1605, the place attracted aristocrats who built chic apartments nearby. Victor Hugo lived at #6 (p. 141).

4. RUE DES ROSIERS. Return to rue des Francs-Bourgeois. Turn left onto rue Mahler and right onto rue des Rosiers to reach the main Jewish neighborhood. Since before World War II, when the Nazis sent over 75% of Parisian Jews to concentration camps, the city's Jewish population has been on the decline (p. 141).

5. FALAFEL. Facing off from either end of rue des Rosiers are Paris's best falafel stands: L'As du Falafel and Chez Hannah. Both do takeout, so you can keep walking.

6. RUE VIEILLE DU TEMPLE AND RUE SAINT-CROIX DE LA BRETTONERIE. At the other end of rue des Rosiers, pause on rue Vieille du Temple. Enjoy Orthodox Jewish bookshops and swanky clothing boutiques. On rue St-Croix de la Bretonnerie, trendy meets chic when it comes to shopping. The street is the epicenter of the Marais's thriving gay community.

THE MARAIS (3ÈME, 4ÈME)

The Marais is Paris's comeback kid, and no Paris pilgrim should miss it. With a name that literally translates to "swamp," its origins are easy to discern—in short, it was all bog. In the 13th century, the area began to find its bearings when monks drained the land to provide building space for the Right Bank. Henri IV's construction of the **place des Vosges** at the beginning of the 17th century heralded the coming of *hôtels particuliers*—and the luxury and scandal that comes with fashionable living. During the Revolution, former royal haunts gave way to slums and tenements; the majority of the *hôtels* fell into ruin or disrepair. In the 1960s, the Marais was once again revived when it was declared a historic neighborhood. Since then, more than 30 years of gentrification, renovation, and fabulous-ization has restored the Marais to its pre-Revolutionary glory. Palatial mansions have become exquisite museums, and tiny winding streets have been adopted by hip bars, avant-garde galleries, and unique boutiques. **Rue des Rosiers,** in the heart of the 4ème, is still the center of the city's Jewish population, though the steady influx of clothing stores threatens its existence. Superb kosher delicatessens neighbor Middle Eastern and Eastern European restaurants, and the Marais remains lively on Sundays, when much of the city is closed. The Marais is unquestionably the center of gay Paris, with its hub around the intersection of **rue Sainte-Croix de la Brettonerie** and **rue Vieille-du-Temple.** Though heavy tourism has recently encroached upon the Marais's personality, the district retains its signature charm: an accessible mix of old and new, gay and straight, cheap and chic, hip and historic.

 RIVE GAUCHE (LEFT BANK). The *"gauche"* in Rive Gauche once signified a secondary, lower-class lifestyle, flaunted by the impoverished students who stayed there. Today, the Left Bank's appeal is ensured by its inexpensive cafes, great shopping and sightseeing, and timeless literary caché.

LATIN QUARTER AND SAINT-GERMAIN (5ÈME, 6ÈME)

Named for the language used in the 5ème's prestigious *lycées* (high schools) and universities before 1798, *le quartier latin* buzzes with energy. The 5ème has been in the intellectual thick of things since the founding of the **Sorbonne** in 1263 (p. 143); its hot-blooded student population has played a role in uprisings from the French Revolution to the riots of May '68. In the 6ème, cafes on the legendary **boulevard Saint-Germain** were the stomping grounds of bigwigs like Camus, Hemingway, Picasso, and Sartre. Truth be told, the Latin Quarter has lost some of its rebellious vigor. The reasons aren't easy to pin down. Some cite the replacement of the old cobblestones—used by protesting students as projectiles in the old days—or the commodification of areas like **boulevard Saint-Michel,** which now overflows with chain stores. Despite the quarter's watered-down spirit, its bars (p. 171) and bookshops (p. 163) are some of Paris's best. The Latin Quarter is also the heart of that quintessentially Parisian passion: art-house cinema. The area's final claim to fame is its street-side pastimes; **place de la Contrescarpe** and **rue Mouffetard,** both in the 5ème, are superb for people-watching, and the Mouff has one of the liveliest street markets in Paris. As for food, you'll probably have to drop some cash if you want more than a *crêpe*, and the area's accommodations aren't any more financially forgiving. However, if money is no object, there is terrific boutique shopping to be had to the west and south of **Église Saint-Germain-des-Prés** (p. 144).

INVALIDES (7ÈME)

Between the grass of the **Champ de Mars** and the fashionable side streets surrounding **rue de Sèvres,** the 7ème offers both the most touristy and the most intimate sights in Paris. The area became Paris's most elegant residential district in the 18th century, though many of the neighborhood's stunning residences have been converted to foreign embassies. The completion of the **Eiffel Tower** (p. 145) sparked outrage in 1889, but it has since secured its reputation as a Parisian landmark. Meanwhile, the **National Assembly** and the **Hôtel National des Invalides** add historical substance and traditional French character to this section of the Left Bank. The 7ème offers dynamic art museums—including the **Musée Rodin** (p. 158)—and much more.

CHAMPS-ÉLYSÉES (8ÈME)

The Champs-Élysées area is past its prime. Its boulevards are still lined with the vast mansions, expensive shops, and grandiose monuments that keep the tourists coming, but there's little sense of sophistication, progress, or style. The Champs-Élysées was synonymous with fashion in the 19th century, but now it houses mostly charmless establishments. Much of the neighborhood is occupied by office buildings and car dealerships, and these areas are comatose after dark. Only the Champs itself throbs late into the night, thanks to flashy nightclubs, cinemas, and the droves of tourists that spill onto its sidewalks. A stroll along **avenue Montaigne**, on **rue du Faubourg Saint-Honoré,** or around the **Madeleine** will give a taste of what life in Paris is like for those with money to burn. The northern part of the neighborhood, near the **Parc Monceau,** is a lovely, quiet area for walking, as are the manicured, tree-lined streets of **Passy, Auteuil,** and **Chaillot,** southwest of the Champs.

OPÉRA (9ÈME)

The 9ème is an example of Paris's cultural extremes. The lower 9ème gleams with the magnificent **Palais Garnier** and the haute couture in Paris's world-famous department stores, the **Galeries Lafayette** (p. 165) and **Au Printemps.** The upper 9ème, near the northern border with the 18ème, offers a striking contrast: lowbrow porn shops, X-rated cinemas, and the world's oldest profession define the neon-lit **Pigalle** neighborhood. Separating these two sectors is a sleepy, residential neighborhood—the 9ème's geographical center. The area known as **Étienne-Marcel** has fabulously cheap clothing and great sales in more expensive stores. The Opéra Comique, now the **Théâtre Musicale,** is between bd. des Italiens and rue de Richelieu.

CANAL SAINT-MARTIN AND SURROUNDS (10ÈME)

Revolutionary fervor once gripped **place de la République,** but Haussmann doused their moxie with some clever urban planning. Since then, the 10ème has quieted down. In general, the area is one of striking juxtapositions—regal statues scrawled with graffiti and peaceful, sunny squares next to boulevards packed with trashy goods. Most travelers only visit the 10ème for the Gare du Nord and Gare de l'Est, but, even though the 10ème doesn't draw tourists, parts of it are well worth exploring. Good, cheap restaurants are everywhere, and the blossoming area near **Canal Saint-Martin** makes for pleasant wandering.

 LET'S NOT GO. The 10ème is far from tourist sights, and areas may be unsafe at night; be extra cautious around the bd. St-Martin, rue du Faubourg St-Denis, and west of pl. de la République along rue du Château d'Eau.

BASTILLE (11ÈME, 12ÈME)

As its name attests, the Bastille (bah-steel) area is most famous for hosting the Revolution's kickoff on July 14, 1789. Hundreds of years later, the French still storm this neighborhood nightly in search of the latest mixed drink, culinary innovation, or up-and-coming artist. Five Métro lines converge at Ⓜ République and three at Ⓜ Bastille, making the Bastille district a transport hub and center of action—the hangout of the young, fun, and frequently drunk. The 1989 opening of the **Opéra Bastille** on the Revolution's bicentennial was supposed to breathe new cultural life into the area, but the party atmosphere has yet to give way to galleries and string quartets. With numerous bars along **rue de Lappe,** original dining options on **rue de la Roquette** and **rue Jean-Pierre Timbaud,** and designer boutiques throughout, the Bastille is great for unwinding after a day of museums. The area is still a little rough, and the wide commercial boulevards that run through it lack the charm of many arrondissements, but interesting establishments can be found throughout this hot spot. North of the Bastille, on **rue Oberkampf** and **rue Ménilmontant,** neighborhood bars provide the perfect end to a pub crawl. **Place de la Nation,** farther south, was the setting for Louis XIV's wedding in 1660 and the site of revolutionary fervor in 1830 and 1848. Its northwestern fringes are funky—the **viaduc des Arts, rue de la Roquette,** and **rue du Faubourg Saint-Antoine** are lined with galleries and stores—and its core is working-class. For a taste of nature, head to the 12ème, which borders the expansive **Bois de Vincennes,** or try the Yitzhak Rabin Garden in the **Parc Bercy.**

 LET'S NOT GO. While the area is generally safe during the day, pl. de la République and bd. Voltaire are best avoided after sunset. Be careful around Gare de Lyon, especially at night, and near av. du Maine's northern end.

BUTTE-AUX-CAILLES AND CHINATOWN (13ÈME)

Until the 20th century, the 13ème was one of Paris's poorest arrondissements, with conditions so terrible that Victor Hugo set parts of *Les Misérables* in the neighborhood. Traversed by the **Bièvre,** a stagnant stream clogged with industrial refuse, the 13ème was also the city's worst-smelling district. Thankfully, in 1910, the Bièvre was filled in and environmentalists won a campaign to close the neighborhood's tanneries and paper factories. Construction began in 1996 on Mitterrand's ultramodern **Bibliothèque de France,** ushering in a new wave of development aimed to transform the 13ème's *quais* into Paris's largest cultural center. Recent projects include dormitories for over 20,000 University of Paris VII students and the **MK2 entertainment complex.** Several immigrant communities make for a thriving Chinatown. Rising over the Seine, the **Pont de Bercy** connects the proletariat 13ème to the youthful 12ème.

MONTPARNASSE (14ÈME, 15ÈME)

Named after Mount Parnassus, the famous Greek mountain of lore, Paris's 14ème revels in its bohemian reputation. During the 1920s, the *quartier* became a haven for the "Lost Generation"—intellectuals and political exiles trying to cope with life after WWI. Famed Montparnasse residents F. Scott Fitzgerald, Ernest Hemingway, Man Ray, and Henry Miller conversed the night away in popular cafes like **Le Select** and **Le Dôme.** These legendary artists no longer roam the Montparnasse neighborhood—mostly because they're dead—but the area's affordability continues to attract artists and students. Unlike its neighbor to the east, the 15ème has never been the stuff of legends. Today, the city's most densely populated arrondissement has been predominantly middle-class for decades. The modern **Parc André Citroën** attracts families on weekends, but aside from this, the 15ème has no tourist sights to speak of; its atmosphere is often crowded, busy, and—around **Gare Montparnasse**—very industrial (a.k.a. ugly). As a result, the 15ème is one of Paris's least touristed areas, and streetwise travelers can benefit from low room rates and affordable restaurants. Locals frequent the many shops on **rue du Commerce**, the cafes at the corner of **rue de la Convention** and **rue de Vaugirard**, and the specialty shops along **avenue Émile Zola.**

PASSY AND AUTEUIL (16ÈME)

When Notre Dame was under construction, this now-elegant suburb was little more than a cluster of tiny villages in the woods. With Haussmann's architectural revolution, however, the area was transformed. The villages of Auteuil to the south, Passy in the east, and northernmost Chaillot banded together, joining the city to form what is now the 16ème. Today, the manicured, tree-lined streets of this elegant *quartier* provide a peaceful respite from the mobbed sidewalks of the neighboring 8ème. The 16ème offers some of the best views of the **Eiffel Tower,** framed by immaculate Art Nouveau and Art Deco architecture. There's also an impressive density of museums that showcase everything from cutting-edge contemporary art to second-century Asian statuary. The upper 16ème is populated with mansions, while the lower half is more modest.

BATIGNOLLES (17ÈME)

The 17ème is a diverse district where bourgeois turns working-class and back again within a block. The eastern and southern parts share the bordering 8ème and 16ème's aristocratic bearing, while the *quartier*'s western edge resembles the tawdrier 18ème and Pigalle. Removed from central Paris's suffocating crowds, the 17ème resonates with authentic charm. Thanks in large part to its multicultural population, the 17ème offers a variety of restaurants spanning the price spectrum. Parents and young children stroll through the tree-lined **Village Batignolles,** while a hip clientele frequents the area's bars at night.

MONTMARTRE (18ÈME)

Montmartre glows with the luster of its bohemian past. Named "Mount of the Martyr" for St-Denis—who was beheaded there by the Romans in AD 260—the hill was a rural village covered with vineyards, wheat fields, windmills, and gypsum mines for centuries. In the late 19th and early 20th centuries, Paris's rebellious artistic energies centered here. During the Belle Époque, Montmartre's picturesque beauty and low rents attracted bohemians like painter Henri Toulouse-Lautrec and composer Erik Satie as well as performer and impresario Aristide Bruant. Toulouse-Lautrec immortalized Montmartre by painting its disreputable nightspots, like the infamous **Bal du Moulin Rouge.** Filled with cabarets like **Le Chat Noir** and proto-Dada artist groups like Les Incohérents and Les Hydropathes, the *butte* (ridge) became the Parisian center of free love, intoxicated fun, and liberated *fumisme*—the satirical jabbing of social and political norms. A generation later, the *butte* welcomed innovators Apollinaire, Modigliani, Picasso, and Utrillo. Today, artsy Montmartre best embodies the stereotyped Parisian dream; nostalgic history on **rue Lepic,** pseudo-artistic schmaltz lingering in **place du Tertre,** and a dab of provocative sleaze from **boulevard de Clichy** lure numerous tourists. The *quartier* appears to transcend its metropolis, however, with functional vineyards, an official arboretum in its cemetery, and a timeless panorama of the city from the **Basilique du Sacré-Coeur.**

LET'S NOT GO. Pl. Pigalle and Ⓜ️Barbès-Rochechoart are notorious for shady dealings, which become apparent at an early hour. The area is heavily policed, but travelers—particularly young women and those traveling alone—should still exercise caution. At night, Ⓜ️Abesse is a safer bet than Anvers, Pigalle, and Barbès-Rochechoart.

BUTTES CHAUMONT (19ÈME)

The 19ème and the 20ème, both primarily working-class, have recently flourished as new centers of Parisian bohemia. Between the romantic **Parc des Buttes Chaumont** and the **Cimetière du Père Lachaise**, performance spaces, artsy cafes, and provocative galleries have joined the neighborhood's ethnic eateries, markets, and shops. Historically lacking the artistic patronage that brought Montmartre fame, today the 19ème battles for cultural recognition; its modern **Cité de la Musique** (p. 168) and **Cité de la Science** encourage citizens' creative appreciation with frequent concerts and interactive museums. Home to Asian, Greek, Jewish, North African, and Russian communities, the 19ème and 20ème arrondissements include Paris's most dynamic neighborhoods.

 LET'S NOT GO. Be careful at night, particularly in the emptier northwestern corner of the 19ème, along rue David d'Angers, bd. Indochine, av. Corentin Cariou, and rue de Belleville, and by the *portes* into the area.

BELLEVILLE AND PÈRE LACHAISE (20ÈME)

The 20ème's population swelled in the mid-19th century, when Hausmann's architectural reforms drove working-class Parisians from the central city. Thousands migrated east to **Belleville** (the northern part of the 20ème), **Charonne** (the southeastern), and **Ménilmontant** (the southern). By the late Second Republic, the 20ème had become a "red" arrondissement, characterized as proletarian and radical. Some of the heaviest fighting during the Commune suppression took place in its streets. Caught between the *versaillais* troops to the west and the Prussian lines outside the city walls, the Commune fortified the Parc des Buttes-Chaumont and the Cimetière du Père Lachaise but soon ran out of ammunition. On May 28, 1871, the Communards abandoned their last barricade and surrendered (see **Life and Times,** p. 63). Following the government's retributive massacres, the surviving workers adopted the fairly isolated 20ème as their home. Today, the arrondissement is still working-class, with busy residential areas and markets that cater to locals rather than visitors.

📃 LOCAL TRANSPORTATION

The **Régie Autonome des Transports Parisiens (RATP)** coordinates a network of subways, buses, and commuter trains in and around Paris. For info, consult La Maison de la RATP, 190 rue de Bercy (across the street from Ⓜ️Gare de Lyon), the Bureau de Tourisme RATP, pl. de la Madeleine, 8ème (☎01 40 06 71 45; Ⓜ️Madeleine; open daily 8:30am-6pm), or www.ratp.fr.

FARES AND PASSES

Individual tickets for the RATP cost €1.60 each, or €12 for a carnet of 10. Each Métro ride takes one ticket. The bus takes at least one, sometimes more, depending on connections you make and the time of day.

PARIS

If you're staying in Paris for several days or weeks, a **carte orange** can be economical. Bring an ID photo (taken by machines in most major stations) to the ticket counter and ask for a weekly *carte orange hebdomadaire* (€17) or the monthly *carte orangemensuelle* (€56). These cards have specific start and end dates (the weekly runs M-Su, the monthly starts on the 1st of the month). Prices quoted here are for passes in Zones 1 and 2 (the Métro and RER) and work on all Métro, bus, and RER modes of transport. If you intend to travel to the suburbs, you'll need to buy RER passes for more zones (they go up to 5).

If you're only in town for a day or two, try the **carte mobilis** (☎08 91 36 20 20; €5.80 for a day pass in Zones 1 and 2), which provides unlimited Métro, bus, and RER transportation within Paris. **Paris Visite** tickets are valid for unlimited travel on bus, Métro, and RER. They also give discounts on sightseeing trips, museum admission, and at stores like Galeries Lafayette—though the discounts do not always outweigh the cost. (Available at the airport, Métro, and RER stations. 1-day pass €8.50, 2-day €14, 3-day €19, 5-day €28.)

STATION SAVVY. The following Métro stations can be dangerous at night: Barbès-Rochechouart, Pigalle, Anvers, Châtelet-Les Halles, Gare du Nord, and Gare de l'Est. Remain vigilant; when in doubt, take a bus or taxi.

MÉTRO

In general, the metro system is easy to navigate, and trains run swiftly and frequently. Métro stations are marked with an "M" or with the "Métropolitain" lettering designed by Art Nouveau legend Hector Guimard; for each listing in the guide, *Let's Go* indicates the corresponding Métro station with an ⓜ. Paris boasts one of the world's most impressive subway systems, with approximately 375 stations. Trains run from 5:30am, and the last ones leave the end-of-the-line stations for the center of the city at about 12:15am. Connections to other lines are indicated by orange *correspondance* signs, exits indicated by blue *sortie* signs. Transfers are free if made within a station, but it is not always possible to reverse direction on the same line without exiting the station. **Hold onto your ticket until you exit the Métro,** and pass the point marked *limite de validité des billets.* If you're caught without one, you must pay a hefty fine. Do not count on buying a Métro ticket late at night; some ticket windows close by 10pm.

RER

The **Réseau Express Régional (RER),** the RATP's suburban train system, passes through central Paris. The RER travels much faster than the Métro. There are five RER lines, marked A-E, with different branches designated by a number. The new E line—called the Eole (Est-Ouest Liaison Express)—links Gare Magenta to Gare St-Lazare. Within Paris, the RER works the same as the Métro, requiring the same ticket. Trips to the suburbs require special tickets. You'll need your ticket to exit RER stations. Insert your ticket just as you did to enter, then pass through. Like the Métro, the RER runs 5:30am-12:30am.

BUS

Although slower and often costlier than the Métro, a bus ride can be a cheap sightseeing tour and an introduction to the city's layout. Bus tickets are the same as those used in the Métro; they can be purchased in Métro stations or on the bus. Inspectors may ask to see your ticket; hold onto it until you get off.

Most buses run daily 7am-8:30pm, although those marked **Autobus du nuit** continue until 1:30am. Still others, named **Noctilien,** run all night. Night buses (€1.60) run from Châtelet to the *portes* of the city every hour on the half hour

12:30-5:30am (1-6am from the *portes* into the city). Look for bus stops marked with a bug-eyed moon sign. Check out www.noctilien.fr or ask at a major Métro station or at Gare de l'Est for more info.

RATP's **Balabus** (☎01 44 68 43 35) stops at virtually every major sight in Paris (Bastille, St-Michel, Louvre, Musée d'Orsay, Concorde, Champs-Élysées, Charles de Gaulle-Étoile; whole loop takes 1hr.). The circuit requires three standard bus tickets and starts at La Défense or the Gare de Lyon.

TAXIS

If you have a complaint or left personal belongings behind, contact the taxi company or **Service des Taxis de la Préfecture de Police** (☎01 55 76 20 00; ⓂConvention). **Tarif A,** the basic rate, is in effect within Paris 10am-5pm (€0.90 per km). **Tarif B** is in effect Monday through Saturday 7pm-7am, all day Sunday, and during the day from the airports and immediate suburbs (€1.20 per km). **Tarif C** is in effect from the airports 7pm-7am (€1.40 per km). The base fee is €2.20 and the minimum charge €5.60. Wait for taxis at the nearest taxi stand; taxis will not stop if you attempt to flag them down on the street. Taxis take three passengers; there is a €2.90 charge for a fourth. Some take credit cards (MC/V). Companies include: **Taxis 75** (☎ 01 78 41 65 05), **Aero Taxi** (☎01 64 17 13 78), **Alpha Taxis** (☎01 53 60 63 50), and **Taxis G7** (☎ 01 47 39 47 39).

CARS

Traveling by car in Paris is only reasonable if your plans include significant travel outside the city. Parisian drivers are merciless. *Priorité à droite* gives the right of way to the car approaching from the right, regardless of the size of the streets, and Parisians exercise this right even in the face of grave danger. Technically, drivers are not allowed to honk within city limits unless they are about to hit a pedestrian, but this rule is often broken. The legal way to show discontent is to flash your headlights. A map of Paris marked with one-way streets is indispensable for drivers. Parking is expensive and hard to find. For info on car-rental agencies, licenses, and insurance, see **Essentials,** p. 35.

TWO-WHEELERS

Thanks to frequent Métro strikes, **bike** shops have come to the rescue of stranded citizens and an emergent cycling community has approached its dream of an auto-free Paris. If you have never ridden a bike in heavy traffic, don't use central Paris as a testing ground. Ask for a helmet (not legally required, but always a good idea) and inquire about insurance. Motorized two-wheelers, called *motos*

TOP TEN LIST

MÉTRO STATIONS

1. Concorde has mosaic-covered walls. Each tile displays a different letter. Take a stab at solving the world's largest word search (actually a series of long quotes). 1*er.*

2. Cluny La Sorbonne has signatures of the Sorbonne's luminaries all over the ceiling. 5*ème.*

3. Arts et Metiers is covered entirely in copper, reminiscent of Captain Nemo's submarine—or plumbing, depending on how you look at things. 3*ème.*

4. Louvre features replicas of the museum's artwork. 1*er.*

5. Montparnasse-Bienvenüe is a mega-station where you can choose your speed of moving sidewalk on the *trattoir roulant rapide* (fast-rolling sidewalk). 15*ème.*

6. Bibliotheque Nationale Francois Mitterand remains at the edge of innovation with the racy new automated line 14 and stairs covered in an array of foreign languages. 13*ème.*

7. Varenne displays replicas of Rodin sculptures. 7*ème.*

8. Châtelet, is a large, grimy, and disorienting station, but the musicians are sure to brighten your commute. 1*er.*

9. Palais Royal boasts a lavishly bejeweled entrance. 1*er.*

10. Porte Dauphine has a florid Art Nouveau entrance, designed by Hector Guimard. 16*ème.*

or *mobylettes,* are everywhere in Paris. Everyone seems to own one, and just as many people seem to have been injured on one. If you want to sacrifice safety for the speed and style of a **scooter,** you can rent one; no special license is required, but a helmet definitely is.

Vélib (www.en.velib.paris.fr). Self-service bike rental. Over 1450 terminals and 20,000 bikes in Paris. Buy a subscription (day €1, week €5, year €29) and rent bikes from (and drop them off at) any terminal in the city. Rentals under 30min. free. Available 24hr.

Roulez Champions, 5 rue Humblot, 15ème (☎01 40 58 12 22; www.roulezchampions. com). ⓂDupleix. Bikes €5 per 2hr., €15 per day. Open Mar.-Oct. Tu-Sa 10:30am-1pm and 3:30-7:30pm, Su 10am-7pm; Nov.-Feb. Tu-Sa 10:30am-1pm and 3:30-7pm.

◪ PRACTICAL INFORMATION

TOURIST AND FINANCIAL SERVICES

Tourist Offices:

Bureau Gare d'Austerlitz, 13ème (☎01 45 84 91 70). ⓂGare d'Austerlitz. Open M-Sa 8am-6pm.

Bureau Gare de Lyon, 12ème (☎01 43 43 33 24). ⓂGare de Lyon. Open M-Sa 8am-6pm.

Bureau Tour Eiffel, Champs de Mars, 7ème (☎08 92 68 31 12). ⓂChamps de Mars. Open daily May-Sept. 11am-6:40pm.

Montmartre Tourist Office, 21 pl. du Tertre, 18ème (☎01 42 62 21 21). ⓂAnvers. Open daily 10am-7pm.

Tours:

Bateaux-Mouches (☎01 42 25 96 10, info 40 76 99 99; www.bateaux-mouches.fr). ⓂAlma-Marceau. 70min. tours in English. Departures every 30min. 10:15am-1pm and 2-10:40pm (no boats 1-2pm) from the Right Bank pier near Pont d'Alma.

Paris à Velo, c'est Sympa!, 37 bd. Bourdon, 4ème (☎01 48 87 60 01). ⓂBastille. 3hr. bike tours leave at 10am, 3pm. €30, under 26 €26.

Currency Exchange:

American Express, 11 rue Scribe, 9ème (☎01 53 30 99 00; parisscribe.france@kanoofes.com). ⓂOpéra or RER Auber. Exchange counters open M-Sa 9am-6:30pm; member services open M-F 9am-5pm, Sa 9am-noon and 1-5pm.

Thomas Cook, 26 av. de l'Opéra, 1er (☎01 53 29 40 00; fax 47 03 32 13). ⓂGeorges V. Open M-Sa 9am-10:55pm, Su 8am-6pm.

LOCAL SERVICES

GLBT Resources: SOS Homophobie, 63 rue Beaubourg, 3ème (☎01 48 06 42 41). Open M-F 8-10pm.

Laundromats: Ask at your hostel or hotel for the closest laundry facilities. **Multiservices,** 75 rue de l'Ouest, 14ème (☎01 43 35 19 51). Wash €3.50, dry €2 per 20min. Open M-Sa 8:30am-8pm. **Laverie Net A Sec,** 3 pl. Monge, 5ème. Wash €4 per 6kg, dry €1 per 9min. Soap €1. Open daily 7:30am-10pm.

EMERGENCY AND COMMUNICATIONS

Crisis Lines:

Poison: ☎01 40 05 48 48. In French, but some English assistance is available.

SOS Help! (☎01 46 21 46 46). An anonymous, confidential hotline for English speakers in crisis. Open daily (including holidays) 3-11pm.

Rape: SOS Viol (☎08 00 05 95 95). Open M-F 10am-7pm.

Pharmacies:

British and American Pharmacy, 1 rue Auber, pl. de l'Opéra, 9ème (☎01 42 65 88 29). ⓂOpéra or RER Auber. Sells hard-to-find Anglophone brands in addition to French products. English-speaking staff. Open daily 8am-8:30pm.

Pharmacie Beaubourg, 50 rue Rambuteau, 3ème (☎01 48 87 86 37). ⓂRambuteau. Open M-Sa 8am-8pm, Su 10am-8pm.

Pharmacie des Halles, 10 bd. de Sébastopol, 1er (☎01 42 72 03 23). ⓂChâtelet-Les Halles. Open M-Sa 9am-midnight, Su 9am-10pm.

Pharmacie Gacha, 361 rue des Pyrénées, 20ème (☎01 46 36 59 10). ⓂPyrénées or Jourdain. Open M-F 9am-8pm, Sa 9am-7pm.

Medical Services:

American Hospital of Paris, 63 bd. Victor Hugo, Neuilly (☎01 46 41 25 25). ⓂPort Maillot, then bus #82 to the end of the line.

Centre Médicale Europe, 44 rue d'Amsterdam, 9ème (☎01 42 81 93 33). ⓂSt-Lazare. Open M-F 8am-7pm, Sa 8am-6pm.

Hôpital Bichat, 46 rue Henri Buchard, 18ème (☎01 40 25 80 80). ⓂPort St-Ouen. Emergencies.

SOS Dentaire, 87 bd. Port-Royal, 13ème (☎01 40 21 82 88). RER Port-Royal. No walk-ins. Open daily 9am-6pm and 8:30-11:45pm.

SOS Médecins (☎01 48 07 77 77). Makes house calls.

SOS Oeil (☎01 40 92 93 94). Eye care. Open daily 6am-11pm.

Internet Access:

Cyber Cube, 5 rue Mignon, 6ème (☎01 53 10 30 50). ⓂSt-Michel or Odéon. €0.15 per min., €30 per 5hr., €40 per 10hr. Open M-Sa 10am-10pm.

easyInternetcafé, 6 rue de la Harpe, 5ème (☎01 55 42 55 42). ⓂSt-Michel. €3 per hr. Open M-Sa 7:30am-8pm, Su 9am-8pm.

Le Sputnik, 14-16 rue de la Butte-aux-Cailles, 13ème (☎01 45 65 19 82; www.sputnik.fr). ⓂPlace d'Italie. Doubles as a hoppin' bar, ensuring socialites form real-world connections. Internet €0.90 per 15min., €25 per 10hr. Scanner use €2. Happy hour daily 6-8pm. Open M-Sa 2pm-2am, Su 4pm-midnight, holidays 4pm-2am.

Taxiphone, 6 rue Polonceau, 18ème (☎01 53 09 95 12). ⓂAnvers. €3 per hr. Open daily noon-10pm.

Post Office: There are post offices in each arrondissement. Most open M-F 8am-7pm, Sa 8am-noon. **Federal Express** (☎08 20 12 38 00). Call for pickup or dropoff at 63 bd. Haussmann, 8ème. ⓂHavre-Caumartin. Open M-F 9am-7:30pm, Sa 9am-5:30pm.

🔥 ACCOMMODATIONS

Accommodations in Paris are expensive—you don't need *Let's Go* to tell you that. At the absolute minimum, expect to pay €20 for a dorm bed in a hostel and €28 for a single in a hotel. It is more economical for groups of two or more to stay in a hotel rather than a hostel, since hotels charge per room and not per person. Paris's hostels tend to have flexible maximum stays. The city has six HI hostels, which offer discounts to members (see **Hostels,** p. 44). The rest of Paris's dorm-style beds are either private hostels or quieter *foyers* (student dorms). English is spoken in most establishments. Rooms fill quickly after morning check-out, so arrive early or reserve ahead—from one week to one month or more in summer. Most hostels and *foyers* include the *taxe de séjour* (€0.10-2 per person per day) in listed prices.

BEFORE YOU GET HOSTEL. If you arrive in Paris without a hostel reservation—or if you arrive in Paris with a hostel reservation that falls through—head for the information desk at a major train station. The employees there will often agree to call hostels and book a room for you.

ÎLE DE LA CITÉ

▨ **Hôtel Henri IV,** 25 pl. Dauphine (☎01 43 54 44 53). ⓂPont Neuf. Named in honor of Henri IV's printing presses, which once occupied the building. Charming views. Spacious rooms, mismatched furnishings, and clean baths. Breakfast included. Showers €2.50. Reserve 1 month ahead, earlier in summer. Singles €29-34, with shower €48; doubles €38-48, with full bath €58; triples €72. MC/V. ❷

CHÂTELET-LES HALLES

1ER ARRONDISSEMENT

▨ **Centre International de Paris (BVJ): Paris Louvre,** 20 rue Jean-Jacques Rousseau (☎01 53 00 90 90). ⓂLouvre or Palais-Royal. 3-building hostel with courtyard. Bright rooms with 2-8 beds are single-sex except for groups. Breakfast included. Lockers €2. Internet €1 per 10min. 3-night max. stay per reservation; extend the reservation once there. Reception 24hr. Rooms held for only 5-10min. after check-in time; call if you'll be late. Reserve 1 week ahead; by phone only. Dorms €28; doubles €30. ❷

Hôtel Montpensier, 12 rue de Richelieu (☎01 42 96 28 50; www.hotelmontpensier-paris.com). ⓂPalais-Royal. Lofty ceilings, bright decor, plush carpets. TVs. Breakfast €8. Shower €4. Internet €10 per 2hr.; Wi-Fi €30 per 24hr. Reserve 1 month ahead in summer. Singles and doubles with sink €67-71, with sink and toilet €74, with full bath €95-109; triples and quads €129-149. AmEx/MC/V. ❺

2ÈME ARRONDISSEMENT

▨ **Hôtel Vivienne,** 40 rue Vivienne (☎01 42 33 13 26; www.hotel-vivienne.com). ⓂBourse, Grands Boulevards, or Richelieu. Hardwood floors and flatscreen TVs. Some rooms with balconies. Breakfast €9. Singles and doubles with shower €60-75, with shower and toilet €87-114, with bath and toilet €90-114. AmEx/MC/V. ❹

Hôtel Tiquetonne, 6 rue Tiquetonne (☎01 42 36 94 58; fax 42 36 02 94). ⓂÉtienne-Marcel. Near Marché Montorgueil. Large rooms. High ceilings. Elevator. Breakfast €6. Hall showers €6. Reserve at least 1 month ahead. Open Jan.-July and from Sept. to mid-Dec. Singles €35, with shower €45; doubles with shower €55. AmEx/MC/V. ❸

THE MARAIS

3ÈME ARRONDISSEMENT

▨ **Hotel Picard,** 26 rue de Picardie (☎01 48 87 53 82; hotel.picard@wanadoo.fr). ⓂRépublique. Welcoming, family-run hotel with superb location. Lovely rooms have baths. TVs in rooms with showers. Breakfast €5. Hall showers €3. Reserve 2 weeks ahead. Singles with sink €44, with sink and shower €65, with full bath €75; doubles €53/83/94; triples €114. 5% discount if you flash your *Let's Go.* MC/V. ❸

Hôtel du Marais, 16 rue de Beauce (☎01 42 72 30 26; hotelmarais@voila.fr). ⓂTemple or Filles du Calvaire. Simple, adequate rooms near an open-air market. Only for students and backpackers. Take the small stairs above the cafe owned by the same friendly man. Turkish-style hallway toilets. 3rd fl. showers €3. Curfew 2am. Singles with sink €25; doubles €35-38. Cash only. ❷

4ÈME ARRONDISSEMENT

▨ **Hôtel des Jeunes (MIJE;** ☎01 42 74 23 45; www.mije.com). 3 small hostels (below) in beautiful old Marais *hôtels particuliers* (mansions). Main welcome desk at Le Fourcy. Arranges airport pickup and dropoff and reservations for sights, restaurants, and shows. Restaurant in a vaulted cellar in Le Fourcy. Public phones. Breakfast and in-room shower included. Lockers free with €1 deposit. Linen included. Internet €0.10 per min. with €0.50 initial fee. 1-week max. stay. Reception 7am-1am. Arrive before noon the 1st day of reservation. Lockout noon-3pm. Curfew 1am. Quiet hours after 10pm. Reserve months ahead online and 2-3 weeks ahead by phone. 4- to 9-bed dorms €29; singles €47; doubles €68; triples €90. MIJE membership required (€3). Cash only. ❷

Maubuisson, 12 rue des Barres. Ⓜ️Hôtel de Ville or Pont Marie. Half-timbered former convent on a silent street by a monastery. Accommodates more individual travelers than groups.

Le Fourcy, 6 rue de Fourcy. Ⓜ️St-Paul or Pont Marie. Large courtyard ideal for meeting travelers.

Le Fauconnier, 11 rue du Fauconnier. Ⓜ️St-Paul or Pont Marie. Ivy-covered, sun-drenched building steps away from the Seine and Île St-Louis. All rooms have showers and sinks.

Grand Hôtel Jeanne d'Arc, 3 rue de Jarente (☎01 48 87 62 11; www.hoteljeannedarc. com). Ⓜ️St-Paul. More like a homestyle inn than hotel. Cozy carpeted rooms with cable TV, toilets, and baths or showers. Breakfast €6. Wi-Fi €2 per day. Wheelchair-accessible room. Reserve 2-3 months in advance, earlier for Sept.-Oct. Singles €60-84; doubles €84-97; triples €116; quads €146. MC/V. ❹

LATIN QUARTER AND SAINT-GERMAIN

5ÈME ARRONDISSEMENT

▨ **Hôtel Marignan,** 13 rue du Sommerard (☎01 43 54 63 81; www.hotel-marignan.com). Ⓜ️Maubert-Mutualité. Clean, freshly decorated rooms can sleep up to 5. Hostel friendliness with hotel privacy. Kitchen. Breakfast included. Hall showers. Laundry. Free Wi-Fi. Singles €47-50, with toilet €55-60, with full bath €75; doubles €60-68/69-80/82-90; triples €75-90/85-105/105-115; quads with toilet €100-125, with full bath €120-140; quints with full bath €105-155. AmEx/MC/V. ❹

Young and Happy (Y&H) Hostel, 80 rue Mouffetard (☎01 47 07 47 07; www.youngand-happy.fr). Ⓜ️Monge. Lively hostel with 21 clean rooms, some with showers and toilets. English-speaking staff. Kitchen. Breakfast included. Linen €2.50; €5 deposit. Internet. Lockout 11am-4pm. Curfew 2am. Apr.-Dec. 6-, 8-, or 10-bed dorms €24; 3-, 4-, or 5-bed €26; doubles €56. Jan.-Mar. €2 less. MC/V. ❷

6ÈME ARRONDISSEMENT

▨ **Hôtel de Nesle,** 7 rue du Nesle (☎01 43 54 62 41; www.hoteldenesleparis.com). Ⓜ️Odéon. Absolutely sparkling. Every room represents a particular figure (e.g., Molière) or locale (e.g., Africa). Ceiling made of bouquets of dried flowers. Garden with duck pond. Laundry. Reserve by phone; confirm 2 days in advance with arrival time. Singles €55-65; doubles €75-100. Extra bed €12. AmEx/MC/V. ❹

Hôtel Stella, 41 rue Monsieur-le-Prince (☎01 40 51 00 25; http://site.voila.fr/hotel-stella). Ⓜ️Odéon. Huge rooms with centuries-old woodwork. Reserve at least 1 month ahead. Singles €45; doubles €55; triples €75; quads €85. Cash only. ❹

INVALIDES (7ÈME)

▨ **Hôtel Eiffel Rive Gauche,** 6 rue du Gros Caillou (☎01 45 51 24 56; www.hotel-eiffel. com). Ⓜ️École Militaire. Family-run. A favorite of Anglophone travelers. Spanish-style courtyard and tastefully decorated rooms. Flatscreen TVs with cable, phones, safes, and full baths. Breakfast €12. Wi-Fi. Singles €95-155; doubles and twins €105-155; triples €115-175; quads €135-205. Extra bed €20. Prices vary seasonally. MC/V. ❺

Hôtel Montebello, 18 rue Pierre Leroux (☎01 47 34 41 18; hmontebello@aol.com). Ⓜ️Vaneau. A bit far from the best sights of the 7ème. Lacks the elegant sophistication of many of the other hotels in this upscale area, but with unbeatable rates and clean,

PARIS

colorful rooms, this hotel ranks high in the categories that really count. Breakfast €5. Reserve at least 2 weeks ahead. Singles and doubles with shower or bath €35-42; with shower or bath and toilet €44-55. Extra bed €17. ❸

CHAMPS-ÉLYSÉES (8ÈME)

Hôtel Europe-Liège, 8 rue de Moscou (☎01 42 94 01 51; fax 43 87 42 18). ⓂLiège. Cheerful, very clean rooms, each with TV, hair dryer, phone, and shower or bath. Breakfast €7. Wi-Fi. Reserve 3-4 weeks ahead. Singles €75; doubles €90. AmEx/MC/V. ❺

OPÉRA (9ÈME)

▨ **Perfect Hôtel,** 39 rue Rodier (☎01 42 81 18 86 or 42 81 26 19; www.paris-hostel.biz). ⓂAnvers. Lives up to its name. Rooms with balcony by request. Caring staff. Well-stocked kitchen, free coffee, and a beer vending machine (€1.50). Be careful in neighborhood after dark. Breakfast included. Reception 24hr. Reserve 1 month ahead. Singles €44, with toilet €60; doubles €50/60. Extra bed €19. Cash only. ❸

Woodstock Hostel, 48 rue Rodier (☎01 48 78 87 76; www.woodstock.fr). ⓂAnvers. Beatles-decorated VW Bug adorns the lobby wall. Communal kitchen and hostel (but definitely not hostile) cat. Breakfast included. Linen €2.50; €2.50 deposit. Internet and Wi-Fi €2 per 30min. 2-week max. stay. Lockout 11am-3pm. Curfew 2am. Reserve ahead. High-season 4- or 6-bed dorms €22; doubles €50. Low-season 4- or 6-bed dorms €19; doubles €22. Cash only. ❷

CANAL SAINT-MARTIN AND SURROUNDS (10ÈME)

▨ **Hôtel Palace,** 9 rue Bouchardon (☎01 40 40 09 45). ⓂStrasbourg-St-Denis. Clean and centrally located (for the 10ème). Breakfast €4. Reserve 2 weeks ahead. Singles €20-25, with shower €33; doubles €28-30/40; triples €55; quads €65-75. MC/V. ❶

BASTILLE

11ÈME ARRONDISSEMENT

▨ **Hôtel Beaumarchais,** 3 rue Oberkampf (☎01 53 36 86 86; www.hotelbeaumarchais. com). ⓂOberkampf. Spacious hotel worth the money. Eye-popping decor. Each carpeted room has safe, shower or bath, and toilet. Suites include TV room with desk and breakfast table. A/C. Buffet breakfast €10. Reserve 2 weeks in advance. Singles €75-90; doubles €110-130; 2-person suites €150-170; triples €170-190. AmEx/MC/V. ❺

Auberge de Jeunesse "Jules Ferry" (HI), 8 bd. Jules Ferry (☎01 43 57 55 60; paris. julesferry@fuaj.org). ⓂRépublique. 99 beds. Modern, clean, and bright rooms with sinks, mirrors, and tiled floors. Party atmosphere. Kitchen. Breakfast included. Lockers €2. Linen included. Laundry €3. Internet access in lobby. 1-week max. stay. Reception and dining room 24hr. Lockout 10:30am-2pm. No reservations; arrive 8-11am to secure a bed. 4- to 6-bed dorms and doubles €22. MC/V. ❷

12ÈME ARRONDISSEMENT

Centre International du Séjour de Paris: CISP "Maurice Ravel", 6 av. Maurice Ravel (☎01 43 58 96 00; www.cisp.fr). ⓂPorte de Vincennes. Large, clean rooms. Lively atmosphere. Art displays, sizable auditorium, and outdoor pool (€3-4). Guided tours of Paris. Cafeteria and restaurant available. Breakfast, linen, and towels included. Free Internet. 1-week max. stay. 24hr. reception. Curfew 1:30am. Reserve 1-2 months ahead.

8-bed dorms with shower and toilet in hall €20; 2- to 4-bed €26. Singles with full bath €39; doubles with full bath €56. AmEx/MC/V. ❶

BUTTE-AUX-CAILLES AND CHINATOWN (13ÈME)

Centres Internationaux du Séjour de Paris: CISP "Kellermann", 17 bd. Kellermann (☎01 44 16 37 38; www.cisp.fr). ⓂPorte d'Italie. 363-bed hostel looks like a retro spaceship on stilts. Cafeteria (buffet €11), laundry service, and TV lounge. Breakfast included. Free Wi-Fi and parking. Reception 24hr. Check-in noon. Check-out 9:30am. Reserve 1 month ahead. 8-bed dorms €20; 2- to 4-bed €26. Singles with full bath €39; doubles with full bath €56. MC/V. ❶

MONTPARNASSE

14ÈME ARRONDISSEMENT

▩ **Hôtel de Blois,** 5 rue des Plantes (☎01 45 40 99 48; www.hoteldeblois.com). ⓂMouton-Duvernet, Alésia, or Gaîté. Flowers adorn rooms with clean bathrooms, lush carpets, hair dryers, phones, and TVs. Welcoming owner keeps scrapbook of previous guests' thank-you notes. 5 floors; no elevator. Breakfast €6.50. Wi-Fi €5 per hr., €26 per day. Reception 7am-10:30pm. Check-in 3pm. Check-out 11am. Reserve ahead. Singles and doubles with shower and toilet €55-70, with bathtub €75-85. AmEx/MC/V. ❹

▩ **FIAP Jean-Monnet,** 30 rue Cabanis (☎01 43 13 17 00, reservations 43 13 17 17; www.fiap.asso.fr). ⓂGlacière. Like a standard college dorm. 500-bed student center. Spotless rooms with bath and phones. 2 restaurants, outdoor terrace, and *discothèque* every W and F night. Breakfast included. Internet €5 per hr. Wheelchair-accessible. Reception 24hr. Check-out 9am. Curfew 2am. Reserve 2-4 weeks ahead; hostel often booked for summer before June. Be sure to specify if you want a dorm bed. 3- to 4-bed dorms €32; 5- to 6-bed €25. Singles €55; doubles €70. MC/V. ❷

15ÈME ARRONDISSEMENT

▩ **Aloha Hostel,** 1 rue Borromée (☎01 42 73 03 03; www.aloha.fr). ⓂVolontaires. Frequented by international crowd. Varnished doors and cheery checkered sheets. Free city tour daily 10am. Breakfast included. Linen €3, deposit €7. Towels €3/6. Internet €2 per 30min.; free Wi-Fi. Reception 24hr. Lockout 11am-5pm. Curfew 2am. Reserve 1 week ahead. Apr.-Oct. dorms €23; doubles €50. Nov.-Mar. €4 less. Cash only. ❷

Three Ducks Hostel, 6 pl. Étienne Pernet (☎01 48 42 04 05; www.3ducks.fr). ⓂFélix Faure. Courtyard palm trees, beach-style shower sheds, airy rooms, and bar. Small 4- to 12-bed dorm rooms and a modest kitchen. Breakfast included. Linen €3.50. Towels €1. Internet €2 per 3hr. Reception 24hr. Lockout noon-4pm. Reserve online 1 week ahead, earlier for doubles. In summer 4- to 12-bed dorms €19; 3-bed €21; doubles €46. In winter 4 to 12-bed dorms €23; 3-bed €25; doubles €52. MC/V. ❶

PASSY AND AUTEUIL (16ÈME)

Hôtel Boileau, 81 rue Boileau (☎01 42 88 83 74; www.hotel-boileau.com). ⓂExelmans. Far from most sights. Clean, carpeted rooms with flatscreen TVs, full bath (some brand-new), and phones. Breakfast €9-11.50. Internet. Reserve 1 month in advance June-Sept. Singles €70-77; doubles €80-95; twins €92-98; triples €125-130. Extra bed €15. AmEx/MC/V. ❺

BATIGNOLLES (17ÈME)

▩ **Hôtel Champerret Héliopolis,** 13 rue d'Héliopolis (☎01 47 64 92 56; www.champerret-heliopolis-paris-hotel.com). ⓂPorte de Champerret. Superb staff. 22 brilliant

THE HIDDEN DEAL

MARCHÉ MADNESS

Eating in Paris can get expensive. Why not take time to enjoy one of Paris's many delicious, inexpensive food markets? Though most are closed Monday, here's a sampling of markets throughout the week:

On Tuesdays, get lost in **Marché Daumesnil**, bd. de Reuily, 12ème, the longest continuous market in Paris, at 1385m. (Ⓜ️Daumesnil. Open 7am-2:30pm.)

On Wednesdays, try **Marché des Barbes**, bd. Chapelle, across from Lariboisière Hospital, 18ème, a favorite of chefs for its superior produce. (Ⓜ️Barbes-Rochechouart. Open 7am-2:30pm.)

Marché Saxe-Breteuil, av. de Saxe, 7ème, rules Thursdays. Savor artisanal cheeses under the Eiffel Tower—how French! (Ⓜ️Segur. Open 7am-3pm.)

On Fridays, the traditional **Marché Mouffetard**, rue Mouffetard, 5ème, is full of idiosyncratic regulars, whose lively banter has been known to break into song. (Ⓜ️Place Monge. Open 7am-1pm.)

Environmentalists rejoice on Saturdays; **Marché des Batignolles**, Terre Plein on bd. des Batignolles, 8ème, sells organic produce. (Open 8am-3pm.)

On Sundays, be sure to stop by the distinctly exotic **Marché de l'Aligre**, pl. Aligre, 12ème, which features unique vendors from around the world. (Ⓜ️Ledru-Rollin. Open Tu-Su 8am-1pm.)

rooms, each with hair dryer, phone, shower, and TV; several with little balconies opening onto a terrace. Breakfast €9.50. Free Wi-Fi. Wheelchair-accessible. Reception 24hr. Reserve 2 weeks ahead via email, fax, or phone. Singles €77; doubles €90, with bath €96; triples with bath €108. Check website for discounts of up to 15%. AmEx/MC/V. ⑤

MONTMARTRE (18ÈME)

🏨 **Le Village Hostel,** 20 rue d'Orsel (☎01 42 64 22 02; www.villagehostel.fr). Ⓜ️Anvers. A quiet repose. All rooms with toilets and showers. Lovely views. Kitchen, stereo, telephones, and TV in lounge. Breakfast included. Internet and Wi-Fi €2 per 30min., €3.50 per hr. 1-week max. stay. Reception 24hr. Lockout 11am-4pm. Reserve online 1 month ahead. 4-, 6-, or 8-bed dorms €24; doubles €60; triples €81. MC/V. ❷

Hôtel Caulaincourt, 2 sq. Caulaincourt (☎01 46 06 46 06; www.caulaincourt.com). Ⓜ️Lamarck-Caulaincourt. Formerly artists' studios. Simple rooms. Skyline views. Breakfast included. Towels €1. 30 min. free Internet, €2 per hr. thereafter; free Wi-Fi. Lockout 11am-4pm. Curfew 2am. Reserve online 1 month ahead. 4- to 6-bed dorms €25; singles with shower €50, with full bath €60; doubles €63/73; 2-bed doubles €66/76; triples with full bath €89. Extra bed €10. MC/V. ❷

BUTTES CHAUMONT (19ÈME)

Crimée Hôtel, 188 rue de Crimée (☎01 40 36 75 29; www.hotelcrimee.com). Ⓜ️Crimée. Sterile business-conference feel. Spotless rooms with A/C, bath, and TVs. Breakfast €7. Free Wi-Fi. Reception 24hr. Check-in and check-out noon. Reserve 2 weeks ahead. Singles €68-70; doubles €70-73; triples €85; quads €100. Extra bed €12. AmEx/MC/V. ⑤

BELLEVILLE AND PÈRE LACHAISE (20ÈME)

Eden Hôtel, 7 rue Jean-Baptiste Dumay (☎01 46 36 64 22; fax 46 36 01 11). Ⓜ️Pyrénées. Clean rooms, each with TV. Dogs welcome. Breakfast €5. Hall showers €4. Free Internet and Wi-Fi. Reserve 1 week ahead. Singles €42-49, with bath €57; doubles with bath €60. Extra bed €10. MC/V. ❸

Auberge de Jeunesse "Le D'Artagnan" (HI), 80 rue Vitruve (☎01 40 32 34 56; www.fuaj.org). Ⓜ️Porte de Bagnolet. Claims to be France's largest youth hostel. 435-bed backpacker's colony. Flashing neon lights and free in-house cinema. Restaurant and bar. Breakfast included. Lockers €2-4 per day. Linen included. Laundry €3. Internet and Wi-Fi €2 per hr. 4-night max. stay.

Reception 24hr. Lockout noon-3pm. Reserve online. 9-bed dorms €20; 3-, 4-, and 5-bed €22. Under 10 ½-price, under 5 free. IYHA membership required; €11-18. MC/V. ❷

🗷 FOOD

French cooking is universally renowned and has influenced cuisine around the world. The preparation and consumption of food are integral to French daily life. When in doubt, spend your money on food in Paris. Skip the museum, sleep in the dingy hotel, but **eat well.** That said, don't approach French dining with the assumption that chic equals *cher;* while three-star restaurants are a valued Parisian institution, you don't have to pay their prices for excellent cuisine. Bistros provide a more informal and often less expensive option. Even more casual are *brasseries,* often crowded and convivial, best for large groups and high spirits. The least expensive option is usually a *crêperie,* where you can often eat for less than you would pay at McDo. The offerings of specialty food shops—*boulangeries, pâtisseries,* and *traiteurs*—make delicious, inexpensive picnic supplies and cheap meals on the go, while a number of North African and Middle Eastern restaurants serve affordable dishes.

AFRICAN
🗷 404 (129)	3ème ❸
Babylone Bis (129)	2ème ❷
La Table d'Erica (131)	6ème ❸

AMERICAN/ANGLO
🗷 Chez Haynes (133)	9ème ❷
🗷 The James Joyce Pub (136)	17ème ❷
McCoy Café (132)	7ème ❷

ASIAN
🗷 Le Cambodge (133)	10ème ❷
Chez Fung (135)	15ème ❷
Kintaro (129)	2ème ❸
Le Lotus Blanc (132)	7ème ❸
Le Pré Verre (131)	5ème ❸
Tricotin (134)	13ème ❷
Wassana (136)	18ème ❷

CAFES/SALONS DE THÉ
Angelina's (129)	1er ❷
L'Apparement Café (129)	3ème ❸
Aux Artistes (135)	15ème ❸
🗷 Le Bar à Soupes (134)	11ème ❷
Café de France (135)	13ème ❸
🗷 Café de l'Industrie (134)	11ème ❷
Café des Lettres (132)	7ème ❸
🗷 Café Flèche d'Or (137)	20ème ❷
🗷 La Fournée d'Augustine (136)	17ème ❷
🗷 Georges (130)	4ème ❹
🗷 Ladurée (132)	8ème ❸
Mariage Frères (130)	4ème ❺
La Mer à Boire (137)	20ème ❶
Palais des Thés (129)	3ème ❷
Place Numéro Thé (128)	Île de la Cité ❷
🗷 Refuge Café (134)	12ème ❸

CRÊPERIES/ICE CREAM
🗷 Amorino (128)	Île St-Louis ❶
🗷 Berthillon (128)	Île St-Louis ❶
La Bolée Belgrand (137)	20ème ❷
Briezh Café (130)	4ème ❷
🗷 Crêperie Plougastel (135)	14ème ❸
myberry (130)	4ème ❶
🗷 Ty Yann (132)	8ème ❷

FRENCH
🗷 Bélisaire (135)	15ème ❹
Brasserie d'Île St-Louis (128)	Île St-Louis ❹
🗷 Le Caveau du Palais (128)	Île de la Cité ❹
🗷 Chartier (133)	9ème ❷
🗷 Chez Gladines (134)	13ème ❷
🗷 Chez Janou (129)	3ème ❸
🗷 Les Cocottes (132)	7ème ❸
🗷 Le Comptoir du Relais (131)	6ème ❸
🗷 L'Ébauchoir (134)	12ème ❸
Le Perraudin (130)	5ème ❸
🗷 Refuge des Fondus (136)	18ème ❷
Resto-Flash (133)	10ème ❸
Le Scheffer (136)	16ème ❸

INDIAN
Anarkali Sarangui (133)	9ème ❷
Tandoori (135)	15ème ❷

MARKETS
Batignolles Organic Produce (136)	17ème ❶
Belleville Outdoor Market (137)	19ème ❶
Marché Bastille (134)	11ème ❶
Marché Beauvau St-Antoine (134)	12ème ❶
Marché Berthier (136)	17ème ❶
Marché Biologique (132)	6ème ❶
🗷 Marché Monge (130)	5ème ❶

PARIS

Marché Mouffetard (131)	5ème ❶	La Boulangerie Mauclerc (137)	19ème ❷
Marché Popincourt (134)	11ème ❶	Debauve et Gallais (132)	7ème ❷
Marché Président-Wilson (136)	16ème ❶	L'Épicerie (128)	Île St-Louis ❷
🔳 Marché St-Quentin (133)	10ème ❶	Fauchon (132)	8ème ❹
		La Maison du Chocolat (133)	9ème ❶
MEDITERRANEAN		Poilâne (131)	6ème ❶
Chez Marianne (130)	4ème ❷	🔳 Stéphane Secco (132)	7ème ❶
Little Italy Trattoria (130)	4ème ❸	🔳 Tang Frères (134)	13ème ❶
Le Samson (135)	13ème ❸		
		TRENDY/INTELLIGENTSIA	
MEXICAN AND SPANISH		Bubbles (130)	4ème ❶
🔳 Ay, Caramba! (137)	19ème ❸	Café de Flore (131)	6ème ❸
La Bodega (136)	18ème ❷	La Coupole (135)	14ème ❹
Chez Papa (135)	14ème ❸	Les Deux Magots (131)	6ème ❷
		Le Procope (131)	6ème ❹
MIDDLE EASTERN			
Aquarius Café (135)	14ème ❷	**VEGETARIAN AND VEGAN**	
🔳 L'As du Falafel (130)	4ème ❶	Bioboa (129)	1er ❷
Babylone (134)	11ème ❶	Le Grenier de Notre-Dame (131)	5ème ❷
Chez Omar (129)	3ème ❸	Joy in Food (136)	17ème ❸
🔳 Comptoir Méditerranée (130)	5ème ❷	🔳 Piccolo Teatro (130)	4ème ❷
		🔳 La Victoire Suprême (130)	4ème ❸
SPECIALTY			
La Bague de Kenza (134)	11ème ❶		

ÎLE DE LA CITÉ

🔳 **Le Caveau du Palais,** 17-19 pl. Dauphine (☎01 43 26 04 28). Ⓜ️Cité. Hearty French fare like *foie gras* and *côte de boeuf*. Elegant dining room with timbered ceiling and stone walls. *Entrées* €9-20. *Plats* €18-50. Open M-F noon-2:30pm and 7-10:30pm. Reservations necessary for dinner and recommended for lunch. AmEx/MC/V. ❹

Place Numéro Thé, 20 pl. Dauphine (☎01 44 07 28 17). Ⓜ️Cité. Casual restaurant-*salon de thé* with a terrace looking out onto the tree-lined pl. Dauphine. Light lunch fare and noteworthy desserts such as the coulis with *fromage blanc* (€5). Exotic teas €5. *Chocolat chaud à l'ancienne* €6. Open M-Tu and Th-F noon-5:30pm. MC/V. ❷

ÎLE SAINT-LOUIS

🔳 **Berthillon,** 31 rue St Louis en l'Île (☎01 43 54 31 61). Ⓜ️Cité or Pont Marie. Reputed to have the best ice cream and sorbet in Paris. Family-run institution since 1954. Flavors like blood orange and honey nougat. Single scoop €2, double €3, triple €4. Open from Sept. to mid-July W-Su 10am-8pm. Closed 2 weeks in Feb. and Apr. Cash only. ❶

🔳 **Amorino,** 47 rue St Louis en l'Île (☎01 44 07 48 08; www.amorino.fr/boutiques.htm). 22 other locations. Ⓜ️Pont Marie. 20 gelati and *sorbetti* flavors (includes the Nutella *l'Inimitable!*). Cups €3-8. Cones €3-5. Open daily noon-11pm. Cash only. ❶

L'Épicerie, 51 rue St Louis en l'Île (☎01 43 25 20 14). Elegant, creative concoctions of everything from *foie gras* to mustard. Over 80 types of tea line the walls of this tiny store. Perfumed sugars (€5), infused olive oils (€8), and variety of jams (€8) make perfect presents. Past patrons include Bill Clinton. Open daily 11am-9pm. MC/V. ❷

Brasserie de l'Île St-Louis, 55 quai de Bourbon (☎01 43 54 02 59). Ⓜ️Pont Marie. Old-fashioned *brasserie* and island institution known for Alsatian specialties such as *choucroute garnie* (sausages and pork on a bed of sauerkraut; €18). Typical cafe fare €7-30. Outdoor *quai* seating. Open daily noon-midnight. MC/V over €15. ❹

CHÂTELET-LES HALLES

1ER ARRONDISSEMENT

Angelina's, 226 rue de Rivoli (☎01 42 60 82 00). ⓂConcorde or Tuileries. RER Neuilly-Porte Maillot. Also at 2 pl. de la Porte Maillot, 17ème (☎01 42 60 82 00). Favorite of Audrey Hepburn and Coco Chanel. Belle Époque frescoes, mirrored walls, and marble tables from 1903 inception. Touristy, but worth it for the ▩**chocolat à l'ancienne dit 'l'africain** (€7). Pastries €5-7. Open daily 9am-7pm. AmEx/MC/V. ❷

Bioboa, 3 rue Danielle Casanova (☎01 42 61 17 67). ⓂPyramides. Small, stylish "food spa." Freshly made food to eat in or take away. 80% of ingredients are organic. Smoothies €5-8. Veggie or beef burger €10-11. Open M-Sa 11am-6pm. MC/V. ❷

2ÈME ARRONDISSEMENT

Babylone Bis, 34 rue Tiquetonne (☎01 42 33 48 35). ⓂÉtienne-Marcel. Zebra skin on the walls and banana leaves on the ceiling. Antillean and African cuisine includes *aloko* (fried bananas; €5.50) and stuffed crab (€9). Late-night destination for musicians: pictures of Snoop Dogg and Marvin Gaye on the walls. Open daily 8pm-8am. MC/V. ❷

Kintaro, 24 rue St-Augustin (☎01 47 42 13 14). ⓂOpéra. Popular Japanese restaurant with everything but sushi. Great noodle bowls (€8-10) and an array of menu combinations (€13-18). Sapporo beer €5. Open M-Sa 11:30am-10pm. MC/V over €23. ❸

THE MARAIS

3ÈME ARRONDISSEMENT

▩ **Chez Janou,** 2 rue Roger Verlomme (☎01 42 72 28 41). ⓂChemin-Vert. Classic Provençal bistro. Lively atmosphere. Try the ratatouille or the goat cheese and spinach salad (both €9). Chocolate mousse (€9) brought in an enormous self-serve bowl. Over 80 kinds of *pastis*. Packed every night. Open M-F noon-3pm and 7:45pm-midnight, Sa-Su noon-4pm and 7:45pm-midnight. Reservations always recommended. MC/V. ❸

▩ **404,** 69 rue des Gravilliers (☎01 42 74 57 81). ⓂArts et Métiers. Sophisticated family-owned Maghreb restaurant. Sit in the airy terrace in the back at lunch. Mouthwatering couscous (€14-24) and *tagines* (€14-18). Vegetarian options. Open M-F noon-2:30pm and 8pm-midnight, Sa-Su noon-4pm and 8pm-midnight. AmEx/MC/V. ❸

L'Apparemment Café, 18 rue des Coutures St-Gervais (☎01 48 87 12 22). ⓂSt-Paul. Make-your-own gourmet salads (€12-16) and Su brunch (reserve ahead; €16-21). Art exhibits on display. Open M-Sa noon-2am, Su 12:30pm-midnight. MC/V. ❸

Palais des Thés, 64 rue Vieille du Temple (☎01 48 87 80 60; www.palaisdesthes.com). ⓂSt-Paul. 4 other locations around the city. Specialty shop sells over 200 organic teas (€8-135 per 100g) collected by the owners from 20 countries in Asia, Africa, and South America. Open M-Sa 10am-8pm. AmEx/MC/V. ❷

Chez Omar, 47 rue de Bretagne (☎01 42 72 36 26). ⓂArts et Métiers. One of the better Middle Eastern places. Come at 7:30pm for a relaxed ambience, later to see the local intelligentsia. Couscous with vegetables €12. Spectacular *steak au poivre* €18. Open M-Sa noon-2:30pm and 7-11:30pm, Su 7-11:30pm. Cash only. ❸

4ÈME ARRONDISSEMENT

🔲 **L'As du Falafel,** 34 rue des Rosiers (☎01 48 87 63 60). Ⓜ️St-Paul or Hôtel de Ville. "The best falafel in the world," according to Lenny Kravitz. Kosher stand. Falafel special €5. Lemonade €4. Open M-Th and Su noon-midnight, F noon-7pm. MC/V. ❶

🔲 **La Victoire Suprême du Coeur,** 29-31 rue du Bourg Tibourg (☎01 40 41 95 03; www. vscoeur.com). Ⓜ️Hôtel de Ville. Run by the devotees of Sri Chinmoy. Classics like seitan "steak" with mushroom sauce (€14). Vegan options. 2-course *menu* €14. Open M-Tu and Th-F noon-3pm and 6:30-10:30pm, Sa noon-11pm, Su 11am-5:30pm. ❸

🔲 **Piccolo Teatro,** 6 rue des Ecouffes (☎01 42 72 17 79). Ⓜ️St-Paul. Romantic vegetarian hideout. *Plats* €8-12. Open daily noon-3pm and 7-11pm. AmEx/MC/V. ❷

🔲 **Georges,** Centre Pompidou, 6th fl. (☎01 44 78 47 99). Ⓜ️Rambuteau or Hôtel de Ville. A cafe almost more impressive than the museum. Unbeatable views. Splurge on a *plat* (king crab *omelette* €25). Champagne €8-12. *Gateau au chocolat de costes* €12. Dress to impress. Open M and W-Su noon-2am. Reserve for dinner. AmEx/MC/V. ❹

Mariage Frères, 30 and 35 rue du Bourg-Tibourg (☎01 42 72 28 11). Ⓜ️Hôtel-de-Ville. Branches at 13 rue des Grands-Augustins, 6ème (☎01 40 51 82 50), and 260 rue du Faubourg St-Honoré, 8ème. 500 tea varieties (€7-15 per 100g) and a book detailing the history of each. Brunch €30. Open daily 10:30am-7:30pm. AmEx/MC/V. ❺

Bubbles, 4 rue Mahler (☎01 40 29 42 41; www.bubbles-dietbar.com). Ⓜ️St-Paul. "Diet bar" best known for thick smoothies (banana, cocoa, and Nutella €5) and fruit juice concoctions (orange, carrot, and ginger €5). Open M-Sa 9:30am-8pm. MC/V. ❶

Chez Marianne, 2 rue des Hospitalières St-Gervais (☎01 42 72 18 86). Unbeatable *assiettes composés* with choice of 4, 5, 6, or 10 dishes (€12, €14, €16, and €26). Extensive wine list. Homemade hummus, falafel, *kefta*, tahini, *tzatziki*, grape leaves, and more. Baklava €5. Open daily noon-midnight. AmEx/MC/V. ❷

Little Italy Trattoria, 13 rue Rambuteau (☎01 42 74 32 46). Ⓜ️Rambuteau. Enticing *salumeria* (deli). Antipasti for 2 €22. Fresh pastas €8-15. Pitcher of wine €7-8. Open daily noon-3:30pm and 7-11:30pm. MC/V. ❸

Briezh Café, 109 rue Vielle du Temple (☎01 42 74 13 77; www.breizhcafe.com). Ⓜ️Filles du Calvaire. Relaxed Breton *crêperie* full of surprises. High-quality ingredients (organic veggies, raw milk, *normand* sausage). *Galettes* €3-11. *Crêpes* €4-8. Open W-Su noon-11pm. Reservations recommended. AmEx/MC/V. ❷

myberry, 25 rue Vieille du Temple (☎01 42 74 54 48; http://myberry.fr). Ⓜ️Hôtel de Ville. Based on Pinkberry. Light, tangy frozen yogurt with a variety of toppings (€1 each). Free Wi-Fi. Small €3, medium €3.50, large €4.50. Fresh fruit juice €4-5. Open daily noon-midnight; closes earlier in winter. MC/V over €15. ❶

LATIN QUARTER AND SAINT-GERMAIN

5ÈME ARRONDISSEMENT

🔲 **Comptoir Méditerranée,** 42 rue du Cardinal Lemoine (☎01 43 25 29 08; www.savan-nahcafe.fr). Ⓜ️Cardinal Lemoine. Savannah Café's little sister, run by the same welcoming owner. More Lebanese deli than restaurant, Serves fresh, colorful dishes. Select from 18 hot or cold options to make your own plate (€6.50-11.50). Sandwiches €4.20. Homemade lemonade €2.50. Espresso €1.70. Open M-Sa 11am-10pm. MC/V. ❷

🔲 **Marché Monge,** pl. Monge. Ⓜ️Monge. Busy but easy to navigate. Everything from cheese and flowers to jewelry and shoes in these stalls. Open W, F, Su 8am-1pm. ❶

Le Perraudin, 157 rue St-Jacques (☎01 46 33 15 75; www.restaurant-perraudin.com). RER Luxembourg. Simple and elegant. French favorites like *boeuf bourguignon*. *Plats* €16-29. 3-course *menu* €30. Open M-F noon-2:30pm and 7-10:30pm. MC/V. ❸

Le Pré Verre, 8 rue Thenard (☎01 43 54 59 47; www. lepreverre.com). ⓂMaubert-Mutualité. Packed with locals. French-Asian fusion. Daily changing menu on chalkboards. Only market-fresh ingredients. Challenge your taste buds with a white chocolate mousse salad. Lunch *formule* €14. 3-course *menu* €28. Open Tu-Sa noon-2pm and 7:30-10:30pm. ❸

Le Grenier de Notre-Dame, 18 rue de la Bûcherie (☎01 43 29 98 29). ⓂSt-Michel. Haven for vegans. Macrobiotic and vegetarian specialties with an edgy French spin. Autumn salad €16. 3-course lunch *formule* €16, dinner €18. Open daily noon-11pm. MC/V. ❷

Marché Mouffetard, rue Mouffetard. ⓂMonge. Cheese, meat, and fish at specialty stores. Fruits and veggies at stalls outside St-Medard church. Highly reputed *boulangeries*. Open Tu-Sa 8am-8pm, Su 8am-4pm. ❶

6ÈME ARRONDISSEMENT

🔳 **Le Comptoir du Relais,** 5 carrefour de l'Odéon (☎01 44 27 07 97). ⓂOdéon. Local-heavy and hyper-crowded. Focus on pork and other meats. *Foie gras* on toast €11. Open M-F noon-6pm and from 8:30pm, Sa-Su noon-11pm. Reserve ahead for weekday dinner; reservations not accepted for weekends. MC/V. ❸

La Table d'Erica, 6 rue Mabillon (☎01 43 54 87 61; www.tableerica.free.fr). ⓂMabillon. Creole gem. 3-course *menu* €13. *Calou Créole* (stew of spinach, okra, chicken, and seafood) €16. Open Tu-Sa noon-2:30pm and 6:30-11pm. AmEx/MC/V. ❸

Poilâne, 8 rue du Cherche-Midi (☎01 45 48 42 59; www.poilane.fr). ⓂVaneau. One of Paris's best breadmakers. Watch the baking process. Famous sourdough loaf €3.80. Melt-in-your-mouth apple tart €2. Open M-Sa 7:15am-8:15pm. MC/V over €20. ❶

Café de Flore, 172 bd. St-Germain (☎01 45 48 55 26). ⓂSt-Germain-des-Prés. Big shots like Apollinaire, Bardot, Breton, Camus, Picasso, and Thurber all sipped the morning brew here. Classic Art Deco seating upstairs; check out Sartre and Beauvoir's famous booth. Coffee €5.50. Pastries €5-10. *Salade flore* €15. Open daily 7:30am-1:30am. AmEx/MC/V. ❸

Les Deux Magots, 6 pl. St-Germain-des-Prés (☎01 45 48 55 25). ⓂSt-Germain-des-Prés. Home to literati from Mallarmé to Hemingway since 1885. Now favored mostly by tourists. Sandwiches €7-14. Coffee €4.20. Open daily 7:30am-1am. AmEx/MC/V. ❷

Le Procope, 13 rue de l'Ancienne Comédie (☎01 40 46 79 00). ⓂOdéon. Founded in 1686, making it the 1st cafe in the world. Voltaire drank 40 cups a day here while writing *Candide*. Marat came here to plot the Revolution. Now a seafood restaurant. 2-course *menu* €26. Open daily 10:30am-1am. AmEx/MC/V. ❹

THE BIG SPLURGE

A BITE IN THE DARK

It's no secret that Paris's cuisine is some of the world's best; what sets the restaurant **Dans le Noir** apart from the gourmet crowd is that you can't see your meal.

Founded in 2004 by Édouard de Broglie and Étienne Boisrond, the restaurant has charged itself with awakening senses other than sight by serving patrons in total darkness. After passing through a series of heavy curtains, diners are led to their table by the restaurant's staff. While you're free to order *à la carte*—the menu consists of inventive takes on traditional French cuisine; the more adventurous will opt for *le menu surprise*—you won't know what's on your plate until you taste it.

You may wonder how your servers are able to move through the dining room so easily. They're used to it—Dans le Noir employs only blind waiters. In addition to its ambitions of sensory awakening, the restaurant has partnered with the Association Paul Guinot to help the blind find employment. Combining a disorienting, exciting experience with social change, Dans le Noir is money well spent.

51 rue Quincampoix, 4ème (☎01 42 77 98 04; www.danslenoir. com). ⓂHôtel de Ville. *2-course menu €37, 3-course menu €43. Student discounts. Reserve 3-5 days ahead.*

Marché Biologique, on bd. Raspail between rue du Cherche-Midi and rue de Rennes. ⓂRennes. Everything from 7-grain bread to tofu patties. Open Su 9am-2pm. ❶

INVALIDES (7ÈME)

🔲 **Les Cocottes,** 135 rue St-Dominique (☎01 45 50 10 31). ⓂSolférino. A simpler, less expensive version of Christian Constant's popular haute cuisine establishments. Fresh, beautifully presented, and comfortingly delicious food. Try *cocottes* (€12-15), cast-iron skillets filled with pig's feet and pigeon or fresh vegetables. Don't miss La Fabuleuse Tarte (€9). Open daily noon-2:30pm and 7:15-11pm. AmEx/MC/V. ❸

🔲 **Stéphane Secco,** 20 rue Jean-Nicot (☎01 43 17 35 20). ⓂLa Tour-Maubourg. Another location at 25 bd. de Grenelle, 15ème (☎01 45 67 17 40). Formerly Poujaran. This *boulangerie-pâtisserie* is the perfect place to stop before a picnic. Creative salads, quiches, *tartes* (€3 for a *petit*), rich desserts (macaroons €1-2), and bread with everything from herbs to apricots (€1-3). Open Tu-Sa 7:30am-8:30pm. Cash only. ❶

Café des Lettres, 53 rue de Verneuil (☎01 42 22 52 17). ⓂSolférino. Scandinavian cafe serves fresh, healthful fare. Leather armchairs and sunny courtyard with statues. Smoked salmon and *blinis* €21. Open July-May M-F noon-2:30pm and 8-10:30pm; June M-F noon-2:30pm and 8-10:30pm, Sa-Su noon-7pm. AmEx/MC/V. ❸

Debauve et Gallais, 30 rue des Sts-Pères (☎01 45 48 54 67; www.debauve-et-gallais. com). ⓂSt-Germaine-des-Près or Sèvres-Babylone. Also at 33 rue Vivienne, 2ème (☎01 40 39 05 50). Favorite of royals like Marie Antoinette since 1800. Historic building designed by Napoleon's architects. Chocolates produced without additives, dyes, or sweeteners. Flavors like peach and almond, nougat, and Earl Grey tea. Velvety chocolate bars in a variety of flavors (€5). Open M-Sa 9:30am-7pm. AmEx/MC/V. ❷

Le Lotus Blanc, 45 rue de Bourgogne (☎01 45 55 18 89). ⓂVarenne. Chef Pham-Nam Nghia has been perfecting Vietnamese dishes for over 25 years. Excellent specialties *à la vapeur* (€7-15) and *grillades*. *Menus* €10-33. Open Sept.-July M-Sa noon-2:30pm and 7:30-11pm. Reserve ahead. AmEx/MC/V. ❸

McCoy Café, 49 av. Bosquet (☎01 45 56 00 00). ⓂÉcole Militaire. American comfort food: burgers (€5-7), bagels (€5-7), and cheesesteak (€6). Attached grocery store home to Betty Crocker, Oreos, Ritz, Pepperidge Farm, Pop Tarts, and even beef jerky. Marshmallow fluff €4. Open daily 8am-8pm. ❷

CHAMPS-ÉLYSÉES (8ÈME)

🔲 **Ty Yann**, 10 rue de Constantinople (☎01 40 08 00 17). ⓂEurope. Breton chef and owner Yann cheerfully prepares outstanding *galettes* (€8-10) and *crêpes*. Decorated with Yann's mother's pastoral paintings. Chew on *La vaniteuse* (€8), with sausage sauteed in cognac, Emmental cheese, and onions. Create your own *crêpe* €6-7. Takeout 15% less. Open M-F noon-3:30pm and 7:30-10:30pm, Sa 7:30-10:30pm. MC/V. ❷

🔲 **Ladurée,** 16 rue Royale (☎01 42 60 21 79; www.laduree.com). ⓂConcorde or FDR. Also at 75 av. des Champs-Élysées, 8ème (☎01 40 75 08 75); 21 rue Bonaparte, 6ème (☎01 44 07 64 87); 62 bd. Haussmann, 9ème (☎01 42 82 40 10). Ever wanted to dine inside a Fabergé egg? Rococo décor attracts a jarring mix of well-groomed shoppers and tourists. Among the 1st Parisian *salons de thé*. Infamous mini macaroons in 16 varieties (€2). Boxes of Chocolats Incomparables from €18. Open M-Sa 8:30am-7pm, Su 10am-7pm. Lunch served until 3pm. AmEx/MC/V. ❸

Fauchon, 26-30 pl. de la Madeleine (☎01 47 42 60 11; www.fauchon.com). ⓂMadeleine. Paris's favorite gourmet food shop comes with gourmet prices. *Traiteur/ pâtisserie/épicerie/charcuterie* has it all. Among Paris's finest wine cellars. Creative box of chocolates €23 for 250g. *Épicerie/confiserie* open M-Sa 9:30am-8pm, *boulangerie* 8am-6pm, *traiteur/pâtisserie* 9am-9pm, tearoom 9am-7pm. AmEx/MC/V. ❹

PARIS

OPÉRA (9ÈME)

Chez Haynes, 3 rue Clauzel (☎01 48 78 40 63). ⓂSt-Georges. Paris's 1st African-American-owned restaurant opened in 1949. Louis Armstrong, James Baldwin, and Richard Wright enjoyed the delicious New Orleans soul food. Ma Sutton's fried honey chicken €14. Sister Lena's BBQ spare ribs €16. Soul food Tu-Sa, Brazilian Su. Live music F-Sa nights; cover €5. Open Tu-Su 7pm-midnight; hours vary. AmEx/MC/V. ❷

Chartier, 7 rue du Faubourg-Montmartre (☎01 47 70 86 29; www.restaurant-chartier.com). ⓂGrands Boulevards. Parisian fixture since 1896; the waitstaff adds up the bill on each table's paper tablecloth. Staples like *steak au poivre* (€8.50) and *langue de veau* (sheep's tongue; €9.80). Side dishes €2.50. Open daily 11:30am-10pm. AmEx/MC/V. ❷

Anarkali Sarangui, 4 pl. Gustave Toudouze (☎01 48 78 39 84). ⓂSt-Georges. Rare North Indian restaurant with pleasant outdoor seating and a brightly decorated interior. Tandoori and curries €7.50-13. Open Tu-Su 11am-2:30pm and 7-11pm. MC/V. ❷

La Maison du Chocolat, 8 bd. de la Madeleine (☎01 47 42 86 52; www.lamaisonduchocolat.com). ⓂMadeleine. Chain with branches in Cannes, London, New York City, and Tokyo. Branches at: Carrousel du Louvre, 99 rue de Rivoli, 1er (☎01 45 44 20 40); 19 rue de Sèvres, 6ème (☎01 45 44 20 40); 52 rue François, 8ème (☎01 47 23 38 25); 225 rue du Faubourg St-Honoré, 8ème (☎01 42 27 39 44). Exquisite chocolates (box of 2 €3) and a distilled chocolate essence drink (€4-6). Mouthwatering chocolate éclairs €4. Open M-Sa 10am-7:30pm. AmEx/MC/V. ❶

CANAL SAINT MARTIN AND SURROUNDS (10ÈME)

Le Cambodge, 10 av. Richerand (☎01 44 84 37 70). ⓂRépublique. Inexpensive and delicious Cambodian restaurant. Good vegetarian options. *Plats* €7-10. M-Sa noon-2:30pm and 8-11:30pm. No reservations; wait up to 90min. MC/V. ❷

Marché St-Quentin, 85 bis bd. de Magenta. ⓂGare de l'Est or Gare du Nord. Outside: a huge construction of iron and glass, built in the 1880s, renovated in 1982, and covered by a glass ceiling. Inside: stalls of all varieties of produce, meat, cheese, seafood, and wine. Open Tu-Sa 8am-1pm and 3:30-7:30pm, Su 8am-1pm. ❶

Resto-Flash, 10 rue Lucien Sampaix (☎01 42 45 03 30). ⓂJacques Bonsergent. Kosher; regulated by the Beth Din of Paris. Standards like *côte de veau* (€18) at slightly elevated prices. Takeaway sandwiches €8. Open M-F 11:30am-3:30pm. MC/V. ❸

CAFE FOR THOUGHT

La Closerie des Lilas—a Parisian staple since 1847—was the haunt of great thinkers throughout the 20th century. The cafe's location near the famous Bullier Ball made the restaurant a popular destination for socialites. Yet it was Émile Zola and Paul Cézanne who established the restaurant as an intellectual haven. In the 20th century, poet Paul Fort hosted gatherings at La Closerie that drew such artists Verlaine and Apollinaire.

Ernest Hemingway immortalized La Closerie in his novel *The Sun Also Rises,* which follows Americans from the Lost Generation in their travels through France and Spain. The novel was loosely based on Hemingway's experiences at La Closerie as a member of the expat community that included writers F. Scott Fitzgerald and Gertrude Stein. Hemingway emphasized his admiration for the establishment: "The only decent cafe in our neighborhood was La Closerie des Lilas, and it was one of the best cafes in Paris."

Although popularity has perhaps made La Closerie des Lilas somewhat passé, the restaurant is representative of Paris's ability to foster intellectual thought and artistic collaboration.

172 bd. St-Germain, 6ème (☎01 45 48 55 26; www.cafe-de-flore. com). ⓂSt-Germain-des-Prés.

BASTILLE

11ÈME ARRONDISSEMENT

Le Bar à Soupes, 33 rue Charonne (☎01 43 57 53 79; www.lebarasoupes.com). ⓂBastille. Small, bright cafe. Big bowls of delicious, freshly made soup (€5-6). 6 varieties change daily. €9.50 lunch *menu* is an astonishing deal; it comes with soup, a roll, wine or coffee, and cheese plate or dessert. Friendly staff will make your day. Gooey *gâteau chocolat* €4. Open M-Sa noon-3pm and 6:30-11pm. MC/V. ❷

Café de l'Industrie, 15-17 rue St-Sabin (☎01 47 00 13 53). ⓂBreguet-Sabin. Happening cafe. Diverse menu. *Vin chaud* €4.50. Salads €8.50-9. Popular brunch platter (served Sa-Su; changes weekly) €12-15. Open daily 10am-2am. MC/V. ❷

La Bague de Kenza, 106 rue St-Maur (☎01 43 14 93 15). Also at 173 rue du Faubourg St-Antoine, 11ème. Piles of creatively sweet Algerian pastries chock-full of nuts, honey, and/or dried fruits (€1.50-2.20). Fruit-shaped marzipan €2.20. Algerian bread €2.10-3.50. Open M-Th and Sa-Su 9am-10pm, F 2-10pm. AmEx/MC/V over €16. ❶

Babylone, 21 rue Dava (☎01 47 00 55 02). ⓂBastille. Tiny and bar-like. Order a falafel (€4-5), shawarma (€5-6), or falafel and shawarma (€5-6) sandwich. Beer €2.50. Open M noon-4pm, Tu-Sa noon-4pm and 7-11:30pm. Cash only. ❶

Marché Bastille, bd. Richard-Lenoir from pl. de la Bastille to rue St-Sabin. ⓂBastille. Produce, cheese, mushrooms, bread, and meat. Open Th and Su 7am-2:30pm. ❶

Marché Popincourt, bd. Richard-Lenoir between rue Oberkampf and rue de Jean-Pierre Timbaud. ⓂOberkampf. Fresh produce and meats. Open Tu and F 7am-2:30pm. ❶

12ÈME ARRONDISSEMENT

L'Ébauchoir, 45 rue de Citeaux (☎01 43 42 49 31; www.lebauchoir.com). ⓂFaidherbe-Chaligny. Funky, lively French restaurant. Daily changing menu features delicious concoctions of seafood and meat. Vegetarian dishes upon request. Impressive wine list. *Entrées* €8-15. *Plats* €17-25. Desserts €7. Lunch *menu* €15. Open M 8-11pm, Tu-Sa noon-11pm. Kitchen open noon-2:30pm and 8-11pm. MC/V. ❸

Refuge Café, 54 av. Daumesnil (☎01 43 47 25 59). ⓂGare de Lyon. Whimsical, ivy-covered cafe-restaurant seems to be out of a fairy tale. Art exhibits every month. Salads €11-15. *Plats* €15-23. *Formules* €14-22. Open M-Sa 8am-midnight. ❸

Marché Beauvau St-Antoine, pl. d'Aligre between rue de Charenton and rue Crozatier. ⓂLedru-Rollin. Among Paris's most diverse markets, lined with Muslim halal butcher shops and delis. Open Tu-Sa 8am-1pm and 4-7:30pm, Su 8am-1pm. ❶

BUTTE-AUX-CAILLES AND CHINATOWN (13ÈME)

Chez Gladines, 30 rue des 5 Diamants (☎01 45 80 70 10). ⓂPlace d'Italie. Intimate seating. Southwestern French and Basque specialties (€7.30-12). Well-deserved acclaim draws crowds; to avoid them, come before 7:30pm or after 11pm. Large salads €6.50-9. Beer €2. Espresso €1. Open M-Tu noon-3pm and 7pm-midnight, W-F noon-3pm and 7pm-1am, Sa-Su noon-4pm and 7pm-midnight. Cash only. ❷

Tang Frères, 48 av. d'Ivry (☎01 45 70 80 00). ⓂPorte d'Ivry. Also at 174 rue de Choisy. ⓂPlace d'Italie. A sensory overload, this huge shopping center in the heart of Chinatown contains a bakery, *charcuterie*, fish counter, flower shop, and grocery store. Exotic fruits (durian €7.80 per kg), cheap Asian beers (can of Kirin €0.85; 6-pack of Tsingtao €3.80), rice wines (€3.50 per 500mL), and sake (€5-6.80). Noodles, rice, soups, spices, teas, and tofu in bulk. Open Tu-Sa 10am-8:30pm. MC/V. ❶

Tricotin, 15 av. de Choisy (☎01 45 84 74 44). ⓂPorte de Choisy. 2 large, cafeteria-style rooms. Delicious food from Cambodia, Thailand, and Vietnam. Start with the spring rolls

(€4.90) before trying the sure-to-please *vapeur* (dim sum) dishes, such as the steamed shrimp ravioli (€3.80). Open daily 9am-11:15pm. MC/V. ❷

Café de France, 12 pl. d'Italie (☎01 43 31 19 86). ⓂPlace d'Italie. Chill, hip vibe. Locals commiserate over a glass of wine (€3) and *brasserie*-style food (€12-15). Come for the desserts; 🔳**chocolate mousse** (€4.50) will have you shamelessly licking your spoon clean. *Entrées* €6.50-12. Espresso €2. Open daily 6:30am-2am. MC/V. ❸

Le Samson, 9 rue Jean-Marie Jego (☎01 45 89 09 23). ⓂPlace d'Italie. Greek-influenced. Moussaka €12. Lunch *menu* €12. 3-course dinner *menu* M-F and Su €14-25, Sa €17-25. Open daily noon-2:30pm and 7-11:30pm. MC/V. ❸

MONTPARNASSE

14ÈME ARRONDISSEMENT

🔳 **Crêperie Plougastel,** 47 rue du Montparnasse (☎01 42 79 90 63). ⓂMontparnasse-Bienvenüe. Ambience and prompt staff set this cozy *crêperie* apart. Dessert *crêpes* feature homemade caramel. *Formule* (generous mixed salad and choice of 2 *galettes* and 5 dessert *crêpes*) €15. *Cidre* €2.90. Open daily noon-11:30pm. MC/V. ❸

Aquarius Café, 40 rue de Gergovie (☎01 45 41 36 88). ⓂPernety. Celebrated local favorite. Protein-heavy vegetarian *plats*. Creative Middle Eastern cuisine. 3-course lunch *menu* €11. Open M-Sa noon-2:30pm and 7-10:30pm. MC/V. ❷

Chez Papa, 6 rue Gassendi (☎01 43 22 41 19). ⓂDenfert-Rochereau. Spanish-influenced. Supplement a hot dish (€13-27) or salads (€8-10) with the delicious 🔳**pain sur la planche aux deux fromages** (toasted bread draped with chèvre and cheese from Auvergne; €8.60). Open daily 11am-1am. AmEx/MC/V. ❸

La Coupole, 102 bd. du Montparnasse (☎01 43 20 14 20; www.lacoupoleparis.com). ⓂVavin. Staple since 1927. Art Deco chambers have attracted Einstein, Hemingway, Piaf, and Picasso. Touristy and unabashedly overpriced, but worth a splurge on a hot chocolate (€4.10) or *croque monsieur* (€6). Open M-Th and Su 8-11am and 11:30am-1am, F-Sa 8:30-11am and 11:30am-1:30am. AmEx/MC/V. ❹

15ÈME ARRONDISSEMENT

🔳 **Bélisaire,** 2 rue Marmontel (☎01 48 28 62 24). ⓂVaugirard. Fit for aristocratic celebrations. Options on chalkboard menus rotate seasonally. Salmon and lobster ravioli are to die for. Packed daily. 3-course lunch *menu* €22. 5-course dinner *menu* €40. Open daily noon-2pm and 8-10:30pm. Reservations are a must. MC/V. ❹

Aux Artistes, 63 rue Falguière (☎01 43 22 05 39). ⓂPasteur. Lively venue attracts a mix of students, professionals, and artists. Despite surfboards and American license plates on the walls, the food adheres to traditional French cafe dictates. *Menus* €11-14. Open M-F noon-2:30pm and 7:30pm-midnight, Sa 7:30pm-midnight. Cash only. ❸

Chez Fung, 32 rue Frémicourt (☎01 45 67 36 99). ⓂCambronne. Authentic, superb Malaysian cuisine—though the small portions may leave you hungry. Specialties include *rojak* Malaysian salad (shrimp, vegetables, and fresh fruit; €14). 3-course lunch *menu* M-F €15. Open M-Sa noon-2pm and 7:30-10pm. MC/V. ❸

Tandoori, 10 rue de l'Arivée (☎01 45 48 46 72). ⓂMontparnasse-Bienvenüe. Lunch *menu* (M-F €10) includes grilled chicken or lamb *plat* with bread, cheese, veggies, basmati rice, and dessert. Musical soirees W-F nights feature live, traditional Indian music; reserve ahead. Open M-Sa noon-2:30pm and 7-11pm. MC/V over €16. ❷

PASSY AND AUTEUIL (16ÈME)

Le Scheffer, 22 rue Scheffer (☎01 47 27 81 11). ⓂTrocadéro. Stronghold of traditional French cuisine. Slow service around lunchtime and suspicion of tourists add to the authenticity. *Plats* include *steak-frites* (€19) and *confit de canard maison garni de pommes sautées* (€15). Open M-Sa noon-2:30pm and 7:30-10:30pm. ❸

Marché Président-Wilson, av. du Président Wilson between rue Debrousse and pl. d'Iéna. ⓂIéna or Alma-Marceau. The smart alternative to exorbitantly priced restaurants. Agricultural and dairy products, meat, fish, exotic breads, rich pastries, and ready-to-eat Chinese and Middle Eastern fare. Open W and Sa 7am-2:30pm. ❶

BATIGNOLLES (17ÈME)

🖼 **La Fournée d'Augustine,** 31 rue des Batignolles (☎01 43 87 88 41). ⓂRome. Lines out the door at lunch. Closet-size *pâtisserie* bakes an absolutely fantastic baguette (€1). Fresh sandwiches (€3-4) range from light fare like goat cheese and cucumber to the more substantial grilled chicken and veggies. *Pain au chocolat* €1.10. Lunch *formule* €5.80-7. Open M-Sa 7:30am-8pm. AmEx/MC/V over €10. ❷

🖼 **The James Joyce Pub,** 71 bd. Gouvion-St-Cyr (☎01 44 09 70 32; www.kittyosheas.com). ⓂPorte Maillot. Stained-glass windows dedicated to Joyce and other Irish wordsmiths. Traditional Irish meals like stew with bacon and cabbage or ham with spuds and cheese (€10). Swells to capacity during televised rugby matches. An informal tourist office for middle-aged and young Anglophone expats. Jazz brunch Sa-Su noon-3pm. Live DJ F-Sa 10pm. Open mike Su 9:30pm. Beer €4.50-7. Open daily noon-2am. Kitchen open M-F noon-3pm and 7-10:30pm, Sa-Su noon-3pm. AmEx/MC/V. ❷

Joy in Food, 2 rue Truffant (☎01 43 87 96 79). ⓂPlace de Clichy. Vegetarian *omelettes, pâtés,* salads, tarts, and organic wine at this cozy, macrobiotic restaurant. Apple crumble €4. Lunch *formule* €11. 3-course *menu* €14. Open M-F noon-2:30pm. MC/V. ❸

Marché Berthier, bd. de Reims between rue de Courcelles and rue du Marquis d'Arlandes, along pl. Ulmann. ⓂPorte de Champerret. Among Paris's cheapest produce markets. North African and Middle Eastern specialties like fresh mint and Turkish bread, plus standard inexpensive goods and produce. Open W 7am-2:30pm, Sa 7am-3pm. ❶

Batignolles Organic Produce Market, on the traffic divider along bd. des Batignolles, between the 8ème and 17ème. ⓂRome. For those looking to live green while traveling, this market brings in the best organic produce around. Open Sa 9am-2pm. ❶

MONTMARTRE (18ÈME)

🖼 **Refuge des Fondus,** 17 rue des 3 Frères (☎01 42 55 22 65; www.lerefugedesfondus. com). ⓂAbbesses. Only 2 main dishes: *fondue bourguignonne* (meat fondue) and *fondue savoyarde* (cheese fondue). Wine served in baby bottles. Leave your Freudian hang-ups at home and join the family-style party at 2 long tables. *Menu* €17. Open daily 5pm-2am. Kitchen open 7pm-2am. Cash only. ❷

La Bodega, 54bis rue Ordener. ⓂJules Joffrin. Informal bar-restaurant specializes in Latin American cuisine with a Spanish twist. Limited seating. Sandwiches €2.30-4.50. *Assiette du jour* €5-9. Mixed drinks €5. Open Tu-Su noon-2am. Cash only. ❷

Wassana, 10 rue Ganneron (☎01 44 70 08 54). ⓂPlace de Clichy. Gold-decorated dining room and delicious Thai food. Lunch *menu* (€12) includes Thai chicken curry in coconut milk or beef in Thai herbs. Many vegetarian options. *Entrées* €6.50-10. *Plats* €9-17.50. Open M-F noon-2:30pm and 7-11:30pm, Sa 7-11:30pm. AmEx/MC/V. ❷

BUTTES CHAUMONT (19ÈME)

▨ **Ay, Caramba!,** 59 rue de Mouzaïa (☎01 42 41 23 80; http://restaurant-aycaramba. com). ⓂPré-St-Gervais. Bright yellow Tex-Mex restaurant in a drab, residential neighborhood transforms chic Parisian dining into a homegrown fiesta. Patrons salsa to live Latino singers F-Sa nights. Tacos €18. Margaritas €7. *Nachos rancheros* €7. Open Tu-Th 7:30pm-midnight, F-Su noon-3pm and 7:30pm-midnight. AmEx/MC/V. ❸

La Boulangerie par Véronique Mauclerc, 83 rue de Crimée (☎01 42 40 64 55). ⓂLaumière. Bakes divine bread in 1 of France's 4 remaining wood-fire ovens. Organic ingredients. Paris's cheapest Su brunch (€11). Pastries, like amazing blueberry crumble, €3-4. Croissant €1.20. Open M and Th-Su 8am-8pm. MC/V over €15. ❷

Belleville Outdoor Market. ⓂBelleville. Middle Eastern-influenced market provides an exhilarating experience. Produce, spices, and much more. The place to find dates and figs. Beware of pickpockets. Open Tu and F 7am-2pm. ❶

BELLEVILLE AND PÈRE LACHAISE (20ÈME)

▨ **Café Flèche d'Or,** 102 bis rue de Bagnolet (☎01 44 64 01 02; www.flechedor.fr). ⓂAlexandre Dumas. In a defunct train station. Bar-cafe-performance space with internationally inspired dishes. Wander from the Netherlands (cheese, eggs, and sausage *tartine;* €12) to New York (bagel with coleslaw, and smoked salmon; €14). Bar/cafe open daily 10am-2am. Kitchen open on performance nights 8pm-midnight. MC/V. ❷

La Mer à Boire, 1-3 rue des Envierges (☎01 43 58 29 43; http://la.meraboire.com). ⓂPyrénées. Multipurpose cafe-bar offers spectacular views and simple, delicious food. Hosts art exhibits and occasional concerts. Brie and raisins or honey and goat cheese served on warm bread with corn, lentils, and tomato salad €10. Tapas €5 each. Wine €2-7.50. Open M-Sa noon-1am. Kitchen open noon-2pm and 7:30-9pm. MC/V. ❶

La Bolée Belgrand, 19 rue Belgrand (☎01 43 64 04 03). ⓂPorte de Bagnolet. Creative *crêpes* like the "Hot Dog." Lunch *menu* €11. *Crêpes* €3.10-7.50. 10% off takeout. Open Tu-Sa noon-2:30pm and 7-10:30pm. MC/V over €15. ❷

◉ SIGHTS

To see most of what makes Paris Paris—medieval passageways, sidewalk cafes, and majestic churches—doesn't require much more than open eyes and a penchant for wandering. From **Notre Dame** (next page) on Île de la Cité to the **Père Lachaise Cemetery** (p. 153) in the 20ème, the City of Light brims with history and splendor. Most sights in Paris are either free or reasonably priced, so anyone can get a gorgeous eyeful while saving enough to splurge on a fancy Parisian dinner (always keep your priorities in mind). Expect many of the more popular sights to be particularly crowded in the summer and know that the **Eiffel Tower** (p. 145) will be mobbed almost all the time. Most sights are open daily, but many have alternative weekend hours during French school holidays.

GUARD YOUR GOODS. Popular sights draw crowds, and crowded areas are rife with pickpockets. Be on alert, especially when you're shuffling through the tourist throngs, for those looking to lighten your load.

ÎLE DE LA CITÉ

▨**SAINTE-CHAPELLE.** When light pours through the floor-to-ceiling stained-glass windows in the **Upper Chapel,** illuminating frescoes of saints and martyrs, it's one of the most stunning sights in Paris. The 15 windows date from 1136 and contain 1113 religious scenes; read from bottom to top, left to right (ending with the rose-shaped window in the back), they narrate the Bible from Genesis to the apocalypse. Built in 1241, the cathedral is the foremost example of Flamboyant Gothic architecture. *(6 bd. du Palais, within Palais de la Cité. ⓂCité. ☎01 53 40 60 97; www.monum.fr. Open daily Mar.-Oct. 9:30am-6pm; Nov.-Feb. 9am-5pm. Last entry 30min. before close. Candlelit classical music concerts Mar.-Nov. Check www.fnac.fr for details. €8, seniors and ages 18-25 €5, under 18 free. Concerts €16-25. Cash only.)*

NOTRE DAME. Once the site of a Roman temple to Jupiter, the ground upon which Notre Dame stands witnessed more than its share of historical moments. Since Maurice de Sully began its 1163 construction—marking the birth of the Gothic style—the cathedral has provided the setting for royal weddings—including that of Henri of Navarre to Marguerite de Valois in 1572—and major trials—such as Joan of Arc's for heresy in 1455. Secularists renamed the cathedral the "Temple of Reason" during the Revolution; it was later reconsecrated and was the site of Napoleon's coronation in 1804. However, the building soon fell into disrepair and was used to shelter livestock for two decades until Victor Hugo's 1831 novel *Notre-Dame de Paris (The Hunchback of Notre Dame)* revived the cathedral's popularity and inspired its restoration.

Notre Dame has recently been released from a massive cleaning project, revealing a glittering, scaffold-free exterior. The oldest part of the cathedral can be found above the **Porte de Sainte-Anne** (on the right), mostly dating from 1165-1175. Flying buttresses support the vaults of the ceiling from outside, allowing light to fill the cathedral. The **Crown of Thorns,** believed to have been worn by Christ, is presented only on the first Friday of every month at 3pm. The cathedral's **Crypte Archéologique** houses temporary art exhibits and artifacts that were unearthed in the construction of a parking garage. Several years of sandblasting have brightened the two **towers**—home to the cathedral's fictional resident, Quasimodo the hunchback—once again revealing the **rose windows** and rows of **saints and gargoyles** that adorn the cathedral. In the South Tower, a tiny door opens onto the **13-ton bell** that even Quasimodo couldn't ring: it requires the force of eight people to move. *(ⓂCité. ☎01 42 34 56 10, crypt 55 42 50 10, towers 53 10 07 00. Cathedral open daily 7:45am-7pm. Towers open June-Aug. M-F 10am-6:30pm, Sa-Su 10am-11pm; Sept. and Apr.-May daily 10am-6:30pm; Oct.-Mar. daily 10am-5:30pm. Last entry 45min. before close. Treasury open M-F 9:30am-6pm, Sa 9:30am-5pm, Su 1-1:30pm and 6-6:30pm. Last entry 15min. before close. Crypt open Tu-Su 10am-6pm. Last entry 5:30pm. Mass M-F 8, 9am, noon, 6:15pm, Sa 6:30pm, Su 8:30am, 10am high mass with Gregorian chant, 11:30am international mass, 12:45, and 6:30pm. Free recital by a cathedral organist 4:30pm. Vespers sung Sa-Su 5:45pm. Free. Towers €8, ages 18-25 €5, under 18 free. Treasury €3, ages 12-25 €2, ages 5-11 €1. Crypt €4, over 60 €3, under 26 €2, under 12 free. Audio tours €5 plus ID deposit; includes visit of treasury. Tours begin at the booth to the right as you enter.)*

PALAIS DE JUSTICE. The Palais has seen a long line of fascinating trials of famous personalities, including Sarah Bernhardt's divorce from the Comédie Française, Mata Hari's death sentence, Émile Zola's trial after the Dreyfus affair, Dreyfus' declaration of innocence, and the trial of Philippe Pétain after WWII. All trials are open to the public, and the theatrical sobriety of the interior is worth a quick glance. *(4 bd. du Palais, within the Palais de la Cité. Enter at 6 bd. du Palais. ⓂCité. ☎01 44 32 51 51. Courtrooms open M-F 9am-noon and 1:30pm-end of last trial. Free.)*

MÉMORIAL DE LA DÉPORTATION. This haunting memorial commemorates the 200,000 French victims of concentration camps. The focal point is a tunnel lined with 200,000 quartz pebbles, reflecting the Jewish custom of placing stones on the graves of the deceased. *(ⓂCité. Open daily Apr.-Sept. 10am-noon and 2-7pm; Oct.-Mar. 10am-noon and 2-5pm. Free.)*

ÎLE SAINT-LOUIS

QUAI D'ANJOU. Some of the island's most beautiful and luxurious *hôtels particuliers* line quai d'Anjou, between Pont Marie and Pont de Sully. No. 37 was home to Lost Generation writer John Dos Passos, no. 29 housed the Three Mountains Press, which published books by Hemingway and Ford Madox Ford and was edited by Ezra Pound, and no. 9 was the address of Honoré Daumier, Realist painter and caricaturist, from 1846 to 1863, during which time he painted *La Blanchisseuse (The Washer Woman)*, now hanging in the Louvre. Charles Baudelaire, poet and author of the famous *Fleurs du Mal*, lived 1843-45 in the **Hôtel Lausan** (a.k.a. Hôtel Pimodoran) at no. 17. *(ⓂPont Marie.)*

CHÂTELET-LES HALLES

1ER ARRONDISSEMENT

JARDIN DES TUILERIES. Sweeping down from the Louvre to pl. de la Concorde, the Jardin des Tuileries was built for Catherine de Medici in 1564 in order to assuage her longing for the promenades of her native Florence. Even Napoleon considered it worthy of his massive parties and celebrations. Sculptures by Rodin and others stand amid the garden's scattered cafes and courts. In the summer, the rue de Rivoli terrace becomes an amusement park with children's rides, food stands, and a huge Ferris wheel. *(ⓂTuileries. ☎01 40 20 90 43. Open daily June-Aug. 7am-11pm; Sept. and Apr.-May 7am-9pm; Oct.-Mar. 7:30am-7:30pm. Amusement park open from July to mid-Aug. English tours from the Arc de Triomphe du Carrousel.)*

PLACE VENDÔME. Pl. Vendôme was begun in 1687 by Louis XIV. Designer Jules Hardouin-Mansart intended the buildings to house embassies, but bankers built lavish private homes for themselves instead. Today, the smell of indulgence is still in the air: bankers, perfumers, and jewelers (including Cartier, at no. 7) line the square. Notable residents include Hardouin-Mansart (no. 9) and Chopin, who died at no. 12. *(Rue de Castiglione. ⓂTuileries.)*

PALAIS-ROYAL. The once regal and racy Palais-Royal was constructed for Cardinal Richelieu between 1628 and 1642 by Jacques Lemercier. In 1781, a broke duke of Orléans rented out the buildings around the palace's formal garden, turning the complex into an 18th-century shopping mall with boutiques, restaurants, theaters, wax museums, and gambling joints. Today, the palace again holds boutiques and cafes in its galleries, while the rest (inaccessible to the public) houses government

LA VIE EN CHOCOLAT

For four days each October, the City of Lights and Love adopts an additional title—the City of Chocolate. The Salon du Chocolate, held in the Paris Expo at the Porte de Versailles, is a celebration of all things cocoa. Over 100,000 visitors flock to the festival each day in order to experience an entire series of choco-centric events: from basic cooking classes and chocolate tastings to a showcase of chocolate sculptures and a fashion show of clothing made completely out of chocolate.

One hundred and thirty chocolatiers from all over the world gather to exhibit their skills and teach the masses about every aspect of chocolate-making. There are even dance performances that celebrate chocolate from all over the world. On the last day of the festival, the best international chocolate makers come together to compete for chocolate awards in the *"espace cacao."*

To curb feelings of guilt from indulgence at the festival, the cacao show hosts discussions on topics justifying the importance of a chocolaty diet, including "Chocolate is Good for Your Heart." Characterized by a whirlwind of delectable dancing, luscious tastings, sweet smells, and mouthwatering lectures, the Salon du Chocolate is a satisfying sensory overload and—though crowded—well worth the visit. Check out www.chocoland.com for more information on this year's festival.

offices. The inside garden and galleries retain a royal air. *(Palace closed to the public. Fountain, galleries, and garden open daily June-Aug. 7am-11pm; Sept. 7am-9:30pm; Oct.-Mar. 7:30am-8:30pm; Apr.-May 7am-10:15pm. Free.)*

ÉGLISE DE SAINT-EUSTACHE. Eustache (Eustatius) was a Roman general who adopted Christianity upon seeing the sign of a cross between the antlers of a deer. As punishment, the Romans locked him and his family into a brass bull that was placed over a fire until it became white-hot. Construction of the church in his honor began in 1532 and dragged on for over a century. Cardinal Richelieu, Molière, and Mme. de Pompadour were all baptized in the Église de St-Eustache. Louis XIV received communion in its sanctuary, and Mozart chose to have his mother's funeral in this magnificent church. Outside the church, Henri de Miller's 1986 sculpture *The Listener* depicts a huge stone human head and hand. *(Above rue Rambuteau. ⓂLes Halles. ☎01 42 36 31 05; www.saint-eustache.org. Open M-F 9:30am-7pm, Sa 10am-7pm, Su 9am-7pm. Mass Sa 6pm, Su 9:30, 11am, 6pm.)*

LES HALLES. Beginning as a small food market in 1135, Les Halles received its first face-lift in the 1850s with the construction of large iron-and-glass pavilions to shelter the vendors' stalls. In 1970, authorities moved the old market to a suburb near Orly and replaced the pavilions with a subterranean shopping mall, the **Forum des Halles** (see **Shopping,** p. 165). The forum and gardens attract a large crowd, especially during the summer months and winter holiday season. Descend from one of the four main entrances to discover over 200 boutiques and three movie theaters. *(ⓂLes Halles.)*

2ÈME ARRONDISSEMENT

Paris's ▉**passages and galeries** are considered the world's first **shopping malls.** The *galeries* that surround the **Jardins du Palais Royal** are Paris's most famous, but others in the 1er and 2ème are also worthwhile. They house upscale clothing boutiques, cafes, gift shops, and antique bookstores. Try **Passage Choiseul,** 23 rue Augustin, **Galerie Colbert,** 6 rue des Petits Champs, **Passage du Claire,** 2 pl. du Claire, and **Passage Brady,** 46 rue Fauberg St-Denis.

BIBLIOTHÈQUE NATIONALE: SITE RICHELIEU. Site Richelieu was the main branch of the Bibliothèque Nationale de France (National Library of France) until 1998, when most of the collection was moved to the new book-shaped Site Mitterrand in the 13ème. Now, the fortress houses collections of stamps, money, photography, medals, maps, and manuscripts. Scholars must pass through a strict screening process—involving lasers and polygraph tests—to enter the main reading room, but temporary exhibits are open to the public. *(58 rue de Richelieu. ⓂBourse. Info line ☎01 53 79 87 93 or 53 79 59 59, tours 53 79 86 87; www.bnf.fr. Library open M-F 9am-6pm, Sa 9am-5pm. Books available only to researchers who prove they need access to the collection. Galleries open only when there are exhibits Tu-Sa 10am-7pm, Su noon-7pm. Admission depends on exhibit; usually €5-7, students €4-5, under 18 free.)*

THE MARAIS

3ÈME ARRONDISSEMENT

ARCHIVES NATIONALES. The most famous documents of the National Archives are on display in the **Musée de l'Histoire de France,** ensconced in the plush 18th-century Hôtel de Soubise. The rotating themed exhibits (2-3 per year) feature historic documents such as the Treaty of Westphalia, the Declaration of the Rights of Man, Marie Antoinette's last letter, letters between Benjamin Franklin and George Washington, and a note from Napoleon to his empress Josephine. Also open to visitors are the apartments of the princess de Soubise, sculpted with mythological motifs and featuring works by Boucher. *(60 rue des Francs-Bourgeois. ☎01 40 27 60 96, group reservations 40 27 62 18. Open M and W-F 10am-12:30pm and 2-5:30pm, Sa-Su 2-5:30pm. €3, Su, ages 18-25, and seniors €2.30, under 18 free.)*

4ÈME ARRONDISSEMENT

■PLACE DES VOSGES. The magnificent pl. des Vosges, at the end of rue des Francs-Bourgeois, is Paris's oldest public square and one of its best spots for a picnic or an afternoon siesta. The central park, **square Louis XIII**, with manicured trees and elegant fountains, is surrounded by Paris's most beautiful 17th-century Renaissance mansions. All 36 buildings that line the square were constructed in the same design by Baptiste de Cerceau; each has arcades on the street level, two stories of pink brick, and a slate-covered roof. In the 18th century, Molière, Racine, and Voltaire filled the grand parlors with their *bon mots*, and a seven-year-old Mozart played a concert here. Follow the arcades around the perimeter of pl. des Vosges for an elegant promenade, window-shopping, and a glimpse at the plaques that mark the homes of famous residents. The corner door at the right of the south face of the *place* (between no. 5 and 7) leads into the garden of the **Hôtel de Sully.** *(Ⓜ Chemin Vert or St-Paul.)*

CENTRE POMPIDOU. Commissioned by President Pompidou in the early 70s, the Pompidou is considered to be both an innovation and an eyesore. The design features color-coded electrical tubes (yellow), water pipes (green), and ventilation ducts (blue) along the building's exterior. The **Salle Garance** hosts a film series, and the **Bibliothèque Publique d'Information** is a free, non-circulating library packed with students. Don't miss the ■**spectacular view** from the top of the escalators, accessible with museum admission or by dining at the rooftop restaurant, **Georges.** *(Ⓜ Rambuteau or Hôtel de Ville. Open M and W-Su 11am-10pm.)*

RUE DES ROSIERS. The heart of the Jewish community of the Marais, rue des Rosiers is packed with kosher shops, butchers, bakeries, and falafel counters. The mix of Mediterranean and Eastern European Jewish cultures gives the area a unique flavor. Until the 13th century, Paris's Jewish population lived around Notre Dame, but when Philippe-Auguste expelled them from the city limits, many families moved to the Marais. Today, the Marais's Jewish community thrives, with two **synagogues** designed by Art Nouveau architect Hector Guimard. *(25 rue des Rosiers and 10 rue Pavée. Ⓜ St-Paul.)*

HÔTEL DE VILLE. The Hôtel de Ville is probably the most extravagant building in Paris that isn't a palace. Poised on a marshy embankment *(grève)* of the Seine, the medieval square served as a meeting ground for angry workers, giving France the useful phrase *en grève* (on strike). Pl. de Hôtel de Ville almost never sleeps: strikers continue to gather here, and the square hosts concerts, special TV broadcasts, and light shows. Every major French sporting event—Rolland Garros, the Tour de France, and any game the Bleus ever play—is projected onto a jumbo screen in the *place*. *(Info office 29 rue de Rivoli. Ⓜ Hôtel de Ville. ☎01 42 76 43 43 or 42 76 50 49. Open M-F when there is an exhibit 9am-7pm; otherwise 9am-6pm. Group tours available with reservations; call for available dates.)*

LATIN QUARTER AND SAINT-GERMAIN

5ÈME ARRONDISSEMENT

PLACE SAINT-MICHEL. The Latin Quarter meets the Seine at this monumental locale where the 1871 Paris Commune and the 1968 student uprising began. Although locals rarely deign to venture here, tourists pose for photos in front of the square's centerpiece, a majestic 1860 **fountain** featuring St-Michel slay-

DISTANCE: 3.5km/2¼ mi.

TIME: 4½hr.

WHEN TO GO: Quand vous avez envie de flâner un peu.

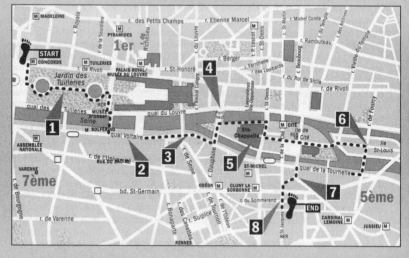

1. JARDIN DES TUILERIES. Like the nearby sidewalks of the Champs-Élysées, this garden features broad pathways perfect for people-watching. Unlike the Champs, it has not been taken over by traffic, fast-food joints, and car dealerships (p. 139).

2. QUAI VOLTAIRE. Head for the Seine and cross pont Royal, then turn left on quai Voltaire. Name an artist, any artist. That artist probably lived on this block. Baudelaire, Wagner, Delacroix, and Sibelius are a few examples. Check the plaques on the buildings for others (p. 145).

3. SEINE BOOKSELLERS. Working out of stands along the Seine, these vendors may be the best source in Paris for cheap used books, old magazines, and 19th-century comics.

4. PONT NEUF. Paris's oldest bridge links Île de la Cité to the Right and Left Banks. If you've brought a significant other along, it's the best place in the city to 🖼 **make out.**

5. SAINTE-CHAPELLE. Walk down the island and turn inward at bd. du Palais. Built in the 13th century to house relics of Christ, the chapel now serves as the foremost example of Gothic architecture, with hundreds of magnificent panels of stained glass (p. 137).

6. BERTHILLON AND AMORINO. Walk to the far end of the island on rue Lutèce. Cross the bridge onto Île St-Louis. Behold the great ice-cream rivalry—Berthillon is the heavyweight, but Amorino, which offers more generous helpings, makes for a scrappy challenger (p. 128).

7. SHAKESPEARE & CO. Cross pont de Tournelle and make a right on quai de la Tournelle. This English-language bookshop published *Ulysses* in 1922; its role as a Parisian literary hub has not changed (p. 163).

8. NATIONAL MUSEUM OF THE MIDDLE AGES. One of Paris's best museums is housed in a medieval mansion. With the famed *Dame à la Licorne (Lady with the Unicorn)* tapestries, it can be easy to miss the wood-carved Romanesque altarpieces or the dazzling manuscripts that fill out the collection (p. 157).

ing a demon. Booksellers and university presses surround the *place*, ready to indulge all literary appetites (see **Shopping**, p. 163). Modern stained glass and spiraling columns decorate the Gothic **Église Saint-Séverin**. *(1 rue des Prêtres-St-Séverin.* ☎ *01 42 34 93 50.)* The **Musée de Cluny** (p. 157) houses an extraordinary collection of medieval art, tapestries, and manuscripts. (Ⓜ*St-Michel.)*

SORBONNE. Founded in 1257 by Robert de Sorbon as a dormitory for poor theology students, the Sorbonne has since diversified its curriculum and earned a place among the world's most esteemed universities. Growing in power and size, the Sorbonne often defied the French throne, even siding with England during the Hundred Years' War. Today, the French government controls the Sorbonne, integrating the college into its extensive public education system. The Sorbonne comprises four of the University of Paris's 13 campuses: **Paris I, Paris III, Paris IV,** and **Paris V.** Befitting its elite status, the Sorbonne remains closed to the public through 2011, when the **Chapelle de la Sorbonne** will re-open after lengthy restoration. *(45-47 rue des Écoles.* Ⓜ*Cluny-La Sorbonne or RER: Luxembourg.)*

COLLÈGE DE FRANCE. Created by François I in 1530 as an alternative to the Sorbonne, the Collège de France—or the "Collège Royal"—lies behind its more prestigious counterpart. The humanist motto **Doce Omnia** (Teach Everything) is emblazoned in mosaics in the interior courtyard. Courses at the college—given in the past by such luminaries as Henri Bergson, Pierre Boulez, Michel Foucault, and Paul Valéry—are free and open to all. Lecture schedules are posted around the courtyard. *(11 pl. Marcelin-Berthelot.* Ⓜ*Maubert-Mutualité.* ☎ *01 44 27 11 47; www.college-de-france.fr. Open Sept.-July. Courses Oct.-May.)*

PANTHÉON. Among Paris's most impressive buildings, the Panthéon displays geometric grandeur and a historical nod to the dead. Some of France's greatest citizens are buried in the Panthéon's crypt, including Marie and Pierre Curie, Jean Jaurès, Louis Braille, Voltaire, Jean-Jacques Rousseau, Émile Zola, and Victor Hugo. An inscription in stone across the Panthéon's front declares, *"Aux grands hommes la patrie reconnaisante"* ("To the great men, a grateful fatherland"). The Panthéon's other main attraction is a famous science experiment: **Foucault's pendulum.** The pendulum's plane of oscillation stays fixed as the earth rotates around it, confirming the Earth's rotation. Louis Napoleon III was among those present at its February 1851 unveiling. *(Pl. du Panthéon.* Ⓜ*Cardinal Lemoine or RER: Luxembourg.* ☎ *01 44 32 18 04. Open daily Apr.-Sept. 10am-6:30pm; Oct.-Mar. 10am-6pm. Last entry 45min. before close. Crypt open daily 10am-6pm. Dome visits Apr.-Oct. Dutch-, English-, French-, German-, Russian-, and Spanish-language tours. Conservative dress required. €7.50, ages 18-25 €4.80, under 18 free; Oct-Mar. 1st Su of the month free.)*

RUE MOUFFETARD. South of pl. de la Contrescarpe, rue Mouffetard hosts one of Paris's oldest and liveliest street markets (p. 131). The stretch up rue Mouffetard, past pl. de la Contrescarpe and onto rue Descartes and rue de la Montagne Ste-Geneviève, is the quintessential Latin Quarter stroll, attracting a mix of Parisians and visitors. Hemingway lived on "the Mouff" at 74 rue du Cardinal Lemoine while poet Paul Verlaine died in the same neighborhood at 39 rue Descartes. (Ⓜ*Cardinal Lemoine, Place Monge, or Censier Daubenton.)*

JARDIN DES PLANTES. The Jardin des Plantes has 260,000 sq. m of carefully tended flowers and lush greenery. Opened in 1633 by Louis XIII's doctor, the gardens originally grew medicinal plants to promote His Majesty's health. The gardens also include the fantastic **Musée d'Histoire Naturelle** (p. 158) and the **Ménagerie Zoo.** During the 1871 siege of Paris, starving Parisians ate a few of the elephants; it wasn't cake, but at least they got fed. An info hut adjacent to pl. Valhubert provides free maps and brochures. (Ⓜ*Gare d'Austerlitz, Jussieu, or Censier-*

Daubenton. ☎01 40 79 37 94; www.mnhn.fr. Garden open daily in summer 7:30am-7:45pm; in winter 7:30am-7:30pm. Zoo open Apr.-Sept. M-Sa 9am-6pm, Su and holidays 9am-6:30pm; Oct.-Mar. daily 10am-5pm. Garden free. Zoo €7, students and ages 4-13 €5, under 3 free.)

6ÈME ARRONDISSEMENT

▪JARDIN DU LUXEMBOURG. Parisians flock to these spectacular formal gardens—despite the truly violent winds—to sunbathe, stroll, and read by the rose gardens and central pool. Beware of ostentatious PDAs: kissing and touching in public is a la mode in Paris. The gardens themselves have been through many eras and uses; a residential area in Roman Paris, the site of a medieval monastery, and later the home of 17th-century French royalty, they were liberated during the Revolution and are now open to all. One of the loveliest spots in the *jardin* is the **Fontaine des Médicis,** a vine-covered grotto complete with a fishpond and Baroque fountain sculptures. In 2005, a Swedish artist added a new touch to the ancient fountain: a **giant nose.** A mammoth force of gardeners tends the grounds—each spring they plant or transplant 350,000 flowers and move 150 palm and orange trees out of winter storage. (Ⓜ*Odéon or RER: Luxembourg. Entrance at bd. St-Michel. Open daily sunrise-sunset. Guided tours in French depart from pl. André Honorat June every W; July-Oct. and Apr.-May 1st W of each month.)*

THÉÂTRE DE L'ODÉON. Paris's oldest and largest theater was bought by Louis XVI and Marie Antoinette for the **Comédie Française,** Molière's celebrated theater troupe, in 1782. As the Revolution approached, the Comédie Française splintered over political loyalties. Republican members moved to the Right Bank, into the company's current location near the Louvre. The actors who remained behind were jailed under the Reign of Terror and the theater closed. The theater was later considered cursed after two fires and a chain of flops left it nearly bankrupt, but the Odéon's fortunes changed after WWII, when it became a venue for experimental theater. *(ⓂOdéon.)*

ÉGLISE SAINT-SULPICE. The Neoclassical facade of Église St-Sulpice dominates the square of the same name. Designed by Servadoni in 1733, the church is both unfinished and in need of a restoration. Look for the Delacroix frescoes in the first chapel on the right (*Jacob Wrestling with the Angel* and *Heliodorus Driven from the Temple*) and Jean-Baptiste Pigalle's *Virgin and Child* in a rear chapel. *(50 rue Vaugirard. ⓂSt-Sulpice or Mabillon. ☎01 42 34 59 60; www.paroisse-saint-sulpice-paris.org. Open daily 7:30am-7:30pm. Guided tour in French Su 3pm.)*

BOULEVARD SAINT-GERMAIN. Most famous as the former literati hangout of Existentialists (who frequented the **Café de Flore,** p. 131) and Surrealists (who preferred **Les Deux Magots,** p. 131), bd. St-Germain is torn between nostalgia for its past and unabashed delight with all things fashionable. It is home to scores of cafes, both new and old, where expensive coffee is *de rigeur.* The boulevard and the many side streets around rue de Rennes have become a serious shopping area, filled with designer boutiques. *(ⓂSt-Germain-des-Prés.)*

ÉGLISE SAINT-GERMAIN-DES-PRÉS. The Église St-Germain-des-Prés is the oldest church in Paris, and it shows: the only remaining decorations on the church's exterior are pink and white hollyhocks growing on one side. Completely redone in the 19th century, the magnificent interior is painted in shades of maroon, deep green, and gold—enough grandeur to counteract the building's modest exterior. Especially striking are the royal blue and gold-starred ceiling, frescoes (by a pupil of Ingres) depicting the life of Jesus, and decorative mosaics along the archways. In the second chapel—on the right after the apse—a stone marks the interred heart of 17th-century philosopher René Descartes. *(3* *pl. St-Germain-des-Prés. ⓂSt-Germain-des-Prés. ☎01 55 42 81 33. Open daily 8am-7:45pm. Info office open M 2:30-6:45pm, Tu-F 10:30am-noon and 2:30-6:45pm, Sa 3-6:45pm.)*

INVALIDES (7ÈME)

◪**EIFFEL TOWER.** Gustave Eiffel, who also engineered the Statue of Liberty, wrote of his tower, "France is the only country in the world with a 300m flagpole." The Eiffel Tower was designed in 1889—a monument to engineering that would surpass the Egyptian pyramids in size and notoriety. Parisians were not impressed: after the tower's completion, writer Guy de Maupassant ate lunch every day at its ground-floor restaurant—the only place in Paris, he claimed, from which he couldn't see the offensive thing. It wasn't until the tower's inauguration in March 1889 as the centerpiece of the **World's Fair** that Parisians finally came around. Since the expo, locals and tourists alike have reclaimed the monument in over 150 million visits. The top floor, with its unparalleled view, is especially deserving of a visit. From dusk until 2am (Sept.-May 1am), the tower sparkles with light for 10min. on the hour. *(ⓂBir-Hakeim or Trocadéro. ☎01 44 11 23 23; www.tour-eiffel.fr. Elevator open daily from mid-June to Aug. 9am-12:45am, last entry 11pm; from Sept. to mid-June 9:30am-11:45pm, last entry 11pm. Stairs open daily from mid-June to Aug. 9am-12:45am, last entry midnight; from Sept. to mid-June 9:30am-6:30pm, last entry 6pm. Elevator to 1st fl. €5, under 12 €2.50, under 3 free; 2nd fl. €8/4.50/free; summit €12/7/ free. Stairs to 1st and 2nd fl. €4, under 25 €3, under 3 free.)*

ÉGLISE DU DÔME. In the reign of Napoleon's nephew, Louis-Napoleon, the mosaic floor of the Église du Dôme was destroyed to build the huge, circular crypt for Napoleon I. Completed in 1861, ◪**Napoleon's tomb** consists of six concentric coffins made of materials ranging from mahogany to lead. Names of significant battles are engraved in the marble floor surrounding the coffins; oddly enough, Waterloo isn't there. Upstairs, a display case holds the hat and gray coat that defined Napoleon's actual wardrobe. In 1989, the 107m high Église du Dôme was regilded, making the glorious Hôtel des Invalides the only monument in Paris to glint with real gold—12kg of gold, to be exact. *(Esplanades des Invalides. ⓂInvalides or St-François-Xavier. ☎01 44 42 37 72; www.invalides.org. Open Apr.-Sept. M and W-Su 10am-6pm; Oct.-Mar. M and W-Su 10am-5pm, Tu 10am-9pm. Closed 1st M of the month. Last entry 30min. before close. €8, students under 26 €6, under 18 free. Tu after 5:30pm €6, under 26 free. Audio tour included; €1 supplement for free admission.)*

QUAI VOLTAIRE. The quai Voltaire, known for its beautiful views of the monuments along the Seine, boasts an artistic heritage more distinguished than any other block in the city. Voltaire himself spent his last days at no. 27. No. 19 was home to Baudelaire while he wrote *Les Fleurs du Mal*, to Richard Wagner as he composed *Die Meistersinger*, and to Oscar Wilde while he was in exile. Eugène Delacroix and Jean Auguste Dominique Ingres had their studios at no. 9-11, followed by Jean-Baptiste-Camille Corot. *(ⓂRue du Bac.)*

CHAMPS-ÉLYSÉES (8ÈME)

◪**PARC MONCEAU.** The signs say *"pelouse interdite"* (keep off the lawn), but on sunny days everyone pretends to be illiterate. Lying behind gold-tipped, wrought-iron gates, the Parc Monceau is an expansive urban oasis especially popular with families. There's plenty of shade, courtesy of the **largest tree in Paris:** an oriental *platane*, 7m thick and two centuries old. A number of architectural oddities—covered bridges, Dutch windmills, Roman ruins, and in-line skating rinks—make this a kids' romping ground. *(ⓂMonceau or Courcelles. Open daily Apr.-Oct. 7am-10pm; Nov.-Mar. 7am-8pm. Last entry 15min. before close.)*

ARC DE TRIOMPHE. Situated atop a hill, the arch offers a stunning view down the Champs-Élysées to the Tuileries and Louvre. In 1758, architect Charles François Ribart envisioned the spot as a monument to France's military prowess—in the form of a giant, bejeweled elephant. Fortunately, construction of the monument was not undertaken until 1806, when Napoleon imagined a less kitschy tribute modeled after the triumphal arches of victorious Roman emperors like Constantine and Titus. Since then, the arch has been a magnet for various triumphant armies, and is now dedicated to all French soldiers and veterans. **The Tomb of the Unknown Soldier,** illuminated by an eternal flame, has lain under the arch since November 11, 1920. Its marker memorializes the 1,500,000 Frenchmen who died during WWI. Visitors can climb up to the terrace observation deck for a brilliant view of the **"Historic Axis,"** from the Arc de Triomphe du Carrousel and the Louvre Pyramid at one end to the Grande Arche de la Défense at the other. *(ⓂCharles de Gaulle-Étoile. Use the pedestrian underpass on the right side of the Champs-Élysées facing the arch. Buy your ticket in the pedestrian underpass before going up to the ground level. Open daily Apr.-Sept. 10am-11pm; Oct.-Mar. 10am-10:30pm. Last entry 30min. before close. Wheelchair-accessible. €9, ages 18-25 €5.50, under 17 free.)*

AVENUE DES CHAMPS-ÉLYSÉES. Radiating from the huge rotary surrounding the Arc de Triomphe, the Champs-Élysées seems to be a magnificent celebration of pomp and glory. While it was the center of Parisian opulence in the early 20th century—with flashy mansions towering above exclusive cafes—the Champs has since undergone a kind of democratization, as commercialization has diluted its glamor. Shops along the avenue now range from designer fashion to car dealerships: the behemoth Louis Vuitton flagship store stands across from an even larger Monoprix, a low-budget all-purpose store. Despite its slip in sophistication, the Champs continues to be known as the most beautiful street in the world. With rents as high as €1.25 million a year for 1000 sq. m of space, the Champs is the **second-richest street in the world.** The Champs continues to host major French events: it features the largest parade in Europe on **Bastille Day** as well as the final stretch of the **Tour de France.** *(ⓂCharles de Gaulle-Étoile.)*

PLACE DE LA CONCORDE. Paris's largest and most infamous public square is the eastern terminus of the Champs-Élysées. In the center of the *place* is the **Obélisque de Luxor.** The obelisk, which dates back to the 13th century BC and recalls the royal accomplishments of Ramses II, was erected here in 1836. Today, it forms the axis of what many Parisians call the **"royal perspective"**—from the Louvre, the straight-line view of pl. de la Concorde, the Arc de Triomphe, and the Grande Arche de la Défense tells the history of Paris century by century, from the reign of Louis XIV to the Revolution, Napoleon's reign, and, finally, all the way to the celebration of commerce. Constructed between 1757 and 1777 by Louis XV to commemorate his monarchy, Concorde quickly became ground zero for public grievances against the monarchy. In fact, Louis XVI met his end near the statue symbolizing Brest, while the obelisk marks the spot where Marie Antoinette, Charlotte Corday (Marat's assassin), Lavoisier, Danton, and Robespierre all succumbed to the sharp reality of death. With its monumental scale and heavy traffic, the *place* is not pedestrian-friendly. Around the *place* stand eight statues representing France's major cities: Brest, Bordeaux, Lille, Lyon, Marseille, Nantes, Rouen, and Strasbourg. *(ⓂConcorde.)*

OPÉRA (9ÈME)

OPÉRA GARNIER. The exterior of the Opéra Garnier—with its multicolored marble facade, sculpted golden goddesses, and ornate columns and friezes—is one of Paris's most impressive sights. It's no wonder that Oscar Wilde once swore he saw an angel floating on the sidewalk while sitting next door at the Café de la Paix. Designed by Charles Garnier in the style of the Second Empire, the Opéra emphasizes both the era's ostentation and its lack of a definitive style. After 15 years of construction, the Opéra opened its doors in 1875. The interior is decorated with Gobelin tapestries, mosaics, and an eight-ton chandelier whose counterweight fell on an 1896 audience. The incident, along with rumors of a spooky lake beneath the building, inspired **Le Fantôme de l'Opera** (*The Phantom of the Opera*), Gaston Leroux's 1910 novel incarnated in several films before bursting into song with Andrew Lloyd Webber's 1986 mega-musical. Pay a visit to the **Phantom's box**, no. 5. The Opéra's five-tiered auditorium has 2200 red velvet seats and a ceiling painted by Marc Chagall in 1964; the balconies were constructed so that audience members could watch one another as well as the show on stage. The Opéra has become mainly a ballet venue, but also houses a library and museum where temporary exhibits on theatrical personages are held during the year. The museum's permanent collection includes sculptures by Degas and scale models of famous opera scenes. (ⓂOpéra. ☎08 92 89 90 90; www.operadeparis.fr. Concert hall and museum open daily 10am-5pm. Last entry 30min. before close. Concert hall closed during rehearsals; call ahead. 90min. tours in English July-Aug. daily 11:30am, 2:30pm; Sept.-June W and Sa-Su 11:30am, 2:30pm. €8, students and under 25 €4, under 10 free. Tours €12, students €9, under 10 €6, seniors €10. See also p. 168.)

CANAL SAINT-MARTIN AND SURROUNDS (10ÈME)

PORTES SAINT-DENIS AND SAINT-MARTIN. The Porte St-Denis looms triumphantly at the end of rue du Faubourg St-Denis. Built in 1672 to celebrate the victories of Louis XIV, the gate imitates the Arch of Titus in Rome. The site of the arch was once a medieval entrance to the city; today it serves as a traffic rotary and a gathering place for pigeons and loiterers alike. In the words of André Breton, *"C'est très belle et très inutile"* ("It's very beautiful and very useless"). The Porte St-Martin at the end of its *rue*, constructed in 1674, is a variation on a similar theme. A herculean Louis XIV dominates the facade, wearing nothing but a wig and a smile. (ⓂStrasbourg-St-Denis.)

BASTILLE

11ÈME ARRONDISSEMENT

PLACE DE LA BASTILLE. Today, this busy intersection mainly ignores its past—except on Bastille Day, when the whole city parties in its honor. At the center of the square is a monument of winged Mercury holding a torch of freedom, symbolizing France's movement toward democracy. (ⓂBastille.)

BASTILLE PRISON. After it was made a state prison by Louis XIII, internment in the Bastille—generally reserved for heretics and political dissidents—was the king's business and, as a result, often arbitrary. But it was hardly the hellhole that the revolutionaries who tore it down imagined it to be—the Bastille's titled inmates were allowed to furnish their suites, bring their own servants, and receive guests: the *cardinal de Rohan* held a dinner party for 20 in his cell. Notable prisoners included the mysterious Man in the Iron Mask (made famous by Alexandre Dumas), the *comte de Mirabeau*, Voltaire (twice), and the *marquis de Sade*, who wrote the notorious *Justine* here. On July 14, 1789, an angry Parisian mob stormed this symbol of royal tyranny, sparking the French Revolution. They only liberated a dozen or so prisoners—but nobody was counting. Two days later, the Assemblée Nationale ordered the prison demolished.

Today, all that remains is the ground plan of the fortress, still visible as a line of paving stones in the pl. de la Bastille. *(Ⓜ Bastille.)*

12ÈME ARRONDISSEMENT

OPÉRA BASTILLE. President Mitterrand made a bold move when he plunked the Opéra Bastille down in the working-class neighborhood around pl. de la Bastille. While the "People's Opera" has been described as an airport and a huge toilet, it has helped renew local interest in the arts. The guided tour offers a behind-the-scenes view of the largest theater in the world. The immense granite and glass auditorium, which seats 2703, comprises only 5% of the building's surface area. The rest of the building houses exact replicas of the stage (for rehearsal purposes) and workshops for both the Bastille and Garnier operas. The Opéra employs almost 1000 people, from techies to actors to administrators to wig- and shoe-makers. *(130 rue de Lyon. Ⓜ Bastille. ☎01 40 01 19 70; www.operadeparis.fr. Open M-Sa 10:30am-6:30pm. 1hr. tour almost every day; call ahead for schedule. Tours €11, students and over 60 €9, under 18 €6. For performances, see p. 168.)*

BUTTES-AUX-CAILLES AND CHINATOWN (13ÈME)

QUARTIER DE LA BUTTE-AUX-CAILLES. Historically a working-class neighborhood, the Butte-aux-Cailles (Quail Knoll) district resembles a mini village in the heart of a big city, with old-fashioned lampposts and cobblestone streets. The *quartier* sprawls from rue de la Butte-aux-Cailles and rue des Cinq Diamants, southwest of pl. d'Italie. One of the first to resist during the 1848 revolution, the neighborhood became the unofficial headquarters of the *soixante-huitards*, the student and intellectual activists behind the 1968 Paris riots. The area is home to funky new restaurants and drinking holes among its old standards. The arrondissement's nascent gentrification has attracted artists, intellectuals, and trendsetters, but this process remains slow-moving. *(Ⓜ Corvisart.)*

QUARTIER CHINOIS (CHINATOWN). The core of Paris's Chinatown lies south of rue Tolbiac, in the blocks surrounding av. Choisy and d'Ivry. Home to a large population of Cambodian, Chinese, Thai, and Vietnamese immigrants, this vibrant community offers Paris's best Asian food. Area eateries focus on *plats à la vapeur*—steamed. *(Ⓜ Porte d'Ivry, Porte de Choisy, Tolbiac, and Maison Blanche.)*

BIBLIOTHÈQUE NATIONALE DE FRANCE: SITE FRANÇOIS MITTERRAND. The last, most expensive of Mitterrand's Grands Projets (see **Life and Times,** p. 72), this library opened in 1996; since 1537, every book published in France has entered the national archives. Most of the Bibliothèque Nationale's 13-million-volume collection, including **Gutenberg Bibles** and first editions from the Middle Ages, have been transferred to the Site Mitterrand. Dominique Perrault designed the library's four L-shaped towers to look like an open book from above. Inside the imposing library, you'll find large **underground reading rooms.** Multiple galleries show temporary multimedia exhibits on themes in French history. *(Quai François Mauriac. Ⓜ Quai de la Gare or Bibliothèque François Mitterrand. ☎01 53 79 59 59; www.bnf.fr. Upper study library open Tu-Sa 10am-8pm, Su 1-7pm. Lower research library open M 2-8pm, Tu-Sa 9am-8pm, Su 1-7pm; closed 2 weeks in Sept. 16+. €3.30; 15-day pass €20; annual membership €35, students €18.)*

MONTPARNASSE

14ÈME ARRONDISSEMENT

CIMETIÈRE MONTPARNASSE. The beautiful Montparnasse Cemetery opened in 1824 and has served as the burial ground for some of the city's most famous former residents. Jean-Paul Sartre, Andre Citroën, Charles Baudelaire, Simone de Beauvoir, Serge Gainsbourg, Samuel Beckett, Émile Durkheim, Alfred Dreyfus, Robert Desnos, Eugène Ionesco, Guy de Maupassant, and sculptors Constantin Brancusi and Frédéric Bartholdi hold permanent real estate here. *(3 bd. Edgar Quinet. Ⓜ️Edgar Quinet. ☎01 44 10 86 50.)*

CATACOMBS. Originally excavated to provide stone for building Paris, the catacombs now attract tourists the world over. The former quarry was converted into a mass grave in 1785—the city's solution to the awful stench elicited by its overcrowded cemeteries. Paris's "municipal ossuary" now comprises dozens of winding tunnels and hundreds of thousands of bones. After a long, dizzying descent down a spiral staircase, it's a half-kilometer walk to the catacombs themselves. While barred gates and signs rule out any possibility of getting lost, the dim lighting and frequent turns can make for a surprisingly isolated experience. The catacombs are dark, chilly, and damp—morbid proverbs carved into the walls will hardly warm you up. The 45min. self-guided tour finishes with a long climb—another narrow spiral staircase of 83 steps—that spits you out two Métro stops from where you started. *(1 av. du Colonel Henri Roi-Tanguy. Ⓜ️Denfert-Rochereau; exit near Ⓜ️Mouton Duvernet. ☎01 43 22 47 63. Open Tu-Su 10am-4pm. €7, over 60 €5.50, ages 14-26 €3.50, under 14 free.)*

 DOWN UNDER. Only 200 visitors are allowed underground at once, so the catacombs often have long, slow-moving lines. Arrive as early in the morning as possible to avoid being bored to death while waiting.

CITÉ UNIVERSITAIRE. Built in the 1920s to promote cultural exchange between international students, the Cité Universitaire—with its topiary mazes and *mansarde* roofs modeled after the Château de Fontainebleau (p. 181)—now serves double duty as a residential campus and a tourist attraction. The building's marble halls house the info desk and cafeteria. While the living quarters are closed to the public, the grounds are open for exploration daily from 7am to 10pm. Behind the **Maison Internationale,** you'll find people picnicking and practicing tai chi. *(Main entrance 17 bd. Jourdain. Ⓜ️Porte d'Orléans, RER: Cité Universitaire, or bus #88. ☎01 44 16 64 00; www.ciup.fr. Grounds open daily 7am-10pm. Maison Heinrich Heine cafeteria open M-F 7am-2pm, Sa-Su 8am-2pm. Guided tours 1st Su of the month; reserve ahead at ☎01 43 13 65 96. Grounds free. Tours €8, students €3, Cité residents free.)*

15ÈME ARRONDISSEMENT

🎔PARC ANDRÉ CITROËN. Landscapers Alain Provost and Gilles Clément created this futuristic park in the 1990s after the Citroën automobile plant's closing. This Parisian jungle contains multilevel fountains, greenhouses, and a "wild" garden whose plants change annually. Compulsive email-checkers can take advantage of the park's three free Wi-Fi zones. Hot-air balloon rides launch from the central garden and offer spectacular aerial views. *(Ⓜ️Javel or Balard. ☎01 44 26 20 00; www.ballondeparis.com. Open in summer M-F 8am-9:30pm, Sa-Su 9am-9:30pm; in winter M-F 8am-5:45pm, Sa-Su 9am-5:45pm. Guided tours leave from the Jardin Noir; €3-6.)*

INSTITUT PASTEUR. Founded by the French scientist Louis Pasteur in 1888, the Institut Pasteur is now a center for biochemical research, development, and treatment. The institute has turned Pasteur's somber but magnificent home into a museum; inside are the instruments Pasteur used to discover an anthrax vaccine and a cure for rabies. The institute remains under the scientific spotlight as the lab where doctors first isolated HIV in 1983. Visitors may visit Pasteur's tomb, an awesome marble and mosaic construction, during the 45min.

museum tour. *(25 rue du Docteur Roux. ⓂPasteur. ☎ 01 45 68 82 83; www.pasteur.fr. Open Sept.-July M-F 2-5:30pm. Box office in a small building next to the museum. Tour times can be erratic. €3, students €1.50; with English- or French-language tour and film €5/2.50.)*

TOUR MONTPARNASSE. Standing 59 stories (209m) tall and completed in 1969, the Tour Montparnasse looks jarringly out of place amid Montparnasse's otherwise subdued 19th-century architecture. Shortly after the tower's creation, the city forbade the construction of similar monstrosities, designating the outer reaches of the La Défense district (p. 153) as the sole home for future *gratte-ciels* (skyscrapers). The Tour boasts an incredible 360° view of Paris, from which you can see for 40km on a clear day. *(33 av. du Maine. Enter on rue de l'Arrivée. ⓂMontparnasse-Bienvenüe. ☎ 01 45 38 52 56. Open M-Th and Su 9:30am-10:30pm, F-Sa 9:30am-11pm. Last entry 30min. before close. €9.50, students €6.80, ages 7-15 €4.)*

PASSY AND AUTEUIL (16ÈME)

PALAIS DE TOKYO. Built for the 1937 World Expo, this austere, Neoclassical, and arguably ugly *palais* is home to the world-class ▧**Musée d'Art Moderne de la Ville de Paris** (see **Museums,** p. 157), which offers free admission to its permanent collection. The west wing houses the excellent *site de création contemporaine,* which exhibits today's hottest and most controversial art. *(11 av. du Président Wilson. ⓂIéna. ☎ 01 47 23 54 01; www.palaisdetokyo.com. Open Tu-Su noon-midnight. €6, under 25, seniors, and members of groups of 10+ €4.50, artists and art students €1.)*

PLACE DU TROCADÉRO. In the 1820s the duke of Angoulême built a memorial to his victory in Spain at Trocadéro. For the 1937 World's Fair, Jacques Carlu added two mirror-image white stone buildings called the **Palais de Chaillot,** block-like and situated in the shape of an arch, as well as an austere veranda between them. Guarded by Henri Bouchard's 7.5m bronze Apollo, the terrace offers the ▧**best view of the Eiffel Tower** and surrounding city, day or night. *(ⓂTrocadéro.)*

BATIGNOLLES (17ÈME)

CIMETIÈRE DES BATIGNOLLES. Stuck behind a noisy *lycée* and plagued by honking cars from the Périphérique, the cemetery's inhabitants would seem to have a hard time resting in peace. Less glamorous than Paris's other graveyards, the Cimetière des Batignolles nevertheless can claim verse poet Paul Verlaine and Surrealist authors André Breton and Benjamin Peret among its interred. *(8 rue St-Just. ⓂPort de Clichy. ☎ 01 53 06 38 68. Open Mar. 16-Nov. 5 M-F 8am-6pm, Sa 8:30am-6pm, Su and holidays 9am-6pm; Nov. 6-Mar. 15 M-F 8am-5:30pm, Sa 8:30am-5:30pm, Su and holidays 9am-5:30pm. Conservation Bureau open M-F 8am-noon and 2-5:30pm; request free map inside. Last entry 15min. before close. Free.)*

MONTMARTRE (18ÈME)

▧**BASILIQUE DU SACRÉ-COEUR.** This ethereal basilica, with its signature white onion domes, was commissioned to atone for France's war crimes in the Franco-Prussian War. The chosen site, atop the "mount of martyrs," had religious as well as historical significance; home to St-Denis, Paris's first bishop, it was where St-François-Xavier and St-Ignatius of Loyola founded the **Society of Jesus** (Jesuits) in 1534. A Benedictine abbey claimed the hill until the French Revolution, when, desiring a clean cut from their past, the revolutionaries beheaded its abbess and destroyed the nunnery. Construction on Sacré-Coeur began in 1876 and ended in 1914, and it was consecrated five years later. The basilica inspired even greater devotion in WWII, when 13 bombs exploded in its vicinity, miraculously without injuring anyone. Sacré-Coeur's architecture appears similarly divine. Inside the basilica, the striking mosaics attract large numbers of tourists. Beneath the basilica, the crypt contains pieces of the heart of Alexandre Legentil, who was the first to vow to build a national church atop Montmartre. To the left of the crypt's entrance, a spiral staircase leads up to the top of Sacré-Coeur's dome. After a tiring, slightly claustrophobia-inducing climb, you can marvel at the view, which stretches 50km on clear days. *(35 rue du Chevalier-de-la-Barre. ⓂAnvers, Abbesses, or Château-Rouge. ☎01 53 41 89 00; www.sacre-coeur-montmartre.fr. Basilica open daily 6am-11pm. Crypt open daily 9am-5:30pm. Dome open daily 9am-6pm. Mass daily 10pm. Wheelchair-accessible. Free. Dome €5.)*

AU LAPIN AGILE. A favorite of Guillaume Apollinaire, Max Jacob, Amedeo Modigliani, and Americans Charlie Chaplin and Ernest Hemingway, this establishment was known as the **"Cabaret des Assassins"** until André Gill decorated its facade with a painting of a *lapin* (rabbit) balancing a hat on its head and a bottle on its paw. The cabaret gained renown as the "Lapin à Gill" (Gill's rabbit). By the time Picasso began to frequent the establishment, walking over from his studio at 49 rue Gabrielle, the name had contracted to the "Lapin Agile." Today, the cabaret has become touristy, but you can still sip a *cerises maison* (€7) while taking in a mix of French *chanson* and comedy. *(22 rue des Saules. ⓂLamarck-Caulaincourt. ☎01 46 06 85 87; www.au-lapin-agile.com. Shows Tu-Su 9pm-2am; €24, students Tu-F and Su except holidays €17. See p. 167.)*

★TIP★ MOUNTING MONTMARTRE. A simple stroll does not exist in Montmartre; rather, its stone staircase *"rues"* and sloping cobblestone hills provide a physique-toning climb. The standard approach is from the south, via ⓂAnvers or Abbesses—although other directions provide interesting, less crowded uphill hikes. From ⓂAnvers, the short walk up rue de Steinkerque to the ornate, switchbacked stairway attracts large numbers of tourists. The longer, more peaceful climb from ⓂAbbesses—fans may recognize this as Amélie's Métro stop—passes by several worthwhile cafes and shops. A glass-covered **funicular** ascends every 10min. from the base of rue Tardieu to atop Montmartre. Operated by the RATP, the funicular functions similar to a ski lift and can be ridden with a normal Métro ticket. (Open M-F and Su 7:35am-12:40am, Sa 7:35am-11:35pm. €1.50 or Métro ticket.) The **Syndicat d'Initiative de Montmartre,** pl. du Tetre (☎01 42 62 21 21), offers 2hr. **walking tours** of historic Montmartre for €10 per person.

LES VIGNES. A Montmartre staple since Gallo-Roman times, the vineyards were known in the 16th century for the diuretic wines they produced. Now this lone surviving winery is one of **Paris's last remaining vineyards.** Montmartre's *vignes* have remained intact more for tradition than function, producing only a few dozen bottles of wine per year. Every October, the vineyard hosts the **Fête des Vendanges;** this boisterous weekend festival of wine-drinking, dancing, and folklore is the only time that the wine produced on the grounds is sold to the public. *(Rue des Saules. ⓂLamarck-Caulaincourt. Closed to the public except during the Fête des Vendanges, Oct. 9-11, 2009; see www.fetedesvendangesdemontmartre.com for more info.)*

BAL DU MOULIN ROUGE. No cabaret or nightclub has achieved the stardom—or notoriety—of the Bal du Moulin Rouge, immortalized by Henri de Toulouse-Lautrec's paintings, Jacques Offenbach's music, and Baz Luhrmann's Hollywood blockbuster. At the turn of the century, Paris's bourgeoisie came to the Moulin Rouge to play at being bohemian. Following WWI, the area around **place Pigalle** became a renowned red light district. Today, despite the

HELPING THROUGH HUMOR

At the age of 26, Michel Colucci adopted the name Coluche and—like so many others with only one appellation—embarked on an entertainment career. Sure enough, the man with the razor-sharp political wit quickly became one of France's most beloved comedians. He ran for president in 1981—"I'll quit politics when politicians quit comedy"—but dropped out of the race when polls showed that he actually had a chance of winning. Before a motorcycle accident ended his life in 1986, Coluche founded the charity **Restos du Coeur** (Restaurants of the Heart) and, in doing so, left a permanent mark on France.

Restos du Coeur is a network of soup kitchens and other volunteer activities. Their emphasis on fostering personal relationships between those who volunteer and those who receive aid, along with their good humor, has set them apart as a uniquely positive force of goodwill. Volunteers can work in the kitchens, provide face-to-face companionship, or help combat illiteracy, but they have to be able to do it for a few months. Coluche knew the importance of dedication and supporting the community; it almost made him president.

Paris office at 4 cité d'Hauteville (☎01 53 32 23 23; www.restos-ducoeur.org).

famous reconstructed windmill, there's not much to see from the street. If you're looking to splurge on one of the splashy cabaret shows, see **Entertainment**, p. 167. *(82 bd. de Clichy. Ⓜ Blanche. ☎01 53 09 82 82; www.moulin-rouge.com.)*

BUTTES CHAUMONT (19ÈME)

◪**PARC DE LA VILLETTE.** Cut in the middle by Canal de l'Ourcq and Canal St-Denis, Parc de la Villette separates the Cité des Sciences from the Cité de la Musique. Dominating the park, the steel-and-glass **Grande Halle** hosts frequent concerts, films, and plays. Twenty-six funny-shaped red buildings called *folies* dot the park at regular 120m intervals; they serve purposes from first-aid center to hamburger stand. Before the Grande Halle, the **information Villette folie** distributes free maps and brochures. In July and August, La Villette hosts a free open-air **film festival** that features a diverse international program. Finally, the **Promenade des Jardins** links several thematic gardens, including the **Garden of Dunes and Wind,** reminiscent of a seashore, the **Garden of Childhood Fears,** which resonates with spooky sounds, and the roller coaster **Dragon Garden.** *(211 av. Jean Jaurès. Ⓜ Porte de Pantin. General info ☎01 40 03 75 75, Trabendo 42 01 12 12, Zénith 42 08 60 00; www.villette.com. Info office open M-Sa 9:30am-6:30pm. Free.)*

◪**CITÉ DES SCIENCES ET DE L'INDUSTRIE.** The Cité des Sciences et de l'Industrie houses the fabulous **Explora Science Museum,** (p. 162) arguably the best destination for kids in Paris. The enormous **Géode** outside the Cité, a mirrored sphere mounted on a flower bed, looks like a gigantic disco ball thanks to the 6433 polished stainless-steel triangles coating its exterior. Inside, **Omnimax movies** on natural phenomena play on a 1000 sq. m hemispheric screen. The **Argonaute submarine** details the interesting history of submersibles from Jules Verne to present-day nuclear-powered subs. Between the Canal St-Denis and the Cité, **Cinaxe** features innovative movies filmed from the first-person perspective; hydraulic pumps simulate every bump and curve as you explore the world in Formula One cars, low-flying planes, and Mars land rovers. Lunch beforehand is not recommended. *(Ⓜ Porte de la Villette. ☎01 40 05 80 00, Géode 40 05 12 12, Cinaxe 40 05 12 12; www.cite-sciences.fr. Open M 10:30am-7:30pm, Tu-Su 10:30am-9:30pm; hours may vary. Argonaute open Tu-Sa 10am-5:30pm, Su 10am-6:30pm. Shows every hr.; €11, under 25 M-F except holidays €9; 2 films €15. Cinaxe open Tu-Su 11am-1pm and 2-5pm; shows every 15min. Argonaute €3, including audio tour. Cinaxe €4.80.)*

BELLEVILLE AND PÈRE LACHAISE (20ÈME)

PÈRE LACHAISE CEMETERY. With its elaborate sarcophagi, the Cimetière du Père Lachaise has become the final resting place for many legends, including Honoré de Balzac, Baron Haussmann, Molière, Marcel Proust, Jim Morrison, and Oscar Wilde. The cemetery's 44 hectares barely contain the million people buried within them: to make room, the government digs up any grave unvisited in ten years and transports the remains to another cemetery. The **Mur des Fédérés** (Wall of the Federals) has become a pilgrimage site for left-wing sympathizers worldwide. *(16 rue du Repo. ⓂPère Lachaise. ☎01 55 25 82 10. Open from mid-Mar. to early Nov. M-F 8am-6pm, Sa 8:30am-6pm, Su and holidays 9am-6pm; from early Nov. to mid-Mar. M-F 8am-5:30pm, Sa 8:30am-5:30pm, Su and holidays 9am-5:30pm. Last entry 15min. before close. 2½hr. guided tour from Apr. to mid-Nov. Sa 2:30pm. Free. Tour free.)*

PARC DE BELLEVILLE. Built into the hillside, a series of terraces connected by stairs and footpaths comprise this well-landscaped park. From its high vantage points, the park offers spectacular views of Parisian landmarks, including the Centre Pompidou, the Eiffel Tower, and the Panthéon. *(27 rue Piat. ⓂPyrénées.)*

LA DÉFENSE. La Défense is a gleaming space crammed with contemporary architecture, enormous office buildings, and one very geometric arch. Shops, galleries, and gardens cluster around the **Grande Arche de la Défense,** a 35-story building in the shape of a hollow cube. Inaugurated on the French Republic's bicentennial in 1989, it took 300,000 tons of steel, F2.6 billion, and the efforts of 2000 workmen—two of whom died in construction accidents—to complete the 87,000 sq. m building. The arch's walls are covered with white marble and mirrors, which gleam in sunlight—bring your shades, or you'll be squinting. *(Ⓜ/RER: La Défense or bus #73. If you take the RER, buy your ticket before going through the turnstile. ☎01 47 74 84 24. Open Apr.-Sept. daily 10am-6pm; Oct.-Mar. M-F 9:30am-5:30pm. Grande Arche open daily 10am-7pm. Last entry 6:30pm. €7.50, students, under 18, and seniors €6.)*

> **TIP** **A TOWER WITH A VIEW.** The outdoor glass elevators on the Grande Arche de la Défense make for a unique ride, as you will get fantastic views all the way up. The view from the top of the arch, however, is less than spectacular, given the number of tall buildings between it and the far-off center of Paris. It doesn't quite match the views from the Eiffel Tower, the Basilique du Sacré-Coeur, the Parc de Belleville, or the top of the Centre Pompidou.

MUSEUMS

Paris's museums are universally considered among the world's best, and no visitor to the city should miss them. If you're going to be doing the museum circuit while in Paris, you may want to invest in a **Carte Musées et Monuments,** which offers admission to 65 museums in greater Paris. The card is cost-effective if you plan to visit more than three museums or sights every day and will enable you to sail past admission lines. It is available at major museums, tourist office kiosks, and many Métro stations. Ask for a brochure listing participating museums and monuments. A pass for two days is €30, for four days €45, for six days €60. For more info, call **Association InterMusées,** 4 rue Brantôme, 3ème (☎01 44 61 96 60; www.intermusees.com). Most museums are closed on Mondays; the Louvre, Centre Pompidou, and Musée Rodin are closed on Tuesdays.

CHÂTELET-LES HALLES

1ER ARRONDISSEMENT

⊠MUSÉE DU LOUVRE

Ⓜ*Palais Royal-Musée du Louvre.* ☎*01 40 20 53 17; www.louvre.fr. Open M, Th, Sa 9am-6pm, W and F 9am-10pm. Last entry 45min. before close; closure of rooms begins 30min. before close. 1½hr. tours in English, French, or Spanish daily 11am, 2, 3:45pm; sign up at the info desk. €9; W and F after 6pm €6; under 18, unemployed, under 26 F after 6pm, and 1st Su of the month free.*

Filled with priceless objects from the tombs of Egyptian pharaohs, the halls of Roman emperors, the studios of French painters, and the walls of Italian churches, the Louvre is a monument that transcends national and temporal boundaries. Explore the endless exhibition halls; witness new generations of artists at work in the galleries; catch a glimpse—if only a glimpse—of the Louvre's most famous residents; and then come back for more.

Enter through IM Pei's glass pyramid in the center courtyard of the building itself; an escalator descends into the Cour Napoléon, the museum's lobby, where you will find tickets, information, and updated maps. There are three wings that branch off the Cour Napoléon: **Sully, Richelieu,** and **Denon.** Each wing is divided into sections according to the art's period, national origin, and medium. To find out which rooms will be open on your visit, check the website, ask the info desk, or call **museum info** (☎01 01 40 20 53). The collection is divided into seven departments: Oriental Antiquities; Egyptian Antiquities; Greek, Etruscan, and Roman Antiquities; Painting; Sculpture; Decorative Arts; and Graphic Arts. Color-coding and room numbers on the Louvre's free maps correspond to the colors and numbers on the plaques at the entrances to every room. Getting lost is an inevitable part of the Louvre experience, but there are plenty of guides who can point you in the right direction. Visitors can find audio tours at the wing entrances or reserve them online before the visit. They describe over 350 of the museum's highlights. *(Rental €6, under 18 €2; deposit of driver's license, passport, or credit card; available to reserve online.)*

 TIP | **STRAIGHT TO THE ART.** The lines stretching across the courtyard at the Louvre can be disheartening. Instead of entering through the glass pyramids, follow the signs from the Métro to the Carrousel du Louvre or enter through one of the wings off the main courtyard to sail past the rest. The Carte Musée et Monuments will let you skip ticket lines, as will using automatic ticket machines in the Cour Napoléon or buying tickets online. For more time with Mona, try to visit on Monday or Wednesday evening, when the museum is open until 9:45pm, or on a weekday afternoon.

MESOPOTAMIAN COLLECTION. The cradle of civilization, the fertile crescent, and the land of epithets, Mesopotamia is also the birthplace of Western art. The **Victory Stela of Naram Sim** (Room 2) is a highlight. It depicts the Akkadian king ascending the heavens, trampling his enemies along the way, and sporting the crown of a god. The **Winged Bulls of Sargon II** (Room 4) served as guardians of the king's Assyrian palace. Hammurabi's Code holds center stage in Room 3. The modest stela inscribed with 282 laws for his Babylonian civilization is a physical memento of the first public **codified law**—it's such an important democratic gesture that it's easy to overlook the fact that dismemberment was the sentence for minor crimes like petty theft. *(Richelieu; ground floor.)*

GREEKS, ROMANS, AND CO. The **Venus de Milo** (Room 74) is the ultimate classical beauty, even if she is missing her arms. The size-14 lady is always surrounded by enthusiastic camera-waving admirers. Overlooking a nearby stairway, the **Winged Victory of Samothrace** proves that a head is not a prerequisite for Greek masterpieces; beware of the intense crowds. Located on the lower ground floor of the Denon wing is a display devoted to Cycladic art, which employed such a highly geometricized style that the sculptures and idols actually look modern. *(Denon and Sully; 1st fl., ground floor, and lower ground floor.)*

ITALIANS. You probably didn't come for the Cycladic idols; you came for Leonardo da Vinci's **Mona Lisa** (Room 6), the world's most famous image. The lady's mysterious smile is still charming, but there's nothing mysterious or charming about looking at it in person. The crowds are fierce, the painting is hidden in a glass box that constantly reflects camera flashes, and you won't be allowed within 15 ft. We at *Let's Go* don't want to be heretical, but if you're pressed for time you might consider skipping the lady. In the adjacent hall, a group of Renaissance masterpieces awaits—including Leonardo's **Virgin on the Rocks,** Raphael's **Grand Saint Michel,** and Fra Angelico's **Calvary.** Visit as early as possible; this wing is a circus within 30min. of the museum's opening. *(Denon; 1st floor.)*

FLANDERS AND THE NETHERLANDS. A more civilized museum experience awaits on the less crowded second floor. Vermeer's astonishing **Astronomer** and **Lacemaker** occupy Room 38. While the lifelong resident of Delft left behind no clues to his preparatory methods, some scholars believe that he used a camera obscura in composing his works. One can make out subtle effects of light that could not have appeared to Vermeer's naked eye without a little help. This section is also filled with works by Rembrandt, Van Eyck, and Van Der Weyden as well as a monumental 24-painting cycle by Rubens. *(Richelieu; 2nd floor.)*

FRANCE. It is only fitting that a French palace would be filled with wonderful French paintings. The 17th-, 18th-, and 19th-century works that occupy the second floor of the Sully wing can be as fluffy and sugary as a chocolate soufflé, but don't lose interest quite yet. Watch out for Watteau's **Pilgrimage to Cytheria** (Room 36), a melancholy ode to the impermanence of love. La Tour's fascination with hidden sources of light produced the haunting works that occupy Room 28. Once you've had your fill of peace and quiet, head back to the first floor of Denon, where the French heavyweights keep a close eye on the *Mona Lisa.* Large-format works dominate Rooms 75, 76, and 77. Géricault's **Raft of the Medusa,** ripped from the headlines in 1819, depicts the Medusa's abandoned passengers struggling to survive as they try to catch the attention of a passing ship. The second most famous painting in these galleries is Delacroix's **Liberty Leading the People,** in which Liberty, like almost everything in Western art, is symbolized by a partially nude woman. David's enormous paintings **The Coronation of Napoleon, The Oath of the Horatii,** and **Sabine Women** showcase the painter's Neoclassical style. Finally, check out Ingres's body-twisting **Grande Odalisque**—go ahead, try to put your legs like that—and Delacroix's **Death of Sardanopolous.** They are both examples of Orientalism, a product of France's imperial adventures in North Africa. *(Sully, 2nd fl.; Denon, 1st fl.)*

OTHER MUSEUMS OF THE 1ER

▨**MUSÉE DE L'ORANGERIE.** The Orangerie has come a long way from its original role as the greenhouse of the Jardin des Tuileries. Opened as a museum in 1927, the intimate building is home to a phenomenal set of works, collected by two men wholly unconnected to one another—except that they were both married to the same woman (at different times). The collection includes works by Renoir, Cézanne, Modigliani, Rousseau, Matisse, and Picasso. The highlight is Monet's extensive and enormous **Les Nymphéas** *(Water Lilies)*, which cover the walls of two oval-shaped rooms that together form the sign for infinity. Though the museum is crowded after recent renovations, the art is worth every moment spent waiting. *(Southwest corner of the Jardin des Tuileries.* Ⓜ*Concorde.* ☎ *01 44 77 80 07; www.musee-orangerie.fr. Open M, W-Th, Sa-Su 12:30-7pm, F 12:30-9pm. Wheelchair-accessible. €7.50, under 26 €5.50. Audio tours €5, under 26 €3.)*

THE MARAIS

3ÈME ARRONDISSEMENT

◪**MUSÉE PICASSO.** When Picasso died in 1973, his family paid the French inheritance tax in artwork. Twelve years later, the French government put collections on display in the 17th-century **Hôtel Salé.** The museum is the world's largest catalogue of the life and 70-year career of one of the most prolific artists of the 20th century. Arranged chronologically, it leads viewers through the evolution of Picasso's artistic and personal life. From his earliest work in Barcelona to his Cubist and Surrealist years in Paris to his Neoclassical work on the French Riviera, each room situates his art within the context of his life. Follow the Sens de Visite arrows around the building or go your own way. Highlights of the collection include the haunting blue **Autoportrait, Le Violon et la Musique,** the Post-Cubist **Deux Femmes Courant sur la Plage,** and sculptures from the 1930s that experiment with human morphology. Picasso's experiments with abstraction often went hand in hand with his love affairs: check out the many studies of **La Tête d'une Femme,** inspired by his lover Marie-Thérèse Walter; **La Femme Qui Pleure,** based on the Surrealist photographer Dora Maar; and **The Kiss,** painted later in his life while he was married to Jacqueline Roque. The museum also houses paintings from Picasso's personal collection, including those by Cézanne, Matisse, and Renoir. *(5 rue de Thorigny.* Ⓜ*Chemin Vert.* ☎ *01 42 71 25 21; www.musee-picasso.fr. Open M and W-Su Apr.-Sept. 9:30am-6pm; Oct.-Mar. 9:30am-5:30pm. Last entry 45min. before close. €6.50, ages 18-25 €4.50, under 18 and 1st Su of the month free.)*

◪**MUSÉE CARNAVALET.** Housed in Mme. de Sévigné's 16th-century *hôtel particulier* and the neighboring **Hôtel Le Peletier de Saint-Fargeau,** this meticulously arranged museum traces Paris's history from its origins to the present. The chronologically themed rooms follow Paris's evolution as a city, from prehistory and the Roman conquest to medieval politics; 18th-century splendor to Revolution; 19th-century urban, literary, and artistic growth; and Mitterrand's Grands Projets. Highlights include Proust's fully reconstructed bedroom, a piece of the Bastille prison wall, and Sévigné's interior decor itself—check out the **Wendel Ballroom,** painted by Jose-Maria Sert, and the Charles Le Brun ceilings in Rooms 19 and 20. The museum also regularly hosts special exhibits featuring the work of cartoonists, sculptors, and photographers. *(23 rue de Sévigné.* Ⓜ*Chemin Vert.* ☎ *01 44 59 58 58; www.carnavalet.paris.fr. Open Tu-Su 10am-6pm. Last entry 5pm. Free. Special exhibits €7, under 26 €4, under 14 free, seniors €6.)*

GALLERIES. The swank galleries in the Marais, concentrated in the 3ème, display some of Paris's most exciting and avant-garde art. Cutting-edge paintings, sculptures, and photographs peek out of storefront windows along **rue de Perche, rue de Thorigny, rue Debellyme, rue Vieille du Temple, rue Quincampoix, rue des Coutures Saint-Gervais, rue de Poitou,** and **rue Beaubourg.** Especially in summer, the *vernissages* (gallery openings) are some of the most exclusive events in town—look for the crowds of gorgeous model-like women. Most galleries are closed Sundays, Mondays, and the month of August. ◪**Galerie Thuillier** features over 1500 pieces of art each year at 21 annual expositions across two sizable storefronts.

It thrives commercially by displaying a variety of media and styles as well as both temporary and permanent artists. *(13 rue de Thorigny. ⓜSt-Sébastien-Froissart. ☎01 42 77 33 24; www.galeriethuillier.com. Open M-Sa noon-7pm. Exhibition Tu evening 6pm.)* ▧**Fait & Cause** aims at spreading humanist and humanitarian consciousness, mostly through documentary photography. Past artists have included Jacob Riis, Jane Evelyn Atwood, and Robert Doisneau. *(58 rue Quincampoix. ⓜRambuteau or Étienne-Marcel. ☎01 42 74 26 36. Open Tu-Sa 1:30-6:30pm.)* ▧**Galerie Emmanuel Perro-tin,** situated in a courtyard building once occupied by the directors of the Bas-tille prison, displays everything from installation art to sculpture and features artists from around the world. *(76 rue Turenne and 10 impasse St-Claude. ⓜSt-Sebastien Froissart. ☎01 42 16 79 79; www.galerieperrotin.com. Open Tu-Sa 11am-7pm.)*

4ÈME ARRONDISSEMENT

▧**MUSÉE NATIONAL D'ART MODERNE.** The Centre Pompidou's main attrac-tion boasts a collection that spans the 20th century, but the art from the last 50 years is particularly brilliant. It features everything from Philip Guston's adorable hooded figures to Eva Hesse's anthropomorphic sculptures. Those looking to escape the discomfort will want to see Cai Guo-Qang's *Bon Voyage*, an airplane made of wicker and vine hanging from the ceiling and studded with objects confiscated from passengers' carry-on luggage at the Tokyo airport. On the museum's second level, early-20th-century heavyweights like Duchamp and Picasso hold court. Most of the works were contributed by the artists them-selves or by their estates; Joan Miró and Wassily Kandinsky's wife are among the museum's founders. For more on the Centre Pompidou, see **Sights,** p. 141. *(Pl. Georges-Pompidou. ⓜRambuteau, Hôtel de Ville, or RER: Châtelet-Les Halles. ☎01 44 78 12 33; www.centrepompidou.fr. Open M, W, F-Su 11am-9pm, Th 11am-11pm. Last ticket sales 1hr. before close. €12, under 26 €9, under 18 and 1st Su of the month free.)*

MÉMORIAL DE LA SHOAH (MUSEUM OF THE HOLOCAUST). Opened in 2005, the memorial serves as a resource center and archives, but its formal mis-sion is to teach: to form a bridge between the generation that experienced the Holocaust and the generation that did not. Beautifully conceived and intensely moving, the museum accomplishes much more. *(17 rue Geoffroy l'Asnier. ⓜPont Marie or St-Paul. ☎01 42 77 44 72; www.memorialdelashoah.org. Open M-W and Su 10am-6pm, Th 10am-10pm. Tours every Su 3pm or upon request. Wheelchair-accessible. Free.)*

LATIN QUARTER AND SAINT-GERMAIN

5ÈME ARRONDISSEMENT

▧**MUSÉE DE CLUNY.** The Hôtel de Cluny houses the **Musée National du Moyen Âge,** one of the world's finest collections of medieval art, including jewelry, sculp-ture, and tapestries. The *hôtel* itself is a flamboyant 15th-century manor built atop second-century Roman ruins. In the 13th century, the site became home to the Cluny abbots. In 1843, the state converted the *hôtel* into the medieval museum. The museum's collection includes art from Paris's most important medieval structures. Panels of brilliant stained glass from Ste-Chapelle line the ground floor. The brightly lit **Galerie des Rois** contains sculptures from Notre Dame—including a series of marble heads of the kings of Judah, severed dur-ing the Revolution. The museum's medieval jewelry collection includes royal crowns, brooches, and daggers. Perhaps the most impressive work of gold-smithing is the exquisite 14th-century **Gold Rose.** Tucked away among gilded reliquaries is the gruesome sculpture of **the head of Saint-Jean le Baptiste on a platter.** A series of allegorical tapestries, **La Dame à la Licorne** *(The Lady at the Unicorn)*, is the museum's coveted star. Claiming a room all their own, the woven masterpieces depict the five senses. The complete cycle comprises the centerpiece of the museum's collection of 15th- and 16th-century Belgian weaving. Outside, irises, mint, and primroses grow in the **Jardin Médiéval**, a 5000 sq. m replica of a medieval pleasure garden. The museum sponsors chamber music concerts during the summer. *(6 pl. Paul-Painlevé.* Ⓜ*Cluny-La Sorbonne. Info* ☎*01 53 73 78 00, reception 53 73 78 16. Open M and W-Su 9:15am-5:45pm. Closed Jan. 1, May 1, and Dec. 25. Last entry 5:15pm. Garden open in summer M-F 9:30am-9:30pm, Sa-Su and holidays 9am-9:30pm; in winter M-F 9:30am-5pm, Sa-Su and holidays 9am-5pm. Call* ☎*01 53 73 78 16 for info on weekly concerts. Temporarily free; prices TBD. Audio tours €1. Gardens free.)*

INSTITUT DU MONDE ARABE. The Institut du Monde Arabe (IMA) is located in one of the city's most striking buildings, built to look like a ship. On its southern face, ▨**240 Arabesque portals** open and close, powered by light-sensitive cells designed to determine the amount of light necessary to illuminate the building's interior without damaging its art. The spacious museum exhibits third- to 18th-century art from Arab regions of the Maghreb, the Middle East, and the Near East. The extensive public library houses over 85,000 documents and provides free Wi-Fi. The ▨**rooftop terrace** has a fabulous—free—view of Montmartre, Île de la Cité, and the Seine. *(1 rue des Fossés St-Bernard.* Ⓜ*Jussieu.* ☎*01 40 51 38 38; www.imarabe.org. Open Tu-Su 10am-6pm. Closed May 1. Library open July-Aug. Tu-Sa 1-6pm; Sept.-June Tu-Sa 1-8pm. €4, under 26 €3, under 12 free. Library free.)*

MUSÉE D'HISTOIRE NATURELLE. Three science museums actually comprise the Museum of Natural History, all beautifully situated within the Jardin des Plantes. The ultramodern, four-floor **Grande Galerie d'Évolution** illustrates evolution with an ironically Genesis-like parade of naturalistic stuffed animals and numerous multimedia tools. Next door is the less than riveting **Musée de Minéralogie.** The **Galeries d'Anatomie Comparée et de Paléontologie** are at the garden's far end, with an exterior resembling a Victorian house of horrors. Despite some snazzy new placards, the place doesn't seem to have changed much since its 1898 opening; it's almost more notable as a museum of 19th-century grotesquery than as a catalogue of anatomy. *(57 rue Cuvier, in the Jardin des Plantes.* Ⓜ*Gare d'Austerlitz or Jussieu.* ☎*01 40 79 30 00; www.mnhn.fr. Grande Galerie de l'Évolution open M and W-Su 10am-6pm. Musée de Minéralogie open Apr.-Oct. M and W-F 10am-5pm, Sa-Su 10am-6pm; Nov.-Mar. M and W-Su 10am-5pm. Galeries d'Anatomie Comparée et de Paléontologie open Apr.-Oct. M and W-F 10am-5pm, Sa-Su 10am-6pm; Nov.-Mar. M and W-Su 10am-5pm. Grand Galerie de l'Évolution €8, students and ages 4-13 €6. Musée de Minéralogie €7, students under 26 €5. Galeries d'Anatomie Comparée et de Paléontologie €6, students €4, under 4 free.)*

6ÈME ARRONDISSEMENT

MUSÉE ZADKINE. Installed in 1982 in the house and studio of Russian sculptor Ossip Zadkine, this tourist-free museum houses a collection of his work, along with moving contemporary art exhibits. Zadkine, who immigrated to Paris in 1909, worked in styles from Primitivism to Neoclassicism to Cubism; the collection represents all 12 of his creative periods. *(100 bis rue d'Assas.* Ⓜ*Vavin.* ☎*01 55 42 77 20; www.zadkine.paris.fr. Open Tu-Su 10am-6pm. €4, under 26 €2.)*

INVALIDES (7ÈME)

▨**MUSÉE RODIN.** The museum is located in the elegant 18th-century **Hôtel Biron,** where Auguste Rodin lived and worked at the end of his life, sharing it with the likes of Isadora Duncan, Cocteau, Matisse, and Rilke. During his lifetime (1840-1917), Rodin was among the country's most controversial artists, classified by many as the sculptor of Impressionism. Today, he is universally acknowledged as the father of modern sculpture. Besides housing many of Rodin's better-known sculptures, including **Le Penseur,** ◼**Le Baiser,** and **L'Homme au Nez Cassé,** the *hôtel* and its surrounding garden are aesthetically appealing in their own right. The museum also has several works by ◼**Camille Claudel,** Rodin's muse, collaborator, and lover. *(79 rue de Varenne. Ⓜ️Varenne. ☎01 44 18 61 10; www.musee-rodin.fr. Open Tu-Su Apr.-Sept. 9:30am-5:45pm; Oct.-Mar. 9:30am-4:45pm. Last entry 30min. before close. Gardens open Tu-Su Apr.-Sept. 9:30am-6:45pm; Oct.-Mar. 9:30am-5pm. Cafe open Tu-Su Apr.-Sept. 9:30am-5:30pm; Oct.-Mar. 9:30am-4:30pm. €6, ages 18-25 and seniors €4, under 18 and 1st Su of the month free. Special exhibits €7/5. Garden €1. Audio tours €4.)*

◼**MUSÉE D'ORSAY.** If only the unimaginative *Académiciens* who turned the budding Impressionists away from the Louvre salon could see the Musée d'Orsay now. The museum's collection, installed in a former railway station, includes paintings, sculpture, decorative arts, and photography from 1848 until WWI. Visit on Sunday mornings or Thursday evenings to avoid the masses. The *Guide to the Musée d'Orsay* (€15), by museum director Caroline Mathieu, is worth the splurge.

The museum is curated in a chronological fashion from the ground floor to the top floor to the mezzanine. The ground floor, dedicated to Pre-Impressionist paintings and sculpture, contains the two scandalous works that started it all, both by Manet: **Olympia,** whose confrontational gaze and nudity caused a stir, and **Déjeuner sur l'Herbe,** which shockingly portrayed a naked woman accompanied by fully clothed men. At the back, the detailed section study of the **Opéra Garnier** is definitely worth a visit. The top floor includes all the big names in Impressionist and Post-Impressionist art: Monet, Manet, Seurat, Van Gogh, and Degas (his famed dancers and prostitutes are a highlight). In addition, the balconies offer supreme views of the Seine and a jungle of sculptures below. Among the decorative arts on the middle level, Rodin's imperious **Honoré de Balzac** and Pompon's adorably big-footed **Ours Blanc** are not to be missed. Besides the permanent collection, seven temporary exhibition spaces, called *dossiers*, are scattered throughout the building. Call or pick up a free copy of **Nouvelles du Musée d'Orsay** to find out what is currently on display. The museum also hosts conferences, special tours, and concerts. *(62 rue de Lille. Ⓜ️Solférino or RER: Musée d'Orsay. Enter at entrance A off 1 rue de la Légion d'Honneur. ☎01 40 49 48 14; www.musee-orsay.fr. Open June 20-Sept. 20 Tu-W and F-Sa 9:30am-6pm, Th 10am-9:45pm, Su 9am-6pm; Sept. 21-June 19 Tu-W and F-Sa 9:30am-6pm, Th 10am-9:45pm. Last entry 1hr. before close. 1hr. English-*

GIVING BACK

RED HOT FOR CHARITY

Each year on the eve of Bastille Day, the streets of Paris erupt in rowdy celebration. The Bals des Pompiers (p. 176)—parties hosted by local firemen—provide excellent places to join in the merrymaking while contributing to a worthy cause. The drinking and dancing starts at 9am and carries through until 4am the next day.

Around 40 accessible charity balls take place in and around Paris during this preamble to Independence Day. While most of the balls merely ask for a small donation, a few of them require a €3-6 cover charge for admission and a drink—a small price to pay for a night of revelry with heroic men who rush into burning buildings. Proceeds from the event benefit the city fire department.

Most of the events feature live music or entertainment before a DJ steers the crowd into the wee hours of the morning. Rumor has it that the strapping young firemen peruse the crowds at the ball and hand out roses to the most beautiful women they see. Keep in mind that the hosts' attire ranges from fully uniformed to scantily clad. Dress to impress, ladies; charity has never looked so good.

To find more information, visit www.pompiersparis.fr.

language tours usually Tu-Sa 11:30am, 2:30pm; call ahead to confirm. Wheelchair-accessible; call ☎01 40 49 47 14 for info. €7.50, ages 18-25 €5, under 18 free; Tu-W and F-Sa after 4:15pm, Th after 8pm, Su all day €5.50. Tours €6.50, ages 18-25 €5, under 18 free. Audio tours €5.)

◼MUSÉE DE MAILLOL. In an arrondissement with some of the best art museums in Paris, the Musée de Maillol holds its own. Aristide Maillol was a sculptor, artist, and painter who, inspired by Paul Gaugin, focused most of his work on the human—especially female—form. When she was 15 years old, Dina Vierney met Maillol and became his muse, eventually finding her own passion as a collector of modern art. The museum's permanent collection combines the careers of these two possibly romantically involved art lovers; it includes Maillol's work as well as pieces by Couturier, Gaugin, Kandinsky, Matisse, Poliakoff, and Redon, among others. The *musée* displays its permanent collection in a series of temporary expositions. *(61 rue de Grenelle. ⓂRue du Bac. ☎01 42 22 59 58; www.museemaillol.com. Open M and W-Su 11am-6pm. €8, students €6, under 16 free.)*

MUSÉE DE QUAI BRANLY. In 2006, President Chirac offered Paris this new cultural monolith of artifacts from Oceania, the Americas, Asia, and Africa. Designed by Jean Nouvel, the wildly inventive museum is ensconced behind a glass shield (to deflect traffic noise) surrounded by an imitation jungle. Once inside, visitors are greeted by a winding ramp with video displays of nature projected onto the ground. Divided into four geographically themed sections, the museum's collection is exhaustive: 3500 of the 300,000 total pieces fill the dimly lit display cases. Towering totem poles stand next to ceremonial masks the size of a small car; enormous, intricately carved ivory tusks are displayed above quirky and creative statuettes. The **Garden Gallery** hosts special exhibits that include rotating pieces from the permanent collection and loans from other museums. **Quai Branly** hosts consortia, workshops, and lectures in art history, philosophy, and anthropology as well as concerts, dance performances, cinema, and theater. *(27, 37, and 51 quai Branly. ⓂAlma-Marceau. ☎01 56 61 70 00; www.quaibranly.fr. Open Tu-W and Su 10am-6:30pm, Th-Sa 10am-9pm. Last entry 45min. before close. English tours available; call ☎01 56 61 71 72 for info. €8.50, students €6, under 18 and 1st Su of the month free. Temporary exhibits in the Garden Gallery €8.50/6/free.)*

CHAMPS-ÉLYSÉES (8ÈME)

◼MUSÉE JACQUEMART-ANDRÉ. Nélie Jacquemart's passion for art and her husband Édouard André's wealth combined to create this extensive collection, housed in their gorgeous late-19th-century home. During the couple's lifetime, only special guests got a glimpse of their precious collection of Renaissance artwork, which included a **Madonna and Child** by Botticelli, **Saint-Georges and the Dragon** by Ucello, and **Pilgrims at Emmaeus** by Rembrandt. Today, you can wander through the mansion, which houses a collection worthy of the most prestigious museums. *(158 bd. Haussmann. ☎01 45 62 11 59. ⓂMiromesnil. Open daily 10am-6pm. Last entry 30min. before close. €10, students and ages 7-17 €7.30, under 7 free. 1 free child ticket per 3 purchased tickets. English headsets included.)*

PETIT PALAIS. Also called the **Musée des Beaux-Arts de la Ville de Paris,** the Petit Palais offers a mix-and-match of works, from 19th-century sculpture to 17th-century portraiture to Renaissance *objets d'art* to ancient Greek relics—as well as the largest public collection of Christian Orthodox icons in France. Themed displays include 19th-century Impressionist works as well as 17th-century Flemish and Dutch masterpieces. After perusing the collection, don't miss the exotic **garden,** which displays more of the Palais's grandiose architecture. *(Av. Winston Churchill. ☎01 53 43 40 00; www.petitpalais.paris.fr. ⓂChamps-Élysées-Clemenceau* *or Franklin D. Roosevelt. Open Tu-Su 10am-6pm. Last entry 5:45pm. Wheelchair-accessible. Free. Special exhibits €9, ages 14-27 €4.50, under 14 and seniors €6 free. Audio tours €4.)*

OPÉRA (9ÈME)

MUSÉE GUSTAVE MOREAU. This monographic museum, housed in Gustave Moreau's home and *atelier* (studio), opened in 1896, two years before the artist's death. Symbolist master, Matisse and Roualt's instructor, and École des Beaux-Arts professor, Moreau left behind a fantastic body of work, much of which depicts mythological scenes. The museum overflows with more than 6000 drawings, models, sculptures, paintings, and watercolors. Climb the Victorian staircase to find Moreau's famous **L'Apparition,** an opium-inspired painting of Salomé dancing before John the Baptist's severed head. *(14 rue de La Rochefoucauld. ⓜTrinité. ☎ 01 48 74 38 50; www.musee-moreau.fr. Open M and W-Su 10am-12:45pm and 2-5:15pm. €5, under 26 and Su €3, under 18 and 1st Su of the month free.)*

BASTILLE

12ÈME ARRONDISSEMENT

CITÉ NATIONALE DE L'HISTOIRE DE L'IMMIGRATION. It is both appropriate and ironic that the museum on immigration, housed in the **Palais de la Porte Dorée** and built during France's colonial expansion, features not-so-politically-correct friezes of "native culture" on its outside walls. The museum inside, however, is a commemoration of the tumultuous history of immigration in France. The permanent collection traces the arrival and subsequent attempts at integration of immigrants in France, from 1830 to today. *(293 av. Daumesnil. ⓜPorte Dorée. ☎ 01 53 59 58 60; www.histoire-immigration.fr. Open Tu-F 10am-5:30pm, Sa-Su 10am-7pm. Last entry 45min. before close. Wheelchair-accessible. €3, during exhibits €5; under 26 €2/3.50.)*

GALLERIES. ▨**Malhia Kent** is a behind-the-scenes look at fashion in the making. Watch artisans weaving the fabric that becomes haute couture for houses like Dior and Chanel. *(19 av. Daumesnil. ⓜGare de Lyon. ☎ 01 53 44 76 76; www.malhia.fr. Open M-F 9am-6pm, Sa-Su 11am-7pm. Jackets and blazers €190-220.)* At ▨**Vertical**, Amazonian wood is turned into Zen-like art. *(63 av. Daumesnil. ⓜGare de Lyon. ☎ 01 43 40 26 26; www.vertical.fr. Open Tu-F 10am-1pm and 2:30-7:30pm, Sa 11am-1:30pm and 3-7:30pm.)*

MONTPARNASSE

14ÈME ARRONDISSEMENT

▨**FONDATION CARTIER POUR L'ART CONTEMPORAIN.** The Fondation Cartier looks like an avant-garde indoor forest, with a stunning modern glass facade surrounding the natural wildlife and local flora of the grounds. Inside the main building, the gallery hosts exhibits of contemporary art, from Andy Warhol to African sculpture. On Thursdays, art hounds can scope out an eclectic set of dance, music, and theater at the Soirées Nomades. *(261 bd. Raspail. ⓜRaspail or Denfert-Rochereau. ☎ 01 42 18 56 50; www.fondation.cartier.com. Open Tu-Su noon-8pm. Soirées Nomades Th 8:30pm; check website for performance details. Reserve ahead at ☎ 01 42 18 56 72. €6, students and seniors €4.50, under 10 free.)*

PASSY AND AUTEUIL (16ÈME)

▨**MUSÉE D'ART MODERNE DE LA VILLE DE PARIS.** The magnificent Palais de Tokyo is home to one of the world's foremost modern art museums. One room is dedicated to Matisse's enormous **La Danse Inachêvée.** Other rooms are organized around significant movements and showcase works from the likes of Modigliani, Vuillard, Braque, Klein, and Picasso. The museum has fantastic special exhibits of both contemporary art and retrospective displays. *(11 av. du Président Wilson. ⑩Iéna. ☎01 53 67 40 00; www.mam.paris.fr. Open Tu-Su 10am-6pm. Last entry 5:45pm. For guided tours, call ☎01 53 67 40 80. Wheelchair-accessible. Free. Special exhibits €4.50-9; under 27 and seniors €3-6; under 13 free.)*

◼MUSÉE MARMOTTAN MONET. Housed in the former hunting villa of the *duc de Valmy* (later the private home of Jules and Paul Marmottan), this hidden museum holds Impressionist treasures, started from the personal collection of Dr. Georges de Bellio, former physician to Manet, Monet, Pissaro, Sisley, and Renoir. All of the patients have works showcased here, as do Morisot, Gaugin, Daumer, and Caillebotte. The basement has the collection's center-piece: wall-size paintings of the Impressionist's water lilies, weeping willows, and wisterias. *(2 rue Louis-Boilly. ⑩Muette. ☎01 44 96 50 31; www.marmottan.com. Open Tu-Su 10am-5:30pm. Last entry 4:30pm. €8, students under 25 and seniors €4.50, under 8 free; with temporary exhibit €9/5.50/free. Audio tour €3.)*

◼MAISON DE BALZAC. Honoré de Balzac hid from bill collectors (under the pseudonym of M. de Breugnol) in this three-story hillside maison, his home from 1840 to 1847. In this tranquil retreat, he completed a substantial part of *La Comédie Humaine* and wrote many other famous works, such as *A Dark Affair*. Visitors can see the desk and embroidered chair where Balzac supposedly wrote and edited for 17hr. per day. In the **Manuscript Room,** you can observe his excruciating editing process. View over 400 printing-block portraits of his characters, organized into genealogical sequences, in one of the last rooms. *(47 rue Raynouard. ⑩Passy. ☎01 55 74 41 80; www.paris.fr/musees/balzac. Open Tu-Su 10am-6pm. Last entry 30min. before close. Permanent collection free. Guided tours and temporary exhibits €4, seniors €3, students under 26 €2, under 12 free.)*

MONTMARTRE (18ÈME)

◼MUSÉE DE L'EROTISME. Bronze statues in the missionary position, Japani-mation sex cartoons, vagina-shaped puppets—seven floors of steamy creations await visitors at Paris's shrine to sex. The museum celebrates erotic art across all media, from painting to sculpture to video—and even includes King Alfonso XIII of Spain's pornos. *(72 bd. de Clichy. ⑩Blanche. ☎01 42 58 28 73; www.musee-ero-tisme.com. Open daily 10am-2am. €8, students and seniors €5. Groups of 4+ €6 per person.)*

BUTTES CHAUMONT (19ÈME)

◼EXPLORA SCIENCE MUSEUM. Dedicated to making science youth-friendly, the Explora Science Museum is a star attraction, located in the complex's **Cité des Sciences et de l'Industrie.** The museum's intriguing exhibits rock just as much as the buildings' futuristic architecture. Explora also features a **planetarium** (level 2), the **Cinéma Louis Lumière** (level 0) with 3D movies, a modest **aquarium** (level -2), and **Médiathèque,** a multimedia scientific and technical library with over 3500 films. The museum's **Cité des Enfants** offers programs for kids ages 2-12. Most programs are in French, but the interactive exhibits are just as fun for English-speaking explorers. *(30 av. Corentin-Cariou. ⑩Porte de la Villette. ☎01 40 05 80 00; www.cite-sciences.fr. Museum open Tu-Sa 10am-6pm, Su 10am-7pm. Last entry 30min. before close. Médiathèque open Tu-Su noon-6:45pm. 1½hr. Cité des Enfants programs Tu-Su 10:30am, 12:30, 2:30, 4:30pm. €8, under 25 €6, under 7 free. Planetarium supplement €3, under 7 free. Médiathèque free. Aquarium free. Cité des Enfants €6.)*

BELLEVILLE AND PÈRE LACHAISE (20ÈME)

TENNISEUM ROLAND GARROS. This fantastic museum chronicles the history of tennis and the French Open, displaying important artifacts like the Coupe des Mousquetaires (the champion's trophy) and the first jacket, worn by the great René Lacoste, adorned with the now-famous crocodile logo. *(2 av. Gordon-Bennett. Ⓜ Porte d'Auteuil or Michel-Ange Molitor. ☎ 01 47 43 48 48; www.tenniseum.fr. Open from mid-Feb. to Oct. Tu-Su 10am-6pm; from Nov. to mid-Feb. W and F-Su 10am-6pm. Tours Tu-Sa 3pm in English; 2, 5pm in French. €7.50, under 18 €4. Tours €10.)*

⬜ SHOPPING

In a city where Hermès scarves function as slings for broken arms and department-store history stretches back to the mid-19th century, shopping is nothing less than an art form. Be prepared to expend every ounce of your energy out in the boutique battlefield, but rest assured that your efforts will pay off. Almost everything in this city, from the world's most expensive dresses to kitchen appliances, is astoundingly stylish. Those who venture to off-the-beaten-path boutiques in the 18ème or Marais will be rewarded with one-of-a-kind pieces—wearable evidence of your exploits in the fashion capital of the world.

BOUGHT AND SOLDE. Twice a year, Parisians and tourists alike hit the pavement for the shopper's version of the Tour de France. The two great *soldes* (sales) of the year start right after New Year's and at the very end of June. If you don't mind slimmer pickings, the best prices are at the beginning of February and the end of July. If the word *braderie* (clearance sale) appears in a store window, that is your signal to enter.

BOOKS AND MUSIC

▨ **Gibert Jeune,** 15 bis bd. St-Denis, 2ème (☎ 01 55 34 75 75; www.gibertjeune.fr). Ⓜ St-Michel. 7 specialized branches cluster around the Fontaine St-Michel. Books in nearly every language. Open M-Sa 10am-7pm. AmEx/MC/V.

▨ **Abbey Bookshop,** 29 rue de la Parcheminerie, 5ème (☎ 01 46 33 16 24; www.abbey-bookshop.net). Ⓜ St-Michel or Cluny. Laid-back shop overflows with new and used English-language titles, as well as Canadian pride courtesy of expat owner Brian. Impressive basement collection. Happy to take special orders. Open M-Sa 10am-7pm. MC/V.

▨ **Shakespeare & Co.,** 37 rue de la Bûcherie, 5ème (☎ 01 43 25 40 93; www.shakespeareco.org). Ⓜ St-Michel. Terrific English-language bookshop and miniature socialist utopia. Bargain bins outside include French classics. Open daily 10am-11pm. MC/V.

Monster Melodies, 9 rue des Déchargeurs, 1er (☎ 01 40 28 00 39). Ⓜ Les Halles. Downstairs supplies used CDs while upstairs overflows with records. Mostly American pop and rock, but some techno and indie rock. Open M-Sa noon-7pm. MC/V.

L'Harmattan, 16 and 21 bis rue des Écoles, 5ème (☎ 01 40 46 79 10; www.editions-harmattan.fr). Ⓜ Cluny-La Sorbonne. Over 50,000 titles of Francophone literature from Africa, the Antilles, Asia, Latin America, and the Middle East. General catalogue available online. Open M-Sa 10am-12:30pm and 1:30-7pm. AmEx/MC/V.

The Village Voice, 6 rue Princesse, 6ème (☎ 01 46 33 36 47; www.villagevoicebookshop.com). Ⓜ Mabillon. Anglophone bookstore and the center of Paris's English literary life. 3-4 readings, lectures, and discussions every month from Sept. to early July. Open M 2-7:30pm, Tu-Sa 10am-7:30pm, Su 1-6pm. AmEx/MC/V.

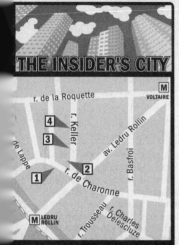

THE INSIDER'S CITY

BEST OF THE BASTILLE

Tucked behind the Bastille are the newest names in Parisian fashion. Up-and-coming boutiques offer threads just as stylish as their Marais counterparts, but at more reasonable prices. The area draws a mix of punk rockers—who frequent the shops that line rue Keller—and trendy young folks.

1. Roucou Paris, 30 bis rue de Charonne. Sleek bags for 60s-style mods. A small wallet is €90, so come ready to spend.
2. Des Petits Hauts, 5 rue Keller. The bright pink exterior is as girly as the clothes inside. Delicate knits in sorbet colors from €40.
3. Anne Willi, 13 rue Keller. The minimalist, pastoral collections on display here are perfect for your inner Zen librarian.
4. Gaële Barré, 17 rue Keller. Unexpected juxtapositions of prints and polka dots adorn tops, dresses, and skirts—all cut in graceful, wispy shapes. Vintage sundress €150.

Les Soeurs Lumière, 18 rue St-Nicolas, 12ème (☎01 43 43 13 15; www.soeurslumiere.fr). ⓂLedru Rollin. Cinema-centered bookstore sells DVDs and the books they're based on. Classics like *The Importance of Being Earnest* and more recent works like *Harry Potter*. Emphasis on English-language titles. Open M-Sa 11am-7pm. MC/V.

Born Bad Record Shop, 17 rue Keller, 11ème (☎01 43 38 41 78). ⓂBastille. Vintage records from a variety of genres, including soul, funk, garage, punk, ska, and more (most €10-20). Also sells comic books and T-shirts (€16-20). Open M-Sa noon-8pm. MC/V.

CLOTHING

▨ **Gabrielle Geppert,** 31-34 Galerie Montpensier, 1er (☎01 42 61 53 52; www.gabriellegeppert.com). ⓂPalais Royal. Favorite of Sharon Stone. Glamorous gold leather and snakeskin bags, rhinestone sunglasses, and fur purses—all by vintage designers like Chanel and Gucci. Exuberant owner handpicks all pieces. Open M-Sa 10am-7:30pm. MC/V.

▨ **Abou d'abi Bazar,** 10 rue des Francs Bourgeois, 3ème (☎01 42 77 96 98). ⓂSt-Paul. Also at 125 rue Vieille du Temple. Feminine fashion in soft, simple, and chic styles. Most items €50-200. Open M and Su 2-7:15pm, Tu-Sa 10:30am-7:15pm. AmEx/MC/V.

▨ **I Heart Ethel,** 47 rue de Turenne, 3ème (☎01 40 29 97 32). Girly boutique with designer-like digs for much less. Flowy *chemises* and going-out tops. Most items €40-110. Open daily 10:30am-7:30pm. AmEx/MC/V.

▨ **Culotte,** 7 rue Malher, 4ème (☎01 42 71 58 89; www.poidsnetparis.com). ⓂSt-Paul. Women's designs range from ripped, printed tees to 40s-style dresses, all handmade. Most items under €100. Open Tu-Sa 12:30-7pm, Su 2-7pm. AmEx/MC/V.

▨ **La Femme Ecarlaté,** 42 av. Bosquet, 7ème (☎01 45 51 08 44). ⓂÉcole Militaire. Left your €3000 evening gown at home? Attentive salespeople will help you select a designer gown to rent. Rentals €150-300. Open Tu-Sa 11am-7pm. Cash only.

Zadig & Voltaire, 15 rue du Jour, 1er (☎01 42 21 88 70; www.zadig-et-voltaire.com). ⓂÉtienne-Marcel. Sleek women's designs. House label does feminine, bohemian-rocker-chic. A big selection of handbags. 7 locations total; hours vary by branch. Main branch open M 1-7:30pm, Tu-Sa 10:30am-7:30pm. AmEx/MC/V.

Vertiges, 85 rue St-Martin, 3ème (☎01 48 87 36 64). ⓂRambuteau. A consignment shopper's heaven—well-organized racks of shirts and skirts (€5), pants (€10), and fabulous leather jackets. Burberry trenches €120. Converse All-Stars €25. Open M-Sa 10am-8pm, Su 11:30am-8pm. Cash only.

Free 'P' Star, 8 rue Ste Croix de la Bretonnerie, 4ème (☎01 42 76 03 72). ⓂHôtel de Ville. Also at 61 rue de la Verrerie, 4ème (☎01 42 78 0 76). Enter as Plain Jane and leave as an 80s star. Wide selection of vintage dresses (€20), velvet blazers (€40), and boots (€30). €10 jean pile. Open M-Sa noon-11pm, Su 2-11pm. MC/V over €20.

Factory's Paris, 3 rue Ste-Croix de la Bretonnerie, 4ème (☎01 48 87 29 10; factorys@noos.fr). ⓂHôtel de Ville. Collared shirts, cargo shorts, and other pieces of the menswear hipster-prep-faux vintage variety. Open M-Sa noon-8pm, Su 2-8pm. AmEx/MC/V.

Loft Design by, 12 rue de Sévigné, 4ème (☎01 48 87 13 07; www.loftdesignby.com). ⓂSt-Paul. 4 other locations around the city. Men's and women's clothing. Well-tailored shirts, fine-gauge sweaters (from €60), and pants (around €85), all in blacks, whites, and grays. Open M-Sa 10:30am-7pm, Su noon-7pm. AmEx/MC/V.

agnès b., 6 and 12 rue du Vieux Colombier, 6ème (☎01 44 39 02 60). ⓂSt-Sulpice. Men's apparel at 12, women's at 6, plus several other locations. Legendary knitwear and other separates in classic cuts and colors. Open daily 10am-7pm. AmEx/MC/V.

Des Petits Hauts, 5 rue Keller, 11ème (☎01 43 38 14 39; www.despetitshauts.com). ⓂLedru-Rollin. Flirty clothes. Flashy shoes and bags. Featured in *Elle Paris*. Open M 1:30-7:30pm, Tu-F 11:30am-7:30pm, Su 11am-7:30pm. AmEx/MC/V.

IN STYLE, IN STOCK. A *stock* is the French version of an outlet store, selling big-name clothes for less—often because it's last season or has small imperfections. Many are on rue d'Alésia in the 14ème, including Cacharel Stock at no. 114 (☎01 45 42 53 04), SR Store (Sonia Rykiel) at no. 112 and no. 64 (☎01 43 95 06 13), and Stock Patrick Gérard at no. 113 (☎01 40 44 07 40). Some other great ones include Stock Kookaï, 82 rue Réamur, 2ème (☎01 45 08 17 91), and Apara Stock, 16 rue Étienne Marcel (☎01 40 26 70 04). Stock Opéra has names like Versace and Dolce & Gabbana and has locations at 9 rue Scribe, 9ème (☎01 40 07 10 20), and 66 rue de la Chaussée d'Antin, 9ème (☎01 40 16 06 00).

DEPARTMENT STORES

🛍 **Galeries Lafayette,** 40 bd. Haussmann, 9ème (☎01 42 82 34 56; www.galerieslafayette.com). ⓂChaussée d'Antin-Lafayette or Havre-Caumartin. Chaotic, but carries it all. High-end labels' ultra-edgy "street wear." 1st fl. food annex, Lafayette Gourmet, has everything culinary. Open M-W and F-Sa 9:30am-7:30pm, Th 9:30am-9pm. AmEx/V.

Forum des Halles, 2ème (☎01 44 76 96 56). ⓂLes Halles or RER: Châtelet-Les Halles. American-style shopping mall. Over 200 stores, including FNAC, Sephora, boutiques, and a 4-story H&M. Open M-Sa 10am-7:30pm (later during *soldes*).

PROS AND CONS. In Paris, pickpocketing is common at department stores, particularly on the escalators. Pickpockets and con artists often work in groups; children are among the most effective extortionists.

BHV, 52-64 rue de Rivoli, 4ème (☎01 42 74 90 00). ⓂHôtel de Ville. Huge, all-encompassing, and unpretentious. Includes Paris's best hardware store. Wheelchair-accessible. Open M-Tu and Th-Sa 9:30am-7:30pm, W 9:30am-9pm. AmEx/MC/V.

Au Bon Marché, 24 rue de Sèvres, 7ème (☎01 44 39 80 00). ⓂSèvres-Babylone. Paris's oldest, most exclusive, and most expensive. From scarves to smoking accessories. Across the street is **La Grande Epicerie de Paris** (38 rue de Sèvres), the celebrated gourmet food annex. Store open M-W and F 9:30am-7pm, Th 10am-9pm, Sa 9:30am-8pm. Épicerie open M-Sa 8:30am-9pm. AmEx/MC/V.

FLEA MARKETS

Le Marché aux Fleurs, pl. Louis Lépine, Île de la Cité. ⓜCité. Year-round covered flower marketplace. Leafy oasis turns into the **Marché aux Oiseaux** (bird market) on Su, attracting children who poke at cuddly furball birds in cages. Open daily 8am-7pm.

Official Market, 18ème (www.parispuces.com). ⓜPorte de Clignancourt or Garibaldi. Divided into 15 sub-markets, each theoretically specializing in a certain type of item. Allow yourself to get lost and then keep browsing. Most official markets have posted individual maps, extremely helpful in navigating the labyrinth of stalls inside. Open M 11am-5pm, Sa 9am-6pm, Su 10am-6pm; most vendors close well before 5pm.

Renegade Market, 18ème. ⓜPorte de Clignancourt. From the moment you exit the metro, you will be surrounded—and hassled—by sellers. Jammed together, the tiny stalls sell flimsy new clothes, cheap woven scarves, wood African masks, fake designer getup, and cheap, colorful jewelry. Some vendors open 5am-9pm.

> **TIP**
>
> **COMMENT DIT-ON "RIP-OFF"?** First-time flea market visitors should note some tips. If you find the Hope Diamond in a pile of schlock jewelry, think again. Be prepared to bargain; sellers don't expect to get their starting prices. Pickpockets love crowded areas, and three-card onte con artists proliferate. Don't be pulled into the game by seeing someone win lots of money; he's part of the con, planted to attract suckers.

GIFTS AND MISCELLANY

Ⓢ Ciné-Images, 68 rue de Babylone, 7ème (☎01 47 05 60 25; www.cine-images.com). ⓜSt-François-Xavier. A cinephile's paradise. Original movie posters from the beginning of film history to the late 1970s. Prices from €30 to €20,000, but it's worth a browse even if you can't afford a thing. Open Tu-F 10am-1pm and 2-7pm, Sa 2-7pm. MC/V.

Ⓢ Pylônes, 57 rue St-Louis en l'Île, Île St-Louis (☎01 46 34 05 02). ⓜPont Marie. 5 other locations. Sells all the crazy items that you'll never really need. Piggy banks €36. Slightly sinister voodoo knife holder €90. Open daily 10:30am-7:30pm. AmEx/MC/V.

Au Vieux Camper, around 48 rue des Écoles, 5ème (☎01 53 10 48 48; www.au-vieux-campeur.fr). 26 locations throughout the 5ème, each specializing in a different outdoor activity. A crunchy backpacker's dream. Books, running gear, canoes, diving equipment, hiking clothes, kayaks, sailing supplies, and tents. Check online for specific store locations. Open M-W and F 11am-7:30pm, Th 11am-9pm, Sa 10am-9:30pm.

SHOES AND ACCESSORIES

Ⓢ Brontibay, 4 rue de Sévigné, 4ème (☎01 42 76 90 80; www.brontibay.com). ⓜSt-Paul. Also at 13 rue Lafayette, 9ème. Vibrant, artistic bags (most €100-200). Printed silk clutches €35. Open M-Sa 11am-8pm, Su 1:30-7:30pm. AmEx/MC/V.

Ⓢ Misia Rêve, 87 rue du Bac, 7ème (☎01 42 34 20 52). ⓜRue du Bac. Accessories for grown-up little girls. Whimsical purses with polka dots and French phrases €15. Leather bags with colorful appliqués from €50. Open Tu-Sa 11am-7:15pm. AmEx/MC/V.

Longchamp, 404 rue St-Honoré, 1er (☎01 43 16 00 16; www.longchamp.com). ⓜConcorde. Branch at 21 rue du Vieux Colombier, 6ème (☎01 42 22 74 75). Flagship store that inspired a trend of classic leather-strapped canvas totes. Leather accessories. Original bags from €48. Open M-Sa 10am-7pm. AmEx/MC/V.

Monic, 5 rue des Francs Bourgeois, 4ème (☎01 42 72 39 15). ⓂChemin Vert or St-Paul. Branch at 14 rue de l'Ancienne Comedie, 6ème (☎01 43 25 36 61). ⓂOdéon. Transgenerational boutique. All types of jewelry €1-300; most under €50. Open M-Sa 10am-7pm, Su 2:30-7pm. AmEx/MC/V.

No Name, 8 rue des Canettes, 6ème (☎01 44 41 66 46). ⓂSt-Sulpice. Stylish sneakers in every color, fabric, and glitter level. Sandals €53-61; sneakers €60-90. Open M and Th 10am-1pm and 2-7pm, Tu-W, F 10am-7pm, Sa 10am-7:30pm. AmEx/MC/V.

ENTERTAINMENT

When it comes to entertainment, Paris satsfies all tastes. The best resources are the weekly bulletins **Pariscope** (€0.40) and **Figaroscope** (€1), both on sale at newsstands. You can also contact **Info-Loisirs,** a recording in English and French that keeps tabs on what's on in Paris (☎08 92 68 31 12, €0.40 per min.).

> **TIP**
>
> **KILLER VIEW.** At almost every theater or concert venue in Paris, there are a few seats—usually in prime seating areas—that are sold just to students at extremely discounted prices (usually €5-12). Look online, check with FNAC (www.fnac.com), or visit a department store to reserve.

CABARET

Bal du Moulin Rouge, 82 bd. de Clichy, 9ème (☎01 53 09 82 82; www.moulin-rouge. com). ⓂBlanche. See **Sights,** p. 151. World-famous cabaret's reviews remain risqué. Be prepared to stand if it's a busy night. Elegant attire required; no shorts, sneakers, or sportswear permitted. Shows nightly 9pm (€99), 11pm (€89; includes champagne). 7pm dinner and 9pm show €145-175. Occasional lunch shows €95-125. MC/V.

Au Lapin Agile, 22 rue des Saules, 18ème (☎01 46 06 85 87; www.au-lapin-agile.com). ⓂLamarck-Coulaincourt. See **Sights,** p. 151. Drinks €6-7. Shows Tu-Su 9pm-2am. €24, M-F and Su students €17; includes 1 drink. MC/V.

CINEMA

You'll find scores of cinemas throughout the city, particularly in the Latin Quarter and on the Champs-Élysées. The notation VO *(version originale)* after a non-French movie listing means that the film is being shown in its original language with French subtitles.

L'Entrepôt, 7 rue Francis de Pressensé (☎01 45 40 07 50, restaurant reservations 45 40 60 70; www.lentrepot.fr). ⓂPernety. 3-screen independent cinema, restaurant with a garden patio, modern art gallery, and trendy bar featuring live jazz Th night and world music F-Sa (9:30pm; cover €7-10). Free weekly debates and lectures. Ciné-Philo, a screening, lecture, and discussion cafe, is held every other Su 2:20pm (€8). Free improv theater fills alternating Su 6:30pm. Su buffet brunch noon-3pm (€25). Check website for other special events. Movie tickets €7, students €5.60, under 12 €4. Complex open daily 9am-midnight. Art gallery open daily 10am-7pm. Bar open M-W and Su noon-3pm and 7:30-10:30pm, Th-Sa noon-3pm and 7:30pm-1am. Kitchen open M-W and Su noon-3pm and 7:30-10:30pm, Th-Sa noon-3pm and 7:30-11pm. AmEx/MC/V.

Musée du Louvre Auditorium, 1er (info ☎01 40 20 53 17; schedules and reservations www.louvre.fr). ⓂLouvre. Concerts and artsy films. Prices vary. Open Sept.-June.

Les Trois Luxembourg, 67 rue Monsieur le Prince, 6ème (☎08 92 68 93 25; www.lestroisluxembourg.com). ⓂLuxembourg. Independent, classic, American, and foreign films, all with French subtitles. €7. Reduced price M-Tu. Cash only.

Cinémathèque Française, 51 rue de Bercy, 12ème (☎01 71 19 32 00; www.cinema-thequefrancaise.com). ⓂBercy. A must for film buffs. 4-5 classics, near-classics, or soon-to-be classics per day. Non-film exhibits include costumes (over 1000), objects, and apparatuses from the past and present world of film. Foreign films usually VO Buy tickets 20min. early. €6, under 26 and seniors €5. Temporary and permanent "collections" open M and W-F noon-7pm, Th noon-10pm, Sa-Su 10am-8pm.

FREE CONCERTS

Free concerts are often held in churches and parks, especially during summer festivals; these are extremely popular, so arrive at the host venue early. The **American Church in Paris,** 65 quai d'Orsay, 7ème, sponsors free concerts. (ⓂInvalides or Alma Marceau. ☎01 40 62 05 00. Concerts Sept.-May Su 6pm.) **Église Saint-Germain-des-Prés** (p. 144) and **Église Saint-Merri,** 78 rue St-Martin, 4ème, also hold concerts; check the information booth just inside the door for times. Concerts take place Wednesday through Sunday in the **Jardin du Luxembourg's band shell,** 6ème (☎01 42 34 20 23); show up early if you don't want to stand. Occasional free concerts are held in the **Musée d'Orsay,** 1 rue Bellechasse, 7ème (ⓂSolférino; ☎01 40 49 49 66).

MUSIC, OPERA, AND DANCE

Connoisseurs will find the thick, indexed *Programme des Festivals* (free at tourist offices) an indispensable guide to seasonal music and dance series.

Cité de la Musique, La Villette, 221 av. Jean Jaurès, 19ème (☎01 44 84 45 00; www.cite-musique.fr). ⓂPorte de Pantin. Modern venue hosts everything from lute concerts to American gospel. Shows 8pm. Tickets generally €10-40. Box office open Tu-Sa noon-6pm, Su 10am-6pm; until 8pm on performance nights. AmEx/MC/V.

Élysée Montmartre, 72 bd. Rochechouart, 18ème (☎01 44 92 45 36; www.elysee-montmartre.com). ⓂAnvers. Rap, reggae, and rock venue. Large dance floor for disco, salsa, and techno nights. Drinks €5-8. Shows €15-40; buy tickets online. AmEx/MC/V.

Opéra de la Bastille, pl. de la Bastille, 12ème (☎08 92 89 90 90; www.operadeparis.fr). ⓂBastille. Opera and ballet with a modern spin. Subtitles in French. Rush tickets 15min. before show for students under 25 and seniors. €7-196. AmEx/MC/V.

Opéra Comique, 5 rue Favart, 2ème (☎01 42 44 45 46 or 08 25 01 01 23; www.opera-comique.com). ⓂRichelieu-Drouot. Operas on a lighter scale. €6-95. MC/V.

Opéra Garnier, pl. de l'Opéra, 9ème (☎08 92 89 90 90; www.operadeparis.fr). ⓂOpéra. Mostly ballet, chamber music, and symphonies. Tickets usually available 2 weeks ahead. Operas €7-160; ballets €6-80. Box office open M-Sa 10:30am-6:30pm. AmEx/MC/V.

Orchestre de Paris, 252 rue du Faubourg St-Honoré, 8ème (☎01 42 56 13 13; www.orchestredeparis.com). ⓂTernes. 119 permanent musicians. Season runs from mid-Sept. to mid-June. Shows 8pm. €10-130. Box office open M-Sa 11am-7pm. MC/V.

THEATER

Fortunately for the non-fluent, much of Parisian theater is highly accessible, thanks in part to its dependence on the classics and in part to its love of a grand spectacle (read: physical humor). Unless you're banking on last-minute rush tickets, make reservations 2 weeks in advance.

▨ **La Comédie Française,** pl. Collette, 1er (☎08 25 10 16 80 or 44 58 14 00; www.comedie-francaise.fr). ⓂPalais Royal. Founded by Molière; the granddaddy of all French theaters. You don't need to speak French to understand most of the jokes. Tickets €11-35. Box office open daily 11am-6pm and 1hr. before shows.

Bouffes du Nord, 37 bis bd. de la Chapelle, 10ème (☎01 46 07 34 50; www.bouffes-dunord.com). ⓂLa Chapelle. Experimental theater produces cutting-edge performances and concerts. Occasional productions in English. Open Sept.-June. Concerts €26, under 26 and over 60 €11. Plays €10-26/10-20. Box office open M-Sa 11am-6pm.

Comédie Italienne, 17 rue de la Gaîté, 14ème (☎01 43 21 22 22; www.comedie-italienne.fr). ⓂEdgar Quinet. French-language adaptations of classic and contemporary Italian comedies. Most shows Tu-Sa 8:30pm, Su 3:30pm. Tickets Tu-Th €15, F-Su and Christmas €21. Box office open M-Sa noon-7:30pm, Su noon-3pm. Cash only.

🔊 NIGHTLIFE

Bars in Paris are either chic nighttime cafes bursting with people-watching potential, house-party-esque joints that are all about rock music and teenage angst, or laid-back neighborhood spots that often double as Anglo havens. In the 5ème and 6ème, bars draw French and foreign students, while the Bastille and Marais teem with Paris's young and hip, queer and straight. The Châtelet-Les Halles area draws a slightly older set, while the outer arrondissements cater to locals in tobacco-stained bungalows and yuppie drinking holes. Paris also harbors a ton of quality **jazz bars,** the best of which are listed in this chapter. **Clubbing** in Paris is less about hip DJs and cutting-edge beats than it is about dressing up, getting in, and being seen. Drinks are expensive, and Parisians drink little beyond the first round (included in most cover charges). Many clubs accept reservations, which means that on busy nights there is no available seating. It is advisable to dress well and be confident—but not aggressive—about getting in. One of Europe's most queer-friendly cities, Paris boasts a plethora of GLBT nightlife hot spots, both calm and cruisy. The **Marais** is the center of GLBT life in Paris. **Les Mots à la Bouche,** 6 rue Ste-Croix de la Brettonnerie, 4ème (☎01 42 78 88 30; www.motsbouche.com), Paris's largest queer bookstore, serves as an unofficial information center for GLBT life.

CHÂTELET-LES HALLES

1ER ARRONDISSEMENT

▨ **Le 18 Club,** 18 rue Beaujolais (☎01 42 97 52 13; www.club18.fr). ⓂPyramides. The oldest gay club in Paris is still going strong. Mostly male crowd dances to lighthearted pop music. Intimate bar and dance floor. Mixed drinks €6-9. Cover €10; includes 1 drink. Open W and F-Sa midnight-6am.

▨ **Banana Café,** 13 rue de la Ferronerie (☎01 42 33 35 31; www.bananacafeparis.com). ⓂChâtelet. *Très branché* (way cool). 1er's most popular GLBT bar. Scantily clad men pole dance amid tropical decor. Legendary theme nights. "Go-Go Boys" Th-Sa midnight-dawn. Beer €5.50. Mixed drinks €8. Cover F-Sa €10; includes 1 drink. Happy hour 6-9pm; 2 for 1 drinks. Open daily 5:30pm-6am. AmEx/MC/V.

▨ **Au Duc des Lombards,** 42 rue des Lombards (☎01 42 33 22 88; www.ducdeslombards.com). ⓂChâtelet. Murals of Ellington and Coltrane cover the exterior of this premier jazz joint. Still the best in French jazz. 3 sets each night. Beer €3.50-5. Mixed drinks €8; prices vary depending on show. Music 10pm-1:30am. Cover €19-25, students €12 if you call in advance, couples €30 in advance. Open M-Sa 5pm-2am. MC/V.

Le Baiser Salé, 58 rue des Lombards (☎01 42 33 37 71; www.lebaisersale.com). ⓂChâtelet. Cuban, African, and Antillean music featured together with modern jazz and funk in a welcoming, mellow space. African music festival in July. Beer €6.50-11.50.

Mixed drinks €9.50; prices vary depending on show. Jazz concerts start at 10pm, music until 2:30am (typically 3 sets). Free jam sessions M at 10pm with 1-drink min. Cover around €20. Happy hour 5:30-8pm. Open daily 5pm-6am. AmEx/MC/V.

Café Oz, 18 rue St-Denis (☎01 40 39 00 18; www.cafe-oz.com). ⓜChâtelet. Also at 1 rue de Bruxelles (☎01 40 16 11 16) and 8 bd. Montmartre (☎01 47 70 18 52), both 9ème. Huge, friendly Australian bar with long wood tables and obliging bartenders. Popular with study-abroaders. Pints €7. Mixed drinks €8. Cover Sa €10; includes 1 drink and coat check. Open M-Th and Su 5pm-3am, F 5pm-6am, Sa 1pm-6am. MC/V.

2ÈME ARRONDISSEMENT

Le Champmeslé, 4 rue Chabanais (☎01 42 96 85 20; www.lachampmesle.com). ⓜPyramides. Paris's oldest and most famous lesbian bar. Both men and women enjoy the popular cabaret shows (Sa 10pm) and monthly art exhibits. Beer €5 before 10pm, €7 after. Mixed drinks €8/10. Open M-Sa 3pm-sunrise.

THE MARAIS

3ÈME ARRONDISSEMENT

■ **Andy Wahloo,** 69 rue des Gravilliers (☎01 42 71 20 38). ⓜArts et Métiers. Moroccan-themed lounge bar. Paint-bucket seats. Patrons smoke hookah to the beat of DJs spinning tunes on the terrace. Beer €5-6. Mixed drinks €9-10. Happy hour 5-8pm; beer and mixed drinks €5. Open M-Sa 5pm-2am, Su 11am-5pm. AmEx/MC/V.

■ **L'Estaminet,** 39 rue de Bretagne (☎01 42 72 34 85), inside the Marché des Enfants Rouges. ⓜTemple. Tiny, clean-scrubbed, and airy wine bar is a place for relaxation. Delightful selection of inexpensive wines by the glass (€3-3.50) or bottle (€5-25). Traipse through the market and pick up something to munch on. MC/V.

Le Connétable, 55 rue des Archives (☎01 42 77 41 40). ⓜArts et Métiers. 3-level bar-restaurant-theater in a former *hôtel particulier*. Nightly concerts 8:30, 10pm; come early. Beer and wine €4-7. Mixed drinks €8. Dinner *menu* €21. Open M-F noon-3pm and 7pm-4am, Sa-Su 7pm-4am. Food served noon-3pm and 7-11pm. AmEx/MC/V.

Le Dépôt, 10 rue aux Ours (☎01 44 54 96 96; www.ledepot.com). ⓜÉtienne-Marcel. The queen of Paris's gay clubs. Find a boy toy in the "cruising" area while watching porn on mounted TVs. Women not welcome (exceptions include Pride Week). Cover M-Th €8.50, Su before 11pm and F €10, Sa €12; includes 1 drink. Open daily 2pm-8am. V.

4ÈME ARRONDISSEMENT

■ **Le Yono,** 37 rue Vieille du Temple (☎01 42 74 31 65). ⓜSt-Paul or Hôtel de Ville. Channels Casablanca with its stone interior, hidden balcony, slowly spinning ceiling fan, and shadow-casting palm leaves. Mellow upstairs with dancing below. Happy hour 6-8pm; mixed drinks €8.50, beer €4. Open daily 6pm-2am. MC/V.

■ **Amnésia Café,** 42 rue Vieille du Temple (☎01 42 72 16 94). ⓜSt-Paul or Hôtel de Ville. Largely queer crowd lounges on plush sofas in a classy wood-paneled interior. 1st fl. cafe, 2nd fl. lounge, and basement club with music from 9pm. Espresso €2. Kir €4. Mixed drinks €7.50-10. Open daily 11am-2am. V.

■ **Raidd Bar,** 23 rue du Temple. ⓜHotel de Ville. The Marais's most hip and happening GLBT club. Disco globes and sexy topless bartenders. After 11pm, performers strip down in glass shower cubicles. Mixed drinks €8. Disco night Tu; 80s and house W; DJ VIP Th; club F-Sa; 90s Su. Happy hour 5-9pm; drink size doubles. The club enforces a strict door policy; women must be accompanied (read: out-numbered) by a few good-looking (read: drop dead gorgeous) men. Open daily 5pm-5am. V.

La Belle Hortense, 31 rue Vieille du Temple (☎01 48 04 71 60; www.cafeine.com). ⓂHôtel de Ville. Literary bar/gallery/cafe draws intellectuals. Walls of books and mellow music. Hosts exhibits, readings, lectures, signings, and discussions. Free Wi-Fi. Wine from €4 per glass, €8 per bottle. Open daily 5pm-2am. MC/V.

Open Café, 17 rue des Archives (☎01 42 72 26 18). ⓂHôtel de Ville. Popular GLBT-friendly bar. Draws a crowd of loyal customers. Always crowded. Terrace seating and sleek metal decor. Most patrons are men, but women are welcome. Beer €3.50-6.50. Mixed drinks €7.50. Happy hour 6-10pm; ½-price beer only. Open M-Th and Su 11am-2am, F-Sa 11am-4am. MC/V.

LATIN QUARTER AND SAINT-GERMAIN

5ÈME ARRONDISSEMENT

▨ **L'Académie de la Bière,** 88 bis bd. de Port Royal (☎01 43 54 66 65; www.academie-biere.com). ⓂVavin. 12 kinds of beer on tap and over 300 more in bottles. Beer €6-9. Happy hour 3:30-7:30pm. Open M-Th and Su 10am-2am, F-Sa 10am-3am. MC/V.

▨ **Le Caveau des Oubliettes,** 52 rue Galande (☎01 46 34 23 09). ⓂSt-Michel. Mellow, funky vibe. Upstairs bar (La Guillotine) has sod carpeting and a real guillotine. Downstairs cellar is a jazz club. Cellar used to be a "cave of the forgotten," where criminals were locked up. Drinks €5-9. Free *soirée boeuf* (jam session) M-Th and Su 10pm-1:30am: Pop rock M, swing Tu, groove W, funk Th, blues Su; free concerts F-Sa. Happy hour daily 5-9pm. Open daily 5pm-2am, later on weekends.

Le Piano Vache, 8 rue Laplace (☎01 46 33 75 03; www.lepianovache.com). ⓂCardinal Lemoine or Maubert-Mutualité. Dim, poster-plastered bar with cow paraphernalia from its butcher-shop days. Often shown in music videos. Crowd ranges from alternative-trendy students to 30-something intellectuals to hotties like ▨ **Johnny Depp.** Beer €3.50, before 9pm €2.50. Live Jazz concerts M. Theme nights 9pm-2am. Open M-F noon-2am, Sa-Su 9pm-2am.

Le Petit Journal St-Michel, 71 bd. St-Michel (☎01 43 26 28 59; www.petitjournalsaintmichel.com). ⓂCluny-La Sorbonne or RER: Luxembourg. Another early jazz stronghold with a mostly middle-aged clientele. Performers include New Orleans and big band acts. Drinks €7-9. Concerts 9:15pm. Obligatory 1st drink €17-20, students €11-15; includes 1 drink. Open Sept.-July M-Sa 9pm-1:15am. MC/V.

NO WORK, ALL PLAY

PANIC AT THE DISCO

Throughout France, clubbers are flailing their arms and contorting their bodies to fast-paced beats under flashing strobe lights. Don't bother calling *le médecin;* that skinny boy isn't having a seizure, he's having a good time. Meet Tecktonik, the dance craze that has been spreading from its origin in the Parisian club Metropolis to the rest of France and neighboring European countries. Born in 2000, the dance has become so hugely popular that teachers are complaining that their students will no longer sit still in class.

While Tecktonik is primarily a blend of hip-hop and techno moves, it borrows steps from other genres as well—the only real rule seems to be to move quickly, passionately, and all over the place. Tecktonik largely owes its popularity to YouTube and other video-sharing sites that allow young people to watch and perfect the new moves at home before heading out to test them in the club.

Tecktonik's rapid diffusion has resulted in major capitalization. Tecktonik is now a copyrighted brand, a haircut, and a fashion trend. Travelers looking to get in on the action should consider donning the signature half-mohawk and half-mullet, slipping into a pair of cigarette jeans, and prepping with a few how-to videos.

Le Caveau de la Huchette, 5 rue de la Huchette (☎01 43 26 65 05; www.caveaudela-huchette.fr). ⓂSt-Michel. Once a meeting place for secret societies; downstairs you can still see the execution chambers of Danton and Robespierre's victims. Now very popular, if touristy. Wine €6. Beer €6-7. Mixed drinks €10. Bebop dance lessons Sept.-June. Live music 10pm-2am. Cover €13, students €9; free after 2am. Open M-W and Su 9:30pm-2:30am, Th-Sa 9:30pm-sunrise. AmEx/MC/V.

6ÈME ARRONDISSEMENT

▨ **Le 10 Bar,** 10 rue de l'Odéon (☎01 43 26 66 83). ⓂOdéon. A classic student hang-out where Parisian youth indulge in (somewhat stereotypical) philosophical discussion. Either that or they're getting drunk and making inside jokes. Jukebox plays everything from Édith Piaf to Aretha Franklin. Famous sangria €3.50. Open daily 6pm-2am. MC/V.

INVALIDES (7ÈME)

▨ **Le Club des Poètes,** 30 rue de Bourgogne (☎01 47 05 06 03; www.poesie.net). ⓂVarenne. Old-style and timbered. Restaurant by day, poetry club at 9-10pm each night. A troupe of readers and comedians bewitches the audience with poetry from Villon, Baudelaire, Rimbaud, and others. If you arrive after 10pm, wait to enter until you hear clapping or a break in the performance. Wine €4-8. Lunch *menu* €15. Open Sept.-July Tu-Sa noon-3pm and 8pm-1am. Kitchen open until 10pm. MC/V.

CHAMPS-ÉLYSÉES (8ÈME)

▨ **buddha-bar,** 8 rue Boissy d'Anglas (☎01 53 05 90 00; www.buddha-bar.com). ⓂMadeleine or Concorde. Too cool for capital letters. Perhaps the most glamorous and exclusive drinking hole in the city; Madonna drops by when she's in town. 2 dim, candlelit levels. 3-story Buddha. Creative mixed drinks €16-17. Beer €8-9. Sake €8. Wine €8-11. Open M-F noon-3pm and 6pm-2am, Sa-Su 6pm-2am. AmEx/MC/V.

Le Queen, 102 av. des Champs-Élysées (☎01 53 89 08 90; www.queen.fr). ⓂGeorge V. A renowned Parisian institution where drag queens, superstars, tourists, and go-go boys get down to the rhythms of a 10,000-gigawatt sound system. Women have better luck with bouncer if accompanied by at least 1 male. All drinks €10. Disco M; Ladies' Night W; house Th-Sa; 80s Su. Cover M and F-Sa €20, Tu-Th and Su €15; includes 1 drink. Bring ID and come in small groups. Open daily midnight-sunrise. AmEx/MC/V.

CANAL SAINT-MARTIN AND SURROUNDS (10ÈME)

LET'S NOT GO. While it's relatively safe during the day, the 10ème becomes a haven of pickpocketing and prostitution after sundown, so *Let's Go* recommends avoiding the area if at all possible.

New Morning, 7-9 rue des Petites Écuries (☎01 45 23 51 41; www.newmorning.com). ⓂChâteau d'Eau. The entrance—a small metal door—is easy to miss; look closely. Dark, smoky, and crowded. 400-seat former printing plant now plays host to some of the biggest American headliners. All the greatest names in jazz have played here—from Chet Baker to Stan Getz and Miles Davis. Continues to attracts big names. Buy tickets from the box office, any branch of FNAC, or the Virgin Megastore. Drinks €6-10. Most concerts 9pm. Tickets €16-20. Open Sept.-July daily from 8pm. MC/V.

BASTILLE

11ÈME ARRONDISSEMENT

▨ **Le Pop In,** 105 rue Amelot (☎01 48 05 56 11). ⓂSt-Sébastien Froissart. Neighborhood bar and rock club with the air of a 90s house party. Favorite hangout of young, carefully bedraggled cool kids. Beer €3-5.50, cheaper before 9pm. Pop, rock, folk, and indie folk concerts Tu, W, and Su at 9pm in the tiny basement. Open Tu-Su 6:30pm-1:30am.

▨ **Wax,** 15 rue Daval (☎01 40 21 16 18). ⓂBastille. Always free and fun. In a concrete bunker with retro orange, red, yellow, and white couches. Beer €5-7. Mixed drinks €10. Disco/funk W and Su; R&B Th; house Sa-Su. Open daily 9pm-sunrise. MC/V over €15.

▨ **Le Bar Sans Nom,** 49 rue de Lappe (☎01 48 05 59 36). ⓂBastille. Laid-back oasis. Older crowd. Dim, seductive lounge with huge bohemian wall hangings. Famous for creative mixed drinks (€9-10), posted on oversized wood menus; don't leave Paris without trying the mojito. Beer €5-6.50. Shots €6.50. Free tarot-card reading Tu 7-9pm; come early. Open Tu-Th 6pm-2am, F-Sa 6pm-4am. MC/V over €12.

Favela Chic, 18 rue du Faubourg du Temple (☎01 40 21 38 14; www.favelachic.com). ⓂRépublique. Franco-Brazilian joint wildly popular with locals. Eclectic decor and colorful clients. Long line snaking out the door on weekends. Mixed drinks €9. Cover F-Sa €10; includes 1 drink. Open Tu-Th 7:30pm-2am, F-Sa 7:30pm-4am. MC/V.

Jacques Mélac, 42 rue Léon Frot (☎01 43 70 59 27; www.melac.fr). ⓂCharonne. Cozy, family-owned wine bar and bistro with strong local following since 1938. 35 wines, at least 2 of which are made in Mélac's vineyards. Mid-Sept., Mélac lets children harvest, tread upon, and extract wine from grapes growing in the bar's storefront. Wine €3 per glass, bottles €15-38. Salads €8-12. Cheese and *charcuterie* €13-15. Open Sept.-July Tu-Sa 9am-3:30pm and 8-10:30pm. MC/V.

Nouveau Casino, 109 rue Oberkampf (☎01 43 57 57 40; www.nouveaucasino.net). ⓂParmentier or Ménilmontant. From electropop to hip hop to rock. Occasional art exhibits and video shows. Cover €5-10. Open from midnight-sunrise during events.

12ÈME ARRONDISSEMENT

▨ **Barrio Latino,** 46-48 rue du Faubourg St-Antoine (☎01 55 78 84 75; www.buddhabar.com). ⓂBastille. Latin, less famous counterpart of buddha-bar (opposite page). 4 floors of lounge chairs and low tables. Giant dance floor heats up around 11pm. Shove the flip-flops in the closet; the bouncers are picky about footwear. Mixed drinks €10-15. Su brunch is an institution among stylish locals (noon-4pm; €29); includes free salsa lesson (2:30pm). DJ 10pm. Cover €20. Open daily noon-2am. AmEx/MC/V.

China Club, 50 rue de Charenton (☎01 43 46 08 09; www.chinaclub.cc). ⓂLedru-Rollin or Bastille. 2 levels of sophisticated socializing, 1 level of high-class clubbing. Upstairs restaurant/piano bar/smoke lounge atmosphere, with high ceilings, marble floors, and lounge chairs; downstairs, Club Chin Chin features red velvet and dimmed lights. Mixed drinks €10-15. 3-course dinner *menu* €40-45. Restaurant open daily 8pm-2am. Club open Th-Sa 10pm-5am. Dinner reservations recommended. AmEx/MC/V.

Le Baron Rouge, 1 rue Théophile-Roussel (☎01 43 43 14 32). ⓂLedru-Rollin. Laidback, cool crowd mingles around enormous wine barrels that serve as tables. Boisterous bartender will suggest wines (a steal at €1-3 a glass). *Assiettes* €5-14. Open Tu-Th 10am-3pm and 5-10pm, Sa 10am-2pm, Su 10am-4pm. MC/V.

BUTTE-AUX-CAILLES AND CHINATOWN (13ÈME)

▨ **La Dame Canton,** Porte de la Gare (☎01 53 61 08 49 or 01 44 06 96 45; www.damedecanton.com). Starting in the early afternoon, couples and groups populate the picnic

Parisian Hipsters Need a Home

Paris has played host to youth subcultures for decades. After WWII, garishly dressed Zazous frequented the burgeoning nightclub scene, swinging to jazz, bebop, and ragtime music. But big

"The new millennium has witnessed Paris's failure... to foster youth culture."

bands and jukeboxes eventually gave way to turntables in 1953 when Régine Zylberberg—the owner of Le Whisky à Gogo—established the modern-day standard for nightclubs and *discothèques* with loud, seamless music. Rock soon replaced jazz as the anthem of youth, and *Zazous* yielded to the latest trends. *Branchés*—a subculture marked by fashionable attire and a similar disregard of the *petit bourgeois* values of hard work and financial advancement—filled the void.

Youth culture made waves in Paris in May of 1968 when a series of student strikes swept the nation in a challenge to conservative morality. The themes of sexual liberation and youth empowerment emphasized by these riots translated to the club scene. Clubbing culture blossomed at the onset of the 70s as crazy parties mixed unconventional aspects of music; eclectic pop icons Mick Jagger, Santana, Kraftwerk, and the New York Dolls provided the soundtracks and inspired fashions of such affairs.

The 80s ushered in the mythic era of Le Palace—a theater turned nightclub that became a haunt of the *branché* scene. Les Bains Douches—yet another club that catered to the subculture—opened just a few months later. Paris had become a hipster playground. Meanwhile, Jean Paul Gautier indulged Parisian youth with clothing collections inspired by pop culture and street fashion; the *branché* lifestyle became more commercialized as businesses realized the potential of the young market.

The following decade saw the hipster crowd transform from disdainful nihilists to ambitious imitators. *Branché* trends flooded popular culture, and the message of the lifestyle gave way to its fashions. Daft Punk, Cassius, and Bob Sinclar comprised the playlist at cultivated hipster parties while simultaneously saturated the airwaves of mainstream radio. *Branché* was no longer a respected youth crowd—in fact, the term came to denote a mocking, pejorative attitude about the fads associated with hipsters. With the dissolution of such an established, fashion-forward subculture that thrived on underground music, the avant-garde slowly ceased to be the driving force behind Parisian culture.

The new millennium has witnessed Paris's failure to absorb minimal techno and therefore a breakdown of Paris's ability to foster youth culture. Few musical artists have emerged from the city of late, and clubs that dare play innovative dance music struggle financially. In fact, on June 14, 2007, Le Pulp—a lesbian club and staple hipster hangout—closed permanently. A year later, Le ParisParis—another nightlife pillar that had welcomed hipsters from all horizons—closed as well. As budget airlines and high-speed trains make London and Berlin increasingly accessible, the fate of Parisian nightlife is depressingly unsure.

An underground dance music genre that mixes disco, techno, punk rock, and glitch music is a brief ray of hope for a hipster presence in Paris. But as representative artists like Justice gain a larger following in the UK rather than in their mother country, the neo-dandy, avant-garde youth presence for which Paris is known seems to be waning.

Samuel Ronsin earned a Bachelor of Science in mathematics and a master's in theoretical economics at the École Normale Supérieure. After an exchange program at Harvard, his other interests—including fine art and electronic music—brought him to Berlin to pursue writing and video projects.

tables and beach chairs on the terrace. Also a restaurant; *menu* starts at €24. Pirate ship behind the bar hosts concerts at 8pm and "DJ parties" on weekends. Tickets available at FNAC. Cover €5. Open Tu-Th 7pm-2am, F-Sa 7pm-5am. MC/V.

 Batofar (☎01 53 60 17 30; www.batofar.fr), facing 11 quai François-Mauriac. ⓜQuai de la Gare or Bibliothèque Nationale de France. This 45m long, 520-ton barge/bar/club has made it big with a variety of music—mainly electronic, hip hop, reggae, and house. Attracts a friendly crowd. Live artists daily. Cover €8-15; usually includes 1 drink. Open M-Th 11pm-6am, F-Sa later; hours change for special film and DJ events. MC/V.

La Folle en Tête, 33 rue de la Butte-aux-Cailles (☎01 45 80 65 99). ⓜPlace d'Italie. Artsy *axis mundi* of the 13ème. Exotic instruments line the walls of this beaten-up hole in the wall. Beer €3. Ti'Punch €6. Happy hour 6-8pm; mixed drinks €5, kir €3. Open M-Sa 6pm-2am, Su 5pm-midnight. MC/V over €15.

PASSY AND AUTEUIL (16ÈME)

Duplex, 2 bis av. Foch (☎01 45 00 45 00; www.leduplex.com). ⓜCharles de Gaulle-Étoile. Weekends bring businessmen and their arm candy. From techno to R&B to hip hop to house. Contains the expensive Le Living restaurant (open Tu-Sa 8:30-11:30pm; DJ Sa 9pm-midnight). All drinks Tu-W and Su €10, Th €9, F-Sa €11. Themed nights. Cover Tu-Th and Su €15, F-Sa €20; includes 1 drink. Sa women free before midnight. Open Aug. 26-July 29. Tu-Su 11pm-sunrise. MC/V.

BATIGNOLLES (17ÈME)

 L'Endroit, 67 pl. du Docteur Félix Lobligeois (☎01 42 29 50 00). ⓜRome. Hip, young crowd haunts this snazzy diner-esque bar in an idyllic spot on a tree-lined *place*. The alcohol is kept on a giant rotating shelf. Wine €4-5. Beer €3-5. Mixed drinks €8-10. Open daily 10am-2am, often later F-Sa. MC/V.

MONTMARTRE (18ÈME)

> **!** **LET'S NOT GO.** Tourists traveling alone, especially women, should avoid ⓜPigalle, Anvers, and Barbès-Rochechouart at night.

La Fourmi, 74 rue des Martyrs (☎01 42 64 70 35). ⓜPigalle. Artsy atmosphere with a zinc bar and industrial-trendy decor, complete with burnt orange walls, a mosaic-tiled floor, and a chandelier made of green chianti bottles. A hyper-hip, energetic, and scrappy young crowd takes refuge here. Hosts rotating art exhibits. Beer €3-7. Wine €5-7. Mixed drinks €7-9. Open M-Th 8am-2am, F-Sa 8am-3:30am, Su 10am-1:30am. MC/V.

Folies Pigalle, 11 pl. Pigalle (☎01 48 78 55 25; www.folies-pigalle.com). ⓜPigalle. The largest, wildest club in the Pigalle *quartier*. Not for the faint of heart. A former strip joint popular with both gay and straight clubbers. Perhaps the most trans-friendly club in the city. Mostly house and techno. Soirées Transsexuelles Th; all types welcome. Cover €20; includes 1 drink. Open M-Th and Su midnight-8am, F-Sa midnight-11am. AmEx/MC/V.

BUTTES CHAUMONT (19ÈME)

Café Chéri(e), 44 bd. de la Villette (☎01 42 02 02 05). ⓜBelleville. Cheap drinks and outdoor seating. Indie atmosphere. Beer from €5; comes with free chips. Nightly DJ sets (pop and electronic) from 7pm. Open daily 8am-2am. MC/V.

BELLEVILLE AND PÈRE LACHAISE (20ÈME)

▓ **Café Flèche d'Or,** 102 bis rue Bagnolet (☎01 44 64 01 02; www.flechedor.fr). Ⓜ Porte de Bagnolet. Live concert venue. Cool, intense, and a little rough around the edges. Music ranges from reggae to hip hop to electropop to Celtic rock. Art videos, dance classes, and crazy theater on the tracks below the terrace. Also a restaurant; see **Food,** p. 137. Beer €4-6. Mixed drinks €8-20. DJ set Th-Sa midnight-6am. Free entry for concerts 8pm-2am. Open W-Sa 10am-3am, Th-Sa 10am-6am. MC/V.

✻ FESTIVALS

For information on festivals, check out www.paris-touristoffice.com. *Let's Go* lists its favorite *fêtes* below. This isn't even close to all of them—just the ones that promise to keep you fat, happy, drunk, or all three. Check listings in *Time Out* and *Pariscope* (at any newsstand) for updates and details on all events.

Fête de la Musique, June 21 (☎01 40 03 94 70). Also called "Faîtes de la Musique" ("Make Music"). Summer solstice celebration gives everyone the chance to make as much racket as possible, as Paris's usual noise laws don't apply for the duration of the festival. The Métro runs all night to transport tired revelers home.

Gay Pride, last Sa in June (www.gaypride.fr). For info, call the **Centre Gai et Lesbien** (☎01 43 57 21 47), **Le Duplex** (☎01 42 72 80 86), or **Les Mots à la Bouche** (☎01 42 78 88 30; www.motsbouche.com). Check posters in the Marais bars and cafes.

▓ **Fête du Cinéma,** late June (www.feteducinema.com). Started in 1984, this festival brings cheaper movies to all Parisians. Purchase 1 ticket at regular movie price (€6-8) and receive a passport for unlimited showings (during the 3-day festival) of participating films for €2 each. Arrive early for popular favorites and expect long lines. Full listings of movies and events can be found online, at theaters, or in Métro advertisements.

▓ **Bastille Day (Fête Nationale),** July 14. France's independence day. Festivities begin the night before, with traditional street dances at the tip of Île St-Louis. Free **Bals des Pompiers** (Firemen's Balls) take place inside every Parisian fire station the night of July 13 and/or 14 9pm-4am, with DJs, bands, and cheap alcohol (€5). For info, contact the **Sapeurs Pompiers,** 1 pl. Jules Renard, 17ème (☎01 47 54 68 22). Dancing and concert at pl. de la Bastille. Be careful: young children sometimes throw fireworks into the crowd. July 14 begins with the army parading down the Champs-Élysées at 10:30am (be prepared to get in place by 8 or 9am) and ends with fireworks at 10:30-11pm. For the parade and fireworks, Métro stations along the Champs and at the Trocadéro close. Paris becomes a nightmarish combat zone with firecrackers underfoot; avoid the Métro and deserted areas if possible. Vive la France!

Jazz à la Villette, early Sept. (☎01 40 03 75 75 or 44 84 44 84; www.villette.com). Ⓜ Porte de Pantin. Parc de la Villette celebrates jazz from big bands to new international talents. Seminars, films, and sculptural exhibits. Performers have included Herbie Hancock, Ravi Coltrane, Taj Mahal, and BB King. Marching bands parade every day, and an enormous picnic ends the festival. Concerts €18, under 26 €15.

▶ DAYTRIPS FROM PARIS

VERSAILLES

By sheer force of ego, the Sun King converted a hunting lodge into the world's most famous palace, Versailles (vehr-SYE). The sprawling château and gardens testify to Louis XIV's absolute power, their luxury allowing him to entertain, govern, and relax. A century later, Louis XVI and Marie Antoinette's escalated extravagance led to lolling—not lounging—heads (see **Life and Times,** p. 61).

 TRANSPORTATION AND PRACTICAL INFORMATION

Public Transportation: RER trains beginning with "V" run from Ⓜ**Invalides** or any stop on RER **Line C5** to the Versailles Rive Gauche station (30-40min., every 15min., round-trip €5.60). Buy your RER ticket before going through the turnstile to the platform; when purchasing from a machine, look for the Île-de-France ticket option. While a Métro ticket will get you through these turnstiles, it will not get you through RER turnstiles at Versailles and could ultimately result in a significant fine. From RER: Versailles, turn right down av. du Général de Gaulle, walk 200m, and turn left at the big intersection on av. de Paris; the entrance to the château is straight ahead.

Tourist Office: 2 bis av. de Paris (☎01 39 24 88 88; www.versailles-tourisme.com), on the left before the château courtyard. Info on local accommodations, events, restaurants, and sightseeing buses. Also sells tickets for historical guided **tours** of the town. Open Apr.-Sept. Tu-Su 9am-6pm; Oct.-Mar. M 11am-5pm, Tu-Su 9am-6pm.

👁 **SIGHTS**

PALACE OF VERSAILLES

☎01 30 83 78 89; www.chateauversailles.fr. Château open Tu-Su Apr.-Oct. 9am-6:30pm; Nov.-Mar. 9am-5:30pm. Last entry 30min. before close. Various other passes and guided tours also available. For group discounts and reservations, call ☎08 10 81 16 14. Admission to palace and self-guided tour through entrance A €8, after 3:30pm €6, under 18 free.

> **TIP**
>
> **LET THEM WAIT IN LINE.** Avoid the heavy crowds—especially in July and August—by arriving early. Figuring out how to get into the château is the hardest part, as there are half a dozen entrances. Most visitors enter at Entrance A, on the right-hand side in the north wing, or Entrance C, in the archway to the left. Both locations rent audio tours for €6-10. From Entrance D, at the left-hand corner as you approach the palace, you can choose between 17 different English- or French-language guided tours, each exploring a different area or theme. After the tour, you can explore the rest of Versailles on your own, without waiting in the general admission line.

CHÂTEAU. Start your visit in the **Musée de l'Histoire de France,** created in 1837 by Louis-Philippe to celebrate his country's glory. Along its textured walls hang portraits of men and women who shaped French history. The 21 rooms, arranged in chronological order, lay out a historical context for the château, helpful for those not taking a guided tour.

Up the main staircase to the right, the king heard mass in the dual-level **royal chapel.** To the left of the staircase, a series of gilded drawing rooms in the **State Apartments** are dedicated to Roman gods like Hercules, Mars, and the ever-present Apollo—unsurprisingly, the Sun King identified with the sun god. The ornate **Salon d'Apollo** was Louis XIV's throne room. French citizens demonstrated great respect for the king's prestige, bowing or curtsying when passing the throne, even when it was empty. The **War and Peace Drawing Rooms** frame the recently renovated **Hall of Mirrors,** originally a terrace until Mansart added a series of mirrored panels and windows to double the light in the room and reflect the gardens outside. These mirrors were the largest that 17th-century technology could produce.

YOU THINK YOU KNOW, BUT YOU HAVE NO IDEA. The Versailles court was the nucleus of noble life, where France's aristocrats vied for the king's favor, a minutely choreographed public spectacle—but things there were less luxurious than one might imagine. Courtiers wore rented swords and urinated behind statues in the parlors, wine froze in the drafty dining rooms, and dressmakers invented the color puce (literally, "flea") to camouflage the bugs crawling on the noblewomen. The king also lacked the necessary funds to keep all his fountains flowing at once; instead he had his gardeners turn the water on and off to correspond to his guest's pre-chosen walking path, giving the illusion that all the fountains functioned continuously.

The **Queen's Bedchamber,** where royal births were public events in order to prove the legitimacy of the heirs, appears almost identically to how the queen last left it on October 6, 1789. A version of *Le Sacre de Napoléon* by David, which depicts Napoleon's self-coronation, dominates the **Salle du Sacré** (also known as the **Coronation Room**). The **Hall of Battles,** installed by Louis-Philippe, is a monument to 14 centuries of France's military.

GARDENS. The Versailles gardens are a spectacular example of obsessive landscaping with neatly trimmed rectangular hedges lining the geometric *bosquets* (groves). The best way to visit the park is during the spectacular summer festival, ⊠**Les Grandes Eaux Musicales.** Weekends and holidays from April to September, almost all the fountains are turned on at the same time, and chamber music groups perform among the groves.

Any self-guided tour of the gardens must begin, as the Sun King commanded, on the **terrace.** To the left of the terrace, the **Parterre Sud** graces the area in front of Mansart's **Orangerie,** once home to 2000 orange trees; the temperature inside still never drops below 6°C (43°F). In the center of the terrace lie the fountains of the **Parterre d'Eau.** Past the **Bassin de Latone** and to the left is one of the gardens' undisputed gems: the fragrant, flower-lined sanctuary of the **Jardin du Roi,** accessible only from the easternmost side facing the **Bassin du Miroir.** Near the grove's south gate lies the magnificent **Bassin de Bacchus,** one of four seasonal fountains depicting the Roman god of wine crowned in vine branches reclining on a bunch of grapes. Behind it, the **Bosquet de la Salle de Bal** features a semicircle of cascading waterfalls and torch holders enabling royals to host late-night balls; a large clearing in the middle provided ample space for dancing and merrymaking. Working your way north toward the center of the garden brings you to the exquisite **Bosquet de la Colonnade,** where the king used to take light meals amid 32 violet and blue marble columns, sculptures, and white marble basins. The north gate to the **Colonnade** exits onto the 330m long **Tapis Vert** (Green Carpet), the central mall linking the château to the garden's conspicuously central fountain, the **Bassin d'Apollon.**

On the garden's north side, you'll find the incredible **Bosquet de l'Encelade.** When the fountain is on, a 25m high jet bursts from Titan's enormous mouth, which is plated with shimmering gold and half buried under rocks. The **Bassin de Flore** and the **Bassin de Cérès** show their ladies reclining in their natural habitats—a bed of flowers and wheat sheaves, respectively. The **Parterre Nord** overlooks some of the garden's most spectacular fountains. The **Allée d'Eau,** a fountain-lined walkway, provides the best view of the **Bassin des Nymphes de Diane.** The path slopes toward the sculpted **Bassin du Dragon,** where a beast slain by Apollo spurts water 27m into the air. Next to it, 99 jets of water issue from sea horns encircling Neptune in the **Bassin de Neptune,** the gardens' largest fountain; make your way here at 5:20pm for a truly spectacular fountain

PARIS

finale. *(Gardens open daily Apr.-Oct. 8am-8:30pm; Nov.-Mar. 8am-6pm. Free. Grandes Eaux Musicales Apr.-Sept. Sa-Su and holidays €8, students and under 18 €6, under 6 free.)*

TRIANONS AND MARIE ANTOINETTE'S HAMEAU. Down the wooded path from the château, the **Petit Trianon** was built between 1762 and 1768 for Louis XV and his mistress Mme. de Pompadour. In 1867, Empress Eugénie, one of Marie Antoinette's few admirers, turned the house into a museum devoted to the hapless queen. If you exit the Petit Trianon, turn left, and follow the marked path, you will arrive at the libidinous **Temple of Love,** a domed rotunda with 12 white marble columns and swans. Marie Antoinette held many intimate parties in the small space illuminated by torchlight. The queen was perhaps at her happiest and most ludicrous when spending time at the **hameau,** her own pseudo-peasant "hamlet" down the path from the Temple of Love. Inspired by Jean-Jacques Rousseau's theories on the goodness of nature, the queen fashionably aspired to a so-called "simple" life. She commissioned Richard Mique to build a 12-building compound comprised of a dairy farm, gardener's house, and mill all surrounding a quaint artificial lake. Marie-Antoinette could play at a glorified country life, imagining that the starving Third Estate must not really suffer all that much. **The Queen's Cottage,** at the hamlet's center, includes ornate furniture, marble fireplaces, and walk-in closets where Marie-Antoinette kept her monogrammed linens. The stone and pink-marble **Grand Trianon** was intended as a château-away-from-château for Louis XIV. Reachable only by boat from the Grand Canal, the king could take a breather from court life. Stripped of its furniture during the Revolution, the mini château was later restored and inhabited by Napoleon and his second wife. *(Shuttle trams, www.train-versailles.com, from the palace to the Trianons and the hameau leave from the North Terrace. 50min.; 1-4 per hr; round-trip €6, ages 11-18 and handicapped visitors €4.50, under 11 free. Audio tours for the garden ride €1.20. Alternatively, the walk takes 25min. Both Trianons open daily Apr.-Oct. noon-6:30pm; Nov.-Mar. noon-5:30pm. Last entry 30min. before close. Apr.-Oct. €9, 2hr. before close €5, under 18 free; Nov.-Mar. €5, under 18 free.)*

CHARTRES

Nothing compares to Chartres. It is the thinking of the Middle Ages itself made visible.
—Émile Male

Were it not for a scrap of fabric, the cathedral and town of Chartres might still be a sleepy hamlet.

IN RECENT NEWS

NON! NON! NON!

The French might love their *futbol,* but the country's true national sport is an angrier one: protest. Protesting is a way of life for the country that celebrates the storming of the Bastille and its turbulent political history.

In 2008, thousands of students took to Paris's broad boulevards chanting, "Non! Non! Non!" in protest of government plans to cut back on state-funded university faculty. The downsizing is part of newly elected President Nicolas Sarkozy's broader plan of greater fiscal conservatism. In the past, French students have done something their modern American counterparts only dream of and have actually gone on strike, refusing to attend classes and boycotting university events. Common points of contention include tuition increases, educational methods, and, according to some, just plain boredom.

Travelers should beware of this social unrest, as students aren't the only protesters. Transportation workers have been known to go on strike throughout the country, often causing delays and shutdowns in subways, trains, and buses. While such travel interruptions can be frustrating, be sure to keep your cool and take measures to avoid protests themselves, as violence has been known to erupt. As Marie Antoinette would say, you don't want to be there when they start yelling, "Off with their heads!"

But the cloth the Virgin Mary supposedly wore when she gave birth to Jesus made Chartres a major medieval pilgrimage center. The spectacular cathedral that towers over the city isn't the only reason to visit: the *vieille ville* is also a masterpiece of medieval architecture that almost lets you forget the zooming highways that have encroached upon it. Chartres's tangle of streets might confuse you, but getting lost can only be enjoyable.

TRANSPORTATION AND PRACTICAL INFORMATION

Trains: Frequent trains from **Gare Montparnasse,** Grandes Lignes, on the Nogent-le-Rotrou line (50-75min.; round-trip €25, under 25 and seniors €20, under 12 €13).

Tourist Office: Pl. de la Cathédrale (☎02 37 18 26 26; www.chartres-tourisme.com). Finds accommodations (€2 surcharge) and supplies visitors with a free and helpful map that includes a walking tour and a list of restaurants, hotels, and sights. Open Apr.-Sept. M-Sa 9am-7pm, Su and holidays 9:30am-5:30pm; Oct.-Mar. M-Sa 9am-6pm, Su and holidays 9:30am-5pm. Closed Jan. 1 and Dec. 25.

Tours: Chart'train (☎02 37 25 88 50) runs 35min. narrated tours (in French and English; from late Mar. to early Nov.). Tours begin in front of the tourist office every hr. 10:30am-6pm. €6, under 12 €3. English-language walking tours (1hr.) depart from the tourist office July-Aug. every Sa at 4:15pm (€5, under 14 €3.50, young children free). Audio tour of the *vieille ville* (1hr.) €5.50, €3 for the 2nd hr.

FOOD

Le Moulin de Ponceau, 21-23 rue de la Tannerie (☎02 37 35 30 05; www.lemoulinde-ponceau.fr). Classic French restaurant. *Menu dégustation* €51. 3-course *menu* €38. *Plat* €20. Open Apr.-Sept. M-Sa 12:15-2pm and 7:30-9:30pm, Su 12:15-2pm; Oct.-Mar. M-Tu and Th-F 12:15-2pm and 7:30-9:30pm, W and Sa 7:30-9:30pm, Su 12:15pm. Make reservations before visiting Chartres—you'll regret it if you don't. AmEx/MC/V. ❹

SIGHTS

CATHÉDRALE DE CHARTRES

☎02 37 21 75 02. Open daily 8:30am-7:30pm. Mass M and W-Th 11:45am, 6:15pm; Tu and F 8am, 6:15pm; Sa 11:45am, 6pm; Su 9:15 (in Latin), 11am, 6pm (in the crypt); closed during mass. Tours from Easter to early Nov. M-Sa noon, 2:45pm; call ☎02 37 28 15 58 for info on winter tours. Call the tourist office for info on concerts in the cathedral, the student pilgrimage in late May, Chartres in Lights in mid-summer, and other events. €10, students €5. English-language audio tours available at the gift shop €3.50-6.50; ID deposit.

The best-preserved medieval church in Europe miraculously escaped major damage during the French Revolution and WWII. A patchwork masterpiece of Romanesque and Gothic design, the cathedral was constructed by generations of masons, architects, and artisans. Its grand scale dominates the town, and its place in French history is equally prominent. English-language tours of the cathedral are given by ▨**Malcolm Miller,** an authority on Gothic architecture who has been leading tours for over 40 years. His presentations on the cathedral's history and symbolism are intelligent, witty, and enjoyable for all ages.

SANCTA CAMISIA. The year after he became emperor in AD 875, Charlemagne's grandson—unfortunately named Charles the Bald—donated the Sancta Camisia to Chartres, the cloth believed to have been worn by the Virgin Mary when she gave birth to Christ. Thousands journeyed to the church to kneel before the sacred relic in hope that it would heal them and answer their prayers. The powers of the relic were confirmed in AD 911 when the cloth supposedly saved the city from invading Goths and Vikings. Today, the relic is preserved behind glass and is on display in the back of the church on the left-hand side.

STAINED GLASS. When books were rare and the vast majority of people illiterate, the cathedral served as a multimedia teaching tool. Most of the 172 stained-glass windows date from the 13th century and were preserved through both World Wars by heroic town authorities, who dismantled over 2000 sq. m of glass and stored the windows pane by pane in Dordogne. The windows feature a stunning color known as "Chartres blue," which has not been reproduced in modern times. Stories read from bottom to top, left to right.

TOUR JEHAN-DE-BEAUCE. The adventurous, the athletic, and the non-claustrophobic can climb the narrow staircase to the cathedral's north tower for a stellar view of the cathedral roof, the flying buttresses, and the city below. If you don't make it all the way to the top, the first viewing platform offers a slightly obstructed but impressive sight. *(Open May-Aug. M-Sa 9:30am-noon and 2-5:30pm, Su 2-6pm; Sept.-Apr. M-Sa 9:30am-12:30pm and 2-5pm, Su 2-5pm; closed Jan. 1, 5, and Dec. 25. Last entry 30min. before close. €6.50, ages 18-25 €4.50, under 18 free.)*

CRYPT. Visitors may enter the 110m long subterranean crypt only as part of a guided tour. Parts of the crypt, including a well down which Vikings tossed the bodies of their victims during raids, date back to the ninth century. *(☎02 37 21 56 33. French-language tours 30min. June 22-Sept. 21 11am, 2:15, 3:30, 4:30, 5:15pm; from Sept 22 to Oct. and from Apr. to June 21 M-Sa 11am, 2:15, 3:30, 4:30pm; Nov.-Mar. M-Sa 11am and 4:15pm. €2.70, students €2.10, under 7 free.)*

OTHER SIGHTS

◪ÉGLISE SAINT-AIGNAN. Rebuilt in the 16th century, this church has magnificent ceiling frescoes. It offers summer concerts and exhibits. *(Rue des Greniers. Open M-F 10am-noon and 2-5:30pm, Sa 2-5pm. Mass M and Sa 9am, Tu-F 7am, Su 10:30am.)*

MUSÉE DES BEAUX-ARTS. This museum is housed in the former Bishop's Palace, which is itself an impressive sight. The palace houses a wildly eclectic collection of painting, sculpture, and furniture in addition to a harpsichord collection. *(29 Cloître Notre-Dame. Behind the cathedral. ☎02 37 36 41 39. Open May-Oct. M and W-Sa 10am-noon and 2-6pm, Su 2-6pm; Nov.-Apr. M and W-Sa 10am-noon and 2-5pm. Closed Jan. 1, May 1 and 8, Nov. 1 and 11, and Dec. 25. Last entry 30min. before close. €2.50, students and seniors €1.50, under 12 free.)*

FONTAINEBLEAU

More digestible and less crowded than Versailles, the Château de Fontainebleau achieves nearly the same grandeur while preserving a distinct charm among the great royal châteaux. French kings hunted on these grounds since the 12th century, when the exiled Thomas Becket consecrated Louis VII's manor chapel. In 1528, François I rebuilt the castle to be closer to the game he loved to hunt and introduced Renaissance art to France with masterfully rendered galleries and frescoes he commissioned for his gallery. A patron of the arts, François sought out Italian artists to design his Fontainebleau, among them Leonardo da Vinci. Since then, Fontainebleau has hosted a number of epic events; in 1814, *par exemple*, Napoleon signed his abdication and bade goodbye to the empire from the central courtyard, now called the Cour des Adieux in his honor.

⊟ ☷ TRANSPORTATION AND PRACTICAL INFORMATION

Trains from Gare de Lyon on the *banlieue sud-est* line (45min., every hr., €16 round-trip; keep your ticket to be validated on the train). At Gare de Lyon, follow signs to the Grandes Lignes and buy your ticket from the Billets Île de France counter. From the station, Veolia (☎01 64 22 23 88) runs **buses** (€1.50) after each train arrival from Paris; take bus A (dir.: Château-Lilas) and get off at the château stop in front of the tourist office. Otherwise, the château is a 25min. walk through Avon and Fontainebleau; follow signs from the station.

> **Tourist Office:** 4 rue Royal (☎01 60 74 99 99; www.fontainebleau-tourisme.com). Turn right from château entrance and left up rue Royal. Finds accommodations, organizes tours of the village, sells audio tours of the château's exterior, and distributes maps of Fontainebleau and Barbizon. Open May-Oct. M-Sa 10am-6pm, Su 10am-1pm and 2-5:30pm; Nov.-Apr. M-Sa 10am-6pm, Su 10am-1pm.

◨ FOOD

The bistros immediately surrounding the château are not the only dining in Fontainebleau. Walk into town on rue de Ferrare, and you'll find quality establishments serving up traditional French cuisine. There are also many *pâtisseries*, *boulangeries*, *crêperies*, and pizzerias along **rue Grande** and **rue de France.**

> **Le Caveau des Ducs,** 24 rue de Ferrare (☎01 64 22 05 05; www.lecaveaudesducs.com). A medieval-style bistro serving up traditional fare; expect *foie gras, terrine,* salmon, and *magret de canard. Menus* €24-41. Classic desserts €7-8. Giant salads €10-20. Open daily noon-2pm and 7-10:30pm. AmEx/MC/V. ❹

◔ SIGHTS

CHÂTEAU DE FONTAINEBLEAU

> ☎01 60 71 50 60 or 71 50 70; www.musee-chateau-fontainebleau.fr. *Château open M and W-Su Apr.-Sept. 9:30am-6pm; Oct.-Mar. 9:30am-5pm. Gardens and courtyard open M and W-Su May-Sept. 9am-7pm; Oct. 9am-6pm; Nov.-Feb. 9am-5pm. Last entry 45min. before close. Call ahead for tour schedule. Wheelchair-accessible. Free. Audio tour €8, ages 18-25 €6, under 18 €1. Admission to Musée Chinois de l'Impératrice Eugénie is included, but it is sometimes closed due to low staffing; call ahead. AmEx/MC/V.*

GRANDS AND PETITS APPARTEMENTS. Throughout the eight centuries that French kings lived here, Fontainebleau experienced a number of epic historical events and impressive architectural innovations, all of which have been documented in the decor of the **Grands Appartements.** The **Celebration Gallery** and **Gallery of Plates** both commemorate Fontainebleau's noteworthy history, the former through large frescoes and paintings, the latter through 128 porcelain plates fitted into the woodwork. The castle's most famous room, the **Galerie de François I** both glorifies the king's royal egotism and serves as a testament to his patronage of the arts. Peppered with Fs, the royal *fleurs de lis,* and François's personal salamander emblem, the *galerie* boasts vivid mythological frescoes glorifying François's line and French royalty. Meanwhile, Henri II's legacy pervades throughout ballroom; note the Hs for Henri, and the entwined Cs for his wife Catherine de Medici—which also resemble Ds for Diane de Poitiers, his mistress. The **Gallery of Diana** holds 16,000 volumes from Napoleon's original library, while every queen and empress of France since Marie de Medici has slept in the gold-and-green **Empress's Bed Chamber;** the gilded wood bed was built for Marie Antoinette. Napoleon—in all his humility—outfitted the **Throne**

Hotel
ARMSTRONG
Paris

The Armstrong offers excellent value and is a favourite for backpackers. It has a direct metro to the Eiffel Tower and the Champs-Elysées, and there is a fast train service to Disneyland Paris.

With its multi-lingual staff, cosy fully licensed bar, 24-hour in-house internet café, sauna and private car park, the Hotel Armstrong is an ideal choice for visiting the City of Lights.

36 rue de la Croix Saint Simon
75020 PARIS

Tel. :33 (0) 1 - 43 70 53 65
Fax :33 (0) 1- 43 70 63 31

www.hotelarmstrong.com
info@hotelarmstrong.com

Room with maroon and gold; today it is the only throne room in France that is still furnished. He also had two bedrooms, though he rarely slept. The first, a monument to both his narcissism and eroticism, is sandwiched between two mirrors, while the second is more austere, containing a narrow military bed. In the emperor's private room—known today as the **Abdication Chamber**—Napoleon signed off his empire in 1814 before bidding farewell to his troops in the château's entry courtyard. The tour ends with the impressive 16th-century **Trinity Chapel**, with soaring vaulted ceilings and more Italian frescoes illustrating the *Redemption of Man*. The **Petits Appartements** feature the private rooms of Napoleon and Empress Josephine as well as the impressive **Map Room** and **Galerie des Cerfs;** they can be seen only by guided tour.

MUSÉE NAPOLÉON. The Musée Napoléon features an extensive collection of the emperor's personal effects, including his toothbrush, tiny shoes, field tent, and gifts from European monarchs. (☎01 60 71 50 60. *Only open to guided 1hr. tours in French; average of 8 per day, but call ahead for exact tour schedule.*)

⬛GARDENS. Fontainebleau's serene **Jardin Anglais** and **Jardin de Diane** shelter quiet grottoes guarded by statues of the huntress Diana. The **Étang des Carpes,** a carp-filled pond, can be explored by rowboat. (☎01 64 22 92 61 or 81 50 09 20. *Boat rental availability irregular. Coach drive through the park €4, children €3.*) On the outskirts of the garden is a 1200m canal perfect for picnicking. The **Forêt de Fontainebleau** is a wooded 20,000-hectare preserve with hiking trails, bike paths, and rock climbing. Find maps at the tourist office or in the château.

CHANTILLY

The French don't call whipped cream "Chantilly" for nothing—this 14th- to 19th-century château is as whimsical and fluffy as the delicious dessert allegedly invented on its grounds. An amalgam of Gothic extravagance, Renaissance geometry, and flashy Victorian ornamentalism, the triangle-shaped château is surrounded by a moat, lakes, canals, and the elegant Le Nôtre gardens. Between the architecturally masterful Grandes Écuries (stables) and the world-class Musée Condé, it's a wonder that Chantilly has stayed a hidden treasure for so long. The whole package makes for a delightful foray into the French countryside; just 30min. from the city, visitors can stroll through the dense woodland surrounding the castle.

🚆 🛈 TRANSPORTATION AND PRACTICAL INFORMATION

Trains: run from Gare du Nord RATP (Grand Lignes) to Chantilly Gouvieux (35min.; every hr. 6am-10pm; round-trip €14, under 25 €11). Schedule varies seasonally. The château is a scenic 25min. walk from the train station—go straight up rue des Otages about 50m, and the well-marked path (1.5km) runs through the woodland opposite. Alternatively, by road (2km), turn left on av. du Maréchal Joffre and right on rue du Connétable, the town's main street. There is also a free but irregular shuttle service; catch it to the left as you exit the train station (M-Sa every hr. until 6pm).

Taxis: ☎03 44 57 10 03. €6 from the tourist office to the château.

Tourist Office: 60 av. du Maréchal Joffre (☎03 44 67 37 37; www.chantilly-tourisme. com). From the train station, walk straight up rue des Otages. Bike rental €10 per ½-day, €15 per day. Open May-Sept. M-Sa 9:30am-12:30pm and 1:30-5:30pm, Su 10am-1:30pm; Oct.-Apr. M-Sa 9:30am-12:30pm and 1:30-5:30pm.

█ FOOD

Rue du Connétable runs through the middle of the town of Chantilly to the Grandes Écuries, offering a number of reasonable dining options—cafes, *crêperies*, and *boulangeries*. Near the entrance to the château grounds, you'll find ice-cream and sandwich stands. The château also has a pricey restaurant.

Le Hameau (☎03 44 57 46 21 or 03 44 56 28 23), in the château gardens. From the château, bear left and go down the stairs toward the fountains; turn right and walk along canal des Morfondus. Cross the canal by 1 of the 2 wood-planked bridges, and the restaurant will be to the right once you clear the woods. Fresh farm-style fare includes cheese, salads, *gesiers, magret de canard, pâté, terrines,* and *foie gras.* The █**assiette gourmande** (€22) is a nice sampler. Desserts (from €5) include Chantilly with fruit, Chantilly with ice cream, Chantilly with pie, or just Chantilly. Beer €5. Open from mid-Mar. to mid-Nov. daily noon-6pm. Reserve ahead in summer. MC/V. ❹

◉ SIGHTS

CHÂTEAU DE CHANTILLY

☎03 44 62 62 62; www.domainedechantilly.com. Open Apr.-Nov. M and W-Su 10am-6pm; Nov.-Mar. M and W-F 10:30am-12:45pm and 2-5pm, Sa-Su and holidays 10:30am-5pm. Gardens open Apr.-Nov. M and W-Su 10am-8pm; Nov.-Mar. M and W-F 10:30am-12:45pm and 2-6pm, Sa-Su and holidays 10:30am-6pm. Gardens €5, students, seniors, and disabled persons €4, ages 4-12 €3. Combined ticket for château and gardens €10/8/4. Passe Domaine for château, gardens, and Musée Vivant du Cheval €17, students €14, ages 4-17 €7. Petit trains with 30min. tour of gardens and grounds in French and English €5, ages 4-17 €3. Audio tours €2. Guided visit to private apartments €5; reserve ahead. AmEx/MC/V.

CHÂTEAU AND MUSÉE DE CONDÉ. Chantilly's biggest attraction lies inside the château: the spectacular Musée Condé houses the duke of Aumale's private collection of premodern paintings and is, along with the Louvre, one of only two museums in France to boast three Raphaels. The skylit picture galleries contain 800 paintings, 3000 drawings, and hundreds of engravings, sculptures, and tapestries—among them works by Titian, Corot, Botticelli, Delacroix, Reynolds, Watteau, and Ingres. Marble busts and drawings of royals and nobles attest to the château's illustrious litany of owners: the powerful noble Montmorency family and the royal Bourbon and Condé princes. Following the duke's will, the paintings and furniture are arranged as they were over a century ago, in the distinctive 19th-century frame-to-frame (academic) style. But the museum's absolute gem is the tiny velvet-walled **sanctuary;** this hidden gallery contains what the duke himself considered the finest works in his collection: illuminated manuscripts by Jean Fouquet, a painting by Fra Filippo Lippi, and two Raphaels. Alas, the museum's two most valuable pieces, a Gutenberg Bible and the illuminated manuscripts of the *Très Riches Heures,* are too fragile to be kept in public view—but a near-perfect digitized facsimile of the latter can be seen in the illustrious library, second only to the Bibliothèque Nationale in prestige. The rest of the château's *appartements* can be visited only by taking a guided tour in French.

GARDENS. Maps of the gardens suggest a walking tour of the grounds, but wandering is just as effective. A bike can help you explore the château's sprawling 115 hectares of parks and grounds. Directly in front of the château, the gardens' central expanse is designed in the French formal style, with neat rows of carefully pruned trees, stately statues, and geometric pools. To the left, hidden within a forest, the Romantic English garden attempts to recreate untamed nature. Here, paths meander around pools where lone swans glide across the surface. Windows carved into the foliage allow you to see fountains in the formal garden as you stroll. To the right, the gardens hide an idyllic play-village *hameau* (hamlet), the inspiration for Marie Antoinette's hamlet at Versailles. Farther in, a statue of Cupid reigns over the "Island of Love." Recent additions include the ⚄kangaroo enclosure—the 15 or so wallabies gathered in the far right corner of the formal gardens—and a labyrinth, near the hamlet; both represent a move back toward the former royal flare.

GRANDES ÉCURIES. Another great—if slightly less sweet-smelling—draw to the château is the Grandes Écuries (stables), whose marble corridors, court-yards, and facades are masterpieces of 18th-century French architecture. Commissioned by Louis-Henri Bourbon, who hoped to live here when he was reborn as a horse, the Écuries boast extravagant fountains, domed rotundas, and sculptured patios that are enough to make even the most skeptical believe in reincarnation. From 1719 to the Revolution, the stables housed 240 horses and hundreds of hunting dogs. Now they are home to the **Musée Vivant du Cheval,** an extensive collection (supposedly the largest in the world) of all things equine. In addition to the stables' 30 live horses, donkeys, and ponies, the museum displays saddles, merry-go-rounds, and a horse statue featured in a James Bond film. The museum also hosts equestrian shows (1st Su of the month at 4pm) and daily dressage demonstrations. The **Hippodrome** on the premises is a major racetrack: France's premier horse races are held here in June. *(On rue du Connétable; enter through the Jeu de Paume gate, to the right. ☎03 44 57 13 13; www.museevivant-ducheval.fr. Open July-Aug. M and W-F 10:30am-5:30pm, Sa-Su 10:30am-6pm; Sept.-Oct. and Apr. M and W-F 10:30am-5:30pm, Sa-Su 10:30am-6pm; Nov. and Jan.-Mar. M and W-F 2-5pm, Sa-Su 10:30am-5:30pm; Dec. M and W-Su 10:30am-5pm; May-June M-F 10:30am-5:30pm, Sa-Su 10:30am-6pm. Educational demonstration equestrian shows Apr.-Oct. daily 11:30am, 3, 4:30pm; Nov.-Mar. M-F 3pm, Sa-Su 11:30am, 3, 4:30pm. Museum €8.50, students €7.50, children €6.50. Hippodrome matches €3; ask for a schedule at the tourist office.)*

LE POTAGER DES PRINCES. The Princes' Kitchen Garden is a cultivated two-hectare expanse of greenery modeled on the château's original 17th-century working garden. First designed by Le.Nôtre as a pheasantry in 1682, it was later converted into a "Roman pavilion" of terraced gardens. Abandoned during the Revolution's pruning of excess, the gardens were restored in 2002 to their former verdant glory, this time as a public attraction. Catering mostly to children, the garden is arranged in themed areas, including a fantasy region replete with bridges and grottoes, a romantic and aromatic rose garden, and a menagerie that features goats, squabbling chickens, and over 100 varieties of pheasant. It also hosts occasional concerts and plays by the likes of Shakespeare and Marivaux in summer; check the website for details. *(300m from the stables down rue du Connétable toward the town, turn on rue des Potagers; garden is at the end of the road. ☎03 44 57 40 40; www.potagerdesprinces.com. Open from mid-Mar. to mid-Oct. M and W-Su 2-7pm. Last entry M and W-F 5:30pm, Sa-Su 6pm. €8, ages 13-17 €7, ages 4-12 €6.)*

GIVERNY

Drawn to the verdant hills, woodsy haystacks, and lily-strewn Epte River, painter Claude Monet and his eight children settled in Giverny in 1883. By 1887, John Singer Sargent, Paul Cézanne, and Mary Cassatt had placed their easels beside Monet's and turned the village into an artists' colony. Today, the vistas depicted by these artists remain undisturbed. In spite of the tourists, who come to retrace the steps of the now-famous Impressionists who found inspiration here (see **Life and Times,** p. 73), Giverny retains its rustic tranquility.

⬛ TRANSPORTATION

Buses and Trains: Trains run regularly from Gare St-Lazare to **Vernon,** the station nearest Giverny. Round-trip around €24, ages 18-25 €18. The fastest way from Vernon to Giverny is by bus (☎08 25 07 60 27; 10min., 4 per day Tu-Su, €4), which leaves every day for Giverny just a few minutes after the train arrives in Vernon.

Bike Rental: ☎02 32 21 16 01. From many restaurants opposite the Vernon station for €10 per day, plus deposit.

👁 SIGHTS

FONDATION CLAUDE MONET. From 1883 to 1926, Claude Monet resided in Giverny. His home, with its thatched roof and pink crushed-brick facade, was surrounded by ponds and immense gardens—two features central to his art. Today, Monet's house and gardens are maintained by the Fondation Claude Monet. From April to July, the gardens overflow with wild roses, hollyhocks, poppies, and fragrant honeysuckle. The **Orientalist Water Gardens** contain the water lilies, weeping willows, and Japanese bridge recognizable from Monet's paintings. Inside the house, with its big windows and pastel hues, the original decorations have been restored or recreated. Highlights include the artist's cheerful, brimming kitchen and his collection of 18th- and 19th-century Japanese prints. *(84 rue Claude Monet.* ☎*02 32 51 28 21; www.fondation-monet.com. Open Apr.-Oct. Tu-Su 9:30am-6pm. €5.50, students and ages 12-18 €4, ages 7-12 €3. Gardens €4.)*

MUSÉE D'ART AMÉRICAIN. The modern Musée d'Art Américain, near the Fondation Monet, is the sister institution of the Museum of American Art in Chicago. It houses a small number of works by American expats like Theodore Butler and John Leslie Breck, who came to Giverny to study Impressionist style. Outside the museum, a garden designed by landscape architect Mark Rudkin features an array of flowers separated by large, rectangular hedges. While not as impressive as Monet's garden, this smaller labyrinth is worth the free visit. It affords a scenic view of **Giverny Hill,** the inspiration for many Impressionist *oeuvres.* *(99 rue Claude Monet.* ☎*02 32 51 94 65; www.maag.org. Open Apr.-Oct. M holidays and Tu-Su, 10am-6pm. €5.50; students, seniors, and teachers €4; ages 12-18 €3; under 12 and 1st Su of the month free. Audio tours €1.50.)*

VAUX-LE-VICOMTE

Nicolas Fouquet, Louis XIV's minister of finance, began building Vaux-le-Vicomte in 1641; upon its completion 20 years later, Fouquet threw an extravagant party in honor of the Sun King. After novelties like elephants wearing crystal jewelry and whales in the canal, the evening concluded with an exhibition of fireworks that featured the king and queen's coat of arms and ⬛**pyrotechnic squirrels** (Fouquet's family symbol). But the housewarming bash was the beginning of the end for Fouquet. Since his appointment to the office in 1653, the ambitious young minister of finance had fully replenished the failing royal treasury. His own lavish lifestyle, however, sparked rumors of embezzlement that were nourished by jealous underlings. Shortly after the *fête,* Louis XIV ordered Fouquet's arrest. In the words of Voltaire, "At six o'clock in the evening, Fouquet was king of France; at two the next morning, he was nothing." In a trial that lasted three years, Fouquet was found guilty of embezzlement and banished from France. Louis XIV overturned the sentence in favor of life imprisonment—the only time in French history that the head of state overruled the court's decision in favor of a more severe punishment. Fouquet was to remain imprisoned at Pignerol, in the French Alps, until his death in 1680.

TRANSPORTATION AND PRACTICAL INFORMATION

Take the RER (D line) to Melun from Châtelet-Les Halles, Gare de Lyon, or Gare du Nord (30min.-1hr., round-trip €14). Catch a shuttle to the château (Sa-Su, €6-8 round-trip) or take a taxi (€15). The château staff will call you a cab for the return trip. By car, take A4 and exit at Troyes-Nancy by N104. Head toward Meaux on N36 and follow the signs. The château is about 50km from Paris.

Tourist Office: Service Jeunesse et Citoyenneté, 2 av. Gallieni (☎01 60 56 55 10; www.ville-melun.fr), by the train station in Melun. Information on accommodations and sightseeing. Open Tu-Sa 10am-noon and 2-6pm.

Tours: Several tour companies run trips from Paris to the château; call ahead to book a trip. **ParisVision** (☎01 42 60 30 01; www.parisvision.com) offers regularly scheduled trips (€25-154). Dinner and visit to candlelight shows May-Oct. €154.

> **TIP**
>
> **A MYSTERY WRAPPED IN AN ENIGMA.** The Fouquet intrigue has been repeatedly dramatized by the popular and literary imagination. Alexandre Dumas, for example, retells the story in *Le Vicomte de Bragelonne*. Some have postulated that Fouquet was the legendary "man in the iron mask," and, though evidence refutes the claim, the film *The Man in the Iron Mask* (1999) was filmed in part at Vaux-le-Vicomte.

⊙ SIGHTS

CHÂTEAU DE VAUX-LE-VICOMTE

☎01 64 14 41 90; www.vaux-le-vicomte.com. Open Mar. 15-Nov. 9 M-F 10am-1pm and 2pm-5:30pm, Sa-Su 10am-5:30pm; Dec. 23-Jan. 7 daily 10am-5:30pm. Candlelight visits July-Aug. F 8pm; from Sept. to mid-Oct. and May-June Sa 8pm. Fountains open Apr.-Oct. 2nd and last Sa of each month 3-6pm. Château, gardens, and carriage museum €13, students, ages 6-16, and seniors €10, under 6 free. Castle dome €2. Candlelight visits €16, students, ages 6-16, and seniors €14. Château audio tour with historical presentation in English €2.50. Golf carts, for rent to the right of the garden from the entrance, €18 per hr. AmEx/MC/V.

While Vaux doesn't appear ostentatious when viewed from the front, it is quite Baroque in the back. The garden-side facade is covered with ornate Fs, squirrels, and the family motto, *"quo non ascendet"* ("what heights might they not reach"). The interior is even more opulent. **Madame Fouquet's Closet,** once lined with tiny mirrors, was the decorative precedent for Versailles's Hall of Mirrors, while the **Room of the Muses** is one of Le Brun's most famous decorative and detailed displays. The artist had planned to crown the cavernous, Neoclassical **Oval Room** (or Grand Salon) with a fresco entitled **The Palace of the Sun,** but Fouquet's arrest halted all decorating activity, and only a single eagle and a patch of sky were painted in to fill the space. Fouquet's successor and great enemy, Colbert, removed even more of his predecessor's mark, seizing the tapestries that once bore Fouquet's squirrels and replacing them with his own adders. Meanwhile, the **King's Bedchamber** boasts a marble-and-gold ceiling featuring cherubs and lions circling Le Brun's *Time Bearing Truth Heavenward*.

GARDENS. The classical French garden was invented at Vaux-le-Vicomte by Le Nôtre, the Sun King's gardener, who became famous for forcing nature to conform to strict geometric patterns. Vaux's multilevel terraces, fountained walk-

PARIS

ways, and fantastical *parterres* (low-cut hedges and crushed stone arranged in arabesque patterns) are still the most exquisite example of 17th-century French gardens. The collaboration of Le Nôtre with Le Vau and Le Brun ensured that the same patterns and motifs were repeated with astonishing harmony in the gardens, the château, and the tapestries inside. But not all is visibly seamless: Vaux owes its most impressive *trompe l'oeil* effect to Le Nôtre's adroit use of the laws of perspective. From the back steps of the château, it looks as if you can see the entire landscape at a glance, but, as you walk toward the far end of the garden, the grottoes at the back seem to recede, revealing a sunken canal known as **La Poêle** (the Frying Pan), which is invisible from the château. The **Round Pool** and its surrounding 17th-century statues mark an important intersection: to the left, down the east walkway, are the **Water Gates,** the backdrop for Molière's performance of *Les Fâcheux*. Closer to the château along the central walkway is the **Water Mirror,** which was designed to reflect the building perfectly. A climb to the **Farnese Hercules** earns the best vista of the grounds. The tremendous Hercules sculpture at the top was at the center of Fouquet's trial; in an age when kings enjoyed divine rights to their royalty, the beleaguered Fouquet likened himself to Hercules, the only mortal to become a god. For those who don't want to venture that far, a visit to the castle's dome is worth the bird's-eye view of the garden as well as the castle's complex. The old stables, **Les Equipages,** also house a surprisingly extensive carriage museum. But by far the best way to see Vaux's gardens is during the ⬛**visites aux chandelles** (candlelit visit), when the château and grounds are lit up by thousands of candles and classical music plays through the gardens in imitation of Fouquet's legendary party; arrive around dusk to see the grounds in all their glory.

DISNEYLAND RESORT PARIS

Seriously? Are you sure you didn't miss a single Parisian treat or attraction? Remember **museums** (p. 153)? They're fun! Fine: www.disneylandparis.com.

LOIRE VALLEY
(VAL DE LOIRE)

Welcome to the land of castles, where fairy tales were born and where floppy-eared hunting hounds still bound eagerly through the woods. Captured on postcards, posters, and 3D puzzles, the châteaux of the Loire Valley are deeply historic, breathtakingly beautiful, and shamelessly extravagant. During the Renaissance, many were converted into residential palaces, framed by spectacular gardens and heaped with artistic masterpieces. Today, the rolling hills of the "Garden of France" are perfect for an afternoon bike ride, while their fertile soil nurtures some of the nation's best wines. Visitors wander through the gardens and gilded salons of the region's many castles, which include Chenonceau (p. 215), whose arches span the Cher River, Cheverny (p. 204), replete with romance, and Chambord (p. 204), the champion of pomp. The southern Loire Valley benefited from the lavish attentions of Charles VII's financier, Jacques Coeur. Before being imprisoned for embezzlement, the extravagant Coeur built a string of châteaux through the heart of Berry, most of which are vacant and open to visitors. Found along the Route Jacques Coeur, they are easily accessible from Bourges (p. 233) or the medieval St-Amand-Montrond (p. 238).

The cities of the Loire are more than just convenient bases for exploring the châteaux; they are exciting destinations in their own right. In Saumur (p. 219), truffles are practically worth their weight in gold. Fun, affordable Tours (p. 209) offers student-centered nightlife. Amboise (p. 206) is home to Leonardo da Vinci's final residence and resting place. Most of these towns have their own castles, which rise above centuries-old cobblestone streets that may just charm you to the point of giving the clichés a second chance.

HIGHLIGHTS OF THE LOIRE VALLEY

PROPOSE in the gallery of Chenonceau (p. 215); it doesn't get much more romantic.

FACE YOUR DOOM at the world-renowned Apocalyptic Tapestry in Angers (p. 227), in which St-Jean battles evil and a seven-headed Satan gobbles down babies.

MARVEL at the mix of beauty and scandal at Fontevraud-l'Abbaye (p. 223).

ORLÉANS
☎ 02 38

The lively city of Orléans (ohr-lay-ahn; pop. 200,000) still recalls its historical prominence as the thriving capital of the Loire Valley. The city once served as an intellectual capital as well, when artists and great thinkers flocked here in the thirteenth century. Many streets are named in honor of the famous Joan of Arc, who was dubbed "Maid of Orléans" after she liberated the city from a seven-month English siege in 1429, which led to the French to victory in the Hundred Years' War. Now, skirted by sprawling commercial and suburban quarters, Orléans nevertheless boasts a charming *vieille ville* with well-preserved marble Renaissance architecture. Crowded cobblestone streets buzzing with life and a friendly, small-town feel make Orléans more than a gateway to the romantic Sully-sur-Loire, Germigny, and St-Benoît-sur-Loire châteaux.

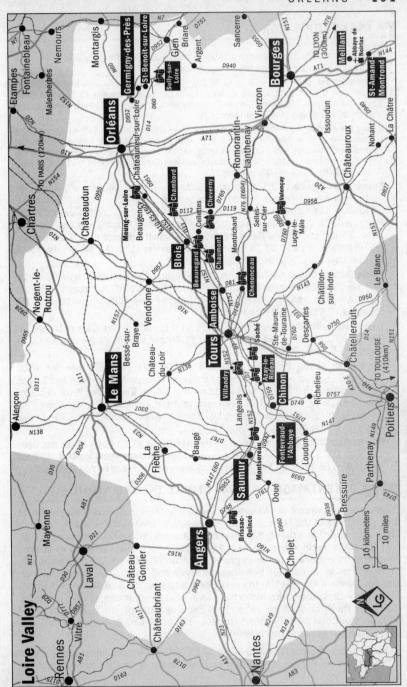

■ TRANSPORTATION

Trains: A trolley shuttles passengers between the 2 train stations every 30min. (€1.20). Tramway A also runs between the stations every 4min. (€1.30).

Gare d'Orléans, pl. Albert I (☎08 21 01 26 29), in the *centre-ville.* Info office and ticket booths open daily 5:30am-8:30pm. Trains to: **Blois** (40min.; at least 15 per day; €9.70, under 26 on weekday mornings €7); **Nantes** (2hr.; M-F 3 per day, Sa-Su 2 per day; €35); **Paris Austerlitz** (1hr., every hr., €13); **Tours** (1hr., every 30min., €18).

Gare Les-Aubrais, rue Pierre Semard (☎02 38 79 91 00), a 40min., 2.5km walk north of the *centre-ville* or 5min. ride with on tram A. Walk north on rue du Faubourg Bannier, make a right onto rue de Joie, then take a left onto rue Louis Labonne. Stay on the left when the road forks and continue onto rue Lamartine, which turns into rue Pierre Semard; the station will be on your left. Trains to **Paris** (1hr., every 30min., €13).

Buses: **Gare Routière,** 2 rue Marcel Proust, connects to the Gare d'Orléans. Info desk open July 11-Aug. 15 M-F 11:30am-1pm and 4:30-6pm; Aug. 16-July 10 M-F 7:30-9am, 11am-1pm, and 1:30-7pm, Sa 10:30am-1:30pm. Les Rapides du Val de Loire (☎02 38 53 94 75; www.ulys-loiret.com) at the Gare Routière runs buses to **Sully** (1hr., 13 per day, €2) via **Germigny** and **Saint-Benoît-sur-Loire** (1hr., 8-10 per day, €2). Transbeauce (☎02 37 18 59 00) runs to **Chartres** (1hr.; M-F 4-8 per day, Sa-Su 2-3 per day; €12). Tickets sold on bus.

Public Transportation: SEMTAO, 2 rue de la Hallebarde and pl. d'Arc (☎08 00 01 20 00; www.semtao.fr), outside the Gare d'Orléans and under pl. d'Arc shopping mall, runs city buses. Info desk open M-F 6:45am-7:15pm, Sa 8am-6:30pm. 1hr. ticket €1.30, carnet of 10 €12, day pass €3.40.

Taxis: **Taxi Radio d'Orléans** (☎02 38 53 11 11), outside the Gare d'Orléans, at the Carrefour Parking exit. €2.10 base; €1.40 per km during the day, €1.90 at night. €5.50 min. Open 24hr.

Car Rental: Ecoto, 19 av. Paris (☎02 38 77 92 92). From €29 per day; €800 deposit. 21+; must have been licensed for 3+ years. Open M 8am-noon and 2-6pm, Tu-F 9am-noon and 2-6pm, Sa 9am-10am and 4-6pm. **Rent A Car,** 3 rue des Sansonnières (☎02 38 62 33 97, www.rentacar.fr), a 4min. walk up the street from Ecoto; keep right when the road splits. Some English spoken. From €30 per day. Open daily 8am-noon and 2-6:30pm.

Bike Rental: CAD, 95 rue du Faubourg Bannier (☎02 38 81 23 00). €11 per day. Open Jan.-Oct. M-F 9am-noon and 2-7pm, Sa 9am-5pm. **Orléans-Cyclo-Touriste,** 180 rue des Murlins (☎02 38 55 11 38; boisseaud@wanadoo.fr). Prices vary by season.

■ ORIENTATION AND PRACTICAL INFORMATION

Most spots of interest in Orléans are located in the *vieille ville*, which sits on the north bank of the Loire, a 2min. walk south of the Gare d'Orléans. To reach the *centre-ville* from the station, first head through the *centre commercial.* Follow the tram tracks down **rue de la République,** which leads to **place du Martroi,** a large square marked by an impressive statue of Joan of Arc on horseback. Here, rue de la République becomes **rue Royale** and runs to the river, intersecting **rue Jeanne d'Arc** and the lively **rue de Bourgogne.** Both of these pedestrian streets are decorated with historical landmarks, restaurants, shops, and bars. To reach the tourist office, take rue d'Escures from pl. du Martroi to pl. de l'Étape. Continue past the Hôtel Groslot onto pl. St-Croix; the tourist office is across the street from the cathedral.

Tourist Office: 2 pl. de l'Étape (☎02 38 24 05 05; www.tourisme-orleans.com), next to the Musée des Beaux Arts. Walking tours (€4-6) of the *vieille ville*'s cathedrals, crypts,

Orléans

ACCOMMODATIONS
Auberge de Jeunesse (HI), **14**
Hôtel de l'Abeille, **3**
Hôtel Bannier, **1**
Hôtel Charles Sanglier, **6**

FOOD
Au Don Camillo, **5**
Bar des Tribunaux, **4**
Mijana, **10**
Les Musardises, **2**
Le Vol-Terre, **13**

NIGHTLIFE AND ENTERTAINMENT
L'Atelier, **11**
La Datcha, **9**
Le Decibel, **12**
Paxton's Head, **7**
Moog, **8**

and nighttime sights are available depending on the season; call for more info. Also runs a small tourist train with tours of Orléans daily 10am-5pm. €5, ages 3-12 €3. English, Spanish, and German spoken. Open daily June 9:30am-1pm and 2-6:30pm; July-Aug. 9am-7pm; May and Sept. 9:30am-1pm and 2-6pm; Oct.-Jan. M-Sa 10am-1pm and 2-5pm; Feb.-Apr. M-Sa 10am-1pm and 2-6pm.

Budget Travel: Thomas Cook Voyages, 34 rue de la République (☎02 38 42 11 80; www.thomascook.fr). Open M-F 9:30am-12:30pm and 2-6:30pm, Sa 9:30am-12:30pm and 2-6pm. AmEx/MC/V.

Banks: Banks with 24hr. **ATMs** line rue de la République and pl. du Martroi but otherwise don't provide tourist services. To cash traveler's checks or get the best exchange rates, head to the main post office (next page).

English-Language Bookstore: Librairie Paes, 184 rue de Bourgogne (☎02 38 54 04 50). Also carries books in German, Italian, Portuguese, Russian, and Spanish. Call or stop by to order books not in stock. Open Tu-Sa 10am-12:30pm and 1:30-7pm. MC/V.

Youth Center: Centre Régional d'Information Jeunesse (CRIJ), 5 bd. de Verdun (☎02 38 78 91 78; www.informationjeunesse-centre.fr). An invaluable resource for info on studying, jobs, housing, volunteer opportunities, and travel. 1hr. of free Internet access (M-F 2-6pm). Open M-W and F 10am-1pm and 2-6pm, Th and Sa 2-6pm.

Resources for the Disabled: Association des Paralysés de France, 11 rue Robert le Pieux (☎02 38 43 28 53; www.apf.asso.fr). City mobility help and info.

Laundromat: Laverie Bourgogne, 176 rue de Bourgogne. Wash €5 per 5kg, dry €1 per 9min. Open daily 7am-9pm.

Police: 63 rue du Faubourg St-Jean (☎02 38 24 30 00).

Crisis Line: Rape crisis line ☎08 00 05 95 95.

Red Cross: ☎08 00 85 88 58.

Pharmacy: ☎15. Line open daily 7am-9pm. After 9pm, call police.

Hospital: Centre Hospitalier Régional, 1 rue Porte Madeleine (☎02 38 51 44 44).

Post Office: Pl. du Général de Gaulle (☎02 38 77 35 14). **Currency exchange** available. Open M-F 8:30am-7pm, Sa 8:30am-12:15pm. **Postal Code:** 45000.

🏠 ACCOMMODATIONS

Hôtel de l'Abeille, 64 rue Alsace-Lorraine (☎02 38 53 54 87; www.hoteldelabeille. com). 1 block from the station, across bd. Alexandre Martin. Owned by the same family since 1919. 29 spacious, comfortable rooms with antique furniture, (non-functional) fireplaces, and fresh flowers fit for Marie Antoinette. Continental breakfast €8.50, in bed €9.50. Wi-Fi in lobby. Singles with shower €47, with full bath €51; doubles €62-66/69-79; triples and quads €95-110. AmEx/MC/V. ❹

Hôtel Charles Sanglier, 8 rue Charles Sanglier (☎02 38 53 38 50; www.hotelsanglier. orleans.neuf.fr). Boasts friendly service and a location in the heart of the city. 60s-style rooms are newly renovated. Some have balconies overlooking rue de Bourgogne. All have bath and cable TV. Breakfast in bed €6. Reservations recommended. Singles €45-51; doubles €55-60. Extra bed €12. Cash only. ❸

Hôtel Bannier, 13 rue du Faubourg Bannier (☎02 38 53 25 86). Turn right on bd. Alexandre Martin as you exit the station; the hotel is 2 blocks away. Wallet-friendly option with 17 clean and well-equipped rooms with wood paneling, some overlooking a quiet yard. Also serves as a *brasserie*. Breakfast €4.30. Reception M-Th 7:30am-9pm, F-Sa 7:30am-10pm. Singles and doubles €31-37; triples €31-47; quads €55. ❷

Auberge de Jeunesse (HI), 7 av. Beaumarchais (☎02 38 53 60 06). From the train station, take tram A to Université-L'Indien (35min.). Take a left down av. de Président John Kennedy, then another left onto rue de Beaumarchais. The hostel is behind Tribune A of the Stade Omnisport. The cheapest option around, but quite a trek from town. Rooms are bare but clean. Bunk beds and shared bathrooms. Breakfast and Wi-Fi included. Parking available. Wheelchair-accessible. Reception M-F 8am-noon and 4-7pm. 4-bed single-sex dorms €12; singles €20.30. Cash only. ❶

🍴 FOOD

In late summer and fall, locals feast on fresh *gibier* (game), once hunted in nearby forests. Street vendors crowd **place du Martroi** peddling regional specialties, such as *andouillette de Jargeau* (tripe sausage) and *saumon de Loire* (Loire salmon). Local cheeses, like *frinault cendré* (Camembert's mild cousin), complement fresh river fare, and buttery *sablés* cookies make for a nice dessert. Orléans's most important culinary contributions are its tangy wine vinegars. Gris Meunier or Auvergnat wines or nearby Olivet's pear and cherry brandies are a delicious finishing touch to any meal.

The extensive **Carrefour** supermarket, in the back of a mall behind the train station at pl. d'Arc, is close to the *centre-ville*. (Open M-Sa 8:30am-9pm. AmEx/ MC/V.) **Les Halles Châtelet,** pl. du Châtelet, is an enclosed ensemble of shops and food stands across the street from Galeries Lafayette, where hungry travelers and locals alike can make a meal of the produce, cheese, bread, and meat sold at various booths. (Open Tu-Sa 7:30am-7:30pm, Su 7:30am-1:30pm. Cash only.) *Brasseries* and bars around Les Halles Châtelet and **rue de Bourgogne** are the best bet for bargain food and a lively atmosphere. Sandwiches with *frites* and Turkish shawarma (kebab) are a good deal (€4-7). Chinese, Indian, and Middle Eastern restaurants lie between **rue de la Fauconnerie** and **rue de l'Université.**

Mijana, 175 rue de Bourgogne (☎02 38 62 02 02; www.mijanaresto.com). A charming Lebanese couple prepares gourmet cuisine, including vegetarian options such as falafel, *baba ghanoush,* and hummus (€7.50 each). An intimate, hospitable, cultural immersion with Lebanese music. Wine and tables named for friends and family. Sandwiches €4-6. Appetizers €7.20-8.50. *Plats* €14-17. Lunch specials include the *menu traditionel* (€18). Open M-Sa noon-1:30pm and 7-10pm. AmEx/MC/V over €15. ❸

Le Vol-Terre, 253 rue Bourgogne (☎02 38 54 00 79). For those tempted by the philosophy of *bio* (organic) food, this small but lively restaurant epitomizes the French culinary aesthetic: clean, healthy, real. Salads (€12-14) use a variety of ingredients, including grilled salmon, lentils, and goat cheese. Lunch specials (€8-12) include appetizers and coffee or a glass of wine. Menu in Braille. Open M-Th noon-2pm and 7:30-11pm, F noon-2pm and 7:30-11:30pm, Sa noon-2pm and 7:30pm-midnight. MC/V ❷

Au Don Camillo, 54 rue Ste-Catherine (☎02 38 53 38 97). A trendy, 2-story hangout offering thin-crust pizzas (€7-9.60) and a surprising variety of salads (€8-10). A favorite of younger locals and tourists alike for its filling portions and fair prices. *Plat du jour* €11. Lunch and dinner pizza or pasta *menus* with salad and drink €11-14. House *menu* €22. Open daily noon-3pm and 7pm-midnight. AmEx/MC/V. ❸

Bar des Tribunaux, 29 rue de la Bretonnerie (☎02 38 62 71 86). This lunch-only cafe is always justifiably packed with lawyers from the Palais de la Justice across the street. Offers an appealing local atmosphere, energetic waitstaff, and a French oldies playlist to set the mood. Salads €8-10. Traditional fish and meat dishes €7-15. *Plat du jour* €8.50. Open M-F 8am-7pm. Kitchen open until 2pm. AmEx/MC/V. ❷

Les Musardises, 38 rue de la République (☎02 38 53 30 98). A classy *salon de thé,* complete with uniformed waitresses and large embellished mirrors. Window displays with regional treats like *macarons d'Orléans* and *chocolat Cyrano,* as well as savory snacks (€3 and up), lure passersby without fail. If undaunted by the intensely yellow interior—and still hungry after a wedge of cake—stay and try the chef's special *plat du jour* (€8.40), served only at lunch. Tea €3. Cakes €4-6. Chocolate €5 and up. Open M-Sa 8am-7:20pm, Su 8am-12:30pm. MC/V. ❷

👁 SIGHTS

Most of Orléans's highlights—including the **Église Saint-Paterne,** remarkable for its stained-glass artwork ranging from the 11th century to modern times—are near pl. St-Croix, where, in 1429, Joan of Arc marched the triumphant French army down the city's oldest—and now hippest—street, **rue de Bourgogne.** For more information about special exhibitions, concerts, and festivals in Orléans, pick up the brochure *Week-end* at the tourist office.

CATHÉDRALE SAINT-CROIX. With towering Gothic buttresses and dramatic arches, this cathedral is Orléans's crown jewel; its 88m spire is visible from almost any spot in town. Originally erected in the 13th century, the cathedral took two centuries to complete. Two golden leopards cowering at Joan of Arc's feet greet visitors in the north wing, while the hand of God opens directly above the altar. *(Pl. St-Croix. Open daily Oct.-Apr. 9:15am-5pm; May-Sept. 9:15am-6pm. In summer mass Su 10:30am. Contact tourist office for tours. Free, often with organ concerts.)*

HÔTEL GROSLOT D'ORLÉANS. Built in 1550 for bailiff Jacques Groslot, this Renaissance mansion was the king's local residence for 200 years and Orléans's city hall until the 1790s. One room is filled with Joan of Arc memorabilia, and another was the final resting place of 16-year-old François II, who died of an ear infection in 1560. Unblemished by its history, the regally furnished rooms now host many of Orléans's receptions and weddings. A peaceful 19th-century garden provides respite from the busy city. *(Pl. de l'Étape, left of the Musée des Beaux Arts. Walk up the stairs to the entrance on the left. ☎ 02 38 79 22 30; hotelgroslot@ville-orleans.fr. Open July-Sept. M-F and Su 9am-7pm, Sa 5-8pm. Oct.-June M-F and Su 10am-noon and 2-6pm, Sa 5-7pm. Contact tourist office for tours. Call ahead for English guides. Brochure €1.)*

MUSÉE DES BEAUX ARTS. This fine collection in a modern building next to the cathedral boasts Italian, Flemish, and French painting and sculpture from the last five centuries. As with most places in Orléans, Joan of Arc has a strong presence; note the large painting of the heroine on horseback in the main lobby. In addition to a particularly strong collection of 17th- and 18th-century French art, the museum hosts modern art and archaeological exhibits. Collection includes paintings by Van Dyck, Boucher, Delacroix, and Gauguin. *(1 rue Fernand Rabier, to the right of the tourist office. ☎ 02 38 79 21 55; www.ville-orleans.fr. Open Tu-Sa 9:30am-12:15pm and 1:30-5:45pm, Su 2-6:30pm. €3, students under 25 and seniors over 65 €1.50, under 16 free. 1st Su of the month free.)*

PARC FLORAL DE LA SOURCE. Originally created to host the International Flower Show of 1967, this 12-hectare park contains the mysterious source of the Loire River, a petting zoo, and a butterfly reserve of 50 exotic species that flutter amid tropical flora. The picnic areas and playgrounds are ideal for a family outing—especially during the annual Easter egg hunt. For €2 extra, travel around the park in the *petit train. (By car, take RN-20 dir.: Vierzon-Bourges and exit at St-Cyr-En-Val. By tram, take tram A dir.: Hôpital and exit at Université-Parc Floral—a 30min. trip. From Gare d'Orléans, take a right, cross the tracks, and walk down the path to the park entrance. ☎ 02 38 49 30 00; www.parc-floral-la-source.com. Open daily from Apr. to mid-Oct. 10am-7pm; from mid-Oct. to Mar. 2-5pm. Butterfly reserve open Apr.-Oct. Ticket booth closes 1hr. prior to closing. €6, ages 6-16 €4, under 6 free. Butterfly reserve €2.60-4 extra.)*

MAISON DE JEANNE D'ARC. This two-room museum is located in the house where the saint stayed during her short sojourn in Orléans. An automated narration reconstructs the seven-month siege with miniature models of the ancient city, creating a unique interactive learning experience. The third floor is dedicated to Joan's helpers and patrons in Orléans. *(3 pl. Charles de Gaulle, across from the post office. ☎ 02 38 52 99 89. Headsets available with narration in English, French, German, Italian, and Spanish. Open Tu-Su May-Oct. 10am-12:30pm and 1:30-6:30pm; Nov.-Apr. 1:30-6:30pm. €2, students €1, under 16 and groups of 10+ free)*

OTHER SIGHTS. Popular with local schoolchildren and nature enthusiasts, the **Musée des Sciences Naturelles** makes natural history surprisingly fun with its hands-on exhibits. Make sure to visit the *cabinet des curiosities*, which features skeletons and stuffed bats with an operatic accompaniment. Live fish brighten the otherwise gloomy aquarium on the first floor, and a greenhouse on the fourth floor provides a relaxing—if humid—finale. *(6 rue Marcel Proust. ☎ 02 38 54 61 05. Open daily 2-6pm. €3, students €1, under 16 and school groups free. 3rd Su of the month free.)* **Musée Historique et Archéologique de l'Orléannais**, housed in the courtyard of the **Hôtel Cabu**, collects odd tidbits such as glass portraits of King Louis XIV and an anonymous cross-eyed ecclesiastic as well as a sculpture of Joan of Arc that gives new meaning to the word "bust." *(Sq. Abbé Desnoyers. ☎ 02 38 79 21 55. Open July-Aug. M-Sa 9:30am-12:15pm and 1:30-5:45pm, Su 2-6:30pm; May-June and Sept. Tu-Sa 1:30-5:45pm, Su 2-6:30pm; Oct.-Apr. W 1:30-5:45pm, Su 2-6:30pm. €3, students €1.50,* *under 16 free. Admission to Musée Historique included with admission to Musée des Beaux Arts. Call the tourist office for tour reservations. Tours €3.80, in languages other than French €5.)* The **Centre Jeanne d'Arc**, at the **Médiathèque d'Orléans,** a modern building on pl. Gambetta, has a library with over 16,000 documents related to the city's heroine. *(☎02 38 52 99 89; www.jeannedarc.com.fr. Open Tu-W and F-Sa 10am-6pm, Th 1-8pm.)*

NIGHTLIFE

The campus of Orléans's university lies on the town's outskirts, so the city's central nightlife is liveliest on weekends. Like most French towns, Orléans has a token pub-crawl street, **rue de Bourgogne,** with bars to suit all tastes and ages.

L'Atelier, 203 rue de Bourgogne (☎02 38 53 08 27). Small, rustic, and lively bar offers free concerts, debates, readings, and exhibitions. The cheap prices are permanent: they've been etched into the wall and wood staircase. Regulars—garrulous artists and musicians—are eager for conversation or a game of cards. Mixed drinks from €2.50. Open M-Sa 5:30pm-2am, Su 4-10pm. MC/V.

La Datcha, 205 rue Bourgogne (☎02 38 81 00 11). This bar—nicknamed the "barslave"—offers 27 different vodka drinks named after Soviet bloc cities ("Julianov" €6) and related cultural spinoffs ("Big Lebowski" €6). Popular with a laid-back, young crowd. Dark wood pillars, tables decorated with graffiti, and ever-present funk music create a trendy vibe. Open M-Sa 5pm-2am. MC/V.

Paxton's Head, 264-266 rue de Bourgogne (☎02 38 81 23 29). Sophisticated bar with suave leather couches, monogrammed carpets, and occasional live jazz. Though the posh gilded fireplace and dark felt walls may suggest high prices, the pub caters to a varied crowd and the TV draws rowdy fans during soccer matches. Owner will open private rooms in the back for large groups. Pool tables. Beer on tap €2.50-9.20. Mixed drinks €7-7.70. Karaoke Th-Sa 10pm. Open daily 3pm-3am. MC/V.

Moog, 38 rue de l'Empereur (☎02 38 54 93 23). Classy crowd enjoys hard liquor (€2.50) under sultry red lighting amid stainless-steel decor and sassy pop tunes. The terrace, with its orange chairs, is oddly reminiscent of a playground. Beer from €5. Mixed drinks €6.80. Open M-Sa July-Aug. 6pm-2am; Sept.-June 6pm-1am. MC/V.

Le Decibel, 229 rue de Bourgogne (☎02 38 77 28 71). Punk music floods the street as an eclectic clientele sips drinks at the outdoor tables. A cafe by day, this bar serves as a great warmup for a night on the town or a post-disco hangout. Wi-Fi available. Beer €2-4.50. 4th drink free. Mixed drinks €3.50-5. Student nights Th-Sa. Cover varies nightly. Open M-Sa 8am-1am. MC/V.

FESTIVALS

Fête de Jeanne d'Arc , in Apr. or May. Parades, music, and food in commemoration of the heroine's miraculous victory over the British.

Jazz d'Orléans (www.orleans.fr/orleansjazz), in June. Orléans hosts international guest musicians. Tickets €10-20, under 26 €10; some daytime concerts free.

Fête de Loire (☎02 38 24 05 05), during the last week of Sept. in odd-numbered years. Fireworks, theatrical events, and nautical displays along the banks of the Loire.

Semaines Musicales Internationales d'Orléans (SMIO), on weekends in Nov. and Dec. Features performances by the Orchestre National de France.

Marché de Noel, in the weeks leading up to Christmas. Candied apples and other local holiday goodies for sale on pl. du Martroi.

LOIRE VALLEY

🔁 DAYTRIPS FROM ORLÉANS

A day's drive eastward along the Loire reveals these three small villages, each from a different era of French history. An early bus (6:40am, €2) departs from **Orléans Routiere** (across from the train station) and stops at all three.

SULLY-SUR-LOIRE. Described by Voltaire as "the most likeable of castles," this white-turreted château 40km southeast of Orléans has been visited by the likes of Charles VII, Joan of Arc, and Louis XIV. Particularly noteworthy is the suite dedicated to the Greek goddess of the soul, Psyche, which was constructed during the Enlightenment and includes 17th-century tapestries bearing the Sully family's coat of arms. The château, meticulously maintained by the family until the 1960s, has recently undergone extensive renovations. Climb up to the chamber of the guards to steal a glimpse of the peaceful Loire stretching through the countryside. Throughout the year, themed tours are given in French; call ☎02 38 78 04 04 for reservations. The 17th-century forest surrounding the château offers a welcome respite from the summer crowds. A historical festival is held outside the castle on the third weekend in May. In mid-June, the grounds stage the **Festival de Sully et du Loiret,** a world-famous classical music festival. Also check out *Week-end* for summer specials like the beach rugby tournament or open-air film festivals at the château. *(Les Rapides du Val de Loire buses run to Bonny-sur-Loire via Sully-sur-Loire (45-80min., at least 4 per day, €2). At the bus stop, the Sully tourist office provides a free brochure. ☎02 38 36 23 70; www.sully-sur-loire.fr. Château open Tu-Su Apr.-Sept. 10am-6pm; Oct.-Dec. and Feb.-Apr. M 10am-6pm, Tu-Su 10am-noon. Forest open daily 8am-sunset. ☎02 38 36 36 86. €7, families €5. Free with prior visit to Chambrol and Gien. Festival reservations ☎0800 45 28 18; www.festival-sully.com.)*

GERMIGNY. About 30km southeast of Orléans lies the Carolingian church of Germigny-des-Prés. Originally constructed in AD 806 by order of Bishop Théodulfe, one of the most prominent "men of letters" in Charlemagne's court, it was thoroughly restored in the late 18th century and is among the three oldest churches in France. Enhancing the simple re-plastered interior are the original pillar headings and a startling ninth-century "golden" mosaic in the demi-cupola of the oratory. Hidden for "protection" behind a white wash, the mosaic was rediscovered in 1830 by a group of children who were playing underneath it. *(Les Rapides du Val de Loire buses run from Orléans to Germigny (45min., 1-3 per day 6:45am-6:30pm, €2). Church ☎02 38 58 27 97, www.tourisme-loire-foret.com. Church open daily Apr.-Oct. 9am-7pm; Nov.-Mar. 10am-5pm. Museum open daily Apr.-Oct. 9am-12:30pm and 2-7pm; Nov.-Dec. and from mid-Feb to Mar. 10am-noon and 2-5pm. Guided tours for groups over 15 with reservation. Church free. Museum €2, ages 10-18 €1, under 10 free.)*

SAINT-BENOÎT-SUR-LOIRE. A Romanesque basilica 35km southeast of Orléans, St-Benoît is home to a community of Benedictine monks. An important cultural center in the ninth through 12th centuries, it is still a pilgrimage site—St-Benedict's 1000-year-old relics lie in an iron casket in the candlelit crypt. Above, Philip I lies on an original fourth-century Roman marble mosaic, transported to the Fleury Abbey at his own bidding. During the French Revolution, the order almost disbanded as the number of monks dwindled to 10. Today, 40 monks live the ascetic life at the historic landmark. The monks offer six services a day, including Gregorian chants and a tour of the basilica every Sunday. *(Les Rapides du Val de Loire buses run from Orléans to Germigny (50min., 1-3 per day 6:45am-6:30pm, €2). Church ☎02 38 35 72 43. Open daily 6:30am-10pm. Abbey office open M-F 9-11:40am and 2-5:50pm. Services M-Sa 6:30am, noon, 2:30, 6:10, 9pm; Su 7:15, 11am, 3, 6:10, 9pm. French tour Su 3:15pm; €3. Write to Monastère de Fleury, 45730 St-Benoît-sur-Loire, to book ahead.)*

LOIRE VALLEY

BLOIS
☎**02 54**

Teenaged hipsters strut down the narrow streets in Blois (blwah; pop. 51,000), a town that showcases centuries worth of French architectural styles. A former medieval capital, Blois was home to Kings François I and Louis XIII and served as the site from which Joan of Arc gathered the army that would liberate Orléans. Today, Blois is a base for visits to Chambord and Cheverny—two of the Loire Valley's most famous châteaux; each is a short bike or bus trip away.

TRANSPORTATION

Trains: Pl. de la Gare (☎08 92 35 35 35). Open M-Sa 5:30am-8:15pm, Su 7:15am-10pm. Trains to: **Amboise** (20min., 15 per day, €6.20); **Angers** (1hr., 9-11 per day, €24) via Tours; **Orléans** (30-50min., 14 per day, €9.70); **Paris** (1hr., 8 per day, €26) via Orléans; **Tours** (40min., 8-13 per day 8am-7pm, €9.20).

Buses: Point Bus, 2 pl. Victor Hugo (☎02 54 78 15 66; www.tub-blois.fr). Open M 1:30-6pm, Tu-F 8am-noon and 1:30-6pm, Sa 9am-noon and 1:30-4:30pm. Transports Loir-et-Cher (☎02 54 58 55 44; www.tlcinfo.net) sends buses from the train station to **Chambord** and **Cheverny** (from mid-May to early Sept. 3 per day; €12; students, under 12, and over 65 €9; reduced entry to châteaux with bus ticket). Buy tickets on board. Open M-F 9am-noon and 2-6pm. For schedules contact TLC or the tourist office.

Taxis: Taxis Radio, pl. de la Gare (☎02 54 78 07 65). €5-6 from the station to the *vieille ville*, €26 to the castles. Open 24hr.

Bike Rental: Bike in Blois, 8 rue Henri Drussy (☎02 54 56 07 73; www.locationde-velos.com), near pl. de la Résistance. Standard bike €14 per day, tandem €38; price reduced for extra days. Open M-F 9:15am-1pm and 3-6:30pm, Su 10:30am-1pm and 3-6:15pm. Cash only. **Cycles LeBlond,** 44 Levée des Tuileries (☎02 54 74 30 13; cycle.leblond@caramail.com). To the left of pl. de la Résistance. €9 per ½-day, €12 per day, €25 per 3 days. Open daily 9am-9pm. Cash only.

ORIENTATION AND PRACTICAL INFORMATION

The château and *centre-ville* are 5min. from the train station, left down **avenue Jean Laigret.** Between the château and **rue Denis Papin** is a bustling pedestrian quarter. When in doubt, descend: all roads lead to the river and town center.

Tourist Office: Pl. du Château (☎02 54 90 41 41; www.bloispaysdechambord.com). Provides free maps of the city and biking routes in the Loire Valley, info on châteaux, tickets for bus circuits, and a reservation service (€2.30). Offers excellent themed tours of the area (€5-7; call office for reservations). Open Apr.-Sept. M-Sa 9am-7pm, Su and holidays 10am-7pm; Oct.-Mar. M-Sa 9:30am-12:30pm and 2-6pm, Su 10am-4pm.

English-Language Bookstore: Librairie l'Abbé, 9 rue Porte Chartraine. Open M 2-7:15pm, Tu-F 9:30am-7:15pm, Sa 9am-7:15pm. MC/V.

Library: Bibliothèque Abbé Grégoire, pl. Jean Jaurès (☎02 54 56 27 40). Internet €0.20 per 5min., €2.40 per hr; max 1 hr. No email or chatting. Open M-Tu and F 1-6:30pm, W and Sa 10am-noon and 2-5pm.

Youth Center: Bureau d'Information Jeunesse (BIJ), 7 av. Wilson (☎02 54 78 54 87). Free Internet access; no chatting. Computer reservations recommended. Brochures on accommodations, job info, cultural events, health, sports, and travel tips. Open M-Tu and Th-F 1-6pm, W 9am-noon and 1-6pm.

Laundromat: 6 rue St-Lubin and 1 rue Jeanne d'Arc. Wash €4.30 per 6kg, dry €1 per 10min. Open daily 7am-9pm.

Police: 42 quai St-Jean (☎02 54 90 09 00).

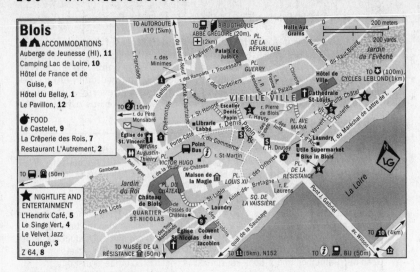

Blois

🔺🏠 **ACCOMMODATIONS**
Auberge de Jeunesse (HI), **11**
Camping Lac de Loire, **10**
Hôtel de France et de
  Guise, **6**
Hôtel du Bellay, **1**
Le Pavillon, **12**

🍴 **FOOD**
Le Castelet, **9**
La Crêperie des Rois, **7**
Restaurant L'Autrement, **2**

⭐ **NIGHTLIFE AND
ENTERTAINMENT**
L'Hendrix Café, **5**
Le Singe Vert, **4**
Le Velvet Jazz
  Lounge, **3**
Z 64, **8**

Red Cross: ☎02 54 55 65 45.

Pharmacy: Pharmacie des 3 Clefs, 30 rue Denis Papin (☎02 54 74 01 35). Open Tu-F 9am-7pm, Sa 8:30am-7pm.

Hospital: Centre Hospitalier de Blois, Mail Pierre Charlot (☎02 54 55 66 33; www.ch-blois.fr).

Post Office: 2 rue Gallois (☎02 54 57 17 17). **Currency exchange** available. Open M-F 8am-7pm, Sa 8am-12:30pm. **Postal Code:** 41000.

🏠🏠 ACCOMMODATIONS AND CAMPING

🛏 **Hôtel du Bellay,** 12 rue des Minimes (☎02 54 78 23 62; http://hoteldubellay.free.fr), at the top of porte Chartraine, to the right of the Old Quarter. Rustic old house, hidden away in a quiet, centrally located nook of the city. Clean rooms. Breakfast €5. Reservations recommended at least 3 weeks ahead. Singles and doubles with sink €25, with toilet €27, with shower €28, with full bath €37; triples and quads €54-62. MC/V. ❷

Le Pavillon, 2 av. Wilson (☎02 54 74 23 27; fax 02 54 74 03 36), on the Loire, across the Pont Gabriel. Walk 5min. or bus #3A from the train station. Bright, comfortable, simply furnished rooms, half of which overlook the Loire and châteaux. Foosball tables in downstairs *brasserie*. Recently renovated. Breakfast €6.50. Singles and doubles with sink €28, with shower and toilet €35; triples €45-55; family suite €65. Cash only. ❷

Hôtel de France et de Guise, 3 rue Gallois (☎02 54 78 00 53; fax 02 54 78 29 45). Ideal location next to the château. 50 elegant rooms—half of which overlook the château—awash in decadent 19th-century splendor. Glass chandeliers and reproductions of Impressionist works by Van Gogh, Renoir, and Monet adorn the hallways, and imposing paintings of the château greet breakfasters in the large dining area. All rooms with TV, phone, Wi-Fi, and bath; some with fireplaces and balconies. Breakfast in bed €7. Singles €45-52; doubles €52-65; family suites €82. MC/V. ❹

Auberge de Jeunesse (HI), 18 rue de l'Hôtel Pasquier (☎/fax 02 54 78 27 21), 5km west of Blois. Take bus #4 (dir.: Les Grouets) to Auberge de Jeunesse (10min., every 30min. 7am-7:35pm) or walk along the Loire (1hr.). 2 large single-sex rooms with 12 bunks each. Spacious and well-equipped kitchen and a common room. Hot showers and toilets in the yard. Nearby dining options scarce, save for a *boulangerie* down the road. Breakfast €3.60. Reception 6:45-10am and 6-10:30pm. Lockout 10am-6pm. Curfew 10:30pm. Open from Mar. to mid-Nov. Dorms €11. Cash only. ●

Camping Lac de Loire, (☎02 54 78 82 05; fax 02 54 78 62 03). From the station or *centre-ville,* take bus S7 to Lac de Loire (20min., July-Aug. 3 per day, €1.10). 2min. bike ride from the *centre-ville.* 220 sites, swimming pool, minigolf (€2), and tennis courts (€6 per hr.). Safe and family-friendly. Hot showers free. Reception July-Aug. 8:30am-noon and 4-7pm; June and Sept. 8am-noon and 2-8pm. Open June to mid-Sept. July-Aug. €15-18 per 2 people; €15-18 per tent; €15-18 per car. June and Sept. €13 per 2 people; €13 per tent; €13 per car. €5 per extra person. Electricity €3. AmEx/MC/V. ●

◘ FOOD

Traditional *blésois* restaurants line **rue Saint-Lubin** and **place Poids du Roi,** while relatively inexpensive Chinese, Italian, and Greek restaurants surround the lively **place de la Résistance.** An **Intermarché** supermarket is at 16 av. Gambetta (open M-Sa 9am-7pm) and a **8 à Huit** is at 11 rue du Commerce (open M-Sa 8am-8pm and Su 8am-noon). Behind Église St-Nicolas, **place Louis XII** bustles with an open-air food and clothing market. (Open Sa 8am-1pm.)

Le Castelet, 40 rue St-Lubin (☎02 54 74 66 09). A local fave by day and tourists' choice at night. Medieval regional specialties (cider-marinated chicken with seasonal vegetables, €13) and local wines, such as the *touraine amboise* (glass €14) can be enjoyed in the homey, rustic interior or on the outdoor terrace. The good-humored owner gladly helps customers' menu decisions and explains the preparation of each dish. Vegetarian *menu* available. *Plats* €10-15. *Menus* €15-29. Open M-Tu and Th-Sa noon-1:45pm and 7-9:45pm. Dinner reservations strongly recommended. MC/V. ❸

La Crêperie des Rois, 3 rue Denis Papin (☎02 54 90 01 90). *Crêperies* are a dime a dozen in most French towns, but this antique-decorated restaurant offers the widest selection in Blois. For a unique savory twist, try the "Texas" (steak, egg, tomatoes, and potatoes; €8.25) or the more exotic "Martinique" (pineapple, ham, cheese, and egg; €6.50). Dessert *crêpes* €0.90-8.50. Open Tu-Su noon-2pm and 7-10pm. MC/V. ●

Restaurant L'Autrement, 5 rue du Pont du Gast (☎02 54 58 89 08), behind St-Vincent. Outgoing waiters serve a variety of affordable pizzas (€7-10), salads (€8), pastas (€8.50-10), and bargain *formules* (*entrée du jour* and *plat du jour;* €8) on colorful cracked-glass tables. Brick bar caters to a diverse clientele. Open Tu-Th noon-3pm and 7-10:30pm, F-Sa noon-3pm and 7-11:30pm. MC/V. ❷

◔ SIGHTS

CHÂTEAU DE BLOIS. Called a "panorama of French architecture" because of the four periods that influenced its construction (Gothic, Renaissance, 16th century, and Classical), the château is the pride of Blois. Home to Louis XII and François I, Blois's château was as prominent in the 15th and early 16th centuries as Versailles became in later years. The motto of François I, *"Nutrisco et extingo"* ("I feed on fire and I extinguish it"), explains carved and painted fire-breathing salamanders, an icon found throughout the entire Loire Valley. As for the porcupines, they were the trademark of Louis XII, who embodied the French saying *"Qui s'y frotte, s'y pique"* ("Those who bother him will suffer the consequences"). The newest wing, part of the château's third major expansion, is a monument to French Classicism. It now houses two museums: the recently renovated **Musée des Beaux-Arts,** featuring a gallery of 16th- to 19th-century paintings, and the **Musée Lapidaire,** exhibiting sculpted rock pieces taken from nearby 16th- and 17th-century châteaux. Don't miss the four secret cabinets in the royal study, where Alexandre Dumas told Catherine de Medici to store her

P 10 PLACES TO FIND THE "SENTIMENT DE L'EXISTENCE"

ean-Jacques Rousseau championed the phrase *"sentiment de
'existence,"* the fulfillment found
iving in the moment. So kick back
n Rousseau's stomping ground
and enjoy the *dolce far niente—*
he sweetness of doing nothing.

_. Daydream atop of the **Denis
Papin stairs** in Blois—the height
may just leave you lightheaded.
2. Meditate by the Loire from the
aised **boardwalk** in Amboise.
_. Take in solitude in a sea of
vheat on the way to **Beauregard.**
_. Feel on top of the world as you
conquer the Loire and ascend to
he **Château de Chaumont.**
_. Gawk at Napoleon's magnifi-
cent cedar in the courtyard of the
Musée des Beaux-Arts in Tours.
_. Stroll down the **quai Maynaud**
and watch the sun slip behind
Saumur's splendid château.
_. Sink into Cathédrale St-Louis's
shadow in the **Jardin de l'Evêché**
and lose your senses in the view
of Blois's *vieille ville.*
_. Let your desire for material
goods melt away as you observe
passersby in designer jeans in Le
Mans's **place de la République.**
_. Sit at the bank of the moat near
Sully-sur-Loire's **château** and
ponder your reflection in the water
raversed by Jeanne d'Arc.
_0. Contemplate good and evil as
heir eternal struggle unfolds at
he Tapisserie de l'Apocalypse in
he **Château d'Angers.**

numerous poisons. Finally, you may want to take the 25min. carriage tour of the city, which departs from the château entrance. (☎02 54 90 33 33; www.ville-blois.fr. Open daily July-Aug. 9am-7pm; Apr.-June and Sept. 9am-6:30pm; Oct.-Mar. 9am-noon and 2-5:30pm. Ticket booth closes 30min. before château. Admission to château and museums €7.50, students under 25 €5, under 17 €3. Historical French tours depart from courtyard May-Sept. every hr.; call ahead to request 20min. English presentation in courtyard. Free with admission. Carriage tours daily July-Aug. 11am-7pm; Sept.-June 2:30-6:30pm. €6, under 12 €4. Light show daily June-July 10:30pm, Aug.-Sept. and from mid-Apr. to late May 10pm. €7, students €5, under 17 €3. English show W. Ticket to château and light show €11.50, students €8.50, under 18 €5.50. Ticket to château and Maison de la Magie €13/8.50/5.50. Ticket for all 3 attractions €17/11/9. MC/V.)

MUSÉE DE LA RÉSISTANCE, DE LA DÉPORTATION, ET DE LA LIBÉRATION. This museum is a powerful memorial to local French Holocaust victims and the city of Blois during WWII. The stories alone—including those about the US pilot who nearly crashed into the Château of Chambord and the circus elephants that were used to pull down crumbling houses in the town center—make it worth the visit. The museum is staffed by WWII veterans and Resistance members, who give excellent tours. (1 pl. de la Grève. ☎02 54 56 07 02. Open M-F 9am-noon and 2-6pm, Sa 2-6pm. €3, students and under 18 €1. For guides in English, call ahead. Translations of tours available.)

MAISON DE LA MAGIE. Beside the château, this museum entertains with mildly amusing films, optical illusions, and displays dedicated to famous *blésois* magician Robert Houdin (Houdini's stage name was a tribute to him). The **hallucinoscope,** a large optical illusion device, is the most popular attraction. The *spectacle* (magic show), performed three to four times a day, provides lighthearted entertainment—especially for children. (1 pl du Château. ☎02 54 90 33 33; www.maisondelamagie.fr. Open July-Aug. daily 10am-12:30pm and 2-6:30pm; Apr.-June and Sept. Tu-Su 10am-12:30pm and 2-6pm. Free guided tours with reservation. 1hr. shows July 20-Aug. 20 11:15am, 2:45, 4, 5:15pm; Aug. 20-July 2011:15am, 3:15, 5:15pm. €7.50, students under 25 €6.50, ages 6-17 €5, under 6 free.)

VIEILLE VILLE. The most relaxing and authentic Blois attractions may be its hilly streets and ancient staircases. Bars and bakeries on **rue Saint-Lubin** and **rue des Trois Marchands** tempt those en route to the 12th-century **Abbaye Saint-Laumer,** now the **Église Saint-Nicolas.** (Open daily 9am-6:30pm. Mass Su 9:30am.) The winding streets east of **rue Denis Papin** are especially beautiful. Meanwhile, 500 years of expansions have endowed **Cathédrale Saint-Louis**—one of Blois's architectural jewels—with a beautiful mix of architectural styles. *(Open daily 7:30am-6:30pm. Crypt open June-Aug.)* A spectacular view from the **Jardin de l'Evêché,** behind the cathedral, reaches over the rooftops of the old quarter, stretching along the brilliant Loire. On your way down, rest at the top of the Denis Papin stairs and watch the city unfold into the distance.

NIGHTLIFE

Nightlife in Blois may be somewhat toned down, but there is a decent variety of places to finish the night off right. Not too far from the center of the action, **rue de Foulerie** has its own set of less touristy restaurants and bars, whose crowds spill into the street in the summer.

Le Velvet Jazz Lounge, 15 rue Haute (☎02 54 78 36 32), just off rue Denis Papin. Holds weekly jazz concerts in a casually classy bar with high-vaulted ceilings that testify to its past as a 13th-century abbey. Blois's 1st nonsmoking establishment. Reservations for concerts recommended. Beer €2.50-5. Mixed drinks €6.50-8.50. Concerts held 1st and/or last F of every month 8-11pm; cover €8-10, sometimes free. Open Tu-Su 3pm-2am; *salon de thé* open 3-7pm. AmEx/MC/V.

Le Singe Vert, 8 rue de Foulerie (☎02 54 78 18 87). This jungle-themed bar serves pint-size glasses of every mixed drink imaginable to the young crowd of regulars who tear up the dance floor. 2 goldfish guard the counter. Guest DJs spin a mix of tunes. Mixed drinks €6-9.50. Concerts and themed parties like Salsa Night keep the scene fresh. Open June-Sept. M and W-Su 7pm-2am; Oct.-Apr. Th-Su 7pm-2am. MC/V.

Z 64, 6 rue Maréchal de Lattre de Tassigny (☎02 54 74 27 76). Around midnight, most—if not all—20-somethings in Blois flock to the neon lights of this downtown club overlooking the Loire. Furnished with velvet zebra-patterned couches, Egyptian-like decor, and a large screen showing music videos. Mixed drinks €6.50-9. €4.50 min. drink purchase. Open Th-Sa 10:30pm-5am. MC/V.

L'Hendrix Café, 1 rue du Puits Châtelet (☎02 54 58 82 73). Posters of rock icons decorate this popular and boisterous bar. Hang among young local goths and rockers and sip a "Led Zeppelin" or "Pink Floyd." Beer €2.30-5. Mixed drinks €7 and up. Terrace cover €0.20. Open June-Sept. daily 3pm-3am; Oct.-Mar. M-Tu and Th-Su 3pm-3am. MC/V.

FESTIVALS

Halle aux Grains (☎02 54 90 44 00), Oct.-Apr. Blois hosts world-class jazz and classical musicians, dancers, and actors. Schedules available by phone. Performances Tu-F 1:30-6:30pm, Sa 2-5pm. Tickets €19-23, students €16-21.

Tous sur le Pont (☎08 92 68 36 22; www.toussurlepont.com). Now in its 3rd year, this music festival rocks Blois during 1st half of July. 2008 featured Alpha Blondy. Open daily 9am-7pm. Festival Pass €34.

DAYTRIPS FROM BLOIS

Transports Loir-et-Cher (TLC) buses, outside the Blois train station, run a châteaux circuit to Chambord and Cheverny (5hr. with 2hr. for each castle, €9.20). For those who prefer to go at their own pace, the châteaux are within relatively easy biking distance through spectacular views of forests and wheat fields. From Blois, it's 18km to Chaumont, 15km to Cheverny, and 10km to Beauregard. Green signposts along the roads mark the châteaux and towns. Cyclists should stay off major highways whenever possible. The tourist office branch across from the Château de Blois distributes maps of safe and efficient routes.

LOIRE VALLEY

The **Regional Tourism Committee** (☎02 54 78 62 52; www.loire-valley-travel.com) offers one-week cycling packages and walking tours of the Loire Valley.

▨CHEVERNY

To bike or drive to the château, head across the Loire on Pont Gabriel and continue straight on av. Wilson. For a long (16-20km) but scenic route, veer toward Chailles when the road splits to Chambord and Chailles. 4km down, turn toward Celletes. Follow signs to Château Troussay and then Cheverny. Alternatively, take D765 south for 12km. Château ☎02 54 79 96 29; www.chateau-cheverny.fr. Open daily July-Aug. 9:15am-6:45pm; Apr.-June and Sept. 9:15am-6:15pm; Oct. 9:30am-5:30pm; Jan.-Mar. and Nov.-Dec. 9:45am-5pm. €7, students €6. Call for guided tours in English, German, and Spanish. The same bus that leaves from the SNCF station to Chambord continues to Cheverny (€9.20).

Ever since its completion in 1634, Cheverny (shay-vayr-nee) has been privately owned by the Hurault family, whose members have served as financiers and officers to the kings of France. The marquis, his wife, and their three children currently live in the castle, which in 1922 became one of the first privately owned châteaux to open its doors to visitors. Murals, armor, and elegant tapestries recounting romantic stories cover every inch of wallspace in the luxurious **Chambre du Roi.** In the dining room, a series of paintings by Jean Monier recreates the story of Don Quixote. The portrait of Jeanne d'Aragon in the salon is attributable to the world-famous Renaissance painter Raphael. Fans of Hergé's *Tintin* books may recognize Cheverny's Renaissance facade as the inspiration for the design of Captain Haddock's mansion, Moulinsart. A gallery of Hergé's art and comics is adjacent to the château's souvenir shop. As well known as the château itself, Cheverny's kennels are home to 120 English-Poitevin hounds still used in hunting expeditions. The *repas de la meurte de chiens* offers a unique opportunity to see these hounds gulp down their chicken and duck dinner at their master's command in less than 60 seconds. (Open from Apr. to mid-Sept. M-F 5pm.) Next to the kennels, in the trophy room, thousands of antlers surround a striking stained-glass window depicting the hunt.

Luxurious—and expensive—**Camping Les Saules ❷** is located 2km south on the road to Contres. Swimming pool and bike rental are onsite, with an 18-hole golf course nearby. (☎02 54 79 90 01; www.camping-cheverny.com. Open daily Apr.-Oct. 8:30am-8:30pm. €16-26 per site, depending on the season; includes 2 people, 1 car, tent, or caravan. €4.50 per extra person, ages 4-10 €2.)

▨CHAMBORD

Take the TLC bus just left of the Blois SNCF station (45min.; May-Sept. 9:10, 11:10am, 1:42pm; €11.20, students €9) or bike 2hr. To bike or drive, cross the Loire and ride 1km on av. Wilson. At the roundabout, go straight until St-Gervais-la-Forêt, then turn left onto D33. Château ☎02 54 50 40 00; www.chambord.org. Open daily from mid-July to mid-Aug. 9am-7:30pm; from Apr. to mid-July and from mid-Aug. to Sept. 9am-6:15pm; Oct.-Mar. 9am-5:15pm. Last entry 30min. before closing. July-Aug. €9.50, ages 18-25 €6.50, under 17 free; Sept.-June €8.50. €2 discount with bus ticket. MC/V.

Built by François I between 1519 and 1545 as a hunting lodge and party house, Chambord (shahm-bohr) is perhaps the largest and most extravagant of the Loire châteaux. A testament to the monarch's desire to flaunt his growing power, the castle could accommodate his entire court—up to 10,000 people. With 426 rooms, 365 chimneys, 282 fireplaces, and 77 staircases, the castle is a surprising synthesis of forms inherited from past centuries and innovations from Renaissance Italy. The Greek-cross floor design used for the keep (the main tower) was formerly reserved for sacred buildings, but 25-year-old François co-opted it in his quest for self-deification. In the center of the castle, he built a spectacular double-helix staircase, the design of which is attributed to

Leonardo da Vinci. The staircase's hollow, high interior mimics cathedral architecture. The chapel in the château's right wing is echoed in François's bedroom in the left. Apparently the king insisted on being worshipped—even in bed.

The ornamentation of Chambord represents the first Italian Renaissance influence on French architecture. François stamped Chambord with 200 of his trademark stone salamanders, commissioned 14m tapestries of his hunting conquests, splayed his initials across the large stone chimneys on the rooftop terrace, and scattered the royal *fleurs de lys* liberally throughout the chambers. Despite the effort, François graced Chambord with his presence for only 72 days, dying before his fantastic dream was completed. In the 17th century, a new wing was built for Louis XIV. Busts of Molière and Lully—who performed in the castle in 1669—adorn his room's antechamber. Rooms are labeled in English, but more detailed explanations of the château are available through an audio tour (€5) in many languages. Also available are 30min. historical presentations, guided tours (€5, students €4), and French tours (€6.50) of the castle as well as a variety of guided excursions into the surrounding forest.

There's an **ATM** next to the snack shops outside the tourist office. To explore surrounding forests, rent a **boat** or **bike** through **Traineur de Loire** near the château. The boat tour around the castle (€8.50, students €6.50; with castle entrance €14/13) affords a panoramic view of the château. (☎02 54 33 37 54. 2-person boats €14 per hr., 3-person €15 per hr., 4-to 5-person €16 per hr. Bikes €6 per hr., €12 per ½-day, €15 per day. Tandem €13 per hr. €14 for 15min. boat ride and bottle of wine. Open daily July-Aug. 10am-7:30pm; Sept.-Oct. and Apr.-June 10am-6pm. MC/V.) Medieval shows take place on castle grounds in summer. (☎02 54 20 31 01. July-Aug. daily 11:45am, 4:30pm. €9, under 18 €7). Campers can trek to **Huisseau-sur-Cosson ❶**, 6 rue de Châtillon, 5km southwest of Chambord on D33. (☎02 54 20 35 26. Open May-Sept. daily 9am-noon and 3-8pm. €4 per person, under 7 €3; €3.50 per tent. Electricity €3.)

🏛 CHAUMONT

Chaumont is accessible by a 1hr. bike ride or 20min. car ride from Blois (16km on N152, dir.: Tours). By bike, make a right after crossing Pont Gabriel and follow D751 to Chaumont. Tourist office directions may suggest you take N152, but it is a large highway. The train that goes from Blois to Tours also runs through Onzain (10min.; M-F 10 per day, Sa-Su 9 per day; €4). From there, it's a 15min. walk to the castle. From the station, head toward the Auberge du Moulin, cross the bridge, and turn right. The Chaumont tourist office, 24 rue Maréchal Leclerc (☎02 54 20 91 73), across the bridge from N152, rents bikes (€8-10 per ½-day, €15 per day). Open W-F 9:30am-7pm, Su 9:30am-1pm and 1:30-6pm. Château ☎02 54 51 26 26; www. domaine-chaumont.fr. Open daily from early May to mid-Sept. 9:30am-6:30pm; late Sept. and from Apr. to early May 10am-6pm; Oct.-Mar. 10am-12:30pm and 1:30-5pm. Last entrance 30min. before closing. Wheelchair-accessible. €7.50, students €5.30, under 12 free.

Built on a precipice, Chaumont (shoh-mohn) peeks out from a shield of pines as though painted into the sky. Originally built in the 10th century by the *comte de Blois* to protect his territories from his rival, the *comte d'Anjou*, the castle stands strikingly—and strategically—overlooking the Loire. The marriage of Denise de Fougères to Sulpice d'Amboise delivered Chaumont into the Amboise family's hands. Following Henri II's death in 1559, his widow Catherine de Medici bought the castle in revenge against Diane de Poitiers, Henri's mistress, who resided in the nearby Château of Chenonceau—a royal architectural jewel that Catherine had coveted for years. She then forced Diane to move from Chenonceau to Chaumont. While Chaumont is not the most lavish of the Loire châteaux, it is one of the most creatively decorated, with intricate designs on the tile floor and paneled ceilings. Throughout the visit, the history of the castle unfolds, ending with a billiard and sitting room furnished in the style of the 1920s. The grounds and gardens of Chaumont are spectacular, as is the view of the Loire Valley. Gardeners from around the world also compete annually in Chaumont's **international garden festival.** The festival is a favorite with children. (☎02 54 20 99 22; www.chaumont-jardins.com. Festival open daily from May to mid-Oct. 9:30am-dusk. Gardens €9, students €6.50, ages 6-18 €3.50. Festival and château €15.Ticket booth closes at 7pm.)

BEAUREGARD

A 1hr., 10km bike ride from Blois. Follow directions to Cheverny, but take a left off D765. A taxi from Blois costs €18. Château ☎02 54 70 40 05. For English assistance, call ☎02 54 70 36 74. Open July-Aug. daily 9:30am-6:30pm; Sept. and Apr.-June daily 9:30am-noon and 2-6pm; Oct.-Nov., from mid-Dec. to early Jan., and from early Feb. to Mar. M-Tu and Th-Su 9:30am-noon and 2-5pm. €6.50, students and ages 7-18 €4.50, under 8 free. Gardens €4.50. Tours are available every hr. in French. Information sheets available in multiple languages.

Before François I unleashed his fantasies on Chambord, he designed Beauregard (boh-ruh-gahr) as a hunting lodge 10km south of Blois for his uncle René, nicknamed the Bastard of Savoie. Though the château belonged to nobility, it is cozier than its flashy cousin and is nestled in a sea of wheat fields, sheltered by cool pines. The portrait gallery, which was commissioned by Paul Ardier, treasurer to Louis XIII, is the world's largest. Today, this collection of 327 wall-to-wall paintings, called the **Galerie des Illustres,** is a who's who of European powers—including the likes of Philippe de Valois, Louis XIII, Elizabeth I, and Christopher Columbus. Though unfurnished, the **Cabinet des Grelots** (Chamber of Bells), in the south wing, is covered with remarkable oak paneling, skillfully carved by Jean du Thier, who also worked for Diane de Poitiers. Added in 1996, **Le Jardin Des Portraits,** behind the château, is a classic French garden, with floral sections arranged by color. To the right of the château are the preserved *glacières*, caves that were once used to collect ice in winter in order to serve cold beverages and sorbets in summer at the request of Catherine de Medici.

AMBOISE ☎02 47

Compared to other Loire Valley towns, Amboise (am-bwahz; pop. 12,000) is tiny, but its peaceful, intimate surroundings ensure the town's popularity with visitors—indeed, tourism is its lifeline. One of the oldest cities in the Loire Valley, Amboise was home to Charles VIII, Louis XI, Louis XII, Catherine de Medici, and François I. Amboise's most famous resident was actually Italian: Leonardo da Vinci spent his final years here. The town's castle, mysterious cave dwellings, and breathtaking views of the Loire more than make up for its shamelessly overpriced restaurants and accommodations. Budget options do exist for those willing to hunt for them.

▐ TRANSPORTATION

Trains: 1 rue Jules Ferry (☎02 47 23 47 23). Open M-F 6:15am-9pm, Sa 7:15am-9pm, Su 9am-9:15pm. To: **Blois** (20min., 10 per day, €6.80); **Orléans** (1hr., every hr., €14); **Paris** (2hr., every hr., €28); **Tours** (20min., 24 per day, €5.20).

Buses: Fil Vert (www.touraine-filvert.com). Departs the tourist office for **Chenonceau** (30min., 2 per day, €3) and **Tours** (35min., 1-2 per day, €3).

Taxis: 12 quai du Général de Gaulle (☎02 47 45 19 55).

Bike Rental: Loca Cycles, 2 bis Jean-Jacques Rousseau (☎02 47 57 00 28), off quai du Général de Gaulle as you walk toward the château. €14 per day, €37 per 3 days; passport deposit. Open Mar.-Oct. daily 9am-12:30pm and 2-7pm. Cash only.

LOIRE VALLEY

⚞⚟ ORIENTATION AND PRACTICAL INFORMATION

Tourist Office: Quai du Général de Gaulle (☎02 47 57 09 28; www.amboise-valdeloire. com). Take a left from the station and follow rue Jules Ferry until it ends, then take a right. Cross the 1st bridge to your left and pass the residential Île d'Or. Cross the 2nd bridge and turn right immediately; the office is 30m down in a circular building across from the shops. Ask about discounts on châteaux admission. Posts hotel vacancies and makes reservations (€2.50); to avoid the fee, call the hotline (☎02 47 23 27 42).

Tours: Information on self-guided walking tours available at the tourist office. Call to reserve. Daily group tours for at least 20 people available; €7, students €6. Some tours in English. Call ahead for guided individual tours. Open M-Sa 9am-1pm and 2-6:30pm; hours change frequently; call ahead for updated info.

Youth Center: Pôle Jeunesse, 19 rue d'Île d'Or (☎02 47 30 55 98; pij.amboise@wana-doo.fr), across the street from **Île d'Or Camping** (see this page). Free **Internet** (M-F 2-5pm). Open M and W-F 9am-noon and 2-5pm, Tu 2-5pm.

Laundromat: LavCentre, 5 allée du Sergent Turpin, across the road from the tourist office. Wash €3.50 per 7kg, dry €1 per 10min. Open daily 7am-9pm. Last wash 8pm.

Police: 1 bd. Anatole France (☎02 47 30 63 70).

Hospital: Hôpital Robert Debre, rue des Ursulines (☎02 47 23 33 33).

Internet Access: Free at the **Pôle Jeunesse** (above). **Cyber Café,** 119 rue Nationale (☎02 47 57 18 04). €1 per 15min., €3 per hr. Sandwich, drink, and 1hr. of Internet access noon-2pm €5. Open M and Su 3-10pm, Tu-Sa 10am-10pm.

Post Office: 20 quai du Général de Gaulle. Facing the tourist office, turn left and walk 3 blocks. **Currency exchange** available. Open M-F 8:30am-12:30pm and 2-6pm, Sa 8:30am-12:30pm. **Postal Code:** 37400.

⌂⌂ ACCOMMODATIONS AND CAMPING

▨ **Hôtel Café des Arts,** 32 rue Victor Hugo (☎/fax 02 47 57 25 04), at the foot of the castle. Vibrantly decorated rooms have bunk beds and sinks. Well-maintained bathrooms in the hall. Reception M and W-F 9am-11pm, Sa-Su 9am-midnight. Open Apr.-Feb. July-Aug. singles €25; doubles €36; triples €58; quads €70. Sept.-Feb. and Apr.-June singles €25; doubles €33; triples €47; quads €58. MC/V. ❷

Centre International de Séjour Charles Péguy (HI), Île d'Or (☎02 47 30 60 90; www.mjcamboise.fr). Follow rue Jules Ferry from the station, cross the 1st bridge on your left, head downhill, and take the 1st right. Clean, colorful, and inviting hostel doubles as a youth center. For a Loire view, ask for a 3rd fl. room. TV, game, and dining rooms can be reserved for groups. Breakfast €3. Linen €3. Reception 10am-noon and 2-8pm. Reservations highly recommended. 1- to 4-bed dorms €12. Cash only. ❶

Hôtel Belle-Vue, 12 quai Charles Guinot (☎02 47 57 02 26; fax 30 51 23). 3-star hotel offers tastefully furnished rooms with wood beds. Despite the name, only half of the rooms have a view. Breakfast €9.50. Reception daily 7am-11pm. Singles €49; doubles €59-69; triples €78; quads €88. MC/V. ❹

▨ **Île d'Or Camping,** Île d'Or (Oct.-Mar. ☎02 46 57 23 37). Clean, well-maintained campground feels more like an outdoor hotel. Multilingual staff, pool (€2.20), minigolf, restaurant, and great Loire views from the *île*. Shower €1.50 for non-guests. Reception July-Aug. 7am-9pm; Sept. and Apr.-May 8:30am-12:15pm and 2:30-7:30pm; June

8am-12:15pm and 2:30-7:30pm. July-Aug. €2.50 per person, children €1.70; sites €3.30. Electricity €2.10. Prices lower Sept.-June. MC/V. ❶

🔲 FOOD

At the base of the château, **rue Victor Hugo** and **rue Nationale** are lined with *brasseries* and *boulangeries*. For a cheap picnic on the Loire banks, stop by **Marché Plus,** 5 quai du Général de Gaulle. (Open M-Sa 7am-9pm, Su 9am-1pm. AmEx/MC/V.) Friday and Sunday mornings, a market unfolds along the riverbanks.

▨ **Café des Arts,** 32 rue Victor Hugo (☎/fax 02 47 57 25 04), on the ground floor of the namesake hotel. Good-humored staff serves sandwiches (€3.10-5), hot snacks (€4-7.50), and salads (€2-9). Concerts, art exhibits, and book readings attract a young, amiable crowd. Open M and W-F 9am-9pm, Sa-Su 10am-10pm. MC/V. ❶

Chez Hippeau, 1 rue François 1er (☎02 47 57 26 30). Locals put up with tourist crowds for delicious regional treats. Classy terrace and sleek interior. Proud owner happily guides guests through the menu. Large salads €12-16. *Menus* €16-25. Open daily July-Aug. noon-3:30pm and 7-10:30pm; Sept.-June noon-2:30pm and 7-9pm. MC/V. ❸

Art Thé, 6 pl. Michel Debré. Plenty of books and hearty breakfasts (€7.50) welcome you to the warm, shabby-chic cafe where customers play board games and sip tea. Ice cream €2.50. Coffee €3. Open daily 9am-7pm. Cash only. ❶

👁 SIGHTS

CHÂTEAU ROYAL D'AMBOISE. Perched atop a precipice overlooking the Loire, this château was once considered one of France's most beautiful. In its glory days, the château housed as many as 4000 people. In 1560, a failed Protestant conspiracy to kidnap the young King François II from the influential Catholic family de Guise led to grisly murder: some of the rebel Huguenots were tossed into the Loire in sacks, while others were decapitated or hung on the château balcony, now described by smiling tour guides as the "Balcony of the Hanging People." The **Logis du Roi,** the main part of the château, still holds carved chairs fashioned to prevent surprise attacks from behind. Most of the château was destroyed or sold off during Napoleon's reign; the current building has been heavily restored. The impressive **Tour des Minimes** attests to the castle's original size; descend to its less frequented twin, the **Tour Hertault,** as you exit the château's gift shop to get an insider's view of the castle. For an outstanding, more popular view, ascend the **Tour Cavalière** and gaze at the Loire below. The jewel of the visit, however, is the ▨**Chapelle Saint-Hubert,** an unassuming Gothic chapel next to the château, which holds Leonardo da Vinci's remains. Dim light, delicate stained-glass windows, fresh flowers, and a stone likeness of Leonardo's face pay the artist graceful homage. Perhaps less graceful is the glimpse up the king's stone skirts as you enter the chapel. Be on the lookout for summer theater productions that take place in the castle in summer months. (*Between rue Victor Hugo and rue de la Concorde.* ☎02 47 57 00 98. www.chateau-amboise.com. *Open daily July-Aug. 9am-7pm; Sept. 9am-6pm; from early to mid-Nov. and Mar. 9am-5:30pm; from mid-Nov. to Jan. 9am-12:30pm and 2-4:45pm; Feb. 9am-12:30pm and 1:30-5pm; Apr.-June 9am-6:30pm. Wheelchair-accessible. €9, students €7.50, ages 7-14 €5.30. MC/V.*)

▨**MAISONS TROGLODYTIQUES.** These centuries-old houses are built into hollowed-out cliffs along narrow, sinuous rue Victor Hugo. Constructed at the same time as the château, these hollows belonged to modest factory workers who grew gardens on the roofs and carved additional rooms into the rock. Today, many of the houses are vacant; to peer into abandoned hollows, walk up the cul-de-sac rue Leonard Perrault.

CAVEAU DES VIGNERONS. Built within the walls of the château, Caveau des Vignerons offers free tastings of locally made wine, goat cheese, *foie gras*, and preserved meats. (*Pl. Michel Debré. ☎ 02 47 57 23 69. Wine €5.50-25 per bottle. Foie gras €6-21. Goat cheese €2.70-6.50. Open daily Apr.-Nov. 10am-7pm. MC/V.*)

CLOS LUCÉ. Amboise's quirkiest attraction rests 400m up rue Victor Hugo. Leonardo da Vinci's most generous patron, François I, gave the artist this Renaissance manor and its sprawling gardens. The king used an underground tunnel between the château and Clos Lucé to visit the artist. Leonardo's bedroom, library, and drawing room have been somewhat unconvincingly restored to resemble their 16th-century selves, while replicas of Leonardo's drawings—including a sketch of the world's first machine gun—rest in the cellar near the tunnel's entrance. (*☎ 02 47 57 00 73. Open daily July-Aug. 9am-8pm; Sept.-Oct. and Apr.-June 9am-7pm; Nov.-Dec. and Feb.-Mar. 9am-6pm; Jan. 10am-5pm. July-Aug. €12.50, students €9.50, under 18 €7; Sept.-Dec. and Feb.-June €9/7/6. Gardens closed in low season. MC/V.*)

🍷 🌿 NIGHTLIFE AND FESTIVALS

The enormous and imaginative drinks at **Le Shaker,** 1 rue de l'Entrepont, on Île d'Or, come shaken—not stirred—and test even the highest tolerances. A young, rowdy crowd from nearby campgrounds and hostels gathers in the evenings to drink amid the gorgeous backdrop of the Loire and château's silhouette. (*☎02 47 23 24 26. Beer €3-6. Mixed drinks €7.50-8. Snacks €6-8. Open June-Sept. M-Th 6pm-3am and F-Sa 6pm-4am. MC/V.*)

> **Les Courants** (*☎02 47 57 09 28; www.lescourants.com*) in early summer. Popular music, film, and art festival. Amboise's parks burst with tents and campers as French youth come to hear their favorite French ska, jazz, and rock bands. Tickets €15-40.

> **Brass Band Festival,** 2nd weekend of June. Marching tunes and classical music. Tickets €6-15. Call the tourist office for more info.

TOURS   ☎02 47

According to Balzac, Tours (toor; pop. 142,000) is "laughing, in love, fresh, flowery, and perfumed better than all the other cities of the world." Although Balzac might have been confusing his birthplace with his idea of the perfect woman, Tours has charmed travelers and locals alike since the Roman era. Born out of the chaos of the Hundred Years' War, the city reigned as the heart of the French kingdom in the 15th and 16th centuries. During WWII, Tours sustained enormous losses, and few monuments remain to attest to its former status. Today, joggers fill the paths along the banks of the Loire, and after sunset, the city's 30,000 students take over the cafe-lined boulevards and the animated pl. Plumereau (**"place Plum"** to locals). Famous for its lack of a local accent, this capital of *"le bien-parlé"* ("the well-spoken") is the best place to perfect your French during a visit to the valley's châteaux.

▣ TRANSPORTATION

> **Trains:** Pl. du Général Leclerc. Info office open M-Sa 5:50am-9:30pm, Su 5:50am-11:30pm. To **Paris** (3hr., every hr., €29), **Poitiers** (50min., 6 per day, €16), and **Saumur** (40min., 12 per day, €11) via **Saint-Pierre-des-Corps.** TGV runs to **Bordeaux** (4hr., every hr., €46), **Paris** (1hr., every hr., €55), and **Poitiers** (1hr., 13 per day, €19).

> **Public Transportation:** Fil Bleu, 5 rue de la Dolve (*☎02 47 66 70 70*), near the train station. Office open M-F 7:30am-7pm, Sa 8:30am-1:30pm. Buses run daily 6am-8:30pm

and occasionally at night; map and bus schedules available from the Fil Bleu office. Tickets €1.50, weekly passes €14 with photo ID.

Taxis: Taxis-Radio, 13 rue de Nantes (☎02 47 20 30 40). €1.40 per km during the day, €2.10 at night. 24hr.

Car Rental: Avis (☎02 47 20 53 27), in the train station. From €91 per day. Under-25 surcharge €25. Open M-F 8am-12:30pm and 1:30-6:30pm, Sa 9am-noon and 2-6pm. AmEx/MC/V.

Bike Rental: Détours de Loire, 35 rue Charles Gîles (☎02 47 61 22 23; www.loca-tiondevelos.com). Bike return at different locations along the Loire, including Blois and Chinon. High season €14 per day, low season €11. Tandem €38 per day. Open M-Sa 9am-1pm and 2-7pm, Su 9:30am-12:30pm and 6-7pm. MC/V.

✦ ⓘ ORIENTATION AND PRACTICAL INFORMATION

Place Jean Jaurès, with its two grandiose fountains, is the intersection of four boulevards in the *centre-ville*. The commercial **rue Nationale,** once part of the main road between Paris and Spain, runs north to the Loire, while **avenue de Grammont** reaches toward the Cher River to the south. **Boulevard Béranger** and **boulevard Heurteloup** run west and east, respectively, from pl. Jean Jaurès. The pedestrian *vieille ville,* the lively **place Plumereau,** and most historical sights are a 10min. walk northwest of pl. Jean Jaurès toward the Loire.

Tourist Office: 78-82 rue Bernard Palissy (☎02 47 70 37 37; www.ligeris.com). Free accommodations booking and reservations for château tours. The ▧**Carte Multi-Visites** (€9; valid for 1 year) provides access to 5 museums and a city tour—be sure to ask about it, as they keep this secret bargain under wraps. Internet access €1 per 15min. Open from mid-Apr. to mid-Oct. M-Sa 8:30am-7pm, Su 10am-12:30pm and 2:30-5pm; from mid-Oct. to mid-Apr. M-Sa 9am-12:30pm and 1:30-6pm, Su 10am-1pm.

Tours: Schedules at the tourist office. 2hr. walking tours from mid-July to mid-Aug. M-Th and Sa-Su 10am; from mid-Aug. to Nov. and from Apr. to mid-July Su 10am. €5.50, ages 6-12 €3. 2hr. nighttime walking tours July-Aug. F 9:30pm. €9/7. Themed tours €5.50/4.50. Call ahead for tours in English and for up-to-date schedules.

Banks: 24hr. **ATMs** can be found all along rue Nationale, including at **BNP Paribas,** 86 rue Nationale (☎08 92 70 57 05), near rue des Minimes. Open M 2-5:45pm, Tu-F 9am-12:15pm and 1:30-6pm, Sa 9am-12:45pm.

English-Language Bookstore: La Boîte à Livres de l'Étranger, 2 rue du Commerce (☎02 47 05 67 29). Open M 10am-7pm, Tu-Sa 9:30am-7pm. MC/V.

Youth Center: Bureau d'Information Jeunesse (BIJ), 78-80 rue Michelet (☎02 47 64 69 13). Free Internet access with daily sign-up. Open Tu and Th 1-6pm, W 10am-noon and 1-6pm, F 1-4pm.

Laundromat: Lavo 2000, 17 rue Bretonneau (☎02 47 73 14 69). Wash €3.80 per 8kg, dry €1 per 10min. Open daily 7am-8:30pm.

Police: 70-72 rue de Marceau (☎02 47 33 80 69).

Hospital: Hôpital Bretonneau, 2 bd. Tonnellé (☎02 47 47 47 47).

Internet Access: Free at **BIJ** (see above) and at the **tourist office** (see above). **Top Communications,** 68-70 rue du Grand Marché (☎02 47 76 19 53). €0.50 per 10min., €2 per hr. Open daily 10am-midnight.

Post Office: 1 bd. Béranger (☎02 47 60 34 05). **Currency exchange** available. Open M-F 8am-7pm, Sa 8am-noon. Branch office at 92 rue Colbert. **Postal Code:** 37000.

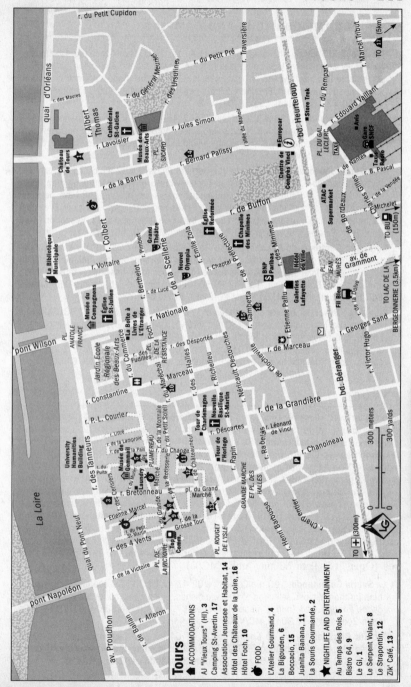

Tours

▲ ACCOMMODATIONS
AJ "Vieux Tours" (HI), 3
Camping St-Avertin, 17
Association Jeunesee et Habitat, 14
Hôtel des Châteaux de la Loire, 16
Hôtel Foch, 10

● FOOD
L'Atelier Gourmand, 4
La Bigouden, 6
Boccacio, 15
Juanita Banana, 11
La Souris Gourmande, 2

★ NIGHTLIFE AND ENTERTAINMENT
Au Temps des Rois, 5
Bistro 64, 9
Le GI, 1
Le Serpent Volant, 8
Le Strapontin, 12
Zik' Café, 13

ACCOMMODATIONS AND CAMPING

Hôtel Foch, 20 rue du Maréchal Foch (☎02 47 05 70 59; hotel-foch.tours@wanadoo. fr). Family atmosphere, spacious, tastefully decorated rooms, and clean baths in an unbeatable location. Owners are extremely knowledgeable about Tours and more than willing to spin you a yarn. Breakfast €6.50. Parking €5. Singles €20-34; doubles €23-46; triples €37-58; quads €51-58. MC/V. ●

AJ "Vieux Tours" (HI), 5 rue Bretonneau (☎02 47 37 81 58; www.ajtours.org). 146 rooms in former student dorm. Rooms with sinks and balconies. Shared bathroom and kitchen. TV lounge on every floor. Breakfast included. Internet €1.50 per 15min., €3 per hr. Free Wi-Fi. Reception daily 8am-noon and 5-11pm. Dorms €19. MC/V. ●

Association Jeunesse et Habitat, 16 rue Bernard Palissy (☎02 47 60 51 51; ajn.ufjt. tours@numericable.fr). Centrally located hostel with warm staff offers long-term housing for workers and students. Large, renovated rooms are pristine and have personal baths. Kitchen on 1st and 3rd fl. Ping-pong tables and small gym with pool. Breakfast €2; other meals €6. Laundry (wash €3; dry €2). Free Internet access. Reception M-Sa 8am-7pm. Singles with shower €20; doubles with bath €30. MC/V. ●

Hôtel des Châteaux de la Loire, 12 rue Gambetta (☎02 47 05 10 05; www.hotelde-schateaux.fr). Rooms with garish floral wallpaper and bedspreads. Amiable staff and elegant lobby make up for lack of taste elsewhere. Each room has shower or bath, toilet, and cable TV. Breakfast €7. Parking €6.50. Open from mid-Feb. to mid-Dec. Singles €45-55; doubles €45-64. Extra bed €6. AmEx/MC/V. ●

Camping St-Avertin, 61 rue de Rochepinard, St-Avertin (☎02 47 27 27 60). Take bus #5 from rue Nationale to Cottier (30min., every 15min., €1.50), make a left over the bridge, and follow the signs. Tennis, volleyball and swimming nearby. Small sites with limited shade. Reception 8am-10pm. Curfew 10pm. In summer, reserve 1-2 months ahead. Open from Apr. to mid-Oct. €4 per person, under 10 €2.50; sites €3.60; €6 per car; €7 per RV. Electricity €3-4.80. AmEx/MC/V. ●

FOOD

Rue Colbert and the streets around **place Plumereau** have dozens of pleasant outdoor options, including many *crêperies* with *menus* under €12. Bistros and pubs crowd **place Jean Jaurès.** Be sure to try the melt-in-your-mouth *macarons à l'ancienne* and anything *aux pruneaux* (with prunes). The light, fruity white wines of Vouvray, Monmousseau, and Montlouis are all worth a sip. In the summer, **place des Halles,** the indoor food market (open M-Sa 7:30am-noon and 2-7pm, Su 7:30am-1pm), extends outdoors Wednesday and Saturday mornings 7am-noon. The *marché gourmand,* **place de la Résistance,** sells gourmet products on the first Friday of the month (4-10pm). A **marché traditionnel** sells fresh produce Tuesdays (8am-noon) in front of the tourist office. Find groceries at the **ATAC** supermarket, 5 pl. du Maréchal Leclerc (open M-Sa 7:30am-8pm; AmEx/MC/V) or at the supermarket in **Galeries Lafayette,** north of pl. Jean Jaurès. (Open M-Sa 9am-7:30pm. AmEx/MC/V.)

La Souris Gourmande, 100 rue Colbert (☎02 47 47 04 80). Cheese lovers congregate here for the delicious selection of *fromage* dishes, which make up for the kitschy bovine decor. Fondue €14 (min. 2 people). *Crêpes* €7. *Omelettes* €8.50-9.50. Open Tu-Sa noon-2pm and 7-10:30pm. MC/V. ●

Juanita Banana, 13 rue du Change (☎02 47 64 91 12). Customers get hooked on dishes like *foie gras* bathed in Coca-Cola (€17). Monthly, themed menu and decor. Salads €12. *Plats* €10-22. Open Tu-Sa 10am-3pm and 6pm-2am. MC/V. ●

L'Atelier Gourmand, 37 rue Étienne Marcel (☎02 47 38 59 87). Enjoy international variations on traditional dishes on the terrace in the heart of vieux Tours. Offers an affordable lunch *menu* that comes with dessert (€11) and makes fine cuisine budget-accessible. Art exhibits on display. *Entrées* €8-12. *Plats* €15-18. Desserts €6. Open M and Sa 7:30-10pm, Tu-F noon-2pm and 7:30-10pm. MC/V. ❸

La Bigouden, 3 rue du Grand Marché (☎02 47 64 21 91). Stands out among *crêperies* near pl. Plumereau. The Camembert and jam *crêpe* (€4.90) is a local favorite. *Galettes* €5-7.80. Desserts €1.70-7.20. Open M-Tu and F-Sa noon-2pm and 7-11pm, Th and Su 7-11pm. Reservations recommended in summer. MC/V. ❷

Boccacio, 9 rue Gambetta (☎02 47 05 45 22). Tucked-away pizzeria off rue Nationale with sleek brick decor. Locals come for crisp, wood-oven-baked pizzas (€9-11) and thick tiramisu (€5). Lunch *menus* €12-14. Open M noon-2:15pm, W noon-2:15pm and 7:30-11pm, Th noon-2pm and 7-9:30pm, F-Sa noon-2pm and 7:30-10pm. MC/V. ❸

👁 SIGHTS

Don't forget to pick up a **Carte Multi-Visites** (€9; valid for 1 year), which offers access to Tours's five museums and a guided tour of the city (p. 210).

📷CATHÉDRALE SAINT-GATIEN. Though not much is known about St-Gatien, this Gothic edifice with elaborate tracery was erected in his name. As the cathedral was built and rebuilt a total of five times over 1100 years, the intricate facade combines centuries of architectural caprice. The two Renaissance spires are unusually asymmetrical—the south is significantly shorter. It allegedly symbolizes royal power, while the north spire stands for spirituality—a not-so-subtle commentary on the balance between the two. The **Psalette Cloister,** on the north end of the cathedral, holds a model of François I's staircase from the Château de Blois and was the location of a scene in Balzac's *La Comédie Humaine.* (*Pl. de la Cathédrale. Cathedral ☎02 47 70 21 00, cloister ☎02 47 47 05 19. Cathedral open daily 9am-7pm. Free. Bimonthly free concerts throughout the year. Cloister open May-Sept. M-Sa 9:30am-12:30pm and 2-6pm; Oct.-Mar. Th-Sa 9:30am-12:30pm and 2-5pm; Apr. daily 10am-noon and 2-5:30pm; €3, students and under 18 €2.80.*)

📷MUSÉE DE COMPAGNONS. The ancestor of France's infamous unions, the Compagnons is a semi-secret society that produces the nation's most talented craftsmen. Though legend claims the Compagnons have been in existence since King Solomon first gathered men to build the Temple of Jerusalem, their origins can only be officially traced back as far as the Middle Ages, when the French first started building cathedrals. Discover their centuries of legacy and impressive handiwork—like a sugar palace the size of a table. (*8 rue Nationale. ☎02 47 21 62 20. Open from mid-June to mid-Sept. M and W-Su 9am-12:30pm and 2-6pm; from mid-Sept. to mid-June 9am-noon and 2-6pm. €5, students and seniors €3, under 12 €2.*)

MUSÉE DES BEAUX-ARTS. A succession of stunning salons, the Musée des Beaux-Arts is located in what was once the archbishop's palace. The architecture and outdoor gardens are as much of an attraction as the art within. The upper floors house art from the 17th to 19th centuries, including works by Delacroix, Monet, and Rodin. Outside, an impressive **📷Lebanese cedar,** planted during Napoleon's reign, stretches its tortuous branches over 800 sq. m. (*18 pl. François Sicard, next to the cathedral. ☎02 47 05 68 73; musee-beauxarts@ville-tours.fr. Museum open M and W-Su 9am-12:45pm and 2-6pm. Gardens open daily in high season 7am-8:30pm; in low season 7am-6pm. 1st Su of the month free. €4, seniors €2, students free.*)

MUSÉE DU GEMMAIL. Located in an ivy-strewn courtyard, this unique museum is dedicated to an art form that originated in Tours in the 1950s. *Gemmail* is a form of glass mosaic that, unlike stained glass, uses no metal in welding. Works range from original pieces to interpretations of classics, including Leonardo da Vinci's *Mona Lisa* (p. 155) and Picasso's *Deux Femmes*. Don't miss the pieces in the 12th-century underground chapel, accessible through the door below the entrance. (*7 rue du Murier. Off rue Bretonneau, near pl. Plumereau. ☎02 47 61 01 19. Open Mar.-Oct. Tu-Su 2-6:30pm. €6, students €4, ages 13-18 €3, under 12 €2.*)

TOWERS OF BASILIQUE SAINT-MARTIN. The **Tour de l'Horloge** and **Tour de Charle-magne** reveal the incredible proportions of the fifth-century Basilique St-Martin. The two towers, fenced off due to their fragility, are all that remain following neglect and pillage after the Revolution. St-Martin, the city's first bishop, now rests in the Nouvelle Basilique St-Martin, an ornate *fin-de-siècle* church designed by Victor Laloux, the architect of the Musée d'Orsay in Paris. (*Entrance on Rue Descartes. ☎02 47 05 63 87. Open daily 8am-8pm. Mass daily 11am.*)

OTHER SIGHTS. You may be surprised to find no châteaux drenched in Renaissance pomp in this Loire Valley city. Tours's châteaux did not withstand the test of time; only one **tower** is left over from the glory days. Henri III had his archrival's son, the second Duke of Guise, imprisoned here during the Wars of Religion, but the duke escaped by tricking his guards into hopping on one foot as he ran away. The tower now holds free temporary art exhibits throughout the year. (*☎04 27 70 88 46.*) For a breath of fresh air, head to **Lac de la Bergeonnerie** (also called Lac de Tours), a 10min. bus ride away on line #1.

🎵 🎦 ENTERTAINMENT AND NIGHTLIFE

The most happening nightlife is on **place Plumereau**, where lively cafes and bars overflow with chatty students in the summer. Three clubs on the square cluster together, while **rue du Commerce,** off pl. Plumereau, booms with busy bars. For the more theatrically inclined, **The Olympia,** 7 rue de Lucé (☎02 47 04 50 50), and **Le Grand Théâtre de Tours,** 34 rue de la Scellerie (☎02 47 60 20 00; www.tours.fr), put on productions year-round.

🎖 **Au Temps des Rois,** 3 pl. Plumereau (☎02 47 05 04 51). A doll, a barrel, T-shirts, and old theater posters hang from the ceiling at this local favorite known for its hip music and cheap prices. Enjoy a beer (€2.50-7) and mingle with an international crowd in the city's liveliest district. Open daily 8:30am-2am. AmEx/MC/V.

Bistro 64, 64 rue du Grand Marché (☎02 47 38 47 40). Jazz lovers meet up at this mellow bar, housed in one of Tours's restored medieval buildings. Enjoy concerts (Sept.-June Th 9:30pm) and a boisterous atmosphere while sipping on one of their famously plentiful mojitos (€5). Beer €4. Open M-Sa 11am-2am, Su 3pm-2am. Cash only.

Le Strapontin, 23-25 rue de Châteauneuf (☎02 47 47 02 74). Blood-red decor designed by the artist-owner is punctuated by oversized cartoons and original furnishings. A classy crowd sips fair-trade mixed drinks (€6.20) in time with an electronica soundtrack. Open M-Sa 5pm-2am. MC/V.

Le Serpent Volant, 54 rue du Grand Marché (☎02 47 38 59 10). This intimate, intellectual bar is a local favorite. An affable literary crowd enjoys occasional book readings, chess tournaments, slam poetry, and open-mike nights. Beer €2.30-5. Mixed drinks €3-4.50. Open M 5pm-2am, Tu-Sa 11am-2am. Cash only.

Zik' Café, 5 rue des 3 Écritoires (☎02 47 38 81 00). Caters to music lovers of all stripes. Locals can sometimes play DJ and spin their own mixes amid more typical rock, reggae, and electro. Because of the club's tucked-away location, visitors may feel most comfortable arriving in groups at night. House punch €2.50. Pint of beer €2.50. Mixed drinks €3. Happy hour 6-8:30pm. Open M-Sa 5pm-2am. MC/V.

Le GI, 13 rue Lavoisier (☎02 47 66 29 96). House, disco, and techno throb in blue and black lighting for a gay crowd of all ages. Mirrors and a zebra motif set the scene on the

1st fl. as the sounds of themed *soirées* blast from the basement. Mixed drinks €8-10. 18+. Cover F €7, Sa €10; includes 1 drink. Open W-Su 11:30pm-5am. MC/V.

✦ FESTIVALS

Acteurs-Acteurs (☎02 47 38 29 29; www.ciecanolopez.fr). A spring film and theater festival. Less redundant than it sounds.

Fêtes Musicales en Touraine (☎02 47 21 65 08; www.fetesmusicales.com), 10 days in late June. A celebration of classical music. €12-23 per night.

Jazz en Touraine (☎02 47 50 72 70; www.jazzentouraine.com), 10 days in Sept.

▉ DAYTRIPS FROM TOURS: NEARBY CHÂTEAUX

CHÂTEAUX HOPPING. Dozens of beautiful castles lie within 60km of Tours. Most châteaux have free guided tours and performances during the summer. Few châteaux are accessible by public transportation, but travelers have other options. Renting a car provides the most freedom, but often at prohibitive prices. Biking is cheapest. With several dropoff locations along the Loire and an office in Tours, **Détours de Loire** (☎02 47 61 22 23; www.locationdevelos.com) offers convenience and competitive prices for bicycles (€14 per day). It's hard to cover more than two châteaux per day by bike. For those in a hurry, plush minibuses depart from Tours every day at 9am or 1pm and visit 2 to 3 châteaux in half a day (€20-33) or 4 to 5 in a full day (€44-50). Some reputable companies are listed below:

Alienor, 35 rue Charles Gîles (☎06 10 85 35 39). Staffed by very friendly English-speaking tour guides. Tours €18-47.

Saint-Eloi Excursions (☎06 70 82 78 75; www.saint-eloi.com). ½-day excursions €20-33, full-day €44-50.

Acco-Dispo Excursions (☎06 82 00 64 51; www.accodispo-tours.com). ½-day excursions €20-33, full-day €44-50.

Quart de Tours (☎06 30 65 52 01; www.quartdetours.com). ½-day excursions €20-34, full-day €44-50.

Touraine Evasion (☎06 07 39 13 31, www.tourevasion.com). ½-day €18-26, full-day €43-49. Some tours include wine tasting.

The Loire Valley is known not only for its royal châteaux, but also for its superlative wines. Cellars often offer free *dégustations*. Ask for a copy of the *Route des Vignobles*, free at the tourist office, which contains a comprehensive list of the 618 wine cellars. **The Wine Tour,** also run by Alienor (see above) offers tours of some of the region's most famous vineyards. By bus, take #61 (20min., M-Sa 7 per day, €1.50) from pl. Jean Jaurès to Les Patis. (☎06 10 85 35 39. Red wine tour €60, lunch included; white wine tour €35.) In Montlouis, across the river to the south, 10 *caves* pour palatable dry whites. Trains run from Tours to Les Patis (10min., M-Sa 3 per day, €2.40).

▉ CHENONCEAU

Trains run to Chenonceau from Tours (30min., 8 per day 9am-9pm, €5.90). The station is in front of the château entrance. Fil Vert buses leave for Chenonceau from the post office in Amboise (25min., M-Sa 1 per day, €1.50) and Tours (1hr., M-Sa 2 per day, €1.50). Biking may be most convenient from Amboise. Château ☎02 47 23 90 07; www.chenonceau.com. Open daily July-Aug. 9am-8pm; Sept. and June 9am-7:30pm; Oct. 1-Oct. 27 9am-6:30pm; Oct. 28-Nov. 4 9am-6pm; Nov. 5-Feb. 9 9:30am-5pm; Feb. 10-Mar. 15 9:30am-6pm; Mar. 16-Mar.

31 9:30am-7pm; Apr.-May 9am-7pm. Light show 9:30-11pm. Castle €10, students €7.50. Entry to Château des Dames wax museum €9. IPod audio tour in 12 languages €12.

Perhaps France's most elegant château, Chenonceau (shuh-nohn-soh) arches gracefully over the Cher River. Take the less traveled pedestrian walk for a view of the donkeys' field, the 16th-century farm, and the flower garden. This *château des dames* (castle of the ladies) owes its beauty to centuries of female designers. Royal tax collector Thomas Bohier originally commissioned the Venetian-inspired château. During his stint in the Italian Wars (1513-21), his wife Katherine oversaw the château's practical design, which features Italian staircases and four rooms branching from a central chamber. In 1547, King Henri II gave the château to his mistress, Diane de Poitiers, in line with official court rules, for her "great and commendable services." Endowed with beauty, intelligence, and a thirst for wealth and fame, Diane turned the castle into a profitable venture, considerably boosting its value by adding luxurious gardens and an arched bridge over the Cher so she could hunt in the nearby forest. Later, Henri's wife, Catherine de Medici, forced Diane to give up the castle in exchange for Chaumont (p. 205). She designed her own gardens and the magnificent two-story gallery atop Diane's bridge as a way to assert her superiority over her late husband's mistress. You may notice that Diane's chambers are stamped with Hs and Cs, the initials of the royal couple. When intertwined, these initials form the letter D (for Diane), an ambiguity that amused Henri more than it did his wife. The 60m long gallery is lit by 18 windows (nine on each side) overlooking the Cher and often hosts art exhibitions. During the world wars, the gallery served as a hospital. Perhaps the most peculiar chamber is that of Louise de Lorraine; its black paneling was meant to accommodate the 12 years during which she mourned the mysterious death of her husband, Henri III. In the 18th and 19th centuries, the Dupin family—who still owns the château today—lightened the mood, welcoming such visitors as Voltaire, Rousseau, and Flaubert. The nearby **La Cave des Domes** offers wine tastings for €2.50. (Open daily 10:30am-1pm and 2-6:15pm.)

◪VILLANDRY

Trains depart Tours for Savonnières (10min., 3 per day, €2.90). In June, Sept.-Oct., Fil Vert makes 2 trips W and Sa from Halte Routière to the tourist office in Villandry (9:05am; 1:05pm, return 12:42; 5:32pm; €1.50); July-Aug., the bus makes both trips daily. See previous page for bus tours to the château. From Tours, cyclists can travel 15km west along D16, which winds past Villandry. Drivers should take D7. Château ☎02 47 50 02 09; www.chateauvillandry.com. Open daily July-Aug. 9am-6:30pm; Sept.-Oct. and from late Mar. to June 9am-6pm; Chrismas and holidays 9:30am-4:30pm; Feb. 9am-5pm; early Mar. 9am-5:30pm. Gardens open daily July-Aug. 9am-7:30pm; Sept. and from late Mar. to June 9am-7pm; Oct. 9am-6:30pm; early Nov. and Feb. 9am-5:30pm; early Mar. 9am-6pm. Free tours in French. Château and gardens €9, students €5. Gardens only €6/3.50. The tourist office, across from the château, has maps and train schedules. ☎02 47 50 12 66. Open July-Aug. M-Sa 10am-7pm, Su 10am-noon and 1-7pm; Sept.-Oct. and Jan.-Mar. M-Sa 9:30am-12:30pm and 2-6pm; from Nov. to mid-Dec. M-Sa 9:30am-12:30pm and 2-5pm; Apr.-June daily 9:30am-12:30pm and 2-6pm.

Villandry (veel-ahn-dree) lives up to its claim of having the most beautiful, geometrically intricate gardens in France. With 125,000 flowers and 85,000 vegetables (all weeded by hand), it is certainly among the largest. Built on the banks of the Cher River by Jean le Breton, minister to François I, the château was falling to pieces when a Spanish couple stumbled upon it in the 1920s. It was love at first sight between the couple and the château; the Carvallos decided to dedicate their lives to reconstructing the gardens and renovating Villandry. Save some euro and settle for a walk through Villandry's main attraction—the gardens, which can be more enlightening than the castle itself.

The elegant grounds are designed according to three historical styles. The *Potager*, filled with aromatic and medicinal herbs, follows medieval tradition. The middle level unfolds in symmetric patterns typical of the Renaissance— each of its four square "gardens of love" is an allegory for a different type of love: tender, passionate, fickle, and tragic. The upper level, lined with lime groves, contains a Classical swan pool, with waterfalls that irrigate the rest of the grounds. An overgrown labyrinth completes the botanical experience.

AZAY-LE-RIDEAU

Trains run from Tours to the town of Azay-le-Rideau (25min.; M-F 9 per day 7:35am-7:30pm, Sa 5 per day 9am-6:30pm, Su 3 per day 2-9pm; €4.90). Turn right from the station and head left on D57 for 20min. Buses run from the Tours train station to the tourist office (50min., 3 per day 6:40am-5:50pm, €5.40). Château ☎ 02 47 45 42 04. Open daily July-Aug. 9:30am-7pm; Sept. and Apr.-June 9:30am-6pm; Oct.-Mar. 9:30am-12:30pm and 2-5:30pm. Last entry 45min. before close. Light show daily from early to mid-July 9:45-10:15pm; from mid-July to mid-Aug. 10pm; from mid-Aug. to mid-Sept. 9pm. Château and gardens €7.50, groups of 20 people €5.70 each, ages 18-25 €4.80, under 18 free; light show €9/7/5/free. The tourist office is at 4 rue du Château (☎ 02 47 45 44 40; www.ot-paysazaylerideau.fr). Open July-Aug. M-Sa 9am-7pm, Su 10am-6pm; Sept. and May-June M-Sa 9am-1pm and 2-6pm, Su 10am-1pm and 2-5pm; Oct.-Apr. M-Sa 9am-1pm and 2-6pm.)

Surrounded by acres of trees and grass atop a dreamy island in the Indre River, the floating château at Azay-le-Rideau (ah-zay-luh-ree-doh) stands on the ruins of a fortress. The village acquired the nickname "Azay-le-Brûlé" (Azay the Burned) during the Hundred Years' War, when Charles VII, insulted by a castle guard rooting for the British, razed it to the ground in revenge. The corrupt financier Gilles Berthelot bought the land and built a new castle on the ruins of the old—with state money. Though smaller than François I's Chambord (p. 204), the château was intended to rival its contemporary in beauty. Berthelot succeeded so thoroughly that he had to flee the country before the king could have him executed, leaving his wife and his beloved, unfinished castle. In symbolic punishment, François I seized the château as royal property.

Azay's Renaissance style is apparent in the furniture and the ornate Italian second-floor staircase carved with the faces of 10 Valois kings and queens and lit by open windows. Portraits of the royal family and other members of the 16th- and 17th-century French aristocracy hang on the walls. The Gothic influence appears in the *grande salle* (grand drawing room), where 16th-century tapestries still hang. Before leaving Azay, take a romantic stroll through the misty grounds and listen to the croaking of the frogs that inhabit the moat.

CHINON

Trains and buses run from Tours to Chinon (45min.; M-F 8 per day, Sa 4 per day, Su 3 per day; €8.20). SNCF buses also leave the Tours station for Chinon (M-F 3 per day, Su 1 per day; €8.20). To drive from Tours, take D751 southwest (dir.: Azay-le-Rideau).

Resting between the banks of the Vienne River and the crumbling château where Richard the Lionheart drew his last breath, Chinon (shee-nohn) was one of the most important cities in France under the reign of Henri II, king of England and Anjou. Its glory days left behind a charming town whose narrow, cafe-filled streets rest at the foot of the hill crowned by Chinon's former fortress. In honor of native son and great Renaissance philosopher-writer François Rabelais, the town's streets and establishments bear his characters' names. Vineyards that produce the region's renowned red wines and the distinctive *confiture de vin de Chinon*, a delicious wine jam, surround Chinon.

For a charming stroll from town, take the less traveled **Impasse du Roberdeau** past ivy-covered ramparts to reach the ruins of Chinon's 10th-century château, scheduled to be under extensive restoration until early 2009. The grounds host three fortresses connected by underground tunnels. The 14th-century **Tour de l'Horloge** has withstood the Hundred Years' War, the Wars of Religion, and the French Revolution without a blemish, protected by the popular legend that anyone who captures the bell tower will die a horrible death. Its bell, called Marie Javelle, has allegedly struck every half-hour since 1399. The **Musée de Jeanne d'Arc**, which occupies the three-story tower, is dedicated to the young warrior, who met with the dauphin in the *grande salle* of the château in 1429. As the story goes, the dauphin, to make sure she was not a fake, hid in the crowd while a guard sat in his throne. Joan picked out the true dauphin, dispelling all doubts Charles VII might have had about her intuition. Slideshows detailing Joan's military campaigns are screened in French. (☎02 47 93 13 45; www.cg37.fr. Open daily Apr.-Sept. 9am-7pm; Oct.-Mar. 9:30am-5pm. Ticket office closes 30min. earlier. For free tours in English, French, or German, call ahead. €3.50, students and under 16 €2. MC/V.)

After visiting the castle, enjoy a wine tasting at **Caves Plouzeau**, 94 rue Haute St-Maurice, in the heart of the *vieille ville*. Marc Plouzeau conducts 🏠**free tours** in a *cave* (wine cellar) beneath the château. (☎02 47 93 32 11; www.plouzeau. com. Open Apr.-Sept. Tu-Sa 11am-1pm and 3-7pm; Oct.-Mar. Sa 11am-1pm and 3-7pm.) The **Caves Painctes de Chinon,** rue Voltaire, form a network of underground tunnels and cellars beneath Chinon's castle. With chandeliers constructed from empty wine bottles and a natural fountain, this *cave* was where Rabelais stored his wine. (☎02 47 93 30 44; www.caves-painctes.abcsalles.com. Tours July-Aug. Tu-Su 11am, 3, 4:30, 6pm. €5; includes *dégustation*.)

On the third Saturday in August, all of Chinon turns out for **Marché à l'Ancienne**, which features regional foods like *fouaces* (a popular medieval pastry immortalized by Rabelais in one of his novels) and a parade of citizens costumed in late-19th-century garb. The **Avoine Zone Blues** brings jazz, blues, and rock groups from France and elsewhere in the first weekend of July. (☎02 47 98 11 15. Tickets from €30, students from €15; some concerts free.) **Cinéma Le Rabelais,** 31 bis pl. du Général de Gaulle, plays French and American films nightly. (☎08 92 68 47 07. Tickets €7.50, students €6.)

Stroll along **rue Voltaire** and near **place de l'Hôtel de Ville** to find the best cheap meals in town. In a 15th-century house, quiet **La Bonne France ❸**, 4 pl. de la Victoire, offers regionally themed *formules*, such as the "Provence" or "Touraine" (€15), as well as tasty €26 *menus*. (☎02 47 98 01 34. Open M-Tu and F-Su noon-1:30pm and 7-9pm, Th noon-1pm. MC/V.) Find a **Shopi** supermarket at 22 pl. de l'Hôtel de Ville (open M-Sa 7:30am-7:30pm, Su 8:30am-12:30pm; AmEx/MC/V) and an open-air market Thursdays (open 7am-1pm) on **place Jeanne d'Arc** and Sundays (open 7am-1pm) on **place de l'Hôtel de Ville.**

Bikes are available at **Detours de Loire,** 12 pl. Jeanne d'Arc, which offers several pickup and dropoff locations along the Loire, including Blois and Tours. (☎02 47 93 36 92; www.locationdevelos.com. Bikes €15 per day. Tandems €40 per day. Open daily 9am-7pm. Cash only.) **L'Étape en Chinonais,** 27 rue Jean-Jacques Rousseau, in front of the tourist office, also rents bikes. (☎02 47 95 92 08; www. loirevelonature.com. €8 per ½-day, €15 per day. Open Tu-Su 9am-8pm. MC/V.) To reach the **tourist office,** pl. d'Hofheim, from the station, take a left and walk beside the river along rue Descartes—which becomes quai Jeanne d'Arc—for 20min., then turn right at Rabelais's statue onto pl. de l'Hôtel de Ville. Continue onto pl. du Général de Gaulle and turn onto rue Jean-Jacques Rousseau at the back right corner of the square. The office is on the left. (☎02 47 93 17 85. Accommodation service €2.50. Walking tours May-Sept. €4.70, students €2.50.

Night tours €5/3. *Petit train* tour July-Aug. 6 times per day; €5.50. Office open May-Sept. daily 9am-7pm; Oct.-Apr. M-Sa 10am-12:30pm and 2-6pm.)

SAUMUR ☎02 41

A *petite ville* spliced by the sprawling Loire, Saumur (soh-moor; pop. 35,000) is a tiny town with big-city style. Best known for its wine, mushrooms, and equestrian tradition, the city has also profited from an abundance of *tuffeau* in the past two centuries, the stone used to build the Loire châteaux. Damp, chilly caves bear witness to years of stone excavation and endow the region with an environment primed for mushroom cultivation. In addition to *champignons de Paris* (button mushrooms), Saumur's fertile soil nurtures high-quality vine-yards. However, this wide palette of discoveries is somewhat tempered by the fact that many sights are only accessible by car or infrequent buses.

▐ TRANSPORTATION

Trains: Av. David d'Angers, 10min. from pl. Bilange. Take bus #11 from Pôle Balzac (dir.: Gare SNCF/St-Lambert; €1.30). Ticket office open M-Sa 6:05am-8:45pm, Su 8:05am-9:45pm. Or walk 10min. into the *centre-ville*. SNCF trains run to **Angers** (30min., 10 per day, €7.80); **Nantes** (1hr., 14 per day, €18-21); **Paris** (1-3hr., 20 per day, €34-58); **Poitiers** (2hr., 8 per day, €25); **Tours** (40min., 10 per day, €7.90-13).

Buses: Agglobus, 19 rue FD Roosevelt (☎02 41 51 11 87). Office open M 2-6pm, Tu-F 9am-noon and 2-6pm, Sa 9am-noon. Buses M-Sa 7am-7pm. Tickets €1.30.

Car Rental: Europcar, 40 av. du Général de Gaulle (☎02 41 67 30 89). From €60 per day. 21+. Under-25 surcharge €30. Open M-F 8am-noon and 2-6pm, Sa 9am-noon and 2-6pm. AmEx/MC/V. **Hertz,** 78-80 av. du Général de Gaulle (☎02 41 67 20 06). From €41 per day. 21+. Under-25 surcharge €35. Open M-F 8:15am-noon and 2-6:15pm, Sa 8:30am-noon and 2-5:30pm. AmEx/MC/V.

Bike Rental: Détours de Loire, 1 rue David d'Angers (☎02 41 53 01 01; www.loca-tiondevelos.com). Several pickup and dropoff locations along the Loire, including Blois and Tours. Bikes €14 per day. Tandems €39 per day. Open M-Sa 9:30am-12:30pm and 4:30-7:30pm, Su 9:30am-12:30pm. Cash only.

✈▐ ORIENTATION AND PRACTICAL INFORMATION

Tourist Office: Pl. de la Bilange (☎02 41 40 20 60; www.saumur-tourisme.com), across 2 bridges from the train station. Multilingual staff books accommodations, offers city **tours** by carriage (1hr.; every hr. July-Aug.; €6, under 11 €4) and by boat on the Loire (☎06 61 92 08 74; €8, under 12 €4.50; sunset tour €9/5), as well as equestrian tours of the city in summer. Open mid-May to Sept. M-Sa 9:15am-7pm, Su 10:30am-5:30pm; Oct. to mid-May M-Sa 9:15am-12:30pm and 2-6pm, Su 10am-noon.

Laundromats: 12 rue du Maréchal Leclerc. Wash €3.50 per 7kg. Open daily 7am-9:30pm. Also at 16 rue Beaurepaire. Wash €3.80 per 7kg. Open daily in high season 7:30am-10pm; in low season 7:30am-9:30pm.

Police: 415 rue du Chemin Vert (☎02 41 83 24 00).

Urgent Care: Route de Fontevraud (☎02 41 53 30 30).

Internet Access: Conseil Micro Service, 69 quai Mayaud (☎02 41 67 15 30; www.conseil-micro-service.com). €1.90 per 30min. Open Tu-Sa 10am-6pm, Su 2-6pm.

Post Office: Pl. du Petit Thouars and across from the train station (☎02 41 40 22 08). **Currency exchange** available. Both open M-F 8:30am-6pm, Sa 8:30am-noon. **Postal Code:** 49400.

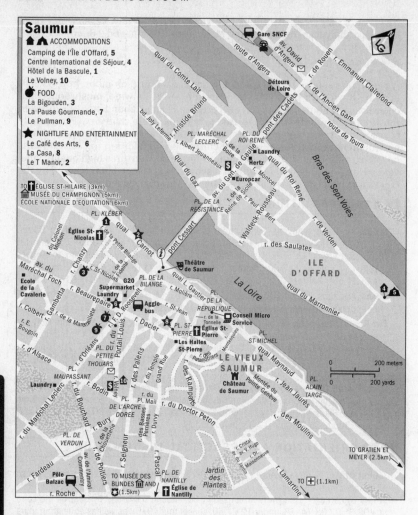

Saumur

🏠🏕 ACCOMMODATIONS
Camping de l'Île d'Offard, **5**
Centre International de Séjour, **4**
Hôtel de la Bascule, **1**
Le Volney, **10**

🍴 FOOD
La Bigouden, **3**
La Pause Gourmande, **7**
Le Pullman, **9**

⭐ NIGHTLIFE AND ENTERTAINMENT
Le Café des Arts, **6**
La Casa, **8**
Le T Manor, **2**

LOIRE VALLEY

🏠🏕 ACCOMMODATIONS AND CAMPING

Camping de l'Île d'Offard (☎02 41 40 30 00; www.cvtloisirs.com). 4-star site at the tip of the Île d'Offard. Shares reception with **CIS** (below). Unbeatable views of the Loire, as well as a pool, tennis courts, a playground, a restaurant, a snack shop, minigolf, and brand-new bungalows named after nearby wine villages. Restaurant open daily 6-9:30pm. *Plats* €4-10. Ask reception for free tickets to Gratien et Meyer and other *caves*. Laundry. Internet €8 per hr. 2 people with car €16-26, €4-5 per extra adult, €2-2.50 per extra child; 4- to 6-person tent €40. Electricity €3.50. MC/V. ❶

Centre International de Séjour (CIS), rue de Verden (☎02 41 40 30 00; www.cvtloisirs.com), on Île d'Offard. Bare (but sizable rooms) with bunk beds. Ask reception for free tickets to local *caves*. Large common rooms and kitchen. Shared bath in hall. Light breakfast included. Internet €8 per hr. Reception July-Aug. 8am-9pm; Sept. and June 8:30am-12:30pm and 2-7pm; Oct. and Mar.-May 9am-noon and 2-7pm. Reservations recommended. 8-bed dorms €15.80; 2- to 4-bed dorms with shower €24 for 1st person, €11 per additional person. 10% off stays over 5 nights. MC/V. ❶

Le Volney, 1 rue Volney (☎02 41 51 25 41; www.levolney.com), to the left of the post office. Rustic charm within walking distance of the *centre-ville*. Cheerful owners offer the best deal in town. Spacious rooms feature tasteful antique furnishings and pristine bathrooms. Breakfast €7. Wi-Fi. Reception 7am-10pm. Open Sept.-June. Singles and doubles with TVs, phones, toilets, and sinks €35, with shower or bath €42-52; quads €55-62. Extra bed €6. AmEx/MC/V. ❸

Hôtel de la Bascule, 1 pl. Kléber (☎02 41 50 13 65), near Église St-Nicolas on quai Carnot. Bright bedrooms with high ceilings, TV, and sparkling clean showers or bathrooms. Some rooms have river views. Breakfast €5.50. Reception M-Sa 7am-7pm. Rooms €37-45. Extra bed €6.10. MC/V. ❸

◖ FOOD

Saumur is renowned for its sparkling *crémant de Loire* wine and bountiful mushrooms. **Place Saint-Pierre** and its offshoots have great options for a light lunch, the most popular time to eat out in Saumur. Stock up at the indoor market **Les Halles** at the far end of pl. St-Pierre (open Tu-F 8am-12:30pm and 3-7pm, Sa 7am-1pm and 3-7pm, Su 9am-12:30pm) or try its outdoor equivalents on **avenue du Général de Gaulle** (open Th 8am-1pm) and **place Saint-Pierre** (open Sa 8am-1pm). The **G20** supermarket, 6 rue Roosevelt, sits inside a shopping center. (☎02 41 53 71 20. Open M-Sa 9am-7:30pm, Su 9am-12:30pm. AmEx/MC/V.)

▨ **Le Pullman,** 52 rue d'Orléans (☎02 41 051 31 79). Intimate, family-run restaurant. Decorated like a 1920s Orient Express dining car, complete with baggage compartments and scenic window views. Terrace is delightfully green in summer. Great lunch deals keep customers coming back. Lunch specials €8-10. *Plats* €7.40-14. *Menus* €14-27. Open M and Th-Su 10am-4pm and 7-10pm, Tu 10am-4pm. MC/V. ❸

▨ **La Bigouden,** 67 rue St-Nicolas (☎02 41 67 12 59). Pink-clad table and fresh flowers add to the already sentimental mood set by sweet *crêpes* with romantic names like the Belle Angèle (sautéed apples, Corinthian grapes, and honey; €6.30) and the Mont Blanc (chestnut cream, French double cream, and almonds; €6.30). Over 35 savory (€7-10) and dessert (€2.70-7) *crêpes*. Salads €3-9. Open July-Aug. daily noon-1:30pm and 7-9:30pm; Sept.-June M and Th-Su noon-1:30pm and 7-9:30pm. MC/V. ❷

La Pause Gourmande, 39 rue d'Orléans (☎02 41 38 32 52). Small but popular lunch spot run by a young Parisian couple. Traditional French fare at reasonable prices. Fresh salads €6. *Plats* €9-14. *Menus* €13-30. Open M 7-9pm, Tu-W and F-Sa noon-2pm and 7-10pm, Th noon-2pm. Lunch reservations recommended. MC/V. ❷

◔ SIGHTS

Unfortunately, many of the city's most interesting sights can only be reached by car or by somewhat unreliable buses. Exercise caution if biking to these destinations, as most country roads lack sidewalks or bike paths.

MUSÉE DU CHAMPIGNON. Located in dark caves that were once *tuffeau* mines, this museum explores the history of mushroom cultivation in the Saumur region. A variety of mushroom species grows in its dank interior—from classic white button mushrooms to colorful velvet shank—and lends the caves a pungent smell. In October, a month-long mushroom festival takes place in the museum. A *dégustation* of local produce (€2-4.50) and fresh varieties of mushrooms, such as *champignons de Paris* (€4 per kg, others €14 per kg), are available at reception. Museum patrons can also ask for regional mushroom recipes. Don't forget to bring an extra layer, as the caves are kept at a brisk 14°C. *(Route de Gennes, Ste-Hilaire-St-Florent. Take bus #5, dir.: Villemole, to the stop bearing the museum's name. ☎ 02 41 50 31 55; www.musee-du-champignon.com. Open daily from Feb. to mid-Nov. 10am-7pm. €7.30, students €6, under 18 €5.50.)*

ÉCOLE NATIONALE D'EQUITATION. In 1763, Louis XV chose Saumur as the location for his distinguished cavalry training camp, thereby establishing this town as France's top center for refined horsemanship. Since 1815, when the École became a civilian national riding school, Saumur has continued the Cadre Noir tradition. The black uniforms distinguish riders from other, lesser-trained, blue-clad cavalry. Students and *écuyers* (professional riders) alike compete internationally and often go on to train budding equestrians around the country. The palatial premises, located 15min. from the *centre-ville* by car, contain over 50km of training grounds, 400 horses, and one of Europe's best veterinarian clinics. Tours pass through the facilities and training grounds; morning visits often include a 30min. viewing of daily warm-ups. *(☎ 02 41 53 50 60; www.cadrenoir. fr. Take bus #31, dir.: St-Hilaire, to Alouette, then follow signs (25min. walk). No sidewalk; exercise caution. Grounds accessible by tour only. 1hr. tour every 30min. Apr.-Sept. M 2-4:30pm, Tu-F 9:30-11:30am and 2-4:30pm, Sa 9am-noon. €7.50, under 18 €4.50. Daily training routines and shows year-round €15, under 18 €8. Call for more info.)*

GRATIEN ET MEYER. Saumur's effervescent wines have been in demand since the 12th century, when the Plantagenêt kings left for England and took their favorite casks with them, demanding a constant supply from then on. Countless wine cellars on the outskirts of Saumur offer tours and tastings. This well-known vineyard, perched atop a steep hill with a spectacular view of the valley, presents its cellars and small museum in a 40min. tour in English or French. The visit ends with a tasting of its award-winning vintages. Over five million bottles are kept in galleries dating from the Middle Ages. *(Route de Montsoreau. Take bus #1, dir.: Fontevraud, from Pôle Balzac to Beaulieu and walk up the hill. ☎ 02 41 83 13 32; www. gratienmeyer.com. Store open Apr.-Oct. daily 9:30am-6pm. Nov.-Mar. open only to groups of 10 or more by reservation. Visits 10-11am and 2-5pm; tours depart every hr. €3, under 18 free.)*

MUSÉE DES BLINDES. Commonly known as "the tank museum," Saumur's 200-piece armed-vehicle collection is the world's largest. The museum traces the evolution of 20th-century warfare—to the delight of the 10-year-old boys who visit from far and wide. An ex-tobacco factory now curated by a lieutenant colonel and brimming with intimidating killing machines, this museum is not for the faint of heart. Keep an eye out for the **Schneider,** France's first tank; the camouflaged **Tiger I,** a monstrous German cruiser; and the **Leclerc,** the world's best-designed tank. Hidden among the massive machines are more subtle vehicles of war, including the Nazi bicycle. *(1043 route de Fontevraud. 40min. walk from the centre-ville, or take bus #34, dir.: Chemin Vert, to Fricotelle and walk left 100m. ☎ 02 41 83 69 95; www.musee-des-blindes.asso.fr. Open daily May-Sept. 10am-6pm; Oct.-Apr. M-F 10am-5pm, Sa-Su 11am-6pm. 30min. group visits. €6, students €4.50, under 18 €3.50.)*

OTHER SIGHTS. Three 12th- to 15th-century **churches** brighten downtown Saumur, and a soothing **Jardin des Plantes** is tucked between av. du Docteur Peton and rue Marceau, on the other side of the château. The picturesque **Pont Cessart** provides a panorama of the château towering above the city.

🎵 📻 ENTERTAINMENT AND NIGHTLIFE

Late-night crowds gather in **place Saint-Pierre** next to the illuminated cathedral and in the numerous Irish pubs at **place de la République,** but for the most part

Saumur has few nightlife options. Next to the tourist office, the 19th-century **Théâtre de Saumur** (☎02 41 83 30 83) hosts everything from *galas de danse* to jazz concerts. Catch the latest flicks at **Cinéma le Palace,** 13 quai Carnot. (☎08 92 68 00 73; www.cinefil.com. Tickets €8; matinees, W, and under 18 €6.20.)

 Le Café des Arts, 4 rue Beaurepaire (☎02 41 51 21 72). Shoot some darts at this large and popular bar in the *centre-ville,* strung with Christmas lights and furnished with heavy black leather. The exotic "beer cocktails" (€2.50-4), including the "Singapour" (Malibu, cherry, pineapple, and, of course, beer), are popular with locals. Open M-Th 8:30am-9:30pm, F-Sa 9:30am-2am. MC/V.

Le T Manor, 14 quai Carnot (☎02 41 51 24 09). Enter the green wrought-iron gates to this mellow after-hours garden hangout with calm beats and a panorama of the languid Loire. The kitchen serves classic French dishes, varying on a daily basis, at affordable prices during the day (*menu* €9.90) while the bar caters to both young and old at night. Beer €2.50. Open daily 2pm-midnight. Cash only.

La Casa, rue du Marché (☎02 41 40 36 02). A classier crowd dances among dark wood furnishings. Offers salsa lessons, ballroom dance, themed parties, and singles and poker nights. Beer €2.80-3.20. Mixed drinks €5-7. Open Tu-Su 5pm-2am.

FESTIVALS

International Festival of Military Music and the Festival des Géants (☎02 41 51 25 69), in late June. A march of oversized puppets storms Saumur in even years.

Carrousel (☎02 41 40 20 66), in late July. Horse performances, including an equestrian dressage demonstration by the elite Cadre Noir. Organized by the École de la Cavalerie and the École Nationale d'Équitation. Tickets €17-35. Saumur also hosts many free equestrian events each year, including several polo matches. Call the Cadre Noire at ☎02 41 53 50 50 for more info.

La Grande Semaine de Saumur (☎02 41 53 50 50; www.cadrenoir.fr), in the 3rd week of Sept. The Cadre Noir shows off its horsemanship.

DAYTRIPS FROM SAUMUR

ABBAYE DE FONTEVRAUD

The best way to reach the abbey is by car, but the #1 bus makes the 17km trip from the Pôle Balzac to Fontevraud Mairie (☎08 00 50 77 82; 25min., M-Sa 2 per day, €1.50; call ahead to for particular times). Last return from Fontevraud M-F at 6:12pm, Sa 1:05pm. ☎02 41 51 87 97; www.abbayedefontevraud.com. Open daily June-Sept. 9am-6:30pm; Oct. and Apr.-May 10am-6pm; Jan.-Mar. 10am-5:30pm. €7.90, students €5.90. Tours free with admission; offered in English July-Aug. The tourist office, pl. St-Michel (☎02 41 51 79 45) dispenses free maps. Themed tours of Fontevraud July-Aug. €7.90. Open Easter-Sept. M-Sa 9:30am-1:30pm and 2-7pm. 1 stop before Fontevraud, in Montsoreau, there are troglodyte cliff dwellings and a well-kept château. Call the Montsoreau tourist office (☎02 41 51 70 22) for more info.

One of the largest—and oddest—monastic complexes in Europe, the imposing Abbaye de Fontevraud (ah-bay duh fohn-teh-vroh) has awed visitors for over nine centuries. Robert d'Arbrissel, who built the abbey in the forest of Fontevraud in 1101, failed to be canonized because he founded a community around the controversial practice of *"martyr blanc,"* or *"syneisaktisme,"* a particularly grueling act of faith wherein men and women sleep naked together, thus arousing each other only to practice ignoring their worldly desires. Church officials, unamused with the scandalously naughty reputation attached to Arbrissel's now-defunct religious traveling group, gave him land on the condition that he clean up his act and keep his clothes on. To increase his monks' humility, Arbrissel demanded that women rule the order, if not in the "terrestrial" world, then at least in the "spiritual" one. Needless to say, this power was somewhat abused in the creation of questionable rules such as those governing daily wine intake (0.5L for women, 0.25L for men). Of Fontevraud's 36 abbesses, over half were of royal—including Bourbon—blood. Under the rule of these noble ladies, the abbey was coquettishly expanded in the style of the royal Loire châteaux—covered with their initials and portraits. Its chapter house is a prime example: 16 abbesses intrude upon painted scenes of Christ's sufferings, the women having added themselves as they came to power to the point of painting over earlier portraits. Following the Revolution, the abbey became a prison and remained so from 1804 until 1963, housing minor criminals incarcerated for such nefarious crimes as sticking their tongues out at guards. The 12th-century church also serves as a Plantagenêt necropolis: Henri II and his wife, Eleanor of Aquitaine, imprisoned by her husband for 15 years, are both buried there. Their legendary son, Richard the Lionheart, completes the family burial site. Twenty-one chimneys herald the 12th-century Romanesque kitchens, inspired by sketches brought back from the Crusades. Unique in their fascinating architecture, the chimneys were designed to clear the kitchen of smoke as effectively as possible while accommodating seven simultaneously burning fires. An English booklet and signs help visitors along, but the 1hr. tour gives the best summary of the abbey's extensive history.

ANGERS ☎ 02 41

Bustling with shops, bars, and excellent restaurants, cosmopolitan Angers (ahn-jhay; pop. 156,000) is a sophisticated city still in touch with its illustrious royal roots. From behind the imposing walls of their fortress, the medieval dukes of Anjou once ruled over the surrounding territory as well as an insignificant island across the channel called Britain. Today, alongside its 13th-century château and cathedral and its world-famous apocalyptic tapestry, the "city of flowers" offers first-class art museums housed in edifices as refined as the pieces residing within. Those who find themselves overwhelmed by upscale boutiques on the main thoroughfares should venture down Angers's quiet side streets to discover the soul of the city.

▌ TRANSPORTATION

Trains: Angers St-Laud, pl. de la Gare. Info desk open M-Sa 6am-9:15pm, Su 8:45am-7pm. To: **Le Mans** (40min., 15 per day, €15); **Nantes** (1hr., every hr., €14); **Orléans** (3hr., 8 per day, €27-29) via **Saint-Pierre-des-Corps; Paris** (3-4hr., 15 per day, €39-46); **Poitiers** (2-3hr., 7 per day, €26-30) via **Saint-Pierre** or **Tours** (1hr., 10 per day, €16). TGV trains run to **Le Mans** (€18), **Nantes** (€17), and **Paris** (€47).

Buses: AnjouBus (☎08 20 16 00 49) sends buses from outside the train station on esplanade de la Gare for **Rennes** (3hr., 2 per day, €14) and **Saumur** (1hr., 2 per day, €7.20). Schedules vary seasonally; check with the ticket office. Open M-Sa 6:30am-7:30pm. COTRA (☎02 41 33 64 64; www.cotra.fr) buses run from the train station and provide local service from pl. Lorraine. Open M-F 7:45am-6:30pm, Sa 8:45am-5:30pm. Tickets €1 from booth or machine, €1.30 on board.

Taxis: Allo Anjou Taxi (☎02 41 87 65 00). €1.40 per km. 24hr.

Car Rental: Avis (☎02 41 88 20 24). From €124 per day. 21+. Under-25 surcharge €25. Open M-F 7:30am-7pm, Sa 8am-noon and 2-6pm. **Europcar** (☎02 41 87 87 10). From €90 per day. 21+. Under-25 surcharge €33. Open M-F 7:30am-7pm, Sa 8am-noon and 2-6pm. Both in the train station.

Bike Rental: At the tourist office. €10 per ½-day, €14 per day.

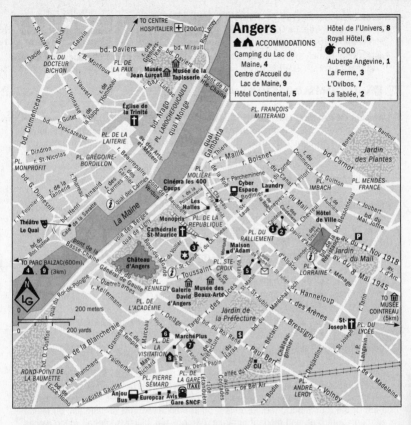

Angers

▲▲ ACCOMMODATIONS

Camping du Lac de
 Maine, 4
Centre d'Accueil du
 Lac de Maine, 9
Hôtel Continental, 5

Hôtel de l'Univers, 8
Royal Hôtel, 6

◆ FOOD

Auberge Angevine, 1
La Ferme, 3
L'Ovibos, 7
La Tablée, 2

▚ ▐ ORIENTATION AND PRACTICAL INFORMATION

Most restaurants and nightlife hot spots are on the pedestrian streets leading into **place du Ralliement**. To reach the château from the train station, follow rue de la Gare, then turn right at pl. de la Visitation onto rue Targot.

Tourist Office: 7 pl. Kennedy (☎02 41 23 50 00; www.angersloiretourisme.com), just across from the castle. Follow directions to the château (above) to rue Targot, then turn left at the traffic light onto bd. du Roi-René. Organizes **tours** of the city (€7.50, students and under 18 €5.50), reserves accommodations, offers currency exchange (€4.20 fee), and provides free maps. Particularly helpful with historical info. Open May-Sept. M-Sa 9am-7pm, Su 10am-7pm; Oct.-Apr. M 2-6pm, Tu-Sa 9am-6pm, Su 10am-1pm.

Youth Center: Centre d'Information Jeunesse, 5 allée du Haras (☎02 41 87 74 47). Info on employment, lodging, outdoor activities, and cultural events. Free Internet for research only; 30min. limit. Open M-Tu and Th-F 1-6pm, W 10am-6pm, Sa 10am-noon.

Laundromat: 15 rue Valdermaine. Open daily 7am-10pm.

Police: 33 rue Nid de Pie (☎02 41 22 94 00).

Hospital: 4 rue Larrey (☎02 41 35 36 37).

Medical Emergency: ☎02 41 35 37 12.

Internet Access: Free at the **Centre d'Information Jeunesse** (above). **Cyber Espace,** 25 rue de la Roë (☎02 41 24 92 71). €1 per 15min., €3 per hr. Open M-Th 9am-10pm, F-Sa 9am-midnight, Su 2-8pm.

Post Office: 1 rue Roosevelt (☎02 41 20 81 82), off rue Corneilles. **Currency exchange** available. Open M-F 9am-6:30pm, Sa 9am-12:30pm. **Postal Code:** 49100.

ACCOMMODATIONS AND CAMPING

Camping du Lac de Maine, av. du Lac de Maine (☎02 41 73 05 03; www.lacdemaine. fr). Take bus #6 to Camping du Lac de Maine and follow signs. 4-star site is perhaps a better deal than attached hostel. Offers a pool, foosball, ping-pong, clean bathrooms, free hot showers, laundry and bike rental (€9 per day). Reception July-Aug. 8am-7pm; Sept.-June 8am-12:30pm and 2-7pm. Open from late Mar. to mid-Oct. 2 people with tent and car €12-17, extra adult €3, extra child €2. Electricity €3.50. Bungalows that feel more like luxury condos €153-572 per week. MC/V. ❶

Hôtel Continental, 12-14 rue Louis de Romain (☎02 41 86 94 94; www.hotellecontinental.com), near pl. du Ralliement in the *centre-ville*. Offers bright rooms with double beds, TV, phone, and sleek furnishings. Buffet breakfast €8.50. Free Wi-Fi. Singles with shower or bathtub €57-66; doubles €68/73; triples €77. AmEx/MC/V. ❹

Royal Hôtel, 8 bis pl. de la Visitation (☎02 41 88 30 25; fax 81 05 75). Don't be deterred by the fake-marble lobby—this place offers spacious rooms with double beds, big windows, and cable TV. Breakfast €6. Free Internet access in lobby. Reception M-Sa 6:45am-midnight, Su 7:15am-midnight. Singles €30-42; doubles €31-51, with private shower or bath €51; triples €56. AmEx/MC/V. ❷

Hôtel de l'Univers, 2 pl. de la Gare (☎02 41 88 43 58; www.citotel.com/hotels/univ_ fr), across from the train station. 45 well-kept rooms with comfortable double beds, telephones, and cable TV. Breakfast €6.40. Hall shower €5. Singles and doubles with sink €33, with shower €44-46, with bath €60-68. AmEx/MC/V. ❷

Centre d'Accueil du Lac de Maine, 49 av. du Lac de Maine (☎02 41 22 32 10; www. lacdemaine.fr). Take bus #6 or 16 to Lac de Maine (dir.: Accueil; 15min.; every 10min., last bus 12:45am from pl. du Ralliement; €1.30). Cross the street and turn right; take a left at the roundabout; the hostel is a 5min. walk away, next to calm Lac du Maine. All rooms with bath and modern furniture. TV room, bar, billiards, pinball, video games. Breakfast included. Free Internet access. 10-day max. stay. Reserve at least 3 weeks in advance. 3- to 5-bed dorms €18; singles €38; doubles €41. AmEx/MC/V. ❶

FOOD

Angers caters to its student population with everything from *crêpes* to Chinese food, particularly along **rue Saint-Laud, rue Saint-Aubin,** and **boulevard Maréchal Foch.** The **Monoprix** grocery store on the ground floor of Les Halles, on pl. de la République, has its own bakery. (Open M-Sa 8:30am-9pm.)

La Tablée, 1 rue David d'Angers (☎02 41 05 12 50). Serves *crêpes* and salads among rotating art exhibits. Authentic Breton feel. Traditional *crêpes* €2.40-5.20. Meat and fish *crêpes* €6.50-13. Desserts €2.40-6. Open M-Th noon-2pm and 7-9:30pm, F noon-2pm and 7-10pm, Sa noon-2pm and 7-11pm. MC/V. ❷

La Ferme, 2 pl. Freppel (☎02 41 87 09 90). Locals and tourists alike pack this family-run "farm." Delicious regional wines, meats, cheeses, and classics like *coq au vin* (€12) and *magret de canard* (€15). Enjoy a lovely view of the cathedral from the terrace. Appetizers and salads €5-10. *Plats* €9-12. Wine by the glass from €2. Lunch *menu* €13. Dinner *menus* €18-35. Open M-Tu and Th-Sa noon-2pm and 7-10pm. Reservations recommended on weekends. AmEx/MC/V. ❸

Auberge Angevine, 9 rue Cordelle (☎02 41 20 10 40; www.auberge-angevine.com). For a divine dining experience, try this chapel-turned-restaurant, complete with its original stained-glass windows. The unique medieval atmosphere, inspired by the Angers of 1462, is worth the price. Student *formule* (M-F; €11) comes highly recommended. *Menus* €12-38. Open Tu-Su noon-2pm and 7:30-10:30pm. AmEx/MC/V. ❸

L'Ovibos, 3 rue d'Anjou (☎02 41 87 48 90). Grills a variety of steaks and meats, complemented by an equally diverse array of salads, all in a ranchero setting. Salads and *menus* are named for US locales: pick a region and dig in. Salads €6-9. *Plats* €5.60-18. *Menus* €9-18. Open M-Sa noon-2pm and 7-11pm. MC/V. ❷

⊙ SIGHTS

Angers is famous for the tapestries that decorate its major sights. It is also home to beautiful parks, including the **Jardin du Mail,** which offers terrific *promenades*, and the **Jardin des Plantes,** a botanical wonder dating from 1901 with provocative sculptures that surround a tranquil pond. Cross the **Pont de la Basse Chaine** at the floor of the château and head into **Parc Balzac** to catch a romantic view of the château and the old city lights above the waters of La Maine.

 ANGERS FOR POCKET CHANGE. Travelers who want a thorough visit to Angers should stop by the tourist office and pick up the **City Pass,** which offers admission to over 10 sites and some guided tours. (€14 for a day pass, €21 for 2 days, €26 for 3 days.) Extra perks include free bus rides and parking as well as discounts at the tourist office and cinema. Check out www.angersloiretourisme.com for more info.

CHÂTEAU D'ANGERS. Seventeen towers and an imposing 900m by 15m wall guard this eerie fortress that was erected over Gallo-Roman ruins in the 13th century. Tucked into an inner courtyard, the duke of Anjou's flamboyant Gothic mansion lacks the Disneyland character of some of France's more touristy châteaux. Beside the château stands a 15th-century chapel with a humble interior covered in fading red frescoes. These intricate buildings make it easy to forget that the château served as a prison for seven centuries and as an asylum until the 1940s. Angers's prized possession is the ⊠**Tapisserie de l'Apocalypse.** Completed in 1375 during the Hundred Years' War, its 74 scenes depict St-Jean's visions of the battle between good and evil while its symbols of John (France) and a menacing, lion-like monster (England) also allude to a political conflict. *(2 promenade du Bout du Monde, on pl. Kennedy. ☎02 41 86 48 77. Open daily May-Aug. 9:30am-6:30pm; Sept.-Apr. 10am-5:30pm. Last entry 45min. before closing. Free tours in French leave from the chapel 5 times per day. €7.50, ages 18-25 €4.80, under 18 free.)*

MUSÉE JEAN LURÇAT. Formerly one of France's ancient hospitals, this museum now houses one of Angers's woven masterpieces. The 80m **Chant du Monde** (Song of the World) offers a symbolic historical journey that includes a depiction of the WWII atomic bombings. The neighboring **Musée de la Tapisserie Contemporaire** has a permanent textile collection, which highlights pieces by Jean Lurçat and Grau-Garriga. The tapestries, including Thomas Gleb's *Zohar*, should not be missed. *(4 bd. Arago. ☎02 41 24 18 45. Open June-Sept. daily 10am-6:30pm; Oct.-May Tu-Su 10am-noon and 2-6pm. €4 for both museums, ages 18-25 €3, under 18 free.)*

MUSÉE COINTREAU. This factory, owned by the Cointreau family, has been making Angers's prized native liqueur since 1849. The exhibit includes documents related to the liqueur's production, advertisements, and a 10min. historical film. *(Bd. des Bretonnières, St-Barthélemy-d'Anjou. Take bus #7 to Cointreau. ☎02 41*

31 50 50; www.cointreau.fr. Visit by guided tours only; must reserve ahead. €6-9.50, including free tasting. Prices vary depending on season.)

GALERIE DAVID D'ANGERS. This restored 11th-century abbey, now beneath a soaring glass roof, holds a collection of 19th-century David d'Angers sculptures. D'Angers produced 23 vibrant, life-size figures and over 50 busts of major literary and historical characters, such as Victor Hugo and Balzac, both of whom were friends of the artist. *(34 bis rue Toussaint. ☎ 02 41 05 38 90. Open June-Sept. daily 10am-6:30pm; from late Oct. to May Tu-Su 10am-noon and 2-6pm. €4; students €3; under 18 and architecture, tourism, and art history students free.)*

CATHÉDRALE SAINT-MAURICE. The 12th-century building is a stylistic hodge-podge—with a Norman porch, a 13th-century chancel intersecting a fourth-century Gallo-Roman wall, and some of France's oldest stained glass. Atop the cathedral's main entrance, a trumpeting angel rises above an illuminated *vitrage* from 1944. The church's single nave, with heavily decorated vault, is in the classic style of the Angevin Plantagenet (Anjou) dynasty. As with any sight in Angers, the church also has a rotating exhibit of rare tapestries. *(Pl. Chappoulie. ☎ 02 41 87 58 45. Open daily 8:30am-7pm. Mass daily 9:30am, 7pm.)*

OTHER SIGHTS. The **Musée des Beaux-Arts** houses a small collection on the city's history, complete with relics uncovered in the region. The upper floors feature paintings from the 14th to 20th centuries. Arranged by century, the second floor houses earlier art, primarily from the Italian Renaissance. Temporary exhibits offer contemporary paintings, sculptures, and graphic art to the tapestry-weary. *(14 rue du Musée. ☎ 02 41 05 38 00. Open June-Sept. daily 10am-6:30pm, Oct.-May Tu-Su 10am-6pm. €4, students €3.)* Though dominated by modern architecture and flashy cafe umbrellas, the **vieille ville** retains some 16th-century stone houses. The timber-framed **La Maison d'Adam** is the city's oldest and grandest medieval residence. Originally called the "House of the Tree of Life" because of the sculpture on the corner, its name was changed when a scandal erupted 200 years ago, sparked by the theft of two wood figures of Adam and Eve from the tree. On its bottom floor, the **Maison des Artisans** sells handcrafted gifts from the region; the upper floors contain private residences. *(1 pl. St-Croix, on the corner of rue Montault. ☎ 02 41 88 06 27. Open M 2-7pm, Tu-Sa 9:30am-7pm.)*

🎵🎭 ENTERTAINMENT AND NIGHTLIFE

The discos have been exiled to the suburbs, but cafes along **rue Saint-Laud** are always packed, and bars on student-dominated **rue Bressigny** get down before the sun does. Music echoes through the streets from behind dark red doors at **Cinéma Les 400 Coups,** 12 rue Claveau, which shows international films. (☎ 02 41 42 87 39. €7.50, students €6, Su 11am matinee €5.) The **Théâtre Le Quai,** across the river from the château, presents cutting-edge avant-garde plays all year. (☎ 02 41 22 20 20. Tickets €5-15. Open daily noon-6pm.)

🎆 FESTIVALS

Festival d'Anjou, info office at 1 rue des Arènes (☎ 02 41 88 14 14; www.festivaldanjou. com), from mid-June to early July. Renowned comedy and drama troupes perform at one of the largest theater festivals in France. €20-30 per show, students €15.

Angers l'Été (☎ 02 41 05 41 48), in July and Aug. International musicians and prestigious jazz bands perform. Tickets available for purchase at the tourist office, 7 pl. Kennedy. €9.50, students €7.50.

LE MANS

☎02 43

Though Le Mans (luh mahn; pop. 146,100) may not be the most beautiful city in the Loire Valley, its central location, lively *brasseries*, spacious squares filled with young hipsters, and old Roman *centre-ville* make it worth exploring. Currently undergoing massive reconstruction, the city has many unsightly areas, but pedestrian pathways preserve the *vieille ville*, one of the most enchanting in the entire region. Most travelers will want to make Le Mans a daytrip, but for car-racing fans, the city is worth a night's stay.

▐ TRANSPORTATION

Trains: Bd. de la Gare. Ticket windows open M-F 6am-8pm, Sa 6am-7pm, Su 8:15am-9:30pm. To: **Nantes** (1hr., 20 per day, €24-27); **Paris** (1-3hr., at least 10 per day, €26-47); **Rennes** (1hr., 10 per day, €25-27); **Tours** (1hr., 6 per day, €9-14).

Buses: SNCF (☎08 91 70 58 05) sends buses from the station to **Saumur** (2hr.; M-Sa 2 per day, Su 9:10pm; €15). SETRAM, 65 av. du Général de Gaulle (☎02 43 24 76 76), carts pedestrians around the city during the day. Info office open M-F 7am-7pm, Sa 8:30am-6:30pm. Buses run 5:30am-8pm. Ticket €1.40, carnet of 10 €9; sold on bus or in office. MC/V. The city's Hi'bus lines take over until 1:30am every night.

Taxis: Radio Taxi, 188 route de Beauge (☎02 43 24 92 92).

Car Rental: Rent A Car, 102 av. du Général Leclerc (☎02 43 24 50 50). Weekday deals from €39. Open M-F 8:30am-noon and 2-6:30pm, Sa 9am-noon. AmEx/MC/V. 2nd branch located across from the train station, where there is also an **Avis** (☎02 43 24 30 50). From €95. 21+. Under-25 surcharge €25. Open M-F 7:30am-7pm, Sa 9am-noon and 2-6pm. AmEx/MC/V.

▐ PRACTICAL INFORMATION

Tourist Office: Rue de l'Étoile (☎02 43 28 17 22; www.lemanstourisme.com), in the 17th-century Hôtel des Ursulines. Walk down av. du Général Leclerc from the train station and stay right on av. François Mitterrand. Distributes free maps and brochures and runs French **tours** of the city (M-F 4:30pm) and cathedral (Su 3pm) in summer (€5.50, under 18 €3). English tours available by reservation. Open July-Aug. M-Sa 9am-6pm, Su 2-6pm; Sept.-June M-F 9am-6pm, Sa 9am-noon and 2-6pm, Su 10am-noon.

Beyond Tourism: France Bénévolat, 5 rue des Jacobins (☎02 43 87 50 40). Volunteer restoration with **Rempart** (☎01 42 71 96 55; www.rempart.com) during the summer. See **Beyond Tourism,** p. 83.

English-Language Bookstore: Thuard Librairie, 24 rue de l'Étoile (☎02 43 82 22 22). Open M-F 9am-7pm, Sa 9am-7:30pm. MC/V.

Youth Center: TVille du Mans Service Jeunesse, 13 rue de l'Étoile (☎02 43 47 38 95). Offers student tips, sports trips, info on jobs and housing, and a brochure of cultural events in the area. Open M, W, F 10am-noon and 1:30-6pm, Tu and Th 1:30-6pm, Sa 2-6pm. Closed Sa during school holidays.

Laundromat: Lav'Ideal, 4 pl. l'Éperon. Wash €3.70, dry €1.10. Open daily 7am-9pm.

Police: 6 rue Coeffort (☎02 43 78 55 00).

Hospital: 194 av. Rubillard (☎02 43 43 43 43).

Medical Emergency: ☎02 43 51 15 15.

Post Office: 13 pl. de la République (☎02 43 39 14 10). **Currency exchange** available. Open M-F 8am-7pm, Sa 9am-12:30pm. **Postal Code:** 72000.

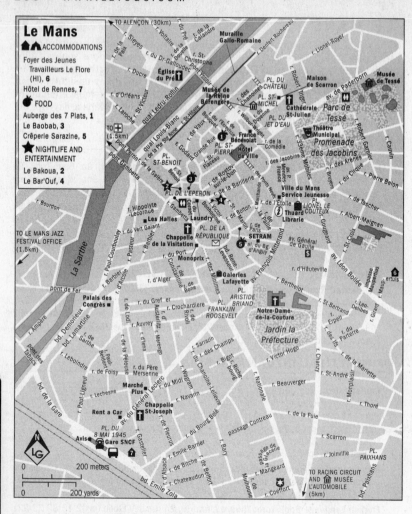

Le Mans

▲⌂ ACCOMMODATIONS

Foyer des Jeunes
  Travailleurs Le Flore
  (HI), **6**
Hôtel de Rennes, **7**

🍴 FOOD

Auberge des 7 Plats, **1**
Le Baobab, **3**
Crêperie Sarazine, **5**

★ NIGHTLIFE AND
  ENTERTAINMENT

Le Bakoua, **2**
Le Bar'Ouf, **4**

🏠 ACCOMMODATIONS

Plenty of hotels line bd. de la Gare, but most accommodations lack that Loire
Valley charm. Better deals can be found farther from the station.

Foyer des Jeunes Travailleurs Le Flore (HI), 23 rue Maupertuis (☎02 43 81 27 55). A
25min. walk from the train station and just blocks from the *centre-ville*. Hospitable staff
tends small but comfortable triples with shower as well as spacious singles, both at
unbeatable prices. Also a local dorm and youth center. TV lounge on every floor. Breakfast included M-Sa 5-8:30am. Cafeteria €5.25-6.50 per meal. Linen €3. Free Internet.
Wheelchair-accessible. 4 night max. stay. €15 per person. Cash only. ❶

Hôtel de Rennes, 43 bd. de la Gare (☎02 43 24 86 40), across from the train station.
A quiet escape from the busy surrounding streets and the even farther pl. de la Répub-

lique. Breakfast €6.40. Reception M-Sa 7am-11pm, Su 7am-noon and 5:30-11pm. Singles and doubles €39, with bath €47; triples with bath €55. MC/V. ❸

🍴 FOOD

Renowned for its poultry, Le Mans's regional cuisine usually includes *pintade* (guinea fowl) and *canard* (duck). The succulent *marmite sarthoise*, a warm casserole of rabbit, chicken, ham, carrots, cabbage, and mushrooms in a bath of *jasnière* wine, is a gourmand's dream. The most affordable *brasseries* used to line **place de la République** before the construction site scared away the diners. If you're willing to pay in the old Roman quarter, try one of the pleasant restaurants along **Grande Rue** or behind **place de l'Éperon** in the *vieille ville*. Fresh produce can be found at the outdoor market on **place des Jacobins.** (Open W and Su 7am-1pm, F 8am-6pm.) There's a **Monoprix** supermarket at 30 pl. de la République (open M-Sa 8:30am-8:30pm; MC/V) and a **Marché Plus** at 68 av. du Général Leclerc (open M-Sa 7am-9pm, Su 9am-1pm; MC/V).

🏅 **Auberge des 7 Plats,** 79 Grande Rue (☎02 43 24 57 77). Choose from 7 appetizers, 7 *plats,* and 14 desserts in a rustic dining room. Ask to be seated downstairs under the high vaulted ceiling carved into medieval stone or try the top floors for more privacy. Free *calvados* spirit with your coffee. Lunch *formules* €12-15. Dinner *menus* €20-28. Open Tu 7-10pm, W-Sa noon-1:30pm and 7-10pm. MC/V. ❸

Le Baobab, 4 rue de la Vieille Porte (☎02 43 24 84 85). Ivoirian owner serves up fresh, budget-friendly, and authentic African delicacies amid festive yellow decor and Senegalese tribal masks. The *assiette de cracros* (plantains in tomato cream sauce; €6.50) is a must. *Entrées* €6.50-16. *Menus* €18-23. Open Tu-Sa 7-11pm. MC/V. ❹

Crêperie Sarazine, 3 rue de la Perle (☎02 43 24 22 11). Hidden in a nook behind pl. de la République, this bright and cheery place offers exotic *crêpes* and a peaceful respite from the rowdy teenage city. For a savory bite, try the Forrestière (mushrooms, ham, Emmental cheese, and cream; €8). Satisfy a sweet tooth with the Créole (dark chocolate, shredded coconut, liqueur; €5.60). Open Tu-Sa noon-2pm and 6-10pm. MC/V. ❷

🔆 SIGHTS

Unlike those of most cities in the valley, Le Mans's main attractions date to antiquity or the Middle Ages. These include churches like the **Maison-Dieu,** founded by Henry Plantagenêt, and the Romanesque **Notre Dame-de-la-Couture,** up av. du Général Leclerc from the station. The **billet inter-musée** (€6, students €3) is available for purchase at any museum and includes visits to two of the following: Musée de Tessé, Musée Vert, or Musée de la Reine-Bérengère.

🏛**VIEILLE VILLE.** Behind thick Roman walls and the Sarthe River, the city's *vieille ville* is one of the most authentic-feeling in France. Fifteenth- to 17th-century houses line the winding streets, and crumbling pillars that once served as street signs—the **Pilier Rouge** and the **Pilier aux Clefs**—mark the corners. Historical tours depart from the Pilier Rouge. *(2hr. M-F 10:30am. €5.50, students €3. Book ahead for private English tours.)* In the summer, after sundown, fantastic figures illuminate the cathedral and the Roman walls in **La Nuit des Chimères.** *(2hr., July-Aug. daily. Free.)* Housed in three 15th-century residences, the **Musée de la Reine Bérengère** displays artifacts from Le Mans's past, including original 16th-century weathervanes. A well-preserved 18th-century *métier à tisser* (loom) in the attic is perhaps the most impressive piece, while the museum's 16th-century facade, depicting the Virgin Mary with the angel Gabriel, is as interesting as the museum's contents. *(7-11 rue de la Reine Bérengère. ☎02 43 47 38 80. Open Tu-Su*

July-Sept. 10:30am-12:30pm and 2-6:30pm; Oct.-June 2-6pm. €2.80, students €1.40, under 18 free; Su ½-price. Night tours by torch light €8, under 18 €4.)

CATHÉDRALE SAINT-JULIEN. Built and rebuilt between the 11th and 15th centuries, the facade of Le Mans's cathedral tells the city's story. Legend has it that Charles VI, seized by a fit of insanity on a visit to Le Mans in 1392, was patiently nursed back to health in the cathedral by St-Julien, who gave the building his name. Donations from the grateful king helped build the great chancel, which doubled the cathedral's size and added the impressive flying buttresses. A Celtic menhir (stone monolith) dating to 5000 BC still rests against the cathedral's western wall; nicknamed the "belly button of Le Mans," its phallic form was believed to enhance fertility. Much of the stained glass dates to the 11th century, while other *vitrages* pay colorful tribute to Joan of Arc. The cathedral feels oddly unfinished: in 1832, lightning struck, destroying its main spire. The cathedral is currently trying to raise the €2.5 million needed to regain its full 15th-century elegance. *(Pl. des Jacobins. Included in the city tour. Open daily from July to mid-Sept. 8am-7pm; from mid-Sept. to June 9am-noon and 2-5:30pm. Tours given by tourist office Su 3pm. Wheelchair-accessible. €5.50, under 18 €3.)*

MURAILLE GALLO-ROMAINE. The stocky fourth-century walls hugging the city's southwestern edge helped make the town of Vindinium (Le Mans's original name) a strong protection base against the "barbarous" tribes of ancient Roman times. Intricate mosaics in 14 different patterns called *lozanges*—intended to proclaim Roman refinement—adorn the exterior. Punctuated by three arched gates and 10 massive towers, the 1.3km wall is the longest and perhaps best-preserved Roman fortification in France. Steep staircases leading to the *vieille ville* penetrate the robust stretch of molded stones.

MUSÉE AND PARC DE TESSÉ. The thoroughly modernized interior of this 19th-century former bishop's palace holds 14th- to 20th-century paintings—including some by Le Sueur—with a special emphasis on the Italian Renaissance. In the depths of the museum lie Egyptian artifacts from 1230 BC, including a reproduction of the underground tomb of Nofetari, one of the wives of Pharaoh Ramses II. The tomb of Sennefer—the mayor of Thebes around 1400 BC—contains a dizzying replica of the cave's original ceiling, accompanied by atmospheric lighting. Call ahead for guided tours in English and French. *(2 av. Paderborn, a 15min. walk from pl. de la République. Take bus #3, dir.: Bellevue, from rue Gastelier by the station or from av. du Général de Gaulle to Musée. ☎02 43 47 38 51. Open July-Aug. Tu-Su 10am-12:30pm and 2-6:30pm; Sept.-June Tu-Sa 9am-noon and 2-6pm, Su 10am-noon and 2-6pm. €4, students €2, under 18 free; Su ½-price.)* Behind the museum lies the spacious **Parc de Tessé,** where open-air concerts are hosted every weekend in the summer. Though it bustles with families and students during the day, the park becomes dangerous and should be avoided at night.

RACING CIRCUIT AND MUSÉE AUTOMOBILE. Le Mans has a world-famous automobile tradition: Amédée Bollée and his sons allegedly invented the steam and the gas car here in the 20th century. The 4km stretch of racetrack south of the city is a must-see for car enthusiasts. Since 1923, the circuit has hosted the annual **24 Heures du Mans,** a grueling test of endurance held in June. *(Tickets ☎02 43 40 24 75 or 72 72 24; www.museeauto24h.sarthe.com. Tickets to the track sold at the museum; €2.)* The massive **Musée Automobile de la Sarthe** traces the evolution of auto racing with vintage and high-tech models, including the slick Socema Gregoire that Bollée drove for 18hr. to introduce to Paris in 1952. Over 140 vehicles are displayed in this giant futuristic garage. *(At the corner of rue de l'Étoile and av. François Mitterrand. Take bus #7 to Raineries to the end of the line. 30min., every 10 min., €1.40. Schedules at SETRAM office. Take a right onto rue de Laigné, following signs to the museum.*

☎02 43 72 72 24. Open June-Aug. daily 10am-7pm; Sept.-Dec. and Feb.-May daily 10am-6pm; Jan. Sa-Su 10am-6pm. €8, students and ages 12-18 €5, ages 7-11 €2.)

🎵 🎭 ENTERTAINMENT AND NIGHTLIFE

Le Mans packs most of its nocturnal revelry into the side streets around **place de la République.** A younger scene is down **rue du Docteur Leroy,** where bars resonate with techno and rock beats. **Rue des Ponts Neuf** has its share of lively bars, decorated with everything from model cars to film projections. Cannes festival winners, independent films, and lesser-known international productions are featured nightly at **Les Cinéastes,** 42 pl. des Comtes du Maine. (☎02 43 51 28 18. €6.80, students €5.80, under 13 €3.80.)

Le Bakoua, 5 rue de la Vieille Porte (☎02 43 23 30 70), off pl. de l'Éperon. Caribbean-themed club draws large, youthful crowds with calypso and DUB music (a mix of electro and reggae), comedy hours, and inexpensive, rum-based tropical concoctions. A small rickety staircase leads to the teenage scene on the 2nd fl. Punch €2. Beer €2.70. Mixed drinks €4-8. Open M-Sa 6pm-2am. MC/V.

Le Bar'Ouf, 8 rue Victor Bonhommet (☎02 43 24 19 01). Attracts a varied crowd with its obscure music, artsy vibe—enhanced by a mosaic floor and recycled ceiling ornaments—and weekly concerts. Free Wi-Fi. DJ or concerts Th and Sa 10pm-1:30am. Beer €2-3.20. Shots €2.50-3.50. Mixed drinks €5.70. Open M-F noon-2am, Sa 2pm-2am. MC/V.

🌿 FESTIVALS

Europa Jazz Festival, 9 rue des Frères Gréban (☎02 43 23 78 99; www.europa.jazz.fr), from mid-Apr. to mid-May. Hosts contemporary jazz artists.

Le Mans Fait son Cirque (☎02 43 47 36 57), in late June. Parades and circus events storm pl. des Jacobins. Past events include "La Grande Marche," when tightropers crossed the *place* 30m in the air. €2-4 for tent events; most other events free.

Les Soirs d'Eté, Th and F in July and Aug. 50 free theater, comedy, and musical performances throughout the city. Pick up a *L'Affiche* supplement at the tourist office for info.

BOURGES ☎02 48

In the heart of the lower Loire Valley, Bourges (boorjh; pop. 75,000) attracts countless visitors with its flamboyant Gothic architecture, half-timbered houses, and medieval streets. Bourges's extravagant wealth originated in 1433, when Jacques Coeur, financier of Charles VII, chose the city as the site for his palatial home. The city has since become famous for its established music festival, Le Printemps de Bourges, hosted every April. Bourges makes a convenient base for daytrips to the secluded châteaux tucked into the thick forests and rolling vineyards of the surrounding region.

🚩 TRANSPORTATION

Trains: Pl. du Général Leclerc (☎08 92 35 35 35). Info office open M-Sa 6:05am-8:30pm, Su 7:30am-8:30pm. Ticket office open M-Th 5:50am-8:25pm, F 5:50am-9:20pm, Sa 6:25am-7:35pm, Su 7:40am-9:05pm. To: **Lyon** (3hr., 3 per day, €36); **Nevers** (45min., 8 per day, €7.80); **Paris** (2hr., 8 per day, €28); **Tours** (1hr., 4 per day, €20). Many trains require a change at nearby **Vierzon.**

Buses: Rue du Champ de Foire (☎02 48 24 36 42). Office open M-Tu and Th-F 8-9:30am and 4-6pm, W and Sa 8am-noon. Most buses stop at the train station.

Public Transportation: CTB (☎02 48 27 99 99) **buses** serve all areas of the city. All schedules are posted at the bus stops and available at the tourist office or 1 pl. de la Nation. Tickets €1.25, carnet of 10 €9.

Taxis: ☎02 48 24 50 00. €5 from the train station to tourist office. 24hr.

Car Rentals: Hertz, 4 av. Henri Laudier (☎02 48 70 22 92), near the train station. From €46 per day. 21+. Under-25 surcharge €35 per day. Open M-F 8am-noon and 2-6pm. AmEx/MC/V. **Avis,** 23 av. Henri Laudier (☎02 48 24 38 84). From €47 per day. Open M-F 8am-noon and 2-6pm, Sa 8am-1pm. AmEx/MC/V. **Ucar,** 21 av. Jean Jaurès (☎02 48 70 63 33), halfway between the station and the *centre-ville.* 21+. Under-25 insurance fee doubles. Open M-Sa 8am-noon and 2-6pm. MC/V.

Bike Rental: Narcy, 39 av. Marx Dormoy (☎02 48 70 15 84; narcyvelo@nerim.net). €7 per ½-day, €8 per day; ID deposit. Open Tu-Su 9am-noon and 2-6pm. MC/V.

🔢 PRACTICAL INFORMATION

Tourist Office: 21 rue Victor Hugo (☎02 48 23 02 60; www.bourges-tourisme.com), near the cathedral. From the station, cross the street and follow av. Henri Laudier into the *vieille ville,* where it becomes av. Jean Jaurès. Bear left onto rue du Commerce and continue straight as it becomes rue Moyenne (18min.). Or catch bus #1 (dir.: Val d'Auron) to Victor Hugo. Helpful staff provides an excellent map of the city and info on museums and festivals. When planning daytrips, ask for brochures **La Route Jacques-Coeur, Route des Vignobles,** and **Route de la Porcelaine.** Accommodations booking €1. Office open Apr.-Sept. M-Sa 9am-7pm, Su 10am-6pm; Oct.-Mar. M-Sa 9am-6pm, Su 2-5pm.

Tours: Le Petit Train Touristique de Bourges (☎02 48 23 02 61). A 45min. tour of the city. Leaves from tourist office; call for times. €7, children under 11 €3. Call office for times. Self-guided illuminated tours July-Aug. nightly; Sept. and May-June Tu-Sa.

Youth Center: Bureau Information Jeunesse (BIJ), 8 bd. de la République (☎02 48 24 77 19; bij@bourges.fr), on the 2nd level of Halle St-Bonnet. Open M 2-5:30pm, Tu and Th-F 9am-12:30pm and 2-5:30pm, W 9am-noon and 2-6pm.

Laundromat: Lavmatic, 117 rue Édouard Valliant, with annex locations at 15 bd. Juranville and 79 rue Marcel Haeselen (☎06 72 77 32 05). Open 8am-8:30pm. Cash only.

Police: 6 av. d'Orléans (☎02 48 23 77 17).

Crisis Line: Medical SOS Médecin (☎02 48 23 33 33).

Pharmacy: Pharmacie du Progrès, 27 rue Moyenne (☎02 48 24 00 41), near the post office. Open M 2-7pm, Tu-F 9am-12:30pm and 2-7pm, Sa 9am-12:30pm. MC/V.

Hospital: 145 rue François Mitterrand (☎02 48 48 48 48).

Internet Access: Médiathèque, bd. Lamarck (☎02 48 23 22 50; www.mediatheque-bourges.fr), 10min. from the tourist office. Free; 30min. limit. Open July-Aug. Tu-F 12:30-6:30pm, Sa 9am-noon; Sept.-June Tu-W and F 12:30-6:30pm, Th 12:30-8pm, Sa 10am-5pm. **Le Tie Break,** 78 rue Jean Baffier (☎02 48 67 94 58), 12min. from the tourist office. €4.80 per hr. Open M-F 11am-10:30pm, Sa 3-10pm, Su 4-8pm. MC/V.

Post Office: 29 rue Moyenne (☎02 48 68 82 82). **Currency exchange.** Open M-F 8am-6:30pm, Sa 8am-12:30pm. **Postal Code:** 18000.

🏠 🏕 ACCOMMODATIONS AND CAMPING

While hotels in the *centre-ville* are relatively pricey, cheaper options can be found a 10-15min. walk away. Summer visitors should reserve ahead.

Le Cygne, 10 pl. du Général Leclerc (☎02 48 70 51 05; www.hotel-lecygne.com), across from the train station. Rooms with large windows off sherbet-colored hallways are comfortable and come equipped with showers, toilets, Wi-Fi (€8 per 3hr.), and TVs.

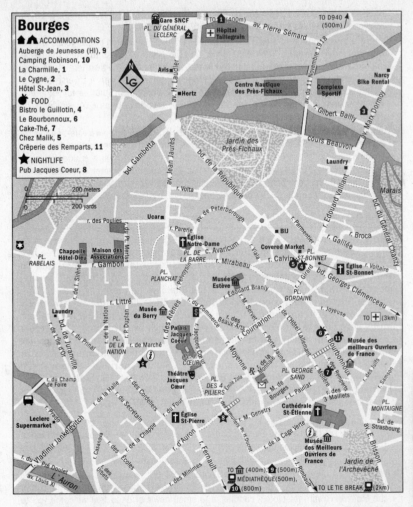

Bourges

ACCOMMODATIONS
Auberge de Jeunesse (HI), **9**
Camping Robinson, **10**
La Charmille, **1**
Le Cygne, **2**
Hôtel St-Jean, **3**

FOOD
Bistro le Guillotin, **4**
Le Bourbonnoux, **6**
Cake-Thé, **7**
Chez Malik, **5**
Crêperie des Remparts, **11**

NIGHTLIFE
Pub Jacques Coeur, **8**

Rooms do not have phones. Elevator and attached restaurant. Breakfast €6.50. Singles and doubles €37-45; triples and quads €50-58. MC/V. ❸

Auberge de Jeunesse (HI), 22 rue Henri Sellier (☎02 48 24 58 09; bourges@fuaj. org), a 15min. walk from the *centre-ville.* From the station, take av. Henri Laudier, which becomes av. Jean Jaurès, to pl. Planchat. Follow rue des Arènes, which becomes rue Fernault and then rue René Ménard. Turn left at rue Henri Sellier. Hostel is on the right, behind a brown and white building (25-30min.). Or take bus #1 (dir.: Golf) or 2 (dir.: Hôpital) to Auron. Clean, colorful 2- to 5-bunk rooms, some with showers. Kitchen. Free parking. Breakfast €3.50. Reception 8-10am and 6-10pm. Dorms €16. Cash only. ❶

Hôtel Saint-Jean, 23 av. Marx Dormoy (☎02 48 24 13 48; hotelstjean.bourges@wana-doo.fr). Located 10min. from both the train station and the *centre-ville* and down the street from the bike shop. Lets small, carpeted rooms with TVs, phones, and clean baths. In need of a few renovations. Elevator. Breakfast €6.50. Reception 7am-10pm. Singles €35; doubles €45; triples €55. MC/V. ❸

Centre International de Séjour: La Charmille, 17 rue Félix-Chédin (☎02 48 23 07 40; www.lacharmille.asso.fr). From the station, use the metal overpass to cross the tracks and walk 5min. up rue Félix-Chédin. The hostel will be on the left. Next to a skate park. Clean, dorm-like rooms with shower. Loud, social atmosphere with a diverse array of guests—mostly young families, teenagers, and 20-somethings. Suitable for long-term stay. Breakfast included. Lunch and dinner €9.50. Laundry. Dorms €14; singles €20. 1-time membership fee €4.40, good for a year. MC/V. ❶

Camping Robinson, 26 bd. de l'Industrie (☎02 48 20 16 85; www.ville-bourges.fr). Follow directions to Auberge de Jeunesse (above). Turn right at the end of rue Henri Sellier onto bd. de l'Industrie. Landscaped riverside campground near a residential area, 20min. from the *centre-ville.* Nearby swimming pool open in summer. Reception June-Aug. 7am-10pm; from Sept. to mid-Nov. and from mid-Mar. to May 8am-9pm. €3.70 per person, children €2, €3.70 per tent. Electricity €3-7.50. AmEx/MC/V over €15. ❶

◻ FOOD

The dining in Bourges is a main attraction, especially during **Le Printemps de Bourges,** when restaurants are filled with the atmosphere enhancer of free live music. Both locals and tourists flock to the outdoor tables of restaurants on **place Gordaine** and **rue des Beaux-Arts** during the spring and summer. The elegant restaurants on **rue Bourbonnoux** or **rue Girard** serve tasty regional cuisine in timber-framed dining rooms. Look for specialties like *poulet en barbouille* (chicken roasted in aromatic red wine), *crottin de chavignol* (the area's most famous goat cheese), and *oeufs en meurette* (eggs in red wine). The largest market is held on **place de la Nation** (Sa morning); another livens up **place des Marronniers** (Th until 1pm). There is a smaller, permanent covered market at **place Saint-Bonnet,** though it moves outdoors on Sunday mornings. (Open Tu-Th 8am-12:45pm and 3:30-7:30pm, F-Sa 8am-1pm and 3-7:30pm, Su 8am-1pm.) The **Leclerc** supermarket, rue Prado off bd. Juranville, next to the bus station, boasts an enormous selection. (Open M-Sa 8:30am-7:20pm. MC/V.)

Chez Malik, 7 rue Jean Girard (☎02 48 24 59 85). Serves huge portions of couscous (€10-18) in an African-themed interior. Big-screen TV shows the sporting match of the moment. Staff serves up a vast menu of flavorful lamb, beef, and chicken combos (€9.90-19). Open Tu-Sa noon-2pm and 7:30-10:30pm. MC/V. ❷

Cake-Thé, 74 bis rue Bourbonnoux (☎02 48 24 94 60; www.cak-t.com). An intimate, storybook tearoom lodged in a lavender-lined courtyard between rue Bourbonnoux and rue Molière. Floral tablecloths, candles, and small bowls of dried fruit welcome you to this *salon de thé,* where delicious desserts (€4-5) and exotic teas (€3-4) provide a sweet, satisfying escape. The selection of books and magazines makes the cafe a place to spend the entire afternoon. Open M and Su 3-7pm, Tu-Sa 11am-7pm. MC/V. ❶

Bistro Le Guillotin, pl. Gordaine (☎02 48 65 43 66). Serves excellent, traditional bistro food. Dining room lined with posters of Le Printemps Festival is always packed. Meat and fish specialties prepared in full view at the charcoal grill. Superb selection of local wines. Check times for the **Café Théâtre** located on the 2nd fl. *Entrées* €12-18. Begins serving daily at noon and 7pm; closing times vary. MC/V. ❸

Crêperie des Remparts, 59 rue Bourbonnoux (☎02 48 24 55 44; www.creperiedes-remparts.com), just past pl. Gordaine along rue Bourbonnoux. Blue-and-white facade stands out among timber-framed neighbors. Delicious *crêpes* and *galettes* (€2-8) in the dining room or shaded courtyard. Open Tu-Sa noon-2pm and 7-10pm. MC/V. ❶

Le Bourbonnoux, 44 rue Bourbonnoux (☎02 48 24 14 76). On a quiet street of half-timbered houses. Serves regional fare in a bright, upscale atmosphere. *Canard* (duck) plays a central role in the dishes and decor; figurines line the walls. *Menus* €13-35. Open M-Th noon-2pm and 7:30-9:15pm, Sa 7-9pm, Su noon-2pm. AmEx/MC/V. ❹

🄶 SIGHTS

Bourges's past has endowed its cobblestone *vieille ville* with numerous museums, an enchanting palace, and a gargantuan cathedral, all of which are clustered close enough to tour in a single afternoon. The city's many parks, including the rose-filled **Jardin de l'Archevêché** and the peaceful **Jardin des Prés-Fichaux,** provide plenty of places for a lovely stroll or a picnic.

█CATHÉDRALE SAINT-ÉTIENNE. This enormous 13th-century cathedral is a masterpiece of Gothic architecture, with gargoyles and flying buttresses reminiscent of Paris's Notre Dame (p. 138). A soaring vaulted ceiling creates a cavernous interior illuminated by light from windows high above the nave. Impressive brass chandeliers hang along the entire length of the interior. In the back right corner stands the **Astronomical Clock,** a 15th-century invention by Jean Fusoris. Aside from its stunning craftsmanship, the clock was designed to show time, phases of the moon, and positions of the zodiac. The small brass Meridian line on the floor is struck at exactly noon every day. The cathedral's **Great Tower,** a copy of one of the Louvre's towers, symbolizes royal power. Entrance to the church is free, but tickets are required to visit the cathedral's crypt or northern tower. *(Cathedral open daily Apr.-Sept. 8:30am-7:15pm; Oct.-Mar. 9am-5:45pm. Tours led by parishioners available June-Sept. 10:30am-12:30pm and 4-6pm. Mass Tu-Sa 6:30pm, Su 11am. Tours of crypt and tower July-Aug. M-Sa 9:30am-12:30pm and 2-6pm, Su 2-6pm; Sept. and Apr. M-Sa 9:45-11:45am and 2-5:30pm, Su 2-5:30pm; Oct.-Mar. M-Sa 9:30-11:30am and 2-4:45pm, Su 2-4:45pm; May-June M-Sa 9:30-11:30am and 2-6pm, Su 2-6pm. €6.50, ages 18-25 €4.50, under 18 free; tower alone €5/3.50/free.)*

PALAIS JACQUES-COEUR. Commissioned in 1443 by Jacques Coeur, finance minister to Charles VII, this palace was intended to flaunt Coeur's personal fortune to high-society guests. Coeur was imprisoned for embezzlement in 1451, years before the palace's completion, and the building passed through many hands until it was finally purchased by the state and restored in 1923. Today, the palace lies unfurnished but remains an example of the flamboyant architectural style of the late Middle Ages. The exterior is dotted with gargoyles, and the interior is decorated with carved mantelpieces and vaulted ceilings. Take note of the ceilings in the attic and second gallery, which are especially unusual and beautiful. *(10 bis rue Jacques-Coeur. ☎02 48 24 79 42. Open daily July-Aug. 9:30am-noon and 2-7pm; Sept.-Oct. and May-June 9:30am-noon and 2-6pm; Nov.-Mar. 9:30am-noon and 2-5pm. Mandatory guided tour in French. Short English text available. Tours every 45min. Free.)*

OTHER SIGHTS. The █**Musée des Meilleurs Ouvriers de France** pays homage to superior local craftsmanship. Each year, the French government bestows a medal of honor, the **Meilleur Ouvrier,** on artists or professionals who produce exceptional work in fields ranging from hairstyling to leatherwork; the museum chronicles the award's history and highlights recent winners who specialize in the year's featured craft. Roof ornamentation is the trade for 2009. *(Pl. Étienne Dolet. ☎02 48 57 82 45. Open Tu-Sa 10am-noon and 2-6pm, Su 2-6pm.)* The **Musée Estève** displays modern paintings, tapestries, and drawings by the local artist. Brochures are available in English and French. *(13 rue Édouard Branly. ☎02 48 24 75 38. Open M and W-Sa 10am-noon and 2-6pm, Su 2-6pm.)* The **Musée du Berry** showcases prehistoric, Gallo-Roman, and medieval artifacts excavated from the region along with displays of ceramic work and 19th-century farming implements. *(4 *rue des Arènes.* ☎ *02 48 70 41 92. Open July-Aug. M and W-Sa 10am-12:30pm and 1:30-6pm, Su 2-6pm; from Sept. to early Jan. and Apr.-June M and W-Sa 10am-noon and 2-6pm; from early Jan. to Mar. M and W-Sa 10am-noon and 2-5pm.)*

🔊 NIGHTLIFE

Nightlife in Bourges is fairly subdued. There is late-night dancing at **Le Daumier,** but most locals hang out in the plentiful bars and pubs in the *vieille ville*.

Pub Jacques Coeur, 1 rue d'Auron (☎ 02 48 70 72 88). Stone-walled hangout fills with a laid-back, mixed-age crowd that comes for billiards, DJs, and frequent live music. Waitresses in Jameson whiskey skirts, a large selection of international beers, and fun drinks like Les Astrologies (one for every sign) provide a unique twist on the typical pub atmosphere. Open M 10am-8pm, Tu-Sa 10am-2am. V.

🎆 FESTIVALS

Le Printemps de Bourges (☎ 02 48 27 28 29; www.printemps-bourges.com). Over 100,000 ears perk up in Apr. for this musical celebration. Most tickets €7-28; some informal folk, jazz, classical, and rock concerts free.

Les Nuits Lumière de Bourges, at sunset May-Aug. daily; Sept. Tu-Sa. This self-guided tour of the city presents Bourges in a whole new light. The tour begins with music and a slideshow on local history, then follows a route through Bourges lit by glowing blue lampposts. Classical music plays while representations of medieval and Renaissance artwork are illuminated on major monuments, creating a fantastical effect. Tours start at nightfall in the **Jardin de l'Archevêché** and last about 2hr. Free.

Un Eté à Bourges (☎ 02 48 24 93 32; www.bourges.fr), every night from mid-June to mid-Sept. Free concerts and performances reign throughout Bourges.

BulleBerry Festival Bande Dessinée (Bubbleberry Comic Book Festival; ☎ 02 48 23 02 60; www.bulleberry.com). Cartoonists and their fans converge on Bourges's historic sites during a weekend in early Oct. for displays and discussion.

🔲 DAYTRIPS FROM BOURGES: ROUTE JACQUES COEUR

Jacques may have left his *coeur* in Bourges, but his ego spilled far into the surrounding countryside. The **Route Jacques Coeur** consists of 13 châteaux, along with a 12th-century abbey, stretching from La Buissière in the north to Culan in the south. Less ostentatious than those of the Loire, these castles see far fewer tourists each year. Many of the families who made them famous still live in the châteaux. Most of the châteaux in this section can be seen only by guided tour. English brochures are often available, but English tours are uncommon.

The châteaux make for fun daytrips, but most can be reached only by car or bike; routes are well marked. If you plan to stay overnight, book lodging in advance. The tourist offices in Bourges (p. 233) and St-Amand-Montrond (below) have free English maps of the route and info on excursions.

SAINT-AMAND-MONTROND

To get to St-Amand from Bourges, take the train (50min.; M-Sa 8 per day, Su 3 per day; €9) or drive south on N144 or A71. From there, a short bike or car ride takes you to nearby sights.

Forty-five kilometers south of Bourges lies St-Amand-Montrond (sehn ah-mahn mohn-trohn), a starting point for explorations of the southern part of the route. Though the châteaux and stretches of forest are the real draw, St-Amand itself makes for an interesting half-day visit. The tourist office arranges a walking tour in French that takes visitors past the city's churches, **Paroisse de Saint-Amand** and the **Église des Carmes.** The ruins of the medieval **Forteresse de Montrond** can be seen from afar—or up close if you reserve ahead. (☎02 48 96 79 64. From mid-June to mid-Sept. 3 tours per day or call to schedule a visit.)

The **tourist office,** pl. de la République, provides free maps highlighting sights both within the city and in its surroundings. From the train station, follow av. de la Gare straight through the roundabout; continue on as it becomes av. Jean Jaurès and, later, rue Henri Barbusse. After 20min., the road runs into pl. de la République; the tourist office is on the left. (☎02 48 96 16 86. Open July-Aug. M-Sa 9am-noon and 2-7pm, Su 10am-12:30pm; Sept. and June M-Sa 9am-noon and 2-7pm; Oct.-May M-Sa 9am-noon and 2-5pm.) For a taxi, call ☎06 09 94 69 34. Bike rental is available at **Cycles HANTZ,** a branch of **Vélo & Oxygen,** 72 av. du Général de Gaulle. Head toward the tourist office from the station and, when av. Jean Jaurès becomes rue Henri Barbusse, turn left onto rue 14 Juillet. At the T intersection with N144, turn left (dir.: Bourges) and walk for 5min. The shop is on the right. (☎02 48 96 00 80. Open M 2-7pm, Tu-Sa 9am-noon and 2-7pm. Bikes €5 per hr., €10 per 4hr., €13 per 8hr.; €120 or ID deposit. MC/V.)

▧CHÂTEAU DE MEILLANT

If you plan on seeing the Abbaye de Noirlac and the château by bike, go to the abbey first; otherwise you'll bike 7km uphill. To get to the town of Meillant from St-Amand, take rue Nationale, starting near the tourist office, and head north to D10. ☎02 48 63 32 05. Open daily July-Aug. 9:30am-6pm; from Sept. to mid-Nov. and Mar.-June 9:30am-noon and 2-6pm. Visit only by guided tour in French; English translation available. Château and gardens €7, students €5.50, ages 5-15 €5. Call for group rates. MC/V.

A beautiful but difficult 8km bike ride from St-Amand through the Forêt de Meillant leads to the impressive Renaissance Château de Meillant (shah-toh duh may-yahn). In the 15th century, it was purchased by the Amboise family, who imported Italian architects, sculptors, and decorators to adorn the castle with extravagant Renaissance accents. Its ornate stone carvings are especially visible on the **Tour du Lion,** a turret partially designed by Leonardo da Vinci. Excellent guided tours of the château in French highlight features of its architecture and interior decoration, describe the living habits of past inhabitants, and explain the incredible range of art and weapons in the castle. The babbling brook and winding paths around the château provide many spots for visitors to admire its exterior. A small building near the castle contains miniature models of castle life from the Middle Ages to the 18th century.

ABBAYE DE NOIRLAC

To reach the abbey from St-Amand, take rue Henri Barbusse to rue 14 Juillet. After crossing the river, turn left onto N144 (dir.: Bourges); the well-marked turnoff for the abbey is on the left. Be careful crossing the wide road if you are biking. ☎02 48 62 01 01; www.abbayede-noirlac.fr. Open daily July-Aug. 9:45am-6:30pm; Sept. and Apr.-June 9:45am-12:30pm and 2-6:30pm; Oct.-Mar. 9:45am-12:30pm and 2-5pm. Ticket office closes 1hr. before abbey. Call ahead for schedule of French tours or to arrange an English guided tour; English explanations also available. Call for dinner reservations at least 15 days ahead. Groups of 20 or more only; €50 per person. Admission €7, students €4.50. MC/V.

Just 3km west of St-Amand-Montrond lies the isolated Abbaye de Noirlac (ah-bay duh nwahr-lahk), a peaceful haven for city-weary travelers. The former Cistercian abbey now has vacant stone rooms with simple stained glass. The cloister at the center is framed by Gothic arcades. Most of the monks' chapter house dates from its 12th-century construction; the rest was renovated in the 18th century. The abbey also exhibits regional arts. During June and July, the popular **L'Été de Noirlac** energizes the abbey with excellent live music. (☎02 48 48 00 27; www.festivaldenoirlac.com. Tickets €12-22.) For larger groups, the abbey will host a special dinner of traditional fare.

LOIRE VALLEY

VÉLO ROUTE

After about an hour of riding uphill, I was having trouble seeing through my sweat. Yet the sight of the beautiful Château Menetou-Salon rising through the trees was enough to keep me motivated. I began singing "I Believe I Can Fly."

At the château, I was greeted by a Renaissance maid who (without breaking character despite the fact that we were the only two people in the castle) informed me that the next tour was not for another 2hr. and that I would have to leave. I reluctantly left, only to watch the clouds turn black. By the time I returned to the castle for my tour—I was still the only one around—it was definite that there would be a storm. Luckily, the Renaissance maid had a cell phone, and after a quick call she informed me that, yes, there would be a big storm and all the buses had left. But would I like my tour?

Faster than lightning (I hoped), I remounted my faithful steed and set off in a race against the skies. I developed a plan to huddle under my rubber tires in the nearby vineyard if the storm got closer.

I made it back in less than half the time it took me to ride there. I was only 15min. from the city when the rain came. Cut to me on a busy highway, struggling with a rental bike, helmet-less, and dripping wet. That Renaissance maid had it in for me.

—*Abigail Crutchfield*

◪MENETOU-SALON AND MAUPAS

To get to Menetou-Salon, take D940 (av. du Général de Gaulle in Bourges) north for 5km, continue straight through the roundabout, and bear right onto D11, following the signs. Menetou-Salon ☎02 48 64 80 54. Open daily July-Aug. 10am-7pm; May-June and Sept. 2-6pm. Visit by tour only; call ahead for tour times. Tours in French with English brochure available; ends with free wine tasting. 1 hr. €8.50, students €6, under 7 free. AmEx/MC/V. To get to Maupas from Menetou-Salon, follow the signs to Parassy and Morogues as the road passes through 7km of scenic, vineyard-covered countryside. The château is on the left, about 1km before Morogues. From Bourges, take rue de la Charité east as it becomes N151. Take a left on D955 and another left on D46. Enter through the white gates on the curbside. Maupas ☎02 48 64 41 71. English brochures available. Open Palm Sunday-June M-Sa 2-7pm, Su 10am-noon and 2-7pm; July-Sept. daily 10am-noon and 2-7pm; from early to mid-Oct. daily 2-6pm; from mid-Oct. to mid-Dec. Su 2-6pm. Tours available by reservation from mid-Dec. to May. Call ahead for English tours. €8, students €6.50, ages 7-12 €4.50. Wine tasting for groups €8. Cash only.

Closer to Bourges, Maupas and Menetou-Salon combine to make an ideal but tough daytrip if traveling by bike; get an early start to ensure enough time. Situated 20km north of Bourges, Menetou-Salon (mehn-too-sah-lohn) is the closer of the two châteaux. From Bourges, the cityscape is quickly replaced by hills and vineyards, which are often difficult for bikers. Many of these *vignobles* (vineyards) offer tours and sell their wine on site. Jacques Coeur bought the Menetou-Salon castle in 1448, but his subsequent imprisonment—as well as the later revolution—left the castle in ruins. In the 19th century, the prince of Arenberg stepped in to finish it. Though the current prince lives in the US, he visits his château often to hunt. The staff is always prepared for his arrival; they fill the rooms with fresh flowers daily. Tour guides dressed in Romantic-era costumes lead visitors through the interior, pointing out antiques and showing off the prince's vintage car collection.

The small but exquisitely preserved 13th-century castle of Maupas (moh-pah) is decorated with antique tapestries, and *faïences* (ornamental crockery) collected by Jerome Agard de Maupas, whose family has lived there since 1688. The tour showcases a collection of 887 painted plates from around the world, a Louis XIV-style canopy bed, 19th-century dollhouses, and the flag of the *comte de Chambord*—the last royalist Bourbon pretender to the throne, who insisted upon replacing the *tricoleur* with the monarchy's white fleur-de-lis.

We'd rather be traveling.

LET'S GO
BUDGET TRAVEL GUIDES
www.letsgo.com

BRITTANY
(BRETAGNE)

French culture has an undeniable presence in Brittany's *centre-villes*, *crêperies*, and châteaux, but the region still holds fast to a separate cultural identity ingrained in a history of independence. Its Celtic roots date back to pre-Roman times when Bretons settled the region. Since then, France has repeatedly tried to win over the province, finally succeeding in 1491 when the duke's daughter, Anne de Bretagne, married two successive French kings to protect her beloved Brittany from war with Paris. The region's cultural autonomy is most noticeable in omnipresent black-and-white Breton flags, street signs written in the Celtic language of Brezhoneg, and the traditional costumes that embellish festivals. The sweetest part of Breton culture though, is the cuisine—especially pastries like the sticky *kouing-amann* and the plum-filled *far breton*.

For its modern visitors, Brittany has something to satisfy every taste, from the millennia-old rows of Neolithic menhirs (monoliths) at Carnac (p. 279) to the centuries-old château of Nantes (p. 281), to the budding nightlife of Rennes (below). Meanwhile, the province's exceptional natural beauty is visible in the stunning seascapes of its offshore islands and in the woodland streams of Pont-Aven (p. 275), which inspired Paul Gauguin and other 19th-century artists to found a new school of painting. In the summer, locals and tourists enjoy the beaches of sun-drenched St-Malo and Quiberon (p. 276). Even in low season—when the churches, beaches, and cliffs become eerily romantic—these seaside destinations are far from dormant.

HIGHLIGHTS OF BRITTANY

ESCAPE the mainland and head to the rugged cliffs and rolling pastures of the western-most point in France: Île d'Ouessant (p. 268).

SUNBATHE in St-Malo (p. 250), which offers the same sandy beaches as the Côte d'Azur—without the high prices.

MIX UP a cocktail of old and new in Rennes, a lively university town where you can party until dawn in centuries-old buildings and even a former prison.

RENNES
☎ 02 99

Two hours from Paris, Rennes (ren; pop. 213,000) has the cosmopolitan attitude of the French capital and the independent spirit of the Breton countryside. The cityscape is a melange of the medieval half-timbered houses, ornate Neoclassical facades, and colorful nightclubs that line winding cobblestone streets and hidden alleys. Unlike Brittany's coast, Rennes is most alive from September to June, when its 60,000 students are in town and the quintessentially French youth culture is palpable from the moment you step off the train.

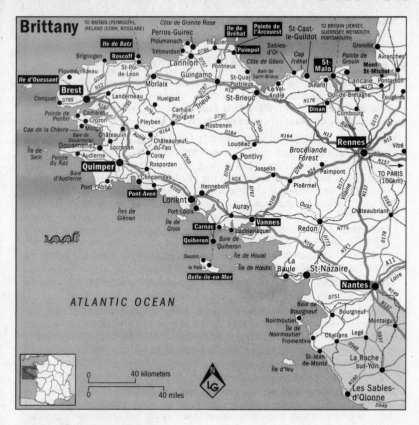

Brittany

TO BRITAIN (PLYMOUTH),
IRELAND (CORK, ROSSLARE)

Côte de Granite Rose

Perros-Guirec

Ploumanach

Île de Bréhat

Pointe de
l'Arcouest

St-Cast-
le-Guildot

TO BRITAIN (JERSEY,
GUERNSEY, WEYMOUTH,
PORTSMOUTH)

Granville

Île de Batz

Trébeurden

Tréguier

Paimpol

Sables-
d'Or

Cap
Fréhel

Pointe de
Grouin

Avranches

Brignogan

Roscoff

St-Pol-
de-Léon

Trégastel

Pontrieux

Côte de Goëlo

St-Malo

Mont-
St-Michel

Ploudalmézeau

Lannion

Guingamp

St-Quay-
Portrieux

Baie de
Saint-Brieuc

Dinard

Cancale

Pontorson

Île d'Ouessant

Brest

Landerneau

Morlaix

Huelgoat

St-Quay

Le Val-
André

St-Brieuc

Dinan

Dol-de-Bretagne

Fougères

Conquet

Pointe de
Penhir

Camaret

Crozon

Carhaix-
Plouguer

Rostrenen

Combourg

Vitré

Cap de la Chèvre

Morgat

Châteaulin

Pleyben

Loudéac

Broceliande
Forest

Rennes

Baie de
Douarnenez

Douarnenez

Locronan

Châteauneuf-
du-Fao

Pontivy

TO PARIS
(100km)

Île de
Sein

Pointe
du Raz

Audierne

Coray

Rosporden

Josselin

Ploërmel

Châteaubriant

Quimper

Baie
d'Audierne

Pont-l'Abbé

Concarneau

Hennebont

Oust

Pont-Aven

Lorient

Port-Louis

Auray

Redon

Îles de
Glénan

Île de
Groix

Carnac

Vannes

Locmariaquer

Quiberon

Baie de
Quiberon

Île de Houat

Sauzon

le Palais

Île de Hœdic

La
Baule

St-Nazaire

Belle-île-en-Mer

Nantes

ATLANTIC OCEAN

Baie de
Bourgneuf

Bourgneuf

Montaigu

Noirmoutier

Île de
Noirmoutier

Challans

Legé

Fromentine

St-Jean-
de-Monts

Île d'Yeu

La Roche
sur-Yon

Les Sables-
d'Olonne

0   40 kilometers

0   40 miles

N

🔲 TRANSPORTATION

Trains: Pl. de la Gare. Info and ticket office open M-Th 5:40am-9:05pm, F 5:40am-9:15pm, Sa 6:45am-8:05pm, Su 7:40am-10:05pm. To: **Brest** (2hr., every hr., €30-40); **Caen** (3hr., 4 per day, €33); **Nantes** (1-2hr., 6-11 per day, €22); **Paris** (2hr., every hr., €53-65); **St-Malo** (1hr., 15 per day, €15); **Tours** (2-3hr., every hr., €37).

Buses: 16 pl. de la Gare (☎08 10 35 10 35; www.gare-routière-rennes.fr), to the right of the train station's north entrance. Illenoo (☎02 99 30 87 80; www.illenoo.fr) serves **Dinan** (1hr.; M-Sa 5 per day, Su 4 per day; €3) and **St-Malo** (2hr.; M-Sa 5 per day, Su 3 per day; €3); ages 10-26 tickets 20% off. Anjou Bus (☎08 20 16 00 49; www.cg49.fr) goes to **Angers** (2hr., 2 per day, €14). Regional buses run to **Mont-St-Michel** (1hr.; 4 per day; €11, under 25 or over 60 €9).

Public Transportation: Star, 12 rue du Pré Botté (☎08 11 55 55 35; www.star.fr). Office open M-F 7am-7:30pm, Sa 9am-6:30pm. **Buses** run M-Sa 5:15am-12:30am, Su 7:25am-midnight. Buy tickets on board, at the bus office, or at *tabacs*. A Métro line runs through the heart of Rennes and accepts the same ticket. Tickets €1.10, day pass €4.

Taxis: At the train station and on pl. de la République (☎02 99 30 79 79). 24hr.

Bike Rental: Guedard, 13 bd. Beaumont (☎02 99 30 43 78). €13 per day. Open M 2-7pm, Tu 9am-12:30pm and 2-7pm, F 10am-7pm, Sa 9am-6:30pm. AmEx/MC/V.

◼◼ ORIENTATION AND PRACTICAL INFORMATION

Avenue Jean Janvier, at the north exit of the station, runs over the Vilaine River, which separates the train station from the *vieille ville.* Turn left and walk along **quai Chateaubriand** to reach **place de la République,** the city's cultural center. To the north on **rue d'Orléans** lies **place de la Mairie,** in the heart of the *vieille ville.*

Tourist Office: 11 rue St-Yves (☎02 99 67 11 11; www.tourisme-rennes.com). From pl. de la République, turn right onto rue George Dottin, then right on rue St-Yves. The office is on the right. Free maps, directions, public toilets, and lists of hotels, restaurants, and shops. 1-2hr. **tours** of *centre-ville* in French July-Aug. daily, Sept.-June 1-3 per week. In English or Spanish Aug. 2 per week. €6.80, students €4, under 7 free. Ticket office for tours, festivals, and concerts. Open July-Aug. M-Sa 9am-7pm, Su 11am-1pm and 2-6pm; Sept.-June M 1-6pm, Tu-Sa 10am-6pm, Su 11am-1pm and 2-6pm. **France Randonnée,** 9 rue Portes Mordelaises (☎02 99 67 42 21; www.france-randonnee. fr). Info on Grande Randonnée (GR) trails (several daylong to weeklong hikes), as well as shorter walks. Open from mid-Mar. to mid-Oct. M-F 10am-12:30pm and 2-6pm, Sa 10am-1pm; from mid-Oct. to mid-Mar. M-F 10am-12:30pm.

Consulate: US, 30 quai Duguay Trouin (☎02 23 44 09 60; fax 35 00 92). Open by appointment only.

English-Language Bookstore: Operated by the **Institut Franco-Américain,** 7 quai Chateaubriand (☎02 99 79 89 22; www.ifa-rennes.org). Brittany's largest English-language bookstore. Open Tu 10am-noon and 1-6pm, W 10am-noon and 1-6:30pm, Th 1-6:30pm, F 1-5:30pm, Sa 10am-1pm. **Comédie des Langues,** 25 rue de St-Malo (☎02 99 36 72 95; www.comediedeslangues.fr). Books in a number of languages (including English, German, Italian, Portuguese, and Spanish). Open M-F 9:30am-7pm, Sa 10am-6pm.

Youth Center: Centre Régional Information Jeunesse Bretagne (CRIJB), Maison du Champ de Mars, 6 cours des Alliés (☎02 99 31 47 48; www.crij-bretagne.com). Info on summer jobs, vacations, and safety. Geared toward locals. Free anonymous counseling Sept.-June. Internet free for research. Personal Internet use for members €1 per hr.; nonmembers €2 per hr.; annual membership €4. Open July-Aug. Tu noon-9pm, W-F noon-7pm, Sa-Su 2-7pm; Sept.-June Tu 10am-9pm, W-F 10am-6pm, Sa 2-6pm.

Laundromats: 18 rue du Robien (☎02 99 38 86 62), near the hostel. Also a cafe. Open Tu-W 11am-8pm, Th-F 11am-1am, Sa 1pm-1am, Su 3pm-1am. Branches at 23 rue de Penhoët (open daily 7am-8pm), 59 rue Duhamel (open daily 7am-10pm), and 3 pl. de Bretagne (open daily 7am-10pm).

Police: 22 bd. de la Tour d'Auvergne (☎02 99 65 00 22).

Pharmacy: Pharmacie de la Gare, 9 pl. de la Gare (☎02 99 30 83 27), across from the train station. Open M-F 8:30am-7:30pm, Sa 9am-12:30pm.

Hospital: Centre Hospitalier Régional Hôtel Dieu, 2 rue de l'Hôtel Dieu (☎02 99 28 43 21).

Internet Access: Taxiphone Cyber Cafe, 58 rue de St-Malo (☎02 99 36 94 63). Photocopies and international telephones. €1.20 per 30min. €2 per hr. Open daily 10am-11pm. Cash only. Also in many cafes around pl. Ste-Anne.

Post Office: Pl. de la République (☎02 99 78 43 32). Open M-F 8:30am-7pm, Sa 9am-12:30pm. **Currency exchange,** fax, photocopies, and Western Union available. Branch at 24 pl. Hoche (☎02 23 20 02 05). Open M 10am-6pm, Tu-F 8:45am-12:15pm and 1:45-6pm, Sa 8:45am-12:15pm. **Postal Code:** 35000.

BRITTANY

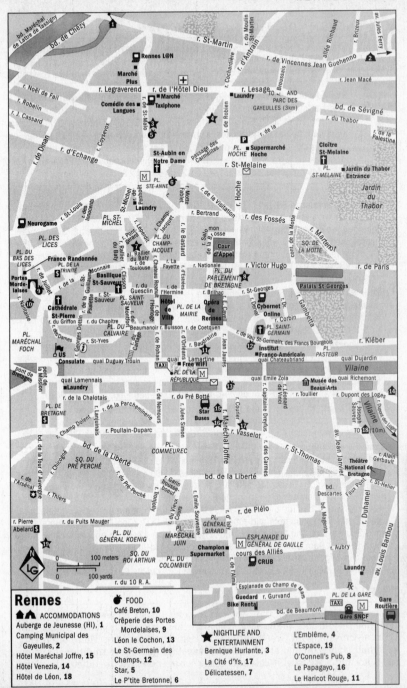

Rennes

♠♠ ACCOMMODATIONS
Auberge de Jeunesse (HI), 1
Camping Municipal des
Gayeulles, 2
Hôtel Maréchal Joffre, 15
Hôtel Venezia, 14
Hôtel de Léon, 18

🍎 FOOD
Café Breton, 10
Crêperie des Portes
Mordelaises, 9
Léon le Cochon, 13
Le St-Germain des
Champs, 12
Star, 5
Le P'tite Bretonne, 6

**★ NIGHTLIFE AND
ENTERTAINMENT**
Bernique Hurlante, 3
La Cité d'Ys, 17
Délicatessen, 7

L'Emblême, 4
L'Espace, 19
O'Connell's Pub, 8
Le Papagayo, 16
Le Haricot Rouge, 11

ACCOMMODATIONS AND CAMPING

Hotels cluster near the train station and the south bank of the Vilaine; cheaper options tend to be slightly farther away. Reserve ahead, especially for stays during the first week of July when the *Tombées de la Nuit* festival hits town.

> **SLEEPING AROUND.** Brittany's tourism department, **Breizhtrotters**, offers a "stay five get one free" deal for regional hostels. The **Pass Bretagne** is accepted at 21 hostels in Brittany, including those in Rennes, Quimper, Quiberon, St-Malo, and Nantes. No more than two consecutive nights at the same hostel can be counted for the pass. For more info, inquire at hostels or check out www.breizhtrotters.com. For hostel info, contact the **Fédération Unie des Auberges de Jeunesse** (☎02 99 89 87 27; www.fuaj.com).

Auberge de Jeunesse (HI), 10-12 canal St-Martin (☎02 99 33 22 33; rennes@fuaj. org). From the station, take the Métro (dir.: Kennedy) to Ste-Anne. Walk to the right of the church on rue de St-Malo, which turns into canal St-Martin. Cross the bridge; the hostel is on the right. Simple 2- to 4-bed rooms with lockers and showers, some with canal views. Kitchen, common room with TV, and cafeteria. Breakfast included. Laundry (wash €3, dry €2). Internet €0.50 per 30min. Reception 7am-11pm. Lockout M-Sa 10am-3:30pm, Su 10am-1pm. Night guard after 1am. Dorms €17. MC/V. ❶

Hôtel Maréchal Joffre, 6 rue Maréchal Joffre (☎02 99 79 37 74; fax 78 38 51). Small, simple, and quiet rooms above a tiny lunch counter in the *centre-ville*. Breakfast €5. Reception M-Sa 24hr., closed Su 1-8pm. Open mid-August to mid-July. Singles €25, with shower and toilet €34; doubles €38; triples €38-44. AmEx/MC/V. ❷

Hôtel Venezia, 27 rue Dupont des Loges (☎02 99 30 36 56; hotel.venezia@wanadoo. fr), on an island in the Vilaine River. Bright, cozy rooms. Some have rugs and marble mantels. Frequented by university administrators and professors. All rooms with TVs. Breakfast €5. Reception 7am-11:30pm. Reservations recommended. Singles €28-36, with shower and toilet €38-46; doubles €38/48. Extra bed €10. AmEx/MC/V. ❸

Hôtel de Léon, 15 rue de Léon (☎02 99 30 55 28; www.hotel-de-leon.fr). Escape the crowds with spacious, clean, budget-friendly rooms close to the *centre-ville*. Breakfast €6. Singles with toilet €32, with full bath €36; doubles €36-41; triples €47. MC/V. ❷

Camping Municipal des Gayeulles, rue Maurice Audin (☎02 99 36 91 22; www.camp-ing-rennes.com), in Parc des Gayeulles. Take bus #3 (dir.: St-Laurent) from pl. du Colombier or pl. de la République to Piscine/Gayeulles (M-Sa every 10min., Su every 40min.; last bus midnight). Follow the path around the pool on the right until the paved road; turn left and follow signs. Deep in the Parc des Gayeulles, with additional sites in July and Aug. Snack bar. The only drawback is the distance from the *centre-ville*. Internet €1 per 30min. Reception from mid-June to mid-Sept. daily 7:30am-1pm and 2-8pm; from mid-Sept. to Oct. and from Apr. to mid-June daily 9am-12:30pm and 4:30-8pm; Nov.-Mar. M-Sa 8-9am and 6-8pm. Gates closed from mid-June to mid-Sept. 11pm-7am; from mid-Sept. to mid-June 10pm-7am. €3.50 per adult, under 10 €1.50, €2.50-5.50 per tent; €1.50 per car; €6.40-7.30 per caravan. Electricity €3. AmEx/MC/V. ❶

FOOD

Rennes's culinary center, northwest of the city, boasts an astounding quantity of ethnic restaurants; **rue de Saint-Malo** alone has Haitian, Lebanese, Indian, and Chinese cuisine, with Greek and Italian restaurants nearby. There are plenty of kebab stands on and around **place Sainte-Anne**, and more traditional restaurants around **place Saint-Michel** and in the *centre-ville*. On the other side of the city, *brasseries* and *crêperies* line **rue Saint-George.** The city's largest market is on **place des Lices** (open Sa 7am-1pm); others are held from Tuesday to Sunday throughout the city (ask at the tourist office for a list). Local supermarkets include a **Champion,** 20 rue d'Isly, in a mall near the train station (open M-Sa 9:30am-8pm), a **Supermarché Hoche,** 9 pl. Hoche (open M-Sa 8am-9pm, Su 9am-noon), and a **Marché Plus,** 43 pl. de la Rance, in an apartment complex off rue de St-Malo near the hostel (open M-Sa 7am-9pm, Su 9am-noon). There are several local grocery stores along **rue Jean Janvier** by the train station.

▨ **Le St-Germain des Champs (Restaurant Végétarien-Biologique),** 12 rue du Vau St-Germain (☎02 99 79 25 52). Friendly chefs serve lunch at this popular organic and vegetarian spot accented with plants, cloth lanterns, excavated fossils and crystals, and nature photos. Lunch *plats* €10- €19. Open M-Sa noon-2:30pm. MC/V. ❸

Crêperie des Portes Mordelaises, 6 rue des Portes Mordelaises (☎02 99 30 42 95). Startlingly blue and pink, this small authentic *crêperie* is one of the city's best—as student crowds will attest. Salads €5.90. Carefully crafted *galettes* and *crêpes* €3-10. Open Aug.-June M-Sa 11:30am-2pm and 6:30-11pm. MC/V. ❷

Star, 3 pl. Ste-Anne (☎02 99 79 07 34). One of the best (and cheapest) *kebaberies* around pl. Ste-Anne. Enjoy the delicious *sauce blanche* while people-watching from the tables outside. Huge *kebab-frites* plus drink €6. *Plats* €5.50-9.50. Cash only. ❷

Café Breton, 14 rue Nantaise (☎02 99 30 74 95). A stylish restaurant serving an ever-changing menu of market-fresh cuisine in a warm, dimly lit dining room. Salads €5-10. *Plats* €10-15. Desserts €4-6. Open M noon-3pm, Tu-W noon-3pm and 7:30-10pm, Th-Sa noon-3pm and 7-11pm. Closed part of Aug. Reservations recommended. ❸

Léon le Cochon, 1 rue Maréchal Joffre (☎02 99 79 37 54; www.leonlecochon.com). Enticing local dishes fuse modern and traditional at this elegant restaurant. The restaurant's swinish theme, emphasized by the giant "chef pig" statue and pig paintings, extends to the menu, although there are plenty of other options. Lunch *formule* €15. *Plats* €9-20. Open M-Th noon-2pm and 8-10:30pm, F-Sa 8-11pm. AmEx/MC/V. ❸

La P'tite Bretonne, 8 rue St-Malo (☎02 99 79 65 64). A summer seaside cottage comes to mind at this relaxing *crêperie* off pl. Ste-Anne. For a brief repose from the hectic street dancers, kick back artisan ciders (€3) or try the "Maya" *crêpe,* a toasted apple *flambé* (€6). *Galettes* from €1.40; sweet *crêpes* from €1.80. Lunch *formule* €8.50. Open Tu-Sa noon-2pm and 7-11pm. MC/V. ❷

RENNES ON A BUDGET. Like many university towns, Rennes can be especially wallet-friendly. A relaxing walk past the rosebushes of the **Jardin du Thabor** (this page) comes at no charge. For nighttime entertainment, check out the **Orchestra de Bretagne** (p. 250), which gives free summer concerts. On Wednesdays in July, head back to the garden for **Les Mercredis du Thabor** (this page), traditional Breton music and dance performances that are colorful, dynamic, and—you guessed it—free. Also, don't miss free exhibits at the art space across from the Parliament building (see p. 249).

◎ SIGHTS

The beautiful *vieille ville* is a medieval village with a young flair. Half-timbered buildings—now filled with bars and modern storefronts—dot the old city from pl. Ste-Anne and pl. St-Michel to pl. du Calvaire and narrow rue St-Georges.

▨**JARDIN DU THABOR.** These lush grounds—some of France's most beautiful—feature fountains, imposing trees, neat flower beds punctuated by statues, an aviary of parakeets, and a former duelists' rendezvous that is now a

THE BIG SPLURGE

BEYOND GLUTTONY

The medieval capital of Bretagne understands the art of eating. Whether it's grilled sausages and sweet *barbe à papa* (cotton candy—literally, Dad's beard) at a festival or flambéed chocolate *crêpes* in one of the city's bistros, Rennes will not disappoint when it comes to food. While it's easy to keep the wallet full with cheap and delicious kebabs and *galettes,* one special event makes it hard for even the most budget-conscious to resist the splurge.

From mid-May to early June, chefs vie for the honor of culinary genius in the **Festival Gourmand.** The contest's theme varies yearly; in 2008 chefs were faced with the prompt, "Surprise us with dishes based on Brittany's seasonal produce." Ravenous visitors can experience the heat of the kitchen for themselves with cooking classes and demonstrations led by four-star chefs that take place over the course of the festival. Sessions typically last 3hr. and can run up to €95 per person—gourmet meal included, of course!

One of the festival's most notable events is the *soirée* at Château d'Apigné, 5km from Rennes. The evening's menu is filled with local ingredients and wines in an authentic 19th-century setting. Reservations well in advance are a must. Seats tend to go for around €40 person. For more info, contact the Rennes tourist office, 11 rue St-Yves (☎02 99 67 11 11; www.tourisme-rennes.com).

performance stage lovingly referred to as "hell." The target-shaped rose garden holds 980 varieties of the *fleur d'amour.* A small gallery on the north side of the gardens exhibits local artwork. (☎02 99 28 56 62. Entrances at pl. St-Melaine, rue de la Palestine, rue de Paris, and bd. de la Duchesse Anne. Open daily June-Aug. 7:30am-8:30pm; Sept.-June 7:30am-6:30pm.) On Wednesdays in July, **Les Mercredis du Thabor** brings Breton song and dance to the gardens. (☎02 99 30 06 87; http://skeudenn.ouestfrance.fr. Free shows at 8:30pm.)

MUSÉE DES BEAUX-ARTS. Rennes's art museum is among Rennes's hidden gems. It features art from ancient Egyptian to modern abstract works, but has few well-known pieces. The Baroque collection is impressive, especially Rubens's *The Tiger Hunt.* The museum also wades in Picasso's Surrealist period of the 20s with *The Bather,* considered one of his most abstract depictions of a woman. (20 quai Émile Zola. ☎02 23 62 17 45; www.mbar.org. Open Tu 10am-6pm, W-Su 10am-noon and 2-6pm. €4.30, students €2.20, under 18 free. Special exhibits €5.40/2.70/free.)

PARC DES GAYEULLES. Gayeulles's expansive forests are interspersed with an indoor pool, several lakes (with paddle boats in the summer), sports fields, tennis courts, minigolf, and a campground. Many great walking and bike paths cut through the park; maps are posted at regular intervals. The park is home to a working farm for children and an animal reserve. (15min. bus ride; see Camping Municipal directions, p. 246. ☎02 99 28 56 62. Open July-Aug. 8am-8:30pm; Sept.-June 8am-5:45pm. Free.)

CATHÉDRALE SAINT-PIERRE. Construction on this cathedral was interrupted by the Revolution and the building was left unfinished until 1844. Standing on a site previously occupied by a pagan temple, a Roman church, and a Gothic cathedral, the church is a 19th-century masterpiece, with a massive Neoclassical facade and huge columns inside holding up the painted and gilded ceiling. The one noticeable 20th-century addition is its altar, a large block of green bronze. The fifth chapel on the right houses the cathedral's treasure: a delicately carved 16th-century wooden altarpiece that traces the life of the Virgin Mary. (Open daily 9:30am-noon and 3-6pm. Closed to visitors during high mass Su 10:30-11:30am.) Across the street, tucked in an alleyway bearing the same name, the unassuming **Portes Mordelaises** are the last vestige of the medieval city walls.

OTHER SIGHTS. Pick up a copy of *Le Circuit des Têtes de l'Art* at the tourist office for detailed information on the month's art exhibits, which include several free shows, especially in summer.

In late June, check out **Sortie des Artistes,** 8 galérie du Théâtre, a gallery that hosts free exhibits. *(www.sortiedesartistes.fr. Open W-Sa 2pm-8pm.)*

🎵 NIGHTLIFE

After the sun sets, the city's population seems to double, and the party doesn't calm down until dawn. Much of the action centers on **place Sainte-Anne, place Saint-Michel,** and **place des Lices.** Don't stop there—hot nightspots pervade the city, with some great bars and *discothèques* south of the Vilaine. When heading outside the *centre-ville,* however, be careful and travel in groups.

BARS

▨ **Le Haricot Rouge,** 10 rue Baudrairie. A "lucky" accordion hangs above the bar at this intimate after-hours hub near pl. de la Mairie. Clientele spills onto the terrace in the summer. Beer €2.60. Pints €5. Free Wi-Fi. Open Tu-Sa 11am-1am. MC/V.

La Cité d'Ys, 31 rue Vasselot (☎02 99 78 24 84). Named for a legendary Breton city, this bar is full of mythic atmosphere, enhanced by Celtic knots and crosses. 2 floors are linked by a twisting spiral staircase; even the bar is a spiral. Live traditional music twice a month. Coreff beer €2.40. Open M-F noon-1am, Sa-Su 2pm-1am. AmEx/MC/V.

O'Connell's Irish Pub, 6-7 pl. du Parlement de Bretagne (☎02 99 79 38 76). Anglophones, Anglophiles, and locals alike come for pints of Beamish (€6), poured by Irish expats. Live Irish jigs Su 8:30pm. Beer €2.50-6. Whiskey €3.10-5.20. Happy hour M 7-10pm, Th 7pm-1am. Open M-Sa 11am-1am, Su 5pm-1am. MC/V.

Bernique Hurlante, 40 rue de St-Malo (☎02 99 38 70 09). Welcomes a diverse crowd in an intimate, funky space with modern art and a mosaic on the back wall. The house specialty is the "rum surprise" (€3.50)—it's as unique as the bar itself. Beer €2.40-5. Open Aug. Tu-Sa 6pm-1am; Sept.-July Tu-Sa 4pm-1am, Su 6pm-1am. AmEx/MC/V.

L'Emblême, 24 rue d'Antrain (☎02 99 38 71 88). A small, welcoming bar with eclectic decor and a red and black floor. Theme nights Sa. Open M-Sa 5pm-1am. MC/V.

Le Papagayo, 10 rue Maréchal Joffre (☎02 99 79 65 13). An unassuming lunch counter by day, this tropical spot is a party after dark—especially on the twice-monthly theme nights. Beer €2.30-5. Champagne €7. Open M-Sa 7am-1am. MC/V.

CLUBS

▨ **Délicatessen,** 7 impasse Rallier du Baty (☎02 99 78 23 41), near pl. St-Michel. Housed in a former prison, this club has swapped jailhouse rock for electronica. Drinks €6, after 1:30am €10. Cover Tu-Th €5, after 1:30am €10; F-Sa €10/15; includes drink. Women free before 1:30am. Mandatory coat check €2, bags €5. Open Tu-Sa midnight-5am.

L'Espace, 45 bd. de la Tour d'Auvergne (☎02 99 30 21 95). Enter through the blue corridor. After 2am, a lively, young crowd grinds to thumping music under video screens. Strobe lights and disco balls fill the stage, cage, and 2 floors. Shots €5. Beer €6-8. Mixed drinks €10. Cover Th-F €10, Sa €13; students Th before 1am free, Th after 1am and F-Sa €8; includes 1 alcoholic or 2 non-alcoholic drinks. Mandatory coat check €2, bags €5. Happy hour Th 11:30pm-1am. Open Th-Sa 11pm-5am. MC/V.

🎇 FESTIVALS

Consult the tourist office for a guide to upcoming theater, dance, and classical music performances and for festival tickets and info.

Festival Les Mythos (☎02 99 79 26 07; www.festival-mythos.com), in Apr. A celebration of *contes* (fairy tales) and other oral traditions.

Fiertés (www.marche.inter-lgbt.org), in mid-June. A jovial annual festival packed with parades, art exhibits, concerts, and dance *soirées*.

Les Tombées de la Nuit (☎02 99 32 56 56; www.tdn.rennes.fr), 1 week in early July. A riot of music, theater, mime, dance, and interactive performances overtakes the city.

Orchestre de Bretagne (☎02 99 27 52 75; www.orchestra-de-bretagne.com), in summer. Performs free concerts.

Rencontres Transmusicales (☎02 99 31 13 10; www.lestrans.com), in early Dec. The city fills with renowned international musicians and bands.

SAINT-MALO   ☎02 99

Scenic St-Malo (sehn-mah-lo; pop. 53,000) deserves its reputation as a prime tourist destination. It combines the best of France's northern villages: rich history, delicious seafood, postcard-perfect vistas, and brilliant beaches. Though 80% of the town was destroyed in 1944, stone-by-stone reconstruction has made it difficult to distinguish the old from the new. The town's ramparts and towers fortify the scenic *vieille ville* and overlook miles of gorgeous coast.

▐ TRANSPORTATION

Trains: Between av. Aristide Briand and rue d'Alsace. Ticket office open M-F 5:30am-8pm, Sa 5:30am-7:45pm, Su 7:30am-8:50pm. Trains run via **Dol** to: **Caen** (3hr., 2-4 per day, €28); **Dinan** (1hr., 5 per day, €9); **Paris** (4hr., 14 per day, €60-75); **Pontorson** (1hr., 2-3 per day, €8); **Rennes** (1hr., 14 per day, €13).

Buses: Esplanade St-Vincent (☎02 99 40 85 96), next to the tourist office. Illenoo (☎02 99 19 70 80; www.illenoo.fr) runs to **Mont-St-Michel** (2hr., 2 per day, €4.50) via **Pontorson.** Tibus (☎08 10 22 22 22; www.cotesdarmor.fr) runs to **Dinan** (1hr., 3-4 per day, €2) and smaller towns to the west. Office (☎02 99 40 19 27) in the train station has info on all buses. Open daily 8:45am-1:30pm and 2:30-6:30pm.

Ferries: Gare Maritime du Naye and Gare Maritime de la Bourse. Open daily 7:30am-6pm. Brittany Ferries (☎08 25 82 88 28, www.brittanyferries.com) serves **Portsmouth** (9hr., 1 per day, €60-75). See **Getting There: By Boat,** p. 30. Condor Ferries (☎08 25 13 51 35; www.condorferries.com) runs to **Jersey** (1hr., 1-3 per day, €34-63) and **Guernsey, UK** (2hr., 1-2 per day, €34-68).

Public Transportation: Keolis, esplanade St-Vincent (☎02 99 56 06 06), by the tourist office. **Buses** run locally and serve **Cancale** (30min., 7-14 per day). Tickets available at the office or on board. Office open M-F 8:15am-12:15pm and 1:45-6pm, Sa 8:15am-noon; varies seasonally. Information also available at train station. Most bus lines run daily July-Aug. 7am-midnight; Sept.-June 6am-8pm. Tickets €1.10 (valid 1½hr.), carnet of 10 €9; day pass €3.

Taxis: Taxi Malouins (☎02 99 81 30 30) or **Taxi Petit** (☎02 99 21 06 01). At esplanade St-Vincent and the train station.

Bike Rental: Les Vélos Bleus, 19 rue Alphonse Thébault (☎02 99 40 31 63; www.velosbleus.fr). €9 per ½-day, €12 per day; €150 deposit. Open daily 9am-noon and 2-6pm; reduced hours in low season and on weekends.

Windsurfer Rental: Surf School St-Malo, 2 av. de la Hoguette (☎02 99 40 07 47; www.surfschool.org), along Grande Plage de Sillon. Rental €25 for 1st hr., €17 thereafter; €42 per ½-day; €79 per day. Lessons €35 per hr. Open daily July-Aug. 9am-6pm, Sept.-June 9am-noon and 1:30-6pm. Reception open until 5:30pm. AmEx/MC/V.

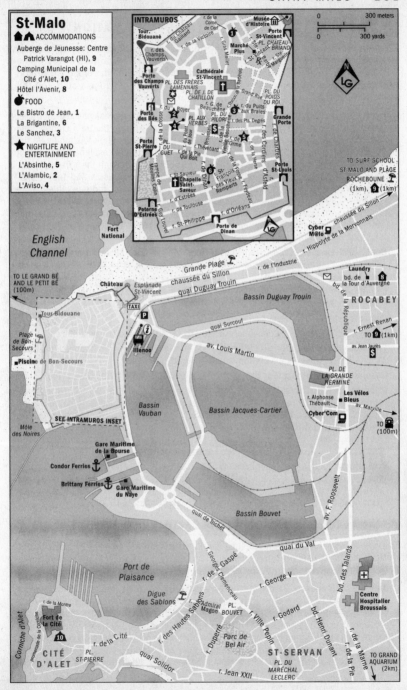

St-Malo

🏠🏠 ACCOMMODATIONS

Auberge de Jeunesse: Centre
  Patrick Varangot (HI), **9**
Camping Municipal de la
  Cité d'Alet, **10**
Hôtel l'Avenir, **8**

🍎 FOOD

Le Bistro de Jean, **1**
La Brigantine, **6**
Le Sanchez, **3**

★ NIGHTLIFE AND
  ENTERTAINMENT

L'Absinthe, **5**
L'Alambic, **2**
L'Aviso, **4**

INTRAMUROS

r. de la
Corne de Cerf

Tour
Bidouane

Musée
d'Histoire

PL. CHÂTEAU-
BRIAND

Porte
St-Vincent

Marché
Plus

r. du Château
Gaillard

r. des
Champs
Vauverts

r. de la Victoire

Gros Mollet

Porte
des Champs
Vauverts

Cathédrale
St-Vincent

PL. DES FRÈRES
LAMENNAIS

PL. DE J. DE
CHATILLON

Grand Rue

PL. DU
POIDS
DU ROI

Porte
des Bés

r. Boyer

r. G. de
Beauchêne

r. du Puits
aux Braies

PL. DU
PILORIE

r. des Pts. Degrés

Grande
Porte

PL. AUX
HERBES

r. du Pélicot

r. de la Crosse

Porte
St-Pierre

PL. DU
GUET

Moulins Collin

r. du Point du Jour

r. Thévenard

r. des Cordiers

r. des Lauriers

r. de l'Orme

r. de la
Herse

Porte
St-Louis

rampe de la

r. de la Pie
Qui Boit

r. de Dinan

St.
François

r. des Vieux
Remparts

r. de la Fosse

Feydeau

Chapelle
Saint-
Saveur

r. St-Sauveur

r. d'Estrées

Poterne
D'Estrées

r. de Toulouse

r. St-Philippe

r. d'Orléans

Porte de
Dinan

TO SURF SCHOOL
ST. MALO AND PLAGE
ROCHEBOUNE
(1km) **9** (1km)

chaussée du Sillon

r. Hippolyte de la Morvonnais

Cyber
M@la

Fort
National

English
Channel

Grande Plage

chaussée du Sillon

r. de l'Industrie

Laundry
bd. de
la Tour d'Auvergne **8**

ROCABEY

TO LE GRAND BÉ
AND LE PETIT BÉ
(100m)

Château

Esplanade
St-Vincent

quai Duguay Trouin

Bassin Duguay Trouin

bd. de la République

r. Ernest Renan

9 (1km)

Tour Bidouane

TAXI

Illenoo

quai Surcouf

av. Louis Martin

av. Jean Jaurès

Plage
de Bon-
Secours

Piscine de Bon-Secours

PL. DE
LA GRANDE
HERMINE

r. Alphonse
Thébault

Les Vélos
Bleus

av. Marville

SEE INTRAMUROS INSET

Bassin
Vauban

Bassin Jacques-Cartier

Cyber'Com

TO
(100m)

Môle
des Noires

Gare Maritime
de la Bourse

Condor Ferries

Brittany Ferries

Gare Maritime
du Naye

Bassin Bouvet

av. F. Roosevelt

quai de Trichet

quai du Val

Port de
Plaisance

Digue
des Sablons

r. de la Montre

r. Georges Gaspé

r. de Clemenceau

Admiral
Magon

PL.
BOUVET

r. Ville Pepin

r. Godard

George V

bd. des Talards

Centre
Hospitalier
Broussais

Fort de
la Cité

10

CITÉ
D'ALET

r. de la Cité

PL.
ST-PIERRE

r. des Hautes Salons

quai Solidor

r. Duperré

Parc de
Bel Air

ST-SERVAN

PL. DU
MARÉCHAL
LECLERC

r. Jean XXII

r. de la Marne

r. de la Pie

bd. Henri Dunant

TO GRAND
AQUARIUM
(2km)

BRITTANY

0   300 meters
0   300 yards

⚡ 🔋 ORIENTATION AND PRACTICAL INFORMATION

The *intra-muros*, or old walled city, atop a rocky peninsula at the northernmost point of the town, is the heart of St-Malo's shopping and restaurant district. The harbor entrance is to the south, while the large, sandy beach runs east. Inland and eastward lies a less expensive but less colorful area where you'll find the train station, the youth hostel, and cheaper restaurants and hotels.

Tourist Office: Esplanade St-Vincent (☎08 25 13 52 00; www.saint-malo-tourisme. com), just outside the city walls. Turn right on the road outside the train station, then left onto av. Jean Jaurès at the roundabout. Make a left onto rue de l'Astrolabe. At the roundabout, make a right onto av. Louis Martin and follow it to esplanade St-Vincent (15min.). Alternatively, take bus #C1 or C2 (dir.: St-Vincent). From the *gare maritime*, turn left onto chaussée Eric Tabarly, which becomes quai St-Louis and then esplanade St-Vincent. Free city guide contains a map, walking tours, and tide tables; more detailed map (€0.50), list of accommodations, and the quarterly *L'Omnibus* (a list of concerts) also available. Open July-Aug. M-Sa 9am-7:30pm, Su 10am-6pm; Sept. and Apr.-June M-Sa 9am-12:30pm and 1:30-6:30pm, Su 10am-12:30pm and 2:30-6pm; Oct.-Mar. M-Sa 9am-12:30pm and 1:30-6pm.

Bank: BNP Paribus, 18 av. Jean Jaurès. Open M-F 8:30am-12:10pm and 2-5:30pm. Branch inside the *intra-muros* at 9 rue Broussais. Open M and F 9am-12:30pm. ATMs accessible daily 6am-10pm.

Laundromat: 27 bd. de la Tour d'Auvergne. Wash €3.50-8, dry €1 per 10min. Open daily 7am-9pm.

Public Toilets: Pl. des Frères Lamennais (€0.30).

Police: 3 pl. des Frères Lamennais (☎02 99 20 69 40), next to the post office.

Pharmacy: 8 rue Vincent (☎02 99 40 86 47), across the street from Marché Plus. Open M 2-7:30pm, Tu-Sa 9am-12:30pm and 2-7:30pm.

Hospital: Centre Hospitalier Broussais, 1 rue de la Marne (☎02 99 21 21 21).

Internet Access: Cyber M@lo, 68 chausseé du Sillon (☎02 99 56 07 78; cyberst-malo@yahoo.fr). €2.50 per 30min., €4 per hr. Open from mid-June to mid-Sept. M-Sa 10am-11pm, Su 3-8pm; from mid-Sept. to mid-June Tu-Th 11am-9pm, F-Sa 11am-11pm, Su 3-8pm. **Cyber'Com,** 26 bis bd. des Talards (☎02 99 56 05 83). €2.10 per 30min. Open M-Tu and F 9am-noon and 1:30-6pm, W 1:30-6pm, Th 10am-noon and 1:30-7pm. Also at **L'Alambic** (see **Entertainment,** p. 254).

Post Office: 1 bd. de la République (☎02 99 20 51 78). **Currency exchange,** fax services, and photocopying available. Open M-F 8am-6:30pm, Sa 9am-12:30pm. Branch at pl. des Frères Lamennais (☎02 99 40 89 90), next to the police station. Open M-F 9am-noon and 2-5:30pm, Sa 9:30am-noon. **Postal Code:** 35400.

🏠 🛏 ACCOMMODATIONS AND CAMPING

Rooms inside the walls of the city don't come cheap, but there are budget options within a few minutes' walk outside. Reserve at least a few days ahead, especially in summer, when the town becomes a magnet for beachgoers.

Auberge de Jeunesse: Centre Patrick Varangot (HI), 37 av. du Révérend Père Umbricht (☎02 99 40 29 80; www.centrevarangot.com). From the train station, take bus #5 (dir.: Croix Désilles) or 10 (dir.: Cancale). On foot from the station, turn right and follow the road for 10min. Turn right on av. Pasteur, which becomes av. du Révérend Père Umbricht. Keep right at the Auberge de Jeunesse sign (30min.). Large stone building 3 blocks from beach. Plain rooms with large windows. Popular with school groups. Tennis, volleyball, and basketball courts. Bar and common room with TV. Kitchen with individual refrigerators (€1.50). Accepts the **Pass Bretagne** (p. 246). Breakfast included. Laundry €4. Free Wi-Fi. Bike rental €11 per ½-day, €15 per day. Wheelchair-accessible. Reception 8am-11pm. July-Aug. dorms €17, with showers and toilets €19; singles €26. Sept.-June dorms €15, with showers and toilets €18; singles €28. MC/V. ❶

Hôtel l'Avenir, 31 bd. de la Tour d'Auvergne (☎02 99 56 13 33), 5min. from the station, 10min. from the *vieille ville.* Simple rooms with blue walls and linens. Above a quiet bar. Breakfast €5.50. Reception 7:30am-8:30pm. Singles €23, with showers €28; doubles €26/32; triples €60. Extra bed €5. Prices slightly higher July-Aug. Cash only. ❷

Camping Municipal de la Cité d'Alet (☎02 99 81 60 91; www.ville-saint-malo.fr/campings), southwest of the city. Take bus #6 (dir.: Quelmer/La Passagère) to Alet. Head uphill and left at the ruins of Cathédrale St-Pierre onto allée Gaston Buy; the campground is 50m ahead. 300 scenic sites near the beach. Reception May-Sept. M-F 9am-12:30pm and 3-6pm, Sa-Su 8:30am-7pm; hours extended July-Aug. Gates closed 11pm-7am; after 8pm see the night guard. 2 people and tent €13; 2 people and caravan with electricity €17. Extra person €5.80, ages 2-12 €2.70. MC/V. ❶

🍴 FOOD

Generic, overpriced restaurants huddle just within the *intra-muros.* Outdoor markets (8am-1pm) are held inside the walls and on **place Bouvet** in St-Servan (both open Tu and F) and on **boulevard de la Tour d'Auvergne** (M, Th, Sa). There is a **Marché Plus** supermarket at 10 bis rue Ste-Barbe, underground near the entrance to the city walls at Porte St-Vincent (open M-Sa 7am-9pm, Su 9am-1pm), and a **Champion** supermarket on av. Pasteur near the hostel. (Open June-Sept. M-Sa 8:30am-8pm, Su 9:30am-noon; Oct.-Apr. M-F 8:30am-12:30pm and 2:30-7:30pm, Sa 8:30am-7:30pm, Su 9am-noon.)

Le Sanchez, 9 rue de la Vieille Boucherie (☎02 99 56 67 17). Gluttonous servings of gelato worth the long line. Order to go and get more for less. 1 scoop €2, 2 scoops €3, 3 scoops plus toppings €4.80. Open from mid-June to mid-Sept. daily 8:30am-midnight; from mid-Sept. to Mar. M-Tu and Th-Su 8:30am-7:30pm; from Apr. to mid-June daily 8:30am-7:30pm. MC/V over €15. ❶

La Brigantine, 13 rue de Dinan (☎02 99 56 82 82). Offers cheap but satisfying *galettes* (€1.80-9.40) and *crêpes* (€1.90-6.50). Open July-Aug. daily noon-10pm; Sept.-June M and Th-Su noon-2pm and 7-10pm. MC/V. ❶

Le Bistro de Jean, 6 rue de la Corne de Cerf (☎02 99 40 98 68). Freshest market fare is given traditional French bistro treatment. Chalk menu changes daily. Appetizers €7.50-15. *Plats* €14-28. Desserts €6.60. Lunch *menus* €14-19. Open M-Tu and Th-F noon-1:45pm and 7-9:45pm, W and Sa 7-9:45pm. AmEx/MC/V. ❸

👁 SIGHTS

The town's ramparts, on the northern side of the city, look out over the beach toward a series of small, fortified islands that once guarded St-Malo's harbor. At low tide, pebbly causeways strewn with stranded mollusks emerge from the sea, giving access to the two closest islands, **Fort National** and **Grand Bé;** check the tide schedules at the tourist office before you visit. Those who prefer dry excursions should heed the posted warnings not to set out for any islands if the tide is within 10m of the causeway.

FORT NATIONAL. This island fortress was designed in the 17th century by the French military's master architect, Vauban, to protect St-Malo from the English. He seems to have done his job well, as the fort has never been taken by sea. The top of the stony fortress offers a fabulous view of the bay and the city. (☎06 72 46 66 26. Open June-Sept. daily. Hours depend on the tides; ask the tourist

BRITTANY

GET YOUR BRET-ON

Brittany is one of few regions in which French doesn't hold a language monopoly. Instead, it competes with Brezhoneg (Breton), which descends from the language of the original Celtic inhabitants of Brittany. Here are the most helpful words to know:

1. Breizh: Brittany. Often appears in compounds, like Breizhtrotters.
2. Ty, also spelled Ti: Translates approximately to "the house of," like *chez*. You'll commonly see it in restaurant names.
3. Penn: Not a Quaker, but a rocky point. These are everywhere along the Breton coast, so you'll see this word a lot on maps.
4. Pesk: Fish. Given the importance of seafood in the Breton diet, this word is vital to survival.
5. Kouing-aman: Another regional specialty, this time a sweet treat—a deliciously sticky pastry.
6. Kroaz: Cross. One of the few Breton words that sounds like its English equivalent, and a reminder of the historic power of Catholicism in the region.
7. Krampouezh: *Crêpe.* The importance is self-explanatory.
8. Tour-tan: Lighthouse. This will help you locate some of the most beautiful sights along Brittany's jagged coastline.
9. Glav: Rain. Hopefully, you won't hear this word too often. The forecast you want to hear is **heol,** which means sun.
10. Yec'hed mat: Cheers! The most important phrase.

office. Tours in French at low tide. Pamphlets in English, German, Italian, and Spanish. €4, ages 6-15 €2.)

LE GRAND BÉ. The curious rocky seclusion of Le Grand Bé, west of Fort National and near the piscine de Bon-Secours, offers a moment of solitude. The only permanent resident is St-Malo's native son and French Romantic author Chateaubriand (1768-1848), who asked to be buried where he could hear nothing but the wind and waves. Farther out to sea is **Le Petit Bé,** defended by another, smaller fort. Tours are available, but the causeway leading to Le Petit Bé from Le Grand Bé isn't exposed at every low tide. (☎ 06 08 27 51 20; www.petit-be.com. Hours depend on the tides; ask the tourist office for details. €5, under 8 free.)

GRAND AQUARIUM. The collection of fish, arranged thematically by habitat, and the 360° wraparound shark tank are some highlights of this sight. The aquarium's pride and joy is the **Nautibus,** an underwater ride. (Av. du Général Patton. Take bus #C1 or C2, dir.: St-Servan or Découverte, from the station or the tourist office. ☎ 02 99 21 19 00; www.aquarium-st-malo.com. Open daily from mid-July to mid-Aug. 9:30am-10pm; late Aug. and early July 9:30am-8pm; Sept. and Apr.-June 10am-7pm; Oct.-Mar. 10am-6pm. Closed 3 weeks in Nov. and 3 weeks in Jan. Last entry 1hr. before close. €18, ages 4-14 €13, under 4 free.)

CATHÉDRALE SAINT-VINCENT. St-Malo native Jacques Cartier, famous for his Canadian explorations, is buried in this 12th-century cathedral, which has been carefully restored following heavy damage in WWII. The distinctively modern 20th-century iridescent stained-glass windows have an undeniable kaleidoscopic allure. (Open daily 9:45am-6pm. Mass Tu-Sa 6:30pm, Su 10, 11:30am, 7pm.)

CHÂTEAU. The city's château, on the northeast corner of the ramparts, dates back to the 14th century. It is home to the town hall and the **Musée d'Histoire,** which fills two huge towers with artifacts illustrating St-Malo's maritime history. Climb to the top of the watchtower for the city's best views. (☎ 02 99 40 71 57; musee@ville-saint-malo.fr. Open Apr.-Sept. daily 10am-12:30pm and 2-6pm; Oct.-Mar. Tu-Su 10am-noon and 2-6pm. €5.20, students €2.60.)

🎭 NIGHTLIFE

Pick up *L'Omnibus*, a brochure that lists local concerts, at the tourist office.

L'Alambic, 8 rue du Boyer (☎ 02 99 40 86 41). Distillery equipment hangs from the ceiling. Young crowd.

Internet €1 per 10min. Beer €2.50-4. Hard liquor €6. DJ F-Sa from 9pm. Open daily May-Oct. 10am-2am; Nov.-Apr. 11am-1am.

L'Absinthe, 1 rue de l'Orme (☎02 99 40 85 40). Attracts a varied clientele to a spacious 4-floor, wood-paneled interior with red lights and comfortable nooks. Beer €2.50-4.50. Frozen margaritas €3.50. Whiskey €5.50. Open daily 5pm-2am. MC/V.

L'Aviso, 12 rue du Point du Jour (☎02 99 40 99 08). Serves 300 types of beer (from €3.70) and 15 kinds of whiskey to a predominantly middle-aged crowd. Open daily July-Aug. 5pm-3:30am; Sept.-June 5pm-3am.

❊ FESTIVALS

Étonnants Voyageurs (☎02 99 31 05 74; www.etonnants-voyageurs.net), at the end of May or beginning of June. Preeminent international literary and film festival in France.

Festival des Folklores du Monde (☎02 99 40 42 50), 1st week of July. International folk music and dance performances.

Route du Rock (☎02 99 54 01 11; www.laroutedurock.com), 2nd weekend in Aug. Rock, techno, and pop music performances.

Quai des Bulles (☎02 99 40 39 63; www.quaidesbulles.com), during the last weekend in Oct. A celebration of comic books.

◗ BEACHES

It's hard to go wrong with the world-famous beaches in St-Malo. On the western side of the *intra-muros*, best accessed by stairwells that lead down from the walls, **plage de Bon-Secours** is sheltered on both sides by rocky outcroppings. It features the curious **piscine de Bon-Secours,** three cement walls that hold in a pool's worth of salt water even at low tide, complete with a diving platform. To the east is the larger **Grande Plage,** a vast expanse of sand. Farther up the coast is the romantic **plage Rochebonne.** On the other side of the old city, to the south and protected from the sea by a marina, lies the more family-oriented **plage des Bas Sablons,** popular with waders and school groups.

DINAN ☎02 96

Dinan (dee-nahn; pop. 11,000), on a hill above the Rance River, has all the charms of a medieval Breton village—cobblestone streets, local artisans, and traditional *crêperies.* Outside the ramparts, the river valley and countryside compose a natural beauty as appealing as the town's architecture.

▐ TRANSPORTATION

Trains: Pl. du 11 Novembre 1918. Open M 7:20am-7pm, Tu-Sa 9am-7pm, Su 11am-7:20pm. To **Paris** (3hr., 6 per day, €632) via **Rennes** (1hr., 8 per day, €13) and **St-Malo** (1hr., 6 per day, €8.30) via **Dol.**

Buses: Tibus (☎02 96 39 21 05; www.cotesdarmor.fr). Open M-F 8am-noon and 2-6pm. Leave from the train station and pl. Duclos Pinot for **St-Malo** (1hr., 3-8 per day) and **Dinard** (1hr.; M-F 3 per day, Sa 1 per day). €2 for all destinations.

Taxis: ☎02 96 39 06 00. At the train station.

❊ ▐ ORIENTATION AND PRACTICAL INFORMATION

Tourist Office: 9 rue du Château (☎02 96 87 69 76; www.dinan-tourisme.com). From the station, bear left across pl. du 11 Novembre 1918 onto rue Carnot, then right onto rue Thiers, which brings you to pl. Duclos Pinot. Turn left to go inside the *vieille ville* walls and bear right onto rue du Marchix, which becomes rue de la Ferronnerie. Pass parking lots on pl. du Champ and pl. Duguesclin to the left; the tourist office is ahead on the right. Multilingual staff provides a free walking-tour city map, an excellent historical guide (€3.50), and a reservations service (€2). Open July-Aug. M-Sa 9am-7pm, Su 10am-12:30pm and 2:30-6pm; Sept.-June M-Sa 9am-12:30pm and 2-6pm.

Tours: Available from the tourist office in French July-Aug. daily 3pm; Sept. and Apr.-June Sa 3pm. Tours in English July 17-Aug. 21 Th 5pm. €5, under 18 €3.

Bank: BNP Paribus, 3 pl. Duclos Pinot. Open Tu-F 9am-12:20pm and 2-6pm, Sa 9am-1pm.

Public Toilets: Underground at pl. du Guesclin. Free.

Police: 16 pl. du Guesclin (☎02 96 87 74 00).

Pharmacy: 4 rue de l'Apport (☎02 96 39 21 31). Open M 10am-12:30pm and 2-7pm, Tu-Sa 9am-12:30pm and 2-7pm.

Hospital: Rue Chateaubriand (☎02 96 85 72 85).

Internet Access: Free Wi-Fi at **Le Patio** (see **Nightlife**, p. 258).

Post Office: Pl. Duclos (☎02 96 85 83 50). **Currency exchange** available. Open M-F 8:30am-6pm, Sa 9am-12:30pm. **Postal Code:** 22100.

ACCOMMODATIONS

Auberge de Jeunesse "Moulin du Méen" (HI; ☎02 96 39 10 83; dinan@fuaj.org), in Vallée de la Fontaine-des-Eaux. From the train station, turn left, then turn left across tracks. Take a right onto rue du Clos du Hêtre, which becomes rue de l'Écuyer and then route de Dinard. Follow the tracks and signs downhill for 2km. Turn right on rue de la Fontaine des Eaux and continue through wooded lanes for another 2km (20-30min.). Clean 1- to 8-bed rooms and communal kitchen. Accepts the **Pass Bretagne** (p. 246). Breakfast €3.60. Free Internet access. Bike rental €6 per ½-day, €10 per day; ID deposit. Reception July-Aug. 8am-noon and 5-9pm; Sept.-June 9am-noon and 5-8pm. Camping €6 per person. Dorms €13. MC/V. ❶

Hôtel du Théâtre, 2 rue Ste-Claire (☎02 96 39 06 91). Prime location above a quiet bar in the heart of the *vieille ville.* Large windows with flower boxes brighten rooms. Breakfast €5. Reception 9am-9pm. Singles and doubles €23, with showers and toilets €29; triples with showers and toilets €39. AmEx/MC/V. ❷

Hôtel de la Gare, pl. de la Gare (☎02 96 39 04 57; fax 39 02 29), next to the train station, 10min. from the *vieille ville.* Large and clean rooms over a corner bar. Breakfast €5. Shower €2. Reception M-Sa 7am-8pm, Su 7am-2pm. Singles and doubles €27, with showers and toilets €34; quads with bath €65. AmEx/MC/V. ❷

FOOD

Simple bars and *brasseries* line the streets linking **rue de la Ferronnerie** with **place des Merciers,** especially narrow **rue de la Cordonnerie.** A **Monoprix** supermarket is at 7 pl. du Marchix. (Open M-Sa 9am-7:30pm.) There is also a **Marché Plus** at 28 pl. Duclos. (Open M-Sa 7am-9pm, Su 9am-1pm.) On Thursdays, head to the outdoor market (open 9am-1pm) on **place du Champ Clos,** near the tourist office, to grab some fruit and a box of the town's specialty cookies, *gavottes* (dried, crystallized *crêpes*). Small restaurants and cafes cluster outside the ramparts, especially along the port, which is down the steep rue du Jerzual from the *vieille ville.* In the *vieille ville,* you'll find *crêperies* at every turn.

▨ **ArThé,** 19 rue de l'Apport (☎02 96 87 48 45). *Salon de thé* and curiosity shop overflows with 100s of intricate porcelain teapots and collectibles from around the world. 65 varieties of exquisite tea (€4.20-6). Open Tu-Su 10:30am-7pm. ❶

Crêperie le Roy, 15 rue de la Lainerie (☎02 96 39 29 72). English-speaking staff serves up filling *galettes* (€2.40-7.90), sweet *crêpes* (€2.30-7.20), and dinner salads (€8.20-8.50). Open M and W-Su 11:30am-3pm and 6:30-9:30pm. ❶

Taj Mahal, 9 rue Ste-Claire (☎03 96 85 43 30; www.restaurant-indien-dinan.com). Authentic Indian delights and vegetarian options. *Entrées* €5-11. *Plats* €12-16. Lunch *menu* €11. Dinner *menu* €18-22. Open daily noon-2pm and 7-11pm. AmEx/MC/V. ❸

👁 SIGHTS

RAMPARTS. Spanning nearly 3km, the town's ramparts are the longest and oldest in Brittany and a sight in themselves. Their remains completely encircle the *vieille ville*, but if all you see is the 13th-century **Porte du Guichet**—which marks the original entrance to the Château de Dinan—you'll still get the picture.

CHÂTEAU. Formerly a military stronghold, ducal residence, and dungeon, the château today houses a small and unimpressive museum of local art and history in its five-floor *donjon* (keep). It's worth the visit just to wander around the keep itself; helpful placards on each floor note what each room was originally used for. A great view awaits those who make it up all 150 steps of the 34m tower. The museum also includes the 15th-century **Tour de Coëtquen,** across the Porte du Guichet from the keep. Along with the occasional temporary exhibit, its dank, drafty basement houses dimly lit medieval tomb statues. *(☎02 96 39 45 20. Open daily June-Sept. 10am-6:30pm; Oct.-Dec. and Feb.-May 1:30-5:30pm. €4.40, students and ages 12-18 €1.70, under 12 free. Cash only.)*

BASILIQUE SAINT-SAUVEUR. This basilica was built by a local noble grateful to have been spared in the Crusades. The Romanesque facade, which dates back to 1120, features a winged lion and bull above the doorway and four eroded statues on the side arches. Within are seven wood altars made by local craftsmen as well as the heart of French military hero Bertrand du Guesclin.

ÉGLISE SAINT-MALO. Completely desecrated during the French Revolution and rebuilt in 1803, the Église St-Malo contains a remarkable 19th-century English organ with blue and gold pipes and a massive Baroque altar. Check out the 20th-century stained glass depicting scenes from medieval life in Dinan. *(Grande Rue. Mass M-Th 8am, F 10am, Su 10:30am.)*

TOUR DE L'HORLOGE. The 15th-century Tour de l'Horloge commands a brilliant view of Dinan's streets and the Rance Valley. The bells ring every 15min. *(Rue de l'Horloge. ☎02 96 87 02 26. Open daily June-Sept. 10am-6:30pm; Apr.-May 2-6pm. Pamphlets available in English. €2.90, students and ages 12-18 €1.90, under 12 free.)*

🎭 NIGHTLIFE AND FESTIVALS

Every other year (next in 2010), Dinan hosts the two-day **Fête des Remparts** during the second half of July. Partygoers don medieval garb for jousting tournaments. (☎02 96 87 94 94; http://perso.wanadoo.fr/fete-remparts.dinan. Presentations daily 10am-10pm. All-day access €10, under 10 and those in medieval costume free; tournaments €10, ages 5-9 €6.) Mid-July is also when the annual **Rencontres Internationales de Harpes Celtiques** hits town. The weeklong festival features Celtic harp concerts and traditional Breton dancing performances.

▨ Le Patio, 9 pl. du Champ Clos (☎02 96 39 84 87). The best ambience in town, with a backlit bar and leopard-skin chairs reflected in its wall-length mirror. Restaurant in the back with deep leather armchairs and a lovely secluded garden. Beer €3-6. *Apéritifs* €2.20-6.50. Open June-Sept. daily 11am-2am; Oct.-Apr. Tu-Su 11am-2am. MC/V.

L'Absinthe, 15 pl. St-Sauveur (☎02 76 87 39 28), near the basilica. Feels like an old-fashioned speakeasy, with soft jazz and exposed-brick walls. Beer €2.50. *Apéritifs* €2-6. Open Mar.-Sept. daily 9am-10pm; Oct.-Feb. Tu-Sa 9am-10pm.

PAIMPOL   ☎02 96

With a port packed with impressive yachts and sailboats, Paimpol (pem-pohl; pop. 8300) has made a visible transition from fishing village to seaside vacation spot. Though it offers few sights of its own, the town provides easy access to the beautiful islands, cliffs, beaches, and hiking trails on this stretch of French coast. Meanwhile, its seafood, *crêperies*, regional specialty shops, and surprisingly vibrant nightlife give it a festive atmosphere with strong Breton flavor.

▐ TRANSPORTATION

Trains: Av. du Général de Gaulle. Open M-F 6:30-7am and 8am-7pm, Sa 8am-7pm, Su and holidays 8:30am-7pm. To **Rennes** (2hr., 4 per day, €26) via **Guingamp.**

Buses: Tibus (☎08 10 22 22 22) serves the **Côtes d'Armor.**

Bike Rental: Intersport, zone de Kerpuns (☎02 96 20 59 46), at the mall on rue Raymond Pellier. €7 per ½-day, €12 per day, €55 per week; under 18 €5/8/40. Open M-Sa 9:30am-12:15pm and 2-7pm. AmEx/MC/V.

▯ PRACTICAL INFORMATION

Tourist Office: 19 rue du Général Leclerc (☎02 96 20 83 16; www.paimpol-goelo. com). From the train station, turn right on av. du Général de Gaulle, follow it to the roundabout, and turn down the 2nd street on the right; the office is on the left. Pl. de la République after 2009. Offers **tours** in French during the summer (€3-6, under 12 free; reserve ahead). Open July-Aug. M-Sa 9:30am-7:30pm, Su 10am-1:30pm; Sept.-June M-Sa 9:30am-12:30pm and 1:30-6:30pm.

Bank: BNP Paribus, 5 pl. du Martay. Open Tu-F 8:45am-12:15pm and 2-6pm, Sa 8:30am-12:30pm.

Laundromats: Au Lavoir Pampolais, 23 rue du 18 Juin 1940 (☎02 96 20 96 41), near the station. Wash €4.50-10, dry €1 per 10min. Open daily 7am-10pm. Branch on rue de Labenne, near the port. Wash €3.20-9, dry €1 per 10min. Open daily 7am-10pm.

Public Toilets: By the train station. Open 7am-10pm. Free.

Police: 2 rue Jean Moulin (☎02 96 20 80 17), off rue Raymond Pellier.

Pharmacy: 6 rue Georges Brassens (☎02 96 20 80 31), near Marché Plus. Open M-Sa 9am-12:30pm and 2-7pm.

Hospital: Chemin de Malabry (☎02 96 55 60 00).

Internet Access: Cybercommune, Centre Dunant (☎02 96 20 74 74; http://cybercommune.paimpol-goelo.com), on the corner of rue Henry Dunant and rue Pierre Feutren. €5 per hr. Open M 2-6:30pm, Tu-Sa 9:30am-12:30pm and 2:30-6:30pm.

Post Office: 10 av. du Général de Gaulle (☎02 96 20 82 40). **Currency exchange** available. Open M and W-F 8am-noon and 1:30-5:30pm, Tu 8am-12:30pm and 1:30-5:30pm, Sa 8am-12:30pm. **Postal Code:** 22500.

🏠 🏕 ACCOMMODATIONS AND CAMPING

Hôtel Berthelot, 1 rue du Port (☎02 96 20 88 66), off quai Morand. Look for a giant blue "H" sticking out of a pink facade. Cheapest hotel for miles around. Cheerful staff. Tidy, spacious rooms. Breakfast €5. Reception 7:30am-8:30pm. Singles and doubles €31, with shower €38, with bath €42, with bath and TV €44. MC/V. ❷

Le Terre-Neuvas, 16 quai Duguay-Trouin (☎02 96 55 14 14; fax 20 47 66), over a restaurant with the same name (see **Food,** this page). Cheapest stay on the water-front. Rooms with showers, toilets, TVs, and phones. Breakfast €5. Free Wi-Fi. Reception 8am-11pm. Reserve ahead in summer. July-Aug. singles €34, with harbor view €40; doubles €42/48. Sept.-June singles €32, with view €38; doubles €40/46. MC/V. ❷

Hôtel Le Goëlo, 4 quai Duguay-Trouin (☎02 96 20 82 74; www.legoelo.com). Comfort-able rooms, each with TV, shower, and toilet; some with harbor views. Breakfast €7. Wi-Fi €2.50 per hr., €5 per 3hr. Wheelchair-accessible. Reception 7am-11pm. Reserve 3-4 days ahead in summer. July-Aug. singles and doubles €51-67; triples €80; quads €90. Sept.-June singles and doubles €45-57; triples €75; quads €80. AmEx/MC/V. ❹

Camping Municipal de Cruckin, rue de Cruckin (☎02 96 20 78 47; fax 20 75 00), 30min. from town. From the station, turn right on av. du Général de Gaulle and right again at the roundabout onto rue du Général Leclerc. Follow the street as it twists several kilometers uphill through 4 name changes; take a left on rue de Cruckin. The entrance is 100m down the hill on the right. Sparse hedges separate 130 plots. Laundry €4, dry €3.50. Bike rental €3-4 per ½-day, €4-6 per day; €150 deposit. Wheelchair-accessible. Reception July-Aug. daily 8:30am-8pm; Sept.-Oct. and Apr.-June M-Sa 9am-12:30pm and 4:30-7:30pm, Su 9-10:30am and 6-7:30pm. Gates closed 10pm-8am. Open Apr.-Oct. July-Aug. €3.30 per person, under 7 €2.10; sites €7.10. Sept.-June €2.90 per person, under 7 €1.50; sites €5.60. Electricity €3.10. AmEx/MC/V. ❶

🍴 FOOD

The market throughout the **vieille ville** provides picnic supplies (Tu morning), as does the **Marché Plus** supermarket, 11 rue St-Vincent, left at the roundabout from the train station. (Open M-Sa 7am-9pm, Su 9am-1pm.) Find seafood along **quai Morand** and *crêperies* along **rue des Huit Patriotes.**

Le Penn Ty, 20 rue des 8 Patriotes (☎02 96 55 11 41). Great *galettes* (€1.70-8.90). Salads €4.90-8.90. *Menus* €7.90-20. Open July-Aug. M-Tu and Th-Sa 11:30am-3pm and 6:30-11pm; Sept.-June daily 11:30am-3pm and 6:30-11pm. AmEx/MC/V. ❷

Le Terre-Neuvas, quai Duguay-Trouin (☎02 96 55 14 14). Elegant seafood dishes ranges from traditional *moules-frites* (mussels and fries; €10) to gourmet *plats* (€14-22). *Menus* €9-31. Open daily noon-2pm and 7-10pm. MC/V. ❸

🧭 SIGHTS

ABBAYE DE BEAUPORT. The ruins of this abbey lie hidden from the road under layers of vegetation. Built in 1202, the abbey has found new charm in its disrepair; grass and flowers sprout from its flying buttresses. The multilingual book-guided tour is included with admission, gives a complete account of the abbey's history, and describes each of the structure's sections in detail. During the summer, the abbey puts on an award-winning light show, which illuminates the ruins. (*Chemin de l'Abbaye, 30min. from Paimpol. Follow directions to the campground but continue past rue de Cruckin to the next major left turn; the abbey is at the end of the lane. ☎02 96 55 18 54; www.abbaye-beauport.com. Open daily from mid-June to mid-Sept. 10am-7pm; from mid-Sept. to mid-June 10am-noon and 2-5pm. Last entry 30min. before close. 4-6 tours in French* *per day. Light show July-Aug. W and Su 10pm-1am. Tours Apr.-Aug. €5, students €4, ages 11-18 €3, ages 5-10 €2; Sept.-Mar. €4.50/4/2/1. Light show €8, ages 5-18 €4.)*

🔲 🌿 NIGHTLIFE AND FESTIVALS

Every other year in early August (next in 2009), the **Fête du Chant de Marin** (Festival of Sailors' Songs) draws sailor-musicians for three days of dancing, boating, and general merriment. (☎02 96 55 12 77; www.paimpol-festival.com.) Paimpol is small, but it knows how to party. As the sun sets, crowds head to bars on side streets off the port, or to **quai de Kernoa** on the waterfront.

🔳 **Le Pub**, 3 rue Islandais (☎02 96 20 82 31). Heavy oak door can't contain the revelry inside. Disco opens upstairs, and drink prices rise at 1am. Beer €3-7. Mixed drinks €5.40-8. Irish folk music Th 9:30pm. Cover for disco €10, includes 1 drink. Open July-Aug. daily 9:30pm-5am; Sept.-June Th-Su 9:30pm-5am. AmEx/MC/V.

Zanzi'Bar, 10 quai de Kernoa (☎02 96 20 75 15). Reggae music, thatched jungle hut decor, and toy giraffe accents set the scene. Occasional themed nights. Beer €2.30. Hard cider €2.20. Open daily July-Aug. 3pm-2am; Sept.-June 5pm-1am. AmEx/MC/V.

Le Corto Maltese, 11 rue du Quai (☎02 96 22 05 76). Locals love its mix of classic rock, flashing lights, and Belgian and Irish beers on tap. Monthly concert in the summer. Beer €2.30. Irish coffee €6.50. Open from mid-May to mid-Sept. daily 10am-2am; from mid-Sept. to mid-May Tu-Su 10am-1am. AmEx/MC/V.

🔳 DAYTRIPS FROM PAIMPOL

POINTE DE L'ARCOUEST AND ÎLE DE BRÉHAT

To get to Pointe de L'Arcouest, take a Tibus bus (☎02 96 20 94 58) from Paimpol (15min.; M-Sa 6 per day, Su 2 per day, more July-Aug.; €2). Drivers follow clearly marked GR34. Les Vedettes de Bréhat (☎02 96 55 79 50; www.vedettesdebrehat.com) runs boats to Île de Bréhat (10min.; 5-16 per day; round-trip €8.50, ages 4-11 €7, with bike €15 more). For a few extra euro, take a 45min. circuit of the island from the sea (€13, ages 4-11 €9.50). For a taxi, call Taxi Les Alizes at Pointe de l'Arcouest (☎02 96 20 49 76).

Six kilometers north of Paimpol, the peninsula ends in a tumble of pink granite called the Pointe de l'Arcouest. While the cape itself is a worthy destination, it usually serves as a jumping-off point for the Île de Bréhat. The surrounding blue-green waters offer some of France's best kayaking; the Centre Nautique de Loguivy-de-la-Mer, 5km from the Pointe, rents **kayaks** and **catamarans.** (☎02 96 20 94 58; www.voile-kayak-mer.com. Kayak rental with guide €30 per ½-day, €49 per day. Catamarans €40 per 2hr. Open M-Sa 9am-noon and 2-5:30pm.)

Two kilometers out at sea lies the Île de Bréhat—a mesh of rocky pink beaches, small tracts of farmland, flower-draped cottages, and fields of elbow-high grass. The Île de Bréhat is actually the largest landmass in an archipelago of 96 islets, some of them so minute that they amount essentially to single rocks. Only 3.5km in length, Bréhat (bray-hah) is divided in the center by a small bridge. The southern half contains the *bourg* (town center) and the port, while the rugged northern half is mostly farmland, with a few scattered houses and the island's two lighthouses. To get the most out of your visit, take an early boat, then head north to avoid the crowds. Plan to take at least half a day to see the island; the trip from Paimpol to the island takes about 45min., and the island itself deserves at least 3hr. of exploration.

Follow signs from the *bourg* to the tiny, orange-roofed **Chapelle Saint-Michel.** Perched on a hilltop on the west side of the island, the chapel offers a marvelous view of the island's green fields and rock-speckled bay. The natural beauty of this panorama is only matched by the eroded pink granite rock piles at the island's northern tip, where the ⬛**Phare du Paon** lighthouse sits. According to legend, when unwed women throw a pebble between the rocks, the number of bounces indicates the years that they must wait until marriage. The lighthouse and its scenic surroundings are worth the 40-50min. walk from the *bourg*.

To reach the **tourist office**—the Syndicat d'Initiative—follow the main road to the main square; the office is on the right. The staff sells a map (€0.20) of the island with six suggested paths. (☎02 96 20 04 15; syndicatinitiative.brehat@ wanadoo.fr. Open July-Aug. M-Sa 10am-1pm and 2-4:15pm, Su 10am-1pm; Sept.-Oct. and Apr.-June M-Tu and Th-Sa 10am-1pm and 2-4:15pm, Su 10am-1pm; Nov.-Mar. M and Th 10am-1pm and 2-4:15pm, Sa 10am-1pm. **Public toilets** next door are free. The best way to tackle the island is by foot or bicycle; paths to major sights are clearly marked. Of the many options for **bike** rental, the closest to the port lies at the end of the walkway leading to the boats, marked by the sign "Vélos à Louer." (€6 per 2hr., €10 per 5hr., €15 per day; under 18 €5/8/13. Helmets included. Open Apr.-Sept. daily 9am-6pm, depending on ferry schedules. MC/V.) In the *bourg*, you can find similarly overpriced restaurants and a **8 à Huit** supermarket. (Open M-Sa 9am-8pm, Su 9am-6pm.) The island's cafes primarily sell *crêpes*, sandwiches, ice cream, and *frites*.

ROSCOFF ☎**02 98**

With a bevy of seafood restaurants, a central port, and several beaches, Roscoff (ross-koff; pop. 3550) is a city of the sea. The town has been everything from a base for pirates and smugglers to the birthplace of *thalassothérapie* (sea-water therapy), a treatment popular in France today. Roscoff's strong nautical character and proximity to Île de Batz make it worth a quick stop.

📧🚻 **TRANSPORTATION AND PRACTICAL INFORMATION.** SNCF **trains** and buses run via Morlaix (30-45min., 4-6 per day, €5.30) to Brest (2hr., 5 per day, €15), Paris (5hr., 4 per day, €69), and Rennes (4hr., 4 per day, €34). The station is open daily 8:15am-6:40pm. Penn-ar-Bed **buses** (☎02 98 76 24 58; www. viaoo29.fr) leave from stops in the *centre-ville* and at the ferry terminal for Morlaix (1hr., M-Sa 5 per day, €2) and Quimper (2hr., 1 per day, €2). **Ferries** depart from the Port du Bloscon, outside of town. Brittany Ferries (☎08 25 82 88 28; www.brittanyferries.com) serves Plymouth, ENG (5-6hr., 1-2 per day, €124), and Cork, IRE (10-11hr., 1 per week, €309). Irish Ferries (☎02 98 61 17 17; www.irishferries.com) serves Rosslare, IRE about twice per week. Irish Ferries offers Eurail discounts up to 30%. Clear signs mark the way to the *centre-ville* from the train station or ferry terminal.

The **tourist office,** 46 rue Gambetta, offers transportation schedules, maps with suggested walking tours, a visitor's guide, a list of *chambres d'hôte*, accommodations booking, and Internet access—all free. (☎02 98 61 12 13; www.roscoff-tourisme.com. Open July-Aug. M-Sa 9am-12:30pm and 1:30-7pm, Su 10am-12:30pm; Sept.-June M-Sa 9am-noon and 2-6pm.) There is a **laundromat** at 3 rue Jules Ferry. (Wash €4-8, dry €1 per 10min. Open daily 7:30am-9pm.) Free public **toilets** are near the tourist office, at the train station, and at the ferry terminal. **Police** are at 16 rue Jules Ferry (☎02 98 19 33 74). **Internet** is available at the tourist office and at **Boulangerie Centrale,** 6 rue Gambetta, with purchase. (☎02 98 69 72 61. Open July-Aug. daily 7am-7pm; Sept.-June M and W-Su 7am-7pm.) The **post office,** 19 rue Gambetta, offers **currency exchange.** (☎02 98 69 71 28. Open July-Aug. M-F 9am-12:30pm and 1:30-5:30pm, Sa 9am-12:30pm; Sept.-June M-F 9am-noon and 2-5pm, Sa 9am-12:30pm.) **Postal Code:** 29680.

ACCOMMODATIONS AND CAMPING. At ⊠Hôtel d'Angleterre ❸, 28 rue Albert de Mun, a delightful staff offers large rooms with Breton furniture in an old mansion. A sunroom with wicker chairs looks over a backyard garden. Enjoy the restaurant, TV room with pool table, and sunny sitting room with chessboards. (☎02 98 69 70 42; fax 69 75 16. Breakfast €7. Reception 8am-11pm. Open Mar.-Oct. July-Aug. singles and doubles €35, with toilet €45, with bath or shower €57; Sept.-Oct. and Apr.-May €28/37/50. *Demi-pension* €38 per person, with toilet €41, with bath or shower €48. Extra bed €16. MC/V.) Roscoff's only campground is **Camping de Perharidy "Aux 4 Saisons" ❶**, near allée des Chênes Verts, 30min. from the train station. From the station, turn left on rue Ropartz Morvan, right on rue des Capucins, left on rue Laënnec, and right on rue de la Baie. Turn left at the coast, following route du Laber past the Jardin Louis Kerdilés, and then right; the campgound will be on your left. About 200 spots by the beach have access to a volleyball court, minigolf, bowling, hot showers, and laundry. (☎02 98 69 70 86 or 06 07 41 28 53; www.camping-aux4saisons. com. Reception daily July-Aug. 9am-noon and 2-8pm; from Sept. to mid-Oct. and Apr.-June 9-11:30am and 5:30-7:30pm. Reserve ahead. Open from Apr. to mid-Oct. July-Aug. 2 adults, car, and tent €11; €3.10 per extra person, children €1.80. From Sept. to mid-Oct. and Apr.-June 2 adults, car, and tent €8.70; €2.80 per extra person, children €1.70. Electricity €2.60-4.30. Cash only.)

FOOD. Restaurants serving seafood *menus* (€13-25) line the port. There is a market (W 9am-1pm) on **quai Auxerre** and a **Casino** supermarket a 15min. walk out of town on the right side of rue du Pontigou. (Open M-F 9am-12:30pm and 2-6pm, Sa 9am-6pm, Su 9am-noon; longer hours July-Aug.) One of Roscoff's most distinctive *crêperies*, **Ti Saozon ❶**, 30 rue Gambetta, just past the tourist office, feels like a traditional Breton home. (☎02 98 69 70 89. *Galettes* and *crêpes* €3-8.50. Open M-Sa from 6:30pm. Reservations recommended.) **Le Surcouf ❸**, 14 rue Amiral Réveillère, dishes up fresh seafood in a simple but elegant interior. (☎02 98 69 71 89; www.jalima.fr. *Plat du jour* €9. Seafood *plats* €14-19. Lunch *menu* €11. Dinner *menus* €16-27. Open July-Sept. M-Th and Sa-Su noon-2:15pm and 7-9:30pm, F noon-2pm and 6:30-9:30pm; Oct.-June M-Tu, Th, Sa-Su noon-2:15pm and 7-9:30pm, F noon-2pm and 6:30-9:30pm. AmEx/MC/V.)

SIGHTS. Boasting a panoramic view of the Bay of Morlaix, **Le Jardin Exotique** is a well-tended jungle featuring over 3000 species of tropical flora. From the tourist office, walk to the dock and turn right. Follow quai d'Auxerre, bear left on rue Jeanne d'Arc, and continue through pl. de Keradraon onto rue Plymouth. Turn right on rue de Great Torrington and then left, following the signs. (☎02 98 61 29 19; www.jardinexotiqueroscoff.com. Open daily July-Aug. 10am-7pm; Sept.-Oct. and Apr.-June 10:30am-12:30pm and 2-6pm; Nov. and Mar. 2-5pm. Guided tours July-Aug. W at 3pm. €5, students and seniors €4, ages 12-18 €2.) The 16th-century **Église Notre Dame de Croaz-Batz** looks like an enormous sandcastle with turreted spires and a Renaissance-style belfry. Twin stone cannons carved into the church's main tower point toward the sea, symbolically defending the city. (Open daily 9am-noon and 2-6pm.) On the far right side of the port is the **Pointe Sainte-Barbe,** with spiraling stone steps that lead to a white chapel. Look out over a local shellfish farm for a view of Roscoff's port and the rocky islands of the Bay of Morlaix. The **Circuits Pedestre** guide on the back of the tourist center map suggests pleasant walking tours (6-12km, 1-3hr.).

ÎLE DE BATZ   ☎**02 98**

Fifteen minutes off the coast of Roscoff sits Île de Batz (eel duh bahtss; pop.
500, in summer 3500), a windswept sanctuary of natural beauty only 3.5km
long and 1.5km wide. Small farms and cottages stand in acres of green grass
dotted with duck ponds, while winding paths lead through the countryside and
along an unspoiled coastline. The island's many small beaches, said to have
some of the finest sand in France, are perfect spots for a secluded dip.

TRANSPORTATION AND PRACTICAL INFORMATION. Three allied **ferry**
companies—Armein (☎02 98 61 77 75), Armor Excursions (☎02 98 61 79 66),
and CFTM (☎02 98 61 78 87)—connect Roscoff and Batz (10-15min.). Boats
leave from Roscoff's port at high tide and from the walkway at the harbor at
low tide. (From late June to Aug. every 30min., last boat from island 7:30pm;
from Sept. to late June 8-10 per day, last boat from island 6pm. Round-trip
€7.50, ages 4-11 €4.) Circle the island or tour the Bay of Morlaix for a few
more euro. (Tours July-Aug. 1hr. island circuit Su 3pm; €11, ages 4-11 €6. 2-5hr.
Bay of Morlaix circuit daily 2:30pm; €13, under 18 €6.) There are a number of
places to rent **bikes** on the island, including Vélos le Saoût, immediately off
the ferry dock. (☎02 98 61 77 65. €3 per hr., €9 per ½-day, €10 per day. Hours
depend on ferry schedules, but generally 9am-8pm.)
   The island's tiny **tourist office** is in the town hall from September to June,
then moves to the port in July and August. To get to the town hall, turn left out
of the port and follow signs. The staff provides a small but sufficient guide,
complete with 2hr. walking tours, and a map. (☎02 98 61 75 70; www.iledebatz.
com. Open July-Aug. M-F 10am-1pm and 2-5pm, Sa 9:30am-1pm; Sept.-June M-F
9am-noon and 1:30-4:30pm, Sa 10am-noon.) The Île de Batz **post office,** with **currency exchange** and fax services, is in the *centre-ville;* look for signs. (☎02 98 61
76 46. Open July-Aug. M-F 9am-noon and 1:30-4:30pm, Sa 9am-noon; Sept.-June
M-F 9:30am-noon and 1:30-4pm, Sa 9:30am-noon.) **Postal Code:** 29253.

ACCOMMODATIONS AND CAMPING. The cheapest bed for miles
around can be found at **Auberge de Jeunesse Marine (HI) ❶.** To reach the hostel
from the port, take the uphill road to the left of the hotel. Signs mark the path
to the hostel (5-10min.). Hidden at the top of a hill, the five-building complex
has the rustic air of a private lodge and access to a secluded beach. (☎02 98
61 77 69; www.aj-iledebatz.org. Breakfast included. Linen €4. Reception daily
July-Aug. 6:30-8:30pm; Sept.-Oct. and Apr.-June 6:30-7:30pm. Open Apr.-Oct.
Dorms €15; cots €14; *demi-pension* €23; *pension complète* €32. Cash only.) The
rooms at the *chambres d'hôte* **Ty Va Zadou ❸,** overlooking the port, are filled with
charming Breton hospitality. From the ferry, head left toward town. This stone
house with light blue shutters sits atop a hill next to the church. A pleasant
proprietress oversees homey, carefully color-coordinated rooms, all with bath.
Vacationers reserve up to a year in advance, so plan ahead. (☎02 98 61 76 91.
Breakfast included. Reception 9am-10pm. Open from Feb. to mid-Nov. Singles
€40; doubles €60; 2-room family suite €80.) The grassy **Terrain d'Hérbergement
de Plein Air ❶,** an open field on the beach near the lighthouse, is the sole legal
campground on the island, but it only allows tents. There's no permanent
reception—a dues collector will come by. (☎02 98 61 75 70. Open from mid-
June to mid-Sept. €2.50 per person, children €1, €1.50 per tent. Cash only.)

FOOD. From the port, bear left and follow signs to the **8 à Huit** supermarket, near the island's highest point. (Open Tu-Sa 9am-12:30pm and 2:30-7:30pm,
Su 10am-12:30pm.) Dining options on the island are rather limited, but a few

BRITTANY

restaurants and *crêperies* greet voyagers coming off the ferry at the port. With a terrace facing the sea, **La Cassonade ❷** offers elegant service and budget prices. Try the house specialty, Ilienne (€9)—a *galette* with scallops and leek purée. (☎02 98 61 75 25. *Galettes* and *crêpes* €2.90-9. Open Apr.-Sept. and school vacations daily 9am-10pm. MC/V.) **Kastell Gwenn ❷**, in the *centre-ville*, serves generously sized pizzas (€7-14) in a relaxed atmosphere. (☎02 98 61 76 34. Open M-W and F-Sa 9am-8:30pm, Th 9am-noon, Su 9am-1pm. AmEx/MC/V.)

◙◪ SIGHTS AND HIKING. The best way to see Île de Batz is to take the **sentier côtier,** 14km of easy-to-follow trails that line the coast, running past the rugged *côte sauvage* along small, sandy beaches, over massive rocks, and past inland lakes. The 4hr. hike is not difficult. Find the trails from any point on the island by taking the nearest road to the coast or by following signs from the port. The tourist office's guidebook has maps for easy 2hr. hikes.

At the southeast tip of the island, signs lead to the tranquil **◪Jardin Georges Delaselle,** a horticultural masterpiece featuring exotic plants from every continent except Antarctica. The garden is arranged around several different *paysages* (landscapes)—including a cactus garden, a palm grove, and the **Nécropole,** a grassy lawn dotted with Bronze Age tombs. (☎02 98 61 75 65. Open July-Aug daily 1-6:30pm; Sept.-Oct. and Apr.-June M and W-Su 2-6pm. 1hr. tours Su 3pm. 2hr. tours July-Aug. Tu 10am. €4.50, students and seniors €3.50, ages 10-16 €2, under 10 free. 1hr. tours €7; 2hr. tours €8.) For a great view of the island and Roscoff, climb the 198 steps of the **lighthouse,** which was built between 1832 and 1836 out of native granite. (Open daily July-Aug. 1-5:30pm; early Sept. and late June M-Tu and Th-Su 2-5pm; closed in poor weather. €2, under 18 €1.) Slightly inland, just before the garden, stand the ruins of the 12th-century **Église Saint-Paul,** renamed the **Chapelle Sainte-Anne** after the patron saint of the island's sailors. During the **Fête de Sainte-Anne,** the year's largest celebration, a parade proceeds from the town church to the chapel's ruins, where an open-air mass is held before a huge bonfire on the dunes (last Sa in July).

BREST
☎ **02 98**

Brest (brehst; pop. 153,000) became a wasteland in 1944 when Allied bombers drove out the occupying German fleet. Reconstructed in modern style, the city boasts a lively urban atmosphere with a twist of seaside flavor. Tourists and locals alike throng its enormous Océanopolis aquarium.

▟ TRANSPORTATION

Trains: Pl. du 19ème Régiment d'Infanterie. Ticket office open M-F 5:20am-7:30pm, Sa 6am-6:30pm, Su 8am-7:50pm. To: **Morlaix** (30min., 13-20 per day, €12); **Paris** (4hr., 10 per day, €66); **Quimper** (30min., 6 per day, €15); **Rennes** (2hr., 10 per day, €35).

Buses: Penn-ar-Bed, (☎02 98 44 46 73; www.viaoo29.fr), next to the train station. Open M-F 6:50am-12:30pm and 1-7pm, Sa 8:45am-1:15pm and 2:30-7pm, Su 1:30-2:30pm and 5:15-7pm. To **Quimper** (1hr.; M-Sa 5 per day, Su 2 per day; €6, under 26 €3), **Roscoff** (1hr.; 5 per day; €2, under 26 €1.50), and smaller towns in the region for €2. Tickets are valid for 1hr. on the Bibus system (below).

Public Transportation: Bibus, 33 av. Georges Clemenceau (☎02 98 80 30 30; www.bibus. fr). Open M-F 8:15am-6:15pm, Sa 9am-5pm. Runs **buses** daily Sept.-June 6am-8pm; night lines hourly M-Th and Su 9-11pm, F-Sa 9pm-midnight. Service reduced July-Aug.; check schedules and maps available at the bus and tourist offices. Buy tickets (€1.20) and 24hr. passes (valid midnight-midnight; €3.30) on board; get carnets of 10 (€9.10) or weekly passes (valid M-Su; €9.40, must have student ID) at the office.

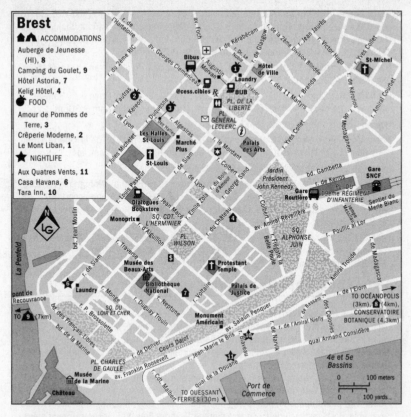

Brest

▲⌂ ACCOMMODATIONS
Auberge de Jeunesse
  (HI), **8**
Camping du Goulet, **9**
Hôtel Astoria, **7**
Kelig Hôtel, **4**

🍎 FOOD
Amour de Pommes de
  Terre, **3**
Crêperie Moderne, **2**
Le Mont Liban, **1**

★ NIGHTLIFE
Aux Quatres Vents, **11**
Casa Havana, **6**
Tara Inn, **10**

Taxis: ☎02 98 42 11 11. At the train station.

Bike Rental: Available at the tourist office July-Aug. €2 per hr., €8 per day.

✈🛈 ORIENTATION AND PRACTICAL INFORMATION

To the right of the train station, av. Georges Clemenceau leads to the central **place de la Liberté,** an open square with fountains in front of the *hôtel de ville.* This is both the *centre-ville* and the main terminal for its bus system. **Rue de Siam,** running south from the place to the sea, is the most vibrant street in the city, with boutiques lining either side. **Rue Jean Jaurès,** north of the place, is also prime shopping territory; exercise caution in the area at night. Ferries leave for nearby isles from **port du Commerce.**

Tourist Office: Pl. de la Liberté (☎02 98 44 24 96; www.brest-metropole-tourisme.fr). Multilingual staff. Visitor's handbook, free maps, info on sights and **tours,** free hotel and ferry reservations, and advice on trips to Île d'Ouessant. Open July-Aug. M-Sa 9:30am-7pm, Su 10am-noon; Sept.-June M-Sa 9:30am-6pm.

English-Language Bookstore: Dialogues, pl. Roull (☎02 98 44 88 68; www.librairiedia-logues.fr), with entrances on rue de Siam and rue Louis Pasteur. An immense bookstore with an English-language section. Free Wi-Fi. Open M-Sa 9:30am-7:30pm.

Youth Center: Bureau Information Jeunesse (BIJ), 4 rue Augustin Morvan (☎02 98 43 01 08; www.bij-brest.org), off pl. de la Liberté. Offers info on jobs and internships. Free Internet. Open July and late Aug. M-F 10am-noon and 1:30-4:30pm; Sept.-June M-Tu 1:30-6pm, W-F 9:30am-noon and 1:30-6pm, Sa 9:30am-noon.

Bank: BNP Paribus, 28 rue d'Aiguillon. Open Tu-F 8:30am-12:15pm and 1:45-5:45pm, Sa 8:50am-12:30pm.

Laundromats: 8 pl. de la Liberté. Wash €3.20-7, dry €1 per 10min. Open daily 8am-8pm. Also at 7 rue de Siam. Wash €3-7, dry €1 per 10min. Open daily 8am-9:30pm.

Police: 15 rue Colbert (☎02 98 43 77 77).

Pharmacy: 29 av. Georges Clemenceau (☎02 98 44 19 47), off pl. de la Liberté. Open July-Aug. M-F 9:30am-7:30pm; Sept.-June M-F 8am-8pm, Sa 9:30am-1pm.

Hospital: 2 av. du Maréchal Foch (☎02 98 22 33 33).

Internet Access: Free at the **BIJ** (see **Youth Center,** above) and at **Dialogues** (see **English-Language Bookstore,** above). **@ccescibles,** 31 av. Georges Clemenceau (☎02 98 46 76 10; www.accescibles.fr). Computer or Wi-Fi €1 per 15min., €3.50 per hr. Open M-Sa 11am-1am, Su 2-11pm.

Post Office: 90 rue de Siam (☎02 98 33 73 06), on esplanade du Général Leclerc. **Currency exchange,** faxing services, and photocopier available. Open M-F 8am-7pm, Sa 8am-noon. **Postal Code:** 29200.

🏠 🏕 ACCOMMODATIONS AND CAMPING

Auberge de Jeunesse (HI), 5 rue Kerbriant (☎02 98 41 90 41; www.aj-brest.org), 4km from the train station, near Océanopolis. From pl. de la Liberté, take bus #3 (dir.: Océanopolis; M-Sa 6:30am-8:30pm, Su 9:45am-8:30pm) or night bus #N25 or #N27 to Palaren. Turn right, walk under the overpass, and take the 2nd right. Walk uphill and turn left to reach the hostel. Palm trees and a nearby beach create a tropical resort atmosphere. Spacious rooms with modern furnishings in several buildings. Experienced staff provides helpful info, including ferry discounts. Stone fireplace, TV room, and common room with piano, foosball, ping-pong, and pool tables. Bicycle garage and kitchen also available. Breakfast included. Luggage storage. Laundry. Free Wi-Fi in the common areas. Key deposit for late entry (€50). Reception July-Aug. 7:30-10am and 5pm-midnight; Sept.-June 7:30am-10am and 5-11pm. Lockout 10am-5pm. Curfew July-Aug. midnight; Sept.-June 11pm. Dorms €17; *demi-pension* €27. MC/V. ❶

Hôtel Astoria, 9 rue Traverse (☎02 98 80 19 10; www.hotel-astoria-brest.com). Central, quiet location. Classy, spotless rooms with TVs. Breakfast €7. Showers €4. Free Wi-Fi. Reception daily 7am-11pm. Reserve 1 week ahead, especially July-Aug. Singles and doubles €29, with shower and toilet €45-50, with bath €53-54. AmEx/MC/V. ❷

Kelig Hôtel, 12 rue de Lyon (☎02 98 80 47 21; lucas.pascale@wanadoo.fr), near the train station. 25 large rooms with showers, TVs, wood wardrobes, and comfortable beds. Breakfast €7. Laundry €8. Free Wi-Fi. Reception M-F 7am-9:30pm, Sa 8am-7pm, Su 8am-12:30pm. Singles with shower €35, with shower and toilet €45-50; doubles €38/48-53; triples €55-60. AmEx/MC/V. ❸

Camping du Goulet, route de Ste-Anne du Portzic (☎02 98 45 86 84). From downtown, take bus #28 (dir.: Plouzané) to Cosquer (20-25min.). At night, take bus #N26 (dir.: Plouzané) via Technopôle (M-Th and Su 1 per night, F-Sa 3 per night). Seems like a luxury resort with pool, waterslides, bar, and clean facilities. Reception July-Aug. 8am-8pm; Sept.-June 9:30am-noon and 2:30-7pm. 2 adults and car €13-23; €2.50-5 per extra person, under 7 €2. Electricity €3-3.50. AmEx/MC/V. ❶

FOOD

Markets are held every day in various locations, such as the traditional and organic markets on **rue du Moulin à Poudre** (open Tu 4-8pm, Sa 8:30am-12:30pm), the enormous market on **place Saint-Louis** (open Su 8:30am-12:30pm), and a slightly pricier indoor market at **Les Halles Saint-Louis,** one block from rue de Siam (open M-Sa 7am-1pm and 4-7:30pm, Su 7am-1pm). *Pâtisseries* and kebab counters can be found on and around **rue Jean Jaurès** and **rue de Siam;** for more filling meals, try the end of rue de Siam near the port. A handful of restaurants and bars clusters to the southeast at **port du Commerce.** For groceries, head to **Marché Plus,** 59 rue Louis Pasteur, just off rue de Siam (open M-Sa 7am-9pm, Su 9am-1pm), or the basement of **Monoprix,** 49 rue de Siam (open M-Sa 8am-8pm).

Le Mont Liban, 8 pl. de la Liberté (☎02 98 80 12 76). Couples rendezvous for 2-person meze (€40-52) and other Middle Eastern delicacies. Lots of vegetarian dishes. Lunch *menus* €8.50-16. Open M-F noon-2pm and 7:30-10pm, Sa 7:30-11pm. MC/V. ❸

Crêperie Moderne, 34 rue Algésiras (☎02 98 44 44 35). Locals enjoy classic *galettes* and *crêpes* (€1.80-10.50). Double your portion for only a little extra. Open M-Sa 11:30am-2:30pm and 6:30-10:30pm. MC/V. ❶

Amour de Pomme de Terre, 23 rue des Halles St-Louis (☎02 98 43 48 51), hidden behind the indoor market. Potato lovers will revel in the abundance of their favorite vegetable. *Plats* €15-28. Lunch *menus* €8.50-19. Open M noon-2pm and 7-10pm, Tu-Th noon-2pm and 7:30-10:30pm, F noon-2pm and 7:30-11pm, Sa noon-2pm and 7-11:30pm, Su noon-2pm and 7:30-10pm. MC/V. ❸

SIGHTS

CHÂTEAU. Brest's château was the only major building to survive the bombings of WWII. In its 1700 strife-filled years, the world's oldest active military institution has been defended by Roman, Breton, English, French, and German troops. Much of the fortress still serves as a French naval base, but several towers house the **Musée de la Marine,** an eclectic collection of naval art and artifacts. Impressive wood prow carvings and model ships appear alongside historical placards detailing the story of the château's construction. (☎02 98 22 12 39; www.musee-marine.fr. Open daily Apr.-Sept. 10am-6:30pm; Oct.-Mar. 1:30-6pm. Last entry 1hr. before close. Tours 2-3 times per day July-Aug. €5, students €3.50, under 18 free. Tours €2.)

MONUMENT AMÉRICAIN. Also known as the **Tour Rose** (Pink Tower), this rose-colored monument overlooks the port du Commerce and commemorates the US Navy's 1917 and 1918 supply convoys. (Rue de Denver.)

OCÉANOPOLIS. This aquarium presents a huge exhibit of sea creatures in three pavilions. The temperate pavilion highlights the marine life of Brittany and the Iroise Sea (which surrounds Île d'Ouessant), while the polar pavilion contains a panoramic theater that opens onto a penguin playland. Finally, the tropical pavilion exhibits a coral reef and sizable shark tank. Arrive early to beat the crowds. (Port de Plaisance. ☎02 98 34 40 40; www.oceanopolis.com. Take bus #3 (dir.: Océanopolis; daily every 30min. until 7:30pm) from pl. de la Liberté. Open from mid-July to Aug. daily 9am-7pm; Sept.-Dec. and Feb.-Mar. Tu-Sa 10am-5pm, Su 10am-6pm; Apr.-June daily 9am-6pm. Wheelchair-accessible. €16, ages 4-17 €11. Audio tour €4. MC/V.)

CONSERVATOIRE BOTANIQUE DE BREST. This public garden and conservatory stretches through 2km of exotic plant life, bamboo groves, and bubbling brooks. (Take bus #3 to Palaren. Head left at the roundabout, uphill onto route de Quimper, and right at the sign. ☎02 98 02 46 00; www.cbnbrest.fr. Gardens open daily May-Oct. 9am-8pm;

BRITTANY

Nov.-Mar 9am-6pm. Free. Greenhouses open from July to mid-Sept. M-Th and Su 2-5:30pm; from mid-Sept. to mid-Nov. and Easter-June W and Su 2-5:30pm. Self-guided booklet tours available in English and French. €3.50, ages 10-16 €2.)

🔊 🎇 NIGHTLIFE AND FESTIVALS

On Thursdays in summer, the popular **Jeudis du Port** concerts liven up port du Commerce with Breton music, rock, and jazz. (From mid-July to late Aug. Th 7pm-1am. Free.) Every four years, next in 2012, Brest hosts a major **Fête Maritime Internationale** (☎02 98 32 20 08; www.brest2008.fr), assembling antiquated boats from around the world into a single unique fleet. Visitors can go aboard vessels at anchor or stay on firm ground for musical performances and shipbuilding demonstrations on the *quais*.

Nightlife centers on **port de Commerce,** the near side of the **pont de Recouvrance,** and the streets near **place de la Liberté.** Avoid the neighborhoods on the other side of the pont de Recouvrance after dark.

🍹 **Casa Havana,** 2 rue de Siam (☎02 98 80 42 87). Lively Latin music and bright red walls. Beer €2.50. Mixed drinks €5.80-6.80. Tapas €2.90. Desserts €3.10. Salsa lessons M-W; beginners 7:30pm (free), intermediate at 9:30pm (€5). Salsa nights Th and the 1st Sa of the month. DJ Th-Sa 8pm. Open daily 3pm-1am. AmEx/MC/V.

Aux Quatres Vents, 18 quai de la Douane (☎02 98 44 42 84). Nautical portside bar with decor of intricate model ships, tables covered with maps, and a boat hanging from the ceiling. Beer €1.70-4. Grog €2.30. Open daily 9am-1am. AmEx/MC/V.

Tara Inn, 1 rue Blaveau (☎02 98 80 36 07), near port du Commerce. Kir €2.20. Beer €2.30-2.90. Celtic-themed venue features choice local musicians on Th nights. *Jazz manouche* the last Su of every month. Breton music 1st Su of every month. Open M-F 11am-1am, Sa-Su 3pm-1am. MC/V.

ÎLE D'OUESSANT   ☎02 98

The westernmost point in metropolitan France, windswept Île d'Ouessant (eel dwess-ahn; *Enez Eussa* in Breton; pop. 950) is an island settlement of hardy Breton villagers and a peaceful refuge for hikers, cyclists, and nature lovers. Just an hour-long boat ride from the nearest point on the mainland, the island is a wide-open expanse of green and golden pasture, mysterious rock formations, blue-green waters, and grazing sheep and cattle. The island's only town, Lampaul, is tucked away on the western side of the island.

🔲 TRANSPORTATION

Ferries: Penn-ar-Bed (☎02 98 80 80 80; www.viaoo29.fr). Runs from **Brest** (3hr.; at least 1 per day, more Apr.-Sept.). Also serves the islands of Molène and Sein. Reservations required at least a day in advance; reserve a week ahead July-Aug. Round-trip €33-34, ages 4-16 €18-20, ages 1-4 €2. 15% student discount. Boats dock at Port du Stiff, 3.5km from Lampaul.

Buses: Ouessant Voyages (☎06 81 04 31 04). Service from the port to the central church (5-10min.; €2, round-trip €3.50). Some companies also offer a 2hr. guided tour in French of the island; €12.

Bike Rental: 3 companies rent bikes for identical prices at the port and in Lampaul. 1-speed bikes €7 per ½-day, €10 per day, €37 per week; mountain bikes €10/14/50. Helmets available. Reserve in advance at the Brest tourist office to get a mountain bike for the price of a 1-speed bike.

▚ PRACTICAL INFORMATION

Tourist Office: Near the church in the *centre-ville* (☎02 98 48 85 83; www.ot-ouessant. fr). Sells a pedestrian guide (€2.50). Map with bike-friendly roads. Open July-Aug. M-Sa 9am-7pm, Su 10am-noon; Sept.-June 10am-noon and 1:30-6pm, Su 10am-noon.

ATMs: At **SPAR** and **8 à Huit** supermarkets (see **Food,** this page).

Public Toilets: By the tourist office. Bring your own toilet paper.

Police: ☎02 98 48 81 61. Only operate on the island July-Aug.

Pharmacy: Down the hill from the church and around the corner to the left (☎02 98 48 81 59). Open M-Sa 9am-12:30pm and 5-7pm, Su 9am-12:30pm.

Post Office: To the left of the church and 30m downhill, across from the 8 à Huit (☎02 98 48 81 77). **Currency exchange** available. Open M and F 9am-noon and 2-5pm, Tu-Th 9am-noon and 2-4:30pm, Sa 9am-noon. **Postal Code:** 29242.

▚ ▚ ACCOMMODATIONS AND CAMPING

Auberge de Jeunesse d'Ouessant (☎02 98 48 84 53; ajouessant@club-internet.fr), 5min. from the *centre-ville.* Take the stairs to the right of the SPAR supermarket across from the church and turn right on the 1st road (not at the top of the stairs). Follow the road as it bears left; the hostel is ahead on the right. 43 beds, a communal kitchen, and a dining area. Breakfast included. Linen €4.10, students and under 26 €3.70. Reception 8am-noon; phone ahead for late arrival. Dorms €17, students and under 26 €15; *demi-pension* €29/26; *pension complète* €41/37; singles €30. ❶

Le Fromveur (☎02 98 48 81 30; fax 48 85 97), in the *centre-ville.* Pastel rooms with TVs, showers, and toilets. TV and exercise room. Popular restaurant downstairs serves the local catch of the day (*menus* €13-32). Breakfast included. Reception 8:30am-10pm. Open from Feb. to mid-Nov. Singles and doubles €40-56; quads €90-98. MC/V. ❸

Camping Municipal (☎02 98 48 84 65), 2km from the port along the main road. Campground is on the left 300m before the church in Lampaul. The bus from the port stops here; ask the driver. A low stone wall separates the campground from the countryside's rolling hills. Showers €1.65. Laundry €5.80. Reception July-Aug. 7am-11pm; Sept. and Apr.-June 9am-noon; hours vary, so call ahead. Night guard 11pm-7am. Open Apr.-Sept. €2.90 per person, under 7 €1.30; €2.90 per tent. Cash only. ❶

▚ FOOD

A **SPAR** supermarket is next to the tourist office (open M-Sa 8:30am-7:30pm, Su 9am-12:30pm), and a **8 à Huit** supermarket lies just downhill. (Open July-Aug. M-Sa 8:30am-7:30pm, Su 9:30am-12:30pm; Sept.-June M and W-Sa 8:30am-7:30pm, Tu and Su 9:30am-12:30pm.) There is also a local grocery store, **Le Marché des Îles,** on the road to the *bourg,* 50m before the campground. (Open M-Sa 8:30am-8pm, Su 9am-1pm and 5-7pm.)

▨ **Crêperie Ti A Dreuz** (☎02 98 48 83 01), just past the 8 à Huit on the left. Filling *galettes* and *crêpes* (€1.60-7.10), including some vegetarian options. Try their specialty, the Ouessantine (€6.70), filled with potatoes, cream, Emmental cheese, and savory *silzig* (Ouessant sausage). 2 sunny rooms with traditional decorations look over a garden. Open July-Aug. daily 11:30am-3:30pm and 7-11pm; Sept. and Apr.-June daily noon-2pm and 7-9pm; Oct.-Mar. Tu-Su noon-2pm and 7-9pm. MC/V. ❶

Ty Korn (☎02 98 48 87 33), across from the church in Lampaul. Marine delights in a small room decorated like a ship deck. Fish and meat *plats* €15-20. *Formules* €13-18. Dinner *menu* €29. Open Tu-Sa noon-1:30pm and 7:30-9:30pm, Su 12:15-1:30pm. MC/V. ❸

THE LOCAL STORY

LIGHTHOUSES ON THE ROCKS

On the edge of the westernmost point in France—Île d'Ouessant—stands the Creac'h lighthouse. Despite its imposing beauty, the lighthouse has fallen out of use and is closed to the public due to the dangers of structural rot.

Lighthouses have long been a symbol of France's *patrimoine* (heritage). It was, after all, Frenchman Augustin-Jean Fresnel who invented the crystal lens as a substitute for mirrors in lighthouses. But the stately structures are disintegrating from both harsh weather and disuse. With the advent of GPS, the formerly vital role of lighthouses has drastically diminished. While French law still requires lighthouses and beacons to shine a light visible 30 mi. out to sea, there is no statute that will save the old, beautiful ones.

France still has a Department of Lighthouses and Signals in its Ministry of Infrastructure, whose leaders are pushing to save some of the 150 distinctive lighthouses in the country. The state, however, perceives the structures to be traffic signals rather than cultural or architectural jewels.

Tourism is a beacon of light in the preservation of many deteriorating lighthouses as sightseers continue to help generate necessary maintenance funds.

SIGHTS AND FESTIVALS

In August, Ouessant hosts the **Salon International du Livre Insulaire** (☎06 81 51 12 87; www.livre-insulaire.fr), a literary conference with an island theme. Off the main road leading to the Pointe de Pern, side roads lead to Ouessant's two museums. A joint ticket allows entry to both (€7, ages 8-14 €4.30).

ECOMUSÉE AND MAISON DU NIOU. The island's culture and history museum displays a collection of local artifacts in a traditional, mid-19th-century *ouessantine* home. *(1km northwest of Lampaul. ☎02 98 48 86 37. Open daily Apr.-Sept. 10:30am-6:30pm; Oct. and Jan. 1:30-5pm; Nov.-Dec. 1:30-4pm; from Feb. to mid-Mar. 10:30am-5:30pm; from mid-Mar. to Apr. 1:30-5:30pm. Printed guide in English available. Weekly tours in French in the summer. €3.50, ages 8-14 €2.20. Tours €0.90.)*

MUSÉE DES PHARES ET BALISES. Housed in the **Phare du Créac'h**, reputedly Europe's most powerful lighthouse, this museum explores the history of maritime signaling. Models illustrate the evolution of lighthouses, but the most impressive artifacts are giant lighthouse lenses that send flashing signals across the museum's interior. Behind the museum, pinnacles of stone stand against the crashing waves. A few wet paths that wind down towards the ocean offer a breathtaking seascape. *(☎02 98 48 80 70. Open daily Apr.-Sept. 10:30am-6:30pm; Oct., Jan., Mar. 1:30-5:30pm; from Nov. to mid-Dec. 1:30-5pm; Feb. 10:30am-6pm. Last entry 30min. before close. Weekly guided tours in French. €4.30, ages 8-14 €2.80. Tours €1.20.)*

OUTDOOR ACTIVITIES

Biking is forbidden on footpaths and along the coast. Cyclists should stick to the relatively flat roads that lead to all major sights. The tourist office's booklet of coastline hiking paths (€2.50) is helpful and includes details of all of the ruins and rocks along each of the four 1-3hr. coastline routes. If you only have time to choose one path, take the 12km (3hr.) northwest trail or the paved road (45min.) to the **Pointe de Pern.** Curious rock formations march into the sea toward a lighthouse standing alone in the water.

QUIMPER   ☎02 98

The quintessential Breton city, Quimper (kam-pehr; pop. 63,000) is filled with local tradition, from its hand-painted *faïence* (earthenware) to its 13th-century cathedral. Ubiquitous placards (in Breton and in French) mark sights of historical

Quimper

ACCOMMODATIONS
Camping Municipal, **6**
Auberge Jeunesse
de Quimper (HI), **5**
Hôtel le Derby, **7**

FOOD
C.com, **3**

Gandhi, **4**
Le Saint Co., **2**

NIGHTLIFE
Café XXI, **1**
An Pointín Still, **8**
St-Andrew's Pub, **9**

interest, making a stroll along the flower-lined footbridges over the Odet River both charming and enlightening. Quimper renews its strong connection with Breton culture each year in August at the weeklong Festival de Cornouaille, when the town explodes in celebration—complete with traditional garb, concerts, and dancing in the large town square.

TRANSPORTATION

Trains: Pl. Louis Armand, off av. de la Gare. Open M 4am-12:20am, Tu-Th 5am-12:20am, F 5am-1:20am, Sa 6am-12:20am, Su 7:10am-1am. To: **Nantes** (2hr.; M-F 6 per day, Sa-Su 4 per day; €32); **Paris** (4hr., 5 TGV per day, €73); **Quiberon** (2hr., 4 per day, €19) via **Auray**; **Rennes** (2hr., 14 per day, €31).

Buses: Next to the train station (☎02 98 90 88 89; www.viaoo29.fr). Open July-Aug. M-Sa 7am-7:15pm, Su 10:30am-3pm; Sept.-June M-Sa 7am-7:15pm, Su 4:45-7:45pm. To **Brest** (1hr.; M-Sa 4-6 per day, Su 2 per day; €6, under 26 €3), **Pont-Aven** (1hr.; M-Sa 4-7 per day, Su 2-3 per day; €2, under 26 €1.50), and **Roscoff** (2hr.; July-Aug. 1 per day; €2, under 26 €1.50).

Public Transportation: QUB (Quartabus), 2 quai Odet (☎02 98 95 26 27), across the river from pl. de la Résistance. Office has schedules and a map of the bus lines; extensive roadwork has altered some routes. Open M-F 9am-12:15pm and 1:30-6:30pm, Sa

9am-noon and 1:30-5:30pm. Buses run M-Sa 6:15am-8:30pm, Su 1:30-8pm (3 lines only). Fewer buses July-Aug. Tickets €1, carnet of 10 €9.20; day pass €3.

Taxis: Radio-Taxi Quimperois (☎02 98 90 21 21), at the train station.

Car Rental: Avis (☎02 98 90 31 34), next to the train station. Open M-Th 8am-noon and 2-7pm, F 8am-noon and 1:30-7pm, Sa 8am-noon and 1-6pm, Su 1:30-6pm. **Hertz,** 19 av. de la Gare (☎02 98 53 12 34), across the street from the train station. Open M-F 8am-noon and 2-7pm, Sa 8am-noon and 2-6pm.

Bike Rental: Torch VTT, 58 rue de la Providence (☎02 98 53 84 41). €15 per day, €70 per week; €300-500 deposit. Reserve at least 1 day ahead. Open Tu-F 9:30am-12:30pm and 2:30-7pm, Sa 9:30am-12:30pm and 2:30-6:30pm. MC/V.

◼➐ ORIENTATION AND PRACTICAL INFORMATION

In the heart of the Cornouaille region, Quimper is separated from the sea by miles of rich farmland. To reach the *centre-ville* from the train station, turn right onto av. de la Gare, bearing left as the road forks, and continue onto bd. Dupleix. With the river on your right, follow it to pl. de la Résistance (10-15min.). The *vieille ville* is across the river to the right.

Tourist Office: 7 rue de la Déesse (☎02 98 53 04 05; www.quimper-tourisme.com), pl. de la Résistance, at the back of the parking lot. Multilingual staff provides hotel booking service and free map; larger, more detailed map €1. Ask about the **Pass Quimper** (€10). Open July-Aug. M-Sa 9am-7pm, Su 10am-1pm and 3-6pm; Sept. and June M-Sa 9:30am-12:30pm and 1:30-6:30pm, Su 10am-1pm; Oct.-Mar. M-Sa 9:30am-12:30pm and 1:30-6pm; Apr.-May M-Sa 9:30am-12:30pm and 1:30-6:30pm.

Tours: Available from tourist office. 1hr. city tour in French, in English for groups only by reservation. €5.20, students and under 26 €2.60. Call for schedule.

Bank: BNP Paribus, 26 rue du Parc. Open Tu-F 8:30am-12:15pm and 1:45-5:45pm, Sa 8:50am-12:30pm.

English-Language Bookstore: Librairie de Mousterlin, 19 rue du Frout (☎02 98 64 37 94; www.librarie-de-mousterlin.fr). Small English section; mostly classics. Open July-Aug. M-Sa 9:30am-7pm; Sept.-June M 3-7pm, Tu-Sa 10:30am-7pm.

Laundromats: Point Laverie, 47 rue de Pont l'Abbé, 5min. from the hostel. Wash €3.40-7, dry €0.80 per 10min. Open daily 8am-10pm. **Laverie de la Gare,** 6 av. de la Gare. Wash €4-7.20, dry €0.50 per 6min. Open daily Apr.-Oct. 8am-9pm; Nov.-Mar. 8am-8pm. **Lavomatique,** 9 rue de Locronan. Wash €3.50-7.20, dry €1 per 10min. Open daily 7am-9pm.

Public Toilets: At the tourist office (free), les Halles (€0.20), and the bus station (€0.50).

Police: 3 rue Théodore Le Hars (☎02 98 65 60 00).

Pharmacy: 24 pl. St-Corentin (☎02 98 95 00 20), across from the cathedral. Open M-Sa 8:45am-7:30pm.

Hospital: Hôpital de Cornouaille, 14 av. Yves Thépot (☎02 98 52 60 60).

Internet Access: Available at **C.com** (see **Food,** opposite page).

Post Office: 37 bd. de l'Amiral de Kerguélen (☎02 98 64 28 25). **Currency exchange** available. Open M-F 8am-6:30pm, Sa 8am-noon. Branches on chemin des Justices and on the corner of rue Falkirk. Open M 1:30-5:30pm, Tu 9-11:45am and 1:45-5:30pm, W-F 9am-12:45pm and 1:30-5:30pm, Sa 9am-noon. **Postal Code:** 29000.

◼➐ ACCOMMODATIONS AND CAMPING

The tourist office has info on local *chambres d'hôte.* For July and August, make reservations as early as possible—especially for the Festival de Cornouaille.

Auberge de Jeunesse de Quimper (HI), 6 av. des Oiseaux (☎02 98 64 97 97; quimper@fuaj.org). From pl. de la Résistance, cross the river and turn left on quai de l'Odet. Turn right onto rue de Pont-l'Abbé and continue through the roundabout; the hostel is just past Lycée Chaptal on the left (20-25min.). By bus, take #1 (M-F; bus A Su) from pl. de la Résistance (dir.: Kermoysan) to Chaptal (last bus 7:30pm). No-frills hostel with dorm-style furniture and a young, English-speaking staff. Kitchen, dining room, and common room with TV and foosball. Bike garage. Accepts **Pass Bretagne** (p. 246). Breakfast €3.50. Reception July-Aug. 8-11am and 5-8pm; Sept. and Apr.-June 8-11am and 5-8pm; call if arriving later. Lockout 11am-5pm. Code for late entry. Open Apr.-Sept. Dorms €12; singles €14. Cash only. ❶

Hôtel le Derby, 13 av. de la Gare (☎02 98 52 06 91; fax 53 39 04), across from the station. Each modern room has a shower, toilet, and TV. Breakfast €5.60. Free Wi-Fi in downstairs bar. Reception daily 7am-8pm. May-Sept. singles €31; doubles €41; triples €48. Nov.-Apr. singles €28; doubles €38; triples €45. MC/V. ❷

Camping Municipal, 4 av. des Oiseaux (☎02 98 55 61 09; www.mairie-quimper.fr), next to the hostel. Secluded location. Reception June-Sept. M 1-7pm, Tu and Th 8-11am and 3-8pm, W 9am-noon, F 9-11am and 3-8pm, Sa 8am-noon and 3-8pm, Su 9-11am; Oct.-May M-Tu and Th-Sa 9-11am and 2:30-7:30pm. €3.40 per person, under 7 €1.70; €0.80 per tent; €1.70 per car; €1.50 per caravan. Electricity €3. Cash only. ❶

🍴 FOOD

The lively covered market at **Les Halles,** on rue St-François, has bargains on produce, seafood, meats, and cheeses; get there early, as some vendors shut down in the afternoon. (Open daily 9am-7pm.) An open-air market is also held twice a week outside Les Halles (open W and Sa 7am-9pm), while **Kerfeunteun** hosts an organic market. (Open F from 4pm.) There is a **Monoprix** across the river from the tourist office on quai du Steir (open M-Sa 9am-7pm) and a **Shopi** grocery downstairs at 20 rue Astor. (Open M-Sa 8am-8pm, Su 9:30am-12:30pm.) Closer to the hostel, there's a **Proxi** on quai de l'Odet. (Open M-Sa 7:30am-8pm, Su 8:30am-12:30pm; longer hours July-Aug.)

C.com, 9 quai du Port au Vin (☎02 98 95 81 62), across from Les Halles. Delicious smells and young, stylish clientele fill 2 sunlit floors. Delicious muffins €2. Salads €7-7.50. Build-your-own sandwiches from €4. *Plat du jour* €7.90. Internet €1 per 15min., €3 per hr. Free Wi-Fi with purchase. Open M-Sa 8am-7pm. MC/V. ❶

Gandhi, 13 bd. de l'Amiral de Kerguélen (☎02 98 64 29 50), near the train station. Delicious curries and tandoori-grilled meats amid tastefully exotic decor. Vegetarians will find a refreshingly wide selection. *Plats* €8.40-15. Lunch *menu* €8.70-14. Dinner *menu* €19. Open daily noon-2:30pm and 7-10:30pm. MC/V. ❷

Le Saint Co., 20 rue du Frout (☎02 98 95 11 47), around the corner from the cathedral. Tasty salads €10-12. Steak and fish *plats* €10-34. *Menus* €20-26. Open M-F noon-2pm and 7-10pm, Sa noon-2pm and 7-11pm. AmEx/MC/V. ❸

🏛 SIGHTS

The **Passeport Culturel** (available at tourist office; €10) gets you into your choice of four of the following: the Musée des Beaux-Arts, Musée Départemental Breton, Faïenceries de Quimper HB-Henriot, Centre d'Art Contemporain, Musée de la Faïence, and the tourist office city tour.

CATHÉDRALE SAINT-CORENTIN. The twin spires of Cathédrale St-Corentin, built between the 13th and 15th centuries, rise high above the center of the old quarter. The stone figure of legendary *quimperois* king Gradlon the Great on horseback stands between the spires, watching over the city. The

BRITTANY

PRICEY POTTERY

Fine pottery and Quimper have had a long history together. The abundant rich clay deposits of the Odet River are ideal for pottery production, and many fragments of earthenware that date back to 3000 BC have been found throughout the city. In 1690, Jean-Baptiste Bousquet founded the first factory that made *faïence*—a fine, tin-glazed pottery—in the historic district of Locmaria. By the end of the 18th century, there were three separate *faïenceries* in Quimper; by 1968, they had combined into one factory, HB-Henriot.

Faïence does not come cheap. Prices range from €25 for the trademark double-handled bowl to hundreds and thousands of dollars for custom-made pieces. However, each piece is really a unique work of art—shaped, glazed, and painted by hand. Their designs show a strong Breton influence; the classic *"le petit Breton"* dates from the 1870s and features a man in traditional Breton costume. Older Quimper *faïence* is strongly sought after by collectors worldwide. As a testament to the importance of *faïence* production in Quimper, the city has incorporated a floral HB-Henriot design into its official logo.

Beware that many tourist shops and street vendors carry "two-eared" bowls that are neither HB-Henriot nor *faïence*. They carry the hefty price tag, but not the historical or cultural significance.

cathedral's interior is surprisingly bright, with a beautiful pink-tile ceiling; the most curious feature, however, is the floor plan, which features a unique bend in the traditional cross-shaped footprint. *(Open May-Oct. M-Sa 8:30am-noon and 1:30-6:30pm, Su 1:30-6:30pm; Nov.-Apr. M-Sa 9am-noon and 1:30-6pm, Su 1:30-6pm. Mass M-F 9am; Sa 9am and 6:30pm; Su 8:45, 9, 10am, 6:30pm. Detailed guide in English €1.50.)*

MUSÉE DÉPARTEMENTALE BRETON. In the former bishop's palace beside the cathedral, this museum offers exhibits on local history, archaeology, and ethnography. A display of traditional Breton clothing is a highlight. *(1 rue du Roi Gradlon. ☎02 98 95 21 60; www.cg29.fr/culture/mdb.htm. Open June-Sept. daily 9am-6pm; Oct.-May Tu-Sa 9am-noon and 2-5pm, Su 2-5pm. €4, students and ages 18-26 €2.50, under 18 free.)*

FAÏENCERIES DE QUIMPER HB-HENRIOT. This factory is the production site for Quimper's world-renowned hand-painted earthenware. Guided half-hour tours in French and English take visitors inside the workshop to see artisans shaping and painting each piece. The adjoining boutique sells pricey but beautiful finished products. Closed due to lack of funds, the museum hopes to re-open in April 2009. *(Rue Haute. ☎02 98 90 09 36; www.hb-henriot. com. Tours in French and English M-Sa 10:15am-4pm, depending on demand. Brochure available in English. Boutique open M-Sa 9:30am-7pm. €5, ages 8-14 €2.50.)*

MUSÉE DES BEAUX-ARTS. Across from the cathedral, this museum houses Breton-themed paintings as well as other European work. A permanent exhibit remembers *quimperois* poet-painter Max Jacob, a friend of Picasso and victim of the Holocaust. A temporary exhibit for 2009 will feature works by Gauguin. *(40 pl. St-Corentin. ☎02 98 95 45 20; http://musee-beauxarts.quimper.fr. Open July-Aug. daily 10am-7pm; Nov.-Mar. M and W-Sa 10am-noon and 2-6pm, Su 2-6pm; Apr.-June M and W-Su 10am-noon and 2-6pm. Wheelchair-accessible. €4, students and ages 13-26 €2.50.)*

NIGHTLIFE

An Poitín Still, 2 av. de la Libération (☎02 98 90 02 77). The bright red walls and rowdy clientele will make your Coreff (€2.30) taste even better. Beer €2.20-5.40. Wild Irish music performed live F 10pm. Open M-Sa 3pm-1am, Su 5pm-1am. AmEx/MC/V.

Café XXI, 38 pl. St-Corentin (☎02 98 95 92 34), across from the cathedral, next to Musée des Beaux-Arts. Metallic bar creates a glamorous atmosphere. Mixed drinks €6-6.50. Lunch (€7-14) served noon-3pm. Open July-Aug. M-Sa 9am-1am; Sept.-June M-Th 9am-9pm, F-Sa 9am-1am. AmEx/MC/V.

St-Andrew's Pub, 11 pl. du Stivel (☎02 98 53 34 49), just across the river from rue de Pont l'Abbé. Old-school comfort, a riverside terrace, and the inviting leather interior provide the perfect setting for a relaxed drink and conversation. Food (€3.20-6.40) served all hours. Beer €2.40-4.70. Whiskey €4.90-7.30. Mixed drinks €7. Open daily 11am-1am. AmEx/MC/V.

FESTIVALS

Festival de Cornouaille (☎02 98 55 53 53; www.festival-cornouaille.com), 3rd week in July. Weeklong summer gala fills the town with lively Breton music, dancing, and costume. 3000 performers march the length of the city in the grand parade on the final Su, when the queen of Cornouaille is crowned. Schedule and prices vary. Tickets (€6-20) required for some performances.

Semaines Musicales (☎02 98 95 32 43; www.semaines-musicales-quimper.org), from early to mid-Aug. Orchestras and choirs perform in the Théâtre de Cornouaille, the cathedral, and smaller churches in town. Every year, the festival pays homage to a different selection of famous composers and musicians. €21-23, ages 12-25 €6.

DAYTRIPS FROM QUIMPER

PONT-AVEN

Pont-Aven and Quimper are connected by Penn-ar-Bed buses (☎02 98 90 88 89; www. viaoo29.fr). Line #14A, dir.: Quimper-Quimperlé; 1½hr.; 2-9 per day; €2, under 26 €1.50.

Fed up with Impressionism, Paul Gauguin triggered a new artistic movement that emphasized pure color and simplified figures while rejecting perspective. His inspiration was Pont-Aven (pohnt-ah-vahn). Today, this small Breton town remains a vibrant artists' colony, with galleries on nearly every street. *Biscuiteries* that sell the town's famous *galettes*, *madeleines*, and *palets* (various types of butter cookies) are almost as prevalent. To watch the cooks at work, visit **Biscuiterie de Pont-Aven,** 8 rue du Général de Gaulle, where an open window is all that separates the baking studio from the shop. (☎02 98 09 14 20. Open daily July-Aug. 9am-7:30pm; Sept.-June 9:30am-12:30pm and 2:30-6:30pm.)

For a refreshing break from civilization, venture into Pont-Aven's tranquil natural surroundings. A free map at the tourist office details a number of hikes passing by spots that inspired Gauguin and others. From the *centre-ville*, cross the bridge and take two quick rights to the **Promenade Xavier Grall,** a series of bridges bordered by greenery and gracefully drooping trees that hover over the swift Aven River. Farther upstream is the **Chaos de Pont-Aven,** a cluster of flat boulders around which the river swirls. A pleasant stroll amid thriving farmland and tree-lined avenues leads to the **Chapelle de Trémalo.** (Open daily July-Aug. 10am-6:30pm; Sept.-June 10am-5:30pm.) The 16th-century Gothic church is an isolated retreat and houses the 17th-century wood painted crucifix that inspired Gauguin's *Le Christ Jaune*. After seeing the environs, view the paintings they incited at the **Musée de Pont-Aven,** pl. de l'Hôtel de Ville, up the street to the left when facing the tourist office. The museum showcases a collection of works by Gauguin, Sérusier, and other adherents of the Pont-Aven school as well as temporary exhibits of regional work. June through September 2009 will bring a collection of Maurice Denis's work to the museum. A 12min. film in French, shown every 45min., is a good introduction to the artistic movements fostered in Pont-Aven. (☎02 98 06 14 43; musee.pont-aven@wanadoo.fr. Open daily July-Aug. 10am-7pm; Sept.-Oct. and Apr.-June 10am-12:30pm and

2-6:30pm; Nov.-Dec. and Feb.-Mar. 10am-12:30pm and 2-6pm. July-Aug. €6, students €4, under 18 free; Sept.-June €4/2.50/free.)

There are a few cafes and restaurants around the *centre-ville*. There is an **Ecomarché** supermarket (open daily 9am-7pm) up rue Émile Bernard, where the bus from Quimper arrives. The **tourist office**, 5 pl. de l'Hôtel de Ville, a block from the bus stop on pl. Gauguin, offers a free handbook on local art galleries, a practical guide and walking-tour map, a guidebook on Pont-Aven art history (€0.50), and 1hr. **tours** of the town in French. (Easter-Sept. Tu, Th, Sa at 11am. €4.50, ages 12-25 €3.50.) The office also provides information on the **Fleurs d'Ajonc Folk Festival,** which takes place on the first Sunday in August. (☎02 98 06 04 70; www.pontaven.com. Open July-Aug. M-Sa 9:30am-7pm, Su 10am-1pm and 3-6:30pm; Sept.-June M-Sa 10am-12:30pm and 2-6pm, Su 10am-1pm.)

QUIBERON ☎02 97

Though it lacks significant museums and monuments, the small peninsula of Quiberon (kee-buh-rahn; pop. 7221) has more than its fair share of beaches and sunshine. Besides ample opportunities for sunbathing, surfing, kayaking, and sailing, the town also makes a good base for daytrips to the stunningly beautiful Belle-Île-en-Mer and the mysterious menhirs of Carnac.

▉ TRANSPORTATION

Trains: Station open July-Aug. daily 8:35am-6:35pm; Sept.-June M-Sa 9:15am-12:25pm and 2:15-5:30pm. Trains run Apr.-Sept. to **Auray** (45min., 6-10 per day, €2.80); connections serve **Brest, Paris, Quimper,** and **Rennes.**

Buses: TIM (☎08 10 10 10 56; www.morbihan.fr) departs from Quiberon's port and train station. To **Auray** (1hr., €6.30) and **Carnac** (45min., €3.80). Both destinations July-Aug. 1 per day; Sept.-June M-Sa 7-9 per day, Su 1-4 per day.

Taxis: ☎06 07 09 01 27.

Bike Rental: Cyclomar, 47 pl. Hoche (☎02 97 50 26 00). Bikes €8 per ½-day, €11 per day, €45 per week. Scooters €26-35 per ½-day, €38-49 per day. Helmet included. Cash, check, or ID deposit. Open July-Aug. daily 8:30am-11pm; Sept.-June Tu-Sa 8:30am-12:30pm and 2-5pm. Train station annex open July-Aug. daily 8:30am-7:30pm MC/V.

▉ PRACTICAL INFORMATION

Tourist Office: 14 rue de Verdun (☎08 25 13 56 00; www.quiberon.com). From the train station, cross the parking lot and turn left. Walk down rue de la Gare and bear right on rue de Verdun. Staff offers a free city guide with a map and a handbook of walking tours. Open early July M-Sa 9am-1pm and 2-6:30pm, Su 10am-1pm; from mid-July to Aug. M-Sa 9am-1pm and 2-7pm, Su 10am-1pm; Sept.-June M-Sa 9am-1pm and 2-6pm.

Bank: BNP Paribus, pl. de la République, just off rue de Port Maria. Open Tu-F 9am-12:40pm and 1:45-5:50pm.

Laundromat: Rue de Port Maria, near the beach. Wash €4-7, dry €1 per 10min. Open daily 9am-8pm.

Police: 147 rue du Port de Pêche (☎02 97 50 07 39).

Pharmacy: 12 rue de Verdun (☎02 97 50 07 79). Open July-Aug. M-Sa 8:45am-12:45pm and 2-7:45pm; Sept. and Apr.-June M 2-7:30pm, Tu-Sa 9am-12:30pm and 2-7:30pm; Oct.-Mar. M 2-7:30pm, Tu-F 9am-12:30pm and 2-7:30pm, Sa 9am-12:30pm.

Hospital: Centre Hospitalier Bretagne Atlantique (☎02 97 01 41 41), in Auray.

Internet Access: Le Nelson, 20 pl. Hoche (☎02 97 50 31 37), between the beach and the tourist office. Wi-Fi and 1 computer. Free with purchase. Open daily 4pm-2am.

Post Office: Pl. de la Duchesse Anne (☎02 97 50 11 92). **Currency exchange** available. Open from mid-July to Aug. M-F 8:30am-6pm, Sa 8:30am-noon; from Sept. to mid-July M-F 8:30am-12:30pm and 2-5:30pm, Sa 8:30am-noon. **Postal Code:** 56170.

ACCOMMODATIONS AND CAMPING

Auberge de Jeunesse "Les Filets Bleus" (HI), 45 rue du Roch Priol (☎02 97 50 15 54), close to the *centre-ville* and beach. From the station, cross the parking lot and turn left onto rue de la Gare. Turn left onto rue de Port Haliguen at the church, right at the roundabout onto bd. Anatole France, and left onto rue du Roch Priol (15min.). 3 rustic 4- to 6-bed rooms open onto an outdoor picnic area. Camping and spots in a communal tent also available. Accepts **Pass Bretagne** (p. 246). Kitchen. Breakfast €3.50. Reception July-Aug. M-Sa 9am-noon and 6-9pm, Su 6-9pm; Sept. and Apr.-June M-Sa 9am-noon and 6-8pm. Reserve ahead July-Aug. Open Apr.-Sept. Camping €6.10 per person. Cots in communal tent €7.70; dorms €11. ❶

Hôtel de l'Océan, 7 quai de l'Océan (☎02 97 50 07 58; www.hotel-de-locean.com). Waterfront location. Well-furnished rooms, some facing the harbor. Sunny bar with wicker chairs and *quai*-side views great for people-watching. Breakfast €7. Wi-Fi in bar €5 per hr. Reception 8am-9pm. Open from mid-Apr. to mid-Nov. Singles from €38; doubles €50-80; quads €110. Extra bed €12. AmEx/MC/V. ❹

Camping Bois d'Amour, rue St-Clément (☎02 97 50 13 52; fax 50 42 67), just off plage du Goviro. Well-tended site has a heated pool, bar, restaurant, and TV room. Staff organizes daily events like karaoke. Laundry (wash €5, dry €3). **Cyclomar** has bikes to rent on-site. Reception daily July-Aug. 9am-noon and 2-8pm; Sept.-June 9am-12:15pm and 3-6:30pm. Gates closed 11pm-7am. Open Apr.-Sept. €3-9 per person, under 10 €2-5; €6-17 per tent or caravan with car. Electricity €5. MC/V. ❶

FOOD

The traditional Quiberon cure for a sweet tooth is the lollipop-like *niniche*, available by the beach. For groceries, there's a **Marché Plus,** 2 rue de Verdun. (Open M-Sa 7am-9pm, Su 9am-1pm.) Produce markets appear on **place du Varquez,** behind the town hall (open Sa 6:30am-1pm), and on **rue de Port Haliguen** (open from mid-June to mid-Sept. W 6:30am-1pm).

La Paillote, 30 rue de Verdun (☎02 97 29 51 32). Jungle-themed eatery with bamboo-backed chairs and stuffed tigers. Pizzas fresh from the wood-fire oven. La N'Importe Quoi (The Whatever; €10) is stacked with whatever toppings the chef is in the mood to add. Pizza €6-12. Open May-Nov. daily noon-2pm and 7-10pm; Oct.-Apr. M-Tu and Th-Su noon-2pm and 7-10pm. Hours vary. MC/V over €15. ❷

La Criée, 11 quai de l'Océan (☎02 97 30 53 09). Fresh catches from the connected fish market. *Plateau gargantua* (€50)—an awesome array of oysters, crab, and other sea creatures—generously serves 2. *Menu* €21. Open Tu-Sa from 12:15pm for lunch and from 7:15pm for dinner, Su from 12:15 for lunch. MC/V. ❹

Aux Armes de Bretagne, 54 rue de Port Haliguen (☎02 97 50 01 20). Over 240 different *crêpes* (€2.50-8.50) and *galettes* (€2.50-12). Open Apr.-Sept. Tu noon-1:30pm, W-Su noon-1:30pm and 7-9pm. MC/V. ❶

NIGHTLIFE AND FESTIVALS

In early April, the **Semaine Océane** takes the town by storm with dance, music, and plays along the waterfront; ask at the tourist office for more info.

BRITTANY

Barantyno's, 4 pl. Hoche (☎02 97 50 18 87). Try the house special, the Mojito Royale (€8), made with champagne. Beer €2.50-5. Mixed drinks €4.50-8. Monthly theme nights. Open Apr.-Nov. daily 1:30pm-2am; Nov.-Mar. W-Su 1:30pm-2am. MC/V.

Hacienda Café, 4 rue du Phare (☎02 97 30 51 76), off pl. Hoche. Black lights and disco lights illuminate the dance floor filled with young *quiberonnais*. Beer €3-5. Mixed drinks €7. Open May-Sept. daily 10pm-4am; Oct.-Apr. F-Sa 10pm-4am. Cash only.

Le Suroît, 29 rue de Port Maria. Attracts an older crowd. Beer €5. Mixed drinks €10. Open July-Aug. daily 11:30pm-5am; Sept.-June F-Sa 11:30pm-5am. AmEx/MC/V.

■ BEACHES

Heed signs marked "Baignades Interdites" (Swimming Forbidden)—rip tides are particularly dangerous in these waters. Green flags mean safe supervised swimming; orange/yellow means dangerous swimming; red means swimming prohibited. The aptly named ■**Côte Sauvage** stretches a wild, windy 10km along the western edge of Quiberon. The views from the road are amazing, but coastal footpaths give you an even better look at the waves and jagged rocks—be careful in the slippery tidal zone. Make the trip at low tide to witness the coastal rocks and formations at their finest. For a safe beach day near the *centre-ville,* follow sun-worshipping tourists, frolicking families, and carefree teenagers to **Grande Plage.** Smaller beaches on the east side of the peninsula offer more tranquil spots for sunbathing.

▶ DAYTRIPS FROM QUIBERON

BELLE-ÎLE-EN-MER

SMN, in Quiberon, sends ferries to Belle-Île (45min.) from the gare maritime of Port Maria (☎08 20 05 60 00; www.smn-navigation.fr). 5-13 per day; round-trip €26-27, under 25 €16, seniors €20-22. Bikes €16. Renting a car or taking the bus shuttles are the easiest ways to get around. Taol Mor Buses run from Le Palais to Belle-Île's other main towns 4-7 times per day: Bangor (30min.), Locmaria (25min.), and Sauzon (20min.). Tickets are available on the bus or at Point Taol Mor, quai Bonelle, in Le Palais (☎02 97 31 32 32). €2.50, ages 4-12 €1.70; 2-day pass €11/7.

This island's name—Beautiful Isle in the Sea—is a simple statement of fact. With its unique rock formations, crashing seas, and fields of green and gold, Belle-Île-en-Mer (bel-eel-ahn-mare) is naturally breathtaking. A few scattered menhirs date man's presence on the island back to prehistoric times; since then, monks, sailors, pirates, and German POWs have all been temporary residents. Although the island is a convenient daytrip from Quiberon, it is quite large (20km long) and can warrant an overnight stay.

The island's best-known wonders are the ■**Aiguilles de Port Coton,** pinnacles of stone memorialized by Monet in several paintings. Around their bases, the water foams against the rocks; the port owes its name to these waves, which are whipped by the winds to be as fluffy as cotton. Ferries from Quiberon dock in **Le Palais,** the island's biggest town, under the shadow of the massive **Citadelle Vauban.** Built in 1549 by Henri II and expanded under Louis XIV, the fortress was only captured twice—by the English during the Seven Years' War and by the Germans in WWII. Today, its walls protect a museum of memorabilia from Belle-Île's celebrity visitors and residents, including Sarah Bernhardt and Claude Monet. Don't miss the great view of the port and the ocean from the ramparts. The **arsenal,** a large rectangular building, often hosts concerts and temporary exhibits; its top floor showcases nautical artifacts. (☎02 97 31 84 17. Citadel open daily July-Aug. 9am-7pm; Sept.-Oct. and Apr.-June 9:30am-6pm;

Nov.-Mar. 9:30am-noon and 2-5pm. Tours in French July-Aug. M-F 3 per day, Su 1 per day. €6.50, ages 7-16 €3.50, under 7 free. Tours €8/5/free.)

Belle-Île's natural treasures lie scattered along the coast. **Plage de Donnant**, on the windy western coast, is the most popular beach. Equally gorgeous is the secluded **plage Port Maria**—by the town of Locmaria on the southeastern shore—and the much larger powder-white **plage Grands Sables**, the longest beach on the island, southeast of Le Palais. Head 6km northwest from Le Palais to the postcard-worthy portside town of **Sauzon**. Pastel-hued houses line the port, facing rock cliffs on the other side. Across the island, waves crash inside the **Grotte de l'Apothicairerie**, surrounded by cliffs on three sides. While access to the grotto is currently restricted, the site still offers a spectacular panorama of the rocky coastline; just be careful to stay well back from the unguarded cliff edges. From late July to mid-August, **Lyrique-en-Mer** brings classical concerts and opera to the island. (☎02 97 31 59 59; www.belle-ile.net. Tickets €8-50 for operas, €5-10 for concerts. Master classes free. Buy tickets online.)

There is a **Super U** supermarket in Le Palais. (Open M-Sa 8am-1pm and 3:30-7:30pm, Su 8am-1pm.) Several companies in Le Palais offer **bike** rental, including Cyclotour, quai Bonnelle, near the tourist office. (☎02 97 31 80 68. Bikes €8 per ½-day, €10 per day; check, ID, or passport deposit. Open daily July-Aug. 8:30am-7pm; Sept.-Oct. and Mar.-June 9am-noon and 2-7pm.) The Palais **tourist office,** quai Bonnelle, is on the dock's left end. The staff offers a guide to the island, which includes info on sailing and kayaking, and a helpful map (both free). Hiking and biking guides (€7 each, €10 for both) in French are also available. (☎02 97 31 81 93; www.belle-ile.com. Open July-Aug. M-Sa 8:45am-7:30pm, Su 8:45am-1pm; Sept. and Apr.-June M-Sa 9am-12:30pm and 2-6pm, Su 10am-12:30pm; Oct.-Mar. M-Sa 9am-12:30pm and 2-6pm.)

CARNAC

TIM buses (☎08 10 10 10 56; www.morbihan.fr) run Sept.-June from Quiberon to Carnac 7 times per day (45min., €3.80); July-Aug., the bus runs only once per day, making it easier to take the train from Quiberon to Plouharnel-Carnac (30min.; 6-10 per day; €2.80, round-trip €5) and then bus #1 or 18 from Plouharnel-Carnac to Carnac (7min., 12 per day, €2). 2 bus stops serve Carnac's 2 tourist offices: Carnac-Ville, in the old centre-ville and closer to the menhirs, and Carnac-Plage, by the main tourist office and the beach. The offices are about a 15min. walk apart; La Carnavettte, a free local shuttle, connects them (5min., every 15min. July-Aug. daily 10am-12:30pm and 1:30-8:30pm).

The fields of ancient megaliths in Carnac (kahr-nak) are the largest and best-preserved prehistoric site of their kind in Europe. These lines of tall stones, erected by Neolithic man between 5000 and 2200 BC, run 4km along the edge of this summer vacation town. Though their original purpose is still unknown, today they make a great break from the beaches as a daytrip from Quiberon.

Carnac holds just under 2800 menhirs (the 18th-century term invented to describe these curious standing stones). The closest to town are the **Alignements du Ménec,** a 2km plot of over 1000 stones up to 4m tall that neatly parallel the adjacent highway. A few hundred meters east, the **Alignements de Kermario** has another 1000 of Carnac's impressive menhir specimens as well as a dolmen (stone-roofed communal tomb). Farther east, a trail off the main road holds **Quadrilatère,** a tight set of rocks arranged in a rectangle, and the **Géant du Manio,** the largest menhir at Carnac. From October to March, visitors are allowed free access to all of Carnac's sites; from April to September, access is allowed only on guided tours to prevent soil erosion. Get **tour** info and tickets at the **Maison des Mégalithes,** route des Alignements, across from the Alignements du Ménec; to get there from the Carnac-Ville tourist office, take a right onto rue St-Cornély in front of the church, another right on rue de Courdiec, and a left

BRITTANY

at the menhirs onto route des Alignements (10min.). Be careful, as there is no sidewalk at some points. Tours begin 2km from the Maison des Mégalithes, so be sure to allow time to walk to the start site and bring sturdy shoes. (☎02 97 52 89 99; http://carnac.monuments-nationaux.fr. Open daily July-Aug. 9am-8pm; Sept.-Apr. 10am-5pm; May-June 9am-7pm. 1hr. tours in French July-Aug. 3-8 per day; Sept. and June 1-2 per day. 1hr. tours in English from mid- to late July W-F at 3pm; from early to mid-Aug. W-F at 11:30am. €4, ages 12-25 €3, under 12 free.) The Maison also has brochures in several languages and a 10min. film in French about the monuments (both free). Behind the tourist office in the town center, the **Musée de Préhistoire,** 10 pl. de la Chapelle, provides good background information for a visit to the megaliths, with informative exhibits on cultural evolution from the Paleolithic Age to the Roman Empire. (☎02 97 52 22 04; www.museedecarnac.com. Open July-Aug. daily 10am-6pm; Sept. and Apr.-June M and W-Su 10am-12:30pm and 2-6pm; Oct.-Mar. M and W-Su 10am-12:30pm and 2-5pm. 1hr. guided tours of museum in French July-Aug. daily at 11am and 3pm. Wheelchair-accessible. Written guides available in 6 languages. €5, ages 6-18 €2.50. Tours €2.50/1.70.) To return to modern times, head to the **beach;** from the tourist office in the historic center, take av. de la Poste, which becomes av. de l'Atlantique, and follow signs to the *plages* (15min.).

The Carnac-Plage (74 av. des Druides) and Carnac-Ville (pl. de l'Église Carnac-Ville) **tourist offices** offer a free visitor's guide and a free map of the town. (☎02 97 52 13 52; www.ot-carnac.fr. Carnac-Plage open July-Aug. M-Sa 9am-7pm, Su 3pm-7pm; Sept.-June M-Sa 9am-noon and 2-6:30pm. Carnac-Ville open July-Aug. M-Sa 9am-7pm, Su 10am-1pm; Sept. and Apr.-June M-Sa 8:30am-noon and 2-5:30pm.) There are several supermarkets, including a **Proxi,** 15 rue St-Cornély, in the old city center (open July-Aug. M-Sa 8:30am-1:30pm and 4-9pm, Su 8:30am-1pm and 5-9pm; Sept.-June Tu-Sa 8am-1pm and 3-7:30pm, Su 8:30am-1pm and 5-7:30pm), and a **Marché U,** 68 av. des Druides, by the Carnac-Plage tourist office (open M-Sa 8:30am-8pm, Su 8:30am-1pm and 5-8pm).

VANNES

Vannes is connected by TIM buses (☎08 10 10 10 56; www.morbihan.fr) to Quiberon (2hr.; July-Aug. daily 1 per day; Sept.-June M-Sa 7-9 per day, Su 1-4 per day; €9.10) and other local towns. To get to the tourist office and centre-ville from the train station, turn right on av. Favrel et Lincy, then left at the roundabout onto rue Victor Hugo. Take a right onto rue Joseph Le Brix, then a left onto rue Thiers; continue downhill to the tourist office on the right (15min.).

With carefully tended gardens sheltered by medieval ramparts, half-timbered houses overlooking cobblestone streets, and an architecturally eclectic cathedral, Vannes (vahn; pop. 53,800) is as enticing now as it was when the dukes of Brittany chose it as their capital. The city's major attractions can easily be enjoyed in a single day, and regular train service makes it a convenient and relaxing daytrip from Nantes, Quimper, or Rennes.

The city centers on the **Cathédrale Saint-Pierre,** on pl. St-Pierre; the structure's constant reconstructions and renovations since the 12th century have left it an architectural hodgepodge. Its most curious feature is the **Chapelle du Saint-Sacrement,** which juts out of the left side of the building. In July and August, knowledgeable volunteers offer free tours of the cathedral in French; a free brochure available in several languages provides some history. (Open daily 8:30am-7pm except during services. Tours July-Aug. M-F 9am-6pm, Su 1-6pm.) Across from the cathedral is **La Cohue,** pl. St-Pierre; formerly the town's covered market and courtroom, it is now home to the **Musée des Beaux-Arts.** The small permanent collection includes Romantic and Impressionist depictions of Brittany. However, the temporary exhibitions that fill more than half of the museum's space are the main attraction. (☎02 97 01 63 01. Open daily from mid-June to Sept. 10am-6pm; from Oct. to mid-June 1:30-6pm. €6, students €4, under 18 free.) The nearby **Château Gaillard**, rue Noé, showcases anthropological artifacts and temporary exhibits. Hidden away at the back of the second floor is the museum's real treasure: the **Cabinet des Pères du Désert**, a 17th-century wood-paneled room covered with paintings of famous hermits. A single ticket, valid for several months, allows admission to both museums. (☎02 97 01 63 00. Open daily from mid-June to Sept. 10am-6pm; from mid-May to mid-June 1:30-6pm.) Don't miss the comical **Vannes et Sa Femme** (Vannes and His Wife) across from the entrance to the château; the medieval carved wood figures, hanging from a half-timbered house, are an unofficial emblem of the city. Exit the city walls by the 17th-century Porte St-Vincent and turn left to visit the **Jardins des Remparts**. With the medieval ramparts and turrets in the background, these neatly arranged flower gardens by the Marle River make the perfect place for a picnic. Behind the gardens and up the hill lies a larger park, the **Jardin de la Garenne,** with a monument to Vannes residents who died in battle. Every year, Vannes chooses a different period of its history to celebrate during the **Fêtes Historiques,** held on the weekend nearest July 14. The small city comes alive with free street performances, concerts, and historical reenactments.

There's a **Monoprix** on pl. Joseph Le Brix. (Open M-Sa 8:30am-7:50pm.) The **tourist office**, 1 rue Thiers, offers a reservations service (€1) and a city guide, which includes a walking tour of the *centre-ville*. (☎08 25 13 56 10; www.tourisme-vannes.com. **Internet** €3 per 30min., €5 per hr. Open July-Aug. M-Sa 9am-7pm, Su 10am-6pm; Sept.-June M-Sa 9:30am-12:30pm and 1:30-6pm.) Other services include **police,** 2 pl. de la Libération (☎02 97 54 75 00), and a **hospital,** rue du Docteur Joseph Audic-Le Tenenio (☎02 97 62 56 56).

NANTES   ☎02 40

Welcome to Nantes (nahnt; pop 280,000), city of chatty cafes, bohemian night-club revelry, and stylish recuperation among manicured gardens. Climb up to the château for a panoramic view of the city's expansive boulevards. France's sixth-largest city is more than just sights: between visits to the cutting-edge art museum and impeccably restored cathedral, curious travelers will uncover countless treasures hidden along winding sidestreets.

▊ TRANSPORTATION

Flights: Aéroport Nantes Atlantique (☎02 40 84 80 00; www.nantes.aeroport.fr), 10km south of Nantes. **Air France** (☎08 20 32 08 20) flies daily to **Lyon, Marseille, Nice, Paris,** and **London.** TAN (☎08 10 44 44 44; www.tan.fr) **shuttle** runs to the airport from pl. du Commerce and the south side of the train station (25min.; every hr. M-Sa 5:30am-9pm, Su 3:30-9pm; tickets €7, carnet of 4 €16). Schedules available at info desk outside the train station, tourist office, or TAN info booth on pl. du Commerce.

Trains: Gare de Nantes, 27 bd. de Stalingrad. Ticket counters open M-Th 5:30am-9:30pm, F 5:30am-10:30pm, Sa 6am-9:30pm, Su 7am-10pm. **Luggage storage** at north side of station. Open 6:15am-11pm. Backpack €4, larger luggage €6.50-8.50; 3-day max. To: **Angers** (40min.; every 30min. 5am-9pm; €14, TGV €17); **Bordeaux** (4hr., 5 per day, €35-45); **La Rochelle** (1hr., 5 per day, €25); **Paris** (2-4hr., every hr., €54-69); **Rennes** (1hr.; M-F 15 per day, Sa-Su 7 per day; €10-21).

Public Transportation: TAN, 4/6 allée Brancas (☎08 01 44 44 44), on pl. du Commerce. Office open M-Sa 7:30am-7:30pm. Runs **buses** and 3 **tram** lines daily 6am-1:30am. Ticket €1.30, 2-ride ticket €2.30, carnet of 10 €11; day pass €3.40.

Taxis: Allô Taxis Nantes Atlantique (☎02 40 69 22 22), at the train station. 24hr.

Car Rental: A row of agencies near the south exit of the train station includes **Avis** (☎02 40 89 25 50). Open M-F 7am-10:30pm, Sa 8:30am-8:30pm, Su 10:45am-10:15pm. **Europcar** (☎02 40 47 19 38) is down the street. Open M-F 7:45am-10:15pm, Sa 8:30am-12:30pm and 2-6pm, Su 10:30am-12:30pm and 5-8:30pm.

Bike Rental: Check at the tourist office or the NGE office, 18 rue Scribe (☎02 40 02 51 84 94 51) for info on **Ville à Velo,** which rents bikes ("Bicloos") from the city's major parking lots (Graslin, Tour Bretagne, Cité des Congrès, Cathédrale, and Commerce), Île de Versailles, and Camping du Petit Port. €1 per 2hr., €4 per day, €10 per week.

Canoe Rental: Companies on Île de Versailles, including **Contre Courant** (☎06 62 28 60 48). Take tram line #2 (dir.: Orvault Grand Val) to St-Mihiel and cross the bridge to the island. €5 per hr., €14 per day; students €4/11. Open Apr.-Sept. Tu-F 10am-12:30pm and 2-7:30pm, Sa-Su 10am-7:30pm.

✦ 7 ORIENTATION AND PRACTICAL INFORMATION

Nantes's *centre-ville* lies north of **cours Franklin Roosevelt,** a broad avenue running east-west parallel to **place du Commerce,** the city's municipal transportation hub. Cours Franklin Roosevelt passes the château at **place de la Duchesse Anne,** where it becomes **cours John Kennedy** and continues to the train station. The wide **cours des 50 Otages** runs north from pl. du Commerce past the **Tour Bretagne,** a modest skyscraper; a right onto rue de la Barillerie leads to the city's lively pedestrian district around **place du Pilori.**

Tourist Office: 3 cours Olivier de Clisson (☎08 92 46 40 44 or +33 2 72 64 04 79; www.nantes-tourisme.com). Exit the train station at the north end and turn left onto cours John Kennedy. Continue to pl. du Commerce and turn left. Maps and info in English, French, German, and Spanish. 2hr. city **tours** in French with a variety of themes. Open M-W and F-Sa 10am-6pm, Th 10:30am-6pm. Branch at 2 pl. St-Pierre, by the cathedral. City and cathedral tours €9, students €6. Open Tu-W and F-Su 10am-1pm and 2-6pm, Th 10:30am-1pm and 2-6pm.

English-Language Bookstore: Librairie L. Durance, 4 allée d'Orléans (☎02 40 48 09 14; www.librairiedurance.fr). Open M 2-7pm, Tu-Sa 9:30am-7pm. MC/V.

Youth Center: Centre Régional d'Information Jeunesse (CRIJ; ☎02 51 72 94 50; www. infojeunesse-paysdelaloire.fr), on the ground floor of the Tour de Bretagne. Free Internet access (30min. max.). Info on youth discounts, housing, and volunteer and employment opportunities. Open from mid-July to mid-Aug. Tu-Th 10am-5:30pm, F 2-5:30pm; from mid-Aug. to mid-July Tu-Th 10am-6:30pm, F-Sa 2-6:30pm.

Laundromats: 7 rue de l'Hôtel de Ville. Open daily 8:30am-8:30pm. Also at 11 rue Chaussée de la Madeleine. Open M 2:30-8pm, Tu-F 11am-8pm, Sa 3-7pm.

Police: 6 pl. Waldeck-Rousseau (☎02 40 37 21 21). Branch on cours Olivier Clossin, next to the tourist office.

Pharmacy: Pharmacie de la Gare, 2 allée du Commandant Charcot (☎02 40 74 14 04). Open M-F 9am-7:30pm, Sa 9am-1pm.

Hospital: Centre Hospitalier Universitaire, 1 pl. Alexis-Ricordeau (☎02 40 08 33 33; www.chu-nantes.fr).

Internet Access: Free at **CRIJ** (above). **K Point Com,** 15 allée Duguay Trouin (☎02 51 82 27 71), near the tourist office. €0.80 per 15min., €2.50 per hr. Open M-Th and Sa 9:30am-9:30pm, F 9:30am-12:30pm and 2:30-9:30pm, Su noon-9:30pm.

Post Office: Pl. Bretagne (☎02 51 10 57 25). From pl. du Cirque, take the stairs or the elevator at the end of rue de l'Abreuvoir to pl. Bretagne. **Currency exchange** available. Open M-F 8:30am-6:45pm, Sa 8:30am-12:30pm. **Postal Code:** 44000.

BRITTANY

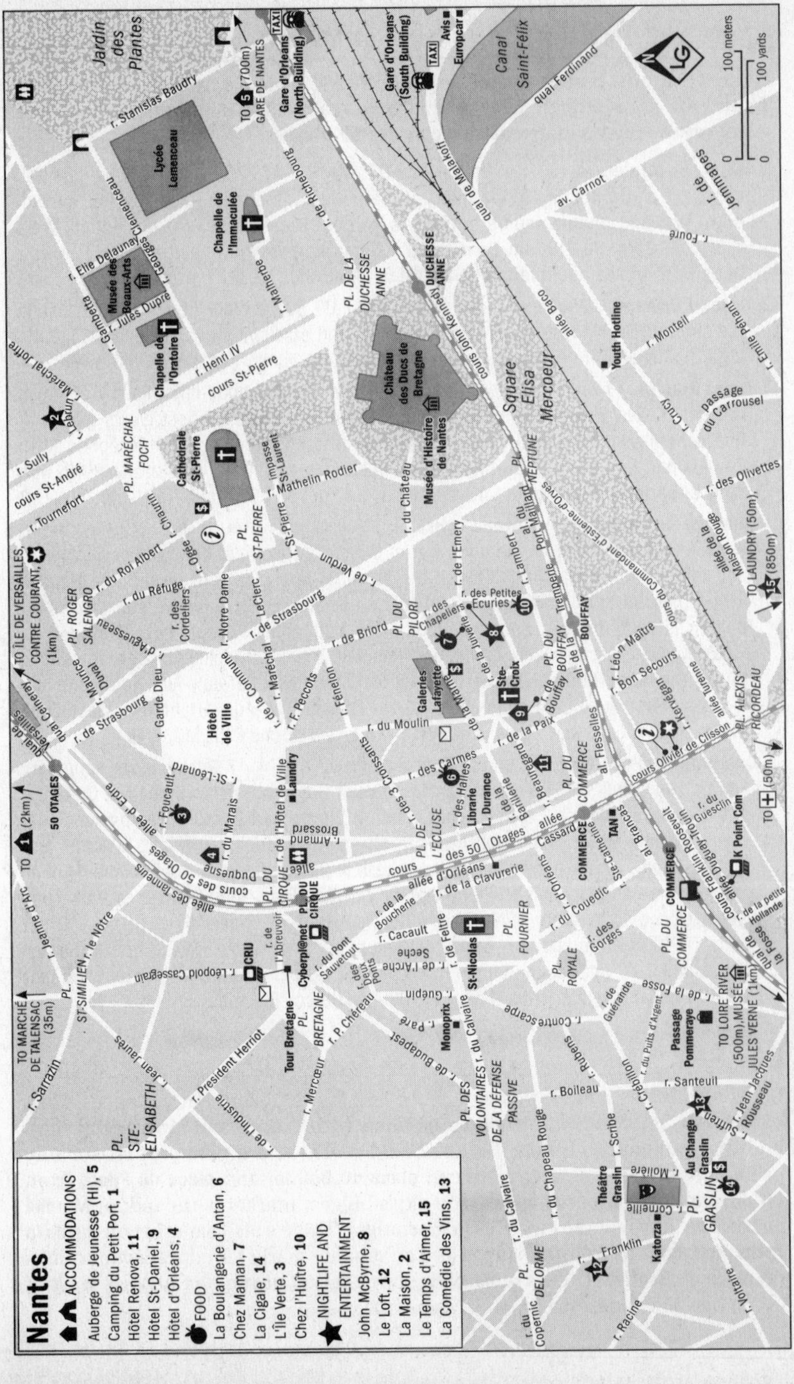
Nantes
ACCOMMODATIONS
Auberge de Jeunesse (HI), 5
Camping du Petit Port, 1
Hôtel Renova, 11
Hôtel St-Daniel, 9
Hôtel d'Orléans, 4
FOOD
La Boulangerie d'Antan, 6
Chez Maman, 7
La Cigale, 14
L'Île Verte, 3
Chez l'Huître, 10
NIGHTLIFE AND ENTERTAINMENT
John McByrne, 8
Le Loft, 12
La Maison, 2
Le Temps d'Aimer, 15
La Comédie des Vins, 13
Jardin des Plantes
Lycée Lemenceau
Musée des Beaux-Arts
Chapelle de l'Oratoire
Chapelle de l'Immaculée
Cathédrale St-Pierre
Château des Ducs de Bretagne
Musée d'Histoire de Nantes
Gare d'Orleans (North Building)
Gare d'Orleans (South Building)
TO 5 (700m) GARE DE NANTES
Canal Saint-Félix
Avis
Europcar
Square Elisa Mercoeur
Youth Hotline
Hôtel de Ville
Galeries Lafayette
Ste-Croix
Librairie L. Durance
Laundry
St-Nicolas
Monoprix
Tour Bretagne
Cyberpl@net
CRIJ
K Point Com
TAN
Passage Pommeraye
Théâtre Graslin
Au Change Graslin
Katorza
TO ÎLE DE VERSAILLES, CONTRE COURANT (1km)
TO 1 (2km)
TO MARCHÉ DE TALENSAC (35m)
TO LOIRE RIVER (500m), MUSÉE JULES VERNE (1km)
TO LAUNDRY (50m), TO 15 (850m)
TO (50m)
PL. MARÉCHAL FOCH
PL. ST-PIERRE
PL. ROGER SALENGRO
PL. DE LA DUCHESSE ANNE
PL. DU PILORI
PL. DU BOUFFAY
PL. NEPTUNE
PL. DU COMMERCE
PL. ALEXIS RICORDEAU
PL. DU CIRQUE
PL. DE L'ECLUSE
PL. FOURNIER
PL. ROYALE
PL. BRETAGNE
PL. ST-SIMILIEN
PL. STE-ELISABETH
PL. DES VOLONTAIRES DE LA DÉFENSE PASSIVE
PL. GRASLIN
PL. DELORME
50 OTAGES
DUCHESSE ANNE
BOUFFAY
COMMERCE
cours des 50 Otages
cours St-Pierre
cours St-André
cours John Kennedy
cours Olivier de Clisson
cours Franklin Roosevelt
quai de Malakoff
quai Ferdinand
quai de Versailles
quai de la Fosse
r. de Strasbourg
r. de Verdun
av. Carnot
r. Henri IV
r. de Jemmapes
r. Crébillon
r. Boileau
r. Santeuil
r. Franklin
r. Voltaire
r. du Calvaire
100 meters
100 yards

BRITTANY

🏠🏕 ACCOMMODATIONS AND CAMPING

Though the most budget-friendly options lie a few blocks from the *centre-ville*, if you look hard enough, a surprisingly agreeable deal might pop up in a side street off the busy squares along **cours des 50 Otages.**

▦ **Hôtel St-Daniel,** 4 rue du Bouffay (☎02 40 47 41 25; www.hotel-saintdaniel. com), off pl. du Bouffay, in the heart of the pedestrian district. Clean rooms, all with bath, TVs, and phones; some overlook a garden. Breakfast €3.50. Reception M-Sa 7:30am-10pm, Su 7:30am-2pm and 7-10pm. Singles and doubles €33-41, with 2 beds €46; triples and quads with bath €51. AmEx/MC/V. ❷

▦ **Hôtel d'Orléans,** 12 rue du Marais (☎02 40 47 69 32), a block from pl. de L'Écluse in the *centre-ville.* Modest rooms have phone, TV, and excellent views. Breakfast €5. Parking €2. Singles €26-37; doubles and triples €42-55; family suites €88. MC/V. ❷

▦ **Hôtel Renova,** 11 rue Beauregard (☎02 40 47 57 03; www.hotel-renova.com), off cours des 50 Otages. Behind a mosaic-adorned facade. Enthusiastic host greets guests at this centrally located hotel. Satellite TV. Breakfast €5. Free Internet. Reception M-Th 7am-10pm, F-Su 7am-11pm. Reserve 1 week ahead. Singles with shower €40, with bath €45; doubles with bath €43-48; triples and quads €55. AmEx/MC/V. ❸

Auberge de Jeunesse "La Manu" (HI), 2 pl. de la Manu (☎02 40 29 29 20; nanteslamanu@fuaj.org). From the north exit of the station, go right down bd. de Stalingrad and left at rue de Manille (15min.); the hostel is in a courtyard on the left. Housed in a former tobacco factory. Industrial feel overshadowed by attentive staff and adorable children in the preschool next door. Clean bathrooms. Accepts **Pass Bretagne** (p. 246). Kitchen, TV room, ping-pong, and foosball. Breakfast included. Luggage storage €1.50. Internet €0.50 per 20min. Wi-Fi €3 per 24hr. Reception July-Aug. 8am-noon and 4-11pm; Sept.-June 8am-noon and 5-11pm. Lockout July-Aug. 10am-4pm; Sept.-June 10am-5pm. Closed last 2 weeks of Dec. 3- to 6-bed dorms €17. MC/V. ❶

Camping du Petit Port, 21 bd. du Petit Port (☎02 40 74 47 94; www.nge-nantes.fr). From pl. du Commerce, take tram #2 (dir.: Orvault Grand Val) to Morrhonnière. Cross the street and walk downhill to the right (15min.). Shaded, well-tended campground with plenty of park space. Reception has info on nearby canoeing, bowling, billiards, and in-line skating. Snack bar, minigolf, and access to the nearby municipal swimming pool. Laundry. Free showers and Wi-Fi. Reception July-Aug. 8am-9pm; Sept.-June 9am-7pm. Gates closed 11pm-7am. June-Sept. €3.50 per person, under 10 €2.30; €4.40 per tent; €6.40 per tent and car; €8.60 per camping-car or caravan; €2.30 per extra car. Oct.-May €2.70 per person; under 10 €1.70; €3.60 per tent; €5.20 per tent and car; €6.80 per camping-car or caravan; €1.90 per extra car. Electricity €3. MC/V. ❶

🍴 FOOD

Local specialties include *poisson au beurre blanc* (fish in butter sauce), Muscadet wine, *muscadines* (chocolates filled with grapes and Muscadet wine), and the trademark Le Petit Beurre cookies. There are plenty of reasonably priced eateries in the area between **place du Bouffay** and **place du Pilori,** from *crêpe* stands to sit-down spots. The city's biggest market is the indoor **Marché de Talensac,** north of the city (Tu-Su mornings). There's also a market on **rue de la Petite Hollande** Saturday mornings and an organic market Wednesday mornings on **place du Bouffay.** There's a **Monoprix** supermarket at rue de Calvaire, west of cours des 50 Otages. (Open M-Sa 9am-9pm.)

Chez l'Huître, 5 rue des Petites Écuries (☎02 51 82 02 02). Inviting bistro offers fresh *huîtres* (oysters; bucket €3.50-14)—slurp them down with the château's towering balconies in view. 3-course *menu* €8-12. Open daily noon-3pm and 6-10pm. MC/V. ❸

La Cigale, 4 pl. Graslin (☎02 51 84 94 94; www.lacigale.com), in an historic monument fashioned in 1895 by *nantais* ceramist Émile Libaudière. Painted ceramic tiles, giant mirrors, and amusing sculptures. Exquisite food with seafood peeled before your eyes. Breakfast €11. *Plats* €10-25. Desserts €6.50-10. Lunch *menus* €14 and €25. Dinner *menus* €19 and €28. Open daily 7:30am-12:30am. AmEx/MC/V. ❸

La Boulangerie d'Antan, 5/7 rue des Carmes (☎02 40 47 59 46). Rustic half-timbered bakery offers sandwiches (€2.45-4), pastries (€1.50-2.50), and tasty, generous quiches (€2.50) to go. Open M-Sa 7am-8pm. AmEx/MC/V over €15. ❶

Chez Maman, 2 rue de la Juiverie (☎02 51 72 20 63). Nearly all the decor—ranging from giant Playmobil® figures to plastic lobsters and a large yellow dinosaur, all illuminated by funky lamps—in this restaurant-antique shop, is for sale. Generous salads. Meat and fish *plats* €13-20. Lunch *menu* €11. Open Tu-Sa noon-2pm and 7-10:30pm. ❷

L'Île Verte, 3 rue Foucault (☎02 40 48 01 26). Combined cafe and bookstore is a vegetarian's dream. Small selection of market-fresh organic salads (€4.20-8.80) and tarts. Takeout available. *Plats* €9.30. Desserts €4.40-5.30. Open Sept.-July M-Tu and Th-Sa 11:45am-2pm. Tea room open 2:30-6:30pm. MC/V over €20. ❷

👁 SIGHTS

 DON'T PASS THIS UP. Consider buying the comprehensive **Pass Nantes,** which offers unlimited rides on public transportation, admission to the château and all the city's museums, a guided tour, and discounts at several stores and recreational activities, such as canoe and bike rental. It's available at the tourist office, airport, youth hostel, and some campgrounds. (€16 for 24hr. access, €27 for 48hr., €32 for 72hr.; under 12 free.)

CHÂTEAU DES DUCS DE BRETAGNE. François II, the last duke of Brittany, built this 15th-century fortress as an imposing ducal residence and a safeguard for the independence of the Breton duchy. It was subsequently used as a prison, an arsenal, and German barracks during WWII. Today, picnickers take advantage of trimmed lawns sunken beside the castle moat, tourists wander the ramparts, and the massive walls guard only the **Musée d'Histoire de Nantes,** whose extensive collection and multimedia exhibits fill 32 rooms. The rooms are themselves historical treasures; many contain elaborate graffiti carved by former prisoners. An interactive virtual balloon tour of the city allows you to travel back in time to 1752 and sail over Nantes to check out several of its neighborhoods. The **Harnachement,** across the château courtyard from the museum, holds excellent temporary exhibits on the history of Brittany. (*4 pl. Marc-Elder.* ☎*08 11 46 46 44; www.château-nantes.fr. Château grounds open daily from mid-May to mid-Sept. 9am-8pm; from mid-Sept. to mid-May 10am-7pm. Guided tours July-Aug. daily; Sept.-June on weekends and occasional weekdays. Free baggage check required. Free admission to grounds. Museum and exhibitions open from mid-May to mid-Sept. daily 9:30am-7pm; from mid-Sept. to mid-May M and W-Su 10am-6pm. Last entry 1hr. before closing. Museum and exhibitions each €5, ages 18-26 €3; both €8/4.80. Audio tours in Breton, English, and French; €3. Tours €4, ages 7-17 €2.40.*)

CATHÉDRALE SAINT-PIERRE. Built between 1434 and 1891, St-Pierre has survived Revolutionary pillagers, WWII bombs, and a 1972 fire. Post-fire restoration gave it a clean, bright interior with soaring Gothic vaults and 20th-century stained glass. Bombs destroyed all but one of the original windows; this lone

NOT YOUR AVERAGE FOUNTAIN

In 2007, Nantes debuted **Estuaire**, a biannual collaboration between international artists that combines installation art in alternative media with a concern for natural phenomena. Estuaire enables artists to exhibit large-scale concepts in a hands-on setting and invites visitors not only to observe art but also to interact with it.

One of the founding exhibits was a project by Danish minimalist sculptor Jeppe Hein that consisted of a bench on the Loire River banks hooked up to a motion detector. When unsuspecting visitors were seated, the sensor would trigger a 20m propulsion of water skyward. With this installation, Hein hoped to make tangible the subtle dialogue between artist and observer. With *Canard de Bain*, artist Florentijn Hofman set up giant rubber duckies on docks along the Loire to signify innocence in a lighthearted attempt to "alleviate global tensions." The ultimate goal of the exhibition is to connect humane efforts with the necessary preservation of earthly resources in a "trail of art."

The next collection of creations will be revealed in early June of 2009. Information and a map of permanent pieces on display since 2007 are available at www. estuaire.info. Info is also available at the Nantes tourist office.

survivor stands in the right transept above the tomb of François II. The tomb itself is an early 16th-century sculpted masterpiece. *(Cathedral open daily Apr.-Oct. 8am-7pm; Nov.-Mar. 8am-6pm. Crypt open Sa 10am-11:30pm and 3-5pm, Su 3-5pm; entry every 30min. Welcome desk open daily 10am-6pm. Free guided visits daily; check at welcome desk for times. Guided visits also provided by tourist office twice weekly in summer. €7, students €4.)*

MUSÉE DES BEAUX-ARTS. Nantes's art museum features a good collection of works by European masters from 13th-century Italian panels to Monet's water lilies. Temporary installations of modern works are housed on the first floor and in the **Chapelle de l'Oratoire,** around the corner from the museum off rue Henri IV. *(10 rue Georges Clemenceau. ☎02 51 17 45 00. Open M, W, F-Su 10am-6pm, Th 10am-8pm. Tours of temporary exhibitions or museum collections July-Aug. W-Th and Su 3pm; Sept.-June W and Su 3pm. Museum €3.50, students €2, under 18 free; after 4:30pm €2; Th 6-8pm and the 1st Su of each month free. Chapelle de l'Oratoire free. Tours €6, students €3.60.)*

OTHER SIGHTS. Outside the *centre-ville* on a hill overlooking the Loire, the small **Musée Jules Verne** honors the science fiction author's life through sketches and artifacts as well as first editions of his novels and posters from the movies they inspired. *(3 rue de l'Hermitage. Take tram #1, dir.: Mitterrand, to Gare Maritime. Cross the tram tracks and take a right at the roundabout onto quai E. Renaud. Bear right and uphill on rue de l'Hermitage; the museum will be on your left. ☎02 40 69 72 52; www.jules-verne.nantes.fr. Open M and W-Sa 10am-noon and 2-6pm, Su 2-6pm. Free tours in French July-Aug. daily 3:30pm; Sept.-June Su 3:30pm. €3, ages 18-26 €1.50, under 18 and 4th Su of month free.)* The **Jardin des Plantes,** across from the train station's north entrance, is a relaxing public garden with fountains and fishponds, many species of trees, and a playground with free lawn chairs. North of the city, the **Île de Versailles** contains a park with Japanese-inspired gardens and a small children's play area. Bridges connect the island to both banks of the Erdre. *(Jardin des Plantes and Île de Versailles open daily from mid-Mar. to mid-Oct. 8:30am-7:45pm; from mid-Oct. to mid-Mar. 11:30am-5:45pm.)*

🎭 🎆 NIGHTLIFE AND FESTIVALS

Nantes plays host to the annual **La Folle Journée,** a classical music festival with short, reasonably priced concerts (☎02 51 88 20 00). Pick up the guide *Aux Heures d'Été* at the tourist office for a listing of summer events from mid-July to mid-August (☎02 51 82 37 70; www.auxheuresete. com). International filmmakers and photographers from Asia, Africa, and South America walk the red carpet at the increasingly popular ■**Festival des Trois Continents** (info ☎02 40 69 74 14) in late November and early December.

Katorza, 3 rue Corneille (☎08 92 68 06 60; www.katorza.fr), shows lesser-known international films in their original language (€9, students €5). Nearby **rue Scribe** is full of late-night bars and cafes. A funky favorite, **quartier Saint-Croix,** near pl. du Bouffay, has bars and cafes on every block. Discos await adventurous travelers farther from the *vieille ville.*

■ **La Maison,** 4 rue Lebrun (☎02 40 37 04 12; www.lamaisonet.com), off rue Maréchal Joffre. Hidden at the back of an alley. Unique decor draws all ages of laid-back hipster. 4 rooms, each furnished like part of a house—from the orange "kitchen" area, complete with dishwasher, to the blue-tiled "bathroom." Free Wi-Fi. Beer €2.50-5.90. Mixed drinks €6. Open daily 3pm-2am. AmEx/MC/V.

John McByrne, 21 rue des Petites Écuries (☎02 40 89 64 46). Irish pub with a festive red-and-green facade and a fittingly jolly crowd. Popular among expats. Packed on weekends; gear up for a noisy drink. Pints €4.60-6. Guinness €6. Irish coffee €6.50. Live Irish music Su 10pm. Open M-Sa 2pm-2am, Su 3pm-2am. AmEx/MC/V.

La Comédie des Vins, 4 rue Suffren (☎02 40 73 11 68). Good-humored bar on a quiet street staffed by wine gurus. Low-key and intimate deck; rustic bar inside heats up at night. Over 40 vintages (€2-4).Open daily noon-midnight. MC/V.

Le Temps d'Aimer, 14 rue Alexandre Fourny (☎02 40 89 48 60; www.letandem.com). Nantes's favorite gay *discothèque.* From the tourist office, take a left on cours Clossin across the river, where it becomes bd. des Martyrs. Take a right onto rue de la Porte Gelée, which becomes rue Fourny. Alternatively, take tram #2 from pl. du Commerce to "Wattignies." Walk up the street toward pl. du Commerce and turn left on rue de la Porte Gelée. Exercise caution in this neighborhood after dark. Beer €7. Liquor €10. Mixed drinks €12. Cover €2; mandatory coat check €2. Open daily midnight-7am.

Le Loft, 9 rue Franklin (☎02 40 48 29 00; www.leloft.net). Multicolored lights, an eclectic mix of dance music, and a crowd that's dressed to impress liven up this chic hot-pink-and-black nightclub. Mixed drinks €6.50. Open W 10pm-4am, Th-Sa 10pm-6am.

NORMANDY
(NORMANDIE)

Normandy's history has always been tied to the sea; as early as AD 911, the Viking raider Rollo sailed in from Norway and established himself as the first duke of Normandy. His descendant William the Bastard confirmed Normandy's naval power when he conquered England in 1066, earning himself a more flattering nickname: William the Conqueror. The English, eager to conquer the closest chunk of France, repeatedly sent their powerful fleets to Normandy during the Hundred Years' War, and in 1431 they captured and burned Joan of Arc in Rouen. By 1450, however, Normandy was safely back in French hands. The English didn't attempt another invasion until June 6, 1944 (better known as D-Day), when they returned—this time in the name of France—with North American allies to liberate Normandy from German control.

Today, Normandy maintains its maritime character and the traces of its tumultuous past with quaint harbors, fresh seafood, and medieval monuments scarred by centuries of warfare. The region is saturated with natural beauty, from breathtaking coastal rock formations and stunning seascapes to rolling countryside dotted with cows. In the larger cities, the atmosphere is livelier; the designer boutiques of Rouen buzz by day, and the clubs of Caen are hopping by night. Take time from the sights to sample Norman culinary specialties— Camembert cheese, fresh seafood, Benedictine *liqueur*, and all things apple.

> **HIGHLIGHTS OF NORMANDY**
>
> **LAND** on the haunting D-Day beaches (p. 313), just as the Allies did in 1944, then visit the Caen Memorial (p. 308), France's best WWII museum.
>
> **IMAGINE** monastic life at the magnificent abbey of Mont-St-Michel (p. 325).
>
> **PEER** over the breathtaking chalk cliffs of Étretat (p. 300).

HAUTE-NORMANDIE

ROUEN

☎ 02 35

Ever since the Viking leader Rollo made it the capital of his new Duchy of Normandy, Rouen (roo-ahn; pop. 450,000)—the "city of a hundred spires"—has been the province's gem. Perhaps best known as the place where Joan of Arc met her fiery end in 1431, Rouen is also famous for its Gothic cathedral, which was immortalized by Monet in his numerous paintings of its facade. Because today's Rouen also houses a hip young population and bustling designer boutiques, it is an attractive stop for both scholarly and fun-loving travelers.

▐ TRANSPORTATION

Trains: Rue Jeanne d'Arc, at pl. Bernard Tissot. Main office open M-Sa 8am-6:30pm; smaller office open M-F 5:30am-10pm, Sa 6:30am-10pm, Su 6:45am-10:30pm;

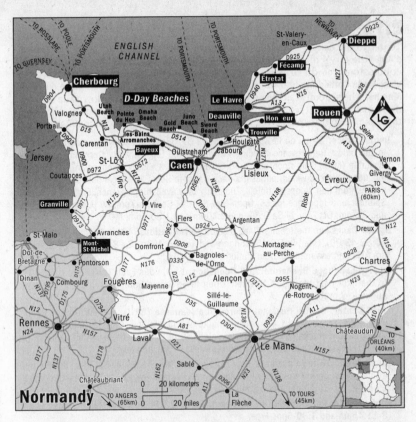

ticket office open M-F 5:10am-9pm, Sa 5:50am-9pm, Su 6:10am-10:30pm. To: **Caen** (1-2hr., 5-9 per day, €22); **Dieppe** (1hr., 6-13 per day, €10); **Le Havre** (1hr., 10-20 per day, €13); **Lille** (2-3hr., 1-3 per day, €30); **Paris** (1hr., every hr., €19.30).

Buses: VTNI/TVS has a station at 11 rue des Charrettes (☎0800 25 07 60 27). Open M-Sa 8am-6pm. To **Le Havre** via **Caudebc-en-Caux** (3½hr.; M-F 7 per day, Sa 6 per day, Su 2 per day) and various towns in the area. All destinations €2.

Public Transportation: TCAR, 9 bis rue Jeanne d'Arc (☎02 35 52 52 52; www.tcar. fr), operates a **subway** and municipal **buses.** Open M-Sa 7am-7pm. Most buses run 6am-10pm. Night bus runs Sept.-June M-Th and Su 11pm-1am, F-Sa 11pm-3:30am. Subway open 5am-11pm. 1hr. ticket €1.40; 1-day pass €3.80, 2-day €5.50, 3-day €7.50; carnet of 10 €10.70.

Taxis: Radio Taxis, 8 av. Jean Rondeaux (☎02 35 88 50 50), across the Seine. At the train and bus stations as well as at the Palais de Justice on rue Jeanne d'Arc. 24hr.

Car Rental: Avis (☎02 35 88 60 94), at the train station. Open M-F 9am-noon and 2-6pm, Sa 9am-noon and 2-5pm.

Bike Rental: Rouen Cycles, 45 rue St-Eloi (☎02 35 71 34 30), between pl. du Vieux Marché and the Seine. Bike rental €20 per day, €30 per weekend, €50 per week. No helmets for rent, but they're on sale for €30-50. Reservations highly recommended. Open Tu-Sa 9am-noon and 2-7pm. MC/V.

ORIENTATION AND PRACTICAL INFORMATION

To get to the *centre-ville* from the station, exit straight and follow **rue Jeanne d'Arc**—the city's main thoroughfare—for several blocks. When it crosses the cobblestone rue du Gros Horloge, you're in the heart of town; a left leads to **place de la Cathédrale** and the tourist office while a right leads to **place du Vieux Marché**, where Joan was burned at the stake. If you continue down rue Jeanne d'Arc instead, you'll reach the Seine and (on the right) the bus station. Although there is public transportation, most sights are within easy walking distance.

Tourist Office: 25 pl. de la Cathédrale (☎02 32 08 32 40; www.rouentourisme.com). In the oldest Renaissance building in Rouen. Free English map. **Currency exchange** available (M-Sa 9am-noon and 1:30-6:30pm) with a €2.50 commission. The French-language guide *Le Viking*, published once a year in Sept., lists local hot spots and businesses from hair salons to hotels. Audio city **tour** available in French, English, German, Spanish, and Japanese for €5. Open May-Sept. M-Sa 9am-7pm, Su 9:30am-12:30pm and 2-6pm; Oct.-Apr. M-Sa 9:30am-12:30pm and 1:30-6pm. MC/V.

Banks: Banks line rue Jeanne d'Arc, including **BNP Paribas**, 40 rue Jeanne d'Arc (☎08 20 82 43 00). Open Tu-F 8:45am-noon and 1:30-5:45pm, Sa 8:45am-1:30pm. There are **ATMs** across from the train station.

English-Language Bookstore: ABC Bookshop, 11 rue des Faulx (☎02 35 71 08 67), to the right past the Église St-Ouen. Open Tu-Sa 10am-6pm. Closed 1st 2 weeks of Aug. MC/V over €15.

Youth Center: Centre Régional Information Jeunesse (CRIJ), 84 and 94 rue Beauvoisine (☎02 32 10 49 49; www.crij-haute-normandie.org). Provides information for young people interested in working, volunteering, or living in the region for 1 month or more. Open Tu-F 10am-6pm; closed for 3 weeks in July and Aug.

Laundromat: 56 rue Cauchoise near pl. du Vieux Marché. Wash €3.70-9, dry €1 per 10min. Open daily 7am-9pm. Alternative on av. Pasteur near pl. de la Madeleine. Wash €3.50-8, dry €1.20 per 8min. Open daily 7am-8pm.

Public Toilets: Rue des Faulx by the Abbatiale. €0.20. Pl. du Vieux Marché. Open Tu-Sa 8-11:45am and 1:30-6pm. Free.

Police: 9 rue Brisout de Barneville (☎02 32 81 25 00), across Seine from *centre-ville*.

Pharmacy: Grande Pharmacie du Centre, 29 pl. de la Cathédrale (☎02 35 71 33 17). Open M 10am-7:30pm, Tu-F 9am-7:30pm, Sa 9am-7pm.

Hospital: Hôpital Charles Nicolle, 1 rue de Germont (☎02 32 88 89 90).

Internet Access: Cyber@Net, 47 pl. du Vieux Marché (☎02 35 07 73 02; www.cybernetrouen.fr). €2 per 20min., €4 per hr. Open M-Sa 10am-8pm, Su 2-7pm. **Compu Net,** 37 rue de la République (☎02 77 76 90 21), near Église St-Maclou. €1 per 15min., €5 per 3hr. if you buy the "Gamer" package. Open M and Su 2:30pm-12:30am, Tu-Th 10:30am-12:30pm, F-Sa 10:30am-3am. **E-mega,** 50 rue de la République. €1 per 15min., €3 per hr. Open M-F 1pm-12:30am, Sa 3pm-2am, Su 3pm-12:30am.

Post Office: 45 bis rue Jeanne d'Arc (☎02 32 76 66 20). **Currency exchange** available. Open M-F 8am-7pm, Sa 8:30am-12:30pm. Branch at 112 rue Jeanne d'Arc (☎02 32 10 55 60), to the left of the train station. Open M-W and F 8:45am-6pm, Th 9:15am-6pm, Sa 9am-noon. **Postal Code:** 76000.

ACCOMMODATIONS AND CAMPING

Accommodations in Rouen range from unique and intimate hotels to standard but convenient chains. If you're planning to spend a weekend in Rouen,

Rouen

ACCOMMODATIONS
Camping Municipal de Déville, 4
Hôtel des Arcades, 8
Hôtel de la Cathédrale, 11

FOOD
Chez Wam, 9
La Couronne, 7
Pommes d'Épices, 2

NIGHTLIFE
Emporium Galorium, 1
L'Euro, 6
L'Insolite, 10
Le Nash, 5
Pub Yesterday, 3

reserve ahead and ask about the **"Rouen, vos Week-ends"** deal—some hotels will give you two nights for the price of one.

☒ **Hôtel de la Cathédrale,** 12 rue St-Romain (☎02 35 71 57 95; www.hotel-de-la-cathe-drale.fr). Prime location by the Cathédrale with 26 adorable rooms, each featuring a different color scheme. *Petite* courtyard with mosaic-topped tables. Extremely accommodating staff. Bar, elevator, and tea room (open 11am-7pm). Buffet breakfast €7.50. Free Wi-Fi. Wheelchair-accessible. Singles €56-76; doubles €66-93; triples €93-115; quads €115. Extra bed €15. AmEx/MC/V. ❶

Hôtel des Arcades, 52 rue de Carmes (☎02 35 70 10 30; www.hotel-des-arcades.fr). Clean, no-frills rooms in the *centre-ville*. TV €4.50. Breakfast €6.50. Public shower €4. Reception M-F 7am-10pm, Sa-Su 7:30am-10pm. Singles €29-36, with shower €40-46; doubles €30-37/41-47; triple with shower €57. Extra bed €6. AmEx/MC/V. ❷

Camping Municipal de Déville, 12 rue Jules Ferry (☎02 35 74 07 59), 4km from Rouen in Déville. Take the subway from the train station (dir: Technopole or Georges Braque) to Théâtre des Arts. Transfer to the TEOR T2 bus line (on the same ticket) toward Mairie V. Schoelcher/Notre Dame de Bondeville. Get off at Mairie de Deville, continue down route de Dieppe for 1 block, and turn left on rue Jules Ferry. Welcoming grassy lawn surrounded by 66 plots. Pets, showers, and cars free. Reception June-Sept. M-F 8am-1pm and 2-8pm, Sa 8am-noon and 2-8pm, Su 9am-noon and 2-8pm; Oct.-May M-F 9:30-11am and 4:30-6:30pm. Closed 1 month around Dec. 15 to Jan. 15. €4.30 per person, under 7 €2.90; €1.70 per tent; €3 per RV. Electricity €2.20. Cash only. ❶

⬛ FOOD

Outdoor cafes and *brasseries* crowd around **place du Vieux Marché,** which also hosts a market with flowers, fish, fruit, and cheese (open Tu-Su 8am-12:30pm). There are more eateries near the Gros Horloge and the Cathédrale de Notre Dame. For self-serve options, try the food section in the back of the **Monoprix** department store on rue du Gros Horloge (open M-Sa 8:30am-9pm) or **Marché Plus** on pl. du Vieux Marché (open M-Sa 8:30am-8:30pm). **Marché U,** 11 pl. du Général de Gaulle (open M-Sa 7am-9pm) sells groceries, stamps, and tickets for public transportation in addition to offering photocopy and fax services.

Pommes d'Épices, 66 rue Bouvreuil (☎02 35 71 73 57), right across from the Tour Jeanne d'Arc. This bustling restaurant with rustic decor offers delicious, elegant, and inexpensive lunches. Menu changes daily; choose from a *formule* of 1 (€10), 2 (€11.50), or 3 courses (€15.50). For dessert, try *pomme d'épices* (warm, syrupy apple chunks served over gingerbread). Open M-F noon-1:45pm. AmEx/MC/V. ❸

La Couronne, 31 pl. du Vieux Marché (☎02 35 71 40 90; www.lacouronne.com.fr). The food and elegant atmosphere of this sophisticated splurge embody French tradition. Housed in the oldest *auberge* in France, this intimate restaurant offers meat dishes and an excellent cheese tray (€15), but its specialty is *canard à la Rouennaise*. Photos and autographs of famous patrons—including Salvador Dalí, Audrey Hepburn, and Cornelius Vanderbilt, to name a few—grace the walls. *Plats* €28-67. Lunch *menu* €25. Dinner *menus* €35-50. Open daily noon-2pm and 7-10pm. AmEx/MC/V. ❺

Chez Wam, 67 rue de la République (☎02 35 15 97 51), near the Abbatiale St-Ouen. Don't be surprised if there's no one at the grill—the cook is often taking a breather outside, but he'll show up in a second or 2 when he sees a customer examining the menu. Kebab with drink €4. Sandwiches and kebabs €1.50-4. Wings, nuggets, or falafel with fries €3.20. Open daily 10am-2am. Cash only. ❶

👁 SIGHTS

The streets of Rouen are lined with picturesque medieval and Renaissance buildings dating to the 14th century. The city also has a number of fascinating museums and churches—each attraction with its own special charm. Notre Dame's mismatched towers and St-Ouen's sloping gardens capture the attention of both the casual observer and the avid art lover or history buff.

▮CATHÉDRALE DE NOTRE DAME. From the delicate stonework of its restored facade to its massive cast-iron spire, this Gothic masterpiece soars skyward in a rising crescendo of architectural extravagance. The 16th-century **Tour de Beurre** (Tower of Butter) on the right was funded by cholesterol-loving parishioners who preferred to pay a dispensation rather than go without the delicious ingredient during Lent. Crane your neck to see the **Lantern Tower**—the tallest cathedral spire in France at 495 ft. aboveground. The beautiful stained glass in the ambulatory dates from 1220-1230 and has survived the Wars of Religion, the French Revolution, and the bomb raids of WWII. Look up in the nave and try to find the keystone that represents Mary and Jesus; according to legend, he who finds it will have his prayers answered. Don't miss the tombs of Richard the Lionheart—containing his lion heart—and Rollo, the first duke of Normandy, inside. *(Pl. de la Cathédrale. Open Apr.-Oct. M 2-7pm, Tu-Sa 7:30am-7pm, Su 8am-6pm; Nov.-Mar. M 2-7pm, Tu-Sa 7:30am-noon and 2-6pm, Su 8am-6pm. Mass Tu-Sa 8, 10am; Su 8:30, 10:30am, noon. Tours in French daily 2:30pm. Free.)*

MUSÉE DES BEAUX ARTS. This magnificent museum presents a broad collection of European (mostly French) art, dating from the 15th century on. Caravaggio's *Flagellation of Christ* stands in a rotunda on the second floor, and the vast Impressionist collection, second in size only to that of the Musée d'Orsay (p. 159) in Paris, proudly displays one of Monet's paintings of the Rouen cathedral. In February and March 2009, the museum will have an exhibit featuring Japanese engravings and prints. From May 16 to August 16, it will be having a special exhibit on the art of Normandy, in collaboration with the Musées des Beaux Arts of Caen and Le Havre. *(Esplanade Marcel Duchamp, on sq. Verdrel. ☎ 02 35 71 28 40; www.rouen-musees.com. Open M and W-Su 10am-6pm. Wheelchair-accessible from rue Jean Lecaunet. €3, students ages 18-25 and group members €2, under 18 free. Extra fee for some special exhibits. €5.35 deal grants admission to the Musée des Beaux Arts and 2 sister museums—the Musée de la Ceramique and the Musée le Secq des Tournelles.)*

MUSÉE FLAUBERT ET D'HISTOIRE DE LA MÉDECINE. Formerly a hospital and later the childhood home of French novelist Gustave Flaubert, this eclectic little museum packs in a formidable number of (occasionally gruesome) objects loosely related to the history of medicine and to the writer himself. Among the objects preserved here are plaster moldings of the heads of Napoleon and the Marquis de Sade, a pregnant mannequin from 1777 once used to teach midwives how to deliver babies, and a room on the history of dentistry with antique drills. Ring the bell if the door's locked when you arrive—if the museum is open, a staff member will let you in. Special exhibits every 2-3 years. *(51 rue de Lecat, next to the Préfecture. ☎ 02 35 15 59 95; www.chu-rouen.fr. Open Tu 10am-6pm, W-Sa 10am-noon and 2-6pm. €3, ages 18-25 €1.50, under 18 free. Guided tour €4.)*

GROS HORLOGE. A gilded 16th-century timepiece, the Gros Horloge (Great Clock) is built into a carved stone bridge that spans its namesake street. While a rotating disk depicting Greco-Roman divinities marks the days, a ball at the top tracks the phases of the moon. A door underneath the bridge leads to a ticket office for audio tours (40min.; available in multiple languages) of the clock tower. The tour showcases the clock master's workshop and living quar-

LOCAL LEGEND

PARDON ME, SAINT-ROMAIN

Every year since 1156, on the morning of Ascension Day, a prisoner is brought before Rouen's parliament. Without a judge, jury, or any sort of a trial, he is set free. By this annual act of mercy, Rouen celebrates the most famous miracle of its patron saint, St-Romain: his heroic defeat of a dragon with the help of a convict.

While serving as bishop of Rouen in the seventh century, St-Romain lived a life of quiet piety; it was not until well after his death in 641 that his fame as a dragon-slayer began to spread. When the saint's remains were moved inside Rouen's walls in the 10th century, they were interred in a flood-prone part of town that subsequently stopped flooding. With this new miracle attributed to St-Romain's intervention, the old legend of his run-in with a dragon recaptured popular imagination.

As the story goes, a dragon emerged from the Seine and sent a flood over Rouen. St-Romain tried to recruit villagers to stop the beast, but only one man—a prisoner—answered his plea. When the two entered the dragon's cave, St-Romain made the sign of the cross, and the beast collapsed.

In order to honor their legendary patron saint and the lone convict who aided him, the people of Rouen continue to annually pardon a prisoner to this day.

ters, the clock mechanism, and the bells as well as exhibits on the history of the clock tower, clockmaking, and the city of Rouen. A trip up the staircase of the 14th-century Gothic belfry is rewarded by a dizzying panorama of the cathedral spires and the city below. (☎02 32 08 01 90; groshorloge@rouen.fr. Open Tu-Su Apr.-Oct. 10am-1pm and 2-7pm; Nov.-Mar. 2-6pm. Adults €6, students 18-25 €3, under 6 free. MC/V.)

ABBATIALE SAINT-OUEN. Once an eighth-century Benedictine abbey, this 15th-century cathedral has since seen many additions—most recently a 19th-century facade. After checking out the cavernous and oddly bare interior, enjoy the view of the exterior from the sloping grounds of the **Jardins de l'Hôtel de Ville,** which provide a picturesque environment for anyone seeking a relaxing afternoon stroll or a lazy game of *pétanque*. The church itself holds just one mass each year (on St-Ouen's Day, Aug. 26) but has monthly concerts, usually featuring the church organist. (At pl. du Général de Gaulle, next to the Hôtel de Ville. Open Apr.-Oct. W-Su 10am-noon and 2-6pm; Nov.-Mar. Tu-Th and Sa-Su 10am-noon and 2-5:30pm. Free.)

OTHER SIGHTS. For those interested in the history of Rouen's most famous heroine, the **Tour Jeanne d'Arc**—the place where the Maid of Orléans was tried before her execution—has exhibitions on castles in Normandy and on the life of Joan of Arc. (Entrance on rue Bouvreuil. Open M and W-Sa 10am-noon and 2-6pm, Su 2-6:30pm. €1.50, students and under 18 free, over 65 and group members €0.75.) A sign marks the spot where Joan was burned in pl. du Vieux Marché, next to the **Église Jeanne d'Arc.** This simple church, built to resemble an upturned ship, features a scaled roof, plain interior, stained glass salvaged from the 15th-century St-Vincent's Church (which stood on the same site), and a long canopy that stretches out into the square. (Open Nov.-Mar. daily 10am-noon and 2-5:30pm; Apr.-Oct. M-Th and Sa-Su 10am-noon and 2-6:30pm. Closed during mass. Mass July-Aug Su 11:30am; Sept.-June M-Sa 6:30pm, Su 11am.

📻 NIGHTLIFE

Emporium Galorium, 151 rue Beauvoisine (☎02 35 71 76 95; www.emporium-galorium.com). A cavernous basement and live concerts (Th-Sa) make this spot one of the loudest and most raucous in the city, especially during the school year. Tu-W €1 shot nights are hard to pass up. Beer €3-3.50, students €2. Mixed drinks €7, students €4. Open Tu-Sa 8pm-3am. AmEx/MC/V.

Le Nash, 97 rue Ecuyère (☎02 35 98 25 24). DJ plays a wide variety of music, including disco and electronica (Th-Sa nights), for a more mature clientele. Scarlet walls, zebra-striped upholstery, lanterns, and flashing colored lights give an exotic flair. Tapas €3.50-5. Beer €3.50-5. Mixed drinks €7. Open daily 6pm-2am. MC/V.

L'Euro, 41 pl. du Vieux Marché (☎06 28 48 66 53). 3 hip floors in an old-fashioned *auberge*, each with its own ambience. Pumping music, sleek bars, cozy nooks, and magenta Louis XV armchairs make this place both chic and comfortable. Beer €4-4.80 and wine €4-6.50. Mixed drinks €8.50-10.50. Open daily 3pm-2am. AmEx/MC/V.

Pub Yesterday, 3 rue Moulinet (☎02 35 70 43 98). Irish music is the perfect soundtrack for a swig of Guinness served by the owner (who is not, by the way, Irish—he just has an insatiable love of Irish things). Whimsical decor upstairs, with more room for revelry in the basement. Beer €3.50. Whiskey €5-7.60. Open daily 5pm-2am. AmEx/MC/V.

L'Insolite, 58 rue d'Amiens (☎02 35 88 62 53). Cozy gay bar invites visitors of all ages (and sexual orientation) into an intimate and classy spot with dim red lighting. Beer €2.80. Mixed drinks €6.50. AmEx/MC/V.

DIEPPE ☎02

The picturesque seaport town of Dieppe (dee-epp; pop. 35,000) became an important channel port after the Norman invasion of England in 1066. But its turbulent history has also witnessed several setbacks, most famously during WWII when Allied Canadian troops suffered a devastating loss to occupying Germans in Operation Jubilee. Today's visitors enjoy seaside vacations on these historically rich lands. The nearest coastal resort to Paris, Dieppe offers long beaches, a hilltop castle, renowned seafood, and a refreshing salt breeze.

◪ TRANSPORTATION

Trains: Bd. Georges Clemenceau. Ticket office open M-F 5:35am-7:40pm, Sa 6:15am-7:20pm, Su 7:30am-8:55pm. Service to **Paris** (2½hr., every hr., €25.70) via **Rouen** (45min., €10).

Buses: Stradibus, 56 quai Duquesne (☎02 32 14 03 03). Serves Dieppe and its outskirts. Tickets €1.15, carnet of 10 €7.50, weekly pass €7.70. Stradibus's Créabus system provides on-call transportation service for registered customers at the same prices. Office open M-F 8am-noon and 1:30-6:30pm, Sa 9am-noon. Single tickets can be purchased on the bus; carnets and passes must be purchased in advance at the office or at *tabacs*. Buses from Voyages Denis/Cars Denis, 10 quai Duquesne (☎02 35 06 86 80), stop at the tourist office on Pont Jehan Ango, serve surrounding towns (€2), and offer trips to other parts of France and Europe.

Ferries: Transmanche Ferries, 7 quai Gaston Lalitte (☎02 32 14 52 05; www.transmancheferries.com), 1km past the Pont Jehan Ango. To **New Haven, ENG** (4hr.; July-Oct. €25-28, Nov.-June €18-25).

Bike Rental: Vélo Service (☎06 24 56 06 27), across from the tourist office on the Pont Jehan Ango. In a converted blue Stradibus. €1 per hr., €3.50 per ½-day, €5.50 per day. Tandems €2/7/11. Open M-F 9am-6pm, Sa 9am-7pm, Su 10am-7pm. Helmets not available. Parental consent for customers under 18. ID and €230 deposit required.

◪◪ ORIENTATION AND PRACTICAL INFORMATION

To reach the *centre-ville* from the train station, walk straight along **quai Berigny** a few hundred feet until it becomes **quai Duquesne**.

Tourist Office: Pont Jehan Ango, quai du Carénage (☎02 32 14 40 60; www.dieppetourism.com). English-speaking staff provides a free city guide and map, guided tours of the city in French on a tramcar (**Petit Train;** 1hr; €6, under 10 €4), and info on available accommodations and events. Open July-Aug. M-Sa 9am-7pm, Su 10am-1pm and 3-6pm; Sept. and May-June M-Sa 9am-1pm and 2-6pm, Su 10am-1pm and 3-6pm; Oct.-Apr. M-Sa 9am-1pm and 2-6pm.)

ATMs: On quai Henri IV.

Laundromats: Lav-O-Clair, pl. Nationale (☎06 08 01 16 80), at the end of rue Notre-Dame. Also at 44-46 rue de l'Épée. Wash €5, dry €1 per 12min. Open daily 7am-9pm.

Public Toilets: On pl. Carnot by the post office (free) and on the beachfront (€0.40).

Police: Bd. Georges Clemenceau (☎02 32 14 49 00), to the left of the train station.

Pharmacy: Pl. du Puits Salé (☎02 35 84 12 62). Open M-F 9am-1pm and 2-8pm, Sa 9am-noon.

Hospital: Av. Pasteur (☎02 32 14 75 00).

Post Office: Bd. Maréchal Joffre (☎02 35 06 99 20). Open M-F 8am-6pm, Sa 8am-12:30pm. Another branch is located on the island, past the Pont Jehan Ango, on quai du Carénage. **Postal Code:** 76200.

ACCOMMODATIONS

Be prepared to pay a little more than usual to stay in Dieppe, especially if you want an ocean view; there are few budget accommodations in the city.

Hotel Crocus Dieppe Falaise, 479 rue de la Providence (☎02 32 14 50 50; www.hotel-crocus-dieppe-falaise.com), in St-Aubin-Sur-Scie. Take the Stradibus line 2 (dir: Val Druel) to the Vasarely stop by the underpass, turn right on the 1st street, and go left at the intersection; the hotel is on the right. English-speaking staff lets clean, bright rooms with TV, A/C, telephone, and private bathrooms with shower. The restaurant downstairs serves a selection of *entrées* (€5-7) and *menus* (€6-10). Breakfast €5.50. Free Wi-Fi. Wheelchair-accessible. Singles and doubles €37; triples €47; quads €57. ❸

Le Relais Gambetta, 95 rue Gambetta (☎02 35 84 12 91), across from the Gambetta stop on Stradibus line 2. This 16-room establishment has seen better days. Guests are mostly students. Pets €5. Breakfast €6. Rooms €31-34; *pension complète* €51, for 2 people €81; *demi-pension* €45, for 2 people €63. Extra bed €9.50. V. ❷

FOOD

There is a market in **place Nationale** in the *vieille ville* (open all day Sa), where vendors sell fresh produce and goods; Tuesday and Thursday mornings see a smaller version with produce only. For groceries, head to **Shopi,** 59 rue de la Barre (open M-Sa 8am-8pm, Su 9am-1pm), or **Marché Plus,** 22 quai Duquesne (open Tu-Sa 7am-1pm, Su 9am-1pm). The restaurants along **quai Henri IV** specialize in seafood, especially Dieppe's famous *moules* (mussels).

Le Festival, 11 quai Henri IV (☎02 35 40 24 29). Serves a pot of mussels for €4.50 at lunch. *Menus* €10-30. Open daily 1:30-3pm and 6:30pm-1am. MC/V. ❷

Café de Tribunaux, 1 pl. du Puits-Sale (☎02 32 14 44 65). Head to the oldest cafe in town for a *croque-monsieur* (grilled ham and cheese sandwich; €5) or a cool drink. Salads €3.50-8. *Entrées* €8.50-13. Open daily 8am-8pm. MC/V. ❶

CRAB 'N' CRUNCH. You may be getting more than you bargained for when you order your next pot of mussels. Pea crabs—small parasites that invade mussels for protection—are often cooked up inside the seafood specialty. They're not toxic, but they do make for an awkward crunch.

👁 SIGHTS

CHÂTEAU-MUSÉE. This 15th-century Château-Musée showcases artifacts that pay homage to Dieppe's maritime history. Several rooms celebrate the *dieppois* tradition of ivory carving, and intricate models of ships are on display. There are also Impressionist paintings of Dieppe, Baroque seascapes, and nautical-themed contemporary art. From the château, take a short walk to the edge of the cliffs for a view of the Channel. (*☎ 02 35 06 61 99. Open June-Sept. daily 10am-noon and 2-6pm; Oct.-May M, W-F, Su 10am-noon and 2-5pm, Sa 10am-noon and 2-6pm. Last ticket sold 1hr. before closing. €3.50; students, ages 12-17, and groups members €2; under 12 free.)*

MEMORIAL TO THE CANADIAN RAID OF 1942. Located in a restored theater on pl. St-Saëns, this small memorial houses authentic army uniforms, a 40min. video (French with English subtitles) with firsthand accounts of the failed raid, and a moving display of black-and-white photographs of survivors from the first major Allied offensive against the Nazis in France. (*☎ 02 35 40 36 65. Open June-Sept. M and W-F 2-6:30pm; from mid-Nov. to mid-Mar. and from mid- to late May daily 2-6:30pm. €2.30, under 16 free, veterans and group members €1.80.)*

CITÉ DE LA MER. Explore the maritime culture of Normandy from the history of shipbuilding and fishing in Dieppe to the geology of the regional cliffs. Children will enjoy observing the aquarium, navigating motorized boats around the pool, or building a Lego ship. (*37 rue de l'Asile Thomas. ☎ 02 35 06 93 20; http://.estran-citedelamer.free.fr. Open daily 10am-noon and 2-6pm. Group tours in English with reservation. Wheelchair-accessible. €5.50, students €4.50, ages 4-16 €3.50, under 4 free. AmEx/MC/V.)*

OTHER SIGHTS. Take some time to relax on Dieppe's gravel beach, which spans over a mile from the harbor to the white *falaises* (cliffs). If the weather is nice, rent a boat and fishing equipment from one of the stores in Le Pollet (ask the tourist office for more information). For the less adventurous, **Promenades en Mer** offers 30min. **boat tours** around Dieppe's cliffs. Boats leave from a dock next to the tourist office. (*☎ 02 32 90 11 91 or 06 09 52 37 38; www.bateau-ville-de-dieppe.com. Call in advance. Wheelchair-accessible. €7, students €6.50, ages 4-12 €5.50.)*

🎐 🎆 NIGHTLIFE AND FESTIVALS

Nightlife in Dieppe is limited on weekends and almost nonexistent on weekdays. Every other September (next in 2010), windy Dieppe hosts the **Festival International de Cerf-Volant** (International Kite Festival), living up to its name as the kite capital of the world.

L'Epsom, 11 bd. de Verdun (*☎ 02 35 84 12 27*). A fairly popular spot with a low-key atmosphere and red upholstered lounge. *Café Litteraire* Th. Live music F. Tapas €3.20-9.50. Tea €3.50-9.50. Dessert €5.50. Mixed drinks €8-10. Open M-Tu and Su noon-1am, Th-Sa noon-2am. MC/V.

L'Abordage, 3 bd. de Verdun (*☎ 02 32 14 48 00*), in the same building as the casino. This pirate-themed venue is great for dancing, mingling, or lounging. Popular among students. Concerts on F-Sa nights; becomes a *discothèque* after 11pm. Beer €6. Mixed drinks €7-9. Sept.-May "tea dance" with live orchestra Su 3-7pm. Cover €10; includes 1 drink. Open M-Th and Su 6pm-3am, F-Sa 6pm-4:30am. AmEx/MC/V.

LE HAVRE   ☎ 02 35

The largest transatlantic port in France, Le Havre (luh ah-vruh; pop. 191,000) wasn't built as a tourist destination. Nevertheless, there are a few bright spots

NORMANDY

amid post-war concrete architecture—in particular, a good museum, a lively university, broad tree-lined boulevards, and some peaceful public parks and gardens. Moreover, Le Havre's cheaper accommodations make it an affordable base for daytrips throughout Normandy.

TRANSPORTATION

Trains: Cours de la République, at intersection with bd. de Strasbourg. Open M-Th 5am-midnight, F 5am-2:30am, Sa 5am-11pm, Su 7:15am-2:30am. Ticket office open M-F 5:20am-7:55pm, Sa 5:40am-7:35pm, Su 7:30am-9:30pm. To **Fécamp** (1hr., 6-12 per day, €7.60), **Paris** (2-3hr., 8 per day, €29), and **Rouen** (1hr., 8-20 per day, €13.30).

Buses: Depart from the *gare routière* (☎02 35 22 34 00), which is connected to the train station. Info office open M-Sa 7am-7pm. Bus Verts (☎08 10 21 42 14; www.bus-verts.fr) serves **Caen** via **Honfleur** (30min.; 4-10 per day; €4.10, under 26 €3.50) and **Deauville** (1hr.; 5-6 per day; €6.20, under 26 €5.20). Cars Périer (☎08 00 80 87 03) runs a line to **Fécamp** (1¾hr., 5-6 per day, €2) via **Étretat** (1hr., 5-6 per day, €2).

Ferries: LD Lines, Terminal de la Citadelle (☎02 35 19 78 78; www.ldlines.com). Open M-F 8am-7pm, Sa-Su 8am-2pm. To **Portsmouth** (daily 5pm, €25) and **New Haven, ENG** (daily 7:30pm, €25).

Taxis: At the train station and across from the Hôtel de Ville (☎02 35 25 81 81).

Bicycles: **Vélocéan**, at the bus station or tourist office. €1 per hr., €3 per ½-day, €5 per day, €8 per weekend, €25 per week. Tandems available. €200 check and ID deposit.

PRACTICAL INFORMATION

Tourist Office: 186 bd. Clemenceau (☎02 32 74 04 04; www.lehavretourisme.com). From the train station, take bd. de Strasbourg to pl. de l'Hôtel de Ville, in the *centre-ville* (10min.). Offers info on nautical activities, a monthly calendar of events, and a free map. Open M-Sa 9am-6:45pm, Su 10am-12:30pm and 2:30-5:30pm.

ATMs: Near the Hôtel de Ville on bd. de Strasbourg and near the station on cours de la République.

Laundromat: 85 rue Casimir Delavigne. Open daily 7am-9pm.

Public Toilets: Pl. de l'Hôtel de Ville (€0.30).

Police: 5 rue Jules Lecesne (☎02 35 19 20 20).

Pharmacy: 35 cours de la République (☎02 35 25 18 74). Open M-F 9am-12:30pm and 2:30-9pm, Sa 9am-12:30pm.

Hospital: 55 bis rue Gustave Flaubert (☎02 32 73 32 15).

Internet Access: Plug In Café, 19 cours de la République (☎02 35 53 11 15; www. leplugin-cafe.com), across from the train station. €1.50 per 15min., €3 per hr. Wi-Fi €1.30 per 15min., €3 per hr. Open M-F 10am-10pm, Sa 2-10pm, Su 2-9pm.

Post Office: 172 bd. Strasbourg (☎02 35 19 55 00). Open M-F 8:30am-6pm, Sa 9am-noon. **Postal Code:** 76600.

ACCOMMODATIONS

There are plenty of two-star chain hotels by the train station, but better deals can be found elsewhere.

The Hôtel Celtic, 106 rue Voltaire (☎02 35 42 39 77; www.hotelceltic.com), close to the Bassin du Commerce and across the street from the Volcan. Each clean, spacious, and well-kept room has shower, TV, and double bed; most have toilets. Breakfast €6.60.

Free Wi-Fi. Reception noon-10pm. Singles €37; with toilet €43-52; doubles €37, with toilet €47-56. Extra bed €12. AmEx/MC/V. ❸

Hôtel d'Yport, 27 cours de la République (☎02 35 25 21 08; fax 24 06 34). From the train station, cross cours de la République and turn right; the hotel is down a narrow street on the left, a block and a half ahead. Hidden from the street in a small courtyard. Small, worn rooms with decent bathrooms. Breakfast €5. Reception 24hr. Singles with shower and toilet €36; doubles €41, 2 beds €46. Monthly rooms €456. MC/V. ❸

▐ FOOD

For groceries, there's a **Super U,** 5 rue de l'Abbé Périer, off av. Foch (open M-Sa 8:30am-8:30pm), and a **Marché Plus,** 156-158 rue de Paris (open M-Sa 7am-9pm, Su 9am-1pm). Buy fresh food at the morning market on **place Thiers,** by the Hôtel de Ville (open M, W, F 7:30am-1:30pm), or the market on **cours République** (open Tu, Th, Sa 7:30am-7pm). There are a few restaurants near the Volcan, by **place de l'Hôtel de Ville** and on the streets surrounding the **quai Lamblardie.**

Côté Jardin, 9 pl. de l'Hôtel de Ville (☎02 35 43 43 04). The attentive waitstaff serves *salades composées* (€9.80), desserts (€2.70-5.30), and a variety of *tartes* (€9.20). Open M 11:45am-2:30pm, Tu-Sa 11:45am-6:30pm. MC/V. ❷

Le Mandarin, 22 rue de Paris (☎02 35 42 28 81), near quai Southampton and the ferry terminal. Overwhelming selection of delicious Asian dishes includes chicken, pork, beef, shrimp, and even frog legs. *Plats* €6-11. *Menus* €13-19. Lunch *menu* €8.50. Open Tu-Su noon-2:30pm and 7-10:30pm. MC/V. ❷

◉ ♫ SIGHTS AND ENTERTAINMENT

MUSÉE MALRAUX. Known for its Impressionist works, this contemporary space displays a collection of paintings by Dufy, Monet, and a host of local artists. The second floor houses pieces by Eugène Boudin depicting Norman seascapes and cows; in addition to creating spectacular artwork, Boudin is credited with introducing Monet to *plein air* (outdoor) painting. Small collections of Baroque art and modern art are also on display. *(2 bd. Clemenceau. ☎02 35 19 62 62; http://musee-malraux.ville-lehavre.fr. Open M and W-F 11am-6pm, Sa-Su 11am-7pm. Wheelchair-accessible. €5, students and members of groups of 6+ €3, under 18 free.)*

VOLCAN. This building—dubbed Le Volcan (The Volcano) for its resemblance to a smooth, white, sunken cinder cone—adds to Le Havre's unusual architecture. Although its bizarre design may be off-putting, Le Volcan is nevertheless a state-of-the-art venue for renowned orchestral works and plays as well as a cinema that screens international new releases, classics, and notable independent films. The complex is composed of two performance halls—Le Grand Volcan and Le Petit Volcan. *(☎02 35 19 10 20; www.unvolcandanslaville.com. Le Grand Volcan info and ticket office open Tu-Sa 2-7pm and 30min. before shows. Le Petit Volcan ticket office open M-F 9am-12:30pm and 1:30-6pm. Wheelchair-accessible.)*

OTHER SIGHTS. Auguste Perret, the 20th-century French architect known for his concrete constructions, made an unusual addition to Le Havre's skyline with the **Église Saint-Joseph,** which looks—both inside and out—like an odd futuristic rocket ship made of cement Legos and lit by multicolored lights. Contemporary black-and-white renderings of religious figures hang at the altar. If you're in need of some fresh air, head to Le Havre's green spaces. The shaded gardens, pleasant gazebo, and stone bridge of **square Saint-Roch,** off av. Foch, provide a refreshingly lush and peaceful oasis, while multiple fountains lend character to the wide-open **place de l'Hôtel de Ville.**

🔁 DAYTRIPS FROM LE HAVRE

DEAUVILLE AND TROUVILLE

Bus Verts (☎ 08 01 21 42 14) sends buses to the train station in Deauville from Le Havre (1hr.; €6.20, under 26 €5.20). Voyages Fournier (☎ 02 31 88 16 73) runs shuttles from pl. du Maréchal Foch, next to the Trouville casino, between the 2 towns (€1.90). For a taxi, call ☎ 02 31 88 35 33 or 87 11 11.

Deauville (doh-veel) and Trouville (troo-veel)—stylish twin towns on the Norman coast—promise travelers fine sand, glittering casinos, and an empty wallet. A stroll along the boardwalk in Trouville affords a view of volleyball courts and the spectacular houses that inspired novelist Gustave Flaubert. In Deauville, where each boardwalk changing room bears the name of a famous movie star, scantily clad beauties lounge on the sands. Joined by the pont des Belges over the Touques River, these sister cities have distinctive identities. The **Casino Barrière de Deauville** has a nightclub and nightly shows. (☎ 02 31 14 31 14. Open M-Th and Su 10am-2am, F 10am-3am, Sa 10am-4am). Residents of Deauville pass the time at two racecourses: **Clairefontaine,** dedicated only to racing (☎ 02 31 14 69 00; www.hippodrome-deauville-clairefontaine.com; races and guided tours in July-Aug. and Oct.; €3; free trotter-driving every morning in July before races; call early to reserve), and **La Touques,** which hosts the occasional polo game as well (☎ 02 31 14 20 00; www.france-galop.com; races in Mar., July-Aug., Oct.-Dec.; M-Sa €3, Su €4, students and seniors €2, under 18 free). Plan ahead; courses are only open a few times a month on race days.

A **market** on the *quai* across from the tourist office in Trouville sells fresh fish, produce, and clothing. (Open W and Su 8am-1:30pm.) For groceries, there's a **Monoprix** in Trouville on the corner of bd. Fernand Moureaux and rue Victor Hugo. (Open M-Sa 9:30am-7:30pm.) Many of the beachfront restaurants offer a perfect view of the horizon at sunset; join the locals as they flock to the terraces to dine during the last light of day. In Trouville, pizzerias, *crêperies,* and seafood restaurants line **rue des Bains** and **boulevard Fernand Moureaux.** In Deauville, try **Mamy Crêpes,** 57 rue Désiré le Hoc, near the tourist office, a lunch counter marked by a wood grandma outside. This *crêperie* serves filling sandwiches (€3-4) and also offers a range of quiches (€3.10), dessert *crêpes* (€2-3.20), and *tartes.* (☎ 02 31 14 96 44. Open M-Tu and Th-Su 9am-10pm. MC/V.)

Cycles Jamme, 11 av. de la République, offers bike rentals down the street from the train station. (☎ 02 31 88 40 22. €4.50 per hr., €10 per ½-day, €13 per day, €40 per week. Scooters €13 per hr., €38 per day. ID and check deposit. Open M-Tu and Th-Sa 9am-12:15pm and 2-6:30pm.) To get to the **Trouville tourist office** from the train station, turn right and cross the pont des Belges. Walk left on bd. Fernand Moureaux for one block. (☎ 02 31 14 60 70; www.trouvillesurmer. org. Open July-Aug. M-Sa 9:30am-7pm, Su 10am-4pm; Sept.-Oct. and Apr.-June M-Sa 9:30am-noon and 2-6:30pm, Su 10am-1pm; Nov.-Mar. M-Sa 9:30am-noon and 1:30-6pm, Su 10am-1pm.) To get to the **Deauville tourist office** from the train station, turn left. At the second roundabout, take the right fork onto rue Désiré le Hoc and follow it through pl. Morny (around the fountain) to pl. de la Mairie. The office provides free maps. (☎ 02 31 14 40 00; www.deauville.org. Open M-Sa 10am-6pm, Su 10am-1pm and 2-6pm.)

ÉTRETAT ☎ 02 35

The former fishing village of Étretat (eh-truh-tah; pop. 1640), an easy daytrip northeast of Le Havre, has captivated the attention of artists, writers, and tourists since the 19th century. Soaring chalk *falaises* (cliffs) and panoramic seascapes make this one of the most breathtaking spots along the English Channel.

TRANSPORTATION AND PRACTICAL INFORMATION. Cars Perier (☎08 00 80 87 03) runs **buses** to Fécamp (45min., 5-6 per day, €2) and Le Havre (1hr., 5-6 per day, €2). **Taxis** wait outside the bus stop (☎06 12 16 48 27). The **tourist office**, pl. Maurice Guillard, behind the bus stop, provides free maps and a guide to hotels and restaurants in the town. (☎02 35 27 05 21; www.etretat.net. Open daily from mid-June to mid-Sept. 9am-7pm; from mid-Sept. to mid-June 10am-noon and 2-6pm.) To reach the water from the tourist office, take rue Monge, which becomes bd. Président René Coty. Find **public toilets** on rue Monge by the bus station and at the beach (free). **Postal Code:** 76790.

ACCOMMODATIONS AND FOOD. Étretat has plenty of hotels, but unfortunately, not many cater to budget travelers, especially near the beachfront. You may be able to find cheap rooms even at pricier hotels if you reserve well in advance. Immaculately clean rooms, each featuring a different literary or film detective at **Detective Hotel ❹**, 6 av. Georges V, offer a fanciful option—but are still more expensive than staying in Le Havre and taking a round-trip bus. The 16 rooms are each equipped with shower, toilets, and flatscreen TV. (☎02 35 27 01 34; www.detectivehotel.com. Buffet breakfast €7. Reception 24hr. Singles and doubles €52-75; quads €70. MC/V.) **Camping le Grandval ❶**, is in a quiet spot bordered by a steep slope of dense forest, a 15min. walk from the tourist office down rue Guy de Maupassant. Some buses from Le Havre and Fécamp stop opposite the site. (☎02 35 27 07 67. Showers included. Laundry. Reception July-Aug. 2-7pm; Sept.-June 9am-noon and 3-7pm. Check-out noon. Gates closed 10pm-7:30am. Open from mid-Apr. to mid-Oct. €3.20 per person, ages 4-10 €2; €3.10 per car with tent, €3.70 per car with RV. Electricity €5-6. AmEx/MC/V.)

Tourists wandering through town will have no trouble finding restaurants on the way to the beach, although skirting down side streets will reward you with a more authentic and budget-conscious experience. Follow signs to **Crêperie Lann-Bihoue ❷**, 45 rue Notre Dame, for a mouthwatering *menu*, which includes both a lunch *crêpe* and a dessert *crêpe* for €9. (☎02 35 27 04 65. *Crêpes* €2.50-9. Open Jan.-Nov. M and Th-Su noon-2:30pm and 7-9:30pm; hours may vary. MC/V over €20.)

THE LOCAL STORY

THE GENTLEMAN THIEF

Created by Étretat native Maurice Leblanc, Arsène Lupin is the hero of a series of detective mystery novels with a popularity as long-lasting and as considerable as Sherlock Holmes in the English-speaking world. In fact, there is a sort of literary rivalry between Arsène Lupin and Sherlock Holmes—or Herlock Sholmes, as Leblanc cunnintly refers to him in several of his short stories.

Arsène Lupin is a gentleman burglar—that is, he is a particularly well-behaved and well-bred thief. He is wealthy in his own right and steals only for amusement and the thrill of adventure rather than for monetary gain. Using a variety of outrageous disguises, his charm, and his devastating good looks (he is—predictably—an incorrigible womanizer), Lupin manages to steal the most unobtainable objects, such as the Mona Lisa and the queen's necklace.

Lupin is also a modern-day Robin Hood; he steals from the rich who don't appreciate their treasures and redistributes the money to the less fortunate. Although he is often on the wrong side of the law, Lupin remains a force for good, defeating—with style and flair—worse villains than he. One of the most popular Lupin novels in the 20-volume original series—*The Hollow Needle*—is set in Leblanc's hometown.

◩ **SIGHTS.** To the west of the pebble beach, the **Aiguille** (Needle) rises up out of the sea beside the great arch of the **Falaise d'Aval.** To the east, the tiny reconstructed **Chapelle Notre Dame de la Garde** sits atop the **Falaise d'Amont,** whose base—as first noted by Guy de Maupassant—curiously resembles an elephant dipping its trunk in the sea. Paths from the beach up to the top of either cliff—sometimes coming within feet of a sheer drop to the ocean below—lead climbers to intense seascape views. Crooked streets crammed with eateries, small shops, and summer visitors wind from **avenue Georges V**—where buses enter town—to the beach. In the other direction, just outside the town center at 15 rue de Maupassant, is **Le Clos Arsène Lupin,** formerly home to crime novelist Maurice Leblanc and now reinvented as the home of his most famous character, the "gentleman burglar" ◼**Arsène Lupin.** Visitors solve a mystery with a 45min. interactive audio tour of the antique home. (☎02 35 10 59 53. Open Apr.-Sept. daily 10am-5:45pm; from Oct. to mid-Dec. and Feb.-Mar. F-Su 11am-5pm. Tours in English and French. €6.75, students €5, ages 6-16 €4.25.)

FÉCAMP   ☎02 35

Though it lacks Étretat's breathtaking beauty, Fécamp (fay-kahm; pop. 23,000), with its quiet harbor, broad beach framed by cliffs, and green slope dotted with cottages, is a pleasant daytrip from Le Havre or Rouen.

◪ **TRANSPORTATION AND PRACTICAL INFORMATION. Trains** (office open M-Sa 9:30am-noon and 1:20-6pm, Su noon-7:10pm) run from bd. de la République to Le Havre (45min., 5-10 per day, €7.40), Paris (2hr., 5-8 per day, €27), and Rouen (1hr., 6-9 per day, €13). Cars Périer **buses** stop at pl. St-Étienne across from the church on av. Gambetta. (☎0800 80 87 03). Buses run to Le Havre (1hr., 5-6 per day, €2) via Étretat. There is a **taxi** stand (☎02 35 28 17 50) across the street from the bus stop on pl. St-Étienne at the top of av. Gambetta.

To reach Fécamp's **tourist office** at quai Sadi Carnot from the train station, take a right and walk to the roundabout. Make another right, and the tourist office is a few hundred feet down, at the corner leading to the pier. The staff offers a free hotel booking service and dispenses maps and nautical info. (☎02 35 28 51 01; www.fecamptourisme.com. Open July-Aug. daily 9am-6:30pm; Sept.-Mar. M-F 9am-6pm, Sa 9:30am-12:30pm and 2-6pm, Su 9:30am-12:30pm; Apr.-June M-F 9am-6pm, Sa-Su 10am-6:30pm.) There is a **BNP Paribus** with an **ATM** at 1 rue Félix Fauré by pl. Charles de Gaulle. (Open Tu-F 8:30am-12:10pm and 1:35-5:15pm, Sa 8:30am-12:10pm and 1:35-4:15pm.) **Postal Code:** 76400.

◪◪ **ACCOMMODATIONS AND FOOD.** Fécamp's lodgings unfortunately don't come any cheaper than the **Hôtel Vent d'Ouest ❸,** 3 av. Gambetta, opposite the bus stop and up the steps from the train station. Spotless, maritime-themed rooms come with showers, TVs, and phones. (☎02 35 28 04 04; www.hotelventdouest.fr. Pets €6. Breakfast €6. Wi-Fi €3 per hr. Reception 7am-11pm. May-Sept. singles €42; doubles €55-58; triples €60. Oct.-Apr. singles €36; doubles €42-45; triples €48. Extra bed €7. AmEx/MC/V.) **Camping Municipal de Reneville ❶,** chemin de Nesmond, is worth the cost; all of its hillside plots have spectacular ocean views. From the train station, turn right on av. Gambetta, which becomes quai Bérigny. Turn left onto rue du Président René Coty, right on rue Georges Cuvier, and left on rue d'Yport. Make a hairpin turn onto chemin de Nesmond. (☎02 35 28 20 97; www.campingdereneville.com. Laundry available. Reception 8:30am-1pm and 2-7:30pm. Gates closed 10pm-7am. Open Apr.-Nov. July-Aug. €12.60 per 2 people and tent; €4.50 per additional person, under 8 €2.30; €15.10 per RV. Sept.-Nov. and Apr.-June €10.10 per 2 people and tent; €4 per additional adult, under 8 €2; €12.60 per RV. Electricity €2.50. AmEx/MC/V.)

There's a **Marché-Plus** supermarket at 83-85 quai Bérigny. (Open June-Sept. M 8:30am-1pm and 3:30-8:30pm, Tu-Sa 7am-9pm, Su 9am-1pm; Oct.-May Tu-Sa 7am-9pm, Su 9am-1pm.) Nearly identical seafood restaurants cluster around **place Nicolas Selle,** at the end of quai Bérigny one block from the ocean. Specializing in seafood and grilled meat, **Le 1900 ❸**, 95 quai Bérigny, offers reasonably priced, filling *formules* (€9-12) and *menus* (€11-35) as well as *à la carte* options for €9-60. (☎02 35 28 01 02. Open daily 10:30am-3pm and 6-11pm. MC/V.) For a snack, swing by **Jean-Paul Martin ❶**, 6 pl. Nicolas Selle, where just €1-3 buy excellent baguettes and pastries. A sandwich, pastry, and drink *formule* costs €5.30. (☎02 35 28 21 99. Open Tu-Su 6:30am-8pm. MC/V.)

◪ SIGHTS. Fécamp became an important place of pilgrimage in Normandy when some drops of *précieux-sang* (Christ's blood) allegedly washed ashore in the trunk of a fig tree. The relic was later housed in the imposing **Église Abbatiale de la Trinité,** pl. du Général Leclerc, built by Richard II of Normandy in 1106 to prove his Christian piety. (Open daily Apr.-Sept. 9am-7pm; Oct.-Mar. 9am-noon and 2-5pm.) Today, Fécamp's main attraction is the magnificent **◪Palais Bénédictine,** 110 rue Alexandre le Grand, home of the famous *Bénédictine liqueur*. The *palais*, a scrambling of architectural styles, is part art museum—with a fantastic collection of medieval and Renaissance work—and part distillery, all housed in a fairy-tale castle. A tour of the *palais* includes a free *dégustation* of the famous liqueur, originally a monastic healing elixir containing 27 herbs and spices invented by a 15th-century Venetian monk. (☎02 35 10 26 10; www.benedictine.fr. Open daily July-Aug. 10am-7pm; from Sept. to mid-Oct. and Apr.-June 10am-1pm and 2-6:30pm; from mid-Oct. to early Jan. and from mid-Feb. to Mar. 10:30am-12:45pm and 2-6pm. Last entry 1hr. before close. Reserve ahead for guided group tours in English or French. €6.50, ages 12-18 €2, under 12 free, families of 2 adults and at least 1 child €14. AmEx/MC/V.)

BASSE-NORMANDIE

Since the mid-19th century, the Parisian elite has flocked to the resorts and thalassotherapy centers (seaside health spas) in the villages along the **Côte Fleurie,** the northeastern coast of Lower Normandy. These days, tourists come from around the world to admire views of the ocean and to shop for regional delicacies like Camembert cheese and *calvados* (apple brandy). Because some of the smaller beach towns between Le Havre and Caen aren't exciting enough to justify their tourist-town prices, hotels and hostels in either city make good budget bases; Bus Verts connections between Le Havre, Caen, Bayeux, and other coastal towns make daytrips a viable option.

HONFLEUR   ☎02 31

Miraculously unharmed by WWII, the harbor town of Honfleur (on-fler; pop. 6000) offers an old-fashioned, quirky charm that fosters an aged population and a close-knit community of artists who often set up their easels in the streets. Middle-aged and elderly tourists flock to Honfleur in the sunny months, mostly to browse the large number of local art galleries and boutiques, sample regional liqueurs, and mill around the picturesque waterfront.

⬛ 🚊 TRANSPORTATION AND PRACTICAL INFORMATION

Buses: Bus Verts (☎08 10 21 42 14) leaves from the *gare routière* at the end of quai Lepaulmier; Line #20 goes to **Caen** (2hr.; 9-15 per day; €7.20, under 26 €6.10; 1hr. express €10.10) and **Le Havre** (30min.; 4-5 per day; €4.10, under 26 €3.50). Office open July-Aug. M-Sa 9:30-11:45am and 1:15-6pm; Sept.-June M-F 9am-12:15pm and 2:15-6:15pm, Sa 9am-12:15pm.

Taxis: ☎06 08 60 17 98. 24hr.

Tourist Office: Quai Lepaulmier (☎02 31 89 23 30; www.ot-honfleur.fr). Take a right out of the bus station and follow quai Lepaulmier 2 blocks. Offers a great map, with several walking tours (2.5-7km) of the town and its forests. Open July-Aug. M-Sa 10am-7pm, Su 10am-5pm; Sept. and Easter-June M-Sa 10am-12:30pm and 2-6:30pm, Su 10am-5pm; from Oct. to mid-Apr. M-Sa 10am-12:30pm and 2-6pm.

Tours: Tram tours (☎02 31 89 28 41) in French only (45min.) leave weekends in May and daily June-Sept. from the bus stop. €5.50, under 18 €4.10.

Postal Code: 14600.

🏠 🏕 ACCOMMODATIONS AND CAMPING

Les Cascades, 17 pl. Thiers (☎02 31 89 05 83), across from the tourist office, with entrances on cours des Fossés and rue de la Ville. Offers 17 airy double rooms in an ideal location. Immaculate bathrooms. Rooms equipped with TVs, telephones, and window boxes; some have skylights. At the elegant seafood restaurant below the hotel, *plats* cost €9.50-14 and *menus* run €13-32. Breakfast €6, children €4. Open Feb.-Nov. Singles and doubles with shower €60. Extra bed €8. AmEx/MC/V. ❹

Camping du Phare, bd. Charles V (☎02 31 89 10 26; www.campings-plage.com), 300m from the *centre-ville*. Arrive early in summer to get a shaded spot. Showers €1.20. Laundry. Reception 8:30am-10pm. Gates closed 10pm-7am. Open Apr.-Nov. €6 per person, under 12 €4; sites €6.70. Electricity €4.05-5.80. Package deal (€20) includes entrance for 4 people, 6 amps of electricity, and access to water. Cash only. ❶

🍴 FOOD

Many relatively pricey and indistinguishable restaurants and *brasseries* along the **quai Sainte-Catherine** and on **place Hamelin** provide a taste of local seafood (*menus* €13-30). For the basics, there is a **Champion** supermarket up rue de la République, near pl. Sorel. (Open July-Aug. M-F 8:30am-1pm and 2:30-7:30pm, Sa 8:30am-7:30pm, Su 9am-1pm; Sept.-June M-F 8:30am-12:30pm and 2:30-7:30pm, Sa 8:30am-7:30pm. MC/V.) Wednesday mornings (8am-1pm), witness **Marché Bio** (organic produce market) on **place Sainte-Catherine,** beside the church; the regular market, which also sells crafts and souvenirs, is held in the same location on Saturday mornings (8am-1pm).

Pom'Cannelle, 60 quai Ste-Catherine (☎02 31 89 55 25). Offers dozens of occasionally bizarre and always delicious flavors of ice cream, including cassis, almond milk, and violet. 1 scoop €2.20, 2 scoops €4. Open daily July-Aug. 9am-midnight; Sept.-June 2-7pm; hours vary. MC/V over €15. ❶

Le Bistrot à Crêpes, 1 quai de Passagers (☎02 31 89 74 96). One of the most affordable options near the water. Serves *crêpes* (€2.50-13.80) and fondue (€14-15). *Menus* €14.50. Open Tu-Su noon-3pm and 6:30-10pm; hours vary. MC/V. ❷

👁 SIGHTS

Honfleur's winding cobblestone side streets hide architectural delights, small antique shops, specialized gift boutiques, and countless art studios. The **Pass Musées** gives access to four of Honfleur's museums and its bell tower. (€9.20, students and ages 10-18 €6.20, under 10 free.)

ÉGLISE SAINTE-CATHERINE. This wood structure—built as a temporary fix after its predecessor was destroyed in the Hundred Years' War—dates back to the 15th century. Its peculiar second nave, built to accommodate the growing population of the town, gives the church the bizarre appearance of two overturned boats. *(Open daily 10am-6pm, except during mass on Su at 10am. Free.)* The church's **bell tower,** across the street, holds a small exhibit of religious art. *(Open Mar. 15-Sept. daily 10am-noon and 2-6pm; Oct.-Nov. M and W-F 2:30-5pm, Sa-Su 10am-noon and 2:30-5pm. €2, free with admission to Musée Eugène Boudin.)*

MUSÉE EUGÈNE BOUDIN. Named in honor of Honfleur's most famous artist, the Musée Eugène Boudin pays tribute to artists who were born or worked in Honfleur and houses a solid collection of Impressionist work as well as some 20th-century art. *(Pl. Erik Satie, off rue de l'Homme de Bois. ☎ 02 31 89 54 00. Open from mid-Mar. to Sept. M and W-Su 10am-noon and 2-6pm; from Oct. to mid-Mar. M and W-F 2:30-5pm, Sa-Su 10am-noon and 2:30-5pm. Wheelchair-accessible. €4.70, students and over 59 €2.90, under 10 free. Audio tours in French or English €2. Cash only.)*

MAISONS SATIE. Housed in the birthplace of prolific composer, musician, and artist Erik Satie, this interactive museum is a crazy trip. After being greeted in a darkened room by a giant illuminated winged pear—Satie's trademark image—grapple through the odd mind of an eccentric artist accompanied by a soundtrack of his compositions. Among the surreal absurdities are a self-playing piano and a robotic monkey butler. *(67 bd. Charles V. ☎ 02 31 89 11 11. Open M and W-Su May-Sept. 10am-7pm; Oct.-Dec. and from mid-Feb. to Apr. 11am-6pm. 45min. audio tour in English or French. €5.40, students and seniors €3.90, under 10 free.)*

NATUROSPACE. To experience the great outdoors—indoors—head to **Naturospace,** the largest butterfly house in France. The location also boasts a greenhouse brimming with tropical plants and exotic birds. *(Bd. Charles V. ☎ 02 31 81 77 00; www.naturospace.com. Open daily Apr.-Sept. 10am-1pm and 2-7pm; Oct.-Nov. and Feb.-Mar. 10am-1pm and 2-5:30pm. Wheelchair-accessible. €7.70, under 14 €5.90.)*

🏔 OUTDOOR ACTIVITIES

For a hike (25min.; sneakers recommended), head to the top of **Mont Joli** by taking rue du Puits up to the winding rampe du Mont Joli (1.5km). The lookout point offers a beautiful view—especially at sunset—over Honfleur and the **pont de Normandie,** a suspension bridge connecting Haute- and Basse-Normandie that boasts the tallest pylons in the world. After admiring the scene, take a right on the road at the top and follow it around to the **Chapelle de Notre Dame de Grâce,** a tiny gem with model boats hanging from the ceiling and votive plaques covering the walls. (Open daily 8:30am-5:15pm except during mass.)

Picnic in the **Jardin Retrouvé** down on the Jetée de l'Ouest and enjoy the fountains, ponds, waterfalls, and tennis courts. (Open daily June-Aug. 8am-9:30pm; Sept.-Oct. and May 8am-7pm; Nov.-Mar. 8am-6pm). Farther along is the broad green expanse of the **Jardin des Personalités** (Garden of Fame), featuring busts of celebrities who have a connection to Honfleur.

CAEN
☎ 02 31

At the end of WWII, three-quarters of Caen (KAI-ehn; pop. 200,000) had been destroyed and two-thirds of its citizens were left homeless. The city of William the Conqueror has since been skillfully restored to its pre-war condition and is now part historical monument, part sizzling university city. It makes a good base from which to explore the D-Day beaches, and, with an abundance of busy bars and outdoor *brasseries*, it has a decidedly younger feel and cheaper prices than its neighbors along the Côte Fleurie.

▐ TRANSPORTATION

Trains: Pl. de la Gare. Ticket office open 5am-8:30pm. To: **Cherbourg** (1hr., 7 per day, €18.80); **Paris** (2hr., 11 per day, €30); **Rennes** (3hr., 2 per day, €32); **Rouen** (1hr., 5-9 per day, €23); **Tours** (3hr., M-F and Su 3 per day, €51) via **Paris St-Lazare.**

Buses: Bus Verts (☎08 10 21 42 14), at the *gare routière* to the left of the train station (open July-Aug. M-Sa 7:30am-7pm, Su 9am-3pm; Sept.-June M 6:30am-7pm, Tu-F 7:30am-7pm, Sa 8:30am-7pm) and a kiosk at pl. Courtonne (open M 7:30am-7pm, Tu-F 7:45am-7pm, Sa 9am-7pm). To **Bayeux** (1hr.; M-F 3 per day; €4, under 26 €3.40) and **Le Havre** (2-3hr.; 3 per day; €10, under 26 €8.50). Express to **Le Havre** (1hr., 2 per day, €14) stops in **Honfleur** (1hr., 2 per day, €10). The **Carte Liberté** gives unlimited rides in a set period. Day pass €11.60, 3 days €22, 1 week €32.

Ferries: Brittany Ferries run to **Portsmouth, ENG** from **Ouistreham,** 13km north of Caen. See **Getting There: By Boat,** p. 30. Bus Verts #1 links Ouistreham to Caen's *centre-ville* and train station (40min.; M-F 24 per day; €2, students €1.70).

Public Transportation: Twisto, the local bus and tram system, supplies schedules and maps at its information office, 15 rue de Geôle (☎02 31 15 55 55; twisto.fr), across the street from the château. Open July 15-Aug. 15 M-F 9am-5pm; Aug. 16-July 14 M-F 8am-6:30pm, Sa 10am-12:30pm and 1:30-5pm; hours vary by season. Smaller kiosk by the Théâtre de Caen open M-F 8am-12:30pm and 1:30-5pm. Tickets €1.30, carnet of 10 €10.10, 1-day pass €3.40, 3-day pass €6.60, weekly pass €12.

Taxis: Abbeilles Taxis Caen, 52 pl. de la Gare (☎02 31 52 17 89). 24hr. Late-night taxi stand at bd. Maréchal Leclerc near rue St-Jean open daily 10pm-3am.

✦ ☐ ORIENTATION AND PRACTICAL INFORMATION

Caen's train station and youth hostel are located relatively far from the *centre-ville* (1km and 3km, respectively). Ambitious travelers can walk from the station, but it's best to take the tram or bus to and from the hostel. Trams stop running just after midnight, so plan accordingly. The two tram lines, A and B, leave from the train station and cut through the *centre-ville;* take either line to St-Pierre (5min.). The St-Pierre stop is on bd. des Alliés, which intersects **avenue du 6 Juin** and **rue Saint-Jean.** These parallel streets run toward the *centre-ville* and border the lively districts between **rue Saint-Pierre** and **rue de l'Oratoire.**

Tourist Office: Pl. St-Pierre (☎02 31 27 14 14; www.tourisme.caen.fr), on rue St-Jean by the Église St-Pierre. Hotel booking, useful brochures, and free maps. *Sortir à Caen,* printed every 3 months, lists concerts and events.

Tours: City tours July-Aug. in French only (1½hr.; Tu-Sa 1-2 per day; €5-6, students €3.50-4.50, under 10 free). Nighttime tours in French from mid-July to Aug. €10-13, students and ages 10-18 €7-9, under 10 free; reservations required. Office open July-Aug. M-Sa 9am-7pm, Su 10am-1pm and 2-5pm; Sept. and Mar.-June M-Sa 9:30am-6:30pm, Su 10am-1pm; Oct.-Feb. M-Sa 9:30am-1pm and 2-6pm, Su 10am-1pm.

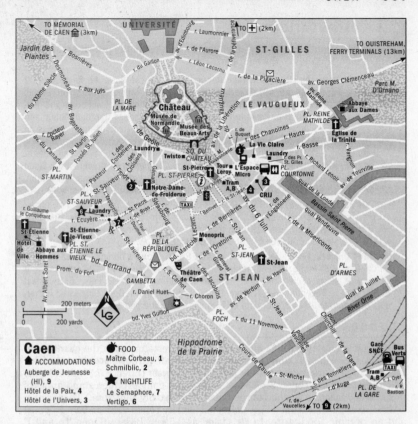

Youth Center: Centre Régional d'Information Jeunesse (CRIJ), 16 rue Neuve St-Jean (☎02 31 27 80 80; www.crij-bn.org), off av. du 6 Juin. Info on events, jobs, and lodging. Photocopiers available. Open M 1-6pm, Tu-Th 10am-6pm, F 10am-5pm.

Laundromats: 17 rue de Prairies St-Gilles (☎06 72 74 57 24). Open daily 7am-9pm. Wash €4 per 8kg, dry €1 per 10min. Also at 16 rue Ecuyère (☎06 80 96 08 26; open daily 7am-9pm) and at 33 rue de Geôle (☎06 60 55 75 60; open daily 7am-9pm).

Public Toilets: Pl. Courtonne, by the Bus Verts kiosk. Free.

Police: 10 rue Thiboud de la Fresnaye (☎02 31 29 22 22).

Pharmacies: Pharmacie Danjou-Rousselot, 5 pl. Malherbe (☎02 31 30 78 00), at the intersection of rue Ecuyère and rue St-Pierre. Open M and Sa 9am-7:30pm, Tu-F 8:30am-7:30pm. Also at 2 bd. des Alliés (☎02 31 27 70 10). Open M-Sa 8am-8pm.

Hospital: Centre Hospitalier Universitaire, av. Côte de Nacre (☎02 31 06 31 06).

Internet Access: L'Espace, 1 rue Basse (☎02 31 93 37 14). 31 computers and DVD Blu-ray rental. €0.80 per 10min., €1.90 per 30min., €5 per 2hr. Open M-F 10am-10pm, Sa 10am-11pm, Su 10:30am-1:30pm and 3-9pm.

Post Office: Pl. Gambetta (☎02 31 39 35 78), past the theater on bd. du Maréchal Leclerc. **Currency exchange** available. Open M-F 8am-7pm, Sa 8:30am-12:30pm. **Postal Code:** 14000.

ACCOMMODATIONS

In Caen, you'll find a couple of well-situated and reasonably priced options, all of which fill up quickly in the summer.

Auberge de Jeunesse (HI): Résidence Robert Rème, 68 rue Eustache Restout (☎02 31 52 19 96; fax 84 29 49). Take bus #5 (dir.: Fleury Cimitière) to Lycée Fresnel. Backtrack for half a block, then turn right on rue Restout; the hostel will be on your left. Alternatively, take tram B to Rostand-Fresnel, walk half a block to the roundabout, and turn right onto rue Armand Marie. Make another right on rue Restout—the hostel is on your left. 3km from the *centre-ville*, but the clean and spacious rooms are worth the trek. 4-person, single-sex dorms with toilets, sinks, and showers. Communal kitchen, cafeteria, and TV room. Photocopy €0.10 per page, fax €0.20 per page. Breakfast €2. Linen €2.50. Laundry €3, dry €1.50. Free Wi-Fi. Wheelchair-accessible. Reception 5-9pm. Check-out 10am. Lockout 10am-3pm. Open June-Sept. Dorms €11. Cash only. ❶

Hôtel de la Paix, 14 rue Neuve St-Jean (☎02 31 86 18 99; fax 08 20 74), off av. du 6 Juin, near the château. Simple, clean rooms with TVs and firm beds. Breakfast €5. Reception 24hr. Singles €29, with toilet €32, with shower and toilet €35; doubles €32/36/39; triples €40/43/47. Extra bed €8. AmEx/MC/V. ❷

Hôtel de l'Univers, 12 quai Vendeuvre (☎02 31 85 46 14; www.hotelunivers-caen.com), off the Bassin St-Pierre. Recently renovated, airy rooms come with TVs, telephones, and showers or baths; pricier ones offer views of the harbor. Free Wi-Fi. Pets €6. Breakfast €6. Free Wi-Fi. Reception M-F 7:30am-10pm, Sa-Su 8:30am-10pm. Singles €37; doubles €42, with toilet €48, with bath €57; triples €62. Extra bed €6. MC/V. ❸

FOOD

Brasseries compete with Chinese and African restaurants in the **quartier Vaugueux** near the château, and there are plenty of cafes around **boulevard Maréchal Leclerc.** Large markets are held at **place Saint-Sauveur** (open F 7:30am-1:30pm) and **place Courtonne** (open Su 7:30am-2:30pm). A daily produce stand appears on **place Courtonne,** at the end of rue Basse. (Open daily 8am-7pm.) There's also a **Monoprix** supermarket at 45 bd. Maréchal Leclerc (open M-Sa 8:30am-8:50pm) and an organic food store, **La Vie Claire,** at 3-5 rue Basse. (Open Tu and F 9:30am-7pm, W-Th 10am-1pm and 3-7pm, Sa 10am-5pm.)

Maître Corbeau, 8 rue Buquet (☎02 31 93 93 00; www.maitre-corbeau.com). Herds of people line up outside this cow-themed eatery at dinnertime. For a cheaper but still filling meal, come for lunch. *Plats* €8-18. Lunch *menu* €9.90. Dinner *menus* €19-24. Fondues €14. Dessert €6. Open M and Sa 7-10:30pm, Tu-F 11:45am-1:30pm and 7-10:30pm. Closed 3 weeks in Aug. Reservations recommended. MC/V. ❸

Schmilblic, 53 rue Froide, off rue St-Pierre. This mom-and-pop lunch counter is a local favorite for its giant, made-to-order sandwiches (€2.80-4), jacket potatoes (large baked potatoes with fillings like ham, cheese, and curry; €4.50), and *crêpes* (€1.10-2.40). Open M-W 10:45am-8pm, Th-F 10:45am-1:30pm. Cash only. ❶

SIGHTS

MÉMORIAL DE CAEN. Hands down the best—albeit the most expensive—of Normandy's WWII museums, the Mémorial de Caen immerses visitors in a powerful exploration of the war, beginning with the "failure of peace" after WWI, then the battles of WWII, the tensions of the Cold War, and finally the modern prospects for peace. Engaging exhibits unfold with a blend of vintage footage, high-tech audio-visuals, historical artifacts, and contemporary art. Explore the

Nobel Peace Prize exhibit in the converted bunker in the basement and the peace gardens designed by different world powers. Allow at least 2hr. to see the museum. Also offers package tours of D-Day beaches. *(Take bus #2 dir.: Mémorial/La Folie to Memorial. ☎02 31 06 06 44; www.memorial-caen.fr. Open from mid-Feb. to from mid-Nov. daily 9am-7pm; mid-Nov. to early Feb. Tu-Su 9:30am-6pm. Last entry 1hr. before close. Mar.-Sept. €17, students, ages 10-18, and seniors €16. Oct.-Feb. €16.50/15.50. AmEx/MC/V.)*

CHÂTEAU. The ruins of William the Conqueror's château sprawl across a hill above the *centre-ville*. The fortress, built in 1060 and expanded over the centuries, was besieged several times during the Hundred Years' War and served as military barracks in 1815. It now hosts museums in its buildings, picnickers on its vast lawns, and tourists on its ramparts, which are open to the public. The free anthropological **Musée de Normandie,** within the château grounds, displays miniature models, jewelry, clothing, and tools tracing the cultural and agricultural evolution of people living on Norman soil from the beginning of civilization to the present day. Outside, the **Jardin des Simples**—an herb garden—sprouts medieval medicinal and culinary plants. *(☎02 31 30 47 60; www.musee-de-normandie. caen.fr. 5-6 temporary exhibits per year housed in the church and the Salle de l'Echequiers. Open June-Sept. daily 9:30am-6pm; Oct.-May M and W-Su 9:30am-6pm. Tours in French for groups by appointment. Wheelchair-accessible. €3, students and group members €2, under 18 free.)* To the right as you enter the château are the spacious, well-lit, and labyrinthine galleries of the **Musée des Beaux-Arts,** which features two large floors of galleries of European art from the 16th century onward as well as temporary exhibits. The year 2009 will usher in an exhibit of Norman art—a collaborative effort with the MBAs of Rouen and Le Havre. *(☎02 31 30 47 70; www.ville-caen.fr/mba. Open M and W-Su 9:30am-6pm. Wheelchair-accessible. Free; entrance fee for temporary exhibits.)*

ABBAYE-AUX-HOMMES. Caen, the seat of William the Conqueror's duchy, owes its first-class Romanesque architecture to William's guilty conscience. After he incestuously married his distant cousin Mathilda despite the pope's condemnation, William tried to get back on the road to Heaven by building several ecclesiastical structures—most notably Caen's twin Benedictine abbeys. The lavish Abbaye-aux-Hommes has functioned as a boys' school and as a shelter for 10,000 of the town's inhabitants during WWII; today, it is the Hôtel de Ville. Damaged during the Hundred Years' War, the structure got an 18th century facelift. A grand staircase and €1 million chandeliers emphasize the abbey's lap of luxury. *(At rue Albert Sorel. ☎02 31 30 42 81. Open to tourists only for 1½hr. tours in French daily 9:30, 11am, 2:30, 4pm; meet in lobby. Additional ½-price, 50min. tours July-Aug. at 10:15am, 3:15, 5:15pm. €2.20, students and seniors €1.10, under 18 free; Su free.)*

JARDIN DES PLANTES. Boasting open grass fields, a gorgeous botanical garden, a greenhouse, and an *orangerie* (orange grove), this is the perfect place for a relaxing afternoon. *(5 pl. Blot; turn left on rue Bosnières from rue Geôle. ☎02 30 48 30 32. Open M-F 8am-sunset, Sa-Su 10am-sunset. Greenhouse open daily 2-5pm. Free.)*

OTHER SIGHTS. Inside the late Romanesque and early Gothic architecture of the adjacent **Église Saint-Étienne** is William's tomb, which was pillaged and stripped of all its contents—save the monarch's left femur—during the Wars of Religion. *(Open M-Sa 8:30am-12:30pm and 1:30-7:30pm, Su 8:30am-12:30pm and 2:30-7:30pm, except during services.)* On the other side of the city sits the **Église de la Trinité of the Abbaye-aux-Dames,** off rue des Chânoines, which houses Mathilda's tomb. Banners that depict famous women surround the church. *(☎02 31 06 98 98. Church open daily until 5:30pm. 1hr. tours in French daily 2:30, 4:30pm. Free.)*

NIGHTLIFE

Bars and clubs line the **quai Vendeuvre** and populate the area between Notre-Dame de Froiderue and the Abbaye aux Hommes.

Vertigo, 14 rue Ecuyère (☎02 31 85 43 12), just past the intersection with rue St-Pierre. Kick off the evening with university students amid medieval decor. The bar closes early but stays packed until closing. Beer €2.30. Mixed drinks €4.80. Happy hour 7-9pm. Open M-Sa 10am-1am. AmEx/MC/V.

Le Semaphore, 44 rue le Bras (☎02 31 39 08 57). Catering to a nocturnal clientele, this bar gets lively (and crowded) from 1am on. Loud music, neon lights, and sleek leather bar stools set the mood. Beer €2.20-3.50, after midnight €2.60-4.20. Mixed drinks €3-4.50/€4.60-7. Happy hour 7-9pm. Open M-Sa 7pm-4am. MC/V.

BAYEUX   ☎02 31

Bayeux (bah-yuh; pop. 28,000) may be most famous for its 900-year-old tapestry narrating William the Conqueror's victory over England, but the lively city offers more than historical needlework. After narrowly escaping the devastation of WWII and surviving both Nazi occupation in 1940 and Allied liberation in 1944, Bayeux today retains its charming architecture and a resplendent cathedral. The city's Old World atmosphere, pleasant—if slightly touristy—pedestrian byways, and manifold D-Day tour operators cater to a map-toting middle-aged crowd, but Bayeux makes an equally appealing base for younger travelers looking to tour WWII sites.

TRANSPORTATION

Trains: Pl. de la Gare. Ticket office open M-Th 6am-8:40pm, F 6am-9:40pm, Sa 6:30am-9:20pm, Su 8:30am-9:20pm. To **Caen** (20min., 23 per day, €5.50), **Cherbourg** (1hr., 12 per day, €14.60), and **Paris** (2hr., 12 per day, €32).

Buses: Bus Verts, pl. de la Gare (☎02 31 92 02 92). Buy tickets on board or at the office. Open June-Aug. M-F 9:30am-1:15pm and 2:30-4:30pm, Sa 10:15am-1:15pm and 2:30-4:30pm; Sept.-May M-Sa 10am-noon. Buses head west to small towns and east to **Caen** (Line 30; 1hr.; M-F 2-3 per day; €4.10, under 26 €3.50). Full-day **Carte Liberté** €11.90. See p. 314 for transport to D-Day beaches.

Public Transportation: Bybus, pl. de la Gare (☎02 31 92 02 92), in the same office as Bus Verts. Runs local buses 7:30am-6pm. Open June-Aug. M-F 9:30am-1:15pm and 2:30-4:30pm, Sa 10:15am-1:15pm and 2:30-4:30pm; Sept.-May M-Sa 10am-noon. Tickets 9-11:30am and 2-4pm €0.75, all other times €0.95; carnet of 10 €7.20, under 20 €6.60. Buy tickets on board, carnets at the office.

Taxis: Taxis du Bessin (☎02 31 92 92 40), at the train station.

ORIENTATION AND PRACTICAL INFORMATION

To get to the *centre-ville* from the train station, bear right to reach bd. Sadi Carnot, then turn left and follow it to a roundabout. Go right at the roundabout up rue Larcher to reach the cathedral. Past the cathedral on rue de Nesmond (which becomes rue de la Maitrise) lies **place Charles de Gaulle.** Several *ponts* (bridges) traverse the **L'Aure River,** which runs through the city.

Tourist Office: Pont St-Jean (☎02 31 51 28 28; www.bayeux-bessin-tourism.com). From rue Larcher, make a right on rue St-Jean; the office is on the left (20min. from train station). English-speaking staff dispenses a city and regional guide with maps and

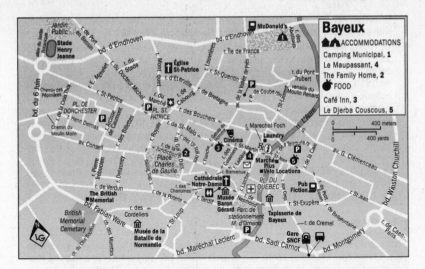

info on D-Day tours. Hotel and D-Day tours reservation service available (€2). Open July-Aug. M-Sa 9am-7pm, Su 9am-1pm and 2-6pm; Sept.-Oct. and Apr.-June daily 9:30am-12:30pm and 2-6pm; Nov.-Mar. M-Sa 9:30am-12:30pm and 2-5:30pm.

ATMs: Available around pl. St-Patrice and up rue St-Martin (becomes rue St-Malo).

Laundromat: 10 rue Maréchal Foch (☎06 08 24 69 98). Wash €3.70-7.10, dry €0.50 per 5min. Open daily 7am-9pm.

Public Toilets: Near the cathedral on rue Leforestier. Free.

Police: 2 pl. St-Patrice (☎02 31 92 02 42; 24hr.). Open M-F 8:30am-noon and 2-6pm, Sa 11am-noon.

Pharmacy: Pharmacie du Pont St-Jean, 1 rue St-Jean (☎02 31 92 07 63). Open M-F 8:30am-12:30pm and 1:30-7:30pm, Sa 8:30am-12:30pm and 1:30-7pm.

Hospital: 13 rue de Nesmond (☎02 31 51 51 51).

Internet Access: Pub Fiction, 14 rue Petit Rouen (☎02 31 10 17 41), close to rue St-Jean. 1 computer. €1 per 15min. Open M-Th 8:30pm-2am, F-Sa 8:30pm-3am. **McDonald's,** bd. Eindhoven at the intersection with av. de la Vallée des Prés, also has free and unlimited Wi-Fi. Open daily 9am-11pm.

Post Office: 14 rue Larcher (☎02 31 51 24 90). **Currency exchange** and photocopying (€0.10 per page) available. **ATM.** Open M-F 8:15am-6:30pm, Sa 8:15am-noon. **Postal Code:** 14400.

ACCOMMODATIONS AND CAMPING

Demand for lodging often exceeds supply in Bayeux, especially during the summer months. It pays to call ahead, but don't expect to find anything cheap. Caen is a much cheaper base for the D-Day beaches. Plan with military precision if you want a room around June 6, the anniversary of D-Day.

Le Maupassant, 19 rue St-Martin (☎02 31 92 28 53; h.lemaupassant@orange.fr). Small, cheerful rooms. On the ground floor, a *brasserie* serves salads (€7-9) and sandwiches (€3-5) on a pedestrian-filled street in the *centre-ville*. Some rooms come with toilets; all have TVs. Breakfast €6. Reception at bar 7:30am-9pm. Singles €29; doubles with shower €40; quads with bath €69. Extra bed €10. MC/V. ❷

The Family Home/Auberge de Jeunesse (HI), 39 rue Général de Dais (☎02 31 92 15 22). Rustic decor and stone courtyards with a British telephone booth and giant chess set add character. Shower and toilet in hall and in some dorms. Breakfast included. Dinner (€10) at 7:30pm. Reception hours sporadic; try calling and looking for the owner if nobody is there. Check-out noon. Dorms €20. Help clean the kitchen and get lunch and a free bed for the night. Cash only. ❶

Camping Municipal, bd. Eindhoven (☎/fax 02 31 92 08 43), within a 12min. walk of the *centre-ville*. From the tourist office, take rue Genas Duhomme to the right off rue St-Martin. Continue straight on av. de la Vallée des Prés. Turn right onto bd. Eindhoven. The campground is on the right. Volleyball, playground, and nearby swimming pool. Laundry (wash €4, dry €2.40). Office open M-Sa 8-10am and 5-7pm, Su 6-8pm. Gates closed 10pm-7am. Open May-Sept. €3.25 per person, under 7 €1.70; sites €4. Electricity €3.30. 10% discount for stays of 5 days or more. AmEx/MC/V. ❶

FOOD

There are markets (open 7am-1pm) on **place Saint-Patrice** (Sa) and **rue Saint-Jean** (W). Down the walkway from the tourist office on rue St-Jean is a **Marché Plus** supermarket. (Open M-Sa 7am-9pm, Su 8:30am-12:30pm.) Most of the town's eateries populate **rue Saint-Martin, rue Saint-Jean,** and their side streets.

Le Djerba Couscous, 67 rue St-Jean (☎02 31 22 51 12). With authentic decoration and a luxurious, intimate upstairs lounge, this Tunisian restaurant maintains a level of unassuming class. Take a break from the usual *pain* and *fromage* to try authentic North African dishes, including astonishingly filling couscous. Plats €8.70-9.50. *Menus* €10-22. Couscous €8.50-21 (including a vegetarian option). Open Tu-Su July-Aug 6:30-10:30pm; Sept.-June noon-2pm and 6:30-10:30pm. AmEx/MC/V. ❸

Café Inn, 67 rue St-Martin (☎02 31 21 11 37). This cozy corner cafe, decorated with teacups and pots, has a quaint cottage feel. Perfect for a lunch break or a snack. Offers salads (€5.70-8), sandwiches (€3.80-4.40), *omelettes* (€4.40-7.40), and pastries (€2.70-4.40). Open M-Sa 9am-7pm. MC/V. ❶

SIGHTS

TAPISSERIE DE BAYEUX. In 1066, Guillaume le Bâtard (William the Bastard) earned himself a more regal nickname by crossing the English Channel with a large cavalry to defeat his distant cousin Harold, who, according to the Norman version of the tale, had stolen the English throne from William. After a grueling 14hr. battle, in which Harold was dramatically killed by an archer, William triumphed in the last successful invasion of England—the Battle of Hastings—to become "le Conquérant" (the Conqueror). In 58 frames, this exquisite tapestry uses striking narrative techniques to illustrate the battle. A mere 50cm tall, but 70m long, the tapestry—now over 900 years old—hangs in all its glory at the **Centre Guillaume le Conquérant.** An edifying exhibit, including an annotated reprint of the tapestry and a film shown in English and French, precedes the viewing of the masterpiece itself. A well-paced audio tour, included in the entry ticket, is available in 14 languages; a children's audio tour is also available in French and English. (*13 bis rue de Nesmond. ☎02 31 51 25 50; www.tapisserie-bayeux. fr. Open daily May-Aug. 9am-7pm; from Sept. to mid-Nov. and from mid-Mar. to Apr. 9am-6:30pm; from mid-Nov. to mid-Mar. 9:30am-12:30pm and 2-6pm. Last entrance 45min. before close. Wheelchair-accessible. €7.70, students and seniors €3.80, under 10 free.*)

CATHÉDRALE NOTRE DAME. The original home of the tapestry, Bayeux's Romanesque-style cathedral was consecrated in 1077. Its central tower contrasts with the simpler twin towers at either side of the entrance. It is a true stylistic melting pot: 13th-century Gothic windows perch above Romanesque arches in the nave; beneath, the 11th-century crypt displays fading 15th-century frescoes. *(Rue de Bienvenue. ☎ 02 31 92 01 85. Open daily July-Sept. 8:30am-7pm; Oct.-Dec. and Apr.-June 8:30am-6pm; Jan.-Mar. 9am-5pm. Closed during mass. Wheelchair-accessible.)*

OTHER SIGHTS. The events of the D-Day landing and the subsequent 76-day struggle for control of northern France are recounted in the **Musée de la Bataille de Normandie.** A stirring film in both English and French dramatizes the Battle of Normandy, while a collection of war artifacts—from tanks to signposts—accompanies the illustration of each phase in the battle. *(Bd. Fabian Ware. ☎ 02 31 51 46 90. Open daily May-Sept. 9:30am-6:30pm; from Oct. to mid-Jan. and Feb.-Apr. 10am-12:30pm and 2-6pm. Last entry 1hr. before close. English-language film every 2hr. €6.50, students €3.80, under 10 free. MC/V.)* The rows of closely set tombstones that line the **British Military Cemetery,** opposite the museum, mark the graves of 4144 Commonwealth soldiers who died in the Battle of Normandy. The **British Memorial** across the street, which names the soldiers without graves, bears the Latin inscription, "We, conquered by William, have freed the homeland of our conqueror."

 FESTIVALS

D-Day Festival, around June 6. Witness spectacular fireworks and musical performances in honor of the WWII invasion.

Fêtes Medievales, 1st weekend in July. Enjoy costume parades and traditional dances at this blast-from-the-past festival.

Festival Gourmand du Cochon de Bayeux, 2nd week of Oct. Indulge in delicacies that celebrate the region's prize breed of pig.

Le Goût du Large, 2nd weekend in Nov. Seafood-lovers should a light breakfast; this maritime festival offers a feast of scallops.

D-DAY BEACHES ☎ 02 31

In 1943, German forces occupying France fortified their defenses with the "Atlantic Wall"—a series of bunkers, and batteries all along France's northern coasts. The Allies learned the difficulty of attacking a major port from the failed 1942 Dieppe raid, in which dozens of Canadians were either killed or taken prisoner. However, convinced that the only way to overthrow Hitler was to take his "Fortress Europe" by sea and desperate to open a second front to relieve the pressure on the eastern front in Russia, Allied commanders decided that Normandy would be their beachhead for the liberation of France. Allied forces set the stage for the infiltration by flooding German intelligence services with false information and planting dummy tanks near Norway to confuse General Rommel and his troops. The action began in the pre-dawn hours of June 6, 1944, when 29,000 troops tumbled onto the coast between the Cotentin Peninsula and Orne. A few hours later, 130,000 more troops arrived by sea; by the end of June 850,000 had landed. The losses incurred on D-Day were devastating to both sides; the Allies alone lost 10,300 troops. The Allied victory was a key precursor to Paris's August 25 liberation and later successes.

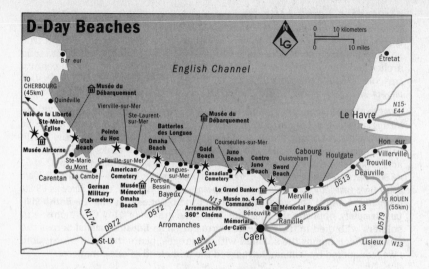

TRANSPORTATION AND ORIENTATION

The Americans who landed at the westernmost beaches—code-named **Utah** and **Omaha**—witnessed the bloodiest battles. **Voie de la Liberté** (Liberty Rd.) follows the US Army's advance to Bastogne, Belgium. British troops landed in the east at **Gold** and **Sword,** and Canadians landed at **Juno.** In the center, between Omaha and Gold, lies **Arromanches,** where the Allies hastily constructed one of two crucial offshore ports.

Bayeux makes the best base for the western and central beaches (Utah, Omaha, and Gold) and is home to companies that offer great guided tours, but Caen has better access by bus to Juno and Sword. The best way to see the sights is undoubtedly by car—not only can you get farther and go at your own pace, but you'll also have the opportunity to stop at any of the countless museums along the route. Even with a car, it is extremely difficult to get to all of the sights in a single day, as the beaches span over 50 mi. For a quick visit, it's best to focus on a single beach or a group of neighboring beaches; if you are careful with your bus connections, Juno and Sword Beaches can both be visited in one day, as can Utah and Omaha. Bus Verts is by far the cheapest way to get from sight to sight and offers many interesting routes, especially from July through August, when service expands. Numerous companies offer guided minibus tours of the major sights. These tours, typically geared toward visitors from a particular country involved in the D-Day invasion, are pricey but educational—quality ranges widely among different tour guides even within the same company, so it's a bit of a gamble. Call in advance to reserve. For the budget-conscious and physically fit, biking to the beaches is a viable option, though cyclists will only be able to visit a limited number of sites. Walking from beach to beach is practically impossible.

Bus Verts (☎08 10 21 42 14), offices in Bayeux and Caen. No-frills bus service throughout Normandy. Special D-Day lines running once a day July-Aug. leave from Caen and Bayeux and visit the 3 beaches (Omaha, Gold, and Juno). Ask at office for complete listing of lines. Tickets €1.55-10.20 (under 26 €1.30-8.70), depending on distance.

From Bayeux: Line #70 serves the area of Omaha Beach, with stops near Pointe du Hoc and the American Cemetery (M-Sa 2 per day). Line #74 serves Gold and Juno Beaches, with stops at Arromanches, Ver-sur-Mer, and Courselles-sur-Mer (M-Sa 3 per day). In July-Aug., line #75 runs from Bayeux to the sights on Gold and Juno Beaches as well as Sword Beach, the easternmost beach by the port of Ouistreham.

From Caen: Line #1 serves Sword Beach. A transfer to line #3 will take you to Juno; another transfer to line #74 can take you on to Gold, but you'll have trouble returning to Caen the same evening.

Tours:

Normandy Sightseeing Tours (☎02 31 51 70 52; www.normandywebguide.com), based in Bayeux. ½- and full-day tours with stops at beaches, various museums, and lesser-known (and often completely unmarked) sights. Enthusiastic and incredibly knowledgeable English-speaking guides. 3hr. morning tours €40, students €35, under 10 €25; 4hr. afternoon tours €45/40/30; 9hr. day tours €75/65/45. Pickup in Bayeux at the train station, at pl. du Québec, or at your hotel. MC/V.

Overlordtour (☎06 70 21 43 42; www.overlordtour.com). Anecdotes and historical photos add flair to tours in English and French. Personalized tours also available. ½-day tour €45, full-day tour €80. Tours depart from pl. du Québec in Bayeux.

Vélos Location, Impasse de l'Islet or 5 rue Larcher (☎02 31 92 89 16), across from the tourist office. Bike rental ½-day €10, full-day €15, week €90; credit-card deposit. Helmets €2. Open daily June-Aug. 8am-9pm; Sept.-May 8am-8pm.

SIGHTS

WESTERN D-DAY SIGHTS

▉POINTE DU HOC. The US Ranger Force at Pointe du Hoc performed the most difficult landing at D-Day. These 225 specially trained Rangers scaled the sheer 30m bluffs on ropes and ladders under the rain of German gunfire and grenades and successfully neutralized a key German naval battery. Expecting to be reinforced within 12hr., the surviving Rangers ended up defending the position alone against German counterattacks for two and a half days, despite having lost the majority of their supplies at sea during the landing. The ground is still pockmarked from the intense shelling that preceded the Rangers' landing, and shattered fragments of concrete bunkers cover the grassy terrain. (☎02 31 51 90 70; www.cc-isigny-grandcamp-intercom.fr. Info office open Apr.-Oct. daily 10am-1pm and 2-6pm; Nov.-Mar. M and F-Su 9am-1pm and 2-5pm. Grounds open daily 9am-6pm.)

▉AMERICAN CEMETERY. On a cliff overlooking Omaha Beach in Colleville-sur-Mer, over 9000 American gravestones stretch in endless rows across a pristine 172-acre coastal reserve. A marble memorial with giant maps of the Allied advance and a 7m bronze statue, **The Spirit of American Youth Rising from the Waves,** face the graves. The **Garden of the Missing,** behind the statue, lists the names of 1557 soldiers whose remains were never recovered. The neat rows of white headstones, which hold only a fraction of those who died in France, are a moving reminder of the June 6 sacrifices. The newly opened visitors center has exhibits commemorating American losses and touchscreen computer catalogs for locating graves. (☎02 31 51 62 00; www.abmc.gov. Open daily from mid-Apr. to mid-Sept. 9am-6pm; from mid-Sept. to mid-Apr. 9am-5pm.)

OMAHA BEACH. Often referred to as "bloody Omaha," this site near Colleville-sur-Mer saw perhaps the most famous—and by far the most disastrous—invasion. Preliminary Allied bombing did little damage here due to stormy weather and poor visibility; as a result, the German defenses were operating near full capacity. Bunkers (still visible on the hills above the beach) along the length of the coast mowed down hundreds of men and destroyed vehicles and equipment. The first waves of men, caught on the barbed wire and obstacles littering the beach, suffered 85% casualties. Little remains on the beach itself to mark the sacrifices made here, but up the road the **Musée Mémorial d'Omaha Beach** presents uniforms, helmets, and equipment as well as dioramas telling the story of the longest day of WWII. *(Av. de la Libération. ☎ 02 31 21 97 44; www. musee-memorial-omaha.com. Open daily July-Aug. 9:30am-7:30pm; Sept. and from mid-May to June 7:30am-7pm; from mid-Feb. to mid-Mar. 10am-12:30pm and 2:30-6pm; from mid-Mar. to mid-May 9:30am-6:30pm. €5.80, students €4.50, ages 7-15 €3.30)*

GERMAN MILITARY CEMETERY. In La Cambe, not far from the American sights, are the often-overlooked graves of 21,300 German casualties—a reminder of the tragic costs of the war on both sides. *(☎ 02 31 22 70 76. Open Apr.-Oct. M-F 8am-7pm, Sa-Su 9am-7pm; Nov.-Mar. M-F 8am-5pm, Sa-Su 9am-5pm.)*

SAINTE-MÈRE-ÉGLISE. During the invasion, many Allied paratroopers of the 82nd Airborne were accidentally dropped into this small town—including John Steele, who hung from the church steeple for 2hr. in the middle of a fierce firefight before being taken prisoner by the Germans. A model paratrooper still hangs from the roof of the church for which the town was named. Despite heavy casualties, the operation was a success after 6hr. of fighting, when the badly outnumbered paratroopers finally broke through heavy German defenses. Inside the church, a stained-glass window shows Mary and Jesus with paratroopers descending on either side. *(☎ 02 33 41 41 48; http://saintemereeglise50.cef. fr. Open daily 9am-6pm except during services. Wheelchair-accessible. The village is accessible by bus from Cherbourg. Tourist office located at 6 rue Eisenhower. ☎ 02 33 21 00 33; www.sainte-mere-eglise.info.)* The parachute-shaped **Musée Airborne** houses one of the original C-47 Douglas planes that dropped the paratroopers as well as a Waco glider used for delivering equipment and a wide range of other war material. *(14 rue Eisenhower. ☎ 02 33 41 41 35; www.airborne-museum.org. Open daily Apr.-Sept. 9am-6:45pm; Oct.-Nov. and Feb.-Mar. 9:30am-noon and 2-6pm. €6, ages 6-14 €3. MC/V.)*

UTAH BEACH. Americans spearheaded the western flank of the invasion near Ste-Marie-du-Mont at Utah Beach, which runs along the coast below Quinéville. Utah was one of the luckiest and most successful D-Day operations. Instead of landing at the intended location, a heavily fortified German strongpoint, the Allied invasion fleet lost its patrol boat and drifted down the coast, eventually reaching the shore in front of a far weaker outpost, over a mile south of its target. As a result, the landings at Utah incurred under 200 casualties. The **Musée du Débarquement** on the beach honors this success; its films and models demonstrate how the 23,000 soldiers and 1790 vehicles came ashore. After perusing manifold miniature models and memorabilia, clamber inside an amphibious DUKW tank. On the grounds nearby stands a large red granite pillar, a monument to the US forces who fought here that day. Unfortunately, the various D-Day sights at Utah are not accessible by public transportation. *(☎ 02 33 71 53 35; www.utah-beach.com. Open daily June-Sept. 9:30am-7pm; Oct. and Apr.-May 10am-6pm; Nov. and Feb.-Mar. 10am-5:30pm. Last entry 45min. before close. Guided tours in French and English available. Wheelchair-accessible. €5.50, students €4, ages 6-16 €2.50. MC/V.)*

EASTERN D-DAY SIGHTS

⬛**ARROMANCHES.** This small town just west of Gold Beach was where the British built **Port Winston** (a.k.a. "Mulberry B"), the floating harbor that supplied the Allied forces until the Cherbourg port was repaired months later. The Allies sank retired ships as breakwaters and towed over 600,000 tons of concrete across the channel in order to build the port. Sixty years later, the hulking ruins of a harbor built in six days and designed to last 18 months remain floating in a broken semicircle just off the coast. **Arromanches 360° Cinéma,** on the cliffs above the remains of the port, screens a wordless 18min. film, *Le Prix de la*

Liberté (The Price of Freedom). The circular screen allows visitors to vicariously fly planes over Pointe du Hoc, wait in pontoons just offshore, and storm the beaches as the troops did on June 6. *(Chemin du Calvaire. ☎ 02 31 22 30 30; www.arromanches360.com. Open daily June-Aug. 9:40am-6:40pm; early Sept. and from mid- to late May 10:10am-6:10pm; from mid-Sept. to Oct. and from Apr. to mid-May 10:10am-5:40pm; Nov. and Mar. 10:10am-5:10pm; Dec. and Feb. 10:10am-4:40pm. Movies at 10 and 40min. past the hr. €4.20, students, ages 10-18, and seniors €3.70, under 10 and veterans free. MC/V.)* **Musée du Débarquement,** on the beach, tells the history of the port. *(Pl. du 6 Juin. ☎ 02 31 22 34 31; www.normandy1944.com. Open June-Aug. daily 9am-7pm; Sept. M-Sa 9am-6pm, Su 10am-6pm; Oct. and Mar. M-Sa 9:30am-12:30pm and 1:30-5:30pm, Su 10am-12:30pm and 1:30-5:30pm; from Nov. to mid-Dec. and Feb. daily 10am-12:30pm and 1:30-5pm; Apr. M-Sa 9am-12:30pm and 1:30-6pm, Su 10am-12:30pm and 1:30-6pm; May M-Sa 9am-7pm, Su 10am-7pm. Guided 1hr. tours. €6.50, students and under 18 €4.50.)* **Gold Beach** is accessible from the nearby town of Asnelles; a lone German bunker, now blocked up, held the British forces at bay here for 6hr. before being silenced by a mortar.

JUNO BEACH. Approximately 14,000 Canadians—some on bicycles—along with 6000 Brits invaded Norman soil at Juno Beach. The last time Canadians had set foot in France, in the 1942 Dieppe raid, they suffered disastrous losses and appalling casualties. Bent on revenge at Juno, Canadians pushed their attacks farther inland than any other Allied units. The **Centre Juno Beach,** located in Courseulles-sur-Mer, tells the story of the war from the Canadian perspective. Nearby, a giant **Croix de Lorraine**—symbol of the "Free French"—marks the spot where General de Gaulle first returned to French soil in 1944. *(Voie des Français Libres. ☎ 02 31 37 32 17; www.junobeach.org. Open daily Apr.-Sept. 9:30am-7pm; Oct. and Mar. 10am-6pm; Nov.-Dec. and Feb. 10am-1pm and 2-5pm. €6.50, students €5, under 8 free. With guided tour of park €9/7/free. MC/V over €15.)* The **Canadian Cemetery,** with just over 2000 tombs, is located at Bény-sur-Mer Reviers, accessible by bus from Caen.

BATTERIE DE LONGUES. In tiny Longues-sur-Mer, 6km west of Arromanches, these heavily fortified bunkers are a somber reminder of the German presence. Naval bombardment on D-Day destroyed the town but left these bunkers and their guns mostly intact. Now the only remaining armed bunkers in the region, the Batterie de Longues are open for visitors to explore. *(☎ 02 31 21 46 87; www.bayeux-bessin-tourism.com. Open Apr.-Oct. daily 10am-1pm and 2-6pm; Nov.-Mar. F-Su 10am-6pm. 1hr. tours in English and French 5 times per day Apr.-Oct. €4, under 10 free.)*

MÉMORIAL PEGASUS. On June 5, 1944, before any other Allied troops had arrived in Normandy, British paratroopers floated from the sky to capture the bridge code-named Pegasus between Benouville and Ranville. They achieved their goal within 10min. of landing and held the bridge until Scottish reinforcements arrived days later. This museum, also known as the **Musée des Troupes Aéroportées Britanniques,** is located at the site of the bridge and recounts the operations of the British Parachute Brigades behind enemy lines on D-Day. The museum grounds hold the actual bridge as well as a full-scale model of the Horsa glider used to transport men and equipment. *(Av. du Major Howard, at the Pegasus Bridge between Benouville and Ranville. Take Bus Verts #1 from Caen to Mairie in Benouville. Take a right at the roundabout 200 ft. away and cross the bridge; the museum is on the left. ☎ 02 31 78 19 44; www.normandy1944.com. Open daily Apr.-Sept. 9:30am-6:30pm; Oct.-Nov. and Feb.-Mar. 10am-1pm and 2-5pm. €6, students and under 18 €4.50.)*

OUISTREHAM. The British anchored the eastern flank of the invasion at Sword Beach, whose easternmost edge is now a popular beach town. The British success is memorialized by ▓**Le Grand Bunker: Musée du Mur de l'Atlantique,** a former German bunker, which was the last part of the town to be captured (it took 4hr. of constant explosives to break the door down). The bunker's rooms have been recreated, complete with infirmary, communications room, weapons storage, and a working range-finding tower. The top of the tower is also open, accessible by iron rungs set in the concrete. (*Av. du 6 Juin.* ☎02 31 97 28 69. *Open daily Apr.-Sept. 9am-7pm; from Oct. to mid-Nov. and Feb.-Mar. 10am-6pm. €7, ages 6-12 €5.*)

CHERBOURG   ☎02 33

Strategically located at the tip of the Cotentin Peninsula, the port of Cherbourg (shehr-boorgh; pop. 90,000) was a major Allied objective following the D-Day invasion; unfortunately, by the time the city was liberated, the Nazis had damaged its port so badly that it was non-functioning for six months. Now in working order, the port shuttles ferries to England and Ireland. Though the seaside city is short on noteworthy sights, it proudly holds a new aquarium and a *vieille ville* that will keep visitors busy.

▉ TRANSPORTATION

Trains: Ticket office open M-Sa 5:30am-7:55pm, Su 7:30am-8:15pm. To **Paris** (3hr., 6 per day, €41) via **Bayeux** (1hr., 9 per day, €15) and **Caen** (1hr., 11 per day, €19); you can also change trains at **Lison** to reach **Rennes** (3hr., 3 per day, €32).

Buses: Zéphir, 40 bd. Schuman (☎02 33 44 32 22). Buses run 6:30am-8pm. There is a stop in front of the STN office. Tickets €1.10, carnet of 10 €9; night buses F-Sa €0.60. VTNI/STN, across the street from the train station. Open M-F 9am-12:30pm and 2-5:30pm. Serves a variety of regional destinations.

Ferries: Brittany Ferries (☎08 25 82 88 28, www.brittanyferries.fr). Office open June-Aug. daily 6am-9:30pm; Sept.-May. reduced hours. To **Portsmouth** and **Poole, ENG** (1-2hr.; from late May to Sept. 2-3 per day, from Oct. to mid-May every other day). Irish Ferries (☎02 33 23 44 44; www.irishferries.com). Office open M-F 9am-noon and 2-6pm. Overnight trip to **Rosslare, IRE** about every other day. Celtic Link (☎02 33 43 23 87; www.celticlinkferries.com). Office open M-Tu and Th-F 9am-1pm and 2-7pm, W 9am-1pm and 2-9:30pm, Su noon-5:30pm. To **Rosslare, IRE** (3 per week). All ferries depart from Gare Maritime Transmanche, a 45min. walk from the *centre-ville* along bd. Maritime. See **Getting There: By Boat** (p. 30) for more information.

Taxis: At the train station and at the *gare maritime* (☎02 33 53 36 38).

◆▉ ORIENTATION AND PRACTICAL INFORMATION

Tourist Office: 2 quai Alexandre III (☎02 33 93 52 02; www.ot-cherbourg-cotentin.fr). Distributes excellent free maps, a regional event calendar, a list of *chambres d'hôte* (€25-60) and campgrounds, and a city guide. Organizes hikes and bus tours in summer; reservations required. Open July-Aug. M-Sa 9am-6:30pm, Su 10am-12:30pm; Sept.-May M-Sa 9am-12:30pm and 2-6pm; June M-Sa 9am-12:30pm and 2-6:30pm. Annex at the *gare maritime* (☎02 33 44 39 92). Open Apr.-Oct.; hours vary.

Bank: BNP Paribus, 1 rue Gambetta. Open Tu-F 9am-12:30pm and 1:45-6pm, Sa 8:45am-1pm.

Laundromat: 62 rue au Blé. Wash €3.50-7, dry €0.40 per 5min. Open daily July-Sept. 7am-9pm; Oct.-June 7am-8pm.

Public Toilets: Rue des Halles, just off pl. Général de Gaulle. Open M-Sa 9am-6pm.

Police: 2 rue du Val de Saire (☎02 33 88 76 76).

Pharmacy: Pharmacie Goffin, 1 pl. du Général de Gaulle (☎02 33 20 41 29). Open M-F 9am-12:30pm and 2-7:30pm, Sa 9am-12:30pm and 2-7pm.

Hospital: 46 rue du Val de Saire (☎02 33 20 70 00).

Internet Access: Archesys, 16 rue de l'Union (☎02 33 53 04 93). €0.50 per 6min.; min. €1. Open Tu-F 11:30am-10pm, Sa 11:30am-midnight, Su 2-10pm. Also available at the **Auberge de Jeunesse** (below) for guests.

Post Office: 1 rue de l'Ancien Quai (☎02 33 08 87 01), on pl. Divette. **Currency exchange** available. Open M-F 8am-7pm, Sa 9am-noon. Branch at 4 rue de Commerce (☎02 33 10 12 50). Open Tu-F 8:45am-12:15pm and 1:30-6pm, Sa 9am-noon. **Postal Code:** 50100.

ACCOMMODATIONS

Auberge de Jeunesse (HI), 55 rue de l'Abbaye (☎02 33 78 15 15; cherbourg@fuaj.org). From the tourist office, turn left on quai de Caligny and then left on rue de Port, which becomes rue Tour Carrée and rue de la Paix. Bear left on rue de l'Union, which runs into rue de l'Abbaye (10min.). From the train station, take bus #3 or 5 to Arsenal (last bus around 7:30pm), cross the street, and head back half a block. This modern hostel has neat 2- to 5-person rooms, each with sink and shower. Recently renovated kitchen, bar, foosball table, and pool table. Breakfast included. Internet €0.50 per 30min. Reception 9am-1pm and 6-11pm. Check-out 10am. Dorms €20. MC/V. ❶

Hôtel de la Gare, 10 pl. Jean Jaurès (☎02 33 43 06 81; fax 43 12 20), across the street from the station. Easy to find but far from the *centre-ville*. An amiable, English-speaking staff lets basic rooms with satellite TV and phones. Breakfast €6-7. Reception 8am-10pm. July-Aug. singles and doubles with shower €33-36, with shower and toilet €41-44; triples €53-62. Sept.-June singles and doubles with shower €28-31, with shower and toilet €36-39; triples €48-57. MC/V. ❸

FOOD

There is a market on **place du Théâtre** (open daily 8am-1pm; small market Tu and Sa, larger market Th) and a huge **Carrefour** supermarket on quai de l'Entrepôt, across the street from the station (open M-Th and Sa 8:30am-9pm, F 8:30am-9:30pm). *Brasseries* and kebab counters (€3.50-8) line **rue de la Paix** between the hostel and pl. de la République.

Crêperie Ty-Billic, 73 rue au Blé (☎02 33 01 11 90). A tourist-free haven with a casual but elegant atmosphere. The *menu* is a full meal of 2 *galettes*, 2 *crêpes*, and a cider for €12-15.50. *Galettes* and *crêpes* €1.90-7.60. Salads €6.30. Open July-Aug. M 7-11pm, Tu-Sa 11am-2pm and 7-11pm; Sept.-June M-Sa 11am-2pm and 7-11pm. MC/V. ❶

L'Antidote, 41 rue au Blé (☎02 33 78 01 28), in a secluded stone courtyard surrounded by hanging paper lanterns. Indulge in delicious meat and fish *plats* (€10-20), exquisite desserts (€5.50-6.50), and a wide selection of wines. *Menus* €19-29. Open Tu-Sa 11:30am-3pm and 7-11pm. Bar open Tu-Sa 10am-1pm. MC/V. ❸

SIGHTS

CITÉ DE LA MER. The site's 11m tall champagne-glass-shaped aquarium—the tallest in Europe—holds 3500 creatures, while smaller tanks feature exotic attractions like black seahorses and fluorescent blue jellyfish. A large touch tank has four different species of rays. The biggest attraction at the Cité, though, is the 128m **Le Redoutable,** the first French nuclear submarine ever built, now open to visitors with an audio tour available in Dutch, English, French, and German. The main entrance to the Cité includes a **tourist office, public toilets, post office, restaurant,** and **bar.** *(In the old gare maritime, halfway between the tourist office and the ferry terminal.* ☎02 33 20 26 69; www.citedelamer.com. *Open daily July-Aug. 9:30am-7pm;*

Sept. and May-June 9:30am-6pm; Oct.-Dec. and Feb.-Mar. 10am-6pm. Last entry 1hr. before close. Apr.-Sept. €18, ages 6-17 €13, under 6 free; Oct.-Mar. €16/11/free.)

BASILIQUE DE LA TRINITÉ. Decorated with intricate latticework and elaborately carved pillars, this basilica features a blend of architectural styles several centuries in the making. Above the altar stands a dramatic statue of the baptism of Christ; to the right, there is a 16th-century Danse Macabre bas-relief. *(8 pl. Napoléon, off quai de Caligny. ☎02 33 53 10 63. Open daily 9am-6:30pm.)*

NIGHTLIFE AND FESTIVALS

The streets around **place Central** and **rue de la Paix** are filled with late-night eateries, pool houses, and bars. Crowds congregate nightly to dance, imbibe creative mixed drinks, and discuss rotating art exhibits at laid-back **Art's Café**, 69 rue au Blé. (☎02 33 53 55 11. Beer €2.50. Wine €2.10. Mixed drinks €5-6. Occasional live concerts and DJ F-Sa. Free Internet for patrons. Open June-Sept. M-Sa noon-2am; Oct-Apr. M-Th noon-1am, F-Sa noon-2am. AmEx/MC/V.)

Festival des Cinémas d'Irlande et de Grande Brétagne (☎02 33 93 38 94), around the 1st week in Apr. Celebrate cinema from across La Manche at this annual film fest.

Charivarue: Festival dans l'Espace Publique (☎02 33 88 43 73; www.charivarue.com), 1st week in July. Circus-like spectacles take center stage at select theaters.

GRANVILLE   ☎02 33

In 1439, expatriate Lord Jean d'Argouges sold his family's fief—the rocky peninsula of Granville acquired as a marriage dowry—to the English. It became a base from which the English spent 30 years trying to overtake the impenetrable Mont-St-Michel. The seaside charms of Granville (grahn-veel; pop. 12,700) include a beautiful beach, a *haute-ville* with incredible views of the harbor, and relaxed nightlife. Relatively inexpensive and untouristed, the city is a popular base for daytrips to Mont-St-Michel and the Chausey Islands.

TRANSPORTATION

Trains: Pl. Pierre Sémard, off av. Maréchal Leclerc. Ticket office open M 5:40am-7pm, Tu-Sa 9:05am-7:30pm, Su 9:10am-8pm. To **Cherbourg** (3hr., 4 per day, €22) via **Coutances** or **Lison.**

Ferries: Manche Îles Express (☎08 25 13 30 50; www.manche-iles-express.com) at the *gare maritime.* To **Jersey, UK** (1hr.; Apr.-Sept. daily, Oct.-Apr. F-Su; €34-38, ages 4-16 €21-23). Prices rise July-Aug; family discounts available. Compagnie des Îles Chausey (☎02 33 50 16 36) sails to the **Chauseys** (1hr.; May-Sept. daily; round-trip €22, students €11, ages 5-14 €14, under 5 €5), as does Jolie-France (☎02 33 50 31 81, in winter 50 31 31; jolie-france@wanadoo.fr). Reservations recommended. Apr.-Sept. 1-5 per day, Oct.-Mar. several per week; round-trip €21, ages 3-14 €13, under 3 €5.

ORIENTATION AND PRACTICAL INFORMATION

To reach the *centre-ville* from the train station, walk downhill on av. Maréchal Leclerc, which becomes rue Couraye and ends at pl. du Général de Gaulle.

Tourist Office: 4 cours Jonville (☎02 33 91 30 03; www.ville-granville.fr), around the corner on the right as soon as you reach pl. du Général de Gaulle. Offers a helpful city guide with a map and the *Calendrier des Manifestations*—a list of summer events. Open July-Aug. daily 9am-noon and 2-6pm; Sept.-June M-Sa 9am-noon and 2-6pm; hours vary, so be sure to call ahead.

Tours: Available through the tourist office, in French. July-Aug. Th-Sa 3pm; €2.50.

Bank: BNP Paribus, 101 rue Couraye. Open Tu-F 8:45am-noon and 1:30-5:45pm, Sa 8:45am-12:30pm. **ATMs** on av. Maréchal Leclerc.

Laundromat: 10 rue St-Sauvier. Wash €3.20-4, dry €1 per 12min. Open daily 7am-9pm.

Public Toilets: Outside the train station and by the post office. Free.

Police: Rue du Port (☎02 33 91 27 50).

Hospital: Rue des Menneries (☎02 33 91 50 00).

Pharmacy: 2 rue Coraye (☎02 33 50 00 80). Open M-F 9am-12:30pm and 2-7:30pm, Sa 9am-12:30pm and 2-7:15pm.

Internet Access: La Citrouille (see **Nightlife,** next page).

Post Office: 8 cours Jonville (☎02 33 91 12 30). **Currency exchange** available. Open M-F 9am-12:30pm and 1:30-6:30pm, Sa 9am-12:30pm. **Postal Code:** 50400.

⌐ ACCOMMODATIONS

Auberge de Jeunesse (HI), bd. des Amiraux (☎02 33 91 22 62; www.crng.fr), in the Centre Nautisme complex. From the train station, turn right onto av. Maréchal Leclerc and follow it downhill. Just before the *centre-ville,* turn left onto rue St-Sauveur. Turn right when the road forks and look for the Centre Nautisme (nautical center) signs straight ahead, beyond the roundabout. Comfortable dorms with ocean views. Pool tables, ping-pong, TV room, and cafeteria. Sailing (€23-42 per hr.), kayaking (single €11, double €15), windsurfing (€20), and parasailing (€15) also available. Breakfast €2.30. Linen €4.50 for nonmembers. Laundry. Reception 9am-noon and 2-7pm. 4-bed dorms €15; 2-bed dorms €20; singles €24. AmEx/MC/V. ●

Hôtel Michelet, 5 rue Jules Michelet (☎02 33 50 06 55; fax 50 12 25). Comfortable rooms, some with balconies. Breakfast €6.50. Reception M-Sa 7:30am-10pm, Su 7:30am-12:30pm and 6-10pm. Singles and doubles €30, with toilets €36, with toilets and showers €45, with toilets and bathtubs €55. Extra bed €9. AmEx/MC/V. ❷

Hôtel Terminus, 5 pl. Pierre Sémard (☎02 33 50 02 05; fax 50 73 35), across from the train station. Spacious rooms in need of refurbishment. All with toilets and TVs. Breakfast €6. Free Wi-Fi. Reception 8am-10:30pm. Singles and doubles €22-30, with showers €30-37, with bath €37; triples €40-47; quads €42-51. AmEx/MC/V. ❷

⌐ FOOD

There are markets on **cours Jonville** (Sa 9am-3pm, mornings only in winter) and on **place du 11 Novembre 1918** (W 8am-1pm). For groceries, head to **Marché Plus,** 107 rue de Couraye. (Open M-Sa 7am-9pm, Su 9am-1pm.) Skip the pricey restaurants in town and opt for one of the small *crêperies* in the *haute-ville* near the Église de Notre-Dame. Kebab and ice-cream stands cluster near the beach, and there are plenty of *boulangeries* and *pâtisseries* along rue Couraye.

☒ La Gourmandise, 37 rue St-Jean (☎02 33 50 65 16), in a romantic spot in the *haute-ville*. La Granvillaise (apples, apple sorbet, and *calvados;* €8) flambéed right at the table. *Galettes* €2.40-9.80. *Crêpes* €2.30-8. Open July-Aug. daily 12:15-2:30pm and 7-9:30pm; Sept.-June M-Sa 12:15-2:30pm and 7-9:30pm. MC/V. ●

Monte Pego, 13 rue St-Sauveur (☎02 33 90 74 44), near the hostel. Italian pastas and brick-oven pizzas (€8-12). Open M-Sa noon-2:15pm and 7-10pm. MC/V. ❷

NORMANDY

👁 🏊 SIGHTS AND BEACHES

Granville's most popular beach stretches northward from the *vieille ville* and features a swimming pool replenished by the tide. At high tide, though, the beach and swimming pool are completely submerged. You'll also find stretches of sand near the hostel on the opposite side of the peninsula. From May to September, boats leave daily for the **Chausey Islands,** a sparsely inhabited archipelago (for ferry info, see **Transportation,** p. 320). The idyllic natural beauty of the islands makes them a relaxing daytrip.

HAUTE-VILLE. Ambling cobblestone streets and charming, old-fashioned architecture complement the *haute-ville's* real draw: a stunning view of the water, beaches, and surrounding village below. Several stairways lead up to the *haute-ville;* the easiest to find is beside the casino on the beachfront, which stretches to a German bunker guarding the harbor. There are wheelchair-accessible ramps to the *haute-ville* by pl. Pleville. In the center of the *haute-ville* stands the somber **Église Notre Dame du Cap-Lihou,** where classical music concerts are held occasionally in the summer. *(Pl. du Parvis Notre Dame.)*

MUSÉE RICHARD ANACRÉON. Anchored at the eastern edge of the *haute-ville,* this museum features modern art and a rare-book collection, including first editions of Apollinaire, Cocteau, and Colette. *(Pl. de l'Isthme, at the top of the stairs from the casino. ☎ 02 33 51 02 94. Open June-Sept. Tu-Su 11am-6pm; Oct.-Dec. and Feb.-May W-Su 2-6pm. Wheelchair-accessible. €2.60, students and under 18 €1.40, under 10 free.)*

MUSÉE CHRISTIAN DIOR. The childhood home of Granville's most famous son, this museum showcases exhibits that honor Christian Dior's *couture* career. In the gardens, designed by Dior himself, you can smell perfumes and check out the teahouse, which features fashion documentaries. The rose-threaded terrace gives way to a spectacular ocean view. *(Follow the coastal path from the beach promenade to the stairs below the cliff top. ☎ 02 33 61 48 21; www.musee-dior-granville.com. Open from May to late Sept. daily 10am-6:30pm. Wheelchair-accessible. €6, students and seniors €4, under 12 free. Gardens open daily July-Aug. 9am-9pm; Sept.-June 9am-8pm. Free.)*

🎭 🎆 NIGHTLIFE AND FESTIVALS

On the last Sunday of July, Granville hosts the **Grand Pardon de la Mer,** a religious maritime holiday, which ends in a candlelight procession. Writers come for the **Journées des Livres,** a book fair held during the first weekend of August. A lively five-day **Carnaval** commences on the Friday before Mardi Gras.

🎬 **La Citrouille,** 8 rue St-Sauveur (☎ 02 33 51 35 51). Big-screen TV and Internet access (€3 per hr.). Occasional live concerts. Beer €2.30. Hard liquor €4.70. Open July-Aug. daily 8:30am-2am; Sept.-June M 5pm-2am, Tu-Sa 8:30am-2am. MC/V over €15.

Bar les Amiraux, bd. des Amiraux (☎ 02 33 50 12 83; www.les-amiraux.com), across from the hostel. Seating on the patio or inside in the cave-like nooks behind the bar. Beer €2.40. Hard liquor €3-7. Wine €2.50-3.50. Open July-Aug. M-Sa 1pm-2am, Su 3pm-2am; Sept.-June M-Th 1pm-1am, F-Sa 1pm-2am, Su 3pm-1am. MC/V.

MONT-SAINT-MICHEL ☎ 02 33

It's little wonder that pilgrims in the Middle Ages considered Mont-St-Michel (mohn-sehn-mee-shell; pop. 50) to be an image of paradise on earth or that the English expended such effort trying to capture it in the Hundred Years' War. From the moment the abbey comes into view across the causeway, it inspires visions of medieval grandeur and timeless majesty. A trip inside the millennium-old abbey, with or without a tour, is an indispensable part of the experience, but no less intoxicating are the views from its fortified walls. Expanses of sandy marshland seem to extend into the horizon, with the perfectly preserved Mont standing out in idyllic isolation.

TRANSPORTATION

Trains: Pl. de la Gare, Pontorson. Open M-Th and Sa 9:15-11:45am and 2:30-7:05pm, F 9:15-11:45am and 2:45-7:30pm, Su 1:30-7:10pm. To: **Caen** (2hr., 2 per day, €23); **Dinan** (1hr., 2-3 per day, €8.10); **Granville** (1hr.; M-F 3 per day, Sa-Su 2 per day; €9); **Paris** (4hr., 1-3 per day, €45) via **Caen; St-Malo** (1hr., 2-3 per day, €7.40) via **Dol.**

Buses: Veolia Manéo (☎0800 15 00 50; www.cg50.fr). Buses leave Mont-St-Michel from the entrance at Porte de l'Avancée and leave Pontorson from pl. de la Gare. **Shuttles** between Pontorson and the Mont run 7 times per day; more July-Aug. The 1st bus from Pontorson is at 6:54am, and the last bus from the Mont is around 6:20pm. €2; tickets available on board. Its subsidiary Illenoo (www.illenoo.fr) runs to **Rennes** (1hr.; M-Sa 6 per day, Su 1 per day; €3) and **St-Malo** (1hr., 2-3 per day, €2.50).

ORIENTATION AND PRACTICAL INFORMATION

Mont-St-Michel, on the border between Brittany and Normandy, is a small island connected to the mainland by a causeway. **Grande Rue** is its only major street. **Pontorson,** 9km due south down D976, has the closest train station and affordable hotels; there's also a supermarket and cheap cabins at the campground across the causeway, 1.8km from the Mont. There's no public transportation off the Mont after 8pm, so plan ahead if you're making a daytrip. Biking to or from Pontorson takes about 1hr. on terrain that is relatively flat but not always bike-friendly; the path next to the Couesnon River is the best route.

Tourist Offices:

Mont-St-Michel: (☎02 33 60 14 30; www.ot-montsaintmichel.com). Helpful multilingual staff in a tiny office to the left of the entrance has info on sites and lodging. A free *horaire des marées* (tide table) will tell you if the vista from the ramparts will be of ocean water or sandy flats. **Currency exchange** available. Open July-Aug. daily 9am-7pm; Sept. M-Sa 9am-6pm, Su 9am-noon and 2-6pm; Oct.-Mar. M-Sa 9am-noon and 2-6pm, Su 10am-noon and 2-5pm; Apr.-June M-Sa 9am-12:30pm and 2-6:30pm, Su 9am-noon and 2-6pm.

Pontorson: Pl. de l'Hôtel de Ville (☎02 33 60 20 65; www.mont-saint-michel-baie.com), off rue St-Michel. Offers free maps and info on walking tours, accommodations, and the Mont. **Internet** €4.50 per 30min., €8 per hr. Open M-Th 9:15-11:45am and 2:30-7pm, F-Sa 3:45-7:30pm, Su 1:30-7:30pm.

Bank: BNP Paribus, 3 pl. de l'Hôtel de Ville. Open M-F 8:45am-12:15pm and 1:30-5:45pm, Sa 8:45am-12:30pm.

Laundromat: Rue St-Michel (☎02 33 49 60 66), in Pontorson, next to the Champion. Wash €4-10, dry €1 per 10min. Open daily 7am-9pm.

Public Toilets: By the Mont tourist office (€0.40). At Pontorson train station (free).

Police: ☎06 07 28 29 14. In July-Aug., available on the Mont (☎02 33 60 14 42), to the left of the Porte de l'Avancée before you enter. Also in Pontorson at 2 chaussée de Ville Chérel (☎02 33 89 72 00).

Hospital: Emergency services at 7 chaussée de Ville Chérel in Pontorson (☎02 33 60 72 00) and in Avranches (☎02 33 89 40 00).

Internet Access: On the 2nd fl. of **Hôtel de la Croix-Blanche,** Grand Rue (☎02 33 60 14 04), on the Mont, and a few doors down at the **Auberge Saint-Pierre** (☎02 33 60 14 03). Also at the **Pontorson tourist office** (above).

Post Office: Grande Rue (☎02 33 89 65 00), about 100m inside the walls. **Currency exchange** available. Open July-Aug. M-Sa 9am-5:30pm, Su 9am-12:15pm and 1:15-5:30pm; from Sept. to mid-Nov. and Mar.-May M-F 9am-noon and 2-5pm; June M-F 9am-5:30pm, Sa 9am-4pm. In Pontorson, 18 rue St-Michel (☎02 33 89 17 76), across from the tourist office. Open M-F 8:30am-noon and 2-5:30pm, Sa 8:30am-noon. **Postal Code:** 50170.

ACCOMMODATIONS AND CAMPING

Forget about staying on the Mont unless St-Michel himself is bankrolling the visit. Even 2km away at the other end of the causeway, hotels generally cost more than €40. However, the campground there—which offers dorms—is affordable. Pontorson has cheap hotels, a hostel, and regular bus service, making it a good base for daytrips to the Mont. Granville and St-Malo are also potential bases. There are also a number of campsites and *chambres d'hôte* in the vicinity (see tourist offices for more details). Reserve ahead; tourists fill the hotels faster than the rising tide fills the bay.

▨ **Camping du Mont-St-Michel** (☎02 33 60 22 10; www.le-mont-saint-michel.com), 1.8km from the Mont on route du Mont-St-Michel. Get off at Caserne, the stop before the Mont, on Manéo line 6 from Pontorson. Closest affordable lodging to the Mont, with spotless dorms and great facilities. Excellent views of the Mont—especially at night. Next to a supermarket. Laundry €4.30, dry €1.80. Wi-Fi at adjoining **Hôtel Motel Vert** (€3 per 30min., €5 per hr.). Bike rental €5 per hr., €8.30 per ½-day, €17 per day. Reception 24hr. Check-out 2pm. Gates closed 11pm-6am. Open from Feb. to mid-Nov. €4.10 per person, children €2.40; sites €6.30. Electricity €9. Dorms €8.60. MC/V. ❶

▨ **Camping Haliotis,** chemin des Soupirs and rue du Général Patton (☎02 33 68 11 59; fax 58 95 36), in Pontorson, next to the hostel. 3-star grounds are a luxurious mini-resort, with cabins and campsites. Heated pool, hot tub, sauna, tennis and volleyball courts, game room, bar, playground, and fishing. Breakfast €5. Laundry €3, dry €2. Free Wi-Fi. Bike rental €5 per ½-day, €9 per day. Reception 7:30am-10pm. Open Apr.-Nov. €4.50-6 per person, children €2-3.50; €5-7 per tent and car or RV. Electricity €2.50-3. Cabins €25 and up. Prices rise July-Aug. MC/V. ❶

Auberge de Jeunesse Centre Duguesclin (HI), rue du Général Patton (☎02 33 60 18 65; aj.pontorson@wanadoo.fr), in Pontorson. From the train station, turn right onto the main road, then left on rue Couesnon. Take the 3rd right on rue St-Michel. At the roundabout, take a left onto rue du Général Patton. Hostel is on the right past the campground entrance. 4- to 6-person single-sex dorms. Lounge and kitchen. Some rooms have showers and toilets. Breakfast €3.20. Reception July-Aug. 8am-10pm; Sept. and Apr.-June 8am-noon and 5-9pm. Open Apr.-Sept. Dorms €14. Cash only. ❶

Hôtel le Grillon, 37 rue du Couesnon (☎02 33 60 17 80), in Pontorson, right after rue St-Michel. 5 quiet, clean rooms behind a *crêperie*. All with showers; some with skylights. Breakfast €5. Reception daily 8am-midnight. Reservations recommended. Singles and doubles €29, with toilets €32. Extra bed €5. MC/V. ❷

Hôtel de l'Arrivée, 14 rue du Docteur Tizon (☎/fax 02 33 60 01 57), in Pontorson, across from the train station. Tidy rooms. Breakfast €5.50. Reception July-Aug. daily 8am-10pm; Sept.-June Tu-Su 9am-10pm. Singles and doubles €22, with showers €29-30, with showers and toilets €37; triples €44; quads €67. MC/V. ❷

FOOD

If at all possible, plan a picnic lunch for the Mont, since food inside the walls is OK at best and sells at tourist-inflated prices; the causeway or the gardens above the town make beautiful lunch spots. Arrive prepared, as there are no grocery stores on the Mont; the nearest one—**Super Marché** (☎02 33 60 09 33; open daily 8am-8pm.)—is 2km away, at the entrance to the causeway next to the Camping du Mont-St-Michel. Pontorson has a market (W 9am-1pm) on **rue Couesnon** and at **place de la Mairie,** as well as a **Champion** supermarket just outside of town at 2 route du Mont-St-Michel. From the Pontorson train station parking lot, take a right on the main road, which becomes bd. du Général de Gaulle. The Champion will be on your right at the edge of town (10min.). From the hostel and campground, turn left, then left again at the roundabout. (Open daily M-Sa 7am-7:30pm, Su 9am-noon.) If you do wind up buying food on the Mont, be prepared to spend at least €16 for a lunch *menu;* alternatively, lunch counters sell unimpressive hot dogs, sandwiches, and *crêpes* to tourists for €3-8.

> **La Sirène,** Grande Rue (☎02 33 60 08 60). Serves fresh salads (€3.20-8.40), *galettes* (€2.50-8.60), and *crêpes* (€2.10-7.80). Wi-Fi €10 per hr. Open daily June-Aug. 9am-10:30pm; Sept.-May 9am-7pm. AmEx/MC/V. ❶
>
> **Le Grillon,** 37 rue Couesnon (☎02 33 60 17 80), in Pontorson. Dinner and dessert *crêpes* (€1.90-7.10), fresh salads (€2.50-6.60), and multi-course *menus* (lunch €9.50, dinner €16). Open M-W and F-Su noon-2:30pm and 7-9:30pm. MC/V. ❷

⊙ SIGHTS

Legend holds that the **Baie de Saint-Michel** was created by a wave that carved three islands: Tombelaine, Mont Dol (now both located inland due to the gradual silting of the bay), and Mont Tomba (meaning "mound" or "tomb"). Tomba was reputedly so appealing that Heaven wanted a piece of it. In AD 708, Archangel Michael supposedly appeared to St-Aubert, bishop of Avranches, and asked him to build a place of worship on the island. The bishop proved rather unresponsive; Michael reportedly had to put a flaming finger through Aubert's skull before the bishop heeded his vision and erected the first small church on the Mont's summit. In the 10th century, a Benedictine abbey was established on the Mont, and the four crypts supporting the abbey church were built. The Mont soon became a spiritual destination as important as Rome and Jerusalem to French pilgrims. In the 14th and 15th centuries, Mont-St-Michel was fortified against a 30-year English attack. When church property was appropriated wholesale in the French Revolution, the Benedictines were driven out of Mont-St-Michel. The abbey became a penitentiary, housing around 700 political prisoners. Finally, in 1863, the prison closed, and Mont-St-Michel became a national monument. Today, the abbey is home to a small community of monks—no longer Benedictines, but rather Brothers and Sisters of Jerusalem.

Mont-St-Michel's **Grande Rue,** the main thoroughfare leading up to the abbey at the summit, is lined with tourist traps. None of the "museums" or gift shops on Grande Rue is worth the money or time; just keep climbing until you reach the abbey and the scenic viewpoints on the town's ramparts.

 SWEET SOLITUDE. To experience the Mont's magnificence, avoid visiting during the crowded summer months, even if it means missing some tours. If you must come then, don't take the main road to the top; instead, take the stairway on the right just after the Porte du Roy or enter through the little-used entrance by the police station to the left of the main entrance.

ABBEY. Mont-St-Michel's winding Grande Rue ends at the abbey entrance. A wide stairway leads up to the ticket office in the former almshouse of the abbey; keep climbing to the welcome desk, which offers pamphlets for self-guided tours in several languages. These steps also lead to the west terrace—the entrance to the abbey church. This is a prime lookout for views of the bay and the departure point for tours. The church is a product of ingenious planning, considering the incredible constraints of its hilltop location. The entire edifice rests on only 200 sq. m of solid rock; the choir, both sides of the transept, and the entire nave are held up by pillared crypts below the church floor. The adjacent cloister, framed by a unique arrangement of columns, rests on the top floor of **La Merveille** (the Marvel), a 13th-century, three-story Gothic monastery. Also on the top floor is the refectory, where the monks took their meals in silence as the life stories of saints were read. Descending to the cathedral's crypts, you pass by the **Salle des Hôtes**, where noble guests were lodged. Directly under the abbey's choir is the **Crypte des Gros Piliers,** whose pillars measure 6m in circumference. Under the southern transept is the **Chapelle Saint-Martin,** used as a cistern when the abbey became a prison; next door, the abbey's ossuary—once filled with the bones of deceased monks—was converted into a supply depot. It holds a giant wheel, powered by two to four men walking inside it; this was once used to pull supplies up the side of the walls on a sled. The visit continues through the **Chapelle Saint-Étienne,** the chapel of the dead, where deceased monks rotted down to bones before being moved to the ossuary. The abbey gardens, clinging to the side of the rock, surround the compound's exit. *(☎02 33 89 80 00. Open daily May-Aug. 9am-7pm; Sept.-Apr. 9:30am-6pm. Last entrance 1hr. before closing. Tours of abbey daily; 2 in English, 8 in French; more in the summer. Tours of crypts daily July-Aug.; Sept.-June Sa-Su. 1hr. Mass daily 12:15pm; entry for service noon-12:15pm only. €8.50, ages 18-25 €5; 1st Su of the month free. Tours free. Audio tour €4. MC/V.)*

TIDES. From various overlooks, you can see the immense tidal basin surrounding the Mont. The tides here are the largest in Europe; when the earth, moon, and sun are aligned, the water can rush some 15km from low tide to high tide in just 4hr., moving as fast as a galloping horse and completely flooding the beaches along the causeway. These *grandes marées* (great tides) happen about twice a month, as predicted by schedules available at the tourist office. You must be inside the abbey 2hr. before in order to watch the rising tide.

 THE UNKINDEST TIDE. Pay attention to the tide warnings. The tides here are some of the strongest, and it's dangerous to go swimming (especially alone) if you are unfamiliar with them.

ILLUMINATION. At night, the illuminated Mont is best seen from either the causeway entrance or from across the bay. In summer, a separate night entrance opens into the abbey, offering an unforgettable view of the pitch-black skies above the bay. *(July-Aug. M-Sa 7-11:30pm. Last entrance 10:30pm. Included with regular admission.)* The Mont also puts on sound-and-light shows after dark in July and August. Unfortunately, there is no public transportation off the Mont after sundown; if you aren't staying on the Mont overnight, you'll have to walk or rent a bike—make sure you have a flashlight or bike light.

THE NORTH

Every day, thousands of tourists pass through the channel ports of the Côte d'Opale on their way to Britain, yet few manage more than a quick glimpse of the surrounding regions, leaving the northern regions of Flanders, Pas-de-Calais, and Picardy undiscovered. When you're fleeing the ferry ports, don't miss the area's hidden gems: the windmills and gabled homes of the once-Flemish Flanders possess gingerbread charm. Lille (below), a large and lively metropolis, has a strong Flemish flavor and a world-class art collection.

Pas-de-Calais's chalk cliffs loom along the Brit-accented coast; the village of Montreuil-sur-Mer (p. 341) seems to belong to a fairy tale, while the busy channel port of Calais (p. 343) is a setting of brash reality. Farther inland, sheep graze near collapsed war bunkers on still-active minefields in Arras (p. 334). Even after five decades of peace, relics from the two World Wars haunt northern France. German-built observation towers still peer over dunes—testimonials to the resilience of this region—while scores of tombstones bear witness to the terrible tolls exacted at Arras, Cambrai, and the Somme.

In Picardy, seas of wheat are sprinkled in spring and summer with red poppies. A once royal and now Parisian retreat, this area is home to lush forests, France's largest Gothic cathedral, and dazzling châteaux.

HIGHLIGHTS OF FLANDERS, PAS-DE-CALAIS, AND PICARDY

TAKE A DIP into culture at Lille's amazing modern art museum, La Piscine (p. 331)—a public pool that has been transformed into a sleek exhibition space.

SOAK UP the bucolic charm of tiny Montreuil-sur-Mer (p. 341), where Victor Hugo set much of *Les Misérables*.

MEANDER through Amiens's cobblestone Quartier St-Leu (p. 346), where canals converge at flower-filled squares.

FLANDERS

LILLE   ☎03 20

Boasting a plethora of noteworthy restaurants, fabulous shopping, and a thriving nightlife scene, Lille (leel; pop. 220,000) has many of Paris's draws without the expensive price tag. Once the feared industrial colossus of the north, Lille has evolved into a lively metropolis, its stylish modern architecture melding with the older cobblestone cityscape. Over 100,000 students flock to Lille each year and keep the city's bars and *discothèques* busy until dawn. In the summer, a calmer atmosphere presents vacationers with relatively untouristed museums and cobblestone streets lined with ice-cream shops.

⌐ TRANSPORTATION

Flights: Aéroport de Lille-Lesquin (☎03 20 49 68 68; www.lille.aeroport.fr). Allo Navette (☎08 91 67 32 10, €0.30 per min.) **shuttles** leave from rue le Corbusier at Gare Lille Europe. Every hr. M-F 5am-10pm, Sa 5am-6pm, Su 10am-10pm; €4.60, students €3.

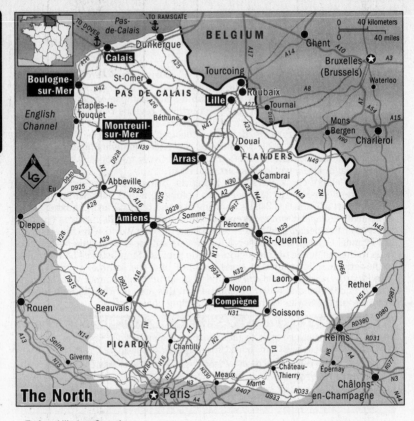

The North

Trains: Lille has 2 stations.

Gare Lille Flandres, pl. de la Gare. Ticket office open M-F 5:30am-9pm, Sa 6am-9pm, Su 7:15am-9pm. **Currency exchange** available M-F 8am-6:30pm, Sa 10am-5pm, Su 10am-4pm. **Luggage storage** available. To **Arras** (40min., 19 per day, €9.40), **Paris** (1hr., 20 per day, €37-51), and **Brussels, BEL** (1hr., 1-3 per day, €18-24).

Gare Lille Europe, av. le Corbusier. Ⓜ Gare Lille Europe. Open daily 5:30am-12:15am. TGVs run to the south of France and **Paris** (1hr., 6 per day, €37-51). Eurostar (☎08 92 35 35 39) runs to **Brussels, BEL** (40min., 15 per day, €18-24), and **London, ENG** (1hr., 15 per day, €110-175).

Buses: Eurolines, 23 Parvis St-Maurice (☎03 20 78 18 88; www.eurolines.eu). Open M-Th 9:30am-6pm, F 10am-8pm. Buses from Gare Lille Europe to **Amsterdam, NTH** (5hr., 2 per day, €51); **Brussels, BEL** (1hr., 3 per day, €22); and **London, ENG** (5hr., 1-4 per day, €61).

Public Transportation: Transpole **bus** terminal is next to Gare Lille Flandres. **Métro** and **trams** serve the town and its periphery daily 5:12am-12:12am. Tickets €1.25, carnet of 10 €11; day pass €3.50. Office open Sept.-June M-F 7:30am-6pm.

Taxis: Taxi Union (☎03 20 06 06 06). **Taxi Gare** (☎03 20 06 64 00). Both 24hr.

✈🛈 ORIENTATION AND PRACTICAL INFORMATION

Lille is like a spider web: streets disperse in all directions from the town's many squares. It's best to carry a map, especially when tackling vieux Lille.

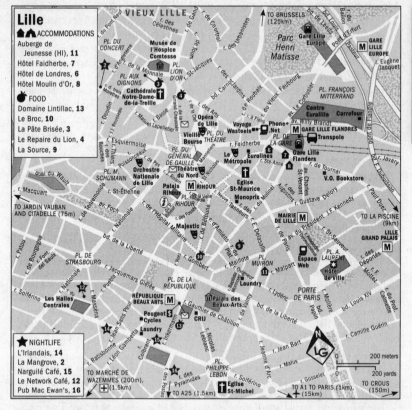

Lille

⌂⌂ ACCOMMODATIONS

Auberge de
 Jeunesse (HI), **11**
Hôtel Faidherbe, **7**
Hôtel de Londres, **6**
Hôtel Moulin d'Or, **8**

🍴 FOOD

Domaine Lintillac, **13**
Le Broc, **10**
La Pâte Brisée, **3**
Le Repaire du Lion, **4**
La Source, **9**

★ NIGHTLIFE

L'Irlandais, **14**
La Mangrove, **2**
Narguilé Café, **15**
Le Network Café, **12**
Pub Mac Ewan's, **16**

The newer part of town, with wide boulevards and 19th-century buildings, culminates in the **Marché de Wazemmes.** The city's largest shopping district is in
the primarily pedestrian area off **place du Théâtre.** Lille, like any big city, can be
unsafe, so be vigilant with your belongings and person at all times.

Tourist Office: Pl. Rihour (☎03 59 57 94 00; www.lilletourism.com), inside the Palais
Rihour. Ⓜ Rihour. From Gare Lille Flandres, go straight on rue Faidherbe for 2 blocks.
Turn left through pl. du Théâtre and pl. du Général de Gaulle. Make a right at the Théâtre
du Nord and walk into pl. Rihour; the office is ahead. Provides maps (€0.50) and **currency exchange.** Also sells the **Lille Metropole City Pass,** which provides unlimited
public transportation and discounts. 1-day pass €18, 2-day €30, 3-day €45. Call for
pharmacie de garde. Open M-Sa 9:30am-6:30pm, Su 10am-noon and 2-5pm.

Tours: The tourist office offers tours via bus, bike, Segway, and cell phone. Useful guidebook (€2) with 5 walking tours is also available. Tours in English and French €7.50-20.
For something more freestyle (and free), flip to p. 332 for **Padding Around Lille.**

Budget Travel: Voyage Wasteels, 25 pl. des Reignaux (☎03 20 06 87 66). Open M-F
9am-12:30pm and 1:30-6:30pm, Sa 9am-1pm.

Bookstore: VO, 36 rue de Tournai (☎03 20 14 33 96; lalibrairie.vo@wanadoo.fr). Large
English book section. Open Tu-Sa noon-7pm.

Youth Center: Centre Régional Information Jeunesse (CRIJ), 2 rue Nicolas Leblanc (☎03 20 12 87 30). Info on work and long-term lodging. Internet €0.15 per 5min., €15 per 10hr. Open Tu and Th 1-7pm, W 10am-6pm, F 1-6pm, Sa 10am-12:30pm.

Laundromat: 2 rue Ovigneur. €2.80 per 5-6kg. Open daily 7am-8pm. **Espace Web Cyberlaundry,** 14 rue Alexandre Desrousseaux (☎03 20 85 07 73). €3 per 7kg, €3.50 per 10kg. Internet available. Open daily 8am-7:30pm.

Police: Pl. Augustin Laurent (☎03 20 49 56 66), in the Hôtel de Ville. Call for the **pharmacie de garde.**

Hospital: 2 av. Oscar Lambret (☎03 20 44 59 62). Ⓜ CHR-Oscar Lambret.

Internet Access: At the **CRIJ** and **Espace Web Cyberlaundry** (both above). **Phone+.Net,** 27 pl. des Reignaux (☎03 20 40 96 07). €0.80 per 15min., €3 per 1hr. Open M-F 9am-midnight, Sa-Su 9am-1am.

Post Office: 8 pl. de la République (☎03 20 36 10 23). Ⓜ République. **ATM** and **currency exchange** available. Open M-F 8am-7pm, Sa 8:30am-12:30pm. Branches on bd. Carnot, near pl. du Théâtre (open M-F 9am-6pm) and on the corner of rue Nationale and rue Jean Roisin (open M 10am-6:30pm, Tu-F 9am-6:30pm, Sa 10am-1pm and 2-4pm). **Postal Code:** 59000.

▀ ACCOMMODATIONS

One- and two-star hotels in the €30-40 range cluster around **Gare Lille Flandres,** while more expensive accommodations dot **place du Théâtre** and **place du Général de Gaulle.** Many of Lille's budget options are run-down or face noisy streets; to guarantee a comfortable stay, you may want to spring for one of the pricier options listed below. As most of these hotels serve a business clientele, try to reserve a month ahead and inquire about lower prices on weekends.

Auberge de Jeunesse (HI), 12 rue Malpart (☎03 20 57 08 94; lille@fuaj.org). Ⓜ Mairie de Lille. Take the left exit from Gare Lille Flandres, turn left onto rue de Tournai, and make a right at rue du Molinel. Head straight for 2 blocks and turn left onto rue de Paris. After 3 blocks, rue Malpart will be on your right. No-frills hostel in a quiet location with dorms named after European cities. Lots of international boarders. TV room, kitchen, and bar. Dorms are often left unlocked; take valuables with you when you leave the room. Breakfast included. Luggage storage €1.50 per day. Free Internet and Wi-Fi. Reception 1am-11am and 3pm-midnight. Check-out 10am. Lockout 11am-3pm. Open from late Jan. to mid-Dec. Dorms €18. MC/V. ❶

Hôtel Moulin d'Or, 15 rue du Molinel (☎03 20 06 12 67; www.hotelmoulindor.com), near the train station. Offers a level of comfort that usually costs much more. Rooms are decorated with large painted flowers on the walls, and all have bath, TVs, hair dryers, and phones. Breakfast €8. Free Wi-Fi. Reception 7am-4pm and 5-9:30pm. Check-out 11am. June-July singles and doubles €57-67; triples €82-92. Aug.-May singles €57-67; doubles €77-82; triples €82-92. MC/V. ❹

Hôtel Faidherbe, 42 pl. de la Gare (☎03 20 06 27 93; fax 55 95 38). Modestly sized rooms, most with TVs. Breakfast €5. Reception 24hr. Check-out 11am. Singles and doubles with tub €33-40, with full bath €47. Extra bed €10. AmEx/MC/V. ❷

Hôtel de Londres, 16 pl. de la Gare (☎03 20 12 09 10; www.hoteldelondres.com), near the train station. Tidy rooms with carpets, vegetable decor, and TVs. Some rooms overlook pl. de la Gare. Breakfast €6.10. Free Wi-Fi. Reception 24hr.; ring bell downstairs if glass door at the top of the stairs is closed. Check-out 11am. Singles with shower €50-60, with toilet €55-70; doubles with shower and toilet €67. AmEx/MC/V. ❹

THE NORTH

🖰 FOOD

Lille is known for Maroilles cheese, *genièvre* (juniper berry liqueur), and, of course, *moules* (mussels). Find the cheese in any *épicerie*, the liqueur in *brasseries* on **rue Gambetta,** and the mussels, well, everywhere. **Rue Léon Gambetta** boasts a slew of cheap kebab joints and leads to **Marché de Wazemmes,** pl. de la Nouvelle Aventure. (Open Tu and Su 8am-2pm, F-Sa 8am-7pm.) EuraLille, next to the Eurostar station, has an enormous **Carrefour** supermarket. (☎03 20 15 56 00. Open M-Sa 9am-10pm.) There is a **Monoprix** in the Centre Commercial off rue des Tanneurs. (☎03 28 82 92 20. Open M-Sa 9am-10pm.)

🖾 **Le Broc,** 17 pl. de Béthune (☎03 20 30 16 00). Cheese-heavy dishes that range from fondues to *crêpes* and salads. Fondue €14-15 per person. *Plats* €7.40-16. Open M-F noon-1:45pm and 7-10:30pm, Sa noon-2pm and 7-11pm. MC/V. ❸

🖾 **La Pâte Brisée,** 63-65 rue de la Monnaie (☎03 20 74 29 00). Cozy teashop that serves quiches, salads, and dessert *tartes*. Those with an indecisive or especially indulgent sweet tooth should opt for the *assortiment des tartes sucrées* (€8.10; includes drink). *Menus* €8.50-20. Open M-F noon-10:30pm, Sa-Su noon-11pm. Lunch *menu* available noon-2pm, dinner 7-10pm. MC/V. ❷

Domaine Lintillac, 7 rue Inkermann (☎03 20 55 44 44). It's always duck season at this homey restaurant that specializes in fantastic *canard* dishes—and nothing else. With such a specific focus, it's no surprise that the quacky *plats* (€8.80-12) are so creative and delicious. Open Tu-Su noon-2pm and 7-10pm. MC/V. ❷

Le Repaire du Lion, 6 pl. Lion d'Or (☎03 20 74 20 36). Classic brick-and-wood *crêperie* boasts over 100 different *galettes* (€2.60-9), sweet *crêpes* (€2.40-6.50), and meal-size salads (€6.20-6.50). Open M-Sa 11:45am-2:15pm and 7-11pm. MC/V. ❶

La Source, 13 rue du Plat (☎03 20 57 53 07). Organic-food store downstairs sells vegetarian specialties like heavily spiced rice dishes. Upstairs restaurant serves creative vegetarian and other organic lunch *menus* (€8.50-15), all of which come with a 1.5L bottle of water and a pitcher of hot tea. Store open M-Th and Sa 8am-7pm, F 7am-9pm; restaurant open M-F noon-2pm. AmEx/MC/V. ❷

🖰 SIGHTS

🖾**PALAIS DES BEAUX-ARTS.** France's second-largest art collection sits in this 19th-century mansion, surrounded by the gardens of pl. de la République. Sculptures and ceramics fill the museum's lower levels; 15th- to 20th-century French and Flemish paintings hang in the hallways upstairs. Rubens's colossal *La Descente de Croix* is a must-see, and a calming set of Monet's oils is tucked away in a room of Impressionist works. Guides to each room are available in English and French. (*Pl. de la République. ⓜRépublique. ☎03 20 06 78 00. Open M 2-6pm, W-Su 10am-6pm. €10, students €7. French tours €4; call ahead for schedule.*)

🖾**LA PISCINE.** Still lifes have replaced lifeguards in this museum, which is situated in a former municipal bathhouse and displays its eclectic art collection around a renovated indoor pool. Shower stalls showcasing ceramics and textiles serve as nifty segues between the central hall's sculpture garden and alcoves of 19th- and 20th-century paintings. Look out for Claudel's marble bust of a bright-eyed *ingénue;* the stunning statue won the hearts of the town's citizens, who pooled their money together to bring the piece to the museum. Every 15min., a short snippet of audio recorded from an indoor pool plays loudly throughout the building, a ghostly reminder of the funky museum's past. (*23 rue de l'Espérance. Note that the rue de l'Espérance on which the musée is found is not the same rue de l'Espérance on the tourist office map. It's easiest to stick to the Métro. Take line 2 to ⓜGare*

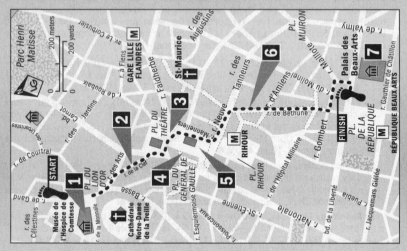

PADDING AROUND LILLE

1. MUSÉE DE L'HOSPICE DE COMTESSE. This museum is relatively untouristed, but the former hospital and orphanage houses an intriguing collection of statues displayed in period rooms. Look for the globe displaying the constellations as they were the day the Sun King was born. (32 rue de la Monnaie. Open M 2-6pm, W-Su 10am-12:30pm and 2-6pm.)

2. RUE DE LA CLEF. This quintessential *vieille ville* street is a charming cobbled walk filled with offbeat boutiques and tiny cafes for shoppers and people-watchers.

3. VIEILLE BOURSE. In the courtyard that once served as Lille's stock exchange, a different sort of paper product is now being haggled over: used books. Interesting old postcards, comics, and maps can also be found at bargain prices. (opposite page).

4. SALON DE THÉ DAGNIAUX. Grab some tasty ▧**Belgian waffles** and homemade ice cream at this stylish tea room, which offers yummy Flemish flavors such as the cinnamon-cookie speculoös. (56 pl. du Général de Gaulle. Open M noon-7pm, Tu-Sa 11am-7pm.)

5. PLACE DU GÉNÉRAL DE GAULLE. Lille's central hub is lined with Flemish facades, cafes, and shops. The central fountain is perfect for people watching.

6. RUE DE BÉTHUNE. Pass by pl. Rihour to the quiet rue de la Clef. The most popular boutiques, cinemas, and terrace restaurants crowd this lively center. Pop into The Majestic to check up on its regular screenings of classic films.

7. PALAIS DES BEAUX ARTS. This grand, well-designed museum houses a host of 15th- to 20th-century masterpieces. Check out this month's featured temporary exhibit and don't miss Monet's *Parliament de Londres* in the Impressionist wing (previous page).

Jean Lebas. Follow av. Jean Lebas; turn right on rue des Champs and left on rue de l'Esperance. The museum is on the right. ☎03 20 69 23 60. Open Tu-Th 11am-6pm, F 11am-8pm, Sa-Su 1-6pm. €3.50, students of architecture and design €2.50; F all students free.)

OTHER SIGHTS. The ▓**Vieille Bourse,** the old stock exchange, built between 1652 and 1653, epitomizes the Flemish Renaissance Baroque. The dignified structure now plays host to regular markets at which hundreds of postcards, letters, maps, and old books are sold. *(Pl. du Général de Gaulle. Markets open Tu-Su 9:30am-7:30pm.)* The **Citadel** on the city's north side was redesigned in the 17th century by military genius Vauban and is still used by the French military today. *(Open with tour in French Su 3pm. Make reservations at the tourist office.)* The **Jardin Vauban,** an English garden designed in 1865, has a carousel and carnival games.

🎵 ▓ ENTERTAINMENT AND FESTIVALS

Every year, the **Marché aux Fleurs** carpets the *centre-ville* at the end of April, while the huge flea market, **La Braderie,** occupies the city's squares on the first weekend of September (10am-midnight). The tourist office has information on film festivals, held at **Le Métropole,** rue des Ponts de Comines (☎08 92 68 00 73), and the **Majestic,** 54 rue de Béthune (☎03 28 52 40 40; student tickets €6).

Théâtre du Nord, pl. du Général de Gaulle (☎03 20 14 24 24; www.theatredunord.fr). Hosts plays and concerts Sept.-June. Find schedules at the tourist office. Prices vary, most student tickets €8.50.

Orchestre Nationale de Lille, 3 pl. Mendes France (☎03 2 012 82 40; www.onlille. com). €18-30, students €10.

Opéra de Lille, 2 rue des Bons-Enfants (☎03 28 38 40 40; www.opera-lille.fr). Hosts concerts and musicals. From €8, students from €5.

💲 NIGHTLIFE

Lille has thriving nightlife, with a spread of bars throughout the city that cater to all tastes. College students fill the pubs on **rue Solférino** and **rue Masséna.** Across town, the *vieille ville* offers trendier clubs and a less raucous scene. Look for the free magazine *Going Out*, often displayed near the entrance of bars, which lists up-to-date nightlife information.

Pub Mac Ewan's, 8 pl. Sébastopol (☎03 20 42 04 42). Draws an energetic barley-loving crowd with its 140 beers (from €2). Open M-Th 11am-2am, F-Sa 11am-3am. MC/V.

Nargullé Café, 151 rue Solférino (☎03 20 63 91 05). Hookah bar with couches and plush pillows. Beer from €3.40. Mixed drinks from €7. Hookah €9.20. Open June-July M-Th 7pm-1am, F 7pm-2am, Sa 4:30pm-2am, Su 7pm-midnight. Aug.-May M-Th 4:30pm-1am, F 4:30pm-2am, Sa 2pm-2am, Su 4:30-11:30pm. MC/V.

Le Network Café, 15 rue Faisan (☎06 70 23 06 41; www.network-cafe.net). Admits only regulars on weekends. Packed dance floor. Laid-back lounge encourages socializing—hence the name. Dress to impress. Open Tu-Su 10:30pm-8am. MC/V.

La Mangrove, 36 rue d'Angleterre (☎03 20 51 88 89). Tropical-themed *rhumerie* (rum distillery) has a lively dance floor. Sporadic concerts. Beer from €2.40. Mojitos €6. Mixed drinks €6. Salsa nights and DJs Th-Sa from 10pm. Open M-Sa 5pm-3am. MC/V.

L'Irlandais, 160-162 rue Solférino (☎03 20 54 92 15). Popular Irish pub with a jovial crowd. Small dance floor. Beer €3. Open daily 5pm-3am. MC/V.

THE NORTH

PAS-DE-CALAIS

ARRAS ☎ 03 21

Gabled townhouses and Flemish arcades lend a regal atmosphere to Arras (ah-rah; pop. 44,000), but the architecture can't hide the town's battle-plagued history. In WWI, the town suffered severe damage as the site of a long series of trench altercations, aptly named the Battle of Arras. Visit this scruffy survivor for its nearby war monuments, and you'll also discover its small-town appeal. Though Arras is over 100km from the ocean, its spirit remains close to the surf: restaurant menus are loaded with seafood specialties, and the sprawling outdoor cafes on the town's two squares seem like beach boardwalks.

▐ TRANSPORTATION

Trains: Pl. du Maréchal Foch. Ticket office open M-F 7am-8pm, Sa-Su 8am-8pm. To: **Amiens** (1hr., 12 per day, €11); **Lille** (45min., 20 per day, €9-11); **Lyon** (3hr., 3 per day, €78); **Paris** (50min., 12 per day, €28-41).

Public Transportation: ARTIS (☎03 21 51 40 30), next to the train station. Open July-Aug. M-F 8am-noon and 2-6pm, Sa 8am-noon; Sept.-June M-F 7:30am-12:30pm and 1:30-6:30pm, Sa 8am-noon. Tickets for local **buses** €1, carnet of 10 €7.

Taxis: Taxi Alain (☎03 21 23 27 74). **Taxi Alliance** (☎03 21 23 69 69). 24hr.

Car Rental: Avis, 4 rue Gambetta (☎03 21 51 69 03), near the train station. Open M-F 8:30am-noon and 2-6pm, Sa 9am-noon and 4-6pm. 21+; must have had license for 1 year. AmEx/MC/V.

✈ ▐ ORIENTATION AND PRACTICAL INFORMATION

Arras is bounded by **boulevard du Général Faidherbe** to the east and **rue Gambetta** to the southwest. Both meet at **place du Maréchal Foch.** The *centre-ville* consists of three large squares: **Grand'Place, place des Héros,** and **Petite Place.**

Tourist Office: Pl. des Héros (☎03 21 51 26 95; www.ot-arras.fr), in the Hôtel de Ville. From the station, walk across pl. du Maréchal Foch onto rue Gambetta. Continue for 5 blocks, then turn right on rue Désiré Delansorne. English-speaking staff offers a free map, a brochure with local hikes, and a city pass to Arras's main sights (€19, students €10). Ask for the free *Arras Pays,* a guide to local events. Open from Apr. to mid-Sept. M-Sa 9am-6:30pm, Su 10am-1pm and 2:30-6:30pm; from mid-Sept. to Mar. M 10am-noon and 2-6pm, Tu-Sa 9am-noon and 2-6pm, Su 10am-12:30pm and 2:30-6:30pm.

Tours: The tourist office offers tours of nearby memorials. Call for schedules, themes, and prices. Self-guided audio tours in Dutch, English, and French €6, students €3.20.

Laundry: Superlav, 17 pl. d'Ipswich, next to the Église St-Jean-Baptiste. Wash €3.50 per 5-6kg, €7.50 for 16kg; dry €1 per 10min. Open daily 7am-7pm.

Police: In the Hôtel de Ville (☎03 21 23 70 70).

Hospital: Bd. Georges Besnier (☎03 21 21 10 10). Call for the **pharmacie de garde.**

Post Office: 13 rue Gambetta (☎03 21 22 94 94). **Currency exchange** available. Open M-F 8:30am-6:30pm, Sa 8:30am-12:30pm. **Postal Code:** 62000.

▐ ACCOMMODATIONS

▨ **Auberge de Jeunesse (HI),** 59 Grand'Place (☎03 21 22 70 02; fax 07 46 15). Prime real estate in the middle of Grand'Place. Perfect for those looking to head out at night;

only a few stumbling steps from the bar to your bed. Kitchen and TV room. Breakfast €3. Reception 8-11am and 5-10pm. Open Feb.-Nov. Dorms €12. MC/V. ❶

Hôtel les Trois Luppars, 47 Grand'Place (☎03 21 60 02 03; fax 24 24 80). Guests enjoy modern conveniences in the oldest house in Arras, including a sauna. Large, white stucco rooms overlook the Grand'Place, while smaller quarters face an enclosed courtyard. Each room has bath, TV, and safe. Breakfast €8. Reception 6am-11pm. Check-out noon. Singles €60-70; doubles €75-80; triples €75-80; quads €80. AmEx/MC/V. ❹

Le Passe Temps, 1 pl. Maréchal du Foch (☎03 21 50 04 04), across from the station. Cheapest hotel rooms in town. Above a *brasserie*. Each has a large double bed, small desk, and TV. Breakfast €6.10. Reception M-Sa 7am-midnight. Singles and doubles €32-34, with shower €36-38, with bath €40-42. MC/V. ❷

🍴 FOOD

There is a **Monoprix** supermarket across from the post office at 30 rue Gambetta (open M-Sa 8:30am-7:50pm), an open-air market on **place des Héros** (open W and Sa 8am-1pm), and specialty shops in the pedestrian shopping area between the post office and the Hôtel de Ville. Inexpensive cafes line pl. des Héros and the pedestrian area, elegant restaurants adorn the **Grand'Place,** and *friteries* (hamburger stands) can be found on **rue la Taillerie,** the alley between the *places.*

La Cave de l'Écu, 54 Grand'Place (☎03 21 50 00 39). In a brick cellar with bird decor. Try an elaborate salad (€9.50-15) or create your own (€10). Free-range chicken (€13) rounds out the bird theme. *Galettes* and *crêpes* €3-9.50. *Menus* €19-25. Open daily noon-2:30pm and 7-10:30pm. AmEx/MC/V. ❸

Le Bateau du Ch'ti, 17 pl. des Héros (☎03 21 23 20 38). Hearty seafood specialties and colossal salads in a dining room of maritime paraphernalia. Salads €8-14. *Plats* €8-16. Open from mid-Apr. to mid-Sept. M-F noon-2:30pm and 7-10pm, Sa-Su noon-2:30pm and 7-11pm; from mid-Sept. to mid-Apr. M and Su noon-2:30pm, Tu-F and Sa noon-2:30pm and 7-10pm. MC/V. ❷

Le Saint-Germain Grill, 14 Grand'Place (☎03 21 51 45 45). *Crêped*-out travelers will rejoice at this unabashedly American-style restaurant. Its claim to having the "best ribs in town" is right on—and not just because it has the only ribs in town. Classic ribs €14. Open daily noon-2pm and 7-10pm. AmEx/MC/V. ❸

👁 SIGHTS

On the outskirts of the *vieille ville*, military monuments and memorials dot the area around the **Vauban Citadel,** a site accessible only by tour on Sundays. (Map at the tourist office. Tours from late July to Aug. 3:30pm. €4.80, students and under 18 €3.20.) See **Daytrips from Arras** (next page) for more extensive information on WWI and WWI sights and tours.

HÔTEL DE VILLE. Amid shops, bars, and cafes, the ornate Hôtel de Ville is a faithful replica of the 15th-century original that reigned over pl. des Héros until its destruction in WWI. Its 75m belfry offers the best view of Arras; an elevator takes you within 43 steps of the top. *(Access through the tourist office. Open May-Sept. M-Sa 9am-6:30pm, Su 10am-1pm and 2:30-6:30pm; Oct.-Apr. M 10am-noon and 2-6pm, Tu-Sa 9am-noon and 2-6pm, Su 10am-12:30pm and 2:30-6:30pm. €2.70, students €1.80.)*

LES BOVES. Beneath the town hall, these labyrinthine tunnels were bored into the site's soft chalk in the 10th century. Over the decades, the passageways have been used as chalk mines, wine cellars, and headquarters for Allied troops awaiting the Battle of Arras during WWI. Now, each spring they are decorated with flowers for a "Boves Garden" exhibit. The tourist office leads 40min. tours; inquire at the office. (☎03 21 51 26 95. Tours €4.70, students and under 18 €2.70.)

CATHÉDRALE AND ABBAYE SAINT-VAAST. Beyond the Hôtel de Ville, the 18th-century Cathédrale and seventh-century Abbaye St-Vaast stand on the hill where St-Vaast used to pray. The cathedral's Gothic interior contains Corinthian columns alongside Art Deco touches. Look for the seven statues of saints taken from the Pantheon. (Open from mid-May to mid-Oct. daily 10:30am-12:30pm and 2-6pm; from mid-Oct. to mid-May M-Sa 2:30-5:30pm. Guided tours available through the tourist office from mid-June to mid-Sept. Sa 3pm. €4.80, students and under 18 €3.20.) Inside the abbey, the **Musée des Beaux-Arts** displays a small but interesting collection. Highlights include the skeletal sculpture of Guillaume Lefrançois and Baglione's series of the eight muses at the top of the stairs. (22 rue Paul Doumer. ☎03 21 71 26 43. Open M and W-Su 9:30am-noon and 2-5:30pm. Last entry 5pm. €4, students €2.)

◧ ※ NIGHTLIFE AND FESTIVALS

For a few weeks in July and August, the town dumps tons of sand in Grand'Place to create **Arras on the Beach.** The festival includes wild beach parties, sporting events, DJs, and live music. Locals play beach volleyball or build sandcastles on this bizarre makeshift shore. Contact the tourist office for specific dates.

> **Vertigo,** 12 rue la Taillerie (☎03 21 23 18 00). Chic lounge. DJ spins house every weekend. Relaxed vibe gives way to an energetic crowd at night. Beer from €2.20. Mixed drinks from €8. Open M-Th noon-1am, F-Sa noon-2am, Su 2pm-1am. MC/V.

> **Le Couleur Café,** 35 pl. des Héros (☎03 21 71 08 70). A Caribbean-themed hangout; a life-size pirate statue greets patrons at the door. Beer from €2.30. Open Tu-Th 11am-1am, F 11am-2am, Sa 10am-2am, Su 4pm-1am. MC/V.

▣ DAYTRIPS FROM ARRAS

▨**Salient Tours** offers minibus tours of the WWI memorials surrounding Arras. Half-day tours cost €35 (students €30) and are the cheapest way to see many of the memorials. Tours leave from the Arras train station, though you can arrange for pickup at your hotel for no additional fee. Tour guides are extremely knowledgeable about the sights' history and have fascinating primary source documents available for examination. The Vimy and Somme memorials are covered in separate tours. Salient mainly visits the memorials below, though you can request to visit other sites. Somme tours depart at 9:15am and return at 1pm. Vimy tours depart at 1:15pm and return at 5pm. (Tours@salienttours. com; www.salienttours.com. Reservations required.)

VIMY MEMORIAL

The Vimy Memorial is 3km from the town of Vimy, 12km northeast of Arras. From Arras, Vimy is a 15min. car ride along N17. If you don't have a car and choose to go without the tour (the cheapest visiting option), catch a taxi in Arras (€20 each way). Walking along the highway to Vimy takes 50min. and can be dangerous. Monument ☎03 21 50 68 68. Open daily sunrise-sunset. Tunnels ☎03 21 48 98 97. Open May-Oct. daily 10am-6pm. Free tours in English and French every 45min. Reservations recommended (☎03 22 76 70 86); tours fill up fast. Museum ☎03 21 50 68 68. Open daily May-Oct. 10am-6pm; Nov.-Apr. 9am-5pm.

In April 1917, Canadian troops overtook German forces at the strategic Vimy Ridge, a feat that other Allied troops had failed to accomplish. Today, the Vimy Memorial stands as a gift to the Canadian government honoring the more than 66,000 Canadian soldiers who were killed during WWI. The two pylons of the monument bear the names of 11,000 soldiers killed in the battle. Sculpted figures surround the edifice: the most poignant is that of a woman, *Canada Weeping for Her Children*, carved from a single 30-ton limestone block.

The surrounding park, crisscrossed by German and Canadian trenches, is morbidly beautiful; hills and craters carved out by shells and mines are now covered by grass and sheep. Explore the trenches, but be sure to stay on the marked paths, as there are still active mines in the fenced-off areas. Today, the town of Vimy employs several full-time mine defusers, who are kept busy with the area's frightening number of remaining explosives. Herds of sheep—or, rather, sacrificial lambs—graze the land so that people don't risk their lives mowing the grass. To the shock of curators, an enormous mine was recently discovered under the women's washroom in the visitors center of the park—but don't head for the bushes yet; it has since been defused. A film at the monument's museum recounts the details of the excavation.

A free underground tour of the crumbling tunnels, given by Canadian students, starts at the kiosk near the trenches. Details highlighted during the tour hint at the realities of life on the front lines. The small museum near the monument recounts the battle and Canada's role in the war.

BATTLE OF THE SOMME MEMORIALS

If you choose to go by car, pick up the useful brochure The Visitors' Guide to the Battlefields of the Somme, available at tourist offices throughout the département; however, the tour provides more information than you'll find at the memorials and is cheaper than renting a car. The following sights are listed in the order they are visited on the tour.

When the French concentrated their forces in an attempt to halt the German advance, they left British and Commonwealth forces on the northern front, along the Somme *département*. After sustaining heavy casualties at Verdun, the French asked their allies to create a northern diversion at the Somme to spread out the German forces. The Battle of the Somme, designed for this purpose, began on July 1, 1916, and was one of the least successful battles of the war for the Allies. Anticipating such an attack, the entrenched German command had substantially fortified its position with a clever layered trench system. The lines barely moved for six months, during which the Allies suffered heavy losses, until Germany voluntarily left the region for strategic reasons. All in all, over one million men were mobilized along the front, and 330,000 casualties were sustained, 58,000 on the first day alone. Cemeteries and monuments pay tribute to those who were lost in the misguided attacks of 1916; some commemorate the more successful repulsion that finally came in 1918.

▨NEWFOUNDLAND PARK. Just outside Beaumont-Hamel, the Newfoundland Park and its enormous hilltop caribou statue facing the battlefield commemorate the loss of nearly an entire regiment of troops from the Canadian province of Newfoundland. An identical statue rests in Newfoundland, facing toward the Somme in reverence. The Allies planned to bombard the Germans for seven days, then set off an 18-ton underground mine to divert attention and initiate a "surprise" attack. On July 1 (after the seven days), the Newfoundland regiment was ordered to walk carefully across 500m of barbed wire, only to discover the bombardment had failed completely—but by then it was too late. The Germans had hidden safely in fortified underground bunkers and, upon seeing the soldiers, opened fire; nearly 700 Allies died in the first half-hour of the attack, at the hands of only five or six German machine-gunners; only 78 men survived. The current park is maintained by the Canadian government, which offers free tours of the trench-marked land in English and French. You may want to slather on insect repellent before you arrive here; the fields are often swarmed with thousands of pesky "thunder bugs." (☎ *03 22 76 70 86.*)

THIEPVAL VISITOR CENTER. The Thiepval Visitor Center offers a great introduction to the multiple stages of the battle with a small museum, film, and narrative display leading to the monument outside. If you choose to visit the memorials by car, this is a good place to start and gain the background you would otherwise receive on the tour. (☎03 22 74 60 47; fax 74 65 44. Open daily May-Oct. 10am-6pm; Nov.-Apr. 9am-6pm. Closed for 2 weeks over Christmas and New Year's. Free.) The 45m **Franco-British War Memorial,** dedicated to the dead and missing of the Battle of the Somme, just outside Thiepval, is the largest British war memorial in the world. It bears the names of over 73,000 soldiers who were lost on the front from 1915 to 1918 and who have no known grave. (Open sunrise-sunset.)

ULSTER MEMORIAL TOWER. Completed in 1921, the memorial stands outside Thiepval. It commemorates the 36th Division troops from Northern Ireland, the only soldiers successful in taking their objectives on July 1—before being subjected to the full force of a German counterattack and losing 5500 men. The tower itself is a replica of Helen's Tower, a large, stoic landmark in Clandeboye, Ireland, that stands where the soldiers trained before the war. The memorial offers tours of the mine-filled Thiepval Woods, which cannot be visited otherwise. If you're making a day of visiting the memorials, stop here for lunch. (☎03 22 74 81 11. Open Tu-Su 10am-6pm. Tour of woods Tu and Sa 11am, 3pm.)

MUSÉE SOMME 1916. This museum is housed in a tunnel that sheltered the French and British during WWI and was used again in 1939 as a bomb shelter. The museum recreates life in the trenches in the July 1916 offensive front and displays photos and objects that narrate the Battle of the Somme. (☎03 22 75 16 17; www.somme-trench-museum.co.uk. Open daily June-Sept. 9am-6pm; Oct.-Dec. and Feb.-May 9am-noon and 2-6pm. Guided tours available; reserve ahead. €5, students and under 18 €3.)

NATIONAL MEMORIAL AND SOUTH AFRICAN MUSEUM. This museum and memorial commemorates South African soldiers in both WWI and WWII. Nearly 4000 South African men were killed in an attack on July 15, 1916. The surrounding woods were also destroyed, and the sole **tree that survived the attack** is as moving as the beautiful etched glass on display in the memorial museum. To find the tree, walk behind the museum to the left. (☎03 22 85 02 17. Open daily from Apr. to mid-Oct. 10am-5:45pm; from mid-Oct. to Mar. 10am-3:45pm.)

CHANNEL PORTS (CÔTE D'OPALE)

The ports of Pas-de-Calais aren't the most scenic spots, but they bring fun-seeking travelers and happy honeymooners alike to France's northern coasts. Prime Coppertone season is the best time to visit the coast's lively beaches.

CHUNNELING TO BRITAIN. Ferries from Calais cross to **Dover,** while Boulogne serves **Dunkerque** and **Ramsgate.** Eurostar trains zip through the tunnel from **London** and **Ashford,** stopping outside **Calais** on their way to **Brussels, Lille,** and **Paris.** Le Shuttle carries cars through the Chunnel between Ashford and Calais. For details on operators, schedules, and fares, see **Getting There: By Boat** (p. 30) and **Getting There: By Train** (p. 32).

BOULOGNE-SUR-MER ☎03 21

The busy harbor of Boulogne-sur-Mer (buh-lohn-yuh-suhr-mayr; pop. 45,000) is the city's lifeblood, but Boulogne's most interesting diversions reside in its secluded *haute-ville* and by its white, sandy shores. The city appeals to beach bums and château enthusiasts alike, and the amazing aquarium is not to be missed by anyone. With a cool sea breeze, summer floral displays, and towering red-brick ramparts, Boulogne is the more aesthetically attractive of the two channel ports. A local summer escape, Boulogne is sleepy in the low season.

TRANSPORTATION

Trains: Gare Boulogne-Ville, bd. Voltaire. Info office open M-Sa 6:15am-7:30pm, Su 6:15am-8:50pm. Ticket office open M-Sa 8:45am-7pm. To **Calais** (30min., 13 per day, €7.20), **Lille** (2hr., 11 per day, €21; TGV 1hr., 2-3 per day, €24), and **Paris** (2-3hr., 11 per day, €58).

Buses: BCD, in Gare Boulogne-Ville. To **Calais** (40min., 4 per day, €7.20) and **Dunkerque** (1hr., 4 per day, €12).

Public Transportation: TCRB, 14 rue de la Lampe (☎03 21 83 51 51). Sends **bus #10** from the train station and pl. de France to the *haute-ville* (get off at Dernier Soy; €1.10). Most buses (€0.70-1.10) go through pl. de France.

Taxis: Calais (☎03 21 91 25 00), at the train station.

ORIENTATION AND PRACTICAL INFORMATION

The **Liane River** separates the ferry terminal from everything else. To reach the central **place de France** from the train station, turn right on bd. Voltaire. Turn left onto bd. Danou and follow it to the *place*. The streets between **place Frédéric Sauvage** and **place Dalton** form the *centre-ville*, while the *vieille ville* is at the top of the hill, up rue de la Lampe, which becomes Grande Rue.

ASSENT TO THE ASCENT. Plan to visit all of your destinations in Boulogne-sur-Mer's fortified *vieille ville* consecutively. Unless you are an enthusiastic hiker, one trip up the very steep hill is trying; climbing it twice unnecessarily is masochistic. The walk from the train station is shorter than an ascent from the waterfront, but the gradient is much steeper.

Tourist Office: 24 quai Gambetta (☎03 21 10 88 10; www.tourisme-boulognesurmer. com), past pl. de France and the roundabout. English-speaking staff offers bus info, a reservations booking service, and a free map. *Guide Touristique,* in English and French, lists nearly every establishment in town. Open M-Sa 9:30am-12:30pm and 1:45-6:30pm, Su 10am-1pm and 3-6pm.

Bank: Crédit Agricole, 26 rue Nationale (☎08 10 81 06 96). 24hr. **ATM** and **currency exchange** available. Open Tu-W 8:45am-12:15pm and 1:30-5:30pm, Th 9:15am-12:15pm and 1:30-4:15pm, F 8:45am-12:15pm and 1:30-6:45pm, Sa 8:45am-12:15pm and 1:30-5pm.

Laundromat: 62 rue de Lille (☎03 21 80 55 15), in the *haute-ville.* Wash €4 per 6kg. Open daily 7am-8pm.

Police: 9 rue Perrochel (☎03 21 99 48 48). Call for the **pharmacie de garde.**

Hospital: Allée Jacques Monod (☎03 21 99 33 33).

Internet Access: Syrius, 23 rue des Religieuses Anglaises (☎03 21 46 33 12). €3 per hr., €5 per 2hr. Open M-Sa 10am-8pm. Cash only.

Post Office: Pl. Frédéric Sauvage (☎03 21 99 09 09). Open M-F 8:30am-6pm, Sa 8:30am-12:30pm. **Postal Code:** 62200.

⌂ ACCOMMODATIONS

Auberge de Jeunesse (HI), pl. Rouget de Lisle (☎03 21 99 15 30; fax 99 15 39), across from the train station. Tidy, well-decorated 2- to 4-bed rooms, each with bathroom that doesn't lock. Kitchen. Breakfast included. Free Internet and Wi-Fi. Reception Mar.-Sept. daily 8am-midnight; Oct.-Dec. M-F 9am-11pm, Sa-Su 9am-noon and 5-11pm. Check-out 11am. 24hr. code access. Reserve ahead in summer. Dorms €21, ages 4-11 €12; €5 more per person to ensure a private room. MC/V. ❶

Hôtel Alexandra, 93 rue Thiers (☎03 21 30 52 22; fax 30 20 03), between the train station and the ferry port. Classy hotel offers clean and spacious rooms with showers, TVs, and beautiful bedspreads. Breakfast €6. Free Wi-Fi. Reception 7am-11pm. Check-out noon. June-Sept. singles and doubles €55-60; triples €72; quads €85. Oct.-May singles and doubles €52-57; triples €69; quads €82. MC/V. ❹

▢ FOOD

There is an excellent market on **place Dalton** (open W and Sa 6am-1pm), and daily fish markets reel customers in along **place Gambetta.** A **Champion** super-market, bd. Danou, is in the Centre Commercial de la Liane. (Open M-Sa 8:30am-8pm.) Small restaurants line **rue de Lille** in the *haute-ville*, as well as **rue du Doyen** in the *centre-ville*. Booming *brasseries* fill **place Danton.**

Restaurant de la Haute Ville, 60 rue de Lille (☎03 21 80 54 10). Cute dining room and flower-strewn courtyard. *Île flottante* (a light, fluffy dessert) €5. *Menu végétarien* €13. Open Tu-Su noon-10pm. MC/V. ❷

Le Doyen, 11 rue du Doyen (☎03 21 30 13 08). Offers regional seafood dishes in an intimate dining room. Tangy *feuilleté de fruits de mer* (seafood platter; €5.90). *Plats* €13-18. Open M-F noon-2pm and 7-9:30pm, Sa noon-2pm and 7-10pm. Reservations strongly recommended. MC/V. ❸

La Scala, 16 pl. du Général de Bouillon (☎03 21 80 49 49). French and Italian cuisine. Outdoor terrace packed on sunny days. Basic, gargantuan pizza (€5). *Menus* from €9. Open daily noon-10:30pm. MC/V. ❷

◉ ▲ SIGHTS AND OUTDOOR ACTIVITIES

Enjoy Boulogne's sparkling surf with a windsurfer or catamaran from **Le Yacht Club Boulonnaise,** 234 bd. Ste-Beuve. (☎03 21 31 80 67; www.ycboulogne.net. Windsurfers €20 per hr. Catamarans €35 per hr. Open Mar.-Nov. M-Sa 9am-5pm.)

◾**NAUSICAÄ: CENTRE NATIONAL DE LA MER.** Boulogne celebrates its main source of commerce at this aquarium. You'll find everything on the food chain—from plankton to sharks—as you move through the building's labyrinthine layout. Exhibits remind visitors of the need to ◾**respect the environment.** Ironically, seafood cafes exist throughout the aquarium, with signs reading, *"La mer vient à votre table"*—literally, "the sea comes to your table." *(Bd. Ste-Beuve. ☎03 21 30 99 99; www.nausicaa.fr. Open daily July-Aug. 9:30am-7:30pm; Sept.-Dec. and from late Jan. to June 9:30am-6:30pm. July-Aug. €17, students and ages 3-12 €11; Sept.-Dec. and from late Jan. to June €15/10. Audio tours in multiple languages €3. English brochure €3.)*

CHÂTEAU-MUSÉE. This 13th-century castle showcases a worldly exhibition, including an Egyptian mummy and 550 Grecian urns—France's second-largest collection of such relics, after the Louvre's cool 25,000. *(Rue de Bernet. ☎03 21 10 02 20; chateaumusee@ville-boulogne-sur-mer-fr. Open M and W-Sa 10am-12:30pm and 2-5pm, Su 10am-12:30pm and 2:30-5:30pm. €2, under 18 free. Audio tours in English and French €2.)*

BASILIQUE DE NOTRE DAME. This 19th-century structure sits above a 12th-century crypt, the second-largest in France. Father Haffreingue, an amateur architect, built this church following the Revolution, when the previous basilica was destroyed. (*Rue de Lille.* ☎03 21 99 75 98. *Open daily Apr.-Aug. 9am-noon and 2-6pm; Sept.-Mar. 10am-noon and 2-5pm. Crypt open Tu-Su 2-6pm. Free. Crypt €2, under 18 €1.*)

🎵 NIGHTLIFE

Neon-lit pubs fill the pedestrian *centre-ville*, particularly at **place Dalton.**

O Sud, 20 bis rue du Doyen (☎03 21 83 97 05; www.restaurantosud.com). Stylish alcove with plush pillows. Tapas (available until 10:30pm) from €2.30; 3 for €6.50. Mixed drinks €6.50. Open M-F and Su 11am-midnight, Sa 11am-1am. MC/V.

WoolPack Inn, 14 pl. de la Résistance (☎03 21 31 62 20), in the *haute ville*. Open Tu-Su 5pm-2am. MC/V.

Bar Hamiot, 1 rue Faidherbe (☎03 21 31 44 20), down the hill by the port. Classic *brasserie*. Beer from €2. Open daily 6am-midnight. AmEx/MC/V.

MONTREUIL-SUR-MER   ☎03 21

Though its name is misleading (there has not been a drop of salt water here since the 13th century, when the ocean began to recede), tiny Montreuil-sur-Mer (mahn-truhy-suhr-mehr; pop. 2430) is as idyllic as one might imagine. Victor Hugo chose to set a large portion of *Les Misérables* in this charming provincial town, which continues to pay homage to the masterpiece with an annual performance of the story. Summer festivals stir things up in the town, but the surrounding countryside offers a constant sense of calm. Maintaining a simple appeal as a relatively untouristed destination, Montreuil will encourage romance in even the most *misérable* of visitors.

🚆 TRANSPORTATION

Trains: Just outside the citadel walls (☎03 21 06 05 09). Open M-F 5:45am-8pm, Sa 9:30am-noon and 1-6:20pm, Su 2:45-7:40pm. To: **Arras** (1hr., 7 per day, €13); **Boulogne** (30min., 7 per day, €6.80); **Calais** (1hr., 5 per day, €12); **Lille** (2hr.; M-F 5 per day, Sa-Su service limited; €17).

Bike Rental: ETS Vignaux, 73 rue Pierre Ledent (☎03 21 06 00 29). Look for a sign that reads "Giant Bikes." €10 per ½-day, €15 per day; €200 deposit. Open Tu-Sa 9am-noon and 2-7pm. AmEx/MC/V.

🛈 PRACTICAL INFORMATION

Tourist Office: 21 rue Carnot (☎03 21 06 04 27; www.tourisme-montreuillois.com). From the station, climb the stairs and turn right onto av. du 11 Novembre. Continue under the Porte de Boulogne and bear right on Parvis St-Firmin. Turn right at the sign for "Auberge de Jeunesse" onto rue des Bouchers, follow it to its end, and take a left on the footpath by the statue of Notre Dame; the office is straight ahead. English-speaking staff distributes a free map, a guide that details the town's 6 churches, and brochures in English and French. Open July-Aug. M-Sa 10am-6pm, Su 10am-12:30pm and 3-5pm; Sept.-Oct. and Apr.-June M-Sa 10am-12:30pm and 2-6pm, Su 10am-1pm; Nov.-Mar. M-Sa 10am-12:30pm and 2-5pm.

Currency Exchange: Crédit du Nord, 37 pl. du Général du Gaulle (☎03 21 90 92 20). **ATM.** Open Tu-F 1:45-6pm; exchanges available Tu-F 8:45am-12:15pm, Sa 8:50-noon.

NOT SO MISÉRABLE

Victor Hugo's *Les Misérables* is renowned throughout the world, but few cities celebrate it with quite as much passion as the little village of Montreuil-sur-Mer. This northern town has good reason to embrace the novel—a significant portion of the story is set within its boundaries. It is here that the famous Jean Valjean lives and works at the beginning of the story, here that he adopts his costar Cosette, and here that he first flees his archrival Javier.

Locals proudly inform visitors that Victor Hugo visited Montreuil-sur-Mer in 1837 and spent a brief—but meaningful—afternoon in town napping on the ramparts, eating lunch at the Hôtel de France, and writing a letter to his wife. Although he was only around for a few hours, it was apparently enough to convince him that the town would be the perfect setting for a historical romance.

When Victor Hugo visited, the town was reputedly divided into two sections according to class. The poor *misérables* lived in the "lower town," while the bourgeois dined in fancy cafes in the "high town." This dramatic separation was possibly yet another influence that inspired Hugo. If Montreuil-sur-Mer incited a classic novel in just a few hours, just imagine what your daytrip will provoke.

Laundromat: Laverie Montreuilloise, 44 rue Pierre Ledent (☎06 35 90 25 89). Wash €3.50 per 6kg. Open daily 8am-8pm.

Police: Pl. Gambetta (☎03 21 81 08 48).

Hospital: Rang-du-Fliers (☎03 21 89 45 45).

Post Office: Pl. Gambetta (☎03 21 06 70 00). Open M-F 8:30am-noon and 1:30-5pm, Sa 8:30am-noon. **Postal Code:** 62170.

ACCOMMODATIONS AND CAMPING

B&B Madame Renard, 4 av. du 11 Novembre (☎03 21 86 85 72), up the stairs from the train station. Large rooms in a 3-story house. Fireplaces in common rooms. Secluded garden. Convenient for backpackers who don't want to lug their packs up to the city. Breakfast included. Reservations recommended. Singles with sink and shared bath or shower €35, with private bath €40; doubles €45. Extra bed €10-15. Cash only. ❸

Auberge de Jeunesse "La Hulotte Citadelle" (HI), rue Carnot (☎03 21 06 10 83), inside the citadel. Summer-camp-style accommodations. Sweeping views make up for the hike. Guests can enjoy the citadel for free. Kitchen. Reception 10am-noon and 2-6pm. Reservations recommended. Open from Mar. to mid-July and from mid-Aug. to Oct. Dorms €11. Cash only. ❶

Camping La Fontaine des Clercs, 1 rue de l'Église (☎03 21 06 07 28). Plots by the Canche River. Local *boulanger* visits the site M-Tu and Th-Su at 8:45am with fresh breakfast for sale. Reception 9-10am, noon-1pm, 6-7pm. Check-out noon. Curfew 10pm. Open Feb.-Nov. 1 or 2 people with car or tent €15; extra person €3.50. Electricity €3.50. AmEx/MC/V. ❶

FOOD

Find restaurants and a **Shopi** supermarket (open M-Sa 8:30am-7:30pm, Su 9am-noon) at pl. du Général de Gaulle; *boulangeries* are on the surrounding streets. A market floods **place du Général de Gaulle** Saturdays 8am-1pm.

Le Jéroboam, 1 rue des Juifs (☎03 21 86 65 80). Classy restaurant named after the term for a 3L wine bottle. Gourmet meals in a room decorated with wine barrels, crates, and corks. *Plats* €20-54. Lunch *menu* €17. Dinner *menus* €25. Open July-Aug. M 7-9:15pm, Tu-Sa noon-1:45pm and 7-9:15pm; Sept.-June Tu-Sa noon-1:45pm and 7-9:15pm. MC/V. ❹

Taverne de l'Écu de France, 5 Porte de France (☎03 21 06 01 89), off pl. du Général de Gaulle. Regional specialties, including *moules* (mussels; €10). Summer salad (€11) is deliciously filling. Open M-Tu and F-Su noon-2pm and 8:30-10pm. MC/V. ❷

👁 🏔 SIGHTS AND OUTDOOR ACTIVITIES

Club Canoë-Kayak, 4 rue Moulin des Orphelins, offers canoe and kayak excursions. (☎03 21 06 20 16; ckmontreuil@wanadoo.fr. ½-day sessions from €10, full-day €25. Open May-Aug. daily 9:30am-5:30pm. Reservations required.)

RAMPARTS. The 3km long ramparts overlook grassy hills, verdant groves of the Canche valley, and distant villages. The **Promenade des Remparts** footpath follows their entire length. *(Free.)*

CITADEL. The 16th-century citadel in the *haute-ville* sits on the site of the old royal castle. Allegedly, Vauban (who designed or redesigned most French fortresses) was unimpressed with the original's safety features and ordered renovations in the 17th century. *(Open with tour from late July to early Aug. daily 10am-noon; from mid-Aug. to Nov. and from mid-Apr. to late July M and W-Su 10am-noon and 2-6pm; from Mar. to mid-Apr. daily 10am-noon and 2-5pm. Free English guides available. €2.50, under 18 €1.25.)*

🍸 NIGHTLIFE

▨ **West Indies,** 25 rue Pierre Ledent (☎03 21 81 95 92). Part *rhumerie* (rum distillery), part tapas bar, and part shrine to Che Guevara. Serves 140 types of rum (€4.50-45) and the popular Hemingway's Special mojito (€8) to rugged locals. Tapas (€3.90-5.50) served on the weekend. Open M-F 6:30pm-1am, Sa 6:30pm-2am. AmEx/MC/V.

▨ **Crêperie et Artisinat,** rue du Clape en Bas (☎06 23 71 17 28). Come early (4pm) to see local artists working in the adjoining studios. Soundtrack ranges from the *"formidable hommage à la légende Elvis"* to Celtic folk. *Crêpes* and *galettes* €2-8. Free concerts Th 9:30pm, Su 5pm; pick up a concert schedule at the bar or tourist office. Open daily from mid-June to Sept. 4pm-midnight. Cash only.

🎇 FESTIVALS

Les Misérables Son et Lumière, from late July to early Aug. *Les Misérables* light show features 300 actors in period costume, horses, and fireworks. €18, ages 5-12 €12.

Les Malins Plaisirs (☎03 21 98 12 26), Aug. Stages operatic, theatrical, and musical performances. Call the tourist office to reserve tickets. €14-18, under 25 €9-14.

Day of the Street Painters, Aug. 15. Artists haunt the ramparts and the *haute-ville* to paint landscapes of Montreuil, which are displayed in pl. Verte in the afternoon.

Festival des Soupes, Bouillons, et Pains, late Oct. Celebrate soup, stock, and bread at the citadel. €5; includes bowl and unlimited soup and bread.

CALAIS ☎03 21

Calais (kah-lay; pop. 80,000)—with its slew of restaurants, bars, and clubs—caters to vacationers at all hours. The beach draws loads of locals and travelers throughout the summer; with the Chunnel nearby, English can be heard everywhere. While Calais doesn't offer much architectual eye candy, the swath of shoreline promises spirited nightlife when the weather is warm.

⌐ TRANSPORTATION

Trains: Calais has 2 stations.

Gare Calais-Ville, bd. Jacquard. Ticket office open M 5am-7:30pm, Tu-Sa 6am-7:30pm, Su 8:30am-7:30pm. Info office open M-Sa 9am-7pm. To: **Boulogne** (30min., 11 per day, €7.20); **Dunkerque** (1hr., 2 per day, €7.70); **Lille** (1hr., 16 per day, €16); **Paris** (3hr., 6 per day, €30-60). Free Balad'In **buses** connect the ferry terminal, pl. d'Armes, and the station (every 30min.).

Gare Calais-Fréthun, near Chunnel entrance. Eurostar and TGV trains serve **Paris** and **London.**

Buses: BCD (☎03 21 83 51 51). To **Boulogne** (40min.; M-F and Su 5 per day, Sa 2 per day; €7.20) and **Dunkerque** (40min.; M-F 6 per day, Sa 3 per day; €7.70).

Public Transportation: OpaleBus, 68 bd. Lafayette (☎03 21 19 72 72). Info office open M-F 9am-noon and 1:30-6:30pm, Sa 9am-noon. **Bus** #3 (dir.: Blériot/VVF) runs from the station to the beach, hostel, and campground (M-Sa 7am-7:45pm, Su 10:10am-7:40pm; €1.10).

Taxis: At the train station (☎03 21 97 35 35 or 97 13 14). 24hr.

ⓘ PRACTICAL INFORMATION

Tourist Office: 12 bd. Georges Clemenceau (☎03 21 96 62 40; www.calais-cotedopale. fr). From the train station, cross the street, turn left onto the bridge, and continue onto bd. Georges Clemenceau; the office is on the right. English-speaking staff offers free maps and accommodations booking. Open June-Aug. M-Sa 10am-1pm and 2-6:30pm, Su 10am-1pm; Sept.-May M-Sa 10am-1pm and 2-6:30pm.

Tours: Run by the tourist office. **Petit train** runs July-Aug. daily 10:30, 11:30am, 2, 3, 4, 5, 6pm; €5, under 12 €2.50. Walking tours depart from Hôtel de Ville July-Aug. Tu-Sa 10am, 2pm; €2.

Currency Exchange: Available at the post office and the ferry and Hovercraft terminals, 5 bd. Georges Clemenceau. Open M-F 9:30am-12:30pm, Sa 10am-12:30pm.

Laundromat: Lavorama, 48 pl. d'Armes. Wash €2.80 per 5kg. Open daily 7am-9pm.

Police: Pl. de Lorraine (☎03 21 19 13 17). Call for the **pharmacie de garde.**

Hospital: 11 quai du Commerce (☎03 21 46 33 33).

Internet Access: **Médiathèque Louis Aragon,** 16 rue du Pont Lottin (☎03 21 46 20 40). €1 per hr. Open Tu 10am-noon and 1:30-7pm, W-Sa 10am-noon and 1:30-5pm.

Post Office: Pl. d'Alsace (☎03 21 85 52 85). **Currency exchange** available. Open M-F 8:30am-6pm, Sa 9am-noon. **Postal Code:** 62100.

⌂⌂ ACCOMMODATIONS AND CAMPING

▨ **Centre Européen de Séjour/Auberge de Jeunesse (HI),** av. du Maréchal de Lattre de Tassigny (☎03 21 34 70 20; www.auberge-jeunesse-calais.com), near the beach. From the train station, turn left and follow rue Royale past pl. d'Armes. Cross the bridge and turn left at the roundabout onto bd. du Général de Gaulle. Turn right onto rue Alice Marie and bear left at the fork. The hostel is the 3rd building on the left (20min.). Alternatively, take bus #3 from the station to Pluviose, 1 block from the hostel. From the ferry, take a shuttle bus to pl. d'Armes. Spacious rooms with meticulously clean shared bathrooms. Pool table, bar, cafeteria, and library. Breakfast included. Wi-Fi €2 per 12hr. Reception 24hr. Check-out 10am. Singles €26; doubles €42. AmEx/MC/V. ❷

Hotel Victoria, 8 rue du Commandant Bonninque (☎03 21 34 38 32; fax 97 12 13), an extension of rue de Thermes. Close to the lighthouse. Heavily wallpapered rooms with TVs. Breakfast €5. Reception 8am-11pm; code access after 11pm. Singles and doubles €31-44, with toilet €44-57; triples and quads €41-44/48-50. AmEx/MC/V. ❷

Hôtel Pacific, 40 rue du Duc de Guise (☎06 62 23 40 26; www.cofrase.com/hotel/pacific). Bright, sizable rooms with bath. Breakfast €6.50. Reception 7:30am-11pm. Check-out 11am. Reserve 1 month ahead in summer. Singles €39-48; doubles €55; triples €63; quads €90. AmEx/MC/V. ❸

Camping Municipal de Calais, av. Raymond Poincairé (☎03 21 97 89 79 or 06 60 46 19 93). Small sites with little privacy packed with RVs. Reception July-Aug. 7am-9pm; Sept. and Apr.-June 8am-noon and 2:30-8pm. Gates closed 10:30pm-6am. Reservations required July-Aug. and recommended otherwise. Open from mid-Apr. to Oct. €3.70 per person, children €3.20; sites €2.60. Electricity €2.05. ❶

◖ FOOD

Calais cuisine is understandably seafood-centric; most restaurants offer regional seafood platters. Any *pâtisserie*—especially those on **boulevard Jacquard**—will have a *gâteau Calais*, composed of rich coffee butter cream, a crumbly cookie base, and a thick layer of icing (€1.50-2). Morning markets are held on **place Crèvecoeur** (open Th and Sa 8:30am-12:30pm) and **place d'Armes** (open W and Sa 8:30am-12:30pm). A **Match** supermarket is located at 50 pl. d'Armes. (☎03 21 34 33 79. Open June-Sept. M-Sa 9am-7:30pm, Su 8:30-11:30am; Oct.-May M-Sa 9am-7:30pm.) Restaurants and *brasseries* line **rue Royale** and **boulevard Jacquard.** Cheaper-than-usual *glaciers* (ice-cream stands) dot the shore.

◰ Tonnerre de Brest, 16 pl. d'Armes (☎03 21 96 95 35). Extensive selection of *crêpes* and *galettes* (€2.70-10) in a maritime-themed setting. Lunch *menu* (*galette, crêpe,* and wine, beer, or cider) €11. *Menus* €10-18. Open July-Aug. daily 11:30am-2:30pm and 6-11pm; Sept.-June Tu-Su 11:30am-2:30pm and 6-11pm. MC/V. ❷

Histoire Ancienne, 20 rue Royale (☎03 21 34 11 20). Classy dining room with black leather chairs and unique artwork. Vegetarian options and a tasty regional *toques d'Opale menu* (€26). Change out of beachwear before arriving. *Plats* €17-23; vegetarian *plats* €17. Open M noon-2pm, Tu-Sa noon-2pm and 6-10pm. Closed 3 weeks in Aug. Reservations recommended for dinner. AmEx/MC/V. ❸

Au Coq d'Or, 31 pl. d'Armes (☎03 21 34 79 05). A knight in full armor greets diners. Outgoing waitstaff serves regional cuisine. *Plats* €10-23. Regional *menu* served M-F (€14). Open daily noon-10pm. MC/V. ❸

◉ ◮ SIGHTS AND OUTDOOR ACTIVITIES

▨BEACH. In the summer, head to Calais's fantastic beach—the town's main attraction. The beach becomes less crowded with hyper children and pickup soccer games as you walk farther from rue de la Mer. *(Follow rue Royale as it becomes rue de la Mer. Continue to the end and turn left along the shore away from the harbor.)*

▨MUSÉE DE LA SECONDE GUERRE MONDIALE. Housed in an old German WWII naval bunker in the Parc St-Pierre, this museum illustrates the fascinating history of Calais's important naval role during the war with old uniforms, weapons, photographs, and newspapers. *(☎03 21 34 21 57. Open daily May-Sept. 10am-6pm; Oct.-Nov. and Feb.-Apr. M and W-Su 11am-5pm. Wheelchair-accessible. €6, students €5, families €14. Group rates available. Free audio tour in Dutch, English, French, and German.)*

THE BURGHERS OF CALAIS. Rodin's evocative sculpture is framed by the Hôtel de Ville's flowered lawn. The statue depicts six burghers who surrendered the keys to Calais during the Hundred Years' War, offering their lives to England's King Edward III in exchange for those of the starving townspeople. Edward's French wife Philippa pleaded for mercy, and the burghers were spared.

PHARE DE CALAIS. This 58m lighthouse with a draining 271-step climb has the best view in town (though the industrial Calais is not the most breathtaking sight to behold). On clear days, the Dover cliffs are visible from the top. A museum at the base explains the history of the structure. *(Pl. Henri Barbuisse. ☎03 21 34 33 34; www.pharedecalais.com. Open June-Sept. M-F 2-6:30pm, Sa-Su 10am-noon and 2-6:30pm; Oct.-May W 2-5:30pm, Sa-Su 10am-noon and 2-5:30pm. €4, ages 5-15 €2.)*

MUSÉE DES BEAUX ARTS ET DE LA DENTELLE. Housed in a hideous building, this museum displays artwork and a collection of *dentelles* (lace) from all eras—including a sexy lingerie display. *(☎03 21 46 48 40. Open M and W-F 10am-noon and 2-5:30pm, Sa 10am-noon and 2-6:30pm, Su 2-6:30pm. Wheelchair-accessible. Free.)*

🎵 NIGHTLIFE

A hearty spirit invigorates pubs on **rue Royale** and **rue de la Mer,** especially where they meet **place d'Armes.** *Discothèques* along **rue Royale** stay open late.

Last Night, 10 rue de la Mer (☎03 21 34 73 24). 81 different mixed drinks (from €4), flashy neon lights, and tons of techno. Beer from €2. Open daily from June to mid-Sept. 2pm-2am; from mid-Sept. to May 2pm-1am. AmEx/MC/V.

PICARDY

AMIENS
☎03 22

At the heart of Amiens (ah-mee-ehn; pop. 139,200) lies France's largest Gothic cathedral, over twice the size of Paris's Notre Dame. This impressive structure may be the city's claim to fame, but Amiens's particular charm comes from its more modest features: a canal-lined pedestrian *quartier,* a museum devoted to native son Jules Verne, and an array of youthful pubs. Beneath its quaint facade, Amiens is a surprisingly modern commercial center—yet its parks and nearby hiking trails provide a perfect escape from city life.

▐ TRANSPORTATION

Trains: Gare du Nord, pl. Alphonse Fiquet. Ticket office open M-F 5:15am-8:30pm, Sa 5:45am-8:15pm, Su 6am-10:15pm. Info office open M-F 6:35am-9:30pm, Sa 10am-1pm and 2-7pm, Su 2-9:30pm. To: **Boulogne-sur-Mer** (1hr., 8 per day, €18); **Calais** (2hr., 1 per day, €22); **Lille** (1hr., 11 per day, €18); **Paris** (1hr., 23 per day, €19); **Rouen** (1hr., 3 per day, €17).

Buses: Rue de la Vallée (☎03 22 92 27 03), down the staircase that faces rue du Vivier. To **Beauvais, Mers-les-Bains,** and other regional destinations. €1.50-14.

Public Transportation: Ametis, 10 pl. Alphonse Fiquet (☎03 22 71 40 00). Open July-Aug. M-F 7am-6:45pm, Sa 8am-4:15pm; Sept.-June M-F 6:45am-7:15pm, Sa 8am-4:30pm. Buses run 5am-9pm. Buy individual tickets (€1.20) on board and carnets of 10 (€9.90) or day passes (€3.40) at the office. All buses stop within a few blocks of the station.

Taxis: ☎03 22 91 30 03. 24hr.

Car Rental: Avis, 11 rue St-Martin aux Waides (☎03 22 91 31 21). From €50 per day. 25+. Open M-F 8:30am-noon and 2-6pm, Sa 9am-noon and 4-6pm. AmEx/MC/V.

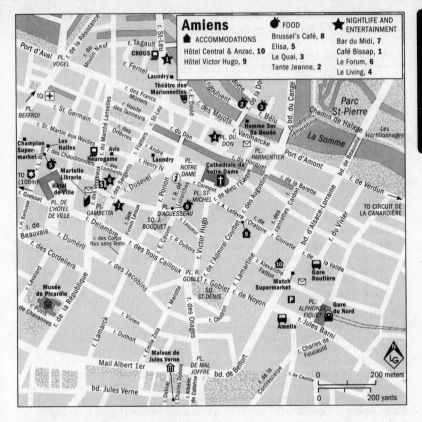

Amiens

🏠 ACCOMMODATIONS

Hôtel Central & Anzac, **10**
Hôtel Victor Hugo, **9**

🍎 FOOD

Brussel's Café, **8**
Elisa, **5**
Le Quai, **3**
Tante Jeanne, **2**

★ NIGHTLIFE AND ENTERTAINMENT

Bar du Midi, **7**
Café Bissap, **1**
Le Forum, **6**
Le Living, **4**

🛈 PRACTICAL INFORMATION

Tourist Office: 40 pl. Notre Dame (☎03 22 71 60 50; www.amiens.com/tourisme). From the station, turn right onto bd. d'Alsace-Lorraine and left onto rue Gloriette. Continue 3 blocks, through pl. St-Michel and onto rue Cormont. The office is ahead on the left, next to the cathedral. English-speaking staff offers reservation service (€3), free maps, and info on suggested hiking circuits. Open Apr.-Sept. M-Sa 9:30am-6:30pm, Su 10am-noon and 2-5pm; Oct.-Mar. M-Sa 9:30am-6pm, Su 10am-noon and 2-5pm.

Tours: Run by the tourist office. Cathedral tours Apr.-Oct. M-F and Su 4pm, Sa 11am; Nov.-Feb. Su 3pm; Mar.-Apr. Su 3pm. City tours in French Sa 3pm. €5.50, students €4, under 12 €3. Call ahead for a bilingual guide; multiple languages available.

Bookstore: Martelle Libraire, 3 rue des Vergeaux (☎03 22 71 54 54). Small English section. Open M-Sa 10am-7pm. MC/V.

Youth Center: CROUS, 25 rue St-Leu (☎03 22 71 24 00; www.crous-amiens.fr). Info on lodging, work, and study opportunities. Free Internet. Open M-F 8:30am-5pm.

Laundromats: Net Express, 10 rue André (☎03 22 72 33 33). Wash €3 per 7kg. Open daily 8am-6pm. **Laverie des Majots Salon Lavoir,** 15 rue des Majots (☎06 66 55 84 74). Wash €3 per 7kg, €5.50 per 10kg. Open daily 8am-9pm.

Police: Pl. Léon Gontier (☎03 22 22 25 50). Call for the **pharmacie de garde.**

Hospital: Hôpital Nord, pl. Victor Pauchet (☎03 22 66 80 00). Take bus #10 (dir.: Collège César Frank).

Internet Access: Free at **CROUS** (above). **Neurogame,** 16 rue Chaudronniers (☎03 22 72 68 79). €3.50 per hr., €5 per 2hr. Open July-Aug. M-Sa 10am-10pm; Sept.-June M-Sa 10am-midnight, Su 2-8pm.

Post Office: 7 rue des Vergeaux (☎03 22 97 04 04). Open M-F 8:30am-7pm, Sa 8:30am-1pm. Branches at 35 pl. Alphonse Fiquet (open M-F 8am-7pm, Sa 8am-noon) and 14 pl. Parmentier (open Tu-F 10am-1:30pm and 2:30-6pm, Sa 8am-5pm). **Postal Code:** 80000.

ACCOMMODATIONS

Hotels with the cheapest rooms (€30-40) cluster around the train station; options in the *centre-ville* are pricier. Amiens has no hostel or campground.

Hôtel Victor Hugo, 2 rue l'Oratoire (☎03 22 91 57 91; fax 92 74 02). Quiet, central location. Each room with bath or shower and TV. Breakfast €6.50. Free Wi-Fi. Reception 24hr.; call if arriving after 11pm. Singles and doubles €42-65. MC/V. ❹

Hôtel Central and Anzac, 17 rue Alexandre Fatton (☎03 22 91 34 08; www.hotel-centralanzac.com). Small rooms with soft beds and large windows. Note the interesting stained glass in the entrance. Breakfast €5.50. Wi-Fi €10 per 3hr. Reception 24hr.; call if arriving 10:30pm-6:30am. Singles €33, with shower €38, with bath €48-52; doubles €39/44/54-58; triples €64; quads €74. AmEx/MC/V. ❷

FOOD

Quai Bélu is packed with canal-front cafes and restaurants. Kebab stands cluster around the station and between the river and the cathedral; *brasseries* surround the Hôtel de Ville. A **Match** supermarket is in the mall to the right of the station (open M-Sa 8:30am-8pm), and a **Champion** supermarket is in the basement of the shopping center next to Les Halles (open M-Sa 8:30am-8pm). Amiens's main market takes over **place Parmentier** on Saturday morning (see **Sights,** below), while smaller markets are on **place Beffroi.** (Open W and Sa.)

Tante Jeanne, 1 rue de la Dodane (☎03 22 72 30 30; www.restaurant-tantejeanne.com). Homestyle restaurant with cathedral view. Sweet *crêpes* and gourmet *galettes* €7-16. Open M-F noon-2pm and 7-10pm, Sa-Su noon-10pm. MC/V. ❷

Le Quai, quai Bélu (☎03 22 72 10 80; www.restaurant-le-quai.com). Most popular place along the river. Classy purple restaurant specializes in extravagant seafood. *Plats* €11-24. Dinner *menus* from €16. Open daily noon-2pm and 7-11pm. Reserve ahead for a table next to the Somme. AmEx/MC/V. ❸

Elisa, 4 rue des Chaudronniers (☎03 22 72 62 24). Elisa's motto of "Fast and Good" defines her cafe. Filling vegetarian lasagna €6.50. Linger a while in comfortable purple chairs. *Plats* €6.50. Salads €4-5. Open daily 9am-7pm. ❷

Brussel's Café, 1 pl. d'Aguesseau (☎03 21 91 46 69). Pub-like cafe. Basic menu of sandwiches, *omelettes,* and salads. Surprisingly un-touristed. Terrace faces pl. Jules Bocquet. *Plats* €8-14. Open M-Sa 7:30am-11pm. MC/V. ❷

SIGHTS AND OUTDOOR ACTIVITIES

CATHÉDRALE DE NOTRE-DAME. Though Amiens's signature monument is France's largest Gothic cathedral, it doesn't necessarily feel enormous from inside—until you realize that you've walked roughly the length of an Olympic-size track and still haven't covered it all. The structure features soaring columns and majestic stained-glass windows, but its showcase of religious artwork and funerary monuments makes it feel like an intimate museum. The cathedral was built in the 13th century to house a relic of **John the Baptist's head**, which sits at the rear of the cathedral. Allied troops made the mournful **Weeping Angel** in the ambulatory behind the choir famous during WWI when they mailed home thousands of postcards of it. The **labyrinth** on the floor of the cathedral dates back to 1288; people used to complete the labyrinth on hands and knees as an acceptably holy alternative to the more difficult pilgrimage to Jerusalem. The **towers** provide a birds'-eye view of the city, but the 302-step ascent is difficult; tours are "not recommended for people with fragile constitutions." In the summer and at Christmas, the front portals are lit up at night to display their original color. (☎ 03 22 80 03 41. Open daily Apr.-Oct. 8:30am-6:15pm; Nov.-Mar. 8:30am-5pm. Towers open to the public July-Aug. M and W-Su 2:30-5:15pm; Sept. and Apr.-June Sa-Su 2:30-5:15pm. Tours of the towers July-Aug. M and W-Su 11am; Sept. and Apr.-June M and W-F 3, 4:30pm; Oct.-Mar. M and W-Su 3:45pm. Nightly illuminations June 10:45pm; July 10:30pm; Aug. 10pm; Sept. 9:45pm; Dec.-Jan. 7pm. The tourist office holds tours in French; see Practical Information (p. 347) for details. The office also distributes audio tours at their office next door. €6.50, students €4.50, under 18 free. Tours €3, under 18 free. Audio tours €4, 2 or more €3 each.)

◪MAISON DE JULES VERNE. The author of the acclaimed novel *20,000 Leagues Under the Sea* wrote most of his fantastical works in this extraordinary *maison*. The first floor shows Verne's home as it was in the late 19th century, complete with ghostly audio of old salon parties. Meanwhile, visitors partake in the author's fictional adventures upstairs. A surprising life-size diorama of a ship echoes with the sound of roaring waves in the *voyage nautique* room. Colorful old posters depict drawings of Verne's heroes, and maps scattered throughout the museum trace their expeditions. Look for the large collection of nifty old-fashioned board games inspired by *Around the World in 80 Days*. (2 rue Charles Dubois. ☎ 03 22 45 45 75; www.amiens.com/julesverne. Open M and W-F 10am-12:30pm and 2-6pm. Call ahead to reserve a guide. €5, students €3.50, ages 8-18 €2.50, under 8 free.)

QUARTIER SAINT-LEU. The most attractive area of Amiens lies north of the cathedral, crisscrossed by branches of the Somme. Cobblestone streets border canals in this self-proclaimed "Little Venice of the North." Nearby, *hortillon-ages* (market gardens) spread into the marshland. Walk along the path starting in the Parc St-Pierre, or tour the waterways on a traditional *barque à cornets*, a boat used by gardeners in the early 1900s. Don't miss the creepy statue, *Homme sur Sa Bouée (Man on His Buoy)*, visible from the bridge on rue de la Dodane. (☎ 03 22 92 12 18. 45min. boat tours in French leave from 54 bd. Beauvillé Apr.-Oct.; call for hours. €5.30, ages 11-16 €4.40, ages 3-10 €2.60. MC/V.)

MUSÉE DE PICARDIE. This museum houses a little bit of everything, including a floor of archaeological relics, works from the Roman age up to the 20th century, and a collection of French paintings and sculptures. See eye to eye with many famous faces in the spectacular room of busts. A small display of modern art includes gems by Balthus and Masson; in the *rotonde des empereurs*, marble statues of Apollo, Diana, and Mars loom in a haunting alcove display. (48 rue de la République. ☎ 03 22 97 14 00. Open Tu-Su 10am-12:30pm and 2-6pm. Wheelchair-accessible. Ask for guides in English. €5, students €3, ages 6-18 €2.50; special group rates.)

PARC SAINT-PIERRE. The gardens, picturesque bridges, and ample picnic space promise an enjoyable day. Soccer fields, running trails, and volleyball and basketball courts are a draw for athletes. (Open daily sunrise-sunset.) Popular with bicyclists, joggers, and families, the **Circuit de la Canardière** begins in Parc St-Pierre and continues for a 13.5km circuit along the Somme. To enter the trail, walk across the small Passerelle Samarobriva footbridge from bd. du Cange. Take a right on chemin de Halage, which becomes the well-marked trail. Pick up a free map of the trail at the tourist office.

🎵 🎭 ENTERTAINMENT AND FESTIVALS

The **Théâtre de Marionnettes**, 31 rue Édouard David, off rue Vanmarcke, stages shows in the **Chés Cabotans d'Amiens** theater; swing by the lobby during the day to view various exhibitions of the marionettes for free. Check www.ches-cabotans-damiens.com for schedules and exhibition times. (☎03 22 22 30 90. €10, students €6, under 12 €5. Open Tu-Sa 10am-noon and 2-6pm, Su 2-6pm.)

Fête dans la Ville, 3rd week in June. Concerts and circus performers in the streets.

Les Couleurs de l'Été, from June to Aug. Sand, hammocks, beach chairs, and mini waterfalls fill pl. Jules Bocquet and pl. Gambetta.

Festival du Jazz, in Nov. Distinguished international musicians perform in concert.

Festival International du Film (www.filmfestamiens.org), in Nov. Screens diverse dramas and documentaries. Draws a suitably international crowd.

🎷 NIGHTLIFE

Café Bissap, 50 rue St-Leu (☎03 22 72 51 50). Named for the African hibiscus flower drink, this *rhumerie afrotropical* serves rum from around the world, a selection of South African wine, and mixed drinks with an island flair. Snakeskin, African instruments, and exotic plants compose the decor. Beer from €2.60. Rum from €4. Mixed drinks from €6.50. Open M-W 4pm-1am, Th-F 4pm-3am, Sa 6pm-3am, Su 6pm-1am.

Bar du Midi, 2 rue des Sergents (☎03 22 91 72 64). Cluttered with old concert posters, this noisy bar hosts hip local youths from *midi* on. Beer from €2.20. Mixed drinks €5-5.50. Open M noon-1am, Tu-F 9am-1am, Sa 3pm-1am, Su 4pm-1am. MC/V.

Le Living, 3 rue des Bondes, off pl. du Don. Closet-size bar in a great location. Metallic chairs, smooth beats, and an affable staff. Beer from €2.50. Mixed drinks from €6.50. Open M 7pm-1am, Tu-Sa 7pm-3am. MC/V.

Le Forum, 18 pl. Gambetta (☎03 22 92 44 45). Stylish, neon-lit bar has comfortable leather booths that seat laid-back crowds. A mix of locals and tourists fill director-style chairs on the patio. Beer from €2.70. Open M-Sa 8am-1am. MC/V.

COMPIÈGNE ☎03 44

In the Middle Ages, Compiègne (kohm-pee-ehn; pop. 45,000) was a favorite summer haven among royalty. Louis XV and his lineage flocked to the Château de Compiègne, as did Napoleon I and III. Today, the hamlet is a retreat favored by Parisians, and its royal pedigree is still shamelessly apparent in opulent landmarks and imperial gardens. Compiègne offers the conveniences and entertainment of city life with the quiet atmosphere of a small country town.

🚍 TRANSPORTATION

Trains: Pl. de la Gare, across the river from the *centre-ville*. Info office open M 9am-7:45pm, Tu-F 9am-8pm, Sa 9:50am-7:30pm. Ticket window open M-Sa 4:50am-9:10pm, Su 6:35am-10pm. To **Paris** (45-80min., 22 per day, €13).

Public Transportation: TIC (☎03 44 40 76 00). **Buses** run M-Sa 6am-8pm, some until 10pm. Free schedules and maps at the tourist office.

Taxis: ☎03 44 83 24 24.

Bike Rental: ☎06 07 54 99 26. No storefront; delivers to hotels or tourist office (free). Sets up on Carrefour Royal on weekends during the summer. €17 per day; ID deposit.

🛈 PRACTICAL INFORMATION

Tourist Office: In the Hôtel de Ville (☎03 44 40 01 00; www.compiegne-tourisme.fr). From the station, cross the parking lot, turn right, cross the bridge, and follow rue Solférino to pl. de l'Hôtel de Ville. English-speaking staff provides info on biking trails, as well as a detailed forest map (€9.50). Open Easter-Oct. M-Sa 9:15am-12:15pm and 1:45-6:15pm, Su 10am-12:15pm and 2:15-5pm; Oct.-Easter M 1:45-5:15pm, Tu-Sa 9:15am-12:15pm and 1:45-5pm.

Tours: Tourist office offers themed city tours in French May-Oct. Su 3:30pm. Schedule varies; call ahead for details. €5.

Laundromat: Blanc-Bleu, 15 rue de Paris. Wash €3.50 per 6kg. Open daily 7am-9pm.

Police: 2 pl. de la Croix Blanche (☎03 44 36 37 37), in the Quartier des Capucins. Call for the **pharmacie de garde.**

Hospital: 8 av. Henri Adnot (☎03 44 23 60 00).

Internet Access: L'Evasion, 5 rue St-Martin (☎03 44 40 21 34), near the Hôtel de Ville. €4 per hr., students €3.50. Open Tu-Sa 11am-7pm.

Post Office: 42 rue de Paris (☎03 44 36 31 80). **ATM** available. Open M-F 8:30am-6:30pm, Sa 8:30am-12:30pm. **Postal Code:** 60200.

🛏 ACCOMMODATIONS

Many moderately priced hotels surround the **train station** and **rue Solférino.** Unfortunately, there are no hostels or campgrounds in the city.

Hôtel de Flandre, 16 quai de la République (☎03 44 83 24 06 or 83 24 40; www.hoteldeflandre.com), off pl. de la Gare. Large rooms, some with balconies overlooking the river. TVs receive a few American channels. Breakfast €8. Wi-Fi €2 per 2hr., €7 per 24hr. Wheelchair-accessible. Reception 7am-midnight. Singles €30, with shower or bath €50-55; doubles €35/60-65; triples €61. MC/V. ❷

Armor Hôtel, 4 rue Solférino (☎03 44 36 06 55; www.armorhotel.net). Spacious rooms, each with bath, flatscreen TV, and minibar. Breakfast €7. Free Wi-Fi. Reception M-F 7:15am-12:15pm and 2-9pm, Sa 8:15am-12:15pm and 3-8pm, Su 8:15-11:15am and 7-8pm; code access for later arrivals, inform reception in advance. Check-out noon. Singles €52-54; doubles €59-61. Extra bed €10. MC/V. ❹

🍴 FOOD

Food, like everything else in Compiègne, is concentrated around **place de l'Hôtel de Ville,** toward **rue des Domeliers** and along both sides of the **Oise River,** near the train station. Restaurants also fill the pedestrian district between **rue Solférino** and **place du Marché.** There's a **Monoprix** supermarket at 33 rue Solférino. (☎03 44 40 04 52. Open M-Sa 8:30am-8:30pm, Su 9am-noon. AmEx/MC/V.)

🍽 **Le Bouchon,** 4 rue d'Austerlitz (☎03 44 20 02 03). Indulge in warm comfort food at its best. Most of the meaty meals are served over a large bowl of beans. Large dinner salads €10-13. Regional *plats* €7-15. Open daily noon-2pm and 7-10pm. MC/V. ❸

🍽 **La Friandine,** 22 rue Jean Legendre (☎03 44 40 04 06). Homey diner atmosphere. Stuffed *galettes* and dessert *crêpes* (€3.50-16) pack a serious punch. Meal-size salads €7.80-11. Open Tu-Su noon-2pm and 7-10:30pm. AmEx/MC/V. ❷

Le Palais Gourmand, 8 rue du Dahonmey (☎30 44 40 13 13). Elegant restaurant serves regional dishes like *foie gras de canard* (€13) and outstanding desserts like tiramisu and a trio of *crèmes brûlées. Plats* €15-18. Desserts €6.90-10. *Menus* €24-48. Open Tu-Sa noon-2pm and 7-10pm, Su noon-2pm. MC/V. ❸

SIGHTS AND HIKING

VILLE DE COMPIÈGNE

CHÂTEAU DE COMPIÈGNE. Formerly one of three royal residences for France's kings, this château is the most famous landmark in town. Reconstructed in the 18th century at Louis XV's command, the château became a favorite retreat of Napoleon I and Napoleon III. A tour of the *grands appartements* reveals sumptuous living quarters with lush bedrooms and a library that would make any bookworm drool. Look for the marble table into which an admonished young noble carved the date of his punishment in 1868 and the leopard-carpeted *salle* where Napoleon met his second wife. In addition to the gilded chambers and halls, the complex contains the first Renault automobile in its **Musée de la Voiture,** which showcases floors of chariots, classic cars, bicycles, and motorcycles. *(Pl. du Général de Gaulle. ☎03 44 38 47 02; chateau.compiegne@culture.gouv.fr. Open M and W-Su 10am-6pm. Last entry 5:15pm. The museum and château are often only accessible by thorough French tours; call to ask about seeing the château without the tour. 1hr. tours every 20-30min. Reduced hours for the grands appartements tours Nov.-Feb. Wheelchair-accessible. Both tours €6.50, students and ages 18-25 €4.50, under 18 free; 1st Su of the month free.)*

PARC DU CHÂTEAU. Behind the palace, the Parc du Château includes miles of breathtaking royal gardens designed by Berthault under Napoleon I. With shaded promenades, impeccably tended *jardins,* and open green expanses, the park's natural beauty rivals the opulence of its neighboring château. *(Entrance to the right of the château. Open daily from mid-Apr. to mid-Sept. 8am-6:45pm; from mid-Sept. to Oct. and from Mar. to mid-Apr. 8am-6pm; Nov.-Feb. 8am-5pm.)*

MUSÉE DE LA FIGURINE. This museum displays over 100,000 historic and military figurines, offering a quirky diversion from Compiègne's grandeur. Hand-painted soldiers in full battle array shine with remarkable detail, while 8 in. giants sport tailored cloaks and hats. Look for the spectacular 4m by 4m scale representation of the Battle of Waterloo. *(28 pl. de l'Hôtel de Ville. ☎03 44 40 72 55. Open Mar.-Oct. Tu-Sa 9am-noon and 2-6pm, Su 2-6pm; Nov.-Feb. Tu-Sa 9am-noon and 2-5pm. Wheelchair-accessible. €2, students €1, under 18 free; 1st Su of the month free.)*

ÉGLISE SAINT-JACQUES. History buffs interested in more than miniature recreations, rejoice; this 13th-century church is where Joan of Arc prayed the morning she was captured in 1430. *(Pl. St-Jacques.)*

FORÊT DE COMPIÈGNE

The misty trails of the Forêt de Compiègne provide a maze of peaceful hiking trails and winding bike routes that span different skill levels. Ask at the tourist office for a detailed map of these well-marked paths (€9.50).

CHÂTEAU DE PIERREFONDS. A 12km stroll through the center of the forest ends at the dazzling Château de Pierrefonds. Bought by Napoleon I and marvelously restored by Viollet-le-Duc under Napoleon III, the medieval-style château is breathtaking. You can walk the ramparts, view the gallery, and visit the cavernous knight's hall to get a sense of royal medieval life. *(☎03 44 42 72 72; www.monum.fr. Château open May-Aug. daily 9:30am-6pm; Sept.-Apr. Tu-Su 10am-1pm and 2-5:30pm. Last entry 45min. before close. €6.10, students ages 18-25 €4.10, under 18 free.)*

WAGON DE L'ARMISTICE. An alternate hiking route passes by the Wagon de l'Armistice. The museum recounts the history of the railway car in which the

German army conceded defeat in WWI. The wagon witnessed the French do the same in 1940. (☎03 44 85 14 18. Open daily from Apr. to mid-Oct. 9am-12:30pm and 2-6pm; from mid-Oct. to Mar. 9am-noon and 2-5:30pm. €3, ages 7-14 €1.50, under 7 free.)

🎵 🎭 ENTERTAINMENT AND NIGHTLIFE

Théâtre Impérial, 3 rue Othenin, presents opera, ballet, and drama performances. (☎08 25 00 06 74; www.theatre-imperial.com. Tickets €8-68; major discounts with the €15 *carte jeune*. Office open July-Aug. M-F 8:30am-12:30pm and 2-6pm; Sept.-June M-F 8:30am-12:30pm and 2-6pm, Sa 9am-noon and 2-5pm; also open 1hr. before every show. MC/V.) Bars and pubs liven up the pedestrian district and the streets around **place de l'Hôtel de Ville,** especially near **rue des Lombards.**

Le Must, 17 bis rue des Lombards (☎03 44 86 36 28). ▧**Jean-Baptiste** serves fancy mixed drinks (€5-8) along with fruit and candy at a sleek bar. Beer from €3. Unofficial dress code is trendy. Open M-W and Su 9:30pm-1am, Th-Sa 9:30pm-3am. MC/V.

Le Cachot, 2 rue des Lombards (☎03 44 40 48 66). Neon-glowing dance floor and a cabana-like bar cater to the mobs on weekends. Mixed drinks from €5. Open daily June-Aug. 11pm-3am; Sept.-May 10pm-3am. AmEx/MC/V over €16.

Le St-Clair, 8 rue des Lombards (☎03 44 40 58 18. www.lesaintclair.skyblog.com). Cafe-pub caters to a slightly older crowd. Beer from €2.90. Mixed drinks from €5.80. Karaoke F-Sa 9pm-3am. Open M-Tu and Su 11am-1am, W-Sa 11am-3am. MC/V.

🎆 FESTIVALS

Salon des Oeufs Décorés, Mar. 20-21, 2009. International exhibit of amazingly detailed Easter eggs in the Salle Tainturier, rue de Clamart. €6, under 12 free.

Concours Complet International (☎03 44 40 18 50; www.cci-compiegne.com), in Apr. Among the biggest equestrian competitions in the world. In the Hippodrome, above the Parc du Château. Free for spectators.

Foire aux Vins, mid-May. Wine fair brings free wine *dégustations* and exhibits to pl. St-Jacques. Call tourist office for more information.

CHAMPAGNE

Brothers, brothers, come quickly! I am drinking stars!
  —Dom Pérignon

Associated with both sophisticated celebration and Dionysian revelry, the fizzy pop of a champagne cork always hits a seductive note. While champagne is reserved for special occasions in most of the world, in Champagne itself bubbly flows constantly, dripping with glamor and luxury.

According to European law, the word "champagne" may be applied only to wines made from grapes from this region and produced according to a rigorous, time-honored method. The process involves the blending of three varieties of grapes (Pinot Noir, Pinot Meunier, and Chardonnay), two stages of fermentation, and frequent realignment of the bottles by *remueurs* (highly trained bottle-turners who can turn up to 50,000 bottles per day) to facilitate the removal of sediment. So fiercely guarded is the name that when Yves St-Laurent created a new perfume called "Champagne," the powerful *maisons* sued to force him to change it—and won. Though at first Dom Pérignon, a Benedictine monk, had to convince his compatriots to try his sweet nectar, few modern-day visitors need additional incentive to come to Champagne to see—and taste—the *méthode champénoise*. Travelers visit the region's *caves* (wine cellars), at their best in lavish towns like Reims (this page) and Épernay (p. 361). Even local cuisine tends to center on the drink, as most regional dishes are drenched in champagne-based sauce.

The grape-fed high life may buoy Champagne economically, but the smaller towns surrounding the vineyards also have distinct character. Come to the region for the giddy luxury of its namesake beverage and the boisterous *joie de vivre* of its signature towns, but don't miss out on the historical landmarks: the grand Cathédrale de Notre Dame in Reims (p. 358), traditional site of French coronations since its construction in 1311, and the ornate 18th-century architecture of the self-satisfied champagne *maisons* of Épernay (p. 363).

HIGHLIGHTS OF CHAMPAGNE

MAKE THE MOST of your toast at Épernay's Moët & Chandon (p. 363), producers of the legendary Dom Pérignon.

QUENCH your thirst at the Champagne Pommery (p. 360) in Reims, home of the 75,000L wine cask that was a showstopper at the 1904 World's Fair.

STROLL among the picturesque streets and half-timbered houses of beautifully preserved, cork-shaped Troyes (p. 365).

REIMS ☎ 03 26

Reims (ranss; pop. 191,300) is the largest and best-known city in the Champagne region. It's fitting that Reims, with its reputation for celebration, is where France once transformed its princes into kings. The city has hosted the coronations of 26 French monarchs, and its ornate cathedral still houses a vial of the oil used to anoint Clovis, France's first king, in AD 486. Today, from the underground champagne *caves* to its lively street-side cafe terraces, the city exudes

glamor and style. There are countless attractions at every turn—and plenty of bubbly to go around when the town's amusements have run dry.

TRANSPORTATION

Trains: Bd. Joffre. Ticket office open M-F 6am-8:15pm, Sa 6:45am-8:15pm, Su 8:45am-10:15pm. Info office at pl. Myron T. Herrick. Open M-F 9am-7pm, Sa 10am-6pm. To **Épernay** (30min., 11 per day, €5.10) and **Paris** (1hr., 11 per day, €23).

Buses: Next to the train station. To **Troyes** and **Châlons-en-Champagne.** Schedules at the tourist office.

Public Transportation: Transport Urbains de Reims (TUR) buses stop at the train station. Info office at 6 rue Chanzy (☎03 26 88 25 38; www.tur.fr). Open M-F 7:30am-7:30pm, Sa 10am-7pm. Buses run 6:35am-9:45pm; some until midnight. Buy individual tickets (€1) and day pass (€3) on bus, carnet of 10 (€8.60) from TUR office.

Taxis: ☎03 26 47 05 05. 24hr.

Car Rental: Avis, cour de la Gare (☎03 26 47 10 08). From €120 per day, with 250km. 21+; must have had license for 1 year. Open M-F 8am-12:30pm and 2-7pm, Sa 8am-12:30pm and 2-6pm. AmEx/MC/V. **Europcar,** 76 bd. Lundy (☎03 26 04 52 82). From €65 per day, with 100km. 21+; must have had license for 1 year. Open M-Sa

8am-noon and 2-7pm. AmEx/MC/V. **Hertz,** 26 bd Joffre (☎03 26 47 98 78). From €121 per day, with 250km. 21+; must have had license for 1 year. Open M-F 8am-noon and 2-7pm, Sa 8am-noon and 2-6pm. AmEx/MC/V.

Bike Rental: Centre International de Séjour, chaussée Bocquaine (☎03 26 40 52 60; www.cis-reims.com). €10 per ½-day, €15 per day, €25 per weekend; €80 deposit or photocopy of credit card. MC/V.

ORIENTATION AND PRACTICAL INFORMATION

In Reims, activity centers on **place Royale** and **place du Forum.** The major thoroughfare, **rue de Vesle,** begins at the river, becomes rue Carnot, and runs through pl. Royale, turning into rue Cérès and later av. Jean Jaurès.

Tourist Office: 2 rue Guillaume de Machault (☎03 26 77 45 00; www.reims-tourisme. com), beside the cathedral, near pl. Royale. From the train station, cross bd. Joffre, continue onto rue du Colonel Driant, and bear left onto rue Thiers. Turn right onto cours Jean-Baptiste Langlet and follow it until it becomes rue du Trésor; turn right on rue Guillaume de Machault, and the office will be on your right. Free map, brochures in many languages, and free same-night accommodations service. Ask for the student guide *Le Monocle* (in French). Office open from mid-Apr. to mid-Oct. M-Sa 9am-7pm, Su 10am-6pm; from mid-Oct. to mid-Apr. M-Sa 9am-6pm, Su 11am-6pm.

Tours: Tourist office provides audio tours of the town in 6 languages, including English; €5. Nighttime walking tour of Reims in French July-Aug. F-Sa 9:30pm; from Sept. to mid-Oct. F-Sa 9pm; from mid-Apr. to May Sa 9pm; June Sa 9:30pm. Tour of Basilique St-Rémi in French July-Aug. F 2pm. Tour of cathedral in French July daily 3:30pm; Aug. daily 10:30am, 3:30pm; Easter-June Sa-Su 2:30pm. €6.50, under 12 free.

Budget Travel: Voyage Wasteels, 26 rue Libergier (☎03 26 79 88 03). ISICs (see **Essentials,** p. 11) and cheap flights. Open M-F 9:30am-6:30pm, Sa 10am-6pm.

Youth Centers: Centre Régional Information Jeunesse (CRIJ), 41 rue Talleyrand (☎03 26 79 84 79). English-speaking staff. Message board with fliers advertising seasonal work, including camp-counselor positions and field work during the harvest. Free Internet with a no-email policy (some travelers report that it is loosely enforced). Free Wi-Fi. **CROUS,** 34 bd. Henri Vasnier (☎03 26 50 59 00; www.crous-reims.fr). Provides assistance with housing and work or study opportunities in the area. Open M-F 8:30am-noon and 1:30-5pm, services for foreign students 9-11:30am and 2-4pm.

Laundry: Lavomatique, 49 rue Gambetta. Open daily 7:30am-9pm. €3 per 5.5kg.

Police: 40 bd. Louis Roederer (☎03 26 61 46 26). Call for the **pharmacie de garde.**

Hospital: 47 rue Cognac Jay (☎03 26 78 78 78).

Internet Access: Free at **CRIJ** (above). **Clique & Croque,** 19 rue Chanzy (☎03 26 86 93 92), set back from the street in Passage du Commerce. €4 for 1st hr., €3.60 for 2nd, €3 for 3rd. Open M-Sa 10am-midnight, Su 2-8pm.

Post Office: 2 rue Cérès (☎03 26 77 64 80), pl. Royale. Open M-F 8:30am-6pm, Sa 8:30am-noon. **Currency exchange.** Also at 2 rue Olivier Métra, near Porte Mars (☎03 26 50 58 01; open M-F 8am-7pm, Sa 8am-noon), and at 9 pl. Stalingrad, close to the hostel (☎03 26 86 69 30; open M noon-7pm, Tu-F 10am-7pm, Sa 10am-5pm). Branches have reduced summer hours; **ATMs** at all locations. **Postal Code:** 51100.

ACCOMMODATIONS

Pricier hotels cluster at the top of **place Drouet d'Erlon** toward bd. du Général Leclerc, while somewhat inexpensive options lie in the region above the cathedral, near the Mairie and west of **place Drouet d'Erlon.**

CHAMPAGNE

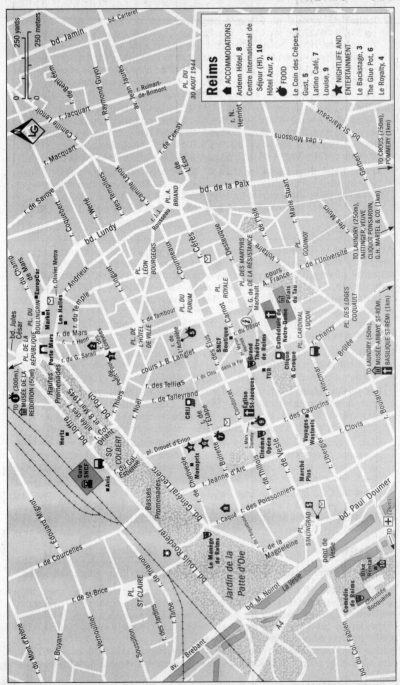

Reims

▲ ACCOMMODATIONS
Ardenn Hôtel, 8
Centre International de Séjour (HI), 10
Hôtel Azur, 2

● FOOD
Le Coin des Crêpes, 1
Gust, 5
Latino Café, 7
Louise, 9

★ NIGHTLIFE AND ENTERTAINMENT
Le Backstage, 3
The Glue Pot, 6
Le Royalty, 4

Centre International de Séjour/Auberge de Jeunesse (HI), chaussée Bocquaine (☎03 26 40 52 60; fax 47 35 70). Park-side setting. Polished rooms. Mix of back-packers and school groups. When returning late at night, take chaussée Bocquaine instead of the path next to the highway, as it can be unsafe. Kitchen. Breakfast included. Laundry. Internet €4.20 per 30min; free Wi-Fi. Wheelchair-accessible. Reception 24hr. Gates closed 10pm-7am. 4- to 5-bed dorms €16, with toilet and shower €19; singles €28/41; doubles €42/56; triples with shower €66. MC/V. ❶

Hôtel Azur, 9 rue des Écrevées (☎03 26 47 43 39; www.hotel-azur-reims.com), near the train station and the Hôtel de Ville. Simple, colorful, and florally scented rooms along a quiet side street. Each room has a recently renovated shower or bath. Breakfast €7. Free Wi-Fi. Reception M and Sa-Su 8:30am-9:30pm, Tu-F 7am-9:30pm. Reserve ahead in summer and fall. Singles €45-52; doubles €60-64; triples €75. MC/V. ❹

Ardenn Hôtel, 8 rue Caqué (☎03 26 47 42 38; www.ardennhotel.fr), near pl. Drouet d'Erlon. Clean, simple rooms with bath and TVs; top-floor rooms have huge skylights. Breakfast €5.50. Reception M-Sa 10am-midnight, Su 10am-noon and 4pm-midnight. Singles €31-41; doubles €47-49; triples and quads €59. Extra bed €8. MC/V. ❷

FOOD

At the heart of Reims, **place Drouet d'Erlon,** you will also find its stomach; *boulangeries* and sandwich shops compete for space with cafes and classier restaurants. Slightly cheaper restaurants can be found on some of the surrounding side streets. Kebab stands line **rue de Vesle,** while *pâtisseries* line **rue Gambetta.** There's a **Monoprix** supermarket at 21 rue Chativesle, in espace d'Erlon (open M-Sa 9am-8pm; MC/V), and a smaller **Marché Plus** at 131 rue de Vesle (open M-Sa 7am-9pm, Su 9am-1pm and 3-7pm; AmEx/MC/V). The main market is on **place du Boulingrin,** near Porte Mars. (Open Sa 6am-1pm.)

Louise, 15 rue Marx (☎03 26 78 00 61). Stylish restaurant with hot-pink trimmings. Delicious *galettes* (€6.90-9) and *crêpes* (€2.30-5.90) piled high with toppings. Ambient dance beats. Salads €6.50-8.80. Open M noon-2pm, Tu-Sa noon-10pm. MC/V. ❷

Le Coin des Crêpes, 123 av. de Laon (☎03 26 83 99 74). Classic street-corner *crêperie* away from the touristy bustle of the *centre-ville.* Extensive selection of regional *galettes* and *crêpes* (€2.50-14) with ingredients like Camembert and *foie gras.* Salads €6-9. Open Tu-Th noon-2pm and 7-10:30pm, F-Sa noon-2pm and 7-11pm. MC/V. ❷

Gust, 7 rue de l'Arbalète (☎03 26 40 23 20). Large modern sandwich shop with customizable salads and an array of pastries. The best—and most stylish—sandwich you'll get in town (served until 6pm). Lunch *menu* (€8) includes salad bar, quiche, and bottled water. Sandwiches and salads €3.80-5.40. Open M-Sa 8am-7pm. MC/V. ❷

Latino Café, 33 pl. Drouet d'Erlon (☎03 26 47 48 89). Brightly decorated restaurant under a hotel pulses with Latin music. The perfect place to grab a snack after hitting the bars. Fajitas and quesadillas €10-16. Large dinner salads €9-12. Open daily 8:30am-3am. Kitchen open until 2:30am. MC/V. ❷

SIGHTS

The most popular sights near the *centre-ville* are all within walking distance.

CATHÉDRALE DE NOTRE DAME. Too lazy to quarry his own stone, the bishop who commissioned this colossal Gothic creation deconstructed the protective walls surrounding the city for building materials; fearing attack, the people appealed to the king, who famously declared, "God will be the guard." The cathedral has since witnessed the crowning of 26 French kings, beginning with Clovis in AD 498. The current church's facade, begun in 1211, boasts 2307 statues of angels, prophets, and saints. More recently, the building witnessed the

CHAMPAGNE

reconciliation between President de Gaulle and German Chancellor Adenauer in 1962. While WWI bombing destroyed most of the original stained glass, the newest windows include spectacular sea-blue tableaux by Marc Chagall. Low-hanging chandeliers make the enormous church seem more intimate. (*☎03 26 47 55 34. Open daily 7:30am-7:30pm. The tourist office gives tours (p. 356) in French and offers audio tours in English and other languages. Tours €5.50, under 12 free. Audio tours €5.)*

MUSÉE DE LA REDDITION. Germany signed its surrender to the Allies on May 7, 1945, in a schoolroom across the railroad tracks from the *centre-ville*—now the small but fascinating Musée de la Reddition. A short film (in English, French, or German) with actual footage of the surrender, along with several galleries of photos and timelines, introduces the preserved room plastered with maps where the American, British, French, and German heads of state sat. The Soviets were out of town, which is why another more famous (but, as the *musée* would say, less important) surrender was signed on Stalin's soil several days later. Nothing here is sleek or showy, but, as a historical time capsule, the place itself is powerful. (*12 rue Franklin Roosevelt, north of the train station. ☎03 26 47 84 19. Wheelchair-accessible. Open M and W-Su 10am-noon and 2-6pm, Tu 2-6pm. €3, students and under 15 free, ages 15-18 €1.50. €3 pass includes admission to 4 other museums in Reims.)*

PALAIS DU TAU. Next to the cathedral, this former archbishop's residence turned museum got its name from its original floor plan, which resembled a "T." With relics from old coronation ceremonies, the palace's exquisite collection offers an immersion into Reims's regal history. Don't miss the showstoppers: Charles X's sumptuous 50 ft. robes and the creepy gargoyles rescued from crumbling portions of the old cathedral's facade. The **Salle de Tau,** adorned in majestic tapestries, was where France's newly crowned kings celebrated their ascension to the throne with lavish feasting and partying. (*2 pl. du Cardinal Luçon. ☎03 26 47 81 79. Open Tu-Su May-Aug. 9:30am-6:30pm; Sept.-Apr. 9:30am-12:30pm and 2-5:30pm. Call for information about guided tours. €6.50, ages 18-25 €4.50, under 18 free.)*

OTHER SIGHTS. Near the Taittinger *caves,* the **Basilique Saint-Rémi** rises above a lavender garden. This Romanesque church was built around the tomb of St-Rémi, the bishop who baptized Clovis, France's first king. Almost entirely destroyed during WWI, it has since returned to its former glory. Its location near the champagne *maisons* makes it a convenient place to picnic in between tours. (*Pl. St-Rémi. Open daily in summer 8am-9pm; in winter 8am-5pm. Son et lumière July-Sept. Sa 9:30pm.)* Around the corner, the small **Musée-Abbaye Saint-Rémi** houses an extensive collection of religious art, military uniforms, and artifacts from the Merovingian and Carolingian eras. Look for a mournful statue of Mercury's head, salvaged from a public edifice in AD 3. (*53 rue Simon. ☎03 26 85 23 36. Open M-F 2-6:30pm, Sa-Su 2-7pm. €3; 1st Su of the month free.)* Rising over pl. de la République on the other side of town, the **Porte Mars** is Reims's largest Roman arch, badly damaged by WWI fighting. The ancient monument is decorated with reliefs of Romulus and Remus, who gave the city his name.

CHAMPAGNE CAVES

Excluding a trip to Épernay (p. 361), this is the best opportunity you'll have to swim in bubbly decadence. Four hundred kilometers of *crayères* (Roman chalk quarries) and 200km of more modern French-built *caves* shelter the bottled treasure. All the champagne *caves* are at least a 25min. walk from downtown. Some tours (all available in English) require reservations at least one day ahead. While Pommery and Ponsardin ostensibly require reservations, solo visitors often have little trouble joining a tour; larger groups would be wise to follow the rules. The cellars are kept at 10°C; bring a sweater.

THE LOCAL STORY

CHAMPAGNE DREAMS

In the champagne-soaked city of Reims, Let's Go picked up some insider information from Géraldine Théron, a champagne connoisseur of the Taittinger maison.

LG: What makes champagne distinctly different from other categories of sparkling wine?

A: The weather here in Champagne is quite cold and humid, with a very short summer. That climate affects how the grapes grow, which in turn gives a particular taste to the champagne. The soil that the grapes grow in is also particular; it's chalky, very soft, and very porous, which gives a mineral taste to the champagne. The method used to make champagne can be used everywhere—but champagne is only champagne if it comes from this region.

LG: How does one become a champagne taster or blender?

A: Champagne tasters and blenders have to do specialized studies and become experts when it comes to wine. I think they have a special talent in their palate and in their nose. It's something you have when you are born—just like people who can sing. It's a gift.

LG: What makes Taittinger champagne unique from other labels?

A: It has a unique style in the taste; it is light and very elegant. Taittinger is a big name with a famous reputation, but it's still a family business.

CHAMPAGNE POMMERY. The most impressive tour is at Champagne Pommery. Mme. Pommery took over her husband's business in 1858 and became one of France's foremost vintners. Carvings by Gustave Navlet line the *caves*, and Pommery hosts a different contemporary art exhibit each year. The art is interspersed throughout the tour, which creates a fun, unique *musée-et-maison* blend. The firm also owns one of the world's largest *tonneaux* (vats), carved by Émile Gallé; it was sent to the 1904 World's Fair in St-Louis as a 75,000L gesture of goodwill. Some of the art works and the vat are on display in the lobby for those who choose not to spring for a tour. *(5 pl. du Général Gouraud. ☎03 26 61 62 56; www.pommery.com. Open daily from Apr. to mid-Nov. 10am-7pm; from mid-Nov. to Mar. 10am-6pm. Last tour 1hr. before close. Tours in English, French, and German. Reservations recommended. €10-17, under 12 free; includes tour and various dégustations. AmEx/MC/V.)*

TAITTINGER. Perfect for anyone unfamiliar with champagne production, this tour provides an informative overview with the process. On certain days, visitors may witness the *dégorgement* process by which sediment is removed from aged bottles. The maison's distinctive *caves* snake along the underground remains of the destroyed Abbaye St-Nicaise. See the **world's largest champagne bottle and crystal champagne glass** and peruse a display of Taittinger bottles designed by modern artists. *(9 pl. St-Nicaise. ☎03 26 85 84 33. Open from mid-Mar. to mid-Nov. daily 9:30am-1pm and 2-5:30pm; from mid-Nov. to mid-Mar. M-F 9:30am-1pm and 2-5:30pm. Last tour 1hr. before close €10, students and ages 12-17 €8, under 12 free; includes short movie, tour, and dégustation. AmEx/MC/V.)*

VEUVE CLICQUOT PONSARDIN. A chic, comprehensive tour passes through the innovative Mme. Clicquot's ornate *salon* before delving into cellars carved from ancient chalk mines, which contain some of her original barrels. The visit finishes with a *dégustation* in a stylish modern lounge. *(1 pl. des Droits de l'Homme. ☎03 26 89 53 90; www.veuve-clicquot.com. Open Apr.-Oct. M-Sa 10am-6pm; Nov.-Mar. M-F 10am-6pm. 1hr. tours in English and French by reservation only; Dutch, German, Italian, and Spanish may also be available. €7.50, under 16 free; includes tour and dégustation. MC/V.)*

G.H. MARTEL & CO. A smaller champagne *maison*, this company offers intimate tours and *dégustations* in small groups. *(17 rue des Créneaux, across the street from the Basilique St-Rémi. ☎03 26 82 70 67; www.champagnemartel.com. Open daily 10am-7pm. Last tour at 5:30pm. 1hr. tours in English, French, and German. Reserve ahead. €8; includes tour and 3 dégustations. MC/V.)*

BUBBLY FOR THE ROAD. If you're out to purchase a souvenir bottle of champagne, don't assume that a famous brand is cheapest in its *maison*'s boutique. Compare prices at local wine stores and supermarkets—you'll often discover the bottles featured in your *dégustation* for fewer euro. If you're traveling by car, look for the small, independent *maisons* outside major towns. If the white, gold, and blue flag of the Champagne region is flying, the *maison* is open to visitors—and they'll usually offer you a free *dégustation*. Since these producers typically sell only to clients directly, they offer the best deals.

♫ 🎆 ENTERTAINMENT AND FESTIVALS

During the summer, Reims hosts the celebrated **Flâneries Musicales d'Été,** with over 80 concerts in six weeks. Esteemed classical musicians share the bill with smaller jazz groups and guitar soloists. (☎03 26 77 45 12; www.flaneriesreims. com. From late June to early Aug. Contact the tourist office for more info. Many performances free; some concerts €10-12, students and under 18 €8-10.)

Comédie de Reims, 3 chaussée Bocquaine (☎03 26 48 49 00; www.lacomediedereims.fr). Follow the sidewalk covered with names of famous playwrights to this regional acting school and theater. Stages regular performances and workshops. Tickets €10-13, students €5-7. Open Sept.-June M-F noon-7pm, Sa 1-7pm.

Cinéma Opéra, 3 rue Théodore Dubois (☎08 92 68 01 22). International films in their original languages. Tickets €7.40-7.60, under 16 €5.40; students M-F €6. Ticket office open daily 1:30-10pm.

Grand Théâtre de Reims, 13 rue Chanzy (☎03 26 50 03 92; www.grandtheatredereims. com). Operas and ballets. Open Oct.-June Tu-Sa 2:30-6:30pm.

Le Manège de Reims, 2 bd. du Général Leclerc (☎03 26 47 30 40; www.manegedereims.com). Dance shows, performance art, and music. *Les dimanches des curiosités* (special themed performances) on Su. Tickets €5.50-20.

🍸 NIGHTLIFE

At night, people fill the cafes and bars on **place Drouet d'Erlon** and **rue de Vesle.** Touristy crowds on **place Drouet d'Erlon** are lively and stay out late.

Le Royalty, 67 pl. d'Erlon. Hip bar with an enormous drink menu. Terrace covered with large orange and white couches. Popular French music adds to the chill atmosphere. Beer from €3. Mixed drinks €6-8. Smoothies €6. Open daily 10am-3am. MC/V.

The Glue Pot, 49 pl. d'Erlon (☎03 26 47 36 46). Popular English-style pub with food at all hours and comfy leather chairs on its outdoor terrace. Beer from €2.80. 10% price increase after 10pm. Open daily noon-3am. MC/V.

Le Backstage, 13 rue de Sarrail. Small *brasserie* away from the town's main drag. Decorated with jazzy posters. Beer from €2.30. Mixed drinks from €4. Open M-Th 7:30am-12:30am, F 7:30am-1:30am, Su 10am-1:30am. MC/V.

ÉPERNAY ☎03 26

Every town has its main street, but few could trump Épernay's av. de Champagne. An endless cascade of opulent mansions, the avenue holds the world's most celebrated champagne maisons, making Épernay (ay-pare-nay; pop. 26,000) the region's showcase. Firms Moët & Chandon, Perrier-Jouet, and Mercier collectively store 700 million bottles of the sparkling spirit in 100km of tunnels beneath the town. At the heart of the Route Touristique du Champagne, Épernay also serves as an excellent base for exploring the surrounding vineyards and châteaux, which offer gorgeous natural diversions once the bubbly buzz has worn off. However, such luxury comes at a price: Épernay caters to scads of wealthy tourists willing to spend and thus offers few budget values for the thrifty traveler—although it's worth a day of splurging.

TRANSPORTATION

Trains: Cour de la Gare, 2 blocks from pl. de la République. Ticket office open M-Th 6:10am-1:30pm, F 6:10am-7:55pm, Sa 7:40am-2:50pm, Su 12:10-7:25pm. To **Paris** (1hr., 18 per day, €25), **Reims** (30min., 16 per day, €5.60), and **Strasbourg** (3hr., 3 per day, €40).

Buses: STDM (☎03 26 65 17 07). Serves **Paris, Reims,** and small towns in Champagne. Ask at the tourist office for a schedule and map.

Public Transportation: Sparnabus, rue E. Duchâtel (☎03 26 55 55 50), at the *gare routière.* Open M 2-6pm, Tu-F 9am-noon and 2-6pm, Sa 9am-noon. Tickets €1.20.

ORIENTATION AND PRACTICAL INFORMATION

There are two streets called **rue Gambetta**—one near the tourist office and one across the water. Be sure not to confuse them.

Tourist Office: 7 av. de Champagne (☎03 26 53 33 00; www.ot-epernay.fr). From the station, walk straight through pl. Mendès France onto rue Gambetta or rue Jean Chandon-Moët. Walk 1 block to pl. de la République and turn left on av. de Champagne (5min.). English-speaking staff provides free maps, a guide to local festivals, info on *caves,* and suggestions for *routes champénoises* (see **Maisons de Champagne,** opposite page). Open from Easter to mid-Oct. M-Sa 9:30am-12:30pm and 1:30-7pm, Su 11am-4pm; from mid-Oct. to Easter M-Sa 9:30am-12:30pm and 1:30-5:30pm.

Laundromat: 8 av. Jean Jaurès. Wash €5, dry €1. Open daily 7am-8pm.

Police: 7 rue Jean Chandon-Moët (☎03 26 56 96 60). Call for **pharmacie de garde.**

Hospital: 137 rue de l'Hôpital (☎03 26 58 70 70).

Internet Access: Cyberm@nia, 11 pl. des Arcades. €3 per 1hr., €5 per 3hr. Open M-Sa 2-11pm, Su 2-8pm. MC/V.

Post Office: Pl. Hugues Plomb (☎03 26 53 31 65). **ATM** and **currency exchange** available. Open M-F 8:30am-6:30pm, Sa 8:30am-noon. **Postal Code:** 51200.

ACCOMMODATIONS AND CAMPING

Hôtel St-Pierre, 1 rue Jeanne d'Arc (☎03 26 54 40 80; www.villasaintpierre.fr), past pl. d'Europe. From the station, follow the directions for the tourist office. When you reach pl. de la République, take rue du Général Leclerc to rue St-Thibault. Turn left and continue straight as it becomes av. Paul Chandon; the hotel is on the left, at the corner of rue Jeanne d'Arc (10min.). 3 floors of spacious, antique-furnished rooms. Breakfast €6. Reception 7am-10pm. Check-out 11am. Reservations recommended. Singles and doubles €21-24, with shower €30-36. AmEx/MC/V. ❶

Hôtel de la Cloche, 3-5 pl. Mendès France (☎03 26 55 15 15; hotel-de-la-cloche.c.prin@ wanadoo.fr). Colorful, comfortable rooms with TVs. Oh-so-surprising champagne decor. Breakfast buffet €7.50. Reception 9am-10pm. Check-out noon. Singles and doubles with shower or bath €48-58; triples €54-58. AmEx/MC/V. ❸

Camping Municipal Épernay, allée de Cumières (☎03 26 55 32 14; camping.epernay@ free.fr), near the station. By the Marne. Sites divided by tall hedges. Volleyball, tennis, and ping-pong. Laundry. Wheelchair-accessible. Reception June-Aug. 7am-10pm; Sept.

and Apr.-May 8am-8pm. Open from mid-Apr. to Sept. €3.50 per person, children €1.80; €2.80 per tent, €2 per car. Electricity €3. AmEx/MC/V over €15. ❶

🍴 FOOD

The streets around **place des Arcades** and **place Hugues Plomb** are dotted with *charcuteries* and *boulangeries*. There's a horde of pizza and kebab eateries on **rue Gambetta** and a **Marché Plus** supermarket at 17 pl. Hugues Plomb, near the post office. (☎03 26 51 89 89. Open M-Sa 7am-9pm, Su 9am-1pm.) **Halle Saint-Thibault,** near pl. de l'Europe, hosts a market. (Open W-Sa 8am-noon.)

La Cave à Champagne, 16 rue Gambetta (☎03 26 55 50 70. www.la-cave-a-champagne.com). Incorporates the adored local product into nearly all its dishes, from *foie gras à la champagne* to salmon in champagne butter. *Menus* €17-44. Open M-Tu and Th-Sa noon-2pm and 7-10pm, W 7-10pm. Reservations recommended. MC/V. ❸

L'Kenavo, 20 rue Jean Moulin (☎03 26 51 00 25). Best and quirkiest *crêperie* around. Stuffed badgers and foxes look on in an Alsatian interior. Range of regional specialties and fairly pricey *galettes* (€9.50-14), but the dessert *crêpes* are nearly meals themselves. *Crêpes* €4.20-8.70. Open Tu-Su noon-1:30pm and 7:30-9pm. MC/V. ❸

Les Palmerales, 19 rue de Reims (☎03 26 32 54 42). Cozy Moroccan restaurant. Flavorful meats and vegetables atop heaps of couscous (€10-19). Gigantic portions are easily serve 2. Open daily noon-2:30pm and 7-10:30pm. MC/V. ❸

⚡ MAISONS DE CHAMPAGNE

The name says it all: ▦**avenue de Champagne** is a long strip of palatial *maisons de champagne* pouring bubbly for hordes of visitors. The tours below are all offered in English or French; no reservations are required for most of the *maisons,* though without reservations you may have to wait up to an hour for the next tour. All include a *petite dégustation* (16+, at Moët & Chandon 18+) and offer more extensive (and expensive) tastings as well. Without springing for a tour, the only thing visitors get to see at the maisons are liquor-lined boutiques and lush lobbies. *Caves* are maintained between 10 and 12°C; bring a sweater. Each firm's tour may give more or less the same explanation of the champagne-making process, but everything, from the dress of the guides to the design of the lobby, reflects the status and character of the producer. For a cheap alternative to the big *maisons,* ask the tourist office about *l'esprit de champagne,* a free presentation and sampling given in the tourist office by several small companies. *(Presentations offered July-Aug. Th-Sa 10:45am-noon and 3-6pm; from Sept. to mid-Oct. and June F-Sa 10:45am-noon and 3-6pm.)*

▦**MOËT & CHANDON.** The granddaddy of them all, Moët & Chandon—the producer of legendary champagne Dom Pérignon—has been "turning nature into art" since 1743. The tour and tasting are worth every euro—and with a slogan like "Be fabulous," what else would you expect? The mansion is filled with the old-money opulence one would expect, from the elegant carvings that line the inside of ancient *caves* to the stately mansion rooms decorated for Napoleon I, a close friend of the Moët & Chandon family. The 1hr. tour details the process of champagne production and gives the history of champagne, highlighting M&C's superior standards at every turn. The polished *caves* are the most beautiful in town, filled with statues and an ornate cask given as a gift by Napoleon I. The 5min. film is a thoroughly amusing bit of highbrow self-promotion. *(20 av. de Champagne. ☎03 26 51 20 20; www.moet.com. Open from Apr. to mid-Nov. daily 9:30-11:30am and 2-4:30pm; from mid-Nov. to Mar. M-F 9:30-11:30am and 2-4:30pm. Tours €13-25, ages 10-18 €8, under 10 free. Reservations required. AmEx/MC/V.)*

MERCIER. If Willy Wonka were to design a champagne *maison*, it would be the Mercier *maison;* in fact, the eccentric founder, Eugène Mercier, is very similar to Roald Dahl's favorite chocolate maker. Always an innovator, Mercier once offered *dégustations* in hot-air balloons and was the first to feature electricity in his *caves*. Less famous than nearby Moët—but equally classy—Mercier is the self-proclaimed maker of the "most popular champagne in France." An advertising scheme that entailed sending a blimp-size cask of champagne to the 1889 World's Fair exposition in Paris brought Mercier from rags to riches. The extravagant wood vat, which took second place only to the Eiffel Tower, now sits in the maison's foyer. The *maison* offers a 30min. tour that begins with a ride in a musical glass elevator past bubbly-sipping mannequins. Visitors then embark on a roller-coaster-style ride through its *caves*. *(70 av. de Champagne. ☎03 26 51 22 22; www.champagne-mercier. fr. Open from mid-Mar. to mid-Nov. daily 9:30-11:30am and 2-4:30pm; from mid-Nov. to mid-Dec. and from mid-Feb. to mid-Mar. M and Th-Su 9:30-11:30am and 2-4:30pm. Wheelchair-accessible. €8-15, ages 12-16 €3.50, under 12 free. MC/V.)*

DE CASTELLANE. Across the street from Mercier, de Castellane offers a less romantic tour than those of M&C and Mercier but gets into the nitty-gritty of champagne production. Whereas M&C and Mercier only allude to modern advancements in wine making, this tour walks visitors through the whole mechanical process. Visitors during the week can observe factory workers unloading, corking, and labeling. Lucky groups may get to witness the *dégorgement* (sediment-removal process) that takes place sporadically throughout each month. A ticket also buys admission to a rather dry museum of mannequins enacting the production process, a random yet thorough exhibit on label-making, and access to a 237-step tower with sweeping views of the region. All are good ways to kill time while waiting for the next tour, though they're not worth going out of your way to visit. *(57 rue de Verdun. ☎03 26 51 19 11. Open from Apr. to late Dec. daily 10am-noon and 2-6pm; Mar. Sa-Su 10am-noon and 2-6pm. Last morning tour 11:15am; last evening tour 5:15pm. Tours in Danish, English, French, German, Danish, and Spanish. €8, extra dégustations €6-8 per glass. AmEx/MC/V.)*

🎷 NIGHTLIFE

The quality of Épernay's nightlife ebbs and flows with the energy (and level of intoxication) of its generally older tourists; don't bank on a lively night out. However, Épernay is one of the few places where you can sip champagne in style at 9:30am without attracting stares. Try **place de la République, place Mendès France,** or **place Hugues Plomb** for youth-filled bars and pubs.

Le Central, 15 pl. de la République (☎03 26 59 19 93). Big eatery downstairs and upstairs bar with comfortable chairs. Beer from €2.50. Mixed drinks from €6.50. Bar open Tu and Th-Su 8pm-1am. Kitchen open M-Tu and Th-Su noon-midnight. MC/V.

Club St-Jean, 12 rue Pierre Semard (☎03 26 55 26 42), across from the train station. Small *discothèque* with a DJ who spins French and international hits. Students and tourists come and go; most of the regulars are 30+. Beer from €4. Mixed drinks from €6. Open M-Th 10:30pm-4am, F-Sa 10:30pm-5am. MC/V.

The Garden Club, 5 av. Foch (☎03 26 54 20 30). Plays a techno-free soundtrack featuring music from the 70s to the present. Attracts a slightly older crowd. Stylish terrace with a pool in the back. Beer from €3.50 until 9pm; from €5.50 9pm-4am. Mixed drinks €5.50/8. Open M-Sa 5pm-4am, Su 7pm-4am. MC/V.

TROYES
☎ **03 25**

Troyes (trwah; pop. 60,900) is a stylish city that prides itself on living the good life. Delicious cuisine combined with massive amounts of bubbly make this city a gastronomic delight, while noteworthy museums entertain between meals. Despite its superficial sheen, the city boasts an extensive intellectual history: it was here that Chrétien de Troyes wrote *Parsifal*, Jewish scholar Rashi translated the Bible and the Talmud, and a local shoemaker's son grew up to become Pope Urban IV. Today, Troyes benefits from a well-preserved *vieille ville* and a lively urban atmosphere—all contained within a city appropriately shaped like a *bouchon de champagne* (champagne cork).

▐ TRANSPORTATION

Trains: At the intersection of av. Maréchal Joffre and rue du Ravelin (☎08 36 35 35 35). Ticket office open M-Sa 5:40am-8:40pm, Su 6:30am-8:40pm. Info office open M-Sa 9:30am-6:20pm. To **Mulhouse** (3-3½hr.; M-F 8 per day, Sa-Su 7 per day; €38), **Lyon** (4-5hr.; M-F 12 per day, Sa-Su 9 per day; €44, TGV via Paris €73-90), and TGV to **Paris** (1hr.; M-F 16 per day, Sa-Su 13 per day; €22).

Buses: Turn left out of the train station and enter through the door to your left in the next building, which is labeled *"gare routière."* SDTM TransChampagne (☎03 25 71 28 42) runs to **Reims** (2hr., M-Sa 2 per day, €22).

Public Transportation: TCAT buses (☎03 25 70 49 00; www.tcat.fr), in front of Les Halles market. Open M-F 8am-12:45pm and 1:30-7pm, Sa 8am-12:45pm and 1:30-6:30pm. Service every 12-23min. Purchase tickets on bus (€1.30, 3 for €3.30); Mini Turbo tickets available at the office or in *tabacs* (12 for €11).

Taxis: Taxis Troyens (☎03 25 78 30 30), across from the bus and train stations, in front of the Grand Hôtel. Open M-Th and Su 4am-1am, F-Sa 24hr.

Car Rental: Budget, 10 rue Voltaire (☎03 25 73 27 37). €52 per day with 250km included; €650 or credit-card deposit. 21+. Open M-F 8am-noon and 2-7pm, Sa 8:30am-noon and 2-6:30pm. AmEx/MC/V.

Bike Rental: Available at **Les Comtes de Champagne** (see **Accommodations,** p. 367). €8 per ½-day, €12 per day, €20 per 2 days, €60 per week; €250 or credit-card deposit. Book 1 day in advance. Discount for hotel guests. AmEx/MC/V.

◢◣ ☑ ORIENTATION AND PRACTICAL INFORMATION

The train station is just three blocks from the edge of the *vieille ville*. The main tourist office is to the right of the train station's exit, on the corner of bd. Carnot; a branch office is on rue Mignard, facing the St-Jean church.

Tourist Office: 16 bd. Carnot (☎03 25 82 62 70; www.ot-troyes.fr) and on rue Mignard (☎03 25 73 36 88). Free city maps, English brochures (€0.50), and free accommodations service with 1st night's deposit (MC/V). Bd. Carnot branch open Apr.-Oct. M-Sa 9am-12:30pm and 2-6:30pm; Nov.-Mar. M-Sa 9am-12:30pm, Su 10am-1pm. Rue Mignard branch open daily from July to mid-Sept. 10am-7pm; from mid-Sept. to Oct. and Apr.-June M-Sa 9am-12:30pm and 2-6:30pm, Su 10am-noon and 2-5pm.

Tours: Available from the tourist office. Audio tours €5.50, students and seniors €3. Themed tours from the Mignard tourist office; check weekly listing. From July to mid-Sept. English and French; from mid-Sept. to June French only. €5.50, students €3. Horse-drawn carriage tour every 45min. July-Aug. Sa 10:15-11:45am and 3-6:45pm; €7, students and seniors €5. The **Pass'Troyes** (€12) includes champagne and chocolate tastings, an audio or personal tour, and admission to major sights.

CHAMPAGNE

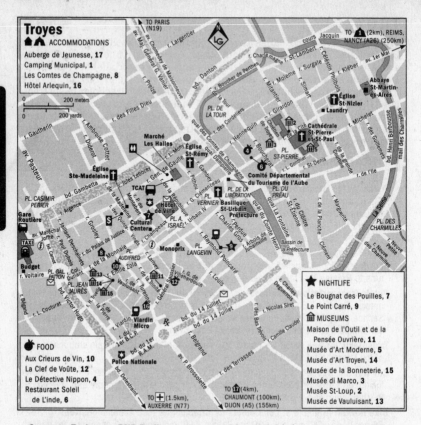

Troyes

ACCOMMODATIONS
Auberge de Jeunesse, **17**
Camping Municipal, **1**
Les Comtes de Champagne, **8**
Hôtel Arlequin, **16**

NIGHTLIFE
Le Bougnat des Pouilles, **7**
Le Point Carré, **9**
MUSEUMS
Maison de l'Outil et de la
Pensée Ouvrière, **11**
Musée d'Art Moderne, **5**
Musée d'Art Troyen, **14**
Musée de la Bonneterie, **15**
Musée di Marco, **3**
Musée St-Loup, **2**
Musée de Vauluisant, **13**

FOOD
Aux Crieurs de Vin, **10**
La Clef de Voûte, **12**
Le Détective Nippon, **4**
Restaurant Soleil
de L'inde, **6**

Currency Exchange: BNP Paribas branches at 53 rue du Général de Gaulle and 58 rue Émile Zola. Open M-F 8:45am-noon and 1:30-5:30pm, Sa 8:45am-noon. **SNVB** banks at 5-7 rue Raymond Poincaré and 39 rue Paul Dubois. Open M-F 8:30am-noon and 1:15-5:55pm, Sa 9am-12:15pm. **ATMs** can be found in the *centre-ville*, particularly around the tourist office and pl. Alexandre Israël.

Laundromat: Laverie St-Nizier, 107 rue du Révérend Père Lafra (☎06 14 66 11 29), near the cathedral. Wash €3.50 per 7kg, dry €0.50 per 6min. Open daily 24hr.

Police: Near the Hôtel de Ville (☎03 25 42 34 21).

Pharmacy: Pharmacie de garde posted in window of rue Mignard tourist office.

Hospital: 101 av. Anatole France (☎03 25 49 49 49).

Internet Access: Le Point Carré, 27 rue Raymond Poincaré (☎03 25 81 63 44). Look for the sign that reads "Cyber Café." €0.10 per min., €2 per hr. Free Wi-Fi with purchase of a drink. Ask about the 10% student discount. Open M-W 10:30am-midnight, Th-Sa 10:30am-1:30am, Su 2pm-midnight. **Viardin Micro,** 10 rue Viardin. €2 per hr. Open M 2-7pm, Tu-Sa 9:30am-noon and 2-7pm. MC/V.

Post Office: 38 rue Louis Ulbach (☎03 25 43 77 77). Open M-F 8am-7pm, Sa 9am-12:30pm. **Currency exchange.** Branch office at 2 pl. du Général Patton (☎03

25 45 29 00), 1 block to the right down bd. Carnot from the train station. Open M-F 9am-noon and 2:30-6pm, Sa 9am-noon. **Postal Code:** 10000.

🏨 🏕 ACCOMMODATIONS AND CAMPING

🏨 **Les Comtes de Champagne,** 56 rue de la Monnaie (☎03 25 73 11 70; www.comtesde-champagne.com). This 16th-century mansion has a courtyard and themed rooms decorated with stylish old magazine ads. All but the least expensive rooms have TVs, toilets, and phones. Breakfast €6.50. Wi-Fi in the lobby. Reception 7am-10pm. Reservations recommended. Singles €27-32; doubles from €33; triples from €61; quads from €67; rooms with kitchenette €66-87. Some rooms fit 5-6; extra bed €6. AmEx/MC/V. ❸

🏨 **Hôtel Arlequin,** 50 rue de Turenne (☎03 25 83 12 70; www.hotelarlequin.com). Welcoming home away from home with color-coordinated rooms, A/C, large windows, and high ceilings. Suites with double rooms attached available for families. Unbeatable suites for 3+ guests. Breakfast €7.50-8.50. Wi-Fi. Reception M-Sa 8am-12:30pm and 2-10pm, Su 8am-12:30pm and 6:30-10pm. Reservations recommended 1 week in advance, especially in summer. Singles and doubles with shower €41, with bath €55-58; triples with shower or bath €72; quads €82. Extra bed €5.50. AmEx/MC/V. ❸

Camping Municipal de Troyes, 7 rue Salengro (☎03 25 81 02 64; www.troyescamping. net), on N77, 2km from town. Take bus #1 (dir.: Pont Ste-Marie) to this well-stocked 3-star site. Includes showers, toilets, TV, restaurant, and laundry as well as a trampoline and playground. Reception 9am-10pm. Open from Apr. to mid-Oct. €4.40 per adult, children €3.20; €6-7 per tent; €6-7 per car. MC/V. ❶

Auberge de Jeunesse (HI), 10430 chemin Ste-Scholastique (☎03 25 82 00 65; www. fuaj.org/aj/troyes). Take local bus #8 from Les Halles (dir.: Château de Rosièrest) to Liberté. Following the signs, continue down rue de la Liberté. Take a left on rue Jules Ferry and a right on chemin Ste-Scholastique. This spacious converted abbey, open year-round and clean as a whistle, holds 104 beds. The catch is that it's 5km from the center of town, and buses can be confusing and inconsistent. Bus #8 only runs to the necessary Liberté stop at certain times of the day, so be sure to ask your bus driver before hopping on board, or you could end up hiking a long distance. Breakfast €3.50. Reception 8am-9pm. 5- and 6-bed dorms with shower €14. MC/V. ❶

🍴 FOOD

The area from **rue Champeaux** south to **rue Émile Zola,** known as the **quartier Saint-Jean,** is the best place to enjoy a scenic and savory meal. Cafes, restaurants, *brasseries,* and *crêperies* line these pedestrian streets just west of pl. Alexandre Israël, which also is the center of *troyenne* nightlife. A walk down **rue du Général Saussier** or **rue de Turenne** leads to the smaller **quartier Vauluisant,** which boasts its own pedestrian avenue with delightful dining options. Inexpensive kebab joints line the less attractive **rue du Général de Gaulle** and **rue de la Cité.**

Les Halles, an indoor market on the corner of rue de la République and rue du Général de Gaulle, offers fresh produce, meats, and baked goods from the Aube region; its outdoor flea market offers decently priced clothing. Try the intense *andouillette de Troyes* (tripe sausage) or the rich and creamy *fromage de Troyes.* (Open M-Th 8am-12:45pm and 3:30-7pm, F-Sa 7am-7pm, Su 9am-12:30pm. Many stands accept MC/V.) Grab groceries at the **Monoprix** supermarket, upstairs at 71 rue Émile Zola (☎03 25 73 10 78; open M-Sa 8:30am-8pm) and picnic in pl. de la Libération, along the bassin de la Préfecture.

Aux Crieurs de Vin, 4-6 pl. Jean Jaurès (☎03 25 40 01 01). As the name suggests, this eatery revolves around Troyes's favorite spirit, from the winery and tasting bar up front to the cellar-like dining area decorated with drinking advertisements. Waiters bring a chalkboard menu featuring a small selection of meats and cheeses (€5-10), *plats* (€9-13), and *entrées* (€5.50-18). Meal with a glass of wine €13. 2 champagne samples free with purchase of the **Pass'Troyes** at the tourist office. Open Tu-Sa noon-2pm and 7:30-10pm. Bar open Tu-Sa 11am-midnight. MC/V. ❷

La Clef de Voûte, 33-35 rue du Général Saussier (☎03 25 73 72 07). Though it's decorated with ski posters and snowshoes, this rustic restaurant offers a warm and inviting atmosphere. Cheese lovers will delight in the selection of gratins and fondues (€15-19); sausage fans should order the Andouillette AAAAA (€15), approved by the Association Amicale des Amateurs d'Andouillettes Authentiques. Those interested in lighter fare should try one of the overflowing salads (€7-15). Open M 7:30-10pm, Tu-Th noon-2pm and 7:30-10pm, F-Sa noon-2pm and 7:30-10:30pm. AmEx/MC/V. ❷

Restaurant Soleil de l'Inde, 33 rue de la Cité (☎03 25 80 75 71). Popular with *troyenne* youth, this stylish eatery offers an extensive Indian and Pakistani selection. The *formule rapide* (€9) includes naan, a meat dish, and a dessert. Plentiful vegetarian *plat* options (€7). Open Tu-Su noon-2:30pm and 7-10:30pm. MC/V. ❷

Le Détective Nippon, 21 rue de la Cité (☎03 25 46 19 48). Though its decorations—painted fans and paper lanterns—are painfully predictable, the food at this Japanese restaurant provides a worthwhile change from *troyenne* fare. For hungry scholars, a filling student *menu* (€7) is offered M-F, except F dinner. *Menus* €9-25. Open M-Th noon-2pm and 7-10pm, F noon-2pm and 7-10:30pm, Sa 7-10:30pm. MC/V. ❷

👁 SIGHTS

CATHÉDRALE SAINT-PIERRE-ET-SAINT-PAUL. The sheer size of this Gothic cathedral is only slightly less stunning than its intricate 13th- to 19th-century stained-glass designs, which illustrate everything from the "Parable of Wise and Foolish Virgins" to scenes from the life of Christ. A long history of fires and other disasters has claimed much of the original architecture, making the surviving windows all the more remarkable. Less conspicuous but equally impressive is the cathedral's 18th-century organ, which was declared one of France's most prestigious instruments in 1974 and is now frequently played at concerts. Call the church for concert listings. *(Pl. St-Pierre, down rue de la Cité. Enter via the small entrance to the right of the main doors. ☎03 25 76 98 18. Open M-Sa 10am-1pm and 2-6pm, Su 10am-noon and 2-5pm. Treasury open July-Aug. Tu-Sa 10am-noon and 3-5pm, Su 3-5pm. Mass Su 10:30am. Treasury tours in French. Info cards available in English and German. Free.)*

MUSÉE D'ART MODERNE. This well-designed museum is Troyes's cultural centerpiece, featuring over 2000 works of French art from 1850-1950, including pieces by Degas, Picasso, Rodin, and Seurat. A former bishop's palace, the building and its grounds are almost as much of an attraction as the art itself, and the open courtyards are ideal for a picnic. The museum contains a diverse collection of statues, masks, and paintings from Africa and Oceania—works that inspired many of their European counterparts. *(Pl. St-Pierre. ☎03 25 76 26 80. Open Tu-Su 10am-1pm and 2-6pm. €5, students and under 18 free; 1st Su of month free.)*

MAISON DE L'OUTIL ET DE LA PENSÉE OUVRIÈRE. This collection of over 8000 tools and architectural models from the 18th and 19th centuries, contained in a delightful 16th-century Renaissance-style house, is the largest such display in the world. Elaborately arranged in bizarre geometric patterns, the instruments for working with wood, iron, leather, and stone will impress even those without an interest in "the tools and thoughts of the worker." *(7 rue de la Trinité. ☎03 25 73 28 26; www.maison-de-l-outil.com. Open daily 10am-6pm. €6.50, students under 25 free, families €16. English and German guidebooks available. MC/V over €13.)*

ÉGLISE SAINTE-MADELEINE. This 12th-century structure boasts an intricate display of stained glass, which includes a complete representation of Christ's family tree. Yet the real sight to see is the flamboyant Gothic *jubé* (gallery) made of carved stone, which sits in the middle of the church and divides the nave from the choir. Sift through your pockets for spare change; for €0.50, the attendant will shine a spotlight on the *jubé* to display spectacular shadow effects. Well-labeled information panels in English, French, and German offer fascinating trivia about the architecture. *(Rue de la Madeleine. ☎ 03 25 73 82 90. Open M-Sa 9:30am-12:30pm and 2-5:30pm, Su 2-5:30pm.)*

BASILIQUE SAINT-URBAIN. At night, this basilica's spear-like spires stand illuminated, but its flying buttresses are best seen in daylight. When Jacques Pantaléon became Pope Urban IV, he commissioned the Gothic structure to be built at the site of his father's old cobbler shop. The original 13th-century choir and transept remain, while stained-glass windows depicting Pantaléon's childhood were added as late as the 19th century. The choir has held Urban IV's remains since 1935. *(Pl. Vernier, off rue Georges Clemenceau. ☎ 03 25 73 13 37. Open M-Sa 9:30am-12:30pm and 2-5:30pm, Su 2-5:30pm. Su mass 9:30, 10:30, 11am, 6pm.)*

OTHER SIGHTS. At the city's second largest museum, the **Musée Saint-Loup,** stuffed vultures lurk above a forest of taxidermal animals, the basement houses a geology exhibit, and portraits of old French royalty rest in luxury on the top floors. *(Rue de la Cité. ☎ 03 25 76 21 68; www.ville-troyes.fr. Open Tu-Su 9am-noon and 1-5pm. €4, students and under 18 free.)* A small building across from the Cathédrale St-Pierre-et-St-Paul houses both the **Musée di Marco** and its associated cafe. The museum features works by Angelo di Marco, who became famous for his hyper-realistic, pulp style of comic-book illustrations. The gallery features only a sampling of his drawings, but a movie about his life (in French only) showcases other pieces. *(Pl. de la Cathédrale. ☎ 03 25 40 18 27; www.museedimarco.com. Open Apr.-Sept. Tu-Su 10:30am-6:30pm; Oct.-Mar. W-Su 10:30am-6:30pm. €5, groups of 10 or more €4 each.)* The **Musée Vauluisant,** which houses both the **Musée d'Art Troyen** and the **Musée de la Bonneterie,** displays a collection of 16th- to 17th-century sculptures from the Troyes school and a 19th-century artisan's textile workshop. With wood floors and winding stone stairwells, the building and the herb garden in the courtyard are as worthy of attention as the art. *(4 rue de Vauluisant. ☎ 03 25 73 05 85. Open Tu-Su 9am-noon and 1-5pm. €3, students and under 18 free.)*

▶ NIGHTLIFE

Troyes may be small, but even the most jaded locals admit that it's a city *qui bouge bien* (a city that's happening). The most concentrated swath of nightlife is around **rue Champeaux** and **rue Molé** off pl. Alexandre Israël.

Le Point Carré, 27 rue Raymond Poincaré (☎03 25 81 63 44). Part bar, part cyber-cafe, this spot caters to a crowd of young, laid-back regulars. Decorated with American film stills and lit with red lanterns at night, the bar is funky yet relaxed. Customers sometimes use the piano and acoustic guitar for sporadic jam sessions. Open M-W 10:30am-midnight, Th-Sa 10:30am-1:30am, Su 2pm-midnight. MC/V.

Le Bougnat des Pouilles, 29 rue Paillot de Montabert (☎03 25 73 59 85), off rue Champeaux. Festive during the school year and relaxed during vacations, this bar welcomes a varied crowd. Enjoy a drink on the outdoor terrace or in the dark, leopard-print-furnished interior. Monthly concerts and themed nights; occasional displays of local artwork. Beer from €3. Mixed drinks from €5. Open M-Sa 5pm-3am. MC/V.

❄ FESTIVALS

Troyes's cultural center, the **Maison du Boulanger,** 42 rue Paillot de Montabert, has information on festivals, exhibits, and concerts. (☎03 25 43 55 00. Open M-F 9am-noon and 2-6pm, Sa 10am-noon and 2-5pm.)

Ville en Musique (☎03 25 43 55 00), from mid-June to mid-Aug. A series of free summer performances that range from modern French rock to classical organ tunes. Stop by the cultural center for more info.

Troyes at Night, July-Aug. daily; Sept. and Apr.-June F-Sa. A free sound-and-light spectacle guides visitors through the *centre-ville* streets at 10pm.

Festival des Nuits de Champagne (☎03 25 72 11 65, reservations 40 02 03; www. nuitsdechampagne.com), a weekend of concerts in Oct. Check website for more info.

⚠ OUTDOOR ACTIVITIES

Over 12,500 acres of freshwater lakes dot the region around Troyes. The sparkling **Lake Orient** welcomes sunbathers, swimmers, and windsurfers, while the wilder waters of **Lake Temple** are reserved for fishing and birdwatching. Those in search of adventure might favor **Lake Amance,** which is populated by speedboats and water-skiers. The **Comité Départemental du Tourisme de l'Aube,** 34 quai Dampierre, offers free brochures on local and regional outdoor activities as well as campsites and cheap camp-style lodgings. (☎03 25 42 50 00. Open M-F 9:30am-12:30pm and 1:30-6pm.) The tourist office has bus schedules for the Troyes-Grands Lacs routes. In July and August, the **Courriers de l'Aube** takes travelers to Lake Orient three times per day. (☎03 25 71 28 40. €5.60.) There is also a 42km bike path between Troyes and Port Dienville, along Lake Amance. In Dienville, camping is available at **Camping du Tertre** (☎03 25 92 26 50).

ALSACE, LORRAINE, AND FRANCHE-COMTÉ

An unfortunate history seems to be the only common thread linking the extremely distinct regions of Alsace, Lorraine, and Franche-Comté. Bordering Belgium, Switzerland, and Germany, these regions formed an eastern frontier that served as spoils in numerous Franco-German wars—most recently, WWII. Today, a battle-ridden past has given way to a more tranquil state of affairs; travelers seeking a hip sojourn or historical vacation can visit the region's cosmopolitan cities, which possess an international feel with a Germanic flair.

Though Alsace and Lorraine are commonly referred to as "Alsace-Lorraine," the two regions are less similar than their hyphenation suggests. To the east, the cities of Alsace cluster beside the Rhine, against the border of their former fatherland. German influence pervades daily life, from the half-timbered houses to the potato-heavy cuisine. Meanwhile, Lorraine unfolds to the west amid wheat fields and gentle plains. Its elegant cities are distinguished by tree-lined boulevards and stately Baroque architecture. In Nancy, the region's cultural capital, streets display turn-of-the-century Art Nouveau pieces.

Vineyards that produce the regional *vin jaune* (yellow wine) mark Franche-Comté's landscape, but the region is also a perfect base for hiking in the summer and for cross-country skiing in the winter; meanwhile, the city of Besançon is a student and hipster haven. Boasting a tumultuous history that gave way to rich diversity, the northwestern coast of France promises to please.

HIGHLIGHTS OF ALSACE, LORRAINE, AND FRANCHE-COMTÉ

BE MOVED by the Chapelle de Notre Dame-du-Haut (p. 385), a WWII memorial chapel and architectural marvel by Le Corbusier.

BIKE the Route du Vin to take in the rustic beauty—and intoxicating delights—of Kaysersberg (p. 394), an untouristed town tucked between green mountains.

ADMIRE Art Nouveau at its best at the Musée de l'École de Nancy (p. 376), where paintings and sculptures were inspired by the most famous muse of all: nature herself.

LORRAINE

NANCY ☎ 03 83

Nancy (nahn-see; pop. 106,000) first flourished when it played home to Duke Stanislas, whose passion for urban planning transformed the sprawling city into a model of 18th-century Classicism, complete with broad plazas and fountains. At the turn of the 20th century, *Nanciens* created the Nancy School of Art Nouveau, which took its inspiration from the natural world. The glow of Nancy's beautiful cityscape at night serves as further artistic inspiration.

Flights: Aéroport de Metz-Nancy Lorraine, route de Vigny (☎03 87 56 70 00). **Shuttles** (☎03 87 78 57 57) run to the train station (35-40min., 10 per day, €4). To: **Clermont-Ferrand; Lyon; Marseille; Nice; Paris; Toulouse.**

Trains: 3 pl. Thiers. Ticket office open M-F 5:40am-8:30pm, Sa-Su 6:30am-8:30pm. Info office open M-F 6am-9:30pm, Sa 6:30am-9:30pm, Su 6:30am-10pm. To **Metz** (40min., 9 per day, €5), **Paris** (1-3hr., 27 per day, €42), and **Strasbourg** (1hr., 20 per day, €23). Visit SNCF, 18 pl. St-Epvre, for info and reservations. Open M 12:30-6pm, Tu-F 9:30am-1pm and 2-6pm. AmEx/MC/V.

Buses: Rapides de Lorraine Buses, 52 bd. d'Austrasie (☎03 83 32 34 20). Depart from the train station. Open M-Sa 7am-7:30pm.

Public Transportation: STAN, 3 rue du Docteur Schmitt (☎03 83 30 08 08; www.reseau-stan.com). Additional info office at pl. de la République. Both open M-Sa 7am-7:30pm. Most buses stop at pl. de la République next to the train station and at Point Central on rue St-Georges. Buy individual tickets (€1.20) on board; find carnets of 10 (€8.70) or 2-day passes (€3.80) at the office. Buses 5:30am-8pm; some run until midnight.

Taxis: Taxi Nancy, 2 bd. Joffre (☎03 83 37 65 37).

Car Rental: Avis (☎08 20 61 17 03), at the train station. From €138 per day. 21+; drivers must have had license for 1 year. Open M-F 8am-9pm, Sa 8:30am-12:30pm and 1:30-5pm, Su 6-9pm. **Europcar,** 18 rue de Serre (☎03 83 37 57 24). From €152 per day. 21+; drivers must have had license for 1 year. Open M-F 8am-noon and 1:30-6:30pm, Sa 8am-noon and 2-6pm.

Bike Rental: At the *gare*, Entrée Thiers. (☎03 83 32 50 85). €3 per ½-day, €5 per day. Open M-F 7:30am-7:30pm, Sa-Su 9am-6pm.

Place Stanislas lies at the heart of the city. From the train station, walk straight through pl. Thiers and turn left onto **rue Mazagran.** Continue until you see a stone archway on your right and pass through onto rue Stanislas. Continue for four blocks until you reach pl. Stanislas. The grid-like layout of the *centre-ville* is fairly easy to navigate, but be sure to carry a map when wandering through the small streets north of pl. Stanislas and west of the train station.

> **TIP**
> **MAKE A PASS AT NANCY.** Pick up Le Pass Nancy (€13) at the tourist office for an audio tour, reduced admission price for all of Nancy's museums, reduced bike-rental fee, a round-trip bus or tram ticket, and a movie ticket.

Tourist Office: Pl. Stanislas (☎03 83 35 22 41; www.ot-nancy.fr), in the Hôtel de Ville. English-speaking staff offers free city and bus maps. Open Apr.-Oct. M-Sa 9am-7pm, Su 10am-5pm; Nov.-Mar. M-Sa 9am-6pm, Su 10am-1pm.

Tours: Tourist office leads themed 1-2hr. tours of the city in French Sa 2:30pm. €7, students €4, under 6 free. English tours available for groups by email reservation. Audio tour in English €6. 1hr. minibus tour of Art Nouveau sights in French July-Sept. Sa 2:30, 4:15pm, Su 11:30am; Oct. and May-June Sa 2:30, 4pm. €8, students and under 16 €4. Ask about self-guided walking tours of Art Nouveau sights. **Petit train** tours depart from pl. de la Carrière (☎03 89 73 74 24; www.petit-train.com). Available in 10 languages. 40min.; May-Sept. 5 per day 10am-4pm; €6, ages 6-14 €4.

Bookstore: Hall du Livre, 38 rue St-Dizier (☎03 83 35 53 01). Small section of books, newspapers, and magazines in English. Open M-Sa 9am-8pm, Su 11am-7pm. MC/V.

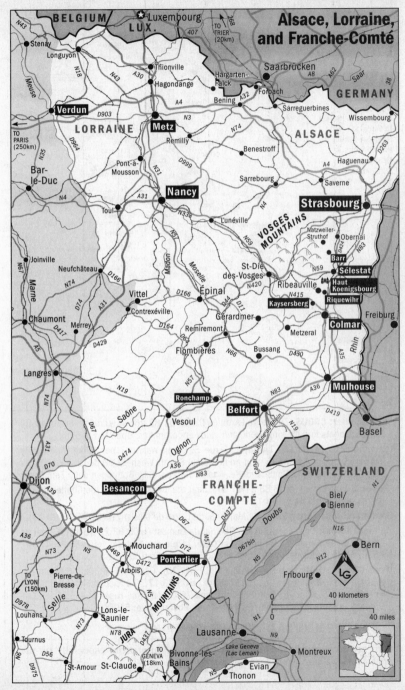

Alsace, Lorraine, and Franche-Comté

BELGIUM
Luxembourg
LUX.
TO TRIER (20km)
Stenay
Longuyon
Thionville
Hagondange
Bening
Forbach
Saarbrücken
Hargarten-Falck
Sarreguebines
GERMANY
Saar
Verdun
Metz
Remilly
N3
Sarrebourg
Wissembourg
TO PARIS (250km)
LORRAINE
ALSACE
Haguenau
Benestroff
Pont-à-Mousson
Bar-le-Duc
Saverne
Nancy
Strasbourg
Toul
Lunéville
VOSGES MOUNTAINS
Natzweiler-Struthof
Obernai
Joinville
Neufchâteau
St-Dié-des-Vosges
Barr
Sélestat
Haut Koenigsbourg
Vittel
Épinal
Ribeauvillé
Riquewihr
Contrexéville
Kaysersberg
Chaumont
Gérardmer
Colmar
Freiburg
Merrey
Remiremont
Metzeral
Langres
Flombières
Bussang
Mulhouse
Ronchamp
Belfort
Basel
Vesoul
Besançon
SWITZERLAND
Biel/Bienne
Dole
Bern
Mouchard
Pontarlier
TO LYON (150km)
Pierre-de-Bresse
Arbois
Fribourg
N
LG
Lons-le-Saunier
JURA MOUNTAINS
0   40 kilometers
0   40 miles
Louhans
Tournus
St-Amour
St-Claude
TO GENEVA (18km)
Divonne-les-Bains
Lausanne
Lake Geneva (Lac Leman)
Montreux
Evian
Thonon

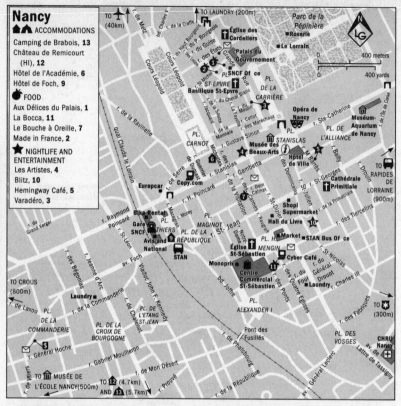

Nancy

ACCOMMODATIONS

Camping de Brabois, **13**
Château de Remicourt (HI), **12**
Hôtel de l'Académie, **6**
Hôtel de Foch, **9**

FOOD

Aux Délices du Palais, **1**
La Bocca, **11**
Le Bouche à Oreille, **7**
Made in France, **2**

NIGHTLIFE AND ENTERTAINMENT

Les Artistes, **4**
Blitz, **10**
Hemingway Café, **5**
Varadéro, **3**

Youth Center: CROUS, 75 rue de Laxou (☎03 83 91 88 26; www.crous-nancy-metz.fr). Helps students find housing, work, and study opportunities. Open M-F 2-5pm.

Laundromats: Le Bateau Lavoir, 124 rue St-Dizier. Wash €3 per 6.5kg. Open daily 7:45am-9:30pm. **Laverie,** 5 rond-point Marcel Simon. Wash €2.60 per 5kg, €3.20 per 7kg. Also 30 rue de la Commanderie. Wash €3.30 per 8kg. Both open daily 7am-9pm.

Police: 38 bd. Lobau (☎03 83 17 27 37), near the intersection with rue Charles III. Call for the **pharmacie de garde.**

Hospital: CHRU Nancy, 29 av. du Maréchal de Lattre de Tassigny (☎03 83 18 09 13).

Internet Access: Copy.com, 3-5 rue Guerrier de Dumast (☎03 83 22 90 41). €2 per hr. Open M-Sa 9am-9pm, Su 2-8pm. **Cyber Café,** 11 rue des 4 Églises (☎03 83 35 47 34). €5.40 per hr., students €4.60. Open M and Sa 11am-9pm, Tu-F 9am-9pm, Su 2-8pm.

Post Office: 10 rue St-Dizier (☎03 83 39 75 20). Open M-F 8:30am-6:30pm, Sa 8:30am-noon. Branches at 66 rue St-Dizier (☎03 83 17 39 11; open M noon-6:30pm, Tu-F 8:30am-6:30pm, Sa 8:30am-4pm) and 75 Grande Rue (open M 1-5:30pm, Tu-F 9am-12:30pm and 2-5:30pm, Sa 9am-4pm). **Postal Code:** 54000.

ACCOMMODATIONS AND CAMPING

There are several budget hotels around the train station, especially on **rue Jeanne d'Arc,** a 15min. walk from pl. Stanislas.

Château de Remicourt (HI), 149 rue de Vandoeuvre (☎03 83 27 73 67; aubergeremicourt@mairie-nancy.fr), in Villers-lès-Nancy. From the station, take bus #126 (dir.: Villers Clairlieu; 2-3 per hr.) to St-Fiacre. Walk downhill and take your 1st right onto rue de la Grange des Moines, which becomes rue de Vandoeuvre. Far from the *centre-ville*, but sunny rooms and the nearby park make it worth the trek. Breakfast included. Reception M-Sa 9:30am-9pm, Su 5:30-9pm. Check-out 9:30am. Dorms €15. AmEx/MC/V. ❶

Hôtel de l'Académie, 7 rue des Michottes (☎03 83 35 52 31). Despite an unappealing exterior, this hotel offers clean rooms with showers. Breakfast €3.50. Reception 7am-10pm; otherwise call ahead. Check-out 11am. Reservations recommended. Singles €20-28; doubles €28-39. Extra bed €6.50. AmEx/MC/V. ❷

Hôtel Foch, 8 av. Foch (☎03 83 32 72 53; hotelfoch.nancy@wanadoo.fr), next to the train station. 5min. from pl. Stanislas. Rooms are small and simply decorated, but the top floors offer beautiful views. All rooms with bath. Breakfast €6. Wi-Fi €5 per 2hr. Reception 24hr. Check-out noon. Singles and doubles €45-51; triples €69-87. Prices can go down on weekends; call ahead or email for latest rates. AmEx/MC/V. ❹

Camping de Brabois, av. Paul Muller (☎03 83 27 18 28; www.campeole.com), near the Centre d'Accueil. Take bus #122 or 126 (dir.: Villers Clairlieu) to Camping. Far from the *centre-ville*, but hillside location offers great views. Tennis courts, grocery store, showers, and laundry. Internet €2 per 15min. Wheelchair-accessible. Reception daily July-Aug. 7:30am-10pm; Sept.-Oct. and Apr.-June 8am-12:30pm and 2-9pm. Open from Apr. to mid-Oct. July-Aug. 2 people with tent €12-14; extra person €4.50-5.10, children €3-3.30. Sept.-Oct. and Apr.-June 2 people with tent €11; extra person €4, children free. Electricity €4. AmEx/MC/V over €15. ❶

▣ FOOD

Nearly all the *pâtisseries* on **place Stanislas** sell Nancy's signature *bergamote*—a bitter hard candy flavored by the same spice used in Earl Grey tea. The town is also famous for its ham-and-cheese *quiche lorraine*. The covered *marché central* is off rue St-Dizier in **place Henri Mengin** (open Tu-Sa 7am-7pm). During the summer, there is an outdoor market next to the covered *marché* selling mostly cheap clothing; unfortunately, this market is also frequented by many beggars. A **Shopi** supermarket is at 26 rue St-Georges (☎03 83 35 08 35; open M-Sa 8am-8pm), and a larger **Monoprix** is in the Centre Commercial St-Sebastian off pl. Henri Mengin (☎03 83 17 78 71; open M-Sa 8:30am-8:30pm). Restaurants spill from **rue des Maréchaux** onto **place Lafayette** and up **Grande Rue** to **place Saint-Epvre**. There are *crêpe* stands behind pl. Stanislas on **terrace de la Pépinière** and cheap kebab joints along and around **rue Stanislas.**

▣ **Le Bouche à Oreille,** 42 rue des Carmes (☎03 83 35 17 17). Funky and antique-filled. Enormous portions of cheese-based cuisine. Extensive menu of fondues, *tartiflettes* (a skillet of cheese, potatoes, and meat), *omelettes*, and salads. Fondue €14-15 per person; 2-person min. Lunch *menu* €11. Dinner *menu* €18. Open M and Sa 7-10:30pm, Tu-F noon-1:30pm and 7-10:30pm. AmEx/MC/V. ❸

▣ **Aux Délices du Palais,** 69 Grande Rue (☎03 83 30 44 19). A tiny, hip eatery serving amped-up comfort food. Locals swivel on cow-print stools while chowing down on lasagna with Roquefort and chicken with mushrooms. Gourmet salads are small but sure to please, with toppings ranging from warm goat cheese to *blini* and gingerbread. *Plats* and salads €9. Open M-F noon-1:30pm and 7-9:30pm, Sa 7-9:30pm. Cash only. ❷

La Bocca, 33 rue des Ponts (☎03 83 32 74 47). A date-worthy Italian restaurant with heart-shaped velvet chairs and zebra-print accents. Unlimited toppings for the popular make-your-own pizza (€11) range from mussels to pineapple—as long as you sign the disclaimer; proprietors take no responsibility for the possibly strange taste of your

Zoo ■

3 **Roserie** **4**
Parc de la Pépinière
PL. DE LA CARRIÈRE

Cours Léopold

r. La Fayette

PL. STANISLAS

r. Ste-Catherine

PL. CARNOT

2

Hôtel de Ville

r. Stanislas
r. Gambetta
r. H. Poincaré
r. St-Didier
r. St-Georges
r. de la Visitation
r. St-Julien
r. St-Jean
r. des Tiercelins

Market

1

PRIME FOR A PICNIC

You can get a gourmet meal in almost any city in France. But what better place than Nancy, birthplace of the École de Nancy—known for its focus on all things flora and fauna—to get down and dirty with your food? (Just kidding about the dirty part.) Grab a blanket and some moist towelettes, and enjoy your *pique-nique*.

1. The covered market. Pick up necessities, like homemade chocolate or perfectly ripe raspberries.

2. Place Stanislas. Savor your *entrée* while lounging next to a majestic gilded fountain.

3. Roserie de Parc de la Pépinière. Time for the main course. Let all your senses be dazzled as you dine in this neat garden.

4. The zoo. Eat dessert while being entertained by the adorable monkeys—just don't feed the animals.

"curieuse" creation. *Plat du jour* €8.50. Dinner *menu* €18. Open Tu-Sa 8am-10:30pm. MC/V. ❸

Made in France, 1 rue St-Epvre (☎03 83 37 33 36). Popular takeout joint. Prides itself on its fresh artisan bread and crisp vegetables. Lines of locals spill out the door. Smoothies €3. Sandwiches €2.60-5.60. Open M-Sa 11:30am-9pm. MC/V. ❶

◎ SIGHTS

◪**PLACE STANISLAS.** This square, open only to pedestrians, is the city's cultural center. Its three Neoclassical pavilions were commissioned in 1737 by Stanislas Leszczynski, the former king of Poland, to honor his nephew, Louis XV. The finely molded **Portes d'Or** (Golden Gates) dazzle during the day. From pl. Stanislas, pass through the **Arc de Triomphe** to find the tree-lined **place de la Carrière,** a former jousting ground with Baroque architecture.

◪**MUSÉE DE L'ÉCOLE DE NANCY.** A trip through this school's lushly decorated rooms feels like a walk through the wilderness: Émile Gallé's butterfly glassworks seem to belong in a fairy-tale forest. The entertaining auido tour helps the less art-savvy understand the significance of the works. No visit is complete without a stroll through the gardens. *(36-38 rue du Sergent Blandan; the museum will be on your right. Take bus #122, dir.: Villers Clairlieu, or 123, dir.: Vandoeuvre Cheminots, to Painlevé. Turn left onto rue du Sergent Blandan. ☎03 83 40 14 86; www.ecole-de-nancy.com. Open W-Su 10:30am-6pm. French tours F-Su 3pm €6, students €4, under 18 free; W students free; 1st Su of month 10am-1:30pm free for all. Free audio tours in English, French, and German.)*

PARC DE LA PÉPINIÈRE. This park is one of the most popular and relaxing places in the city. Expanses of rigorously controlled flowers and trees give way to a zoo, an outdoor cafe, and a miniature golf course. The aromatic **Roserie** displays vibrant flowers from around the world. Be sure to see Rodin's famous (and controversial) sculpture of Claude Gellée *(Le Lorrain)*, which features Apollo among galloping horses. To the shock of its commissioners, Gallée looks confused, awkward, and distorted. The statue is located directly north of the main entrance. *(North of pl. de la Carrière, near pl. Stanislas. Open daily June-Aug. 6:30am-10:30pm; Sept.-Oct. and Apr.-May 6:30am-9pm; Nov.-Mar. 6:30am-8pm. Free.)*

MUSÉE DES BEAUX-ARTS. This Baroque building showcases art from 1380 to the present, with a focus on modern works. Exhibits include gems by Delacroix, Monet, Picasso, and Rodin as well as a fantastic exhibit of Art Nouveau Daum glasswork.

(3 pl. Stanislas. ☎03 83 85 30 72. Open M and W-Su 10am-6pm. Wheelchair-accessible. €6, students €4, under 18 free; W students free; 1st Su of month 10am-1:30pm free for all. Tours in French €1.60. Free audio tours in English, French, and German.)

MUSÉUM-AQUARIUM DE NANCY. This recently renovated building holds hundreds of colorful fish, sea urchins, and other underwater dwellers in small tanks on the ground floor, organized by region, while the second floor contains a **zoology museum** filled with stuffed animals and a temporary exhibit hall. You may not want to visit during school hours, as you'll likely have to fight through schools of students to reach the schools of fishes. *(34 rue Ste-Catherine. ☎03 83 32 99 97; www.man.uhp-nancy.fr. Open daily 10am-noon and 2-6pm. Free guided tours in French W at 2:15pm. €3.80, ages 12-18 €2.30; W students free.)*

OTHER SIGHTS. While its interior is classically plain, the **Cathédrale Primitiale** is notable for its 18th-century painted dome, which depicts a chaotic ensemble of saints, angels, and major biblical figures. *(Rue St-Georges, past rue Montesquieu. Open daily 8am-7pm.)* North of pl. Stanislas, the 19th-century **Basilique Saint-Epvre** boasts brilliant windows from around the world. It also hosts free evening concerts of classical and organ music. *(Pl. St-Epvre, off Grande Rue. Concert dates and times vary; check with the tourist office for more details. Open daily 8am-7pm.)*

🎵 🌺 ENTERTAINMENT AND FESTIVALS

The **Opéra de Nancy et de Lorraine,** pl. Stanislas, presents productions from February to July. *(☎03 83 85 33 11. Tickets €5-55, student discount available; 15min. before show €5-41. Box office open Tu-Sa 1-7pm.)* The **theater** also holds ballets and symphonies year-round. *(☎03 83 85 69 01; www.ballet-de-lorraine.com. Tickets €15-30, students €10-20. Box office open M-F 10am-1pm and 2-6pm.)*

Festival International de Chant Choral (☎03 83 27 56 56; www.chantchoral.org), May 20-24, 2009. 2000 singers from around the world perform in concert.

Jazz-Pulsations (☎03 83 35 40 86; www.nancyjazzpulsations.com), in Oct. 2-week festival features performances by international musicians. Tickets €50; higher at the door.

🍷 NIGHTLIFE

Quirky bars and cafes line **Grande Rue** and **place Stanislas**. A young and very laid-back crowd makes for plenty of fun places to head out to with friends or to explore as a solo traveler. Check www.nancybynight.com for update-to-date info on bars, clubs, concerts, and theater events.

- **Blitz,** 76 rue St-Julien (☎03 83 32 77 20). Smoky lounge style at its best. Red-velvet interior. Beer from €2.30. Mixed drinks from €5. Open July-Aug. M 5:30pm-2am, Tu-Sa 2pm-2am, Su 5:30pm-1am; Sept.-June M 5:30pm-2am, Tu-Sa 2pm-2am. V.

- **Hemingway Café,** 5 rue Maurice Barrès (☎03 83 30 04 04). Lined with bookcases, the bar at Hemingway attracts crowds of students who salivate over the house mojitos. Beer from €2.50. Mixed drinks from €5. Open M-Sa 2pm-2am. MC/V.

- **Varadéro,** 27 Grande Rue (☎03 83 36 61 98). Cuban-style bar with a live DJ, revolutionary vibe, and lots of 20-somethings ready to dance long into the night. Shots €1.50. Beer from €2. Mixed drinks €6. Open Tu-Sa 9pm-2am. MC/V.

- **Les Artistes,** 36 rue Stanislas (☎03 83 30 54 92). Students arrive here in the early afternoon to sip tea (€2.50) or popular (for good reason) milkshakes (€3.50) and don't leave until closing. 2 floors of comfy couches. Microbrew beer from €3.90. Mixed drinks from €4.60. Happy hour daily 6-9pm; certain drinks ½-price, pitchers of sangria €6. Open M-Sa 8am-2am, Su 1pm-2am. MC/V.

Le Mezcalito, 49 Grande Rue (☎03 83 57 98 08). Bright blue, gay-friendly. Outdoor tables provide the perfect spot to sip drinks in the early evening. Techno music and exhibits by local artists inside entertain the eyes and ears. Beer from €2.50. Mixed drinks from €7. Open M-F 6pm-2am, Sa-Su 3pm-2am. AmEx/MC/V.

METZ ☎03 87

Though it's been more than a century since Metz (mehts; pop. 128,000) ceded to the Germans following the Franco-Prussian war, the city still bears the marks of its vacillating nationality. Neo-Romanesque architecture—characteristic of the German Empire—stands beside many of the city's quintessentially French monuments. Now home to a *très chic* student population and a set of über-contemporary art exhibition halls, Metz is the thriving capital of Lorraine.

⌐ TRANSPORTATION

Trains: Pl. du Général de Gaulle. Ticket window open M-F 5:55am-8:15pm, Sa 6:10am-8:15pm, Su 8:20am-8:55pm. Info office open M-Th and Sa 5:40am-9pm, F 5:40am-9:15pm, Su 5:40am-9:45pm. To: **Lyon** (5hr., 4 per day, €50); **Nancy** (40min., 3 per hr., €5); **Paris** (1-3hr., 10 per day, €39-50); **Strasbourg** (1hr., 10 per day, €21); **LUX** (1hr., every hr., €14).

Buses: Les Rapides de Lorraine, 1 rue Louis Débonnaire (☎03 87 63 65 65; www. tim57.fr), sends buses to small towns in the region. Take the underpass to the right of the train station below the tracks, turn left, and continue straight into the *gare routière*. Ticket window open July-Aug. M-Tu and Th-F 8:30am-12:30pm and 1-4pm, W 8:30am-12:30pm; Sept.-June M-Tu and Th 7:30-11am and 2-5pm, F 7:30-11am and 2-4pm. To **Verdun** (1hr., 4 per day, €6.20).

Public Transportation: TCRM, 1 av. Robert Schuman (☎03 87 76 31 11; www.tcrm-metz.fr). Office open July-Aug. M-F 9:15am-5pm; Sept.-June M-F 7:30am-6:30pm, Sa 9am-4:45pm. Most lines run M-F 6am-8pm, Sa-Su less often. Line #11 runs 10pm-midnight. Individual tickets (€1.20) available for purchase on board; carnets of 10 (€8.60) and day passes (€4.30) available at the office.

Taxis: At the train station (☎03 87 56 91 92). 24hr.

Car Rental: Avis (☎03 87 50 60 30), at the train station. Open M-F 8am-noon and 2-7pm, Su 5-8pm. **Europcar** (☎03 87 62 26 12). Open M-F 9am-noon and 3-7pm.

Bike Rental: Mob d'Emploi (☎03 87 74 50 43), across from the train station, in the small tower. €5.50 per ½-day, €8 per day, €18 per week; €100 and photocopy of ID deposit. Helmets available upon request. Open M-F 6am-8pm. Branch at rue d'Estrées (☎03 87 66 50 87). Open Mar.-Nov. daily 9am-6pm; Dec.-Feb. M-F 9am-6pm.

▟ ⁊ ORIENTATION AND PRACTICAL INFORMATION

Tourist Office: 2 pl. d'Armes (☎03 87 55 53 76; www.tourisme.mairie-metz.fr), between the cathedral and the Hôtel de Ville. From the station, take a right on rue Vauban, then left on rue des Augustins, which becomes rue de la Fontaine, pl. du Quarteau, and pl. St-Louis. Continue on until you reach pl. St-Simplice and turn left onto rue de la Tête d'Or, which becomes rue du Petit Paris. Make a right onto rue Fabert; the office is straight ahead. Alternatively, take minibus line A or B to pl. d'Armes from the stop to the right of the train station (€0.70). English-speaking staff books lodgings (€1.50 and 10% paid at the office). Free Wi-Fi. **Currency exchange.** Open M-Sa 9am-7pm, Su 10am-5pm.

Tours: Tourist office leads 1hr. tours in French of the cathedral (M-Sa 3pm) and the city (M-Sa May-Sept. 3, 4pm; Oct.-Apr. 4pm). €5 per tour, €7 for both; students and ages

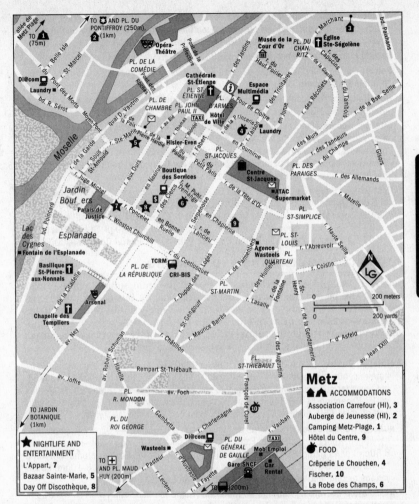

ALSACE, LORRAINE, AND FRANCHE COMTÉ

Metz

ACCOMMODATIONS

Association Carrefour (HI), **3**
Auberge de Jeunesse (HI), **2**
Camping Metz-Plage, **1**
Hôtel du Centre, **9**

FOOD

Crêperie Le Chouchen, **4**
Fischer, **10**
La Robe des Champs, **6**

NIGHTLIFE AND ENTERTAINMENT

L'Appart, **7**
Bazaar Sainte-Marie, **5**
Day Off Discothèque, **8**

12-25 €2.50/3.50; under 12 free. English, German, or French audio tour available (€7, with passport deposit). A 45min. **petit train** (☎03 87 73 03 08) takes visitors through the city and more remote gardens. English, French, and German. Departs from the cathedral; ask tourist office for times. €5.50, under 18 €3.50. Night tours depart from the tourist office July-Aug. at 10pm (1½hr., €8).

Budget Travel: Agence Wasteels, 3 rue d'Austrasie (☎03 87 50 54 46; www.wasteels. fr). Open M-F 9am-noon and 2-6pm, Sa 9am-noon. Branch at 2 rue de Grand Cerf (☎03 87 18 44 34). Open M 2-6:30pm, Tu-F 9:30am-6:30pm, Sa 9:30am-5pm.

Bookstore: Hisler-Even, 1 rue Ambroise Thomas (☎03 87 74 27 76). Open M-Sa 10am-7pm.

Youth Center: Centre de Renseignement et d'Information, Bureau Information Jeunesse (CRI-BIJ), 1 rue de Coëtlosquet (☎03 87 69 04 50; www.cribij.fr), upstairs in a nondescript office building. Info on concerts, hiking and outdoor activities, lodging, study, travel, tourism, and job openings. Free Internet; reserve ahead by phone during the school year. Open M noon-4pm, Tu-Th 9am-4pm, F 9am-noon.

Laundromat: 22 rue du Pont des Morts (☎03 87 63 49 57). Wash €4. Open daily 7am-8pm.

Police: 45 rue Belle Isle (☎03 87 16 17 17), near pl. de Pontiffroy. Call here for the **pharmacie de garde.**

Hospital: Centre Hospitalier Regional Metz-Thionville, 1 pl. Philippe de Vigneulles (☎03 87 55 31 31), near pl. Maud Huy.

Internet Access: Free at **tourist office** and **youth center** (above). **Espace Multimédia,** 2 rue du Four du Cloître (☎03 87 36 56 56). Free. Photo ID and passport-size photo necessary. Reserve ahead to use computer. Wi-Fi 2hr. max. Open M 1-6pm, Tu-Sa 9am-6pm; closed 1st M of month. **Di@com,** 20 rue Gambetta (☎03 87 63 08 85). €3 per hr., with student ID €2. Open M-Sa 10am-9pm, Su 11am-9pm.

Post Office: 9 rue Gambetta (☎03 87 56 74 30). **Currency exchange** available. Open M-F 8am-7pm and Sa 8:30am-12:30pm. Branches at Centre St-Jacques (☎03 87 37 99 00; open M-F 9am-7pm, Sa 9am-noon and 1:30-5pm), 1 rue de la Pierre Hardie (☎03 87 37 75 74; open M-F 9am-7pm, Sa 9am-5pm), and 39 pl. St-Louis (☎03 87 18 47 74; open M 2-6pm, Tu-F 9am-6pm, Sa 9am-noon). **Postal Code:** 57000.

🏠 🏕 ACCOMMODATIONS AND CAMPING

Relatively inexpensive hotels cluster around the train station, while pricier ones fill the pedestrian district. Metz attracts many business travelers, so reserve a few weeks ahead. For weekend stays, many hotels offer two nights with breakfast for the price of one; ask for the *Bon week-end en ville* promotion conducted through the tourist office. (24hr. advance reservation required; offer depends on the availability of rooms at any given hotel.)

🏨 **Hôtel du Centre,** 14 rue Dupont des Loges (☎03 87 36 06 93; www.perso.wanadoo.fr/hotelducentre-metz), in the heart of the *vieille ville.* 19th-century building with a winding lavender staircase. Well-decorated rooms with bath and TVs. Breakfast €6-8. Free Wi-Fi. Reception M-F 6:30am-10pm, Sa-Su 7:30am-9pm. Check-out 11am. Singles and doubles €59; triples €63; quads €75. Extra bed €8. AmEx/MC/V. ❹

Auberge de Jeunesse (HI), 1 allée de Metz Plage (☎03 87 30 44 02; www.ajmetz.free.fr), 15min. from the *vieille ville.* From the station, take bus #3 (dir.: Metz-Nord; last bus 8:30pm) or #11 (dir.: St-Eloy; last bus midnight) to Pontiffroy. No-frills rooms with wood bunks. Kitchen. Breakfast included. Free Wi-Fi. Reception 8-10am and 5-10pm. Reservations recommended. 2- to 6-bed dorms €16. AmEx/MC/V. ❶

Association Carrefour/Auberge de Jeunesse (HI), 6 rue Marchant (☎03 87 75 07 26; www.carrefour-metz.asso.fr). Take minibus A or B from the station to pl. d'Armes. Take a right on En Fournirue and a left onto rue Taison, which becomes rue des Trinitaires and then rue Marchant. Bright, clean rooms. Popular with large groups. Restaurant and TV room. Breakfast included. Lockers €1 per day; inquire at reception. Laundry facilities available. Internet €1 per 15min., €3 per hr. Reception 24hr. Check-out 10am. 3- and 4-bed dorms €18; singles and doubles €22. AmEx/MC/V. ❶

Camping Metz-Plage, allée de Metz-Plage (☎03 87 68 26 48; campingmetz@mairie-metz.fr), bordering the river. Enter from rue de la Piscine, behind the hospital on rue Belle Isle. A large grassy plot with views of the river. Great location minutes from the *centre-ville.* Small snack bar and TV room. There's a giant public pool next door. Showers and laundry. Free Wi-Fi. Wheelchair-accessible. Reception 7am-noon and 2-10pm. Open May-Sept. €3 per person, children €1.50; €3 per tent; €6-8 per car; €14-16 per RV. Prices from May to mid-June and Sept. 10% less. Electricity free. AmEx/MC/V. ❶

▣ FOOD

Local *pâtissiers* throw the region's yellow *mirabelles* (plums) into everything from tarts to preserves. *Boulangeries* and other cheap eateries cluster in the pedestrian district on **rue Coislin** and near the hostel on **rue du Pont des Morts.** Restaurants line **place Saint-Jacques** and **rue Dupont des Loges.** The **Centre Saint-Jacques,** off pl. St-Jacques, has specialty stores, cheap eateries, and an **ATAC** supermarket in the basement. (☎03 87 74 02 90. Open M-Sa 8:30am-7:30pm. MC/V.) The biggest market is near the **cathedral** (open Sa 7am-1pm). Thursday mornings (7am-1pm), a small market takes place near the **train station.** Kebab stands occupy every corner of pl. St-Jacques and the surrounding streets.

La Robe des Champs, 14 rue Marguerite Puhl-Demange (☎03 87 36 32 19). Don't let the pearl-draped chandeliers deceive you; this classy restaurant's signature baked-potato *plats* (€8.50-19) are anything but dainty. Open M-F 11:30am-2:30pm and 6:30-10pm, Sa 11am-3pm and 6:30-11pm. AmEx/MC/V. ❸

Crêperie Le Chouchen, 10 rue Taison (☎03 87 18 50 50). The Lorraine *crêpe,* smothered in *mirabelles,* jam, ice cream, and liqueur, is a delicious blend of the region's flavors. *Crêpes* €2.50-9. Open daily noon-2pm and 7-10pm. MC/V. ❷

Fischer, 6 rue François de Curel (☎03 87 36 85 97), near the train station. Sandwich shop layers its meats on some of the best bread in town—the fluffy baguettes turn standard sandwiches (€3.10-3.90) into standouts. Beats nearby competitors hands down. Salads €5-6. Lunch *menu* €7.50. Open M-F 7am-6:30pm, Sa 7am-4:30pm; seating area closes 30min. before takeout window. MC/V. ❶

◔ SIGHTS

◨CATHÉDRALE SAINT-ÉTIENNE. This golden 13th-century cathedral, the third-tallest in France at 42m, is known by locals as the "lantern of God." The church also boasts the largest collection of stained glass in the world—6500 sq. m ranging from the 13th to 20th centuries. Don't miss Marc Chagall's modern windows in the western transept and the **Chapelle de Saint-Sacrament** near the welcome desk; his stunning designs feature jagged geometric fragments of brightly hued stained glass. (*Pl. d'Armes.* ☎03 87 75 54 61. Open daily June-Sept. 8am-7pm; Oct.-May 8am-6pm. Crypt and treasury open M-Sa 10am-noon and 2-5pm, Su 2-5pm. Closed to tourists during mass, Su 9am. 1½hr. tours in French July-Aug. F-Su 2:30pm; Apr.-June by reservation only. Crypt and treasury each €2, students €1. Tours €4.)

◨ESPLANADE AND GARDENS. At the other end of rue des Clercs from pl. d'Armes sits the esplanade, a pavilion overlooking the lake and parks of the Moselle Valley. The pavilion has colorful flora and a colossal fountain, but these features pale in comparison to the manmade **Lac aux Cynges.** There, the beautifully simple **fontain de l'Esplanade** shoots streams of water to lofty heights in artistic, mesmerizing patterns. In summer, the illuminated fountains spurt in time to music for **Les Eaux Musicales du Lac aux Cygnes.** (*From late June to early Sept. 2-3 times per week at nightfall. Ask at tourist office for specific dates. Free.*) Paddle or pedal your way around the nearby mouth of the **Moselle** with rentals from **La Flottille.** (*1 quai des Régates.* ☎03 87 36 86 71. Pedal boats for 2 people €9.50 per 30min.; motorboats for 2 people €17 per 30min. Call ahead for hours. Cash only.*) One kilometer south of the esplanade, swans preen at the **Jardin Botanique,** a botanist's heaven. (☎03 87 55 54 00. Garden open daily 8am-sunset. Greenhouse open Apr.-Sept. M-F 9am-6:45pm, Sa-Su 9-11:30am and 2-6:45pm; Oct.-Mar. M-F 9am-4:45pm, Sa-Su 9-11:30am and 2-4:45pm.)

OTHER SIGHTS. The **Arsenal** hosts contemporary art exhibits at its own minimalist gallery as well as at two of Metz's nearby historical landmarks—the basilica and chapel. *(3 av. Ney.)* France's oldest church, **Basilique Saint-Pierre-aux-Nonnains,** was erected by the Romans in AD 380 to accommodate large baths and a sports arena. After it suffered a devastating fire in the fifth century, it was restored as a chapel in the sixth century. Little is left but the church's sandy brick walls, which provide a striking contrast with the ever-changing and often bizarre modern art exhibits held inside. *(☎03 87 39 92 00; www.mairie-metz.fr/arsenal. Open from mid-June to late Sept. M-Sa 1-6pm, Su 2-6pm; from Oct. to mid-June Sa 1-6pm, Su 2-6pm.)* The **Chapelle des Templiers,** a pint-size rotunda situated between the Arsenal and the basilica, fits fewer works of art but makes for a nice transition between the two larger spaces. *(Open from mid-June to late Sept. M-Sa 1-6pm, Su 2-6pm.)* Built over a swamp across town, **Place de la Comédie** served a less than comedic function during the Revolution: its main attraction was the guillotine, where 63 men were beheaded. Built in 1751, Metz's **Opéra-Théâtre** is the oldest functioning theater in France. *(4-5 pl. de la Comédie.)*

🎵 🌸 ENTERTAINMENT AND FESTIVALS

The **Opéra-Théâtre** hosts various operas and ballets. (☎03 87 55 51 43, tickets 75 40 50; http://opera.ca2m.com. €10-39, students €5-13. Ticket office open M-F 9am-12:30pm and 3-5pm. MC/V.) Concerts and guest lecturers regularly come to the modern performance hall at the **Arsenal.** (☎03 87 39 92 00, reservations 74 16 16; www.mairie-metz.fr/arsenal. €18-40, students €15-36. Ticket office open Tu-Su 1-6:30pm; exhibition gallery open Tu-Sa 1-6pm and Su 2-6pm. MC/V.) Bargain shoppers love Metz's twice-monthly *marché aux puces* (flea market), one of France's largest. Dates vary, so check with the tourist office for the latest schedule. (☎03 87 55 66 00; www.fim-metz.com. Open Sa 6am-noon.)

Metz en Fête (www.mairie-metz.fr), in July. Free outdoor concerts and theatrical performances in the cathedral.

Grandes Fêtes de la Mirabelle, in late Aug. Huge street party held in honor of the plum.

Marché de Noël, in Dec. Over 100 market stalls open on pl. St-Louis and pl. de Gaulle.

🌙 NIGHTLIFE

Metz has a solid supply of lively bars and a few good clubs. At night, students pack the bars and cafes at **place Saint-Jacques** and **place Saint-Louis.**

DO—Day Off Discothèque, 7 rue Poncelet (☎03 87 78 62 96). Downstairs couches are perfect for an intimate chat, while a small bar upstairs echoes the diverse dance soundtrack blaring from the lounge. Student crowd loves frequent themed nights. Beer from €3.50. Mixed drinks €8-10. Cover €10, often lower W-Th; includes 1 drink. Women free before midnight. Open W-Sa 10:30pm-5am. AmEx/MC/V.

L'Appart, 2 rue Haute Pierre (☎03 87 18 59 26; www.l-endroit.com). Stylish gay bar—popular with both men and women—gets wild with loud music and dancing (often atop the long metallic bar). Beer from €2.70. Mixed drinks from €7.50. Theme nights Su; check online for schedule. Open Tu-Su 8pm-2:30am. AmEx/MC/V.

Bazaar Sainte-Marie (BSM), 2 bis-4 rue Ste-Marie (☎03 87 21 05 93). A quirky bar filled with comfy sofas, colorful tapestries, and old carpets. Locals come to sit, smoke, chat or ■ **make out for hours.** Perfect for laid-back types looking for an alternative to pubs and clubs. Beer from €2. Mixed drinks from €5.80. DJ plays house, groove, and funk F-Sa. Open M 2pm-2am, Tu-Th 10am-2am, F-Sa 10am-3am. MC/V.

VERDUN

☎ 03 29

The specter of war haunts the city of Verdun (vehr-duhn; pop. 22,000), which was the last eastern stronghold stopping the WWI German advance on Paris. In 1914, German offensives pressed into Verdun, inaugurating four years of trench warfare that would devastate an entire generation. French and German forces held their ground as battle lines budged merely a few feet with each costly assault. In the 1916 Battle of Verdun, one of WWI's most horrific conflicts, each side lost nearly 400,000 men. Though Verdun's *centre-ville* is now a serene and scenic hub, eerie reminders of the battle remain on the outskirts of town, where the ground is still pocked from trench warfare. In spite of its violent past, the city was christened "World Capital of Peace, Freedom, and Human Rights" in 1987. In terms of tourism, all of Verdun's best sights can be covered in a day or two; unfortunately, they're most easily accessible by car.

▐ TRANSPORTATION

Trains: Pl. Maurice Genevoix. Ticket office open M 4:45-11:45am and 1:30-6:35pm, Tu-F 5:45am-12:45pm and 1:30-6:35pm, Sa 9:45am-noon and 2:15-6:35pm, Su 12:30-7:30pm. To **Metz** (1hr., 3 per day, €6) and **Paris** (1-3hr., 4 per day, €32).

Buses: Les Rapides de la Meuse (☎08 20 85 01 50, €0.12 per min.). Depart from the parking lot at the end of rue du 8 Mai to surrounding towns. SNCF buses leave from the train station for **Metz** (1hr., 3 per day, €6).

Taxi: Magny (☎06 81 95 26 98). 24hr.

Car Rental: AS Location, 22 rue Louis Maury (☎03 29 86 58 58). Open M 7:45-11:30am and 2:30-6:15pm, Tu 8:30-11:30am and 2:30-6:30pm, W 9-11am and 2:30-6:15pm, Th 8:30-11:30am and 2:30-6pm, F 8-11:30am and 2:30-6:30pm, Sa 9-10am and 4:30-6pm. AmEx/MC/V.

Bike Rental: Véloland, av. du Metz (☎03 29 86 12 43). €10 per ½-day, €15 per day; passport deposit. Open Tu-F 9am-noon and 2-7pm, Sa 9am-noon and 2-6:30pm. MC/V.

▐ PRACTICAL INFORMATION

Tourist Offices: Pl de la Nation. In an ironic twist, the "World Capital of Peace" has 2 competing tourist offices directly across the street from each other, with nearly identical services. From the station, walk to the roundabout straight ahead and follow av. Garibaldi as it ends, curves to the right, and becomes rue Frères Boulhaut. Walk through Porte Chaussée and cross the bridge on the left (10min.). Both offices have English-speaking staff and provide maps of the city. The office next to the park (☎03 29 86 14 18; www. verdun-tourisme.com) offers a free, poorly labeled map; the office across the street has a better map (€0.50). Open July-Aug. daily 9am-7pm; Sept.-Nov. and Mar.-June 9:30am-12:30pm and 1:30-6pm; Dec.-Feb. 10am-12:30pm and 2-5pm.

Tours: Both tourist offices offer 4hr. tours of the battlefields and monuments—the best deal for those visiting these historical locations without a car. If you have a car, you may want to explore on your own; the tour provides little info besides what can be easily found in the English brochures at each location. The office next to the park offers tours in English in addition to the French tours offered by both. Tours May-Sept. daily 2pm; €26, ages 8-16 €16, ages 4-7 €7.50, under 4 free. Tours can fill quickly; call ahead.

Laundromat: 2 rue Raymond Poincaré. Open daily 6:30am-9:30pm. Wash €4 per 6kg.

Police: 2 rue Chaussée (☎03 29 86 00 17). Call for the **pharmacie de garde.**

Hospital: 2 rue d'Antohouard (☎03 29 83 84 85).

Post Office: Av. de la Victoire (☎03 29 83 45 58). **ATM** and **currency exchange** available. Open M-F 8am-7pm, Sa 8am-noon. **Postal Code:** 55100.

🏠 🏕 ACCOMMODATIONS AND CAMPING

Auberge de Jeunesse (HI), pl. Monseigneur Ginisty (☎03 29 86 28 28; verdun@fuaj. org), beside the cathedral. From the station, head right on rue Louis Maury to rue de la Belle Vierge (10min.). A converted seminary. Winding staircase leads to 4- and 6-bed rooms with wood bunks and bathrooms. 2-story 11-bunk room offers views of the city. Kitchen, bar, and foosball. Breakfast €3.50. Free daytime luggage storage. Wheelchair-accessible. Reception M-F 8am-12:30pm and 5-11pm, Sa-Su 8-10am and 5-9pm. Check-in 5pm. Check-out 10am. Dorms €13. MC/V. ❶

Hôtel Montaulbain, 4 rue de la Vieille Prison (☎03 29 86 00 47; fax 84 75 70), near pl. du Maréchal Foch. High ceilings and large beds lend a sense of luxury. Some rooms have antique furniture; all with bath. Breakfast €5.50. Reception 7am-10pm. Check-out 11am. Reservations recommended July-Aug. Singles €30, with toilet €38; doubles €35/40-42; triples €48; quads €50. Extra bed €10. MC/V. ❷

Hôtel Les Colombes, 9 av. Garibaldi (☎03 29 86 05 46; fax 83 75 25), 1 block from the train station. Simple rooms. €60 room is surprisingly luxurious, with shower, bath, and celestial-themed decor. Breakfast €5.50. Reception 7am-9pm. Single with toilet €26; doubles with full bath €35-60; triples and quads €45. MC/V. ❷

Camping Les Breuils, allée des Breuils (☎03 29 86 15 31; www.camping-lesbreuils. com), 1km from town, past the Citadelle Souterraine. Turn right onto av. du Général Boichut, and take the 1st left. Bar, grocery store, pool, and laundry. Reception July-Aug. 7:30am-10pm; Sept. and Apr.-June 8am-noon and 2-10pm. July-Aug. €5.50 per person; Sept. and Apr.-May €4.40; June €5. Sites €4.50. Electricity €4. MC/V. ❶

🍴 FOOD

Verdun's contribution to confection is the *dragée*, a sugar-coated almond first engineered by a 13th-century apothecary; according to local legend, the sweet *bonbons* foster fertility. The treats can be found just about anywhere in town. The main covered market is on **rue de Rû** (open F 7:30am-12:30pm). Stock up at the **Match** supermarket a block away from the station on rond-point des États-Unis. (Open M-Sa 8:30am-7:30pm, Su 8:30am-12:30pm.) Verdun generally lacks quality restaurants and cafes; the best places can be found in the area along **rue Chaussée** and **rue des Rouyers** and by the canal on **quai de Londres.**

Marie la Crêpe, 54 rue des Royeurs (☎03 29 84 20 70). Crispy *galettes* (€3-8.60) and sweet *crêpes* (€2.60-8.30) fill your stomach without emptying your wallet. Place-mat doodlers can try for a spot on the wall among other talented patrons. Open July-Sept. daily noon-10pm; Oct.-June Tu-Su noon-2pm and 6-9pm. Cash only. ❶

Le Boucher du Quai, 19 quai de Londres (☎03 29 86 72 01). Good food, riverside location, and an attentive staff. Sandwiches €3.50-4.70. Pasta €7.50-8.40. Open daily noon-2pm and 7-10pm. MC/V over €10. ❶

👁 SIGHTS

MONUMENT À LA VICTOIRE. Towering over Verdun's pedestrian district, the soldier of the Monument à la Victoire exudes strength and persistence. The colossal sculpture stands on an old chapel—the Église de la Magdeleine. The pyramid-like stairs that lead up to the monument summon the grandeur of an ancient ziggurat. Inside the tiny chapel, three enormous volumes display records of the names of soldiers who fought here. (*☎03 29 84 37 97. Brochures available in English, French, and German. Open daily July-Aug. 9:30am-12:30pm and 2-6:30pm; Sept.-Oct. and Apr.-May 9:30am-noon and 2-5:30pm; June 9:30am-12:30pm and 2-6pm. Free.)*

CITADELLE SOUTERRAINE. This fortress that once sheltered groups of 10,000 front-bound soldiers offers a reconstructed exhibit on trench warfare. The official *petit train* tour (the only means of entering) plunges visitors into the citadel's underground galleries and depicts the lives of soldiers and nervous generals through realistic—though slightly corny—talking holograms. The citadel is a chilly 7°C; dress accordingly. *(Av. du 5ème RAP, down rue de Rû. Open daily July-Aug. 9am-6:30pm; Sept. and Apr.-June 9am-6pm; Oct.-Nov. 10am-noon and 2-6pm; Dec. 10am-noon and 2-5pm. Tours in Dutch, English, French, German, Italian, and Spanish. 30min. tours in French every 5min., in English every hr. Wheelchair-accessible. €6, ages 5-15 €2.50. MC/V over €12.)*

OTHER SIGHTS. Verdun's pre-war constructions include the 10th- to 12th-century **Cathédrale Notre Dame.** Its crypt, unearthed during WWI bombings and renovated thereafter, features a set of beautiful modern stained-glass windows. **Les Heures Musicales,** a series of choir and organ concerts, fill the cathedral in June and July. *(Rue de la Belle Vierge. ☎03 29 86 87 88, for concert info 86 20 00; www.accv.fr. Concert times vary; call tourist office for details. Cathedral open daily Apr.-Sept. 8:45am-7pm; Oct.-Mar. 8:45am-6pm.)* Built in 1200, the **Porte Chaussée,** quai de Londres, has served as a prison, a guard tower, and an exit for WWI troops. On rue Frères Boulhaut, a copy of Rodin's triumphant **La Défense** faces a parking lot; the Netherlands created the replica for the town after the Battle of Verdun. **Parc Municipal Japiot,** across from the tourist office, is home to tall roses by the banks of the Meuse as well as some excellent picnic benches.

🎵 NIGHTLIFE AND FESTIVALS

Le Son et Lumière de la Bataille de Verdun recreates the Battle of Verdun with over 300 actors and 1000 projectors. The show is impressive, but the site is unfortunately not served by public transportation. Bring warm clothing; it gets very cold at night, even in the middle of July. (*☎03 29 84 50 00; www.spectacle-verdun.fr. June-July F-Sa nights. Call the tourist office for tickets. June €15, ages 12-18 €9, under 12 free; July €18/€9/free.)* The sounds of **L'Été Musicale** waft up the river from quai de Londres Saturday nights throughout July and August.

For a night out, stick around the **quai de Londres** and neighboring **rue Chaussée** for the best nightlife. The pubs around the river fill up most evenings.

L'Estaminet, 45 rue des Rouyers (*☎03 29 86 07 86). German *bierstube* plays jazz and blues. Beer from €2.50. Open M-F 2pm-2am, Sa 3pm-3am. MC/V.

Le Lapin Qui Fume, 31 rue des Gros Degrès (*☎03 29 86 15 84). Endearingly gritty green-lit tavern with friendly service, loud music, and cheap beer. Beer from €2. Mixed drinks from €4. Open Tu-Su 11am-2am. MC/V.

La Planet, 1 rue des Gros Degrès (*☎03 29 86 02 86). Small *discothèque* livens up after Verdun's bars have closed for the night. Beer €5. Mixed drinks €7. Cover men €7, women free. Open Th 11pm-4am, F-Sa 11pm-5am. AmEx/MC/V.

◢ DAYTRIPS FROM VERDUN

WWI MEMORIALS
Many sites near Verdun commemorate the battle of 1916. The 4hr. bus tour conducted by the tourist offices (p. 383) visits the 4 memorials listed below, describing each in French. The

office also offers a €13 pass (in addition to the price of the tour) to all of the mentioned monuments. Touring the entire 25km circuit on your own requires a car.

After Alsace and parts of Lorraine were annexed by Germany in 1871, Verdun found itself within 40km of the German border. In a panic, France built 38 forts to protect Verdun and the surrounding area. But when the forts began to crumble under German cannon attacks, French General Joffre ordered the disarmament of all fortifications in 1915, redirecting his troops toward the offensive lines. The abandoned forts became the targets of German General Falkenhayn's 1916 offensive. German troops captured the immense concrete **Fort de Douaumont,** whose supported position, lookout, and 3km of passageways made it an invaluable acquisition. The French shelled it for the next eight months in an attempt to dislodge the German garrison. Their persistence paid off, and in October 1916 the Germans fled under fire; a detachment of French-led Moroccan troops then reclaimed the fort. Visitors to the fortress can still see the ruin resulting from the assault, which also tragically resulted in over 100,000 French deaths. The dark and grimy conditions of the fort's old toilets and disinfection room hint at their former squalor, while the shell-firing room, bedrooms, and *boulangeries*—each only steps apart from each other—offer a brief glimpse of daily life as a soldier. Sporadically, the fort rings with a sonic recreation of a single exploding shell. These effects underscore the terrors of the 1916 battle more powerfully than Verdun's other monuments. (☎03 29 84 41 91; www.meuse.fr. Open daily Apr.-Aug. 9am-6:30pm; Sept.-Nov. 10am-1pm and 2-6pm; Dec. and Feb.-Mar. 10am-1pm and 2-5pm. Free informational brochures available in English, French, and German. €3, under 16 €1.50.)

The central and most moving monument is the **Ossuaire de Douaumont,** a crypt situated above a cemetery. Aglow with the blood-orange hues from its stained-glass windows, the crypt's granite walls bear the names of hundreds of soldiers who were never found. A small chapel in the middle of the crypt allows visitors a quiet moment to reflect, as the enormous halls are often filled with equally enormous crowds. Outside, windows at the base of the monument reveal the ashes and bones of 130,000 unknown non-French soldiers. (☎03 29 84 54 81; www.verdun-douaumont.com. Open daily May-Aug. 9am-6:30pm; Sept. 9am-noon and 2-6pm; Oct. and Mar. 9am-noon and 2-5:30pm; Nov. 9am-noon and 2-5pm; Apr. 9am-6pm. Brochures available in English. Historical film contains a few graphic scenes. Ossuary free. Film and tower €4, under 18 €3.) Nearby, the **Tranchée des Baïonettes** holds the bodies of members of France's 137th regiment, who died while taking cover from enemy fire. The precise events of the assault are not known, but some speculate the troops may have been buried alive. The only sign of the men was the points of their bayonets protruding from the ground; the tips of two guns can still be seen in the dirt.

The little town of **Fleury** was at the epicenter of the battle and changed hands 16 times during the war. The fighting devastated the town, and the surrounding farmland was unusable for generations. Stones have been placed where former houses used to sit, while white-painted plots of land signify the town's old streets. You can still see the remains of trenches in the rippled grass. Fleury's former railway station is now the **Memorial de Verdun** museum, which houses old weapons, uniforms, and an exhibit on the development of medicine during the war. The basement recreates a devastated trench, with old helmets, shattered trees, remnants of artillery, and barbed wire. (☎03 29 84 35 34. Open daily from Apr. to mid-Sept. 9am-6pm; from mid-Sept. to Dec. and Feb.-Mar. 9am-noon and 2-6pm. €7, students and ages 11-16 €3.50, under 11 free. MC/V over €14.)

ALSACE

STRASBOURG   ☎ 03 88

Clinging to the edge of Alsace, a few kilometers from the German border, Strasbourg (strahss-boorg; pop. 270,000) is a French city with a truly international
character. The prize of centuries of Franco-German border wars, Strasbourg
maintains a near even mix of the two countries' cultural bearings. In the *vieille ville, winstubs* (vin-shtoobs; Alsatian restaurants), and *pâtisseries* rest
amicably side by side, and you're as likely to hear German as French. Hordes
of visitors come from across the continent to tour the European Parliament,
study at the local university, and soak up the rich sights and museums. The
city's broad avenues and zipping trams cater to its youthful diversity, while its
serene canals, pastel facades, and gargantuan cathedral possess an arresting
Old World beauty. Visitors can easily explore the city by foot, as miles of flat
paths and numerous lush parks make Strasbourg a pedestrian's dream.

TRANSPORTATION

Flights: Strasbourg-Entzheim International Airport, route de Strasbourg (☎03 88 64
67 67; www.strasbourg.aeroport.fr), 15km from Strasbourg. **Air France,** 7 rue du Marché (☎08 20 82 08 20), and other carriers fly to **London, Lyon,** and **Paris.** Allô CTS
(☎03 88 77 70 70) **shuttle buses** run from the airport to the Strasbourg tram stop
(Baggarsee) on Line A, a 20min. tram ride from the *centre-ville* (12min.; 3 per hr. from
the airport 5:45am-10:45pm, to the airport 5am-10:30pm; €5.20, round-trip €9.70).

Trains: Pl. de la Gare. Info office open daily 4am-1:15am. Ticket office open M-Sa
5:45am-8:50pm, Su 7am-9:10pm. To: **Paris** (4hr., 24 per day, €47; TGV 2hr., €63);
Frankfurt, DEU (2-4hr., 13 per day, €52); **LUX** (2-3hr., 10 per day, €33); **Zurich, CHE**
(3hr., 4 per day, €40-47). SNCF buses run to surrounding towns from the station; check
station or tourist office for schedules.

Public Transportation: Compagnie des Transports Strasbourgeois (CTS), 14 rue de
la Gare aux Marchandises (☎03 88 77 70 11, bus and tram info 77 70 70; www.
cts-strasbourg.fr). 5 **tram** lines run 4:30am-12:30am. Find tickets (€1.30, round-trip
€2.50) on board and carnets of 10 (€12) and day passes (€3.50) at the CTS office, 56
rue du Jeu des Enfants. Open M-F 8:30am-6:30pm, Sa 9am-5pm.

Taxis: Taxi 13, 30 av. de la Paix (☎03 88 36 13 13; www.taxi13.fr). Also gives 1hr. city
tours with audio commentary in English, French, or German (1-4 people €33) and service to the Route du Vin. **Alsace Taxi** (☎03 88 22 19 19). 24hr.

Car Rental: Europcar, 16 pl. de la Gare (☎08 25 85 74 79). From €95 per day. 21+.
Open M-F 8am-noon and 2-7pm, Sa 8am-noon and 2-5pm. AmEx/MC/V. **Hertz,** 10 bd.
de Metz (☎03 88 64 69 50). **Avis** (☎08 20 61 17 00), **Budget** (☎03 88 64 69 40),
and **Europcar** (☎08 25 00 41 01) are all at Strasbourg-Entzheim International.

Bike Rental: Vélocation, 10 rue des Bouchers (☎03 88 24 05 61), near the cathedral. €8 per day; €100 check deposit and photocopy of ID. Open July-Aug. M-F
9:30am-12:30pm and 1:30-7pm, Sa-Su 9:30am-noon and 2-7pm; Sept.-June M-F
9:30am-12:30pm and 1-5pm. MC/V. Also at **CIARUS** (see **Accommodations,** p. 390).

ORIENTATION AND PRACTICAL INFORMATION

The *vieille ville* is a lemon-shaped island in the city center bordered to the
north by a large canal and to the south by the **Ill River.** To get there from the train
station, follow rue du Maire-Kuss across Pont Kuss and make a quick right onto

quai Desaix and then an immediate left onto Grande Rue, which becomes rue Gutenberg. Turn right at pl. Gutenberg, then left down rue Mercière toward the cathedral. The **tourist office** is to the left of the cathedral entrance. Continue to quai Desaix, which becomes quai de Turkheim, to reach **La Petite France**, a neighborhood of old Alsatian houses, restaurants, and narrow canals.

Tourist Office: 17 pl. de la Cathédrale (☎03 88 52 28 28; www.ot-strasbourg.fr), near the cathedral. English-speaking staff offers accommodations booking (€2 plus 1st night's deposit) and a free map; better map €1. The **Strasbourg Pass** (€12, ages 4-18 €5.70) quickly pays for itself, covering the costs of a visit to 1 museum, ascent to the cathedral platform, a boat tour of the city, bike rental for ½-day, and a view of the astronomical clock, in addition to other ½-price offers. Open daily 9am-7pm. **Bas-Rhine ADT,** 9 rue du Dome (☎03 88 15 45 88; www.tourisme67.com), has info on the Route du Vin. Open July-Aug. M-F 9:30am-6pm, Sa 9am-noon and 1-5pm; Sept.-June M-F 10am-noon and 2-5pm. Smaller branch at pl. de la Gare (☎03 88 32 51 49).

Tours: The tourist office organizes a variety of tours.

Walking: Tours of the *vieille ville* and the cathedral in French and German. See office for schedule. €6.80, students and ages 12-18 €3.40. English audio tours €5.50.

Petit Train: Leaves from pl. de la Cathédrale. 40min. tour of the *centre-ville*. Daily every 30min. from May to mid-Sept. 9:30am-7pm; from mid-Sept. to mid-Oct. and Apr. 10am-5:30pm; from mid- to late Oct. 10am-5pm. €5.20, ages 4-12 €2.70.

Boat: Departs from behind the landing stage of the Palais Rohan. Daily Apr.-Oct. every 30min. 9:30am-9pm; Nov. and Jan.-Mar. 4 per day 10:30am-4pm; Dec. every 30min. 9:30am-5pm. Evening tours available May-Sept. 9:30, 10pm. €7.60, students and ages 3-18 €3.80. 15% family discount (includes 1 adult and 3 children).

Consulates: US, 15 av. d'Alsace (☎03 88 35 31 04; fax 24 06 95), next to Pont John F. Kennedy. Open M-F 9:30am-noon and 2-5pm. Other nations' consulate information available at tourist office.

English-Language Bookstore: ⬛**The Bookworm,** 3 rue de Pâques (☎03 88 32 26 99), between rue du Faubourg de Saverne and rue du Marais Vert. Selection of fiction, non-fiction, and dictionaries as well as a small selection of secondhand books for €1-2. English-speaking staff always ready to greet the weary traveler with some advice about the city. Open Tu-F 9:30am-6:30pm, Sa 10am-6pm. AmEx/MC/V.

Youth Centers: CROUS, 1 quai du Maire-Dietrich (☎03 88 21 28 00; www.crous-strasbourg.fr). Info on employment, housing, and study opportunities. Open M-F 9am-noon and 1:30-4pm. **Centre d'Information Jeunesse (CIJ),** 7 rue des Écrivains (☎03 88 37 33 33; www.cija.org). Info on jobs and housing. 1 computer with free Internet access (research only). Open M and W-F 9am-noon and 1-5pm, Tu 1-5pm.

Laundromats: Wash'n Dry, 15 rue des Veaux. Wash €7 per 16kg, dry €2 per 30min. Open daily 7am-9pm. **Lavomatique,** 29 Grande Rue. Wash €4 per 8kg. Open daily 7:30am-8pm.

Police: 11 rue de la Nuée Bleue (☎03 88 15 37 17). **Police Nationale,** 34 route de l'Hôpital (☎03 90 23 17 17).

Pharmacy: Association SOS Pharmacie (☎03 88 61 03 83). 24hr.

Hospital: Hôpital Civil de Strasbourg, 1 pl. de l'Hôpital (☎03 88 11 67 68), south of the *vieille ville* across the canal.

Internet Access: L'Utopie, 21-23 rue du Fossée des Tanneurs (☎03 88 23 89 21). €1 per 15min., €3 per 1hr. Wi-Fi available. Open M-Sa 6:30am-11:30pm, Su 8am-10pm. **Net.sur.cour,** 18 quai des Pêcheurs (☎03 88 35 66 76). €1 per 30min., €2.20 per hr. Wi-Fi available. Open M-Sa 9:30am-8:30pm, Su 1:30-7:30pm.

Post Office: 5 av. de la Marseillaise (☎03 88 52 35 50). Open M-F 8am-7pm, Sa 8am-noon. Also at cathedral (open M-F 8am-6:30pm, Sa 9am-5pm), 1 rue de la Fonderie (open M-F

ALSACE, LORRAINE, AND FRANCHE COMTÉ

Strasbourg

ACCOMMODATIONS
A.J. Réné Cassin (HI), 13
Camping la Montagne Verte, 14
CIARUS, 1
Hôtel le Grillon, 3

FOOD
Au Poitron, 12
Au Pont St-Martin, 8
Le Hanneton (Chez Denis), 10
El Pimiento, 4
Le Troc'afé, 2

NIGHTLIFE AND ENTERTAINMENT
Les Brasseurs, 6
Bar Exils, 9
Elastic Bar, 11
Le Gayot, 5

8am-6:30pm, Sa 8:30am-noon), and 1 pl. de la Gare (open M-F 8:30am-6:30pm, Sa 8:30am-noon). **ATM** and **currency exchange. Postal Code:** 67000.

ACCOMMODATIONS AND CAMPING

Centre International d'Accueil de Strasbourg (CIARUS), 7 rue Finkmatt (☎03 88 15 27 88; www.ciarus.com), 15min. from the train station. From the train station, take rue du Maire-Kuss to the canal, turn left, and follow quai St-Jean. Turn left on rue Finkmatt; the hotel will be on your left. Big, bright hostel houses international boarders of all ages. Small, tidy rooms have metallic bunks, ample shelving, and baths. TV room, ping-pong, cafeteria, and bar. Disco night W. Make-your-own-*crêpes* night Th. Breakfast included; lunch and dinner €5-7. Free Wi-Fi. Wheelchair-accessible. Reception 24hr. Check-in 3:30pm. Check-out 9am. Reservations recommended. 6- to 8-bed dorms €21, during parliamentary sessions €24; 3- to 4-bed dorms €25/28; 2-bed dorms €28/31. Singles €44/47; family rooms €21/24 per person. MC/V. ❶

Hôtel le Grillon, 2 rue Thiergarten (☎03 88 32 71 88; www.grillon.com), 1 block from the train station. Dark wood trimmings and cheerful pink walls. Large, clean hallway bathrooms, an Internet cafe (€1 per 15min.), and a hip bar. TV in all but the cheapest rooms. Breakfast €7.50. Reception 24hr. Check-out noon. Reservations recommended. Singles €33, with shower €43-58; doubles €40/50-65. Extra bed €13. MC/V. ❷

Auberge de Jeunesse René Cassin (HI), 9 rue de l'Auberge de Jeunesse (☎03 88 30 26 46; fax 30 35 16), 2km from the train station. Take bus #2 (dir.: Campus d'Illkirch) to Auberge de Jeunesse. Clean rooms. Quiet, beautiful canal-side setting. TV room, kitchen, and bar. Breakfast included. Internet €1.20 per 15min. Wi-Fi €5 per day. Reception 7am-noon, 1-7:30pm, 8:30-11pm. Code access after 1am. Open Feb.-Dec. 3- to 6-bed dorms €19; singles €34; doubles €47. MC/V. ❶

Camping la Montagne Verte, 2 rue Robert Forrer (☎03 88 30 25 46; www.aquadis-loisirs.com), near the René Cassin hostel. Take bus #2 (dir.: Campus d'Illkirch) to Nid de Cigognes. Turn right onto rue du Schokeloch and right again onto rue Robert Forrer. Spacious riverside campground with minimal privacy; sites are divided by a small white fence or not at all. Tennis and basketball courts, and bar. Laundry. Reception 8:30am-9:30pm. Closed to cars after 10pm. Open from mid-Mar. to Oct. and from late Nov. to early Jan. €3.90 per person, under 10 €2; sites €5.60. Electricity €4.30. MC/V. ❶

> **TIP**
>
> **PARLIAMENTARY, MY DEAR WATSON.** The European Parliament brings hordes of visitors to Strasbourg—especially when it is in session—and hotel prices increase accordingly. Likewise, room prices can decrease as much as €10 per night when the politicians are out of town. Go to www.europarl.europa.eu to find the schedule of sessions.

FOOD

Local restaurants are known for *choucroute garnie* (sauerkraut with meats), but you can find delicious sausages at stands throughout the city. Other specialties include the ubiquitous *tarte flambée* (thin-crust pizza with a cream-sauce base; €5-8) and a vast array of wines from the **Route du Vin.** The streets around the cathedral are filled with reasonably priced restaurants, while cafes line **rue du Vieux Seigle** and **rue du Vieux Marché aux Grains.** Less touristy restaurants can be found around **rue de la Krutenau.** In **La Petite France,** you'll find small *winstubs*—classic (and somewhat pricey) Alsatian taverns with a German flavor, characterized by timber exteriors, checkered tablecloths, and menus full of countless combinations of carbohydrates, melted cheese, and salted meats. Cheap kebab and sandwich joints cluster around the train station and on **Grande Rue.** Markets are held at **boulevard de la Marne, place de Bordeaux** (both open Tu and Sa 7am-1pm), and **place Broglie** (open W and F 7am-6pm). Supermarkets are scattered around the *vieille ville;* an **ATAC** is at 47 rue des Grandes Arcades, off pl. Kléber. (☎03 88 32 51 53. Open M-Sa 8:30am-8:30pm. MC/V.)

◪ **Le Hanneton (Chez Denis),** 5 rue Ste-Madeleine (☎03 88 36 93 76). Pieffel Denis, the attentive host and chef at this *winstub,* prepares Alsatian favorites. Dozens of Alsatian *sorcières* (witch dolls) hang overhead. Traditional *choucroute à l'alsacienne* (€15) is a heaping pile of sauerkraut with 5 meaty toppings. *Tartes flambées* €6.50-7.50. Open Tu 7-11pm, W-Su noon-2pm and 7-11pm. Reservations recommended. MC/V. ❸

◪ **El Pimiento,** 52 rue du Jeu des Enfants (☎03 88 21 94 52), by pl. Homme de Fer. At this chill, dimly lit tapas restaurant, you may forget that Spain is a country away. *Ensalada de pimientos* (salad with roasted peppers and olive oil) €3. Chorizo sausage €3.50. Tapas €2.30-7. Open M-Sa 11:30am-2:30pm and 6:30pm-1am. MC/V. ❶

Au Potiron, 24 rue Ste-Madeleine (☎03 88 35 49 86). Specializes in vegetarian pasta and pizza (€7.50-11). Even the decorations—pictures of vegetables—are health-conscious. 4-cheese pizza, loaded with gorgonzola, feta, Gouda, and Emmenthal, €9.50. Salads €8-9.50. *Menu du jour* €11. Open M-Sa noon-2pm and 7-10:30pm. MC/V. ❷

Au Pont St-Martin, 13-15 rue des Moulins (☎03 88 32 45 13). Popular, consummately German *winstub,* featured on postcards of La Petite France. Canal-side location. *Tartes flambées* €7-9. Beer from €2.70. Lunch *menu du jour* €9. Dinner *menus* €18. Open M-F 10am-3pm and 6-10:30pm, Sa-Su noon-10:30pm. AmEx/MC/V. ❸

Le Troc'afé, 8 rue Faubourg de Saverne (☎03 88 23 23 29). A popular lunch spot that's all about atmosphere. Filled with enormous funky paintings, American movie posters in French translation, and old advertisements. Standard Alsatian fare and pastries. The perfect place to nurse a cup of coffee. Beer from €2. *Plat du jour* €8. Sa brunch noon-2:30pm. Open M-F 7:30am-9:30pm, Sa 11am-8pm. AmEx/MC/V. ❷

🕓 SIGHTS

◪**CATHÉDRALE DE STRASBOURG.** Completed in 1439, this towering 142m structure took 260 years to build. As the story goes, German literary giant Goethe scaled its 332 steps regularly to cure his fear of heights. If you look to the southern transept of the cathedral's prized spire, the **Pilier des Anges,** you'll find a stunning depiction of the Last Judgment. Behind the spire, the massive **Horloge Astronomique** attests to the wizardry of 16th-century Swiss clockmakers. At 12:30pm, tiny apostles march out of the face, and a rooster greets St-Pierre. Beware of pickpockets around and within the cathedral. (☎03 88 21 43 34. Cathedral open M-Sa 7-11:40am and 12:40-7pm, Su 12:45-6pm. Info desk open M-F 9:45-11:45am and 2-5pm. Tower open July-Aug. 9am-7:15pm; Sept. and Apr.-June 9am-6pm; Oct. and Mar. 9am-5:30pm; Nov.-Feb. 9am-4:30pm. Tours in French July-Aug. M-F 3pm. Tickets available 9-11:30am and 11:45am-12:25pm. Arrive 30min. early July-Aug. Tickets to horloge film and performance available at 11:35am, film noon. Free film on cathedral every 11min. in southern wing. Tower €4.60, students and ages 5-18 €2.30. Tours €3. Horloge film €2, under 18 €1.50.)*

◪**LA PETITE FRANCE.** The old tanners' district, in the southwest corner of the *centre-ville,* is characterized by steep-roofed houses with carved, pastel-colored facades—all surrounded by waterways. Locals flock to this neighborhood to chat in sidewalk cafes over the sounds of accordion music and the gurgling of the river. A host of restaurants and *winstubs* make this a perfect—though sometimes pricey—dining spot and an ideal location for a date. The area is bordered by "covered bridges," which have kept their name although they haven't had roofs since the 18th century. Four towers and the remains

GIVING BACK

SHOPPING FOR A CAUSE

Thanks to the Association des Aveugles et Handicapés Visuels d'Alsace et de Lorraine, shoppers can load up on souvenirs and contribute to a worthy cause at the same time. Based in Strasbourg, the association has created specialty shops that carry regional products. All of the shops' proceeds go directly to the blind community, providing funds for a community home, a sports and leisure center, and the increased accessibility of guide dogs. The stores also create employment opportunities for the blind; many of the association members either work directly in the stores or help create the products that they sell.

The stores' most popular items are traditional woven baskets (€10-25), which are ideal for blending in with the locals as you browse Alsace's plentiful outdoor markets. If baskets are too Dorothy for your style, the shops also contain a huge variety of other regional goods, including wine, beer, candy, soaps, and packets of perfumed flowers. The *lait de rose* shower gel smells unbelievably divine and helps the memory of France linger long after that last *tarte flambée* has been devoured.

27 rue de la 1ère Armée (☎03 88 36 03 77; www.aveugles-alsace-lorraine.asso.fr). Open Tu-F 10am-noon and 2-6pm, Sa 10am-noon. MC/V.

of the 14th-century city walls also surround the district, while farther west the **Vauban dam** offers a terrace with a view. *(Open daily 9am-7:30pm.)*

PALAIS ROHAN. This magnificent 18th-century building houses three small museums. The **Musée des Arts Décoratifs,** once a residence for cardinals, was looted during the Revolution, then refurbished for Napoleon in 1805. The gold-encrusted ceilings and expanses of marble are stunning, but the highlight of the building is the demure library, where majestic portraits and staid marble busts overlook bookshelves along the hall's perimeter. The museum offers a free informative English guidebook. The impressively comprehensive **Musée Archéologique** illustrates the history of Alsace from 600,000 BC to AD 800 with old tools, relics, and an unsettling number of skeletons. It also displays samples from Alsace's collection—the largest in the world—of early and middle Neolithic tombs. Upstairs, the **Musée des Beaux-Arts** displays a solid art collection from the 14th to the 19th centuries, including works by Botticelli, El Greco, Giotto, Goya, Raphael, Rubens, and Van Dyck. *(2 pl. du Château. ☎03 88 52 50 00. Open M and W-Su 10am-6pm. Each museum €6, students €3; 1st Su of month free.)*

MUSÉE D'ART MODERNE ET CONTEMPORAIN. Opened in 1998, Adrien Fainsilber's glass and steel behemoth, which resembles a smaller version of Paris's Centre Pompidou, holds a collection of late-19th- and 20th-century paintings, including Impressionist, Surrealist, and Cubist works. Highlights include gems by Dufy, Ernst, Gauguin, Kandinsky, Monet, and Picasso. The collection is distinctive for its creative arrangement; in a ground-floor foyer, a version of Rodin's stoic *Thinker* sits among violently colorful post-millennium paintings. *(1 pl. Hans Jean Arp. ☎03 88 23 31 31. Open Tu-W and F-Sa 11am-7pm, Th noon-10pm, Su 10am-6pm. €5, students €2.50, under 18 free; 1st Su of month free.)*

L'ORANGERIE. Strasbourg's most spectacular park, L'Orangerie was designed by the famed Le Nôtre in 1692 after he polished up Versailles. The park seems to have something for everyone: promenades, gardens, and pagodas are perfect for a leisurely stroll or a brisk jog, while a zoo and a miniature farm filled with traditional Alsatian storks provide diversions for children. L'Orangerie also boasts go-carts, a pond with waterfalls, and Le Nôtre's original concrete-lined skateboard park. *(Take bus #6, dir.: Pl. des Sports, from pl. des Halles to L'Orangerie.)*

OTHER SIGHTS. The **Palais de l'Europe** houses the Council of Europe and the European Parliament in a spectacular modern complex off av. de l'Europe, at the northwest edge of L'Orangerie. Across the canal from the Council, the **Human Rights Building,** designed by Richard Rogers in 1995, houses the European Court of Human Rights. Its shape is meant to simulate a ship following the curve of the river, while the building's facade is intended to evoke the scales of justice. *(The Council of Europe gives tours by reservation. ☎03 88 41 20 29.)* The **Musée Alsacien,** inside a quintessentially Alsatian half-timbered house, showcases everyday life in Alsace since the Middle Ages. A model of a small synagogue showcases Jewish history in the area. *(23-25 quai St-Nicolas. ☎03 88 52 50 01. Open M and W-Su July-Sept. 10am-6pm; Oct.-June noon-6pm. €4, students €2, under 18 free; 1st Su of the month free.)* The **Kronenbourg Brewery,** though no longer functional, gives visitors a taste of Germany, with tours including a short film in English, French, or German. You'll get a look at the different stages of brewing and a *dégustation. (68 route d'Oberhausbergen. Take tram to Ducs d'Alsace. ☎03 88 27 41 59; www.brasseries-kronenbourg.com. Open May-Sept. and Dec. M-Sa; Oct.-Nov. and Jan.-June M-F; hours vary. By reservation only. €2.50.)* **Heineken** offers free tours of its brewery in English, French, and German, but only for groups with advance reservations. *(4 rue St-Charles, Schiltigheim. ☎03 88 19 57 55. Call to schedule M-F 8am-noon and 1:30-4:30pm.)*

🎵 🎇 ENTERTAINMENT AND FESTIVALS

The **Orchestre Philharmonique de Strasbourg** performs at the Palais de la Musique et des Congrès, behind pl. de Bordeaux. (☎03 88 37 67 67; www.strasbourg-meeting.com. Performances Oct.-June. Student tickets ½-price or less.) The **Théâtre National de Strasbourg,** 1 av. de la Marseillaise, puts on performances from September to June. (☎03 88 24 88 24; www.tns.fr. €16-25, students €14-16. MC/V.) The **Opéra du Rhin,** 19 pl. Broglie, features opera and ballet in its 19th-century hall. (☎03 88 75 48 00. Tickets €11-75, students under 26 ½-price; rush tickets from €10/5.50.) Summer in Strasbourg centers on **place de la Cathédrale,** which becomes a stage every afternoon and evening for performers, including a troupe of musicians, flame-eaters, acrobats, and mimes. The cathedral hosts organ concerts throughout the summer. (Free concerts June-Sept. Su 5:30pm. Organ recitals F 8:30pm. €10, students €5.) A nightly *son et lumière* (sound and light show) in July and August brings the austere facade of the cathedral to life with dazzling colors, accompanied by music (10:30pm-1am).

> **Festival de Musique de Strasbourg,** 2 weeks in June. Attracts Europe's best classical musicians. For more info on the Festival de Musique and the Festival de Jazz (below), contact Wolf Musique, 24 rue de la Mésange (☎03 88 36 30 48; www.jazzdor.com).
>
> **Festival de Jazz,** 1st 2 weeks of July. Draws big names of the jazz world. Tickets €26-65; student tickets available at reduced prices.
>
> **Street Performance Festival,** 9 days in mid-Aug. Clowns, musicians, and acrobats bombard Strasbourg's squares. Special performances in pl. du Marché aux Poissons and pl. des Tripiers nightly 5:30, 9pm; call the tourist office for details.
>
> **Musica** (☎03 88 23 47 23; www.festival-musica.org), from mid-Sept. to early Oct. Contemporary music festival hosts an array of popular concerts, operas, and films.

🎉 NIGHTLIFE

Strasbourg specializes in friendly bars rather than throbbing clubs. **Place Kléber** attracts a student scene, while **rue des Frères** and the tiny **place du Marché Gayot** fill up quickly after 10pm with a diverse, slightly older crowd. The area between **place d'Austerlitz** and **place de Zurich,** across the canal from the *vieille ville,* is lively until the wee hours. It is best to visit these areas in groups at night.

Bar Exils, 28 rue de l'Ail (☎03 88 32 52 70), near the cathedral. Casually hip bar stays crowded until closing. Loud music fills the main room, while the small outdoor terrace and back billiards room offer a more subdued scene. Wi-Fi available. Over 40 different beers from €2; after 10pm €2.50. Open M-F noon-4am, Sa-Su 2pm-4am. MC/V.

Les Brasseurs, 22 rue des Veaux (☎03 88 36 12 13; www.au-brasseur-strasbourg. com). Trendy microbrewery serves 4 different homebrews (on tap from €2, after 9:30pm €2.40; bottles from €4.10) and *tartes flambées* (€4.90-8.10) in a dark red and wood interior. Free concerts on weekend nights (F-Sa 9:30pm). Piano bar W. Happy hour 5-6:30pm. Open daily 11:30am-1am; service ends 12:30am. MC/V.

Elastic Bar, 27 rue des Orphelins (☎03 88 36 11 10). Takes grunge to heart with graffiti decor. Among the city's most energetic scenes on weekend nights. Regulars shout over loud music. Beer from €2.60. Open M-W 5:30pm-3am, Th-Sa 5:30pm-4am. MC/V.

Le Gayot, 18 rue des Frères (☎03 88 36 31 88). Expansive terrace opens onto the lively pl. Marché Gayot and fills up early with 30-somethings. Mojitos €8.50. Beer €3.10. Mixed drinks from €6.10. Open June-Aug. M-F noon-12:30am, Sa-Su noon-1am; Sept.-May M-Sa noon-1am. MC/V.

ROUTE DU VIN (WINE ROUTE)

The vineyards of Alsace flourish in a 150km strip called the Route du Vin (root doo vehn), which runs along the foothills of the Vosges Mountains. The Romans were the first to ferment Alsatian grapes, but the Alsatians have perfected the process, now selling over 150 million bottles every year. Hordes of wine-loving and largely middle-aged tourists are drawn to the medieval villages along the route by gorgeous houses and wineries that offer free *dégustations*. With over 60 wine-producing towns, the route offers an authentic Alsatian experience. Yet each town has a different attraction; some—such as Kaysersberg—combine wine-sipping with small-town charm, while others—like Barr—allow for grittier treks through massive vineyards.

Consider staying in Colmar (p. 400) or Sélestat (p. 397)—larger towns that anchor the southern route—and daytripping to the smaller, pricier towns. Buses run frequently from Colmar to surrounding towns, but transportation to northern towns is more difficult. You can explore the route by car if you're willing to pay the steep rental fees in Strasbourg or Colmar. Biking, especially from Colmar, requires the stamina to endure lengthy, often hilly journeys, but the trails are well marked. Trains connect Sélestat, Molsheim, Barr, Colmar, and Mulhouse. The absence of good sidewalks makes walking unpleasant.

The best source of info on regional *caves* is the **Centre d'Information du Vin d'Alsace,** 12 av. de la Foire aux Vins, at the Maison du Vin d'Alsace in Colmar. (☎03 89 20 16 20; fax 20 16 30. Open M-F 9am-noon and 2-5pm.) Tourist offices in Strasbourg (p. 388) or along the route dispense helpful advice and distribute the detailed *Alsace Wine Route* brochure.

KAYSERSBERG ☎03 89

If you only have time for one town on the route, make it Kaysersberg (ky-suhrss-burg). Relatively untouristed and tucked between green mountains, the town offers a complete immersion into rustic tranquility.

TRANSPORTATION AND PRACTICAL INFORMATION. Kaysersberg has no train station, but Kunegel **buses** (☎03 89 24 65 65; www.l-k.fr) run to **Colmar** (35min.; July-Aug. 4-6 per day, Sept.-June 8 per day; €3.15). The stop in

Colmar is in front of the train station; some buses also stop at the Unterlinden Théâtre. The **tourist office,** 39 rue du Général de Gaulle, is in the Hôtel de Ville, down the street from the Porte Haute stop. (☎03 89 78 22 78; www.kaysersberg.com. Open from mid-June to mid-Sept. M-Sa 9am-12:30pm and 2-6pm, Su 10am-12:30pm; from mid-Sept. to mid-June M-Sa 9:30am-noon and 2-5:30pm. Free brochures in English, French, and German. Guided **tours** in French July-Aug. M and F 9pm. €5, under 16 free. Free **Internet** for up to 20min.)

◘ **FOOD.** Compared to the other towns on the route, Kaysersberg offers few wine *caves,* though the restaurants that line **rue du Général de Gaulle** and **rue des Forgerons** serve local bacchanalian specialties. Nearly every eatery serves the popular *tarte flambée.* Head to **Bretzel Chaud du Moulin ❶,** 60 pl. du Premier RCA for the locally cherished *kougelhopf* (€2-8), a sweet pastry that looks like an upside-down muffin. (☎03 80 47 39 23. Open Tu and Th-Su 10am-7pm.)

◪ ⚜ **SIGHTS AND FESTIVALS.** The ruined **château** on the hill is a 10min. climb from the tourist office. Its open peak provides stunning views of the surrounding vineyards and Kaysersberg's beige and pink facades. Overgrown vines create a romantic feel on the stony path up the hill, but steer clear of the poison ivy that rears its itchy head on parts of the walk. Before heading down to the central **Hôtel de Ville,** stop in at the **Musée Albert Schweitzer,** 126 rue du Général de Gaulle, located across the street from the Porte Haute bus stop. This tiny museum contains memorabilia tracing the life and achievements of the late Dr. Schweitzer—winner of the 1952 Nobel Peace Prize. The three rooms of the museum don't take more than a few minutes to see, but the cost is justified; all museum proceeds benefit a hospital in Lambaréné. (☎03 89 47 36 55. Open from Apr. to mid-Nov. daily 9am-noon and 2-6pm. €2, under 18 €1.) The glassblowing studio **Verrerie d'Art de Kaysersberg,** 30 rue du Général de Gaulle, offers free viewings of its workshops and explanations of its traditional glass-blowing methods. (☎03 89 47 14 97. Open Feb.-Dec. Tu-W and F-Sa 10am-12:30pm and 2-6pm, Th 10am-12:30pm. Free brochures in English.) Christmas season brings Kaysersberg's greatest *fête,* **Préludes de Noël,** with painting exhibitions, markets, and concerts for four weekends leading up to the big day (11am-8pm).

RIQUEWIHR   ☎**03 89**

One of the most popular villages along the route is the 16th-century village of Riquewihr (rick-wuhrr). The town's *vieille ville* is simple to navigate, centralized along rue du Général de Gaulle. Old-fashioned cobblestone streets lend Riquewihr a sense of calm, which seems to persist even as summer tourists swarm in. Almost every shop sells macaroons—a favorite local pastry for good reason. If you have a sweet tooth, be sure to get a taste of the local flavor.

◪⁊ **TRANSPORTATION AND PRACTICAL INFORMATION.** Pauli Autocars (☎03 89 78 11 78; www.pauli.fr) runs **buses** from the train station in Colmar (30min.; Sept.-June 9 per day, July-Aug. 5 per day; €3.15). To reach the **tourist office,** 2 rue de la Première Armée, take the bus to Poste and walk through the gate of the Hôtel de Ville and up the hill; the tourist office is on the left and has free maps. The office also gives walking **tours** of the *vieille ville* in French. (☎03 89 49 08 40; www.ribeauville-riquewihr.com. Tours from mid-July to Aug. M 6pm, F-Sa 9:30pm. Office open May-Sept. and Dec. M and W-Sa 9:30am-noon and 2-6pm, Tu 10am-noon and 2-6pm, Su 10am-1pm; Oct. and Apr. M and W-Sa 9:30am-noon and 2-6pm, Tu 10am-noon and 2-6pm; Nov. and Jan.-Mar. M-F 10am-noon and 2-5pm, every other Sa 10am-noon and 2-5pm.)

⚑ CAMPING. Pitch a tent at the four-star **Camping Intercommunal ❶**, 1.5km from the *centre-ville*. (☎03 89 47 90 08; campingriquewihr@wanadoo.fr. Open Mar.-Dec. Reception July-Aug. 8:30am-noon and 1-9pm; Sept.-Dec. and Apr.-June 8:30am-noon and 3:30-7pm. Apr.-Oct. €3.60 per adult, children €1.70; Nov.-Dec. €3.30/1.60. Sites €4. Electricity €3.50-4. Cash only.)

◉ ✿ SIGHTS AND FESTIVALS. The town's best sight is the ▧**Tour des Voleurs** (Tower of Thieves), rue des Juifs, which served as a prison until the 18th century. The eerily enthralling torture chamber still holds its signature weapon: a rope-and-pulley estrapade that would hang prisoners by their wrists until their arms were disjointed. An audio tour in the chamber gives all the gruesome details. The last room of the museum, sponsored by several anti-torture political groups, alerts visitors to the continuing perils of torture in the modern world. (Open Apr.-Nov. daily 10:15am-12:30pm and 2-6:30pm. €2.50, under 10 free.) Riquewihr also has a **petit train** that tours the city walls and vineyards, leaving from the town hall. (☎03 89 73 74 24. Commentary in Danish, Dutch, English, French, German, Italian, Japanese, and Spanish. 30min.; every hr. 10am-7pm; €6, under 18 €4.) Markets take place every Friday on **rue des Trois Églises** (open 8am-noon). In nearby Ribeauvillé, the **Foire aux Vins** (Wine Fair) comes to town at the end of July. On the first Sunday of September, the streets of Riquewihr are filled with classic Alsatian songs at the **Minstrel's Festival.**

BARR ☎ 03 88

Of the Route du Vin towns, Barr (bahrr), on the slopes of Mont Ste-Odile, seems most invested in its grapes: 2min. from the *centre-ville*, you can sip a glass of white wine while strolling among the rows of vines where its grapes were nourished. With fewer crowds and touristy gift shops than other towns on the route, Barr appears peacefully untouched.

To reach *caves* in the *vieille ville*, turn onto rue du Docteur Sultzer from pl. de l'Hôtel de Ville. Behind you sits the austere **Église Protestante,** which serves as the starting point for the ▧**sentier viticole** (vineyard trail). The highlight of any trip to Barr, this path winds 2km through fields of glistening grapes. Walk the trail on your own or join a **tour** led by local viticulturists (call the tourist office). The tourist office leads free tours of Barr's wine caves, but most *maisons* expect you to buy something after the complimentary *dégustation*. (☎03 88 08 52 50. Tours in French July-Aug. Th 4pm. Call ahead. Free.) The local *vigniers* pull out their best bottles for the **Foire aux Vins,** or wine fair, in the second week of July, while the **Fête des Vendanges** during the first weekend in October brings music, markets, and—of course—more wine.

Trains to Barr run from Sélestat (25min., 10 per day, €3.20) and Strasbourg (50min., 14 per day, €6). Buy a return-trip ticket before you leave; the Barr station (open M-F 5:15am-8:10pm) does not sell tickets. The **tourist office,** pl. de l'Hôtel de Ville, offers a city guide, available in French and English. From the train station, turn right on rue de la Gare and left on av. des Vosges. Continue past the roundabout, bear left, and avoid what becomes rue de l'Hôpital de la Gare. Continue for several blocks onto rue St-Marc. Take a right, veer left through pl. du Marché aux Pommes de Terre, and walk straight until the end of rue des Boulangers. Turn right onto rue des Bouchers; the tourist office is on the left. (☎03 88 08 66 65; www.pays-de-barr.com. Open July-Aug. M-Sa 9am-12:30pm and 2-6pm, Su 10am-noon and 2-6pm; Sept.-Oct. and Apr.-June M-Sa 9am-noon and 2-6pm, Su 2-6pm; Nov.-Mar. M-Sa 9am-noon and 2-6pm.)

ALSACE, LORRAINE, AND FRANCHE COMTÉ

SÉLESTAT ☎ **03 88**

Halfway between Colmar and Strasbourg, Sélestat (say-leh-stah; pop. 17,500) lacks the crowds of other stops along the route. Once part of the Holy Roman Empire and a center of Renaissance humanism, Sélestat is a relaxed hamlet with unique museums and stunning churches. The town has an infectious sense of tradition: every Tuesday morning since 1435, thousands of Alsatians have flooded the streets for Sélestat's weekly food and clothing market. Visitors to the tiny town can cover its gems in a weekend; those looking for affordable lodgings or exciting nightlife should explore Sélestat as a daytrip.

▐ TRANSPORTATION

Trains: Pl. de la Gare. Ticket office open M 6am-7pm, Tu-F 7am-7pm, Sa 8:30am-5pm, Su 11:20am-6:50pm. To **Colmar** (15min., 38 per day, €4), **Paris** (3hr., 15 per day, €95), and **Strasbourg** (30min., 54 per day, €7.10).

Buses: Run from the station to a number of surrounding towns. Tourist office provides a complete guide of bus companies and schedules.

Taxis: Several companies (☎03 88 92 05 49, 92 10 00, or 08 94 46) with similar fares run 24hr. Useful for daytrips to Haut Koenigsbourg.

Bike Rental: At the tourist office (below). €13 per day, €55 per week; €150 deposit.

▐ PRACTICAL INFORMATION

Tourist Office: Bd. du Général Leclerc (☎03 88 58 87 20; www.selestat-tourisme.com), in the Commanderie St-Jean, close to the *centre-ville*. From the train station, walk straight on av. de la Gare and through pl. du Général de Gaulle to av. de la Liberté. Turn left onto bd. du Maréchal Foch, which becomes bd. du Général Leclerc after pl. Schaal. The office is a few blocks down on the left. Staff doles out expert advice and guides in English, French, and German as well as a free map (more detailed map €1). Open July-Aug. M-F 9:30am-12:30pm and 1:30-6:30pm, Sa 9am-12:30pm and 2-5pm, Su 10:30am-3pm; Sept.-June M-Tu and Th-F 9am-noon and 2-5:45pm, W 9:30am-noon and 2-6pm, Sa 9am-noon and 2-5pm; later hours during festivals.

Tours: Themed French tours from the tourist office July-Aug. M-Th and Su. €5-7.

Police: Bd. du Général Leclerc (☎03 88 92 10 17). Call for the **pharmacie de garde.**

Hospital: 23 av. Pasteur (☎03 88 57 55 55), behind the train station.

Internet Access: ▧**Bazook'Kafé**, 3 rue Ste-Foy (☎03 90 57 20 66, www.bazook.net). Flatscreen monitors, wireless keyboards, and large bowl chairs create a sleek feel. €1.50 per 30min. Open daily 7am-1:30am.

Post Office: 7 rue de la Poste (☎03 88 58 80 10), near the Hôtel de Ville. **ATM.** Open M-F 8am-noon and 1:30-6pm, Sa 8am-noon. **Postal Code:** 67600.

▐ ▐ ACCOMMODATIONS AND CAMPING

Hôtel de l'Ill, 13 rue des Bateliers (☎03 88 92 91 09), on a residential street in the *vieille ville*. From the train station, take av. de la Gare and turn right on av. de Gaulle. Go halfway around pl. du Général de Gaulle, which becomes av. de la Liberté, rue du 4ème Zouaves, and finally rue du Président Poincaré. Make a left onto rue de l'Hôpital and follow it to pl. du Marché aux Choux; rue des Bateliers is on the right. 15 cheerful pastel rooms, each with bath and TV. Breakfast €5. Reception 7am-9pm. Check-out 10am. Singles €33; doubles €42; triples €50; quads €60. AmEx/MC/V. ❷

Auberge des Alliés, 39 rue des Chevaliers (☎03 88 92 09 34; www.aubergedesallies. com). From the train station, follow the directions for the Hôtel de l'Ill until rue du Président Poincaré. Take a left on rue des Chevaliers; the hotel is 2 blocks down on the left. Color-coordinated rooms above a restaurant in the *vieille ville*. All rooms have bath and TVs. Breakfast €8. *Menu du jour* €14. Free Wi-Fi. Reception 7am-10pm. Reservations recommended. Singles €48-50; doubles €55-65. Extra bed €5. AmEx/MC/V. ❹

Camping Les Cigognes, rue de la 1ère DFL (☎03 88 92 03 98), on the southern edge of the *vieille ville*. Near tennis courts, parks, and a lake. Located on a grassy field, but has a distinctly suburban feel. Wheelchair-accessible. Reception July-Aug. 8:30-11am and 2:30-8:30pm; Sept. and Apr.-June 9-11am and 3-7pm. Open Apr.-Sept. July-Aug. €3.60 per adult; under 10 €2.90; sites €11. Sept. and Apr.-June €1.80 per adult; under 10 €1.50; sites €8.90. Electricity included. Cash only. ❶

🍴 FOOD

Boulangeries and restaurants line **rue des Chevaliers** and **rue des Clefs.** A market fills the *centre-ville* with breads, meats, and produce as well as clothing, books, and toys. (Open Tu 8am-noon.) Another market for regional specialties fills **place Albert Ehm** (Sa morning), and a third fills the **arsenal Saint-Hilaire,** rue des Chevaliers, with produce and goods crafted by local artisans (Sa morning).

▨ **À L'Improviste,** 13 bd. du Général Leclerc (☎03 89 82 81 81). Creative cuisine in an exotic dining room. From the *salade d'avocat au poulet caramalisée* (avocado and chicken salad; small €7, meal €13) to the *magret de canard aux framboises* (duck breast with raspberries; €16), each original dish bursts with fresh flavor. Open M-Tu 11:45am-2pm, W-Sa 11:45am-2pm and 7-10pm. MC/V. ❸

JP Kamm, 15 rue des Clefs (☎03 88 92 11 04). A local favorite, with a dazzling selection of pastries and ice cream. Pizzas and quiches €3.70-5.40. Salads from €4.50. Ice cream from €4.60, to go from €2.30. Open Tu and Th-F 8am-7pm, W 8:30am-7pm, Sa 8am-6pm, Su 8am-1pm. Terrace service Tu-F until 6:30pm, Sa until 5:30pm. MC/V. ❶

Melina Crêperie, 14 rue de la Grande Boucherie (☎03 88 58 48 36). Crispy *galettes* and plate-size *crêpes* (€2.50-7.10) overflow with toppings. While the food isn't extraordinary, the nostalgic ambience can't be beat. Sit at a table made out of an old-fashioned sewing machine and enjoy the weekday lunch *menu* (€11). Open Tu 7am-1:30pm and 6:45-9pm, W-Sa noon-1:30pm and 7-9pm, Su 7-9pm. MC/V. ❷

👁 SIGHTS

MAISON DE PAIN. Located in a bread-makers' guild, this museum provides a history of bread-making from 12,500 BC to the present, accompanied by the aromas of fresh loaves baking on the ground floor. Head to the *boulangerie* downstairs to ▨**twist your own pretzels.** (*7 rue du Sel. ☎03 88 58 45 90; www.maisondu-pain-d-alsace.com. Open Jan. and Mar.-Nov. Tu-F 9:30am-12:30pm and 2-6pm, Sa 9am-12:30pm and 2-6pm, Su 9am-12:30pm and 2:30-6pm; Dec. daily 10am-7pm. Closed from Christmas to Feb. €4.60, students €3.80, ages 16-18 €1.60, under 16 free. AmEx/MC/V.*)

BIBLIOTHÈQUE HUMANISTE. According to legend, Sélestat was founded by a giant. His thigh bone—a mammoth tusk, according to skeptics—can be found at the town's library. The austere, one-room collection of books from Sélestat's 15th-century humanistic boom includes only five tables of text but spans from 13th-century annotated translations of Ovid to the 16th-century *Cosmographie Introductio*—the first book to mention America by name. The painstaking calligraphy and detailed ink prints are nothing short of marvelous. (*1 rue de la Bibliothèque; entrance on pl. Gambetta. ☎03 88 58 07 20. Open July-Aug. M and W-F 9am-noon and*

2-6pm, Sa 9am-noon and 2-5pm, Su 2-5pm; Sept.-June M and W-F 9am-noon and 2-6pm, Sa 9am-noon. €3.80, students and seniors €2.30. Audio tour in English €1.65.)

ÉGLISE SAINT-GEORGES. This church houses Max Ingrand's modern 1960s stained-glass windows, which contrast starkly with the choir's detailed 14th-century biblical *tableaux.* Built during the 13th and 14th centuries, the church sits on the site where Charlemagne spent Christmas in AD 775—as Sélestat's proud citizens never fail to mention. *(Rue de l'Église, at the north end of the vieille ville.)*

ÉGLISE SAINTE-FOY. Surrounded by ivy-covered homes, this 12th-century church was constructed by Benedictine monks but later occupied by Jesuits. The church harbors an eclectic set of hard-to-spot artwork: a humble Roman bas-relief near the baptistry, two striking mosaics of the Ganges and Euphrates Rivers on the church floor, and an exterior pair of grimacing lion statues—symbolic of the imperial Hohenstaufen family (a line of Germanic kings). Search for your zodiac sign; all 12 are arranged in the mosaics on the floor. *(Pl. Marché aux Poissons. Informative guides in English, French and German €1.)*

■ ※ NIGHTLIFE AND FESTIVALS

Bars and pubs cluster on **rue des Chevaliers;** for a livelier time, visit the winstubs of **rue du Président Poincaré,** along the southern wall of the *vieille ville.*

Home to the first recorded European Christmas tree, Sélestat decks itself in evergreen for the weeks leading to December 25.

Corso Fleuri (☎03 88 58 85 75; www.corso-selestat.fr), 2nd weekend in Aug. Street musicians play music throughout the day, and stilt-walkers strut through the town at this flower festival. Evening brings fireworks, a public ball, and the festival's most celebrated tradition: a cascade of floats decorated with over 500,000 dahlias. 2009 marks the 80th anniversary of the festival. €6, students €5.50, under 12 free.

Sélest'Art (☎03 88 58 85 75; www.ville-selestat.fr), Sept.-Oct. 2009. A biennial showcase of Alsatian and European art. For more information, contact the Office de la Culture de Sélestat et Sa Région (☎03 88 58 85 75).

◪ DAYTRIPS FROM SÉLESTAT

HAUT KOENIGSBOURG. On a rocky outcropping far above the **plaine d'Alsace,** this highly touristed château is an early 20th-century masterpiece of medieval restoration. When the people of Sélestat presented Germany's Kaiser Wilhelm II with the ruins of a 12th-century Hohenstaufen fortress demolished in the Thirty Years' War, he rebuilt a château on its site. The castle he created delights streams of tourists with its dungeon, collection of medieval weaponry, hunting trophies, ornately carved green furnaces, and splendid architecture. The decadent **Salle des Fêtes** (Party Room) is particularly dazzling. On clear days you can see Strasbourg's famous cathedral in the distance; on cloudier visits you can still gawk at the villages and fields below. *(By car from Sélestat, take A35 to Exit 17 via Kintzheim or 18 via St-Hippolyte, then take N59 via Lièpvre. A taxi is about €20 each way from Sélestat. The Sélestat tourist office runs several buses to and from the château July-Aug. daily; Sept.-Nov. Sa-Su. Inquire at the office for specific departure times; round-trip €4. ☎03 88 58 22 66. Open daily June-Aug. 9:30am-6:30pm; Sept. and Apr.-May 9:30am-5:30pm; Oct. and Mar. 9:45am-5pm; Nov.-Feb. 9:45am-noon and 1-5pm. Dungeon tours July-Aug. 10:45am, noon, 1:45, 3, 4:15pm. Free 1hr. tours of château in French July-Aug. every 20min. 10am-noon and 1:30-5pm; Sept. and Apr.-June 11am, 2:30, 4pm; Oct.-Mar. 11am, 2:30pm. Entrance to the château €7.50, students €5.70, under 18 free. Free English tours available by arrangement. Free brochures in English, French, and German. Medieval musical €7.50, ages 18-25 €4.80, under 18 free; Oct.-Apr. 1st Su of month free. Audio tour €4 with ID deposit.)*

COLMAR ☎03 89

The largest town on the Route du Vin, Colmar (kohl-mahrr; pop. 68,000) possesses a unique charm, despite its reputation as a temporary stop on the way to quainter villages. Hometown of Statue of Liberty sculptor Bartholdi, the city has its own smaller version of Lady Liberty. Though the city is a great base for exploring route towns, Colmar itself hosts a smattering of worthwhile diversions, including a museum that holds the 16th-century *Isenheim Altarpiece*—arguably the most celebrated piece of Alsatian artwork. Otherwise, the peaceful, pastel-painted *vieille ville* makes for a scenic visit.

▐ TRANSPORTATION

Trains: Pl. de la Gare. Open daily 4am-1am. Ticket office open M-F 6am-8pm, Sa 8:30am-7pm, Su 8:30am-8:15pm. To: **Lyon** (4-5hr., 9 per day, €42); **Mulhouse** (20min., 42 per day, €7.10); **Paris** (5hr., 2 per day, €52); **Strasbourg** (30min., 12 per day, €10).

Buses: Companies on pl. de la Gare run lines to small towns on the **Route du Vin** (6am-7pm). Check the tourist office for detailed info.

Public Transportation: Trace, rue des Unterlinden (☎03 89 20 80 80), in a covered *galerie* to the right of the tourist office. Open M-F 7:30am-noon and 1:30-6pm. **Buses** run 6am-8pm. Tickets €1.05, carnet of 10 €7.80. Somnabus provides infrequent night service (M-Sa 9pm-midnight).

Taxis: Pl. de la Gare (☎03 89 27 08 31). 24hr.

Bike Rental: ColmarVélo, pl. Rapp (☎03 89 41 37 90), near av. de la République. €5 per ½-day, €6 per day; €50 and ID deposit. Helmet only upon request. Open daily 8:30am-12:15pm and 1:15-7:15pm. Cash only.

▐ PRACTICAL INFORMATION

Tourist Office: 4 rue des Unterlinden (☎03 89 20 68 92; www.ot-colmar.fr). From the train station, turn left on av. de la République in front of the large fountain and continue while it becomes rue Kléber and curves right through pl. du 18 Novembre into pl. Unterlinden. English-speaking staff has small, free maps. Larger, detailed maps €3.50. Cash-only **currency exchange.** Free, same-night reservations service with a night's deposit. Check window for **pharmacie de garde.** Open July-Aug. M-Sa 9am-7pm, Su 10am-1pm; Sept.-Oct., Dec., and Apr.-June M-Sa 9am-6pm, Su 10am-1pm; Nov. and Jan.-Mar. M-Sa 9am-noon and 2-6pm, Su 10am-1pm.

Tours: Available from the tourist office. Tours in French and German highlight the *vieille ville*, Bartholdi, and Judaic history.

Laundromat: 1 rue Ruest. Wash €3.70 per 5kg. Open daily 7am-9pm.

Police: 2 rue de la Cavelerie (☎03 89 29 47 00).

Hospital: Hôpital Pasteur, 39 av. de la Liberté (☎03 89 12 40 00).

Internet Access: Infr@ Réseau, 12 rue du Rempart (☎03 89 23 98 45). €2 per 30min., €3 per hr. Open July-Aug. M-Sa 10am-11pm, Su 2-11pm; Sept.-June M-Sa 10am-8:30pm, Su 2-8pm. Wi-Fi available at **ISA** (below).

Post Office: 36-38 av. de la République (☎03 89 24 62 62), across from Champs de Mars. **ATM** and **currency exchange.** Open M-F 8am-6:30pm, Sa 8:30am-noon. Branch at 21 rue du Nord. Open M-F 8:30am-6:30pm, Sa 9am-noon. **Postal Code:** 68000.

ACCOMMODATIONS AND CAMPING

Auberge de Jeunesse (HI), 2 rue Pasteur (☎03 89 80 57 39). Take bus #4 (dir.: Europe) to Pont Rouge. On Su, take Bus B (dir.: Ingershiem) to Pont Rouge. Standard dorm accommodations at bargain prices. Breakfast included. Linen €4. Reception Apr.-Sept. 7-10am and 5-10:30pm; Oct.-Mar. 7-10am and 5-11pm. Lockout 10am-5pm. Curfew Apr.-Sept. midnight; Oct.-Mar. 11pm. Reservations recommended June-Aug. Open from mid-Jan. to mid-Dec. 6- to 8-bed dorms €13; singles €17; doubles €26. MC/V. ●

Hôtel Primo, 5 rue des Ancêtres (☎03 89 24 22 24; www.hotel-primo.com). Lets cheap rooms in a wing of a larger building. Rooms are clean but spartan. Breakfast buffet €6. Internet €3 per 30min., €5 per hr. Free Wi-Fi. Reception 24hr. Check-out 11am. Singles €29, with shower and toilet €39-59; doubles €29/59. MC/V. ❷

Hôtel Colbert, 2 rue des 3-Epis (☎03 89 41 31 05), 5min. from the *vieille ville,* Offers large, tidy rooms with A/C and bath. Close proximity to the train station is a mixed blessing; many rooms face loud, frequently used tracks. Breakfast buffet €7. Free Wi-Fi. Reception 24hr. Singles from €39; doubles €59; triples €69. AmEx/MC/V. ❸

Camping de l'Ill, route de Neuf-Brisach (☎03 89 41 15 94; www.camping-alsace.com), 2km from town. Take bus #1 (dir.: Horbourg-Wihr) to Plage de l'Ill. On a river with a beautiful view of the Vosges. Reception 8am-noon and 2-9pm. Open from mid-Mar. to mid-Dec. €3.40 per person, children €2.10; sites €4.15. Electricity €8. MC/V. ●

FOOD

Colmar has a wealth of gastronomic goodies for the thrifty diner. There is a **Monoprix** supermarket at pl. Unterlinden (open M-Sa 8am-8pm; AmEx/MC/V) and markets on **place Saint-Joseph** (Sa morning) and at the intersection between **rue des Écoles** and **rue des Vignerons** (Th morning).

La Pergola et Sa Taverne, 28 rue des Marchands, (☎03 89 41 36 79). Cozy restaurant decorated with pink pigs. Mouthwatering menu features Alsatian specialties, including *roestis* (potato and cheese garnished casserole; from €12), *brouillards* (whipped egg and potato dish; €8.50-17), and *tarte flambée* (€12) with Muenster cheese. Try the *flammizza*—a mix between a pizza and a *tarte flambée* with toppings (€9.80-15). Open M-W and F-Su 11:30am-2:30pm and 6-10pm. MC/V. ❷

Djerba la Douce, 10 rue du Mouton (☎03 89 24 17 12). Huge portions of Tunisian cuisine. Owner performs impromptu drum concerts. Couscous €10-18. Grilled meats €10-17. Open M-Sa noon-2pm and 7-10pm. AmEx/MC/V. ❸

Le Croissant Doré, 28 rue des Marchands (☎03 89 23 70 81). Charming restaurant on a cobbled pedestrian street. Delicious desserts (€2.80-3.10), quiches, and *tartes flambées* (€6.80-8). Teas €2.50. Open Tu-Sa 8:15am-7pm, Su 10am-7pm. Cash only. ❷

ISA, 70 Grand'Rue (☎03 89 23 66 30). Diverse dishes served up in a crisp, modern atmosphere. Soups and salads €6.50-9.50. *Plats* €11-18. Desserts €4-5. Open M-Th 8am-6:30pm, F 8am-10:30pm, Sa 9am-10:30pm. MC/V. ❷

SIGHTS

MUSÉE D'UNTERLINDEN. Converted from a 13th-century Dominican convent, this museum showcases a collection of religious art, including Mathias Grünewald's and Nikolaus Haguenauer's *Isenheim Altarpiece* (1500-16), which depicts scenes from Christ's life in stunning detail. The collection also encompasses a section of tiny 15th-century woodblock prints, a wine cellar, and works by Monet and Picasso, all arranged around a courtyard. (*1 rue des Unterlinden.* ☎03 89 20 15 58; www.musee-unterlinden.com. Open May-Oct. daily 9am-6pm; Nov.-Apr.

M and W-Su 9am-noon and 2-5pm. Last tickets sold 30min. before close. €7, students and ages 12-17 €5, under 12 free. Free audio tours in English, French, and German. MC/V over €14.)

ÉGLISE DES DOMINICAINS. This church's minimalist interior reflects the monks' strong attachment to spiritual austerity. Today, it's a showroom for Martin Schongauer's exquisite 1473 *Virgin in the Rose Bower*, a richly colored panel overwhelmed by an ornate Neo-Gothic frame. *(From the Musée d'Unterlinden, turn right onto quai de la Sinn. Follow it until you reach pl. des Dominicains. Open June-Oct. M-Th and Su 10am-1pm and 3-6pm, F-Sa 10am-6pm; Nov.-Dec. and Apr.-May daily 10am-1pm and 3-6pm. Last tickets sold 15min. before close. €1.50, students €1, ages 14-16 €0.50.)*

MUSÉE BARTHOLDI. This museum honors the noted French sculptor Frédéric Auguste Bartholdi (1834-1904), best known for a 47m statue of his mother entitled *Liberty Enlightening the World*—more often called the Statue of Liberty. The giant plaster ear on display was a full-size practice model of Lady Liberty's left lobe. The miniature lions in another room are scaled-down replicas of the majestic *Lion de Belfort*—Bartholdi's most renowned sculpture still on French soil. *(30 rue Marchands. From Église des Dominicains, take a right and follow the pedestrian road to rue des Serruriers. Take a left on pl. de l'École and an immediate left again onto rue des Marchands. The museum is on the right. ☎ 03 89 41 90 60. Open Mar.-Dec. M and W-Su 10am-noon and 2-6pm. €4.50, students €2.90, under 12 free. Cash only.)*

MUSÉE DU JOUET ET DES PETITS TRAINS. Entering the Museum of Toys and Little Trains, might lead visitors to think that they've stumbled upon Santa's toy factory. Its collection includes a life-size diorama of Cinderella in her horse-drawn carriage, hundreds of Barbie dolls, and a 1000m network of button-activated model trains. Look for the creepily beheaded "Sleeping Pretty" doll. *(40 rue Vauban. ☎ 03 89 41 93 10; www.museejouet.com. Open July-Aug. daily 10am-7pm; Sept. daily 10am-noon and 2-6pm; Oct.-Nov. and Jan.-June M and W-Su 10am-noon and 2-6pm; Dec. daily 10am-6pm. Marionette shows 11am, 3, 4, 5pm. €4.50, students and ages 8-18 €3.50.)*

OTHER SIGHTS. Painted Easter-egg colors, Colmar's traditional **Alsatian houses** cluster in the **quartier des Tanneurs** and **la petite Venise** (little Venice). On rue des Têtes, 105 grotesque stone heads stare out from the **Maison des Têtes**, a must-see for its sheer absurdity. It also contains an elegant but expensive restaurant. The 13th- to 14th-century **Collégiale Saint-Martin**, pl. de la Cathédrale, boasts German stained glass and a multi-hued exterior that dazzles in the sunlight.

◪ NIGHTLIFE

Colmar can be sleepy at night; most clubs are a cab ride away. Traditional pubs and bars dot the *vieille ville*, particularly around the **cathedral** and **Grand'Rue.**

Café des Arcades, 10 Grand'Rue (☎03 89 41 00 00). Early evening drinkers sip mixed drinks (€7) on the terrace. Night owls chill on comfy couches inside. Beer from €2.60. Open M-F 9am-1:30am, Sa 11am-1:30am, Su 3pm-1:30am. MC/V.

Le Murphys, 48 Grand'Rue (☎03 89 29 06 66). Loud Irish music, wood bar stools, and an extensive beer list might make you think that you're in Ireland. Beer from €2.70. Wine €2.20. Open daily 11am-1:30am. MC/V.

▨ FESTIVALS

Soirées Folkloriques, Tu 8:30pm from May to mid-Sept., except during the Festival International de Colmar. Free folk music concerts and dancing in pl. de l'Ancienne Douane.

Festival International de Colmar (info ☎03 89 20 68 97, tickets 41 05 36; www.festival-colmar.com), 1st 2 weeks of July. Features 24 concerts by some of the best names in classical music. Annual theme pays homage to one of the great composers. Tickets €4.50-57, students €3-20.

Festival d'Orgue, Tu 8:45pm from late July to Aug. Collégiale St-Martin's organists perform in concert. €10, students €7; €3 more for opening concert.

Foire aux Vins d'Alsace (☎03 90 50 50 50; www.foire-colmar.com), 10 days in mid-Aug. The region's largest wine fair. Tastings and exhibitions during the day, while popular European bands hold concerts at 9pm. Festival entrance 11:30am-1:30pm €1, 1:30-5pm €4, after 5pm €6. Concerts €20-43.

MULHOUSE   ☎03 89

Once a wealthy industrial powerhouse, Mulhouse (moohl-howss; pop. 118,000) is now a thriving cultural center. Unique for its set of museums devoted to modern technological marvels, Mulhouse provides a refreshing respite from the region's ubiquitous Gothic churches and 17th-century architecture. From its hip, young nightlife to its city vibe, Mulhouse's *coeur* may be a mechanical one—but this is one pacemaker that will get you going.

◨ TRANSPORTATION

Trains: 10 av. du Général Leclerc. Office open M-Sa 5:30am-8:30pm, Su 8am-8:30pm. To **Paris** (4hr., 18 per day, €51) via **Belfort** (45min., 16 per day, €8.10), **Strasbourg** (1hr., 14 per day, €18), and **Basel, CHE** (20min., 28 per day, €6.20).

Public Transportation: ☎03 89 66 77 77; www.solea.info. **Buses** run from the train station and Porte Jeune, north of the pedestrian district. Most routes 5am-8pm; evening routes 8pm-midnight. Buy tickets at the office in the SNCF station (open M-F 7:15am-12:15pm and 1:45-6:45pm) or at the Porte Jeune office (open M-F 7:30am-12:30pm and 1:30-6:30pm, Sa 9am-12:30pm). Individual tickets available on the bus. €1.20, 2 rides €2.20, carnet of 10 €9.20, day pass €3.80. If you are taking the **tram** (bus lines #1 and 2), buy your ticket from the machine on the platform.

Taxis: Taxis Radio Mulhouse (☎03 89 45 80 00). 24hr.

Car Rental: Hertz, 94 rue de Bâle (☎08 45 86 18 61). Open M-F 8am-noon and 2-6:30pm, Sa 8am-noon and 3:30-6:30pm. MC/V.

⚅ PRACTICAL INFORMATION

Tourist Office and Tours: 9 av. Foch (☎03 89 35 48 48; www.tourisme-mulhouse.com), 2 blocks from the station. Cross any bridge and turn right onto rue du 17 Novembre and left onto av. Foch. The office is on your left. White signs from the station direct cars while yellow signs direct walkers. English-speaking staff offers a free reservation booking service and free (poorly labeled) town maps. Open M-F 9am-noon and 2-6pm. Tours in French July-Aug. Tu and Sa 10:30am. €4, under 12 free. Main office is farther from the station, in the Hôtel de Ville off pl. de la Réunion. (☎03 89 66 93 13). Open July-Aug. daily 10am-7pm; Sept.-June M-Sa 10am-6pm, Su 10am-noon and 2-6pm.

Laundromat: 3 bis rue des Halles (☎06 62 86 55 43), off pl. de la Paix. Wash €4 per 7kg. Open daily 7am-8pm.

Police: 12 rue Coehorn (☎03 89 60 82 00), off bd. de la Marseillaise. Call for the **pharmacie de garde.**

Hospital: 20 rue du Dr. Laënnec (☎03 89 64 64 64), behind the station.

Internet Access: Brasserie Le Convivial, 5 rue de la Sinne (☎03 89 46 11 06). €2.50 per hr. Open M-Tu and Th-Sa 7am-1:30am, W 5pm-1:30am, Su 9am-1:30am.

Post Office: 3 pl. de Gaulle (☎03 89 56 94 11). **ATM** and **currency exchange** available. Open M-F 8am-7pm, Sa 8am-noon. Branch at pl. de la Réunion (☎03 89 46 83 11) with an **ATM**. Open M 1-6pm, Tu-F 9am-6pm, Sa 9am-noon. **Postal Code:** 68100.

🏠 🏕 ACCOMMODATIONS AND CAMPING

Hôtel St-Bernard, 3 rue des Fleurs (☎03 89 45 82 32; stbr@evhr.net), halfway between the train station and the *centre-ville*. Family-run hotel has bright rooms with showers and TVs. The dog for whom the hotel is named lazes in the lobby and welcomes guests. Small library. Breakfast €7.50. Free Internet. Reception M-Sa 7am-9pm, Su 7am-1pm and 5-9pm. Singles €34; doubles €38-54. Extra bed €10. MC/V. ❷

Auberge de Jeunesse (HI), 37 rue d'Illberg (☎03 89 42 63 28; ajmulhouse@ifrance. com). From the train station, take tram #1 (dir.: Rattachement) to Port Jeune. Transfer to tram #2 (dir.: Coteaux) and get off at Palace des Sports. Walk to the left and take your 1st right at the corner of the park; the *auberge* is the blue building at the end of the street on your right. Offers basic but clean 2-, 4-, and 6-bed rooms with co-ed bathrooms. Kitchen and bar. Breakfast included. Reception 8am-noon and 5-11pm. Lockout noon-5pm. Dorms €19. MC/V. ❶

Camping de l'Ill, rue Pierre de Coubertin (☎03 89 06 20 66). From the station, turn left and follow the path next to the river. Cross the small footbridge and, when you get to a large park, walk straight for 5min.; the site will be on your right (20min.). On-site grocery store. Tent rental €2.20. Reception 8am-noon and 3-9pm. Open Apr.-Oct. July-Aug. €4.90 per person, under 10 €3.70; sites €4.90. Sept.-Oct. and Apr.-June €3.70 per person, under 10 €1.90; sites €3.70. Electricity €3.70. MC/V. ❶

🍴 FOOD

The cheap kebab joints, gyro shops, and *friteries* along **rue Wilson** and **avenue de Colmar** are packed with students. A **Monoprix** supermarket is at the corner of rue du Sauvage and rue des Maréchaux. (Open M-Sa 8:15am-8pm. AmEx/MC/V.)

Auberge au Vieux Mulhouse, 8 rue des Archives (☎03 89 45 84 18), in pl. de la Réunion. Sunny cafe serves up La Mulhousienne—a pork and sauerkraut platter with spicy horseradish (€15). *Plats* and salads €7-16. Weekday lunch *menu* €11.50. Open M-Th and Su 11am-10:30pm, F-Sa 11am-11pm. MC/V. ❷

Le Maharadjah, 8 rue des Tanneurs (☎03 89 56 48 21; www.maharaja.fr). Unassuming facade conceals an intimate dining area decorated with large Hindu statues. Generous, flavorful *plats* include chicken tikka masala (€14) and curried potatoes *alu saag* (€12). Ask for extra spicy if you're looking for something with a kick. Vegetarian specialties €11-14. Meat *plats* €12-17. Weekday lunch *menu* €9. Open M 6:45-11:30pm, Tu-Su 11:45am-2pm and 6:45-11:30pm. AmEx/MC/V. ❸

👁 SIGHTS

Mulhouse's historic district centers on **place de la Réunion**. Most museums are outside the *vieille ville* and accessible only by bus.

█**CITÉ DU TRAIN (MUSÉE FRANÇAIS DU CHEMIN DE FER).** Housing a cornucopia of colossal trains, this theatrical museum celebrates France's long-standing love affair with the railway. Films detail the history of French trains since 1929, while mannequins narrate relevant scenes from cinema and literature. Peer into the perfectly restored compartments of an Orient Express train and walk into the small tunnel to gaze up at a train's complicated underbelly. Every hour, a massive 1949 steam engine—the last of its kind—chugs away in place. *(2 rue Alfred de Glehn. Take bus #20 from the station to Musées; 2 per hr. On Su, use bus #62. ☎03*

8942 83 33. Open Apr.-Oct. daily 10am-6pm; Nov.-Dec. and Feb.-Mar. daily 10am-5pm; Jan.-Feb. M-F 1-5pm, Sa-Su 10am-5pm. Wheelchair-accessible. €10, students and ages 7-17 €7.60, under 7 free. Joint ticket to train and auto museums €18, students and under 18 €13. MC/V.)

MUSÉE NATIONAL DE L'AUTOMOBILE. The 400 top-of-the-line automobiles on display at this museum range from an 1878 steam-driven Jacquot à Vapeur to futuristic electric cars. Even those with little interest in the technical aspects of the vehicles will be wowed by the cars' flashy aesthetics. The *chefs d'oeuvres* (masterpieces) room is undeniably impressive. Look out for the famous Bugatti Royale as well as cars owned by the likes of Charlie Chaplin and Emperor Bao Da. (192 av. de Colmar. Take bus #10 north to Musée Auto or tram #1 to Musée de l'Automobile. ☎03 89 33 23 23; www.collection-schlumpf.com. Open Apr.-Oct. daily 10am-6pm; Nov.-Dec. and Feb.-Mar. daily 10am-5pm; Jan.-Feb. M-F 1-5pm, Sa-Su 10am-5pm. Wheelchair-accessible. €11, students and ages 7-18 €8, under 7 free. Joint ticket to train and auto museums €18, students and under 18 €13. Free audio tours in English. MC/V.)

ELECTROPOLIS. Every facet of this museum is electrifying, from its exaggerated introductory recording about "a day in the life with electricity" to a movie about lightning gods. The final exhibit is the **Grand Machine,** a generator that supplied the city with electricity for 46 years. (55 rue du Pâturage, next to the railway museum. ☎03 89 32 48 50; www.edf.electropolis.mulhouse.museum. Open Tu-Su 10am-6pm. Wheelchair-accessible. Audio in English. €8, students and ages 6-18 €4, under 6 free. MC/V.)

TEMPLE SAINT-ÉTIENNE. When construction of this Protestant cathedral began in 1859, St-Étienne demanded that its steeple rise higher than that of the Catholic church. All that's left of the 10th-century structure, demolished in 1851, are the 14th-century windows that now line the galleries. (☎03 89 66 49 06. Open May-Sept. M and W-F 10am-noon and 2-6pm, Sa 10am-noon and 2-5pm, Su 2-6pm. Free.)

MUSÉE DE L'IMPRESSION SUR ÉTOFFES. An homage to the printed textile industry that took root in Mulhouse in 1746, this museum offers a trip into the intricate world of hand printing, dye-making, and mechanization. For €5, print a T-shirt using 200-year-old hand-carved blocks. (14 rue Jean-Jacques Henner. ☎03 89 46 83 00. Open Tu-Su 10am-noon and 2-6pm. €6, students €3, ages 12-18 €2, under 12 free.)

NIGHTLIFE

Mulhouse's *centre-ville* is typically crowded at night. **Rue Henriette** buzzes with pub chatter late into the night, and the area between **rue du Sauvage** and **place de la Réunion,** especially down **rue des Tondeurs,** boasts many nightlife options.

O'Bryan Pub, 5 pl. des Victoires (☎03 89 56 25 58), off rue du Sauvage. Students and older locals compose the clientele. Beer from €2.50. Mixed drinks €6.50. Open M-Sa 10am-1:30am, Su 3pm-1:30am. MC/V.

La Salle des Coffres, 74 rue du Sauvage (☎03 89 56 34 98), outside the *vieille ville.* Metallic staircase connects 2 floors of dancing. Cover F-Sa €16 for 2 drinks, €9 for 1 drink; students €6, without drink. Open Tu-Sa 10pm-4am.

FESTIVALS

Fête de la Danse, in mid-June. Locals take to the streets to salsa, tango, cha-cha, and groove to music from around the world. Contact the tourist office for more info.

Festival Automobile de Mulhouse (☎03 69 77 67 77), in mid-July. Brings together car lovers from around Europe. Includes drive-in movies, an auction, and a parade— all centered on an annual theme.

Bêtes de Scène (☎03 89 32 94 10; www.noumatrouff.fr), in mid-July. 4 days of concerts by fringe rock bands, reggae groups, and underground DJs. Day passes €12-15; festival pass €25; some events free.

FRANCHE-COMTÉ

BELFORT   ☎03 84

Though Belfort (bel-fohr; pop. 52,000) houses the factories that produce TGV trains and Peugeot automobiles, the industrial development has not penetrated its *vieille ville*, which remains full of bustling shops and hosts France's largest open-air rock festival. The town now has few attractions besides a sprawling mountaintop citadel and the enormous lion statue below, but it is a great base for a trip to the surprisingly awesome Chapelle Notre-Dame du Haut.

TRANSPORTATION

Trains: Av. Wilson. Station open M-F 4:20am-11:30pm, Sa 3:50am-11:30pm, Su 4:20am-11:30pm. Ticket office open M-F 5:30am-8pm, Sa 8:30am-6:30pm, Su 8:50am-8pm. To: **Besançon** (1hr., 25 per day, €14); **Mulhouse** (30min., 16 per day, €8.10); **Paris** (2hr., 17 per day, €46); **Strasbourg** (1hr., 7 per day, €21).

Buses: CTRB, 9 Faubourg des Ancêtres (☎03 84 21 08 08; www.ctrb.fr). Office open M-F 9am-12:15pm and 1:45-6pm, Sa 9am-noon. Lines run 6am-8pm throughout the city. Tickets €1.05, day pass €5.50.

Taxis: 90000 BELFORT (☎06 07 47 42 24) or **Taxis Fabbri** (☎06 85 99 30 34). 24hr.

Car Rental: Avis, 21 av. Wilson (☎03 84 28 45 95). Open M-F 8am-noon and 2:30-6pm, Sa 8am-noon. AmEx/MC/V.

Bike Rental: At the tourist office. €4-5 per ½-day; 1st full day €7, €5 thereafter; €42 per week. ID and €250 deposit.

ORIENTATION AND PRACTICAL INFORMATION

To get from the station to the tourist office, walk left down av. Wilson and keep right as it curves onto Faubourg de France. Turn left on Faubourg des Ancêtres and follow it to rue Clemenceau; the office, set back from the road, is to the right of the massive Caisse d'Épargne.

Tourist Office: 2 bis rue Clemenceau (☎03 84 55 90 90; www.ot-belfort.fr). Distributes *Spectacles*—a free guide to restaurants and clubs—as well as free maps. Open from late June to Aug. M-F 9am-noon and 1:45-6:30pm, Sa 9am-noon and 1:45-6pm; from Sept. to late June M-F 9am-noon and 1:45-6pm, Sa 9am-noon and 1:45-5:30pm.

Youth Center: Belfort Information Jeunesse, 3 rue Jules Vallès (☎03 84 90 11 11). Internet €1.50 per hr.; reservations recommended. Open M 1:30-6pm, Tu-F 10am-noon and 1:30-6pm, Sa 2-5pm.

Laundromat: 60 Faubourg de Montbeliard. Wash €5 per 7kg. Open daily 7am-9pm.

Police: Rue du Manège (☎03 84 58 50 00). Call for the **pharmacie de garde.**

Hospital: 14 rue de Mulhouse (☎03 84 57 40 00).

Post Office: 19 Faubourg des Ancêtres (☎03 84 22 93 77). **ATM** and **currency exchange** available. Open M and W-F 8:30am-6:30pm, Tu 9am-6:30pm, Sa 8:30am-noon. **Postal Code:** 90000.

FRUGAL FRANCHE. Those traveling in Franche Comté should consider buying **SNCF's VISI'ter Pass** (€10), which can be used by up to five people. The first three people travel at half-price; the last two get round-trips for €1. Visit www.ter-sncf.com/franche_comte for more info. (Pass valid July-Aug. daily; Sept.-June Sa-Su and holidays. Valid only for travel within Franche-Comté and for round trips from Franche-Comté to Dijon.)

ACCOMMODATIONS

Belfort has a smattering of one- and two-star hotels but few truly budget places. Find info on camping at the tourist office or on its website.

Hôtel au Relais d'Alsace, 5 av. de la Laurencie (☎03 84 22 15 55; www.arahotel.com). Perhaps France's most welcoming hotel. The lobby decorated with pictures and souvenirs left by adoring guests. Hand-pressed linens and freshly squeezed orange juice at breakfast speaks to the attentive care of the owners. Brightly colored rooms have toilets, showers, TVs, and phones. 2nd fl. windows have great citadel views. Breakfast €6.30. Reception M-Sa 7am-10pm; call ahead if arriving on Su. Singles €33-40; doubles €40; triples €45-55; quads €55-65. MC/V. ❷

Résidence Madrid (HI), 6 rue Madrid (☎03 84 21 39 16; www.ufjt.org/adresse/belfort-madrid), 10min. from the station. From the train station, turn left onto av. Wilson, left on rue Michelet, and right onto rue Parisot, which becomes av. du Général Leclerc. Rue Madrid is on the left. Be cautious on the street at night. Caters to an international crowd. Dorm-style rooms and singles. Co-ed toilets and clean showers. Breakfast €4.80. Free Wi-Fi in the lobby. Reception hours vary but are usually 8:30am-12:30pm and 2:30-7:30pm. Dorms €16. MC/V. ❶

FOOD

Be sure to try a *belfore*—a fluffy raspberry-almond meringue tart. Finding food is delightfully easy anywhere in the *vieille ville*, especially along **Faubourg de France,** which runs from the river to the train station. Cafes, *boulangeries*, and restaurants cluster around **place d'Armes.** For groceries, head to **Petit Casino,** 1 rue Léon Blum, by the hostel. (☎03 84 21 20 88. Open M-F 7am-12:30pm and 3-7pm, Sa 7am-noon. MC/V.) **Monoprix,** at the corner of bd. Carnot and av. Foch, is another option. (☎03 84 21 47 67. Open M-Sa 8:15am-8pm. AmEx/MC/V.)

Gazelle d'Or, 4 rue des 4 Vents (☎03 84 58 02 87; www.lagazelledor.fr), off pl. d'Armes. Hearty Moroccan *plats* and vegetarian options. Specializes in creative couscous dishes. *Plats* €9.50-18. Open M-Sa noon-2pm and 7-10pm. MC/V. ❷

Aux Crêpes d'Antan, 13 rue du Quai (☎03 84 22 82 54), near the cathedral. Yellow-and-blue Provençal-themed *crêperie* serves up a formidable selection of *crêpes* and *galettes* (€2.80-11) filled with meats or sweets. Pleasant outdoor seating on terrace. Open daily noon-2:30pm and 7-10:30pm. MC/V. ❶

SIGHTS

A joint admission pass for the Belfort Lion statue, Musée d'Histoire, Grand Souterrain, Musée Beaux-Arts, Musée d'Art Moderne, Donation Jardot, and Tour 46 is €8 for adults, €6 for students and seniors.

MEDIEVAL CHÂTEAU. Atop any list of Belfort's attractions—and atop the hill overlooking the town—is the city's medieval château, which served as a military fortress during the Thirty Years' War but now shelters a scenic hodgepodge of historical attractions. An entertaining 1hr. audio tour of the grounds, included in the price of admission, recounts the state's turbulent history. (☎ 03 84 22 84 22. Open daily Apr.-Sept. 10am-6pm; Oct.-Mar. 10am-5pm. Last entry 5:30pm. €5, students and seniors €4.50, ages 11-18 €3.50. Includes visit to the lion.)

BELFORT LION. This giant monument pays tribute to the failure of the Prussians' 1870-71 siege and to the pride of the citizens of Belfort. Sculptor Frédéric Auguste Bartholdi—the Alsatian native who crafted the Statue of Liberty—carved the lion out of pink Vosges sandstone. Photos and other representations of the lion that appear throughout the city don't do justice to the real thing; be sure to pay a visit. (On the château grounds. Platform open daily June-July 9am-7pm; Aug.-Sept. 9am-6pm; Oct.-Mar. 10am-noon and 2-5pm; Apr.-May 9am-noon and 2-7pm.)

DONATION MAURICE JARDOT. This chic museum houses an impressive rotating collection by modern greats like Picasso, Braque, Léger, and Chagall. (8 rue de Mulhouse. ☎ 03 84 90 40 70; www.mairie-belfort.fr. Open July-Aug. M and W-Su 10am-6pm; Sept. and Apr.-June daily 10am-noon and 2-6pm; Oct.-Mar. daily 10am-noon and 2-5pm. Wheelchair-accessible. €4, students €2.50, under 18 free. AmEx/MC/V.)

NIGHTLIFE AND FESTIVALS

The *centre-ville*, particularly along **Faubourg de Montbeliard,** hosts several popular bars. Even on calm nights, locals flock to **Bistrot des Moines,** 22 rue Dreyfus Schmidt, a lively bar and restaurant with an extensive beer selection served from creative bar taps. Intimate round booths line the sides. (☎ 03 84 21 86 40. Beer from €2.20. Open M-F 10:30am-1am, Sa 10:30am-2am. MC/V.)

The tourist office has a free guide with info on summer concerts and festivals. During these events, reserve accommodations well in advance.

Grand Marché aux Puces, Mar.-Dec. 1st Su of every month. An enormous flea market takes over the *vieille ville.*

Festival International de Musique Universitaire (☎ 03 84 22 94 44; www.fimu.com), early June. Over 2000 musicians hit town for a 3-day extravaganza offering over 200 free concerts ranging from classical and jazz to rock and world music.

Les Eurockéennes (☎ 08 92 68 36 22, €0.40 per min.; www.eurockeennes.fr), 1st weekend in July. 90,000 music fans from all over Europe descend upon Belfort for France's largest open-air rock festival. The 2008 lineup featured Girl Talk, Cat Power, Ben Harper, The Offspring, and nearly 60 other acts. Get tickets early. Day pass €37; festival pass €85-95. Tickets sold at FNAC stores and at the tourist office.

Château Events, July-Aug. The château hosts free jazz concerts (W 8:30pm) and free screenings of musical comedy films (F 9:45pm).

Entrevues (☎ 03 84 22 94 44), last week of Nov. Film festival showcases young directors and retrospectives.

OUTDOOR ACTIVITIES

The tourist office has pamphlets with information on hiking and biking trails in and around Belfort. One popular route circles Bessoncourt, 4km to the east. The town is also the departure point for the daunting E5 trail from the Adriatic to the Atlantic. Follow one of the *petites randonnées* around the area for a fairly flat circuit (10-14km, 3-5hr.). North of town, three major long-distance trails—the GR5, GR7, and GR59—meet at the towering summit of the 1247m **Ballon d'Alsace.** The taxing hike to Ballon's peak culminates in panoramic views of the glacial **Doller Valley** and **Rhine** and **Saône Valleys.**

Lac du Malsaucy, west of Belfort, offers hiking, swimming, sunbathing, and fishing. Boats, nautical bicycles, and mountain bikes can be rented from the

Base de Loisirs du Malsaucy, rue d'Evette (☎03 84 29 21 13). Nearby **Maison de l'Environnement** (☎03 84 29 18 12) has exhibits on everything from frogs to weather patterns. Throughout the summer, puppeteers, acrobats, comedians, and musicians perform lakeside. Free outdoor movies are shown on Tuesdays at 10pm from late July through August. To get to the lake, take bus #17 from town. For more info on fishing in and around Belfort, contact the **Fédération du Territoire de Belfort pour la Pêche** (☎03 84 23 39 49; www.federationpeche.fr/90).

🎿 DAYTRIPS FROM BELFORT

RONCHAMP

To reach Ronchamp, take the SNCF train from Belfort (20min., 4-6 per day, €4). Buy your return tickets in Belfort; the Ronchamp station does not sell them. To reach the chapel from the train station, follow rue de la Gare left, turn left onto rue Le Corbusier, and go left again onto rue de la Chapelle. Climb the steep road for 1.5km. For those without a car, bike, or the desire for a moderately difficult hike, call Taxi Guy Bourgogne (☎03 84 20 65 66; 24hr.). The ride is about €6 each way from the train or bus stop.

A 20min. train ride west, in the tiny village of Ronchamp (rhon-sham), stands Le Corbusier's famous 1954 🎿**Chapelle Notre-Dame du Haut,** on the site of a disastrous 1944 German attack. The mushroom-shaped chapel, which draws architecture students and pilgrims from all over the world, was built as a testament to hope in the wake of WWII's devastation. Its sloping lines, receding walls, and sparsely decorated candlelit interior "create a space of silence, prayer, peace, and interior joy." The asymmetrical pews and inscribed stained glass are truly unique. (☎03 84 20 65 13. Open daily Apr.-Sept. 9:30am-7pm; Oct. and Mar. 10am-5pm; Nov.-Feb. 10am-4pm. Wheelchair-accessible. €3, students €2, ages 5-12 free. Guided tours €25.)

BESANÇON ☎03 81

The capital of rural Franche-Comté, Besançon (bess-ahn-sahn; pop. 123,000) boasts a wealth of museums, bargain restaurants, classy boutiques, and hot nightlife. The town's population of international students provides a constant infusion of energy and personality, and its gay scene is one of the best in France. Tucked in a horseshoe-shaped bend in the Doubs River, Besançon enjoys the beauty of the countryside and the sophistication of cities many times its size.

NO WORK, ALL PLAY

BATTLE OF THE BANDS

Music lovers rejoice for the Festival International de Musique Universitaire, which takes place in Belfort over the course of three days during late May or early June. The festival features over 2500 musicians and singers and brought in an estimated 80,000 visitors in 2008. The audience enjoys a weekend of nonstop free concerts in and around the *vieille ville*, while the musicians—all students or amateurs—get a chance to show off what they've got.

In order to perform at the concert, musicians must submit an application form complete with photographs of the band and a recording of their music. A committee then decides which groups or individuals have the talent and image necessary to perform. Any and all music genres are welcome to apply; performances range from classical to pop to hip hop.

Such a range of sound naturally has something to please just about everybody, and as a result the crowds swarm to Belfort and pack into every hostel and hotel available. Finding accommodations during the festival can be a fierce battle, so if you plan to take advantage of this free musical wonderland—or hope to perform yourself—be sure to book early.

For more information, check online at www.fimu.com or call ☎03 84 22 94 42.

ALSACE, LORRAINE, AND FRANCHE COMTÉ

▣ TRANSPORTATION

Trains: Gare de la Viotte, av. de la Paix. Ticket office open M-F 5:10am-9:30pm, Sa 5:40am-8pm, Su 6:25am-9:30pm. To: **Belfort** (1hr., 24 per day, €14); **Dijon** (1hr., 34 per day, €13); **Lyon** (2hr., 8 per day, €25); **Paris** (2hr., 9 per day, €49-60); **Strasbourg** (3hr., 9 per day, €30). Gare de la Mouillère, av. de Chardonnet, runs 1 train line to **Morteau** and **Switzerland**.

Buses: Monts Jura (☎08 25 00 22 44), in the train station. Open M-F 8:30am-noon and 2:30-6:30pm, Sa 8:30am-noon. #104 runs to **Pontarlier** (1hr., 8 per day, €7.50).

Public Transportation: Ginko, 4 pl. du 8 Septembre (☎08 25 00 22 44; www.ginko-bus.com). Open M-Sa 10am-7pm. Night buses run sporadically until midnight. Tickets €1.20, carnet of 10 €9.80; day pass €3.50. Buy individual tickets on bus, carnets at *tabacs*, and day passes on bus or at tourist office.

Taxis: ☎03 81 88 80 80.

✦ ▣ ORIENTATION AND PRACTICAL INFORMATION

Most areas of interest in Besançon lie within the turn of the **Doubs River**.

Tourist Office: 2 pl. de la 1ère Armée Française (☎03 81 80 92 55; www.besancon-tourisme.com). From the train station, cross the parking lot and head down the stairs. Follow av. de la Paix straight ahead and continue as it turns into av. Foch. Walk down the hill. Bear left at the river. Follow av d'Helvétie to pl. de la 1ère Armée Française at the 2nd bridge; the office is in the park to the right. Ignore the signs that point to the tourist office; they are for cars and will take you out of your way. Offers the free student guide *La Besace* and free accommodation booking. **Currency exchange** available. Open June-Sept. M 10am-7pm, Tu-Sa 9:30am-7pm, Su 10am-5pm; Oct. and Apr.-May M 10am-6pm, Tu-Sa 9:30am-6pm, Su 10:30am-12:30pm; Nov.-Mar. M 10am-12:30pm and 1:30-5:30pm, Tu-Sa 9:30am-12:30pm and 1:30-5:30pm, Su 10:30am-12:30pm.

Tours: Available from the tourist office. May-Sept. tours in French. €6, students €4. *Petit train* tours Apr.-Sept. in French. €5.60, students €3.10. Check with the tourist office for departure points and times.

Bookstore: Campo Novo, 50 Grande Rue (☎03 81 65 07 70). Small selection of books in English. Open M 10am-7pm, Tu-Sa 9:30am-7pm. MC/V.

Youth Center: Centre Régional d'Information Jeunesse (CRIJ), 27 rue de la République (☎03 81 21 16 16; www.jeunes-fc.com). Info on internships, jobs, school opportunities, and apartments for people under 25; mostly in French. HI cards. Free Internet and Wi-Fi. Open July-Aug. M 1:30-6pm, Tu-F 10am-noon and 1:30-6pm; Sept.-June M and Sa 1:30-6pm, Tu-F 10am-noon and 1:30-6pm.

Laundromat: Laverie Automatique, 54 rue Bersot (☎06 18 84 12 79). Wash €3.50 per 5-6kg, €4 per 7kg, €6 per 10kg. Open daily 6am-9pm. **Salon Lavoire GTI,** 54 rue Battant. Wash €3.50 per 5kg, €4 per 7kg. Open daily 7am-7pm.

Police: 2 av. de la Gare d'Eau (☎03 81 21 11 22), near pl. St-Jacques. Call for the **pharmacie de garde.**

Hospital: Centre Hospitalier Universitaire, 2 pl. St-Jacques (☎03 81 66 81 66).

Internet Access: At **CRIJ** (above). **Id PC,** 28 rue de la République (☎03 81 81 26 25), across from the CRIJ. €3 per hr. Open Tu-Sa 9:30am-noon and 2-7pm. **M-Ro@d,** 29 rue Ronchaux. €3 per hr. Also offers printing, photocopy, and fax services. Open July-Aug. M-F 10am-noon and 2-5pm, Sa 10am-noon and 2-6pm; Sept.-June M-F 9:15am-6:30pm, Sa 10am-noon and 2-5pm.

Post Office: 23 rue Proudhon (☎03 81 65 55 82), off rue de la République. **ATM** and **currency exchange** available. Open M-F 8am-7pm, Sa 8:30am-12:30pm.

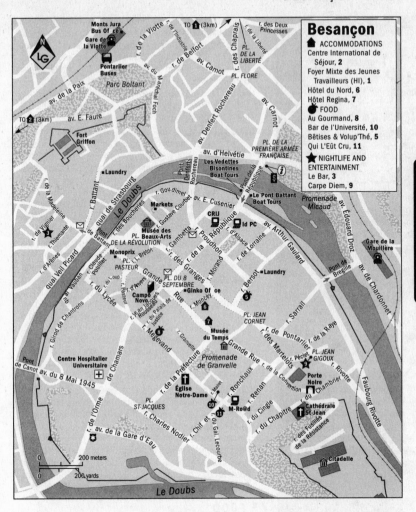

Branches at pl. du 8 Septembre (open M 2-5pm, Tu-F 9:30am-noon and 1:30-5pm) and 1 rue Battant (☎03 81 25 23 22; open M-F 9am-noon and 1:30-6:30pm, Sa 9am-12:30pm). **Postal Code:** 25000.

🏠 ACCOMMODATIONS

Besançon's hostels are a trek from the *vieille ville* (15-30min. by bus or a 45min.-1hr. walk) but offer excellent bargain facilities. The Foyer and the Centre are easily accessible by bus lines, but the ride is longer at night.

Foyer Mixte des Jeunes Travailleurs (HI), 48 rue des Cras (☎03 81 40 32 00; fax 40 32 01). Take bus #5 (or night line A; 3-5 per hr., €1.15) from pl. Liberté (dir.: Orchamps) to Les Oiseaux, down the street from the hostel. To get to pl. Liberté from the train station,

FRANCE ON FILM

So you've packed your bags, bought your maps, and read *Let's Go: France* from cover to cover, but you've still got 20hr. before your flight. What better way to spend it than watching 10 quintessentially French films back to back?

1. Amélie (2001). We had to put this modern classic first. Once you watch this disarming love story/mystery/chase flick starring the undeniably charming Audrey Tautou as a waitress all alone in the big city, you'll know Paris like the back of your hand.
2. La Règle du Jeu (1939). Many believe this Jean Renoir upstairs-downstairs satire to be the best film ever made—anywhere. Renoir broke away from the current trend toward obsessive naturalism, painstakingly revising a script that harks back to turn-of-the-century French theater.
3. Les 400 Coups (1959). François Truffaut's semi-autobiographical classic is a simultaneously heartbreaking and adorable portrait of juvenile delinquency in the streets of Paris. If *Les 400* is too bleak, consider the lighthearted *L'Argent du Poche* (1976), also by Truffaut, for the double bill. Or make it an outright marathon with a jaunt through Paris in Albert Lamorisse's iconic *The Red Balloon* (1956).
4. À Bout de Souffle (1960). Stylish Jean Seberg stars opposite Jean-Paul Belmondo in Jean-Luc Godard's part-thriller, part-slapstick answer to *Les 400 Coups.*

take a left on rue de la Viotte, then the 1st right on rue de l'Industrie. Turn left onto rue de Belfort, which leads to pl. de la Liberté. The stop is on rue de la Liberté. Houses an international student crowd. Ping-pong and foosball. Clean single rooms with private toilets and showers. Breakfast included before 8am. Cafeteria meal M-Sa €7, Su €4. Free Internet and Wi-Fi. Reception 8:30am-8pm. Oct.-Mar. fewer rooms available. Singles €23 for the 1st night, following nights €18. AmEx/MC/V. ❷

Hôtel du Nord, 8 rue Moncey (☎03 81 81 34 56; www.hotel_du_nord_besancon.com), in the *vieille ville*. Rooms with windows overlooking the street offer excellent people-watching. All are tastefully decorated, with big closets, satellite TV, and spacious, sparkling bathrooms. Breakfast €6. Free Wi-Fi. Reception 24hr. Check-out noon. Reservations recommended. Singles and doubles with shower or bath €39-51; triples and quads with shower or bath €53-69. AmEx/MC/V. ❸

Centre International de Séjour, 3 av. des Montboucons (☎03 81 50 07 54; www.cis-besancon.com). From the train station, take rue Foch across the parking lot and down the hill; the bus stop is on your left. Take bus #4 (dir.: Founottes or Temis) or bus #8 (dir.: Campus) to Intermarché. From the stop, walk back uphill and turn left on av. des Montboucons; the hostel is in the Pole Sportif complex on the left. Spacious rooms. Caters to international students. Restaurant, TV room, and foosball. Breakfast €4.80. Reception 7am-1am. Check-in noon. Check-out 9am. Singles €26, with bath and TV €30-32; doubles €30/33-38. MC/V. ❷

Hôtel Regina, 91 Grande Rue (☎03 81 81 50 22), in a courtyard set back from the *centre-ville*. Large, color-coordinated rooms, many of which overlook a garden. Relaxing terrace furnished with wicker chairs. All rooms with wood floors and bath. Decorated with sketches and pictures of the city. Most expensive rooms have kitchenettes. Breakfast €6.50. Reception 24hr. Reservations recommended. Singles €36-46; doubles €41-53; triples €58-63; quads €79. AmEx/MC/V. ❸

🍴 FOOD

Besançon's dining options are plentiful and reasonably priced to accommodate the city's large student population. **Rue Claude Pouillet, place de la Révolution,** and **rue des Granges** dish out tempting options at steep prices, while out-of-the-way eateries around the university cater to the student budget and to vegetarian diets. For a do-it-yourself meal, try the **Marché Beaux-Arts** near the Musée des Beaux-Arts, in the square between rue Goudimel and rue Gustave Courbet. (Open Tu and F 7am-7pm.) Groceries are available at **Monoprix**, 12 Grande Rue. (☎03 81 65 36 36. Open M-Sa 8:30am-8pm. AmEx/MC/V.)

Sharp cheddar-like *comté fromage* is Besançon's specialty. Wash it down with *vin jaune*, one of the more famous *Arbois* wines. *Charcuteries* along **rue des Granges** sell *saucisse de Morteau*, a regional sausage specialty, while *chocolatiers* tempt with *boulets de la Citadelle* or *noisettines*—layered chocolate, nut, and sugar confections.

▨ **Au Gourmand,** 5 rue Megevand (☎03 81 81 40 56). An astonishing array of meat-and-potato dishes at low prices. Retro clocks and a collection of colorful carafes make it feel like an eccentric friend's kitchen. Hearty salads €6-8. Rice and pasta dishes €6.50-7.80. Open Tu-F 11:30am-1:45pm and 6:45-8:30pm, Sa 6:45-8:30pm. Reservations recommended. MC/V. ❷

▨ **Bêtises & Volup'Thé,** 2 rue Bersot (☎03 81 50 83 45). This enchanted-garden-themed eatery is perfect for a girls' night out. The salad with heart-shaped toppings is particularly adorable. Serves exotic teas (€2.50-3), extravagant salads (€8-13), and milkshakes in miniature planters (€4). Vegetarian *menu* €13. 3-course *menus* from €12. Open daily 11am-10pm. Kitchen open noon-2pm and 6-10pm. MC/V. ❷

Qui L'Eût Cru, 3 rue Chifflet (☎03 81 83 25 18). New Age eatery for the adventurous vegetarian. Artistic and deliciously fresh *plats du jour* (lunch €13, dinner €20-25). Meat option available at dinner. Open Tu-Sa 10am-3pm and 7:30-11pm. AmEx/MC/V. ❸

Bar de l'Université, 5 rue Mainet (☎03 81 81 68 17). Large cheap sandwiches (€3-5) and free Wi-Fi draw local students—laptops in hand—to this red and yellow eatery. Cafe by day and popular student bar at night. Beer from €2. Open daily 9:30am-1am. MC/V. ❶

⬡ SIGHTS

Besançon's *vieille ville* is an expansive but walkable circuit; it takes 10min. to walk the length of the main **Grande Rue**—if you don't stop to gawk at the Renaissance buildings along the way.

▨**CITADELLE.** A military masterpiece designed during Louis XIV's reign by the Sun King's go-to architect, Vauban, this Renaissance-style citadel now holds several museums. Getting there requires a steep, grueling trek from the town, but the visit is worth every step. Summer visitors can take a free *navette* that runs between the *centre-ville* and the citadel. (*July-Aug. daily every 10-20min., 9am-7pm.*) The ▨**Musée de la Résistance et de la Déportation** commemorates the 100 members of the French Resistance who were shot at the citadel in 1944 during the German occupation of Besançon. Vivid photographs and relics of the dead leave nothing to the imagination. Twenty rooms hold a

5. La Science des Rêves (2006). This fantastical indie flick, starring the irresistible Gael García Bernal *(The Motorcycle Diaries)* from Michel Gondry (director of *Eternal Sunshine of the Spotless Mind*), rivals Amélie in the heartwarming romance department. Gondry's film follows timid Stéphane (Bernal) in and out of his dream world as he makes one faltering move after another in an attempt to woo his next-door neighbor.

6. Les Diaboliques (1955). Alfred Hitchcock once cited this eerie thriller as one of his major influences. Backstabbing, blackmail, and betrayal run rampant in this boarding-school murder mystery. The French do those twists and turns better than anyone.

7. Les Parapluies de Cherbourg (1964). A sugary, Technicolor delight, this musical has it all: star-crossed lovers, swinging 60s wardrobes, and literally thousands of umbrellas.

8. Au Revoir les Enfants (1987). Yet another moving film to add to France's coming-of-age canon, this time by Louis Malle and set in a Vichy-era boys' boarding school.

9. Ratatouille (2007). Fine, it's not French cinema per se, but this Pixar production is flat-out one of the best movies of the 21st century. Additionally, it stars some incredible French food.

10. French Kiss (1995). We have weaknesses, too!

chronological display of the terrors of WWII. Free audio tours in English and German play survivors' recorded accounts as well as explanations of some of the items exhibited. Children under 10 are advised not to visit the museum. Most artifacts are in French, though extensive information cards in English and German are available in each room. A number of smaller exhibits are on display in the **Natural History Museum,** including an illustration of Darwin's theory of evolution that showcases "unfit" taxidermal animals. The **Insectarium** next door is fascinating, but not for the weak-stomached; a kitchen exhibit reveals the buggers that hide inside cupboards. An **aquarium, climatorium, zoo,** and **noctarium** make a significant attempt to be interactive; at the fish "petting pool," children harass dozens of fish crammed into a tiny tank. More conventional is the informative **Espace Vauban,** which chronicles the life of the citadel's famous architect with informational cards in English. Those with the strength for further climbing can ascend the **Tour de la Reine** for a spectacular view of the city below. (☎ 03 81 87 83 33; www.citadelle.com. Open daily July-Aug. 9am-7pm; Sept.-Nov. and Apr.-June 9am-6pm; Dec.-Mar. 10am-5pm. Most sites wheelchair-accessible. In high season €7.80, students and 1hr. before close €6.50, ages 4-14 €4.50; in low season €7.20/6/4. Includes entrance to every museum and facility. Be sure to buy your tickets at the entrance to the park near the parking lot before you ascend. Audio tour €2.20.)

MUSÉE DU TEMPS. Captain Hook would have hated this ticking homage to time, where hands-on exhibits cater to young explorers, teaching the principles of physics that underlie mechanical and quartz-based clockmaking. First-floor halls hold clocks dating back to Galileo's era, while whimsical upstairs rooms present high-tech devices, games, and experiments. After glancing at the glistening showcases of quartz, ascend to the observation deck to see Besançon's Renaissance buildings; with only the old, intricate roofs visible, the city seems frozen in the past. (Palais Granvelle, 96 Grande Rue. ☎ 03 81 87 81 53; musee-du-temps@ besancon.com. Open Tu-Sa 9:15am-noon and 2-6pm, Su 10am-6pm. Free tour in French Su 3pm. Wheelchair-accessible. M-F €5, Sa €2.50, Su free; students with ID free. Ticket includes admission to the Musée des Beaux-Arts. Free English and German guides available at desk.)

MUSÉE DES BEAUX-ARTS ET D'ARCHÉOLOGIE. France's oldest museum, which began with Abbé Boisot's small collection of art in 1694, houses an exceptional anthology of more than 6000 works by Ingres, Matisse, Picasso, Renoir, and others. Its clever chronological layout ascends a ramp that winds through intimate halls—leading visitors from ancient Egyptian relics to modern oils. (1 pl. de la Révolution. ☎ 03 81 87 80 49. Open M and W-F 9:30am-noon and 2-6pm, Sa-Su 9:30am-6pm. Tours in French for groups only; reserve at tourist office. Wheelchair-accessible. €5, students with ID free; Su and holidays free. Includes entrance to Musée du Temps. AmEx/MC/V.)

CATHÉDRALE SAINT-JEAN. Beneath the citadel, this graceful cathedral boasts the **Horloge Astronomique,** a 30,000-part 19th-century clock that would knock the springs out of any clock at the Musée du Temps. Its 57 faces provide information about all facets of the universe, such as the planets and eclipses. The clock is only shown during a 10min. tour that culminates in the hourly awakening of the wood religious figures at the top. The cathedral also features the **Rose de Saint-Jean**—an 11th-century white marble altar. (Cathedral ☎ 03 81 83 34 62. Open M and W-Su 9am-6pm except during mass. Free. Horloge ☎ 03 81 81 12 76; www.monum.fr. Tours Feb.-Sept. M and Th-Su every hr. 9:50-11:50am and 2:50-5:50pm. Tours €3, under 18 free.)

DOUBS RIVER. Vedettes de Besançon runs boat cruises on the Doubs and the citadel canals from Pont de la République, near the tourist office. (☎ 03 81 83 02 41; www.vedettes-panoramiques.com.fr. Operates Apr.-Oct. daily. 1hr.; 3-4 per day; €10, ages 4-12 €8.50. Dinner cruises by reservation July-Aug.) **Bateaux de Besançon,** on the other side of the bridge, offers similar cruises. (☎ 03 81 68 13 25; www.sautdudoubs.fr. Operates

Apr.-Oct.; Nov.-Mar. for groups by reservation only. 1hr.; 4-5 per day; €10, under 18 €8. July-Aug. M-F 10am, 2:30, 4:30pm; Sa-Su 10am, 2:30, 4:30, 6pm. Sept.-June call for times.) The tourist office has information on other cruises down the Doubs.

◪ NIGHTLIFE

Besançon's international students pack bars and *discothèques* until the early morning on weekends and filter into pubs on calmer nights. Students overflow onto the streets between **rue Claude Pouillet** and **place Jouffroy d'Arbans**. Small, intimate *brasseries* crowd the pedestrian section of town.

Carpe Diem, 2 pl. Jean Gigoux (☎03 81 83 11 18). An outgoing owner runs this tiny watering hole according to his philosophy of *"le rôle sociale du pub"*—bringing together all ages and creeds for genial conversation and idea-swapping. Most solo patrons pore over novels or their own masterpieces beneath eclectic decorations that range from exotic instruments to Jameson whiskey brand towels. Events, films, and concerts held regularly; some are organized, others improvised. Beer from €3. Open M-Th 8:30am-1am, F-Sa 8:30am-2am, Su 9am-2am. MC/V.

Le Bar, 15 rue de Vignier (☎03 81 82 01 00; www.lebar.info). Decorated with homo-erotic art, the upstairs bar is a casual pre-club spot until about 2am, when everyone heads over to *discothèque* Le Privé. Downstairs is another story: from the all-porn video room to lockable "pleasure rooms," the theme is sex—and everyone is exploring. Clientele is mostly male; some bring female friends. Beer €4. Mixed drinks from €4. Open M-Th 8pm-1am, F-Sa 9pm-2:30am, Su 9pm-2am. MC/V over €15.

❋ FESTIVALS

The tourist office publishes several comprehensive lists of events; make sure to get a *Les Temps Chauds de l'Été* guide for up-to-date summer information.

Jazz en Franche-Comté (☎03 81 83 39 09; www.aspro-impro.fr), from mid- to late June. Unites international jazz musicians. Tickets €10-18, students €5-12; some events free.

Les Temps Chauds de l'Été, in July and Aug. Theater performances, music and dance expositions, and film screenings. Many events are free. Call the tourist office for info.

Les Concerts de Granvelle, F nights in July and Aug. Brings free musical acts to Palais Granvelle. Call tourist office for info.

Festival International de Musique (☎03 81 82 08 72; www.festival-besancon.com), in mid-Sept. Orchestras from across Europe perform favorites and recent compositions in 85 concerts, many of which are free. Ticketed events €12-45, students €5-20.

JURA MOUNTAINS

The Jurassic Period derived its name from the Jura mountain range—formerly an ocean floor with abundant paleontological treasures. Travelers often overlook the mountains, flocking instead to the younger, pointier Alps to the south. Smoothed by time, the Jura provide slightly easier—but no less scenic—hiking, biking, and skiing trails. Relatively un-touristed towns in the area provide convenient bases for exploration and have some of the lowest prices in France.

PONTARLIER   ☎03 81

A storied tradition of absinthe production made Pontarlier (pon-tar-lee-ay; pop. 18,400) a psychedelic place to hallucinate until the infamous liquor was banned in 1915. Nearly 100 years later, the town still seems a bit hungover; a slow, relaxed atmosphere pervades as locals spend most of their time sitting in cafes shooting the breeze. As France's second-highest town (837m), Pontarlier now serves as a base for hiking, horseback riding, skiing, and biking in the Jura or for a trip to Switzerland, just 12km away.

TRANSPORTATION AND PRACTICAL INFORMATION

Trains: Pl. de Villingen-Schwenningen. Ticket office open M-F 4:50am-12:25pm and 1:30-8:40pm, Sa 4:50am-12:25pm and 1:25-8:30pm, Su 7:20am-12:30pm and 1:30-8:40pm. To **Dijon** (1½hr., 7-9 per day, €24-30) and **Paris** (3-4hr., 7-9 per day, €53-67).

Buses: Monts Jura (☎03 81 39 88 80), in front of the train station. To **Besançon** (1hr., 6 per day, €7.50). Schedules posted on the door of the Ponta Bus office, rue Remparts, next to the post office. Open M 3-6pm, Tu-F 9am-noon and 3-6pm.

Tourist Office: 14 bis rue de la Gare (☎03 81 46 48 33; www.pontarlier.org). From the train station, take rue de la Gare—the road on the far left side of the roundabout. The office is a block down at the intersection of rue Marpaud. Free maps, info on outdoor activities, and *Guide Pratique*, a list of cheap mountain lodgings. Internet €1 per 15min.; free Wi-Fi. GPS device rental €3 per ½-day, €10 per day. Open July-Aug. M-Sa 9am-7pm, Su 10am-noon; Sept.-June M-Sa 9am-12:30pm and 1:30-6pm.

Laundromat: 13 rue du Moulin Parnet. Wash €3 per 5kg. Open daily 7am-9pm.

Police: 19 Rocade Georges Pompidou (☎03 81 38 51 10). Call for the **pharmacie de garde**.

Hospital: 2 Faubourg St-Étienne (☎03 81 38 54 54).

Post Office: 17 rue de la Gare (☎03 81 38 49 44). Open M-F 8:30am-6:15pm, Sa 8:30am-12:15pm. **Postal Code:** 25300.

ACCOMMODATIONS AND CAMPING

Auberge de Pontarlier (FUAJ), 21 rue Marpaud (☎03 81 39 06 57; pontarlier@fuaj. org). From the station, walk straight down rue de la Gare and take your 1st left onto rue Marpaud; the hostel is down the street on your left (5min.). Renovated in 2008. Bright rooms in an unbeatable location. 2- or 4-bed dorms come with toilets and showers. Social TV room. Breakfast included. Wheelchair-accessible. Reception daily 7am-10pm. Reservations recommended July-Aug. Dorms €19. Cash only. ❶

Hôtel de France, 8 rue de la Gare (☎03 81 39 05 20). Colorful rooms with TVs. Breakfast €5. Reception Tu-Su 7am-9:30pm. Phone ahead if arriving M. Singles with hall shower €22, with shower €32; doubles €30; triples €37; quads €58. AmEx/MC/V. ❷

Camping du Larmont, rue du Tolombief (☎03 81 46 23 33; lelarmont.pontarlier@ wanadoo.fr). From the station, turn right onto Rocade Georges Pompidou, cross the river, and bear left on rue de l'Industrie. Take 1st right onto av. de Neuchâtel and follow signs (20-25min.). 3-star site with a stunning view. TV, game room, and bar. Reception July-Aug. daily 8am-10pm; Sept.-June M-Sa 9am-noon and 5-7pm, Su 9am-noon. July-Aug. €3.20 per person, children €2; €7.50 per tent and car. Sept.-June €3.20 per person, children €2; €6.50 per tent and car. Chalets for 2 July-Aug. €60; Sept.-June €53. Weekly chalets July-Aug. €405; Sept.-June €315. Extra bed €5. Electricity July-Aug. €4; Sept.-June €6. 6-person max. MC/V. ❶

FOOD

Although it may not pack the hallucinogenic punch that once made it famous, a modern version of absinthe Pontarlier is available at most bars and cafes for €3-4. Buy groceries at the **SPAR** supermarket, 75 rue de la République. (☎03

81 46 51 22. Open M-F 8:30am-12:30pm and 2-7:30pm, Sa 8:30am-7:30pm, Su 9am-noon. AmEx/MC/V.) Outdoor markets appear Thursday and Saturday mornings at **place Jules Pagnier.** Good restaurants are concentrated around **rue de la République** or on **rue Jeanne d'Arc** and **rue Sainte-Anne.**

Le Gambetta, 15 rue Gambetta (☎03 81 46 67 17). 20 varieties of pizza. Toppings include ham, eggs, tuna, and potatoes. Shave €1.50 off the bill by ordering a "mini," barely smaller than the hefty regular portions. Pizza from €6, design-your-own €9. Salads €6.50-7.50. Open Oct.-Aug. W-Su noon-1:30pm and 7-9:30pm. MC/V. ❷

La Pinte Comtoise, 4 rue Jeanne d'Arc (☎03 81 39 07 35). Sample the *menu régional* (€13), which features smoked Haut-Doubs ham and local *saucisse de Morteau.* For vegetarians, a fondue of regional *comté* cheese (€12 per person; min. 2 people) provides a rare meat-free taste of Franche-Comté cuisine. Open M and Th-Su noon-1:30pm and 7-9pm, Tu noon-1:30pm. MC/V. ❸

Le Grand Café Français, 36 rue de la République (☎03 81 39 00 72). A popular lunch spot in the heart of town. Affordable *plats du jour* (€7.70) and *Flamenkuch*—a pizza-like dish with onions, ham, and cheese (€7.80)—bring in the masses. Open M-Sa June-Sept. noon-2pm and 4-9:30pm; Oct.-May noon-2pm. AmEx/MC/V. ❷

◎ SIGHTS

CHÂTEAU DE JOUX ET MUSÉE D'ARMES ANCIENNES. The massive 1000-year-old castle houses dungeons and a collection of rare arms. During the **Festival des Nuits de Joux,** from late July to mid-August, the château hosts music, theater, and general merriment. (☎03 81 69 47 95, festival info 39 29 36; www.chateaudejoux.com. Open daily July-Aug. 9am-6pm; from Sept. to mid-Nov. and Apr.-June 10-11:30am and 2-4:30pm. €5.80, students €4.70, ages 6-14 €3. Shows €18, under 12 €11.)

MUSÉE MUNICIPAL DE PONTARLIER. This museum showcases a minor exhibit on local archaeology and a bizarre collection of 19th-century toilets and bedpans. Its real draw is the old hand-painted posters advertising *la fée verte* (the green fairy) and other assorted absinthe-related drinking paraphernalia. (2 pl. d'Arçon. ☎03 81 38 82 14. Open M and W-F 10am-noon and 2-6pm, Sa-Su 2-6pm. Wheelchair-accessible. €3.40, students €1.75, under 12 free.)

DISTILLERIE LES FILS D'ÉMILE PERNOT. After you've learned the story of the scandalous serum at the *musée*, walk down the street and try some absinthe for yourself at the distillery. Founded in 1890 by Émile Pernot to make Pontar-lier's *apéritif mythique*, the distillery now produces tamer tonics, such as the scrumptious *liqueur du sapin* (pine liquor). Visits to the distillery are wonderfully casual and mostly involve wandering around and watching employees at work. Tastings of hallucinogenic-free absinthe are available. (44 rue de Besançon. ☎03 81 39 04 28. Open M-F 8am-noon and 2-6pm. Reservations required for Sa tours and groups. Tours and tastings free; available in English and French.)

LE PONEY CLUB. Enjoy horseback riding for all skill levels at this farm. Geese, ducks, dogs, and turkeys roam freely, so keep an eye out for animal crossings. (Rue du Toulombief, next to the campground. ☎03 81 46 71 67. Pony rides €5 per 30min., €7 per hr. Horse rides €6.50 per 30min., €10 per hr. For guided rides, call ahead.)

⚐ OUTDOOR ACTIVITIES

The Jura Mountains are home to 106km of cross-country skiing trails, which locals and visitors alike traverse in winter. Nine trails on two slopes (**Le Larmont** and **Le Malmaison**) span every skill level. Find a free trail map at the tourist office. (Daily pass for cross-country skiing €6, under 17 €3.50; downhill skiing €11, under 12 €8. MC/V.) Le Larmont (☎03 81 39 44 19; www.cc-larmont.fr), the ski area nearest to Pontarlier, offers toboggan and snowshoe trails. **Sport et Neige,** 7 rue Mervil Zone des Grands Planchants, is the closest store that rents ski equipment. Yet, Sport still a long trek from town, and it's only practical if you have a car. (☎03 81 39 04 69; www.sportetneige.com. Downhill skis €10 per day, €45 per week; under 18 €8/40. Cross-country skis €15 per day, under 18 €8. Open M 2-7pm, Tu-Sa 9:30am-noon and 2-7pm. MC/V.) South of Pontarlier, at **Métabief Mont d'Or,** ski until sunset. (☎03 81 49 13 81. Lift tickets €19 per day, under 12 €15. MC/V.) The Jura are much colder than the Alps, but snow quality is not always reliable; call the tourist office for conditions.

In the summer, skiing gives way to fishing, hiking, and mountain biking. There are two mountain-bike departure points in Pontarlier, one to the north, just off rue Pompée, and one to the south, about 2km west of Forges. Hikers can try the **GR5,** an international 262km trail accessible from Larmont. The tourist office sells a map (€3) with departure points for biking and hiking trails, including one near the train station at pl. St-Claude and one at Pont de la Fauconnière. More detailed maps can be found at **Librairie Rousseau,** 20 rue de la République. (☎03 81 39 10 28. A small selection of English books also available. Open M 2-7pm, Tu-Sa 9am-noon and 2-7pm. MC/V.)

BURGUNDY
(BOURGOGNE)

With rich green vineyards punctuated by brightly colored village rooftops, this agricultural region has long fostered a strong identity and an independent spirit. This sovereign attitude was best demonstrated during the Hundred Years' War when the Burgundians betrayed the young Joan of Arc by siding with the English—or rather, against the French.

The heartland of Roman Gaul in the first century BC, this fruitful region was finally conquered in the AD fifth century by the the namesake Germanic tribe of Burgundians. By the Middle Ages, the duchy of Burgundy had grown fat off the land, building magnificent cathedrals and palaces, collecting priceless works of art, funding powerful monasteries, and creating a legacy of world-class winemaking. The ducal palace and museums of Dijon—the regional capital—stand as vivid reminders of a time when Burgundian dukes wielded more power than the puny Parisian monarchy.

Taste a source of regional pride by sampling the wines produced in this fertile area; Louis XIV called Burgundian wine *"le vin des rois, le roi des vins"* ("the wine of kings, the king of wines"). Today, a bicycle ride through the rolling hills of the Côte d'Or reveals some of the world's finest vineyards, haunted by connoisseurs in search of the perfect Pinot Noir.

HIGHLIGHTS OF BURGUNDY

CONTEMPLATE monastic life at the impeccably restored 12th-century monastery Abbaye de Fontenay (p. 425) during a daytrip from Dijon.

DELIGHT in the city of Dijon (below), whose Musée des Beaux Arts and Palais de Ducs commemorate its former power and attest to its current capital status.

GET LOST in a wine stupor at one of the family-owned vineyards along the Route des Grands Crus (p. 426), including Marsannay-la-Côte and Gevrey-Chambertin.

DIJON   ☎ 03 80

While Dijon (dee-jhon; pop. 150,000) is synonymous with the pungent mustard that it has produced for centuries, the town hardly survives on Grey Poupon alone. Now Burgundy's regional capital, the city was once the center of secular power for all of France, and its grandeur lives on in fine museums and splendid churches. Unlike the Côte d'Or wineries nearby, which retain a rustic enchantment, Dijon is thoroughly modern, and a large international student presence makes it a great place for a night out. Though it lacks Parisian glamor, Dijon offers something for everyone—from haute cuisine to high culture, from pulsating clubs to peaceful *salons de thé*.

⊏ TRANSPORTATION

Trains: Cours de la Gare, at the end of av. du Maréchal Foch. Ticket office open daily 5am-11pm. Info office open M-W 6:30am-9pm, Th-F 6:30am-9:30pm, Sa 6:30am-9pm, Su 7:15am-9:30pm. To: **Beaune** (25min.; 26 per day, fewer Sa-Su; €6.40); **Clermont-**

BURGUNDY

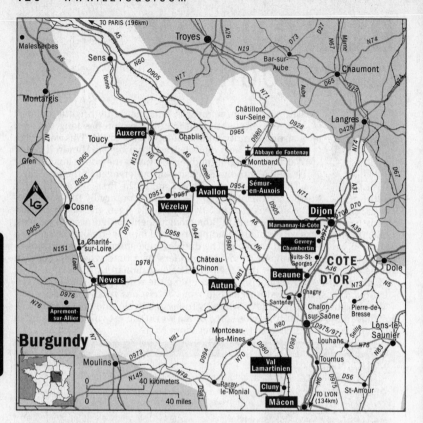

Burgundy

Ferrand (4-5hr.; 10-12 per day, 2 TGV; €44); **Lyon** (2-2½hr.; 14 per day, 4 TGV; €25); **Nice** (6-8hr., 6-8 per day, €88); **Paris** (1-3hr.; 3-4 per day, 12-15 TGV; €52).

Buses: TRANSCO, 21 cours de la Gare (☎03 80 42 11 00; www.cg21.fr), connected to the train station, left of the exit. Ticket and info office open M-Th 5:45am-9pm, F 5:45am-9:30pm, Sa 5:30am-8pm, Su 9am-9pm. Schedule posted outside the terminal. Tickets available on the bus. To **Beaune** (1hr., 6 per day, €6.30) via **Gevrey Chambertin** (10min., every hr. 6am-8pm, €1.80) and to various stops in the Côte D'Or.

Public Transportation: Divia, pl. Grangier (☎0800 10 20 04; www.divia.fr). Office open M-F 7:30am-6:45pm, Sa 8:30am-6:30pm. **Buses** run 6am-9pm; limited night service until 12:30am. Tickets €1, carnet of 10 €7.40; day pass €3.20, 1-week pass €8.90. Buy individual tickets on board; carnets and passes are available at the office.

Taxis: Taxi Dijon (☎03 80 41 41 12) or **Taxi 2000** (☎03 80 54 34 54). Outside the train station. 24hr.

Car Rental: 7 bis cours de la Gare. **Hertz** (☎03 80 53 14 00). From €60 per day. Under-25 surcharge €34. Open M-F 8am-noon and 1:30-6:30pm, Sa 8am-noon and 2-5pm. AmEx/MC/V. **National** (☎03 80 53 09 08). From €76 per day. Under-25 surcharge €24. Open M-F 8am-12:30pm and 2-6:30pm, Sa 9am-noon. AmEx/MC/V.

Bike Rental: Available at the tourist office (below). €12 per ½-day, €18 per day, €50 per 3 days; passport photocopy and credit-card deposit.

THE PRICE IS RIGHT FOR THE CITY OF LIGHTS. Those staying in Dijon over a weekend can take advantage of reduced train ticket prices to Paris—on Saturdays, *aller-retour* fares dip as low as €15. Schedules make for the perfect daytrip: trains leave early and return late the same day.

ORIENTATION AND PRACTICAL INFORMATION

The main axis of the *vieille ville*, **rue de la Liberté,** runs roughly from **place Darcy** (recognizable by its arch, Porte Guillaume) and the tourist office to **place Saint-Michel.** From the train station, follow av. du Maréchal Foch. **Place de la République** is the central roundabout for roads leading out of the city.

Tourist Office: 34 rue des Forges (☎08 92 70 05 58, €0.34 per min.; www.dijon-tourism.com). Offers a free detailed map of the city and accommodations booking (☎03 80 44 11 59; www.reserver-dijon.fr). Open from May to mid-Oct. M-Sa 9am-7pm, Su 9am-12:30pm and 2:30-5pm; from mid-Oct. to Apr. M-Sa 10am-6pm, Su 9am-12:30pm and 2:30-5pm. Branch at pl. Darcy. Open M-Sa 9am-12:30pm and 2:30-6pm.

Tours: Tourist office organizes themed city tours, some in English (daily July-Aug; €6, students €3, under 18 €1), and vineyard tours (www.wineandvoyages.com; €55-65). Reserve in advance.

Luggage Storage: At the train station. €4 per bag per 24hr. Open July-Aug. M-F 8am-7:15pm; Sept.-June M-F 8am-7:15pm, Sa-Su 9:30am-12:15pm and 1:45-5:45pm.

English-Language Bookstore: Librairie Privat, 17 rue de la Liberté (☎03 80 44 95 44). Small selection of books in English. Open M-Sa 9:30am-7pm.

Youth Center: Centre Régional d'Information Jeunesse de Bourgogne (CRIJ), 50 rue Berlier (☎03 80 44 18 35; www.crijbourgogne.com). Info on lodging, classes, grape-picking, summer jobs, and travel; mostly in French. Open M 2-6pm, Tu-F 10am-6pm.

Laundromats: 36 rue Guillaume Tell (☎06 32 08 88 32). €4 per 7kg. Open daily 6am-9pm. 55 rue Berbisey. Wash €3.50 per 7kg, dry €2 per 28min. Open daily 7am-8:30pm.

Police: 2 pl. Suquet (☎03 80 44 55 00). Call for the **pharmacie de garde.**

Medical Services: Centre Hospitalier Régional, 2 bd. du Maréchal de Lattre de Tassigny (☎03 80 29 30 31). **SOS Médecins** (☎03 80 59 80 80, €0.12 per min.). **Médecin de garde** (☎03 80 40 28 28). **Dentiste de garde** (☎03 80 46 01 02).

Internet Access: Cybersp@ce 21, 46 rue Mongue (☎03 80 30 57 43). €0.10 per min., €4 per hr. Open M-Sa 11am-midnight, Su 2pm-midnight.

Post Office: Pl. Grangier (☎03 83 50 62 19), near pl. Darcy. **Currency exchange.** Open M-Tu and Th-F 8:30am-7pm, W 9am-7pm, Sa 8:30am-12:30pm. **Postal Code:** 21000.

ACCOMMODATIONS AND CAMPING

Hôtel Le Jacquemart, 32 rue Verrerie (☎03 80 60 09 60; www.hotel-lejacquemart.fr), centrally located on a side street near Église Notre-Dame. A classy lobby and winding staircase lead to tidy rooms blooming with floral decorations. Breakfast €5.90. Reception 24hr. Reservations recommended. Singles €29, with shower or bath €43-53; doubles €32/52-64; triples €59-69; quads €72-74. AmEx/MC/V. ●

Hôtel Victor Hugo, 23 rue des Fleurs (☎03 80 43 63 45; hotel.victor.hugo@wanadoo.fr). Simple, impeccably neat rooms with TV. Some have garden views. Breakfast €6. Reception 24hr. Reservations recommended. Singles €31, with shower and toilet €35-39; doubles €39-49; quads €81. Extra bed €7. AmEx/MC/V. ●

Foyer International d'Étudiants, 6 rue du Maréchal Leclerc (☎03 80 71 70 00). A very long walk (30-40min.) or bus #3 from Sévigné (from the train station, take a right on rue Remy and then a left on bd. de Sévigné; the stop will be on your right; dir.: St-Apollinaire la Fleuriée or Val Sully) to Billardon (20min.), on rue Moulin. Rue du Maréchal Leclerc is 1 block ahead on the right. A colorless, dorm-like hostel with an international crowd. Spacious rooms with desks, mini-fridges, and sinks. Common co-ed bathrooms, kitchen, ping-pong, tennis courts, piano, and TV rooms. Cafeteria open from Oct. to early June daily. Laundry. Reception 24hr. Singles €16; doubles €22. MC/V. ❶

Camping Municipal du Lac, 3 bd. Kir (☎03 80 43 54 72; www.camping-dijon.com). Take bus #3 (dir.: Fontaine d'Ouche) from the station to CHS La Chartreuse. From the stop, take an immediate right and follow the underpass to the campground. Grassy sites within walking distance of a large lake. Barbecue, restaurant, laundry and Wi-Fi. Reception July-Aug. 8am-8pm; Sept.-Oct. and Apr.-June 8:30am-12:30pm and 2:30-8pm. Gates closed 10pm-7am. Open from Apr. to mid-Oct. Reservations recommended. July-Aug. €3.40 per person, under 7 €2; sites €5. From Sept.-Oct. and Apr.-June €2.50 per person, under 7 €1.50; sites €3.70. Electricity €3.50. MC/V. ❶

🍴 FOOD

Dijon's reputation for haute cuisine is well deserved but, unfortunately, reflected in its high restaurant prices. **Rue Berbisey, rue Monge, rue Musette,** and **place Émile Zola** feature restaurants that serve meals for €15-20. Pedestrian **rue d'Amiral Roussin,** behind pl. de la Liberté, provides outdoor dining in a 17th-century setting. A colorful market takes place in the pedestrian area around **Les Halles,** extending to **place François Rudé** (open Tu and F mornings, Sa all day). Les Halles is also host to several small specialty stores, including cheese and chocolate shops. Cheap kebab joints are located throughout the *centre-ville* (kebabs €3-5) and around the train station. There's a **Monoprix** at 11 rue Piron, off pl. Jean Macé. (☎03 80 30 26 60. Open M-Sa 9am-8:45pm.)

La Mère Folle, 102 rue Berbisey (☎03 80 50 19 76). A large painting of "the crazy mother" watches as patrons enjoy traditional *bourguignon* fare worth every euro. Try the rich, flavorful *poulet à la Gastro Gérard* (chicken in a white wine, Gruyère, and mustard sauce; €13). For a taste of the exotic, try ostrich with *escargots* (€14). Salads €11. *Plats* €11-14. 2-course *menu* €15. Open M, Th, Su noon-2pm and 7-11pm; W 7-11pm; F noon-2pm and 7-11:30pm; Sa 7-11:30pm. MC/V. ❸

La Petite Marché, 27-29 rue Musette (☎03 80 30 15 10). Above a health-food store. Organic and vegetarian fare, like the fruit-filled *salade exotique* (€8.50), along with some meat dishes, like *steak haché* (€8). Salads €6.50-8.50. *Plat du jour* plus appetizer or dessert €11. *Tartes* €5.50. Open M-Sa 9am-2pm. MC/V. ❷

Les Moules Zola, 3 pl. Émile Zola (☎03 80 58 93 26). As its name so subtly suggests, this popular restaurant serves heaping bowls of mussels swimming in sauces—like creamy regional mustard or the spicy Spanish tomato—with huge helpings of *frites* (€11-13). Huge seafood salads €6.80-10. Open June-Aug. daily noon-2pm and 7-10pm; Aug.-May W-Su noon-2pm and 7-10pm. ❷

Brasserie des Grands Ducs, 96 rue de la Liberté (☎03 80 30 25 30). The *quiche lorraine* (€5.10) is tasty, but the menu's jewels are ice-cream sundaes like lemon sorbet and vodka (€6.80). Open M-Th and Su 6:30am-midnight, F-Sa 6:30am-2am. MC/V. ❷

👁 SIGHTS

Dijon's major sights are all contained within a few blocks in the *centre-ville*. The Palais des Ducs de Bourgogne is the city's most celebrated landmark, but other sights make for more entertaining diversions. In 2004, Dijon's mayor

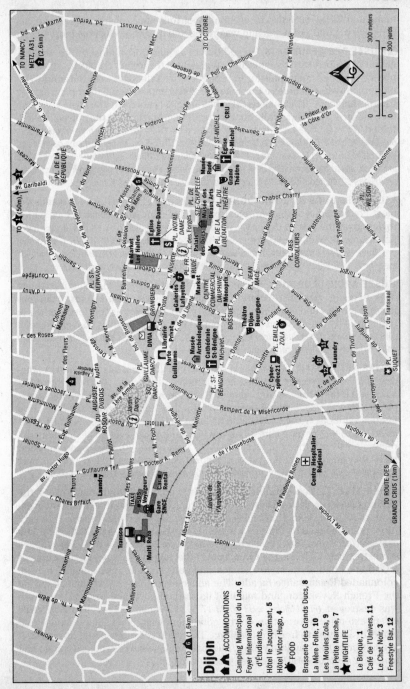

BURGUNDY

300 meters
300 yards

Dijon

mandated ▓**free admission** to all municipal museums; unsurprisingly, he has proven a popular politician and was re-elected in 2008. Relish the bargain!

▓**MUSÉE DES BEAUX ARTS.** In addition to a collection of mostly 15th- to 20th-century European art, the museum's highlight is the **Tomb of the Dukes,** which displays two gilded memorials for the 15th-century Valois dukes of Burgundy. The modern art wing includes a Cézanne and 20th-century technicolor paintings by Charles Lapicque. The museum also has special tours throughout the year; one focuses on death in art, while another leads visitors through the museum blindfolded. *(Pl. de la Libération. Enter by cours de Bar. ☎ 03 80 74 52 70; www.musees-bourgogne. org. Open M and W-Su May-Oct. 9:30am-6pm; Nov.-Apr. 10am-5pm. Modern art wing open M and W-Su May-Oct. 9:30-11:45am and 1:45-6pm; Nov.-Apr. 10-11:45am and 1:45-5pm. Special tours in French; ask at the information desk for times and prices. Permanent collection free; temporary exhibitions €2, students €1. Audio tours in English, French, and German €3.90.)*

PALAIS DES DUCS DE BOURGOGNE. At the center of the *vieille ville* stands the most conspicuous vestige of ducal power, the 52m **Tour Philippe le Bon,** which towers over the rest of the city. Climb the 600-year-old tower's 316 steps for a panoramic view of the *vieille ville. (Pl. de la Libération. ☎ 03 80 74 52 71. Tours from mid-Apr. to mid-Nov. daily every 45min. 9am-noon and 1:45-5:30pm; from mid-Nov. to mid-Apr. every hr. W 1:30-3:30pm, Sa-Su 9-11am and 1:30-3:30pm. €2.30, students €1.20.)*

MUSÉE ARCHÉOLOGIQUE. In the converted 11th-century Benedictine Abbey of St-Bénigne, view the evolution of the Côte d'Or's manmade art, from prehistoric jewelry and Gallo-Roman sculpture to 17th-century pottery. For those uninspired by the museum's collections, the courtyard offers a lovely, shaded place to relax. *(5 rue du Docteur Maret. ☎ 03 80 48 83 70. Open M and W-Su 9am-12:30pm and 1:30-6pm. Free. Temporary exhibits €6, under 18 €5.)*

ÉGLISE NOTRE-DAME. Built over a span of only 20 years, this "miniature cathedral" has an intricately detailed and unified Gothic style. To the right of the altar, you'll find 13th-century stained glass, among the oldest surviving examples in France. The **Horloge à Jacquemart** atop the church tower, one of the city's famous symbols, was captured and brought to Dijon by Philippe le Hardi after a 1382 victory over the Flemish. As you leave the church via rue de la Chouette, remember to rub the well-worn *chouette* (owl) with your left hand for good luck—but don't look at it, or it won't work. *(Pl. Notre Dame. ☎ 03 86 41 86 76; www. notre-dame-dijon.net. Information pamphlet available in many languages; worth the €0.50.)*

OTHER SIGHTS. Recognizable by its brightly colored Burgundian towers, the Gothic **Cathédrale Saint-Bénigne** was constructed in the sixth century over the tomb of its namesake. Don't miss the spectacular—and enormous—18th-century organ designed by Charles Joseph Riepp. *(Pl. St-Bénigne. ☎ 03 80 30 39 33. Open daily 9am-7pm. Crypt open M 10am-6pm, Tu-F 9:30am-6pm, Sa 9:30am-4pm, Su 2-6pm. €2 with informative brochure.)* While the **Église Saint-Michel** has the dark, vaulted interior of a Gothic cathedral, its style changed mid-construction, resulting in a hybrid, colonnaded Renaissance facade. The church suffered severe damage during the French Revolution, and much of its stained glass and original sculpture was destroyed. *(Pl. St-Michel. ☎ 03 80 63 17 80.)* Founded in 1747, **Moutarde Maille** offers extensive information on the condiment that made Dijon a household name, in addition to free *dégustations.* This shop is serious about its mustard; in addition to the standard yellow, they offer unique flavors such as mango and melon. *(2 rue du Chapeau Rouge. Open M-Sa 9am-7pm. MC/V.)*

♪ ▓ ENTERTAINMENT AND FESTIVALS

In July, Dijon's **Estivade** brings revelry to its streets and auditoriums. Pick up *L'Été on Continue* at the tourist office for info. (☎03 80 74 53 33. Tickets €8.) The city devotes a week in late summer to the **Fêtes de la Vigne** and the **Folklorla-des Internationales,** celebrations of grapes that feature over 20 foreign dance and music troupes. (☎03 80 30 37 95; www.fetesdelavigne.com. Tickets €10.)

> **Grand Théâtre,** pl. du Théâtre (Info ☎03 80 60 44 44, tickets 42 44 44; www.fnac.com), next to St-Michel. Presents operas from mid-Oct. to mid-May. Tickets €15-48, students €5.50-10. Office open M-F 10am-6pm, Sa 10am-4pm.

> **Théâtre Dijon Bourgogne-Parvis Saint-Jean,** rue Danton (☎03 80 30 12 12; www.tdb-cdn.com). Performances Oct.-June typically M and W-Th 7:30pm, Tu and F 8:30pm, Sa 5pm. Tickets €20, students and under 26 €12. Info office open July M-F 1-7pm; from late Aug. to June M-F 1-7pm, Sa and performance nights 11am-4pm.

▓ NIGHTLIFE

Rue Berbisey is lined with bars and cafes, and *brasseries* stay open late around **Les Halles** and **place de la Libération.**

> ▓ **Le Broque,** 1 rue du Général Fauconnet (☎03 80 73 81 14; www.lebroque.com). Unpretentious 2-story bar. Dance floor stays hopping late. Patrons jive on bar tops and croon along to songs. Beer from €2. Open Tu-Sa 10pm-2am, Su 9pm-2am. MC/V.

> **Le Chat Noir,** 20 av. Garibaldi (☎03 80 73 39 57; www.lechatnoir.fr). Chic *discothèque* adorned with stylish cat decor. Cavernous ground floor plays techno and house, while a livelier basement blasts hits from decades past. Expect a line at the door. Mixed drinks from €8. Open W-Th 11:15pm-5am, F-Sa 11:15pm-6am. MC/V.

> **Free Style Bar,** 104-106 rue Berbisey (☎03 80 30 05 16). A student hangout that gets packed on weekends. Waiters entertain by juggling bottles and serving up flaming shots (€3-4), which come in every alcoholic combination imaginable. Drink menu boasts some creative concoctions, such as the Kamasutra (vodka, Southern Comfort, cranberry juice, blue caraçao, and banana juice; €7). Open M-Sa 6pm-2am.

> **Café de l'Univers,** 47 rue Berbisey (☎03 80 30 98 27). The galaxy painted on the windows of this rock-and-roll bar offers just a taste of what lies inside. Decor includes an enormous Betty Boop. A slightly older clientele sips drinks on the terrace, but students fill the basement for weekly concerts. Beer from €2.50. Open daily 5pm-2am.

▓ DAYTRIPS FROM DIJON

▓ABBAYE DE FONTENAY

To get to Fontenay from Dijon, take the train to Montbard (45min., 4-5 per day, round-trip €22) and then a taxi to the abbey (€21 round-trip). If there aren't any at the station, call ☎03 80 92 18 57 or 92 31 49. Most passengers who head to the taxi stand at Montbard are also visiting the abbey—share a cab to cut costs. ☎03 80 92 15 00; www.abbayedefontenay.com. Open daily from Apr. to mid-Oct. 10am-5:30pm; Nov.-Mar. 10am-noon and 2-5pm. Entrance fee includes 1hr. tour in French. Most visitors choose to forgo the tour and instead use multilingual pamphlets from the info office. €8.90, students €4.20.

If ever a single location could make a traveler yearn for the seclusion of monastic life, the Abbaye de Fontenay (ah-bay du fohn-tuh-nay) would be it. Converted into a paper mill in the 18th century, it was restored in the early 20th century and now exists almost exactly as it did in the 12th century. From the majestic Romanesque church—known for its stunning Virgin of Fontenay statue—to the simple yet spacious dormitories that often hold art exhibitions and the beautiful gardens, this out-of-the-way stop is worth the time, money, and effort it takes to get there. In May 2008, the abbey inaugurated a recreation of the 12th-century forge. The whole abbey is now a UNESCO World Heritage Site. Adjacent to the grounds is a museum that holds the enormous papal proclamation of the founding of Fontenay.

CÔTE D'OR ☎ 03 80

The 60km of well-tended slopes that run from Dijon to the tiny village of Santenay, 20km south of Beaune, have nurtured grapes since 500 BC. Limestone-laced soil, perfect rainfall rates, and ample sunshine make the region a viticulturist's dream—not to mention some of the world's best real estate. The Côte d'Or is divided into two regions, which by law can only bottle and sell wine from two kinds of grapes: the red pinot noir and the white Chardonnay. The Côte de Nuits, stretching south from Dijon through Nuits-St-Georges to the village of Corgoloin, is known for subtle, sophisticated reds. The Côte de Beaune, farther south, is known particularly for its white wines.

▐ TRANSPORTATION

The most intimate way to see the vineyards near either Beaune or Dijon is to **bike** the Route des Grands Crus; bike-rental shops in both cities arrange tours of varying lengths. From downtown Dijon, follow the signs toward Beaune to highway N74 and follow signs for the Côte d'Or. Renting a car in Dijon or Beaune (from €60 per day) is the fastest way to the grapes. TRANSCO **buses** (☎03 80 42 11 00) run frequently from Dijon to Beaune (1hr.; M-Sa 7 per day, Su 3 per day; €6.30) and stop at all the great names in between, including **Gevrey-Chambertin** (30min., 19 per day, €1.80). Many buses are wheelchair-accessible. Call ahead or visit the Dijon or Beaune bus stations for schedules.

▐ ACCOMMODATIONS

Lodging on the Côte is expensive: reserving a room at one of the many village *chambres d'hôtes* is usually the cheapest option, and Dijon is the cheapest base. The tourist offices in Beaune and Gevrey-Chambertin have comprehensive lists of bed and breakfasts, in addition to the *Bourgogne Hôtes* guide, which lists almost every hotel and campsite in the region. In Gevrey-Chambertin, bunk at **Marchands ❷**, 1 pl. du Monument aux Morts, a B&B with a country feel. (☎03 80 34 38 13; dmarc2000@aol.com. Reservations recommended in summer. Singles €30; doubles €40-45; triples €55-60; quads €70-75. MC/V.)

▐ ROUTE DES GRANDS CRUS

The city traffic on this flat, 60km road fades out a few kilometers outside Dijon, as the route winds through Chenove, Marsannay-la-Côte, Couchey, Fixin, Brochon, and Gevrey-Chambertin—each village more enchanting than the one before. The countryside's vast vineyards are speckled with church spires and fields of flowers. Family-owned *caves* (wine cellars) along the route offer free *dégustations*, but most businesses will expect you to buy something.

MARSANNAY-LA-CÔTE

Only 20min. by bike from Dijon, Marsannay-la-Côte (mahr-sah-nay-lah-koht), known as the "door to the Côte d'Or," is the only town on the Côte that produces *rosé* wines in addition to reds and whites. The peaceful village feels a world away from urban Dijon—and the Defense Association for the Quality of Life in Marsannay-la-Côte has been campaigning heavily to keep it that way.

To sample the local specialties, try the ▨**Château de Marsannay,** which hosts a tour of its grounds followed by a candlelit wine *dégustation* in the deep *caves.* *Sommeliers* (wine stewards) take visitors through this personalized tasting of the château's wines—including a *rosé* and a *premier cru* red. (☎03 80 51 71 11; chateau.marsannay@kriter.com. Open Apr.-Oct. daily 10am-noon and 2-6:30pm; Nov.-Mar. M-Sa 10am-noon and 2-6:30pm. 1hr. tours €10; includes *dégustation.* Wines for purchase from €6.) To reach the château from Dijon, follow signs for Marsannay-la-Côte and the château or take Divia bus #15 (dir.: Marsannay Château) to the last stop. The Marsannay-la-Côte **tourist office,** 41 rue de Mazy, has a list of winemakers in the region and houses a museum that offers a taste of the life of a 19th-century winemaker. (☎03 80 52 27 73; www.ot-marsannay. com. Open June-Sept. M-Sa 9am-12:30pm and 2-6:30pm, Su 9am-1pm; Oct. and Mar.-May M-F 9:30am-12:30pm and 2-6pm, Sa 9am-12:30pm and 2-5:30pm; Nov.-Feb. M-F 9am-12:30pm and 2-6pm, Sa 9am-12:30pm and 2-5:30pm.)

GEVREY-CHAMBERTIN

Perhaps the finest vineyards in all of France surround Gevrey-Chambertin (jhay-vree-sham-bayr-tehn), 11km south of Dijon, home to nine of Burgundy's 33 *grands crus* (best grown). The ▨**Château de Gevrey-Chambertin** is the perfect place to unwind after a long bike ride. Its gracious proprietors will take you through their family-owned 10th-century château, which was built to protect the wine and villagers (in that order) and was later handed over to the monks of Cluny in the 13th century. The monks turned the château's winemaking into a tradition, and workers still use their original methods. The house is filled with old frescoes and 17th-century furniture. The tour ends with an informative 3D animation detailing the château's evolution over time. (☎03 80 51 84 85; www.chateau-de-gevrey-chambertin.com. Open Mar.-Oct. Sa-Su 10am-noon and 2-6pm. Tours in English by request. Tours €6, ages 7-11 €3, under 7 free; includes *dégustation.*) Wine lovers should not miss the **Festival Musical des Grands Crus de Bourgogne,** held on weekends in September, which pairs tastings of just-harvested vintages with classical music. Student tickets to combined tastings and shows are as low as €8. Ask the tourist office for more info.

Getting to Gevrey-Chambertin from Dijon by bike takes about an hour; by foot, it's a 2hr. hike. To get to the château from the bus stop, go left up the hill and take your next right. The Gevrey-Chambertin **tourist office,** 1 rue Gaston Roupnel, offers a free map with a list of vineyards, Internet access (€1 per 15min.), and tours and tastings on Fridays from June through August. (2hr. tour with lunch €8, under 16 €4. 2hr. tour €4, ages 12-16 €2.50, under 12 free. Reservations recommended for lunch tours. Call the tourist office for times.) Many vineyards require reservations for tours; contact the tourist office for details. (☎03 80 34 38 40. Open May-Sept. M-F 9:30am-12:15pm and 1:30-6pm, Sa 9:30am-12:30pm and 1:30-5:30pm, Su 10am-12:30pm and 1:30-4pm; Oct.-Apr. M-Sa 9:30am-12:30pm and 1:30-5:30pm.)

BEAUNE   ☎03 80

Beaune (bone; pop. 23,000) encapsulates the France that nearly every tourist longs for—winding cobblestone roads filled with *boulangeries*, restaurants serving regional delicacies, and an approximate wine-bottle-to-person ration of 10 to 1. However, the atmosphere in Beaune is decidedly bourgeois, and the prices at the restaurants and hotels can make it inaccessible for budget travelers. Those unwilling to splurge are best off spending an hour or two here for a presentations at the Musée du Vin before renting a bike and putting their newfound knowledge into practice on the Route du Vin.

BURGUNDY

TRANSPORTATION

Trains: Av. de Lyonnais. Info office open M-F 10am-noon and 2-7pm. Ticket office open M-F 5:30am-8:30pm, Sa 5:45am-8pm, Su 6:15am-8:30pm. To **Dijon** (20-35min.; 26 per day, 3 TGV; €6.40-8.10), **Lyon** (1-2hr., 10 per day, €21), and **Paris** (2hr., 14 per day, €45-55).

Buses: TRANSCO (☎03 80 42 11 00). To **Dijon** (1hr., 2-7 per day, €6.30) from several stops, including the train station. Schedule at the tourist office.

Taxis: Allô Beaune Taxi (☎06 11 83 06 10). 24hr.

Car Rental: ADA, 26 av. du 8 Septembre (☎03 80 22 72 90). ½ a block down from the train station. From €55 per day with 250km included. 21+; must have had license for 1 year. Open M-F 8am-noon and 2-6pm, Sa 8am-noon and 2-4pm. MC/V.

Bike Rental: Bourgogne Randonnées, 7 av. du 8 Septembre (☎03 80 22 06 03; www.bourgogne-randonnees.com), near the station. English-speaking staff offers free maps, free luggage storage, great advice on routes, and wonderful private tours of nearby vineyards. Bikes €4 per hr., €17 per day, €32 per 2 days, €90 per week; credit-card deposit. Open M-Sa 9am-noon and 1:30-7pm, Su 10am-noon and 2-7pm. MC/V.

ORIENTATION AND PRACTICAL INFORMATION

Streets run in concentric rings around the **Collégiale Notre Dame.** Most sights lie within the circular ramparts enclosing Beaune's *vieille ville.* To get there from the station, head straight on av. du 8 Septembre, which becomes rue du Château. Turn left onto rue Thiers and follow it as it becomes rue Poterne and then rempart Madeleine. Turn right onto rue de l'Hôtel-Dieu, which leads to the Hôtel-Dieu and the tourist office's automated branch, 1 rue de l'Hôtel-Dieu.

Tourist Office: 6 bd. Perpreuil (☎03 80 26 21 30; www.ot-beaune.fr). From the train station, turn left onto bd. Jules Ferry and continue straight when it becomes bd. Perpreuil; the office is on your left (5min.). Staff provides maps and lists of *caves,* reserves rooms, and sells the **Pass Beaune,** which provides discounts to most of the town's major attractions. Open from Apr. to mid-Nov. M-Sa 9am-7pm, Su 9am-6pm; from mid-Nov. to Mar. M-Sa 9am-6pm, Su 10am-12:30pm and 1:30-5pm.

Police: 5 av. du Général de Gaulle (☎03 80 25 09 25).

Hospital: 120 av. Guigone de Salins (☎03 80 24 44 44), northeast of the *centre-ville.*

Internet Access: Baltard Café, 14 pl. des Halles (☎03 80 24 21 86), next to Hôtel-Dieu. €1 per 15min. Wi-Fi. Open daily 7am-9pm.

Post Office: Bd. St-Jacques (☎03 80 26 29 50). **Currency exchange** available. Open M and W-F 8am-6:30pm, Tu 8am-12:30pm and 1:30-6:30pm, Sa 8:30am-12:30pm. **Postal Code:** 21200.

ACCOMMODATIONS AND CAMPING

Visitors swarm Beaune from April to November; reserve at least a week ahead and beware that there are no true budget hotels within the *vieille ville.*

Hôtel le Foch, 24 bd. Foch (☎03 80 24 05 65), on the other side of the ramparts from the train station. Rooms with TVs and sinks. Breakfast €6.50. Reception 7am-9pm. Singles and doubles €28, with shower €33-38; triples €45; quads €48. MC/V. ❷

Hôtel Rousseau, 11 pl. Madeleine (☎03 80 22 13 59). 50-year-old hotel retains an antique ambience. Some rooms face a quiet courtyard. Breakfast included. Shower €3. Reception 7:30am-11:30pm. Singles €30, with toilet €40, with bath €52; doubles €38/48/55; triples €55-62. Cash or check only. ❷

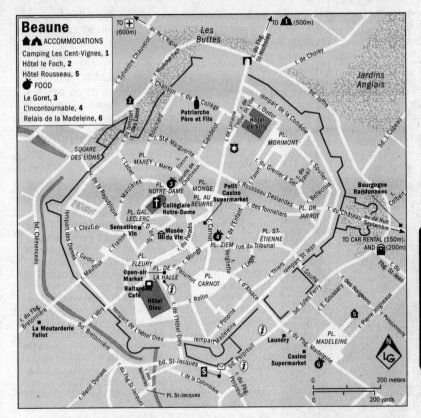

Beaune

🏠⛺ ACCOMMODATIONS

Camping Les Cent-Vignes, **1**
Hôtel le Foch, **2**
Hôtel Rousseau, **5**

🍎 FOOD

Le Goret, **3**
L'Incontournable, **4**
Relais de la Madeleine, **6**

BURGUNDY

Camping les Cent-Vignes, 10 rue Dubois (☎03 80 22 03 91), 500m from the *centre-ville*. From pl. Monge, walk away from the *centre-ville* on rue Lorraine. Signs point the way as you walk down rue du Faubourg St-Nicholas and turn left on rue Dubois; the campground is on your right. Popular with both rugged bikers and those who want to relax in the *vieille ville*. Gravel or grass sites separated by hedges. Grocery store, laundry, restaurant, ping-pong, and tennis available on-site. Reception 8am-noon and 1-9:30pm. Open from mid-Mar. to Oct. €3.60 per person, under 7 €1.80; €4.40 per car. Electricity €3.70. MC/V. ❶

🍴 FOOD

The restaurants around **place Madeleine** and **place Carnot** serve the cheapest *menus*. There is a **Casino** supermarket at 28 rue du Faubourg Madeleine (☎03 80 26 25 25; open M-Sa 8:30am-7:30pm, Su 9am-noon) and a **Petit Casino** on rue Carnot (open Tu-Sa 9am-7:30pm, Su 8am-12:30pm). There is an open-air market on **place de la Halle** Wednesday and Saturday mornings.

🖼 **Relais de la Madeleine,** 44 pl. Madeleine (☎03 80 22 07 47). A cut above the rest. Large portions of specialties like pistachio duck *pâté*, peppered trout, and *mousse au chocolat*—all of which can be sampled as part of a 4-course *menu. Menus* from €14. Open M-Tu and F-Su noon-2pm and 7-10pm, Th noon-2pm. AmEx/MC/V. ❸

THE BIG SPLURGE

THE WRONG CONDIMENT

No matter how many baguettes I eat, I will always be a foreigner. Despite my attempts to assimilate into French culture, there some tics that I will never master:

1. Eating French fries with mayonnaise. The French, ignoring everything that is taught about fats and lipids in junior-high health class, eat their *frites* with globs of straight mayonnaise. Gross.

2. I cannot taste the difference between a champagne that is "unctuous" and one has a "pronounced attack." I truly admire the French for their amazingly developed palates and take full responsibility for my own pathetic, cultureless taste buds.

3. I own sneakers, and I will not part with them. I admire the beautiful French women who can not only stay skinnier than me while eating french fries with mayonnaise but can also walk faster than me in 4 in. heels.

4. Despite three years of college French classes, I cannot pronounce the names of many of the towns that I visit. "Beaune" is not "bee-une," "be-a-une," or "bee-on." It's "bone." One syllable.

Luckily, the French are a forgiving people. With that in mind, I will contentedly eat my ketchup, drink €2 *rosé*, and admire the beautiful Hôtel Dieu from the lowly position of my Nikes.

—Sarah Ashburn

L'Incontournable, 29 rue Carnot (☎03 80 26 14 95). Channels the spirit of the local wine *caves* with its intimate basement seating area and stone walls. Lunch *menu* (€13) comes with *plat du jour*, dessert, glass of wine, and espresso. *Menus* from €22. Open Tu-Sa noon-1:30pm and 7-10:30pm. MC/V. ❹

Le Goret, 2 rue Maizières (☎03 80 22 05 94). Specializes in everything pig—from regional pork dishes to the pig dolls in the windows. Offers a few meat-free options, such as the deliciously thick tomato soup (€6). *Plats* and meal-size salads €7-10. Open Tu-Sa 11am-2pm and 7pm-1am. Kitchen open until 10pm. Bar open until 2am. MC/V. ❷

👁 SIGHTS

HÔTEL-DIEU. In 1443, Nicolas Rolin, chancellor to the duke of Burgundy, built the Hôtel-Dieu as a hospital to help the city recover from the famine that followed the Hundred Years' War; patients were treated here until 1971. In the courtyard, visitors ogle the tiled rooftops; inside, they marvel at the **Salle des Pôvres**, a room that once held dozens of patients. The Hôtel-Dieu's treasures are its 16th-century tapestries—which tell "the story of the human condition"—and Roger van der Weyde's *The Last Judgment*—a polyptych, or work consisting of connected carved panels. Most info placards are in English. *(2 rue de l'Hôtel-Dieu. ☎03 80 24 45 00. Ticket office open daily from late Mar. to mid-Nov. 9am-5:30pm; from mid-Nov. to mid-Mar. 9-11:30am and 2-5:30pm. €6, students €4.80, ages 10-18 €2.80, under 10 free. With Musée du Vin and Musée Beaux Arts €10/6.60/4.10/free. Tours in French July-Aug. 4 per day, €1.80. Call for times.)*

LA MOUTARDERIE FALLOT. Fallot Mustards presents a hands-on historical presentation of the famous yellow condiment. In an hour-long tour, professional guides, animated films, and audio recordings explain the mustard-making process. Finish the visit by mixing your own mustard and comparing it to flavors of the Fallot brand. *(31 Faubourg Bretonnière. ☎03 80 26 21 33; www.fallot.com. Tours M-Sa 10, 11:30am. Extra afternoon visits July-Aug.; call the tourist office for times. €10, available at the tourist office.)*

OTHER SIGHTS. Beaune is packed with wineries offering *dégustations* and tours, but some of the best value for your money can be found at **Patriarche Père et Fils.** The largest of the *caves*, Patriarche Père et Fils offers 1hr. tours and tastings for €10. *(5-7 rue du Collège. ☎03 80 24 53 78 Open daily 9:30-11:30am and 2-5:30pm. All proceeds to charity.)* For those wondering what to taste for, **Sensation Vin** offers a range of interactive wine courses in English and French. *(1*

rue d'Enfer. ☎*03 80 22 17 57; www.sensation-vin.com. 30min. courses €9, 1hr. €19, 2hr. €35.*
Open daily 10am-7pm.) Inside the 15th-century Hôtel des Ducs de Bourgogne, the
Musée du Vin offers a detailed analysis of the Côte's *terroire* (land), from the angle
of sunlight to the composition of the soil to the location of individual vineyard
plots and their characteristics. Winemaking instruments, third-century Gallo-
Roman wine goblets, and even sheet music for drinking songs are on display.
Detailed information is presented in French only, but each room has summary
cards in English. *(Rue d'Enfer, off pl. Général Leclerc.* ☎*03 80 22 08 19. Open Apr.-Nov. daily*
9:30am-6pm, last entry 5:30pm; Dec.-Mar. M and W-Su 9:30am-5pm. €5.40, students €3.50.)

❊ FESTIVALS

Festival International d'Opéra Baroque (☎03 80 22 97 20; www.festivalbeaune.com),
in July. Hosts operas and concerts every weekend. €12-80, students €10-68.

La Fête de la Vente du Vin, 3 days in late Nov. Beaune's moderate level of wine intake
swells to a spirit-soaked party during a celebration of the wine harvest. This family-oriented event promises live music, theatrical performances, and wine booths throughout
the pedestrian district. The festival once encouraged drinking *sans modération* but has
since shifted its focus from quantity to quality.

MÂCON ☎03 85

The following daytrips are accessible via nearby Mâcon, an unimpressive town
that's useful as a base for exploring.

▐▌ TRANSPORTATION AND PRACTICAL INFORMATION

Trains and buses run from **Beaune** to rue Bigonnet in Mâcon (55min., 5 per day,
€15). Check schedules at the station. (Ticket window open M-F 5:05am-7:50pm,
Sa 5:40am-7:40pm, Su 6:10am-8pm.) For a **taxi,** call ☎06 09 34 08 07. **Car rental** is
available at **Avis,** 23 av. Édouard Herriot (☎03 85 38 68 75).

The **tourist office** is located in the *vieille ville.* (☎03 85 21 07 07; www.
macon-tourism.com. Open M-Sa 9:30am-12:30pm and 2-6:30pm.) **Internet**
access is available at the tourist office and at **Café le Bon Accueil,** 35 pl. la Poissonnerie. (☎03 85 38 07 61. Open 8am-2am.)

▐▌ ACCOMMODATIONS AND FOOD

The **Hôtel de Geneve ❶,** 1 rue Bigonnet, offers clean rooms in a great location
just down the hill from the train station and a few blocks from the *centre-ville.*
(☎03 85 38 18 10; www.hotel-de-geneve.com. Singles €48-58; doubles €63-65;
triples €78; quads €96.) The streets of the *vieille ville* are filled with *brasseries*
and bars. **La Maison de Bois ❷,** pl. aux Herbes, offers drinks, desserts, and a
large selection of meats, fish, and salads (€8-10). **Bistrot l'Origan ❷,** 37 pl. Gérard
Genevès, serves delicious pizza (€7-10) and salads. (☎03 85 39 19 22.)

▣ SIGHTS

Although Mâcon best serves as a base town for the surrounding countryside,
the city itself boasts several attractions, including the **Musée Lamartine** (open
Tu-Sa 10am-noon and 2-6pm, Su 2-6pm) and the **Église Saint-Pierre,** a stone
Romanesque Revival cathedral. Both are great ways to pass the time while
waiting for the bus to Cluny or Val Lamartinien.

SIPPING IN STYLE

Burgundy is known throughout the world for superb wines and country villages. The only downside of this stellar reputation is the not-so-stellar cost of exploring these cultural treasures. However, Beaune's **Bourgogne Randonnées** offers tours of Burgundy's vineyards that—while far from cheap—are worth every penny.

Tours cost €69-250 per group and comprehensively examine life in Beaune. The most affordable tour is a half-day extravaganza that includes a bike ride through the countryside, a tour through a local vineyard, and lunch with a *dégustation* (tasting) of six different wines. The most expensive tour is a half-day of driving, walking, or biking through a number of Côte de Beaune villages and vineyards, with a guide to explain everything from the history of the villages to how soil affects the wine's quality.

Sarah Bird, a fluent French and English speaker, leads all the tours with a contagious enthusiasm; she tailors each outing to suit travelers' particular interests. While the price tag on the tours could put quite a dent in the solo traveler's budget, the memorable day will be worth the euro, and you'll return from the vineyards with your thirsts—whether they're for wine or knowledge—quenched.

7 av. du 8 Septembre (☎03 80 22 06 03; www.bourgogne-randonnees.com).

◾ DAYTRIPS FROM MÂCON

CLUNY

It can be challenging to reach Cluny, which has no train station and infrequent buses. Transdev RSL bus #7 runs to Cluny from Mâcon (40min., 6 per day, €4.30). The schedule is at the Mâcon tourist office and the train station. Biking from Mâcon is possible for those up for the 23km trip; take the scenic, car-free Voie Verte path, a stretch of road that covers most of the rolling countryside near Cluny. The path begins at Charnay-les-Mâcon, a 15min. ride from Mâcon; purchase a Voie Verte guide from the Mâcon, Cluny, or Cormatin tourist offices (€1.50). To get from the Cluny bus stop to the tourist office, 6 rue Mercière, walk against traffic on rue Porte de Paris, turn right at pl. du Commerce, and continue for 5min. The office gives out a map and Guide Pratique. (☎03 85 59 05 34. Open July-Aug. daily 10am-6:45pm; Sept. and Apr. M-Sa 10am-12:30pm and 2:30-6:45pm; Oct. M 2-6:30pm, Tu-Sa 10am-12:30pm and 2:30-6pm; Jan.-Mar. M 2:30-5pm, Tu-Sa 10am-12:30pm and 2:30-5pm; May-June daily 10am-12:30pm and 2:30-6:45pm.)

Founded in AD 910 by 12 monks, the **Abbey of Cluny** (kloon-ee) became the most influential church organization in medieval Europe, controlling a network of daughter abbeys. At its height, Cluny and its omnipotent abbots escaped control of local bishops and secular powers and answered only to the pope—nearly a dozen of whom came out of the abbey. A Romanesque building as tall as most Gothic cathedrals, the abbey and its church were looted and used as a quarry during the Wars of Religion and the French Revolution. One-tenth of the complex remains today, giving guests a good idea of its former grandeur. Visitors are aided by several impressive models that reconstruct Cluny's former glory and an excellent 3D video in French that creates the illusion of being inside the completed church. Guided tours take groups past the remaining transept, the ornately decorated Gothic Pope Gelasius facade, and numerous chapels. The central cloister is now home to the **École Nationale Supérieure d'Arts et Métiers,** an engineering school whose students live in the old monk's quarters. Tickets for the abbey are sold at the **Musée d'Art et d'Archéologie.** Entrance to the museum, which provides a good introduction to the abbey, is included in the ticket price. To get to the museum from the tourist office, follow rue 11 Août 1944 to pl. de l'Abbaye. Turn left on pl. du Marché; the ticket office and museum are in the **Palais Jean de Bourbon** up the stairs on the right and past the school. This area, particularly **rue d'Avril** and **rue Lamartine,** is home to the best of the medieval houses that dot the city. (☎03 85 59 15 93; fax 59 82 00. Open daily May-Aug. 9:30am-6:30pm; Sept.-Apr. 9:30am-noon and 1:30-5pm. Abbey tours in French daily. English tours July-Aug. daily; Sept.-June by reservation. Call for schedule. €6.50, ages 18-25 €4.50, under 18 free. MC/V.)

PASS AWAY THE DAY. To facilitate exploration of Mâcon, Cluny, and Cormatin, buy the *pass balad* (€10), which provides unlimited bus travel (until 4pm) and discounts to major museums and sights in the area. (☎03 85 45 86 10. Buy pass on any #7 bus. Available from mid-June to Oct.)

VAL LAMARTINIEN

The Val Lamartinien area is accessible by the same routes as Cluny. The Transdev RSL bus #7 from Cluny (20min., 8 per day 5:20am-7:54pm, €3) or Mâcon (1hr., 6 per day 8am-7:15pm, €6.40) stops next to the Château de Cormatin in Val Lamartinien.

The namesake of lush Val Lamartinien (vahl lah-mar-tin-ee-en), Romantic poet Alphonse de Lamartine (1790-1869), drew inspiration from this bucolic paradise of gently rolling farmlands. The fertile valley is filled with châteaux, most notably the privately owned ◼**Château de Cormatin,** complete with a moat, aviary, maze, and beautiful formal gardens perfect for a stroll. Located in the north wing, the grand staircase was the height of sophisticated Italian style and engineering at the time of its construction (1605-16); in an unadorned display of structure and form, it embodies the Renaissance Neo-Platonic belief in the harmony of universal order. Tours immerse visitors in early-17th-century life, relating architectural and artistic elements of the building to their symbolism and practical functions at the time. (☎03 85 50 16 55, fax 50 72 06. Open daily from mid-July to mid-Aug. 10am-6:30pm; from mid-Aug. to mid-Sept. and from mid-June to mid-July 10am-noon and 2-6:30pm; from late Mar. to mid-June 10am-noon and 2-5:30pm. Tours in French with written English translations every 30min; tours in English available by reservation. €9, students and ages 18-26 €5.50, ages 8-17 €4. Gardens €4, under 8 free.)

AUTUN ☎03 85

With a Roman amphitheater seemingly plopped in the middle of its surrounding fields, Autun (aw-tuhn; pop. 18,000) strikes a balance between its rich past and its thriving modern spirit. Founded around 15 BC by Emperor Augustus as a "sister and rival of Rome," the city is still oddly littered with stony remnants of the empire. Today, history buffs rejoice in Autun's ancient offerings, while others enjoy relaxing in the city's tranquil atmosphere.

◤ TRANSPORTATION

Trains: Av. de la République, on pl. de la Gare. Open M-F 7:05am-12:30pm and 12:50-7pm, Sa 9am-12:30pm and 2:30-6:30pm, Su noon-7:30pm. Ticket office open M-Sa 10am-12:30pm and 2-6:45pm, Su 12:25-7:25pm. To **Avallon** (1-2hr., 2-3 per day, €15), **Dijon** (1-2hr.; M-Sa 7-8 per day, Su 4 per day; via **Chagny** €14.50, via **Etang** €18), and **Paris** (2-2½hr., 5 per day, €55-71).

Buses: Depart from the train station for **Châlon-sur-Saône** (2hr., 3 per day, €10).

Taxis: ☎03 85 52 04 83. 24hr.

⚓ 🛈 ORIENTATION AND PRACTICAL INFORMATION

The main street, **avenue Charles de Gaulle,** runs from the train station to central **place du Champ du Mars.** Head left onto av. de la République from the station and turn right on av. Charles de Gaulle. To get to the *vieille ville* from there, follow the signs from rue aux Cordeliers or rue St-Saulge.

Tourist Office: 13 rue du Général Demetz (☎03 85 86 80 38; www.autun-tourisme. com). Follow av. Charles de Gaulle through pl. du Champ de Mars to the pedestrian streets on the other side. Turn right on rue du Général Demetz; the office will be on your left. Open M 2-6pm, Tu-Sa 9:30am-12:30pm and 2-6pm. Branch at 5 pl. du Terreau (☎03 85 52 56 03), next to the cathedral. Open June-Sept. M-Sa 10:30am-12:30pm and 2:30-6pm, Su 2:30-6pm.

Tours: Tourist office offers themed city tours and nightly summer tours of the *vieille ville.* City tours in English July-Aug. €6.10, under 12 €3.05. Night tours in French July-Aug. 10pm; €8.20, under 16 €6.60. Call the office for tour schedules.

Laundromat: Salon Lavoir, 1 rue Guerin (☎03 85 86 14 12). Wash €4 per 5kg, dry €1 per 15min. Open daily 7am-9pm.

Police: 29 av. Charles de Gaulle (☎03 85 86 01 80). Call for **pharmacie de garde.**

Hospital: 7 bis rue de Parpas (☎03 85 86 84 84).

Internet Access: Elge Inter@ctive, 6 Grande Rue Chauchien (☎03 85 86 13 07). €1 per 15min. Wi-Fi €4 per hr. Open M-F 9am-noon and 2-6:30pm, Sa noon-7pm.

Post Office: 8 rue Pernette (☎03 85 86 58 10). **ATMs** and **currency exchange** available. Open M-F 8:30am-6:30pm, Sa 8:30am-noon. **Postal Code: 71400.**

🏠 🏕 ACCOMMODATIONS AND CAMPING

Hôtel de France, 18 av. de la République (☎03 85 52 14 00; www.hotel-de-france-autun.fr). Across from the train station. Gracious staff lets modestly furnished rooms over a quiet restaurant and bar. The restaurant's hearty 3-course lunch *menu* is a steal at €11. Breakfast €5. Free parking. Reception M-Sa 8am-10pm, Su 8am-3pm. Call ahead if you plan to arrive Su night. Check-out noon. Open Mar.-Jan. Singles and doubles €23-25, with toilet €26, with shower €28-35, with bath €41; triples €35-41; quads €41-48; quints €56. MC/V. ❷

Hôtel du Commerce & Touring, 20 av. de la République (☎03 85 52 17 90). Inviting rooms with TVs and large bathrooms; rooms with tubs are particularly spacious. Breakfast €5. Reception M-Sa 6:30am-11pm, Su by reservation. Open Feb.-Dec. Singles and doubles €27, with shower €34-38, with bath €44; triples and quads €42. MC/V. ❷

Camping Municipal de la Porte d'Arroux (☎03 85 52 10 82; www.camping-autun. com), 20min. from town. From the train station, turn left on av. de la République and follow the signs from rue de Paris. 3-star camping along the banks of Le Ternin river. Grassy sites separated by hedges. Restaurant (open June-Aug.), grocery store, common room with TV and Internet (€8 per hr.), a playground, and a pond for fishing and swimming. Bike rental €5 per ½-day, €10 per day; €100 deposit. Canoe rental €5 per hr., €15 per ½-day, €20 per day; €20 deposit. Office open daily June-Aug. 8am-noon and 4-9pm; Sept.-Oct. and Apr.-June 9-10:30am and 5-8pm. Check-out noon. Open Apr.-Oct. June-Aug. €3.20 per person, children €1.70; €5.70 per tent; €1.80 per car. Sept.-Oct. and Apr.-May €2.90 per tent. Electricity €3. AmEx/MC/V. ❶

🍴 FOOD

For a quick picnic on the ancient steps of the Théâtre Romain, grab supplies at **ATAC** supermarket, 46 av. Charles de Gaulle. (Open M-Sa 8:30am-7pm.) Morning markets are held in **place du Champ du Mars.** (Open W and F 7am-noon.) Restaurants and pizzerias line the streets around the cathedral.

Le Lutri, 1 pl. du Terreau (☎03 85 52 48 44). Terrace in the shadow of the cathedral. Offers cheaper pizzas (€7-11) than its counterparts. Open May-Sept. daily noon-2pm and 7-10pm; Oct-Apr. M and W-Su noon-2pm and 7-10pm. Cash only. ❷

Le Petit Rolin, 12 pl. St-Louis (☎03 85 86 15 55), near the cathedral. Serves *crêpes* and salads for under €10. Romantic garden seating available at night. Dinner *plats* from €13. Weekday lunch *menu* from €12. Open Apr.-Oct. daily noon-3pm and 7-11:30pm; Nov.-Mar. W-Su noon-2:30pm and 7-10:30pm. MC/V. ❷

🄖 SIGHTS

THÉÂTRE ROMAIN. Northeast of the *vieille ville*, this theater is delightfully unrestored. Its remaining stones emerge from the grassy hillside, and picnickers relax where 12,000 enthralled spectators once sat. *(From the cathedral, take rue du Chanoine Triquetat to the opposite end of pl. St-Louis; bear left onto rue Piolin at pl. d'Hallencourt. Turn right on rue du Faubourg St-Pancrace, left on rue St-Branchez, and walk straight past the cemetery; the theater is on the left (25min.).* ☎03 85 52 52 52.) During the first two weekends in August, 600 locals bring chariot races and Roman games to life in the much-hyped Augustodunum show, held in the original theater. Unfortunately, the festivities are in French and might be difficult for an Anglophone to follow. *(*☎03 85 86 80 13. Tickets sold at the tourist office. €14, ages 6-12 €5, under 6 free.)*

PIERRE DE COUHARD. Rue du Vieux Colombier or rue St-Branchez provide the best view of this 30m pyramid-shaped brick structure. The purpose of the pyramid remains unclear, although recent excavations unearthed a 1900-year-old plaque that cursed anyone who disturbed the slumber of the man inside.

CATHÉDRALE SAINT-LAZARE. At the top of the upper city, the cathedral rises above the Morvan countryside; the uphill walk from pl. du Champ de Mars feels like a pilgrimage. The elaborate tympanum (sculpted panel) above the church doors, which depicts the Last Judgment with expressive 12th-century figures, escaped the ravages of the Revolution. Before heading for a drink at one of the bars nearby, look to the right of the tympanum to see the sculpted fate of the drunkard with his barrel—you may opt for a *café au lait* instead. Information cards are available in Dutch, English, French, and German. *(Follow chemin des Manies, a footpath off chemin des Ragots, at the end of rue St-Branchez. Open daily 8am-7pm and 9-11pm. Capital room open until 6:30pm.)*

MUSÉE ROLIN. This museum features the city's true archaeological treasures, including mosaic floors harvested from ruins and 12th- to 15th-century statues and paintings taken from St-Lazare for safekeeping. Get a bird's-eye view of the cathedral without the climb; the museum houses an intricate model of the church. *(5 rue des Bancs, next to the cathedral.* ☎03 85 52 09 76. Open Apr.-Sept. M and W-Su 9:30am-noon and 1:30-6pm; Oct.-Mar. Su 10am-noon and 2:30-5pm. €3.40, students €1.80.)*

OTHER SIGHTS. Several landmarks stand as reminders of Autun's former role as Roman Gaul's largest city. The easiest way to see these sights is on the *petit train*, which leaves from pl. du Champ de Mars and from the tourist office annex near the cathedral. Tours are given in French, but English translations are available. *(50min., from late June to Aug. 7 per day 10am-6pm.)* Check out the first-century **Temple de Janus,** in the fields behind the train station. The two remaining walls, which tower over pastures, offer a framed view of Autun's cathedral. *(From the train station, make a left on av. de la République and another left onto rue de Paris, which becomes rue du Faubourg d'Arroux. Continue ahead, cross the bridge, and turn left onto a* *footpath that goes to the ruins.*) This route to the temple will carry you through the **Porte d'Arroux,** one of the city's two remaining Roman gates. The arches once led the way to the Via Agrippa, the main trade road connecting Lyon and Boulogne and the source of Autun's ancient wealth. Better-preserved **Porte Saint-André** is at the intersection of rue de la Croix Blanche and rue de Gaillon. Autun's ramparts and towers, including the **Tour des Ursulines** by the cathedral, are best seen from the hills above. To get there, take one of the paths off rue du Faubourg St-Blaise past the *vieille ville* and head toward the Pierre de Couhard. As part of the Morvan Valley, Autun provides access to over 2400km of mountain-biking trails. Ask the tourist office for the guide *Le Morvan à VTT* (€13, French only) or call the **Morvan Park Authority** for more information. (☎*03 86 78 79 57.*)

NEVERS ☎03 86

Small medieval rooftops nestled beneath the tower of Cathédrale St-Syr et Ste-Juliette illustrate the skyline of Nevers (nay-vayr; pop 40,000) from across the Loire River. This symbolic religious dominance pervades the city, which is home to the Espace Bernadette—a spiritual haven that draws many pilgrims each year. Settled in the countryside of Burgundy, Nevers is a budding travel destination of medieval streets and Renaissance churches and a charming base from which to explore the surrounding châteaux.

BURGUNDY

TRANSPORTATION

Trains: Av. du Général de Gaulle (☎08 92 35 35 35). Ticket office open M 5:45am-8pm, Tu-F 6am-8pm, Sa 6am-7:30pm, Su 8am-9pm. Trains to **Bourges** (45min., 11 per day, €7.80), **Clermont-Ferrand** (1hr., 8 per day, €24), and **Paris** (2hr., 16 per day, €33).

Buses: Ticket office at 31 av. Pierre Bérégovoy (☎03 86 57 16 39). Open daily 6:45am-8:15pm. Buses depart from rue de Charleville, to your left with your back to the main entrance of the train station. €1 to *centre-ville.* Transit maps available at main office.

Taxis: ☎03 86 59 58 00.

Bike and Canoe Rental: Le Bureau des Guides de la Loire, quai des Eduens (☎03 86 57 69 76; www.l-o-i-r-e.com). Rentals include helmet and repair kit. Helpful owner speaks English and keeps relaxed store hours. Bikes €12.50 per ½-day, €18 per day. Unguided canoe rentals €10 per 2hr. Call ahead to reserve guided trips, available for groups of 6 or more. Daytrip €23-45 per person, €42 per 2 days, €120 per week. Transport from destination included for canoes. Open Apr.-Sept. daily 9am-7pm.

PRACTICAL INFORMATION

Tourist Office: 4 rue Sabatier (☎03 86 68 46 00; www.nevers-tourisme.com). To get to the tourist office from the train station, take av. du Général de Gaulle through pl. Carnot to rue Sabatier. Offers free maps, an English guide listing hotels and restaurants, directions for self-guided walking tours, accommodations booking (€2.30), and info on outdoor excursions. Open Apr.-Sept. M-Sa 9am-6:30pm, Su 10am-1pm and 3-6pm; Oct.-Mar. M-Sa 9am-noon and 2-6pm.

Currency Exchange: Crédit Municipal, 8 pl. Carnot (☎03 86 71 66 86). Open Tu-F 8:15-11:45am and 1:15-5:30pm, Sa 8:15am-12:30pm. There are **ATMs** in the train station, post office, and banks in pl. Carnot, including **Credit Mutual.**

Police: 6 bis av. Marceau (☎03 86 60 53 00). Call for the **pharmacie de garde.**

Hospital: Bd. de l'Hôpital (☎03 86 93 70 00).

Internet Access: City Game, 16 av. du Général de Gaulle (☎03 86 60 47 09; www.cityg-ameinfo.com). €3 per hr. Open M and W 11am-12:30pm and 1:30-8pm, Th 2-6:30pm, F-Sa 11am-12:30pm and 1:30-8pm. Also by appointment F-Sa 8pm-2am. MC/V.

Post Office: 25 bis av. Pierre Bérégovoy (☎03 86 59 87 00). **Currency exchange** and **ATMs.** Open M-F 8am-6:30pm, Sa 8am-noon. **Postal Code:** 58000.

ACCOMMODATIONS

Hôtel de Verdun, 4 rue de Lourdes (☎03 86 61 30 07; www.hoteldeverdun-nevers. com). A 2min. walk down rue Henri Barbusse from pl. Carnot. Overlooks the Parc Salengro and has clean, quiet, and spacious rooms (1 is wheelchair-accessible) with full baths. Each room has its own color scheme and tasteful decor. Some have large bathrooms, and all have cleaning service, phones, and cable. Buffet breakfast €6.50. Wi-Fi. Reception M-Sa 6:30am-9pm, Su 7am-noon. Singles €34-46; doubles €40-52; triples €50-62. Extra bed €10. AmEx/MC/V. ❸

Hôtel Beauséjour, 5 bis rue St-Gildard (☎03 68 61 20 84; www.hotel-beausejour-nevers.com). From the train station, walk left up rue de Charleville and take a sharp right at the intersection onto rue St-Gildard. A personable owner, comfortable rooms, and location across from the Espace Bernadette make for a pleasant stay. All rooms have TVs and phones. Breakfast €6.40. Reception daily 7am-10pm. Singles and doubles with sink €30, with shower €33, with shower and toilet €37-50. Extra bed €10. MC. ❷

FOOD

Brasseries are located throughout the *vieille ville,* but cheaper and more interesting options can be found around **place Carnot.** The tourist office distributes a restaurant guide in French and English that lists reasonably priced *menus.* **Marché Carnot**—the covered market on av. Général de Gaulle and rue St-Didier—is largest on Saturdays and has very fresh produce. (Open Tu-F 7am-12:40pm and 3-6:35pm, Sa 6:30am-2pm.) **Magasin Nevers de Gaulle**—a collection of stores, including a **Champion** supermarket—is located at 12 av. du Général de Gaulle, a half-block from pl. Carnot. (Open M and W-Th 9am-7:30pm, Tu and F 9am-1pm, Sa 8:30am-7:30pm, Su 9am-noon. MC/V.) There is a **Monoprix** supermarket on rue Mitterrand. (Open M-Sa 8:30am-7:30pm, Su 9am-noon. AmEx/MC/V.)

Le Goémon Crêperie, 9 rue du 14 Juillet (☎03 68 59 54 99; le.goemon@wanadoo. fr). Breton-inspired cafe serves up delicious omelettes (€4.50-6), enormous *galettes* (€3-9), and a large assortment of sweet and savory *crêpes* (€2.50-6) like the Popeye (with spinach, of course!). The buttery smells and yummy eats make this stone and timbered dining room the perfect finale after a tough day of biking or sightseeing. Lunch *menu* of appetizer, *galette,* and dessert €9.80. Open Tu-Sa noon-2pm and 7-10pm. ❶

L'Agricole, 10 pl. Carnot (☎03 86 59 40 83). The outdoor tables are always filled with a regular crowd of locals. The cafe's scenic location across from Parc Roger Salengro and the bonus of Wi-Fi make up for the mediocre food. *Menu* €8-14. Open M-Th and Su 7:30am-midnight, F-Sa 7:30am-2am. Last order midnight. MC/V. ❷

Tandem Café, 7 pl. Guy Coquille (☎03 86 59 24 15). The young and fashionable smoke outside this popular local hangout. Offers the basics: salads, *gratinés,* and *tartines.* Good French music and funky, modern decor make this a great place to sip a drink. Also be sure to note the posters on the walls, which offer information about upcoming music events and parties. *Menus* €8-12. Open Tu-Sa 8am-8pm. MC/V. ❷

BURGUNDY

👁 SIGHTS

Nevers's architecture is one of its greatest draws. A blue line extending from the tourist office along the sidewalks provides a self-guided walking tour.

▓CATHÉDRALE SAINT-CYR ET SAINTE-JULIETTE. With its **Tour Boyer** standing 53m above the city, the Cathédrale St-Cyr et Ste-Juliette is the most visible building in Nevers. Although the church is a seemingly average cathedral at first glance, history has bestowed several fascinating architectural oddities upon it. After much of the original building was destroyed in a fire, a Gothic facade was added to the Romanesque rear. The cathedral also boasts unusual stained-glass windows, which were redesigned by modern artists after the originals were blown out during WWII bombings. (☎ 03 68 36 41 04. Open Apr.-Sept. 9am-7:30pm; Oct.-Mar. 9am-6pm. Ask tourist office for schedule of tours. Wheelchair-accessible.)

ESPACE BERNADETTE. Perhaps the most important sight in Nevers, the stone-enclosed convent is the resting place of Ste-Bernadette, a former sister. Within the stone walls, burning incense and complete silence provide a spiritual sanctuary for even the irreligious. Espace Bernadette also welcomes volunteers and provides dorm-like housing, but only for religious pilgrims. (34 rue St-Gildard. ☎ 03 68 71 99 50; www.sainte-bernadette-nevers.com. Open daily Apr.-Oct. 7am-12:30pm and 1:30-7:30pm; Nov.-Mar. 7:30am-noon and 2-6pm.)

PALAIS DUCAL. Opposite the cathedral, fairy-tale turrets ornament the 15th-century Palais Ducal, once the seat of regional government. The modest museum within houses an eclectic collection, including a small aquarium of regional fish, historic paintings, and displays of local porcelain. The exquisite exterior is the real draw. (Enter from tourist office. ☎ 03 68 68 46 00. Open Apr.-Sept. M-Sa 9am-6:30pm, Su 10am-1pm and 2:30-5:30pm; Oct.-Mar. M-Sa 9am-noon and 2-6pm. Free.)

ÉGLISE SAINT-ÉTIENNE. This perfect example of unspoiled Romanesque architecture stands just off rue St-Étienne. Though plain-looking in comparison to the ornate cathedral, Église St-Étienne has, amazingly, not seen any major transformation since its construction in 1068.

🏔 OUTDOOR ACTIVITIES

BIKING AND HIKING

West of the city along D504 lies **Le Bec d'Allier,** the confluence of the Allier and the Loire, France's two most raging rivers. Hikers take advantage of the 1.5km nature trail that leads into the area around Le Bec, starting from the other side of the Loire in the town of Gimouille. To get there by car, exit Nevers by the Pont de la Loire on N7 and take a right onto D976 (dir.: Bourges); signs direct you to the parking lot and trails on the right, about 10min. down the road. By bike, follow the trail that runs beside the **Canal Latéral de la Loire** to **Gimouille,** where you will find a sign with information and a map.

OTHER OUTDOOR ACTIVITIES

Whether you choose to explore the city's outskirts or enjoy its many parks, Nevers is sure to satisfy your thirst for the outdoors. A walk through the rose-lined gardens of the **promenade des Remparts,** which stretch from the Loire River to rue de la Porte du Croux, follows a segment of Nevers's 12th-century fortifications. In the center of the city, just off pl. Carnot, trees shade picnic-ready lawns along the paths of **Parc Roger Salengro,** which wind through a playground, gazebo, and garden. The scenic **Sentier Ver-Vert** footpath stretches 3.5km along the rolling banks of the Loire. To get there, follow route des Saulaies along the river west (dir.: Marzy) to sq. Henri Virlogeux.

The tourist office provides maps and information on outdoor activities suited to Nevers's two rivers. **Le Bureau des Guides de la Loire** (p. 436) rents canoes, bikes, and camping gear and offers guided canoe excursions down the Loire or Allier Rivers for an afternoon or overnight trip.

◨ DAYTRIPS FROM NEVERS

APREMONT-SUR-ALLIER

Apremont-sur-Allier, 16km southwest of Nevers, is accessible by bike or car. To get there, take rue St-Genest over the river and continue straight as it becomes D907. Veer right onto rue Louis Bonnet and right again onto route du Bourges, or D976. Follow D76 until you cross the river again. Turn left onto route de Guerche, then left onto route d'Apremont, which will take you into the village. There is also a vélo route that covers the 1st part of the trip and is highly recommended by the bike shop. To take the vélo route, turn left just after crossing the Loire onto a bike trail that runs along the right side of the campground. Do not enter the campground; instead, follow the trail around the swimming pool (with the pool to your right) until you come to a small bridge. Cross the bridge and turn right onto a road. Stay on this road until you reach a stoplight, at which point make a left. Make a right just after passing the Intermarché. At this point, there will be signs leading to Apremont. The vélo route is a bit more complicated, but the trip is very scenic and avoids traffic.

Set on the banks of the Allier River, the tranquil and unassuming village of Apre-mont-sur-Allier (ah-pruh-mohn suhr ah-lee-ay) seems to be in its own world. Apremont's focal point, ◧**Le Parc Floral,** is a beautiful garden. Butterflies weave through the sundry assortment of flowers and trees, all of which are carefully labeled by name. The view of the castle above makes the floral-scented air feel enchanted. Yet the garden has more to offer than natural beauty. The park also features three follies—decorative accent buildings—that were added in the 1990s as a tribute to 18th-century fashion. Inspired by the drawings of Russian artist Alexandre Serebriakoff, the three follies in Le Parc Floral are a **Chinese Bridge,** a **Turkish Pavillion,** and the **Belvedere**—a gazebo with paintings depicting a round-the-world journey that ends in Apremont. While the castle itself is not open to the public, there is a small museum in the old stables that showcases old-fashioned carriages. Furthermore, the striking view from the castle's hill over vast moors has remained unchanged since the Middle Ages. (☎02 48 77 55 06. Open Mar. 23-Oct. 5 M-F 10:30am-12:30pm and 2:30-6:30pm, Sa-Su 10:30am-6:30pm. €7.50, ages 7-12 €4.50, under 7 free, handicapped €3.50. Museum €1 more. Discount rates for groups over 20 are available.) Between the garden and the castle stands Apremont's only restaurant, **Le Brasserie du Lavoir ❷,** which serves excellent food on an outdoor patio or in the comfortable dining room. (☎02 48 77 55 03. *Plats* €8-14. Salads and sandwiches €3.50-7.)

AUXERRE ☎03 86

High above the banks of the Yonne River, Auxerre (ohg-zayr; pop. 40,000) has thrived on its waterfront location throughout its history. Starting in the first century, the town began to accumulate wealth through trade; today, expensive yachts line the river. Visitors can explore Auxerre via rented mini-boats; those without strong sea legs can walk up the hill to visit Auxerre's abbey and narrow, cafe-crammed alleys. The surrounding area also contains prime fishing locations, superb vineyards, and a lively *centre-ville* with timbered Ancien Régime houses. Most businesses in Auxerre close on Sundays; plan accordingly.

⊏ TRANSPORTATION

Trains: Rue Paul Doumer (☎03 86 46 78 78), across the river from the *centre-ville*. Ticket office open M-F 5:15am-8:30pm, Sa 6:15am-8:30pm, Su 6:45am-9:30pm. To: **Avallon** (1hr.; M-F 6 per day, Sa-Su 3-4 per day; €8.70); **Dijon** (2hr., 12 per day, €23); **Lyon** (3-5hr.; M-F 7-8 per day, Sa-Su 5 per day; €41) via **Dijon; Marseille** (4hr. TGV, 5 per day, €70) via **Laroche-Migennes; Paris** (2hr., 12 per day, €23).

Local Transportation: Allô Le Bus (☎03 86 94 95 00; www.auxerre.com) and the tourist office run local **buses**. Schedules and maps at the tourist office. Buses run M-Sa 7:50am-12:10pm and 1:30-7:10pm. Buy tickets on the bus or at most *tabacs*. €1.10, carnet of 10 €9.

Taxis: ☎03 86 53 32 91. At the train station.

Bike Rental: At the tourist office (below). €4 per hr., €18 per day; ID and €150 deposit.

⁊ PRACTICAL INFORMATION

Tourist Office: 1-2 quai de la République (☎03 86 52 06 19; www.ot-auxerre.fr). From the station, veer left onto rue Jules Ferry and right onto rue Gambetta. Walk to the intersection at pl. Jean Jaurès, cross Pont Paul-Bert, and take a right onto quai de la République; the office is 3 blocks down on the left, after the Passerelle footbridge (12min.). Staff sells the *Auxerre Privilèges* passport (€2), which includes ½-price admission to most town attractions and ½-price bike rentals. Open from mid-June to mid-Sept. M-Sa 9am-1pm and 2-7pm, Su 9:30am-1pm and 3-6:30pm; from mid-Sept. to mid-June M-F 9:30am-12:30pm and 2-6pm, Sa 9:30am-12:30pm and 2-6:30pm, Su 10am-1pm. Annex at 7 pl. de l'Hôtel de Ville (☎03 86 51 03 26). Open from mid-June to mid-Sept. Tu-Sa 10am-12:30pm and 1:30-7pm; from mid-Sept. to mid-Apr. M-F 10am-noon and 1:30-6pm, Sa 10am-noon and 1:30-6:30pm; from mid-Apr. to mid-June Tu-Sa 10am-noon and 1:30-6:30pm.

Tours: In French June-Sept. daily; Oct.-May Sa-Su by reservation. In English July-Aug. by reservation. €5, students €3.

Laundromat: 17 rue Egleny. Wash €3.20 per 5.5kg, dry €0.90 per 10min. Open daily 7am-9pm.

Police: 32 bd. Vaulabelle (☎03 86 51 85 00).

Pharmacy: 114 rue du Pont (☎03 86 52 00 16).

Hospital: 2 bd. de Verdun (☎03 86 48 48 48).

Internet Access: La Maison de la Jeunesse, pl. de l'Arquebuse (☎03 86 72 18 18). Free. Open M-F 10am-noon and 2-6pm. **Média 2,** 17 bd. Vauban (☎03 86 51 04 35). €1.25 per 15min., €4 per hr. Open M-Th 9am-noon and 2-7pm, F 9am-noon and 2-6pm.

Post Office: Pl. Charles-Surugue (☎03 86 72 23 00). **ATMs** and **currency exchange** available. Open M-F 8:30am-6:30pm, Sa 8:30am-noon. Branch at 110 rue du Pont (☎03 86 72 07 20). Open M 1:30-6pm, Tu-F 9:30am-12:30pm and 1:30-6pm, Sa 9:30am-12:30pm and 1:30-5pm. **Postal Code:** 89000.

🏠🏕 ACCOMMODATIONS AND CAMPING

Hôtel le Seignelay, 2 rue du Pont (☎03 86 52 03 48; www.leseignelay.com). Large windows and antique furniture lend rooms a quirky sense of luxury. All but the cheapest rooms come with showers or baths. Buffet breakfast €7. Reception Tu-Su 24hr. Ring bell to enter 9pm-7am. Reserve ahead June-Aug. Open Mar.-Jan. Singles and doubles €30, with shower or bath €53-58; triples €60-67; quads €70. AmEx/MC/V. ❷

Foyer des Jeunes Travailleurs (HI), 16 bd. Vaulabelle (☎03 86 52 45 38). Take rue Jules Ferry to rue Gambetta, turn right, and walk to pl. Jean Jaurès. Cross Pont Bert and turn left on quai de la République. Take the 1st right onto rue Vaulabelle, walk for 10min., take a left at the alley after the Service Citroën, and continue through the parking lot. Turn right and enter the glass door on your left between 2 handicapped parking spots. Hall showers and toilets. Breakfast included. Reception 9am-10pm. Reservations recommended in summer. Singles €16. Cash only. ❶

Camping Mairie, 8 route de Vaux (☎03 86 52 11 15; camping.mairie@auxerre.com), south of town on D163. Follow directions above to rue Vaulabelle. Walk straight for 5min. to the next big intersection and follow signs to the campground. Reception 7am-10pm. Open Apr.-Sept. €2.90 per person; sites €2.60. Electricity €2.35. MC/V. ❶

🍴 FOOD

Markets are held on **place de l'Arquebuse** (Tu and F), in the *centre-ville* (W), and on **place Degas** (Su morning). The **Monoprix** supermarket, 10 pl. Charles Surugue, in the heart of the old town, operates a cheap cafeteria with a three-course lunch *menu* for €6.20. (☎03 86 52 10 67. Store open M-Sa 8:30am-8pm. Cafeteria open M-Sa 11:30am-5:30pm; lunch service 11:30am-2pm.)

Au Grand Gousier, 45 rue de Paris (☎03 86 51 04 80). Packed to the brim with locals and tourists alike. Maintains a traditional French atmosphere, serving local favorites like the daunting *boudin* (blood sausage). *Escargots* from €5.70. *Plats* from €10. Lunch *menu du jour* €11. Dinner *menu* €20. Open M-Tu noon-2pm and 7-9pm, W-Th noon-2pm, F-Sa noon-2pm and 7-9:30pm. MC/V. ❷

👁 SIGHTS

CATHÉDRALE SAINT-ÉTIENNE. Built in 1215, this cathedral is a must-see, featuring detailed stained glass. Its aged facade, which is now being restored, still displays statuettes that were decapitated by Huguenots when they occupied the city in 1567. The **treasury** on the south wall guards relics, manuscripts, and a moving 16th-century tableau of Christ painted by a student of Raphael. *(Cathedral open Apr.-Oct. M-Sa 7:30am-6pm, Su 2-6pm; Nov.-May M-Sa 7:30am-5pm, Su 2-5pm. Crypt and treasury open June-Sept. M-Sa 9am-6pm, Su 2-6pm; Oct.-May M-Sa 10am-5pm. Crypt €3, under 12 free. Treasury €1.90, students free with entry to crypt. 50% off with Auxerre Privilèges passport. Son et lumière show with audio tours in English and German nightly from June to mid-Aug. 10pm; from mid-Aug. to Sept. 9:30pm. €5. Call ☎03 86 52 23 29 for details. AmEx/MC/V.)*

ABBAYE SAINT-GERMAIN. The Gothic abbey, commissioned around AD 500 by Clothilde, attracts pilgrims and tourists to the tomb of the former bishop of Auxerre. While the church contains a **crypt** with some of France's oldest frescoes, the abbey, which now houses a **museum,** better illuminates the history of the *centre-ville*. Featuring St-Germain's preserved tunic, ancient coins, and monastic relics, the museum recreates Benedictine life. *(2 pl. St-Germain. ☎03 86 18 05 50. Open M and W-Su June-Sept. 10am-12:30pm and 2-6:30pm; Oct.-May 10am-noon and 2-6pm. Tours of the crypt in French June-Sept. daily. €2.10, with Auxerre Privilèges passport €1.05, students under 26 free; temporary exhibits €2.50/1.25/free.)*

OTHER SIGHTS. The scenic **Passerelle footbridge,** to the right of Pont Paul-Bert from the train station, is a good starting point for exploring Auxerre. The tourist office offers free multilingual guides to the **Thread of History,** a fading yellow line on the ground that weaves past every monument in the city. Newer bronze arrows embedded into the sidewalks now accompany the line, along with a character called **Cadet Roussel,** who points tourists in the right direction. Visitors wandering near pl. de l'Hôtel will notice the **Tour de l'Horloge,** a turreted 15th-century clock tower, and statues of *auxerrois* celebrities, including Paul Doumer (13th president of France's Third Republic), that dot the area.

🎵 🌺 ENTERTAINMENT AND FESTIVALS

Théâtre of Auxerre, 54 rue Joubert (☎03 86 72 24 20), presents a variety of musical and dramatic events from September to May. Concerts erupt in Auxerre throughout the summer; for more information on concerts or the events listed below, contact the tourist office.

"Garçon, la note!", in July and Aug. This series kicks off Auxerre's concert season. Watch out for performances on the city's terraces. Free concerts M-F 9-11:30pm.

Festival d'Auxerre, in mid-Oct. 5-day festival featuring international films and music.

🔊 NIGHTLIFE

Laid-back pub-crawlers can enjoy the bars that line **rue du Pont,** but none of them stay open much later than midnight. **Place des Cordeliers** is a better bet for a lively time, with a cluster of bars facing the open plaza.

Le Subway, pl. des Cordeliers (☎03 86 51 41 41), on your right when facing the cathedral. Self-dubbed "music cafe." Hip, brightly colored pub keeps the youth up until the wee hours with local musicians and themed parties. Wi-Fi. Open M-Sa 10am-1am, Su 9am-1am. Call for info on upcoming events.

🔺 OUTDOOR ACTIVITIES

Auxerre and the Yonne region are home to some great fishing spots. Contact the **Fédération de Pêche de l'Yonne,** 9-11 rue du 24 Août, for info. (☎03 86 51 03 44; www.peche-yonne.com.) The **Société Mycologique Auxerroise,** 5 bd. Vauban (☎03 86 46 65 96), organizes mushroom-hunting expeditions in the spring and fall.

AVALLON   ☎03 86

Though the oldest section of town contains picturesque 17th-century homes and specialty stores, Avallon (ah-vah-lohn; pop. 8217) isn't exactly every tourist's dream. Centered on its train and bus station, it lacks compelling sights and inexpensive hotels. Yet it offers a central base in the stunning Vallée de Cousin, from which to take breathtaking daytrips to the Morvan surrounding countryside. Worthwhile sites nearby include small Burgundian towns like Vézelay or Sémur-en-Auxois as well as numerous vineyards and châteaux.

▣ TRANSPORTATION

Trains: Pl. de la Gare. Open M-F 6:30am-noon and 1:30-8pm, Sa 5:30am-noon and 2-6:10pm, Su 9:15am-noon and 3:30-6:30pm. To **Autun** (1hr.; M-Sa 3-4 per day, Su 1 per day; €14), **Auxerre** (1hr., 4-5 per day, €8.70), and **Paris** (2-3hr., 4 per day, €28-50).

Buses: Pl. de la Gare. To **Vézelay** (25min.; July-Aug. M-F 9:20am, Sa-Su 10:45am, return daily 5:28pm; Sept.-June 1 bus F evening, returns M morning; €3.70). TRANSCO buses (☎03 80 42 11 00) to **Dijon** (2hr.; M-Sa 3 per day, Su 5:05pm; €17) via **Semur-en-Auxois** (45min.; M-Sa 3 per day, Su 1 per day; €7.40). Schedule at tourist office.

Taxis: ☎03 86 34 04 52. 24hr.

Bike Rental: M. Gueneau, 26 rue de Paris (☎03 86 34 28 11). €16 per day. Helmets not available. Open Tu-Sa 8am-noon and 2-6pm. MC/V.

🛈 PRACTICAL INFORMATION

Tourist Office: 6 rue Bocquillot (☎03 86 34 14 19; www.avallonnais-tourisme.com). From the station, head onto av. du Président Doumer, turn right onto rue Carnot, and swing left onto rue de Paris at the intersection. Walk through pl. Vauban and onto Grande Rue Aristide Briand, which passes through the Tour de l'Horloge and ends at the office (15-20min.). Offers free accommodations service, Internet (€2 per 30min.), and city maps (€0.50). Open from mid-June to Sept. daily 9:30am-1:30pm and 2:30-7pm; Oct.-Mar. M 2:30-6pm, Tu-Sa 10am-12:30pm and 2:30-6pm; from Apr. to mid-June M-Sa 10am-12:30pm and 2:30-6pm; longer hours during holidays and festivals.

Laundromat: 8 rue du Marché, off pl. du Général de Gaulle. Open daily 7am-9pm.

Police: 2 av. Victor Hugo (☎03 86 31 09 50).

Hospital: 1 rue de l'Hôpital (☎03 86 34 66 00).

Internet Access: Café de l'Europe (see **Food,** next page). €4.60 per hr.

Post Office: 9 rue des Odebert (☎03 86 34 91 05). Open M 10am-noon and 1-5:30pm, Tu-Th 8:30am-12:30pm and 1:30-5:30pm, F 8:30am-6pm, Sa 8:30am-12:30pm. **Postal Code:** 89200.

🏠 🏕 ACCOMMODATIONS AND CAMPING

Hôtel de Rocher, 11 rue des Isles Laboume (☎03 86 34 19 03). From the *centre-ville,* follow rue Paris to Grande Rue Aristide Briand, straight onto rue Bocquillot, and past the church. Continue downhill at each fork until rue des Isles Laboume (25min.). Gracious couple manages the town's best budget option. Each room has sink and dresser. Breakfast €5. Showers in the hall (€1). Singles €20; doubles €27. MC/V. ❶

Hôtel St-Vincent, 3 rue de Paris (☎03 86 34 04 53). Intricate wallpaper, cozy quilts, and antique armoires entertain the eye at this snug hotel. Each room has a TV and shower. Breakfast €5.50. Reception M-Sa 8am-11pm at restaurant. Singles from €35; doubles from €40; triples €46; quads €60. MC/V. ❸

Les Capucins, 6 av. du Président Doumer (☎03 86 34 06 52), 5min. from the station. Very professional staff. Each room tastefully furnished with TV, desk, toilet, and shower or bath. Larger suites are particularly elegant, with spacious marble bathrooms. Many rooms have A/C. Restaurant downstairs has full *menus* from €17 and vegetarian *plats* from €12. Breakfast €7. Reception 7:30am-11pm. Reservations recommended. Singles and doubles €40-55; triples €61; quads €69. AmEx/MC/V. ❸

Camping Municipal Sous-Roche (☎03 86 34 10 39), 2km downhill from the *centre-ville.* From the train station, walk straight on av. du Président Doumer, turn left on rue Carnot, and continue straight through the intersection at rue de Lyon. Follow the signs to this quiet campground across the street from a river. Laundry and small grocery store on-site. Reception 8am-noon and 2-7pm. Open from mid-Mar. to mid-Oct. €3 per person, under 7 €1.50; €2 per car; sites €2. Electricity €3. Cash only. ❶

🍴 FOOD

Pick up groceries at the **Petit Casino** supermarket, 31 rue de Paris. (☎03 86 34 50 63. Open Tu-Sa 8am-12:30pm and 3-7:15pm, Su 8:45am-noon.) Morning markets are held on **place du Marché** (Sa) and on **place du Général de Gaulle** (Th).

🍽 **Relais des Gourmets,** 45-47 rue de Paris (☎03 86 34 18 90). Saucy vegetarian and traditional Burgundian fare. Elegant dining room outfitted with full-grown indoor trees.

Unlimited *hors d'oeuvres* buffet €14. Vegetarian *menus* €21. Reservations recommended. Open daily noon-1:30pm and 7-9:15pm. AmEx/MC/V. ❸

La Pizzeria de la Tour, 84 Grande Rue Aristide Briand (☎03 86 34 24 84). A variety of Italian and Burgundian dishes—from pizza to *escargots*—in a half-timbered 15th-century house behind the Tour de l'Horloge. Try the *formule cinéma* (€14), which includes a pizza and a ticket to the local movie theater. Large salads €5-11. Pizzas €7.50-10. Open Tu-Sa 11:45am-2pm and 6:45-10:30pm. MC/V. ❷

Café de l'Europe, 7 pl. Vauban (☎03 86 34 04 45). Watch all of Avallon walk by from the porch of this bustling hangout. Dinner *formule* including salad, *plat du jour,* wine, and coffee from €8. Salads from €5.50. Sandwiches from €5. Pizzas €7-10. Open daily 7am-midnight. Bar open until 2am. MC/V over €16. ❷

👁 SIGHTS

Those with more than a few hours to kill in Avallon should consider a walk through the surrounding countryside. The tourist office provides a free map of an 8km walk covering the area's highlights.

MUSÉE DU COSTUME. Historical narrative meets fashion show with rooms full of 18th- to 20th-century haute couture. Mannequins dressed in their finest sit in the extensive rooms of this mansion, which are decorated as they were when the house belonged to the governor of Burgundy in the 17th century. *(6 rue Belgrand, off Grande Rue Aristide Briand. ☎03 86 34 19 95. Open from mid-Apr. to Nov. daily 10:30am-12:30pm and 1:30-5:30pm. Tours in French. €4, students and under 18 €2.50.)*

VÉZELAY ☎03 86

High above the Vallée de Cousin and seemingly frozen in time, Vézelay (vay-zeh-lay; pop. 457) has distilled all the stereotypical perfections of a French village into its tiny *centre-ville.* From its hilltop perch, the town watches over dense forests, fields of golden wheat, and herds of cattle. The shops along the village's four main streets sell only local Burgundian produce and artisanal creations. Vézelay is one of France's most pristine villages, so budget travelers must contend with high prices and hordes of tourists in the summer, but these are not reasons to miss out on this perfect portrayal of the past.

▣ TRANSPORTATION

Trains: From **Paris** to **Sermizelles** (2hr., 3-4 per day, €27) via **Auxerre** or **Laroche-Migennes.**

Buses: Rapides de Bourgogne buses leave the train station at **Avallon** for Vézelay (July-Aug. M-F 9am, Sa-Su 10:30am, return M-F 5:34pm, Sa 3:58pm; Sept.-June bus leaves F night and returns M morning; €3.70). Les Cars de la Madeleine (☎03 86 33 50 38) **navette** goes from **Avallon** to Vézelay (Sa 11:30am).

Taxis: ☎03 86 34 04 52 or 32 31 88. €24 from Avallon. 24hr.

Bike Rental: AB Loisirs, rue des Graviers (☎03 86 33 38 38; www.abloisirs.com), across from the campsite in nearby St-Père, 2km downhill along D957 toward Avallon. €18 per ½-day, €25 per day. Also organizes outdoor activities, including ½-day trips from St-Père to Sermizelles by canoe, raft, or kayak. Swimming ability is a must; insurance is highly recommended. 2hr. trip M-F €33, Sa-Su €27. Rafting €33-41. ½-day guided cave tour €37. Horseback riding €17 per hr. Open daily 9:30am-6pm.

THE WAY TO VÉZELAY. The lack of a train station might make getting to Vézelay seem dauntingly complicated, but there are plenty of options. You can catch a train to Sermizelles and take **Allo Taxi Vézelay** (☎03 86 32 31 88) for the 10km ride (€17) to Vézelay. A cheaper option is the bus—or even the *navette*, if it coincides with your schedule. Vézelay can also be reached by bike—a great way to explore the nearby countryside. The road from Avallon is a bit hilly, so bring water and prepare to move at the pace of an *escargot*.

🛈 PRACTICAL INFORMATION

Tourist Office: 12 rue St-Étienne (☎03 86 33 23 69; www.vezelaytourisme.com). Internet €2 per 10min. Group **tours** (most in French, some English) by reservation; individual tours July-Aug. Open June-Sept. daily 10am-1pm and 2-6pm; Oct. and Apr. M-W and F-Su 10am-1pm and 2-6pm; Nov.-Mar. M-W and F-Sa 10am-1pm and 2-6pm.

Pharmacy: 25 rue St-Étienne (☎03 86 33 24 85). Open M-Sa 9am-noon and 2-7pm. Check the window for the **pharmacie de garde.**

Post Office: 17 rue St-Étienne (☎03 86 33 26 35). **ATM** and **currency exchange** available. Open M-F 9am-noon and 2-4pm, Sa 9am-noon. **Postal Code:** 89450.

🏠 🏕 ACCOMMODATIONS AND CAMPING

With more than 100,000 visitors passing through each summer, Vézelay's accommodations fill up rapidly. Book a month ahead, particularly in summer. Most lodgings have a few rooms with views of the Morvan countryside.

■ **Maison Les Glycines,** rue St-Pierre (☎03 86 32 35 30), 1 block from the church. 3-star hotel with tall windows, tiled floors, and elegant furnishings. In the town's artistic spirit, each room is named for a French artist or writer. Breakfast €9. Wheelchair-accessible. Reservations required. Singles €35-52; doubles €65-82. Extra bed €15. MC/V. ❸

Auberge de Jeunesse (HI) and **Camping de L'Ermitage** (both ☎03 86 33 24 18). From rue St-Étienne, veer left downhill and bear right on route de l'Étang. Follow the signs; the hostel and campground will be on your left (15min.). 4-6 bed rooms. Kitchen. Reception 5:30-7pm. Lockout 10am-5:30pm. Open Mar.-Nov. Camping €3 per person, children €1.50; €1 per tent. Electricity €2.50. Dorms €8-10. Cash only. ❶

🍴 FOOD

Pick up groceries at the **Vival** supermarket, near the bottom of rue St-Étienne. (Open July-Aug. daily 8:30am-1pm and 2-8pm; Sept.-June M-Sa 8:30am-12:30pm and 3-7pm, Su 9am-12:30pm. MC/V.)

■ **Auberge de la Coquille,** 81 rue St-Pierre (☎03 86 33 35 57; www.coquille-vezelay. com). Try the *menu bourguignon* (€12), which includes a ham-and-egg galette, crêpe with honey, and glass of wine. 3- and 4-course *menus* from €14. Open June-Aug. daily noon-2pm and 7-9pm. Reservations recommended. MC/V. ❸

Le Bouganville, 28 rue St-Étienne (☎03 86 33 27 57). 4-course *menu du jardinier* (€20) includes salad, vegetables, cheese, and dessert. *Noix de joue de porc au pain d'épices* (pork braised in a gingerbread sauce; €13). *Plats* from €9. Open Feb.-Nov. M and Th-Su noon-2pm and 7-9pm. Reservations recommended. MC/V. ❸

La Dent Creuse (☎03 86 33 36 33; www.vezelaytour.net), at the intersection of pl. du Champ de Foire and rue St-Étienne. Pizza menu (€8.50-12) has options like the loaded *bourguignonne* with cream, *champignons*, *escargots*, and eggs. *Menus* €19-25. Open from mid-Mar. to mid-Jan. daily noon-2pm and 7-10pm. MC/V. ❸

◉ SIGHTS

BASILIQUE SAINTE-MADELEINE. All roads in Vézelay converge at this famous hilltop church. An impressive representation of Romanesque and Gothic styles, the church has a sculpted tympanum above the doors to its cavernous interior. Concerts and performances take place in the basilica during the summer; call the tourist office for info. (☎03 86 33 39 50. *Open daily 7am-8:30pm. Closed during mass. Tours in English with reservation. Concert tickets €25. Pamphlets in English €6.*)

OTHER SIGHTS. Caves du Pèlerin—the local winery—offers guided tours and *dégustations.* (*32 rue St-Étienne.* ☎03 86 33 30 84. *French tours from mid-Apr. to mid-Sept. Sa-Su 2:30-5pm. Tours in English by reservation; reserve by at least the Th before your visit. €5, under 18 free. MC/V.*) Head to **Musée Zervos** for a sampling of modern art collected by French art critic Christian Zervos. Several Calder mobiles hang overhead, and works by Ernst, Giacometti, Kandinsky, and Picasso adorn the walls. (*Rue St-Étienne.* ☎ 03 86 32 39 26; www.musee-zervos.fr. *Open from mid-Mar. to mid-Nov. daily 10am-6pm. Last entry 5:20pm. €3, students €2, under 18 free.*)

SÉMUR-EN-AUXOIS   ☎03 80

The towers that protect the *vieille ville* and the seventh-century château of Sémur-en-Auxois (say-moor-ohn-ohk-swah; pop. 5000) have long defined its identity; the name of this 2000-year-old town stems from its Roman title, Sene Muros, meaning "old walls." Overlooking a bend in the Armençon River, the provincial town offers stunning views of the walls and quirky specialty shops, but little else. Thanks to its rooted local community, Sémur-en-Auxois feels thoroughly unspoiled—despite its status as a tourist town.

◧ TRANSPORTATION

Buses: Rue de la Liberté. TRANSCO (☎03 80 42 11 00) runs Rapides de Côte d'Or (☎03 80 78 93 33) buses to **Avallon** (40min.; M-Sa 8:25am, 1:44, 7:50pm, Su 12:46, 7:59pm; €7.20) and **Dijon** (1hr.; M-Sa 7:10am, 1, 6pm, Su 6pm; €11). Schedules at the tourist office.

Taxis: ☎03 80 96 60 18 or 06 07 91 24 93.

Bike Rental: RDX, 3 rue Carnot (☎03 80 97 10 26). €8 per ½-day, €13 per day. Open Tu-Sa June-Aug. 9am-noon and 2-7pm; Sept.-May 9:30am-noon and 2-6:30pm. MC/V.

▣ PRACTICAL INFORMATION

Tourist Office: Pl. Gaveau (☎03 80 97 05 96; www.ville-semur-en-auxois.fr), where rue de la Liberté meets the gates of the *vieille ville.* Has free maps with walking tours, a list of hotels, and an SNCF info and reservation office. Open July-Aug. M-Sa 9:30am-1pm and 1:45-7pm, Su 10am-12:30pm and 3-6pm; Sept.-June Tu-Sa 9am-noon and 2-6pm. SNCF info office open Tu-F 9am-noon and 2-6pm, Sa 9am-noon and 2-5pm.

Tours: Tourist office schedules walking tours of the city, offers free brochures with self-guided itineraries, and runs a 45min. *petit train* in the summer. July-Aug. Tu-Su; call tourist office for times. €4.30, ages 4-12 €2.70.

Laundromat: At the Centre Commercial Champion. Open daily 8am-8pm.

Police: Rue de la Fontaignotte (☎03 80 97 01 11).

Hospital: Av. Pasteur (☎03 80 89 64 64), east of the Centre Commercial.

Internet Access: Cyber KFE, 19 rue de la Liberté (☎03 80 96 64 40), inside the Hôtel du Commerce. €2 per 30min. Open M-F 7:30am-8pm, Sa 8am-8pm. **Carpe Diem** (see **Food,** below). Free with purchase.

Post Office: Pl. de l'Ancienne Comédie (☎03 80 89 93 06). **ATM** and **currency exchange** available. Open M-F 8:30am-noon and 1:30-5:30pm, Sa 8:30am-noon. **Postal Code:** 21140.

ACCOMMODATIONS AND CAMPING

Hôtel du Commerce, 19 rue de la Liberté (☎03 80 96 64 40), near the *vieille ville*. Spacious rooms with bath, TVs, and access to terrace bar make up for peeling paint. Breakfast €6-10. Reception M-Sa 7am-8pm, Su by reservation. Reservations recommended in summer. Singles and doubles €40-55; quads €60. Extra bed €8. AmEx/MC/V. ❸

Camping Municipal du Lac de Pont (☎03 80 97 01 26), 3km south of Sémur. From pl. de l'Ancienne Comédie, follow signs to Hôtel du Lac de Pont; the campground is next to the hotel. Note that the signs are narrow and sometimes hard to find. 3-star spot in the sun next to a scenic lake with tennis courts, a beach, bike rental, laundry, and a mini-mart. Reception 8am-noon and 4-7pm. Open from May to mid-Sept. €3.70 per person, children €1.90; €1.60 per car; sites €1.80. Electricity €2.50. MC/V. ❶

FOOD

For groceries, stop at the **Petit Casino** supermarket, across from the church on rue Notre Dame. (☎03 80 96 61 21. Open Tu-Sa 8am-1pm and 3-8pm, Su 8am-1pm. MC/V.) A weekly market opens along **rue Buffon** (open Su morning).

La Goulue, 15 rue Buffon (☎03 80 97 28 97; www.chezlagoulue.com). Colorful decor. Enormous portions. Tasty *escargot*-topped *crêpe bourguignonne* €15. *Crêpes* from €10. Desserts from €4. 3-course lunch *menu du marché* €12. Open May-Aug. daily 11:30am-2:30pm and 7-10pm; Sept.-Apr. M-Tu and Th noon-2pm, F-Sa noon-2pm and 7-10pm, Su noon-2pm. MC/V. ❸

Entr'act, rue du Vieux Marché (☎03 80 96 60 10). Extra cheesy pizzas and pastas in a homey dining room. Locals enjoy meals on the outdoor terrace. Pizzas €7-10. *Plat du jour* €8.50. Open daily noon-2pm and 7:30-10:30pm. AmEx/MC/V. ❷

Carpe Diem, 4 rue du Vieux Marché (☎03 80 97 00 35). Nautical-themed restaurant and bar. Variety of *crêpes* (€2-3) and well-stocked bar (drinks from €4). Internet free with purchase. *Plat du jour* €7.50. Open Tu-Sa 11am-1:45am, Su 11am-5pm. ❷

SIGHTS AND FESTIVALS

Each year on weekends in late May and early June, Sémur hosts the **Fêtes de la Bague,** which includes a medieval festival with artisan products, music, theater, fireworks, and even horse races through the town. On Thursdays from July to September, **Jeudis de l'Été** hits town, ushering in a series of free concerts and spectacles, such as circus performers. Call the tourist office for details.

COLLÉGIALE NOTRE DAME. In the medieval town, down rue Buffon, mossy gargoyles menace the central *place* from the 15th-century Gothic facade of this church. The interior lacks the polish of other Burgundy cathedrals, but its stained-glass memorial to fallen WWI soldiers makes a peek inside worthwhile. The unusual windows show two soldiers kneeling before Joan of Arc as buildings behind them burn down in vibrant flames. Outside, a 13th-century tympanum on the **Porte des Bleds** faces rue Notre Dame. Behind the church lies a quiet park perfect for a picnic. (☎03 80 97 05 96. *Open daily 9am-noon and 2-6pm.*)

MUSEÉ MUNICIPAL DE SÉMUR-EN-AUXOIS. Filled with sculptures, archaeological relics and oil paintings—not to mention a statue of France's greatest hero, ◾Vercingetorix—this small museum has it all. The collection of enormous snail shells will put the *escargots* on your plate to shame. *(Rue Jean-Jacques Collenot. ☎ 03 80 97 24 25. Open Apr.-Sept. M and W-Su 2-6pm; Oct.-Mar. M and W-F 2-5pm. Free.)*

OTHER SIGHTS. Stroll around the ramparts and the **Armençon River,** a 10min. walk from the *centre-ville*. Romantics can take a walk down to the seldom-touristed **Pont Pinard** for a breathtaking view of the illuminated *vieille ville*. *(From rue du Rempart, walk away from Notre Dame and make a left onto rue du Fourneau, then follow the signs (10min.). Vieille ville illuminated from mid-June to Sept. nightly 10pm-midnight.)*

🎵 🍺 ENTERTAINMENT AND NIGHTLIFE

With only about 300 seats, the **Théâtre Municipale,** 11 rue du Rempart, is France's smallest opera house. Visitors will enjoy the impressive acoustics and architecture *à l'italienne*. (Open only for performances. Check the tourist office for the season's schedule and ticket prices.) To find the most popular bars and *brasseries*, take a walk down **rue Buffon** or **rue de la Liberté**.

Le Domysyl, 13 rue Buffon (☎ 03 80 96 69 05). Playing an eclectic set of tunes ranging from hip hop to bebop, this *brasserie* draws a youthful crowd in an otherwise sleepy town. Food service, mostly consisting of cheese-centric appetizers, available until close. Beer from €2. Open M-F 10am-7pm, Sa 10am-1:30am. MC/V.

BURGUNDY

RHÔNE-ALPES

As the Alps-bound train leaves the rolling countryside and begins its long climb into the mountains, riders abandon their newspapers to watch a stunning transition: hills give way to craggy peaks, calm rivers to rushing torrents, and lazy cows to dashing mountain goats. High in the Alps, vast snowfields and glaciers look down on mountainsides blanketed with wildflowers. The region's stunning beauty draws not only those who want to admire it but also those who want to experience it up close: world-class athletes descend on the area each year to hike, bike, ski, and climb its majestic peaks. A trip to the region isn't complete without at least a glimpse of Mont Blanc—Western Europe's highest peak—but the gentler ranges of the Chartreuse and Vercors, dotted with tiny glacial lakes, provide an equally rewarding visit. Summer and winter visitors will find the most dependable weather and, naturally, the biggest crowds.

The region offers ancient attractions alongside the ultramodern, natural next to manmade wonders. Lyon, France's third-largest city, is the regional hub. In Annecy, architectural achievements take a back seat to those of Mother Nature; the pristine Lac d'Annecy is fringed by mountains, making the city a paradise for hikers and sailors. Higher up in the mountains, skiing is the main attraction, but the hotels in Chamonix and Val d'Isère are also packed in the summer when outdoors enthusiasts come to scale the rugged peaks.

> ## HIGHLIGHTS OF RHÔNE-ALPES
>
> **CHILL** with chamois (the antelope's smaller cousin) as you take in the scenery of Val d'Isère's Vanoise National Park (p. 490), the Alps's premier wildlife preserve.
>
> **ADMIRE** the lake in Annecy (p. 478), where the well heeled and well booted meet for refined relaxation or rugged recreation.
>
> **INDULGE** in gourmet luxury in Lyon (below), arguably France's finest culinary hub.

LYON   ☎ 04

Ultramodern, ultra-friendly, and undeniably gourmet, Lyon (lee-ohn; pop. 453,000) is more relaxed than Paris and claims a few more centuries of history. Its location at the confluence of the Rhône and Saône Rivers and along the Roman road between Italy and the Atlantic made Lyon an easy choice for the capital of Roman Gaul. Today, Lyon has shed its long-standing reputation as a gritty industrial city, emphasizing its beautiful parks, a modern financial sector, and a well-preserved Renaissance quarter. The city is best known as the stomping ground of world-renowned chefs Paul Bocuse and Georges Blanc and as an incubator of contemporary culinary genius.

◩ INTERCITY TRANSPORTATION

Flights: Aéroport Lyon-Saint-Exupéry (☎08 26 80 08 26). Satobuses/Navette Aéroport (☎04 72 68 72 17; www.satobus.com) runs shuttles from the airport to **Gare de la**

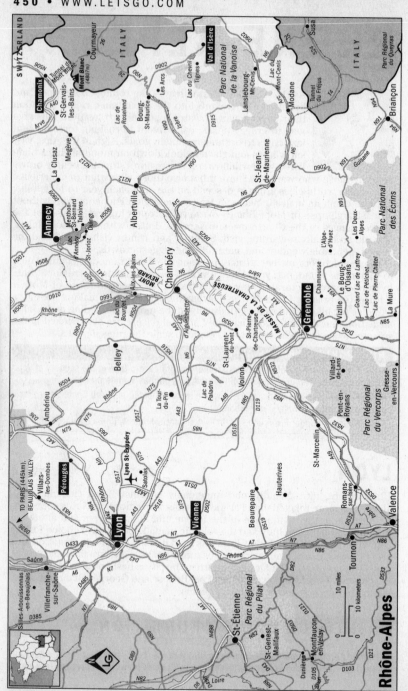

RHÔNE-ALPES

Part-Dieu, Gare de Perrache, and subway stops **Grange-Blanche, Jean Macé,** and **Mermoz Pinel** (every 20min.; €8.60, ages 12-24 €6.50, ages 4-11 €4.30). **Air France,** 10 quai Jules Courmont, 2ème (☎08 20 32 08 20), has 10 daily flights to Paris's **Orly** and **Charles de Gaulle** airports (from €118). Open M-Sa 9am-6pm.

Trains: Gare de la Part-Dieu, 5 pl. Béraudier, on the Rhône's east bank. ⓂPart-Dieu. Info desk open daily 5am-12:45am. Ticket windows open M-Th and Sa 5:15am-11pm, F and Su 5:15am-midnight. Trains terminating in Lyon go to **Gare de Perrache,** pl. Car-not. ⓂPerrache. Open daily 4:45am-12:30am. Ticket window open M 5am-10pm, Tu-Sa 5:30am-10pm, Su 7am-10pm. SNCF trains leave from both stations to: **Dijon** (2hr., every hr., €26); **Grenoble** (1½hr., every hr., €18); **Marseille** (1½hr., every hr., €44); **Nice** (6hr., 3 per day, €62); **Paris** (2hr., 17 per day, €60); **Strasbourg** (5½hr., 6 per day, €49); **Geneva, CHE** (3-4hr., 6 per day, €23). The SNCF office, 2 pl. Bellecour, is near the tourist office. Open M-F 9am-6:45pm, Sa 10am-6:30pm.

Buses: On the lowest level of Gare de Perrache and at Gorge de Loup in the 9ème (both ☎04 72 61 72 61). It's usually cheaper and faster to take the train. Philibert (☎04 72 75 06 06). Eurolines (☎72 56 95 30; www.eurolines.fr), on the main floor of Perrache. Open M-Sa 9am-9pm.

Car Rental: National (☎04 78 53 46 89), Gare de la Part-Dieu. Open M-F 7am-10:30pm, Sa 8:30am-12:30pm and 2-6:30pm, Su 10am-noon and 3-6:30pm. AmEx/MC/V.

Bike Rental: Holland Bikes, 15 rue Aime Collomb (☎04 78 60 28 03; www.holland-bikes.com). Open M 9am-2pm, Tu-Sa 9am-7pm.

✈ ORIENTATION

Lyon is easily navigable thanks to several visible landmarks and two rivers, which divide the city into three sections. Lyon is further divided into nine arrondissements. Bound by the **Saône** to the west and the **Rhône** to the east, the narrow *presqu'île* (peninsula) is the *centre-ville* and home to the 1er, 2ème, and 4ème arrondissements. Here you will find Lyon's two major squares: **place Bellecour,** the largest square in Europe and site of the tourist office, and **place des Terreaux,** with the **Hôtel de Ville** and its giant statue of four horses, 15min. to the north. The 2ème includes the Gare de Perrache, pl. Bellecour, and major pedestrian shopping areas—rue de la République north of Bellecour and rue Victor Hugo to the south. North of the 2ème, the 1er is home to the city hall, giant opera house, Musée des Beaux-Arts, and nocturnal Terraux neighbor-hood with its sidewalk cafes and student-packed bars. Farther north, the *presqu'île* widens into the 4ème and the famous **Croix-Rousse** hill, a residential neighborhood that once housed Lyon's silk industry. To the west of the Saône lies the oldest and most charming part of the city, **vieux Lyon** (5ème), with nar-row cobblestone streets, a cathedral, and Renaissance houses. From here you can walk uphill to reach Roman ruins and unbeatable views of the city below. Most of Lyon's permanent residents, however, live east of the Rhône in the 3ème and 6ème-8ème, home to **Gare de la Part-Dieu,** several universities, the enormous **Parc de la Tête d'Or,** and an ultramodern commercial complex. The **Tour du Crédit Lyonnais**—a reddish-brown skyscraper shaped like a pencil near the train station—is Part-Dieu's most obvious landmark.

Perrache is the more central of Lyon's two train stations, while **Part-Dieu** is larger and operates long-distance trains. Walking alone to or from either sta-tion at night is not recommended. Both are connected to Lyon's **Métro,** which is the fastest way to the **tourist pavilion** on pl. Bellecour; however, for those looking to stretch their legs, Lyon is fairly walkable. To walk from Perrache to the tour-ist pavilion, head straight onto rue Victor Hugo and follow it until pl. Bellecour; the tourist office is on the right (15min.). From Part-Dieu, walk straight on rue

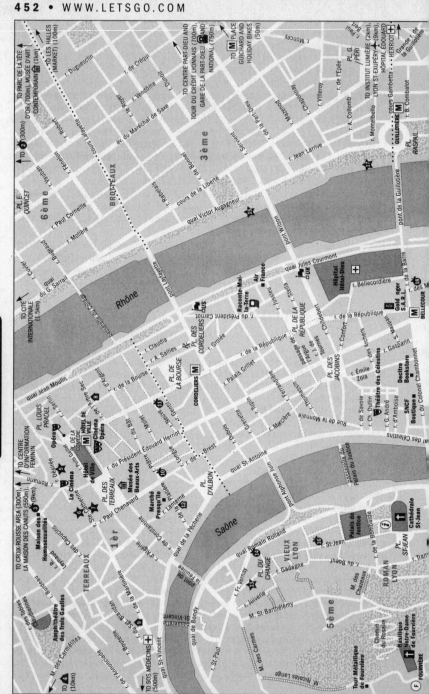

RHÔNE-ALPES

Lyon

ACCOMMODATIONS
Auberge de Jeunesse (HI), **22**
Camping Indigo, **4**
Hôtel d'Ainay, **24**
Hôtel Iris, **8**
Hôtel de la Marne, **26**
Hôtel de Paris, **12**
Hôtel St-Vincent, **9**

FOOD
Bernachon, **2**
Chabert et Fils, **20**
Chez Marie-Danielle, **23**
Chez Mounier, **18**
Léon de Lyon, **10**
La Marronnier, **19**

Le Nord, **11**
Les Paves de St-Jean, **16**
René Nardone Glacier, **15**
Restaurant Paul Bocuse, **3**
Le Sud, **21**

★ **NIGHTLIFE**
Ayers Rock Café and
   Cosmopolitan, **5**
The Shamrock, **6**
Le Sirius, **17**
The Smoking Dog, **13**
Tavern of the Drunken
   Parrot, **7**
Q Boat, **14**

Rhône

Saône

PRESQ'ÎLE

2ème

7ème

PL. BELLECOUR

PL. ANTONIN PONCET

PL. ANTOINE VOLLAN

PL. CARNOT

PL. AMPÈRE

PL. DE LA COMMANDERIE

VIEUX LYON

PERRACHE

Gare de Perrache

Eurolines

Parc Archéologique

Musée Gallo-Romain

Théâtre Romain

Hôpital de l'Antiquaille

MINIMES

AMPÈRE VICTOR HUGO

Le Grand Tour

Musée Historique des Tissus and Musée Lyonnais des Arts Décoratifs

Voyages Wasteels

Canada

Laundry

Centre d'Histoire de la Résistance et de la Déportation

MAISON DE LA DANSE (2km)

TO Ireland (200m),

Streets:
r. G. Dru
r. Janjot
r. Béchevelin
r. de Marseille
r. Sébastien Gryphe
av. Berthelot
r. Pasteur
r. de Bonald
r. Montesquieu
r. d'Aguesseau
r. Salomon Reinach
r. Cavenne
r. de l'Université
r. Chevreul
r. Jaboulay
r. du Professeur Grignard
r. Raulin
r. Étienne Rognon
r. Raoul Servant
quai Claude Bernard
quai Dr. Gailleton
r. Ch. Biennier
r. Sala
r. de la Charité
r. Laurencin
r. des Remparts d'Ainay
r. Mazard
r. Duhamel
r. A. Comte
r. Fr. Dauphin
r. Victor Hugo
r. d'Auvergne
r. Ste-Hélène
r. Jarente
r. Henri IV
r. de Condé
r. Boissac
r. Alphonse Fochier
r. Sala
r. Franklin
r. Bourgelat
r. d'Enghien
r. de Castries
r. G. Plessier
r. du Plat
r. Vaubecour
r. Guynemer
quai M. Joffre
cours de Verdun
r. du Bélier
quai Tilsitt
quai Fulchiron
av. A. Max
av. du Doyenné
Montée du Gourguillon
Montée du Chemin Neuf
r. des Farges
r. de l'Antiquaille
r. Cléberg
r. R. Radisson
Montée du Télégraphe
Bonaparte
pont de l'Université
pont Galliéni
pont Kitchener
autoroute A7
Marchand
passerelle St-Georges

Universités:
Université Lyon II et Lyon III

0   200 meters
0   200 yards

Servient, cross the Rhône on Pont Wilson, and continue on rue Childebert to pl. de la République. Turn left on rue de la République and follow it to pl. Belle-cour. The tourist office will be on the far side of the square (25min.). Although Lyon feels reasonably safe, it is a large city and travelers should beware of pickpockets inside Perrache, at pl. des Terraux, and in pl. Bellecour's crowds.

▐ LOCAL TRANSPORTATION

Public Transportation: TCL (☎08 20 42 70 00; www.tcl.fr). Info offices at both bus stations and all major Métro stops. *Plan de Poche* (pocket map) available from any TCL branch. Tickets valid for Métro, buses, and trams. Tickets €1.60, carnet of 10 €13; student discount includes 10 passes valid for 1 month (€12). Tickets valid 1hr. in 1 direction, connections included. **Ticket Liberté** day pass (€4.40) is a great deal for short-term visitors, as is **PassLyon** (see **Tourist Office,** below). Métro, buses, and trams run 5am-12:20am. Ⓜ T1 connects Part-Dieu to Perrache directly. A night *navette* runs between pl. Tarreaux and local universities (Th-Sa every hr. 1-4am). Funiculars swing between Ⓜ Vieux Lyon, pl. St-Jean, and Fourvière and St-Just until midnight. €2.20.

Taxis: Taxi Radio de Lyon, 15 rue Dumont d'Urville (☎04 72 10 86 86; www.taxilyon. com). Perrache to airport during the day €40, at night €55; airport to Part-Dieu €36/50. 24hr. **Maison des Taxis du Rhone,** 13 rue de Gerland (☎04 72 72 03 03). **Taxis Voyages Courses,** 1 rue Joseph Pillard (☎04 74 69 63 11).

▐ PRACTICAL INFORMATION

Tourist Office: In the pavilion, at pl. Bellecour, 2ème (☎04 72 77 69 69; www.lyon-france.com). Ⓜ Bellecour. Free accommodations booking and map. Buy the **Lyon City Card** for unlimited public transportation as well as admission to museums, tours, and river cruises. 1-day pass €19, 2-day pass €29, 3-day pass €39. Open from mid-Apr. to mid-Oct. M-Sa 9:30am-6:30pm, Su 10am-5:30pm; from mid-Oct. to mid-Apr. M-Sa 10am-5:30pm. MC/V.

Tours: Offered by the tourist office. In French (English in summer). €9, students €5. Audio tours €5 per 1½hr. **Le Grand Tour** (☎04 78 56 32 39; lyon.legrandtour@voyages-naime.com). 1¼hr. tour, with multilingual audio tours. Buy tickets on bus or in hotels. Start at pl. Bellecour. €17, ages 4-11 €8; 2-day pass €20. Last tour of the day €10.

Budget Travel: Voyage Wasteels, 5 pl. Ampère, 2ème (☎04 78 42 09 02). Ⓜ Ampère-Victor Hugo. Open M-F 9:30am-12:30pm and 2-6pm.

Consulates: Canada, 17 rue Bourgelat, 2ème (☎04 72 77 64 07), 1 block from Ⓜ Ampère-Victor Hugo. Open M-F 9:30am-12:30pm by appointment. **Ireland,** 58 rue Victor Lagrange, 7ème (☎06 85 23 12 03). Open M-F by appointment. **UK,** 24 rue Childebert, 2ème (☎04 72 77 81 70). Ⓜ Bellecour. Open M-F 9am-12:30pm and 2-5:30pm. **US,** 1 quai Jules Courmant, 2ème (☎04 78 38 33 03). Open M-F 10am-noon and 2-5pm by appointment only.

Currency Exchange: Goldfinger SARL, 81 rue de la République (☎04 72 40 06 00). No commission. Open M-Sa 9:30am-6:30pm.

English-Language Bookstore: Decitre, 6 pl. Bellecour, 2ème (☎04 26 68 00 12; www. decitre.fr). Helpful English-speaking staff. Open M-Sa 9:30am-7pm. MC/V.

Women's Center: Centre d'Information Féminin, 18 pl. Tolozan, 1er (☎04 78 39 32 25; www.infofemmes.com). Open M-F 9am-1pm and 1:30-5pm.

Laundromat: 19 rue Ste-Hélène, north of pl. Ampère, 2ème. Wash €3.50 per 6kg. Open daily 7:30am-8:30pm. Branch at 51 rue de la Charité, 2ème. Open daily 6am-9pm.

Police: 47 rue de la Charité (☎04 78 42 26 56). ⓜPerrache.

Crisis Lines: AIDS info service (☎04 78 27 80 80).

Pharmacie de Garde: Pharmacie Blanchet, 5 pl. des Cordeliers, 2ème (☎04 78 42 12 42). ⓜCordeliers. Night fee €4.

Hospitals: All hospitals should have English-speaking doctors on call, and Lyon is known for excellent medical service. **Hôpital Édouard Herriot,** 5 pl. d'Arsonval, 3ème. ⓜGrange Blanche. Best for emergencies, but far from the *centre-ville*. More central is **Hôpital Hôtel-Dieu,** 1 pl. de l'Hôpital, 2ème. ⓜBellecour. The central city hospital line (☎08 20 08 20 69) will tell you where to go.

Internet Access: Free Wi-Fi at the **Bellecour McDonald's. Raconte Moi la Terre** (☎04 78 92 60 23), at the intersection of rue Grolée and rue Thomassin, 2ème. ⓜCordeliers. €4 per hr. Open M noon-7:30pm, Tu-Sa 10am-7:30pm.

Post Office: Pl. Antonin Poncet, 2ème (☎72 40 65 22), next to pl. Bellecour. **ATM** and **currency exchange** available. Open M-F 8am-7pm, Sa 8:30am-12:30pm. **Postal Codes:** 69001-69009; last digit indicates arrondissement.

🏠🏕 ACCOMMODATIONS AND CAMPING

France's second-largest financial center (after Paris, *bien sûr*) is filled on most weeknights with businessmen who leave town on the weekends. September is the busiest season in Lyon; it's easier and cheaper to find a place in the summer, but it's still wise to reserve ahead. Rooms under €30 are rare finds. Low-end hotels cluster east of pl. Carnot and prices rise toward pl. Bellecour. There are inexpensive options just north of **place des Terraux**. The accommodations in vieux Lyon, aside from the hostel, tend to break budgets.

■ **Auberge de Jeunesse (HI),** 41-45 montée du Chemin Neuf, 5ème (☎04 72 15 05 50 or 15 05 51; www.fuaj.org). ⓜVieux Lyon. Prime location in vieux Lyon. Terrace offers breathtaking views. Lively bar. Some dorms have private baths. Breakfast included. Laundry €4.10. Internet €4.80 per hr. 6-night max. stay. Reception 24hr. Reservations (by fax only) recommended, especially in summer. Dorms €16. MC/V. ❷

■ **Hôtel Iris,** 36 rue de l'Arbre Sec (☎04 78 39 93 80; www.hoteliris.freesurf.fr). ⓜHôtel de Ville. Convent turned hotel in a prime location near Terreaux. Artistic decor. Breakfast €5. Internet access. Reception 8am-8:30pm. Reserve 2 weeks ahead in summer. Singles and doubles with sink €35-42, with bath €48-50. MC/V. ❸

■ **Hôtel de la Marne,** 78 rue de la Charité (☎04 78 37 07 46; www.hoteldelamarne.fr). ⓜPerrache. Quiet rooms with spacious bathrooms. Homey atmosphere. A/C. Breakfast €6. Free Wi-Fi. Reception 24hr. Singles €51-57; doubles €57-63. AmEx/MC/V. ❹

Hôtel d'Ainay, 14 rue des Remparts d'Ainay, 2ème (☎04 78 42 43 42). ⓜAmpère-Victor Hugo. Some rooms with private baths. No communal showers. Breakfast €4.50. Reception 24hr. Singles €27, with shower €42; doubles €32/48. Extra bed €8. MC/V. ❷

Hôtel de Paris, 16 rue de la Platière, 1er (☎04 78 28 00 95; www.hoteldeparis-lyon. com), near pl. de Terraux. ⓜHôtel de Ville. Small, no-frills rooms. Clean bathrooms. Comfortable lobby adorned with Impressionist drawings of Lyon. Breakfast €6.50. Internet. Reception 24hr. Singles €48; doubles €62-79; triples €87-105. MC/V. ❹

Hôtel Saint-Vincent, 9 rue Pareille, 1er (☎04 78 27 22 56; www.hotel-saintvincent. com), off quai St-Vincent. ⓜHôtel de Ville. Comfortable rooms with wood floors and sparkling clean bathrooms. Breakfast €5.50. Reception 24hr. Reservations strongly recommended. Singles €55; doubles €65; triples €75-85. MC/V. ❹

RHÔNE-ALPES

Camping Indigo, 10km from Lyon (☎04 78 35 64 55; www.camping-indigo.com). ⓂGare de Vaise. From the stop, take bus #89 (dir.: Dardilly) to Gargantua. Campground with a pool, TV, game room, volleyball court, and bar. Internet. Tent sites €13-16. ❶

◖ FOOD

The galaxy of Michelin stars adorning Lyon's restaurants confirms the city's status as France's culinary capital. *Lyonnais* food is bizarre, elegant, and appetizing; however, it can be hard on both the waistline and the wallet. While most dinner *menus* don't dip below €16, equally appealing options can be found at lunch. If you're going to splurge on food, though, there's no better place. For a happy medium between haute cuisine and university canteens, try one of Lyon's many *bouchons*, descendants of the inns where travelers stopped to dine and have their horses *bouchonné* (rubbed down). These cozy restaurants serve delectable local dishes (€16-20) and can be found along **rue Mercière** and **rue des Marronniers** in the 2ème as well as on **rue Saint-Jean** in vieux Lyon. Chinese fast-food joints and *brasseries* line the streets off **rue de la République** in the 2ème, and dozens of kebab joints surround the **Hôtel de Ville.**

There are markets on the **quais** of the Rhône and Saône (open Tu-Su 8am-1pm) and small supermarkets and *épiceries* close to most major squares, including **Bellecour, Saint-Jean,** and **place des Terreaux.** For a homemade *lyonnais* meal, stock up on ingredients at the **Marché Presqu'île** supermarket, 9 rue de la Platière, 1er. (☎04 72 98 24 00. Open M-Sa 9am-8:30pm. MC/V.)

▨ **Le Sud,** 11 pl. Antonin Poncet, 2ème (☎04 72 77 80 00; fax 77 80 01). ⓂBellecour. Specializes in *la cuisine du soleil* (Mediterranean fare). Appropriately decorated with a huge metallic sun. Seafood and pasta from €12. *Menus* €19-22. Open M-Th and Su noon-2:30pm and 7-11pm, F-Sa noon-2:30pm and 7pm-midnight. AmEx/MC/V. ❸

▨ **Le Nord,** 11 rue Neuve, 2ème (☎04 72 10 69 69 or 10 69 68). ⓂCordeliers. Sample Bocuse's traditional *lyonnais* fare in a famed century-old *brasserie*. Attentive service. Upscale yet comfortable. Try the *gauffres* (waffle topped with melted chocolate and whipped cream) if you're in the mood for a treat. *Menus* €20-28. Open daily noon-2:30pm and 7-11pm, F-Sa noon-2:30pm and 7pm-midnight. AmEx/MC/V. ❹

▨ **René Nardone Glacier,** 26 quai de Bondy, 5ème (☎04 78 28 29 09). ⓂVieux Lyon. Huge ice cream selection in a variety of quirky flavors. Take note of the *murs peints* (murals) on the facade of René Nardone's building. €2 per scoop. Ice cream dishes €4-9.50. Open daily 9am-1am. MC/V. ❶

▨ **Chez Mounier,** 3 rue des Marronniers, 2ème (☎04 78 37 79 26). ⓂBellecour. Top-notch cuisine. Lunch *menu* €8. 4-course *menus* €11-20. Open Tu-Sa noon-2pm and 7-11pm, Su noon-1:30pm. MC/V. ❷

▨ **Chabert et Fils,** 11 rue des Marronniers, 2ème (☎04 78 37 01 94; www.chabertres-taurant.fr). ⓂBellecour. A well-loved *bouchon*, 1 of 4 on rue des Marronniers run by the same family. *Museau de boeuf* (snout of cattle) is one of many *lyonnais* concoctions on the €18 *menu*. For dessert, try the exquisite, creamy *guignol* (€5.70), a rum-soaked cake with a hint of orange. Lunch *menus* €8-13. Dinner *menus* €18-35. Open M-Th and Su noon-2pm and 7-11pm, F-Sa noon-2pm and 7-11:30pm. MC/V. ❷

▨ **Chez Marie-Danielle,** 29 rue des Remparts d'Ainay (☎04 78 37 65 60). ⓂAmpère-Victor Hugo. Her collection of awards may be intimidating, but chef Marie-Danielle makes guests feel at home as she whips up superb *lyonnais* fare in a colorful room. Lunch *menu* €15. Dinner *menu* €22. Open M-F noon-2pm and 7:30-10pm. MC/V. ❸

Bernachon, 42 cours Franklin Roosevelt (☎04 78 52 23 65). ⓂFoch. Specializes in pricey, delicious desserts (from €1.20). Open Tu-Sa 8:30am-7pm. MC/V. ❶

Restaurant Paul Bocuse (☎04 72 42 90 90; www.bocuse.fr), 4km out of town. The pinnacle of the *lyonnais* food scene. *Menus* €120-195. MC/V. ❺

Léon de Lyon, 1 rue Pléney, 1er (☎04 72 10 11 12). Famous chef Jean-Paul Lacombe prepares delicious, high-end cuisine. *Menus* €59, €118, and €150. Open Tu-Sa noon-2pm and 7:30-10pm. AmEx/MC/V. ❺

Les Paves de Saint-Jean, 23 rue St-Jean, 6ème (☎04 78 42 24 13). Ⓜ Vieux Lyon. Savory meat dishes are a worthwhile splurge. *Menus* €12-20. MC/V. ❸

La Marronnier, 5 rue des Marronniers, 2ème (☎04 78 37 30 09). Ⓜ Bellecour. Another local *bouchon*. Features filling French *plats,* like black pudding with apples and potatoes. Lunch *menu* €12. Dinner *menus* €15-20. Open M-Sa noon-2pm and 7-11pm. ❸

👁 SIGHTS

VIEUX LYON

While vieux Lyon is the most touristy district, it is also the most charming. Stacked against the Saône at the foot of the Fourvière Hill, vieux Lyon's narrow streets are home to lively cafes, hidden passageways, and medieval and Renaissance homes. The *hôtels particuliers,* with their delicate carvings and ornate turrets, sprang up between the 15th and 18th centuries when Lyon was the center of Europe's silk and printing industries. The regal homes around **rue Saint-Jean, rue du Boeuf,** and **rue Juiverie** have housed Lyon's elite for 400 years.

TRABOULES. The distinguishing features of vieux Lyon townhouses are their *traboules,* tunnels connecting parallel streets through a maze of courtyards, often with vaulted ceilings and spiral staircases. Although their original purpose is still debated, the *traboules* were often used to transport silk safely from looms to storage rooms. During WWII, the passageways proved invaluable as escape routes for the Resistance. Many are open to the public in the morning. A 2hr. tour beginning at the tourist office is the ideal way to explore these hidden treasures; the tourist office also provides a list of open *traboules* and their addresses for self-guided touring. However, inconsistent opening times make the guided tour more appealing. *(Tours in English and French every few days July-Aug. 2:30pm; Sept.-June irregular hours; contact tourist office. €9, students €5.)*

CATHÉDRALE SAINT-JEAN. This large but somewhat lackluster cathedral dominates the southern end of vieux Lyon. Because the building took over 300 years to complete, its architecture features Romanesque and Gothic elements; look for the gradual shift in style where the rows of arches become more rounded. While many of the older stained-glass windows depict Bible stories, some of the newer ones—installed to replace those destroyed during the Nazis' 1944 retreat—are purely geometric. The **Window of Two Adams** is particularly noteworthy, while the pink spiral window at the back is a stunning example of the contemporary glass. Automatons pop out of the cathedral's impressive 14th-century 🔔astronomical clock and reenact the Annunciation every hour between noon and 4pm. *(Open M-F 8am-noon and 2-7:30pm, Sa-Su 8am-noon and 2-7pm. Free.)*

FOURVIÈRE AND ROMAN LYON

Fourvière Hill, the nucleus of Roman Lyon, towers above the *vieille ville.* It is accessible via the rose-lined **Chemin de la Rosaire** (open daily 6am-9:30pm) and, for non-walkers, *la ficelle*— the funicular that leaves from Ⓜ Vieux Lyon.

🔲**BASILIQUE NOTRE DAME DE FOURVIÈRE.** During the Franco-Prussian War, the people of Lyon and their archbishop prayed fervently to the Virgin Mary for protection; the thankful survivors erected this magnificent basilica in her honor. High upon a hill, the building's brilliant white exterior is visible from almost anywhere in the city. With octagonal turrets, the basilica bears some resemblance to a fortress, though many locals maintain that the building's unique architecture makes it look like *un éléphant renversé* (an upside-down elephant). Inside, exquisitely intricate and colorful **mosaics** that wrap around nearly the entire cathedral depict the life of Mary, along with other religious scenes, such as Joan of Arc at Orléans. While many of France's cathedrals seem to blend together in travelers' memories, this basilica is truly unforgettable. For an amazing panorama of the city, ascend the **Tour de l'Observatoire** or the nearby **esplanade Fourvière** and scan for Mont Blanc, 200km east. *(Behind the esplanade at the top of the hill. Chapel open daily 7am-7pm; basilica open daily 8am-7pm. Tower open by tour June-Sept. daily 2:30, 4pm; Apr.-May W and Su 2:30, 4pm. Elevator €2, under 15 €1.)*

MUSÉE GALLO-ROMAIN. This expansive museum educates and fascinates with a vast collection of mosaics and statues. Unique items include a bronze tablet inscribed with a speech by Lyon's favorite son, Emperor Claudius. Most artifacts are labeled in English and French. *(☎04 72 38 81 90; www.musees-gallo-romains. com. Open Tu-Su 10am-6pm. €3.80, students €2.30, under 18 free; Th free for all.)*

PARC ARCHÉOLOGIQUE. This ancient park holds the well-restored 2000-year-old **Théâtre Romain** and the **Odéon.** Visitors are free to explore most of the hilltop ruins on their own. In the summer, enjoy the **Nuits de Fourvière** (see **Festivals,** p. 461), which is hosted at both venues. *(Next to ⓂMinimes/Théâtres Romains. Open daily from mid-Apr. to mid-Sept. 7am-9pm; from mid-Sept. to mid-Apr. 7am-7pm. Free.)*

LA PRESQU'ÎLE AND DES TERREAUX

Monumental squares and statues are the trademarks of the *presqu'île*, the lively area between the Rhône and the Saône. Just to the west lies **place des Terreaux,** a plaza covered with dozens of illuminated fountains. On the eastern edge of the square sits the 17th-century facade of the **Hôtel de Ville,** while on the north side, opposite the Musée des Beaux-Arts, is the magnificent **Fontaine Bartholdi.** The Neoclassical Opéra is lit up in an alluring shade of crimson at night.

▨MUSÉE DES BEAUX-ARTS. Lyon's art museum takes visitors on an artistic whirlwind. The archaeological wing displays Egyptian sarcophagi and Roman busts, while works by Monet, Renoir, and Picasso line the third-floor walls. Other highlights include an Islamic art display and a large French, Greek, and Roman coin collection. The garden in the interior courtyard is open to the public free of charge during museum hours. *(20 pl. des Terreaux. ☎04 72 10 17 40; www.mairie-lyon.fr. Open M, W-Th, Su 10am-6pm, F 10:30am-6pm. Sculptures and antiques closed 11:55am-2:15pm; paintings closed 1:05-2:15pm. €6, students and under 26 free. MC/V.)*

MUSÉE HISTORIQUE DES TISSUS. While the rows of extravagant 18th-century dresses and 4000-year-old Egyptian tunics might not be considered chic today, those interested in fashion and textiles will enjoy this collection of historical fabrics and clothing. Highlights include scraps of Byzantine cloth and silk wall-hangings that resemble stained glass. The ticket price includes admission to the neighboring **Musée des Arts Décoratifs,** housed in an 18th-century hotel. Its rooms showcase an array of clocks, painted plates, silverware, and furniture from the Renaissance to the present. Be sure to check out the wraparound mural of Lyon, painted in 1826, upstairs. *(34 rue de la Charité, 2ème. ⓂAmpère-Victor Hugo. ☎04 78 38 42 00; www.musee-des-tissus.com. Fabric open Tu-Su 10am-5:30pm. Arts Décoratifs open Tu-Su 10am-noon and 2-5:30pm. €5, students €3.50, under 18 free.)*

LA CROIX-ROUSSE AND THE SILK INDUSTRY

Though mass silk manufacturing has left town, Lyon is proud of its former dominance of the industry in Europe. The city's Croix-Rousse district, a steep walk—or smooth Métro ride—from pl. des Terreaux, houses the vestiges of its silk-weaving days. It's here that Lyon's few remaining silk workers perform a different kind of handiwork: reconstructing rare patterns for museum displays. The Croix-Rousse was also the location of the late-19th-century *canut* (silk weavers) revolts—considered the first Industrial Revolution uprising.

◼LA MAISON DES CANUTS. The silk industry of yesteryear lives on at this workshop. The *canuts* specialize in two methods of embroidery that are impossible to automate and still use 19th-century looms. Artisans demonstrate and explain their unbelievably complicated work and recount the evolution of the silk industry. Scarves and ties cost at least €32 in the gift shop, but you can take home a handkerchief for just €8.50. *(10-12 rue d'Ivry, 4ème. ☎04 78 28 62 04. Open Tu-Sa 10am-6:30pm. €5, students €2.50, under 12 free. Tours in French and English on demand daily 11am, 3:30pm and by request for groups of 10 or more.)*

PART-DIEU AND MODERN LYON

Lyon's newest train station and monstrous space-age mall form the core of the ultramodern Part-Dieu district. Locals call the district's commercial **Tour du Crédit Lyonnais** "Le Crayon" (the pencil). Next to it, the seashell-shaped **Auditorium Maurice Ravel** hosts major cultural events.

◼CENTRE D'HISTOIRE DE LA RÉSISTANCE ET DE LA DÉPORTATION. Housed in a building where Nazis tortured detainees during the Occupation, this museum presents a sobering collection of documents, photos, and films about the Holocaust and Lyon's role in the Resistance. Audio tours lead visitors through displays of heartbreaking letters and inspiring biographies. *(14 av. Bertholet, 7ème. Ⓜ Jean Macé. ☎04 78 72 23 11. Wheelchair-accessible. Open W-F 9am-5:30pm, Sa-Su 9:30am-6pm. €4, students €2, under 18 free; includes audio tour in 3 languages.)*

MUSÉE D'ART CONTEMPORAIN. This modern art mecca resides in the **Cité International de Lyon,** an ultramodern complex designed by Renzo Plano that also houses shops, theaters, and Interpol's world headquarters. All of its exhibits are temporary—even the walls are rebuilt for each installation. *(Quai Charles de Gaulle, next to Parc de la Tête d'Or, 6ème. Take bus #4 from Ⓜ Foch. ☎04 72 69 17 17; www.moca-lyon.org. Wheelchair-accessible. Open W-Su noon-7pm. €5, students €3, under 18 free.)*

INSTITUT LUMIÈRE. This museum chronicles the exploits of the brothers Lumière, who invented the motion picture in 1895 (see **Life and Times,** p. 76). The institute's complex also includes a movie theater. *(25 rue du 1er Film, 8ème. Ⓜ Monplaisir Lumière. ☎04 78 78 18 95; www.institut-lumiere.org. Open Tu-Su 11am-6:30pm. €6, students €5, members of groups of 4 or more €4.50. English audio tours €3.)*

PARC DE LA TÊTE D'OR. This massive park, one of the largest in Europe, is as diverse as the surrounding city. Its 259 acres offer a wide range of activities from cycling to boating to touring the zoo. Visitors enjoy the tranquil 60,000-bush rose garden, while children delight in the park's merry-go-round and minigolf course. Wide, shaded avenues also make the park a perfect destination for afternoon strolls. The park's name (Park of the Golden Head) represents the element of mystery that looms over its green expanses: legend has it that a golden head of Jesus lies buried somewhere on its grounds. *(Ⓜ Charpennes or Tram T1 from Perrache, dir.: IUT-Feyssine. ☎04 78 89 02 03. Open daily from mid-Apr. to mid-Oct. 6:30am-10:30pm; from mid-Oct. to mid-Apr. 6:30am-8:30pm.)*

RHÔNE-ALPES

ENTERTAINMENT

For info on summer entertainment and cinema, consult the weekly *Lyon Poche* and *Guides de l'Été de Lyon* or the seasonal *Lyon Libertin* (€2), sold in many *tabacs*. For longer stays, pick up *Le Petit Paumé*, a comprehensive list of all the city's goings-on, available at **l'EM Lyon**, 23 av. de Collongue. **Cinéma Opéra**, 6 rue Joseph Serlin (☎04 78 28 80 08), and **Le Cinéma,** 18 impasse St-Polycarpe (☎04 78 39 09 72), specialize in black-and-white, un-dubbed classics and international films. (€6.50, students €5.50, under 14 €3.50; W €5.50.)

Théâtre des Célestins, 4 rue Charles Dullin, 2ème (☎04 72 77 40 40). ⓂHôtel de Ville. Box office open Tu-Sa 12:15-6:45pm. Tickets €15-32, discounts for under 26.

Opéra, pl. de la Comédie (☎08 26 30 53 25; www.opera-lyon.com). ⓂHôtel de Ville. Tickets €5-95. Pass'Opéra Jeune provides €10 tickets to certain shows for those under 26. Reservations office open Tu-Sa (and M when there's a show) noon-7pm.

Orchestre National de Lyon (☎04 78 95 95 95; www.auditoriumlyon.com). Plays a full season Oct.-June. Tickets €15-45.

Maison de la Danse, 8 av. Jean Mermoz, 8ème (☎04 72 78 18 00; www.maisondeladanse.com). ⓂGrange Blanche. Tickets €10-45.

SHOPPING

Lyon's shopping scene will satisfy both the serious consumer and the casual window-shopper. The **Centre Commercial Part-Dieu**, across bd. Marius Vivier-Merle from Gare de la Part-Dieu, is your typical generic shopping mall, complete with chain clothing stores, food shops, a movie theater, a bowling alley, and a huge Galleries Lafayette. The 1er and 2ème arrondissements, particularly **rue de la République** and the charming **passage de l'Argue,** are centers of upscale brand-name stores. Funky boutiques cluster around **rue Saint-Jean** in vieux Lyon, and 🕮bookstores surround **place Bellecour**. Bargain-hunters will enjoy the massive flea market that sets up on Mondays on the *quais* east of the Saône.

NIGHTLIFE

Nightlife in Lyon is fast and furious. A vast array of riverboat clubs, student bars, Anglophone pubs, and gay establishments make going out in Lyon a constant adventure. There is a row of exclusive joints off the Saône, on **quais Romain Rolland, de Bondy,** and **Pierre Scize** in vieux Lyon (5ème), but the city's best and most accessible late-night spots are the riverboat dance clubs by the east bank of the Rhône. Students buzz in and out of tiny bars on **rue Sainte-Catherine** (1er) until 1am, when they head to the clubs. For a more mellow (but expensive) evening, head to the jazz and piano bars on the streets off **rue Mercerie.** When school's out, the scene is lively only on weekends. The tourist office guide provides a listing of spots that cater to Lyon's gay community, and *Le Petit Paumé* offers superb tips. The most popular gay spots are in the 1er.

🍸 **Ayers Rock Café,** 2 rue Désirée (☎08 20 32 02 03; www.ayersrockcafe.com). ⓂHôtel de Ville. This Aussie bar (run, obviously, by a South African) is a cacophony of loud rock music and wild bartenders who drum on the hanging lights. Packed for rugby matches. Bouncers are selective when the bar is crowded, so dress to impress. Shots €3. Mixed drinks €7. Open July-Aug. M-Sa 9pm-3am; Sept.-June M-Sa 6pm-3am, Su 6-10pm.

Cosmopolitan, 4 rue Désirée (☎08 20 32 02 03; www.cosmopolitanbar.com). Next door to Ayers and managed by the same owners. Atmosphere is less international and more restrained. Serves New York-themed drinks, ranging from "Taxi Driver" to "Greenwich Village." Shots €3. Mixed drinks €7. Student nights Tu, with happy hour all night. Open July-Aug. M-Sa 9pm-3am; Sept.-June M-Sa 8pm-3am. MC/V.

Le Sirius, across from 4 quai Augagneur (☎04 78 71 78 71; www.lesirius.com). ⓂGuillotière. Busiest riverboat on the Rhône. Cargo-ship-themed. Young, international crowd packs the bar for "sirius" dancing on the lower-level dance floor. See website for concert listings. Open Tu-Sa 6pm-3am. MC/V.

The Shamrock, 15 rue Ste-Catherine (☎04 72 07 64 96). ⓂHôtel de Ville. A happening but formulaic Irish pub. Young crowd knocks back pints (€5.20). Live concerts nightly W-Su at 9pm. Happy hour 6-9pm. Open daily 6pm-1am. AmEx/MC/V.

Q Boat, across from 17 quai Augagneur (☎04 72 84 98 98; www.actunight.com). ⓂGuillotière. Electronic and house music on a swanky boat with Art Deco decor. Crowd of chic young professionals. Open W-Sa 5pm-5am, Su 2pm-5am. AmEx/MC/V.

The Smoking Dog, 16 rue Lainerie (☎04 78 28 38 27; www.smoking-dog.fr). ⓂVieux Lyon. A fun, traditional-looking pub with Anglophone bartenders. Mixed drinks €5. Pints €4.50. Legendary "quiz night" Tu 9pm. Open daily 2pm-1am. MC/V.

Tavern of the Drunken Parrot, 18 rue Ste-Catherine (☎06 85 29 51 11). ⓂHôtel de Ville. Boisterous, nautically themed bar. Extremely potent homemade rum drinks (€2) in 28 flavors. Try *piment* (hot pepper). Open daily 6pm-1am. MC/V.

🌿 FESTIVALS

Les Nuits de Fourvière (☎04 72 32 00 00; www.nuitsdefourviere.fr), June-July. Concerts, theater, dance, and film screenings. Recent artists include REM and ▓ **Cat Power.** Tickets from €12 available at the Théâtre Romain or the FNAC on rue de la République.

Festivals du Vieux Lyon (☎04 78 38 09 09), early and mid-Dec. Dancers and artists from around the world showcase their talents on pl. du Petit Collège. Odd-numbered years bring the Contemporary Arts Festival; the dance festival takes place during even-numbered years. Tickets €15-36.

Fête des Lumières, Dec. 8. Light display fills the city while locals place candles in their windows and ascend with tapers to the basilica to honor the Virgin Mary.

🔢 DAYTRIPS FROM LYON

🏙PÉROUGES

Trains run from Lyon (30min.; M-Sa 18 per day, Su 9 per day; €6.50) to Meximieux-Pérouges. From the station, turn left and follow the road around the curve to the roundabout; take a left and continue until the intersection at the Gendarmerie. Turn right at the sign for Pérouges. Walk up the hill and turn right onto a dirt pedestrian road, which leads to the city gates (20min.). Arrive in the morning to avoid the tour groups.

The tiny, historic hilltop hamlet of Pérouges (pay-roojh) is such a source of pride for Europe that it was one of the official sights visited by the foreign leaders who attended the 1996 G7 summit held in Lyon. It only takes a short time in the town to understand why the French government formally deemed it "one of the most beautiful villages in France." Pérouges's streets, called *galets*, are made with age-worn stones collected from nearby rivers, whose shape and muted colors complement the town's masonry. The town's culinary specialty is the ▓**galette de Pérouges** (a large doughy pastry dripping in sugar, butter, cream, and fresh berry syrup), which is served alongside *cerdon* wine. Try them at **Relais de la Tour,** pl. Sutilleul (☎04 74 61 01 03). For a bit of area history, stop in at the small **Musée de Vieux Pérouges,** in the Maison des Princes, which show-cases an assortment of historical documents, antiques, a sculpture garden, and a rotating contemporary art exhibit. The museum turret has a great view of the rooftops below. (☎06 74 61 00 88. Open June-Oct. daily 10am-noon and 2-6pm. €4, under 10 free.) The **tourist office** is just outside the medieval city. (☎04 74 46 70 84. Open May-Aug. daily 10am-5pm; Sept.-Oct. and Mar.-Apr. Tu-F 10am-noon and 2-5pm, Sa-Su 2-5pm; Nov.-Feb. M-F 2-4:30pm.)

BEAUJOLAIS VALLEY

The most beautiful and authentic areas in the Beaujolais are difficult to access by public transportation; trains run between Mâcon and Lyon but stop mostly in uninteresting industrial towns like Villefranche. The best option is to rent a car in Lyon. Pick up the English tourist map highlighting points of interest and various wine routes, along with the helpful Tours: Vistas of the Rhône Region, which outlines 9 suggested driving itineraries. Venturing in by bike is more difficult; rent a bike in Lyon from Holland Bikes (☎04 78 60 28 03) and use one of the midpoint train stops on the Lyon-Mâcon line, such as Belleville-sur-Saône, as a starting point (bikes are welcome on the train). Take the scenic Beaujolais Voie Verte, a car-free path stretching from St-Jean d'Ardières near Belleville to Beaujeu, which offers 7 themed circuits (29-58km) along the way. Hiking brochures with maps are also available at the Lyon tourist office and at many hotels in the area. Ask for Randonnées en Pays Beaujolais.

Every mention of Beaujolais (boh-jhoh-lay) induces a thirst for the cool, fruity wine that this region exports. Between the Loire and the Saône rivers, with Lyon at its foot and Mâcon at its head, the Beaujolais houses an important tex-tile and lumber industry, but its claim to fame undeniably lies in its vineyards. The most touristy spot is **Le Hameau,** a wine museum in the town of Romaneche-Thorins that offers *dégustations,* displays on winemaking, and a 3D movie about the Beaujolais tradition. (☎03 85 35 22 22; www.plaisirsenbeaujolais. com. Open daily Apr.-Oct. 9am-7pm; Nov.-Dec. and Feb.-Mar. 10am-6pm. Apr.-Oct. €16, under 16 free; Nov.-Dec. €13/free.) However, the real draw of the area lies outside of any city or museum. Endlessly rolling vineyards dotted with medieval châteaux await those who venture away from the main *autor-oute.* Devoted wine enthusiasts should ask for a list of serious wine growers from the Lyon tourist office. A visit to the **Château de Corcelles,** not far from Belleville, makes for a lovely detour from the vineyards. Visitors can stroll through the inner courtyard, climb to the second-story chapel, and peer down into the dungeon of this 15th-century castle free of charge. Today, the château's main enterprise lies in the Beaujolais wine it produces from the surrounding countryside; bottles of the specialty spirit are available in the stable turned cellar filled with enormous casks. (☎04 74 66 00 24. Open M-Sa 10am-noon and 2:30-6:30pm.) Any tourist office in the area can provide directions to the castle, along with listings of other points of interest, ranging from gardens designed by Versailles's landscape architect Le Notre to a flower-lined cloister.

VIENNE ☎04 74

In 47 BC, Vienne (vyehnn; pop. 30,000) became a Roman colony—a rare and coveted designation that entitled its inhabitants to all the privileges of Roman citizens. Today, Vienne is little more than a sleepy town on the banks of the Rhône, but the impressive vestiges of its glory days cluster in the *centre-ville* and spread along a stretch of land across the river. In recent years, the town's name has become synonymous with the world-renowned **Festival du Jazz à Vienne,** a wine-soaked party that takes place in June.

▐ TRANSPORTATION

Trains: Pl. de Pierre-Semard. Open M-Sa 5:15am-8pm, Su 5:15am-10pm. To **Lyon** (20-30min., 45 per day, €6).

Buses: At the train station. Open M-F 9am-noon and 2:30-6:30pm, Sa 9am-noon. Ticket €1.10, carnet of 10 €6.90. MC/V.

Taxis: Dubot Taxis (☎04 74 57 69 21), at the train station.

▐ PRACTICAL INFORMATION

Tourist Office: ☎04 74 53 80 30; www.vienne-tourisme.com. From the station, walk straight on cours Brillier to the river; the office is on the left. Staff provides train schedules, accommodations booking, and a *guide pratique* with a map. Detailed city map (€1). Themed walking **tours** of the city in French and English. July-Aug. 2-3 per week 3:30pm; Sept.-June by reservation. €6.50, students €5.50. 2hr. audio tour in English €5. Internet €7.50 per hr. Open July-Aug. daily 9am-6pm; Sept.-June M-Sa 9am-noon and 1-6pm, Su 10am-noon and 2-5pm.

Youth Center: Bureau Information Jeunesse, 2 cours Brillier (☎04 74 53 80 70), next to the tourist office. Offers advice and Internet for young people, travelers, and students. Open M-Tu and Th noon-5pm, W 10am-5pm.

Laundromat: Salon Lavoir, pl. Drapière. Open daily 7am-8pm.

Police: Pl. Pierre Semard, next to the train station.

Pharmacy: 3 pl. François Mitterrand (☎04 74 85 02 70; fax 85 76 15).

Hospital: ☎04 74 31 33 33.

Internet Access: Wi-Fi between pl. du Palais, the Hôtel de Ville, and pl. Du Pilori.

Post Office: In front of the train station. **ATM** and **currency exchange** available. Open M-W 8:30am-noon and 1:30-6pm, Th 8:30am-noon and 2-6pm, F 8:30am-6pm, Sa 8:30am-noon. **Postal Code:** 38544.

▐ ▐ ACCOMMODATIONS AND FOOD

Most hotels in town start at around €50, but cheaper establishments are 8-10km outside of town; the tourist office provides a list and directions. The best bet is Vienne's hostel, located in the middle of the *centre-ville*. To reach the **Auberge de Jeunesse ❶**, 11 quai Rondet, walk 5min. from the tourist office. Dorms overlook the Rhône. (☎04 74 53 21 97; mjcvienne.auberge@laposte.net. Breakfast €3.50. Linen €2.80. Reception from July to mid-Sept. daily 5-9pm; from mid-Sept. to June M-F 5-9pm. Dorms €10. Cash only.)

Cafes and *brasseries* line cours Brillier toward the station, while **cours Romestang** has dozens of *pâtisseries* and *salons de thé*. There's a midsize **SPAR** supermarket around the corner from the train station at 50 cours Romestang. (Open daily 7:30am-9pm. MC/V.)

La Medina, 71 rue de Bourgogne (☎04 71 53 51 35). Popular Moroccan restaurant serves delicious, filling couscous (€11-16). *Menus* €14-18. Open M-Tu 7-10pm, W-Th noon-2pm and 7-10pm, F-Su noon-2pm and 7-11pm. MC/V. ●

Au P'tit Bouchon, 26 rue Voltaire (☎04 74 31 60 95; www.vienne-online.com). Small *brasserie* with a shaded terrace packed with locals. *Plats* €8.50-16. *Menus* €11-30. Open Tu-Sa noon-2pm and 7-10pm. MC/V. ❷

◉ SIGHTS

RUINS. Vienne's best sights represent what remains of its days as a Roman colony. The oldest of the ruins is the ■Gallo-Roman city, across the river at St-Roman-en-Gal, accessible by a walkway from the *quai* or by the bridge at pl. du Jeu-de-Paume. Restored fountains gurgle amid the ancient streets, and elaborate gardens color the foundations of once-palatial estates. The area contains the remains of some of the larger Roman homes, a forum, main streets, public bathrooms, baths, and underground storerooms. Analysis of *amphorae* (ancient storage jars) found here dated the Italian wine inside to around AD 124. The adjoining museum contains cutlery, *amphorae*, coins, and mosaics discovered in the city. (☎04 74 53 74 01. Open Tu-Su 10am-6pm. Museum and sites €3.80, students €2.30; Th free.) The well-preserved **Temple of Augustus and Livia** lies in the heart of the pedestrian district. The temple dates from around 10 BC and was converted to a church during the Middle Ages. On the hillside, the steeply plunging **Théâtre Romain** is thought to have been one of the largest theaters in Roman antiquity; the well-restored amphitheater now hosts outdoor concerts.

MONT PIPET. The flat-topped **Mont Pipet** looms over the amphitheater and offers spectacular views of the valley and its hillside ruins. The church and statue crowning its summit are dedicated to the Virgin Mary and have drawn pilgrims since the 19th century. From the theater, continue 15min. uphill on steep rue Pipet and take a left at the sign.

CHURCHES. Impressive churches fill the *centre-ville*. The **Cathédrale Saint-Maurice** boasts an array of Romanesque capitals and stained glass. *(Open daily 8:30am-6pm.)* **Église Saint-Pierre,** pl. St-Pierre, was built on the ruins of a Gallo-Roman city in the AD fifth century and is now home to an archaeological museum with Roman artifacts. *(☎04 74 85 20 35. Open Apr.-Oct. Tu-Su 9:30am-1pm and 2-6pm; Nov.-Mar. Tu-F 9:30am-12:30pm and 2-5pm, Sa-Su 2-6pm. €2.80.)*

◉ 🎇 NIGHTLIFE AND FESTIVALS

The amphitheater hosts pop, jazz, and classical artists all summer; the tourist office and the theater box office both have schedules. **Jazz à Vienne** (www.jazzavienne.com) takes over the town from late June to mid-July. World-renowned artists perform in concert, usually at 8:30pm, in the amphitheater. Tickets cost €27-30, but *musique gratuite* (free music) bookends the main shows.

> **Cuba de Sol,** 3 rue du Musée (☎04 74 31 56 67). A Cuban scene, complete with Che Guevara murals. Open daily 7:30am-1am. MC/V.

> **Boogaloo,** 1 rue des Carmes (☎04 74 85 20 18). Features an Afro-Caribbean atmosphere and a huge variety of rum. Open Tu-Sa 8am-3pm and 6pm-1am. Cash only.

GRENOBLE
☎04 76

Grenoble (gruh-no-bluh; pop. 168,000) boasts all the spoils that come from its status as a dynamic and diverse university town: great nightlife, charming sidewalk cafes, and shaggy hippies. Immigrant influxes in the 20s and 50s gave Grenoble sizable Italian and North and West African populations, which contribute to its multicultural atmosphere. Throughout the year, a thriving foreign exchange program fills the city with young scholars from all corners of the globe. Grenoble's Rhône Alps setting, however, has made the city a haven not only for students but also for hikers, skiers, and bikers, who flock to Grenoble for its snow-capped peaks and challenging trails.

Grenoble

▲▲ **ACCOMMODATIONS**
Auberge de Jeunesse (HI), **16**
Camping Les 3 Pucelles, **12**
Le Foyer de l'Étudiante, **3**
Hôtel de la Poste, **11**
Hôtel Victoria, **13**

🍴 **FOOD**
Le Couscous, **10**
Karkadé, **8**
Larde Aux Fruits, **9**
Mosaïque Pâtisserie, **2**
Tête à l'Envers, **1**
Le Tonneau de Diogène, **4**

★ **NIGHTLIFE AND ENTERTAINMENT**
Couche-Tard Pub, **5**
365 Café, **7**
London Pub, **6**

Parc Paul Mistral

Cimetière St-Roch

TO ⊕ (1km)

l'Isère

Parc Guy Pape

RHÔNE-ALPES

TO LYON (105km), AÉROPORT DE GRENOBLE ST-GEOIRS

TO ⊡ CASINO (6km)

TO RU (300m)

⌐ TRANSPORTATION

Flights: Aéroport de Grenoble Saint-Geoirs, St-Étienne de St-Geoirs (☎04 76 65 48 48). International flights only. British Airways and easyJet fly to **London, ENG.** Ryanair flies to **Stockholm, SWE.** Buses run between the bus station and the airport (€3.80). Satobus runs to **Aéroport Lyon Saint-Exupéry** every hr. 5am-9pm (€20).

Trains: Gare Europole, pl. de la Gare. Ticket office open M-F 5am-8:45pm, Sa 5am-7:45pm, Su 6am-8:45pm. An SNCF office is on rue de la République, across from the tourist office. Open M-F 9am-6:30pm, Sa 10am-6pm. To: **Annecy** (1½hr., 18 per day, €17); **Lyon** (1½hr., 30 per day, €18); **Marseille** (4-5½hr., 15 per day, €37); **Nice** (5-6½hr., 5 per day, €57); **Paris** (3hr., 9 per day, €70).

Buses: To the left of the train station. Open M-Sa 6:15am-7pm, Su 7:15am-7pm. VFD (☎08 20 83 38 33; www.vfd.fr) runs to **Nice** (7hr., 1 per day, €53) and **Geneva, CHE** (3hr., 1 per day, €27). Frequent service to ski resorts and outdoor areas.

Public Transportation: Transports Agglomération Grenobloise (TAG; ☎04 76 20 66 66; www.semitag.com). Grenoble's **tram** and **bus** network is useful only for transport to and from the *gare;* the *centre-ville* is pedestrian-friendly. Info desk in the tourist office open July-Aug. M-Sa 9am-6pm; Sept.-June M-F 8:30am-6:30pm, Sa 9am-6pm. Lines run 6am-8:30pm, 4 night lines Th-Sa 9pm-midnight; 2 tram lines run daily every 5-10min. 5am-midnight. Tickets €1.30, carnet of 10 €11; day pass €3.50, 5-day pass €12.

Taxis: Taxi Grenoble, 14 rue de la République (☎04 76 54 42 54), next to the tourist office. €68-72 to the airport. 24hr.

Car Rental: Around the train station. **Self Car,** 24 rue Émile Gueymard (☎04 76 50 96 96), across from the station. From €49 per day, €77 per weekend. Insurance included. 21+. Open M-F 7:30am-noon and 1:30-6pm, Sa 8am-noon. MC/V.

✳ ⟁ ORIENTATION AND PRACTICAL INFORMATION

The primarily pedestrian *vieille ville* stretches from the tourist office to the river, bound by the Jardin de Ville and Musée de Grenoble.

Tourist Office: 14 rue de la République (☎04 76 42 41 41; www.grenoble-isere.info). From the train station, turn right onto pl. de la Gare and take the 3rd left onto av. Alsace-Lorraine. Follow the tram tracks through rue Félix Poulat and rue Blanchard; the tourist complex is on the left, before the tracks fork (15min.). Alternatively, tram lines A and B (dir.: Échirolles or Gières) run to Hubert Dubedout-Maison du Tourisme. Hosts local bus office and post office. English-speaking staff offers *Le Guide de l'Étudiant,* a free guide to long-term housing. Also offers a **Grenoble City Pass** that includes entry to 1 museum, a *petit train* ride, a *téléphérique* ride, and a walking tour. Open May-Sept. M-Sa 9am-6:30pm, Su 10am-1pm and 2-5pm; Oct.-Apr. M-Sa 9am-6:30pm, Su 10am-1pm.

Tours: Available from the tourist office. Tours of the *vieille ville* in English and French June-Aug. M-Tu and Th-Sa 10am, W 2:30pm; Sept.-May Sa 10am. €7.50, students and under 18 €5.50. Tours of the Bastille in English and French July-Aug. daily 3pm. €6, under 18 €3. Audio tour €7.50. 40min. multilingual *petit train touristique* leaves from pl. Grenette daily 10am-7pm. €6.

Budget Travel: Voyages Wasteels, 7 rue Thiers (☎04 76 47 07 13; www.wasteels.fr). Student travel packages. Open M-F 9:30am-1pm and 2-6pm, Sa 9am-1pm. MC/V.

GLBT Resources: www.grenoble-lgbt.com.

Laundromat: Lavomatique, 14 rue Thiers (☎04 76 96 28 03). Open daily 7am-10pm.

Hiking Information: Maison de la Montagne, 3 rue Raoul Blanchard (☎04 76 44 67 03; www.grenoble-montagne.com), across from the tourist office. Open M-F

9:30am-12:30pm and 1-6pm, Sa 10am-1pm and 2-5pm. **Weather:** ☎08 92 68 02 38. **Snow info:** ☎08 92 68 10 20.

Police: 36 bd. du Maréchal Leclerc (☎04 76 60 40 40). Call for the **pharmacie de garde.** Take bus #31 (dir.: Malpertuis) to Hôtel de Police.

Hospital: Av. des Maquis du Grésivaudan (☎04 76 76 75 75).

Internet Access: Celsiuscafe.com, 11 rue Gutéal (☎04 76 46 43 36). €1 per 15min., €2.50 per hr. Open daily 9am-11pm.

Post Office: 7 bd. du Maréchal Lyautey (☎04 76 43 51 39). Open M-F 8am-7pm, Sa 8am-noon. Branch at 12 rue de la République (☎04 76 63 32 70), adjacent to the tourist complex. **Currency exchange** available. **ATMs** at both locations. Open from mid-July to Aug. M-F 9am-noon and 1:45-5:30pm, Sa 9am-noon; from Sept. to mid-July M 8am-5:45pm, Tu-F 8am-6pm, Sa 8am-noon. **Postal Code:** 38000.

▌▛ ACCOMMODATIONS AND CAMPING

▨ **Le Foyer de l'Étudiante,** 4 rue Ste-Ursule (☎04 76 42 00 84; fax 42 96 67). Close to the *vieille ville*. Spacious rooms with desks. Backpackers mingle in courtyard. Kitchen, piano, laundry (€2.20), free Internet and Wi-Fi. 1-week min. stay. Reception 24hr. Weekly singles €118; doubles €160. ❶

Hôtel de la Poste, 25 rue de la Poste (☎/fax 04 76 46 67 25). Located on the 1st fl. of an apartment building. Large, nicely furnished rooms feel like home away from home. Kitchen. Reception 24hr. Singles €34; doubles €41. Cash only. ❸

Auberge de Jeunesse (HI), 10 av. des Maquis du Grésivaudan (☎04 76 09 33 52; www. fuaj.org). Take bus #1 (dir.: Pont Rouge) from the corner of rue Alsace-Lorraine and cours Jean Jaurès to Quinzaine, in front of a shopping plaza. Facing the direction from which the bus came, turn left onto av. des Maquis du Grésivaudan; the *auberge* is 3 buildings down on the right. Alternatively, take tram A (dir.: Échirolles) to la Rampe. Walk in the direction from which the tram came, turn left at the 1st intersection, and follow the "Auberge de Jeunesse" signs down av. de Grugliasco through several intersections and past the Casino supermarket (15min.). Clean building with a bar and kitchen. Most of the 2- to 8-bed dorms have private showers and toilets. Laundry €3. Wi-Fi €2 per day. Reception 7:30am-11pm. 24hr. keycard access. Dorms from €18. MC/V. ❷

Hôtel Victoria, 17 rue Thiers (☎04 76 46 06 36; www.hotelvictoria.com). Halfway between the train station and the *centre-ville*. While the 11:30pm curfew isn't ideal for sampling Grenoble's nightlife, the stylish lobby and peaceful, spacious rooms over-looking a courtyard provide a true refuge. Rooms have TVs and Wi-Fi. Breakfast €7. Reception 7am-11:30pm. Open Jan.-July and from Sept. to mid-Dec. Singles €39, with shower €46; doubles €47/55; quads €74. MC/V. ❸

Camping Les 3 Pucelles, 58 rue des Allobroges (☎04 76 96 45 73; www.camping-trois-pucelles.com), 4km from town in Seyssins. From the train station, take tram A (dir.: Échirolles) to Charvat, then take tram C (dir.: Seyssins Le Prisme) to Mas des Îles. Turn left; it's a few blocks down (15min.). Small suburban campground has plots divided by tall hedges and 2 pools. Laundry €3. Reception 8am-1pm and 3-9pm. 1 person, tent, and car €9.50. Extra person €4. Electricity €2.50. Cash only. ❶

▐ FOOD

Grenoble's diverse population has brought an unbeatable array of ethnic cuisine to the city. Asian eateries can be found between **place Notre Dame** and the river and on **rue Condorcet;** North African establishments congregate around **rue Chenoise** and **rue Lionne.** Cheap pizzerias line **quai Perrière** across the river. For more traditional fare, cafes and *brasseries* cluster around **place Notre Dame** and

place Saint-André in the heart of the *vieille ville*. Crowded regional restaurants cater to locals around **place de Gordes**. The most lively of Grenoble's 17 markets can be found on **place Saint-André, place Saint-Bruno, place aux Herbes** (all open Tu-Th 7am-1pm), and **place Sainte-Claire** (open Tu-Th 7am-1pm, F-Sa 3-7pm). There is a large **Marché Plus** at 22 cours Jean Jaurès, near the Alsace-Lorraine tram stop. (☎04 76 12 91 44. Open M-Sa 7am-9pm, Su 9am-noon.) There's a **Casino** with a cafeteria at 46 cours Jean Jaurès, up the street from the HI hostel. (Open M-Sa 8:30am-8pm. Cafeteria open daily 11am-9:30pm.) **Restaurants Universitaires (RUs; ☎**04 76 57 44 00) sell meal tickets (€2.70) during the school year. Grenoble's three RUs are on 5 rue d'Arsonval (open M-F 11:30am-1:30pm and 6:30-7:45pm), 6 pl. Pasteur (open daily 11:45am-1:15pm and 6:30-7:45pm), and rue Maurice Gignoux (open daily noon-1:15pm and 6:30-7:50pm).

☒ **Tête à l'Envers,** 12 rue Chenoise (☎04 76 51 13 42). 7-table gem offers a creative international melange. Chef cooks up whatever looks fresh at the market. *Plats du jour* €11. Dessert platter €9.50. Lunch *menus* €15-17. Open W-F noon-3pm and 7:30pm-1am, Tu and Sa 7:30pm-1am. Reservations recommended. MC/V. ❷

Le Couscous, 19 rue de la Poste, next to Hôtel de la Poste. Guests pack the terrace to fill up on generous portions of the restaurant's namesake dish. Couscous €6.50-17. *Plat du jour* €7.40. Open M 7-11pm, Tu-Su noon-2pm and 7-11pm. MC/V. ❷

Mosaique Pâtisserie, 3 rue Chenoise (☎04 76 01 91 28), across from Tête à l'Envers. An African twist on a French staple. Mint "special-tea" is a refreshing way to get your caffeine fix. Honey- and almond-saturated Tunisian pastries €1-2.50. Salads €4-5. Couscous €7-13. Open daily 8am-10pm. AmEx/MC/V. ❷

Le Tonneau de Diogène, 6 pl. Notre Dame (☎04 76 42 38 40), underneath a bookstore, near the Musée de Grenoble. Walls covered with Nietzsche quotes are the backdrop for a laid-back student scene. Salads €4.50-8.40. *Menu* €7.50. Open from mid-Aug. to early July daily 11:30am-midnight. MC/V. ❶

Karkadé, 6 rue Servan (☎04 76 44 02 78). Intimate Egyptian *salon de thé* serves flavorful *karkadé* (hibiscus flower) tea behind velvet curtains. African instruments and rotating art exhibits surround cushioned benches. Pastries €3. Teas €4. Open Tu 11am-3pm and 6-11pm, W-F 11am-3pm and 6:30-11pm, Sa 6:30-11pm. Cash only. ❶

Larde Aux Fruits, rue Diodore Rahoult. Locals crowd this small, but incredibly popular ice-cream stand. 1 scoop €2, 2 scoops €3. Cash only. ❶

◎ SIGHTS

☒**TÉLÉPHÉRIQUE GRENOBLE-BASTILLE.** These gondolas, the city's icons, depart every 10min. and head for the Bastille, a 16th-century fort sitting 475m above Grenoble. From the top, on a clear day, visitors can look north toward the Lyon valley and its two rivers or east over the mountain ridge to the distant peak of Mont Blanc. From the Bastille, follow signs to the **Grotte de Mandaran,** a long and exciting (read: barely lit) cave—bring a flashlight. Continue 1hr. up to **Mont-Jalla,** where a flower-studded memorial tells the story of the Alpine soldiers who have protected Grenoble for centuries. Starting in the Jardins des Dauphins and ending at the Bastille, the **Via Ferrata** gives Alpine climbers the chance to scale the hill's rock face; the route was the first urban climbing site constructed in the world. Rent equipment at **Borel Sport.** (*42 av. Alsace-Lorraine.* ☎04 76 46 47 46; fax 46 00 75. Ski and snowboard packages €7-17 per day. Open June-Aug. Tu-W and F-Su 10am-noon and 2-6pm; Sept.-May daily 9:30am-12:30pm and 2-7pm. MC/V.) The **Parc Guy Pape** trail offers a pleasant way to bypass the *téléphérique;* its trails wind through gardens, starting in the Jardins des Dauphins and ending at the Bastille (1hr.). Be cautious: the trail has several steep staircases, many of which pass through poorly lit tunnels. *(Quai Stéphane-Jay.* ☎ *04 76 44 33 65. Open July-Aug. M 11am-12:15am, Tu-Su 9:15am-12:15am; Sept. and June M 11am-11:45pm, Tu-Sa 9:15am-11:45pm, Su 9:15am-7:25pm; Oct. and Mar.-May M 11am-7:25pm, Tu 11am-11:45pm, W-Sa 9:30am-11:45pm, Su 9:15am-7:25pm; from Nov. to early Jan. and from late Jan. to Feb. M-Tu 11am-6:30pm, W-Su 10:45am-6:30pm. €4.20, round-trip €6.10; students €3.40/4.85; ages 5-18 €2.80/3.85; over 75 €1.70/2.80; under 5 free.)*

MUSÉE DE GRENOBLE. This museum houses canvases by Rubens, La Tour, and Zurbarán as well as a 20th-century collection, with works by Chagall and a room devoted to Matisse. Local artists' depictions of the mountains are on display just outside the museum's doors. *(5 pl. de Lavalette. ☎ 04 76 63 44 44; www.museedegrenoble.fr. Open M and W-Su 10am-6:30pm. Guided 1½hr. tours in French Sa-Su 3pm. €5, students €2, under 18 free. English audio tour €3. Guided visits €3.)*

VIEILLE VILLE. Built over 17 centuries, Grenoble's *vieille ville* is a motley but charming collection of old squares, stately fountains, and lush parks. Vestiges of the Roman ramparts are visible near the town's historic center, **place Saint-André,** now Grenoble's most popular student hangout. The 13th-century **Collégiale Saint-André** was the traditional burial place for dauphins until 1349. Its soaring bell tower is made from volcanic rock. *(Open daily 8am-5pm.)* Across the street, the **Palais de Justice** boasts a Gothic facade, a Renaissance-style right wing, and 19th-century heraldic shields of Grenoble over its door. The building was erected by dauphin and future king Louis XI in 1453 to house the region's parliament. The **Café de la Table Ronde,** 7 pl. St-André, built in 1739, is the second-oldest coffee shop in France and has been frequented by such famous patrons as Léon Blum and Mussolini. *(☎ 04 76 44 51 41. Open M-Sa 9am-1am.)*

MUSÉE DAUPHINOIS. Transformed from convent to prison to Catholic school to historic site, this regional ethnographic museum contains exhibits on Lyon's traditions. Situated on the north bank of the Isère, the 17th-century building houses four themed exhibitions with impressive multimedia and sound effects. Gens de l'Alpes (People of the Alps) explores the history of the first pioneering settlers who carved out a livelihood in the mountains, while La Grande Histoire du Ski (The History of Skiing) traces the evolution of snow sports, featuring a vast collection of early and modern skis. These two permanent exhibits have English explanations. *(30 rue Maurice Gignoux. Cross Pont St-Laurent and*

FROM THE ROAD

LOST IN TRANSLATION

Hollywood movies and American television may have captivated a market in France, but there's often little rhyme or reason regulating the translation of their titles:

Lolita in Spite of Myself *(Mean Girls):* Vladimir Nabokov and Lindsay Lohan: the perfect pop-culture union.

The Counterattack of the Blondes *(Legally Blond):* Perhaps a little aggressive for a movie about Reese Witherspoon and shoes.

The Little Champions *(Mighty Ducks):* From the Flying V to the quack chant, the *canard* is the heart and soul of this film.

Rambo *(Rambo):* Some words just transcend linguistic and cultural barriers.

The Man Who Would Murmur at the Ears of Horses *(The Horse Whisperer):* Just in case there was any ambiguity in the original title.

A Day with No End *(Groundhog Day):* If you don't get the Groundhog Day reference, this is going to be a long movie.

La Grande Évasion *(The Great Escape):* If they didn't translate this literally, Steve McQueen would've taken everyone down.

The Big Lebowski *(The Big Lebowski):* The French recognize that The Dude does not appreciate name changes.

Lost in Translation *(Lost in Translation):* Apparently this one wasn't.

—Vinnie Chiappini

go up Montée Chalemont. ☎04 76 85 19 01; www.musee-dauphinois.fr. Open June-Sept. M and W-Su 10am-7pm; Oct.-May M and W-Su 10am-6pm. Free.)

MUSÉE D'HISTOIRE NATURELLE DE GRENOBLE. Children in particular will enjoy the interactive games and dioramas of Alpine animals lining the stately hall of this museum. The second floor showcases exotic insects from around the world and glittering gems. Many of the exhibits have English descriptions. *(1 rue Dolomieu. ☎04 76 44 05 35; www.museum-grenoble.fr. Open M-F 9:30am-noon and 1:30-5:30pm, Sa-Su 2-6pm. €2.20, ages 18-25 €1.50, under 18 free; W free.)*

OTHER MUSEUMS. Consult the tourist office for a full list of free museums throughout the city. The **Musée de la Résistance et de la Déportation,** 14 rue Hébert, highlights Grenoble's WWII resistance effort with theatrical exhibits. *(☎04 76 42 38 53; fax 42 55 89. Open July-Aug. M and W-Su 10am-7pm; Sept.-June M and W-F 9am-6pm, Sa and Su 10am-7pm.)* The **Musée de l'Ancien Evêché,** 2 rue Très-Cloîtres, explores the region's history from prehistoric times to the present in the old Bishop's Palace. *(☎04 76 03 15 25. Open M and W-Sa 9am-6pm, Tu 1:30-6pm, Su 10am-7pm.)*

🎵 🌺 ENTERTAINMENT AND FESTIVALS

Grenoble's main **theater** features plays and classical music performances; info and tickets are at the *billetterie* next to the theater on pl. St-André. *(☎04 76 42 96 02. Open Tu-F 10am-noon and 1-6pm, Sa 1-6pm.)* The **MC2, Grenoble's Maison de la Culture,** located at 4 rue Paul Claudel, about 15min. from the *centre-ville,* organizes cultural events and performances. *(☎04 76 00 79 00; www.mc2grenoble.fr. Open Sept.-June Tu-F 12:30-7pm, Sa 2-7pm.)* **FNAC Billetterie,** in a superstore on rue Felix Poulat, across from the church, has info and tickets for most theater events. *(www.fnac.com. Open M-Sa 10am-7pm.)* For movie schedules, consult *Le Petit Bulletin,* free in cinemas and at the tourist office.

Festival du Court Métrage, in early July. Short film festival. Contact the Cinémathèque, 4 rue Hector Berlioz (☎04 76 54 43 51), for more info.

Bastille Day, July 14. Fireworks over the municipal building kick off the festival season.

Cabaret Frappe (☎04 76 00 76 85; www.cabaret-frappe.com), from late July to early Aug. International musicians perform in concert at 7pm (free) and 9pm (€13).

Festival 38ème Rugissants (☎04 76 51 12 92), in late Nov. African and South American music festival features live performances.

🎧 NIGHTLIFE

Most of Grenoble's funky cafes and raucous bars are located in the area between **place Saint-André** and **place Notre-Dame.**

Couche-Tard Pub, 1 rue du Palais (☎04 75 44 18 79). Small bar's walls are covered with customers' scribbled musings. International 20-something crowd mixes it up on the dance floor after downing shots of flavored vodka (€1.60). Beer and mixed drinks €2.50. Student discounts M-W. Happy hour 7-10pm. Open M-Sa 7pm-2am. AmEx/MC/V.

London Pub, 11 rue Brocherie (☎04 76 44 41 90). 2 floors of black lights and English paraphernalia. At midnight, the bar becomes a dance floor. Shots €1.60. Pints from €3. Ladies nights M-W. Happy hour 6-9pm. Open M-Sa 6pm-1am. AmEx/MC/V.

Le 365, 3 rue Bayard (☎04 76 51 73 18; fax 44 65 39). Laid-back artsy haunt. Happy hour 6-8:30pm. Mixed drinks €5-13. Open Sept.-July Tu-Sa 3pm-1am. AmEx/MC/V.

HIKING

Grenoble is surrounded by steep mountains, providing city dwellers with a hiking paradise in their backyard. Trails with starting points accessible by TAG city buses crisscross the countryside. The free and invaluable trail map, *La Carte des Sentiers des Franges Vertes*, available at the **Maison de la Montagne** (p. 466), offers transportation information and highlights points of interest along paths. Many excellent trails are accessible from the top of the *téléphérique.* The #31 bus takes nature lovers to the trailhead of a path through the Alpine countryside. More isolated hikes are accessible only by car or infrequent buses; while getting to these trails can be challenging, their breathtaking beauty is worth the hassle. Hikes have well-marked trails, but taking an **IGN hiking map** is highly recommended (available at local bookstores; €9.50). All bus schedules and maps are available at the TAG info desk in the tourist office.

Le Moucherotte (8.4km, 4hr. round-trip; 731m elevation change). Take VFD bus #5100 (dir.: Lansen) to St-Nizier du Moucherotte (40min., 1-3 per day, €2.90) and turn right toward the church. Follow the road to the left of the church and cemetery to the trailhead of the GR9, across the street from the panoramic viewpoint. This route leads to the summit and is marked by red and white lines. A red and white "X" indicates that you are leaving the trail. Descend by the same route.

Chamechaude (14.2km, 6-7hr. round-trip; 1068m elevation change). Take VFD bus #7140 to Le Sappey-en-Chartreuse (30min., 2-3 per day, €2.90). The bus stops after the church; follow the street to the right downhill. The trailhead is marked with yellow signs on the left. The 1st section of the hike follows GR9 "Tour de Chartreuse," marked with red and white lines on trees and rocks. At Habert Chamechaude, take trail B on the left toward Chamechaude. This trail is marked with yellow paint. The final 15m require a climb up a near-vertical rock face using a wire cable for assistance; it can be dangerous, especially when wet, so exercise caution. Descend along the same route.

SKIING

OISANS

The biggest ski areas are to the east in Oisans. The **Alpe d'Huez,** rising above one of the most challenging legs of the Tour de France, boasts a 3330m vertical drop and sunny, south-facing slopes; 250km of trails span all difficulty levels. (Tourist office ☎04 76 11 44 44; www.alpedhuez.com. Ski area ☎04 76 80 30 30. Lift tickets €38 per day, €192 per week.) Popular with advanced skiers, **Les Deux Alpes** has the largest skiable glacier in Europe, limited summer skiing, and a slope-side youth hostel. Its lift system, including two gondolas, runs up the 2000m vertical slope. (Tourist office ☎04 76 79 22 00; www.2alps.com. Ski area ☎04 76 79 75 01. Reservations ☎04 76 79 24 38. Youth hostel ☎04 76 79 22 80. Lift tickets in winter €35 per day, €172-192 per week; in summer €30/143.)

BELLEDONNE

The Belledonne region, northeast of Grenoble, lacks the towering heights and ideal conditions of the Oisans but boasts lower prices. **Chamrousse** is its biggest and most popular ski area, offering a lively atmosphere and a youth hostel. If conditions are right, there's plenty of good downhill and cross-country skiing at a great value, especially for beginners. (Tourist office ☎04 76 89 92 65; fax 89 98 06. Reservations ☎04 76 59 01 01. Youth hostel ☎04 76 89 91 31; fax 89 96 66. Lift tickets €27 per day, €150 per week.) Only 30min. from Grenoble, the resort makes for an ideal summer daytrip (6 buses per day,

RHÔNE-ALPES

€3.80). Chamrousse maintains four mountain-bike routes of varying difficulty in addition to a 230km network of hiking trails.

VERCORS

The slopes of the Vercors region, south of Grenoble, are popular with locals. In small ski resorts like **Gresse-en-Vercors,** vertical drops are around 1000m. Rock-bottom prices make the area an option for beginners or those looking to escape the hassles of the major resorts. The drive from Grenoble takes 40min. (Tourist office ☎04 76 34 33 40. Lift tickets €16 per day, €82 per week.)

ANNECY ☎04 50

Far from the noisy thoroughfares and high-rises of downtown, the *vieille ville* of Annecy (ahn-see; pop. 53,000)—with its cobblestone streets and turreted castles—feels more like a fairy tale than a modern city. Annecy provides a change of pace from the Alpine countryside; life here revolves around the lakeshore rather than the distant snow-capped peaks. As the sun rises over Lac d'Annecy, one of Europe's purest bodies of water, the lake becomes a deep shade of deep azure, providing a stunning sight for the paragliders above.

▐ TRANSPORTATION

Trains: Pl. de la Gare. Open daily 4:30am-9pm. Ticket window open daily 7:40am-7:30pm. To: **Chamonix** (2½hr., 7 per day, €20); **Grenoble** (1½hr., 8 per day, €16); **Nice** (7-9hr., 6 per day, €86) via **Lyon** (2½hr., 8 per day, €22); **Paris** (4hr., 7 per day, €85).

Buses: Autocars Frossard (☎04 50 45 73 90), next to the train station. Open M-F 7:45-11am and 2-7:15pm, Sa 7:45-11am. To **Geneva, CHE** (1¼hr., 2-3 per day, €10).

Public Transportation: SIBRA (☎04 50 10 04 04; www.sibra.fr). Info booth across from the train station at the corner of rue de la Gare. Open M-F 7:30am-7pm, Sa 9am-noon and 2-5pm. Extensive **bus** service throughout the city; info booth provides schedules. Ligne d'Été bus runs July-Aug. from the train station and stops at the hostel, campground, and summit of Semnoz (dir.: Semnoz; July-Aug. 6 per day 9am-6:15pm; Sept. and June Sa-Su 6 per day 9am-6:15pm). €1.10; carnet of 10 €9.20, students €6.60.

Taxis: At the station (☎04 50 45 05 67). €10 to the hostel, €12 at night. 24hr. **ALTESA** (☎0800 20 91 00) provides transportation for the handicapped. 24hr.

Bike and In-Line-Skate Rental: Roul' ma Poule, 4 rue des Marquisats (☎04 50 27 86 83; www.roulmapoule.com), next to the port. €10-15 per ½-day, €15-28 per day; includes helmet and lock. In-line skates €9 per ½-day, €14 per day. Open daily 9am-7pm. MC/V. **Golf Miniature de l'Imperial,** 2 av. du Petit Port (☎04 50 66 04 99; www.roller-golf-annecy.com), beside plage d'Albigny. €5 per hr., €14 per day. In-line skates €8 per ½-day, €11 per day. 20% discount if you're staying at the Auberge de Jeunesse. Open daily July-Aug. 9am-11pm; Sept.-Oct. and Apr.-June 10am-noon and 1:30-7pm.

▟ ⁊ ORIENTATION AND PRACTICAL INFORMATION

Most activity centers on the lake southeast of the train station and the *vieille ville* just off its shore. A canal runs east-west through the *vieille ville*, which is bounded by the château and by the tourist office in the main shopping area.

Tourist Office: 1 rue Jean Jaurès (☎04 50 45 00 33 or 45 56 66; www.lac-annecy.com). From the train station, walk 1 block down rue de la Gare. Turn left onto rue Vaugelas and follow it for 4 blocks; the office is straight ahead in the Bonlieu shopping mall. Offers a brochure outlining 5 city walking tours in English and French and a Lac d'Annecy map with hiking and biking routes. *Walks and Treks* guide (€6.50) and the regional IGN map

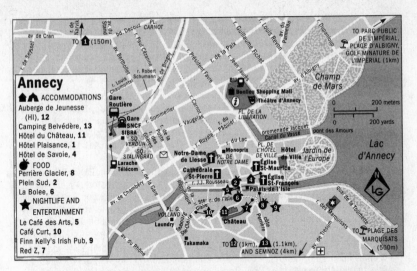

Annecy

♠ ♦ ACCOMMODATIONS
Auberge de Jeunesse (HI), **12**
Camping Belvédère, **13**
Hôtel du Château, **11**
Hôtel Plaisance, **1**
Hôtel de Savoie, **4**

🍴 FOOD
Perrière Glacier, **8**
Plein Sud, **2**
La Bolee, **6**

★ NIGHTLIFE AND ENTERTAINMENT
Le Café des Arts, **5**
Café Curt, **10**
Finn Kelly's Irish Pub, **9**
Red Z, **7**

RHÔNE-ALPES

(€9.50) also detail hiking paths around the lake. Open June-Aug. M-Sa 9am-6:30pm, Su 9am-12:30pm and 1:45-6:30pm; from Sept. to mid-Oct. and Mar.-May daily 9am-12:30pm and 1:45-6pm; from late Oct. to Feb. M-Sa 9am-12:30pm and 1:45-6pm.

Tours: Tourist office offers 2hr. walking tours of the *vieille ville*. July-Aug. tours in French daily 10:30am-3:30pm, in English Tu and F 4pm; Sept.-Oct. and May-June tours in French Th and Sa 9am-3pm. €5.70, under 12 free. **Petit train** tour (30min., €4) leaves from the Centre Bonlieu and stops at the Pont des Amours and the Parc de l'Imperial.

Youth Center: Bureau Information Jeunesse (BIJ), 1 rue Jean Jaurès (☎04 50 33 87 40; infojeunes@ville-annecy.fr), in the Centre Bonlieu. Staff offers advice and info on study opportunities, housing, jobs, and recreational activities. Free Internet, but expect a wait. Open M 3-6pm, Tu-Th 11am-6pm, F 11am-5pm, Sa 10am-noon.

Laundromat: Lav'Confort Express, 6 rue de la Gare, across the canal. Wash €5, dry €0.50 per 5min. Open daily 7am-9pm.

Police: 15 rue des Marquisats (☎04 50 52 32 00). Call for the **pharmacie de garde.**

Hospital: 1 av. de Trésum (☎04 50 88 33 33).

Internet Access: Free at the **BIJ** (above). **Larache Télécom,** 3 av. de l'Industrie (☎04 50 33 08 95), near the train station. €3 per hr. Open daily 9am-10pm.

Post Office: Rue des Glières (☎04 50 33 68 20), down the street from the train station. **ATM** and **currency exchange** available. Open M-F 8:30am-6:30pm, Sa 8am-noon. **Poste Restante:** 74011. **Postal Code:** 74000.

🏠 🏕 ACCOMMODATIONS AND CAMPING

Annecy's priciest hotels are in the *vieille ville* and by the lake, but prices drop along the city's outskirts. Reservations are recommended, especially in ski season and during the Fête du Lac at the beginning of August.

🏠 **Auberge de Jeunesse "La Grande Jeanne" (HI),** 4 route de Semnoz (☎04 50 45 33 19; annecy@fuaj.org). Take the Ligne d'Été (see **Public Transportation,** opposite page). Or take bus #6 (dir.: Marquisats) from the station to Hôpital, in front of the police station. Walk straight on av. de Tresum, away from the lake, and follow the signs to Semnoz. Take a left onto bd. de la Corniche and a right onto chemin du Belvédère for the ascent to the hostel (15min. by bus, 30min. by foot from train station). Makes up for its distance from the *centre-ville* with peaceful location near the Semnoz forest. 4- and 5-bed dorms with modern furnishings, sinks, and showers. Single-sex rooms available. Game room, kitchen, TV room, and bar. Breakfast included. Laundry. Internet €1 per 10min. Reception 7am-10pm. Reservations recommended in summer via Internet at www.hihostels. com; pay ahead. Open from late Jan. to Nov. Dorms from €17. MC/V. ●

◪ **Hôtel du Château,** 16 rampe du Château (☎04 50 45 27 66; hotelduchateau@noos. fr), uphill from the *vieille ville* on the same square as the château. Beautifully kept hotel offers well-furnished rooms with comfortable beds and excellent views. Peaceful distance from the hubbub of the *vieille ville* without sacrificing proximity. All rooms have TVs and bath. Breakfast €7. Wi-Fi. Reception 7:30am-10pm. Singles €49; doubles €60-68; triples €73; quads €83. AmEx/MC/V. ❹

◪ **Camping le Belvédère,** 8 route de Semnoz (☎04 50 45 48 30; camping@ville-annecy. fr), uphill from the hostel. Sites on a hill next to the forest. Grocery store, TV, and hiking trails. Laundry €8.40. Bike rental €6 per ½-day, €10 per day. Reception 8:30am-2pm and 5-8pm. Reservations recommended. Open Mar.-Oct. 1-2 people with tent and car €11-15. Extra person €4.20-5; extra tent €1.70-2.60. Electricity €2.60. MC/V. ●

La Clusaz, route du Col de la Croix Fry (☎04 50 02 41 73; fax 02 65 85), outside the ski resort of the same name. Mostly quads with showers. Reception 8am-noon and 5-9pm. Open from mid-Dec. to mid-Apr. and from mid-June to mid.-Sept. From mid-Dec. to mid-Apr. weekly stays only. *Demi-pension* €32; *pension complète* €38. V. ●

Hôtel Plaisance, 17 rue de Narvik (☎/fax 04 50 57 30 42), off av. de Cran, 7min. from the train station. Quiet, carpeted rooms with comfortable 70s-style furnishings. TV salon and nice breakfast area. Breakfast €3.90. Showers €2. Reception 7am-midnight. Reservations recommended, especially during festivals. Singles and doubles €29, with shower €33, with bath €35; triples €44-56; quads €47. MC/V. ❷

Hôtel de Savoie, 1 pl. St-François (☎04 50 45 15 45; www.hoteldesavoie.fr). Convent turned hotel features small rooms with wood floors. An unbeatable spot in the heart of the *vieille ville* facing the Palais de l'Isle and the canal. Make reservations 1 month ahead in summer and during ski season. Breakfast €7. Reception 7:30am-11:30pm. Singles with sink €28-35; doubles with shower €65-90. AmEx/MC/V. ❷

◖ FOOD

Reasonably priced restaurants in colorful buildings decorate Annecy's *vieille ville;* beware that some restaurant prices are more about location than delicious food. Take a stroll down **Faubourg Sainte-Claire** for an endless variety of *brasseries, glaciers, boulangeries,* cafes, and bars. Lakeside picnics often make for the best and most satisfying meals. Fill your basket with local specialties like *reblochon* cheese at the ◪**market** on **place Sainte-Claire.** (Open Tu, F, Su 8am-noon.) An additional market takes place on **boulevard Taine.** (Open Sa 8am-noon.) A **Monoprix** supermarket fills most of pl. de Notre Dame. (☎04 50 45 23 60. Open M-Sa 8:30am-7:50pm. AmEx/MC/V.)

Plein Sud, quai de l'Isle (☎04 50 51 00 44), on the banks of the canal. Fresh, creative dishes served on bright tables with palm umbrellas. House specialty pizza €10-13. *Menu* €14. Open daily 11am-10pm. Cash only. ❸

La Bolee, 14 rue de l'Isle (☎04 50 45 26 62), near the Palais de l'Isle. This *crêperie bretonne* is always packed, and for good reason. Try the Menhir (hot goat cheese and tomatoes; €8.50) followed by the refreshing Citron (sugar and lemon; €3.90). Savory *crêpes* €8-11. Sweet *crêpes* €2-7. Open daily 11am-midnight. MC/V. ❷

Perrière Glacier, at the corner of quai Perrière and rue Perrière. Prices are on par with the other countless *glaciers*, but Perrière's 56-flavor selection is its true draw. Standard flavors and delicious alternatives, like the Don Vito (vanilla, raspberry, and chocolate). 1 scoop €2; 5 scoops €6.50. Open daily 11am-midnight. Cash only. ●

👁 SIGHTS

VIEILLE VILLE. Bring an extra roll of film (or an extra memory card) for a walk through Annecy's *vieille ville.* While the real attraction lies in its alleyways and flower-lined Venetian canals, there are stops along the way that should not be missed. The 13th-century **Palais de l'Isle** sits with imposing pride in the center of the canal. Most recently, it served as a prison for WWII Resistance fighters, whose impassioned carvings mark the walls. A museum inside walks visitors through Annecy's history, but the château's highlight is its beautiful exterior. (☎ 04 50 33 87 30. Open June-Sept. daily 10:30am-6pm; Oct.-May M and W-Su 10am-noon and 2-5pm. €3.40, students €1.) Beneath the towers of the castle across the canal, **quai Perrière, rue de l'Isle,** and **Faubourg Sainte-Claire** are some of Annecy's most charming streets. Straddling the town's narrowest canal, the large, bare **Église Saint-Maurice** is known for the 15th-century painting (on the left wall near the back) that marks the tomb of Philibert de Monthoux, an Annecy noble. The macabre mural of a decomposing corpse—finished two years before its patron's death—is thought to reflect de Monthoux's anxiety over the Hundred Years' War.

GARDENS. With manicured hedges, fountains, and the occasional swan, the shaded **Jardin de l'Europe** is yet another example of Annecy's appreciation of natural beauty. At its northern side, the **Pont des Amours** (Lovers' Bridge) connects the European gardens to the **Champ de Mars,** a grassy esplanade frequented by picnickers, sunbathers, and soccer players. The gardens have won the national Ville Fleurie (Flower City) contest three times in the last decade.

CHÂTEAU. The unadorned 12th-century château, a short, steep climb from the *vieille ville,* rises over Annecy. Once a stronghold of Genevan counts, the castle and its imposing parapets now house archaeological exhibits of medieval *savoyard* furniture and religious sculpture. (☎ 04 50 33 87 30. Open June-Sept. daily 10:30am-6pm; Oct.-May M and W-Su 10am-noon and 2-5pm. Château €4.80, students €2, under 12 free; Oct.-May 1st Su of the month free. Grounds free.)

🎵 🎆 ENTERTAINMENT AND FESTIVALS

The **Théâtre d'Annecy,** in the Bonlieu Mall, hosts arts events and film screenings, but tickets can be difficult to get at the last minute. (☎ 04 50 33 44 11. Tickets €20-25, students €17-22. MC/V.) Pick up festival schedules at the tourist office.

Festival International du Film d'Animation, in early June. Animation festival.

Fête du Lac (☎ 04 50 33 65 65), 1st Sa in Aug. Annecy's biggest festival. A spectacular fireworks-and-water show lights up the city. Tickets €6-32. MC/V.

Le Retour des Alpages, in mid-Oct. A celebration of local tradition and food.

📷 NIGHTLIFE

Relaxing bars line the canal in the *vieille ville,* creating a scene that tends to revolve more around mellow drinking than wild dancing.

Finn Kelly's Irish Pub, 10 Faubourg des Annonciades (☎ 04 50 51 29 40; www.finn-kellys.com). Play darts, shoot pool, and watch the game with a mix of locals and tourists. Plenty of beers on tap, with an emphasis on the Irish brew Beamish. Large Anglophone crowd for rugby and soccer matches on the big-screen TVs. Free Wi-Fi and Internet with drink purchase. Beer €2.90-4.70. Open M-Sa 4:30pm-2am, F-Su 4:30pm-3am. MC/V.

Café Curt, 35 rue Ste-Claire. Small, laid-back bar where locals chat and people-watch. Known for delicious shots (€2), like white chocolate and cotton candy. Wine €2-3.50. Cognac €5. Sangria from €2. Open daily June-Sept. depending on what the owners "feel like from day to day," roughly 10am-2am; Oct.-May 10am-1am.

Red Z, 14 rue Perrière (☎04 50 45 17 13). Americans might not appreciate the cleverly rhyming name (pronounced Red-Zed). Annecy's flashiest, though slightly touristy, bar and *discothèque.* 20-somethings congregate in the hip interior. Dancing picks up around 11pm and lasts into the morning. Beer €3-5. Mixed drinks €9-14. Live DJs Th-Sa. Open daily Apr.-Oct. 11am-3am; Nov.-Mar. 5pm-3am. MC/V.

Le Café des Arts, 4 passage de l'Isle (☎04 50 51 56 40). An eclectic, local crowd lounges on the terrace along the canal. Beer €2.30-4. Open daily 10am-2am.

 HIKING

HIKES IN ANNECY

Dozens of hiking and biking trails begin on **Semnoz,** a limestone mountain at the southern edge of the city. The **Office National des Forêts** (☎04 50 23 84 10) distributes *Sentiers Forestiers* (€3.10), a map that outlines several routes that begin a 15min. walk from town. One of the better hikes is the **circuit de périmètre,** which begins at the Basilique de la Visitation, 7min. from the hostel and campground. From town, take bus A to its last stop, Visitation. With the basilica on your left, continue uphill on av. de la Visitation until it runs into route de la Petite Jeanne on the left, where you'll find the trailhead, labeled "La Tambourne." From this point, there are several trails into **La Forêt du Crêt du Maure.** Follow the signs for the *circuit de périmètre.* This gently graded trail, marked with blue blazes, follows a meandering circle through the Semnoz forest. The loop terminates at a second trailhead just above the hostel and campgrounds. A short road above the campgrounds leads back to the start.

HIKES AROUND LAC D'ANNECY

Hikes of varying skill levels originate around the perimeter of Lac d'Annecy. Unfortunately, most of the advanced hikes are not easily accessible by public transportation. Those with cars should inquire at the tourist office about hiking up the mountains on the southeastern edge of the lake, including **La Tournette,** the area's highest peak. *Walks and Treks* (€6.50 at the tourist office) is an English guide with directions for 15 hikes around the lake.

To shorten your hike, you can access some towns by bus and boat. Voyages Crolard **buses** depart from the train station and stop in front of the tourist office and near plage d'Albigny, circling the lake. (☎04 50 45 08 12; www.voyages-crolard.com. M-Sa 9 per day, Su fewer; €2.80-3.10.) Compagnie des Bateaux runs several **boat tours** around the lake. For a full tour, their best deal is the ◪**Circuit Omnibus,** a 2hr. loop that makes stops at Veyrier, Menthon, Talloires, Doussard, Duingt, St-Joriez, and Sevrier. (☎04 50 51 08 40. Boats leave Annecy from mid-July to Aug. 9:30, 10:30am, 2:15, 4, 4:45pm; Sept. and from late Apr. to early July 10:30am, 2:15, 4:45pm. €15, under 12 €11.)

MONT VEYRIER AND MONT BARON. The twin peaks of Mont Veyrier and Mont Baron offer unbelievable lake vistas. The easiest way to access this moderate hike (2½hr.; 719m elevation change) is to take Transdev Crolard's **Rive Bus** from the train station to Veyrier (dir.: Talloires; M-Sa 9 per day, Su 4 per day; €2). The tourist office, down the street from the bus stop in the direction of Annecy, provides a simple map and directions; a more detailed IGN map is recommended. To reach the trailhead from the tourist office or bus stop, walk along the road away from Annecy to the church; head uphill to the right of the church's front steps. Go left at the roundabout, through pl. des Écoliers, and turn left immediately on chemin du Péril. Follow this to the trailhead at the entrance to the forest. Soon after entering the forest, veer right at the fork in the trail and follow it until you reach the Chapeau de Napoléon. Turn left and follow the signs for Col des Sauts. The trail becomes flatter and winds through the forest, providing teasing glimpses of the lake. It then renews its ascent up a series of switchbacks and some dangerous rocky terrain. After reaching Col des Sauts, follow the signs toward Mont Veyrier (15min.) and Mont Baron (25min.) on the trail marked with yellow and red lines. Dozens of spectacular viewpoints lie along the path as it follows a ridge to Veyrier. Descend by the same route.

MENTHON, TALLOIRE, AND THE ROC DE CHÈRE. Combine sightseeing, hiking, and beach-hopping with Compagnie des Bateaux's morning boat to Menthon. There, you can visit the town's castle before hopping on a trail that leads to the Roc de Chère, and then into Talloires (2hr.). In Talloires, another hiking loop features a beautiful waterfall and panoramic views of the lake below. A boat from Talloires makes the return trip to Annecy.

Menthon holds the opulent 12th-century **Château de Menthon,** the birthplace of St-Bernard de Menthon, who made his name in the dog-breeding business. His wealthy descendants still live here, but the lower floors—including a walnut-paneled library with a Diderot encyclopedia and a 14th-century bedroom—are open to the public. (☎04 50 60 12 05; www.chateau-de-menton.com. Open July-Aug daily noon-6pm; Sept. and May-June F-Su 2-6pm. €7, children €4. Weekend tours with guides in period dress €8, children €5.)

To get to the trailhead from the port of Menthon, head uphill on route du Port until it reaches rue St-Bernard. Take a right and continue through the *centre-ville* and past the tourist office to pl. des Choseaux. Turn right on route des Bains and continue for 50m until you see the "Les Choseaux" sign on the left. Turn left on chemin du Crêt Martin, then bear onto chemin du Roc de Chère and follow the signs for the Roc de Chère. The gravel road turns to dirt as it enters the forest. Continue in the direction of "Liaison Talloires," marked by yellow arrows. The trail provides views of the lake as it emerges near Talloires's port. Follow the road from the port along the lakeshore as it turns left uphill and goes toward the tourist office. From the Talloire tourist office (☎04 50 60 70 64; open M-Sa 9am-7pm, Su 9am-12:30pm and 2:45-7pm), take a right onto route du Crêt, a right through the roundabout, and a left onto route du Vivier. After 10min., the rocky trail marked with a sign for the **Cascade d'Agnon** branches off to the left. To reach the waterfall, go around a metal barrier on the right-hand branch of the fork in the trail. The path descends into the **Gorge du Nant d'Oÿ.** The trail dead-ends within 15 ft. of the largest waterfall. Be cautious; the trail near the falls can be slippery. Hikers can extend the trip another hour and complete a scenic loop back to the tourist office. From the fork where the trail to the falls begins, take the left branch toward Verel and St-Germain. Continue until the path forks again and follow the sign for Pirraz to the left. After reaching a parking lot, cross the paved road on the right and take chemin de la Pirraz through the village. At the T intersection, turn left onto route de Ponnay. As the road continues uphill, the lake comes into view. At the fork in the road, head left on chemin rural de Ponnay, which leads into the village. At the T intersection, marked with a sign for Ponnay, turn left downhill and left again at the fork in the road. At the St-Germain church, follow the signs for Les Granges and Talloires to return to the *centre-ville.*

RHÔNE-ALPES

⛰ BIKING

Cyclists should check out the 30km *piste cyclable* (bike route) that hugs the level, western shore of the lake and travels through many towns. An entire circuit of the lake can be completed by cycling along the eastern shore's main road (D909A), but be prepared for hills and beware of traffic. The tourist office has a free map of bike routes. Semnoz also has a variety of mountain-biking trails; Sibra runs a special bus (July-Aug. 6 per day) that caters to cyclists starting at the summit (see **Public Transportation,** p. 472).

⛷ SKIING

Cross-country skiers hit the trails at nearby **Semnoz,** but Annecy's closest downhill ski resorts are in the **Massif des Aravis,** a ski area of four stations with 220km of trails and 96 lifts: La Clusaz (32km from Annecy, with 130km of trails and 56 lifts), St-Jean-de-Sixt (29km), Manigod (27km), and Le Grand-Bornand (20km, with 90km of trails and 37 lifts). Transdev Crolard runs **buses** from the Annecy bus station to La Clusaz and Le Grand-Bornand (☎04 50 45 08 12; 1hr., 9 per day). The **Skibus** links Le Grand-Bornand, St-Jean-de-Sixt, and La Clusaz (from late Dec. to mid-Mar. 19 per day, reduced hours from mid-Mar. to Apr.; €3.60, weeklong pass €14). For those planning to ski for several days, the **Forfait Aravis** provides access to runs at all four stations and to the Skibus (2 days €59, under 15 €50; 1 week €174/129). Contact the tourist offices at any of the stations for info. (La Clusaz ☎04 50 32 65 00; www.laclusaz.com. St-Jean-de-Sixt ☎04 50 02 70 14; www.saintjeandesixt.com. Manigod ☎04 50 44 92 44; www.manigod.com. Le Grand-Bornand ☎04 50 02 78 00; www.legrand-bronand.com.) To stay the night in La Clusaz, see p. 474.

🏔 OTHER OUTDOOR ACTIVITIES

Annecy offers outdoors enthusiasts the best of both worlds: visitors can water-ski one day and ascend sheer cliff faces the next. The **Bureau des Guides** (☎06 88 27 93 77; www.annecyguidesmontagne.com) and the staff at **Anglophone Takamaka,** 23 Faubourg Ste-Claire, run mountaineering excursions, including hiking, rock climbing, canyoning, and trips up the nearby Via Ferrata. Those inclined to stay at the water's edge should also consult Takamaka, which offers kayaking, canoeing, water-skiing, sailing, and whitewater rafting outings. (☎04 50 45 60 61; www.takamaka.fr. Canoeing €15 per hr. Water skiing €29 per 15min. Tandem rock climbing €390. Tandem paragliding €75-520. Canyoning €49-64. Sign up the night before. Open July-Aug. M-Sa 9am-6:30pm, Su 1:30-6:30pm; Sept.-June M-F 9am-noon and 2-6pm. MC/V.)

Lac d'Annecy is one of Europe's cleanest and purest; eight mountain streams and one underground source combine to fill the 14km long body of water. Beaches dot the perimeter, and there are two popular swimming spots. The grassy **plage d'Albigny** draws tourists and locals, who dine in lakeside restaurants after long days of windsurfing, sailing, and kayaking. (Open June-Aug. daily 10am-7:30pm; Sept.-May 24hr. June-Aug. €3.50, students and under 12 €2; Sept.-May free.) The **Parc Public de l'Impérial** is an aquatic wonderland next to plage d'Albigny with waterslides, minigolf, sailing, swimming, and a casino. (☎04 50 23 11 82. Open May-Sept. daily 11am-7:30pm. €3.50). The smaller **plage des Marquisats,** 1km south of the city down rue des Marquisats, permits swimming free of charge. The **Club de Voile Française,** on the lake, rents watercraft, while many companies rent out pedal boats on the south side of the Champ de Mars. (€9 per 30min., €14 per hr.) On the other side of Pont des Amours, speedboats take tours of the lake. (€8 per 35min., €16 per hr. Cash only.)

CHAMONIX

☎ 04 50

The train station is named "Chamonix-Mont Blanc" for more than practicality: the towering snow-capped mountain and the city in its shadow have an intimate connection. Chamonix (shah-moh-nee; pop. 10,000) hosted the first Winter Olympics in 1924 and has yet to extinguish the torch. Today, athletes from around the world arrive determined to conquer the rugged peaks. The mountains around Chamonix are a true challenge: steep grades, potential avalanches, and unpredictable weather make this region ill-suited for beginners. However, with adequate planning, expeditions into some of the highest altitudes in Europe are utterly—and literally—breathtaking. Those who glance away from Western Europe's tallest peak will find a welcoming town of chalets, pedestrian streets, hip bars and clubs, and an international population that speaks as much English as French.

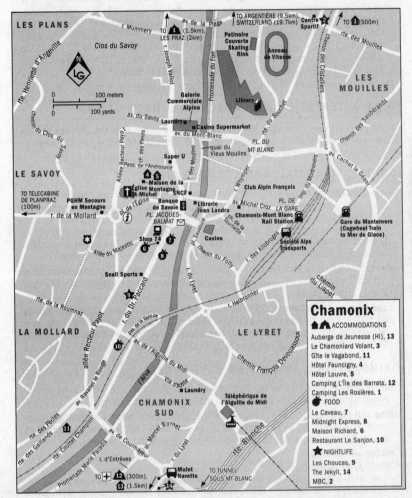

Chamonix

🏠🏔 ACCOMMODATIONS

Auberge de Jeunesse (HI), 13
Le Chamoniard Volant, 3
Gîte le Vagabond, 11
Hôtel Faucigny, 4
Hôtel Louvre, 5
Camping L'Île des Barrats, 12
Camping Les Rosières, 1

🍴 FOOD

Le Caveau, 7
Midnight Express, 8
Maison Richard, 6
Restaurant Le Sanjon, 10

⭐ NIGHTLIFE

Les Choucas, 9
The Jekyll, 14
MBC, 2

RHÔNE-ALPES

◧ TRANSPORTATION

Trains: Pl. de la Gare. Ticket office open daily 6:40am-8:20pm. There is an SNCF office in the SAT office at 13 av. Michel Croz (☎04 50 53 00 95). Open M-F 9am-noon and 2:30-6pm. Most trains connect through St-Gervais on the Martigny line. From St-Gervais to: **Annecy** (1½hr., 8 per day, €13); **Grenoble** (4hr., 1 per day, €26); **Lyon** (3½hr., 7 per day, €29); **Paris** (5-8hr., 6 per day, €75-95); **Geneva, CHE** (4½hr., 2 per day, €51).

Buses: Société Alpes Transports (SAT), at the train station (☎04 50 53 01 15). Ticket office open July-Aug. M-F 7:30-11:30am and 1-6pm, Sa-Su 7:30am-noon and 1-6pm. Call for hours in low season. To **Courmayeur, ITA** (50min.; July-Aug. 6 per day, Sept.-June M-Sa 2 per day; €9.50) and **Geneva, CHE** (1½hr.; July-Aug. 3 per day; Sept.-Nov. and May-June M-Sa 1 per day; Dec.-Apr. M-F 4 per day, Sa-Su 5 per day; €35).

Public Transportation: Mulet Navette circles through town July-Aug. every 10min. 8:30am-6:30pm, with stops at the train station and Chamonix Sud, Sept.-Dec. and May-June every 20min.; free. Chamonix Bus (☎04 50 53 05 55) runs to ski slopes and hiking trails. Follow signs from pl. de l'Église to the main **bus** stop. €1.50. Night bus makes the same circuit every hr. 8:30-11:30pm in the winter; €2. Chamonix hotels and *gîtes* dispense the **Carte d'Hôte,** which provides free bus travel.

Taxis: At the station (☎06 07 02 22 13). €12 to the Auberge de Jeunesse.

◪ 🛈 ORIENTATION AND PRACTICAL INFORMATION

At the intersection of **avenue Michel Croz, rue du Docteur Paccard,** and **rue Joseph Vallot**—each named for a conqueror of Mont Blanc's summit—lies the *centre-ville.* The train station is south of the Arve River.

TOURIST, FINANCIAL, AND LOCAL SERVICES

Tourist Office: 85 pl. du Triangle de l'Amitié (☎04 50 53 00 24; www.chamonix.com). From the station, follow av. Michel Croz through town, turn left onto rue du Docteur Paccard, and take the 1st right onto pl. de l'Église. English-speaking staff has a list of accommodations, hiking map *Carte des Sentiers d'Été* (€4), a hiking guide with map (€14), and info on local bus schedules and weather conditions. Wi-Fi. Open daily from July to mid-Sept. 8:30am-7pm; from mid-Sept. to Dec. 9am-12:30pm and 2-6:30pm.

Bookstore: Librairie Jean Landru, 74 rue Vallot (☎04 50 53 14 41). Small selection of popular English titles. Open daily July-Aug. 8am-7:30pm; Sept.-June 8:30am-12:30pm and 2:30-7pm. MC/V.

Laundromat: Cham'Laverie, 98 via d'Aoste (☎04 50 53 56 48), off av. de l'Aiguille du Midi. Wash, dry, and fold €11. Open M-Sa July-Aug. 9am-1pm and 2-7pm; from late-Dec. to May 9am-8pm. **Laverie Automatique,** 65 av. du Mont Blanc, in the Galerie Commerciale Alpina. Wash and dry €8.50. Open daily 8:30am-6pm.

BIKING, HIKING, AND SKIING RESOURCES

Biking Information: Pick up the free, invaluable English map and guide to mountain-biking itineraries at the tourist office or at mountain-bike rental shops.

Bike and Ski Rental: Dozens of places rent skis, snowboards, bikes, and climbing equipment. Skis should not be more than €8-20 per day or €40-80 per week, depending on quality. Snowboards should not exceed €16 per day and €82 per week.

Hiking Information:

Office de Haute-Montagne (☎04 50 53 22 08; www.ohm-chamonix.com), on the top floor of the Maison de la Montagne, across from the tourist office. Expert staff plans excursions, provides info on *refuges* and cable cars, and sells detailed maps (€4-9.50). Extensive library of route itineraries and recent travel logs. Open July-Aug. daily 9am-noon and 3-6pm; Sept.-Oct. and Dec.-June M-Sa 9am-noon and 3-6pm; Nov. M-F 9am-noon and 3-6pm.

Club Alpin Français, 136 av. Michel Croz (☎04 50 53 16 03; www.clubalpin-chamonix.com). Best source of info on mountain *refuges* and road conditions. Bulletin board matches drivers, riders, and hiking partners. Hikers convene in the office to plan excursions (F 7pm). Members only; email to inquire about membership. Open July-Aug. M-Tu and Th-Su 9am-noon, W 3:30-7pm; Sept.-June M-Tu and Th-Sa 3:30-7pm.

Hiking and Skiing Equipment: There are countless outdoor outfitters in Chamonix's main shopping areas. **Snell Sports,** 104 rue Paccard (☎04 50 53 02 17; www.cham3s.com). Massive stock of skiing, climbing, and hiking gear. Rentals of everything from boots (€9 per day) and backpacks (€8 per day) to a "Mont Blanc" kit of boots, crampons, and ice axes (€18 per day). Open daily in high season 9am-12:30pm and 2:30-7:30pm; in low season 9am-noon and 2:30-7pm. AmEx/MC/V.

Mountain Rescue: PGHM Secours en Montagne, 69 route de la Mollard (☎04 50 53 16 89). 24hr. emergency service.

Skiing Lessons and Info: École du Ski Français, pl. du Triangle de l'Amitié (☎04 50 53 22 57; www.esf-chamonix.com), on the 2nd fl. of the Maison de la Montagne. ½-day group lessons €56; ½-day private lesson for 1-6 people €155; guided group descent to Vallée Blanche for 1-4 people €260. Open Dec.-Apr. daily 8:15am-7pm. MC/V. On the main floor, **Compagnie des Guides** (☎04 50 53 00 88; www.cieguides-chamonix.com) gives climbing lessons and leads guided summer hikes and winter ski trips. Morning climbing sessions €44. Group ski excursions €67 per person per day; 3-day min. Register by 6pm the evening before. Open daily 8:30am-noon and 3:30-7:30pm. MC/V.

Weather Conditions: At the Maison de la Montagne, Club Alpin Français, and the tourist office. Call ☎08 92 68 02 74 for a French report of road and weather conditions.

EMERGENCY AND COMMUNICATIONS

Hospital: Centre Hospitalier, 509 route des Pèlerins (☎04 50 53 84 00). **Ambulance** ☎04 50 53 46 20.

Police: 48 rue de l'Hôtel de Ville (☎04 50 53 75 02).

Internet Access: Free Wi-Fi at the tourist office (opposite page). **Shop 74,** 16 cours du Bartavel (☎04 50 90 73 17). €6 per hr. Free Wi-Fi with drink purchase. Open daily July-Aug. 10am-1pm and 3-7:30pm; Sept.-June 10am-7:30pm. MC/V.

Post Office: Pl. Jacques-Balmat (☎04 50 53 15 90). **Currency exchange** available. Open M-F 9am-12:30pm and 1:30-5:45pm, Sa 9am-noon. **Postal Code:** 74400.

◤◥ ACCOMMODATIONS AND CAMPING

Chamonix's hotels are expensive, but *gîtes* and dorms are quite cheap. The hardest time to get a room is during high season (from mid-June to late August and from late December to April). The area's *refuges* have few facilities and are frequently unattended. The tourist office and Club Alpin have listings of openings and prices. **Centrale de Reservation** (☎04 50 53 23 33; http://reservation. chamonix.com) books hotels for stays of two nights or more.

Gîte le Vagabond, 365 av. Ravanel le Rouge (☎04 50 53 15 43; www.gitevagabond. com), 7min. from the *centre-ville*. A backpacker fave. Young Brits run this friendly *gîte* with rustic bunks and stone walls. Popular bar. Kitchen (€1 to use stove) and climbing wall. Breakfast €5. Linen €5. Laundry €11. Free Wi-Fi. Reception 8-10am and 4:30-10pm. 4- to 6-bed dorms €15; *demi-pension* €35. Credit-card deposit. MC/V. ❶

Auberge de Jeunesse (HI), 127 montée Jacques Balmat (☎04 50 53 14 52; chamonix@fuaj.org), in Les Pèlerins at the foot of Glacier de Bossons. Take the bus from the Chamonix train station or pl. Mont Blanc (dir.: Pèlerins) to Pèlerins École and follow the signs uphill. By train, get off before Chamonix at Les Pèlerins and follow the signs. Alternatively, walk down route des Pèlerins (30min.). Clean, modern 4- and 6-bed rooms. Ask about transportation discounts, ski packages, and equipment rental. Breakfast included. Linen €1. Reception 8am-noon and 5-10pm. Open Dec.-Sept.; closed 2-3 weeks in May. Dorms €18; doubles with shower €22. MC/V. ❶

Le Chamoniard Volant, 45 route de la Frasse (☎04 50 53 14 09; www.chamoniard. com), 15min. from the *centre-ville.* From the station, turn right, go under the bridge, and turn right across the tracks, left on chemin des Cristalliers, and right on route de la Frasse. Rustic *gîte* with wood walls, red-checkered tablecloths, and vintage ski paraphernalia. 4-, 6-, and 8-bed rooms; 1 15-bed dorm. Breakfast €4.90. Linen €4.50. Internet €0.10 per min. Free Wi-Fi. Reception 10am-10pm. Reservations recommended. Dorms €14; *demi-pension* €30. Credit-card deposit. MC/V. ❶

Hôtel Louvre, 95 impasse de l'Androsace (☎04 50 53 00 51; www.hoteldulouvre.fr). Small 1-star hotel in a quiet yet central location. Simple wood-trimmed rooms. Breakfast €6. Reception 8am-noon and 2-9pm. Singles with sink €34, with bath €48; doubles with bath €42-57; triples €54-60; quads €69. MC/V. ❷

Hôtel Faucigny, 118 pl. de l'Église (☎04 50 53 01 17; www.hotelfaucigny-chamonix. com). Family-run. Comfortable rooms in an unbeatable location near the tourist office. Hallways lined with books add to the endearing, family atmosphere. All rooms with full bath. Breakfast €8. Free Wi-Fi. All but singles have TVs. Singles €44-48; doubles €68-79; triples €82-93; quads €98-112. MC/V. ❸

Camping L'Île des Barrats, 185 chemin de l'Île des Barrats (☎04 50 53 51 44), off route des Pèlerins. With your back to the cable car, turn left, pass the roundabout, and continue for 5min.; Barrats is on the right. Crowded, grassy campground with great mountain views. Sites are separated by waist-high hedges. Luggage storage €1 per bag per day. Laundry (wash €5, dry €3). Reception July-Aug. 8am-noon and 2-8pm; Sept. and May-June 9am-noon and 4-7pm. Open May-Sept. €6.40 per person, children €4.80; €5.40 per tent; €2.50 per car. Electricity €3.30. Cash only. ❶

Camping Les Rosières, 121 clos des Rosières (☎04 50 53 10 42; www.campingles-rosieres.com), off route de Praz, close to Les Praz. Follow rue Vallot for 1.2km or take a bus to Les Nants. Open sites with stunning views. Reception 8:30am-12:30pm and 2-8pm. Open June-Sept. 2 people, tent, and car €20. Electricity €3.10-3.30. ❶

Refuge du Lac Blanc (☎04 50 53 49 14). The place to stay for hikers on the Lac Blanc trail (p. 485). Breakfast and dinner included. Reservations required. Rooms €47. ❷

Refuge du Plan de l'Aiguille (☎06 65 64 27 53; http://plandelaiguille.free.fr). Follow the signs 2½hr. from the Mer de Glace. For daytripping hikers on the Lac Blanc trail (p. 485). Open from mid-June to late-Sept. Rooms €13; *demi-pension* €33. ❶

Hôtel Montnevers (☎04 50 53 87 70). Also along the Mer de Glace trail (p. 484). Breakfast and dinner included. Open from mid-June to mid-Sept. Dorms €37. ❸

🍴 FOOD

Chamonix has a wider gamut of restaurants than one might expect. After a hard day on the slopes, it's easy to find a decent, hearty meal in one of the many bars and ski lodges in town. For a more traditional meal, however, head to one of the local bistros for fondue or *raclette*. There's a **Super U** supermarket at 117 rue Joseph Vallot (☎04 50 53 12 50; open M-Sa 8:15am-7:30pm, Su 8:30am-noon; AmEx/MC/V) and a **Casino** supermarket at 17 av. du Mont Blanc, inside the Galerie Commerciale Alpina (☎04 50 53 11 85; open July-Aug. M-Sa 8:30am-6:30pm, Su 8:30am-12:30pm; Sept.-June M-Sa 8:30am-6:30pm; MC/V). A morning market is held on **place du Mont Blanc** (open Sa 7:30am-1pm).

▨ **Le Caveau,** 13 rue du Docteur Paccard (☎04 50 55 86 18). This 300-year-old former wine cellar provides a romantic setting, but the laid-back, English-speaking staff prevents the atmosphere from getting too stuffy. Tasty brick-oven pizzas, *savoyard* specialties, and international and vegetarian dishes. Try the bestseller and house specialty: Swedish meatballs (€14). The garlic bread is widely considered the best in town. Open daily Dec.-Sept. 6:30am-2am; Oct.-Nov. 6:30am-1am. MC/V. ❸

Midnight Express, 23 rue du Docteur Paccard (☎04 50 53 44 10), near the post office. Chamonix mainstay burger joint. Cheap meals and late hours cater to backpackers and clubbers. Try the Double American Midnight burger (€7.50). Burgers with fries €4.20-7.50. Vegetarian options available. Open daily 11:30am-2am. Cash only. ❶

Maison Richard, 8 rue du Docteurr Paccard (☎04 50 53 56 88). Lines spill out onto the street. Try a scoop of "Mont Blanc" ice cream (€1). Open daily 7am-8pm. ❶

Restaurant Le Sanjon, 5 av. Ravanel le Rouge (☎04 50 53 56 44). The best bet for enjoying *savoyard* delicacies. Rustic atmosphere complements its specialty meat, cheese, and potato dishes. *Plats* €14-29. *Menus* €18-24. Open daily 11:30am-10:30pm. ❸

◎ NIGHTLIFE

Chamonix's nightclubs and pubs are especially popular in winter, when people party hard with whatever energy they have left in their ski-weary bodies. Pubs are open year-round, although they are usually empty during the low season and not quite as rowdy during the summer months.

▨ **MBC: Micro Brasserie de Chamonix,** 350 route du Bouchet (☎04 50 53 61 59), 10min. from the *centre-ville*. Canadian-owned microbrewery stays packed with a laid-back crowd that comes for the tasty international fare. 5 homebrewed beers on tap. Pints €5. 1.5L pitchers €14. *Plats* €11-17. Occasional live music; more frequent performances in winter. ½-price wings M night. Open daily in high season 4pm-2am; in low season 4pm-1am. Kitchen open 4-11pm. MC/V.

▨ **The Jekyll,** 71 route des Pèlerins (☎04 50 55 99 70). Anglophone pub draws a crowd with hearty Irish food and big-screen TVs. *Plats* €13-21. Happy hour daily June-Aug. 6-7pm and 11am-midnight; Dec.-May 4-5pm and 11pm-midnight. Boot hour (for those still in ski gear) Dec.-May daily 6-7pm. Pub open daily 4pm-2am. MC/V.

Les Choucas, 206 rue du Docteur Paccard (☎04 50 53 03 23). Revamped chalet offers mix of alpine rusticity and boisterous modern vibe. Cow-skin lounges, 4 vivid big-screen TVs, and a strobe-lit dance floor. Beer €3.10-5.10. Mixed drinks €9-13. Live DJ. Concerts W. Regular *soirées spéciales*. Open daily from late June to mid-Sept. 4pm-4am; from mid-Dec. to mid-Apr. 5pm-4am. MC/V.

◤ TÉLÉPHÉRIQUES

Hikers and skiers will probably need to take a *téléphérique* (cable car) during their stay in Chamonix; others will want to take the ride just for the views. The tourist office and Office de Haute Montagne provide a list of open lifts; many close from early May to late June.

▨ **Aiguille du Midi** (☎08 92 68 00 67). Offers the best views of Europe's highest peaks and the valley below. Open daily July-Aug. 6:30am-5pm; Sept.-Oct. and Dec.-June 8am-5pm. Closed part of May. Tickets €35, under 15 €28. To midpoint **Plan de l'Aiguille** €18/15. AmEx/MC/V.

Helbronner and Glacier Géant. From the Aiguille du Midi summit, continue on to Helbronner, a 4-person gondola that provides views of the **Matterhorn** and **Mont Blanc.** 25min. ride allows visitors to stride along the French-Italian border and the Glacier Géant. May-Sept. €46, under 11 €37; includes the Aiguille du Midi. AmEx/MC/V.

RHÔNE-ALPES

Courmayeur. Descends from Helbronner into **La Palud, ITA,** near the resort town of Courmayeur. Bring a passport and cash—the Italian side doesn't accept credit cards for the cable car. Open July-Aug. 8am-5:30pm; Sept.-Oct. and June 8:30am-1pm and 2-4:20pm. Complete circuit from Chamonix €87, under 15 €70. Verify at the tourist office that the entire route is in operation before setting out.

Le Brévent (☎04 50 53 13 18). Departs from the corner of route Henriette and La Mollard, up the street from the tourist office. Mid-station **Planpraz.** Open daily July-Aug. 8am-6pm; Sept.-June 9am-5pm. To Brévent €15; to Planpraz €10. MC/V.

La Flégère (☎04 50 53 18 58). Stops at namesake plateau in **Les Praz** on the way to **l'Index** (2595m), a starting point for ice climbs. Open daily July-Aug. 7:40am-5:50pm; Sept. and June 8:40am-4:50pm. €15, round-trip €18.

Mer de Glace. Montnevers Railway (☎04 50 53 12 54; www.compagniedumontblanc.fr) departs for Mer de Glace *téléphérique* from a small cabin next to the train station. Runs daily July-Aug. every 20min. 8am-6pm; Sept. and May-June every 30min. 8:30am-5pm; Nov.-Apr. every hr. 10am-5pm. Round-trip €16. MC/V. *Téléphérique* runs to an ice cave. Car descent €4.40; cave admittance €3.40. **Forfait Global** pass (€20, under 11 €16) includes a round-trip train and cable-car ride and admission to the cave.

SKIING

Chamonix is surrounded by skiable mountains. The south-facing side of the valley opposite **Mont Blanc** offers terrain for all abilities and has exceptional views. Extreme skiers head over to the death-defying north face, which has mostly advanced, off-piste, and glacial terrain. Those aiming to ski for only one or two days should buy separate day pass lift tickets at the different ski areas—one area is more than enough for each day. Those planning to stay longer might consider buying the Chamonix Le Pass or the Mont-Blanc Unlimited pass, available at the tourist office or major *téléphériques* (Brévent, Flégère, and Aiguille du Midi). **Chamonix Le Pass** is the cheaper option and gives unlimited access to ski areas in the Chamonix valley, excluding Les Houches (1 week €209, ages 4-15 €167; passport photo required). **Mont-Blanc Unlimited** provides unlimited access to all of the areas covered by Chamonix Le Pass, plus the Aiguille du Midi and Helbronner cable car, the Montnevers train, the Logna-Grands Montets cable car, the Les Houches area, and one day in Courmayeur-Val-Veny, Italy (1 week €255, ages 4-15 €204; passport photo required). Chamonix Le Pass and Mont-Blanc Unlimited passholders also have free access to the local buses that connect the valley's resort villages. Long lift lines at the base make early starts essential, but the crowds tend to thin out at the lifts higher up.

SKIING NORTH OF CHAMONIX

On the northern side of the Chamonix valley, advanced trails, vertical drops, and glaciers help to fuel Chamonix's reputation as a paradise for extreme skiers. **Les Grands Montets** (☎04 50 54 00 71; 3300m), 8km from Chamonix in Argentière, is the *grande dame* of Chamonix's ski spots, boasting some of the most difficult piste and off-piste terrain in the area. While skiers predominate, the resort also caters to snowboarders with a remodeled half-pipe (day pass €37). Directly above Chamonix, the **Vallée Blanche** requires courage and a hearty dose of insanity. From the top of the Aiguille du Midi *téléphérique*, the ungroomed, unmarked, un-patrolled 20km trail runs down a glacier to Chamonix. The best bet is to ski with a guide who knows the area; try the **Compagnie des Guides** (p. 481; from €67 per person). English-speaking guides help create your itinerary and make all the necessary arrangements, from equipment rental to lift reservations. *Let's Go* does not recommend skiing this area alone, but, if you find yourself without a guide, always check conditions before venturing out and log your route with the ski patrol or the Office de Haute Montagne.

SKIING SOUTH OF CHAMONIX

At the end of the valley, near the Swiss border, **Le Tour-Col de Balme** (☎04 50 54 00 58), above the village of Le Tour, is the first of Chamonix's ski areas. Its sunny trails are most suitable for beginning to intermediate skiers, but a new gondola to the town of **Vallorcine** gives experts the chance to make tracks through pine forests (day pass €37). Connected by a cable car, **Brévent** and **Flégère** together constitute Chamonix's largest ski area with runs suitable for novice skiers. Located steps from the tourist office, the Brévent *téléphérique* is particularly convenient. Note that the terrain at the top of the Brévent gondola is advanced; less confident skiers should get off at the middle stop **Planpraz**, the starting point for several easier trails (day pass €37).

◪ HIKING

Chamonix has 350km of marked hiking trails, with terrain ranging from forests to windswept glaciers. The **Carte des Sentiers d'Été** map, available at the tourist office, lists all the mountain *refuges*, departure points, and estimated lengths for trails (€4). Climbers should buy the IGN topographic map, available at the Office de Haute Montagne and local bookstores (€9.50). Terrain is often steep, and using a *téléphérique* is a great way to facilitate a leg of your hike. If you're merely in the market for a walk, meander the trail that follows the **Arve River** through the valley; it begins next to the sports center. While there are hundreds of routes in the mountains, the following are well-known intermediate-level hikes that are easily accessible from Chamonix.

HIKES NORTH OF CHAMONIX

▨ **Grand Balcon Sud.** West of la Flégère, the Grand Balcon Sud—yes, this trail is actually on the north side of the valley—is a spectacular trail that winds its way to **Planpraz**, the mid-station of the Brévent *téléphérique* (2hr.). From there, you can hike or ride back to town or embark on the steep ascent to the **Col de Brévent** (2368m) at the top of the Brévent lift (2hr.). Alternatively, take the steep trail from Planpraz to the brilliant waters of **Lac Cornu** (2hr.) and the pristine **Lacs Noirs** (45min.). Descend via the same route.

Chalet Floria and Petit Balcon Sud (45-50min.). This lower-altitude trail is the perfect introduction to the mountains around Chamonix. Heading out of town toward Les Praz, turn left on rue Mummery, go right through the roundabout, and follow the signs to an uphill track that eventually becomes a narrow trail. The walk ends at a chalet turned restaurant with views of Mont Blanc. The owners allow picnics with drink purchase (€3). To extend this hike, ramble along the relatively flat Petit Balcon Sud, which winds through the forest and overlooks the valley. The trail runs from above the town of Servoz to the west, through Chamonix, and all the way to **Argentière** and is accessible from nearly all of Chamonix's surrounding villages; you can get on and off as you please. To access the trail from Chamonix, take the paved chemin de la Pierre Ruskin to the left of the Brévent *téléphérique*. Signs lead to the Petit Balcon Sud.

Lac Blanc (2hr.). Ascend to Les Praz by taking the Flégère cable car or climbing the ski slopes on the trail that starts behind the nearby golf course (2½hr.). From the station, a number of hikes lead along the craggy range. From the top of the *téléphérique*, follow signs for a breathless ascent to Lac Blanc, whose Alpine waters stay frozen through June. If you're truly in love, stay the night at the *refuge* (p. 482).

RHÔNE-ALPES

HIKES SOUTH OF CHAMONIX

Mer de Glace. A number of picturesque trails surround the Mer de Glace, France's largest glacier. 1 great 2½hr. trip through forests and boulder fields begins 900m beyond the Montnevers train station. Climb under the **télésiège de Planards** until signs appear to Rochets des Mottets. Follow the signs along a wide trail. After reaching the Rochets cabin (1½hr.), turn right onto the steeper trail, which climbs to the Montnevers train station (1hr.). The train whisks tired hikers back to Chamonix, but daytrippers can extend the hike. Head under the tracks toward the glacier's **Hôtel Montnevers** (p. 482) or follow the sign toward the **Refuge du Plan de l'Aiguille** (p. 482).

Grand Balcon Nord (2½hr.). The spectacular, wildflower-studded Grand Balcon Nord trail, constructed in the 20s by famous alpinist Joseph Vallot, winds gently toward the *refuge*. The Balcon Nord may not be passable until late June; ask at the Office de Haute Montagne for up-to-date reports. After reaching the *refuge*, ascend a short trail to the midpoint stop of the Aiguille du Midi cable car and ride down or descend from the refuge along the steep trails; both lead back to Chamonix.

Mont Blanc (4810m elevation change). Experienced mountain climbers, of course, come to Chamonix to ascend Mont Blanc, a 2- or 3-day climb. Don't climb alone. Hikers can get caught in vicious blizzards, even in Aug. The Maison de la Montagne, Compagnie des Guides, and Club Alpin Français all have info on this most classic of Alpine climbs (see **Biking, Hiking, and Skiing Resources,** p. 480).

VAL D'ISÈRE   ☎04 79

Travelers to Val d'Isère (val dee-zayr; pop. 1700) worship its snow, *hautes montagnes*, and native Jean-Claude Killy, who walked away with the gold in every men's downhill event in the 1968 Grenoble Olympics. As an area spokesman, Killy brought the Winter Olympics to Val d'Isère in 1992, permanently transforming the town's main street into a tourist-laden strip of expensive hotels and restaurants. The tradition will continue in 2009, when the town hosts the World Alpine Ski Championships. When Val d'Isère "opens" for the summer in late June, the turquoise Isère River emerges spectacularly from under melting snow, rushing past the wood-and-stone chalets that line the narrow valley. Prices drop, and bikers, hikers, and climbers fill the hotels. The town's second high-season "opening" occurs in early December; it can be eerily quiet during the low season. Expect to hear quite a bit of English in Val d'Isère, which is one of the biggest summertime ski destinations for Anglophones.

⌫ TRANSPORTATION

Trains: Pl. de la Gare in Bourg-St-Maurice. Ticket office open daily 5:10am-9:30pm. Office (☎04 79 06 03 55) is in the Val d'Isère bus station. Open M-F 9:30am-12:30pm and 2:30-6:30pm. To: **Annecy** (3-4hr., 5 per day, €26); **Grenoble** (3hr., 4 per day, €20); **Lyon** (3-4hr., 5-6 per day, €31); **Paris** (5-6hr., 6 per day, €75-95).

Buses: Autocars Martin (☎04 79 06 00 42), at the Val Village bus station, 150m down the main drag from the tourist office. Open July-Aug. and Dec.-Apr. M 9-10:15am and 1-8pm, Th-F 9-11am and 1:30-8pm, Sa 6:45-10am and 12:45-7:30pm. Main office at pl. de la Gare (☎04 79 07 04 49; www.altibus.com), in Bourg-St-Maurice. Open M-F 8am-noon and 2-6:30pm. From Bourg-St-Maurice to: **Lyon** (4hr.; Dec.-May M-F 2 per day, Sa 4 per day, Su 3 per day; €56); **Tignes** (45min.; M-F and Su 3 per day, Sa 7 per day; €13); **Val Village** (45min.; M-F and Su 3 per day, Sa 7 per day; €13); **Geneva, CHE** (4½hr.; Dec.-May M-F 3 per day, Su 4 per day; €52).

RHÔNE-ALPES

Public Transportation: Val d'Isère runs free **navettes** around town during ski season and in July and Aug. **Train Rouge** runs between La Daille, Val Village, and Le Fornet (July-Aug. every 30min. 9am-7:30pm; Dec.-Apr. every 5min. 8:30am-5:30pm, every 20min. 5:30pm-2am), while **Train Vert** runs from the Val Village tourist office to the Manchet Sports complex and Vanoise National Park (July-Aug. every 15min. 8:15am-7pm; Dec.-Apr. every 30min. 10am-8pm).

Taxis: ABC (☎06 18 19 20 00). **Altitude Espace Taxi** (☎06 07 41 11 53).

✈ 🛈 ORIENTATION AND PRACTICAL INFORMATION

The Val d'Isère mega-resort is made up of three villages in a line along the Isère River. **La Daille** lies at the valley's entrance; **Val Village,** uphill from La Daille, is home to most accommodations, restaurants, and the tourist office. An ascent from Val Village leads to **Le Fornet,** a tiny but welcoming slice of wilderness. Unless otherwise stated, listings below are in Val Village, the most substantial of the three towns. Street names are neither used nor clearly indicated, but the town is navigable with the tourist office's invaluable *Practical Guide* map.

Tourist Office: ☎04 79 06 06 60; www.valdisere.com. From the bus station, walk along the main road toward Le Fornet; the office is on the left at the large roundabout (5min.). Distributes *Practical Guide* with map and list of hotels and restaurants in 6 languages. Hiking desk helps plan outdoor excursions. Internet €9 per hr. Open July-Aug. daily 8:30am-7:30pm; Sept.-Nov. and May-June M-F 9am-noon and 2-6pm, Sa-Su 10am-noon and 3-6pm; Dec.-Apr. M-F and Su 8:30am-7:30pm, Sa 8:30am-8pm.

Laundromats: Laverie Automatique (☎06 08 26 92 86), above the Spar supermarket, to the right of the roundabout from the bus station. Open daily 7am-9pm.

Weather, Ski, and Road Info: Call the tourist office or listen to French-language Radio Val (96.1FM; ☎04 79 06 18 66). **Ski Lifts:** ☎04 79 06 00 35. **Ski Patrol:** ☎04 79 06 02 10. **Weather forecast:** ☎08 92 68 02 73.

Police: 600m past the tourist office toward Le Fornet (☎04 79 06 03 41).

Hospital: In Bourg-St-Maurice (☎04 79 41 79 79).

Post Office: Across from the tourist office (☎04 79 06 06 99). **ATM** and **currency exchange** available. Open July-Aug. M and W-F 8:30am-1pm and 2-4pm, Tu 8:30am-1pm and 3-5:45pm, Sa 8:30-11:30am. Winter hours vary. **Postal Code:** 73150.

🏠 🏕 ACCOMMODATIONS AND CAMPING

A budget option for groups is to rent an apartment in one of the many chalets; contact the tourist office for booking assistance. **Val Hôtel** (☎04 79 06 18 90; valhotel@valdisere.com) helps visitors find hotel deals during the ski season. The hotels that stay open in the low season offer rooms for reasonable prices. The cheapest beds are at the *refuges*, **Le Prariond** and **Le Fond Des Fours,** each a 2hr. hike from downtown, and at *gîtes* in Le Fornet.

▧ Chalet Turia (☎04 79 06 06 26; fax 06 16 65), 2.5km from the tourist office, in Le Fornet. Gorgeous wood-trimmed studios for 2, 4, or 10 people in a chalet overlooking the Isère. Studios come with bath, kitchen, TV, and heated floors. One of France's best bargains. Apr.-Nov. €25 per person. Dec.-Mar. weekly rentals only. Dec. and Feb.-Mar. doubles €350; triples and quads €560; 10-person rooms €1750. Jan. doubles €350; triples and quads €460; 10-person rooms €1600. ❷

Hôtel les Crêtes Blanches (☎04 79 06 05 45; www.cretes-blanches.com). Turn right at the roundabout above the bus station. English-speaking staff offers simple, wood-paneled rooms with TVs. Perfect location near the bus stop, chair lifts, and shops, restaurants, and nightlife. Breakfast €7. Reception 8am-8pm. Open Dec.-May. and July-Aug. singles €42-68; doubles €50-86. June singles €68-175; doubles €90-194. MC/V. ❹

Hôtel Sakura (☎04 79 06 04 08; www.sakura7.com). Turn right at the roundabout above the bus station. Rooms have comfortable beds, bath, TV, and kitchen. English-speaking owner builds all the furniture himself. Free Wi-Fi. Reception 8am-8pm. Open July-Aug. and Dec.-May. July-Aug. singles and doubles from €45; triples and quads from €70; quints from €100. Dec.-May singles and doubles €60-125; triples and quads €80-210; quints €100-240. MC/V. ❹

Le Relais du Ski (☎04 79 06 02 06; www.valdisere.com/lerelaisduski), 500m from the tourist office. Clean rooms with bathrooms. Breakfast included. Singles €120-138; doubles €140-172; triples €177-204; quads €204-252. AmEx/MC/V. ❹

Refuge de Prariond (☎04 79 06 06 02; www.prariond.com). During un-staffed months, supplies are provided with payment. Breakfast €6.80. Shower €2.50. Sleepsacks €2.50. Reservations recommended. Staffed from late Mar. to early May and from mid-June to mid-Sept. Dorms €13, students €9; *demi-pension* €35/31. ❶

Refuge du Fond des Fours (☎04 79 06 16 90). Showers €3. Sleepsacks €3.30. Staffed from mid-June to mid-Sept. and from mid-Mar. to mid-May. Dorms €13, students €8.80; *demi-pension* €35/32. ❶

Camping les Richardes (☎04 79 06 26 60; http://campinglesrichardes.free.fr), 1km from the tourist office. Take the Train Rouge to Les Richardes. A fence surrounds this undivided field in a beautiful valley near the *centre-ville*. Showers €1 per 5min. Reception 7:30am-12:30pm and 2-8pm. Open from mid-June to mid-Sept. €3 per person; €1.60 per tent; €1.50 per car. Electricity €1.90-3.80. MC/V over €15. ❶

🍴 FOOD

Restaurants in Val d'Isère tend to be pricey. Hearty regional specialties include fondue and the meat-and-potatoes-heavy *tartiflette* and *raclette*. Cheaper pizzerias around Val Village's bus station offer more standard fare. In the low season, only a few restaurants remain open; ask at the tourist office for a list. A **Spar** supermarket is to the right of the roundabout from the bus station. (☎04 79 06 02 66. Open daily 8am-1pm and 3:30-8pm. MC/V.)

Chevallot (☎04 79 06 29 36), 20m uphill from the bus station. Family-owned *boulangerie*, *pâtisserie*, and *salon de thé*. Gourmet treats such as *tourte au beaufort* (cheese tart), quiche lorraine, *tartiflette*, and sandwiches (€2.30-6.50). Mouthwatering pastries and *fondant chocolat* (€3). Open daily July-Aug. and Dec.-Apr. 6:30am-8pm; Oct.-Nov. and May-June 7am-1pm and 3-7pm. MC/V. ❶

L'Arolay (☎04 79 06 11 68). Le Fornet's only restaurant. Beautiful terrace overlooks the Isère, while the wood-trimmed interior is adorned with festive lights. Fondue €17-22. *Tartiflette* €15. *Raclette* €23. *Plats* €16-24. Lunch *menu* €15. Dinner *menu* €30. Open July-Aug. and Dec.-Apr. daily 10am-10pm. MC/V. ❸

Le Bananas (☎04 79 06 04 23), to the right of the roundabout near the base of the *téléphériques*. Ski instructors and famished skiers pack this rockin' chalet for Tex-Mex and beers. Share the fajitas (€23). *Menus* from €18. Happy hour Dec.-Apr. 7-9pm. Open daily July-Aug. and Dec.-Apr. noon-3pm and 5pm-1am. AmEx/MC/V. ❸

La Casserole (☎04 79 41 15 71), behind the bus station. Savory specialties like *raclette* (€25). Salads €16-19. *Plats* €16-27. Open in summer Tu and Su noon-2pm, W-Sa noon-2pm and 7-9pm; in winter daily noon-2:30pm and 7-10:30pm. AmEx/MC/V. ❸

🎵 🎭 ENTERTAINMENT AND NIGHTLIFE

Ciné Alps Val, across from the bus station, shows American movies. (☎08 92 68 73 33; www.cinealps. fr. Shows daily 2:30, 6, 9pm. €9, under 12 €7.50.)

Typical après-ski bars line the streets of Val Village, but most of the late-night action centers on the roundabout above the Val Village bus station.

> **Lodge Bar** (☎04 79 06 02 01), to the right of the roundabout from the bus station. Attached restaurant, open only in winter, serves famous fondue. Beer €3-5. Happy hour 4:30-7:30pm. Open daily July-Aug. 6pm-2am; Nov.-Apr. 4:30pm-2am. MC/V.

> **Le "XV"** (☎04 79 41 90 55), across from the bus station. Popular après-ski spot. Mostly Anglophone crowd sips drinks on the terrace. Big-screen TVs play sporting events. Beer €2.90. Mixed drinks €6. Open July-Aug. and from mid-Nov. to early May 9am-1:30am.

⛷ SKIING

Skiing is more than an obsession in Val d'Isère—it's a way of life. Over 100 lifts, several of them starting in Val d'Isère and Tignes, provide access to 300km of trails; you can ski for a day without returning to the same base and for a week without repeating a run. Lift tickets are valid on the entire **Espace Killy,** which includes all lifts and runs from Val d'Isère to Tignes, a ski station 7km away. The mountains are typically accessible from late November to early May, with optimum conditions in mid-winter. (Lift tickets available at slope-side offices or www.stvivaldisere.com. €42 per day; discounts for ages 5-13 and over 65.) The **École du Ski Français** (☎04 79 06 02 34; www.esfvaldisere.com), Val d'Isère's largest ski school, offers private and group ski lessons.

BELLEVARDE, PISSAILLAS, AND TIGNES

Most beginner runs start at higher altitudes, near the Marmottes and Borsat lifts on the south side of Bellevarde (take the Bellevarde lift up) and in the Pissaillas area (take the Solaise cable car, then the Glacier and Leissier lifts). Intermediate and advanced skiers frequent the slopes that surround Tignes, while the north side of Bellevarde is known for its expert runs. There's a **snow park** between Val and Tignes. A snowboard trail runs from the top of the Mont Blanc lift to La Daille, where a Funival car whisks boarders back to Bellevarde's summit. From late June to mid-July, Pissaillas and La Grande Motte in Tignes offer summer skiing.

IN RECENT NEWS

SEE 'EM SKI FOR FREE

Although winter in Val d'Isère is always spectacular, this year will bring an amazing event to the mountain village—the Alpine World Ski Championships 2009. The town is well equipped to handle the limelight; Val d'Isere hosted four men's Alpine skiing events in the 1992 winter Olympics and is also the hometown of many skiing legends, such as Henri Oreiller, Jean-Claude Killy, and the Goitschel sisters.

This year promises to be special not only for the city but also for the sport, as Val d'Isère is eliminating audience admission fees—a first in the world of international skiing. All visitors must have an invitation, which can be obtained at www.valdisere2009.org.

In addition to the city's efforts to host a wonderful event (they have even hired Guy Martin, a Michelin-starred chef, to design a special 2009 championship soup), Mother Nature is lending a helping hand. The layout of the competition site is unique and unprecedented in ski history; the two mountains—Bellevarde and Solaise—are positioned face to face, making 90% of the competition open to full view. After last year's hot and hazy summer Olympic events, the Alpine World Ski Championships in Val d'Isère should be refreshing.

OFF-PISTE SKIING

Val d'Isère locals are most proud of the area's off-piste offerings; limitless opportunities for backcountry skiing await thrill-seekers, but these trails are generally quite dangerous, and access is often prohibited. To experience Val d'Isère's off-piste trails, inquire at the École du Ski Français or hire one of the many independent guides in the area (ask the tourist office for a complete list). With or without a guide, always check weather conditions, always leave an itinerary with the ski patrol, and never go alone.

◪ HIKING

With plunging gorges and snow-covered glaciers, the mountains surrounding the Val offer some of the most spectacular hiking in the Alps. The trails are dotted with *refuges*, most of which offer full board in July and August; with proper planning, backpackers can stay in the mountains for days by hiking from *refuge* to *refuge*. *L'Estive*, available at the tourist office, has a complete list of *refuges*. The Val serves as an entrypoint for hikes in ◪**Vanoise National Park,** which extends to the Italian border and is France's premier wildlife reserve. Before setting out for any trip, call ahead to make sure *refuges* and trails are open, check the weather report, and bring warm clothing—snowstorms strike even in summer. Trails around Val are well marked with blazes and signs, but hikers should buy an **IGN map** (€10) and the detailed **Carte des Sentiers de Randonnée** (€5), which describes over 50 routes spanning 100km, at the tourist office. The book details several Vanoise hikes that originate in Val d'Isère.

◪ **Refuge de Prariond and Col de la Galise** (3km, 1¼hr.; 300m elevation change). The hike starts at Pont St-Charles, a 30min. walk from Le Fornet along the main road leaving Val Village. The **Train Rouge** extends its route to Pont St-Charles 2 times per day (to the *pont* 9 and 10am; from the *pont* 4 and 5pm). From the parking lot near the bridge, a marked trail ascends quickly within the 1st km. Upon reaching the **Gorges du Malpasset,** the trail plateaus and continues along the hillside above the Isère and through an alpine meadow to the Refuge de Prariond (see **Accommodations,** p. 488). The trail passes through several streams; be cautious when walking on wet rocks. From the *refuge,* signs point to a more difficult trail that ascends to the **Col de la Galise** (2hr.; 710m elevation change), a small summit that straddles the French-Italian border.

Le Fornet (50min.; 100m elevation change). Easy trail starts at the church in Val Village. Following the signs for Le Fornet, walk though vieux Val to a pedestrian road that joins up with the GR5 before forking again toward Le Fornet.

Refuge du Fond des Fours and the GR5 (1¾hr.; 560m elevation change). Intermediate hike starts at the Manchet entrance to the Vanoise. Take the free Train Vert **shuttle** to Le Manchet (see **Public Transportation,** p. 487) and continue up the road to the park entrance, past the base of the chair lift and old stone farmhouses. From just inside the entrance, follow the trail on the left marked "Refuge du Fond des Fours." The trail rises gradually through a valley before reaching steeper terrain, where it follows a series of switchbacks upward. After descending briefly into a small valley, it goes up another fairly steep rise to the *refuge* (see **Accommodations,** p. 488), in a high valley across from the Méan Martin glacier and alpine lakes. To return to Val, descend via the same path. Another option is to cross the Col des Fours pass and head back to town via the **GR5,** a 7hr. loop that crosses difficult terrain. Continue along the trail to the *refuge,* then turn left onto the path that ascends the line between the 3135m Pelaou Blanc and the 3072m Pointe des Fours (1¼hr.; 450m elevation change). Where the trail ends, turn left on the red-and-white-marked GR5 for a descent on the Col d'Iseran, a popular leg of the Tour de France (3hr., 6km; 900m elevation change).

Lac du Santel (12.25km, 7hr. round-trip; 940m elevation change). This advanced trek starts at the Fornet *téléphérique*. From the station, descend slightly and turn right at the trail marker for the Balcon des Barmettes. There, head right on Trail #36, the Bailletta, which climbs steeply for 800m to the small **Lac de la Bailletta** (2½hr.), reaches a pass, and then descends gradually to the larger Lac de la Sassière.

 LAWS OF THE LAND. Because the Refuge de Prariond, Col de la Galise, Refuge du Fond des Fours, and GR5 are located in Vanoise National Park, there are strict laws in place to protect nature. Similar regulations apply for the Lac du Santel, which is located on the Reserve de la Bailletaz. Familiarize yourself with these laws before heading out and avoid marring your record with a flower-picking offense.

⚑ OTHER OUTDOOR ACTIVITIES

The **Bureau des Guides** (☎04 79 06 05 53) teaches ice climbing (morning session €76) and rock climbing (afternoon session €28) and leads full-day canyoning trips (€64). Nature expeditions are offered for all levels. Advanced climbers should verify routes with guides before setting out. Beginners should check out the Via Ferrata (morning and afternoon sessions €46) in La Daille. This 3hr. climb (360m elevation change) hugs the side of the mountain facing the valley; there is also a more demanding 4-6hr. climb that requires a guide. Make all reservations with the **Bureau des Guides** the night before. (Info desk on the lower level of Killy Sports, next to the tourist office. Open daily 6am-7:30pm.)

For a relaxing trip to the summit of Val d'Isère, take a **téléphérique** over peaks, glaciers, and valleys to the top of the mountain. In the summer, a chairlift runs to Solaise, a small summit surrounded by a lake and easy hiking trails. (July-Aug. €7; Dec.-Apr. ski pass access only.)

RHÔNE-ALPES

MASSIF CENTRAL

Many claustrophobic travelers escape from Paris to the coastal regions of Provence and the Riviera only to find that the rest of Paris has done the same. But the few who slip away to the Massif Central, in the very heart of the country, find unadulterated beauty. The area plays host to a forested chain of extinct volcanoes—a beautiful and mystical landscape. The Auvergne's countryside and wealth of outdoor adventures more than compensate for its tame nightlife. The towering Puy-de-Dôme (p. 497) offers prime views of the volcanic park, though the real hiking and skiing mecca is Le Mont-Dore (p. 498), nestled in the shadow of a string of dormant volcanoes. The Massif's varied terrain also caters to less adventurous travelers; in Le Puy-en-Velay (p. 502), pumice-paved streets wind among Renaissance houses. The real draw for those seeking refuge are the mineral waters of Le Mont-Dore (p. 500) and Vichy (p. 509), better known as France's capital under Nazi occupation. Known for their healing powers, the waters and spas of these cities attract both *curistes* (those who believe in the healing powers of the springs) and the curious. Whether you come seeking relaxation or recreation, the Massif Central is sure to deliver.

HIGHLIGHTS OF THE MASSIF CENTRAL

CLIMB to the top of Le Mont-Dore's Puy de Sancy (p. 501) for a 360° view.

FEEL a little bit closer to heaven at the chapel of St-Michel d'Aiguille (p. 505).

GET INSPIRED at Clermont-Ferrand's Cathédrale Notre-Dame de l'Assomption (p. 496), where 13th-century workers used volcanic rock to build the sky-high spire.

CLERMONT-FERRAND ☎ 04 73

During the Middle Ages, Clermont-Ferrand (clare-mohn-fur-rahn; pop. 141,000) existed as rival cities—Clermont and Montferrand—until Louis XIII merged them in 1630. Clermont got a better deal: the allegedly "combined" city's walls excluded Montferrand. Now the outcast city is nearly forgotten while its illustrious twin has become a lively urban center. During the 20th century, red-roofed Clermont became synonymous with Michelin tires (rubber was first used in bike tires here) and the revered Red and Green Guides, thanks to brothers André and Édouard Michelin. Today, Clermont-Ferrand is a true college town, home to two major universities, nearly 35,000 students, and the comic shops, kebab stands, and tattoo parlors that so often accompany them. While the city itself provides ample entertainment for a short stay, it also makes a perfect base for trips to the surrounding mountains.

▐ TRANSPORTATION

Trains: Av. de l'Union Soviétique (☎04 73 90 22 90). Ticket booths open M-Th 5:20am-8:20pm, F 5:20am-9:20pm, Sa 6am-7:40pm, Su 7am-9:50pm. To **Le Puy** (2hr., 4 per day, €21), **Lyon** (2hr., 8 per day, €29), and **Paris** (3hr., 8 per day, €50).

Buses: Pl. Gambetta (☎04 73 93 13 61). Office open M-Sa 8:30am-6:30pm. To destinations throughout the Auvergne, including **Vichy** (1hr., 1 per day, €9.60). Infrequent service July-Aug.

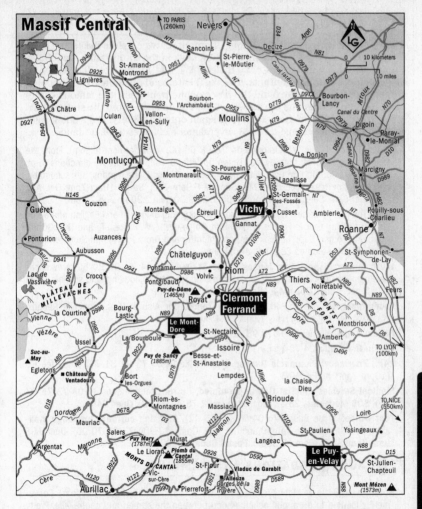

Massif Central

Public Transportation: 24 bd. Charles de Gaulle (☎04 73 28 70 00; www.t2c.fr). **Buses** cover the city 5am-10pm. New **tram** system serves the city 4am-midnight. Tickets to both €1.30, day pass €4.20; available from vending machines throughout the city.

Taxis: Eurotaxis Clermontois, 15-17 rue du Pre la Reine (☎04 73 60 06 00). **Taxi 63,** 40 rue Fontgieve (☎04 73 31 53 15). **Taxis Radio,** 9 allée Pierre-de-Fermat (☎04 73 19 53 53). All 24hr.

Car Rental: Avis, av. de l'Union Soviétique (☎04 73 91 72 94; fax 90 74 11). Branch at 9 rue Eugène Gilbert (☎04 73 29 27 28), in the *centre-ville.* Open M 9:30am-1pm and 2-6:15pm, Tu-F 9am-1pm and 2-6:15pm.

Bike Rental: MooviCité, 20 pl. Renoux (☎08 10 63 00 63; fax 28 99 80). Branch at 43 av. de l'Union Soviétique. €3 per day, €10 per week. Discounts for students, under 25, and over 65. Both open M-F 7am-7pm, Sa 8am-7pm. Cash only.

⊞ 🔣 ORIENTATION AND PRACTICAL INFORMATION

Clermont-Ferrand's *centre-ville* is in Clermont, between **place Delille** and **place de Jaude.** Pick up a map at the information desk in the train station, which is a 15min. walk from the *centre-ville.* Buses #2, 4, and 14 run from the station to pl. de Jaude. Several restaurants, a movie theater, and the monstrous shopping complex **Centre Jaude** surround the *place,* while boutiques, the famous cathedral, and bookstores line the streets of the *vieille ville.* From the station, turn left onto av. de l'Union Soviétique, left again onto bd. Fleury, and a quick right onto av. Carnot. Continue through several name changes to pl. de Jaude.

Tourist Office: Pl. de la Victoire (☎04 73 98 65 00; www.clermont-fd.com). From the train station, turn left onto av. de l'Union Soviétique. Follow the above directions to pl. Jaude to av. Carnot; turn right onto rue St-Gènes (20min.). Great maps, bus schedules, and hiking routes. Office open May-Sept. M-F 9am-7pm, Sa-Su 10am-7pm; Oct.-Apr. M-F 9am-6pm, Sa 10am-1pm and 2-6pm, Su 9:30am-12:30pm and 2-6pm.

Tours: The tourist office offers a self-guided walking tour in French and English and a 2hr. guided walking tour in French of Clermont (July-Aug. M, W, F 3pm, Tu and Th 8:30pm; from early to mid-Sept. M, W, F 3pm) and Montferrand (from July to mid-Sept. Tu, Th, Sa 3pm). €5.90, students €3.20, under 18 free.

Youth Center: Espace Info Jeunes, 5 rue St-Gènes (☎04 73 92 30 50; www.espaceinfojeunes.net). Helpful staff provides info on jobs, travel, lodging, and schools. Wi-Fi €0.50 per 30min. Open M-F 10am-6pm, Sa 10am-1pm.

Laundromat: 57 rue du Port. Open daily 7am-11pm. Also at 6 pl. Hippolyte Renoux. Wash €4 per 7kg. Open daily 7am-8pm. Cash only.

Police: 2 rue Pélissier (☎04 73 98 42 42).

Poison Control: ☎04 72 11 69 11.

24hr. Pharmacy: Pharmacie Ducher, 1 pl. Delille (☎04 73 91 31 77). Night fee €6 (10pm-7am). AmEx/MC/V.

Medical Services: Hôpital Gabriel-Montpied, 58 rue Montalembert (☎04 73 75 07 50). **SOS Médecins,** 28 av. Léon Blum (☎04 73 42 22 22). Open 24hr.

Post Office: 1 rue Busset (☎04 73 30 65 42). **ATM** and **currency exchange** available. Open M-Sa 9am-7pm. Branch at 2 pl. Gaillard (☎04 73 31 70 00). Open M-F 9am-7pm, Sa 8:30am-12:30pm. **Postal Code:** 63000.

🏠 🏨 ACCOMMODATIONS AND CAMPING

Hôtel Ravel, 8 rue de Maringues (☎04 73 91 51 33; hotelravel63@wanadoo.fr). Conveniently located in a tranquil neighborhood between the station and *centre-ville.* Pretty green lobby more stylish than the rooms. Each clean, comfortable room has bath, phone, and TV. Breakfast €6. Singles €39; doubles €47; triples €58; quads €70. MC/V. ❸

Foyer Hôme Dome, 12 pl. de Regensburg (☎04 73 29 40 70; www.ethic-etapes.fr). From the intersection of av. Carnot and av. d'Italie, near the station, take bus #13 (dir.: Perignat) to Regensburg. High-rise building near a quiet residential area. Simple, modern rooms with toilets and showers. Restaurant, kitchen, and computer lab without Internet. Breakfast included. Laundry. 2-night min. stay. Reception 24hr. Singles €19, for stays over 3 nights €17; doubles €38/34. MC/V. ❶

Foyer des Jeunes Travailleurs (Corum Saint Jean), 17 rue Gaultier de Biauzat (☎04 73 31 57 00; www.corumsaintjean.fr). Prime location. Simple dorm-style rooms. Bar, cafeteria-style restaurant, and climbing wall. Some rooms with private showers. Breakfast included. Laundry €3. Free Internet. Reception 24hr. Dorms €20-54. MC/V. ❶

Clermont-Ferrand

ACCOMMODATIONS
Camping Le Chancet, 2
Foyer Hôme Dome, 8
Foyer des Jeunes
Travailleurs, 1
Hôtel Ravel, 4

FOOD
Le 1513, 5
Ahl St-Tropez, 6
Le Pescajoux, 3

MASSIF CENTRAL

200 meters
200 yards

TO AVIS (100m)

Gare SNCF
av. de l'Union Soviétique
r. de Riom
SQ. DE LA JEUNE RÉSISTANCE
r. Jeanne d'Arc
av. Charras
r. Pourchet
TO
r. Victor Hugo
r. d'Alsace
av. d'Italie
r. de Maringues
av. Albert et Elisabeth
r. de Courpière
Covered Market
r. d'Ambert
av. de Grande Bretagne
r. Auguste Audollent
r. des Jacobins
TO MONTFERRAND (2.5km)
Église Godefroy de Bouillon
av. Charras
r. de Billom
PL. DE L'ESPLANADE
bd. Fleury
av. Carnot
r. Delarbre
r. Bansac
r. Paul Collomp
PL. DELILLE
St-Laurent Couronne
bd. Trudaine
cours Sablon
r. des Archers
r. Neyron
r. Robertus
Basilique de Notre-Dame du-Port pl. d'Espagne
Laundry
r. Clausmann
r. Abbé Lacoste
r. du Port
r. Villeneuve
r. de l'Oratoire
r. du Bon Pasteur
imp. St. Austremoine
Église St-Genès
av. des paulines
r. d'Amboise
TO SOS MÉDECINS, HOSPITAL (1.4km)
Musée Lecoq
Chapelle des Capucins
r. Bardoux
bd. Lafayette
Musée d'Archéologie Bargoin
r. Lecoq
r. Deschamps
r. Paradis
r. Bargoin
r. d'Enfer
r. Breschet
r. Antoine d'Auvergne
r. Grégoire de Tours
r. Nve. des Carmes
r. Maréchal Joffre
r. Pascal
r. des Gémeaux
r. de Boulogne
H. Barbusse
r. Thomas
F. Méchier
r. du Terrail
Espace Info Jeunes
r. de la Treille
r. F.P. Leblanc
r. St-Esprit
r. Ballainvilliers
MooviCité
r. Busset
r. Renon
r. Maréchal Juin
r. M. de lattre de Tassigny
Laundry
r. Georges Clémenceau
PL. DE LA VICTOIRE
Cathédrale Notre-Dame-de-l'Assomption
pl. Terrasse
r. St-Genès
r. Marcombes
P. Marcombes
Fontaine d'Amboise
PL. DE LA POTERNE
r. André Moinel
r. St-Hérem
PL. DU MAZET
V. Latour. r. Boirot
r. des 2 Marchés
r. Boucherie
Covered Market
r. St-Pierre
r. Barthélemy
r. St-Pierre
r. Gaultier de Biauzat
Dulaure
TO PARC MONTJUZET
TO
r. Fontgiève (1.5km), r. Barnier
r. Ste-Rose
la Michodière
Voyages Wasteels
PL. GAILLARD
av. des États-Unis
r. de l'Ange
r. St-Dominique
r. des Minimes
r. Lamartine
Église St-Pierre
r. Blatin
r. Ste-Madeleine
gd. Passage
av. Julien
Champion Supermarket
av. Maréchal Foch
r. des Salles
r. Renan
PL. DE JAUDE
Cinéma Le Paris
PL. DE LA RÉSISTANCE
r. Gonod
CENTRE JAUDE
av. Col. Gaspard
r. Duprat
r. Charretière
PL. LOUIS ARAGON
r. D'Allagnat
r. Meissonier
r. Sodacroix
bd. Desaix
bd. du Coche
r. de la Préfecture
r. du Cheval Blanc
r. N. Perret
r. du 11 Novembre
r. des Petits Gras
r. des Chaussetiers
pl. Sugny
pl. Prévote
r. de l'Ente Gras
Barrière de Jaude
TO SNCF BOUTIQUE (200m)
TO
r. Lagarlaye
bd. L. Malfreyt
r. Giscard de la Fonderie
TO
r. Bonnabaud
r. Gilbert
r. Maréchal Foch
TO 2 (6km), PUY-DE-DÔME
TO 1 (50m)
TO 8 (750m)
PL. DE JAUDE

Camping Le Chancet, av. Jean-Baptiste Marrou (☎04 73 61 30 73), 6km outside Clermont, on N89 (dir.: Bordeaux). From the station, take bus #4C (dir.: Ceyrat) to Préguille. Hedges separate spots. Heated pool, minigolf, and biking and hiking excursions in summer. Laundry. Reception 9am-10pm. €2.70-3.10 per person, under 10 €1.80-2.10; sites €3.40-5.60. Prices vary seasonally. Electricity €3.60. AmEx/MC/V. ❶

🍴 FOOD

Clermont-Ferrand's Michelin brothers may have created the most influential French restaurant guide to compensate for a hometown not known for its cuisine. College hangouts are tucked into side streets in the *centre-ville,* fast-food joints cluster on **avenue des États-Unis,** and a few *brasseries* surround the tourist office and cathedral. A **Champion** supermarket takes up much of rue Giscard de la Tour Fondue, past pl. de Jaude. (Open M-Sa 8:30am-8:30pm, Su 9am-12:30pm. MC/V.) Off pl. Gaillard, the **Marché Couvert/Espace Saint-Pierre** stocks local produce, cheese, and meats. (Open M 7am-7pm, Tu-Sa 7am-7:30pm.)

Le Pescajoux, 13 rue du Port (☎04 73 92 12 26). Relaxed dining room decorated with the artist-owner's sculptures and abstract works. Among the largest *crêpe* and *galette* menu you'll ever see—over 100 variations ranging from basic *chocolat* (€3.50) to the more intimidating "XXL" (750g of steak, eggs, and cheese; €14). Open Tu-F noon-2pm and 7:30-11:30pm, Sa 7:30-11:30pm. AmEx/MC/V. ❶

Ah! St-Tropez, 10 rue Massillon (☎04 73 90 44 64), near pl. de Victoire. Tasty gourmet *menus* (€13-24) of—illogically enough—entirely Provençal cuisine. Try the Tian, a vegetable *gratin*. Open Tu-Th noon-2pm and 7:30-10pm, F-Sa 7:30-11pm. MC/V. ❸

Le 1513, 3 rue des Chaussetiers (☎04 73 37 49 36). Tucked inside the stone archway of a fantastically preserved medieval hotel. Intimate atmosphere with 2 private courtyards and small stone-walled dining rooms. *Galettes* €2.50-12. Enormous desserts €2.50-9. *Menu* €14. Open M-F noon-2pm and 6pm-12:30am, Sa-Su noon-12:30am. MC/V. ❷

👁 SIGHTS

Clermont's *vieille ville,* called the **Ville Noire** (Black City) for its many black-stoned buildings, features architecture from the Middle Ages, the Belle Époque, and modern times. Tiny Montferrand doesn't boast much in the way of attractions, but it does feature some well-preserved half-timbered houses, medieval mansions, and a church built of volcanic rock. A combined €6.50 ticket allows entry into any two of the city's four museums. Most museums are free for students and those under 18 and free for everyone on the first Sunday of the month. The best sights, however, lie in the surrounding mountains. To reach Montferrand (a 40min. walk up av. de la République), take the Clermont tourist office's French walking tour (p. 494) or tram line A (dir.: Champratel).

🏛**CATHÉDRALE NOTRE-DAME-DE-L'ASSOMPTION.** First built in AD 450 and later completely reconstructed in Gothic style between 1248 and 1295, this magnificent cathedral rises high above the surrounding buildings and remains a presence wherever you are in the city. Tiny bubbles in the black volcanic stone used in construction made it much lighter, allowing the church's spires to soar to 100m. The combination of the cathedral's gargoyle-covered Gothic exterior, towering height, and jet-black color make the building seem more like an evil citadel than a house of God. Climb up the 252-step tower for unrivaled views of Clermont-Ferrand and a closer look at the gargoyles and flying buttresses. *(Pl. de la Victoire. www.catholique-clermont.cef.fr. Open M-Sa 8am-noon and 2-6pm, Su 9:30am-noon and 3-7pm. Tower open M-Sa 10am-noon and 2-6pm, Su 3-6pm. €1.50.)*

BASILIQUE DE NOTRE DAME DU PORT. This 12th-century church, near the site where Pope Urban II allegedly started the First Crusade, was built in Auvergnat Romanesque style. In May, pilgrims come to see the Black Virgin icon. *(Pl. Notre Dame du Port. ☎04 73 91 32 94. Open daily 8am-7pm. Tours in French July-Aug. W and F 3pm.)*

PARC DE MONTJUZET. This immaculately groomed park covers a hill located high above Clermont, offering panoramic views of the city and its surrounding mountains, including Puy-de-Dôme, which are only bested by those from the cathedral's tower. The Mediterranean garden—one of the park's highlights— seems to be taken straight out of a Van Gogh landscape. The rest of the park features shaded paths, contemporary sculptures, and various playgrounds, making it a perfect spot for people of all ages to enjoy a picnic or afternoon stroll. *(Northwest of the main city. Main entrance and parking on rue du Parc de Montjuzet; secondary pedestrian entrance closer to the vieille ville on rue des Aubepines. A 15min. walk from the cathedral; ask at the tourist office for directions. ☎04 73 42 63 63. Open 7am-8pm.)*

MUSÉE D'ARCHÉOLOGIE BARGOIN. Prehistoric skeletons and North African textiles take a back seat to this small museum's rich collection of Gallo-Roman artifacts. What the array of artifacts lacks in size it makes up for in variety; figurines, glassware, mosaics, sculptures, and relics of Puy-de-Dôme's Temple of Mercury are just some of the items on display. *(45 rue Ballainvilliers. ☎04 73 42 69 70. Open Tu-Sa 10am-noon and 1-5pm, Su 2-7pm. €4.20, students €2.70, under 18 free.)*

♫ ✺ ENTERTAINMENT AND FESTIVALS

Pool tables and cheap beer are the main attractions at bars across from the train station. Check out the *Guide de l'Étudiant Clermont-Ferrand* (available at the tourist office) for complete bar listings.

> **Festival International du Court Métrage** (☎04 73 91 65 73; www.clermont-filmfest. com), from Jan. 30 to Feb. 7, 2009. Over 3000 filmmakers and 130,000 guests gather for the Cannes of short film. Contact **La Jetée,** 6 pl. Michel de l'Hôpital, for more info. 5- to 6-film pass €2.50.

> **Contre-Plongées de l'Été** (☎04 73 42 69 89), in July. Open-air film screenings and live concerts in parks and squares around the city.

◢ DAYTRIPS FROM CLERMONT FERRAND

PUY-DE-DÔME

Although Puy-de-Dôme is only 12km from Clermont-Ferrand, getting there takes planning. A shuttle circulates 3 times per day from the Clermont train station to the summit and 4 times per day to the Vulcania. (☎0800 50 05 24. 35min.; July-Aug. daily, Sept. and May-June Sa-Su and holidays; round-trip €5, students and under 16 €2.50. Includes connecting shuttles to Vulcania.) Cyclists allowed on mountain July-Aug. daily 10am-6pm; Sept.-Oct. and May-June Sa-Su and holidays 10am-6pm. Drivers pay a €6 toll, leave cars at the base, and take a bus to the top (last bus descends 6pm, round-trip €4). Limited free parking at base and summit.

Clermont-Ferrand's greatest attraction may be its proximity to extinct volcanoes, crater lakes, and mountains. Puy-de-Dôme (pwee-duh-dohm), the mountain dominating the region's middle, is part of the **Parc Naturel Régional des Volcans d'Auvergne** (☎04 73 65 64 00). Hikers, bikers, and skiers enjoy the unspoiled terrain of one of France's largest parks. A hiking guide is available at the Clermont-Ferrand tourist office. There are three main sections in the protected area: the **Mont-Dore,** the **Monts du Cantal,** and the **Monts Dômes.**

On a clear day, the sweeping view from flat-topped Puy-de-Dôme (1465m) encompasses the rest of the **Chaîne des Puys,** a lush ridge of extinct volcanoes.

MASSIF CENTRAL

The scenery in late autumn can be particularly spectacular, as a sea of clouds often obscures the plains below so that only isolated peaks protrude into the sky. The ruins of the Roman **Temple de Mercure,** from the first and second centuries, sit on the summit. *Parapente* (paragliding) is quite popular on the summit. (Paragliding flights daily 10am-sunset, depending on weather. Contact the Puy-de-Dôme paragliding director, ☎06 08 32 08 46, for information on hours and weather conditions. €70 per flight. Cash only. Puy-de-Dôme open July-Aug. daily 10am-9pm; Sept.-June hours depend on daylight.) Call ahead (☎04 73 62 12 18) to see if the road to the top is open.

Hikers can take the *navette* to the base of the mountain and make the 45min. ascent up the chemin des Muletiers, a path that climbs 350m vertically before reaching the summit. Though tiring, the hike is reasonable for most. If you miss the *navette*, a longer hike is necessary: take bus #14 to Royat from the stop at pl. Allard. From there, take D68 to reach the first yellow markers that guide the rest of the wide, graveled, 3hr. hike along the PR Chamina to the summit. The hike from Royat is approximately 10km, mostly uphill. Buy the **IGN Chaîne des Puys** map and listen to the weather forecast for the day; conditions change rapidly, affecting access to the summit, guided tours, and paragliding.

LE MONT-DORE ☎04 73

In an isolated valley where the Dordogne River is little more than a trickle, Le Mont-Dore (luh mohn-dohr; pop. 1700) sits at the foot of the largest volcano in a dormant range. Puy de Sancy, the highest peak in the Massif Central, is only 3.5km from the *centre-ville*, making the town a premier ski resort and a hiking mecca. The town brims with chalets and rustic, timbered lodges—with an atmosphere of natural luxury. For centuries, its famous *thermes* have attracted summer *curistes* (spa-goers) seeking rejuvenation in the warm, mineral-rich hot springs that seep through cracks in the lava. Visitors find an interesting melange of these two worlds in the *centre-ville*, where ski and mountain-bike rental shops sit side by side with wine *caves* and lace boutiques.

⬛ TRANSPORTATION

Trains: Pl. de la Gare (☎04 73 65 00 02). Ticket office open M-F 5:25am-7:45pm, Sa 5:25am-7:30pm, Su 9:30am-7:30pm. To **Clermont-Ferrand** (2hr., 2-3 per day, €12) and **Paris** (6hr., 2 per day, €57).

Taxis: Taxi Thierry Barlaud (☎04 73 65 09 32). Taxi Sepchat (☎06 88 19 82 66).

Bike and Ski Rental: Bessac Sports, rue de Maréchal Juin (☎04 73 65 02 25), near the top of the hill. Bikes €12 per ½-day, €18 per full day. Ski packages €13-27 per day. Snowboard packages €16-21. ID deposit. Hiking equipment also available. Open daily May-Sept. 9am-noon and 2-7pm; from early to mid-Dec. and from mid-Jan. to Apr. 9am-noon and 1:30-7pm; from mid-Dec. to mid-Jan. 8:30am-7pm. MC/V.

⬛ ORIENTATION AND PRACTICAL INFORMATION

Le Mont-Dore is bounded by two major streets: **avenue de la Libération** on the west side of the **Dordogne River** and **route de Clermont** on the east side.

Tourist Office: Av. de la Libération (☎04 73 65 20 21). From the station, head up av. Michel Bertrand, through pl. Charles de Gaulle, onto rue Meynadier. Turn right onto allée Georges Lagaye; the office is across the ice-skating rink. English-speaking staff offers city guide, hiking trail map (€7), hiking guidebooks (€7-50), and hotel booking. Open July-Aug.

M-Sa 9am-7pm, Su 10am-noon and 2-6pm; Sept. and May-June M-Sa 9am-12:30pm and 2-6pm, Su 10am-noon and 2-6pm; Oct. M-Sa 9am-noon and 2-6pm.

Laundromat: Pl. de la République. Open daily 9am-8pm.

Police: Av. Michel Bertrand (☎04 73 65 01 70).

Pharmacie de Garde: Alternates between **Pharmacie du Parc,** 17 rue Meynadier (☎04 73 65 02 86; open M-Sa 9am-noon and 2:30-7pm) and **Pharmacie de l'Établissement,** 3 pl. du Panthéon (☎07 43 65 05 21; open M-Sa 9am-12:30pm and 2:30-7:30pm).

Hospital: 2 rue du Capitaine-Chazotte (☎07 43 65 33 33), off pl. Charles de Gaulle.

Internet Access: Sancyber (☎04 73 65 28 84), behind the casino. €2.50 per 30min. Open daily 2-11pm.

Post Office: Pl. Charles de Gaulle (☎07 43 65 37 10). **ATM** and **currency exchange.** Open M-F 8:30am-noon and 2-5:30pm, Sa 8:30am-noon. **Postal Code:** 63240.

ACCOMMODATIONS AND CAMPING

Le Mont-Dore has over a dozen hotels, and rooms start around €20, making it relatively easy to find an affordable bed in town. Even so, reservations are recommended during summer and peak skiing season.

Hôtel Artense, 19 av. de la Libération (☎04 73 65 03 43; www.artense-hotel.com), near the tourist office. Wood-paneled rooms are clean and comfortable. Breakfast €5. Internet access. Reception 8am-7pm. Open Dec.-Oct. Singles and doubles €20-40; triples with bath €40-45; quads €43-53. MC/V. ❶

Castel Medicis, 5 rue Duchatel (☎04 73 65 30 50; www.castel-medicis.com). Rustic ambience. Bright, clean rooms with wood floors. Breakfast included. Internet access. Reception 8am-7:30pm. Singles €34; doubles €38. Extra bed €10. MC/V. ❷

Auberge de Jeunesse "Le Grand Volcan" (HI), route du Sancy (☎04 73 65 03 53; www.auberge-mont-dore.com), a 3km uphill walk from town. From the station, climb av. Guyot-Dessaigne, which becomes av. des Belges. Continue on D983 (through several name changes) into the countryside. The hostel is on the right, after the chairlifts. Take a taxi from town (€10) or the *navette* from the train station and the tourist office (4 per day, last at 5:55pm; €2.30). Cozy ski-lodge atmosphere and tiny but clean 1- to 7- bed dorms. Steps from skiing and hiking trails. Outdoor kitchen, bar, pool table. Breakfast included. Internet €4 per hr. Ski and snowboard packages from €34. Reception 8am-noon and 6-8pm. Dorms €16, ages 5-10 €8, under 5 free. Cash only. ❶

Des Crouzets, av. des Crouzets (☎/fax 04 73 65 21 60), across from the train station. In a hollow on the Dordogne. Well kept but lacks trees or hedges for privacy. Reception M-Sa 9am-noon and 3-6:30pm, Su 9:30am-noon and 4-6pm. Open from mid-Dec. to mid-Oct. €3.10 per person, sites €3.20. Electricity €3.60-4. ❶

FOOD

Le Mont-Dore's setting makes it an ideal spot for mountaintop picnics; you can find St-Nectaire cheese, flavored dry sausage, and other regional products at the specialty shops between **place de la République** and **place du Panthéon.** Another option is the **Spar** supermarket on rue du Cap-Chazzotte. (Open M-Sa 7am-12:30pm and 3-7:30pm, Su 7am-noon and 4-7pm.) Restaurants take a back seat to outdoor pursuits in Le Mont-Dore. However, after a long day on the slopes or trails, small spots serving regional dishes like *truffade*—potatoes with melted cheese—or its creamed cousin *aligot* are ideal. Many restaurants in Le Mont-Dore are affiliated with a hotel and give discounts to guests.

▨ **Café de Paris,** 8 rue Jean Moulin (☎04 73 65 01 77). Classy 1920s salon with a small-town atmosphere. Frequent jazz concerts. *Truffade* €13. *Omelettes* €6. Open Dec.-Oct. daily 8am-8pm. Kitchen open noon-3pm. Cash only. ❷

La Grignote, 35 pl. André (☎04 73 65 09 89; www.lagrignote.com), behind the church. Bicycles, bathrobes, and boxing gloves hang from the ceiling. Quirky couple offers an enormous menu of pizzas (€7-13) and seafood specialties (€13-15). Salads €7-13. *Menus* €16-24. Open July-Aug. daily noon-2pm and 7-9:30pm; Sept.-June Th-Sa noon-2pm and 7-9:30pm, Su noon-2pm. Cash only. ❷

Le Bougnat, 23 rue Georges Clemenceau (☎04 73 65 28 19). Romantic atmosphere. Regional fare. *Plats* €12-17. Open daily noon-1:30pm and 7-8:30pm. AmEx/MC/V. ❸

◐ SIGHTS

ÉTABLISSEMENT THERMAL. Every morning during the thermal season (May-Oct.), *curistes* seeking the healing power of Le Mont-Dore's springs descend upon this establishment—a tradition that has sustained the town for centuries. The eight springs used today were originally channeled by the Romans, who discovered that the water did wonders for their horses' sinuses. Today, a French-language tour of the *thermes* takes visitors through the building's Neo-Byzantine interior and ends with a dose of the celebrated *douche nasale gazeuse*, a tiny blast of carbon and helium that ▨evacuates sinuses better than any sneeze. (*1 pl. du Panthéon.* ☎04 73 65 05 10; fax 65 09 37. Tours from late Apr. to late Oct. M-Sa every hr. 2-5pm; €3.30, ages 10-15 €2.30, under 10 free.)

◪ HIKING

Over 650km of trails run through the region's dormant volcanic mountains, spanning dense forests and grassy mountainsides, passing rushing waterfalls, and running along jagged rocks. Scaling the peaks is relatively easy—the summit of **Puy de Sancy** (1886m) is a manageable 1½hr. climb—and day-long rambles along the grassy ridges bordering the valley overlook the town. Those embarking on an extended hike should confer with the tourist office, which offers maps and good advice. Leave an itinerary of multi-day routes with the *peloton de montagne* (mountain police; ☎04 73 65 04 06 or 65 24 38), on rue des Chasseurs or at the base of Puy de Sancy. A map is a must; while a few of the most popular trails feature yellow signs indicating the distance and direction to nearby destinations, many less-traveled trails are left unmarked. The tourist office, bookstores, and newsstands around town sell the comprehensive **Massif du Sancy Carte de Randonnée** (€7), which includes all the hiking trails within a 20km radius of Puy de Sancy. Hikers should also be sure to consult weather reports—mist in the valley often signifies hail or snow in the peaks.

For all the views without all the exertion, the **téléphérique** (cable car) runs from the base by the hostel to a station just below Puy de Sancy; a 20min. climb up steep wood stairs leads to the summit. (☎08 20 82 09 48. Every 10min. July-Aug. 9am-7pm; Sept. and May-June 9am-12:30pm and 1:30-5pm; Oct.-Nov. schedule varies; Dec.-Apr. 8:45am-4:45pm. €5.60, round-trip €7.30; under 10 €4.20/5.70. MC/V.) Farther north, the **funicular** departs from near the tourist office to **Salon des Capucins,** a rocky outcropping high above town. (Every 20min. daily 9:30am-12:10pm and 2:10-6:40pm. €3.30, round-trip €4.20; under 10 €2.65/3.30. MC/V.) Both can be used to access other hikes or to save weary knees from a final descent. The following recommendations represent only a few hiking possibilities; innumerable routes can be planned. Distances and times given are for round-trip hikes from the trailhead.

▨ **La Grande Cascade** (4km, 2hr.; 222m elevation change). Starts from behind the Établissement Thermal in the *centre-ville* and ends above the falls on the **Plateau de Durbise,** a huge grassy plain high over the town that provides incredible views of the whole Sancy range. Area's largest waterfall—the trail's 30m high namesake—is well worth the hike. In summer, large rocks at the base of the falls provide an ideal setting for picnics or afternoon sunbathing; in winter, ice climbers converge on the spot to scale the frozen falls. From the *thermes*, follow rue des Desportes to the right and climb the stairs of chemin de la Bane on the left; at the top, turn right onto chemin de Melchi-Rose, which runs into route de Besse. After crossing the road, the trail winds up a narrow gorge. A quick climb up the metal stairway to the right leads to the top of the waterfall and the grassy field above. Descend via the same route.

▨ **Puy de Sancy** (6.2km, 3hr.; 555m elevation change). 360° view from the summit of the Massif's highest peak includes the entire region on clear days; views from the trail on the way up are nearly as good. Start at the base and ascend the mountain via Val de Courre, a picturesque cow pasture. Trail begins a few hundred meters to the right of *téléphérique* #2. Follow the wide rocky path in the center of the valley up Puy Redon. Trail veers left and narrows significantly at the top of Redon. Hikers should be careful on this upper section, especially on wet days, as there are no guard rails at the steep dropoffs. Trail heads upward toward the now-visible summit and eventually leads to a series of wood steps and up to a platform at the top. Descend via the same route.

Cascade de Queureuilh and Cascade de Rossignolet (5km, 1-2hr.; 60m elevation change). Easy, flat hike through a forest leads to 2 waterfalls. Queureuilh is arguably more spectacular, falling from a steep 30m cliff face. Follow the same staircase that leads to La Grand Cascade but turn left at the top onto chemin de Melchi-Rose, which runs into av. de Clermont. Turn left onto chemin de Monteyroux, then right onto route des Cascades. Trailhead marked by signs begins 300m up on the right at Prends-Toi-Garde.

Sancy to La Grande Cascade. Experienced hikers with lots of energy left after the climb up Sancy may consider the 8.9km hike along peaks between Sancy and La Grande Cascade. Difficulty rewarded by amazing views. Less traveled, often more peaceful. Beware that the largely unmarked trails are often little more than foot-wide dirt paths or muddy ditches where rainwater has eroded the trail. Trail particularly rugged between Puy des Crebasses and Roc de Cuzeau. From Sancy's summit, head down the path on the opposite side of the platform from where you came up. After 700m, the path branches into 3 trails at Col de la Cabane. Take the leftmost path 300m to Pan de la Grange; at the fork in the road, take the right-hand trail. Walk 2km along the ridge to Puy de Crebasses. When the path branches off again, stay left and continue 1.3km to Roc de Cuzeau. Go downhill and onto the Plateau de Durbise. Follow the path to the road on the opposite side. 1.1km trail to **La Grande Cascade** begins to the left, mostly along the **GR4**. A good map is a must; find one at the tourist office.

⚑ OTHER OUTDOOR ACTIVITIES

Bikers should visit the calm volcanic lakes, such as **Lac Servière** (15km northeast off D983), which pool in nearby craters. Most of the lakes have small pebble beaches suitable for windsurfing, sailing, and swimming. **Lac d'Aydat,** to the northeast, offers calm waters for **pedal boating,** as does **Lac Chambon,** 20km east of Mont-Dore via D996, near Murol. **Lac Pavin,** 25km southeast of town, has plenty of good **fishing.** Le Mont-Dore offers a spectacular winter wonderland. **Skiers** and **snowboarders** encounter pleasantly smaller crowds (and shorter lift lines) than elsewhere in France. A network of ski trails covers much of the **Massif du Sancy;** skiers can also venture down the other side of the valley into ritzy **Super-Besse** on clear days. Ski-rental shops fill the main village; rental packages generally cost €14-24 per day. Lift tickets for the entire Mont-Dore and Super-Besse area cost €19 per half-day and €24 per full day. At the base of Puy de

MASSIF CENTRAL

Sancy lifts is a **ski school** (☎04 73 65 07 43). The area also features an extensive network of cross-country skiing trails; ask at the tourist office or call the central cross-country resort (☎04 73 21 54 32) for information.

▶ DAYTRIPS FROM LE MONT-DORE

LA BOURBOULE. The region surrounding Le Mont-Dore has a number of small, picturesque towns within easy driving or hiking distance. La Bourboule (lah bohr-bool), which can also be reached by *navette* service from Le Mont-Dore, was established in 1875 upon the discovery of its thermal springs and became a widely popular destination in the 20s. The city, just 15min. from Le Mont-Dore, maintains its roaring atmosphere with exquisite, over-the-top Art Nouveau architecture, glamorous plazas, and charming hotels and restaurants. Information on *therme* visits, **shuttles** from Le Mont-Dore, and lodging is available at the **tourist office**, pl. de la République. (☎04 73 65 57 71; www.bourboule. com. Open July-Aug. daily 9am-7pm; Sept. and Apr.-June daily 9am-noon and 1:30-6pm; Oct.-Mar. M-Sa 9am-noon and 1:30-5:30pm, Su 9:30am-12:30pm.)

LE PUY-EN-VELAY   ☎04 71

Jutting crags of volcanic rock pierce the sky near Le Puy-en-Velay (luh pwee-uhn-vah-lay; pop. 20,500). For centuries, the city has served as the starting point for the 1600km Via Podiensis pilgrimage trail, which ends in Santiago de Compostela, Spain. The summer influx of pilgrims, many of them young—as well as tourists who come for Le Puy's famous *lentilles* (lentils) and *dentelles* (lace)—gives Le Puy a vitality uncommon among cities of its size.

▣ TRANSPORTATION

Trains: Pl. du Maréchal Leclerc. Ticket office open M-F 5:30am-7:10pm, Sa 6:10am-7:10pm, Su 10:05am-8:10pm. To **Clermont-Ferrand** (2hr., M-F 5-6 per day, €21) and **Lyon** (1hr., M-F 9 per day, €21).

Buses: Pl. du Maréchal Leclerc, next to the train station. Schedules and info available at the tourist office. To **Langogne** (1hr., M-F 3 per day, €7.80). Buy tickets on board.

Public Transportation: SAEM TUDIP **buses** leave from pl. Michelet. Info, map, and tickets at the tourist office. Runs daily 7am-7:25pm. Buy tickets (€1.10) on board or carnets of 10 (€7.20) at the office.

Taxis: Radio-Taxis, pl. du Breuil (☎04 71 05 42 43). 24hr.

✦ ▤ ORIENTATION AND PRACTICAL INFORMATION

From the station, walk left along av. Charles Dupuy, cross sq. du Docteur Henri Coiffier, and turn left onto bd. du Maréchal Fayolle. A 5min. walk leads to **place Michelet** and **place du Breuil.** Turn right onto rue Porte-Aiguière to reach the tourist office in **place du Clauzel.** Restaurants and stores cluster around this *place*; the cathedral, hostel, and *vieille ville* are uphill to the right.

Tourist Office: 2 pl. du Clauzel (☎04 71 09 38 41; www.ot-lepuyenvelay.fr). Free accommodations booking and Internet access (max. 10min.). Sells *Le Puy-en-Velay et ses Environs à Pied* (€13), which lists 45 local hikes. Open July-Aug. daily 8:30am-7:30pm;

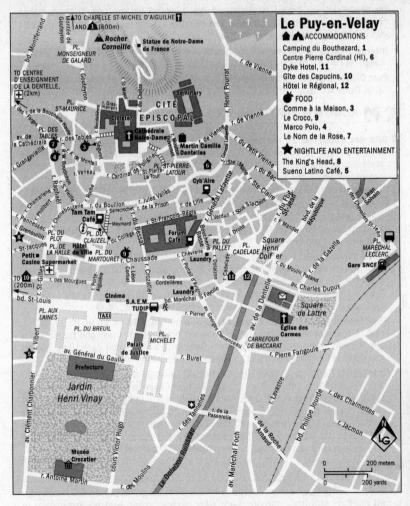

Le Puy-en-Velay

🏠🏠 ACCOMMODATIONS
Camping du Bouthezard, **1**
Centre Pierre Cardinal (HI), **6**
Dyke Hotel, **11**
Gîte des Capucins, **10**
Hôtel le Régional, **12**

🍎 FOOD
Comme à la Maison, **3**
Le Croco, **9**
Marco Polo, **4**
Le Nom de la Rose, **7**

⭐ NIGHTLIFE AND ENTERTAINMENT
The King's Head, **8**
Sueno Latino Café, **5**

MASSIF CENTRAL

Sept. daily 8:30am-noon and 1:30pm-6:15pm; Oct.-Easter M-Sa 8:30am-noon and 1:30-6:15pm; Easter-June daily 8:30am-noon and 1:30-6:15pm.

Tours: Tourist office offers guided walking tours of the city (€5) and cathedral July-Aug. daily 3:30pm; Sept.-June Sa 3pm. Visits to geological sites and guided hiking trips from early July to early Sept. Prices and schedule vary; ask the office for *Visites Guidées.*

Youth Center: Le Point Information Jeunesse, 28 rue Vibert (☎04 71 04 04 46; fax 02 04 33). Offers advice about housing and opportunities for young people. Internet access available. Open M 1:30-5:30pm, Tu 10am-noon and 1:30-6pm, W-Th 9am-noon and 1:30-6pm, F 9am-noon and 1:20-5pm, Sa 9am-12:30pm.

Laundromat: Lav'Flash, 24 rue Portail d'Avignon. €3.70 for 7kg. Open M-Sa 8am-7:30pm, Su 9am-6:30pm.

Police: 1 rue de la Passerelle (☎04 71 04 04 22).

Medical Services: Centre Hospitalier Émile Roux, 12 bd. du Docteur Chantemesse (☎04 71 04 32 10). 24hr. **Clinique Bon Secours,** 67 bis av. du Maréchal Foch (☎04 71 09 87 00). **Ambulance** ☎04 71 09 87 60.

Internet Access: See **tourist office** or **youth center** above. **Forum Café,** 5 rue du Général Lafayette (☎04 71 04 04 98). €0.90 per 30min., €1.50 per hr. Open Tu-Sa 1-6pm.

Post Office: 8 av. de la Dentelle (☎04 71 07 02 00). **ATM** and **currency exchange** available. Open M-F 8am-6:30pm, Sa 8:15am-12:15pm. **Postal Code:** 43000.

🏠 🏠 ACCOMMODATIONS AND CAMPING

🏨 **Gîte des Capucins,** 29 rue des Capucins (☎04 71 04 28 74 or 06 63 09 13 69; www.le-puy.de), off bd. St-Louis, near the *vieille ville*. Immaculate 4- to 6-bed dorms, most with private bath. English-speaking staff fosters a cozy atmosphere with guests' names posted on doors. Communal kitchen. Breakfast €4.60. Linen €1.50. Reception 7am-noon and 5-7pm. Check-out 10am. Dorms €14; apartments €48. Cash only. ❶

Dyke Hotel, 37 bd. du Maréchal Fayolle (☎04 71 09 05 30; fax 02 58 66). The hotel's name, pronounced "deek," refers to the tall outcroppings of volcanic rock in Le Puy. Modern yellow rooms with TVs and showers. Breakfast €6. Free Wi-Fi. Singles €36; doubles €43-48. Extra bed €7.60. MC/V. ❸

Centre Pierre Cardinal (HI), 9 rue Jules Vallès (☎04 71 05 52 40; fax 05 61 24). Hillside location within 5min. of the cathedral. Clean 4-bed dorms and 1 much larger room in former barracks. Kitchen. Breakfast €3.20. Linen €3.20. Reception July-Aug. daily 2-11:30pm; Sept. and Apr.-June M-Sa 2-11:30pm, Su 10am-8pm. Curfew 11:30pm. Closed holidays and weekends Oct.-Mar. Dorms €10. AmEx/MC/V. ❶

Hôtel le Régional, 36 bd. du Maréchal Fayolle (☎04 71 09 37 74, fax 06 85 27 73 77), near pl. Michelet and the train station. Cheapest hotel in town. Clean and simple rooms with TVs and toilets separated by screens. Breakfast €5. Reception 7am-10pm. Singles and doubles €24-28; triples and quads €29-48. AmEx/MC/V. ❷

Camping de Bouthezard, chemin de Bouthezard (☎04 71 09 55 09, fax 06 15 08 23 59), located 400m from Le Puy's *centre-ville*, near Chapelle St-Michel. Walk up bd. St-Louis, continue on bd. Carnot, and, when the road ends, turn right onto av. d'Aiguille; the campground is on the left (15min.). Or, take bus #6 (dir.: Mondon) from pl. Michelet to Parc Quincieu (10min., every hr., €1.05). Clean, pleasant riverside location. Open from mid-Mar. to Oct. Reception July-Sept. 8am-noon and 1-9pm; Oct. and from mid-Mar. to June 8am-noon and 3-9pm. €2.80 per person, €2.70 per tent. Electricity €3.10. ❶

🍴 FOOD

Le Puy-en-Velay has been recognized by the French government for its exceptional cuisine. Quality-controlled *lentilles vertes* (green lentils) are grown in mass quantities throughout the region, and they appear on nearly every menu. Cap off a meal with Verveine, an alcoholic *digestif* with a sweet mint flavor, made from local herbs and honey (€10-22 per bottle). The **distillery** outside of town on N88 offers tours and Verveine *dégustations*. (☎04 71 03 04 11; www. verveine.com. Open July-Aug. daily 10am-12:30pm and 1:30-6:30pm; Sept.-Dec. and Mar.-June Tu-Sa 10am-noon and 1:30-6:30pm; Jan.-Feb. Tu-Sa 1:30-4:30pm. €5.80, students €4.20, under 12 €2.) A **Petit Casino** supermarket, 8 rue St-Gilles, sits near pl. du Plot. (Open Tu-Sa 7:30am-12:30pm and 2:30-7:30pm, Su 8am-12:15pm. MC/V.) On Saturdays (6am-noon), farmers set up fresh produce markets on almost every square. The markets on **place du Plot** and **place de la Halle** sell fresh fruit, cheese, and mushrooms as well as live chickens and rabbits. Inexpensive restaurants can be found on streets off **place du Breuil.**

Comme à la Maison, 7 rue Séguret (☎04 71 02 94 73). Serves superb gourmet *formules du jour* (€17-22) on a secluded stone patio in the garden. Interior channels a modern art gallery. Open daily noon-3pm and 7-11pm. Cash only. ❸

Le Croco, 5 rue Chaussade (☎04 71 02 40 13), around the corner from the tourist office. Cheap eats served in a cheerful yellow interior or on the patio. *Menus* €13-19. Open M-Sa noon-3pm and 7-10pm. MC/V. ❸

Le Nom de la Rose, 48 rue Raphael (☎04 71 05 90 04). Specializes in organic Mexican food. Time-tested favorites like *chili con carne* as well as more unique house specialties like cactus leaf salad, under a cathedral-esque ceiling. Outdoor seating. Vegetarian *plats* €7.50-9.30. *Menus* €15-23. Open daily 12:15-2pm and 7-10:30pm. MC/V. ❷

Le Marco Polo, 46 rue Raphael (☎04 71 02 83 11). Large portions of delicious homemade pasta. Warm orange and red interior decorated with paintings on potato-sack canvases. *Plats* €10-13. *Menus* €17-18. Open Tu-Sa 11:30am-3pm and 7-11pm. ❸

🅜 SIGHTS

Le Puy's essential religious sights draw thousands of pilgrims each year; as a unit, they represent sections of the Bible's apocalyptic Book of Revelation.

🅜 CATHÉDRALE NOTRE-DAME. Legend has it that in the AD fifth century the Virgin Mary healed a woman who came to pray at what is now the **Cité Episcopale,** a collection of religious buildings that tower over the city on a rock known as *le puy.* Now a pilgrimage site, the cathedral has attracted pilgrims and tourists for over 1000 years. The major attractions include the famous statue of **La Vierge Noir** (the Black Virgin), who sits serenely on a tabernacle flanked by two golden angels, and a piece of black slate on which Mary is reputed to have healed the sick woman. The simple stone interior is adorned with unusual crystal chandeliers that reflect the colorful lights from the stained glass above. Especially stunning is the stained-glass dome above *La Vierge Noir.* The church is surrounded by a dense cluster of religious buildings, making it difficult to get a good look at the exterior. However, a walk up the steps on rue des Talbes is rewarded by a stunning view of the beautiful polychromatic facade. To see the entire cathedral, including its dome and huge bell tower, walk up the hill to the **Statue of Notre-Dame.** (*☎04 71 09 79 77; www.cathedraledupuy.org. Open daily 6:30am-7:30pm. Tours in French from early July to late Aug. Free.*)

CHAPELLE SAINT-MICHEL D'AIGUILLE. This chapel sits atop an 80m spike of volcanic rock. Erected in the 10th century by Le Puy's bishop after he returned from a pilgrimage to Compostela, the church's colorful front conceals an interior full of recently restored frescoes. (*☎04 71 09 50 03. Open daily May-Sept. 9am-6:30pm; from Oct. to mid-Nov. and from mid-Mar. to Apr. 9:30am-noon and 2-5:30pm; from Feb. to mid-Mar. 2-5pm. €2.75, students €2.50, under 14 €1.25.*)

STATUE DE NOTRE-DAME DE FRANCE. The pinnacle of the *vieille ville* is the **Rocher Corneille,** a 757m tall core of a volcano. A 23m statue of the Virgin Mary cast from Russian cannons captured during the Crimean War crowns the summit. The structure earned fame in 1942 when 20,000 young people came here to pray for France's liberation. The statue itself is more impressive from the bottom of the hill; a steep climb inside leads only to a small chamber marred by graffiti. (*Open daily July-Aug. 9am-7:30pm; Sept. and May-June 9am-7pm; from Oct. to mid-Mar. 10am-5pm; from mid-Mar. to Apr. 9am-6pm. €3, students with ID and under 18 €1.50.*)

CLOISTER. Attached to the cathedral, the cloister boasts terra-cotta mosaics and striped arches that reflect a Spanish Islamic influence. Beneath flame-red tiling and ornate arcades is the *bestiaire,* a series of grinning faces and mythical beasts carved into the stone around the courtyard. Amid the Byzantine

MASSIF CENTRAL

arches of the *salle capitulaire*, a well-preserved 13th-century fresco depicts the Crucifixion. The entry ticket also allows a peek at the second-level **Trésor d'Art Religieux,** a museum of 13th- to 18th-century art containing impressive life-size wood statues and a small collection of paintings, chalices, and crucifixes. (☎04 71 05 45 52. Both open daily July-Aug. 9am-6:30pm; Sept. and May-June 9am-noon and 2-6:30pm; Oct.-Apr. 9am-noon and 2-5pm. Tours in French 10:30am, 2:30, 3:30pm; English tours available by reservation. Free written explanation in 6 languages. €5, ages 18-25 €3.50.)

MUSÉE CROZATIER. This all-encompassing museum has a different theme for each floor: local craftsmanship, fine arts, archaeology, and natural history. Particularly impressive is an exhibit on Le Puy native Émile Reynaud, who invented the *praxinoscope*—the precursor to the film projector. Another museum highlight is the first-floor statue by Emmanuel Hannaux, *Fleurs de Sommeil.* The museum overlooks the meticulously manicured **Jardin Henri Vinay.** Its shaded pond is the perfect backdrop for a picnic. (Musée ☎04 71 06 62 40. Open from May to mid-Sept. daily 10am-noon and 2-6pm; Oct.-Apr. M and W-Sa 10am-noon and 2-4pm, Su 2-4pm. Garden open daily May-Sept. 7:15am-9pm; Oct.-Apr. 7:15am-7pm. Free.)

🎵 🎬 ENTERTAINMENT AND NIGHTLIFE

There's a **cinema** at 29 pl. du Breuil. (☎04 71 09 00 35. €6.50, students €5.50.) The **Municipal Theater,** pl. du Breuil, hosts plays and dance shows. (☎04 71 09 03 45.) For information on performances in towns around Le Puy, call the **Centre Culturel de Vals,** av. Charles Massot (☎04 71 05 90 12).

The King's Head, pl. du Marché Couvert (☎04 71 02 50 35). An English pub with a personable owner. Excellent beer list (€3.50-9.50). Don't leave without trying a glass of John Martin's (€2.80). Open Tu-F 4pm-1am, Sa 10am-2am. Cash only.

Sueño Latino Café, 26 rue Vibert (☎04 71 02 61 56). In a new location near the Jardin Vinay. Locals chat amiably over Latin rhythms, mojitos in hand. Beer and mixed drinks €2.50-4. Open Tu-Su 3pm-2am. Cash only.

❋ FESTIVALS

The tourist office gives out free copies of *Sortir*, a guide to the festival season, and can provide up-to-date info.

Fête de la Musique, in mid-June. This musical celebration kicks off Le Puy's summer festival season.

Parade of the Black Virgin, Aug. 15. A procession moves through the streets of Le Puy honoring the virgin and her famous statue in the cathedral.

Festival de la Chaise-Dieu (☎04 71 00 01 16; www.chaise-dieu.com), from mid- to late Aug. Choral groups from all corners of the globe perform in concerts in Le Puy and nearby Chaise-Dieu. Tickets €10-77.

Fête Renaissance du Roi de l'Oiseau (☎04 71 09 38 41), in mid-Sept. 400-year-old tradition of Renaissance revelry.

VICHY ☎04 70

On June 22, 1940, the French government signed the armistice at Rethondes, surrendering to the German military and submitting to Nazi occupation. The Nazis replaced Paris with Vichy (vee-shee; pop. 27,000) as the capital of France, selecting the town for its large hotels and modern telephone system. Under the leadership of Philippe Pétain, a WWI hero, Vichy remained the seat of the Nazi-controlled puppet regime from 1940 to 1944. Today, a tiny monument to the citizens deported from Vichy during the Occupation stands in the shadow of a much larger WWI memorial, but the town is otherwise nearly devoid of vestiges of these dark years, suggesting an eerie historical amnesia. Instead, Vichy's lacy ironwork and Belle Époque architecture recall its pre-war days, when the town's mineral-rich hot springs, still popular with *curistes* world-wide, drew royalty, celebrities, and the fabulously wealthy.

▉ TRANSPORTATION

Trains: Pl. de la Gare. Ticket desks open M 5:30am-8:20pm, Tu-Th 5:40am-8pm, F 5:40am-8:20pm, Sa 6:30am-8pm, Su 7:10am-8:30pm. To: **Clermont-Ferrand** (40min., 10 per day, €8.80), **Nevers** (1hr., 6 per day, €16), and **Paris** (3hr., 6 per day, €45).

Public Transportation: Pl. de la Gare, next to the train station. Open M 9am-noon and 2-6pm, Tu-F 8:30-11:30am and 2-6pm; reduced hours July-Aug. Local **buses** run 6:30am-8pm (€1.10). Find schedules at the tourist office and at the Bus Inter kiosk, pl. Charles de Gaulle (☎04 70 97 81 29), near the post office. Open M-Th 8:30-11:30am and 1-6pm, F 8:30-11:30am and 1-5pm. Buy tickets on board.

Taxis: Vichy Taxis (☎04 70 98 69 69). 24hr.

Car Rental: Hertz, 5 av. de Lyon (☎04 70 97 82 82), a 2min. walk from the train station. Open M-F 8am-noon and 2-6:30pm, Sa 8am-noon and 2-5pm. AmEx/MC/V.

▉ PRACTICAL INFORMATION

Tourist Office: 19 rue du Parc (☎04 70 98 71 94; www.vichy-tourisme.com). From the train station, walk down rue de Paris, turn left at the fork onto rue Georges Clemenceau, and turn right onto rue Sornin. The office is across Parc des Sources (10min.). Located in the Hôtel du Parc, which once housed Pétain's government. Provides a good map, list of hotels and restaurants, free accommodations bookings (☎04 70 98 23 83), and info on the town's natural springs in French. Open July-Aug. M-Sa 9am-7pm, Su 2:30-7pm; Sept. and Apr.-June M-F 10am-noon and 1:30-6pm, Sa 10am-noon and 2-6pm, Su 3-6pm; Oct.-Mar. M-F 10am-noon and 2-6pm, Sa 10am-noon and 2:30-5:30pm.

Tours: Tourist office offers daily guided walking tours in French. The tours, which range in theme from Napoleon III's impact on the city to the city's impact on WWII, may be the city's sole acknowledgment of the Occupation. July-Aug. W 3:30pm, Sa 10:30am; Sept. and June W 3:30pm. €6, under 12 free.

Laundromat: 3 bd. Gambetta (☎06 64 75 34 31). €3.50 per 5kg. Open daily 7am-9pm.

Police: 35 av. Victoria (☎04 70 30 17 28).

Pharmacy: La Grande Pharmacie, 48 rue de Paris (☎04 70 98 23 01).

Hospital: Centre Hospitalier, 15 bd. Denière (☎04 70 97 33 33). Open M-Sa 9am-12:15pm and 2-7:15pm.

Internet Access: Échap, 12 rue Source de l'Hôpital (☎04 70 32 28 57). €0.07 per min. Open Tu-Sa noon-midnight, Su 2pm-midnight.

Post Office: Pl. Charles de Gaulle (☎04 70 30 10 75). **ATM** and **currency exchange.** Open M-F 8:30am-12:30pm and 1-6pm, Sa 8:30am-12:30pm. **Postal Code:** 03200.

▉ ▉ ACCOMMODATIONS AND CAMPING

Hôtel du Rhône, 8 rue de Paris (☎04 70 98 63 45; fax 98 77 40), between the train station and the *thermes*. Quiet, comfortable rooms with red carpets and vintage decor;

MASSIF CENTRAL

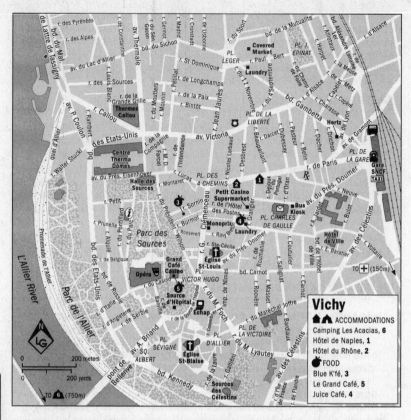

Vichy

▲▲ ACCOMMODATIONS
Camping Les Acacias, **6**
Hôtel de Naples, **1**
Hôtel du Rhône, **2**

🍴 FOOD
Blue K'fé, **3**
Le Grand Café, **5**
Juice Café, **4**

some overlook a private garden. Small breakfast €3, buffet €7. Singles with shower €29-35; doubles €37-58; triples €49-59. AmEx/MC/V. ❷

Hôtel de Naples, 22 rue de Paris (☎04 70 97 91 33; hoteldenaples@orange.fr). Varnished plywood exterior has never been out of—or in—style. Clean rooms in a central location. Breakfast €5.50. Wi-Fi. Rooms €33-38. MC/V. ❷

Camping Les Acacias au Bord du Lac, rue Claude-Decloitre (☎04 70 32 36 22; www. camping-acacias.com). Take bus #7 from the train station (dir.: La Tour d'Abrest) to Charles de Gaulle, then bus #3 to Les Acacias; it's 3.5km on foot. Riverside sites separated by perfectly trimmed hedges. Bar, small market, pool, tennis courts, and laundry facilities. Reception 8am-10pm. Open from Apr. to mid-Oct. €3.90-5 per person, under 7 €2.50-3.60; €4.20-6 per tent. Electricity €3. MC/V. ❶

🍴 FOOD

Cheap eateries line rue de Paris. Many of Vichy's restaurants are affiliated with hotels. To avoid paying top dollar, head to the **Monoprix** supermarket, on the corner of rue Georges Clemenceau and rue Ravy Breton (open M-Sa 8:30am-8pm; Su 9:30am-12:30pm and 2:30-7pm; AmEx/MC/V), or the **Petit Casinos** at the corner of pl. Charles de Gaulle or on rue de l'Hôtel des Postes (both open M-Sa 8:30am-12:30pm and 2:30-7:30pm).

Juice Café, 16 rue Ravy Breton. Friendly British owner whips up luscious fruit smoothies or thick milkshakes (€5-6) and deliciously filling pasta (with pesto or tomatoes; €7-8), in a tropical-themed dining room lined with popular English-language novels. Open June-Aug. M and Su 2-8pm, Tu-Sa 10am-8pm; Sept.-May Tu-Sa 10am-8pm, Su 2-8pm. Cash only. ❷

Le Grand Café, 7 rue du Casino (☎04 70 97 16 45; www.casinodugrandcafe.com), attached to the casino. All-you-can-eat lunch buffet (€18) offers *crudités*, fruit, cheese, *foie gras*, cold cuts, seafood, and desserts. *Plats* €11-18. *Menus* €18-26. MC/V. ❸

Bleu K'fé, 22 passage de l'Amirauté (☎04 70 98 56 04), in the *centre-ville*. Specializes in salads and vegetarian *plats*. Hanging lanterns brighten the namesake color scheme. *Plats* €7.80. 2-course *menu* €12. Open Tu-Sa 9:30am-6:30pm. MC/V. ❷

👁 SIGHTS

The only evidence of Vichy's dark years is a small **memorial** down the street from the tourist office commemorating the 1942 deportation of 6500 Jews to Auschwitz. Significant WWII buildings are not marked. The best way to see the Nazis' Vichy is to take the tourist office's **tour** (p. 507).

SOURCES. Vichy's real attraction springs from its *sources* (springs). Due to volcanic forces, the water circulates for hundreds—even thousands—of years deep underground, collecting dissolved mineral deposits before finally bubbling to the surface. These deposits reputedly endow Vichy's water with certain healing effects for everything from common allergies to indigestion. Just one sip of Vichy's nectar, however, makes one wonder why people keep coming back for more—its putrid taste is nearly insufferable. The town's *sources*, each of which provides water with a distinct chemical makeup and alleged healing effect, are housed in covered fountains at points throughout the city. Close to the *centre-ville*, **Célestins** bubbles up free of charge at the fountain on bd. Kennedy. It is said to be good for the skin and, according to a sign at the *source*, was proven to relieve arthritis by a 1992 Hôpital Cochimin (Paris) study. *(Open Apr.-Sept. M-Sa 7:45am-8pm, Su 8am-8pm; Oct.-Mar. daily 8am-6pm.)* The nearby **Hôpital** *source*, used to cure stomach and intestinal ailments, flows behind the Grand Casino. *(Open M-Sa 6:30am-8:30pm, Su 7:45am-8:30pm.)* All of Vichy's spring waters are on tap in the **Halle des Sources** at the edge of the Parc des Sources. *(☎0800 30 00 63. Open Mar.-Nov. M-Sa 6am-7:30pm, Su 7:45am-7:30pm.)* Regulars bring their own glass encased in a special woven carrying basket available for purchase at Vichy pharmacies for €8.50. Visitors may purchase a less classy plastic cup on-site for €0.20. Two springs are located within the Halle des Sources: **Chomel** is the most popular among the hot-water *sources*, while **Grand Grille** is the most powerful, with only very small doses advised. Visitors can recover with older *curistes* in the **Parc des Sources.** Surrounded by a wrought-iron Art Nouveau promenade and flanked by the Opéra, the space exemplifies Vichy elegance.

OTHER SIGHTS. The beautiful *vitraux* (stained-glass windows) and frescoes of **Église Saint-Louis** merit a visit. The church was given as a gift to the town by Napoleon III in 1865. *(Rue St-Cécile.* ☎*04 70 96 51 20.)* Manicured floral displays, swan-filled ponds, and thick trees shade the English-style gardens in the elegant riverside **Parc de l'Allier,** also commissioned by Napoleon III.

🎵 ENTERTAINMENT

Take a risk at the **Grand Café Casino** in the Parc des Sources. (☎04 70 97 07 40. Open daily 10am-4am.) Treat yourself to a show at the **Opéra,** 1 rue du Casino, with your winnings. (☎04 70 30 50 30. Box office open Tu-Sa 1:30-6:30pm, until curtain on performance nights; by phone only Tu-F 10am-12:30pm. Operas €30-60, under 25 €28-54; concerts €21-42/18-26. MC/V.)

DORDOGNE AND LIMOUSIN

A lack of big cities and waterfronts has kept these regions from the fame they deserve. Most sights are relatively undiscovered, offering a respite from the ceaseless crowds that storm the Loire châteaux. Dordogne and Limousin have long been artistic breeding grounds, producing painter Auguste Renoir, dramatist Jean Giraudoux, and novelist George Sand. Shops and museums throughout the regions proudly display local craftsmanship, particularly those in Limoges (below), where some of the world's finest porcelain is made. The ambling waters of the Dordogne River cut through the regions' rolling hillsides, creating a spectacular backdrop for castles and hilltop cities. Named after the river, the Dordogne—where green countryside is splashed with yellow sunflowers, steep and chalky limestone cliffs, and ducks paddling down shady rivers—boasts exceptional historical remnants of the Neolithic, Roman, and medieval periods, including the most famous cave paintings in the world at Lascaux. Neighboring Limousin is home to vibrant cities, while the southern Lot Valley offers an assortment of French favorites: villages, vineyards, cliffs, and caves.

HIGHLIGHTS OF DORDOGNE AND LIMOUSIN

LOSE YOUR BREATH when you see the spectacular paintings at the caves of the Vézère Valley (p. 530)—no, seriously, human breath ruins the artwork.

GO NUTTY over Brive-la-Gaillarde's Maison Denoix (p. 520), the oldest liquor distillery in France, known for its signature walnut liqueur.

NEVER FORGET the ghost town of Oradour-sur-Glane (p. 517), untouched since Nazis systematically massacred its residents.

LIMOUSIN

Home to substantial cities like Limoges and Brive-la-Gaillarde, the rural region of Limousin has just recently caught up with France's pace. Until the 70s, the majority of non-urban residents still spoke Occitan. Today, Limousin is known for its beef farming, porcelain production, and sleepy villages.

LIMOGES   ☎ 05 55

For centuries, Limoges (lee-mohjhs; pop. 137,500) has manufactured delicate porcelain and enamel for the French upper class. Filled with small, artisan boutiques and museums housing world-famous ceramics, Limoges remains a porcelain mecca to this day. Resting on the right bank of the Vienne River, Limoges's natural scenery rivals the beauty of its earthenware. While parts of Limoges possess a romantic elegance marked by wide boulevards and vast green parks, the rest of the city has a modern, urban sensibility.

▣ TRANSPORTATION

Trains: Gare des Bénédictins, 7 pl. Maison-Dieu (☎08 92 68 82 66 or 05 55 45 10 72), off av. du Général de Gaulle. Restored to its 1920s Art Deco splendor, this is one of Limoges's most beautiful buildings. Info booth open M-F 4:30am-10:30pm, Sa 4:30am-10pm. Ticket office open daily 5:15am-9:45pm. SNCF, rue Othon Péconnet, near pl. de la Motte. Open M-Sa 9am-7pm. To: **Bordeaux** (3hr., 5 per day, €28); **Brive-la-Gaillarde** (1hr., 12 per day, €17); **Lyon** (6hr., 1 per day, €44); **Paris** (3hr., 13 per day, €48); **Poitiers** (2hr., 3 per day, €19); **Toulouse** (4hr., 6 per day, €38).

Buses: Equival, 14 rue de l'Amphithéâtre (☎05 55 10 10 03; www.equival87.fr). Tickets available at the office, at the SNCF station, or on buses. Most buses stop at the train station. Office open M-F 9am-6pm.

Public Transportation: TCL, 10 pl. Léon Betoulle (☎05 55 32 46 46). Open M 1:30-6pm, Tu-F 8:30am-12:30pm and 1:30-6pm, Sa 8:30am-12:30pm. Buy individual tickets (€1.05) on board and carnets of 10 (€9.10) at the station.

Taxis: Taxi AALT Limoges, 16 rue Alfred de Vigny (☎05 55 38 38 38) and **Taxi Vert Limoges,** 197 av. du Général Leclerc (☎05 55 37 81 81). Wait by the station. 24hr.

Car Rental: Avis (☎05 55 79 78 25; www.avis.com), in the train station. Open M-F 9:45am-noon and 4-6pm, Sa 9:45am-noon. **Europcar** (☎05 55 77 64 52), in the train station. Open M-F 10am-1:30pm and 4-6pm, Sa 9:30am-noon and 2-5:30pm.

✴☀ ORIENTATION AND PRACTICAL INFORMATION

Medieval fortresses originally separated Limoges into two villages: **la Cité** and **le Château.** Today, divided by only one city block, the two villages have become the main commercial and tourist sectors of the city. Cobblestone-paved la Cité surrounds the **Cathédrale Saint-Étienne** and runs along the **Vienne River,** holding the municipal museum and gardens, while le Château contains restaurants, clothing boutiques, and porcelain shops.

Tourist Office: 12 bd. de Fleurus (☎05 55 34 46 87; www.tourismelimoges.com), near pl. Wilson. From the train station, walk down av. du Général de Gaulle. Cut across pl. Jourdan onto bd. de Fleurus. English-speaking staff offers free maps, English brochures, and a free guide in French that lists restaurants and accommodations. **Currency exchange** available at steep rates. Open from M-Sa April-Sept. 9am-7pm; Oct-Mar. 9:30am-6pm.

Tours: Offered several times per month; contact the tourist office for a schedule and prices. 1hr. *petit train* tours daily July-Aug. 11:30am, 2:30, 4, 5:30, 9:30pm; Sept. 1-14 and June 9-30 3, 4:30pm. Special holiday tours. €5, ages 3-12 €3.50.

Library: Bibliothèque Francophone Multimédia de Limoges, 2 rue Louis Longequeue (☎05 55 45 96 00; www.bm-limoges.fr), next to the Hôtel de Ville. Free Wi-Fi. Often long lines. Must sign up for free library membership. Internet available W 10am-7pm, Sa 10am-6pm; 1hr. limit.

Laundromats: 31 rue François Chenieux. Wash €3.80 per 7kg. Open daily 7am-9pm. Branch at 14 rue des Charseix. Open daily 8am-9pm.

Police: 84 av. Émile Labussière (☎05 55 14 30 00).

Crisis Lines: SOS Médecin (☎05 55 33 20 00). **Poison Control** (☎05 55 96 40 80).

Hospital: 2 av. Martin Luther King (☎05 55 05 55 55).

Internet Access: Free at the **library** (above). **Tendanceweb.com,** 5 bd. Victor Hugo (☎05 55 10 93 61; www.tendanceweb.com). €2 per 30min., €3 per hr., €7 per 2hr. Open M-Th 10am-4am, F-Sa 10am-6am, Su 2pm-4am. **Pointcyber,** 7 av. du Général de Gaulle (☎05 55 79 03 28; www.pointcyber.com), near the train station and Hôtel de Paris. €2.80 per hr. Open M-Sa 9:30am-midnight, Su 2pm-midnight. **L'Interval,** rue du

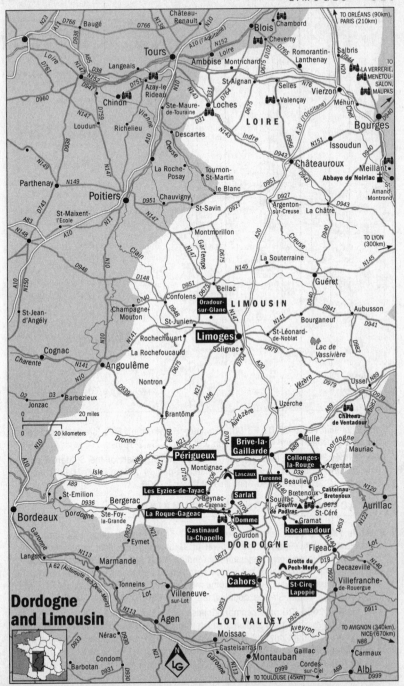

Dordogne and Limousin

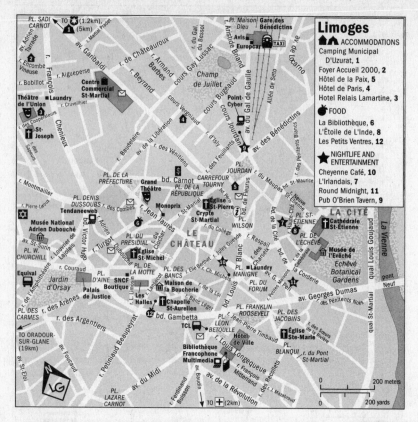

Maréchal Juin (☎05 55 01 23 90; www.interval-cafe.com). Free Internet access and bar service. Open Tu and W-F 9am-noon and 2-7pm, Sa 2-7pm.

Post Office: 39 bis av. Garibaldi (☎05 55 79 81 00), part of the St-Martial shopping complex. **Currency exchange** available. Open M 2-7pm, Tu-F 10am-7pm, Sa 10:30am-12:30pm and 1:30-6pm. **Postal Code:** 87000.

🏠 🏕 ACCOMMODATIONS AND CAMPING

🏨 **Hôtel de Paris,** 5 cours Vergniaud (☎05 55 77 56 96; www.hotelparis87.com). From the train station, walk up av. du Général de Gaulle and turn right onto cours Bugeaud, then right onto cours Vergniaud. A winding wood staircase, Victorian wallpaper, and rooms with double doors, tall windows, and clean bathrooms emphasize that you're getting more bang for your buck. All rooms with TVs and telephones. Breakfast €6. Wi-Fi. Reception 7am-10pm. Singles, doubles, and triples €30-62. AmEx/MC/V. ❷

Foyer Accueil 2000, 20 rue Encombe Vineuse (☎05 55 77 63 97; fjt.accueil-2000@wanadoo.fr). From the train station, head to the right on Champ du Juillet, onto cours Gay Lussac. Turn right onto av. Garibaldi, then left onto rue Aigueperse. Make a right on rue Chénieux and a quick left on rue Encombe Vineuse. The hostel is on the right; look for the Foyer des Jeunes Travailleuses sign. Clean and relatively spacious dorm-like singles and doubles with sinks; some with small refrigerators. Showers and toilets on each floor hall. Communal kitchen, TV room, and elevator. Breakfast included. Reception 24hr. Singles €18; doubles €22. Cash only. ❶

Hôtel de la Paix, 25 pl. Jourdan (☎05 55 34 36 00; fax 32 37 06), on the far side of pl. Jourdan, near the tourist office. Central location overlooking a park. Clean, carpeted rooms with large windows and TV. Breakfast €7. Wi-Fi. Reception 24hr. English- and German-speaking staff. Singles and doubles €41-69. AmEx/MC/V. ❹

Hôtel Relais Lamartine, 10 rue des Coopérateurs (☎05 55 77 53 39; fax 79 46 92), next to Théâtre de l'Union. Walk away from the train station onto av. du Général de Gaulle. At the roundabout, bear right onto cours Bugeaud. Take a right on av. Garibaldi and a quick left on av. de la Libération. Continue to pl. Denis Dussoubs and turn right on rue François Chinieux and left on rue des Coopérateurs (20min.). Crimson, wood-trimmed lobby. Bright breakfast area. Breakfast €4. Reception 24hr. Singles €20, with shower €22, with toilet €26; doubles €27-35. Extra bed €7. Cash only. ❶

Camping D'Uzurat, 40 av. d'Uzurat (☎05 55 38 49 43; www.campinglimoges.fr), 5km north of Limoges. From the train station, take bus #20 (dir.: Beaubreuil; M-Sa 6am-8:30pm) to L'Armand. Walk 50m to the intersection at av. d'Uzurat and turn left; follow signs to campground. Park surrounding Lake Uzurat. Access to tennis courts and trails. Wheelchair-accessible. Reception 8:15am-12:30pm and 2:30-8:10pm. Gates closed 10pm-7:30am. July-Aug. €3.50 per person, ages 3-14 €1.50; sites €7. Sept.-Oct. and Mar.-June €3 per person, ages 2-14 €1; site €5. Electricity €3. MC/V. ❶

🍴 FOOD

The stalls of the central **Halles** indoor market, facing pl. de la Motte, over-flow with fresh cheeses, produce, meat, fish, and baked goods. (Open daily 8am-1pm; fewer stalls open Su.) A larger market (Sa mornings) brightens **place Marceau,** near pl. Sadi Carnot. A **Monoprix** supermarket has entrances at 42 rue Jean Jaurès and 11 pl. de la République. (Open M-Sa 8:30am-8:30pm.) Charming restaurants on and around medieval **rue de la Boucherie** offer gourmet dining. For a cheaper meal, look to **rue Haute-Cité,** near the cathedral, for *crêperies* and *brasseries.* For an even greater variety of flavor, **rue Charles Michels** offers a bit of everything—from Chinese to Moroccan to Tex-Mex.

La Bibliothèque, 7 rue Turgot (☎05 55 11 00 47; fax 11 00 48). Restaurant by day and busy bar by night. Lives up to its name ("The Library") with chic mahogany stools and shelves of leather-bound books, but 20-something patrons are more enticed by the constant stream of music videos flashing on big-screen TVs. Big, tasty pizzas and salads €5-19. Open M-Th 7am-1am, F-Sa 7am-2am. MC/V. ❷

L'Étoile de L'Inde, 7 rue Haute-Cité (☎05 55 32 46 95). Serves tandoori specialties in an elegant French atmosphere with white tablecloths and flowers. *Plats* €6-16. *Menu* €16. Open Tu-Su noon-2pm and 7:30-11pm. MC/V. ❸

Les Petits Ventres, 20 rue de la Boucherie (☎05 55 34 22 90; www.les-petits-ventres. fr). In a converted 15th-century home, with a touch of medieval charm and a peaceful outdoor terrace. Known throughout Limoges for its traditional cuisine. *Plats* €15-25. *Menus* €22-36. Open Tu-Sa noon-2pm and 7:30-10:30pm. AmEx/MC/V. ❹

👁 SIGHTS

🏛**MUSÉE NATIONAL ADRIEN DUBOUCHÉ.** Founded in the 19th century by a wealthy Cognac merchant, this paradise for porcelain connoisseurs houses one of the largest ceramics collections in Europe. Amazingly diverse, it features ceramic pieces from antiquity through the modern era—and from all over the globe—including ornate sculptures, playful figurines, and colorful plates. Par-

DORDOGNE AND LIMOUSIN

ticular emphasis is given to French porcelain, especially pieces from Limoges. A first-floor room walks visitors through the stages of ceramics production. The large Chinese plate with a ⬛dragon in its center, dating from 1345, is one of the most valuable pieces of china in the world. *(8 bis pl. Winston Churchill. ☎05 55 33 08 55; www.musee-adriendubouche.fr. Open M and W-Su July-Aug. 10am-5:40pm; Sept.-June 10am-12:25pm and 2-5:40pm. Free. Free English audio tours.)*

MUSÉE MUNICIPAL DE L'EVÊCHÉ. Also known as the **Musée de l'Émail** (Museum of Enamel), this 18th-century bishop's palace contains the city's collection of 12th-century enameled art. Its display of ceramics cannot compete with that of Dubouché, but its other art, including interesting Egyptian figurines and sarcophagi, make this museum worth a visit. *(Pl. de la Cathédrale. ☎05 55 45 98 10. Open June-Sept. daily 10am-noon and 2-6pm; Oct.-May M and W-Su 10am-noon and 2-5pm. Free.)*

EVÊCHÉ BOTANICAL GARDENS. With a prime spot on a hillside overlooking Vienne and the cathedral, this floral oasis is perfect for a mid-morning stroll. Its themed gardens are perfectly manicured and color-coordinated, and a promenade along the outer walls of the gardens reveals panoramic views of the valley surrounding Limoges. *(☎05 55 45 62 67. Open daily May-Sept. 8am-8:30pm; Oct. and Mar.-Apr. 8am-7pm; Nov.-Feb. 8am-5pm. Tours by appointment.)*

OTHER SIGHTS. The **Cathédrale Saint-Étienne** is one of the few examples of Gothic architecture south of the Loire; it was built on the site of a Roman temple and took over 600 years to complete. *(Pl. St-Étienne in la Cité. Open daily 2:30-5pm.)* For a slice of life as a butcher, visit the **Maison Traditionelle de la Boucherie.** *(36 rue de la Boucherie. ☎05 55 34 46 87. Open July-Sept. daily 10am-1pm and 2:30-7pm. Tours in English and French. Free.)* Across the street, the 15th-century **Chapel Saint-Aurelien** still lights candles to honor the patron saint of butchers. A short walk toward 71 bd. Gambetta reveals a plaque commemorating the birthplace of painter ⬛**Pierre-Auguste Renoir.** While the majority of the city's porcelain boutiques are found on **rue Louis Blanc,** Limoges's famous ceramics also decorate several remarkable structures, including **Les Halles,** the nearby **Pavilion de Verdurier,** and the fountain in front of the **Mairie. Manufacture Bernardaud** offers factory tours for those who want to learn more about porcelain production. *(27 av. Albert Thomas. ☎05 55 10 21 86. Tours June-Sept. daily 9am-7pm; Oct.-May by reservation. €4.)*

🎵 ENTERTAINMENT

On weekdays, the five **Centres Culturels Municipaux** host concerts, theater productions, and films. The **Centre Culturel John Lennon,** 41 rue de Feytiat (☎05 55 06 24 83), caters particularly to young people.

Grand Théâtre, 48 rue Jean Jaurès (☎05 55 45 95 00). Presents 60 ballet, orchestral, operatic, and choral productions each season from Sept. to early June. Box office open Sept.-June daily 10am-6pm. €5-35. MC/V.

Théâtre de l'Union, 20 rue des Coopérateurs (☎05 55 79 90 00; www.theatre-union.fr). Hosts performances from Oct.-May. Box office open Tu-Sa 1-7pm, Su 2-7pm.

🔲 NIGHTLIFE

At night, Limoges's streets seem to empty out, though a handful of popular bars and clubs dot the streets. Many *brasseries* serve as social hangouts in the evening, but most nightlife centers on **rue Charles Michels**—known among locals as *"la rue de la soif"* ("the street of thirst")—and **cours Jourdan.**

Cheyenne Café, 4 rue Charles Michels (☎05 55 32 32 62). Get a glimpse of France's perception of the Wild West at this saloon-themed bar. 20-somethings enjoy hip-hop music. Beer €2-4. Open Tu-W 6pm-1am, Th and Sa 6pm-2am.

L'Irlandais, 2 rue Haute-Cité (☎05 55 32 46 47), near the cathedral. A laid-back atmosphere prevails on the terrace of this Irish-themed restaurant, which transforms into a popular bar at night. Live music in summer F-Sa nights. Pints €4.50-6. Open Tu-W 5pm-1am, Th-F 5pm-2am, Sa 3pm-2am, Su 3pm-1am. AmEx/MC/V over €15.

Round Midnight, 12 av. Gabriel Péri (☎05 55 33 73 58; round.midnight@aliceadsl.fr). Jazz fans (read: 30- and 40-somethings) flock to this small bar. Club boasts an intimate atmosphere, with comfy leather chairs surrounding a small stage. Piano bar 8pm. Concerts 9:30pm. Open Tu-W 7pm-1am, Th-Sa 7pm-2am.

Pub O'Brien Tavern, 6 cours Jourdan (☎05 55 10 96 96), close to the train station and Hôtel de Paris. One of Limoges's most popular Irish pubs. Locals gather to watch football. Open M-W and Su 6:30pm-1am and Th-Sa 6:30pm-2am.

FESTIVALS

Fête de St-Jean, at the end of June. Also known as the **Fête des Ponts,** this celebration brings dancing, musical performances, and fireworks shows to the city.

Festival Urb'Aka (☎05 55 32 08 42 or 45 63 85), the last 3 days in June. Heats up the summer with street performances, fireworks, and concerts.

Festival International des Théâtres Francophones (☎05 55 10 90 10; www.lesfrancophonies.com), at the end of Sept. Features thousands of Francophone performing artists from around the world.

Fête des Petits Ventres, 3rd F of Nov. Don't let the name of the festival deceive you; this food celebration is large enough to satisfy even the hungriest glutton.

DAYTRIPS FROM LIMOGES

ORADOUR-SUR-GLANE

The tiny town of Oradour-sur-Glane—not to be confused with Haute-Vienne's 2 other Oradours— contains 2 distinct sections: the new town and its obliterated predecessor. Equival runs a daily bus (#12) from Limoges (at the train station, pl. des Charentes, pl. des Carmes, or pl. Winston Churchill) to the Centre de la Mémoire (old town) Sept.-June and to both towns July-Aug. (30min., 4-6 per day, €3). Schedules at the Limoges tourist office and train station.

On June 10, 1944, in a heinous act of brutality, Nazi SS troops massacred all the residents of the farming village Oradour-sur-Glane (oh-rah-door suhr glahnn)— without warning or provocation—in their relentless quest to rid the countryside of resistors. The Nazis entered the town at 2pm and corralled the women and children into the church and the men into six barns. At 4pm, a shot was fired, ordering the troops to begin the massacre. The women and children in the church were burned alive; the men were shot, then burned as well. By 7pm, 642 people—including 205 children—had been slaughtered. Most of the SS troops involved in the attack were tried in 1953, found guilty, and immediately freed according to the French government's general amnesty decree. Heinz Barth, commander of the unit, served part of a life sentence in a German jail until he was released due to ill health.

Today, the town remains in hauntingly untouched ruins. Houses with crumbling walls stand watch over the silently rotting remains. Telephone lines dangle eerily over deserted streets lined with rusted skeletons of 50-year-old cars. The village has been preserved so that no one will forget the atrocities that occurred in Oradour and elsewhere under the Nazi regime. Visitors can walk freely along the main thoroughfare and peer into remnants of homes; signs indicate the name and profession of many former residents. A small memorial between the cemetery and town displays bicycles, toys, and watches that were all stopped at the same moment by the heat of the fire. The incredible ⚃**Centre de la Mémoire** places the massacre and the Nazi regime in social and historical context with artifacts, timelines, and an informative 12min. film, all with English subtitles. (☎05 55 43 04 30. Museum and town open daily from mid-May to mid-Sept. 9am-7pm; from mid-Sept. to Oct. and from Mar. to mid-May 9am-6pm; from Nov. to mid-Dec. and Feb. 9am-5pm. Museum €7.50; students, veterans, and ages 10-18 €5.20; under 10 free.)

BRIVE-LA-GAILLARDE ☎05 55

When the courageous citizens of Brive-la-Gaillarde (breeve-lah-gay-yahrd; pop. 50,000) repelled English forces during the Hundred Years' War, they earned their town the nickname "la Gaillarde" ("the Bold"), an appellation reaffirmed in 1944 when Brive—the seat of many secret information networks during WWII—became the first French town to liberate itself from the Germans. Today, Brive's residents maintain their fighting spirit through their support of the town's First Division rugby team, whose jerseys, flags, and bumper stickers dominate almost every street. Relatively tourist-free, Brive has a vibrant atmosphere and peaceful *centre-ville;* the town also provides an inexpensive base for exploring the ancient villages of Limousin.

▐ TRANSPORTATION

Trains: Av. Jean Jaurès. Open M 4:15am-8:35pm, Tu-Sa 5:25am-8:35pm, Su 6:35am-9:35pm. To: **Bordeaux** (2hr., 4 per day, €26); **Limoges** (1hr., 12 per day, €15); **Lyon** (6-9hr., 4 per day); **Sarlat** (1hr., 3-4 per day, €13) via **Souillac; Toulouse** (2hr., 5 per day) via **Montauban.**

Buses: Stop at the train station and in pl. du Maréchal de Lattre de Tassigny.

Public Transportation: STUB (☎05 55 74 20 13). CFTA, pl. du 14 Juillet (☎05 55 17 91 19). Info desk open M-Sa 8:15am-12:15pm and 2-6:15pm. **Buses** serve surrounding areas, including **Collonges-la-Rouge** and **Turenne.** €1.10, carnets of 10 €7.20.

Taxis: ☎05 55 24 24 24. 24hr.

Car Rental: Avis, 58 av. Jean Jaurès (☎05 55 24 51 00). Open M-F 8am-noon and 2-6:30pm, Sa 9-11:30am and 2:30-5:30pm. **Europcar,** 52 av. Jean Jaurès (☎05 55 74 14 41). Open M-F 8am-noon and 2-6:30pm, Sa 8:30am-12:30pm and 2-6pm.

Bike Rental: Sports Bike, 142 av. Georges Pompidou (☎05 55 17 00 84), a 20min. walk down av. Thiers. €14 per day. Open Tu-Sa 9am-12:30pm and 3-7pm. AmEx/MC/V.

▐ PRACTICAL INFORMATION

Tourist Office: Pl. du 14 Juillet (☎05 55 24 08 80; www.ot-brive.com). From the station, walk to the end of av. Jean Jaurès, then down rue de l'Hôtel de Ville toward the cathedral. Cut diagonally across pl. Charles de Gaulle. After the library, veer left onto rue Toulzac, which becomes av. de Paris, and cross the parking lot. Provides maps, an audio tour in English, and bus schedule. City **tours** in English and French for groups of 5+ (€4). Call for schedule. Open July-Aug. M-Sa 9am-7pm, Su 3-7pm; Sept. and Apr.-June M-Sa 9am-12:30pm and 1:30-6:30pm; Oct.-Mar. M-Sa 9am-noon and 2-6pm.

Laundromat: 39 rue Dubois (☎05 55 17 08 67). €3 per 5kg, €3.70 per 7kg. Open daily 6am-9:30pm.

Police: 4 bd. Anatole France (☎05 55 17 46 00).

Crisis Line: ☎05 55 79 25 25.

Pharmacy: 23 av. Paris (☎05 55 74 13 30).

Hospital: Bd. du Docteur Verlhac (☎05 55 92 60 00).

Internet Access: Centre Culturel de Brive, 31 av. Jean Jaurès (☎05 55 74 20 51; www. centreculturelbrive.com). Free.

Post Office: Behind pl. du Maréchal de Lattre de Tassigny (☎05 55 18 33 10). **Currency exchange** available. Open M-F 8am-6:45pm, Sa 8am-noon. **Postal Code:** 19100.

ACCOMMODATIONS

Hôtellerie des Grottes de St-Antoine, 41 rue Edmond Michelet (☎05 55 24 10 60; www.fratgsa.org), 15min. from the *centre-ville*. A peek at the monastic lifestyle; St-Antoine of Padua came here to pray when he lived in Brive. Comfortable, clean rooms. Breakfast included. Free Internet access. Singles €18-30; doubles €28-40. ❶

Auberge de Jeunesse (HI), 56 av. du Maréchal Bugeaud (☎05 55 24 34 00; www. aubergejeunessebrive.com). From the station, walk the length of av. Jean Jaurès and turn onto bd. Maréchal Lyautey, which becomes bd. de Puyblanc. Bear left onto bd. Jules Ferry, and turn right on av. du Maréchal Bugeaud. Clean hall bathrooms, kitchen, and big-screen TV. 2- to 4-bunk rooms. Breakfast €3.50. Wheelchair-accessible. Reception M-F 8am-noon and 2-7pm, Sa-Su 8am-noon and 6-9pm. Dorms €12. ❶

Hôtel Le Chêne Vert, 24 bd. Jules Ferry (☎05 55 24 10 07; www.lechenevert.eu). Well-lit rooms, some with balconies. Breakfast €7. Rooms from €42. AmEx/MC/V. ❸

FOOD

Brive's open-air markets at **place Tassigny** and **place du 14 Juillet** offer clothing, shoes, jewelry, and local produce. (Tu, Th, Sa 8am-noon; Sa smaller market.) Four times a year from December to February, the streets of Brive host **La Fois Grasses,** a market with the delicacies that make Brive famous: geese, ducks, *champignons* (mushrooms), truffles, chocolate, and *foie gras*.

Le Corrèze, 3 rue de Corrèze (☎05 55 24 14 07). Family-run. Large portions of regional fare. 2- and 3-course *menus* €7-12. Open M-Sa noon-2pm and 7-10:15pm. MC/V. ❸

Chez Francis, 61 av. de Paris (☎05 55 74 41 72; fax 17 20 54). Walls and ceiling covered with messages and caricatures drawn by Foire de Livre writers and humorists. *Plats* €9. Open Tu-Sa noon-1:30pm and 6:30-9:30pm. Reservations required. MC/V. ❸

La Saladière, 13 rue de l'Hôtel de Ville. Vegetarian's paradise. *Cabecous* (goat cheese), tomatoes, and green beans are popular ingredients. Salads €6.60-10. Lunch *menus* €8.20-10. Dinner *menus* €15-22. Open M-Sa noon-2pm and 7-10pm. MC/V. ❸

SIGHTS

MUSÉE LABENCHE. Housed in the 16th-century Hôtel de Labenche, the museum's galleries house an impressively varied collection, featuring human skeletons, ancient coins, 17th-century English tapestries, prehistoric artifacts, old accordions, contemporary art, and medieval weapons. All signs are in French. *(26 bis bd. Jules Ferry. ☎05 55 18 17 70; www.musee-labenche.com. Open M and W-Su Apr.-Oct. 10am-6:30pm; Nov.-Mar. 1:30-6pm. Temporary exhibits open Apr.-Oct. 10am-noon and 1:30-6:30pm; Nov.-Mar. 10am-noon and 1:30-6pm. €4.70, students and war veterans €2.50, under 16 free; last Su of month free. Temporary exhibits free. Free English audio tours available.)*

DORDOGNE AND LIMOUSIN

MAISON DENOIX. The oldest liquor distillery in France, this *maison* is most famous for "La Suprême Denoix" *eau de noix* (walnut liqueur). Since 1839, four generations of the Denoix family have produced this famous drink using an unchanged recipe and time-honored methods. Today, free 1hr. tours give an explanation of artisanal methods and a history of the distillery, ending with a fabulous *dégustation. (9 bd. du Maréchal Lyautey. ☎05 55 74 34 27; www.denoix.com. Open July-Aug. and Dec. M-Sa 9am-noon and 2:30-7pm; Sept.-Nov. and Jan.-June Tu-Sa 9am-noon and 2:30-7pm. Guided tours July-Aug. Tu and Th 2:30pm.)*

CENTRE NATIONAL DE LA RÉSISTANCE ET DE LA DÉPORTATION EDMOND MICHELET. Located in its namesake's former home, this museum is dedicated to the Brive native and Resistance leader Edmond Michelet, who survived internment at the Dachau concentration camp for over a year. The museum also displays photographs of women and children on their way to the gas chambers, heartbreaking last letters to loved ones, and mementos displaying Brive's role in the Resistance effort. *(4 rue Champanatier. ☎05 55 74 06 08; www.centremichelet.org. Open M-Sa 10am-noon and 2-6pm. Free. Free audio tours available in English and French.)*

ÉGLISE COLLÉGIALE SAINT-MARTIN. This church's namesake was an icono-clastic Spaniard who introduced Christianity to the largely pagan Brive in the fourth century. Unreceptive town members beheaded Martin in AD 407, but, when the following years saw devastating plagues and foreign invasions, citi-zens agreed to honor him with a local procession. According to legend, a great light followed, and suffering ceased. The church, whose crypt now houses Mar-tin's tomb, honors the saint. *(Pl. Charles de Gaulle.)*

🎵 NIGHTLIFE

After dinner, the streets of Brive's *centre-ville* become relatively deserted, but pockets of nightlife can be found in tucked-away bars and *brasseries*.

Bar Le Toulzac, 8 pl. des Patriotes-Martyrs (☎05 55 17 72 54). Unofficial center for rugby fans; jerseys and team posters decorate the bar. Beer €2-5. Open July-Aug. M-Sa 7am-2am; Sept.-June M 1-9pm, Tu-Th 7am-9pm, F-Sa 7am-2am. Snacks noon-2pm.

Pub le Watson, rue des Échevins (☎05 55 17 07 87). Terrace fills with boisterous beer-drinkers. Pints €4-5.50. Open M-Sa 4pm-2am. AmEx/MC/V.

La Charette, 33 av. Ribot (☎05 55 87 65 73), 25min. walk across the river. 20-some-things dance to techno and disco. Cover €10. Open Tu and Th-Sa until 5am. MC/V.

❄ FESTIVALS

Brive-Plage, last week of June. Manmade beaches host rugby, soccer, and volleyball tournaments by day and concerts by night.

Orchestrades Universelles (☎04 78 36 87 14; www.orchestrades.com), mid-Aug. Orchestras, bands, and choirs from around the world perform at this celebration of classical and jazz music. Daily concerts free until 9pm on the last evening, when a spec-tacular gala celebrates 700 young musicians in l'Espace de 3 Provinces. From €3.

Foire du Livre (☎05 55 18 18 41), early Nov. Masterpieces from over 400 French authors presented in pl. du 14 Juillet and Halle Georges Brassens. Free.

▶ DAYTRIPS FROM BRIVE

TURENNE

Buses run from Brive 2 or 3 times per day; ask at the CFTA office, pl. du 14 Juillet, or at the tourist office for schedules. Buses also stop at Collonges-la-Rouge, but the best option for

those hoping to see both villages is to stop 1st in Turenne. The 8km trip from Turenne to Collonges can easily be made on a bike rented from in Turenne. Buses are the best way to get to Turenne, but driving and biking are possible as well. From Brive, take av. Alsace-Lorraine (D38), and after 10km, at the roundabout, bear right onto D8, which leads to Turenne. Taxis run between Turenne and Collonges. (☎05 55 25 30 30. €19.)

Built dramatically into a steep hillside 15km south of Brive, Turenne (tuh-rehnn) carries a long legacy of power. In the 13th and 14th centuries, it served as the fortified seat of the region's viscount, who controlled more than 1200 villages. In the 17th century, with the Wars of Religion ravaging the country, Turenne became a bastion of Protestantism. However, the town was not invincible; in 1738 Louis XV bought the château and, in an assertion of royal power, had the castle dismantled. Today, Turenne remains virtually untouched by modernization, retaining many vestiges of its considerable heyday. Perhaps the best part of Turenne is the wonderful uphill walk to the château, full of narrow medieval streets cutting between flower-draped houses. On the way to the summit, be sure to stop at **La Collegiale Notre Dame,** a modest church with a touching war memorial and elaborate gold tabernacle. At the château, visitors can tour the keep, ascend the watchtower for an unparalleled view of the region, or explore the small garden. (Open July-Aug. daily 10am-7pm; Sept.-Oct. and Apr.-June daily 10am-noon and 2-6pm; Nov.-Mar. Su 2-5pm. Guide available in English. €3.50, ages 10-18 €2.30, under 10 free.) For a drink or homemade dessert, stop by the château's restaurant, **Le Jardin Perche ❸.** (☎05 55 85 90 66. Open July-Aug. daily 11:30am-6pm; May-June and Sept. by reservation.)

At the base of town, Turenne's **tourist office** offers maps (€1-3.40), guided city **tours** in French (June-Sept. W and F 10:30am, 5pm; €4; reservations recommended), **bike** rental (€10 per day), and English audio tours. (☎05 55 85 94 38. Open July-Aug. daily 9:30am-12:30pm and 2:30-6:30pm; Sept. and Apr.-June Tu-Su 10am-12:30pm and 3-6pm.)

COLLONGES-LA-ROUGES

CFTA runs infrequent buses to the village on line #4 from Brive (M-F 2-3 per day, Sa 2 per day; fewer buses July-Aug.). From the main road, signs point to the town's tourist office (☎05 55 25 47 57 or 25 32 25), which provides maps (€1), extensive hiking guides (€1), and city tours in English and French. French tours July-Aug. 4 per day. English tours by reservation. Open July-Aug. daily 10am-1pm and 2-7pm; Sept.-Oct. and Apr.-June daily 10am-noon and 2-6pm; Nov.-Mar. M-Sa 10am-noon and 2-5pm.

Twenty kilometers southeast of Brive, Collonges-la-Rouge (koh-lonjh-lah-roojh) seems too good to be true: red sandstone buildings are covered with green vines, trellises brim with blooming flowers, and overhanging archways provide refreshing shade from the sun. There's little to do here besides appreciate what has been called France's most beautiful village. Stop into the 12th-century **Église Saint-Pierre;** inside, dull red bricks contrast with the bold green and gold altar. Medieval figurines depicting Odysseus and a young siren are sculpted on the exterior of the **Maison de la Sirène,** which houses a museum.

ROCAMADOUR

While Rocamadour is in the Lot Valley, it is most easily accessible from Brive. Trains from Brive stop at the Rocamadour station, 4km from town on N140 (40min.; M-Sa 6 per day 8:30am-6:25pm, Su 3 per day; last return train 7:50pm; €12). The Brive train station provides schedules and tickets. From the Rocamadour station, a flat, winding road leads into town (45min.). A hiking trail provides a more direct route: with your back to the station, head left down the street for 2min. until you see a wood sign on the right side of the road indicating the trailhead. For a taxi, call ☎05 65 50 14 82. €10.

DORDOGNE AND LIMOUSIN

Tiny Rocamadour (roh-kah-mah-door), a stunning three-layered city carved into large chalk cliffs, overlooks a deep valley. The town was named for St-Amadour, whose perfectly preserved body was unearthed near the chapel in the 12th century. The saint was reputed to have been the biblical Zacchaeus, a thieving tax collector who mended his ways after dining with Jesus. A stop on the road to Santiago de Compostela, Rocamadour continues to host faithful pilgrims come to pray in its chapels, but the town's holy sites and stunning views attract more tourists than religious devotees.

At the top of the city sits the 12th-century **château,** home to the chaplains of Rocamadour and closed to the public. Walk along the ramparts for great views. (€2; coins only.) Zigzagging up a steep pathway to the château is the **Chemin de Croix,** which depicts the 14 Stations of the Cross. The middle section of the cliff is dominated by the **Cité Religieuse,** an enclosed courtyard that encompasses seven chapels, two of which can be visited without a guide. Its nucleus is the **Chapelle Notre Dame,** a silent place of prayer containing a model ship honoring shipwreck victims. Outside the entrance to the chapel is a fading—but nevertheless haunting—fresco depicting death personified, while high up on the cliff to the left of the entrance, wedged into a rock, is the legendary **☒sword in the stone**—which was allegedly wielded by Hector of Troy and used by Roland, an epic hero who served under Charlemagne. **La Basilique Saint-Sauveur,** adjacent to the chapel, attracts visitors to its gilt altar. (☎05 65 33 23 30. Open Apr.-Oct. M-Sa 9am-noon and 2-6pm.) Under Notre Dame and St-Sauveur lies the **Crypte Saint-Amadour,** where the saint's body rested undisturbed until a Protestant tried to set it ablaze during the Wars of Religion. Though apparently immune to the flames, the saint's body could not withstand the assailant's backup plan: an axe. The old **medieval town**—whose streets now host tourist-friendly ice-cream and sandwich shops—occupies the lower level of the city. Your best bet is to start from the château and move downward. The two elevators that connect the city's three levels are not worth the steep prices for those able to ascend on their own. (☎05 65 33 62 44. Elevators operate daily July-Aug. 8am-8pm; Sept.-June 9am-6pm. €2, round-trip €3.)

Rocamadour's surrounding areas offer appealing, family-oriented attractions. The **Grotte des Merveilles,** beside the upper tourist office, is a cave of stalactites and remnants of prehistoric paintings. Guided tours (40min.) in English and French provide more information about the cave art. (☎05 65 33 67 92; www.grotte-des-merveilles.com. Open daily July-Aug. 9:30am-7pm; Sept.-Nov. and Apr.-June 10am-noon and 2-6pm. €6, ages 5-11 €4.) Signs from the upper tourist office point the way (300m) to **La Féerie,** a fantastic model world, complete with realistic trains, cars, and people. Every detail, down to the last doorknob, was constructed by one man over 60,000hr. The 1hr. show in French (with English subtitles) constructs a story highlighting the models' bells and whistles. While the show may be a bit bizarre, the amazing feat of La Féerie is well worth a visit. (☎05 65 33 71 06; www.la-feerie.com. Tickets sold daily from mid-July to late Aug. 9am-noon and 2-7pm; from late Aug. to early Nov. and from Easter to mid-July 10am-noon and 2-6pm. Apr.-Sept. 4-8 shows per day; Oct. 2 per day. €8, under 12 €5.) The **Rocher des Aigles**—home to over 400 birds of 60 different species—shares the plateau with the castle and hosts a 1hr. show with trained birds of prey. (☎05 65 33 65 45; www.rocherdesaigles.com. Open from early to mid-July and from mid- to late Aug. daily 1-7pm, 4 shows; from mid-July to mid-Aug. daily 11am-7pm, 5 shows; Sept. and Apr.-June Tu-Su 1-6pm, 3 shows; Oct.-Nov. Th-F and Su 2-5pm, 1 show. €8, ages 5-14 €4.50.)

Separate **tourist offices** (☎05 65 33 22 00; www.rocamadour.com) serve the cliff's top and bottom layers. Both have guides, accommodations booking, maps (€1), and **currency exchange** at undesirable rates. The upper office is in l'Hospitalet, on route de Lacave, and the lower is in the old Hôtel de Ville. (Neither has consistent hours, but one of the two is open July-Aug. daily 10am-12:30pm and 1:30-6pm; Sept.-Oct. and Apr.-June daily 10am-noon and 2-6pm; Nov.-Mar. M-Sa 10am-noon and 2-5:30pm, Su 2-5:30pm.) A tour on the town's **petit train,** which leaves from Porte du Figuier, provides interesting historical commentary. (☎05 65 33 67 84. Open daily 10am-7:30pm. Tours 30min. Night tours from 7:30pm. Call tourist office for schedule. €5, under 18 €2.50.) Other services include an **ATM** inside the **post office** near the lower tourist office. (☎05 65 33 62 21. Open July-Aug. M-F 10am-noon and 1:30-4:30pm, Sa 10am-noon; Sept.-June M-F 1:30-4:30pm.)

DORDOGNE

Dramatic cliffs and poplar thickets overlook the Dordogne River's lazy waters, which provided a natural boundary between French and English Aquitaine during the Hundred Years' War. In the summer, tourists on bikes and in cars and canoes descend on the picturesque valley—in many places you'll probably hear more English than French. To the north, the terrain ranges from deep vales amid rolling hills to towering white cliffs above fields of tall grass. Renting a car is the wisest option, but biking the Dordogne is feasible if you are prepared for the long distances and steep hills.

PÉRIGUEUX   ☎05 53

High above the Isle River, the towering steeple and five massive cupolas of the Cathédrale St-Front—often a stop on the pilgrimage to Santiago de Compostela—dominate the skyline of Périgueux (pare-ee-guh; pop. 65,000). Beneath the cathedral lies the quiet, colorful, and largely pedestrian *centre-ville*, where narrow streets are lined with myriad shops, cafes, and restaurants featuring the regional specialties. Travelers with cars might want to daytrip to the caves of the Vézère Valley from Périgueux rather than from Les Eyzies-de-Tayac.

▐ TRANSPORTATION

Trains: Rue Denis Papin (☎05 53 06 21 94). Info office open M-F 4:15am-12:30am, Sa 5am-12:30am, Su 6am-11:30pm. Ticket booth open M-Th 5:40am-7:40pm, F 5:40am-8:25pm, Sa 7:10am-7:10pm, Su 7:20am-7:40pm. To: **Bordeaux** (1hr., 12 per day, €18); **Brive-la-Gaillarde** (1hr., 6 per day, €11); **Limoges** (1hr., 12 per day, €14); **Lyon** (6-8hr., 2 per day, €51); **Paris** (4-6hr., 13 per day, €57); **Sarlat** (1hr., 5 per day, €13); **Toulouse** (4hr., 12 per day, €32) via **Agen, Brive,** or **Bordeaux.**

Buses: CFTA Centre-Ouest. Info at the *gare routière*, 19 rue Denis Papin (☎05 53 08 43 13). Open M-F 9am-noon and 2-5pm. To **Angoulême** (1hr.; M, W, F 2 per day, Su 1 per day; €13) and **Sarlat** (1hr.; M-Tu and Th-F 1 per day, W 3 per day; €7.70).

Taxis: Taxi Périgueux, pl. Bugeaud (☎05 53 09 09 09). €5.50 base; €1.30 per km during the day, €1.90 at night. 24hr.

Car Rental: Avis, 18 rue du Président Wilson (☎05 53 53 39 02). From €47 per day. 21+. Open M-F 8am-noon and 2-7pm, Sa 8am-noon and 2-6pm. AmEx/MC/V. **Hertz,** 1 av. Henri Barbusse (☎05 53 54 61 80), across from the train station. Open M-F 8am-noon and 2-7pm, Sa 8am-noon and 2-6pm. AmEx/MC/V.

Périgueux

🏠🏠 ACCOMMODATIONS

Le Barris, **8**
Camping Barnabé-Plage, **5**
Les Charentes, **2**

🍴 FOOD

Au Bien Bon, **7**
L'Olivio, **9**
Le Romarin, **4**

⭐ NIGHTLIFE

Le Mellow, **3**
The Star Inn, **1**
Zanzi Bar, **6**

✦ 🛈 ORIENTATION AND PRACTICAL INFORMATION

The *vieille ville* is bordered by **cours Tourny** and **cours Fénelon** to the north and south, **boulevard Georges Saumand** along the river, and **boulevard Michel de Montaigne** to the east and west. To reach the *vieille ville* and tourist office from the station, turn right on rue Denis Papin and left on rue des Mobiles de Coulmiers, which becomes rue du Président Wilson. After the Monoprix, turn right and walk one block. The office is on the left, beside the **Tour Mataguerre** (15min.).

Tourist Office: 26 pl. Francheville (☎05 53 53 10 63; www.tourisme-perigueux.fr). Free map and info on walking, *petit train*, and bike tours. Open June-Sept. M-Sa 9am-6pm, Su 10am-1pm and 2-6pm; Oct.-May M-Sa 9am-1pm and 2-6pm.

Tours: 1hr. tours from the tourist office provide entry to otherwise inaccessible sights. Tours July-Aug. M 10:30am, 2:30, 3pm; Tu-Sa 10:30am, 2:30, 3, 9pm; Su 3pm. June and Sept. M-Sa 10:30am, 2:30, 3pm; Su 3pm. Oct.-May M-Sa 2:30pm; Su 3pm. €5, students €3.80. Bike tour July-Aug. Tu 10am. €5, students €3.80.

Youth Center: Centre Information Jeunesse (CIJ), pl. du Coderc (☎05 53 53 52 81). Open M, W, F 9am-noon and 2-5pm.

Laundromat: Lav'matic, 20 rue Mobiles de Coulmiers, near rond-point Lanxade on the way to the train station. Wash €3-8, dry €1 per 9min. Open daily 8am-9pm.

Police: Rue du 4 Septembre (☎05 53 06 44 44), near the post office.

Pharmacy: Rue Taillefer (☎05 53 53 38 31). Open M 2-7:30pm, Tu and Th-F 8:45am-12:30pm and 1:30-7:30pm, W 8:30am-12:30pm and 1:30-7:30pm, Sa 8:30am-12:30pm and 1:30-7pm.

Hospital: Centre Hospitalier, 80 av. Georges Pompidou (☎05 53 45 25 25).

Internet Access: La Cyber Tour, 9 cours Fénelon (☎05 53 53 03 52), around the corner from the tourist office. €1 per 15min., €3 per hr. Open M-Th and Sa 9am-10pm, F 9am-1:30pm and 2:30-10pm, Su 3-10pm.

Post Office: 1 rue du 4 Septembre (☎05 53 03 61 12). **Currency exchange** available. Open M-F 8:30am-6:30pm, Sa 9am-noon. **Postal Code:** 24000.

🏠🏕 ACCOMMODATIONS AND CAMPING

Les Charentes, 16 rue Denis Papin (☎05 53 53 37 13; fax 53 97 52), across from the station. Clean, comfortable rooms with endearing 1970s decor. A tiny hotel managed by a friendly couple eager to share Périgueux with its guests. Extensive organic, vegetarian menu in the attached restaurant. Breakfast €6. Reception 7am-10pm. Reservations recommended in summer. Open from mid-Jan. to mid-Dec. Singles with shower €25, with TV €30, with toilet €35; doubles €30/35/40. Extra bed €5. AmEx/MC/V. ❷

Les Barris, 2 rue Pierre Magne (☎05 53 53 04 05; www.hoteldesbarris.com). 5min. from the *centre-ville*. A riverside hotel with spectacular views of the cathedral and *vieille ville*. Comfortable, modern rooms with toilets, showers, and TVs. Breakfast €6. Wi-Fi. Singles €44; doubles €49; triples €54; quads €59; quints €64. MC/V. ❸

Camping Barnabé-Plage, 80 rue des Bains (☎05 53 53 41 45; fax 54 16 62), 1.5km away in Boulazac. From cours Montaigne, take bus #8 (dir.: Cité Bel Air; M-F 1 per hr. 7am-7pm, Sa less frequent; €1.30) to rue des Bains. It may be faster to walk; from Cathédrale St-Front, head downhill and cross Pont des Barris. Turn left after the bridge onto rue des Prés; the street ends at rue des Bains. Take a right and an immediate left on rue des Jardins to reach the entrance (25min.). Shady, tranquil riverside site featuring a bar and minigolf. Reception 9am-midnight. Open Mar.-Oct.; packed in summer. €4 per person; €3.30 per tent; €2.40 per car. MC/V. ❶

🍴 FOOD

The labyrinth of narrow stone streets between **cours Michel Montaigne** and **rue Taillefer** reveals restaurants serving regional culinary treasures—including walnuts, fruit liqueurs, *foie gras*, other duck specialties, and *cèpe* and *girolle* mushrooms. A stroll down **rue Salinière** and **rue Limogeanne** reveals an assortment of *charcuteries*, *pâtisseries*, *boulangeries*, and sandwich shops. There are small morning markets on **place du Coderc** and **place de l'Hôtel de Ville,** and a larger one on **place de la Clautre,** near the cathedral. (Open W and Sa 8am-1pm.) The behemoth **Monoprix** at pl. Bugeaud is impossible to miss. (Open M-Sa 8:30am-8pm. MC/V.) There's a **Marché Plus** at 55 rue du Président Wilson. (Open M-Sa 7am-9pm, Su 8am-1pm. MC/V.)

Au Bien Bon, 15 rue des Places (☎05 53 09 69 94). Exceptional regional cuisine served with a touch of attitude. Tables outside this picturesque medieval building overlook a quiet pedestrian street. Specialties include *magret* (duck steak; €14) and *cèpes*

LET THEM EAT FOIE GRAS

After a sip of fine wine and a bite of a warm, buttery croissant, you completely understand why France is famous for fabulous food. Yet, among the oh-so-delicious crowd, there is one delicacy in France that stands out. *Bienvenue* to the home of *foie gras*.

Although the stuff was first made in Egypt as early as 2500 BC, France has taken over as the world's largest producer of fattened goose or duck liver. The country now produces over 75% of the worlds *foie gras*, 90% of which is produced in the medieval villages of the Dordogne.

The production locations seem fitting, as the process of making *foie gras* is a bit medieval itself. The birds must be prepared by *gavage* (force-feeding) in order to be legally classified *foie gras* in France. The birds are fed cornmeal through tubes in their esophagus to fatten their livers before an untimely death. Animal rights groups like PETA have declared *gavage* to be an unfit treatment of animals. Several countries—including Israel and Turkey—have banned *foie gras* production.

Foie gras's presence on menus in restaurants throughout Sarlat, Brive-la-Gaillarde, and Les Ezyies, however, makes it clear that the controversy in France is virtually ignored. The choice is yours, hungry traveler: take a stand or take your gourmet meal.

(a kind of mushroom) *omelettes* (€12). Lunch *menu* €14. Open M-Th noon-1:30pm, F noon-1:30pm and 7:30-9:30pm, Sa 7:30-9:30pm. MC/V. ❸

Le Romarin, rue de la Clarté (☎05 53 53 27 84), near pl. du Coderc. Another excellent place to sample the Dordogne's cuisine. Small restaurant with a marble-topped bar and a pleasant, laid-back atmosphere. Filling salads (€8) and huge *tartines* (€8.50). *Menus* €13-20. Open May-Sept. daily 8am-10pm. Kitchen open noon-2pm and 7-10pm. ❸

L'Olivio, 14 rue de l'Aubergerie (☎05 53 09 63 88). Pizzeria in a restored medieval house with a wholesome family feel. Salads from €5. Pizza from €7. Open Tu-Sa noon-2:30pm and 7-10pm. MC/V. ❷

⬡ SIGHTS

Périgueux is divided into two distinct historical districts: the Medieval and Renaissance section to the northeast and the Gallo-Roman city to the southwest. Next to the tourist office is the medieval **Tour Mataguerre,** which derives its name from the Occitan (ancient Languedoc) language—*matar*, meaning "to hold at bay," and *guerra*, meaning "war."

◼MUSÉE GALLO-ROMAIN. An intricate walkway passes over the excavated ruins of the Domus de Vésone, once the lavish home of a wealthy Roman merchant. A modern, interestingly beautiful building, the interesting museum boasts a rich collection of Roman artifacts, murals, and stonework. Detailed displays describe Roman life and the design of ancient Périgueux. *(Rue Claude Bernard, next door to the Tour de Vésone. ☎05 53 05 65 60. Open July-Sept. daily 10am-7pm; Sept.-Oct. and Apr.-July Tu-Su 10am-12:30pm and 2-6pm; Nov.-Dec. and Feb.-Mar. Tu-Su 10am-12:30pm and 2-5:30pm. Tours in French July-Aug. daily. €5.70, under 12 €3.70. Tours €1. Audio tour in English €1.)*

CATHÉDRALE SAINT-FRONT. For travelers who have seen one too many Gothic cathedrals, this cathedral offers a break from the ordinary. The visually stunning church—built in the shape of a Greek cross—is crowned by five immense Byzantine cupolas next to a soaring belfry. The interior features beautiful chandeliers, an impressive organ, and an unusually beautiful wood altarpiece. In the 19th century, St-Front was restored by architect Paul Abadie, who used the cathedral as inspiration for his design of the Basilique Sacré-Coeur (p. 150) in Paris. *(Open daily 8am-noon and 2:30-7pm.)*

MUSÉE DU PÉRIGORD. This museum is home to one of France's most important collections of prehistoric artifacts, including fossils from Les

Eyzies, 2m long mammoth tusks, and an Egyptian mummy whose bare toe bones peek out from crusty coverings. It also holds a small collection of art from the medieval through modern periods. *(22 cours Tourny, down rue St-Front from the cathedral. ☎05 53 06 40 70. Open Apr.-Sept. M and W-F 10:30am-5:30pm, Sa-Su 1-6pm; Oct.-Mar. M and W-F 10am-5pm. €4, students €2, under 18 free.)*

TOUR DE VÉSONE. The ruins of this Gallo-Roman tower, built in the AD first century, were once part of a huge temple dedicated to the patron goddess and namesake of Vésone (the name of ancient Périgueux). Although only the crumbling shell of the tower remains, the site still retains a spiritual quality; it was originally a *cella*—the center of worship in Roman temples. About a quarter of the weighty structure was demolished, supposedly by the last fleeing demons of paganism, though it was more likely dismantled to create the city's defensive wall. *(Park grounds open daily Apr.-Sept. 7:30am-9pm; Oct.-Mar. 7:30am-6:30pm.)*

OTHER SIGHTS. Cross the bridge from the Tour de Vésone and turn left down rue Romaine to reach a cluster of architectural vestiges dating from the first century through the High Middle Ages. Flowers sprout through the crevices of the **Château Barrière,** a four-story Late Gothic castle. The Romanesque house next door is an example of the use of *spolia*—the decorative incorporation of ruins in modern buildings. The **Porte Normande** is a fragment of the wall that once surrounded the city to defend against the first Norman and barbarian attacks. On rue Romaine, the 11th-century **Église Saint-Étienne-de-la-Cité,** the city's primary cathedral until it was badly damaged during the Wars of Religion, features two simple but stately cupolas dotted with small Romanesque windows. *(Open daily 9:30am-noon and 2:30-6:30pm.)* A Roman **amphitheater** currently serves as a public park, with luxurious foliage and an inviting fountain. *(Open daily Apr.-Sept. 7:30am-9pm; Oct.-Mar. 7:30am-6:30pm.)*

☕ NIGHTLIFE

Although the streets may be sleepy, Périgueux's night spots liven up when the sun sets. **Place Saint-Silain** and **place Saint-Louis** are the centers of the city's nightlife, with music and outdoor cafes, while **place du Marché au Bois** hosts frequent concerts. Bars line the lively **rue de la Sagesse.**

- **The Star Inn,** 17 rue des Drapeaux (☎05 53 08 56 83; www.thestarinnfrance.com). Classic Irish pub in a Renaissance house. English-speaking owners suggest fun daytrip excursions. Outdoor seating available. English book exchange W afternoons and pub quiz F 10-11pm. Drinks from €2.50. Happy hour M-W 7-9pm. Open July-Aug. M-Tu and Th-Sa 7pm-2am, W noon-2am; Sept.-June daily 7pm-1am. MC/V over €15.

- **Le Mellow,** 4 rue de la Sagesse (☎05 53 08 53 97). Sophisticated and appropriately named. Lounge plays upbeat electronic music and features a sleek cigar bar. Mixed drinks €5.50-6.50. Salsa lessons Th (intermediate 8-9pm, advanced 9-10pm; €5). Salsa party every 3rd Th. Open Tu-Sa 4:30pm-2am. MC/V.

- **Zanzi Bar,** 2 rue Condé (☎05 53 53 28 99). Serves jungle-inspired drinks (from €4.50) and tapas until 10pm (€6). Live music on weekends. Open Tu-Sa 6:45pm-2am. MC/V.

❄ FESTIVALS

Macadam Jazz, Tu nights in July and Aug. Free jazz concerts in the *vieille ville.*

Mimos (☎05 53 53 18 71), 1st week of Aug. Périgueux quiets down for the world's leading international mime festival. Big events charge admission, but there are free performances and workshops all over town. Ticketed events €10, students €8.

DORDOGNE AND LIMOUSIN

LES EYZIES-DE-TAYAC   ☎05 53

With jutting limestone cliffs, lush green forests, and steep hillsides dotted with the medieval châteaux of the lords of Tayac, Les Eyzies-de-Tayac (layz-ay-zee-duh-tay-ak; pop. 900) is the picture-perfect base for travel to the Vézère River's famous caves; many of them, with the exception of Lascaux, are less than 20min. from the *centre-ville* by foot. The nearby Vézère River provides an idyllic setting as it flows past Les Eyzies and into some of France's most picturesque landscapes. The village exhausts the prehistoric theme when it comes to hotels and shops, but rustic restaurants serving duck specialties and Bergerac wines prove that the city is more than just a tourist destination.

⌐ TRANSPORTATION

Trains: ☎05 53 06 97 22. Open M-F 8am-6pm, Sa-Su 10am-6pm. To **Paris** (4-6hr., 4 per day, €60) via **Limoges** (1hr., 4 per day, €30), **Périgueux** (30min., 6 per day, €6.80), and **Sarlat** (1hr.; 2 per day, change at Le Buisson; €7.50).

Taxis: Taxi Tardieu (☎05 53 06 93 06). 24hr. €7 to Combarelle; €5 to Le Grand Roc.

Bike Rental: At the **tourist office** (below). €14 per day; ID or €20 deposit.

✳🛈 ORIENTATION AND PRACTICAL INFORMATION

Facing away from the train station, turn right and walk 500m down av. de la Préhistoire to reach the *centre-ville* (5min.).

Tourist Office: 19 av. de la Préhistoire (☎05 53 06 97 05; www.tourisme-terredecromagon.com). **Internet** €1.50 per 15min. **ATM** and **currency exchange** available. Open July-Aug. M-Sa 9am-7pm, Su 10am-noon and 2-6pm; Sept. and Apr.-June M-Sa 9am-noon and 2-6pm, Su 10am-noon and 2-5pm; Oct.-Mar. M-Sa 9am-noon and 2-6pm.

Tours: Cro-Mignon (☎05 53 07 05 23). Train departs from parking de la Vézère. 40min. tours of the village run 10am-7pm.

Laundromat: Route de Sarlat, past the tourist office and the gas station. Open M-Sa 9am-noon and 2:30-7pm.

Police: Rue le Pigeonnier (☎05 53 30 80 00), in St-Cyprien.

Pharmacy: 1 av. de la Forge (☎05 53 06 97 40). Open M-F 9am-12:30pm and 2-7:30pm, Sa 9am-12:30pm and 2-7pm.

Hospital: In Sarlat (☎05 53 31 75 75).

Post Office: Av. de la Préhistoire (☎05 53 06 94 11), past the tourist office. **Currency exchange** available. Open M-Tu and Th-F 8:30am-noon and 2-4pm, W 9:30am-noon and 2-4pm, Sa 9-11:30am. **Postal Code:** 24620.

⌂🛏 ACCOMMODATIONS AND CAMPING

Les Eyzies-de-Tayac hosts many tourists, so rooms are plentiful but expensive. The tourist office has a complete list of B&Bs in the area (€29-37 for 1-2 people), and **avenue de la Préhistoire** is lined with small hotels and *chambres d'hote*, many of which are moderately priced. Drivers will notice signs along the main roads advertising *fermes* (farms) with camping space (€3-8). Some village homes rent rooms for €25-48 during the summer; look for *chambres* signs, especially on the east end of town.

🏨 **Demaison Chambres d'Hôte,** route de Sarlat (☎05 53 06 91 43), 3min. outside town. From the train station, follow signs to Sarlat; the house is past the laundromat on the right. 12 charming, immaculately clean rooms—all with toilet and bath—in a home on the edge of the forest. Breakfast €5. Reservations required. Singles and doubles €25-36; triples and quads €48. Cash only. ❷

Hôtel des Falaises, 35 av. de la Préhistoire (☎05 53 06 97 35). Spotless, spacious, brightly colored rooms, each with shower and toilet. Larger rooms have a balcony overlooking the garden. More private lodgings available in the annex down the road. Breakfast €5. Reception in the bar downstairs 8am-6pm. Doubles €38-42. Cash only. ❷

Camping La Rivière, route du Sorcier (☎05 53 06 97 14; www.lariviereleseyzies.com), 10min. from the *centre-ville*. From the tourist office, turn left and follow av. de la Préhistoire for 5min. Cross the bridge and turn left at the gas station. Restaurant and pool on location. Laundry, Internet, and bike rental available. Reception 9am-noon and 2-7pm. Open Apr. 5-Nov. 1. €3.10-5 per person; sites €5.30-7.90. Electricity €3.50. MC/V. ❶

🍴 FOOD

From April to October, a market runs the length of town. (Open M 9am-1pm.) The market at **Halle des Eyzies**, just past the *centre-ville* on route de Sarlat, houses stalls selling pricey but high-quality *gâteau aux noix* (walnut cake), *foie gras*, and Bergerac wine. (Open daily from mid-June to mid-Sept. 9:30am-1pm and 2:30-7pm.) These delicacies can also be found in specialty shops along **avenue de la Préhistoire**, the town's main street. Get groceries at **Relais de Mousquetaires**, route de Sarlat. (Open M-Sa 8:30am-12:30pm and 3-7pm.)

Le Chateaubriant, 29 av. de la Préhistoire (☎05 53 35 06 11). Regional specialties at good prices. Sample *foie gras*, duck, and local *fromage de chèvre* (goat cheese) in the sleek dining room or on the peaceful terrace overlooking the park and river. The €11 *menu du jour* is a great value. *Omelettes* with salad €9-11. Grilled meat *plats* €10-13. Open M-Tu and Th-Sa noon-2pm and 7-9pm. MC/V. ❸

La Milanaise, av. de la Préhistoire (☎05 53 35 43 97). Delicious thin-crust pizzas (€6.80-13) with toppings like duck, *foie gras*, and mango as well as salads (€4-14) full of *gésiers* (duck livers) and walnuts. Try a delicious ice cream treat of epic proportions. *Plats* €8.60-15. *Menus* €16-25. Open daily 11am-2pm and 6:30-10pm. MC/V. ❸

La Grignotière (☎05 53 06 91 67), down the street from the tourist office. Cheap drinks, tasty *omelettes* (€5-8), and sandwiches (€3-5). Open daily 8am-10pm. MC/V. ❷

👁 SIGHTS

MUSÉE L'ABRI PATAUD. Sitting on the site of a prehistoric *abri* (shelter) where reindeer hunters lived for over 20,000 years, this museum provides an in-depth explanation of the region's archaeological finds. A selection of the thousands of artifacts recovered from the adjacent excavation site is on display. The 18,600-year-old remains of a teenage girl cradling her infant found on the site is the highlight of the *abri* and may represent a link between Neanderthal and Cro-Magnon man. (☎05 53 06 92 46; www.semitour.com. Open July-Aug. daily 10am-7pm; Sept.-Oct. and Apr. M-F and Su; Nov.-Mar. M-Th 10am-12:30pm and 2-5:30pm. Hours subject to change; call ahead for details. 1hr. tours in French; call for times; reservations required for groups. Tours in English by reservation. €5.80, ages 6-12 €3.80, under 6 free.)

MUSÉE NATIONAL DE PRÉHISTOIRE. In a château overlooking the village, this museum showcases a collection of prehistoric discoveries from the many caves around Les Eyzies. The permanent exhibit offers a high-tech presentation of prehistoric cultures. Displays include the remains of a Neanderthal infant and prehistoric etchings of bison. English explanations are available at the entrance of each room. (*1 rue de Musée.* ☎05 53 06 45 65; www.musee-prehistoire-eyzies. fr. Open July-Aug. daily 9:30am-6:30pm; Sept. and June M and W-Su 9:30am-6pm; Oct.-May M

and W-Su 9:30am-12:30pm and 2-5:30pm. English tours by reservation. Wheelchair-accessible.
€5, ages 18-25 €3.50, under 18 free; with 1hr. French tour €10/8.50/5.)

⚑ DAYTRIPS FROM LES EYZIES: VÉZÈRE VALLEY CAVES

▥LASCAUX

The Lascaux caves are 2km up the road from Montignac, 23km northeast of Les Eyzies on
D706. The train station nearest to Montignac is 10km away at Condat-le-Lardin. Trains run
from Les Eyzies to Condat-le-Lardin via Niversac (45min., 1 per day, €16). Taxis (☎05 53
50 86 61 or 51 80 46) will pick you up from the station. Trans-Périgord (☎05 53 59 01
48) runs 2 buses per day Sept.-June from Périgueux and 3 from Sarlat; call or check at the
stations for times and prices. Making the trip by bike is possible for those who can handle
the hilly countryside and the steep climb from Montignac to Lascaux.

The world's most famous prehistoric cave paintings line the ceilings of Lascaux
(lahss-koh), nicknamed "the Sistine Chapel of prehistory." In 1940, four teenagers chasing after their runaway dog discovered a small hole near some tree
roots. When they came back the next day to explore further, they stumbled into
this ancient cave of wonders. They decided to keep it a secret, but—fortunately
for the rest of the world—they could only stay quiet about their amazing discovery for three days. After welcoming hordes of visitors, Lascaux closed to
the public in 1963 because the humidity from the viewers' breath bred algae
and spurred the formation of microscopic mineral deposits on the paintings
that nature had preserved for 17,000 years. Today, people line up to see **Lascaux II**, a duplicate of the original that offers one of the best guided English
and French cave tours in the valley. This is no second-rate tourist trap; sculptors spent over a decade shaping the new caves' walls to match the contours
of the original precisely, and the new paintings were crafted with the same
techniques as the originals. Lascaux also reveals the surprising sophistication
of the prehistoric artwork. The ancient artists used perspective to give the
paintings depth and often used one line to define the shape of two animals,
giving the huge murals a fascinating unity. (☎05 53 51 95 03; www.semitour.
com. Open July-Aug. daily 9am-7pm; Sept.-Oct. and Apr.-June daily 10am-noon
and 2-6pm; Nov.-Mar. Tu-Su 9am-noon and 2-5pm. Ticket office at pl. Bertran-
de-Born open July-Aug. daily 9am until tickets sell out; Sept.-June sold at cave
entrance. 40min. tour in English, French, German, or Spanish. Reserve ahead
for July-Aug. €8.20, ages 6-12 €6.20, under 6 free.)

In Thonac, Le Thot Espace Cro-Magnon, 6km from Lascaux on D706, serves
as a great introduction to Lascaux and local prehistoric discoveries, painting
a picture of ancient life, from hunting to cave painting. Le Thot also features
the 10% of Lascaux's art not reproduced in Lascaux II, and a small zoo full of
prehistoric animal descendants. (☎05 53 50 70 44; www.semitour.com. Open
July-Aug. daily 10am-7pm; Sept. and Apr.-June daily 10am-6pm; from Oct. to
mid-Nov. 10am-noon and 2-6pm; from mid-Nov. to Feb. Tu-Su 10am-12:30pm
and 2-5:30pm. €5.70, ages 6-12 €3.70; discount with Lascaux II ticket.)

Numerous campgrounds dot the Vézère Valley near Montignac. Five minutes from the *centre-ville* and within walking distance of Lascaux, **Le Moulin
du Bleufond ❶** offers 83 shady spots, a restaurant, a tennis court, a pool, and
Internet access. (☎05 53 51 83 95; www.bleufond.com. Wheelchair-accessible.
Open from Apr. to mid-Sept. €4-5.30 per person, children €2.40-€3.20. Electricity €3.20. AmEx/MC/V.) The Montignac **tourist office,** pl. Bertran-de-Born (☎05
53 51 82 60; www.perigordnoir.com), shares a building with the Lascaux II
ticket office. Free tours in English and French of Montignac's medieval section
are offered on Thursdays at 8:30pm during July and August.

OTHER DAYTRIPS

GROTTE DU GRAND ROC. A 1.5km walk northwest of Les Eyzies (15min.), the Grotte du Grand Roc is a geologic treasure chest. Halfway up the chalk cliffs, the cave commands a spectacular view of the valley. While the tour of the cave is short and only features a small portion of the cave, the millions of stalactites, stalagmites, and *eccentriques*—small calcite accretions that grow neither straight down nor straight up—make the visit a delight. The cave also features troglodyte dwellings that are still inhabited. (☎05 53 06 92 70; www.grandroc.com. Open daily July-Aug. 9:30am-7pm; Sept.-Oct. and Apr.-June 10am-6pm; early Nov. and Feb.-Mar. 10am-12:30pm and 2-5pm. 30min. tour in French every 30min., or in both French and English according to demand. Written guides available in English. €7.50, under 18 €3.50, under 5 free.)

GROTTE DE FONT-DE-GAUME. The last cave in the Aquitaine basin with multicolored paintings still open to the public, Grotte de Font-de-Gaume is 1km east of Les Eyzies on D47 (dir.: Sarlat). Though the spectacular 15,000-year-old friezes—completed over the course of hundreds of years—have faded slightly, they are still visible and display the innovative artistic technique of the ancient painters, who incorporated the natural contours of the cave for depth. Locals discovered the paintings in the 1700s but did not realize their importance until two centuries later, by which time several murals had decayed or been defaced by graffiti. Consequently, the most brilliant colors have been preserved only in the cavern's deeper recesses. The scene of a black reindeer licking the nose of its kneeling red cousin demonstrates expressive use of detail, but the *voûte* (vault) where 12 bison stampede across the ceiling is the undisputed highlight. The cave can be chilly, so bring an extra layer. Cave access is limited to 180 visitors per day; reserve four weeks ahead for visits in July or August and two weeks ahead for September through June. Meanwhile, 50 same-day tickets go on sale at 9:30am; arrive early in summer. (☎05 53 06 86 00; fax 35 26 18. Open from mid-May to mid-Sept. M-F and Su 9:30am-5:30pm; from mid-Sept. to mid-May M-F and Su 9:30am-12:30pm and 2-5:30pm. Visit only by 1hr. tour; tours in French, in English based on demand. €6.50, ages 18-25 €4.50, under 18 free.)

ROQUE SAINT-CHRISTOPHE. Northeast of Les Eyzies on D706 (8km), the Roque St-Christophe is the most extensive cave dwelling ever discovered. Five floors of limestone terraces house 100 cave shelters 80m high and over 400m long. From 40,000 BC until AD 1580, when it was destroyed by a Catholic army attacking the Protestants who sought refuge here, this sanctuary served as a defensive fort and housed over 3000 people. Detailed pamphlets (available in English) guide visitors on a 45min. loop through the complex. Spectacular re-creations of the 11th-century kitchen, armory, and quarry give visitors an idea of what life was like during the Middle Ages. (☎05 53 50 70 45; www.roque-st-christophe.com. Open daily July-Aug. 10am-8pm; Sept. and Apr.-June 10am-6:30pm; from Oct. to mid-Nov and Feb.-Mar. 10am-6pm; from mid-Nov. to Jan. 2-5pm. Last entry 45min. before close. €7, students €6, ages 12-16 €4, ages 5-11 €3.)

ABRI DU CAP-BLANC. Only 12 figures, less detailed than those in Font-de-Gaume, are visible on the sculptured frieze of Abri du Cap-Blanc, northeast of Les Eyzies on D48 (7km). Hunters etched horses, bison, and reindeer onto the thick limestone walls 15,000 years ago. The centerpiece is a 2m long herd of animals. (☎05 53 59 60 30 or 06 86 00; www.leseyzies.com/cap-blanc. Open from mid-May to mid-Sept. M-F and Su 9:30am-5:30pm; from mid-Sept. to mid-May M-F and Su 9:30am-12:30pm and 2-5:30pm. Visit only by 45min. French tour with English translations. €6.50, under 18 free.)

GROTTE DE ROUFFIGNAC. Fifteen kilometers northwest of Les Eyzies in Rouffignac on the road to Périgueux, La Grotte de Rouffignac, also called the **Grotte**

aux Cent Mammouths, houses 250 pieces of prehistoric artwork. Etchings of rhinos and horses are interspersed with striking paintings of shaggy mammoths. The tour (via train) lasts an hour. (☎05 53 05 41 71; www.grottederouffignac.fr. Open daily July-Aug. 9-11:30am and 2-6pm; Sept.-Oct. and Apr.-June 10-11:30am and 2-5pm. Tours in French only. Tickets sold same day from 9am for morning visits, from noon for afternoon visits. Wheelchair-accessible. €6.20, under 18 €3.90.)

I WANT TO RIDE MY BICYCLE. Roque St-Christophe, Abri du Cap-Blanc, and Rouffignac make for a great daytrip by bike. It's easiest and most enjoyable to begin with Abri du Cap-Blanc, go to Roque St-Christophe next, and end with Rouffignac. Take D48 east out of Les Eyzies, D6 west to Roque, D6 (often also D706) to Rouffignac, and D32 back to Eyzies.

GROTTE DES COMBARELLES. Two kilometers from Grotte de Font-de-Gaume, this cave has lost its paintings to humidity, but the etchings in the "Lascaux of engravings" are spectacular even without color. Over 600 realistic carvings depict lions, donkeys, rhinos, and early humans. The six-person tours are wonderfully personalized; reserve well in advance for the summer. (☎05 53 06 86 00. Reservations required. Hours, prices, website, and tour information same as Font-de-Gaume.)

SARLAT ☎05 53

Narrow, twisting alleyways open onto *places* lined with bustling *brasseries*, giving Sarlat (sar-lah; pop. 11,000) the quiet mystery and busy color of a medieval village in full swing. The town was relatively unknown until 1962, when Minister of Culture André Malraux selected it for a massive restoration project. Three years later, a handsomely refurbished Sarlat emerged with its medieval buildings in immaculate condition—making it the perfect setting for films like *Cyrano de Bergerac, Manon des Sources,* and *Ever After.* Sarlat's face-lift has also drawn tourists to the village, but the cobblestone streets and huge wood doors speak louder than large groups of Anglophone tourists. Sarlat's sights are concentrated enough to explore in one day at a relaxing pace, leaving time for excursions to the nearby lower Dordogne and Lascaux (p. 530).

▐ TRANSPORTATION

Trains: Av. de la Gare (☎05 53 59 00 21). Ticket office open M 5:10am-8:15pm, Tu-Th 5:30am-8:15pm, F 5:30am-10:30pm, Sa-Su 7am-8:15pm. To **Bordeaux** (2hr., 5-8 per day 5:30am-7:45pm, €23) and **Périgueux** (3hr., M-Sa 3 per day, €14) via **Le Buisson.**

Buses: Trans-Périgord (☎05 53 02 20 85; www.cg24.fr), at the train station. To **Souillac** (40min., 3 per day, €4.70) and **Périgueux** (1hr., €8.90) via **Montignac.** CFTA, pl. Pasteur (☎05 55 59 01 48), runs a bus to **Périgueux** via **Montignac** (1hr.; Sept.-June M-F 6am, July-Aug. W 7:30am; €11).

Public Transportation: Sarlat Bus (☎05 53 59 01 48). **Bus** line A stops at the train station, line B at the roundabout down rue Dubois. Open M-Sa 8:30am-noon and 2-6pm.

Taxi: Sarlat Taxi (☎05 53 59 06 27). **Allo Allo Taxi Sarlat** (☎05 53 59 02 43).

Car Rental: Europcar, pl. du Maréchal de Lattre de Tassigny (☎05 53 30 30 40; www. europcar.fr). From the train station, walk down rue Dubois and cross the roundabout. Open M-F 8am-noon and 2-6:30pm, Sa 8am-noon and 2-6pm. AmEx/MC/V.

Bike Rental: MultiTravel (☎06 08 94 42 01; www.multitravel.co.uk). Englishman ▓**Joel Caine** offers free delivery and pickup (within a 10km radius of his shop next to Maisonneuve near Castelnaud). Helps with route planning, guided rides, and transfers for

€1.50 per km. €10 per ½-day, €15 per day. Locks and repair kits provided; helmets and maps €1 each. 7th day free. Open daily according to demand. Cash only. **Vélo & Oxygen: Cycles Sarladais,** 16 av. Aristide Briand (☎05 53 28 51 87; www.cycles-sar-ladais.com). €8 per ½-day, €13 per day, €35 per 3 days, €63 per week. Open July-Aug. M-Sa 9am-noon and 2-7pm; Sept.-June Tu-Sa 9am-noon and 2-7pm. MC/V.

🔳🗷 ORIENTATION AND PRACTICAL INFORMATION

Sarlat's *centre-ville* is framed by two main streets; to the north and west is **bou-levard Nessman** and to the south and east is **boulevard Voltaire. Rue de la République** runs north-south, bisecting the town.

Tourist Office: 3 rue Tourny (☎05 53 31 45 45; www.sarlat-tourisme.com). From the station, turn left on av. de la Gare. Take a right at the bottom of the hill onto av. Thiers, which eventually becomes rue de la République. Bear right on rue Lakanal; the tourist office is on the left. Accommodations booking (€2 within Dordogne, €3 otherwise), a list of campgrounds, city **tours,** and a city guide in English. 1-3 French tours per day. English tours June-Sept. W 11am. €5, students and ages 12-18 €3, under 12 free. Open July-Aug. M-Sa 9am-7pm, Su 10am-noon and 2-6pm; Sept. M-Sa 9am-1pm and 2-7pm, Su 10am-1pm and 2-5pm; Oct. M-Sa 9am-noon and 2-6pm, Su 10am-1pm; Dec.-Mar. M-Sa 9am-noon and 2-5pm; Apr. M-Sa 9am-noon and 2-6pm, Su 9am-1pm and 2-5pm; May-June M-Sa 9am-6pm, Su 10am-1pm and 2-5pm.

Laundromat: 10 pl. de la Bouquerie (☎05 53 59 25 96). Wash €4. Open daily 8am-noon and 2:30-6:30pm.

Police: Pl. Salvador Allende (☎05 53 31 71 10). Also across from pl. de la Grande Rigaudie, near the post office.

Hospital: Rue Jean Leclaire (☎05 53 31 75 75; fax 59 17 62).

Internet Access: Easy Planet, 17 av. Gambetta (☎05 53 29 23 48; www.easy-planet. net). English-speaking staff. €6 per hr. Open July-Aug. M-Sa 10am-10pm, Su noon-8pm; Sept.-June M-Sa 10am-7pm. **T Company,** 5, pl. de la Liberté (☎05 53 30 23 31). Free with the purchase of drink. Open M 11am-7pm, Tu-Su 10am-7pm.

Post Office: Pl. du 14 Juillet (☎05 53 31 73 10; fax 31 73 19). **Currency exchange** available. Open M-Sa 8:30am-5:30pm, Sa 8:30am-noon. **Postal Code:** 24200.

🏠🗷 ACCOMMODATIONS AND CAMPING

Sarlat's hotels are quite expensive; the best option is to book a room at one of the *chambres d'hôtes* (€25-50) close to the *centre-ville.* The tourist office has a complete list that also includes *gîtes*, farms, and campgrounds.

🔲 **La Chambre d'Hôtes Le Versau,** 49 route de Pechs (☎05 53 31 02 63; www.versau-sarlat.com), 10min. up the steep chemin du Plantier. Bookshelves in each room. Break-fast included; served in a colorful garden. Reservations required. Singles €24-40; dou-bles €32-44; quads €49-54. Cash only. ❷

🔲 **Chambres d'Hôtes de Charme,** 4 rue Magnanat (☎05 53 31 26 60; www.toulemon. com), off pl. de la Liberté. 3 spacious rooms with high ceilings, stone walls, and beauti-ful wood floors. Building classified as historic monument. Walled garden. Breakfast €6. Doubles July-Aug. €45; Sept.-June €38. Extra bed €8. ❸

Hôtel de la Mairie, 13 pl. de la Liberté (☎05 53 59 05 71; www.hotel-marie-sarlat. com). Large, wood-trimmed rooms with bright decorations and tiled bathrooms. Phones available. Dogs welcome. Breakfast €6. Internet access. Singles and doubles €47-57; triples €62-73; quads €89. AmEx/MC/V. ❹

Maisonneuve (☎05 53 29 51 29; www.campingmaisonneuve.com), 11km from Sarlat. Convenient base for daytrips. Cafe, grocery store, minigolf, ping-pong, pool, and swimming hole. *Gîte* with kitchen, bath, and beds for 10 available. Internet access. Reception 9am-8pm. Open Mar. 23-Oct. 6. €3.90-€5.50 per person; under 7 €2.70-3.80; sites with vehicle €5.30-7.50. *Gîte* €10. Electricity €2.70-3.80. MC/V. ❶

Le Montant (☎05 53 59 18 50; www.camping-sarlat.com), 2.5km from Sarlat. Bar, hot tub, pool, minigolf. Laundry. Internet access. Reception 9am-12:30pm and 1:30-8pm. Reserve ahead July-Aug. Open Apr.-Sept. €3.50-5.50 per person, under 7 €2.10-4; €4-7.90 per tent; €4-7.90 per car. Electricity €2.90-3.60. AmEx/MC/V. ❶

🗋 FOOD

Most regional delicacies—*foie gras, confit de canard* (preserved duck), truffles, walnut oil, and Bergerac wine—can be purchased from their sources in the surrounding countryside or in the rows of shops in town. Sarlat's *pâtisseries* and *confisseries* sell decorated breads, chocolate tarts, and *gâteaux aux noix* (walnut cakes). A lively market packs the *vieille ville* on Saturday (8:30am-6pm), while a smaller market fills **place de la Liberté** each Wednesday (8:30am-1pm). **Église Sainte-Marie,** next to pl. Marché Aux Oies, houses a covered market. (Open from mid-Apr. to mid-Nov. M-Th and Sa-Su 8:30am-2pm, F 8:30am-8pm; from mid-Nov. to mid-Apr. Tu-W and F-Sa 8:30am-1pm.) There's a **HyperChampion** supermarket 15min. from the *centre-ville*, along av. de Selves (open M-Sa 9am-8pm, Su 9am-12:30pm), and a **Petit Casino** at 32 rue de la République. (☎05 53 59 05 25. Open July-Aug. daily 7:30am-12:30pm and 2:30-7:30pm; Sept.-June M-Sa 7:30am-12:30pm and 2:30-7:30pm, Su 7:30am-12:30pm.)

▨ Chez le Gaulois, 3 rue Tourny (☎05 53 59 50 64), near the tourist office. Excellent cuts of meat with side salad and jar of pickles. *Plats* €9.50-11. Open July-Aug. daily noon-2pm and 7-10pm; Sept.-June Tu-Sa 11:30am-2:30pm and 6:30-9:30pm. V. ❷

Auberge des Lys D'Or, 17 rue Albéric Cahuet (☎05 53 31 24 77). Fish and duck specialties served under a timbered ceiling. *Formule* (€10) available until 8pm. *Menus* €13-24. Open daily 11:30am-2pm and 6:30-10pm. ❸

Bar Le Practice, 19 rue de la République (☎05 53 31 67 04). Delicious meat *plats* (€8-9) and *omelettes* (€5-8). Golf-themed mixed drinks like the Bogey (€6.50). Open daily June-Sept. 8am-2am; Oct.-May 8am-1am. MC/V over €15. ❷

👁 SIGHTS

The tourist office's walking tour provides a comprehensive introduction to the city's landmarks. Without a doubt, Sarlat is a city best explored by wandering the alleys and cobblestone streets of the *centre-ville*.

CATHÉDRALE SAINT-SACERDOS. This Neo-Gothic structure is to your right as you exit the tourist office. Originally part of a Benedictine abbey, it was largely rebuilt in the 16th and 17th centuries. Small and sparsely decorated compared to the Gothic behemoths for which France is famous, the cathedral has a more inviting atmosphere. The cathedral's different architectural styles and asymmetry testify to its various construction stages. The hill behind the structure—the stomping ground of local teenagers—is a nice spot to relax.

OTHER SIGHTS. Venture into an open doorway and up a winding stone staircase, and you might discover one of Sarlat's many **art galleries.** The lovingly landscaped **Jardin Public du Plantier,** just outside the *centre-ville* on bd. Henri Arlet, offers refuge from the downtown bustle. It features benches along flower-lined paths that look out onto picture-perfect vistas of Sarlat's rooftops.

DORDOGNE AND LIMOUSIN

◪ ❀ NIGHTLIFE AND FESTIVALS

Nearly every weekend during the summer, street performers and musicians converge on **place de la Liberté**. During the last two weeks of July and the first week of August, Sarlat hosts the **Festival des Jeux du Théâtre,** which features open-air performances, musicals, and panel discussions. (☎05 53 31 10 83. Tickets €15-25. 20% student discount with ID.) In early November, Sarlat hosts many of France's leading filmmakers in its annual **film festival.** Screenings are open to the public at the Cultural Center and CinéRex.

Le Bataclan, 31 rue de la République (☎05 53 28 54 34). Noisy rock and a carefree crowd spill onto the streets. Mixed drinks €2.50-5. Open daily 8am-2am. MC/V.

CinéRex, av. Thiers (☎08 92 68 69 24). Screens foreign films in their original languages. €7.30. Discounts all day M and Tu-F afternoon and evening.

◪ DAYTRIPS FROM SARLAT

CASTELNAUD-LA-CHAPELLE AND CHÂTEAU DES MILANDES

These daytrips are not accessible by public transportation. To get to Castelnaud-la-Chapelle, 12km south of Sarlat on D57, follow rue Faure, which becomes rue de Cahors, then rue Gabriel Tarde. At the roundabout, head down av. de la Dordogne, then follow signs for D57 and Château de Castelnaud. D57 is hilly; bikers might prefer to take a slightly longer but much flatter route with less traffic. At the 2nd roundabout, turn left on D46 toward Vitrac. From Vitrac, follow the roadside signs to Castelnaud. The Château des Milandes is 5km from Castelnaud on D57.

Although the panoramic views of the Dordogne Valley alone make the trip worthwhile, Castelnaud-la-Chapelle (kah-stell-noh-lah-shah-pell) is exciting in its own right. Actors in medieval garb reveal what life was like in the Middle Ages and hold theatrical demonstrations with impressive full-size *trébuchets* outside. (☎05 53 31 30 00; www.castelnaud.com. Open daily July-Aug. 9am-8:15pm; Sept. and Apr.-June 10am-7pm; from Oct. to mid-Nov. and Feb.-Mar. 10am-6pm; from mid-Nov. to Jan. 2-5pm; holidays and school vacation 10am-5pm. July-Aug. 8 French tours per day; English tours M-F 3 per day, Sa 8 per day. Call in advance for low-season English tours and for schedule of demonstrations. €7.60, ages 10-17 €3.80, under 10 free.)

Halfway down the hill from the castle lies the **Eco-Musée de la Noix de Périgord,** a restored farmhouse that celebrates the history of the region's famous walnut industry with exhibits and a documentary film. In the store, nut lovers can purchase homemade walnut products like walnut wine (€5-9). True nut nuts should stop in the small museum and stroll through the walnut grove. (☎05 33 59 69 63; www.ecomuseedelanoix.site.voila.fr. Open daily from Easter to Nov. 10am-7pm. €4, under 18 €3, under 10 free.)

The **Renaissance Château des Milandes** (shah-toh day mill-ahnd) was built by François de Caumont in 1489 to satisfy his wife, who wanted a more stylish home than the outdated fortress of Castelnaud. Centuries later, cabaret singer Josephine Baker fell in love with the neglected château, purchased the property, and created a "world village" to house and care for the children she had adopted on her international tours. A museum devoted to her life now occupies the château, its luxurious rooms showcasing the cabaret star's furniture, glamor shots, and authentic stage costumes. In a truly random acknowledgment of its medieval origins, the château offers a falconry show, complete with handlers in costume. A restaurant and bar are also on-site. (☎05 53 59 31 21; www.milandes.com. Open July-Aug. daily 9:30am-7:30pm; Sept. M-F and Su 10am-7pm; Oct. M-F and Su 10am-6:15pm; Apr.-June M-F and Su 10am-6:30pm.

Apr.-Oct. 2-4 falconry shows per day; call for schedule. Audio tours in French. €7.80, students €6, ages 5-10 and handicapped €5.50, under 5 free.)

DOMME AND LA ROQUE GAGEAC

These daytrips are most easily accessible by car. From Sarlat, take av. de la Dordogne and head southwest at the roundabout on D57 toward Beynac or south on the significantly less hilly D46 (dir.: Vitrac and Domme). Car rentals are available in Sarlat. Découverte et Loisirs minibuses run through the valley several times per week from Sarlat. (☎05 65 37 19 00; www.decouverte-loisirs.com. €30-40. Call for schedule.) For cyclists, Sarlat is the best starting point. It's about 4-10km between each village, and, once along the Dordogne, the bike ride is fairly level, with small hills every few kilometers.

Across from the Domme (dohmm) tourist office, a 45min. cave tour descends into the ◧**Grottes de la Halle.** Discovered almost 100 years ago, this beautiful network of expansive caverns is filled with rows of breathtaking white stalactites and stalagmites that resemble organ pipes. A visit to this natural cathedral affords visitors a detailed explanation of the cave's geological features and a chance to admire the colorful, well-lit formations. (☎05 53 31 71 00. French tours with written English explanations July-Aug. every 20-30min. 10:15am-7pm; Sept. and Apr.-June every 45min. 10:15am-noon and 2-6pm; Oct. and Feb.-Mar. every hr. 2-5pm. Call ahead for English tours. €6.50, students €5.50, ages 5-14 €4.) Explore the dilapidated **Porte des Tours** during a 1hr. guided tour in French. Seventy Templar Knights were imprisoned here in 1307 and tortured for nearly 20 years by King Philip IV, who wanted the secret of their hidden treasure. The artistic graffiti they scratched into the walls with their teeth, hands, and fingernails remains a mysterious combination of Christian iconography and Muslim and Jewish motifs encountered by the Templars during the Crusades. (Accessible by tour only. July-Aug. 2-3 per day; Sept.-Dec. and Feb.-June by reservation. €6.50, students €5.50, ages 5-14 €4.)

The Domme **tourist office** is at pl. de la Halle, in the stone building near the river's edge. (☎05 53 31 71 00; www.ot-domme.com. Tickets for village tours available. Open daily July-Aug. 9am-12:30pm and 2-6pm; Sept. and June 10am-12:30pm and 2-5:30pm.) Domme also offers a 20min. **petit train touristique tour.** (☎05 53 31 71 00; www.domme-perigord.com. July-Aug.)

Downstream, the village of **La Roque Gageac** (lah rohk gah-jhay-ahk) overlooks the Dordogne River. While the town boasts few sights, it offers a relaxing location for a picnic and serves as a good canoeing outpost. A 1hr. tour on a *gabare*, a traditional wood boat, affords a perfect view of the châteaux along the Dordogne. **Norbert** (☎05 53 29 40 44; www.norbert.fr; tours daily Apr.-Oct. every hr. 10am-6pm; €2 audio tours available in English; €8, under 18 €5) and **Caminade** (☎05 53 29 40 95; garbarrecaminade@wanadoo.fr; tours in English and French Easter-Oct. daily 10am-6pm; €8, under 18 €5) boats depart from La Roque Gageac. The 12th-century **Fort Troglodytique Aérien** commands a spectacular view of the Dordogne River Valley. Nestled securely into a cliff, it withstood all English assaults during the Hundred Years' War. (☎05 53 31 61 94. Open daily from Apr. to mid-Nov. 10:30am-7pm; from mid-Nov. to Mar. 11am-5pm. €5, students €4, ages 10-18 €2, ages 6-9 €1, under 6 free.) For more information on any La Roque Gageac's sights, call the **tourist office** (☎05 53 29 17 01).

Campgrounds and companies along the river rent **canoes** and **kayaks.** At the Pont de Vitrac, near Domme, try **Canoës-Loisirs** (☎05 53 31 22 92; www.canoes-loisirs.com). **Canoë-Dordogne** (☎05 53 29 58 50; www.canoe-dordogne.fr) and **Canoë Vacances** (☎05 53 28 17 07; www.canoes-vacances.com) are located in La Roque Gageac. Prices are typically around €11 per half-day and €16 per day.

LOT VALLEY

Winding from Cahors to Cajarc, the fertile Lot Valley is a strip of green that shelters its temperate river and vineyards between steep cliffs. While the area's natural beauty is best taken in at walking pace, infrequent bus traffic makes it easiest to explore the many out-of-the-way wonders by car. Some travelers choose to hitchhike, though *Let's Go* does not advise it. The Cahors tourist office sells hiking maps (€4.60) of the entire Lot Valley.

CAHORS   ☎05 65

Nestled in the crook of the Lot River, Cahors (kah-ohr; pop. 20,000) is a staple in the St-Jacques de Compostela pilgrimage as well as a convenient base for daytrips to the surrounding villages, vineyards, cliffs, and caves. The town itself offers the impressive 14th-century Valentré Bridge and a medieval quarter—both of which can be explored in a leisurely afternoon.

▐ TRANSPORTATION

Trains: Av. Jean Jaurès. Info booth open M and F 6am-6pm, Tu-Th and Sa-Su 8am-6pm. To: **Brive-la-Gaillarde** (1hr., 8-9 per day, €15-17); **Limoges** (2hr., 6 per day, €26-29); **Montauban** (45min., 10 per day, €9.80-12); **Toulouse** (1hr., 9 per day, €17).

Taxi: Allo-Taxi, 742 chemin des Junies (☎05 65 22 19 42). 24hr.

Car Rental: Avis, 26 av. Jean Jaurès (☎05 65 30 13 10), on pl. de la Gare. Open M-F 8am-noon and 2-6pm, Sa 8am-noon. AmEx/MC/V.

▐ PRACTICAL INFORMATION

Tourist Office: Pl. Mitterrand (☎05 65 53 20 65; www.mairie-cahors.fr). From the station, bear right, cross the street, and head up rue Anatole France. At the end of the street, turn left on rue du Président Wilson, then right on bd. Gambetta. The office is around the corner (15min.). Staff reserves accommodations (€0.90) and gives **tours** of the *cité médiévale* and the Pont Valentré in French; €6.50, students and ages 12-18 €4, under 12 free. Open July-Aug. M-F 9am-12:30pm and 1:30-6:30pm, Sa 9am-12:30pm and 1:30-6pm, Su 10am-1pm; Sept.-June M-Sa 9am-12:30pm and 1:30-6pm.

Youth Centers: Bureau Information Jeunesse, 20 rue Frédéric Suisse (☎05 65 23 95 90). Internet (€2 per hr.), printing service, travel planning, and info on housing and summer jobs. Open M-Tu 1-6pm, W 9am-noon and 1-6pm, F 1-5pm. **Les Docks,** 430 allées des Soupirs (☎05 65 22 36 38). Internet €2 per hr. Open Tu-F 2-6pm.

Laundromats: 208 rue Georges Clemenceau. Wash €3.60-7, dry €0.40 per 5min. Open daily 7am-9pm. Also at 265 rue Nationale. Wash €3.40, dry €1 per 10min. Open daily 7:30am-9:30pm.

Police: Pl. Bessières (☎05 65 23 17 17).

Hospital: 449 rue du Président Wilson (☎05 65 20 50 50).

Post Office: 257 rue Wilson (☎05 65 20 61 00). **Currency exchange** available. Open M-F 8:15am-6pm, Sa 8:30am-noon. **Postal Code:** 46000.

▐ ▐ ACCOMMODATIONS AND CAMPING

▨ **Foyer des Jeunes Travailleurs Frédéric Suisse (HI),** 20 rue Frédéric Suisse (☎05 65 35 64 71; fax 35 95 92). From the station, bear right on rue Anatole France and left on rue Frédéric Suisse. 17th-century mansion has co-ed dorms, comfortable private rooms, and large multi-room suites. Toilets and showers in the hall. Breakfast €3.50. Linen €2.90. Reception 9am-noon and 1:30-9pm. If the office is closed, pull the rope. 2- to 10-bunk dorms and singles €10. Cash only. ❶

Le Melchior, 397 av. Jean Jaurès (☎05 65 35 03 38; www.lemelchior.com). A pilgrim favorite. Family-run. Clean, comfortable rooms with baths. Reserve early for bargain singles. Breakfast €5.80. Reception daily 7am-10pm. Singles €35; doubles €43-50; triples and quads €60. Extra bed €8. MC/V. ❸

Camping Rivière de Cabessut, rue de la Rivière (☎05 65 30 06 30; www.cabessut. com). From pl. de la Libération, take the 2nd left onto rue Pelegry and turn right over the bridge. Turn left and walk along the water for 2km (35min.). Or take the free shuttle from the tourist office to Stade and walk 10min. along the river. Large, shaded sites. On-site bar, pool, and minigolf. Laundry. Reception 8am-10pm. Reserve ahead in summer. Open Apr.-Sept. €4 per person, children €2.50; sites €8. Electricity €2. Cash only. ❶

🍴 FOOD

Open-air markets on **place Chapou** (W and Sa 8am-noon) and **Les Halles** (Tu-Sa 8am-12:30pm and 3-7pm, Su 9am-noon) offer fresh produce, local wine, Cabécou cheese, and a friendly atmosphere. The first and third Saturdays of the month, a fair takes over **place François Mitterrand**. A **Casino** supermarket is on pl. Imbert, near the tourist office. (Open July-Aug. M-Sa 9am-12:30pm and 3-7:30pm, Su 9am-12:30pm; Sept.-June M-Sa 9am-12:30pm and 3-7:30pm.)

Le Mephisto, 10 av. Jean Jaurès (☎05 65 53 00 77). Enthusiastic owner and hearty food ensure a warm welcome. *Menus* €9-18. Open M-Sa 7am-9pm. MC/V. ❷

Le Lamparo, pl. de la Halle (☎05 65 35 25 93), in the *cité médiévale*. Pizzas (€7.60-9.50), heaping plates of pasta (€7-8.90), and traditional French meat dishes on a sprawling terrace. *Menu* €12-22. Open M-Th 11:45am-2:15pm and 7-10:30pm, F-Sa 11:45am-2pm and 7-11:30pm. MC/V. ❸

👁 🎆 SIGHTS AND FESTIVALS

In mid-July, Cahors enjoys the four-day **Cahors Blues Festival**. Afternoon and evening blues "appetizers" in cafes and bars are free, while Wednesday and Friday concerts on pl. Bessieres are €20. (☎05 65 20 87 83; www.cahorsbluesfestival. com. Buy tickets online.) The **Festival de Saint-Céré** features classical music in Cahors from late July to mid-August. (☎05 65 38 28 08; www.festival-saint-cere. com. Buy tickets by phone or last-minute at the tourist office.)

PONT VALENTRÉ. This 14th-century structure, credited with staving off invaders during the 1580 siege of Cahors, is by far the city's most impressive sight. Legend has it that its architect, dismayed by construction delays, sold his soul to the devil with the promise that he could have any wish before dawn. He wished for the bridge to be finished and for the devil to bring him water in a strainer. The demon could not grant the second wish and turned to stone. Look carefully to see the devil clutching a corner of the central tower, a detail added by restoration architect Paul Gout. Hike up the trail on the other side of the bridge for a spectacular view of the city.

CATHÉDRALE SAINT-ÉTIENNE. This 12th-century cathedral offers a juxtaposition of Roman and Gothic styles. The structure is topped by two recently uncovered cupolas and boasts vividly restored medieval murals. St-Étienne often hosts classical concerts. (*Pl. Chapou.* ☎05 65 35 27 80. *Open daily 9am-7pm.*)

MUSÉE HENRI MARTIN. In addition to Cahors-themed temporary exhibits, this museum displays some earlier modern art, including Neo-Impressionist interpretations of Cahors by the Toulouse-born and locally renowned Henri Martin. *(792 rue Émile Zola. ☎ 05 65 20 88 66. Open M and W-Sa 11am-6pm, Su 2-6pm. €3, students, seniors, and ages 7-18 €1.50, under 6 free; 1st Su of the month free.)*

MUSÉE DE LA RÉSISTANCE, DE LA DÉPORTATION, ET DE LA LIBÉRATION DU LOT. Located in the former barracks of a military base, this museum recounts Cahors's role in WWII. Each of its three floors is dedicated to one of the name-sake themes. Do not miss the display of detainees' drawings and poems on the second floor. Info is available in English, but a grasp of French is required to fully appreciate the exhibits. *(Pl. Bessières. ☎ 05 65 22 14 25. Open daily 2-6pm. Free.)*

> **🌂TIP** **UNDER MY UMBRELLA (ELLA ELLA).** Umbrellas are surprisingly hard to come by in the rainy regions of Dordogne and Limousin. To avoid getting caught in the rain, always double check the weather forecast before heading out for the day. If you find yourself exploring the streets when the skies open up on you, don't duck into a pharmacy looking for salvation—unless you just want the shelter. Most area pharmacies don't sell umbrellas, but bag stores do. It might even be worth bringing a small umbrella from home to avoid the hassle of finding Louis Vuitton store in a shower.

SAINT-CIRQ-LAPOPIE ☎05 65

One of the most beautiful villages in France—as the sign outside town proudly proclaims—tiny St-Cirq-Lapopie (sehn-sehrk-lah-poh-pee; pop. 207), atop a cliff ledge, has streets so steep that the roof of one 13th-century house begins where its neighbor's garden ends. The beauty of the village attracted such painters as Henri Marin and André Breton, who apparently claimed he would not live anywhere else. St-Cirq was a young local martyr slaughtered in the Middle East during Crusades, while "Lapopie"—which means "nipple" in Old Breton—was first used to describe the suggestive form of the cliff on which the village was founded. Scandalous connotations aside, St-Cirq-Lapopie has been classified as a national historical monument; not a single new building ruins the skyline that the Surrealist Breton loved so deeply.

◪▨ TRANSPORTATION AND PRACTICAL INFORMATION. To get to St-Cirq-Lapopie by car, follow D653 out of Cahors and turn right onto D662 when you reach Vers. SNCF **buses** run past St-Cirq-Lapopie from Cahors on the way to Figeac (#16; 45min.; M-Sa 5 per day, Su 4 per day; €5.30). Get off at Tour de Faure. Walk in the direction from which the bus came, cross the bridge on the left, and hike uphill to town (30min.). The **tourist office**, pl. de Sombral, in the main square, offers walking **tours** in French and a list of hotel vacancies. (☎05 65 31 29 06. Open July-Aug. M-F 10am-1pm and 2-7pm, Sa-Su 10am-1pm and 2-6pm; Sept.-Oct. and Apr.-May daily 10am-1pm and 2-6pm; Nov.-Mar. and June M-Sa 2-6pm.) Kalapca Loisirs, near the campsite, offers **kayak** rental and books two- to six-day trips with camping or *gîte* packages. (☎05 65 30 29 51; www.kalapca.com. Canoes €5 per hr. Kayaks €7 per hr., €10-13 per ½-day. MC/V.)

▐◖ ACCOMMODATIONS AND FOOD. The best beds in St-Cirq are at the *gîte d'étape* and cultural center ▧**Maison de la Fourdonne ❶**, a restored 16th-century house with a stocked kitchenette and timbered common room containing a decorative stone fireplace. Three- to five-bed rooms all have baths; some have balconies. (☎/fax 05 65 31 21 51. Bring sheets. Reception from early Apr. to early Nov. 10:30am-12:30pm and 2:30-7pm. Reservations highly recommended

July-Aug. Open from mid-Mar. to mid-Nov. Dorms €13. Cash only.) **Auberge du Sombral ❹**, in front of the tourist office, offers elegant rooms with tasteful paintings. (☎05 65 31 26 08; fax 30 26 37. Breakfast €8. Singles with shower €50; doubles with shower €70, with bath €78; triples €88. MC/V.) Between the town and the bus stop, the riverside ◼**Camping de la Plage ❶** is close to a small beach as well as kayak and canoe sites. High bushes provide privacy for campers in this crowded site. (☎05 65 30 29 51; www.campingplage.com. Free Wi-Fi. €5 per person; sites €5-7. Electricity €4-5. MC/V.)

For a good meal, try **L'Atelier ❸**, just before the village on the main road into town. Traditional French *plats* are served in a shaded courtyard with a view of the valley. Don't hesitate to doodle on your place mat—generations of drawings are pinned to the walls. (☎05 65 31 22 34. Open Feb.-Dec. M and Th-Su noon-2pm and 7-9:30pm, Tu noon-2pm; hours are "elastic." MC/V.)

◪ **SIGHTS.** Though all of the village's archives were burned during the French Revolution, the cultural center, **Maison de la Fourdonne**, pieces together St-Cirq's rocky history. The center also hosts plays and concerts every Tuesday evening. (☎/fax 05 65 31 21 51. Open Apr.-Nov. Tu-Su 2:30-7pm. Guided tours Tu-Sa 11am or with reservation. Evening shows June-Sept. Tu. €1.50, students €1. Tours €4. Shows €3-5.) Stairs located behind the tourist office lead up to the highest point of the village: the ruins of **Château Lapopie**. Condemned to destruction in 1580 by Henri de Navarre, the castle had proved impervious to sieges for centuries. Today, it offers a stunning panorama of the valley.

POITOU-CHARENTES

Poitou-Charentes could be France's best-kept secret. Distinctly influenced by its proximity to the Atlantic Ocean, it is a brilliant collage of coastal fishing towns, wetland preserves, and untouched islands. The diverse landscapes of Île de Ré (p. 568) and Île d'Yeu (p. 578)—with pine forests, rolling meadows, and brilliantly white beaches—cater to curious cyclists, passionate history buffs, and topless tanners alike. Full of châteaux and medieval towns, the region also offers distinctly modern diversions. Today, though still marked by the vestiges of its intriguing past, La Rochelle (p. 560) welcomes party animals and leisure-seekers alike, with roaring festivals and succulent seafood. Those looking for a lighter side of the region head to the technologically advanced Futuroscope theme park (p. 547) and Angoulême (p. 549), the French capital of comic books. Stop by Les Sables d'Olonne (p. 575) for all manner of outdoor activities—or relax with the locals and go fishing or sunbathing. When all else fails, Cognac (p. 554) can always provide the means for a good time.

HIGHLIGHTS OF POITOU-CHARENTES

STUFF YOURSELF with boatloads of seafood in coastal La Rochelle (p. 560). Walk it off with a hike around the wild countryside of nearby Île de Ré (p. 568) or sleep it off with a nap on one of Ré's sunny beaches.

MARVEL at the region's unique natural beauty as you set off in a canoe from picturesque Coulon (p. 574) into the wetlands preserve of the Marais Poitevin.

INDULGE both your inner sophisticate and inner child with the liquor bouquets at distilleries in Cognac (p. 554) and the comic-spattered walls of Angoulême (p. 554).

POITIERS   ☎ 05 49

The magnificent churches of Poitiers (pwah-tee-ay; pop. 100,000) testify to the power Catholicism held over the city in the early Middle Ages. Though the church left behind a rich history, today these holy sites are probably the city's only magnificent features. In 1432, Charles VII founded the Université de Poitiers, and students now make up over 25% of the population. The city bustles with youngsters during the year but deflates entirely in summer, as fewer tourists pass by on their way to Futuroscope. This loud, polluted commercial metropolis is redeemed by its lively nightlife and cultural events.

▆ TRANSPORTATION

Trains: Bd. du Grand Cerf. Ticket office open M-Th and Sa 6am-9pm, F 6am-10pm, Su 7am-10:20pm. To: **Bordeaux** (2hr., 15 per day, €33); **La Rochelle** (1hr., 15 per day, €20-23); **Paris** (2hr., 20 per day, €48-61); **Tours** (1hr., 10 per day, €15-18).

Public Transportation: Vitalis, 9 av. de Northampton (☎05 49 44 66 88). Open M-F 8:30am-12:15pm and 2-5pm. **Buses** run throughout the city during the day; a night

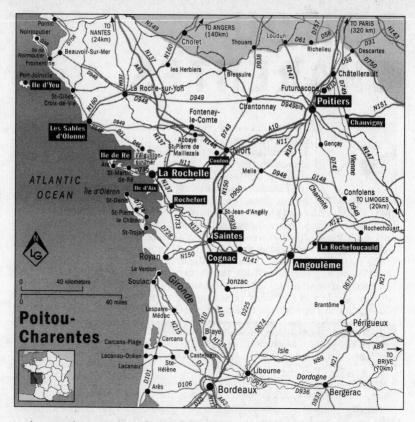

Poitou-Charentes

bus runs the same route infrequently 9pm-1:50am. Timetables are at the tourist office and train station. Buy individual tickets (valid for 1hr., €1.30) on board and carnets of 5 (€4.90, under 25 €4.40) at *tabacs* or at the office.

Taxis: Radio Taxis, 22 rue Carnot (☎05 49 88 12 34), wait outside the train station.

Car Rental: Avis, 133 bd. du Grand Cerf (☎05 49 58 13 00). Open M-F 8am-12:30pm and 1:30-7pm, Sa 1:30-5pm. AmEx/MC/V.

Bike Rental: Atelier Cyclaman, 60 bis bd. Pont Achard (☎05 49 88 13 25), 400m from the station. €9.50 per ½-day, €15 per day; ID deposit. Open Tu-F 9am-12:30pm and 3-7pm, Sa 9am-12:30pm and 2-7pm.

ORIENTATION AND PRACTICAL INFORMATION

Poitiers centers on **place Maréchal Leclerc, place Charles de Gaulle,** and the winding restaurant- and shop-filled streets between. Buses run from the stop opposite the train station to the **Hôtel de Ville** in pl. Maréchal Leclerc. The *centre-ville* and surrounding area are bordered by the rivers **Le Clain** and **La Boivre.**

! LET'S NOT GO. Though a bustling transport hub by day, Poitiers's train station and the poorly lit surrounding streets are best avoided after dark.

Tourist Office: 45 pl. Charles de Gaulle (☎05 49 41 21 24; www.ot-poitiers.fr). Ask for a free English-language walking guide, a guidebook with hiking and biking trail maps (€12), *Laissez-vous conter Poitiers*, a calendar of cultural events, and *Le guide des manifestations*—a free list of the seasons' concerts and shows. Open June 21-Sept. 21 M-Sa 10am-11pm, Su 10am-6pm and 7-10pm; Sept. 22-June 20 M-Sa 10am-6pm.

Tours: The tourist office offers tours in French (1-2hr.) July-Sept. daily 11am, 3pm; themed tours in summer. €5.50, ages 11-25 €4, under 10 free. Free night tours July-Aug. Sa-Su 9pm.

English-Language Bookstore: Librairie de l'Université, 70 rue Gambetta (☎05 49 41 02 05), off pl. du Maréchal Leclerc. Open M-Sa 9am-7:30pm. AmEx/MC/V.

Youth Center: Centre Regionale Information Jeunesse (CRIJ), 64 rue Gambetta (☎05 49 60 68 68), near pl. du Maréchal Leclerc. Helps with jobs, lodging, budget travel, and activity planning. Free Internet access for students. Open Tu-Sa 1-6pm.

Laundromat: Laverie, 180 Grande Rue. Wash €3.50 for 7.5kg, dry €0.50 per 5min. Open daily 8am-8pm.

Police: 38 rue de la Marne (☎05 49 60 60 00).

Hospital: 2 rue de la Miletrie (☎05 49 44 44 44), on the road to Limoges.

Internet Access: Free at CRIJ (above). **Virtual 86,** 21 rue Magenta (☎05 49 53 63 42). €2 per hr. Open M-Sa 10am-2am, Su noon-2am.

Post Office: 2 rue des Écossais (☎05 49 55 52 36). **Currency exchange** available. Open M-F 8:30am-7pm, Sa 8:30am-noon. **Postal Code:** 86000.

ACCOMMODATIONS AND CAMPING

The cheapest singles are located in the less pleasant area near the train station. Beware that nightfall heralds sketchiness; it is worth spending a few extra euro for a room in the *centre-ville*. Make sure not to travel alone after 10pm.

Auberge de Jeunesse (HI), 1 allée Tagault (☎05 49 30 09 70). From the train station, take bus #7 (dir.: Pierre Loti) to Bellejouanne or the Hôtel de Ville near pl. Leclerc (10min., M-Sa every 30min. until 7:50pm, €1.30). Dining area and pool table. Bright, old-fashioned rooms with sinks. Common bath in the hall. Breakfast €3.60. Internet €0.15 per min. Reception M-F 7am-noon and 4-11pm, Sa-Su 7am-noon and 6-11pm. Campsites €6. Dorms €13. AmEx/MC/V. ❶

Hôtel du Chapon Fin, pl. du Maréchal Leclerc (☎05 49 88 02 97; www.hotel-chaponfin. com), across from the Hôtel de Ville. Rooms with classy furniture overlook the square. Breakfast €6. Reception M-Sa 24hr., Su 7am-noon and 7-11pm. Singles and doubles with shower €36, with toilet €47, with bath €52. Extra bed €9. MC/V. ❸

Le Plat d'Étain, 7-9 rue de Plat d'Étain (☎05 49 41 04 80), off pl. du Maréchal Leclerc. Pleasant location. Welcoming staff. Breakfast €7.80. Free parking. Singles €29-30, with shower €45-48, with bath €53-61; doubles €31-32; triples €60-62. MC/V. ❷

Hôtel Central, 35 pl. du Maréchal Leclerc (☎05 49 01 79 79; www.centralhotel86. com). Simple, clean rooms with antique furniture. Top-floor balconies overlook the town's liveliest square. Breakfast €6.50. Singles and doubles with toilet and shower €45, with bath €53; triples €55-60. Extra bed €10. AmEx/MC/V. ❹

Camping du Porteau, rue du Porteau (☎05 49 41 44 88), 2km from town. Take bus #7 from the station (dir.: Centre de Gros) to Porteau (25min., M-F every 30min., €1.30). Small campground, used mostly by caravans, with brand-new IKEA-style facilities. Reception July-Aug. 7am-10pm; Sept. and from late May to June 7:30-11:30am and 2:30-7:30pm. €3 per person, children €2; sites €6. Electricity €3. MC/V. ❶

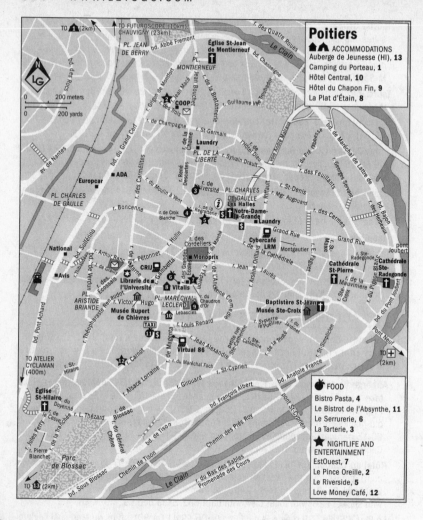

Poitiers

♟♟ ACCOMMODATIONS
Auberge de Jeunesse (HI), **13**
Camping du Porteau, **1**
Hôtel Central, **10**
Hôtel du Chapon Fin, **9**
La Plat d'Étain, **8**

🍎 FOOD
Bistro Pasta, **4**
Le Bistrot de l'Absynthe, **11**
Le Serrurerie, **6**
La Tarterie, **3**

⭐ NIGHTLIFE AND
ENTERTAINMENT
EstOuest, **7**
Le Pince Oreille, **2**
Le Riverside, **5**
Love Money Café, **12**

🍴 FOOD

In Poitiers, it's easy to find local specialties—from macaroons to goat cheese, from the wines of Haut-Poitou to lamb from nearby Montmorillon. The problem is finding a budget-friendly *menu;* most hover around €15-30. Many *brasseries* and hotel bars post adequate three-course *menus* for €12-13, and inexpensive pizzerias line the pedestrian streets between **place Leclerc** and **Notre-Dame-la-Grande** as well as the more student-frequented areas north of the cathedral. There are a few more student-friendly cafes near the conservatory, north of the tourist office around **place de la Liberté.** Most restaurants fill quickly at noon, as their best deals are during lunch. There's a market at **Les Halles,** pl. Charles de Gaulle, which expands to epic proportions on Saturdays (open Tu,

Th, Sa 7am-1pm), and a **Monoprix** supermarket at Ilot des Cordeliers on rue des Grandes Écoles (open M-F 9am-9pm, Sa 9am-8pm; AmEx/MC/V).

🔲 **La Serrurerie,** 28 rue des Grandes Écoles (☎05 49 41 05 14; www.laserrurerie.com). Busy restaurant by day, student bar by night. Quirky decor and a Beatles soundtrack. Generous portions and vegetarian options. Special weekend brunch specials Sa-Su 11:30am-3pm include dessert and wine (€10-15). *Omelettes* €6.80-8. *Plats* €6.50-15. Beer €2.50. Open M-F 8am-2am, Sa 9am-2am, Su 10am-2am. AmEx/MC/V. ❷

Le Bistrot de l'Absynthe, 36 rue Carnot (☎05 49 37 28 44). Will have you seeing green before you even take a shot of its namesake—you can't miss the bright green facade. Regulars enjoy upscale French favorites like *escargots* (€8), *foie gras de canard* (€11), and absinthe (€4.30). Lunch *menu* €7.50-9. Dinner *menus* €19-24. Open M-F noon-2pm and 7:30-10pm, Sa 7:30-10pm. MC/V. ❸

La Tarterie, 14 pl. Charles VII (☎05 49 47 56 93). Wild furniture, colorful lamps, and massive homemade *tartes* (€5.50-8.90) both sweet and savory. Karaoke. Lunch *menu* (€8.90) includes *tarte, salade,* dessert, and coffee. Open M-Sa noon-10pm. MC/V. ❷

Bistro Pasta, 1 bis rue de Croix Blanche (☎05 49 88 92 33). Owned by 3 Neapolitan brothers. Over 35 sauce varieties top hand-rolled pasta. Try the *paiglia e fieno* (cream sauce, ham, eggs, and paprika; €10). Pasta €8.50-15. Live folk music W nights. Open Tu-Th noon-2pm and 7-10:30pm, F-Sa noon-2pm and 7pm-midnight. MC/V. ❸

🄖 SIGHTS

Modern-day Poitiers is unfortunately noisy and polluted, its once-beautiful buildings crumbling and choked with soot. Yet the city remains a haven for church lovers; its religious monuments date from the AD fourth century and are its most impressive attractions. (Open daily 9am-6pm; frequent random closings. Free.) Many hold concerts in July and August; check the *Guide des Manifestations* or *Concerts d'Orgues à Poitiers* for more info.

◾**BAPTISTÈRE SAINT-JEAN.** This AD fourth-century baptistry, sunk 2.5m into the ground, is one of France's oldest Christian structures. Today, the Baptistère museum holds Roman, Merovingian, and Carolingian sarcophagi, which were uncovered during excavations beneath the church in the 50s. The relics were kept by early Christians when Gauls destroyed Poitiers's Roman baths, arches, and amphitheater. St-Jean's interior contains an AD fourth-century baptismal pool that looks like a modern-day hot tub and is surrounded by remarkably well-preserved 12th-century frescoes. *(Rue Jean Jaurès, near the cathedral. Open Apr.-Sept. M and W-Su 10:30am-12:30pm and 3-6pm; Oct.-Mar. M and W-Su 2:30-4:30pm. Informational English pamphlet (€0.50) available. €1.50, under 12 and group members €0.75.)*

◾**NOTRE-DAME-LA-GRANDE.** This small church is one of France's most celebrated structures. Biblical and historical scenes decorate its 12th-century Romanesque facade between exquisitely delicate moldings. Though the crypt is closed to the public, some people stick their arms through the bars of the small door on the right and feel around for potential light switches (on the left) in order to peek into its dank depths. Dim light filters through stained-glass windows, illuminating the church's meticulously painted columns. During the summer, ◾**polychromies** (light shows) project the original colors onto the facade, reviving the medieval splendor of the carvings; seven different light show themes rotate throughout the week. *(Pl. de Gaulle, off Grande Rue. Free 15min. projections daily from mid-June to Aug. 10:30pm; early Sept. 9:30pm.)*

CATHÉDRALE SAINT-PIERRE. In 1160, the construction of the high-arched St-Pierre was funded by Eleanor of Aquitaine and her husband King Henri II, who lived in the present Palais de Justice. The church's **Cliquot organ** (1787-91) is

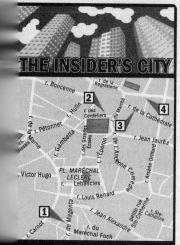

FORSAKEN MASTERPIECES

Poitiers brims with churches and medieval houses, but one of its better kept secrets is a more contemporary art form—graffiti.

1. The abstract images in the square off **rue Magenta**—free-floating teeth, burning cars, and crazed-looking men smoking cigarettes—look like something out of a Hunter S. Thompson book.

2. Check out the boutiques on **rue des Cordeliers**. A flowing sea of chocolate on Benoit Chocolaterie's storefront leaves you drooling for more. Landreau's jewelry shop is a canvas of beautiful women decked out in sparkling diamonds.

3. Head over to rue de la Cathédrale and gaze into the eyes of the menacing ghost face that hovers above. Below, a spaceship attempts a *coup* over the jungle with dunes in the background.

4. Slink into the alley off **Grand Rue** and stand before the door emblazoned with "Tropical Café." Consider the enigmatic object—is it an old Morse code machine? An ancient cash register?

one of only two that survived the Revolution and was the last instrument created under the Ancien Régime. Don't miss the towering angel at the top. The cryptic wood **carvings** that crown the stalls behind the choir are the church's hidden masterpieces. Deciphering them has been a challenge for centuries. *(Pl. de la Cathédrale, off rue de la Cathédrale.)*

ÉGLISE SAINTE-RADEGONDE. Legend has it that, in AD 587, Christ appeared to Radegondea—Thuringian princess and sister-in-law to Clovis—who then fled her violent husband Clothaire to found this very church. Christ predicted her death and allegedly told her she was the most beautiful jewel in his crown, which explains why his statue points to his head. Unfortunately, the crown was stolen in 2006, rendering the statue's head bare, and his gesture somewhat incomprehensible. Christ is said to have left a footprint in the stone floor before vanishing—a print that is still visible today. This church is an important pilgrimage destination—traditionally, pilgrims and believers crawled under Radegonde's tomb in the crypt for good luck. *(Off rue de la Mauvinière, down the street from the cathedral.)*

MUSÉE SAINTE-CROIX. This museum spans four millennia, its contemporary exterior housing everything from prehistoric artifacts to renderings of the plump naked ladies of the 18th century. In the basement is a Roman excavation site with the original walls and foundations of ancient homes. A stone representation of Minerva was found under one of the streets of modern-day Poitiers and is now on display with other Roman paraphernalia. The museum also holds a small sculpture from Rodin and works of his famous muse, Camille Claudel. *(3 bis rue Jean Jaurès. ☎ 05 49 41 07 53. Open June-Sept. M 1:15-6pm, Tu-F 10am-noon and 1:15-6pm, Sa-Su 2-6pm; Oct.-May M 1:15-5pm, Tu 10am-5pm, W-F 10am-noon and 1:15-5pm, Sa-Su 2-6pm. Free guided tours in French only Tu 6-7pm. €3.70, students and under 18 free, groups of 10 or more €2.70,; Tu and 1st Su of the month free. Admission includes entrance to the Musée Rupert de Chièvres.)*

OTHER SIGHTS. Often overlooked, the 11th-century Gothic **Église Saint-Jean de Montierneuf** was originally constructed by the count of Poitiers to purge his sins—which must have been grave indeed to necessitate such a grand building. The church contains some of the city's most striking stained glass. *(To the right of Pl. Montierneuf from the centre-ville.)* Behind skillfully sculpted wood doors, the **Musée Rupert de Chièvres** displays a collection of Dutch and Flemish works, French portraits, and Italian paintings. The portrait of an ecstatic (read: orgasmic) Ste-Madeleine, by Louis Finson, is tucked away at the end of the collection. *(9 rue Victor Hugo. ☎05 49 41 42 21. Open June-Sept. M 1:15-6pm, Tu and F 10am-noon and 1:15-6pm, Th 10am-noon and 1:15-9pm, Sa-Su 10am-noon and 2-6pm; Oct.-May M 1:15-5pm, Tu-F 10am-noon and 1:15-5pm, Sa-Su 2-6pm. €3.70, students and under 18 free; Tu, 1st Su of the month, and June-Sept. free. Admission includes entrance to the Musée St-Croix.)*

🎵 🎭 ENTERTAINMENT AND NIGHTLIFE

In summer, **passeurs d'images** (open-air cinemas) show free films in neighborhoods throughout Poitiers. (☎05 49 44 12 48. July 10:30pm; Aug. 10pm; Sept. 9:30pm.) Nightlife in Poitiers is rowdy during the school year, when students head to pubs and restaurants along the side streets of **place du Maréchal Leclerc.** In summer, a lot of venues close as students leave town. *Café-Concert: Bars avec Animations*, available at the tourist office, lists the city's bars and clubs.

🏅 **Le Pince Oreille,** 11 rue des 3 Rois (☎05 49 60 25 99; www.lepince-oreille.com). Putting its stage to good use, Le Pince hosts a variety of jazz, rock, and reggae bands as well as "open" jam sessions—although you may want to think twice before taking on local music conservatory students. Plush chairs, soft lighting, and a constant stream of cheap beer promotes harmony without pretension. Beer €2.50. Mixed drinks €5-7. Free jam sessions Tu-Th, concerts F-Sa; both at 10:30pm. Open Tu-Sa 5pm-2am. MC/V.

EstOuest, 10 rue l'Éperon (☎05 49 41 13 36). Crowded 2-story pub with a young clientele, popular Francophone music, and pool tables. Vodka Malabar (€2) comes with a plop of popular French bubble gum. Beer from €2.10. Mixed drinks €5.50. Karaoke F midnight. Open M-F 11am-2am, Sa 2:30pm-2am, Su 9pm-2am. AmEx/MC/V.

Le Riverside, 18 ter rue de la Regratterie (☎05 49 41 76 36). Classy gay bar tucked away in a small courtyard near Notre-Dame. For those tired of loud student drinking holes. Massive jugs of Bacardi and vodka cling to the wall behind the bar. Beer €2.40. Homemade punch €2.10. Open M-Sa 11am-2am. MC/V.

Love Money Cafe, 82 rue Carnot, (41 04 33, www.lovemoneycafe.fr). Serves *croquemonsieurs* (€4.40) and other delectable sandwiches (€2.90) and keeps the beer (€1.20) flowing for a young, student crowd on one of the liveliest streets in Poitiers. Perfect start to a night out. Open M-F 7:30am-2pm and 4:30-9pm. Cash only.

✴ FESTIVALS

Les Nuits en Musique, from late June to Aug. Held in the Notre-Dame-La-Grande. Free performances range from period Renaissance songs to world music. Concerts F at 9:30pm. Contact tourist office for more info.

Les Concerts Allumés (☎05 49 03 18 98), in late Sept. A series of light-show concerts throughout the city seeks to unite classical music with imaginative lighting in churches and cathedrals. Tickets €3.50-12.

Rencontres Internationales Henri Langlois (☎05 49 03 18 90; www.rihl.org), in early Dec. Independent screenings popular with international film students. €3 per film.

🎟 DAYTRIPS FROM POITIERS

🎢 FUTUROSCOPE

10km north of Poitiers, near Chasseneuil. Take bus #9 (30min.; M-F every 20min., Sa every 30min., last bus 7:52pm, €1.40) or line E on Su (30min.; 3 per day; last bus 6:43pm) from Poitiers's Hôtel de Ville (Marne) stop or across from the train station. Schedules subject to change. Get off at Parc du Futuroscope and follow directions to the park entrance. By car, follow A10 (dir.: Paris-Châtellerault) to Exit 28. The park is also accessible by TGV from Bordeaux (2hr., 1-2 per day, €36) and Paris (1hr., 2-3 per day, €45). ☎05 49 49 30 08; www.futuro-

scope.com. Open Feb.-Dec. daily 10am-sunset. €33, ages 5-16 €25, under 5 free. All main attractions included in the price except the video games on Cyber Avenue and the Les Yeux Grands Fermés attractions (€5).

Futuroscope is a fun, though somewhat overwhelming, collection of spectacular architecture, high-tech film theaters, virtual reality, and high-definition 3D simulation rides. **La Cité de Numérique** overflows with the latest Xbox 360™ games for visitors—more accurately, teenage boys—to play on plasma screens. IMAX movies take visitors on sappily narrated journeys from the bottom of the ocean to the tops of untouched mountains. Some of the attractions have moving seats, which coordinate with the on-screen adventures to throw you into the action. The toboggan ride down the side of an "erupting" volcano is especially popular with kids. **Les Yeux Grands Fermés** offers tours in French led by blind guides through a pitch-black world, offering visitors a glimpse of life without sight. A portion of the proceeds benefits an association for the visually impaired. A free headset from the Maison de Vienne near the entrance provides the English translation for many films. Hotels and restaurants are in close proximity to the park for those who are enticed to stay longer (after the last bus departs) for the late-night laser show, with images projected onto water and synchronized with music and fireworks.

CHAUVIGNY

SNCF buses leave Poitiers for Chauvigny (dir.: Châteauroux; 30min.; M-Sa 6 per day, Su 4:52, 9:20pm; €4.60). Buy tickets at the SNCF train station in Poitiers. The bus will stop at pl. de la Poste in Chauvigny's modern center. The cité médiévale, encompassing the castle ruins, lies up the hill. To get there, walk back on rue du Marché in the direction the bus came from, turning right onto rue du Petit Pont after the Hôtel de Ville. At the end of the street, turn right and take a left onto rue Poulizard, which leads to the stairs to the cité. The tourist office is on rue St-Pierre, across from the bishop's palace ruins. ☎ 05 49 46 39 01. Open July-Aug. daily 10am-1pm and 2-7pm; Sept. and June Tu-Su 10am-12:30pm and 2-6:30pm; Oct. and Apr.-May Tu-Su 2-6pm, Sa 9am-noon; Nov.-Mar. Tu-F 2-6:30pm, Sa 9am-noon. July-Aug. tours several times per week; €3.10. Call ☎ 05 49 46 35 45 for schedule and to book tours in English.

Chauvigny (shoh-vee-nyee), 23km from Poitiers on N151, boasts a *cité médiévale* unlike any other in Europe: a striking skyline of five 11th- to 13th-century fortresses lines its single outer wall. Among these lies the 12th-century **Collégiale Saint-Pierre,** a bright and perhaps excessively restored church, complete with modern light switches and soft colors. Its renowned column heads engraved with nightmarish figures such as lion-headed dragons, vultures eating naked men, a Babylonian prostitute, and a grinning Satan. Marrying the medieval with the modern, the **Espace d'Archéologie Industrielle** showcases exhibits in its ingenious interior design, the remains of the Gouzon dungeon. Featuring displays about regional quarrying, porcelain-firing, milling, and steam-engine activity, the museum transports its visitors from level to level in a glass elevator; the last stop yields a spectacular 360° view of the city and countryside below. All explanations are in French. (☎05 49 46 35 45. Open from mid-June to Aug. M-F 10am-12:30pm and 2:30-6:30pm, Sa 2:30-6:30pm, Su 11am-6:30pm; Sept.-Oct. and from May to mid-June daily 2-6pm. French tours available; call ahead for a schedule. €4.50, students €3.10, under 14 free. MC/V.) The imposing—though crumbling—walls of the old bishop's palace are now home to **Les Géants du Ciel,** a show that boasts 60 eagles, falcons, vultures, Arctic owls, African storks, and other birds. The highlight of the show is when the flock swoops over the city, just above the heads of the audience. (☎05 49 46 47 48. Open daily July-Aug. 10am-noon and 2-7pm; Sept. and Apr.-June 2-7pm. Shows daily July-Aug. daily 11am, 3, 5pm; Sept. M-F 3pm, Sa-Su 3, 5pm; Apr.-June daily 3, 5pm. €8.50, ages 4-10 €5.50.) A 30min. walk from pl. du Marché, **Saint-Pierre-les-Églises** houses some of Occidental Christianity's oldest frescoes, dated from the eighth to 10th centuries. A large cemetery sits on its remote riverside site. From pl. du Marché, walk down rue du Marché in the direction of Poitiers and take a left onto D749 at the roundabout. Continue straight past the bridge and through the next roundabout; the church is down a small road on the right. (Open July-Aug. daily; Sept.-June call tourist office for reservations.)

To play train conductor for a day, take a ride on **Vélo-Rails,** 10 rue de la Folie. These pedal-powered rail contraptions take passengers on a demanding 17km loop around the Chauvigny valley, along the viaduct that traverses the Vienne River. Reservations must be made at least one day ahead. To get there from pl. de la Poste, walk down rue du Marché, cross the Vienne River, and continue straight as the road becomes rue de Poitiers. After reaching rue de la Verrerie, turn right, then left onto rue de la Folie. (☎05 49 41 08 28. Open daily July-Aug. 10am-7pm, departures 10:30am, 2:30, 7:30pm; Sept.-Oct. and Apr.-June 2-6pm, departure 2:30pm. 2hr. €27 for 2 adults and 1 child.)

In July and August, the **Festival d'Été** fills the city with (occasionally free) concerts, theater, and street performances. Great for families, the Caribbean-themed **Festival Caraïbes Ô** brings reggae and island food in mid-July. The festival offers beach volleyball, dancing, concerts, and vendors. (Call the tourist office for more info; www.festivalcaraibes-o.net. €15 for both festivals.)

ANGOULÊME   ☎05 45

Unmarred by tourist hordes, Angoulême (ahn-goo-lem; pop. 46,000) sits high atop a plateau overlooking the Charente River. Host to missionaries led by John Calvin on a quest to purify Europe by spreading "predestination" in the early 1530s, the city's modern-day celebrities have more lighthearted aims: they're all comic book characters. A fantastic world seems to pounce from comic-book strips right onto the city's hodgepodge architecture and jumbled stone houses. Angoulême will leave weary travelers with a fresh bout of serious fun.

◪ TRANSPORTATION

Trains: Pl. de la Gare. Info office open M-F 7am-1pm and 2:30-8:30pm, Sa-Su 2:30-8:30pm. Ticket windows open M-F 5:40am-8:50pm, Sa 6:40am-8pm, Su 7:40am-9:30pm. To: **Bordeaux** (1hr., 8 per day, €17-25); **Paris** (3hr., 6 per day, €50-65); **Poitiers** (45min.; 10 per day; €10-20, TGV €20); **Saintes** (1hr., 8 per day, €8-15).

Buses: Autobus Citram (☎05 45 95 95 99). Open from mid-July to mid-Aug. M-F 2-6:15pm; from mid-Aug. to mid-July M-F 9:15am-12:15pm and 2-6:15pm. To **Cognac** (1hr., 8 per day, €8.50) and **La Rochelle** (3hr., 2 per day, €18). Buy tickets on board. CFTA Périgord (☎05 53 08 43 13) runs from the train station to **Périgueux** (1hr.; 1 per day M-W, F, Su, and 2nd Th of the month; €14).

Public Transportation: STGA, pl. Bouillaud (☎05 45 65 25 25). Open the 6th-27th of each month M-F 1:15-6pm, Sa 8:45am-12:15pm; the 1st-5th and 28th-31st of each month M-Sa 8:45am-12:15pm and 1:30-6pm. **Buses** run M-Sa 6am-8pm to many of the museums. Tickets €1.30, carnets of 10 €9.10; week pass €11.

Taxis: Radio Taxi (☎05 45 95 55 55), in front of train station.

Car Rental: Europcar, 15 pl. de la Gare (☎05 45 92 02 02). Cars can be returned to other locations throughout France. From €59 per day. 21+. under-25 surcharge €33. 10% student discount on vans only. Open M 8am-noon and 2:30-6:30pm, Tu-F 9am-noon and 2:30-6:30pm, Sa 9am-noon and 2:30-5pm. **ADA,** 19 pl. de la Gare

(☎05 45 92 65 29), across from the station. From €45 per day. Open M-F 8am-noon and 2-7pm, Sa 8am-noon and 2-5pm.

ORIENTATION AND PRACTICAL INFORMATION

Angoulême's *vieille ville* sits encircled by ramparts just south of the Charente River and southwest of the train station. The bustling **rue Hergé**, lined with modern boutiques and swarmed with locals, leads to the *vieille ville* on the south side by the Palais de Justice. It's easy to get lost in its maze of steep streets, which are often on different planes of elevation; check the map outside of the train station before launching yourself into comic book land.

Tourist Office: 7 bis rue du Chat (☎05 45 95 16 84; www.angouleme-tourisme.com), in pl. des Halles. From the train station, follow av. Gambetta right and uphill to pl. Gérard Pérot, and continue up the rampe d'Aguesseau. Turn right up steep bd. Pasteur. Keep close to the rail overlooking the valley; the office is across from the market building. Multilingual staff helps book hotels. Rock-climbing, fishing, and canoeing info. Open July-Aug. M-F 9:30am-7pm, Sa 10am-7pm, Su 10am-1pm and 2-5pm; Sept.-June M-F 9am-12:30pm and 1:30-6pm, Sa 10am-noon and 2-5pm.

Tours: Day and night tours offered through the Hôtel de Ville's **Via Patrimoine** (☎05 45 38 70 79; www.patrimoine-charente.com). Open M-F 9am-noon and 2-6pm. Enter the main gates of Hôtel de Ville and cross the courtyard; the office is on the left. 2hr. daytrips (1hr. tour of the old Château Comtal, 1hr. tour of the *vieille ville*) leave July-Aug. daily 4pm; Sept.-Oct. and Apr.-June Sa-Su 3pm; Nov.-Mar. 3pm on select weekends. Both tours €5, students and ages 12-18 €3.50, under 12 free; 1 tour €4/2.50/free. English-speaking guides are available; call ahead.

Budget Travel: Voyages Wasteels, 2 pl. Francis Louvel (☎05 45 92 21 45). Open M-F 10am-noon and 2-5pm, Sa 10am-12:30pm.

Banks: Banque de France, 1 rue du Général Leclerc (☎05 45 97 60 00), on pl. de l'Hôtel de Ville. Open M-F 8:40am-noon and 1:30-3:30pm.

Youth Center: Centre Information Jeunesse (CIJ), 1 bd. Berthelot (☎05 45 37 07 30; www.info-jeunesse16.com), inside the Espace Franquin building. Internet €0.75

per 15min., €2 per hr. Open from mid-July to Aug. Tu-F 10am-12:30pm and 2-6pm, Sa 2-6pm; from Sept. to mid-July Tu-F 10am-6pm, Sa 2-6pm.

Laundromat: Lavomatique, 3 rue Louis Trarieux, in the heart of the *vieille ville.* Wash €3.50-7, dry €0.50 per 5min. Open daily 7am-9pm.

Police: Pl. du Champs de Mars (☎05 45 39 38 37), next to the post office. Call here for the **pharmacie de garde.**

Hospital: Hôpital de Girac, route de Bordeaux (☎05 45 24 40 40). Take bus #1 (dir.: La Couronne Galands) or 8 (dir.: Nersac Les Epinettes) from the Hôtel de Ville or pl. du Champ de Mars to Girac and follow the signs.

Internet Access: CIJ (above). **Musée de la Bande Dessinée** (next page). Offers access with museum admission or for €2 per hr. **Espace Culture Multimédia** (☎05 45 37 07 32), below the youth center, in the basement of the Espace Franquin building. Up to 2hr. free. Open Tu-W 9am-noon and 2-6pm, Th-Sa 2-6pm.

Post Office: Pl. du Champs de Mars (☎05 45 66 66 00; fax 66 66 17). Branch at pl. Francis Louvel (☎05 45 90 14 30), near Palais de Justice. Both offer **currency exchange.** Both open M-F 8am-6:30pm, Sa 8:30am-noon. **Postal Code:** 16000.

ACCOMMODATIONS

Cheap hotels cluster near the intersection of **avenue Gambetta** and the pedestrian district, which is in the southeastern corner of the *vieille ville.*

Hôtel Saint Martial, 6 bd. Pasteur (☎06 64 38 61 41). The huge blue mural of women staring out onto the Charentes valley that graces the south side of the old building is one of the city's largest comic art pieces. Some rooms have river views. Location can't be beat. Breakfast €5. Free parking. Rooms €30-35. Cash only. ❷

Hôtel d'Orléans, 133 av. Gambetta (☎05 45 95 07 53), across from the train station. Clean, color-coordinated rooms with showers, toilets, and TVs. Lounge and bar. Breakfast €5. Reception 6:30am-10pm. Singles and doubles €39. Extra bed €6. MC/V. ❷

Auberge de Jeunesse (HI), Île de Bourgines (☎05 45 92 45 80; angouleme@fuaj.org), in the Charente. A hike from the *centre-ville.* From the train station, turn right on av. Gambetta and take the 1st right on rue Denis Papin. Cross the railroad tracks and veer left. Take a right on rue de Paris, then a left onto rue Lamaud; pass the church and turn right along the Charente. A footbridge leads onto the island; the hostel is on the left (30min.). By bus, turn right onto av. Gambetta from the train station; the stop is on the left, right after the intersection with bd. de la République. Take bus #7 (dir.: Le Treuil, last bus 8pm, €1.20) to St-Antoine, then take a left along the water. Cross the footbridge and take a left. Large, worn 2-bed rooms with river views. Hosts mainly short-term workers but fills with young international visitors during festivals. Kitchen. Breakfast €3.50. Bike rental available. Reception M-F 8:30am-noon and 5-9pm, Sa-Su by appointment only. Lockout noon-5pm. Dorms €12. MC/V. ❶

FOOD

Pricey restaurants throughout the *vieille ville* feature the local specialty, **cagouilles à la charentaise** (garlic and parsley snails with sausage, smoked ham, and spices), while the flower-shaped *marguerite chocolate*—named for François I's sister, Marguerite de Valois—as well as *cornuelle* (a triangular cake), can be found in all *pâtisseries.* Bars, cafes, and *boulangeries* line **rue de Saint-Martial** and **rue Marengo,** but more inventive eateries crowd the narrow streets of the quadrant formed by **Les Halles, place du Palet, Église Saint-André,** and the **Hôtel de Ville.** The market on **place des Halles,** down rue du Général de Gaulle from the Hôtel de Ville, sells the town's freshest produce. (Open daily

7:30am-1pm.) There's a **Champion** supermarket, 19 rue Goscinny, by the Champ de Mars. (Open M-Sa 8:30am-7:30pm, Su 9-11:45am. MC/V.)

Le Chat Noir, pl. des Halles (☎05 45 95 26 27). Serves seafood salads (€7.50), *crêpes* (€2-4), and bruschetta (€7) on a shaded terrace. Open M-Sa 7:30am-2am. MC/V. ❶

Le Passe-Muraille, 5 rue Ste-Andre (☎05 45 38 61 62). Intimate restaurant with just 8 tables. Daily menu features all things *charentaise*. Try the huge variety plate with eggs, cheese, and *foie gras* (€8). *Foie gras* risotto (€18) and *lasagne canard* (duck lasagna; €15) are also worth a try. Open M-Sa noon-2pm and 5-10pm. AmEx/MC/V. ❸

La Plancha, 20 pl. du Palet (☎05 45 95 29 06). Cozy interior with retro white leather stools and wine barrel tables. Try the house specialty, *tartiflette (*potatoes in cheese fondue and white wine; €15). *Menu* €15. Open M-F noon-2pm and 5-9pm. MC/V. ❸

Le Scoopitone, 33 rue de Genève (☎05 45 38 10 21). Family-run. Famous for brick-oven pizza (€5-8.50). The Anthonio (with tomato, cheese, smoked salmon; €8) is a must-try. *Menus* €11-18. Open daily noon-2:30pm and 6-10pm. MC/V. ❸

👁 ⚑ SIGHTS AND OUTDOOR ACTIVITIES

▨MUSÉE DE LA BANDE DESSINÉE. This museum pays tribute to Angoulême's leading role in the development of *la bande dessinée* (the comic strip). Enter the comic-book realm—complete with giant cardboard characters and cartoon buildings—where exhibits feature French and international cartoons from the 19th and 20th centuries, including favorites like Tintin, Astérix, and Popeye. Free audio tours in a variety of languages enhance pictorial displays. The center also holds a comic-book library and bookstore as well as the art-house cinema **Salle Nemo,** which screens international indie films (€7, students €5); ask at the museum for times. *(121 rue de Bordeaux. Currently undergoing renovations and expected to re-open in 2009 across the river from the Centre Nationale de la Bande Dessinée et de l'Image (CNBDI). From pl. du Champ de Mars and pl. de l'Hôtel de Ville, take bus #3 or 5 to Nil-CNBDI or walk along the ramparts, following the signs (10min.). ☎05 45 38 65 65; www.cnbdi.fr. Open July-Aug. Tu-W and F 10am-6pm, Th 10am-7pm, Sa-Su 2-6pm; Sept.-June Tu-W and F noon-6pm, Th noon-7pm, Sa-Su 2-6pm. €6, students €4.50.)*

MUSÉE DE LA RÉSISTANCE ET DE LA DÉPORTATION. Once home to religious reformer John Calvin, this museum chronicles Angoulême's Resistance during WWII. On the ground floor, a letter from a young Resistance fighter to his mother on the eve of his execution is just a warm-up; horrifying photographs on the second floor document the life and death of the 1180 Jews from the Charente region. Exhibits are in French, with some English explanations. *(34 rue de Genève. ☎05 45 38 76 87. Open M-F July-Aug. 9am-noon and 2-6pm; Sept.-June 2-6pm or by appointment. €2.50, students €1.50, under 16 free.)*

CATHÉDRALE SAINT-PIERRE. The elegant 12th-century cathedral of Angoulême adheres to the Romanesque style, but for one main element: internal columns were omitted to create an uninterrupted view of the interior. The edifice exerted considerable architectural influence during the height of religious power, not only on other diocesan churches but also on more distant buildings like the Loire's Fontevraud and Poitiers's Notre-Dame-la-Grande. In the northern wing lies a recently canonized 19th-century saint, who was murdered during a mission in Korea. *(Pl. St-Pierre. ☎05 45 95 20 38. Open daily 9am-6pm.)*

ÉGLISE SAINT-ANDRÉ. The 12th-century church, initially built in Romanesque style, was reworked in a Gothic design, leaving only the front vestibule of the original work. Today, it holds paintings from the 16th to 19th centuries, a massive altarpiece, and a superb Baroque pulpit made of oak. The facade was redone in the early 19th century and hides the church's magnitude surprisingly well. *(8 rue Taillefer, near pl. Louvet in the vieille ville. Open daily 9am-7pm.)*

OTHER SIGHTS. Childhood heroes such as Lucky Luke and Gaston Lagaffe greet passersby from the *vieille ville*'s windows and murals; a stroll through the streets will acquaint visitors with many a French comic-book celeb. The city's quiet ramparts and green riverside areas complement the relaxed pace. At the bottom of av. du Président Wilson, beneath the park's meandering paths, *cascades* (waterfalls) flow in the **Jardin Vert,** a great place to unwind among unruly grass and trees. The AD fourth-century ramparts that surround the town provide a view of red-roofed houses. To find out about hiking opportunities, call **Randonnée en Charentes,** 22 bd. de Bury. *(☎05 45 38 94 48. Open M-F 9am-noon and 1:30-5:30pm, Sa 10am-noon.)* For water-skiing, call **CAM's.** *(☎05 45 92 76 22. 15min. session €28, ages 10-17 €25, under 9 €17. Open July-Aug. daily 1-8pm.)*

◀ NIGHTLIFE

During the day, the modern **rue Hergé,** lined with brand-name shops and fast-food eateries, is packed with locals, but as the sun sets the crowd moves toward the cafes on **rue Massillon** and **place des Halles.** In the *vieille ville,* **avenue Gambetta** comes alive with bars and restaurants.

- ▨ **Le Bistroc,** 19 rue Raymond Audour (☎05 45 94 22 20). Cartoon characters painted in the windows welcome a fun-loving clientele. *Foie gras canard* €7.50. Cognac, wine, and specialty whiskeys start at €3. Open daily noon-2pm and 8-11:45pm. MC/V.

  The Kennedy, 3 rue de Beaulieu (☎05 45 94 12 41). This rowdy Irish pub isn't afraid to show its pride—giant tucans adorning the gates welcome visitors with, "It's a lovely day for a Guinness." Beer €3. Open Tu-Sa 5pm-2am. Cash only.

  Blues Rock Café, 19 rue de Genève (☎05 45 94 05 98), on pl. des Halles. Lives up to its name with its decor (guitars nailed to the wall) but not its music (mostly pop). Beer €3. Live music Th in summer. Happy hour daily 6:30-9pm with ½-price drinks. Open Apr.-Oct. daily 10am-2am; Nov.-Mar. M-Sa 10am-2am. AmEx/MC/V.

  Cinq Sens, 14 rue Massillon (☎05 45 95 34 24). Hip 20-somethings crowd this bar where everything is "it"—from the modern art on walls to the designer jeans on the clientele. Beer €2-4. Hard liquor €3.20-8. Open Tu-Sa noon-2am. MC/V.

❋ FESTIVALS

Salon International de la Bande-Dessinée (☎05 45 97 86 50; www.bdangouleme. com), last weekend in Jan. Over 200,000 visitors spend 4 days meeting artists, discovering new installments, and admiring comic-strip exhibits throughout town. For tickets, visit the tourist office or www.ticketnet.fr.

Festival Musiques Métisses, 6 rue du Point-du-Jour (☎05 45 95 43 42), mid-June. Live *chaud* music (from south of the equator). Tourist office sells tickets. €20-40 per night.

Jeudi Jeux de Rue, in July and Aug. Open-air theater festival performances and films Th evenings in in the *vieille ville.* Call the tourist office for info. Free.

Circuit des Remparts, 2 rue Fontgrave (☎05 45 94 95 67; www.circuit-des-remparts. com), in mid-Sept. Antique car races and exhibitions in the *centre-ville.* €12.

Piano en Valois (☎05 45 92 11 11), in Oct.-Nov. International pianists participate in 2-week-long installments of concerts. €12-28.

Gastronomades (☎05 45 67 39 30), in mid-Nov. Free cooking lessons and tastings.

Ludoland (☎05 45 21 29 02; www.ludoland.fr), in mid-Nov. Children's festival with the newest toys and video games. €10 per day, under 18 €5.

◪ DAYTRIPS FROM ANGOULÊME

LA ROCHEFOUCAULD

Reach La Rochefoucauld by train (30min.; M-Sa 3 per day, Su 2 per day; €5.40). From behind the station, cross the parking lot and go halfway around the roundabout to the right. Continue 4 blocks through the centre-ville. The château is straight ahead (8min.). The tourist office is at 1 rue des Tanneurs (☎05 45 63 07 45). Open June-Sept. daily 10am-1pm and 3-7pm; Oct.-May M-Sa 9:30am-12:30pm and 2-6pm.

La Rochefoucauld (lah rohsh-foo-koh) has been home to over 43 generations of the aristocratic Foucauld family, members of which included an archbishop and the founder of Caisse d'Épargne (one of France's major banks). The present château, known as the "pearl of Angoumois" and a favorite for wedding pictures, owes most of its elegance to Anne de Polignac, wife of Duke Francis II de Foucauld, who added a Renaissance wing and an elegant chapel to the medieval fortress in 1520. Indeed, the castle seems to have been plucked from the Loire Valley and plopped into the heart of Charente. The magnificent central spiral staircase is said to have been designed by Leonardo da Vinci. On the top floor, visitors can try on colorful costumes that span over six centuries of fashion. **Foucauld de La Roche** (the rock of Foucauld)—the town's namesake, a stone above the banks of the Tardoire River upon which the original fortress was founded—can be explored by descending into the dark and damp caverns underneath the castle, through the second guardroom. (☎05 45 62 07 42. Open Apr.-Dec. M and W-Su 10am-7pm; Jan.-Mar. Su 2-7pm. English tours available. €8, ages 4-12 €4.) Other highlights at the foot of the castle include a well-preserved 14th-century cloister, **Le Couvent des Carmes,** and a church with an impressive and deeply colored stained-glass window, which dates from 1266.

COGNAC   ☎05 45

Cognac (coh-nyack; pop. 20,000) was a sleepy village until the invention of double distillation in the 16th century. French law states that only crops produced in the Cognac region may become the brandy that bears its name. Today, Cognac's main attractions are still its distilleries, which offer tours and tastings; the town returns to its past drowsiness as soon as the *caves* close.

◪◪ TRANSPORTATION AND PRACTICAL INFORMATION

Trains: To **Angoulême** (40min., 5 per day, €9) and **Saintes** (20min., 6 per day, €3-5).

Tourist Office: 16 rue du 14 Juillet (☎05 45 82 10 71; www.tourism-cognac.com). From the station, follow av. du Maréchal Leclerc to the 1st roundabout and take a right. Follow signs to the *centre-ville.* Turn right on rue Bayard and cross pl. Bayard onto rue du 14 Juillet (15min.). 4 *Sentiers de Randonnées* maps available (€2.30 each, €9.20 for all 4). Offers **tours** of a local barrel-making factory. Open July-Aug. M-Sa 9am-7pm, Su 10am-4pm; Sept. and May-June M-Sa 9:30am-5:30pm; Oct.-Apr. M-Sa 10am-5pm.

Banks: CIC Banque, 36 bd. Denfert-Rochereau (☎05 45 36 84 84). 24hr. **ATM.** Open Tu-F 8:45am-12:30pm and 1:45-6pm, Sa 8:45am-12:30pm.

Youth Center: Bureau Information Jeunesse (BIJ), 53 rue Angoulême (☎05 45 82 62 00). Info on jobs, vacations, and housing for young people. Internet €0.90 per 30min., €1.60 per hr. Open M-F 10am-noon and 2-6pm.

Police: 68 bd. Denfert-Rochereau (☎05 45 82 38 48).

Hospital: Rue Montesquieu (☎05 45 36 75 75).

Post Office: 2 pl. Bayard (☎05 45 36 31 70). Open M-F 8am-6pm, Sa 8am-noon. **Postal Code:** 16100.

ACCOMMODATIONS AND CAMPING

Oliveraie, 6-8 pl. de la Gare (☎05 45 82 04 15; www.oliveraie-cognac.com), across from the train station. Nestled under a shady arboretum. Immaculately clean, spacious rooms for the city's best prices. Rooms have TVs, bath, and phones; some have A/C. Discounts for the Hennessy distillery. Breakfast €6.50. Wheelchair-accessible. Reservations recommended. Singles €44; doubles €49; triples €58. Extra bed €8. MC/V. ❸

Le Cheval Blanc, 6 pl. Bayard (☎05 45 82 09 55; www.hotel-chevalblanc.fr), across from the tourist office. Small, newly renovated rooms with A/C, bath, and TVs. Breakfast €7. Free Wi-Fi. Reception M-Sa 7am-12:30pm and 3-10pm, Su 8am-12:30pm and 5-10pm. Singles €46; doubles €52; triples €58; quads €65. AmEx/MC/V. ❹

Cognac Camping, bd. de Châtenay (☎05 45 32 13 32; www.campingdecognac.fr), past Parc François 1er, a 30min. walk from town on D24. In summer, bus lines A-C run here from pl. François I (15min., 2 per day, €1.20); get off at Camping. Well-kept sites with ample foliage, a pool, and laundry (€3). Open May-Oct. July-Aug. sites for 2 €15; sites for 3 €21. Sept.-Oct. and Apr.-June sites for 2 €13; sites for 3 €17. MC/V. ❶

✂ FOOD

Stock up on the basics at **Supermarket Eco,** pl. Bayard, near the tourist office. (Open M-Sa 8am-8pm, Su 9-11:45am. MC/V.) There is an indoor market at **place d'Armes** that sells everything from croissants to spindly octopus legs (open Tu-Su 8am-1pm) and a lively outdoor market all day in the *centre-ville* on the second Saturday of each month. Sampling Cognac's famous brandy doesn't necessarily mean drinking it; restaurants around **place François I** serve pricey meat and dessert specialties drenched in the luxury liqueur.

Le Cellier, 4-6 rue du 14 Juillet (☎05 45 82 25 46), off pl. François I. Local favorite, packed with customers for its generous portions of meat and fish. *Plats* €9-15. Lunch *menus* €9.50-15. Dinner *menus* €16-29. Open July-Sept. M-F noon-2:30pm and 7-10pm, Sa 7-10pm; Oct.-June M-F noon-2:30pm and 7-10pm. MC/V. ❸

Le Dugueslin, 9 rue du 14 Juillet (☎05 45 82 46 22), off pl. François 1. Pizzeria-*crêperie* attracts young visitors and locals with cheap, tasty thin-crust pizza. Salads €3-7. Pizzas €8-13. *Menus* €7-13. Open daily noon-2:30pm and 7-10pm. MC/V. ❷

🍾 **THE GIFT OF DOUBLE DISTILLATION.** Strict regulations require bars and restaurants to obtain a permit to serve cognac. Look for "Le Cognac: L'Esprit du Région" stickers on the door for the green light to imbibe.

👁 SIGHTS

▓**MUSÉE DES ARTS DU COGNAC.** The extremely detailed sensory exhibits in this museum are dedicated to all things cognac, including films featuring scenes with the drink, past marketing campaigns, and even a glass-blowing machine. (*Pl. de la Salle Verte.* ☎05 45 32 07 25; www.musees-cognac.fr. Explanations available in English. Open July-Aug. daily 10am-6:30pm; Sept.-Oct. and Apr.-June M and W-Su 11am-6pm. €4.50, students €3. Admission includes entrance to the Musée d'Art et d'Histoire de Cognac.)

MUSÉE D'ART ET D'HISTOIRE DE COGNAC. This museum recounts the history of Cognac through regional clothing, ceramics, and 20th-century paintings, including Pascal Adolphe Dagnan-Bouveret's remarkable but chilling *Marguerite au Sabbat*, tucked away behind a red curtain on the second floor. *(48 bd. Denfert-Rochereau. ☎05 45 32 07 25; www.musees-cognac.com. Open daily July-Aug. 10am-6:30pm; Sept.-Oct. and Apr.-June M and W-Su 11am-6pm; Nov.-Mar. M and W-Su 2-5:30pm.)*

L'ESPACE DÉCOUVERTE. This museum features a short artistic presentation on the Charente River as well as temporary exhibits and occasional free chocolate tastings. *(☎05 45 36 03 65. Open July-Aug. daily 10am-6:30pm; Sept. and June Tu-Su 10am-6:30pm; Oct. and Apr.-May Tu-Su 10:30am-6pm; Nov. and Mar. Tu-Su 2-6pm. Free. Entrance included with ticket to Musée des Arts du Cognac.)*

🎨 DISTILLERIES

The joy of visiting Cognac comes from traveling from one liqueur producer to the next, touring the cellars, learning the history of each house—and, best of all, tasting the delicate differences between their "VS" (Very Special), "VSOP" (Very Special Old Pale), and "XO" (eXtra Old) cognacs. In the summer, most houses give tours in English; call ahead during the winter. The distilleries listed below, with the exception of Rémy Martin, are located in the *centre-ville*.

■ **Hennessy,** quai Richard Hennessy (☎05 45 35 72 68; www.hennessy-cognac.com). Presentation includes boat ride along the Charente and glimpse of the region's oldest vintages. Reservations recommended. Tours in English and French daily June-Sept. every hr. 10am-5:30pm; Oct.-Dec. and Mar.-May 10am-5pm; Jan.-Feb. by reservation only. Tour with taste of 1 vintage €9, ages 12-18 €7, under 12 free.

Rémy Martin, route de Pons (☎05 45 35 76 66), 5km outside the *centre-ville* toward Merpins. 1hr. luxury experience from the most elite Cognac producer. Sample 2 vintages with gourmet enhancers like chocolate, smoked salmon, and *foie gras*. Individual tours from €25. Open Apr.-Oct. M-Sa 11am-noon and 1:30-6pm. Reservations required. Tours in English by request. Tasting and tour €15, ages 12-18 €8, under 12 free.

Otard, 127 bd. Denfert-Rochereau (☎05 45 36 88 86), in the Château de Cognac, François I's birthplace. 50min. tour led by guides in medieval costume. 2-vintage *dégustation*. Open daily 10am-7pm. Tours July-Aug. daily every 15min.; Sept.-Oct. and Apr.-June daily 11am, 2, 3:30, 5pm; Nov.-Dec. M-F 11am, 2, 4pm; Jan.-Mar. reservations required. €7, students and ages 12-18 €3.50, under 12 free.

Martell, pl. Édouard Martell (☎05 45 36 33 33; www.martell.com). Founded in 1715. Historical tour features replica of an 18th-century export ship and visit to the founder's perfectly renovated cottage. Open Apr.-Oct. M-F 10am-5pm, Sa-Su noon-5pm. Tours in English daily; call for times. €7, students and ages 12-18 €3. Tastings up to €20.

🎊 FESTIVALS

The Hennessy Distillery hosts an annual **film festival;** contact the tourist office for specific dates. Free concerts liven up the *quais* for the annual **Fête du Cognac** in mid-July, around Bastille Day every year (☎05 45 81 21 05; www.lafetedecognac.com). More open-air music follows with **Blues Passion** during the last weekend in July. (☎05 45 36 11 81; www.bluespassion.com. Tickets €30-35.)

🏞 OUTDOOR ACTIVITIES

Cognac's valley promises great hiking among vineyards, fields, and forests; off-trail discoveries include abbeys, châteaux, and a 13th-century crypt. The free *Passion-Vélo* guide has information on local cycling paths. On Parc François I's northern banks, **Base de Pleine Air** offers canoe and kayak rentals. (☎05 45 82 46 24. Rentals €26 per day. Open July-Aug. afternoons only.) Parks in Cognac include the classy **Jardin Public de l'Hôtel de Ville** around the museum (open daily

May-Sept. 7am-9pm; Oct.-Apr. 7am-7pm) and the tree-lined **Parc François I,** northwest of the *centre-ville* on the banks of the Charente.

 NO MORE DRAMA. Be sure to snag a copy of *Poitiers Été* at the tourist office for a full schedule of free summer arts events. The brochure lists everything from dance recitals to outdoor theater in the Parc de Blossac.

SAINTES   ☎ 05 46

Founded by AD first-century Romans, Saintes (sehnt; pop. 27,000) today houses ancient ruins, grand medieval churches, and lively markets. Over the years, massive renovations have made the town a pleasant and pedestrian-friendly escape from the bustling cities in the area.

▣ TRANSPORTATION

Trains: Pl. Pierre Semard. Info and ticket office open M 5:30am-7:30pm, Tu-Th 7:30am-7:30pm, F 7:30am-8:15pm, Sa 8:20am-7pm, Su 8:25am-8:15pm. To: **Bordeaux** (1hr., 5 per day, €18); **Cognac** (20min., 7 per day, €5.20); **La Rochelle** (1hr., 6 per day, €13); **Paris** (2-4hr., 7 per day, €51-63); **Poitiers** (1hr., 8 per day, €21-29).

Taxis: ☎ 05 46 74 24 24. Available at the train station.

Car Rental: Rent-a-Car, 45 av. de la Marne (☎ 05 46 91 87 80). From €30 per day. Open M-F 8:30am-12:30pm and 3-6:30pm, Sa 9am-noon. MC/V. **Europcar,** 41 av. de la Marne (☎ 05 46 92 56 10). From €45 per day, €214 per week; €600 deposit. 21+. Under-25 surcharge €15. Open M-F 8am-noon and 2-7pm, Sa 8am-noon and 2-6pm.

⊞ PRACTICAL INFORMATION

Tourist Office: 62 cours National (☎ 05 46 74 23 82; www.ot-saintes.fr), in Villa Musso. Take a sharp left out of the train station and follow av. de la Marne. Turn right onto av. Gambetta. Cross the bridge at Pont Palissy with the arch on the left and continue straight on cours National for 10min. The office is set back from the street on the right. Open July-Aug. M-Sa 9am-1pm and 2-7pm, Su 10am-1pm and 2-6pm; Sept. and Apr.-June 9:30am-1pm and 2-6pm, 1st and 3rd Su of Sept. 10am-1pm and 2-6pm; Oct.-Mar. M-Sa 9:30am-12:30pm and 1:30-5:30pm.

Tours: Tourist office leads walking tours in French June-Sept. Stops include the cathedral's bell tower (otherwise closed to the public). €3-7.

Laundromat: Laverie Reverseaux, 46 cours Reverseaux (☎ 06 86 91 07 91). Wash €3.30-8.20, dry €1 per 10min. Open daily 7am-9pm.

Police: 1 pl. du Bastion (☎ 05 46 90 30 40).

Hospital: Pl. du 11 Novembre (☎ 05 46 92 76 76).

Internet Access: Cyberzone, 2 rue Alsace-Lorraine (☎ 05 46 74 02 88), near the cathedral. €1 per 15min., €2 per hr. Open M 3-7pm, Tu-Sa 10am-7pm.

Post Office: 6 cours National (☎ 05 46 93 84 53). **Currency exchange** available. Open M and W-F 8:30am-6pm, Tu 9am-6pm, Sa 8:30am-noon. **Postal Code:** 17100.

♠ ⌂ ACCOMMODATIONS AND CAMPING

Hotels fill quickly during festival season from early to mid-July. Cheaper accommodations are on the train station side of the Charente.

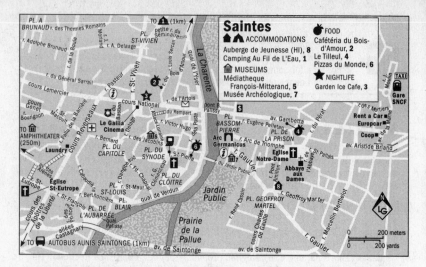

Saintes

▲■ ACCOMMODATIONS
Auberge de Jeunesse (HI), 8
Camping Au Fil de L'Eau, 1

🏛 MUSEUMS
Médiathèque
François-Mitterrand, 5
Musée Archéologique, 7

🍎 FOOD
Cafétéria du Bois-
d'Amour, 2
Le Tilleul, 4
Pizzas du Monde, 6

⭐ NIGHTLIFE
Garden Ice Cafe, 3

▧ Auberge de Jeunesse (HI), 2 pl. Geoffray Martel (☎05 46 92 14 92; fax 92 97 82), next to the Abbaye-aux-Dames. From the station, take a left on av. de là Marne, a right on av. Gambetta, a left on rue du Pérat, and a right on rue St-Pallais. Turn left through the archway into the abbey courtyard. Walk through the courtyard and down the steps; the hostel is on the right. Cozy brick-walled, cabin-like rooms. Spotless bathrooms. Breakfast included; dinner €6-9. Internet €1 per hr. Reserve months ahead. Reception June-Sept. 7am-noon and 5-11pm; Oct.-May 7am-noon and 5-10:30pm. 2- to 6-bed single-sex dorms with bath €16. MC/V. ❶

Camping Au Fil de L'Eau, 6 rue de Courbiac (☎05 46 93 08 00; www.camping-saintes-17.com), 1km from the *centre-ville.* From the station, follow directions to the hostel until av. Gambetta, then turn right onto quai de l'Yser after the bridge. It's 500m ahead to the right. Private pool, minigolf (€4), and shaded sites. Laundry facilities available. Reception July-Aug. 8am-10pm; Sept.-Oct. and Apr.-June 8am-noon and 2-8pm. Gates closed 10pm-7am. €2.20 per child, sites €4.40. Electricity €3.50. MC/V. ❶

🍴 FOOD

Restaurants in Saintes showcase local seafood, *escargots*, and *mojettes* (white beans). Start things off with ▧**Pineau**, cognac's sweeter relative. The pedestrian district by **rue Victor Hugo** has plenty of family-run restaurants and bars. There are markets at **place du 11 Novembre,** off cours Reverseaux (open Tu and F), near Cathédrale St-Pierre (open W and Sa), and on **avenue de la Marne** and **avenue Gambetta** (open Th and Su), all of which are open from 7am to 1pm. On the first Monday of every month, cours National and av. Gambetta host **Le Grand Foire,** an open-air market that sells everything, including clothes, sunglasses, and purses (open from 8am). A huge **Leclerc** supermarket is on cours Charles de Gaulle. (Open M-Th and Sa 8:30am-7:45pm, F 8:30am-8:15pm.)

Le Tilleul, 72 av. Gambetta (☎05 46 74 23 01). Light-green facade and brightly lit bar, in the shade of a lime tree. *Plats du jour* include *faux-filet* (sirloin; €12) and *confit de* *canard* (duck preserved in fat; €17). Lunch *menu* €13. Dinner *menus* €25. Open daily 8am-midnight; kitchen open noon-2:30pm and 7-10:30pm. MC/V. ❸

Cafétéria du Bois d'Amour, 7 rue du Bois d'Amour (☎05 46 97 26 54). True lunchroom atmosphere—lunch ladies, plastic trays, and all. *Entrées* €1-5.50. *Plats* €4.30-7. Open M-Sa 10:30am-3:30pm and 6:30-10pm. 5% student discount. MC/V. ❶

Pizzas du Monde, rue St-Pierre (☎05 46 74 55 56). Huge internationally themed pies loaded with a variety of toppings. 4 pies for the price of 1 at dinner. Pizza €5-13. Open M-Th 11am-2pm and 6-10:30pm, F-Su 11am-2pm and 6-11pm. Cash only. ❷

⚲ SIGHTS

The comprehensive **Pass Saintes** (available at the tourist office; €8) includes admission to all museums, the abbey, and the amphitheater. ❶

◪**SAINT-EUTROPE.** The steps off cours Reverseaux wind through tree-lined fields down to this curious church. As the story goes, its patron saint was a Persian prince who came to Saintes after having allegedly met Jesus in Palestine and converting to Christianity. Soon after his arrival, Eutrope successfully persuaded the governor of Gaul's daughter to convert and live an eternal life of solitude and contemplation—with him. The governor, furious at his daughter's corruption, had St-Eutrope decapitated by the local butchers. His head now lies at the church's altar. The rest of his body is at the site of his murder—the magnificent Romanesque **crypt** beneath. *(Open daily 9am-7pm.)*

AMPHITHEATER. Not far from St-Eutrope lie the sprawling Roman ruins that figure so prominently on all of Saintes's postcards. Built in AD 40, the amphitheater used to seat up to 15,000 spectators. *(☎05 46 97 73 85. Guided tours M-Sa 3, 4pm. €2, ages 10-18 €1, under 10 free. Tours €4, under 16 free. Audio tour in English and French €3. Open June-Sept. daily 10am-8pm; Oct.-May M-Sa 10am-5pm, Su 1:30-5pm.)*

MUSÉE ARCHÉOLOGIQUE. Farther down the river, on esplanade André Malraux, this two-room museum displays a modest collection of ancient Roman funeral monuments as well as jewelry, pottery, and a reconstructed chariot, all dating back to the AD first century. Outside, an impressive—and free—Roman ruins exhibit outshines the interior. *(☎05 46 74 20 97. Open June-Sept. Tu-Sa 10am-6pm, Su 2-6pm; Oct.-May Tu-Sa 10am-5pm. €2, under 16 free.)*

MÉDIATHEQUE FRANÇOIS-MITTERRAND. Hosting an interactive permanent exhibit on Saintes's medi-

THE HIDDEN DEAL

À LA MODE ON THE CHEAP

Lately, young people in the world's fashion capital have perfected the art of dressing down in the name of shabby, hippie chic. While many shops are capitalizing on the second coming of grunge by gauging prices, hole-in-the-wall thrift stores hidden along your route are sure to offer some great bargains.

One particularly curious find is **Emmaüs** in Saintes, a veritable treasure-trove of odds and ends that date from the dawning of the technological age. Equipped with eight-tracks and gold watches that may once have belonged to Louis XIV, this place is better than your grandmother's attic. Your inner flower child will discover a haven of soft, billowing blouses, patched bellbottoms, and John Lennon shades—all at prices that will have you breaking your fives.

If you are more into the business side of dealings and your backpack is wearing you down, consider selling some of your grimy old T-shirts for extra cash. The next fad-seeker will surely pick up where you left off, maybe even passing you on the street without so much as a nod of thanks for the gift you have bestowed upon the world of French fashion.

Emmaüs, 27 rue St-Michel (☎05 46 02 02 03). DVDs €1. Shirts €2. Jeans €5-15. Original Tin-Tin comic books €0.10. Open W-Sa 10am-noon and 2:30-6pm.

eval construction, this media-savvy museum provides audio tours in English and French, as well as a 3D model of the city. After exploring the interior, venture out to the courtyard and ascend the stone staircase for a view of the surrounding Roman-tile rooftops as well as a glimpse of the distant amphitheater among languid lily ponds. If you aren't astonished by the high-tech exhibits, surely the price will change your mind—it's all free. *(Pl. de l'Échevinage, off rue Alsace-Lorraine. ☎ 05 46 93 25 39. Open M-Sa 10am-5pm. Free.)*

OTHER SIGHTS. Built in AD 18 as a gateway into the city, the Roman **Arc Germanicus** rises above the river's right bank in honor of Emperor Tiberius. Originally located in front of a bridge that crossed the Charente, the arc was moved to its present location in 1843, when it began to lose stability due to the river's widening. Rue Arc de Triomphe leads to the Romanesque **Abbaye-aux-Dames,** which now serves as a conservatory and cultural center. Its bright **Salle Capitulaire** displays frequent local artists' exhibits. The bell tower of the connected **Église Notre Dame,** partially funded by Eleanor of Aquitaine, dates from the 12th century. The last abbess allegedly died at the exact moment when the revolutionaries removed the tower's bells in 1791. All explanations are written in French, though English headsets are available. *(☎ 05 46 97 48 48; www.abbayeauxdames.org. Exhibit and ramparts open daily Apr.-Sept. 10am-12:30pm and 2-7pm; Oct.-Mar. 2-6pm. Tours in French from early May to late Sept. 4 per day 2:30-5:30pm. Church free; abbey €2, under 16 free. Concerts €12-48. Tours €3.50. Audio tours €4, available in English and French.)*

🎵 🎆 ENTERTAINMENT AND FESTIVALS

Late in the day, Saintes's cafes and pubs are great places to unwind. The lively, inviting ▧**Garden Ice Cafe,** 63 cours National, hosts a classy crowd and sports a snazzy interior, with leather couches and wall-size mirrors. *(☎05 46 93 19 64. Beer €2.70-5. Theme nights F-Sa. Open daily 7am-2am. MC/V.)* **Le Gallia Cinéma,** pl. du Théâtre, shows two to four movies per week; at least one is usually in English. During the school year, it hosts live theater. *(Movies €7, students €6. Daily screenings 6-10pm. Live theater €15-25.)*

> **Les Oreilles en Éventail** (☎05 46 92 34 26; www.ville-saintes.fr.), 3 days in July. Open-air concerts in the *vieille ville.* Free.

> **Festival de la Paix** (☎05 46 97 04 35; www.festival-de-la-paix.com), 10 days in mid-July. International folk music, food, and dance. Some events free, others €12-27.

> **Festival de Saintes** (☎05 46 97 48 48; ww.abbayeauxdames.org), 10 days in mid-July. Over 35 classical music concerts held at the Abbaye-aux-Dames and other churches. Consult *L'Abbaye aux Dames: Été* at the tourist office for festival info. Tickets €12-48.

LA ROCHELLE ☎ 05 46

One of France's best-protected seaports, La Rochelle (lah roh-shell; pop. 80,000) both thrived and suffered as a coveted Protestant prize during the Thirty Years' War. Given its charming waterfront and relaxed outdoor cafes, it's hard to imagine that La Rochelle was nearly starved into oblivion in 1627 by Cardinal Richelieu and Louis XIII—characters immortalized in Dumas's *The Three Musketeers,* an irate attack on the city's British sympathies. Though the port's medieval architecture remains among vestiges of its turbulent past, La Rochelle now insists on living the good life, with renowned museums and festivals, pristine coastal islands, and excellent seafood restaurants.

TRANSPORTATION

Trains: Bd. du Maréchal Joffre. Office open M-Th and Sa 5am-11:15pm, F 5am-12:45am, Su 6:10am-11:45pm. To: **Bordeaux** (2hr., 6 per day, €25) via **Saintes; Nantes** (2hr., 6 per day, €17-23); **Paris** (3-4hr., 9 per day, €58-72); **Poitiers** (1hr., 12 per day, €20-23).

Buses: Pl. de Verdun. Océcars (☎05 46 00 95 21). To **Saintes** (4 per day, €13) via **Rochefort.** Buy tickets on board or at the office. Info office open M-Th 8:30am-12:30pm and 1:30-6pm, F 8:30am-12:30pm and 1:30-5:30pm.

Ferries: Pl. de Verdun (☎05 46 34 02 22; www.rtcr.fr). Croisières Inter-Îles (☎05 46 44 49 70) sends boats to **Île d'Aix** (1hr.; July-Aug. up to 5 per day, Sept. and May-June 2 per day; €26, ages 4-18 €22, under 4 €6), **Île de Ré** (1hr.; €20, ages 4-18 €15, under 4 €4), and **Fort Boyard** (2hr. tour circles the privately owned fort; €20, ages 4-18 €12, under 4 free). Bus de Mer (☎05 46 34 02 22) shuttles from the old port to **Les Minimes** (July-Aug. every 30min. 9am-11pm, Sept. and Apr.-June every hr. 10am-noon and 2-7pm; €1.50-2). Le Passeur (☎05 46 34 02 22) runs the same route as Bus de Mer (every 5-10min. June-Sept. 7:30am-midnight, Oct.-Mar. 7:30am-8pm, Apr.-May 7:30am-10pm; €0.60).

> **WHERE DID ALL THE WATER GO?** During low tide, La Rochelle's harbor becomes so shallow that it looks like a swampy marshland. No boats can leave before 10am. While waiting to catch a ferry, walk down the boardwalk to witness another curious sight: the quest for *fruits de mer.* Fishermen trudge around the empty harbor in search of tiny snails and oysters to sell at the *marché* at the end of rue des Merciers. After you check out the scavenger hunt, head to the market for a savory treat—straight from the mud.

Public Transportation: Autoplus, pl. de Verdun (☎05 46 34 02 22). Maps and schedules available. Open M-Sa 9:15am-12:15pm and 1:50-6pm. Buses serve the campgrounds, hostel, and *centre-ville* (every 20min. 7am-8pm, €1.30) as well as nearby towns. Tickets for rides within the city sold on board; buy tickets for longer trips at the office.

Taxis: 5 rue des Gonthières and pl. de Verdun (☎05 46 41 55 55).

Car Rental: Several line av. du Général de Gaulle, 100m from the train station. **ADA** (☎05 46 41 02 17; www.ada.fr). Open M-F 8am-noon and 2-7pm. MC/V. **Budget** (☎05 46 41 35 53; fax 41 55 26). Open M-F 8am-12:30pm and 1:35-6:30pm, Sa 9:30am-12:30pm and 1:45-5:45pm. AmEx/MC/V.

Bike Rental: Vélos Municipaux Autoplus (☎05 46 34 02 22), off quai Valin. 1st 2hr. free, €1 per hr. thereafter; ID deposit. Open daily July-Aug. 9am-7pm; May-Sept. 9am-12:30pm and 1:30-7pm. Also at pl. de Verdun, near the bus station. Open M-Sa 9:15am-12:15pm and 1:50-6pm.

ORIENTATION AND PRACTICAL INFORMATION

The heart of La Rochelle spans cafe-lined **quai Duperré** in the *vieux port* to the boutique-filled *vieille ville* inland. South of the *vieille ville* is the more modern *ville en bois* (wood village), which, despite its name, is a complex of industrial buildings and museums that include the excellent aquarium and local university. Farther to the south is a little strip of beachfront, **Les Minimes.**

Tourist Office: Quartier du Gabut (☎05 46 41 14 68; www.larochelle-tourisme.com), at the corner of quai Georges Simenon and quai de la Georgette, across the water from the aquarium. 5min. from the station; head up av. du Général de Gaulle to pl. de la Motte Rouge and turn left onto quai du Gabut. Multilingual staff. Hotel reservations (€2). Open

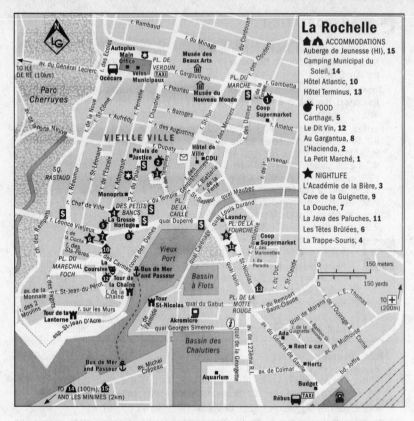

La Rochelle

⌂ ⌂ ACCOMMODATIONS
Auberge de Jeunesse (HI), **15**
Camping Municipal du
 Soleil, **14**
Hôtel Atlantic, **10**
Hôtel Terminus, **13**

🍎 FOOD
Carthage, **5**
Le Dit Vin, **12**
Au Gargantua, **8**
L'Hacienda, **2**
La Petit Marché, **1**

★ NIGHTLIFE
L'Académie de la Bière, **3**
Cave de la Guignette, **9**
La Douche, **7**
La Java des Paluches, **11**
Les Têtes Brûlées, **6**
La Trappe-Souris, **4**

July-Aug. M-Sa 9am-8pm, Su 10:30am-5:30pm; Sept. and June M-Sa 9am-7pm, Su 10:30am-5:30pm; Oct.-May M-Sa 10am-12:30pm and 1:30-6pm, Su 10am-1pm.

Tours: Tourist office runs walking tours of the *vieille ville* July-Aug. daily 10:30am (2hr.; €6, students €4). Horse-and-carriage tours daily 2:30pm (1hr.; €9, under 18 €6). Theatrical night tours from July to mid-Sept. Th 8:30, 9, 9:30pm (2hr.; €10.50, under 18 €7). Reservations required for carriage and night tours. Tours in French only.

Banks: Banque de France (☎05 46 51 48 00), on the corner of rue Réamur and rue Léance Vieljeux. Open M-F 8:30am-noon and 1:30-3:30pm. **Crédit Lyonnais,** 19 rue du Palais. 24hr. **ATMs** available.

Laundromat: Laverie Automatique, 4 bis quai Louis Durand. Wash €4 per 8kg, €7 per 13kg; dry €1 per 8min. Open daily 8:30am-8:30pm.

Police: 2 pl. de Verdun and 14 rue du Palais (☎05 46 51 36 36).

Hospital: Rue du Docteur Schweitzer (☎05 46 45 50 50). English spoken. 24hr. emergency entrance on bd. Joffre.

Internet Access: Akromicro, 15 rue de l'Aimable Nanette (☎05 46 34 07 94; www.akromicro.com), in Le Gabut. €0.05 per min., €2 per hr. Open daily 10am-midnight.

Post Office: 52 av. de Mulhouse (☎05 46 51 25 03), 50m from the train station. **Currency exchange** available. **Poste Restante:** 17087. **Postal Code:** 17000.

ACCOMMODATIONS AND CAMPING

Cheap beds in town are limited, especially during the festival-laden summer months. For July and August, book by June.

Centre International de Séjour, Auberge de Jeunesse (HI), av. des Minimes (☎05 46 44 43 11). From the train station, walk up av. du Général de Gaulle, cross av. 123ème RI to the left of the roundabout, and walk along quai Georges Simenon. Take a left and cross the bridge onto av. Michel Crépeau. Walk along the water for 10min., then turn left to follow av. Michel Crépeau for another 5min. past the campground on the left. Turn right; signs lead to the hostel, which is on the right. Alternatively take bus #10, 17, or 19 (dir.: Port des Minimes) from av. de Colmar, 1 block from the station, to La Sole (M-Sa every 20min. 7am-7:55pm; Su #42A every hr., last bus 6:30pm; €1.20). Take a right onto av. des Minimes; hostel is on the right. Small 2- to 6-bunk dorms and excellent facilities. TV room, cafeteria, and laundry. Breakfast included. Internet €0.50 per 15min. Reception July-Aug. 8am-10pm; Sept.-June 8am-noon, 2-7pm, and 9-10pm. Lockout 10am-2pm. Gates closed midnight-6:30am. Reservations recommended. 4- to 6-bed dorms €17-19, with shower €20; singles €25/27; doubles €21/22. ❶

Hôtel Atlantic, 23 rue Verdière (☎05 46 41 16 68 or 43 81 20; fax 41 25 69). Comfortable rooms. Excellent location near the *vieux port* with views of sunbaked rooftops. Breakfast €5.50. Open from mid-Mar. to Nov. Singles and doubles €32, with shower €48-56, with full bath €60-64; triples €75-85; quads €85. MC/V. ❷

Hôtel Terminus, pl. du Commandant de La Motte Rouge (☎05 46 50 69 69; www.tourisme-francais.com/hotels/terminus). Victorian wallpaper and large windows with cascading white curtains create a romantic ambience. Bright 1st-floor lounge and elegant breakfast area. Rooms have TVs. Breakfast €6.50. Parking. Reception 7am-11pm. Singles €60-69; doubles €64-72; triples and quads €72-80. AmEx/MC/V. ❹

Camping Municipal du Soleil, av. Michel Crépeau (☎05 46 44 42 53; fax 52 25 18), 10min. from the *centre-ville.* Pass Le Gabut and follow av. Michel Crépeau as it curves left or take bus #10 (dir.: Port des Minimes) to Technoforum. Go right and take the 2nd left on rue de la Huguenotte. Veer right onto av. Michel Crépeau, which runs alongside the campground. Green and shaded. Old-fashioned bungalows. Reception 7:30am-11pm. Gates closed 10pm-7am. Open from late June to mid-Sept. 1 person and car €8.70; €3.40 per extra person, €2.50 per extra child. Electricity €3.50. MC/V. ❶

FOOD

For fresh fish, head to the market at **place du Marché** (open daily 7am-1pm). There's a **Monoprix** on rue de Palais, near the clock tower. (Open M-Sa July-Aug. 8:30am-9pm; Sept.-June 8:30am-8pm.) Restaurants pack **rue Saint-Jean du Pérot, rue de la Chaîne,** and the waterfront—though they can be pricey.

La Petite Marché, 4 rue des 3 Fuseaux (☎05 46 34 30 30), behind the Vieux Marché. Students and the organically inclined delight in this tiny bistro's imaginative vegetarian menu. Try the honey-marinated carrots and lentil flour pancakes. Salads €4-12. *Plats* €9. Desserts €3.50. Open M-Sa 10am-3pm and 5:30-9:30pm. AmEx/MC/V. ❷

Le Dit Vin, 12 rue St-Jean du Pérot (☎05 46 27 50 23). The name "says" it all: the place is *divin* (divine). Classy dark red decor. Extensive wine selection. Stands apart from the seafood racket in both style and value. Tasty *entrées* from €6. *Plats* €11-24. Exceptional 3-course dinner *menu* €18. Open M-Sa 7pm-1am. MC/V. ❸

Au Gargantua, 4 rue Léonce Vieljeux (☎05 46 50 57 40). Small student-run takeout spot on the port, tucked between sprawling and expensive tourist attractions. Attracts sleepless clubbers and broke students with fresh pasta to go. Pasta €2-4.50. *Menu* with dessert and drink €6. Open M-Th and Su 11am-3am, F-Sa 11am-5am. MC/V. ❶

POITOU-CHARENTES

L'Hacienda, 22 Petite Rue du Temple (☎05 46 41 03 89). Lebanese sandwich shop. Students gather in the outdoor seating area after a night out. Freshly made kebabs, falafel, and burgers (€3.50-7). *Formules* €5-8. Open daily 10:30am-3am. MC/V. ❶

Carthage, 17 rue Léonce Vieljeux. Family owned. Exquisite meat couscous (€8.50-14) at a small lunch counter or in the breezy adjoining dining room. Don't miss the homemade baklava (€1.60). Open M and W-Su 11am-2am. Cash only. ❸

👁 SIGHTS

La Rochelle's flourishing commerce with Canada and the West Indies endowed it with an impressive port. Three of its original towers are still standing. During WWII, the Germans took advantage of these fortifications, using the town as a submarine base. In fact, the Germans didn't let go of La Rochelle until the general surrender in May 1945, making it the last French city to be liberated. A unique blend of art and architecture—from 17th-century graffiti to contemporary exhibitions—La Rochelle is a city of hidden wonders. A mere €6 buys combined admission to the **Musée du Nouveau Monde, Musée des Beaux Arts,** and **Musée d'Orbigny-Bernon.** Joint tickets are available at the tourist office or at any of the three museums and are valid for one month.

📷**AQUARIUM.** This aquarium is home to a whopping 10,000 marine animals, and 500 different species, kept in habitats that simulate their natural environments—from the French Atlantic coast to the tropical rainforest. Audio tours offered in four languages (€3.50) provide background on the eating and sexual habits of the fish, which accompany awe-inspiring tanks filled with sharks, translucent jellyfish, giant eels, and poisonous anemones. The aquarium makes for a perfect rainy-day activity, but be prepared to deal with crowds of families. Avoid stepping on turtles in the tropical greenhouse, where they roam freely. *(Bassin des Grande Yacht, across the water from the tourist office. ☎05 46 34 00 00. Open daily July-Aug. 9am-11pm; Sept. and Apr.-June 9am-8pm; Oct.-Mar. 10am-8pm. Last entry 1½hr. before close. Wheelchair-accessible. €13, students and under 18 €11.)*

TOUR SAINT-NICOLAS AND TOUR DE LA CHAÎNE. The port's emblematic 14th-century towers once guarded it from attack. When hostile ships approached, guards closed off the harbor by raising a chain between the two towers. Now the 800-year-old chain lies along the dock, at the foot of the aptly named Tour de la Chaîne. After Richelieu won the siege of La Rochelle, he had all of the city's fortifications destroyed except for these towers. Tour St-Nicolas impresses visitors with thick fortifications and a maze of dizzying staircases. According to local legend, Fairy Mesuline—the half-woman, half-eel mermaid ancestor—was flying above the city one night when her apron broke. Stones that magically spilled out formed St-Nicolas's present shape. Initially, La Rochelle's citizens were planning to link the towers with an arch, but these plans were abandoned when they discovered St-Nicolas's foundations were tilted. The Tour de la Chaîne now houses a timeline of the city's history and an exhibit on trade with Canada. *(☎05 46 34 11 81 or 41 74 13. Both towers open July-Aug. daily 10am-7pm; from early to mid-Sept. and from mid-May to June 10am-12:30pm and 2-6:30pm; from mid-Sept. to mid-May Tu-Su 10am-12:30pm and 2-5:30pm. Last entry 30min. before close. €5.70, ages 18-25 €4.80, under 18 free. Combined ticket includes Tour de la Lanterne and ferry passage between the 2 towers; €11, ages 18-25 €7; Oct.-Mar. and 1st Su of the month free.)*

TOUR DE LA LANTERNE. Accessible from the Tour de la Chaîne by a low rampart, this 70m tower is France's oldest lighthouse. Built in the 15th century around the foundations of a 12th-century tower, the structure has a morbid history: its second name, Tour des Prêtres, derives from the 13 priests who were thrown from the steeple during the Wars of Religion. The stone walls along its

162 steps are carved with three centuries' worth of intricate graffiti that provide remarkable historical documentation of shipwrecks and crews, recorded by the tower's British, Dutch, French, and Spanish detainees. One particularly impressive work depicts a 19th-century steam engine with amazing detail. At the summit, only 1m of stone protects visitors from free falls. On a sunny day, the view extends all the way to the Île d'Oléron. (☎ *05 46 41 56 04. Open July-Aug. daily 10am-7pm; from early to mid-Sept. and from mid-May to June daily 10am-12:30pm and 2-6:30pm; from mid-Sept. to mid-May Tu-Su 10am-12:30pm and 2-5:30pm. Last entry 30min. before close. €5.70, ages 18-25 €4.80, under 18 free.)*

VIEILLE VILLE. The pedestrian *vieille ville*, dating from the 17th and 18th centuries, stretches beyond the townhouses of the harbor, romantic arcades lining its meandering streets. The 14th-century **Grosse Horloge** (Great Clock Tower) is worth strolling by; its two-ton Gothic bell once tolled the raising of the chain between the two towers that opened the port each morning. The flamboyant Gothic facade of the Renaissance **Hôtel de Ville,** with a prominent statue of its builder, Henri IV, is also noteworthy. *(2hr. night tour July-Aug. M-Sa 10:30pm. €6, under 10 €4. 1hr. horse-drawn tour July-Aug. M-Sa 2:30pm. €9, under 10 €6.)*

MUSÉE DU NOUVEAU MONDE. This museum examines European perceptions of the New World during the Age of Exploration. More specifically, it traces the history of La Rochelle's commerce with the Antilles. The striking *Mascarade Nuptiale* by Roza Jose Conrado, a painting of entertainers at the 18th-century Portuguese court, sums up the oddity of artifacts contained within the museum. The Fleuriau family, who originally owned the building, made its fortune trading slaves and Caribbean sugar, spices, and coffee. Curtis's ethnographic photogravures (ancient predecessors of the photograph) on the top floor are also not to be missed. *(10 rue Fleuriau. ☎ 05 46 41 46 50. Open Apr.-Sept. M and W-Sa 10am-12:30pm and 2-6pm, Su 2:30-6pm. €3.50, students and under 18 free.)*

MUSÉE DES BEAUX ARTS. This museum houses mostly French works from the 17th century, which feature—surprise, surprise—naked women before utopian backgrounds. There's also a Fromentin series that appears on some of the town's postcards. Look for Paul Signac's 20th-century watercolor of the lively La Rochelle harbor. *(28 rue Gargoulleau. ☎ 05 46 41 64 65. Open M and W-Sa 2-6pm, Su 2:30-6pm. English guidebook available at the desk. €3.50, students and under 18 free.)* Downstairs, **L'Espace Art Contemporaine** contains more exciting temporary exhibits of modern art from local artists. *(☎ 05 46 34 76 55. Open M and W-Sa 2:30-6pm. Free.)*

🎵 🎴 ENTERTAINMENT AND FESTIVALS

La Coursive, 4 rue St-Jean du Pérot, hosts music, theater, and films. (☎ 05 46 51 54 00. Office open Sept.-June M-F 1-6:30pm.) In summer, **quai Duperré** and **cours des Dames** close to cars and open to mimes, jugglers, and an outdoor market. (Open July-Sept. daily 8pm-midnight; May-June Su noon-8pm.)

Festival International du Film de La Rochelle (☎ 01 48 06 16 66; www.festival-laro-chelle.org), last week of June and 1st week of July. The Cannes of the Atlantic. Fans pull all-nighters. 1 film €6; 3 films €15, under 25 €10; all 100 films €85/65.

Théâtre en Été (☎ 06 66 79 60 65), at the end of July. Celebrated theater-fest comes to quai Georges Simenon.

🎫 **FrancoFolies** (☎ 05 46 50 55 57; www.francofolies.fr), in mid-July. Nationally renowned 6-day rock festival draws international Francophone performers. Some afternoon performances €6-7, evening concerts €10-37.

Grand Pavois (☎ 05 46 44 46 39; www.grand-pavois.com), 2nd week of Sept. Boats in the port des Minimes open to the public for one of Europe's biggest "boat salons."

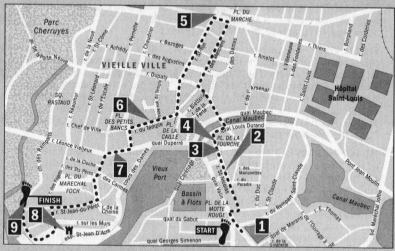

LA ROCHELLE BY FOOT

1. MARCHÉ AUX PUCES (FLEA MARKET). Try your bargain-hunting luck across from pl. de la Motte Rouge, where vendors hawk ancient postcards, cheap jewelry, yellowed paperbacks, and vintage army supplies. (Open Th and Sa 8am-4pm.)

2. RUE SAINT-NICOLAS. Head down toward the canal to window-shop at funky boutiques. Afterward, check out free exhibits in the galleries that line the cobblestone street.

3. LA SOLETTE CAFÉ. Slip into the alley that leads to pl. de la Fourche and lounge under the huge tree while you sip an espresso at this earthy cafe.

4. BOULANGERIE IN PLACE DE LA FOURCHE. Peek into the bakery on the corner as you turn back onto rue St-Nicolas to get a glimpse of boulangers rolling away the day's fare.

5. MARKET ON PLACE DU MARCHÉ. After you cross the canal, bear right up rue des Merciers to take in the aroma of the day's catch: shrimp, octopuses, and other fruits de mer.

6. LE TASTE VIN. Turn right onto rue du Temple and stop in at Le Taste Vin for a free wine tasting. The schedule on the barrel outside lists the region of the day.

7. CARTHAGE. Turn left at pl. des Petits Blanc and right when you reach the water onto rue Léonce Vieljeux. Refuel with a hefty falafel at Carthage, a homestyle Tunisian kebab joint where the lunchtime line stretches around the corner (p. 564).

8. TOUR DE LA LANTERNE. Walk down cafe-lined rue St-Jean du Pérot and turn left on rue des Fagots. Climb to the top of this tower for a breathtaking panoramic view from 50m up (p. 564).

9. PARC CHERRUYES. Backtrack from the tower on rue des Fagots and walk along the water to reach the beach and forests of the parc. Pull up on a grassy knoll and take a load off.

Jazz Entre les 2 Tours (☎05 46 27 11 19. www.larochelle-jazz-festival.com), early Oct.
Marathon (☎05 46 44 42 19; www.marathondelarochelle.com), in late Nov.

☁ NIGHTLIFE

The **cour du Temple**, a lively square just off rue des Templiers, offers a cool place to start off a hot summer night. The tourist office provides *Gay-Friendly La Rochelle*, which lists gay-friendly nightlife. The streets leading to the clubs near the Tour de Lanterne are dark and isolated at night—exercise caution.

■ **Cave de la Guignette**, 8 rue St-Nicolas. No visit to La Rochelle is complete without a stop at this bar, which has lured local fishermen with barrels of wine since 1933. Today, barrels serve as furniture for students, who sip cheap wine (from €1.40) before heading out to dinner. Try "La Guignette," white wine infused with fruit flavors (1L €8.50). Open M 4-8pm, Tu-W 10am-1pm and 4-8pm, Th-Sa 10am-1pm and 3-8pm. Cash only.

La Java des Paluches, 12 rue St-Nicolas (☎05 46 30 54 20). Young laid-back crowd. Warhol-esque artwork, random kitchen furniture, low leather couches, and loud rock. Try the famous mojitos (€6) or any of 50 different types of whiskey—but good luck fighting your way to the bar. Beer €2.50. Bordeaux €6. Open daily 7pm-2am. MC/V.

L'Académie de la Bière, cours du Temple (☎05 46 42 43 78). Loyal older clientele sips beers of all shades *(blondes, brunes, rousse)* in this 2-story bar. Try a "Girafe," a 1m tube of beer (€23). Wine and hard liquor from €2.50. Open daily 10am-2am. MC/V.

La Douche, 14 rue Léonce Vieljeux (☎05 46 41 24 79). "H2O concept" includes showers on the dance floor and cellophane on the ceiling. Live DJs play electro-house. €2 compulsory coat check. Beer €6. Cover €10; includes 1 drink. Open Th-Su 2-5am. MC/V.

Les Têtes Brûlées, 20 rue Verdière (☎05 46 50 57 73). Air-force-inspired bar with WWII memorabilia lightens the mood with satirical quotes scrawled on the walls and large-scale models of Barbie airplanes. Hosts a friendly collection of radical young people. Try a "Bombarder" (€7.50), the house specialty. Beer €2.60. Open daily 6pm-2am. MC/V.

La Trappe-Souris, 5 rue Verdière (☎05 46 29 07 06). Intimate cafe turns into an even cozier bar nightly. Hosts alternative art exhibits. Classic rock. Beer €2.10. Mixed drinks €4. Champagne €6. Open M-Tu and Th-F 10am-2am, W and Sa-Su 3pm-2am. MC/V.

▶ DAYTRIPS FROM LA ROCHELLE

ROCHEFORT

Rochefort is accessible by Océcars, which shuttles between the gare routière and La Rochelle (line #51; 20min.; M-Sa 8 per day, Su 2 per day). Consider investing in the Pass Partout (€8), which includes transportation, museum admission, and a bike for a day. Ask the tourist office in La Rochelle for info. The Rochefort tourist office on av. Sadi Carnot is very helpful. From the train station, follow the centre-ville signs. After the signs stop, veer left past the hospital and follow rue Thiers; turn right on rue Audry de Puyravault and continue past the post office. The tourist office is on the left. (☎05 46 99 08 60. Open July-Aug. M-Sa 9:30am-7pm, Su 10am-6pm; Sept.-June daily 9:30am-12:30pm and 2-6pm.) The office offers the free carte sésame discount, valid at all the city's museums. After paying full price at 1 sight, receive a stamp valid for reduced admission at the rest of the museums.

Modern Rochefort (rohsh-fohr) was a sparsely populated marsh along the Charente River until Louis XIV claimed it for his own in the 17th century and transformed it into France's greatest dockyard. Numerous fortifications were erected around the estuary, including on Île d'Aix, Île de Ré, and Fort Boyard. In homage to their naval past, residents of Rochefort have begun the construction of an exact replica of ■**L'Hermione,** the vessel that sped La Fayette to George Washington's assistance during the American Revolution in 1780. While the original was constructed in six months, this impressive wood giant's recreation has required more than a decade of work. The ship is scheduled to sail to Boston in 2011. Guided tours of the work site demonstrate the craft of 18th-century blacksmiths and carpenters. (☎05 46 87 01 90. Open daily Apr.-Sept. 9am-7pm; Oct.-Mar. 10am-noon and 2-6pm. Tours July-Aug. 9am-7pm; Sept. and Apr.-June 11:30am, 2, 5pm; Oct.-Mar. M-F 2, 4pm, Sa-Su 11:30am, 2, 4pm. €6.50; *carte sésame*, students, and retirees €5; ages 8-18 €3.50; under 8 free. With tour €8, *carte sésame*, students, and retirees €6.50, €3.50, under 8 free.)

An avid imagination masterminded the ◪**Maison Pierre Loti**, 141 rue Pierre Loti, which exhibits the exotic and bizarre collection accumulated by its creator, novelist and actor Loti. Eccentric to the extreme, this rich Rochefort resident transformed the rooms of his house into romanticized simulations of a Turkish lounge, an Islamic mosque, and a Gothic chamber—none of which he ever visited. The museum is open by guided tour only. (☎05 46 99 16 88. Tours in French from July to mid-Sept. daily every 30min. 10-11:30am and 2-6pm; Oct.-June M and W-Sa 10:30, 11:30am, 2, 3, 4pm, Su 2, 3, 4pm. €7.80, *carte sésame* €6.80, students and ages 8-18 €4.) The **Musée National de la Marine**, 1 pl. de la Galissonnière, next to *L'Hermione*, is housed inside the former naval commander's official residence. The museum, dedicated to Rochefort's nautical history, displays a large collection of curious artifacts—from 17th-century ship models to carved coconuts made by prisoners on the ships. (☎05 46 99 86 57. Open daily May-Sept. 10am-8pm; Oct.-Mar. 1:30-6:30pm. €6, under 18 free.) The oddly futuristic 176m steel and iron **Pont Transbordeur**, 10 rue du Docteur Pujos, 2km farther down the Charente, was designed by engineering genius Ferdinand Arnodin, a student of the architect of the Eiffel Tower. Constructed in 1900 with the same materials as the famed tower, the *pont* was built impressively high in order to facilitate the passage of steam and sailboats.

For those who really want to spend the night in Rochefort, the **Auberge de Jeunesse (HI) ❶**, 20 rue de la République, is in a spacious old house just down the street. Equipped with a small kitchen and green courtyard often open for camping, this clean hostel offers brightly colored dorms and singles, some of which open onto a terrace. (☎05 46 99 74 62. Shared baths. Breakfast €3.50. Reservations recommended. Camping €6 per tent. Dorms €16; singles €22; doubles €19. MC/V.) Locals recommend the bistro-grill **Le Cap Nell ❸**, 1 quai Bellot, which overlooks the windy harbor. Sample the fresh seafood, the duck (€5.50), or the *steak flambé au cognac* for €19. (☎05 46 87 31 77. *Menu* €19-21. Open July-Aug. daily noon-2pm and 7:30-10pm; Sept.-June M and Th-Su noon-2pm and 7:30-10pm, Tu noon-2pm. AmEx/MC/V.)

ÎLE DE RÉ ☎05 46

Île de Ré (eel duh ray; pop. 16,000) was initially dubbed "Ré La Blanche" for its former salt trade, but the nickname could easily apply to its 70km of white sand beaches. The 30km long sunny paradise is connected by a 5km bridge to mainland La Rochelle. With ruinous monuments, a landscape of pine forests, farmland, vineyards, and ports—all connected by winding, paved bike paths—Île de Ré is a one-stop shop for the active ecotourist. The population swells in summer as crowds flood the main town of St-Martin-de-Ré and the beaches on the southern coast. Though this popular Parisian getaway is busier than nearby Île d'Aix, easily accessible beaches and nature trails keep it charming and relatively calm even during the summer months.

TRANSPORTATION

If you choose to **drive** across Pont La Pallice, you'll pay steep tolls. (From June to mid-Sept. €19 round-trip; from mid-Sept. to May €10. Motorcycles and scooters €2 year-round.) **Taxis** are available from the train station, but they are expensive (€35-65). Alternatively, **walk** or **bike**; cycling from La Rochelle to Sablanceaux—the first beach on the island after the bridge—takes less than an hour. The ride to the island is a bit tough, but once you arrive the trails offer great coastal views. From pl. de Verdun in La Rochelle, head west on av. du Maréchal Leclerc and follow road signs to Île de Ré until the bike path appears on the left.

Île de Ré

Buses: Autoplus, pl. de Verdun, La Rochelle (☎05 46 34 02 22). Lines #1, 10, and 50 to **Sablanceaux** (€1.50). Make sure the bus is going to Sablanceaux: sometimes lines #1 and 10 stop before crossing the bridge. In early and late summer, buses operate infrequently; in low season, no buses go to Sablanceaux. Rébus (☎05 46 09 20 15). Info office, 36 av. Charles de Gaulle, in St-Martin. Open M-F 9am-noon and 2-5:30pm. From pl. de Verdun to: **La Flotte** (40min., 14 per day, €3); **Les Portes** (1hr., 11 per day, €7); **St-Clement** (1hr., 11 per day, €7); **St-Martin** (50min., 14 per day, €4).

Ferries: Croisières Inter-Îles, 3 promenade des Coureauleurs, La Rochelle (☎08 25 13 55 00; www.inter-iles.com). To **St-Martin** (2 per day in high season; in low season 1 per day; €18, ages 4-18 €15, under 4 €4). Check the island's transportation website, www.service-maritime-iledaix.com, for up-to-date schedules.

Bike Rental: Cycland, rue de Sully, St-Martin (☎05 46 09 08 66). €3.50-5.50 per hr., €6.50-10 per ½-day, €8-15 per day; ID deposit. Open daily July-Aug. 9am-1pm and 2-7pm; Sept.-June 9:30am-12:30pm and 2-7pm. MC/V.

ORIENTATION AND PRACTICAL INFORMATION

Saint-Martin-de-Ré, the island's historical capital, is the best base.

Tourist Office: Quai Nicolas Baudin (☎05 46 09 20 06; www.saint-martin-de-re.fr). Biking trail maps €1. Open July-Aug. M-Sa 10am-7pm, Su 10am-1pm; Sept.-June M-Sa 10am-noon and 2-6pm.

Tours: From mid-June to mid-Sept. walking tours depart the tourist office (1hr.; W 10:30am; €6, under 18 €3) and carriage tours leave from Parking Vauban (1hr.; by reservation only; 1hr. Th 10am; €8.50, under 18 €5). Mayor's office (☎01 45 88 17 00 or 06 81 91 64 15) organizes guided tours of **Fort de la Prée.** Times vary. Open Apr.-Oct. daily 10am-12:30pm and 3-7pm. €5, under 13 €4, under 5 free.

Police: ☎05 46 09 21 17.

POITOU-CHARENTES

Hospital: In St-Martin. Emergency services and **ambulances** July-Aug. ☎05 46 09 20 01; Sept.-June ☎05 46 15 or 18.

Pharmacy: Pharmacie Du Port, 7 rue de Sully (☎05 46 09 20 43). Open July-Aug. M-Sa 9am-12:30pm and 2:30-7:30pm, Su 10am-12:30pm.

Internet Access: At most hotels. Some Wi-Fi near the harbor at St-Martin.

Post Office: Pl. de la République (☎05 46 09 38 20). Offers **currency exchange.** Open M-F 9am-noon and 1:30-4pm, Sa 9am-noon. **Postal Code:** 17410.

ACCOMMODATIONS AND CAMPING

Rates in Ré skyrocket in summer to at least €55 a night; camping is your best bet. Campgrounds between the bridge and St-Martin-de-Ré are crowded in July and August. Reserve ahead for all accommodations in summer. The tourist office lists rooms for rent that tend to run €10 less than most hotels.

St-Martin's Hôtel du Port, 29 quai de la Poithevinière (☎05 46 09 21 21; www.iledere-hot-port.com), across the port from the tourist office. Impeccable rooms, with large windows, TVs, and renovated baths. Breakfast €7.30. Reception 8am-10pm. Singles and doubles €70-95; 3- to 5-person suites €85-150. Extra bed €15. AmEx/MC/V. ❺

L'Hippocampe, 16 rue Château des Mauléons (☎05 46 09 60 68), in La Flotte, 4km east of St-Martin and 9km north of Sablanceaux. Pastel rooms straight out of a Martha Stewart magazine. Most rooms have full baths. Breakfast €6. Reception 8am-11pm. Reservations recommended. Singles and doubles €52-74; triples €98. V. ❸

La Plage, 408 rue du Chaume (☎05 46 29 42 62; www.la-plage.com), near St-Clément. Lively beachside campground. Reservations recommended far in advance. In summer, campers can stay only by the week. Open Apr.-Sept. 2 people with tent and car €18-28; €5.50-11.50 per extra person, children €3.30-11.80. Electricity €5.50. MC/V. ❶

Camping Tamaris, 4 rue du Comte d'Hastrel (☎05 46 09 81 28), in the center of Rivedoux. Popular, thickly forested campground. Open Easter-Sept. 1-3 people €17; €6 per extra person, under 7 €4. Electricity €4. Cash only. ❶

FOOD

Most towns have pizzerias and *crêperies* as well as morning markets, which are listed in Ré's free tourist packet. St-Martin's indoor market is off **rue Jean Jaurès,** by the port. (Open in high season daily 9am-1pm; in low season Tu-Su 9am-1pm.) Just east of St-Martin on the road to La Flotte, there's an **Intermarché,** 4 av. des Corsaires. (☎05 46 09 42 02. Open M-Sa 8:30am-8pm, Su 9-11:45am.) Several *dégustation* houses sit along the bike paths where local fishermen offer their catch of the day. A bucket of oysters tends to run half the price of most restaurants (see **Île de Ré Bike Tour,** p. 572, for specific locations). Tasty, albeit pricey, restaurants surround the port in St-Martin.

Marco Polo, 6-8 quai de Bernonville (☎05 46 09 15 92). Moderately priced Italian cuisine. *Formules* €13-19. *Menu* €19. Open daily noon-3pm and 7-10:30pm. MC/V. ❸

SIGHTS

ABBAYE DES CHÂTELIERS AND MAISON DU PLATIN. Built in 1156, the abbey was destroyed during the Wars of Religion as Ré changed hands between Catholics and Protestants only to be abandoned 400 years later. Many of its stones helped build the Fort de la Prée. Today, the romantic, windswept ruins—the nave's walls and a gaping window frame—stand in a poppy field between Sablanceaux and La Flotte. The **Maison du Platin** details the history of the island's fish and salt industries with photographs and costumed mannequins meant to represent Ré's earliest residents. The museum offers walking tours in French of the old quarters, port, and nearby oyster farms as well as 1hr. bike tours of the abbey. *(Av. du Front de Mer, La Flotte. ☎05 46 09 61 39. Open Apr.-Oct. W-Su 2-6pm. €4, under 13 free. Bike tours €5, under 13 €4.)*

ÉCLUSES À POISSONS. Tours (1hr.) of these medieval fishing beds teach visitors about the island tradition. The beds' stone walls, which lie along the beaches between St-Clément and Sablanceaux, were erected to trap fish with the waning tides. The tour includes walking on shells, so wear boots. *(60 cours des Jarrières in Ste-Marie-de-Ré. ☎05 46 37 47 50. Times vary with tides; call for a schedule.)*

HÔTEL CLERJOTTE. This 15th- to 17th-century Renaissance gallery houses the island's history museum, **Musée Ernest Cognacq.** Temporary exhibits in media from film to paintings and sketches to 3D models reveal the Sun King's extravagant dreams and the tenacity of the engineer who brought them to life. *(Av. Victor Bouthillier. ☎05 46 09 21 22; www.saint-martin-de-re.fr. Open M-F 10am-noon and 2-5pm, Sa-Su 2-5pm. €4, students €2.50; 1st Su of the month free.)*

ÉGLISE SAINT-MARTIN. This imposing 15th-century church sits just uphill from the *quai*. A haul up to the top of the bell tower at sunset is rewarded with a glowing island panorama. *(Open daily July-Aug. 10am-11:30pm; Sept.-June 10am-sunset. Free. Bell tower €1.40, ages 11-15 €0.60, under 10 free. Guided tours €2.50/€1.70/free.)*

OTHER SIGHTS. On the way to St-Martin, stop by **Ars** to admire its 17 windmills, dismantled in the 19th century when an insect plague wiped out one of Ré's chief crops—cereals. Today, sea salt is the island's pride and joy. St-Martin lays claim to a port built by Vauban and a **citadel** commissioned by Louis XIV to protect Ré from the invading English. Today, the citadel is an active prison. In St-Clément-des-Baleines, watch for the blinking red light of the **Phare des Baleines.** Built in 1854, the 57m lighthouse is one of France's tallest. Climb its 257 stairs for a great ocean view. *(☎05 46 29 18 23. Open daily July-Aug. 9:30am-7:30pm; Sept. 10am-6:30pm; Oct.-Mar. 10:30am-5:30pm; Apr.-June 10am-7pm. €3, ages 7-12 €1.50.)*

🔲🔁 BIKING AND BEACHES

It's easy, scenic, and affordable to rent a bike in any island town and pedal along the paths, coastal sidewalks, and wooded lanes spread out across the island. Although trails to St-Martin along the southern half of Île de Ré can be packed, crowds thin out to the north. The *Guide des Itinéraires Cyclables* (€1), available from island tourist offices, describes five 10-22km paths. For a riveting jaunt around the island, check out the 🔲bike tour (next page). One of the island's best trails begins in St-Martin and runs along the northern coast to Ars through a salt marsh and a bird preserve. In winter, 20,000 birds use the sanctuary as a rest stop as they migrate from Siberia and Canada to Africa.

The island's major attractions are, of course, its splendid beaches. Put on some sunscreen—and nothing else—at the bathing suit-optional **plage du Petit Bec** in Les Portes-en-Ré or head to the pine-fringed dunes of **plage de la Conche des Baleines,** near the lighthouse just off Gare Bec.

DANGER, AHOY! The beaches on the northern coast are large and uncrowded—for a reason. The sea off the north coast tends to be dangerous and the shores rocky; for better swimming, try the sandy strip along the southern shore beginning at La Couarde.

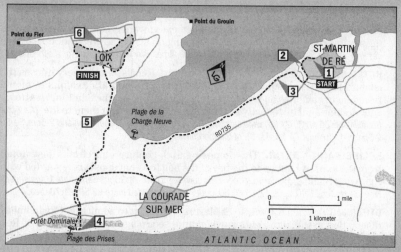

ÎLE DE RÉ BY BIKE

1. From Cycland, head back toward the water and turn left. Load up on snacks for the road at the covered **market,** where islanders peddle fresh produce, sandwiches, and nuts.

2. Follow the signs to "Ars" and "Loix." The road becomes cyclists-only, and after a few minutes of quiet the trees thin out to reveal distant sandy beaches and light-blue water.

3. For an early stop, try one of the oyster houses with *"dégustation"* signs inviting visitors to sample the delicious fresh catch. Once you're full, bike for another 20min., and turn right at the unlabeled arrow as the path veers left into the mainland. Do not continue straight toward Blois, or you will be led away from the coast.

4. After a stretch of ripening vineyards, fields of potatoes, and poppy meadows, turn left at the crossing at rue Chemin de la Griffondine to head into the **Forêt Domaniale.** The road leads to **plage des Prises;** stop off for a short nap under the sun. When you feel recuperated, turn back the way you came and head straight toward Loix at the crossing.

5. On the winding coastal road, take note of the oyster and *bigorneaux* (tiny, much-sought-after snails) reservoirs as well as the long-beaked avocets looking to snag a treat. Geographically, Île de Ré is a migration meeting-point for birds flying south from Siberia and north from Africa. The stretch of marshland and mud flats you see along the ride is a preservation effort by the **Ligue pour la Protection des Oiseaux** (League for the Protection of Birds).

6. After crossing the bridge, follow the narrow, maze-like roads marked by *"centre village"* signs to the **Loix** *place.* Reward yourself with homemade ice cream from one of the stands or lounge at one of the *crêperies* before heading back. To continue the journey, follow signs for "Ars," which run along the south side of the coast to the next city—the more boisterous and touristy **Ars-en-Ré.** Seventeen stately windmills will guide your way.

ÎLE D'AIX

☎ **05 46**

Smaller and less accessible than Ré, windy Île d'Aix (eel-dex; pop. 200) is almost entirely free of the souvenir shops and fast-food stands that populate most beach towns in the region. Just 3km long and barely 600m wide, the island's population grows tenfold in summer when its tiny coves and rocky coastline are flooded with campers and schoolchildren. The best beaches are along the southwest coast near the lighthouses, though Sables Jaunes, nestled between rocky cliffs on the northwest tip, is the most sheltered.

Aix's most striking sight dates to 1815, when the island hosted Napoleon for three days before he surrendered to the English and was exiled to Ste-Hélène. The house he stayed in was transformed into the **Musée Napoléonien** in 1928. Today, it contains a small but impressive collection of portraits and paraphernalia, including 40 clocks stopped at 5:49—his time of death—and a rough draft of his letter of surrender to England. The **Musée Africain** next door, unaltered since the 1930s, presents a hodgepodge of Central African artifacts collected by Napoleon Gourgaud during five expeditions. Napoleon Bonaparte's stuffed dromedary (a type of camel) is also an interesting—if random—piece of the exhibit. (☎ 05 46 84 66 40. Both open July-Aug. daily 9:30am-1pm and 2-5:30pm; Sept.-Oct. and June daily 9:30am-12:30pm and 2-6pm; Nov.-Apr. M and W-Su 9:30am-noon and 2-5pm. One ticket provides admission to both museums. €4.50, ages 18-25 €3, under 18 free. Free on select Su 9:30-11:30am and 2-5pm; check exact dates at the tourist office.) The **Fort Liedot,** commissioned and allegedly designed by Napoleon to help protect the arsenal in Rochefort, housed prisoners, including Algerian president Ben Bella, until the late 70s. Later, it became a children's summer camp. (Open for guided tours July-Aug. 1hr. tours in French available through the tourist office. Daily 11am and 6pm. €3.)

Île d'Aix's only hotel, **Hôtel Napoleon** ❹, will be undergoing renovations until the summer of 2009; for information on prices and amenities, contact the tourist office. Next to the port, quiet **Camping le Fort de la Rade** ❶ offers a picturesque setting inside the battlements of a Vauban fort. (☎ 05 46 84 28 28; fax 84 00 44. Pool available. Reception 9am-noon and 5-7pm. Open Apr.-Sept. €4.10 per person, children €3; €9-15 per tent, depending on location. Sept. and Apr.-June €3.70 per person, children €2.20; €6.70 per tent. MC/V.) Aix's few restaurants tend to be pricey. The bakery on **rue Gourgaud** sells cheap sandwiches, and a little grocery store across the street sells essentials. For an oyster feast, check out one of the *dégustation* houses along the coast at **Les Mathes.** (Oysters, local white wine, and bread typically run €7-9. Open July-Aug. noon-5pm.) Classy **Les Paillotes** ❹, rue Le Bois Joly, serves lamb and seafood in an elegant, shaded courtyard encircled by trimmed evergreens. (☎ 05 46 84 66 24. *Menus* €19-35. Open July-Aug. daily 9am-2am; Sept.-June M-F 9am-4pm, Sa-Su 7pm-2am; often closed M. MC/V.) Cheerful **Pressoir** ❸, down rue Le Bois Joly, has a *formule* of fresh *moules frites* for €9.50. Communal tables add to the rustic feel. The bar is decorated with sketches of French celebrities. (☎ 05 46 84 09 37. *Menus* €22. Open daily 9am-1:45am. Reservations recommended. AmEx/MC/V.)

Aix is one of the only coastal islands with no highway to the mainland; only locals use cars. Croisières Inter-Îles, 3 promenade des Coureauleurs, La Rochelle (☎ 08 25 13 55 00), runs **boats** from La Rochelle to Île d'Aix (€26, under 18 €20). Check the island's transportation website (www.service-maritime-ile-daix.com) for schedules. The **tourist office,** 6 rue Gourgaud, lies beyond the horse-drawn carriages. (☎ 05 46 83 01 82. Open daily July-Aug. 9am-5pm; Sept. and Apr.-June M 10am-noon, Th-Su 10am-noon and 2-5pm.) The horse-drawn carriages lead **tours** of the island in French. (☎ 05 46 84 69 73. 50min. €6.50, under 10 €5.50.) *Crêperies* and snack shops in town rent **bikes** (around €3.50

per hr., €8.50 per day; ID deposit). Pedestrians can walk around the island in a mere two hours, and some of the best spots are only accessible by foot.

COULON
☎ 05 49

The winding streets of tiny Coulon (koo-lohn; pop. 2200) run alongside the canals of the Marais Poitevin, making the town an ideal launch site for a boat ride into the marshland. Stretching from Niort to the Atlantic coast just north of La Rochelle, this "natural" wetland used to flood regularly at high tide—until monks in the AD ninth century decided to irrigate the area to protect their agriculture from salt water. Nicknamed "La Venise Verte" (the Green Venice) today for its serene canals, this tucked-away spot has enchanted painters, writers, and poets alike. Bikers along the banks pass through a maze of narrow creeks, weeping willows, purple irises, and herds of cattle. By the Sèvre Niortaise River, trees form an overhanging canopy while duckweeds carpet the water's surface, making the canals look like fleeting grassy paths.

⊡ TRANSPORTATION. CASA Autocars **buses,** 11-13 chemin du Fief Binard (☎05 49 24 93 47), arrive from Niort's *gare routière* (next to the train station) and its central pl. de la Brèche (30min.; M-Tu and Th-F 5 per day, more W, Sa, and during school vacations; €1.20). Take bus #20 (dir.: Coulon/Marais Poitevin). The best way to delve farther into the Marais is by **boat** or **bike.** Boats are worth the cost and are a unique way to experience the *marais*. There are 14 boat-rental locations along the river. Most travelers explore on their own, but a few places offer guided tours. Stirring the waters releases methane gas trapped below; guides may prod the water to light a fire on the surface. In Coulon, **Le Trigale,** 6 rue de l'Église (☎05 49 35 14 14), supplies private boats and boatmen, though few speak English. (1hr., up to 10 people €25-68.) The adventurous can rent a boat and navigate themselves (1-7hr.; €15-45; MC/V). Other vendors offer similar deals; places down the river are usually €1-2 cheaper.

⊠ PRACTICAL INFORMATION. Head to the **tourist office,** 31 rue Gabriel Auchier, for general info about hiking and bicycling tours and a list of the area's *chambres d'hôtes* and campgrounds. (☎05 49 35 99 29. Open daily July-Aug. 10am-12:30pm and 2-6:30pm; June 10am-12:30pm and 2-6pm; call for low-season hours.) Find an **ATM** at **Crédit Agricole,** pl. de l'Église. The **post office,** 17 rue Gabriel Auchier, next to the tourist office, offers **currency exchange** with advance notice. (☎/fax 05 49 35 90 11. Open M-W and F 9am-noon and 1:40-5pm, Th 10am-noon and 1:40-5pm, Sa 9-11:30am.)

⊡⊠ ACCOMMODATIONS AND CAMPING. Hotels are expensive in Coulon, but many *chambres d'hôtes* are available from €45 for two people. The elegant, green-shuttered, stone **Le Central ❶,** 4 rue d'Autremont, in the *centre-ville*, is the cheapest hotel in town and offers spacious rooms that verge on apartments, with modern bathrooms, tasteful decor, air-conditioning, and TVs. Prices vary according to season and view. (☎05 49 35 90 20; www.hotel-lecentral-coulon. com. Breakfast €8. Reception 8am-10pm. Reservations recommended. Open Mar.-Jan. Singles €49-51; doubles €56-61. AmEx/MC/V.) **Camping de La Garette (l'Îlôt du Chail) ❶** is in a tucked-away grove, 3km south of Coulon, surrounded by three streams and accessible only by bridge. Lines of trees offer shade, while a pool, laundromat, and organized activities in July and August make this modest campground a true family affair. La Garette is just after Coulon on CASA bus #20. Get off at La Garette-Centre des Loisirs and walk in the direction of the bus, past the horse stables, until you reach the campground. (☎05

49 35 00 33. Bikes €4 per hr., €11 per day. Canoe rental available up the river. Reception July-Aug. 8:30am-1pm and 2-8pm; mid-Sept. and June 9:30am-noon and 2:30-7:30pm; Apr.-May 10am-noon and 3-7pm. Open from Apr. to mid-Sept. €3-4 per person, children €2-2.50; €1.50 per car; sites €3-5. Electricity €2.50. MC/V.) A hike through marshy forests starts beside the campground and winds past the tall two-door houses (one for land, one for water) unique to the area.

🔲 🖼 **SIGHTS AND FESTIVALS.** For the avid ecotourist, **La Maison des Marais Mouillés,** pl. de la Coutume, is worth a look. The **Maraiscope,** an endearing presentation of the marshland's history and the museum's highlight, is only given in French. (☎05 49 35 81 04. Open daily July-Aug. 10am-7pm; Sept.-Oct. and Apr.-June 10am-noon and 2-6pm. Guided tours for groups of 15 or more. €5.50, ages 6-16 €3.) Every July, tourists flood the 🖼**Marché sur l'Eau,** the only French market where customers row from one boat stand to the next to buy fresh produce. (For more information and schedules, call the organizing committee at ☎05 49 35 00 13.) In the first week of July, citizens dress in authentic garb and lead a parade of traditional boats down the river for the **Fête du Miget.** The **Rallye Canoë-Kayak** attracts 300 boats and 2000 spectators for a race down the *marais* during the penultimate weekend in June.

LES SABLES D'OLONNE   ☎02 51

Les Sables d'Olonne (lay sah-bluh duh-lohn; pop. 15,500), once a port for the regional capital, Olonne (Gallic for "over waters") was abandoned when the harbor dried up. Les Sables ("the sands") is now a popular vacation spot for French families and teenagers. The favorable waters and weather make it a prime spot for watersports, fishing trips, and marshland hikes. In an unusual mix of climates, this area combines Brittany's cold waters and the Riviera's sprawling sandy beaches—with perhaps a touch of tackiness.

▣ TRANSPORTATION

Trains: Rue de la Bauduère. Open M 5:20am-7:45pm, Tu-F 6:20am-7:45pm, Sa 8:40am-6:30pm, Su 10:30am-7:30pm. To **La Rochelle** (2-3hr., 9 per day, €19) via **La Roche-sur-Lyon, Nantes** (1½hr., 12 per day, €16), and **Paris** (4hr., 6 per day, €64-78).

Buses: Rue de la Bauduère, next to the train station. Office open M-F 8:30am-12:30pm and 2:30-6:30pm, Sa 9:30am-noon. Sovetours (☎02 51 95 18 71) sends buses to **La Rochelle** (3hr., 9am, €24) and **Fromentine** (2hr., 2-4 per day, €12).

Ferries: Compagnie Vendéenne, 11 bis rue Bénatier (☎08 25 13 90 85; www.compagnievendeenne.com), in La Chaume. To **Île d'Yeu** (1hr.; July-Aug. 2-5 per week; round-trip €42, ages 4-18 €28, under 4 €6). TUSCO (☎02 51 32 95 95) serves the beaches. The tourist office has maps and schedules. €1.20, carnet of 10 €8.50.

Taxis: Radiotaxi Sablais (☎02 51 95 40 80). €1.30 per km.

Water Taxis: La Sablaise crosses the small canal dividing Les Sables and La Chaume. Leaves from quai Guiné. €1. Runs June-Aug. daily 6am-9pm; Sept. and Mar.-May Sa-Su 6am-8pm; Oct.-Mar. daily 6am-8pm.

Car Rental: Avis (☎02 51 96 97 78). €69 per day. 21+. Under-25 surcharge €25. Open M-Sa 9am-noon and 2-6pm. AmEx/MC/V.

Bike Rental: Holiday Bikes, 66 promenade Georges Clemenceau (☎02 51 32 64 15; www.holiday-bikes.com). Bikes €10-12 per day; €150 deposit. Scooters €39-43; €800 deposit. Motorbikes €105; €1600 deposit. Open June-Sept. daily 10am-8pm.

POITOU-CHARENTES

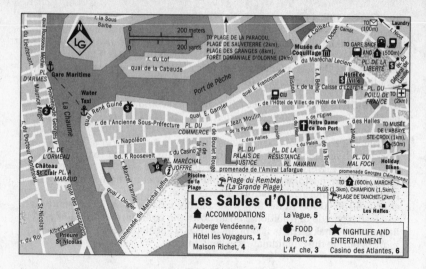

Les Sables d'Olonne

🏠 ACCOMMODATIONS   La Vague, **5**

Auberge Vendéenne, **7**   🍴 FOOD
Hôtel les Voyageurs, **1**   Le Port, **2**   ⭐ NIGHTLIFE AND
Maison Richet, **4**   L' Af che, **3**   ENTERTAINMENT
                                                    Casino des Atlantes, **6**

🛈 PRACTICAL INFORMATION

Tourist Office: 1 promenade du Maréchal Joffre (☎02 51 96 85 85; www.lessablesdol-onne-tourisme.com). From the train station, turn onto av. du Général de Gaulle toward pl. de la Liberté. Continue straight through the park, past the fountain, and onto rue de l'Hôtel de Ville. Take a left on rue Travot. Turn right at the water. Walk along the beach (15min.); the office is in the casino. English spoken. Boat **tours** to Île d'Yeu. Open July-Aug. daily 9am-7pm; Sept.-June M-Th and Sa 9am-12:30pm and 1:30-6pm, F 10am-12:30pm and 1:30-6pm, Su 10:30am-noon and 3:30-5:30pm.

Youth Center and Internet Access: Centre d'Information Jeunesse (CIJ), 34 rue de l'Hôtel de Ville (☎02 51 33 76 29). Apartment and event listings. Open M-Th 9am-noon and 2-6pm, F 9am-noon and 2-5pm.

Laundromat: Lavarie des Salines, 5 rue Nicot (☎06 89 63 45 23). Wash €4 per 7kg, dry €0.50 per 15min. Open daily 7am-9pm.

Police: 1 bd. Blaise Pascal (☎02 51 21 19 91).

Hospital: 75 av. d'Aquitaine (☎02 51 21 85 85).

Post Office: 1 rue Haxo (☎02 51 21 82 82). **Currency exchange** and **Western Union** available. Open M-F 8:30am-6pm, Sa 8:30am-noon. **Postal Code:** 85100.

🛏 ACCOMMODATIONS

Lodgings in Les Sables are expensive, especially in summer; most tourists camp outside of the city and commute to the beaches and shops. Les Sables's campgrounds are listed at the tourist office and are accessible by bus.

Auberge Vendéenne, 36 rue Remparts (☎02 51 32 03 98; www.aubergevendeenne.fr.st), along the water. Simple, clean rooms look out on an inner courtyard. Breakfast €5. Reception 11am-2pm and 6-10pm. Singles €28-39; doubles €33-59, with showers and toilets €43-65; triples with showers and toilets €53-75. Extra bed €5. MC/V. ❸

Maison Richet, 25 rue de la Patrie (☎02 51 32 04 12; www.maison-richet.fr), 50m from the beach and the *centre-ville*. A tropical escape, complete with palm trees, terrace, bright-blue rooms, and straw carpets. Breakfast €8.50. Free Wi-Fi. Reception 3:30-9pm. Open Feb.-Oct. Singles and doubles €48-55, with toilets and showers €55-68; triples €65-80; quads with toilets and showers €75-87. Prices lower in winter. MC/V. ❹

Hôtel les Voyageurs, 16 rue de la Bauduère (☎02 51 95 11 49; http://voyageurshotel. free.fr), across from the train station, 15min. from the beach. Spartan rooms with clean bathrooms. Above a *brasserie.* Buzz if restaurant is closed. Breakfast €6.50. Reception July-Aug. daily 6:45am-9pm; Sept.-June M-F 6:45am-9pm. Closed last 2 weeks of Dec. Singles and doubles with full bath €46-49; family rooms €78. MC/V. ❹

La Vague, 8 rue des Écoliers (☎02 51 32 05 29), just steps from the beach. Cozy rooms above a bar. Breakfast €5. Singles €25-30; doubles €37-40. MC/V. ❷

📷 FOOD

The 19th-century Art Nouveau **Les Halles,** behind Notre Dame de Bon Port, hosts a market. (Open from mid-June to mid-Sept. daily 8am-1pm.) There's a **Champion** supermarket on 93 bd. de Castelnau, 500m north of the beach (open M-Sa 9am-8pm, Su 9am-12:30pm) and a **Marché Plus** on 87 av. Aristand Briand. (Open M-Sa 7am-9pm, Su 9am-1pm.) To take away a gastronomical souvenir, try a can of *thon aux pruneaux et épices* (tuna with prunes and spices). The nearly identical *brasseries* and *crêperies* along **plage du Remblai** serve the cheapest food in town, though many of them have fairly low culinary standards. Try the **Porte de Pêche,** where dozens of restaurants serve the catch of the day.

Le Port, 24 quai Georges V (☎02 51 32 07 52), across the water in La Chaume near the water taxi stop. Specializes in grilled seafood (from €10). Few vegetarian options. *Entrées* €8-13. *Menus* €13-20. Open daily noon-2pm and 7-10pm. MC/V. ❸

L'Affiche, 21 Quai Guiné (☎02 51 95 34 71). Cheery beach posters create a mellow atmosphere at this waterside gourmet restaurant. Fish €11-15. 5-course dinner *menu* and wine €31. Open daily 6-11pm. AmEx/MC/V. ❸

👁📷 SIGHTS AND BEACHES

MUSÉE DU COQUILLAGE. Yard-long Antiguan lobsters welcome visitors to this one-of-a-kind museum, which displays over 45,000 colorful shells, corals, crabs, and even stuffed sharks—all personally collected by a local who dropped out of the army to pursue his collection. (*8 rue du Maréchal Leclerc, near the Porte de Pêche.* ☎*02 51 23 50 00; www.museum-du-coquillage.com. Open May-Aug. daily 9am-8pm; Sept.-Apr. M-Sa 9:30am-12:30pm and 2-6:30pm, Su 2-6:30pm. €7, ages 4-11 €4.*)

MUSÉE DE L'ABBAYE SAINTE-CROIX. This restored 17th-century Benedictine abbey presents an excellent modern and contemporary collection as well as a smaller inventory of regional artifacts and folk art. Most notable are writer-painter Victor Brauner's works and Gaston Chaissac's colorful paintings. Temporary exhibits showcase up-and-coming artists. (*Rue de Verdun.* ☎*02 51 32 01 16; musee-lessables@wanadoo.fr. Open Tu-Su from mid-June to Sept. 10am-noon and 2:30-6:30pm; from Oct. to mid-June 2:30-5:30pm. €4.60, students and under 18 €2.30; 1st Su of month free.*)

OTHER SIGHTS. Along the promontory across the channel from the *centre-ville,* the 15th-century **Château Saint-Clair** has views of the **Tour d'Arundel,** the only pre-18th-century lighthouse on the coast of the Vendée, while **Prieuré Saint-Nicolas,** a restored 18th-century church, is now a contemporary art gallery. Near the *centre-ville,* in front of Les Halles, **Notre Dame de Bon Port** features a rare blend of Gothic and Baroque styles. (*Pl. de l'Église. Open M-Sa 9am-noon and 2:30-6:30pm, Su 9am-noon and 5:45-7:30pm. Mass Su 10:30am.*)

POITOU-CHARENTES

♫ ENTERTAINMENT

On Tuesdays and Thursdays during the summer, **Les Remblais,** the widest strip of the boardwalk, becomes a pedestrian walkway with concerts, outdoor theater, jugglers, clowns, and marionette shows. The nearby **Casino des Atlantes,** 3 bd. Franklin Roosevelt, is most notable for its neon lights and rattling slot machines. On most summer nights, the casino puts on free concerts or dance shows with dinner. (☎02 51 32 05 40. Open daily July-Aug. 10am-4am; Sept.-June 10am-3am. Free concerts 10pm-2am. Restaurant open 7-10pm.)

⚐ OUTDOOR ACTIVITIES

The tourist office distributes a free brochure in French with 10 **hiking** and **biking** trails detailing jaunts that traverse its dunes, forests, and beaches. In July and August, the office also posts daily listings of local tennis tournaments, free concerts, and organized beach volleyball games, which welcome volunteers. Guided boat trips, canoeing, surfing, sailing, diving, and other watersports are also available. The closest trail starts about 1km north of Les Sables's train station. From the station, follow rue de la Baudùère until it crosses rue du Docteur Charcot; signs indicate the beginning of an 18km trail that winds through the tiny villages of countryside to a beautiful church at Olonne-sur-Mer.

    La Grande Plage, otherwise known as **plage du Remblai,** a flat 3km expanse of sand on the outskirts of the *centre-ville,* is the largest and most crowded of Les Sables's shores, with souvenir shops and *crêperies* spilling out onto its banks. A popular surfing spot with great waves, **plage de Tanchet** is right beyond La Grande Plage, behind the Lac du Tanchet, as you walk along the beach away from the tourist office; bus B also runs to Tanchet from the stop at Schwabac. For more solitude, take bus A to La Chaume's **plage de la Paracou** (stop at Le Large), known for its more dangerous, rocky waters. Following the coast north from Paracou, beachgoers will encounter two less crowded beaches with great surf and topless—and often bottomless—sunbathers. **Plage de Sauveterre** is nestled in a forest 4km north of Paracou, while **plage des Granges** is 1km farther. Adventurers may enjoy the **Forêt Domaniale d'Olonne** just east of here, where huge dunes span all the way from dry woodlands into the sea.

ÎLE D'YEU   ☎ 02 51

Île d'Yeu (eel dyuh; pop. 4800) is a breath of fresh air from the tourist hordes in Les Sables, characterized by dark pine forests, secluded sandy beaches, and misty cliffs. Ferries unload French tourists who flood the island every summer; foreigners, however, rarely stumble upon Île d'Yeu on their own. One out of a handful of islands splattered alongside France's Atlantic coast, Île d'Yeu may not be the most popular or picturesque, but its rocky points, tucked-away beaches, and rambling bike paths make it a paradise in its own right.

⬅ TRANSPORTATION.
Direct **ferries** run from Les Sables to Île d'Yeu, but seaside village Fromentine is the easiest base from which to reach the island by ferry. **Buses** leave Nantes and run to the port at Fromentine (2-4 per day, €9-12). Head to the *gare maritime* for **Vedettes Inter-Îles Vendéennes.** (☎02 51 39 00 00; www.ile-yeu.com. 2-4 per day. Round-trip €24-30. Open M-Sa 9am-noon and 2-6pm, Su 9am-noon. MC/V.) **Yeu Continent** (☎08 25 85 30 00; www.compagnie-yeu-continent.fr) is also at the *gare maritime.* (Office open M-F 9:30am-noon and 2-5pm, Sa 9:30-11:30am. Ferries 1hr.; 2-4 per day. Round-trip €31, seniors €25, ages 12-18 €21. MC/V.) **Taxis** are available through **Taxi Joinville** (☎06 07 68 53

96), and **public buses** run to most island destinations. (☎02 51 37 13 93. Schedules vary. €1. Open M-F 8am-12:30pm and 1:30-6:30pm, Sa 9am-12:15pm.) Rent **cars** at **Cantin**, 1 quai de la Mairie, which stores bags and provides maps. (☎02 51 58 48 00. From €65 per day. 21+. Open June-Aug. daily 8:30am-7pm. MC/V.) Biking is the most efficient means by which to explore the numerous paths, and over a half-dozen **bike** rental shops dot the docks near the *gare maritime.* **La Roue Libre,** 4 rue Calypso, rents road and mountain bikes. (☎02 51 59 20 70. Road bikes €10.50 per day; mountain bikes €12 per day. Open July-Aug. daily 8:30am-7:30pm; Sept.-Mar. school holidays only; Apr.-June daily 9am-12:30pm and 2-7pm. MC/V.) **La Trottinette,** on rue de la Chaume, also rents bikes. (☎02 51 58 31 06. Bikes €10.50 per day. Scooters €48 1st day, €30 per day thereafter; €400 deposit; over 16 only. Open Apr.-Sept. daily 9am-7pm. MC/V.)

⚠ PRACTICAL INFORMATION. The **tourist office,** rue du Marché, distributes biking and hiking itineraries with English, German, and Spanish descriptions as well as hotel and transportation info. Get a free map on the island; Fromentine's tourist office charges €1. From the dock, turn right along the waterfront, left onto rue de l'Abbesse, and right onto rue de la République. (☎02 51 58 32 58; www.ile-yeu.fr. Open July-Aug. M-Sa 9am-7pm, Su 9:30am-1pm; Sept. and Apr.-June M-Sa 9am-12:30pm and 2-6pm, Su 9:30am-12:30pm; Oct.-Mar. M-Sa 9am-12:30pm and 2-5:30pm.) Other services include: 24hr. **ATMs** on quai Carnot; **police** (☎02 51 58 30 05); the **hospital** on Impasse du Puits Raimond (☎02 51 26 08 00); **laundry** at La Tornade Bleue, pl. Ketanou, near Hôtel L'Escale (wash €5 per 6kg.; dry €2 per 15min.; detergent €0.40; open daily 8am-8pm); and **Internet access** at **Oyanet Informatique,** 11 rue des Quais. (☎06 15 37 05 16; www.oyanet. com. €1 per 15min. Open M-Sa 10am-1pm and 2:30-7pm, Su 10am-1pm.)

⚑⚐ ACCOMMODATIONS AND FOOD. Though accommodations on Île d'Yeu are expensive, one stands out as worth the cost. The charming two-star **Hôtel L'Escale ❹,** 14 rue de la Croix du Port, is a 5min. walk from the quai at Port Joinville on a quiet street one block from the beach. Brand-new, renovated rooms with flatscreen TVs overlook a grassy courtyard filled with roses and folding chairs. (☎02 51 58 50 28; www.yeu-escale.fr. Breakfast €7.30. Reception 7:30am-1pm and 5-8:30pm. Open Dec.-Oct. Singles and doubles with bath, telephones, hair dryers, and TVs €52-72; triples and quads €68-84. Prices vary by season. Extra bed €7.30. MC/V.) For a place to stay before the ferry leaves Fromentine, try the **Relais des Îles ❸,** 18 av. de l'Estacade, which offers unconsciously rustic rooms behind the town bar. (☎02 51 68 52 11. Breakfast €5. Reception 8am-9pm. Singles with sinks €30, with full bath €45; doubles €40/50. Extra bed €6. MC/V.) The island's crowded but jovial **Camping Municipal ❶,** 1km east of the port, is enclosed by a calm expanse of beach on one side and tennis courts on the other. (☎02 51 58 34 20. Reception M-Sa 9am-1pm and 4:30-8pm. €3.10-4.20 per tent; €6.40 per caravan; extra person €2.50-3.10; €3.50 per car. Electricity €2.) There are seven campsites in Fromentine; its tourist office, pl. de la Gare, has a list (☎02 51 68 51 83). Full of shaded sites, the **Campeole de la Grande Côte ❶,** on the route de la Grande Côte, 1km from Fromentine and the beach, has a pool, bike and grill rental, laundry, a small restaurant, and a full calendar of activities. This popular campground gets crowded in summer, so reserve early. (☎02 51 68 51 89; www.campeole.fr. Reception M-Th 9am-noon and 1:30-5pm, F 9am-noon and 1:30-6pm, Sa-Su 10am-noon and 3-6pm. Open from May to mid-Sept. 2 people with car €13-20. Extra person €4.50-6.10. Electricity €3.90.) Eating out on touristy Île d'Yeu is a rather expensive affair, but fresh food is available from the **outdoor market** on pl. de la Norvege, by the docks. (Open daily 9am-1pm.) The **Casino** supermarket, 31 rue Calypso, is

2min. from the port, past La Roue Libre. (☎02 51 58 57 16. Open July-Aug. M-F 9am-12:30pm and 3:30-7:30pm, Sa 9am-7:30pm, Su 9am-1pm; Sept.-June M-F 9am-12:30pm and 3:30-7:30pm, Sa 9am-7:30pm.)

◙ 🔼 **SIGHTS AND OUTDOOR ACTIVITIES.** Île d'Yeu's tourist office skillfully lays out three easy **bike** circuits of the island, all originating from Port Joinville. The shortest, a 10km path, runs to the island's southern port and back in 2hr. Its highlights are **Port Meule** and 🔲**Pointe du Châtelet,** a seascape vista crowned by a towering cross that overlooks the withering ruins of the 14th-century **Vieux-Château.** The château, once frequently attacked by the English, was used as a fortress in the 16th century until it was ultimately abandoned by Louis XIV, who demanded that it be demolished. This may have been the only one of his orders that wasn't carried out; the crumbling remains stand stubbornly on the craggy coast, accessible only by bike. (Tours in French daily July-Aug. 11am-6pm; from May to mid-June W-Th and Sa-Su noon-5:30pm; late June Tu-Su noon-5pm. €4, ages 7-18 €1.) Just past the Port Meule, a quiet harbor moored with blue-bottomed boats, rests the **Pierre Tremblante,** a sizable boulder that shifts if rubbed the right way. The longest route (5hr.) circles the island, passing Renaissance churches, serene ports, and **plage des Conches.** One of the most popular bike routes (4hr.) travels to the center of the island, stopping 2km southeast of Port Joinville at the 12th-century **church** in St-Sauveur, where stained-glass windows illuminate a cool, dark interior. Along this route lies the sparkling **plage des Sapins,** popular with windsurfers, where a pine tree forest peters out into soft sand. The route then curves around to the south coast, where cliffs rise in all directions. 🔲**Plage Anse des Soux,** nestled between looming cliffs, is the perfect place for a siesta. The path then leads back to Joinville, but bikers can also continue past the town to the **Grand Phare,** a lighthouse on the island's highest hill, for a view of the island from 20m above. Coastal paths are pedestrian-only; signs throughout the island direct bikers.

AQUITAINE AND PAYS BASQUE

At the edge of France and Spain, Aquitaine and the Pays Basque are diverse in both landscape and culture. The English held Aquitaine from the 12th to 15th centuries, and the Pays Basque is the French half of the former kingdom of Navarre, the mountainous ancestral home of the Basque people. The area was joined with the Kingdom of France when its ruler, Henri IV, inherited the French throne in 1598. Today, a small Basque separatist minority still maintains that its land is independent of French and Spanish authority; for the most part, though, most French Basque willingly function in the larger French society while still proudly asserting their strong cultural identity.

Sprawling vineyards dominate Aquitaine, especially near Bordeaux, while the pine forest of Les Landes opens to the windswept west coast known for its stunning beaches, wild waves, and great surfing. In Pays Basque, closer to the Spanish border, the scent of fresh seafood accompanies the clinking of cowbells. An hour or two to the east, tiny villages sit among the towering peaks, lush foliage, and roaring waterfalls of the Pyrenees.

When locals aren't enjoying the beach or mountain trails, they're relishing the regional cuisine. The Pays Basque cooks up some of France's best seafood, along with *jambon cru* (cured ham) and the ubiquitous *piperade* (omelet with green peppers, onions, and tomatoes). In Aquitaine, *Moulard* duck, *Roquefort* cheese, and *Armagnac* (a local brandy) are essentials. Aquitaine flavors its cuisine with the elusive *truffe noir* (black truffle), but its glory is its wine, as the vineyards of Bordeaux produce some of the world's best vintages.

HIGHLIGHTS OF AQUITAINE AND PAYS BASQUE

HANG GLIDE on Europe's tallest sand dune, the Dune du Pilat (p. 590).

HIT THE TRAILS and cross the border while you're at it. Starting from Cauterets, hike into Spain past towering waterfalls in the Parc National des Pyrénées (p. 613).

HAVE A GLASS or buy a bottle at the wineries of St-Émilion (p. 588), an idyllic village where grapes have been crushed since Roman times.

AQUITAINE

BORDEAUX ☎ 05

Though its name is synonymous with wine, the city of Bordeaux (bohr-doh; pop. 235,000) has more to offer than most lushes would expect. Hipsters and tourists—and everyone in between—gather on the elegant streets of the cafe-filled city center, while in the surrounding countryside the legendary vineyards of St-Émilion, Médoc, Sauternes, and Graves draw international renown. The city is filled with history, drenched in culture, and animated with nightlife.

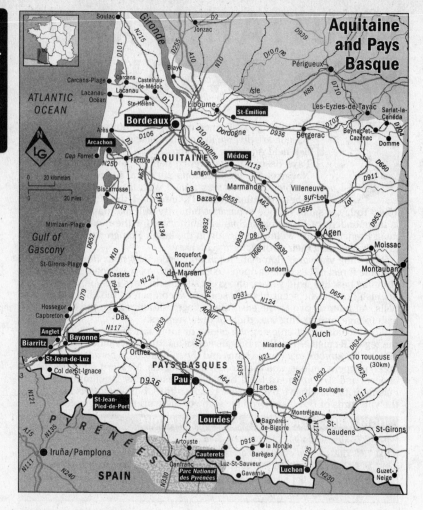

Aquitaine
and Pays
Basque

TRANSPORTATION

Flights: Airport in **Mérignac** (☎05 56 34 50 50), 11km west of Bordeaux. A shuttle connects the airport to the Bordeaux St-Jean train station and pl. Gambetta (40min.; every 45min. 6:45am-9:45pm to the airport, 7:45am-10:45pm to the station; €7, students, seniors, and under 26 €6). **Air France** office in Bordeaux, 37 allée de Tourny (☎08 20 32 08 20), makes reservations and provides schedules. Open M-F 9:30am-6:30pm, Sa 9:30am-1:15pm. AmEx/MC/V.

Trains: Gare St-Jean, rue Charles Domercq. Info office open M-Sa 9am-7pm. To: **Lyon** (8-10hr., 7 per day, €62-154); **Marseille** (6-7hr., 10 per day, €71-75); **Nantes** (4hr., 4 per day, €42); **Nice** (9-12hr., 2 per day, €103-110); **Paris** (3hr., 15-25 per day,

€46-66); **Poitiers** (2-3hr., 10 per day, €36-39); **Rennes** (6hr., 2 per day, €54); **Toulouse** (2-3hr., 11 per day, €31-34).

Buses: Réseau Trans Gironde, pl. de Quinconces (☎05 56 43 68 43). Open daily 7am-7pm. Buses travel to over 50 small towns surrounding Bordeaux.

Public Transportation: The TBC/Connex **bus** and **tram** system (☎05 57 57 88 88; www. infotbc.com) serves the city and suburbs. Maps at the train station. Info offices at 9 pl. Gambetta (open M-F 8am-7:30pm, Sa 9:45am-12:25pm and 2-6pm), at Pavilion de Quinconces (open M-F 7am-7:30pm, Sa 9:45am-12:25pm and 2-6pm), and at Gare St-Jean (open M-F 7am-7:30pm, Sa-Su 8:30am-3pm). 3 tram lines A, B, and C run daily 5am-1am. The *Tickarte Bordeaux Découverte* provides unlimited city bus and tram use (1-day pass €4.10, 2-day €7.10, 3-day €9.20). Individual tickets €1.30.

Taxis: Taxi Télé (☎05 56 96 00 34), in front of the train station. €1.30 per km during the day, €1.96 after 7pm. €30-45 to the airport.

Car Rental: Europcar, cours des Arrivées (☎08 25 00 42 46), connected to the train station. From €76 per day, €282 per week; €650 deposit. 21+. Open M-F 7am-10pm, Sa 8am-7pm, Su 10am-7:30pm. AmEx/MC/V.

Bike Rental: Pierre Qui Roule, 32 pl. Gambetta (☎05 57 85 80 87; www.pierrequiroule.fr). €7 per ½-day, €10 per day, €20 per weekend, €45 per week. In-line skates and pads €6 per ½-day, €9 per day. Open M 2-7pm, Tu-Sa 10am-7pm. MC/V.

 ## ORIENTATION AND PRACTICAL INFORMATION

Bordeaux's transportation hubs, **place Gambetta** and **place des Quinconces,** are in the *centre-ville*, while the bus depot is directly in front of **Gare St-Jean.** Tramway line C runs from the train station to pl. des Quinconces (10min.). To get to pl. Gambetta from the station, take line C to pl. de la Bourse and walk down rue St-Rémi, which becomes rue de la Porte Dijeaux. Bus #16 runs from the bus station to pl. de la Victoire and pl. Gambetta (every 10min. 5am-9pm, €1.30). To get to the *centre-ville* on foot, walk along the run-down but lively cours de la Marne, past Marché des Capucins and onto pl. de la Victoire. From here, turn right under the arch on the pedestrian rue Ste-Catherine, which continues into **vieux Bordeaux,** the hub of the city. To reach the tourist office, continue on rue Ste-Catherine for 15min., cross the wide cours de l'Intendance, and enter pl. de la Comédie as the street becomes cours du 30 Juillet. The tourist office is on the right, a block beyond the Grand Théâtre.

> **! EN GARDE.** Bordeaux can be dangerous; there are many poorly lit, empty streets at night. Be aware of your surroundings and use caution, especially in the neighborhoods to the south of the city center, by the hostel, and around the train station.

Tourist Office: 12 cours du 30 Juillet (☎05 56 00 66 00; www.bordeaux-tourisme. com). Free maps, brochures, and hotel reservations. Open July-Aug. M-Sa 9am-7:30pm, Su 9:30am-6:30pm; May-June and Sept.-Oct. M-Sa 9am-7pm, Su 9:30am-6:30pm; Nov.-Apr. M-Sa 9am-6:30pm, Su 9:45am-4:30pm. Branch at train station (☎05 56 91 64 70) also makes hotel reservations. Open May-Oct. M-Sa 9am-noon and 1-6pm, Su 10am-noon and 1-3pm; Nov.-Apr. M-F 9:30am-12:30pm and 2-6pm.

Tours: Tourist office offers tours in English and French (☎05 56 00 66 24). **Walking** tours daily July-Sept. 10am, 3pm; Oct.-June 10am. €7.50, students and ages 12-18 €6.50, under 12 free. 2hr. **bus** tour W and Sa. Visit the tourist office for seasonal schedules. 1-day bus tours to vineyards from mid-May to Oct. daily around 9:15am (departs from the tourist office). €85, lunch included. Each day features a different vineyard; call in advance for details. AmEx/MC/V.

Budget Travel: Voyage Wasteels, 13 pl. de Casablanca (☎05 56 31 11 74), across from the train station. Open M-F 9am-1pm and 2-6pm, Sa 9:30am-12:30pm. MC/V.

Consulates: US, 10 pl. de la Bourse and 65 cours Alsace Lorraine (☎05 56 48 63 80; fax 05 56 51 61 97). Open only by appointment. **UK,** 353 bd. du Président Wilson (☎05 57 22 21 10; fax 05 56 08 33 12). Open M-F 9:30am-noon and 2-4:30pm. To reach other foreign consulates, contact the tourist office.

American Express: 11 cours de l'Intendance (☎05 00 63 36). **Currency exchange** available. ID required for all transactions. Open M-F 9:30am-6pm.

Youth Center: Centre d'Information Jeunesse d'Aquitaine (CIJA), 5 rue Duffour Dubergier (☎05 56 56 00 56). Info about activities, jobs, long-term accommodation, and GLBT resources. Branch 1 block away, 125 cours d'Alsace Lorraine (☎05 56 56 00 56). Sells train tickets and provides up to 15min. of free Internet. Both open M-Th 9:30am-6pm, F 9:30am-5pm.

Laundromats: 26 rue Docteur Charles Nancel-Penard. Wash €3.50, dry €0.50 per 6min. Open daily 7:30am-8:30pm. 10 rue Lafaure de Monbadon. Wash €3.80-7, dry €1.10. Open daily 7am-9pm.

Police: 23 rue François de Sourdis (☎05 57 85 77 77).

Hospital: Hôpital St-André, 1 rue Jean Burguet (☎05 56 79 56 79).

Internet Access: Free at **CIJA** (see **Youth Center,** above) and free up to 15min. at CIJA branch on av. Alsace Lorraine. **L@Cyb,** 23 cours Pasteur (☎05 56 01 15 15), across from the Musée d'Aquitaine. €0.75 per 15min., €2 per hr. Open M-Sa 9:30am-2am, Su 2pm-2am. **I.Phone,** 24 rue Duplais Gallien (☎05 57 85 82 62), 3 blocks from pl. Gambetta. €0.50 per 15min. Open daily 10am-11pm.

Post Office: 52 rue Georges Bonnac (☎05 57 53 04 00), off pl. Gambetta. Open M-F 8:30am-6:30pm, Sa 8:30am-noon. Branch (☎05 57 14 32 00) with **currency exchange** at the corner of rue St-Rémi and rue des Piliers-de-Tutelle. Open M 2-6pm, Tu-F 10am-6pm, Sa 10am-12:30pm. **Postal Code:** 33000.

ACCOMMODATIONS

Bordeaux's main youth hostel is close to the train station. Despite the convenience, the area is run-down, and the 5-10min. walk from the nearest public transit stop is not safe at night. Great deals slightly farther from the station can be found in the *centre-ville* on the streets around pl. Gambetta and cours d'Albret. Reserve a few days ahead in summer.

Hôtel Studio, 26 rue Huguerie (☎05 56 48 00 14; www.hotel-bordeaux.com). Walk 1 block down cours Clemenceau from pl. Gambetta, turn left on rue Lafaurie de Montbadon, and head left again on rue Huguerie. A backpacker favorite. Tiny, relatively clean rooms have telephone, bath, and cable TV at the lowest prices in the city. Attentive staff makes this hotel feel like home. Breakfast €5. Reception 7am-11pm. Reservations recommended in July and Aug. Singles €19-29; doubles €25-35. AmEx/MC/V. ●

Auberge de Jeunesse Barbey (HI), 22 cours Barbey (☎05 56 33 00 70; fax 05 56 33 00 71). 4 blocks from Gare St-Jean, in the run-down red-light district; travelers, especially those alone, should exercise caution at night. Shiny metal and bright colors characterize modern rooms where all furniture is securely nailed to the floor—sorry, kleptomaniacs! Almost all rooms with shower, some with toilet. TV room, well-equipped kitchen, and foosball table. Breakfast included. Free Internet. 3-night max. stay. Lockout 10am-4pm. Curfew 2am. 2- to 6-person dorm rooms €21. MC/V. ●

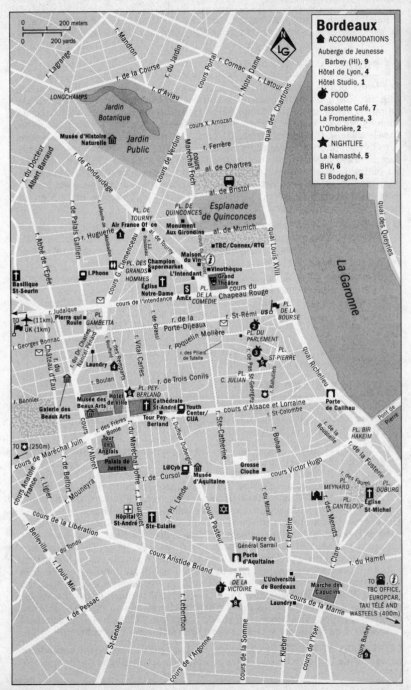

Bordeaux

🏠 ACCOMMODATIONS

Auberge de Jeunesse
  Barbey (HI), **9**
Hôtel de Lyon, **4**
Hôtel Studio, **1**

🍎 FOOD

Cassolette Café, **7**
La Fromentine, **3**
L'Ombrière, **2**

⭐ NIGHTLIFE

La Namasthé, **5**
BHV, **6**
El Bodegon, **8**

Hôtel de Lyon, 31 rue des Remparts (☎05 56 81 34 38). Small, recently renovated rooms with bath, cable TV, and telephone. Reception 7am-11pm. Singles €32-35; doubles €39-45; triples €59-65; quads and quints €69-85. AmEx/MC/V. ❷

FOOD

Bordeaux boasts a range of local specialties. Try oysters straight from the Atlantic, *foie gras* from Les Landes, and beef braised in St-Emilion wine. Restaurants cluster around **rue Saint-Rémi** and **place Saint-Pierre**, while small budget-friendly options line the narrow streets between **place du Parlement** and **place Camille Julian**, to the east of rue Ste-Catherine. *Bordelais* don't usually eat before 9pm in the summer; restaurants typically serve food until 11pm or midnight. Sample local fish and produce at the **Marché des Capucins** (Tu-Su 6am-1pm), off cours de la Marne, and *bio* (organic) produce on **quai des Chartrons** (Th 6am-4pm), at **place Lucien Victor Meunier** (F 6:30am-1pm), and at **place des Martyrs de la Résistance** (Sa 6am-2pm). For prepared goods, try **Champion,** in the Marché des Grands Hommes (open M-Sa 9am-9pm).

L'Ombrière, 14 pl. du Parlement (☎05 56 48 58 83). Busy restaurant in the elegant *centre-ville* serves perfectly prepared French cuisine near a bubbling fountain. For lunch, try a meal-size salad with baked goat cheese (€10) or *foie gras* on toast (€13). 3- and 4-course *menus* €15-23. Open daily noon-2pm and 7-11pm. MC/V. ❸

La Fromentine, 4 rue du Pas St-Georges (☎05 56 79 24 10), near pl. du Parlement. Anything but your average *crêperie*. 2 pots of fresh flowers herald the entrance to this bovine shrine, where the walls are covered with cows and the food is covered with cheese. Variety of salads €2.70-9.80. *Galettes* €5.80-7.80. *Menu* €10-15. Open M-F noon-2pm and 7-10pm, Sa 7-10pm. MC/V. ❷

Cassolette Café, 20 pl. de la Victoire (☎05 56 92 94 96; www.cassolettecafe.com). Bustling kitchen serves an array of local recipes in *cassolettes* (heavy clay skillets). *Plats* €13. Open daily noon-midnight. MC/V. ❸

SIGHTS AND TASTES

Bordeaux is short on blockbuster sights but not on fun and quirky ways to pass the hours between glasses of wine. Admission to all of Bordeaux's museums is free the first Sunday of every month.

MAISON DU VIN/CIVB. Those in town for only a day or two but desperate for the full wine experience should head to the Maison du Vin/CIVB, an immense building that houses industry offices and an extensive wine bar staffed by professionals who guide tastings. The 2hr. "Introduction to Bordeaux Wines" course, available in English as well as French, teaches the art of oenophilia (the love of wines) through a comparative tasting of two reds and two whites. Tickets can be purchased across the street at the tourist office. (*3 cours du 30 Juillet. ☎05 56 00 22 85; http://ecole.vins-bordeaux.fr. Open M-F 9am-5:30pm. Wine-tasting course June-Sept. M-W and F-Sa 10am in English, 3pm in French; €22. MC/V.*) Those appropriately impressed can purchase the goods at two nearby wine shops. **L'Intendant,** a more intimate wine shop across the street, offers an impressive selection of regional wines and a knowledgeable staff. (*2 allée de Tourny. ☎05 56 48 01 29. Open daily 10am-7:30pm. AmEx/MC/V.*) Connoisseurs then venture across the square to buy their high-end bottles and crystal pitchers—not to mention obscure gadgets—at classy **Vinothèque,** a store specializing in all things *vin*. (*8 cours du 30 Juillet. ☎05 56 52 32 05; www.la-vinotheque.com. Open M-Sa 10am-7:30pm. MC/V.*)

CATHÉDRALE ST-ANDRÉ. Sculpted angels and apostles adorn the cathedral's facade, while Gothic windows allow natural light to illuminate the interior. St-

André has been home to many important royal weddings (a.k.a. alliances): that of Eleanor of Aquitaine and the future Louis VII in 1137 and that of Louis XIII and Princess Anne of Austria in 1615—whereupon Louis walked through the "royal portal" on the north side of the church, an entrance that has allegedly not been used since. *(Pl. Pey-Berland. ☎ 05 56 52 68 10. Open M 2-7:30pm, Tu-F 7:30am-6pm, Sa 10am-7pm, Su 9:30am-6pm.)* For a great view of the city, climb the 229 steps of the **Tour Pey-Berland,** which rises 66m into the sky and is topped with a golden statue of the Virgin Mary. For fear that the vibrations of the bells would make the cathedral collapse, masons built the tower 15m from the cathedral. *(☎ 05 56 81 26 25. Open June-Sept. daily 10am-1:15pm and 2-6pm; Oct.-May Tu-Su 10am-12:30pm and 2-5:30pm. Last entry 30min. before closing. €5, seniors and ages 18-25 €3.50, under 18 free.)*

GRAND THÉÂTRE. The austere facade of this 18th-century opera house conceals a breathtakingly intricate Neoclassical interior. To see it, attend an opera, concert, ballet, or play—or give your wallet a break by taking a daytime tour in English. *(Pl. de la Comédie. ☎ 05 56 00 85 95; www.opera-bordeaux.com. Open M-Sa 11am-6pm. 1hr. tours organized through tourist office; frequency depends on theater's production schedule. Opera tickets €8-80, student and under 25 50% discount, over 65 10% discount. Student tickets 48hr. before any show €8. No shows in Aug.)*

ÉGLISE ST-MICHEL. Though the actual church is more often than not closed to the public, Bordeaux's best cityscape can be experienced from atop St-Michel's 114m bell tower. At ground level, you're likely to see even more of the world: a lively flea market selling everything from African specialties to Syrian hookahs sprawls at the tower's base. Note that this area should not be visited alone at night. *(Tower open daily June-Sept. 2-7pm. €2.50, under 12 free. Market open daily 9am-1pm.)*

MUSÉE DES BEAUX ARTS. Originally used as stables for the palace that is now the **Hôtel de Ville,** Bordeaux's art museum owns many great works by painters like Caravaggio, Matisse, Picasso, Renoir, Seurat, and Titian. However, the pieces have not been available to the public for years. The permanent collection is in the two buildings that frame the Hôtel de Ville, while the temporary exhibits are across the street in the **Galeries des Beaux Arts.** Besides the collections, the highlight of the museum is the grandeur of the Hôtel's architecture. *(20 cours d'Albret, near the cathedral. ☎ 05 56 10 20 56. Open M and W-Su 11am-6pm. Permanent gallery free. Tickets for temporary exhibits €5, students €2.50.)*

▣ NIGHTLIFE

With a student population of 70,000, Bordeaux is full of bars and nightclubs. Ask for **Clubs and Concerts,** a free brochure at the tourist office. **Place de la Victoire** and **place Gambetta,** as well as most of the streets between **place des Quinconces** and **place Camille Julian,** are mobbed during the school year and continue to serve as entertainment hot spots during the summer. Travelers should exercise caution when walking around the city at night.

▣ **El Bodegon,** 14 pl. de la Victoire (☎ 05 56 94 74 02). Dominates nightlife in la Victoire, the most popular student-nightlife quarter. DJ plays the latest club hits and plasma screens air the latest soccer match. Also serves food 11am-3pm. Beer on tap €2.80. On W nights, crowds come for karaoke at 10:30pm. Theme nights such as foam parties every weekend. Happy hour 6-8pm. Open M-Sa 7am-2am, Su 2pm-2am. MC/V.

BHV (Bar de l'Hôtel de Ville), 4 rue de l'Hôtel de Ville (☎ 05 56 44 05 08). Flashing lights spin off mirrors in this fashionable and friendly gay bar. Welcomes both men and women and fills up most nights. Beer €4. Mixed drinks €6. Theme nights July-Aug. on Sa. Drag shows Sept.-June Su 10pm. Open daily 6pm-2am. V.

Le Namasthé, 8 rue de la Devise (☎05 56 81 08 68). Gauze curtains, soft cushions, and a wide variety of exotic, non-alcoholic drinks greet guests in this teahouse. Tall lassis (€5) are available in a dozen flavors, while a selection of beers (€5) and wines completes the relaxing experience. Open in summer M-F 7pm-1:30am, Sa-Su 4pm-1:30am.; in winter Tu-F 7pm-1:30am, Sa-Su 4pm-1:30am. MC/V over €10.

⬛ DAYTRIPS FROM BORDEAUX

Bordeaux's world-famous wines have been in relatively high demand since the Romans first conquered the area. However, the marriage of Eleanor of Aquitaine and England's King Henry II in 1152 changed the region's fate considerably. The Plantagenet king refused to be deprived of his claret (as the British call red Bordeaux wine) and thus bestowed special shipping rights on Bordeaux, opening it up to the seemingly unquenchable British market. At first the *Bordelais* simply shipped wines produced farther up the Garonne River, but the money flowing in sparked a local planting mania. Soon Bordeaux gained a monopoly over the market by refusing to ship wines produced elsewhere. Today, the region produces almost 800 million bottles per year.

SAINT-ÉMILION

Trains go to St-Émilion from Bordeaux (40min., at least 10 per day, €7.70). Watch carefully: St-Emilion is the 2nd stop, and the tiny station is poorly marked.

The famed viticulturists of St-Émilion (sehnt-eh-meel-yohn), 35km northeast of Bordeaux, have been refining their technique since Roman times—and it shows. Local winemakers nourish over 5400 acres, gently crushing the grapes to produce two and a half million liters of wine each year. The medieval village's antiquated stone buildings, twisting narrow streets, and religious monuments ensuring a charming, relaxed visit.

To take home a taste of St-Émilion at an affordable price, walk up the main rue Guadet to the *grand cru château* **Clos des Menuts,** on pl. du Chapitre des Jacobins, in the center of town. An aging, maze-like cellar displays vintages over 40 years old, whetting the appetite for the free *dégustation* available aboveground. (☎05 57 74 45 77. Open daily Apr.-Nov. 10am-12:30pm and 2-7pm; Dec.-Mar. 10am-6pm. Free entrance to cellars. Bottles from €6. MC/V.) The **Maison du Vin de Saint-Émilion,** pl. Pierre Meyrat, houses a free exhibit on winemaking with an *olfactif* (nasal) guessing game, offers a 1hr. course on local wines in several languages including English and French, and sells wine at wholesale prices. (☎05 57 55 50 55; www.vins-saint-emilion.com. Open daily Aug. 9:30am-7pm; Apr.-July and Sept.-Oct. 9:30am-12:30pm and 2:30-6:30pm; Nov.-Mar. 10am-12:30pm and 2-6pm. Wine course from mid-July to mid-Sept. daily 11am; €17. MC/V.) The **Église Monolithe,** carved by Benedictine monks over three centuries out of solid rock, is the largest and best-preserved subterranean church in all of Europe. Giant iron clamps keep the church's columns from collapsing under the combined stress of the heavy bell tower—added in the 17th century—and the underground stream running beneath. The damp underground **catacombs,** a burial place for infants and wealthy monks, and the adjacent cave of the hermit Émilion represent only a small part of the 70 acres of underground galleries in the region that have yet to be excavated. To visit the three monuments, you must take one of the guided tours, which depart from the tourist office. (45min. tours every hr. July-Aug. 10am-noon and 2-5pm. English tours 11:30am, 2:30, 4:30pm. €6.50, students €4.10, ages 12-17 €3.20.)

The **tourist office,** on rue du Clocher in pl. des Créneaux, distributes the *Grandes Heures de St-Émilion,* a list of **classical concerts** and **wine tastings** hosted by nearby châteaux. To get to the office from the station, take a right on the main road; from town, walk 2km (20min.) up rue de la Porte Bouqueyre toward the tower. (☎05 57 55 28 28; www.saint-emilion-tourisme.com. Open daily July-Aug. 9:30am-8pm; from mid- to late June and from early to mid-Sept. 9:30am-7pm; from Apr. to mid-June and from mid-Sept. to Oct. 9:30am-12:30pm and 1:45-6:30pm; Nov.-Mar. 9:30am-12:30pm and 1:45-6pm.) The office gives tours in English or French and rents bikes. (Bikes €10.50 per ½-day, €14.70 per day; credit card deposit. Tours May-Sept. Su 3pm or for large groups by appointment; €10, ages 12-17 €6. MC/V.) To visit the vineyards of St-Émilion, pick up a *St-Émilion Guide*, available at the tourist office, containing a list of contact information for local châteaux; some require appointments. The larger wine houses have tours ending in a *dégustation* (€3-6 per person).

MESSAGE ABOUT A BOTTLE. Approximately 10,000 châteaux—the term used in Bordeaux for all wine establishments—dot the region's countryside. This area is easiest to explore by car, as the vineyards spread over 120,000 hectares and most châteaux are only accessible by difficult-to-navigate local roads. Pick up a map of vineyard locations at the tourist office in Bordeaux, which also gives tours of the more popular châteaux in both English and French. (Tours run daily throughout high season, exploring a different region each day—consult the *Bordeaux Tourisme* guide or the office website for more information.) Some château owners offer private tours to wine connoisseurs, but it's important to call ahead or ask the tourist office to call for you. Tours and tastings are often free, but at the end of the visit you're expected to buy a bottle or two.

GRAVES AND MÉDOC REGIONS

To access vineyards in this region without a car, book one of the organized tours that departs from Bordeaux (€25-29) or take the Réseau Trans Gironde Line 705 from the depot in pl. des Quinconces to Pauillac, a particularly renowned village. The bus leaves from pl. des Quinconces (1hr.; M-Sa 10 per day, Su 2 per day; €12-15).

Though St-Émilion's vineyards are best for a first visit, they're not the only worthwhile stop in the area. South of the Garonne, the **Graves** (grahv) region, named for its gravel topsoil, is said to be the birthplace of Bordeaux viticulture. Graves's dry and semi-sweet wines were the drink of choice in Eleanor of Aquitaine's time, and, though the reds of Médoc overtook their popularity in the 18th century, it was not due to a change in quality. Within Graves, at the southeastern end, is the **Sauternes** (so-terhn) region, celebrated for its sweet white dessert wines. The **Médoc** (may-dohk) area north of Bordeaux, between the Gironde Estuary and the ocean, gets its name from the Latin *in medio aquae* (in the middle of the water). Within Médoc is the town of Pauillac, home to 3000 acres of vineyards, including some of the world's most famous premier *cru* reds: Lafite-Rothschild, Latour, and Mouton-Rothschild.

To get to the **tourist office,** take the bus to Hôtel de Ville and walk in the direction from which the bus came. The office, to your left on the banks of the estuary, provides maps, suggests hiking trails, and makes reservations for visits to local châteaux. (☎05 56 59 03 08; www.pauillac-medoc.com. Open M-Sa 9:30am-12:30pm and 2-6pm, Su 10:30am-12:30pm and 3-6pm.)

ARCACHON

The train station, bd. du Gal Leclerc, has service to Bordeaux (1hr., approx. 25 per day, €9.40), in addition to the TGV to Paris (4hr., 1-3 per day, €71). Ticket office open M-F 6am-9:30pm, Sa 8:30am-7:15pm, Su 8:50am-7:20pm.

Anyone looking for a reprieve from wine can relax in Arcachon (ahr-kah-shohn), one of the most beautiful beach towns on the Côte d'Argent (Silver Coast), the thin strip of sand that runs along 200km of France's southern Atlantic seaboard. Created 150 years ago by French aristocrats suffering from poor lungs and boredom, Arcachon remains a classically posh southern French resort town, full of vacationing families in summer and empty except for loafing retirees in the low season. During the high season, the town offers guided tours of the surrounding wildlife parks, making it a perfect daytrip from Bordeaux. The **Bassin d'Arcachon** is known in particular for two sandy landmarks: the **�Dune du Pilat** (or *Pyla*), Europe's highest sand dune, and the **Banc d'Arguin,** a 1000-acre sand bar in the form of a crescent.

Rising from the edge of a pine forest 5km south of town, the 105m high Dune du Pilat looks more like a section of the Sahara than a French beach; the wind races furiously across the face of the dune, creating an ocean of white sand unblemished by vegetation. Every year without fail, the dune moves a few centimeters east; the army barracks that were constructed at the summit in 1942 now litter the water's edge. At the edge of the dune, there is a protected area for wading, although a fierce undertow makes deeper swims dangerous. Farther along the water, there are beaches for the clothed as well as the nude. From the bus stop "Dune du Pilat," head into the park and continue past the shops for about 500m to reach the staircase to the top. **Sand Fly** offers hang gliding from the dune (www.sand-fly.com); inquire at the tourist office.

To save money, French tourists often buy bread from one of the many *boulangers artisanals* and produce from the market on **esplanade Pompidou.** (Open daily 8am-1pm.) Don't leave Arcachon without savoring your pick of the 15,000 tons of oysters gathered here each year. Cafes line av. Gambetta and bd. de la Plage, offering seafood and **moules frites** (mussels and fries; €10-12). **Le Commerce ❸**, 9 av. Gambetta, spills onto the street with wood tables and famished tourists, providing a perfect seaside spot to enjoy shellfish. (☎05 56 83 05 17. Salads €9-13. Meat *plats* €8-15. Fish *plats* €10-11. *Menus* €15-24. Open daily 8am-midnight. AmEx/MC/V.)

City **bus** #1 runs from the train station to "Dune du Pilat," within 5min. of the dune. (☎08 10 20 17 14. 25min.; May-Sept. every hr., fewer Oct.-Apr.; €1.) To reach Arcachon's **tourist office,** pl. Georges Pompidou, turn left from the train station and walk one block. (☎05 57 52 97 97; www.arcachon.com. Open July-Aug. daily 9am-7pm; Apr.-June and Sept. M-Sa 9am-6:30pm, Su 10am-1pm and 2-5pm; Oct.-Mar. M-Sa 9am-5pm.)

PAYS BASQUE

BIARRITZ
☎05 59

The town of Biarritz (bee-ah-reetz; pop. 30,000) is synonymous with glitz—and not just because they sort of rhyme. Once a minor whaling village, Biarritz became an aristocratic playground in the mid-19th century. Its natural beauty has drawn the likes of Napoleon III, Alphonse XIII of Spain, Nicholas II of Russia, and the Shah of Persia. While today Biarritz remains an opulent getaway for jet setters from around the world, its crowded beaches, jagged rocks, and glamorous clubs are still within the reach of budget travelers.

TRANSPORTATION

Flights: Aéroport de Parme, 7 esplanade de l'Europe (☎05 59 43 83 83). On M-Sa, take bus #6 (dir.: Bayonne Gare) from Hôtel de Ville (every 30min. 7am-7:20pm); on Su, take bus C (dir.: Aéroport; buses depart at irregular times). **Ryanair** (☎08 92 23 23 75) flies to **Dublin, Frankfurt, London, Birmingham,** and **Shannon** for €25-170.

Trains: Biarritz-la-Négresse (☎05 59 50 83 07), 3km from town. Information desk open daily 7am-7pm. To: **Bayonne** (10min.; at least 15 per day; €2.30, TGV €4); **Bordeaux** (2hr., at least 10 per day, €22-26); **Paris** (5hr., 12 per day, €40-85); **Pau** (2hr., at least 5 per day, €17); **Toulouse** (4hr., at least 5 per day, €25-40). Additional SNCF ticket office at 13 av. Foch (☎05 59 50 83 34). Open M-F 9am-noon and 2-6pm.

Buses: ATCRB (☎05 59 08 00 33) runs from the sq. d'Ixelles to **St-Jean-de-Luz** (20min., €3) and **Hendaye** (35min., €3). Buy tickets on the bus.

Public Transportation: STAB (☎05 59 52 59 52). Office with schedules on rue Louis-Barthou (☎05 59 24 26 53). Open M-Sa 8:15am-noon and 1:30-6pm. Buses (M-Sa 6am-8:30pm bus #1, 2, or 6; Su 7:30am-8:30pm bus A, B, or C) run to **Anglet** (10min.) and **Bayonne** (25-30min.). 1hr. tickets €1.20, carnet of 5 €4.75, carnet of 10 €9.50.

Taxis: Atlantic Taxi Radio (☎05 59 03 18 18). €1.44 per km during the day, €1.88 at night. €7 minimum fare. €15 to Bayonne. 24hr.

Bike and Scooter Rental: ▓**Rent-a-Bike,** 24 rue Peyroloubilh (☎05 59 24 94 47; www. sobilobiarritz.com). Bikes and in-line skates €15 per day; €153 deposit. Scooters €31 per day; €1525 deposit or credit-card number. Open daily July-Aug. 9am-8pm; Sept.-June 9am-7pm. €10 *Let's Go* discount. MC/V.

Surfboard Rental: Rip Curl Surf Shop, 2 av. Reine Victoria (☎05 59 24 38 40), 1 block from Grande Plage. €10 per ½-day, €15 per day, €85 per week; ID deposit. 1hr. lesson €35, 3 lessons €90, 5 lessons €160. Open daily July-Aug. 10am-8pm; Sept.-June 10am-1pm and 3-7pm.

✴🛈 ORIENTATION AND PRACTICAL INFORMATION

Because the train station is 3km from the *centre-ville*, the STAB and ATCRB buses are the most practical means of reaching Biarritz, arriving near the tourist office from surrounding cities. Buses #2 (dir.: Sainsontan) and 9 (dir.: La Barre or St-Madeleine) run from the train station to the city center and tourist office (every 20min. M-Sa 6:30am-9pm, €1.20). On Sundays, bus B (dir.: Sainsontan) travels the same route (every 30min. 8am-8pm, €1.20). To get there, keep left as you walk out of Biarritz-la-Négresse. You'll find yourself on **allée du Moura**, which becomes **avenue du Président Kennedy.** Turn left onto av. du Maréchal Foch, which continues into the *centre-ville* to pl. Clemenceau (30min.).

Tourist Office: Sq. d'Ixelles (☎05 59 22 37 10; www.biarritz.fr), off av. Édouard VII. English- and Spanish-speaking staff tracks down same-day hotel reservations or campsites for free. Pick up the free *Biarritzscope* for monthly events listings. Open daily July-Aug. 9am-7pm; Sept.-June 9am-6pm.

Tours: The **Petit Train** (☎06 07 97 16 35), departing every 30min. from the Grande Plage (Casino) or the Rocher de la Vierge, offers 30min. guided bus-disguised-as-train rides of the Port des Pêcheurs, the Port Vieux, and the Perspective Côte des Basques. Open daily July-Aug. 8am-11pm; May-June and Sept. 10am-5pm; Apr. and Oct. 10:30am-1pm and 2-5pm; hours depend on weather. €5, ages 3-12 €4.

Currency Exchange: Change Plus, 9 rue Mazagran (☎05 59 24 82 47). No commission. Open July-Aug. M-Sa 9am-6pm; Sept.-June M-F 9am-noon and 2-6pm, Sa 9am-noon. Currency exchange also available at the post office.

Laundromat: La Goutte d'Eau, 4 av. Jaulerry, by the post office. Wash €4-7, dry €1 per 10min. Detergent €0.30. Open daily 7am-9pm.

Beach Information and Emergencies: Grande Plage ☎05 59 22 22 22. Plage Marbella ☎05 59 23 01 20. Plage de la Milady ☎05 59 23 63 93. Plage Miramar ☎05 59 24 34 98. Plage du Port Vieux ☎05 59 24 05 84. Plage de la Côte des Basques ☎05 59 24 92 70.

Police: 3 av. Joseph Petit (☎05 59 01 22 22).

Hospital: Hôpital de la Côte Basque, 13 av. Interne Jacques Loëb (☎05 59 44 35 35), in Bayonne.

Internet Access: Formatic64, 15 av. de la Marne (☎05 59 22 12 79). €4 per hr. Open daily 10am-8pm.

Post Office: 17 rue de la Poste (☎05 59 22 41 20). Open M-F 8:30am-6pm, Sa 8:30am-noon. **Currency exchange** available. **Postal Code:** 64200.

🏠🏚 ACCOMMODATIONS AND CAMPING

Bargains are hard to find in this upscale vacation town. To get the best deals, plan at least a month ahead for stays in July and August or enlist the help of the tourist office. The best prices are off rue Mazagran, around rue du Port Vieux.

■ **Hôtel la Marine,** 1 rue Goélands (☎05 59 24 34 09). The best deal in central Biarritz. Run by an attentive and caring family. Spotless, comfortable rooms decorated with maritime-themed wicker furniture. All with bath. Breakfast in bed €5. Internet €2 per 30min. at computer in lobby; Wi-Fi (€2 per day) available in all rooms. Reception 8am-11pm; front door code allows after-hours access. July-Aug. singles €40-47; doubles €47-52; triples €75. Sept.-June €35-42/40-47/67. AmEx/MC/V. ❸

■ **Auberge de Jeunesse (HI),** 8 rue de Chiquito de Cambo (☎05 59 41 76 00; biarritz@ fuaj.org). A 15min. bus ride or 40min. walk from Biarritz. From the *centre-ville*, take bus #2 (dir.: Gare SNCF) or #9 (dir.: Labourd) to Bois de Boulogne. Continue walking in the direction of the bus and turn right when you see a sign for the hostel; follow the road down the hill. Near a beautiful lake. Laid-back crowd and well-stocked bar. Bright rooms with bunk beds have lockable cabinets, key-card entry, and ensuite bathrooms. Breakfast included. Laundry €3.50, dry €2.50. Internet €0.50 per 10min. Reception July-Aug. 8:30am-12:30pm and 6-10pm; Sept.-June 8:30-11:30am and 6-9pm. Check-out by 11am is strictly enforced. 2- to 4-bed dorms €18.10. AmEx/MC/V. ❶

Camping Biarritz, 28 rue d'Harcet (☎05 59 23 00 12; www.biarritz-camping.fr), 10min. from Milady and 30min. from town. Take bus #9 or follow signs down av. du Président JF Kennedy from the bus station. Quiet, unshaded plots separated by neat hedges. Restaurant, bar, laundry, hot tub, and pool. Internet €3 per 20min., €6 per hr. Wheelchair-accessible. Reception 8am-9pm. Reservations required July-Aug. Open from early May to mid-Sept. From early July to late Aug. tent sites for 2 €23; RV sites €500-600 per week. May-June tent sites for 2 €15; RV sites €230-295. Electricity from early July to late Aug. €4; May-June €2.80. MC/V. ❶

◪ FOOD

In dining, as with everything in Biarritz, style trumps substance; restaurants here can get away with charging gourmet prices for gruel if they provide the right view. The restaurants around **Grande Plage** and **place St-Eugénie** tend to be expensive. Look on rue Mazagran and place Clemenceau for cheap *crêpes* and sandwiches. Several restaurants along rue du Port Vieux, near Le Palmarium, offer good meals at reasonable prices; be aware, though, that the quality of a *prix-fixe* menu is most accurately reflected in its price. The market on **rue des Halles** offers local produce and an abundance of specialties. (Open daily 7am-1pm.) Next door is a **Shopi** supermarket, 2 rue du Centre. (☎05 59 24 18 01. Open M-Sa 9am-12:40pm and 3-7:10pm, Su 9am-12:30pm. AmEx/MC/V.)

■ **Casa Juan Pedro,** Port des Pecheurs (☎05 59 24 00 86). Nestled in the rocky cove, this outdoors-only seafood restaurant boasts a sensational ocean view. Locals crowd the patio. Try *moules à la creme* (mussels in cream sauce; €8) or *merlu à l'espagnol* (Spanish grilled hake; €13). Open daily July-Aug. noon-3pm and 7-11pm; Sept. and Apr.-June noon-2pm and 7:30-10pm. Closed in bad weather. MC/V. ❷

Le Palmarium, 7 rue du Port Vieux (☎05 59 24 25 83). Local favorite in a palm-lined courtyard. Options include pizzas (€8-10) and meat or fish dishes (€8-14), but the best choice is the paella: a house specialty that features a mammoth serving of rice, chicken, and shellfish for €13 (served 7-11pm). Open daily noon-midnight. MC/V. ❷

L'Atalaya, Plateau de l'Atalaye (☎05 59 22 33 34), above the Musée de la Mer. Museum cafe stands out for massive sandwiches of Basque ham and other local *charcuterie* (€5-8) and a view of the Rocher de la Vièrge—but not for the quality of food. Paella €11. *Menu* €8.80. Open daily July-Aug. 9am-10pm; Sept.-June 9:30am-6pm. MC/V. ❷

◉ SIGHTS

Glittery beaches reel in sunbathers, surfers, and everyone in between. In summer, perfect bodies blanket the **Grande Plage,** while those seeking a slightly quieter beach experience head up the beach to **Plage Miramar.** Quiksilver-clad beach bums hit the waves at the **Plage de la Côte des Basques.** Though beaches are the main attraction, Biarritz has its distractions when the sun isn't out.

LA MUSÉE DE LA MER. Water-lovers should take a break from the beach and visit this museum, which features an aquarium on the lower level and museum on the two upper levels. Drop by at 10:30am or 5pm to catch the feeding of the seals. Audio tours in English guide visitors through the exhibits, one of which includes the skull of a blue whale. (☎05 59 22 75 40; www.museedelamer. com. Open June and Sept. daily 9:30am-7pm; July-Aug. daily 9:30am-midnight; Oct.-May Tu-Su 9:30am-12:30pm and 2-6pm. €7.80, students and under 16 €5, under 4 free.)

MUSÉE DU CHOCOLAT. This museum is worth the 15min. trek for the exhibits on the history of chocolate—which include chocolate sculptures—and the free samples of rich hot chocolate. (14 av. Beaurivage. ☎05 59 23 27 72; www.planet-musee-chocolat.com. Guided tours in French for groups only. Wheelchair-accessible. Open M-Sa 10am-12:30pm and 2:30-6:30pm. €6, students and ages 13-18 €5, ages 4-12 €3.50.) The boutique of chocolate-maker **Henriet** sits next door and features a selection of Basque chocolates, like the Rocher Biarritz—almonds and oranges covered in chocolate. (☎05 59 41 54 69. Open daily 10am-12:30pm and 2:30-6:30pm.)

OTHER SIGHTS. The best way to soak in all that Biarritz has to offer is to stroll along the shoreline. Start at ▨**Pointe Saint-Martin,** 10min. north of the center along av. de l'Imperatrice. This promontory not only provides the foundation for a lighthouse, **Le Phare de Biarritz,** but also offers a panoramic view of the coastline. From here, head back toward the center of the city along the beach: you'll be walking down **Plage Miramar,** one of Biarritz's more famous beaches. You can't miss the **Hôtel du Palais,** crown jewel of Biarritz's luxury hotels, 500m down on your left; walk around to the front if you want to get a full view. Constructed in 1854 by Emperor Napoleon III, the E-shaped palace now lets rooms starting at €280 per night. Rock formations provide shelter for small fishing boats in the **Port des Pêcheurs.** Near the port, **BAB Subaquatique** organizes scuba excursions. (☎05 59 24 80 40. Open daily 8am-7pm. Guided dives. First dive €30. Open-water boat excursions for certified divers €42. Diving excursions to the vieux port and nighttime trips available for all experience levels. Cash and traveler's checks only.) Continue down the coast, over the bridge, and through the iconic **Rocher de la Vierge,** a tooth-like rock with a statue of the Virgin Mary, to watch the sunset.

◉ NIGHTLIFE

Weekend evenings kick off at 11pm at the bars that cluster around **Hôtel la Marine** on rue Mazagran, especially at **Le Ventilo, La Marine,** or **La Tireuse.** At 2am, as bars close, young people form long lines outside Biarritz's *boîtes* (clubs).

Casino Barrière de Biarritz, 1 av. Édouard VII (☎05 59 22 77 77). Stands over the Grande Plage in all its Art Deco glory. Red-carpeted ocean of slot machines and craps tables. 18+ ID required. Open July-Aug. M-Th and Su 10am-4am, F-Sa 10am-5am; Sept.-June M-Th and Su 10am-3am, F-Sa 10am-4am. Tables open 8pm-close.

Ibiza, on Grande Plage (☎05 59 24 38 34, www.ibiza-biarritz.com). Small, swanky *boîte* (club) caters to a classy young crowd. Mixed drinks €8. Cover €10. Bar open daily 10pm-2am. Dance club open daily 2-5:30am.

Le Copa, 24 av. Édouard VII (☎05 59 24 65 39). Large tropical bar on main fl. Dance club downstairs plays Latin, techno, and hip-hop. Mixed drinks €9-11. Cover €10. Bar open daily noon-2am; kitchen open 10pm. Dance club open daily 11pm-6am.

San Sebastian, just over the border in Spain. On weekend nights, many head for cheaper, wilder partying until the sun comes up. The tourist office has information on which train and bus lines to use to get back home after your night out.

🌸 FESTIVALS

JAI ALAI TOURNAMENTS

Jai alai is a popular type of Basque *pelota*, a sport played with a ball and racket. For these three events, call the ticketing desk of the tourist office (☎05 59 22 44 66); all are €10-20.

Biarritz Masters Jai Alai Tournament, during 2 weeks in mid-July. Biarritz can't get enough of its native sports.

Gant d'Or, in mid-Aug. Another tournament takes over the town. Both festivals attract a large crowd of tourists and locals.

Trophée du Super Champion, in mid-Sept. The winning teams of the 2 previous tournaments compete for the ultimate triumph.

OTHER FESTIVALS

Roxy Jam, in mid-July. Biarritz pays tribute to its other primary sport: surfing.

Junior Pro Competition, in late Aug. Surfer dudes rejoice at the talented bunch that comes out for this competition.

Le Temps d'Aimer, in Sept. Showcases music, ballet, and art. Tickets at the tourist office. €10-35, students €10.

International Festival of Biarritz (www.festivaldebiarritz.com), in the 1st week of Oct. Celebrates Latin American cinema and culture.

BAYONNE   ☎05 59

Though only a few kilometers from the center of Biarritz, Bayonne (bay-ohn; pop. 42,000), the self-proclaimed chocolate capital of France, takes life at a slower pace than its fashionable neighbor. While parts of the city, particularly around St-Esprit, are dotted with X-rated shops and newer buildings, central Bayonne offers the full charm of a smaller French town: picturesque bridges crossing the Nive River, shuttered half-timbered houses, and an abundance of local spirit. Things pick up in the middle of July and August, as raucous tourists flock to Bayonne for festivals, bullfights, sports matches, and jazz concerts.

🚊 TRANSPORTATION

Trains: Pl. de la Gare. Info office open M 5:35am-8:30pm, Tu-Sa 6:05am-8:30pm, Su 6:15am-8:30pm. To: **Bordeaux** (2hr., at least 10 per day, €22-28); **Paris** (5hr., at least 8 per day, €40-81); **Toulouse** (4hr., at least 10 per day, €37); **San Sebastian, ESP** via **Hendaye** (30min., 15 per day, €8).

Public Transportation: STAB, Hôtel de Ville (☎05 59 52 59 52). Office open M-Sa 8:15am-noon and 1:30-6pm. **Buses** run every 20-30min. M-Sa 6:30am-8pm, Su 6:30am-7pm. Lines #1, 2, and 6 serve **Biarritz** M-Sa; lines A and B serve it Su. Line #2 serves the Anglet tourist office, and line #7 serves Anglet's beaches and forest. 1hr. ticket €1.20, carnet of 5 €4.75, carnet of 10 €9.50.

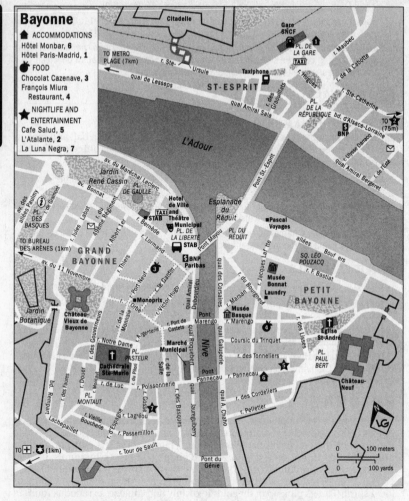

Bayonne

🏠 **ACCOMMODATIONS**
Hôtel Monbar, **6**
Hôtel Paris-Madrid, **1**

🍴 **FOOD**
Chocolat Cazenave, **3**
François Miura
  Restaurant, **4**

⭐ **NIGHTLIFE AND**
  ENTERTAINMENT
Cafe Salud, **5**
L'Atalante, **2**
La Luna Negra, **7**

Taxis: Taxi Bayonne (☎05 59 59 48 48), outside the train station and at pl. Charles de Gaulle. Open 24hr.

ORIENTATION AND PRACTICAL INFORMATION

Two rivers join to split Bayonne in three. **Saint-Esprit,** containing Bayonne's train station, cheap hotels, and Internet cafes, is on the northern side of the Adour River. From here, the **Pont Saint-Esprit**—usually lined with fishermen—connects to budget-friendly **Petit-Bayonne,** home of Bayonne's museums and smaller restaurants. Five bridges span the much narrower Nive to connect Petit-Bayonne to **Grand-Bayonne** on the western bank. This older part of town has a pedestrian zone filled with a maze of side streets. The *centre-ville* is easy to navigate on foot, and an excellent bus system makes Anglet and Biarritz easy to reach.

Tourist Office: Pl. des Basques (☎08 20 42 64 64; www.bayonne-tourisme.com). From the train station, follow the signs to the *centre-ville*. Cross the main bridge to Petit-Bayonne. Continue through pl. du Réduit and cross Pont Mayou to Grand-Bayonne. Take a right on rue Bernède and continue 300m, past the Hôtel de Ville; the street becomes av. Bonnat. The tourist office is on the left. Free city map, hotel reservations, and *Fêtes en Pays Basque* brochures. Organizes 2hr. walking tours of neighborhoods and old ramparts in French (10:30am, 2:30, or 3pm, depending on the day; in English for groups only; call ahead to reserve. €5, under 12 free). Open July-Aug. M-Sa 9am-7pm, Su 10am-1pm; Sept.-June M-F 9am-6:30pm, Sa 10am-6pm.

Budget Travel: Pascal Voyages, 8 allée Boufflers (☎05 59 25 48 48). Open M-F 8:30am-6:30pm, Sa 9am-noon.

Bank: BNP Paribas, 1 pl. de la Liberté (☎08 20 82 00 01). **ATMs** outside.

Laundromat: Atelier Lavopratic, 57 rue Bourgneuf (☎06 82 02 41 55). Wash €3.40, dry €0.40 per 5min. Ironing available. Owner will transfer laundry to dryer for you.

Police: 6 av. de Marhum (☎05 59 46 22 22).

Hospital: 13 av. Interne Jacques Loëb (☎05 59 44 35 35).

Internet Access: Taxiphone, 1 pl. St-Ursule (☎05 59 55 86 34). €0.60 per 15min. Open daily 11am-1:30pm and 3:30-10:30pm.

Post Office: 11 rue Jules Labat, Grand-Bayonne (☎05 59 46 33 60), in a beautiful Art Deco building. **Currency exchange** available. Open M-W and F 8am-6pm, Th 8am-12:15pm and 1:45-6pm, Sa 8:30am-noon. Branch office on the corner of bd. Alsace-Lorraine and rue de l'Este (☎05 59 50 32 90). Open M-F 8:30am-5:30pm, Sa 8:30am-noon. **Postal Code:** 64100.

ACCOMMODATIONS

Reasonably priced lodgings dot St-Esprit's train station area, but expect some noise at night. Hotels fill quickly in festival season, from the end of June to the beginning of October, so reserve ahead. The closest hostels are in **Anglet** (p. 599) and **Biarritz** (p. 590), each a 20min. bus ride away.

Hôtel Paris-Madrid, pl. de la Gare (☎05 59 55 13 98; sorbois@wanadoo.fr), 8min. from Petit-Bayonne. To the left as you exit the train station. Don't let the plaster bunker-like exterior deter you. Large windows make up for dim lightbulbs, and rooms are decorated with old wood furniture. Gracious English- and Spanish-speaking owners are more knowledgeable and forthcoming than most tourist offices. In-room TV €1. Breakfast €4. Shower €1. Reception daily 6:30-12:30am. Singles and doubles €20, with shower €28, with shower and toilet €35; triples and quads with bath €44-49. MC/V. ❶

Hôtel Monbar, 24 rue Panneceau (☎05 59 59 26 80). Wedged above a bar in Petit-Bayonne, this newly renovated 9-room hotel is one of Bayonne's best values. Small rooms with modern furniture are clustered around an indoor courtyard. Each room has toilet, shower, telephone, and TV. Breakfast €4.50. Reception opens 7:30am; closing time varies. Singles and doubles €32; triples €41; quads €51. MC/V. ❷

FOOD

Bayonne offers more than just chocolate; in fact, the indulgence is not as ubiquitous as one would think for the "chocolate capital." Most of the fish and meat dishes reflect a Spanish influence; menus abound with various tapas and *grillades à la plancha* (Spanish-style grilling). The *café-brasseries* of Petit-Bayonne and St-Esprit offer €10-15 local specialties like *jambon de Bayonne* (dry-cured ham) and *poulet à la basquaise* (chicken wrapped in peppers). Three nearly identical cafes at the corner of the quai Admiral Dubourdieu and the

Pont Marengo offer views of the scenic quai de la Nive and serve decent three-course lunch *menus* for €11. Try **Vivaldi** first; it's the third restaurant from the Pont Marengo. Vendors sell meats, fish, cheese, and produce at the indoor **marché municipal,** quai Roquebert. (Open M-Th 7am-1pm, F 7am-1pm and 3:30-7pm, Sa 6am-2pm.) There is also a **Monoprix** supermarket on the corner of rue Orbe and rue Port Neuf. (☎05 59 59 00 33. Open M-Sa 8:30am-8pm. AmEx/MC/V.)

☒ **François Miura Restaurant,** 24 rue Marengo (☎05 59 59 49 89). Worth the splurge, this restaurant stands out among Bayonne's upscale eateries. Patrons dine on sophisticated Basque dishes like squid marinated in pork juice and its own ink (€16) amid white stone walls and modern art. *Plats* €18-21. *Menus* €19-30. Open M-Tu and Th-Sa noon-2pm and 8-10pm, Su noon-2pm. Reservations recommended. AmEx/MC/V. ❹

Chocolat Cazenave, 19 rue Port Neuf (☎05 59 59 03 16). The best of Bayonne's sweets. Specialty is *chocolat mousseux,* a Basque spin on hot chocolate (€5.20). Chocolate available for bulk purchase (€16.50 per 250g). Open daily 9am-noon and 2-7pm. ❷

👁 SIGHTS

MUSÉE BONNAT. This fascinating museum displays the works and art collection of *bayonnais* painter Léon Bonnat (1833-1922). Bonnat, one of the most famous portrait artists of his time, painted haunting portraits of Victor Hugo and Alexandre Dumas, among others. He used the money he earned to buy the paintings and sculptures collected in this museum—luckily for us, his taste was impeccable, and his collection includes works by Degas, Goya, Rembrandt, and Van Dyck. (*5 rue Jacques Laffitte.* ☎05 59 59 08 52. *Open July-Aug. M-Tu and Th-Su 10am-6:30pm, W 10am-9:30pm; May-June and Sept.-Oct. M and W-Su 10am-6:30pm; Nov.-Apr. daily 10am-12:30pm and 2-6pm. €5.50, students €3, under 18 free; July-Aug. W after 6:30pm and Sept.-June 1st Su of the month free. Combined ticket with Musée Basque €9, students €4.50.*)

MUSÉE BASQUE. The world's largest ethnographic museum devoted to the Pays Basque includes everything Basque, from ancient shears that stripped Basque sheep of their wool to modern documentaries about the Guernica bombing. Explanations are in Basque, French, and Spanish. (*37 quai des Corsaires.* ☎05 59 59 08 98; www.musee-basque.com. *Open July-Aug. M-Tu and Th-Su 10am-6:30pm, W 10am-9:30pm; Sept-June Tu-Su 10am-6:30pm. The tourist office leads guided tours in French through the museum; times vary. €5.50, students €3, under 18 free. July-Aug. W after 6:30pm and Sept.-June 1st Su of the month free. Combined ticket with Musée Bonnat €9, students €4.50.*)

OTHER SIGHTS. Turn right when you exit the Musée Basque, veer left onto the Pont Marengo, and walk straight until you see the **Cathédrale Sainte-Marie,** a UNESCO World Heritage site, on your left. (*Open M-Sa 10-11:45am and 3-5:45pm, Su 3:30-6pm.*) Savor the 85 ft. vault in this Gothic cathedral before visiting the **botanical gardens.** The gardens flourish atop the battlements, with 1000 species of Japanese flora, including a miniature bamboo forest. (*To reach the gardens, turn left on rue Notre-Dame as you exit the cathedral, immediately turn right at rue des Gouverneurs, and then duck into the tunnel through the ramparts. Open mid-Apr. to mid-Oct. Tu-Sa 9:30am-noon and 2-6pm.*) Those looking for a more secluded beach than the crowded plots of sand in Anglet or Biarritz should try the **Métro Plage** in Tarnos. Lifeguards are only on duty during July and August, but the beach is beautiful all year. (*Take bus #10 from the train station. 30min., every 20min.-1hr. M-Sa 7:20am-7:25pm.*)

🎵 🎭 ENTERTAINMENT AND NIGHTLIFE

Nightlife is gentle in this town of long afternoons and short evenings. Students line **rue des Cordeliers** in Petit-Bayonne, enjoying cheap drinks in an atmosphere that is more conducive to conversation than dancing. Travelers seeking a more lively scene should take the 10min. bus ride to Biarritz or head over the border to San Sebastian. The orchestra **Harmonie Bayonnaise** gives jazz, pop, and traditional Basque concerts in the pl. de Gaulle gazebo. (July-Aug. Th 9pm. Free.) From September to June, the **Théâtre Municipale**, pl. de la Liberté, hosts musical performances. (☎05 59 55 85 05. Ticket office open Tu-F 10am-2pm and 2:45-5:30pm, Sa 10am-1pm. €15-30, students €2 per 3 tickets.)

   Café Salud, 63 rue Panneceau (☎05 59 59 14 49). Serves good wine and mixed drinks to a young local crowd in a quiet bar of understated elegance. A mojito (€4) or a glass of *vin navarre* (€2) makes the perfect precursor to the slightly more raucous student scene 1 block over. Wheelchair-accessible. Open Tu-Sa 9am-2am. AmEx/MC/V.

   La Luna Negra, rue Gosse (☎05 59 25 78 05). Enter through a red door to find a basement bar with a cornucopia of music genres on its cabaret-style stage. Weekends feature salsa, jazz, storytellers, and more. Beer €2.50-4. Blues Th. Most shows €9, students €7. Shows start 9-9:30pm. Open W-Sa 7pm-2am.

   L'Atalante, 7 rue Denis Etcheverry (☎05 59 55 76 63; www.cinema-atalante.org), in St-Esprit. Shows international films in their original language—with subtitles—and has an appealing bar. Wheelchair-accessible. €6.20, students €4.20. M-F 6pm screening €5.60. Closed 2 weeks in early Aug. Its sister cinema, **L'Autre Cinema,** 3 quai Amiral Sala (☎05 59 55 52 98), shows more English language films at the same price.

🌿 FESTIVALS

Bayonne holds its own in a region known for its festivals. Several **corridas** (bullfights) take place at the **Bureau des Arènes** from July to September; be aware that the matadors actually kill the bull. (☎05 59 46 61 00. Open M-F 10am-1pm and 4-7pm.) For specific dates or more info on the festivals listed below, visit www.bayonne-tourisme.com and www.fetes-de-bayonne.com.

   Foire du Jambon, 3 days before Easter. If the other white meat is your thing, Bayonne is the place to be during the Forum of Ham.

   Journées du Chocolat, in mid-May. The city of chocolate finally lives up to its reputation, letting visitors indulge in a variety of *chocolats artisanals*.

   Marché Mediéval, July 12-14 (www.marchemedieval.org). Experience Bayonne in a whole new era—complete with musical performances and swordfights.

   Fêtes Traditionelles, usually beginning the 1st W of Aug. Locals enjoy 5 days of unrestrained hedonism, with concerts, bullfights, fireworks, and a chaotic cow race. The fête is one of the world's 5 biggest festivals, with over 1 million visitors.

🏛 DAYTRIPS FROM BAYONNE

ANGLET

Anglet, while accessible from Biarritz, is most convenient from Bayonne. From Bayonne, take the #7.1 or 7.2 STAB bus to Mairie Anglet Plages (20min., every 20-25min.). From Biarritz, take bus #2 from the train station and switch to bus #7 at 5 Cantons. On Su and holidays, take bus C from Bayonne or bus B from Biarritz; you'll have to walk from 5 Cantons if you take bus B.

King of the Côte Basque and the French surfing scene, Anglet (ahn-glay) boasts 4km of fine-grained white sand parceled out into nine sparkling beaches. The waves are strongest at **Plage des Cavaliers,** where most of Anglet's surfing competitions are held (the surf is best at low tide), but swimmers all along the coast should be wary of the strong undertow. When in doubt, swim near a lifeguard. (Be aware that there is no lifeguard on duty at Plage du Club, Plage des Dunes, or Plage de la Petite Madrague.)

From the bus stop at Anglet Plages, turn left at the traffic circle and walk 100m toward the ocean, passing several beach-appropriate eateries (Tex-Mex, kebab joints, and *crêperies*). The road ends at av. des Dauphins; continue straight to reach **Plage des Sables d'Or** (lifeguards on duty mid-June to Aug.), where public volleyball courts are available. You can rent surf and ski equipment at **Freestyle**, down the street. (☎05 59 03 27 24; freestyle.surfacademy@wanadoo.com. Surfboards €11 per ½-day, €15 per day, €90 per week. Wetsuits €6-8/8-10/40-50. Skis and snowboards with boots €70-80 per week. 50% deposit required. Open daily 10am-7pm.)

For an outdoors experience away from the beach, get off bus #7 a few stops earlier, at **Douanes**. From there, continue on the promenade de la Barre and follow signs to the **Centre Equestre**. The **Club Hippique** provides **riding lessons** and **horseback tours** of the Forêt du Chilberta. The stables are on rue du Petit Palais, off promenade de la Barre. (☎05 59 63 83 45; contact@chcote-basque.com. 1hr. lesson €20; forest walk €18. Open July-Aug. M-F 9am-noon and 3-7pm, Sa 9am-noon and 3-6pm; Sept.-June M and F 3-7pm, Tu-W and Sa 9am-noon and 3-7pm. Reservations required. MC/V.)

Along the coast, professional surf competitions are held throughout the summer and are free for spectators. Starting at the beginning of August, surfers from around the world gather at La Plage des Cavaliers to compete in several of Anglet's featured surf competitions. In mid-August, pros and amateurs show off their skills at the **Quiksilver Airshow**, a surfer favorite. The qualifying rounds take place at the Sables d'Or. For five days in May, women take over the waves to compete in the longboard and bodyboard divisions of the **Kana Miss Cup**. In mid-September, the **Royal Single Trophée** comes to Marinella Beach, accompanied by concerts. Dates for 2009 are available at www.anglet-tourisme.com.

From the bus stop at Anglet Plages, turn left to reach the **Tourist Office Annex;** the annex has the same services as the main branch in town and is more convenient, as it is located near Anglet's beaches. (☎05 59 03 93 43. Open daily July-Aug. 10:30am-7:30pm; Apr.-June and Sept.-Oct. 10:30am-1pm and 3-6:30pm.)

SAINT-JEAN-DE-LUZ   ☎05 59

St-Jean-de-Luz (sehn-jhahn-d-looz; pop. 13,000) has everything: the red shutters and narrow side streets of Bayonne, a sheltered version of Biarritz's sandy beaches, and a rich Basque tradition that takes over the streets in late-summer festivals. St-Jean has a storied past; the plunder of 17th-century whalers and pirates has left in its wake fine examples of Basque architecture, from the bell tower above Ravel's birthplace to the elaborate interior of the Église St-Jean-Baptiste. The town is pedestrian-friendly, as most sights fit in the 300m stretch between the train station and the beach. Budget travelers will want to visit St-Jean as a daytrip from more affordable Bayonne or Biarritz, as the town offers the perfect place to enjoy a gourmet meal, stroll a quiet beach, and break from the tourist throngs of the rest of the Côte Basque.

◪ TRANSPORTATION

Trains: Bd. du Commandant Passicot (☎08 92 35 35 35). Info office open M-Sa 7:45am-7:30pm, Su 10am-7:30pm. To: **Bayonne** (30min.; 10 per day; €4.20, TGV €6); **Biarritz** (15min.; 10 per day; €2.70, TGV €4.40); **Paris** (5hr., 10 per day, €81); **Pau** (2hr., 7 per day, €18).

Buses: Across from the train station. Office open M-F 9am-noon and 2-6pm. ATCRB (☎05 59 08 00 33) runs to **Bayonne** (1hr., 15 per day, €6) and **Biarritz** (40min., 17 per day, €3). Buy tickets on board.

Taxis: At the train station (☎05 59 26 10 11). €7-9 within St-Jean-de-Luz, €30 to Biarritz. At night, taxis become the only mode of transport to Biarritz.

Car Rental: Avis (☎05 59 26 76 66), at the train station. Possible to return to other locations, including Paris and Bayonne. From €326-500 per week; copy of credit card and driver's license as deposit. Under-25 surcharge €25 per day. Open M-F 8am-noon and 2-6pm, Sa 9am-noon and 2-6pm. AmEx/MC/V.

Bike Rental: Fun-Bike Location (☎05 59 26 75 76), at the train station. Bikes €15 per day, €61 per week; €200 deposit. Scooters €41 per day; €900 deposit. Open July-Aug. daily 10am-7pm; Sept.-June call in advance. MC/V.

🔲 🛈 ORIENTATION AND PRACTICAL INFORMATION

From the train and bus stations, the center of St-Jean-de-Luz is all that stands between you and the beach. To reach the tourist office, use the passageway under the freeway, then turn right and walk to the traffic circle. Turn left again onto av. Jauréguiberry and walk 100m; the office is on your right, at the intersection with bd. Victor Hugo. To reach the beach from the train station, turn left as you exit the passageway; at the traffic circle, follow av. de Verdun to pl. Foch. Rue de la République runs two blocks through pl. Louis XIV then on to the beach; pedestrian rue Gambetta is to the right.

Tourist Office: 20 bd. Victor Hugo (☎05 59 26 03 16; www.saint-jean-de-luz.com). Maps and info on accommodations and excursions. 2hr. town tours in French July-Aug. Tu and Th 10am; Sept.-June Tu 10am. €5, ages 12-18 €2.50, under 12 free. Open July-Aug. M-Sa 9am-7:30pm, Su 10am-1pm and 3-7pm; Sept.-June M-Sa 9am-12:30pm and 2-7pm, Su 10am-1pm; closes at 6pm on weekdays during the winter.

Bank: Société Generale, 9 bd. Victor Hugo (☎05 59 57 90 00). Open Tu-F 8:15am-12:20pm and 1:35-5:10pm, Sa 8:15am-12:25pm. **ATMs** also line bd. Victor Hugo.

Laundromat: Laverie du Port, 5 pl. Foch (☎05 59 85 17 69). Turn left out of the station and follow av. de Verdun at the traffic circle. Wash €4.70-8.20, dry €0.50 per 4min. Full service €17 per 7kg. Open daily 7am-9pm. Full service open Tu-F 9:30am-12:30pm and 2:30-7pm, Sa 9:30am-1pm.

Police: Av. André Ithurralde (☎05 59 51 22 22).

Medical Services: Polyclinique, 7 rue Léonce Goyetche (☎05 59 51 63 63). Private hospital with 24hr. emergency services.

Internet Access: Internet World, 7 rue Tourasse (☎05 59 26 86 92). €1 per 10min. with a €2 min. purchase. Fixed cards for €25 per 5hr., €45 per 10hr. Printing €0.30 per page. Open July-Aug. daily 9am-midnight; Sept.-June M-Sa 10am-6pm.

Post Office: 44 bd. Victor Hugo (☎05 59 51 66 58). Open M and W-F 8:45am-noon and 1:30-5:15pm, Tu 8:45am-noon and 2:15-5:15pm, Sa 8:45am-noon. **Postal Code:** 64500.

🏠 🏕 ACCOMMODATIONS AND CAMPING

Hotels are expensive and fill up rapidly in summer, particularly during festival season, so reserve early. For most budgets, it's not worth the cost to stay in St-Jean-de-Luz proper. Instead, commute from **Bayonne** (p. 595) or **Biarritz** (p. 590), as a fulfilling visit to St-Jean-de-Luz can easily be made in a day. The **Auberge de Jeunesse** in Biarritz and the **Hôtel Paris-Madrid** in Bayonne are particularly convenient, since they are near train stations. There are 14 **campsites ❶** in St-Jean-de-Luz; all are behind plage d'Erromardie. The tourist office has addresses and phone numbers. Take bd. Victor Hugo from the *centre-ville*, continue along the road as it turns into av. André Ithurralde, and veer left on chemin d'Erromardie at a fork in the road (30min.). Or take an ATCRB bus (€1) headed to Biarritz or Bayonne and ask to get off near the camping sites.

> **Hôtel Verdun,** 13 av. de Verdun (☎05 59 26 02 55), across from the station. Unremarkable pastel-colored rooms with large bathrooms. Breakfast €5. Reception 8am-11pm. Singles and doubles €28-45; triples and quads €45-60. MC/V. ❷

🍴 FOOD

St-Jean-de-Luz has the best Basque and Spanish specialties north of the border. Famous seafood awaits in restaurants along **rue de la République** and on **place Louis XIV;** they are tourist-oriented but offer reliable *formules* for around €14. St-Jean-de-Luz's true gems lie in its smaller restaurants, whose more gourmet offerings are outstanding examples of the regional fare. There is a large market at **place des Halles.** (Open from July to mid-Sept. daily 8am-1pm.) For groceries, stop at the **Shopi** supermarket, 87 rue Gambetta. (Open July-Aug. daily 9am-8pm; Sept.-June M-Sa 9am-12:30pm and 3-7:15pm. AmEx/MC/V.)

> ⛄ **Txantxangorri,** 30 rue Chauvin Dragon (☎05 59 26 04 32). Offers a menu of inspired Basque cuisine that could be your best meal in France. Delicacies include a tomato and mozzarella salad with basil oil and balsamic sorbet (€7) and *pavé* of *merlu* (hake fish) in a lentil stew with coddled egg (€14). The excellent *gambas à la plancha* (grilled prawns; €13) make a regular appearance on the changing menu. Lunch *menu* €11. Open Tu-Sa noon-2:30pm and 7:30-10pm, Su 7:30-10pm. MC/V. ❸

> ⛄ **Pil-Pil Enea,** 3 rue Sallagoity (☎05 59 51 20 80). Restaurant on the side streets serves *merlu* (hake fish) and other local specialties rooted in family recipes. Its menu is conservative but superb. *Entrées* €10-20. *Menu* €28. Fish and meat *plats* €15-20, though some specialties run up to €40. Open M-Sa 12:15-2pm and 7:30-10pm. MC/V. ❹

> **Etchebaster Frères,** 42 rue Gambetta (☎05 59 26 00 80). Cherry jam- and cream-filled *gâteaux Basques* (€7-14) tempt passersby from the windows of this small bakery. Owner takes pride in his frosted *gâteaux des rois* (orange flour cakes; €6.50-14). Open July-Aug. Tu-Sa 8:30am-1pm and 3:30-7:30pm, Su 8am-1pm and 4-7pm; Sept.-June Tu-Su 8:30am-12:30pm and 3:30-7pm. MC/V. ❷

👁 SIGHTS

ÉGLISE SAINT-JEAN-BAPTISTE. The spartan stone walls and wood beams of this 15th-century church belie the glory of the interior, whose nave, with its painting and gold sculptures, presides over the altar. Louis XIV married the Spanish princess Maria Teresa in this church. (*Rue Gambetta.* ☎*05 59 26 08 81. Open daily 8am-noon and 2-6:30pm. Mass Sa 7pm; Su 8:30, 10:30am, 6pm.*)

MAISON LOUIS XIV. Owned by the same family for over 350 years, the royal furniture inside this house has been frozen in time—as if awaiting the return of its famous boarder. The museum also houses royal portraits and even the royal sedan chair. (*Pl. Louis XIV.* ☎*/fax 05 59 26 27 58. 30min. guided tour in French leaves at 11am, 3, 4, 5pm. Written explanations in English and audio tours in French available upon request. Open July-Aug. M and W-Su 10:30am-12:30pm and 2:30-6:30pm; Sept. and June M-Sa 10:30am-noon and 2:30-5:30pm, Su 2:30-5:30pm. €5, students and ages 12-18 €3, under 12 free.*)

ECOMUSÉE BASQUE. This museum was made for the uncompromising devotee of Basque culture. The 1hr. audio tour (available in French, English, Spanish, and Basque) includes free samples of Izarra (sweet Basque liqueur) and a documentary about the Basque linen-making method; by the end, you'll be equipped with more knowledge than you'll ever need about Basque work habits. (*3km out of the city along the route of the ATCRB bus (dir.: Biarritz or Bayonne); get off at*

Dubonnet. ☎05 59 51 06 06. Open July-Aug. daily 10am-6:30pm; Sept.-Oct. and Apr.-June M-Sa
10-11:15am and 2:30-5:30pm. Tours every 15min. €6, students €5.50, ages 5-12 €2.50.)

FESTIVALS

Summer in St-Jean-de-Luz is jammed with countless concerts, Basque festivals,
and the much-anticipated championship *cesta punta* (jai alai) match, a game
that features the fastest-moving ball in any sport. (☎05 59 51 65 36; www.ces-
tapunta.com. Qualifying series and finals July-Aug. Tu and F at 9pm. Tickets,
available at the tourist office, €6-19, under 12 free. MC/V with phone reservations.) For information for all the festivals listed below, call ☎05 59 26 02 87 or
check out www.saint-jean-de-luz.com.

Fête de la St-Jean, during a weekend in late June. The biggest annual festival, when
singing and dancing fill the streets. Nearly continuous performances by amateurs and
professionals animate the *fronton* (arena), while spectators sip sangria and sink their
teeth into barbecued Basque dishes.

Toro de Fuego, W and Su at 10:30pm in July-Aug., Heats up summer nights in pl. Louis
XIV with pyrotechnics, dancing, and bull costumes.

Fête du Thon, on the 2nd Sa in July, beginning at 6pm. Locals gather in the *centre-ville* to
eat tuna, dance, and toss confetti. Entrance free. Meals at booths €10.

Nuit de la Sardine, the 2nd Sa in Aug. The homage to fish continues at the Campos-
Berri, next to the *cesta punta* stadium.

BEACHES

To see the coast of St-Jean-de-Luz at its most striking, turn right when you
reach the beach. Follow promenade Jacques Thibaud along the Grande Plage.
As you continue to the Sainte Barbe, the *balade à pied* (footpath) leads you
along the edge of St-Jean's cliffs. From the lookout points, gaze out over the
Nivell River to Hendaye and the Spanish border.

The **Grande Plage,** while an attractive destination for daytrippers looking to
escape the throngs of Biarritz, differs little from beaches elsewhere along the
Côte Basque. It does, however, provide greater accessibility to some of the
Basque region's best sailing and surfing. For information about boat rentals,
contact the tourist office. Those seeking more secluded beaches can take the
ACTRB bus (dir.: Biarritz or Bayonne) to **Acotz,** near several campgrounds,
where there are two beaches popular with surfers.

Billabong, 16 rue Gambetta (☎05 59 26 07 93). A full array of boards and wetsuits.
Wetsuit €7 per ½-day, €12 per day; surfboard €10/15. ID deposit. 2hr. lesson €40.
Open July-Aug. daily 10am-11pm; Sept.-June M-F 10am-12:30pm and 2:30-7pm, Sa
10am-7:30pm, Su 11am-1pm and 3-7pm. AmEx/MC/V.

FISHING

From 1954 to 1956, St-Jean-de-Luz was France's primary tuna supplier. Fishing
boats still leave from **quai de l'Infante** and **quai Maréchal Leclerc,** although they are
not as fruitful as in the past, as overfishing and an encroaching tourist industry
edge out fishing as the primary means of employment here.

Nivelle III (☎06 09 73 61 81), at the docks near Maison Louis XIV. Try a 4hr. fishing
trip (8am-noon) and an afternoon cruise along the Spanish coast (2-4pm). Customers

keep the fish they catch. Trips vary by day May-Sept. but run daily July-Aug. Reservations required. Fishing trip €30, under 11 €20. Afternoon cruise €15/8.

SAINT-JEAN-PIED-DE-PORT   ☎ 05 59

Tucked into the Pyrenean hills, St-Jean-Pied-de-Port (sehn-jahn-pee-ed-duh-pohr; pop. 1417) is the meeting place of three major trails—from Paris, Vezelay, and Puy. The town has been a resting place for pilgrims on the road to the tomb of St-James in Santiago de Compostela, Spain, since the 10th century. Today, St-Jean embodies rural Basque charm, complete with small white houses and red shutters, flower-lined stone-arch bridges, and a medieval citadel. Pilgrims have been replaced by backpackers from all corners of the world seeking to embark on one of many trails through the French and Spanish Pyrenees, which lie only a short distance outside the city walls. The GR10 and the GR65 trails—notoriously challenging for hikers and cross-country skiers—lie nearby, making St-Jean the intersection of backpacking paradise and peaceful small town.

▐◄ ▐? TRANSPORTATION AND PRACTICAL INFORMATION

Trains: Av. Renaud (☎05 59 37 02 00). Info office open M-Sa 6:30am-noon and 1-6:45pm, Su 9am-noon and 2-7pm. To **Bayonne** (1hr., at least 5 per day, €8).

Bike Rental: Garazi Cycles, 32 bis av. du Jaï-Alaï (☎05 59 37 21 79). From the tourist office, turn right and keep left when the road splits; past the traffic circle, look for a shed on the right. Bikes €10 per ½-day, €15 per day; passport or ID deposit. Scooters €18/30; €350 deposit. Motorcycles €35/50; €700 deposit. Open M-Sa 9am-noon and 2-7pm. July-Aug. service available Su by arrangement. MC/V.

Tourist Office: 14 pl. du Général de Gaulle, (☎05 59 37 03 57; www.pyrenees-basques. com). From the station, turn left and then immediately right on av. Renaud, follow it uphill, and turn right at its end. The office will be 40m away on the left. Gives out maps of the town and sells hiking guides (€8) charting 25 regional trails. Open July-Aug. M-Sa 9am-7pm, Su 10am-4pm; Sept.-June M-Sa 9am-noon and 2-6pm, Su 10am-1pm.

Police Station: Rue d'Ugange (☎05 59 49 20 10).

Medical Services: Clinique Luro (☎05 59 37 00 55), in Ispoure.

Post Office: Rue de la Poste (☎05 59 37 90 00). Open M-F 9am-noon and 2-5pm, Sa 9am-noon. **Postal Code:** 64220.

▐ ACCOMMODATIONS

St-Jean-Pied-de-Port is a paradise of budget accommodations. Hotels fill up quickly in the summer, but there is a glut of *gîtes* (rooms rented out in family homes, normally €8-12 per night), thanks to the city's position along the pilgrimage route to **Santiago de Compostela,** Spain. Many are clustered on **rue de la Citadelle.** Contact the tourist office (☎05 59 37 03 57) or the **Amis du Chemin** (☎05 59 37 05 09) to make reservations.

Mme. Etchegoin's Gîte d'Étape, 9 rte. d'Uhart (☎05 59 37 12 08). From the tourist office, turn left, cross the bridge, and take the first right. After you pass the city gates, the street becomes rte. d'Uhart; when the road splits, keep right, following the sign to Bayonne (5min.). 12 spartan but comfortable bunks in an 18th-century house along with 3 attractive *chambres d'hôte* with antique furnishings and hardwood floors. Each room has large bed and either a private or communal shower. Breakfast €5 with dorms, included with rooms. Sheets or sleeping bag €2. Reception 8am-10:30pm. Reserve ahead. Open Mar.-Nov. Dorms €10; singles €30; doubles €38; triples €50. ❶

Camping Municipal 1, av. du Fronton (☎05 59 37 11 19), 5min. from the *centre-ville*. From the tourist office, turn left, then take an immediate left through the wall of the citadel on rue de l'Église. Continue along the river on allée d'Eyheraberry. After 20m, cross the wood footbridge, and the campsite will be on your left. Quiet and plain. Bathrooms and showers free for campers, €2 for visitors. Reception Apr.-Oct. daily 9-11am and 5-7pm. €2.50 per person, €2 per child; €2 per tent; €2 per car. Electricity €2.50. ❶

◖ FOOD

Farmers bring *ardigazna* (tangy dry sheep's-milk cheese) to the market on **place de Gaulle.** (Open M 9am-6pm.) In July and August, local fairs bring produce from nearby villages; ask for the dates at the tourist office. Bread, cheese, and wine are all available at any one of the small shops that line **rue d'Espagne.** There is a **Relais de Mousquetaires** supermarket on the corner of rue d'Espagne and route d'Uhart. (☎05 59 37 00 47. Open M, W, F-Sa 9:30am-12:30pm and 4-7pm; Tu and Th 9:30am-12:30pm. MC/V.) Most budget restaurants in St-Jean-Pied-de-Port serve familiar food of familiarly mediocre quality, but the cafes and *crêperies* along **rue de Zuharpeta** offer acceptable meals and refreshing sangria.

Lizarra Ostatua, pl. Floquet (☎05 59 37 00 99). Homey restaurant is a fantastic break from Gallic portions; the €13 *menu* comes salad, dessert, and an exceptional *plat* overflowing with vegetables and *frites*. Charming matron of the house sits down and chats with her customers. Pizzas €7-9. Paella €10. *Plat du jour* €8.50-11. *Menus* €12-25. Open M-W and F-Su noon-2:30pm and 7-10:30pm. MC/V over €15. ❷

Coté Tarte, 5 rue de l'Église (☎05 59 49 16 78). A charming bric-a-brac boutique that also serves delicious tarts with creative flair. Try the curry tart (with chicken, hot curry, and mushrooms; €8) or the Tatinouille, jammed with vegetables flavored in a rich Tuscan sauce (€9). Tarts €7-11. Open M and W-Sa 11am-6pm. MC/V. ❷

Etche Ona, pl. Floquet (☎05 59 37 01 14). This restaurant—though a bit of a splurge—serves expertly cooked duck, lamb, and rabbit garnished with traditional Basque sauces (all €14). *Plats* €14. *Menu* €29. Open July-Sept. daily 10am-2pm and 7:30-10pm; Oct.-June M-W and Sa-Su 10am-2pm and 7:30-10pm. MC/V. ❸

◖ SIGHTS

Though the Pyrenees are the main draw, the tiny center of St-Jean-Pied-de-Port is worth at least a brief visit. Bounded by the porte d'Espagne and porte St-Jacques, St-Jean's ancient *haute-ville* consists of a single narrow street, rue de la Citadelle, which is bordered by houses made from the regional crimson stone. To reach it, turn right when you leave the tourist office, right again on rue de France, left on rue de la Citadelle, and continue up the hill.

CITADELLE DE VAUBAN. Unquestionably St-Jean's greatest attraction, the citadel is uphill from the *haute-ville*. Built by Pierre de Conty in the 1620s, the fortress was later reinforced by Vauban during the reign of Louis XIV and now towers over the town and surrounding farmland. In the 18th century, the citadel housed soldiers who protected Bayonne and Orthez from Spaniards lurking across the border, at one point garrisoning as many as 2000 men. Though the stronghold's interior has since been converted into a middle school, visitors can still climb to the top to picnic on grassy ramparts and catch a breathtaking view of the town below and the surrounding mountains. *(41 rue de la Citadelle.)*

PRISON DES EVÊQUES. Below the walls of the fortress, this small but beautiful building was built in the 13th century. Its name is actually a misnomer, as no bishops either imprisoned or were imprisoned here; it was used to discipline unruly soldiers during the 19th century and to torture French escapees during Nazi occupation. Today, the prison is a museum dedicated to St-Jacques's pilgrimage. *(41 rue de la Citadelle. ☎ 05 59 37 00 92. Open July-Aug. daily 10am-7pm; Sept.-Oct. and Easter-June M and W-Su 11am-12:30pm and 2:30-6:30pm. €3, under 10 free.)*

📚 HIKING

The most spectacular hikes from St-Jean-Pied-de-Port either require more than a day or are not accessible by public transportation. Nonetheless, one manageable 3hr. hike is worthwhile; striking views of Pau and the surrounding mountains on the second half of the hike are the reward for a less exciting walk along flat roads at the beginning. From the tourist office, turn right, staying left on av. du Jaï Alaï at the fork. Pass straight through the traffic circle and, following signs to **Ispoure,** turn left after the bridge over the river. Continue until you see the small church, the **Église d'Ispoure,** on your right. Turn right toward the church and walk uphill, passing the church, which should now be on your left. Fifty meters past the church, turn left at the intersection marked by a stone cross. Continue to the second intersection and turn left, following the sign to **Etchaine.** Pass a first fork, keeping right along the stream, and after 5min. keep left at the second fork in the road marked by a row of four pine trees on the right. Walk up a steep hill with a stream to your right. At the next fork, continue upward on the gravel road. You'll find yourself in the **Domaine Abotia** vineyard; after around half an hour, you will reach signs pointing back into Ispoure and toward an *aire de pique-nique* (picnic ground). Continue toward the *aire* another 15min. to reach a tranquil clearing, complete with stone-hewn seating, from which to view the entire valley; your total ascent is around 600m. Retrace your steps back to St-Jean or follow the sign back through Ispoure. For a detailed map of the area, see **hike #21** in the tourist office's guidebook.

PAU   ☎ 05 59

Once the seat of the kings of Navarre, Pau (po; pop. 78,000) has transformed into a vibrant and youthful regional hub. Though it may lack the blockbuster sights of bigger cities and pastoral attraction of smaller Pyrenean villages, it has greater rail accessibility than any other city in the region, and a stopover here need not be wasted. The château where King Henri IV was born and raised remains in near-perfect condition—an unchanging testament to the city's history. And, as the capital of the Béarn region, Pau is the center of *béarnais* cuisine and home to more than 150 tempting restaurants.

🚈 TRANSPORTATION

Trains: Av. Gaston Lacoste, at the base of the hill by the château. Info and ticket office open M-Th and Sa 5:15am-8:30pm, F 5:15am-11:30pm, Su 7:15am-11:30pm. To: **Bayonne** (1hr., 7 per day, €15); **Biarritz** (1hr., 6-7 per day, €18); **Bordeaux** (2hr.; 11 per day; €28, TGV €32); **Lourdes** (30min., at least 15 per day, €6.60-8); **St-Jean-de-Luz** (2hr., 6 per day, €18).

Buses: CITRAM, av. Thimonier (☎05 59 27 22 22). Office open M-F 9am-noon and 2-5pm. To **Agen** (3hr., 1 per day, €27.20). Société TPR, 4 rue la Pouble (☎05 59 27 45 98. Office open M-F 9am-noon and 2-6pm. To **Lourdes** (1hr.; M-Sa 5 per day, Su 2 per day; €4, under 6 free).

Public Transportation: STAP, pl. d'Espagne (☎05 59 14 15 16). Tickets €1.10, day pass €2.50, carnet of 8 €5.60. 1st bus in any direction M-Sa 6:30am, Su 1:15pm;

last bus in any direction M-Sa 8:20pm, Su 7:40pm. Pau has little night transport; the Noctambus, run by STAP, circulates on a few routes in the evening, running 2-4 buses 8pm-midnight at the same fares.

Taxis: (☎05 59 02 22 22), at the train station and the airport. Base €2; €1.50 per km during the day, €1.88 at night. €30 from the train station to the airport.

Bike Rental: Romano Sport, 6 rue Jean-Réveil (☎05 59 98 48 56). Mountain bikes (€20 per day), in-line skates (€7 per day), skis (€20 per day, including boots), and mountain equipment. ID deposit. Open daily 9am-noon and 3-7pm. Cash only.

🔧🚺 ORIENTATION AND PRACTICAL INFORMATION

To get to the town center from the station, ride the free **funicular** to bd. des Pyrénées (every 3min. M-Sa 6:45am-12:10pm, 12:35-7:10pm, and 7:35-9:40pm; Su 1:30-7:10pm and 7:35-8:50pm) or zig-zag along the steep path to the hilltop.

Tourist Office: (☎05 59 27 27 08; www.pau-pyrenees.com), at the top of the funicular, across the tree-lined pl. Royale. Open July-Aug. M-F 9am-6:30pm, Sa 9am-6pm, Su 9:30am-1pm and 2-6pm; Sept.-June M-Sa 9am-6pm, Su 9:30am-1pm.

Laundromat: (☎05 59 82 73 60), at the corner of rue Lespy and rue Émile Garet. Open 10am-7pm. Wash €3, dry €0.30 per 4min. Detergent €0.30.

Police: Rue O'Quin (☎05 59 98 22 22).

Hospital: 4 bd. Hauterive (☎05 59 92 48 48).

Internet Access: C Cyber, 20 rue Lamothe (☎05 59 82 89 40), past the post office. Open M-Sa 10am-2am, Su 2pm-midnight. €0.80 per 10min., €4.80 per hr.

Post Office: Cours Bosquet at rue Gambetta (☎05 59 98 98 98). **Currency exchange,** Cyberposte, and copy and fax services available. Open M-F 8:30am-6:30pm, Sa 8:30am-noon. **Postal Code:** 64000.

📍 ACCOMMODATIONS

Low-priced, high-quality accommodations are difficult to come by in Pau; getting one or the other is considerably easier.

Hôtel Regina, 18 rue Gassion (☎05 59 27 29 19). In a quieter section of town, this charming hotel offers clean linoleum-floored rooms with high ceilings, large windows, pink stucco walls, and beautiful bathrooms. A particularly good value for groups of 2-4. Breakfast €5. Reception 8am-11pm. Doubles and triples with bath $35-50. MC/V. ❸

Hôtel Central, 15 rue Léon Daran (☎05 59 27 72 75). The 26 large, spotless rooms tended by an attentive owner are painted with various maritime and pastoral motifs. Each comes with TV and clean bathroom. Saint-Exupéry, author of *Le Petit Prince*, stayed in room #7 before his rise to fame. The main floor features a billiard room and bar with cable TV. Breakfast €7. Reception 7am-10:30pm. Reservations recommended. Singles €39-57; doubles €45-72, with 2 single beds €62-85. Extra bed €10. AmEx/MC/V. ❹

Hôtel de la Pomme d'Or, 11 rue Maréchal Foch (☎05 59 11 23 23; fax 11 23 24). Turn left from the tourist office onto rue Louis Barthou and left again on rue Alred de Lassence. Walk through pl. Georges Clemenceau and turn right onto rue Maréchal Foch. Offers acceptable rooms in the *centre-ville* at the cheapest rates around. Breakfast €4. Reception 24hr. Singles €26, with shower and toilet €34; doubles €38-42; triples with shower €48; quads €53. Cash only. ❷

🍴 FOOD

The region famous for *béarnaise* sauce has no scarcity of specialties: *saumon* (salmon), *brochet* (pike), *oie* (goose), *canard* (duck), and *assiette béarnaise* (a platter of gizzards, duck hearts, and asparagus) all make frequent appearances on *palois* menus. In addition, the large immigrant population in Pau brings with it a suprising variety of good ethnic restaurants, which provide a nice alternative from bistro fare. The area around the château, including **rue Sully** and **rue du Château,** has elegant regional restaurants (*menus* €12-17). Inexpensive pizzerias, kebab joints, and Vietnamese eateries can be found in the pedestrian mall around **place Georges Clemenceau** and on **rue Léon Daran.** A sprawling **Super U** supermarket sits on the lower level of the Centre Bosquet megaplex on cours Bosquet. (Open M-Sa 9am-7:30pm. MC/V.) The equally enormous market at **Les Halles,** pl. de la République, is a maze of vegetable and cheese stalls. (Open M-Sa 6am-1pm and 3:30-7:30pm.) The **Marché Biologique,** pl. du Foirail, sells organic produce. (Open W and Sa 8am-12:30pm.)

Ciel and Chocolat, 11 rue Maréchal Foch (☎05 59 27 44 15). Hip restaurant serves chic food at reasonable prices. €10 lunch *menu* includes a choice of *entrée* or dessert—the €3.50 profiteroles are delicious—and *plat.* Try the *magret de canard au miel* (duck breast; €8). Open M-W noon-2pm, W-Sa noon-2pm and 7:30-10pm. MC/V. ❷

L'Entrecôte, 26 rue Lamothe (☎05 59 27 45 75), near the post office. Locals fight over tables to enjoy generous pizzas (€8-9) that come with a large assortment of toppings. The pizza rocquefort is a house specialty loaded with mushrooms, Roquefort, and ham. Owner brings hot pizzas directly from the oven to your plate. Salads €9. Steaks and other beef dishes €9.50-15. Open daily noon-2pm and 7pm-midnight. MC/V. ❷

L'Isle au Jasmin, 28 bd. des Pyrénées (☎05 59 27 34 82), tucked behind the château. Mint-green beach chairs perched on the lawn are perfect for looking out on a captivating Pyrenean vista. Owner brews the coffee and blends the teas herself, using everything from dried mountain flowers to fresh berries. Coffee €1.40. Teas by the pot €2.50. Cakes and *petits-fours* €1-2. Open daily 10am-8pm; closed in bad weather. Cash only. ❶

SIGHTS

CHÂTEAU D'HENRI IV. After getting off the funicular, turn left along bd. de Pyrénées and admire the mountains to your left and the city to your right. You'll come to the Château d'Henri IV, where the famed first of the Bourbon kings, Henri IV, was born in December of 1553. Originally built as a medieval fortress, it was remodeled by Louis-Philippe in 1838 and again by Napoleon III. The castle has become a national museum that now displays a famous collection of Gobelin tapestries as well as the enormous tortoise shell that served as Henri IV's crib. The château is accessible only through 1hr. guided tours in French, which depart every 15min. Printed English translations of the tour are available upon request. (☎05 62 82 38 02. English tours by appointment. Open daily from mid-June to mid-Sept. 9:30am-12:15pm and 1:30-5:45pm; from mid-Sept to mid-June 9:30-11:45am and 2-5pm. Last tour 1hr. before closing. €5, ages 18-25 €3.20, under 18 free.)

MUSÉE DES BEAUX ARTS. The main attraction of this museum is an enormous tableau of Henri IV's birth. Otherwise, the museum houses a collection of modern art and 17th- to 19th-century European paintings. (Rue Mathieu Lalanne. ☎05 62 27 33 02. English and French guides available if requested in advance. Open M and W-Su 10am-noon and 2-6pm. €3, students €1.50, under 18 free.)

ENTERTAINMENT AND NIGHTLIFE

Not only does the flower-lined bd. des Pyrénées overlook expansive green mountains, but it also features great bars that cater to Pau's young and restless, who overflow onto the sidewalk in the summer.

▨ **Le Garage,** 49 rue Émile Garet (☎05 59 83 75 17). On the corner of rue Langles past the Centre Bosquet, where local 20-somethings congregate. The venue is covered in rugby paraphernalia, and the ambience that of a raucous pub. Pints and mixed drinks from €4. Salads €7. *Plats* €7-9. Open M-F 11:30am-3am, Sa-Su noon-2am. MC/V.

Galway, 20 bd. des Pyrénées (☎05 59 82 94 66). 2-story bar draws a large Anglophone crowd with quality music and beer. Pints from €3.70. Live music twice a month. Open daily 1pm-2am. MC/V.

La Station des Artistes, 8 rue René Fournets (☎05 59 83 83 02). The place to go for gay nightlife. Offers lots of smoke and mirrors as well as a transsexual show Su at 11pm. Open daily 9pm-2am. MC/V.

Cinéma le Méliès, 6 rue Bargoin (☎05 62 27 60 52; www.lemelies.net). Shows foreign flicks and art films, some in English and all subtitled in French. Movies 1:30-10:30pm. Closed 1st 2 weeks of Aug. €6, students €4.80. MC/V.

✳ FESTIVALS

Summer in Pau brings a bounty of festivals. Contact the tourist office or ask for a *Guide des Fêtes* for more information.

Formula 3 Grand Prix de Pau, in June. Cars race around the town to the delight of a horde of spectators.

Tour de France, in mid-July. Bicycles replace cars as the Tour passes through spectator-lined city streets. Don't get trampled!

Ciné Cité, from mid-July to mid-Aug. The Ciné brings free concerts and outdoor films. Salsa, blues, and jazz bands perform at around 9pm and are quickly followed by either a recent film or an old classic.

Pelote Basque, 458 bd. du Fronton (☎05 62 02 00 01; www.pilotak.fr), every M and Th night from mid-July to mid-Aug. Free matches at the distant outdoor fronton (arena) of the new **Complexe de Pelote.** Ask at the tourist office for directions.

LOURDES ☎05 62

In 1858, Bernadette Soubirous first reported seeing visions of the Virgin Mary in the Massabielle Grotto in Lourdes (loord; pop. 17,200). Eventually, the Virgin Mary instructed her to have a chapel built on the spot. Today, over six million visitors from more than 100 countries come annually to this pilgrimage center, carrying rosaries and whispering prayers as they march—or are wheeled—to the Blessing of the Sick. The sesquicentennial (150th) anniversary of Bernadette's vision in 2008, known as the Jubilee Celebration, marked a special time for Lourdes. The Jubilee Way, a path around Lourdes, was created for the occasion to highlight the most important spiritual landmarks of the city.

▉ TRANSPORTATION

Trains: 33 av. de la Gare (☎05 62 46 45 62). Info office open daily July-Aug. 7:05am-9:30pm; Sept.-June 7:05am-6:30pm. To **Bayonne** (2hr., at least 5 per day, €20); **Bordeaux** (3hr., at least 10 per day, €31-37); **Paris** (6-8hr., 5 per day, TGV €81-100); **Pau** (30min., at least 15 per day, €6-8); **Toulouse** (2hr., at least 7 per day, €20-27).

Buses: SNCF buses run from the train station to **Cauterets** (55min., 6 per day, €6.50) The local (☎05 62 94 10 78) runs from all points in the city to the **grotto,** the **Pic du Jer** (from which the funicular departs), and **Lac de Lourdes** (Easter-Oct. daily every 15-30min. 7am-7pm, Sept.-June Tu, Th, Sa 7am-7pm; €1.20).

Taxis: At the train station and the grotto Easter-Oct. (☎05 62 46 14 61).

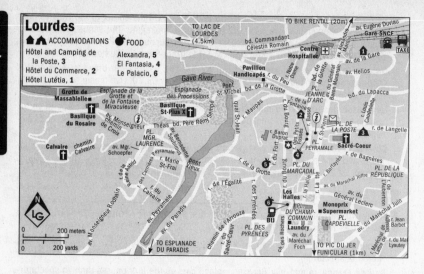

Bike Rental: Cycles Antonio Oliveria, 14 av. Alexandre Marqui (☎05 62 42 24 24). €10 per ½-day, €15 per day, €90 per week; €300 or photo ID deposit. Open Tu-Sa 9:30am-noon and 2-7pm. MC/V.

✴ 🛈 ORIENTATION AND PRACTICAL INFORMATION

The train station is on the northern edge of town, 10min. from the town center. The religious heart of Lourdes is the **grotto,** located 15min. from the station. Follow av. de la Gare to the intersection, turning left onto av. de Maransin. Walking along av. de Maransin, you will cross a small overpass; on the far right side, there is a staircase that gives onto bd. de la Grotte. Follow this boulevard, past the crowds and trinket stores, to the grotto. Continue across the Gave River to reach the Esplanade des Processions, the Basilique St-Pius X, and the grotto.

Tourist Office: Pl. Peyramale (☎05 62 42 77 40; www.lourdes-infotourisme.com). From the station, continue past the bridge and staircase on av. de Maransin; the office is in a glass complex on the right. Maps, info on religious ceremonies, a list of hotels, and brochures. Interactive touch screen outside the office contains most tourist info and is available even after the office closes. Open July-Aug. M-Sa 9am-7pm, Su 10am-6pm; Sept. and from mid-Mar. to June M-Sa 9am-6:30pm, Su 10am-12:30pm; from Oct. to mid-Mar. M-Sa 9am-noon and 2-6pm. Bernadette-related sights are managed by the **Sanctuaires de Notre Dame de Lourdes,** which has a **Forum d'Info** to the left as you approach the basilica (☎05 62 42 78 78). Open daily 8:30am-12:15pm and 1:45-6:30pm; reduced hours in winter.

Youth Center: Forum Lourdes/Bureau Information Jeunesse, 30 pl. du Champ Commun (☎05 62 94 94 00). A helpful youth center with Internet access (€3 per hr.), in a red building behind Les Halles. Open M-F 9am-noon and 1:30-5:30pm.

Laundromat: 42 pl. du Champ Commun. Wash €4.20, dry €0.60 per 5 min. Open daily 8am-8pm. Cash only.

Police: 7 rue Baron Duprat (☎05 62 42 72 72).

Hospital: 3 av. Alexandre Marqui (☎05 62 42 42 42), at the intersection with av. de la Gare. **Emergency services,** 2 av. Alexandre Marqui (☎05 62 42 44 38); disabled services at **Pavillon Handicapés** (☎05 62 42 79 92), to the right after Porte St-Michel.

Post Office: 31 av. de Maransin (☎05 62 42 72 00). Bills-only **currency exchange** available. Open M-Tu and Th-F 8:30am-noon and 1:30-6pm, W 9am-noon and 1:30-6pm, Sa 8:30am-noon. **Postal Code:** 65100.

ACCOMMODATIONS AND CAMPING

Finding a decent room for €25 in Lourdes is relatively easy as hotels compete for the business of hordes of pilgrims. Similar hotels are grouped together—the cheap ones on **rue Basse** and the two-star establishments on **avenue de la Gare, avenue Maransin,** and **boulevard de la Grotte.** Though most budget hotels here are clean, they are often drab. In July and August, it is essential to reserve at least a month ahead to ensure a good rate. The city's reputation as a healing center has induced many proprietors to improve wheelchair-accessibility and construct facilities for the visually and hearing impaired.

Hôtel du Commerce, 11 rue Basse (☎05 62 94 59 23; hotel-commerce-et-navarre@wanadoo.fr), facing the tourist office. Helpful owners take pride in their hotel and it shows: the whole building was recently refurbished, and spotless rooms come with telephones and sparkling bathrooms with toilet and shower. Back rooms overlook the château. Breakfast €4.50. Singles €35; doubles €45; triples €59; quads €73. MC/V. ❷

Hôtel Lutétia, 19 av. de la Gare (☎05 62 94 22 85; www.lutetialourdes.com), near the train station. Clean and comfortable. Each room has telephone, some with TV. Elevator and free parking. Singles €18, with toilet €25, with shower €32; doubles €25-64; triples €58. Students receive free upgrade to the next class of room. MC/V. ❷

Hôtel and **Camping de la Poste,** 26 rue de Langelle (☎05 62 94 40 35), 2min. beyond the post office (follow signs). Backyard campground lets 8 clean rooms in attached hotel. Breakfast €5. Showers for campground €1.30. Open from Easter to mid-Oct. Camping €2.80 per person; €4 per site. Doubles €26, with shower €28; triples €35/38; quads with shower €48. Electricity €2.50. Cash or French check only. Camp ❶, Hotel ❷

FOOD

Find groceries at the **Monoprix** supermarket, 9 pl. du Champ Commun. (☎05 62 94 63 44. Open M-Sa 8:30am-8pm, Su 8:30am-noon.) Produce, flowers, second-hand clothing, books, and cheap pizza are sold at the market in **Les Halles,** pl. du Champ Commun. (Open M-F 6:30am-1:30pm, Sa 5:30am-1:30pm, Su 6am-1:30pm.) On **boulevard de la Grotte,** similar restaurants charge similar prices (€9-12), making it clear that cuisine is not Lourdes's primary attraction. Slightly cheaper *plats* and *menus* can be found around the tourist office and on **rue de la Fontaine.** The somewhat swankier—though still touristy—restaurants that line both sides of the Gave River, have the nicest views in town.

Alexandra, 3 rue du Fort (☎05 62 94 31 43), just off bd. de la Grotte. The best place for a high-quality meal at a reasonable price, with 3-course lunch (€9) and dinner (€12) *menus*. Stone, red plaster, comfort, and elegance characterize this small restaurant, where expertly prepared bistro classics are the specialty. *Plats* €12-20. Open M-F noon-1:30pm and 7-9pm, Sa 7-9pm. AmEx/MC/V. ❷

El Fantasia, 5 rue Basse (☎05 62 94 15 58). Basic, wholesome Moroccan menu to relieve *brasserie*-tired palates. Inspired chicken and lamb couscous dishes (€10.50-16). Open daily 11:30am-2pm and 7-11:30pm. Cash only. ❷

Le Palacio, 28 pl. du Champ Commun (☎05 62 94 00 59). Filling tagliatelle with smoked salmon (€10) and pizza (€6.50-11). Lunch *menu* €10. Dinner *menus*

GIVING BACK

SOUTHERN HOSPITALITY

For six million people each year, Lourdes is a place of spiritual profundity, of healing, and of hope—hope witnessed by the thousands of handicapped and invalid pilgrims who make the trek to the springs in search of wholeness. They are aided by members of the Hospitality of Our Lady of Lourdes, a corps of volunteers that assists in all of the activities that make Lourdes run smoothly.

There are six main services in addition to the volunteers who push invalid pilgrims' wheelchairs. Service St-Jean-Baptiste helps pilgrims make a full immersion in the baths of the spring; Service Notre Dame welcomes visitors at the train station and airport and helps to accommodate sick visitors; Service Marie Ste-Frai aids with wheelchair management; Service St-Joseph ushers during ceremonies; Service St-Michel works with maintenance and logistics; and Service Ste-Bernadette aims to spread Lourdes's message of peace to visitors.

Volunteers must be 18 years of age, be available for at least one week, and provide their own accommodations. If you want to help, contact **Hospitalité Notre-Dame de Lourdes**, Accueil Jean-Paul II (☎05 62 42 80 80; hospitalite-lourdes@wanadoo.fr).

€15-26. Open M noon-2:30pm, Tu and Th-Su noon-2:30pm and 7-10pm. AmEx/MC/V. ❸

👁 SIGHTS

Lourdes offers both religious attractions and the natural beauty of the Pyrenees, although its sights draw more pilgrims than tourists. The handy **Lourdespass** (€30, ages 6-12 €15) can be purchased at the tourist office and provides access to four Bernadette-related museums, the **Fortified Castle** and its museum, the funicular to **Pic du Jer**, and the train that runs through town.

JUBILEE PATH. Most pilgrims or visitors to Lourdes venture to the city to complete this four-stop tour that passes by the most important religious sites in Lourdes. The path begins with the **Parish Church,** where St-Bernadette was baptized. Next is the **Cachot,** the old prison where the Soubirous resided. The **Grotto,** arguably Lourdes's holiest site, is the third stop. Here, visitors from around the world shuffle past the rock where the vision first appeared, touching the rock walls and whispering prayers. Nearby, water from the bubbling spring where Bernadette washed her face is available for drinking, bathing, and bringing home in one of the numerous water bottles for sale (€1-3). Finally, there is the **Hospital Oratory,** where Ste-Bernadette completed her First Communion. *(Church open daily 8:30am-noon and 1:30-6:30pm. Cachot open daily 9am-noon and 2-6pm. Wall open daily from 11am. Hospital Oratory open daily 9:30am-noon and 2-6pm. No shorts, tank tops, smoking, cell phones, or food. Each stop earns another stamp on one's "Jubilee Badge," available free of charge from the kiosk just inside the Sanctuary gates.)*

BASILIQUE DU ROSAIRE, LA CRYPTE, AND UPPER BASILICA. These three religious sights were built triple-decker-style above Bernadette's grotto. Though religiously important, they do not offer much aesthetically. The **Rosaire,** consecrated in 1901, houses a giant statue of the Virgin Mary, while modern mosaics decorate the side chapels. The **upper basilica,** consecrated in 1876, has a more traditional Gothic interior and contains stained-glass windows depicting both biblical salvation history and the 18 Marian apparitions of Lourdes. Between the two sits **La Crypte,** built in 1866, the first of the chapels requested by the Virgin Mary in Bernadette's visions, accessible by a domed passageway. The most remarkable space for prayer is the **Basilique Saint-Pius X,** which is hidden underground in front of the other two basilicas, to the left of the **Esplanade des Processions.** Accessible by several wide passages is its stadium-size concrete echo chamber. Filled with singing voices, the space is inspiring. *(All 3 open daily Easter-Oct. 6am-7pm; Nov.-Easter 8am-6pm. 7 daily masses in French. Mass in English Apr.-Oct. daily 9am at St-Cosmas and St-Damian buildings.)*

PROCESSION OF THE BLESSED SACRAMENT AND THE BLESSING OF THE SICK. These huge affairs are normally held every Saturday and Sunday at 4pm, starting in the Rosaire. One by one, wheelchair-bound or otherwise infirm pilgrims—often escorted by nuns—receive a blessing. Observers can stand, squeeze onto a bench, or watch from the upper basilica's balcony. Non-pilgrim visitors should be prepared for the event's solemnity. All are welcome to join the procession as a "one-day pilgrim" and march along the esplanade. A torch-lit procession blazes from the Rosaire to the esplanade on Friday and Saturday at 8:30pm. Pilgrims from all over the world recite "Hail Mary" in six languages and proudly hold banners proclaiming church names and nationalities. *(For more information, including questions about guided tours, consult the Forum Information of the Sanctuaires de Notre-Dame de Lourdes. ☎05 62 42 78 78; www.lourdes-france.org.)*

⚑ OUTDOOR ACTIVITIES

HIKING

Pic du Jer (☎05 59 94 00 41). Walk toward Les Halles from the tourist office and continue straight for 1.5km to a sign for the funicular on the left. Bus #2 runs from the tourist office to the depot (€2.20 round-trip). Just outside of town, a funicular track climbs 1km up the most interesting secular attraction that Lourdes has to offer. After the 7min. ride, a 10min. hike gives access to a summit observatory with a stunning view of the countryside and the town below. Energetic travelers can hike up the mountain using the map from the ticket booth (1hr.). Beware of rapidly descending mountain bikers. Both funicular and hike are wheelchair-accessible. Open July-Aug. 9am-7pm; Sept.-June 9:30am-6pm. Last ride up 45min. before closing. €9, ages 7-12 €6.50, under 6 free.

LAKES

Lac de Lourdes. Buses D and #3 (July-Aug. daily 9:15am, 5:45pm; Sept.-June Tu, Th, and Sa 9:15am, 5:45pm). These lines tend to be unreliable; check the schedule. By foot, take av. de Maransin toward the train station, passing r. de la Gare on the right, and turn left onto bd. Romain. The street becomes av. Béguere and then av. Jean Prat. Take a left onto chemin du Lac to reach the water. (40min.) Large, peaceful lake 4km from *centre-ville*. Locals dive off the dock and eat ice cream in the neighboring cafe.

PARC NATIONAL DES PYRÉNÉES   ☎05 62

The Parc National des Pyrénées shelters endangered brown bears, lynxes, and 200 threatened colonies of marmots. The area also encompasses 118 lakes and 160 unique plant species on its snowcapped mountains and in its lush valleys. Packed with sulfurous springs and unattainable peaks, the Pyrenees change dramatically with the seasons yet manage to maintain their allure year-round. To get a sense of the mountain range's variety, hikers should explore both the lush French side and barren Spanish side (a 4- to 5-day round-trip). Tiny Cauterets (co-tuh-ray; pop. 1300), perched in a narrow valley between the near-vertical peaks of the gorgeously green Pyrenees, is the logical base from which to explore the Park. Skiers flock to the Cirque du Lys in winter, and spring's melting snow draws wilderness lovers. Serious hikers will enjoy the contrasting French and Spanish sides of the Pyrenees, accessible from Cauterets, while others can try the many day hikes (1-8hr.). Cauterets also attracts less athletic visitors—the town's famous *thermes* offer an array of restorative treatments.

AT A GLANCE: PARC NATIONAL DES PYRÉNÉES

AREA: Narrow 100km long swath along the France-Spain border.

CLIMATE: Misty in France, arid in Spain.

GATEWAYS: Gavarnie; Luz-St-Sauveur; Ainsa, ESP.

ACCOMMODATIONS: *Gîtes* are available in towns along the GR10 for around €11; 1-night camping permitted at least 1hr. away from major highways.

DAY HIKES: Lac de Gaube (6-7hr. round-trip from Cauterets via Pont d'Espagne), Chemin des Cascades (5hr. round-trip from Cauterets).

LONG HIKES: Cirque de Gavarnie, through waterfalls and lush forests (2- to 3-day hike from Cauterets); through Spain (4-5 days from Cauterets).

TRANSPORTATION

Buses: Pl. de la Gare. Office open May-Oct. daily 9am-1pm and 3-6:30pm; Nov.-Apr. Tu-Sa 9am-1pm. SNCF (☎05 62 92 53 70) runs buses to **Lourdes** (1hr., at least 5 per day, €6.60), where travelers can transfer to trains or other buses.

Public Transportation: Bordenave Excursions, 8 pl. Georges Clemenceau (☎05 62 92 53 68, cell 06 71 01 46 86). Runs **shuttle buses** from the Mairie in Cauterets to the park in July and Aug. (8am-6pm every 2hr.; €4, round-trip €6) and provides **taxis** (€14) the rest of the year. Office open daily 9am-noon and 4:30-7pm.

Bike Rental: Le Grenier, 4 av. du Mamelon Vert (☎05 62 92 55 71). €23 per ½-day, €32 per day. Open daily 9am-7pm. MC/V.

Ski Rental: Starski, 12 av. du Général Leclerc (☎05 62 92 55 99). Skis, boots, and poles €12 per day. 10% discount for 6 consecutive days. 10% student discount. Open daily Dec.-Apr. 8:30am-1pm and 2-7pm; May-Oct. 9am-7pm. MC/V.

PRACTICAL INFORMATION

Cauterets Tourist Office: Pl. Foch (☎05 62 92 50 50; www.cauterets.com). From the bus station, follow av. du Général Leclerc uphill. Offers a map and a free *Guide Pratique*. The *Cauterets Spécial Rando Facile* (French only; €5) is the best hiking resource. Open July-Aug. M-Sa 9am-12:30pm and 2-7pm, Su 9am-noon and 3-6pm; Sept.-June M-Sa 9am-noon and 2-6pm, Su 9am-noon.

Parc National Office: Maison du Parc, pl. de la Gare (☎05 62 92 52 56; www.parc-pyrenees.com), in Cauterets. Provides info on the 14 different trails that begin and end in Cauterets. Trails in the park are designed for a range of abilities, from novices to expert backpackers. Maps (day-hike maps €6.40, topographical maps €8.70) are sufficient for most hikes starting from Cauterets. For the Cauterets region, use the Institut de Géographie Nationale Vignemale map #1647. Informational films (Tu and F 5pm) in French feature aerial views of the local mountains. Open July-Aug. M-Sa 9:30am-noon and 2:30-7pm; Sept.-June M-F 9:30am-noon and 3-6pm.

Tours: Bureau des Guides, 8 rue Verdun (☎05 62 92 59 83, cell 06 88 71 90 77; www.lechendesmontagnes.com). Runs **rock climbing, canyoning, hiking,** and **skiing** tours. Medium-difficulty tours €15-40 per person, harder ones €55-150. Open daily 9am-7pm; ring bell and call cell if no one responds.

Police: Av. du Docteur Domer (☎05 62 92 51 13).

Medical Emergency: ☎05 62 92 14 00.

Mountain Rescue: ☎05 62 92 71 82.

Internet Access: Pizzeria Giovanni, 5 rue de la Raillère (☎05 62 92 57 80). €3 per hr. Open daily 10am-2pm and 5-11pm. Also in the basement of the **public library,** 2 esplanade des Oeufs (☎05 62 92 59 96). €5 per hr. Open W and Sa 3-6:45pm, Th-F 4:45-6:45pm; during school vacations W-Sa 3-6:45pm. Free Wi-Fi is available with the purchase of food or drink at **Le Ski Bar** (see **Food,** next page).

Post Office: On the corner of rue Belfort and rue des Combattants (☎05 62 92 53 93). **Currency exchange** and **ATMs** available outside. Open M-F 9am-12:15pm and 2-4:30pm, Sa 9am-noon. **Postal Code:** 65110.

TIP | **HEADING FOR THE HILLS.** Natural wonders await hikers of all levels in the Pyrenees, but no one should go it alone. Before leaving, visit the Parc National office and tell the office where you're headed; they'll keep track of your information in case of emergency. These resources can ensure that your day hike doesn't become a three-day—or three-week—fiasco.

 ACCOMMODATIONS AND CAMPING

Gîtes (about €11 per night) are generally located in towns along the GR10 and are marked on maps as well as trail signs. Reserve at least two days ahead, especially in July and August. The Parc National office will help plan an itinerary while the **Service des Gîtes Ruraux** (☎05 59 11 20 64) in Pau makes *gîte* reservations. Pick up a free listing of *gîtes* from the office in case you need to find one while on the trails. Camping is permitted anywhere in the wilderness for one night (7pm-9am), provided you are more than an hour's hike from the nearest highway. Long-term camping in one place is not allowed. Those looking to stay somewhere for a couple days should find a camp zone near a *refuge*.

▨ **Hôtel le Chantilly,** 10 rue de la Raillère (☎05 62 92 52 77; www.hotel-cauterets.com), in Cauterets. Charming Irish owners offer hiking advice and delicious meals. Rooms on lower 2 floors newly renovated, with large windows, showers, and toilets. Breakfast €6. Reception 7am-10pm. July-Sept. singles and doubles €34, with shower €42; triples from €52. Oct. and Jan.-June singles €30/34; triples from €38. MC/V. ❷

Hôtel Christian, 10 rue Richelieu (☎05 62 92 50 04; www.hotel-christian.fr), in Cauterets. Darts, *bocce,* and a Pyrenean view. Gracious owner's family has run the hotel for generations. All rooms with bath. Breakfast included. Reception 7:30am-10pm. Open Dec.-Sept. July-Aug. singles €55; doubles €69-74; triples €88-93; quads €106-111. Sept.-June singles €49; doubles €66; triples €86; quads €102. AmEx/MC/V. ❹

Gîte d'Etape UCJG, 3 av. du Docteur Domer (☎05 62 92 52 95), 7min. from the Cauterets *centre-ville.* From the Parc National office, cross the parking lot and street and turn left uphill on a footpath underneath the funicular depot. The *gîte* is 5min. down the street. A practical accommodation for real mountaineers. Beds in every setup, from traditional campsites to canvas barracks to small attic bedrooms. Managed by a caring pastor who enjoys introducing guests to one another. Kitchen and shower facilities available. Reception 24hr. Open from mid-June to mid-Sept. Tent sites €4. Dorms €8; space in the *gîte's* tent €6.50, in bungalow €8.50, in apartment €11. Cash only. ❶

Refuge Estom (☎05 62 92 07 18; call 8-10:30am and 7-10pm), near the Lac d'Estom (p. 617). Open June-Sept. Dorms €10, *demi-pension* €28. Cash only. ❶

Refuge des Oulettes (☎05 62 92 62 97). Food and lodging on the Lac de Gaube hike (p. 617). Open Mar.-Sept. Dorms €19, *demi-pension* €40. Cash only. ❶

Refuge Wallon/Marcadau (☎05 62 92 64 28). See **Hiking,** p. 617. Breakfast €5.90. Open from June to late Sept. Dorms €16, *demi-pension* €37. Cash only. ❶

Refuge de Goriz (☎+34 974 34 12 01). On the hike through Spain (opposite page). Call ahead for more info and to reserve.

📷 FOOD

Despite relatively few dining options, Cauterets offers a high percentage of cheap gourmet fare. The local specialty is the *berlingot*, a hard sugar candy originally used by patients visiting the *thermes* to enhance "the cure." Several small restaurants with outdoor seating line **rue Verdun.** The beautifully old-fashioned **Halles** market, near the tourist office on av. du Général Leclerc, has wine, fresh cheese, meat, and sandwiches. (Open June-Sept. daily 8am-1pm and 4-7pm; Oct.-May M-Sa 9am-1pm and 4-7pm, Su 8am-1pm. Hours vary.) Stock up on meats, homemade jams, pizzas, tarts, or quiches at **Au "Mille Pâtes,"** 5 rue de la Raillère. The prepared food and the *charcuterie* is excellent and well priced. (☎05 62 92 04 83. Open daily July-Aug. and Feb. 8am-12:30pm and 4-8pm; Sept.-Dec., Jan., Mar., June Th-Tu 8am-12:30pm and 4-8pm. Cash only.)

🍽 **En Sò de Bedaù,** 11 rue de la Raillère (☎05 62 92 60 21). This wine bar and stone-lined basement restaurant is a diamond in the rough that draws locals with a solid Pyrenean menu. The Medallion de Lutour—a triple serving of wild mountain trout wrapped in smoked asparagus, bacon, and lettuce with a parmesan cream sauce—is the closest that €11 will get you to nirvana. Open July-Aug. daily noon-2pm and 6pm-2am; Sept.-June Tu-Sa noon-2pm and 6pm-2am, Su noon-2pm. MC/V over €10. ❸

Le Ski Bar, pl. Foch (☎05 62 92 53 85). *Crêpes* and every other kind of snack food imaginable—as well as pitchers of sangria—make this a popular spot with hikers. Free Wi-Fi. Snacks €3.50-6. *Plats* €6.50-11. Open July-Aug. daily 7:30am-midnight; Sept.-June M-Tu and Th-Su 7:30am-midnight. AmEx/MC/V over €15. ❷

À la Reine Margot, pl. de la Mairie (☎05 62 92 58 67). More than 30 flavors of candy are prepared by hand and cranked through a candy-making machine to the delight of onlookers. The only *berlingot confiserie* that uses all-natural ingredients also offers free samples. €1.60 per 100g. Open daily July-Aug. 9:30am-12:30pm and 1:30-11pm; Sept.-Oct. and Dec.-June 10am-12:30pm and 3-7:30pm. AmEx/MC/V. ❶

Chez Gillou, 3 rue de la Raillère (☎05 62 92 56 58). This delectable *pâtisserie* specializes in *tourtes myrtilles* (blueberry cakes) and *pastis des Pyrénées* (almond cakes), both worth every cent of €5.50. Open daily Jan.-Apr., from mid-July to Oct., and Dec. 7:30am-12:30pm and 3-7:30pm. AmEx/MC/V. ❶

📷 SIGHTS

SPRINGS. Cauterets's natural sulfur springs have been credited over the years with the cure for everything from sterility to consumption. Now accessible only through a spa-like complex on the edge of town, the water continues to draw legions of the sick, elderly, and overstressed. Massages are available. For info on the *thermes*, contact **Thermes de César.** (*Av. Docteur Domer.* ☎05 62 92 51 60; *www.thermesdecauterets.com. Aerobath-sauna-hydrojet pool €9.50 per 20min., hydromassage jet showers €11 per 20min. Information/reservation desk open M-Sa 8:30am-noon and 2-6pm. Treatments available M-Sa June-Sept. 5-8pm; Oct.-May 4-8pm. Hours vary.*)

OTHER SIGHTS. The park area, **esplanade des Oeufs,** includes a **cinema** and **casino.** The cinema plays French and foreign films (the latter are mostly popular American imports dubbed in French), while the casino features table games and a bar. (*Both* ☎05 62 92 52 14.) The **patinoire** (skating rink) hosts skating nights, according to a changing schedule available at the tourist office. The rink itself can be reached through the parking lot of the train station. (*☎05 62 92 58 48. €8, students and under 18 €5.50; skate rental €2.50.*)

⚑ HIKING

Before setting out on any hike, listen to **Météo-Montagne** for a French weather forecast for nearby mountains (☎08 92 68 02 65; updated twice daily). Below, *Let's Go* recommends a number of hikes leaving directly from Cauterets, each of which is also listed in the *Spécial Rando Facile*, available at the tourist office and in the Parc brochure. If you plan to take the hikes directly from Cauterets, use the Chemin des Cascades (below) to reach the Pont d'Espagne; make sure to add an extra 4hr. round-trip to the given time. Times for day hikes are one-way; for overnight hikes, round-trip.

DAY HIKES

▨ **Le Chemin des Cascades** (2½hr., moderate). Deservedly popular, this waterfall-laden climb begins in Cauterets on a staircase to the right of the casino and ends in the national park at Pont d'Espagne. From here, 3 additional hikes are possible: Lac de Gaube, Refuge Wallon, and Circuit des Lacs. Free trail maps are available in English and French at the Parc office; follow red and white trail markers.

Lac et Refuge d'Estom (3½hr., easy). The trailhead is left of the Thermes de César. Stunning trail leads through a broad valley to a mountain lake. Follow signs to Chemin des Pères, the Fruitière, and Lac d'Estom. After 90min., you'll reach the Fruitière. The Lac d'Estom is 2hr. farther ahead. Once at the lake, the **Refuge Estom** (see **Accommodations,** p. 615) offers an overnight stop.

Col de Riou and Plateau du Lisey (3hr. and 4hr., moderate). Slightly more taxing hikes lead to 2 neighboring peaks, but they do not offer the same striking scenery as some of the other hikes. Ask at the tourist office or Parc National office for more information.

Lac de Gaube (3½hr., moderate). A popular destination, this lake is 1hr. from Pont d'Espagne, making it a possible day hike from Cauterets as well. Take the Chemin des Cascades to the Pont d'Espagne. 2 more hours lead through a glacial valley to the 2km high **Refuge des Oulettes** (see **Accommodations,** p. 615).

Circuit des Lacs (8hr. round-trip, difficult). The longest and most difficult of the day hikes listed here, this remarkable trail will challenge your legs and reward your eyes. The trail turns off the Refuge Wallon/Marcadau route and heads steeply uphill; after about 1hr., follow signs and yellow trail markers to Circuit des Lacs. Take a bus or taxi between Cauterets and the Pont d'Espagne to do this hike in 1 day. Trailhead along the route to the Refuge Wallon/Marcadau. Check with the tourist or Parc office before taking this hike to make sure conditions are good.

OVERNIGHT HIKES

GR10 (Difficult). The Parc National's major route. Meanders across the Pyrenees, connecting the Atlantic with the Mediterranean and looping through most large towns. Both major and minor hikes intersect with and run along it, including Le Chemin des Cascades and Lac du Gaube. Pick up one of the purple maps at the park office (€8.70). Near Cauterets, join the GR10 from one of the minor hikes that intersects it.

Refuge Wallon/Marcadau (12hr., difficult). The journey to this *refuge*, less traveled than the one to the Lac de Gaube, is a manageable day hike from the Pont d'Espagne and allows access to a variety of Pyrenean vistas. The round trip from Cauterets is impossible in 1 day, but hikers can stay at the *refuge* (see **Accommodations,** p. 615).

Spain (4-5 days, difficult). For a sense of the Pyrenees' diversity, explore the Spanish and French sides of the range. Both the red rock of the Spanish side and the misty forests of the French side are accessible on a 4- to 5-day hike from Cauterets. A 1- to 2-day hike from Pont d'Espagne—possible only July-Sept. due to snow in winter—runs up and over the Spanish border. Descend the far side of the Pyrenees to the village of Torla and hop on a bus to the **Refuge de Goriz** (see **Accommodations,** p. 616). A magnificent hike to the snowcapped peaks of **Brèche de Roland,** on the edge of the Cirque de Gavarnie, will start hikers' return to France the following day. Cut the hike short at 4-5 days by taking a bus back from Gavarnie to Luz and then to Cauterets. Confer with the tourist office (☎+34 974 50 07 67) in Ainsa, ESP for reservations at the Spanish *refuges* before attempting this trek. Don't forget your passport!

◢ SKIING

A weekend's worth of skiing is available directly from Cauterets via the **Cirque du Lys** cable car, which departs near the train station. From the tourist office, turn right on av. du Général Leclerc and right again on rue du Pont Neuf; the *télécabine* (lift) station is on the right. **Cirque du Lys** offers 36km of skiing on 21 slopes, including five green (easy) and two black (difficult) trails. (☎05 62 92 13 00; www.cauterets.com. Day pass €26, students €20, ages 6-10 €18.) The Cauterets tourist office has free *plans des pistes* (trail maps). Other resorts in the area are accessible by SNCF **bus** from Cauterets or Lourdes. **Luz-Ardiden** offers downhill and cross-country skiing. (☎05 62 92 30 30. €26.50 per day, students €16.) Farther away, **Barèges** offers 69 slopes. (☎05 62 92 68 86. €29 per day, during school vacations €30.)

LUCHON   ☎ 05 61

Though it lacks Cauterets's picturesque charm and Lourdes's religious sights, Luchon (loo-shawn; pop. 2900) still draws thousands of hikers and skiers as well as a large elderly population seeking a cure at the town's sulfurous springs. Luchon's bounty of cheap food and lodging sweeten the deal. A *télécabine* (lift) takes visitors from the *centre-ville* to the nearby skiing community, **Superbagnères,** a buzzing slope complex in winter. Though a few hikes depart directly from Luchon, they do not approach the variety offered in Cauterets.

▟ ▐ TRANSPORTATION AND PRACTICAL INFORMATION

Trains and Buses: Av. de Toulouse (☎05 61 79 03 36). Open daily 8:15am-noon and 1:30-5pm. Runs an occasional direct train to **Toulouse** or **Paris,** making the SNCF buses to **Montréjeau** (50min., at least 5 per day, €6.30) the primary transport. From Montréjeau, make connections to **Bayonne, Paris, Toulouse,** and other cities.

Tourist Office: 18 allées d'Etigny (☎05 61 79 21 21; www.luchon.com). From the station, turn left on av. de Toulouse and bear right at the immediate fork to follow av. Maréchal Foch. At the traffic circle—marked by statues of lions—cross and bear left, following signs to the *centre-ville*. Av. Maréchal Foch will become av. Carnot and finally the main allées d'Etigny (15min.). The office, 1 block down on the right, distributes information on nearby hikes, mountain bike trails, and ski slopes. Open daily July-Aug. 9am-7pm; Sept. and June M-Sa 9am-12:30pm and 1:30-7pm, Su 9:30am-12:30pm and 2-6pm; Oct.-May M-Sa 8:30am-7pm, Su 8:30am-12:30pm and 2-7pm.)

Laundromat: 33 rue Lamartine. Wash €6-8, dry €1 per 11min. Open daily 8am-11pm.

Police: At the Hôtel de Ville (☎05 61 94 68 81).

Medical Services: 5 cours de Quinconces (☎05 61 79 93 00).

Internet access: Espace Internet, 3 allées d'Etigny (☎05 61 79 01 65), in the Hôtel de Bellevue, across from the tourist office. €2 per 15min., €5 per hr. Open M-Sa 10am-noon and 3-7pm. MC/V.

Post Office: 26 allées d'Etigny (☎05 61 94 74 50), on the corner of av. Gallieni. Open M-F 8:45am-noon and 2-5:45pm, Sa 8:45am-noon. **Postal Code:** 31110.

ACCOMMODATIONS

Hôtel François 1er, 1 allées d'Etigny (☎05 61 79 03 93). Prices are hard to beat. Located above one of Luchon's cheapest *brasseries.* Cozy and clean rooms have colorful curtains, showers, toilets, and phones; some have TVs. Breakfast €4.50. Reception 7:30am-midnight. Singles €25; doubles €30; triples €39. Cash only. ❷

Gîte Skioura (☎05 61 79 60 59; www.gite-skioura.com), uphill from the tourist office on the way to Superbagnères (2km). Call ahead to be picked up or follow cours des Quinconces out of town and up the mountain. On weekday mornings, catch the *car thermal* from the train station to the *thermes* and get off at the Beauregard camping stop (15min., every 30min., free). Keep walking uphill on the highway for 25min. 5 large and extremely clean rooms, each in a separate guesthouse, contain 36 beds. Breakfast €4.50. Linen €3.50. Dorms €21; *demi-pension* €37. Cash only. ❶

FOOD

The town market (open W and Sa 8am-1pm) is at **place Rouy.** A **Casino** supermarket is at 43 av. Maréchal Foch. (Open M-Sa 8:30am-12:30pm and 3-7:30pm, Su 9am-noon. MC/V.) For cheap and filling meals, head to **allées d'Etigny's** *brasseries,* many of which become lively bars late at night.

Le Pub Gourmand, 6 av. Carnot (☎05 61 79 89 00), on the way from the train station to the tourist office. Good food in massive quantities. Features an all-you-can-eat buffet of cold hors d'oeuvres (with dessert; €10) as well as traditional meat *plats* (€10-14). The €14 *menu* is a great deal, with a large salad, delicious salmon, and dessert. Open Dec.-Oct. Tu-Sa noon-2pm and 7:30-9pm, Su noon-2pm. AmEx/MC/V. ❸

Les Plaisirs du Gout, 9 av. Carnot (☎05 61 79 18 95). This *pâtisserie* provides sweet and savory quiches and tarts, including an exquisite *tourte aux myrtilles* (blueberry tart). Most selections under €2. Open daily 6am-1pm and 3-8pm. Cash only. ❶

SIGHTS

THERMES. Enjoy a soak in the *thermes,* but be prepared for the sulfurous smell and medical atmosphere. Fourteen euro buy unlimited afternoon access to the 32°C (90°F) pool and the **Vaporarium,** a natural underground sauna. Inquire at **Vitaline,** the large modern building at the end of allées d'Etigny, next to the bathhouse. (*In the lavish white marble building at the end of allées d'Etigny.* ☎05 61 94 52 52; www. thermes-luchon.fr. Open from mid-Dec. to mid-Oct. Info office open daily 9am-noon and 2:30-7pm. Vaporarium open daily from early July to early Sept. and from mid-Dec. to late Mar. 3:30-8pm; from late Mar. to early July and from early Sept. to Oct. 3:30-7pm. Closed last Su of the month in spring. Tours of the thermes in French only June-Sept. Tu 2pm. €3.50.)

OUTDOOR ACTIVITIES

The tourist office has information about **hiking** paths and mountain **bike** trails that leave from Luchon. For a sunny afternoon hike, try the short walk to the small village of **Cazarilh** (3hr. round-trip). To reach the trailhead from the tourist office, turn left on allées d'Etigny, which quickly becomes av. Carnot. Walk through pl. Joffre to pl. Comminges and make a slight left on rue Nérée Boubée. When you reach the cemetery, turn right on cours de la Casseyde.

Just after the edge of the cemetery, look for a red and white shack to your left; the trail begins there, and a hidden sign points the way to Cazarilh. From the sign, follow the yellow trail markers. A more strenuous, nearly day-long hike leads along the GR10 from Luchon to **Superbagnères** and back (4-5hr. round-trip). From the tourist office, turn left, then left again on rue Gambetta. Continue past the market on your right and turn right when rue Gambetta ends at rue Laity; the first left leads directly to the trailhead. Alternately, the Altiservice runs a *télécabine* (lift) that transports hikers, bikers, and skiers to the top of Superbagnères. (☎05 61 79 97 00. Open daily July-Aug. 9am-12:45pm and 2-6pm; in ski season daily 8:45am-6pm. €5.90, round-trip €7.90.) The tourist office has two free hiking and biking maps. Also check the **Bureau des Guides,** 66 allées d'Etigny, which has info on biking, hiking, rock climbing, canyoning, and skiing. (☎05 61 79 69 38; contact@bureau-guides-luchon.com. ½-day guided hikes €20-100. Canyoning and climbing €30-63. Skiing excursions €60-150. Open May-Oct. daily 9am-noon and 3:30-7pm; Nov.-Apr. by appointment. Cash only.) Consider shopping around for excursion opportunities, since several outdoor companies are within a few blocks of the tourist office. Consult the tourist office's brochure, which contains a leaflet listing the outdoor companies' rates.

LANGUEDOC-ROUSSILLON

Languedoc-Roussillon is in fact two distinct regions, each with its own thriving, independent culture and enough reasonably priced accommodations and eateries to make the area a great opportunity for travelers to see the south of France on a budget. A rogue land once independent of both France and Spain, Languedoc had its own distinct language, the *langue d'oc*, meaning "the tongue of the West." Known as part of Occitania in the Roman era, the region stretched from the Rhône Valley to the Pyrenean foothills. Though it has been part of France since the 12th century, Languedoc preserves its rebellious spirit with frequent strikes and protests, while its *joie de vivre* is apparent in frequent impromptu street performances and large neighborhood parties.

Situated between the Mediterranean coast and the peaks of the Pyrenees, Roussillon inspired Matisse and Picasso and now attracts a mix of young sunbathers and backpackers. At the southwest corner of France, the region was historically part of Catalonia, not France, and Perpignan (p. 640) was the capital of the kings of Majorca. Many inhabitants of Roussillon identify more with Barcelona than with Paris and speak Catalan, a thriving Romance language that sounds like a French-Spanish hybrid. Architecture, food, and nightlife all bear the zest of the region's Spanish neighbors.

HIGHLIGHTS OF LANGUEDOC-ROUSSILLON

ESCAPE the city with three peerless daytrips from Perpignan—to Céret, Villefranche-de-Conflent, and Collioure—and soak up all the cherries, art, and hiking you can take without spending a penny on transportation (p. 645).

GOGGLE at the largest Renaissance painting in the world in Albi's cathedral (p. 631).

PARTY in Montpellier (p. 653), taking advantage of some of France's best nightlife.

TOULOUSE ☎ 05

Known as *la ville en rose* (the pink city), vibrant and zany Toulouse (too-looze; pop. 435,000) is the place to come when all French towns begin to look alike. Graduates of Toulouse's university are reluctant to leave their exuberant yet laid-back city. During the school year, 110,000 scholars fill the cafes and *brasseries* in the narrow streets of the place where Thomas Aquinas discussed Aristotle with fellow theologians. At the heart of Toulouse sits the massive Capitole, whose eight grand columns symbolize the eight headstrong town *capitouls* (councilors) who defied counts and kings to govern the city until the Revolution. An abundance of museums and concert halls makes France's fourth-largest city the region's cultural capital. Family-owned art galleries, independent theaters, and a diverse music scene support the city's free-thinking tradition. Whether it is the Garonne River or the grungy yet charming rue du Taur that makes your heart pound, it's hard not to fall in love with Toulouse.

Languedoc-Roussillon

TRANSPORTATION

Flights: Aéroport Blagnac (☎08 25 38 00 00). **Air France** (☎36 54) flies to **London** (6 per day) and **Paris** (35 per day). Navettes Aérocar (☎05 34 60 64 00; www. navettevia-toulouse.com) serves the airport from the bus station and allée Jean Jaurès (30min., every 20min., €4).

Trains: Gare Matabiau, 64 bd. Pierre Sémard. Ticket office open daily 7am-9:10pm. To: **Bordeaux** (2-3hr., 14 per day, €33); **Carcassonne** (1hr., 15 per day, €13); **Lyon** (4hr., 7 per day, €70); **Marseille** (4hr., 10 per day, €50); **Paris** (6hr., 12 per day, €90).

Buses: Gare Routière, 68-70 bd. Pierre Sémard (☎05 61 61 67 67), next to the train station. Open M-F 8am-7pm, Sa 9am-1pm and 2-6pm, Su 10am-4pm. To: **Albi** (1hr., 4 per day, €13); **Carcassonne** (2hr., 1 per day, €12); **Foix** (2hr., 1 per day, €9.90); **Montauban** (1hr., 4 per day, €7.30). Buy tickets on the bus. Eurolines (☎05 61 26 40 04; www.eurolines.fr), runs buses to most major European cities. Info office open M-F 9:30am-12:30pm and 2-6:30pm, Sa 9:30am-12:30pm and 2-5pm.

Public Transportation: Tisséo Métro, station Jean Jaurès (☎05 61 41 70 70). Trains run M-F and Su 5:25am-midnight, Sa 5:25am-1am; schedule varies. Maps at ticket booths and tourist office. Buy tickets inside the station. €1.40, round-trip €2.50; carnet of 10 €11, ages 18-25 €6.70; 1-week pass €11 (max. 2 rides per day).

Taxis: Capitole Taxi (☎05 34 25 02 50). €1.30 per km during the day, €1.90 at night. €25 from the train station to the airport. 24hr.

Bike Rental: VeloToulouse, in front of the tourist office. €1 per ½-day; €260 deposit. Open M-F 8am-6pm, Sa-Su 10am-6pm. MC/V.

 ## ORIENTATION AND PRACTICAL INFORMATION

While residential Toulouse sprawls along both sides of the Garonne, the thriving student quarter occupies a small area east of the river bounded by **rue de Metz** in the south, **boulevard de Strasbourg** to the north, and **boulevard Carnot** to the east. The huge stone plaza of the Capitole marks the *centre-ville*. The walk from the station to the *centre-ville* is less than 15min.

> **TIP**
>
> **NOTHING TO LOSE.** Those visiting Toulouse for more than a day or two should pick up a **Carte Privilège** at the tourist office. For a mere €10, cardholders get 30% discounts at museums and participating hotels. At most hotels, the card pays for itself in one night. As a final bonus, cardholders receive free *apéritifs* at many of Toulouse's restaurants. The tourist office has a list of participating museums, hotels, and restaurants.

Tourist Office: Donjon du Capitole, rue Lafayette (☎05 61 11 02 22; www.toulouse-tourisme.com), at sq. du Charles de Gaulle. Ⓜ️Capitole or down rue de Bayard from the station. Veer left around pl. Jeanne d'Arc and continue on rue d'Alsace-Lorraine; the office is in the far right-hand corner of the park on the right. City tours in English (July-Aug. Th and Sa), French (M-F), and Spanish (July-Aug. Su). Pick up the free *Guide Pratique*, which lists hotels, restaurants, museums, transportation information, and cultural events. Open June-Sept. M-Sa 9am-7pm, Su 10:30am-5:15pm; Oct.-May M-F 9am-6pm, Sa 9am-12:30pm and 2-6pm, Su 10am-12:30pm and 2-5pm.

Budget Travel: Voyages Wasteels, 36 rue de Taur (☎05 61 12 18 88). Cheap airfares for students. Open M-F 10am-1pm and 2-6pm, Sa 10am-12:30pm and 2-5pm. MC/V. **Nouvelles Frontières,** 2 pl. St-Sernin (☎05 61 21 74 14). Open M-F 9am-7pm, Sa 9am-6pm. AmEx/MC/V.

Consulates: US, 25 allée Jean Jaurès (☎05 34 41 36 50). Open W 9am-noon and 2-5pm by appointment only.

Currency Exchange: C2E Capitole Exchange, 30 rue du Taur (☎05 61 13 64 25). Open M-F 9am-12:30pm and 2-6pm, Sa 10am-noon and 2-5pm.

English-Language Bookstore: The Bookshop, 17 rue Lakanal (☎05 61 22 99 92). Fiction, French history, and guidebooks. Open M 2-7pm, Tu-Sa 10am-7pm. AmEx/MC/V.

Youth Center: Centre Regional Information Jeunesse (CRIJ), 17 rue de Metz (☎05 61 21 20 20; www.crij.org). Info on travel, work, and study. Open July-Aug. daily 10am-1pm and 2-6pm; Sept.-June M-F 10am-6pm, Sa 10am-1pm and 2-5pm.

Laundromats: Le Centre des Lois, 44 rue des Lois (☎06 81 41 17 60). Wash €4, dry €0.50 per 5min. Open daily 7:30am-9pm. **Laverie Bayard,** 10 rue Stalingrad. Wash €2.90-3.30, dry €0.40 per 6min. Open daily 7am-9:30pm.

Police: Commissariat Central, 23 bd. Embouchure (☎05 61 12 77 77).

Late-Night Pharmacy: 70-76 allée Jean Jaurès (☎05 61 62 38 05). Open M-Sa 8pm-8am, Su and holidays 8pm-9am.

Hospital: CHR de Rangueil, av. du Professeur. Jean Poulhès (☎05 61 32 25 33).

LANGUEDOC-ROUSSILLON

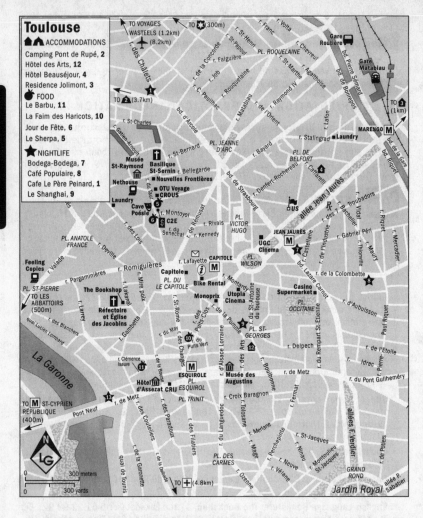

Toulouse

ACCOMMODATIONS

Camping Pont de Rupé, **2**
Hôtel des Arts, **12**
Hôtel Beauséjour, **4**
Residence Jolimont, **3**

FOOD

Le Barbu, **11**
La Faim des Haricots, **10**
Jour de Fête, **6**
Le Sherpa, **5**

NIGHTLIFE

Bodega-Bodega, **7**
Café Populaire, **8**
Cafe Le Père Peinard, **1**
Le Shanghai, **9**

Internet Access: Feeling Copies, 3 rue Valade (☎05 61 22 97 47). €1 per hr. Open M-F 9am-7pm. **Nethouse,** 1 rue des 3 Renards (☎05 61 21 98 42). €3 per hr. Open M-Sa 9am-11pm, Su noon-8pm. Rue du Taur has other establishments with similar prices.

Post Office: 9 rue Lafayette (☎05 34 45 70 82). **Currency exchange** and Western Union. Open M-F 8am-7pm, Sa 8am-noon. **Poste Restante:** 31049 Cedex. **Postal Code:** 31000.

ACCOMMODATIONS AND CAMPING

Residence Jolimont, 2 av. Yves Brunaud (☎05 34 30 42 80; www.residence-jolimont. com). ⓂJolimont. A member of the French youth hostel league. Doubles as a long-term *résidence sociale,* helping 18- to 25-year-olds get on their feet. Large, clean double rooms with shower and toilet. Ping-pong, billiards, and basketball court. Breakfast M-F €2.50. Dinner €8. Free Internet access. Reception 24hr. Dorms €16. AmEx/MC/V. ❶

Hôtel des Arts, 1 bis rue Cantegril (☎05 61 23 36 21; fax 61 12 22 37). ⓂEsquirol. Spacious, tastefully decorated rooms with high ceilings in a central location. Breakfast €6. Reception 7am-11pm. Reservations recommended 2 weeks ahead. Singles and doubles €42, with shower €54-58. MC/V. ❸

Hôtel Beauséjour, 4 rue Caffarelli (☎05 61 62 77 59), off allée Jean Jaurès, near the station. Clean, large, and bright rooms with new beds are a good value. Free Wi-Fi. Reception 7am-11pm. Singles and 1-bed doubles with shower €33, with full bath €35; 2-bed doubles €39/41; triples €44/46. MC/V. ❷

Camping Pont de Rupé, 21 chemin du Pont de Rupé (☎05 61 70 07 35), at av. des États-Unis (N20 north). Take bus #59 (dir.: Fenouillet) from pl. Jeanne d'Arc. Cross the bridge at the stop; the campsite is 200m down on the right. Snack bar and laundry. €15 for 2 people with a tent. €2.90 per additional person. MC/V. ❶

◖ FOOD

What Toulouse lacks in cheap lodging it makes up for with cheap food. Budget travelers should head directly to **rue du Taur** in the student quarter, where cheap eateries serve €5-10 *plats*. Chinese, Lebanese, and Mexican restaurants fill the storefronts on **rue des Filatiers** and **rue Paradoux.** On Tuesdays and Saturdays, **place du Capitole** becomes an open-air market selling organic food as well as everything from shoes to sunglasses to purses. (Open 8am-3pm.) Other food markets are held at **place Victor Hugo, place des Carmes,** and **place Saint-Cyprien.** (Open Tu-Su 6am-1pm.) There's a **Monoprix** supermarket at 39 rue Alsace-Lorraine (open M-Sa 9am-10pm; MC/V) and a **Casino** supermarket, near pl. Occitane, in the Centre Commerciale St-Georges (open daily 8:30am-8pm; MC/V). Students who want a good, hot meal at a low price (€3-4) should head to the *restaurants universitaires* scattered around Toulouse; contact the tourist office for locations. The *brasseries* that crowd **place Wilson** offer €15-25 *menus*.

Jour de Fête, 43 rue du Taur (☎05 61 23 36 48). A neighborhood favorite and student hangout with local art on its walls. *Plat du jour* €6.90. Salads €6.50-7.50. Tapas (selection of 4) €9.50. *Crêpes* €3.50-6.50. Open daily noon-midnight. Cash only. ❷

La Faim des Haricots, rue du Puits Vert (☎05 61 22 49 25), between pl. Capitole and the student quarter. Vegetarian heaven offers a fresh, filling selection of pasta, *tartes*, and creative veggie combinations. €11-14 *menus* let you pick 2-5 selections from the all-you-can-eat salad, tart, soup, and dessert bars; the €16 *menu* adds an *apéritif* and coffee. Open M-W noon-2:30pm, Th-Sa noon-2:30pm and 7-10:30pm. MC/V. ❸

Le Sherpa, 46 rue du Taur (☎05 61 23 89 29). That rare species: a sit-down *crêperie* that's not a rip-off. Any 2 *crêpes* for less than €13. Add an egg to your *crêpe* (€0.20) and fill up while soaking in the hand-painted wall murals. Savory *crêpes* €3.50-6.50. Dessert *crêpes* €1.70-5. Open daily noon-midnight. Cash only. ❷

Le Barbu, 9 rue Clémence Isaure (☎05 61 21 96 62). Offers massive portions under brick arches, with boots hanging on the walls. At dinner, all *plats* (€11-16) come with delicious soup. The adventurous will want to try the *boudin* (blood sausage). Lunch *menus* €11. Open M-F noon-2pm and 8pm-midnight. Cash only. ❸

◖ SIGHTS

Toulouse's best sights are not easily distilled into a list. Young people crowd the streets, creating the feeling of a large city in the concentrated *centre-ville*. Walking or biking is the best way to get around—exploration never goes unrewarded. Toulouse is famous for the red-brick mansions of the town's

CAPITAL CULTURE

Americans are familiar with a certain gamut of intercity rivalries; there are any number of permutations, and they all seem to revolve around competitive sports. But when was the last time New York City and Boston battled it out for whose museums truly kick butt?

For France, the competition is about to get heated come 2013, when the country will again be eligible to present one of its own cities as a "European Capital of Culture" to the European Union. Four heavyweights are waiting to duke it out for the title: Toulouse, Bordeaux, Lyon, and Marseille.

Created in 1985, the title of Capital of Culture has grown into an extremely attractive prize, carrying with it a tourism boom and the chance to remake a city's public image worldwide, much like the Olympic host city selection. With this in mind, it's easy to see how rabid French cities could become. Each contender is planning cultural events like festivals and concerts; Toulouse has already announced a partial schedule including pop star Mika. The final decision will be announced in June 2009, and, though the competition will rub on some old rivalries, it remains within the context of mutual benefit. In the meanwhile, travelers and locals alike can make the most of cities intent on being the best.

wealthy 15th- and 16th-century dye merchants. Multi-sight passes are sold at all museums: visit any three museums for €6, any six for €9.

BASILIQUE SAINT-SERNIN. St-Sernin is the longest Romanesque structure in the world, but its most visible feature is an enormous brick steeple that rises in five ever-narrowing double-arched terraces, much like a massive wedding cake. St-Dominic, head of the Dominican order of friars, made this ornate church his base in the early 13th century. However, in doing so he departed from the ascetic monastic traditions; at the end of the simple, elegant, and huge Romanesque nave lies an altar surrounded by vivid frescoes. Behind the altar's left side is a crypt containing holy relics, from engraved silver chests to golden goblets—some from Charlemagne's time. (☎05 61 21 80 45. Church open daily July-Sept. 8:30am-6:30pm; Oct.-June 8:30am-noon and 2-6pm. Crypt open July-Sept. M-Sa 10am-5pm, Su 11:30am-5pm; Oct.-June M-Sa 10-11:30am and 2:30-5pm, Su 2:30-5pm. €2.)

CAPITOLE. This mammoth brick palace faces a stone plaza that is home to swanky restaurants, occasional political protests, and hundreds of laid-back students taking a break from their books on the stone benches. In short, it's an ideal spot for people-watching. The huge building was once home to the bourgeois *capitouls*, who unofficially ruled the city—which was technically controlled by counts—for many years. All people who marry in Toulouse must pass through its **Salle des Illustres.** Next door, **La Salle Henri Martin** has 10 Post-Impressionist tableaux by Henri Martin, representing Toulouse in all four seasons. (Salles open daily 10am-5pm; slightly later hours in the summer. Free.)

RÉFECTOIRE ET ÉGLISE DES JACOBINS. This 14th-century Romanesque church is so beautiful that in 1368 Pope Urban V decided it was worthy of St-Thomas Aquinas's remains. His ashes take center stage in an tomb lit from below. Be sure to note the interesting ceiling, whose vaults resemble palm trees. The *réfectoire* houses temporary exhibits of world art. (Rue Lakanal. Open daily 9am-7pm. Occasional summer piano concerts. Tickets at tourist office. Cloister and réfectoire exhibition €3, students with ID free.)

OTHER SIGHTS. The Hôtel d'Assezat houses the **Fondation Bemberg,** which displays 35 Bonnards, a modest collection of Dufys, Gauguins, and Pissarros, and the occasional Matisse, Picasso, Braque, and Renoir. The rose-brick building also makes it worth a visit. Guided tours of the museum depart daily at 3:30pm. (Pl. d'Assezat. Fondation ☎05 61 12 06

89. Open Tu-W and F-Su 10am-12:30pm and 1:30-6pm, Th 10am-12:30pm and 1:30-9pm. €4.60, students €2.75.) The huge **Musée des Augustins** bristles with Romanesque and Gothic sculptures—including 15 howling gargoyles—in a renovated Augustinian monastery. Look for the harrowing Rubens painting *Christ Entre les Deux Larrons*, inside the church in one of the insets to the left of the rose window. *(21 rue de Metz, off rue des Arts. ☎ 05 61 22 21 82. Free organ concerts W 8-8:30pm. Open M-Tu and Th-Su 10am-6pm, W 10am-9pm. €3, students with ID free. Temporary exhibitions €7, students €5.)* The **Musée Saint-Raymond** holds a collection of archaeological finds, including a series of Roman portraits discovered in France and a detailed inquiry into life in ancient Toulouse. Artistic and anthropological discoveries are juxtaposed; an ancient road marker from Narbonne to Toulouse stands near fragments of a beautiful mosaic. *(Pl. St-Sernin. ☎ 05 61 22 31 44. Open daily June-Aug. 10am-7pm; Sept.-May 10am-6pm. English text available. €3, students with ID free.)* Across the river, **Les Abbatoirs**—old slaughterhouses converted into a vast art space—houses intermittent exhibits of up-and-coming artists as well as a permanent contemporary collection. Don't skip the basement, which contains the 8m by 13m curtain Picasso painted for the premier of Romain Rolland's play *14 Juillet*. *(Ⓜ St-Cyprien/République. 76 allée Charles de Fitte. ☎ 05 62 48 58 00. Open Tu-Su 11am-7pm. €6, students €3.)*

🎵 🎧 ENTERTAINMENT AND NIGHTLIFE

Toulouse always has something going on, though things are quieter in summer when university isn't in session. Most movie theaters are in and around **place Wilson. UGC,** 9 allée Roosevelt, plays new American releases, sometimes dubbed in French (☎ 08 92 70 00 00). **Utopia Cinema,** 24 rue Montardy, shows international independent films in their original languages (☎ 05 61 23 66 20).

Café Populaire, 9 rue de la Colombette (☎ 05 61 63 07 00). A hot and smoky destination for a motley crowd of fun-loving students. A tray with 13 glasses of beer costs €20 but €13 M 9:30pm-12:45am. Beer €1 every 13th of the month 7-9pm. Happy hour daily 7:30-8:30pm with drink specials. Open M-F 11am-2am, Sa 2pm-4am. Cash only.

Bodega-Bodega, 1 rue Gabriel Péri (☎ 05 61 63 03 63), off bd. Lazare Carnot. A wildly popular destination for young crowds, this 2-floor Spanish-themed club offers food by day and fun by night. When the clock strikes midnight, the atmosphere heats up with Latin music and dancing. Beer €3. Margaritas €6. Min. €6 drink charge Th-Sa starting at 11:30pm. Open M-W and Su 8pm-2am, Th-Sa 7pm-6am. AmEx/MC/V.

Le Shanghai, 12 rue de la Pomme (☎ 05 61 23 37 80). The place for gay nightlife. A sleek club with shiny black walls, mirrors, and red lighting. Mixed drinks €8. Cover €8. Open daily midnight-7am. Cash only.

Cave Poésie, 71 rue du Taur (☎ 05 61 23 62 00; www.cave-poesie.com). Hosts plays and performances. "Open stage" nights, when locals and amateur performers show off their talents, only happen when there is a full moon (begins 8:30-9:30pm, €2). Other plays, poetry readings, and concerts begin regularly at 7:30 and 9:30pm. Pick up a schedule outside the door or at the tourist office. Tickets €12, students €8.

🎉 FESTIVALS

Grand Fénétra (☎ 06 86 55 20 24), last weekend in June. Traditional music and dance groups parade through the streets.

Toulouse d'Eté, from mid-July to mid-Aug. Brings ballet performances and jazz, classical, and gospel concerts to the Jacobins courtyard and the Halle aux Grains at fantastic prices. Tickets are sold at concert halls (€10-12).

Festival International de Piano aux Jacobins (☎05 61 22 40 05; www.pianojacobins. com), 2 weeks in Sept. at 8:30pm. Tickets at the tourist office. €15-32, students €6-9.

🔲 DAYTRIPS FROM TOULOUSE

CASTRES

Castres's train station, av. Albert I (open M-F 6am-8:15pm, Sa 6:45am-8:15pm, Su 8:45-10:15am), has service to Toulouse (1hr., at least 10 per day, €13). Though trains from Albi eventually arrive in Castres via St-Sulpice (2hr.), buses are cheaper and more direct. They run from the bus station, pl. Soult (☎05 63 35 37 31), to Albi (45-55min., at least 5 per day, €12) and Toulouse (1hr., 5 per day, €11).

When Castres (kah-struh) acquired the bones of St-Vincent, the city became an essential pilgrimage stop for those en route to **Santiago de Compostela**. This prominence ended when the basilica was destroyed during the Wars of Religion. Recently, the city compensated by constructing a number of museums; they're worth visiting, but Castres still lacks in breathtaking landscapes.

In front of the Jardin de l'Evêché's groomed shrubs, the **Musée Goya** occupies an ancient Episcopal palace. The museum houses a large collection of Spanish paintings along with works by Catalan and Aragonese masters; the collection's focus is four series of Goya engravings. Look for the gripping *The Disasters of War*, in which Goya depicts the horrors of the Napoleonic wars. (☎05 63 71 59 27. Open July-Aug. daily 10am-6pm; Sept.-June Tu-Sa 9am-noon and 2-6pm, Su 10am-noon and 2-6pm. Tours offered in French July-Aug. 2-3 times each afternoon; ask at museum for exact schedule. Printed information in English. €2.30, under 18 free.) The small **Centre National et Musée Jean Jaurès**, 2 pl. Pélisson, caters to those interested in France's social history—or those who wonder why nearly every town in the country has an av. Jean Jaurès. A brilliant scholar and professor of philosophy, Jaurès led the striking glass-workers of Carmaux in 1892 and vehemently supported Alfred Dreyfus, a Jewish officer framed for treason by the army. The sleek building is packed with political cartoons, photographs, and newspaper articles that recount Jaurès's spirited life and rhetoric as well as occasional temporary art exhibits. (☎05 63 62 41 83. Open July-Aug. daily 10am-noon and 2-6pm; Sept. and Apr.-June Tu-Su 10am-noon and 2-6pm; Oct.-Mar. Tu-Sa 10am-noon and 2-5pm. €1.50, students €0.75.) The Musée Goya and Musée Jaurès sell a €4 ticket to all Castres's museums.

After enjoying what Castres has to offer indoors, don't miss a walk along the **Agout River.** The Agout, famous for sunbathing, makes Castres a magnet for beach bums. For two weeks in early July, the **Extravadanses** festival celebrates Hispanic culture with concerts, exhibitions, and flamenco and ballet performances. Many events are free; tickets to others are available at the tourist office or by calling the Théâtre Municipale. (☎05 63 71 56 58. Open M-F 10:30am-1pm and 2:30-6pm, Sa 10am-noon and 2-4pm.) The city also hosts a **multicultural festival** in mid-August with free concerts and dances.

When hunger strikes, try the market on **place de l'Albinque** (covered and open-air market open Tu-Sa 7am-1pm, Su 7am-noon; organic market open Th 4-8pm). A **Monoprix** supermarket is on rue Sabatier at pl. Jean Jaurès. (Open M-Sa 8:30am-7:30pm. AmEx/MC/V.) For a sit-down meal, try **La Mandragore ❸**, off pl. Jean Jaurès on rue Malpas. The restaurant serves regional cuisine like artichoke ravioli in cream sauce. (☎05 63 59 51 27. Lunch *menu* €13. Dinner *menus* €20-30. Open Tu-Sa noon-2pm and 7-9pm. AmEx/MC/V.) Traditional *nougatines castraises* (€7.20 for 125g)—a delightful almond and meringue confection—are the specialty at **Cormary ❶**, 13 rue Victor Hugo, which also sculpts chocolates, marzipan, and pastries into animal shapes. (☎05 63 59 27 09. Open Tu-Sa 6am-1pm and 1:30-7:30pm, Su 6am-1pm. AmEx/MC/V.)

Getting around Castres is easy: all the sights are within a 5min. walk of one another. To get to the **tourist office,** 2 pl. de la République, from the train station, turn left onto av. Albert I and then, at Carrefour de la Gare, take a right onto bd. Henri Sizaire. At pl. Alsace-Lorraine, turn left along the gardens onto rue de l'Evêché; the office is a block down on the left (20min.). From the bus station, walk across pl. Soult and continue straight on rue Villegoudou, cross the Pont Neuf, and turn left on rue de la Libération. Turn right at rue de l'Hôtel de Ville, then left on rue de l'Evêché; the office is on your right when you reach pl. de la République. (☎05 63 62 63 62; www.tourisme-castres.fr. Open July-Aug. M-Sa 9:30am-6:30pm, Su 10:30am-noon and 2:30-5pm; Sept.-June M-Sa 9:30am-12:30pm and 2-6pm, Su 2:30-4:30pm.)

MONTAUBAN

Accessible from Toulouse by train (25min., 30 per day, €8.20; info office open M-Sa 7am-7:30pm, Su 8am-8:30pm) and by bus (☎05 62 72 37 23; 1hr., 4 per day, €7.30). Trains are twice as fast and nearly 8 times as frequent—well worth the extra €0.90.

Montauban's (mohn-toh-bahn) red-brick buildings make it one of France's three *villes en rose* (pink cities), along with Toulouse and Albi. The city's ochre-tinted architecture dates back to 1144, when the count of Toulouse incited local artisans to sack the wealthy abbey at Montauriol ("Golden Mountain") and use its stones to start present-day Montauban's construction. Never on good terms with Catholicism, Montauban was one of the last bastions of French Protestantism after the 1685 revocation of the Edict of Nantes. To get to the *centre-ville,* walk straight out of the train station onto av. de Mayenne and continue across the bridge (10min.). The **Musée Ingres,** 19 rue de l'Hôtel, will be on the right in the 17th-century bishop's palace. The town's greatest attraction, the museum honors 19th-century Montauban-born painter Jean-Auguste Dominique Ingres. Check out the *Portrait de Caroline Gonse,* on the third floor, for an example of Ingres's mature work. This museum isn't exclusively Ingres— its large collection also features sculptures by Bourdelle, another well-known Montauban native. Don't miss the medieval hall in the lower basement, a remnant of the château built by the Black Prince Edward in 1362. (☎05 63 22 12 91. Open July-Aug. daily 10am-6pm; Sept.-Oct. and Apr.-June Tu-Su 10am-noon and 2-6pm; Nov.-Mar. Tu-Sa 10am-noon and 2-6pm, Su 2-6pm. Tours in French offered through the tourist office by arrangement. Museum July-Oct. €6, students free, seniors €3; Nov.-June €4/free/2. 1st Su of the month free. Tours €7, seniors €4.) If you turn right after exiting the Musée Ingres, **Notre Dame de l'Assomption** will be down the street on your right. Four enormous sculptures of the Evangelists keep solemn watch over the church, and *Le Voeu de Louis XIII,* one of Ingres's most impressive religious works, dominates the left transept. Detailed murals decorate the smaller side chapels, and the entrance facade is the tallest in Europe. (Open daily 9am-noon and 2-5pm.)

During the weeklong **Alors Chante** festival, revelers play traditional French tunes at the **Eurythmie,** beginning the Tuesday preceding Ascension and finishing on that Sunday. (☎05 63 63 66 77. Tickets €20-32.) A **jazz festival** swings through during the third week of July. Big-name concerts, with artists like Lucky Peterson, are ticketed events, but the week before the festival the streets of the *vieille ville* resound with free concerts, usually held at 9pm. (☎05 63 63 56 56; www.jazzmontauban.com. Tickets at tourist office. €20-45, students €15-40.)

Transports Montalbanais, 15 bd. Midi-Pyrénées, runs local **buses.** (☎05 63 63 52 52. 7am-7:20pm. €0.90, carnet of 10 €7.) Taxis are often at the train station. (☎05 63 66 99 99. €2.40 base; €1.40 per km during the day, €1.95 at night. Open daily 6am-midnight.) To reach the **tourist office,** 4 rue du Collège, turn right from the cathedral onto rue Notre Dame and left at bd. Midi-Pyrénées. When the road ends, veer left. (☎05 63 63 60 60. Open July-Aug. M-Sa 9:30am-6:30pm, Su 10am-12:30pm; Sept.-June M-Sa 9:30am-12:30pm and 2-6:30pm.)

ALBI   ☎05 63

The magnificent Cathédrale Ste-Cécile dominates the winding cobblestone streets of Albi (al-bee; pop. 55,000) along the tree-lined Tarn River. The lights of Paris and the Moulin Rouge lured away native son Henri de Toulouse-Lautrec, but his celebrated paintings remain. The Toulouse-Lautrec Museum alone is worth the journey to this small city. Albi enchants with its red-bricked beauty and casual spirit, but budget travelers should be aware that this is not a town of bargains. To save, make Albi a daytrip from the easily accessible Toulouse, which has more affordable food and lodging.

◪ TRANSPORTATION

Trains: Pl. Stalingrad. Open M-F 5:10am-9:25pm, Sa 6:10am-9:25pm, Su 6:10am-10:10pm. To **Castres** (1hr., at least 10 per day, €15) via **St-Sulpice** and **Toulouse** (1hr., at least 15 per day, €12). Check the info office for times.

Buses: Depart from Le Halte, pl. Jean Jaurès (☎05 63 54 58 61), for **Castres** (1hr., M-Sa 8 per day, €2).

Public Transportation: Espace Albibus, 14 rue de l'Hôtel de Ville (☎05 63 38 43 43), runs **buses.** Open M 2-5pm, Tu-Sa 10am-5pm. €1.

Taxis: Albi Taxi Radio, 19 chemin Sapins (☎05 63 54 85 03). Base €2.50; €1.40 per km during the day, €1.60 at night. €6 from the station to the cathedral.

✴ PRACTICAL INFORMATION

Tourist Office: Palais de la Berbie, pl. Ste-Cécile (☎05 63 49 48 80; www.albi-tourisme. com). Turn left from the station onto av. Maréchal Joffre, then left at the 1st intersection on av. du Général de Gaulle. Keep left at pl. Lapérouse and walk into the pedestrian *vieille ville* and onto rue de Verdusse. Once you've reached pl. Ste-Cécile, the office is ahead and to the left. The staff books rooms and offers city guides, tours in French (July-Sept. M-Sa 12:15pm, €4.40), and **currency exchange** on bank holidays. Open July-Aug. M-Sa 9am-7pm, Su 10am-12:30pm and 2:30-6:30pm; Sept. and May-June M-Sa 9am-12:30pm and 2-6:30pm, Su 10am-12:30pm and 2:30-6:30pm; Oct.-Apr. M-Sa 9am-12:30pm and 2-6pm, Su 10am-12:30pm and 2:30-5pm.

Laundromat: 10 rue Émile Grand (☎05 63 54 07 01), off rue Lices Georges Pompidou. Wash €2.80 per 6kg, dry €2.60 per 5.5kg. Open daily 7am-9pm.

Police: 23 rue Lices Georges Pompidou (☎05 63 49 22 81).

Hospital: Rue de la Berchère (☎05 63 47 47 47).

Internet Access: Ludi.com, 62 rue Séré de Rivière (☎05 63 43 34 24). €4 per hr. Open M-Sa 11am-midnight.

Post Office: Pl. du Vigan (☎05 63 48 15 50). **Currency exchange** and **ATMs** available. Open M-F 9am-6:30pm, Sa 9am-12:30pm. **Postal Code:** 81000.

⌂⌂ ACCOMMODATIONS AND CAMPING

Albi's accommodations fill up despite steep prices; be sure to reserve ahead to secure a room, especially for summer weekends. For info on *gîtes d'étape* and rural camping, consult **ATTER** (☎05 63 48 83 01; www.gites-tarn.com).

Hôtel Saint-Clair, 8 rue St-Clair (☎05 63 54 25 66; http://andrieu.michele.free.fr). Elegant hotel has large, immaculate rooms overlooking a courtyard. Annex across the street. Breakfast €7. Free Wi-Fi. Reception 8am-9pm. Singles and doubles with shower and toilet €38-60; triples €55-65; quads €68. MC/V. ❸

Hôtel Lapérouse, 21 pl. Lapérouse (☎05 63 54 69 22; fax 38 03 69), halfway between the train station and the cathedral. Each well-furnished room has a toilet and shower. Attractive outdoor swimming pool. Ask the gracious English-speaking owners for a cheaper, smaller room facing the street. Breakfast €6. Free Wi-Fi. Reception 7am-10pm. Doubles €38-62. AmEx/MC/V. ❸

Hôtel La Régence-George V, 27 av. Maréchal Joffre (☎05 63 54 24 16; fax 49 90 78). Thoughtfully decorated rooms and spotless bathrooms. Soundproof windows. Breakfast €6.50. Wi-Fi €2 per day. Singles €29-46; doubles and triples €34-56. AmEx/MC/V. ❷

Parc de Caussels (☎05 63 60 37 06), east of the *centre-ville,* toward Millau on D999 (2km). Take bus line S4 from the Andrieu stop, just south of pl. Jean Jaurès, to Trois Tarn (M-Sa every hr. 7:30am-7pm). Alternatively, walk (30min.) leaving town on rue de la République. Continue straight through the traffic circle; ignore signs to the campground and keep walking through a 2nd traffic circle. Cross a small bridge, turn left on the path, and walk uphill to the campground on the left. Reception 7am-10pm. Open from Apr. to mid-Oct. 1 person €9; 2 people with car €12. Additional person €3.50. Cash only. ❶

FOOD

Near Albi, the region of **Gaillac** is home to estates that prepare some of the best wines in the southwest. There is a market on **rue Émile Grand** (open Tu-Su 8am-noon) and a flea market at **place du Forail** (open Sa 8am-noon). Stock up on groceries at **Casino,** 39 rue Lices Georges Pompidou. (Open M-Sa 9am-7:30pm. AmEx/MC/V.) Otherwise, the region's food is excellent but comes at a price.

La Table du Sommelier, 20 rue Porta (☎05 63 46 20 10), over the bridge. Carefully prepared cuisine is a welcome alternative to tourist-oriented cafes. Selection changes with the season and incorporates regional ingredients. The courtyard is the perfect place to enjoy your chosen *vin. Dégustations* of up to 5 wines €9-18. Lunch *menu* €13-16. Dinner *menu* €25. Open Tu-Sa 12:15-2pm and 7:15-11pm. MC/V. ❸

La Tête de l'Art, 7 rue de la Piale (☎05 63 38 44 75). Serves regional specialties like *foie gras,* duck salad, and creative grilled meats. *Plats* €15-32. *Menus* €13-39. Open M and Th-Su noon-2pm and 6:30-9:30pm. AmEx/MC/V. ❸

Le Tournesol, 11 rue de l'Ort en Salvy (☎05 63 38 38 14). This popular vegetarian restaurant behind pl. du Vigan has vegan *pâté* as well as hummus and heavenly desserts (€3.50-5.90). *Plat du jour* €9.50. Open Tu-Sa noon-2pm. AmEx/MC/V. ❷

SIGHTS

CATHÉDRALE SAINTE-CÉCILE. This red-brick cathedral is the pride of Albi. Stained-glass windows, lavish gold and blue walls, and graphic frescoed depictions of Hell create an imposing manifestation of the medieval church's power. Built between the 13th and 14th centuries, the cathedral enforced the "one true religion," which flowered after Catharism was rooted out in the Albigeois Crusade. Carvings line the choir walls in intricate, lace-like patterns; don't miss the grapes carved by homesick Burgundian workers. The un-restored fresco covering the entire ceiling, painted in 1512, is the world's largest Italian Renaissance painting. (☎05 63 43 23 43. *Open daily June-Sept. 9am-6pm; Oct.-May 9am-noon and 2-6pm. Mass M-F 6:20pm, Su 11:15am. Free organ concerts from mid-July to Aug. W 5pm, Su 4pm. Tours by the tourist office daily from mid-July to Aug. 10am, 2:30pm; early July and early Sept. 2:30pm. Choir €2. Treasury €2. Tour €6.40. Included audio tour is available in many languages.*)

PALAIS DE LA BERBIE. This 13th-century former bishop's palace was constructed in a defensive style, reflecting the tense relations between the church and the ruling family. The fortress displayed the clergy's wealth and power; it was both the tribunal and prison for those charged by the church. Beautiful gardens and walkways, crafted after the building was converted into a residence, offer splendid vistas of the Tarn River. For the best views of the palace itself, cross the Tarn. The palace now contains the ▓**Musée Toulouse-Lautrec.** The son of the count of Toulouse, Henri de Toulouse-Lautrec moved to Paris to experience the high life of cafes, nightclubs, and brothels. His art captured the pathos of late 19th-century city life. The museum's impressive collection of his oil paintings and ink prints includes all 31 of the famous posters of Montmartre nightclubs. Works by Degas, Dufy, Matisse, and Rodin are displayed on the fourth floor. Major renovations are under way, so expect some changes in 2009. (☎05 63 49 48 70. Open July-Aug. daily 9am-6pm; Sept. and June daily 9am-noon and 2-6pm; Oct. M and W-Su 10am-noon and 2-5:30pm; Nov.-Feb. M and W-Su 10am-noon and 2-5pm; Apr.-May daily 10am-noon and 2-6pm. Gardens open daily 9am-7pm. Tours June-Sept. 11:15am, 4pm. €5, students €2.50. Garden free. Tours €9.40/6.90. Audio tour €3.)

♫ ▣ ENTERTAINMENT AND NIGHTLIFE

When the sun goes down, the crowds come out along **place de l'Archevêché** in front of the Palais de la Berbie and on **Lices Georges Pompidou.**

Café Le Grand Pontie, pl. du Vigan (☎05 63 49 70 75). Enormous and popular. Pizza, special house desserts, beer, and pitchers of local wine. Enjoy rock music near the neon mirrored bar or sit outside. Beer €3.80. Pastas €9.50. Open daily noon-2am. MC/V.

L'Athanor Scène Nationale, pl. de l'Amitié Entre les Peuples (☎05 63 38 55 62), near bd. Carnot. Screens foreign art films. €7, M and W students and seniors €4.70. Ticket office open Tu-Sa 12:30-6:30pm. Movies M-F 6:30, 9pm; Sa-Su 3:30, 6:30, 9pm.

❋ FESTIVALS

La Pause Guitare (☎05 63 60 55 90; www.arpegesettremolos.com), 4 days during the 1st week of July. A series of guitar concerts in pl. St-Cécile and the Théâtre de Verdure. Tickets €5-35, pass €120.

F'Estival de Théâtre (☎05 63 54 99 70), in mid-July. Brings innovative theater to the Théâtre de la Verdure and Théâtre de la Croix Blanche. Tickets from €25, students €21.

L'Histoire du Soir, every W night in Aug. A traveling play, with parts all over Albi. Shows start 9:30pm next to the cathedral. Call the tourist office for more information. Free.

▶ DAYTRIPS FROM ALBI

CORDES-SUR-CIEL

Buses run on school schedules to Cordes. Consult the tourist office for exact times or call carrier Sudcar Rolland (☎05 63 54 18 39; 40min., M-F 2 per day, €5.30; W bus returns in the early afternoon). Alternatively, catch the train from Albi and use the minicar Taxi Barrois (☎05 63 56 14 80; €4.20).

Perched on a hill and surrounded by a crumbling wall 24km from Albi, the center of this tiny city is accessible only by a steep, cobblestone street. Cordes-sur-Ciel (cord-suhr-s'yell), whose former name of Cordes was changed to reflect its position, passes for a city in the sky. Archaeologist Charles Portal preserved much of the town's medieval architecture; wherever you look, there are stone or half-timbered houses. The best thing to do in Cordes is wander around, resign yourself to an overpriced meal, and bask in the quaintness.

Once you've had your fill of charming homes, check out the **Musée de l'Art du Sucre,** 33 grande rue Raymond VII, which sells all kinds of sweets and includes a small but impressive exhibit on the use of sugar as an artistic medium. The subjects displayed include a model of Grande Rue Raymond VII and an ◪**80kg female nude sculpted from a massive block of chocolate.** Try a free sample of the local *croquante cordaise.* (☎05 63 56 02 40. Open Mar.-Oct. daily 10am-12:30pm and 1:30-7pm. €3.) The **Musée de l'Art Moderne,** Maison du Grand Fauconnier, boasts a few works by Miró and Picasso among its five rooms of modern artwork, all accessible by a key given as a ticket. (☎05 63 56 14 79. Open daily June-Sept. 11am-12:30pm and 2-7pm; Oct. and Apr.-May 11am-12:30pm and 2-6:30pm; Nov.-Mar. 2-5pm. €3.50, students €2, under 12 free.) The **Musée Charles Portal,** Portail Peint, 12 grand rue Raymond VII, chronicles the town's history with a collection of the honored explorer's finds. (☎05 63 56 00 52. €2.30, ages 12-18 €1.10, under 12 free.) Across the street, **place de la Bride** once served as the town's defensive platform. Today, it provides a panoramic view of the countryside. Just past pl. de la Bride is the **Puits de la Halle,** a 114m deep well constructed in 1222 by tunneling through an entire mountain; the oasis supplied Albi with water during sieges. To the left, behind the well, sits the **Église Saint-Michel,** whose tower marks the highest point in town.

For a few days around July 14, fire-eaters play to a costumed crowd during the **Fête du Grand Fauconnier,** which offers plays, concerts, magic shows, banquets, and a medieval market. (☎05 63 56 49 13. €8, under 18 €3, those dressed in medieval attire free. Costumes can be borrowed from the festival *costumerie.*) The **Festival Musique** sponsors classical music concerts during late July. (☎05 63 56 00 75. Tickets €25-30, students €10-15.)

A **market** takes place at the bottom of the hill next to the bus stop. (Open Sa 8am-noon.) The **tourist office,** Maison du Pays Cordais, 8 pl. Jeanne Ramel-Cals, offers guided tours and books accommodations for free. From the bus stop in town, the office is 50m ahead and to the left. (☎05 63 56 00 52; www.cordes-sur-ciel.org. 1hr. tours July-Aug.; €4.50, students €3.50, under 18 €1.50. Open July-Aug. daily 9:30am-1pm and 2-6:30pm; Sept. M 2-6pm, Tu-Su 10:30am-12:30pm and 2-6pm; Oct. M and Sa 2-6pm, Tu-F and Su 10:30am-12:30pm and 2-6pm; Nov.-Mar. hours vary; Apr.-June M and Sa-Su 2-6pm, Tu-F 10:30am-12:30pm and 2-6pm.) There is an annex (☎05 63 56 14 79) in the Musée de l'Art Moderne, on top of the hill. A **petit train** runs between the annex in the *haute-ville* and the main branch (May-Sept. daily 9:30am-12:50pm and 2-5:50pm every 20min.; €2.50, under 12 €1.50).

CARCASSONNE   ☎04 68

Carcassonne (car-cah-sohnn; pop. 46,000) has a split personality: on the eastern edge lies La Cité—a fortress that, once upon a time, fell off the page of a fairy tale and onto the bank of the Aube River, while Bastide St-Louis—the center of the contemporary city—is the hub of modern life under the shadow of the medieval fort. Dramatic and perfectly preserved, Carcassonne is one of France's largest tourist attractions for a reason. Experience the town late in the evening, when the floodlit fortress echoes with free concerts. Up to 800,000 daytrippers flock to Carcassonne in July, when Bastille Day brings one of France's most spectacular fireworks displays.

▣ TRANSPORTATION

Trains: Behind Jardin André Chenier (☎04 68 71 79 14). Info office open M 5:15am-9:10pm, Tu-F 5:45am-9:10pm, Sa 6:40am-9:10pm, Su 7am-9:45pm. To: **Lyon**

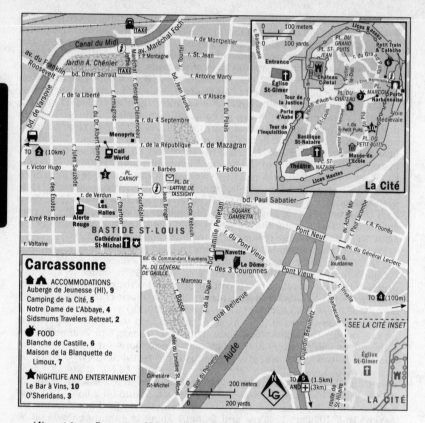

Carcassonne

🏠🏠▲ ACCOMMODATIONS
Auberge de Jeunesse (HI), **9**
Camping de la Cité, **5**
Notre Dame de L'Abbaye, **4**
Sidsmums Travelers Retreat, **2**

🍎 FOOD
Blanche de Castille, **6**
Maison de la Blanquette de
   Limoux, **7**

★ NIGHTLIFE AND ENTERTAINMENT
Le Bar à Vins, **10**
O'Sheridans, **3**

(4hr., at least 5 per day, €55-71); **Marseille** (3hr., 4 per day, €37-41); **Montpellier** (1½hr., at least 7 per day, €20-22); **Nice** (6hr., at least 4 per day, €63); **Nîmes** (2hr., at least 5 per day, €24-29); **Perpignan** (2hr.; at least 5 per day, change at **Narbonne;** €18); **Toulouse** (1hr., at least 5 per day, €14-16).

Buses: Bd. de Varsovie. From the train station, cross the canal and turn right on bd. Omer Sarrut, then left at the fork. Check schedules at the station. Trans'Aude (☎04 68 25 13 74) serves western Roussillon.

Public Transportation: In summer, a **navette** (shuttle; ☎04 68 47 82 22) goes from the train station to the parking du Dome on bd. Camille Pelletan (in the lower city) to the citadel gates and continues to Camping de la Cité. From mid-June to mid-Sept. daily every 25min. 9:30am-12:30pm and 1:30-7:30pm, round-trip €1.50. Agglo'Bus, bd. Camille Pelletan (☎04 68 47 82 22), runs **buses** through the city. To get from the station to the Cité in the low season from pl. Gambetta, turn right and continue on bd. Camille Pelletan to the bus stop at the parking area; take bus #2 (dir.: St-Georges/Montlegun; M-Sa every hr. 7:30am-6:20pm, €1.10). Pick up schedules at the tourist office.

Taxis: Radio Taxi Services (☎04 68 71 50 50). At the train station or across the canal by Jardin André Chenier. €2.60 base; €1.50 per km during the day, €2.30 at night. €8 from station to the Cité. 24hr.

◑ ⃠ ORIENTATION AND PRACTICAL INFORMATION

The **Bastide Saint-Louis,** once known as the *basse-ville* (lower town), is Carcassonne's commercial center. Its main functions are shops, hotels, bars, and the cathedral; from the train station, the shuttle runs to the citadel in the summer. To get from the train station to the Cité on foot (25min.), walk down rue Maréchal Joffre, which turns into rue Georges Clemenceau. Past the clearing of pl. Carnot, turn left on rue de Verdun past the tourist office, sharply bear right through pl. Gambetta, and turn left up rue du Pont Vieux. After the bridge, take a sharp right to reach rue Barbacane, which leads to the citadel entrance.

Tourist Office: 28 rue de Verdun (☎04 68 10 24 30; www.carcassonne-tourisme.com). Free map, English guide, and accommodations booking. Open July-Aug. daily 9am-7pm; Sept.-June M-Sa 9am-6pm, Su 9am-noon. Annexes in the Cité's Porte Narbonnaise (☎04 68 10 24 37) and near the station on Port du Canal (☎04 68 25 94 81).

Tours: French tours of Bastide St-Louis from mid-June to mid-Sept. W-Th 9:30am; €5, under 15 €2. Audio tours €3. Regional excursions €35-40, under 18 €15.

Laundromat: Laverie Le Dauphin, 71 av. Général Leclerc (☎04 68 71 43 65). Wash €3.50-6.50, dry €0.50 per 6min. Detergent €0.30. Open daily 8am-8pm.

Police: Comissariat, 4 bd. Barbès (☎04 68 11 26 00). Call for **pharmacie de garde.**

Hospital: Centre Hospitalier, route de Ste-Hilaire (☎04 68 24 24 24).

Internet Access: Alerte Rouge, 73 rue de Verdun (☎04 68 25 20 39). €3 per hr. Wi-Fi €2 per hr. or free for 1hr. with 1 drink. Open M-Sa 10am-11pm. **Call World,** 32 rue de la République (☎04 68 72 89 00). €3 per hr. Open M-Sa 10am-noon and 2-9pm, Su 3-9pm.

Post Office: 40 rue Jean Bringer (☎04 68 11 71 00). **Currency exchange** available. Open M-F 8:30am-6pm, Sa 8:30am-noon. **Poste Restante:** 11012. **Postal Code:** 11000.

◪ ⬛ ACCOMMODATIONS AND CAMPING

▨ **Auberge de Jeunesse (HI),** rue de Vicomte Trencavel (☎04 68 25 23 16; carcassonne@ fuaj.org). A rare refuge of affordable comfort in the medieval city. Summer excursions (€12) and occasional courtyard concerts. Lockers, showers, and sinks in large, clean 4- to 6-bed rooms. Kitchen, bar, and bike rack. Breakfast included. Laundry €6. Internet €2 per hr. Bike rental €8 per day. Reception 24hr. Lockout 10am-3pm. Reservations recommended; we're talking months ahead for Bastille Day. Bunks €21. MC/V. ❶

Notre-Dame de L'Abbaye, 103 rue Trivalle (☎04 68 25 16 65), 5min. from the Cité. Walk straight after crossing the Pont Vieux from the lower city, continue on rue Hoche, and enter the next building on the left. The cheaper rooms are an absolute steal. Breakfast included. Linen €3. Reception daily 9am-12:30pm and 2-6pm. July 15-Sept. 15 singles €30, with shower and toilet €45; doubles €50/60. Sept 16-July 14 singles €26/40; doubles €44/55. AmEx/MC/V. ❷

Sidsmums Travelers Retreat, 11 chemin de la Croix d'Achille (☎04 68 26 94 49 or 06 16 86 85 00; www.sidsmums.com), 10km south of Carcassonne. Take the bus (dir: Limoux) from the *gare routière* (M-Sa 10:30am, 5:15, 6:15pm; €2.50), which passes through Preixan. Call ahead to catch a ride on the owner's free daily lifts into town. New wood cabins with beds or bunks, comfy couches, and a full bookshelf. Ask about hikes to nearby castles and rivers. It is possible to swap lodging for 3hr. of work per day. Spacious kitchen. Internet €3 per hr. Bike rental €10 per day. Reception 24hr. Reservations recommended. Dorms €19-21; doubles €42-47.50. Cash only. ❶

Camping de la Cité, route de Ste-Hilaire (☎04 68 25 11 77; cpllacite@atciat.com). From the *basse-ville,* cross the Pont Vieux and turn right across the garden down rue Dujardin-Beaumetz. Follow the footpath along the stream and past the sunflower field

(45min., from the Cité 30min.) until you reach a green fence, through which you can see the campground; turn left and follow the path. Alternatively, take the *navette* (€1.50) that goes to the Cité and continues to the campground. Pool, snack bar, and grocery store. Karaoke, dancing, and bike excursions. Laundry. Internet €3 per 30min. Reception July-Aug. 8am-8:30pm; from Sept. to mid-Oct. and from mid-Mar. to June 9am-noon and 2-7pm. From July to late Aug. 2 people with tent €22-23; from late Aug. to early Oct. and from mid-Mar. to June €16-22.40. Electricity €4. Cash only. ❷

🍴 FOOD

The grassy, shady banks of the Aude, near the Pont Vieux, provide ideal picnic sites. If you do eat out, don't pass up Carcassonne's specialty, the rich and meaty white bean stew cassoulet—it's served at nearly every restaurant and is popular even in summer. There's a fruit and veggie market every Tuesday and Thursday in **place Carnot** and a larger version with dried fruit and olive vendors every Saturday (8am-noon). For groceries, pop into the **Monoprix** supermarket, at the intersection of rue Georges Clemenceau and rue de la République. (Open M-Sa 8:30am-8pm, Su 9am-noon. AmEx/MC/V.) Restaurants on **rue du Plô** offer €11-17 *menus;* save room for dessert at one of the outdoor *crêperies* on **place Marcou.** In the winter, restaurants in the Cité tend to have limited hours.

🍴 **Maison de la Blanquette de Limoux,** pl. Marcou (☎04 68 71 66 09). Fill up on the famed *cassoulet castelnaudary,* a delicacy said to date back to a culinary experiment in the 100 Years' War. 3-course *menu,* including cassoulet, 0.25L wine, and an *apéritif,* €14. Open July-Aug. daily noon-2:30pm and 7pm-midnight; Sept.-Nov. 15 and Apr.-June M and Th-Su noon-2:30 and 7pm-midnight, Tu noon-5pm. MC/V over €15. ❸

  Blanche de Castille, 21 rue Cros Mayrevieille (☎04 68 25 17 80). This *salon de thé* serves what seems like the only iced coffee in France (€3.80)—though it barely resembles the American version. *Foie gras* on toast (€12) and tea (€3-4) served on a terrace. Ice cream €3-7. Sandwiches €4.20-8.50. Open July-Aug. daily 8:30am-8pm; Sept.-Oct. and June daily 9am-7pm; Feb.-May Th-Sa 10am-5pm. AmEx/MC/V over €15. ❷

👁 SIGHTS

MEDIEVAL CITY. On a steep hill along the bank of the Aube, Carcassonne's stone gray Cité (pop. 120), capped with a melange of silver cones and flat medieval towers, is a breathtaking sight. The well-preserved walls and fortifications lie on a foundation dating to the first century. After centuries of unsuccessful sieges, Carcassonne finally came under French control in 1226. Thus began the Cité's architectural metamorphosis—a 600-year journey from Roman times to the Renaissance illustrated in the architecture of its 52 watchtowers. The outer ramparts were built by Louis IX and Phillip III. A *petit train* takes visitors around the ramparts with commentary in eight languages, including English and Spanish. (☎04 68 24 45 70. 20min.; May-Sept. daily 10am-noon and 2-6pm; €7, students €6.) A *calèche* (horse-drawn carriage) also crosses the bridge to the town. (☎04 68 71 54 57. 20min.; Apr.-Oct. daily 10am-6pm; €6, under 12 €4.) Both tours depart from the main entrance of the Cité, at the Porte Narbonnaise.

CHÂTEAU COMTAL. Intended to be a palace at the time of its construction in the 12th century, the château was transformed into a citadel after Carcassonne submitted to royal control in 1226. In the 19th century, the castle went through a controversial restoration project, which capped the towers with cone-shaped roofs instead of preserving the medieval architecture. Join a guided tour to visit the château's inner walls, peruse its ramparts, and learn about the various ways in which the fortress prepared a cruel death for attackers. The **Tour**

de la Justice's treacherous staircase was a stairway to heaven for invaders who rushed upstairs only to find themselves trapped at the dead end; special openings from above allowed huge stones to be dropped onto unfortunate climbers. The **Cour du Midi** holds the remains of a Gallo-Roman villa, once home to the troubadours for which Carcassonne's court was famous. *(1 rue Viollet-le-Duc. ☎04 68 11 70 70. Open daily Apr.-Sept. 10am-6:30pm, 1st tour 10:30am; Oct.-Mar. 9:30am-5pm, 1st tour 10:15am. 45min. tours in English, French, and Spanish. From mid-June to mid-Sept. frequent departures. Check the board at the entrance as times change daily. 1hr. tours also available for groups by appointment; €4 extra. €7.50, ages 18-25 €4.80. Audio tour in English, French, German, and Spanish €4, 2 for €6; audio tour does not permit access to ramparts.)*

BASILIQUE SAINT-NAZAIRE. The basilica mixes Gothic and Romanesque styles in a vast interior busy with colorful designs. From July to mid-September, the **Estivales d'Orgue de la Cité** hosts organ concerts every Sunday at 5pm. *(At the end of rue St-Louis. Open M-Sa 9-11:45am and 1:45-6pm, Su 9-10:45am and 2-4:30pm.)*

OTHER SIGHTS. Carcassonne's Cité is filled with small museums, most of which are tourist traps. An exception is the **Musée de l'École**, which displays life-size figures, photographs, and report cards from the late 1800s, when statesman Jules Ferry made primary education free, compulsory, and secular. *(3 rue du Plô. ☎04 68 25 95 14. Open daily July-Aug. 10am-7pm; Sept.-June 10am-6pm. €4, students €3, under 12 free.)* The *basse-ville*—the **Bastide Saint-Louis**—was born when Louis IX, afraid enemy troops might find shelter close to his fortress, burned the houses that clung to the city's walls and relocated residents. To make up for the loss, he gave the homeless townspeople their very own walled fortifications and church, which grew into a community that soon eclipsed the Cité itself. Converted into a fortress after the Black Prince razed Carcassonne in the Hundred Years' War, the *basse-ville*'s **Cathédrale Saint-Michel** still sports fortifications on its southern side. The church's back entrance opens onto a small but meticulously kept garden. *(Rue Voltaire. Open M-Sa 7am-noon and 2-7pm, Su 8:30am-12:30pm.)*

◉ NIGHTLIFE

The evening is the best time for wandering Carcassonne's Cité streets and relaxing in the cafes in **place Marcou**. Bars and cafes at **place Carnot**, in the *basse-ville*, stay open until midnight or later.

Le Bar à Vins, 6 rue du Plô (☎04 68 47 38 38). The best bar in town. A fusion of glitter and electronica, this wine bar meets beer garden draws a mixed crowd of tourists and local youth. The excellent house mojito (€9) alone is worth a stop. Tapas and sandwiches €4.50-12. Wine €2. Beer €2.90-6. Open daily 9am-2am. MC/V.

O'Sheridans, 13 rue Victor Hugo (☎04 68 72 06 58), off pl. Carnot. A friendly Irish pub filled with French and Anglo crowds. Pints €6. Live music Sept.-June every other Th 10pm. Happy hour 6-8pm; whiskey ½-price. Open daily 5pm-2am. MC/V.

✿ FESTIVALS

Festival de la Cité (☎04 68 11 59 15; www.festivaldecarcassonne.com), in July. Brings dance, opera, theater, and concerts to the Château Comtal and the amphitheater. €25-66, most shows students €15.

Festival de la Bastide (☎04 68 10 24 30; www.carcassonne-festivaldelabastide.com), in July. Showcases smaller bands as well as free comedy, music, and dance performances in the squares of the Cité and the Bastide St-Louis. Schedules at tourist office.

Bastille Day, July 14. Deep red floodlights and smoke set the entire Cité ablaze in remembrance of the villages burned by the inquisitorial jury headquartered here during the Tour de l'Inquisition. The fireworks display draws 700,000-800,000 visitors. The banks of the river provide a great view, but do try to avoid getting trampled.

Tournoi de Chevaliers (☎04 68 72 37 40; www.carcassonnetoros.com), in July and Aug. At 3 and 4:45pm, an equestrian show offers mock jousting and battles. Turkey legs, anyone? €10, ages 7-18 €5, under 7 free.

Spectacles Médlévaux, 2 weeks in mid-Aug. The Cité returns to the Middle Ages. Even non-French-speakers will enjoy the nightly 9:30pm show—a multimedia drama in the castle amphitheater that brings the 13th century to life (€2-5, under 7 free).

Fiesta y Toros, the last week of Aug. A celebration of Spanish culture with horse shows, traditional dances, and *corridas* (bullfights; €30).

FOIX ☎05 61

The red-tiled roofs and cobblestone streets of Foix (fwah; pop. 9700) lie in a massive medieval château's shadow. The counts who ruled from this magnificent fortress were not the only ones to leave their mark; nearby caves and grottoes hold paintings by the Ariège region's prehistoric inhabitants. The city is now a base for hiking through the region's thick forests and kayaking down its twisting rivers. Consider renting a car here to visit surrounding areas; public transport to the prehistoric caves and serene Ariège passes is inconvenient.

⊏ TRANSPORTATION

Trains: Av. Pierre Sémard (☎05 34 09 29 00), north of town off N20. Open M 5:40am-12:35pm and 2:15-9:10pm, Tu-F 6:55am-1:30pm and 2-9:10pm, Sa 9:55am-6:10pm, Su 2:25-10:20pm. To **Toulouse** (1-1½hr., 20 per day, €13).

Buses: Salt Autocars, 2 rue des Cheminots, Toulouse (☎05 61 48 61 51). Runs buses between **Toulouse** and **Foix** (2hr., 1 or 2 per day, €11).

Canoe and Kayak Rental: Base Nautique (☎05 61 65 44 19), down the street from Camping du Lac/Labarre (below). €12 per ½-day. Open July-Aug.

⁊ PRACTICAL INFORMATION

Tourist Office: 29 rue Théophile Delcassé (☎05 61 65 12 12; www.ot-foix.fr). Turn right out of the train station, follow the street to the main road (N20), and take it to the 1st bridge on the right. Once over the bridge, take the 2nd left onto rue Théophile Delcassé and walk to the end of the street, about 3 blocks (10min.). The office provides a free small map and tons of info on exploring the region. Open July-Aug. M-Sa 9am-7pm, Su 9:30am-12:30pm and 2-6pm; Sept.-June M-Sa 9am-noon and 2-6pm.

Youth Center: Bureau d'Information Jeunesse (BIJ), 3 rue Longue (☎05 61 02 86 10). **Internet** €5 per hr. Open M, W, F 10am-noon and 1-5pm, Tu and Th 1-5pm.

Laundromat: 22 rue de la Faurie. Wash €5. Open daily 8am-8:30pm.

Police: 2 rue Lakanal (☎05 61 05 43 00).

Hospital: (☎05 61 03 30 30), 5km away in St-Jean de Verges.

Post Office: Allées Villote (☎05 61 02 01 02). **Currency exchange** available. Open M-W and F 8:30am-6:30pm, Th 8:30am-noon and 2-6:30pm, Sa 8:30am-noon. **Postal Code:** 09000.

⋔ ⋔ ACCOMMODATIONS AND CAMPING

▨ **Foyer Léo Lagrange,** 16 rue Peyrevidal (☎05 61 65 09 04; www.leolagrange-foix.com). From the tourist office, turn right onto cours Gabriel Fauré and right again onto rue

Peyrevidal, passing under the pavilion of the Halle aux Grains; the hotel will be on your right. The best option for budget travelers. A cross between a hotel and a hostel, it offers privacy and sociability in 18 clean 1- to 4-bed rooms, each with sink, desk, and private shower. Toilets off the main hallway. Breakfast €5. Linen €3. Free Internet and Wi-Fi. Reception 8am-11pm; call ahead if arriving late. €18-20 per person. Cash only. ❶

Hostellerie de la Barbacane du Château, 1 av. de Lérida (☎05 61 65 50 44; fax 02 74 33), 5min. from the tourist office. Just past the roundabout, to the right on cours Gabriel Fauré. Elegant mahogany beds and sparkling bathrooms. Call ahead for a room with a château view. Elevator. Breakfast €7. Reception Apr.-Dec. 7am-11pm. Singles and doubles €40, with bath €42, with château view €50, with bath and TV €45-72. MC/V. ❸

Camping du Lac/Labarre (☎05 61 65 11 58; www.campingdulac.com), 3km up N20 toward Toulouse. A 3-star lakeside site. Buses from Toulouse stop at the camp. From the train station, go left along N20 until signs for the campground appear on the left. 2 people, car, tent, and electricity from mid-July to mid-Aug. €20; late Aug. and early July €18; Sept. and June €17; Oct.-Apr. €13.50; May €15. ❶

🗗 FOOD

Ariège regional specialties include *truite à l'ariègeoise* (trout) and *cassoulet* (white-bean and duck stew). Moderately priced restaurants line **rue de la Faurie** and **rue des Chapeliers.** For the basics, try the **Casino** supermarket, rue Laffont. (Open M-Sa 8:30am-7:30pm, Su 8:30am-noon.) On Fridays and the last Monday of the month, open-air markets sprout up all over Foix, with meat and cheese at the **Halle aux Grains,** fruit and vegetables at **place Saint Volusien,** and clothing along the **allées de Villote.** (Food 9am-1pm; clothes 9am-4pm.)

Le Jeu de l'Oie, 17 rue de la Faurie (☎05 61 02 69 39). Dinner draws local in this neighborhood favorite. For a taste of Ariège cuisine at unbeatable prices, try the generous *plat du jour* (€6.90). A 2-course *menu* that includes a glass of wine (€8.60) is a bargain. Salads €3.50-8.50. *Plats* €7.30-14. Open July-Aug. Tu-Sa noon-3pm and 7-11pm; Sept.-June Tu-F noon-2:30pm and 7-10:30pm, Sa 7-10:30pm. MC/V. ❷

La Sainte Marthe, 21 rue Peyrevidal (☎05 61 02 87 87). *Plats* range from the smoked duck, walnut, and fried onion salad (€7) to the decadent *magret de canard* (duck breast) with *foie gras* and truffle sauce (€21). Sumptuous profiteroles (€6). House cassoulet €16. Open daily noon-2:30pm and 7:30-10pm. AmEx/MC/V. ❷

🗗 SIGHTS

CHÂTEAU DE FOIX. Perched on a pedestal of jagged rock high above the city, the château is worth visiting even if you don't plan to go inside; walk up the path around the château for a view of Foix and the Pyrenean foothills. The château has three stunning towers, each built in a different century; the 15th-century round tower is the tallest and a particularly impressive fortress. Inside the well-preserved castle, the regional **Musée de l'Ariège** displays a collection of armor, stone carvings, and artifacts from the Roman Empire to the Middle Ages. Don't miss a small novelty collection of ornate carved medieval keys. After its glory days, the castle was used as a garrison and a prison: inside the round tower are graffiti written by desperate prisoners. After the tour, visitors haul themselves up the castle towers for an even better view. *(From the tourist office, turn right on cours Gabriel Fauré, then right again just past the Mairie, on rue St-Jammes. Continue as the road becomes rue Lazema and rue des Chapeliers. Take a left uphill onto rue du Rocher. ☎05 34 09 83 83. Open July-Aug. daily 9:45am-6:30pm; Sept. and June daily 9:45am-noon and 2-6pm; Oct. daily 10:30am-noon and 2-5:30pm; Nov.-Apr. M and W-Su*

LANGUEDOC-ROUSSILLON

10:30am-noon and 2-5:30pm; May daily 9:45am-noon and 2-5:30pm. Free tours in French every hr., in English July-Aug. daily 1pm. €4.30, students €3.20.)

ABBAYE SAINT-VOLUSIEN. Down the hill at pl. St-Volusien, the 14th-century abbey occupies the site of an ancient Roman church and still includes part of the Roman structure. Simple but imposing vaulted ceilings bridge the intricate rose- and beige-colored stone walls in this fine example of Gothic architecture. *(Open daily 8am-8pm. Guided visits M-F 11am and 4-6pm, Sa 11am and 2-4pm.)*

❄ FESTIVALS

Résistances Festival (☎05 61 65 44 23), 1st weekend of July. Brings upward of 75 art films—many of which premiere at Cannes—to Foix. Call the tourist office for more info.

Trad'estiu (☎05 61 65 12 12; www.tradestiu.com), around the 3rd weekend of July. "Traditional summer" arrives in Foix. This festival of traditional music and dance features popular—and free—outdoor performances.

Jazz Festival (☎05 61 01 18 30; www.jazzfoix.com), the weekend after Trad'estiu. Concerts nightly at 9pm and jazz playing from speakers around town. €25 per night, students €20, under 25 €10; week pass €130/80/40.

L'Ariège au Fil du Temps, early Aug. Tu and Th-F at 10pm. An extravagant medieval festival enlivens the area around Foix's château. Villagers come for a sound and light show of Ariège history that includes reenacted battles and more fireworks than some cities use on Bastille Day. For info and tickets, call Théâtre de l'Espinet (☎05 61 02 88 26). €8-23, under 18 €5-12.

▶ DAYTRIPS FROM FOIX

GROTTE DE NIAUX. Lanterns illuminate prehistoric wall drawings of bison, horses, and ibex from around 12,000 BC. Reservations are required to enter the cave. Twenty kilometers south of Foix, the grotto is accessible only by car. Be sure to bring a warm jacket and appropriate footwear. *(☎05 61 05 88 37 in summer, 05 10 10 the rest of the year. Open Apr.-Oct. daily; Nov.-Mar. Tu-Su. €9.40, under 18 €7.)*

RIVIÈRE SOUTERRAINE DE LABOUICHE. An hour-long boat ride floats down the longest navigable underground river in Europe. Six kilometers from town, the small metal boat cruises through galleries of stalactites and stalagmites, lead by clever Anglophone guides. There is no public transportation to this site; a taxi from Foix costs €12 each way (☎05 61 65 12 69). In summer, arrive as early as possible and at least before 3:30pm to avoid crowds. *(☎05 61 65 04 11. Open July-Aug. daily 9:30am-5:15pm; Sept. and Apr.-June daily 10-11:15am and 2-5:15pm; from Oct. to mid-Nov. Sa-Su 10-11:15am and 2-4:30pm. €8.50, students €7.50, under 12 €6.50.)*

PERPIGNAN   ☎04 68

Perpignan (pehr-peen-yohn; pop. 117,000) is a few kilometers from the Mediterranean, 27km from the Spanish border, and 30km from the foothills of the Pyrenees. This is a town of contrasts—from the palm-lined and litter-strewn av. du Général de Gaulle to the tiny streets of the *vieille ville* and the massive Cathédrale St-Jean. Yet Perpignan is, above all, a daytripper's paradise. Free weeklong regional bus passes give access to the remarkable, and otherwise nearly unaffordable, towns of Céret, Villefranche-de-Conflent, and Collioure.

▣ TRANSPORTATION

Flights: Aéroport de Perpignan-Rivesaltes (**PGF;** ☎04 68 52 60 70; www.perpignan. cci.fr), 6km northwest of the *centre-ville,* just outside of town along D117. **Ryanair** (www.ryanair.com) offers the cheapest flights to **London.** Navette Aéroport (☎04 68 55 68 00) runs **shuttles** from the SNCF train station and the *gare routière* to the airport (15min.; M-F 4 per day, Sa-Su 5 per day). Shuttles are synchronized with flights, and the connection is usually guaranteed. Schedule changes frequently; check with tourist office. €4.50, ages 4-10 and group members €3.

Trains: Pl. Salvador Dalí. Ticket window open M-Sa 6:10am-8pm, Su 6:40am-8pm. To: **Carcassonne** (1hr.; 3-7 per day, change at Narbonne; €17); **Lyon** (4-5hr., 5 per day, €62); **Marseille** (4-6hr.; 3 per day, change at **Narbonne;** €38); **Montpellier** (1-2hr.; 8-11 per day, change at Narbonne; €21); **Paris** (5hr., 1-4 per day, €101); **Toulouse** (2-3hr.; 2-7 per day, change at Narbonne; €26).

Buses: Pl. Salvador Dalí (☎04 68 35 29 02), near the train station; due to ongoing construction, this station is only temporary. Ask at tourist office or train station for more info. Office open M-Sa 7am-6:30pm. All buses free with weeklong regional bus pass. To **Céret** (45min.; M-Sa 10 per day, Su 4 per day; €4.40), **Collioure** (45-50min.; M-Sa 10 per day, Su 1 per day; €6.60), and **Villefranche-de-Conflent** (1hr., 8 per day, €9.60).

 PASS FOR A PASS. To obtain a free tourist pass for a week of free regional bus rides, bring your passport and photo to the tourist office.

Public Transportation: Compagnie Transports Perpignan Mediterranée (CTPM), 27 bd. Clemenceau (☎04 68 61 01 13). Open M-F 7:30am-12:30pm and 1:30-6:30pm, Sa 9am-noon and 2:30-5pm. Runs **buses** throughout Perpignan and to **Canet-Plage.** 1st bus in any direction 7am, last bus around 8:30pm. €1.10, round-trip €2, carnet of 10 €7.80. Not covered by weeklong regional bus pass.

Taxis: Accueil Perpignan Taxi (☎04 68 35 15 15), by the train station. €2 per km, more at night and on weekends. €40 to the airport, €30 to Canet-Plage. 24hr.

Car Rental: ADA, 30 bis av. du Général de Gaulle (☎04 68 34 52 89), near the train station. From €74 per day, 250km. 21+; must have had license for 1 year. Open M-Sa 9am-noon and 2-6pm. AmEx/MC/V. **Europcar** (☎04 68 34 89 80), in the train station. From €315 per 5 days, 1750km. 21+. Under-25 surcharge €30 per day. Open M-Sa 8am-noon and 2-6pm. AmEx/MC/V. **Hertz** (☎04 68 61 18 77), at the airport and near the train station; also at 9 av. du Général de Gaulle (☎04 68 51 37 40). From €168 for 3 days, 300km. 21+. Under-25 surcharge €34. Open daily 8am-7pm. AmEx/MC/V.

Bike Rental: Bouti Cycle, 20 av. Gilbert Brutus (☎04 68 85 02 71). €38 per 5 days, €54 per week. Min. 5-day rental; €200 cash deposit. Open Tu-Sa 9am-12:30pm and 2:30-7:30pm. MC/V.

▣▣ ORIENTATION AND PRACTICAL INFORMATION

Perpignan's train station was once referred to as "the center of the world" by off-center Salvador Dalí. The liveliest part of the city is the labyrinth of small streets in the heart of the *vieille ville,* a 10min. walk from the station. The triangular area's three corners are marked by the regional tourist office, pl. de Catalogne toward the train station, and the Palais des Rois de Majorque to the south. Avoid Quartier St-Jacques, near the intersection of bd. Jean Bourrat and bd. Anatole France, at night.

Perpignan

ACCOMMODATIONS
Auberge de Jeunesse La Pépinière (HI), **4**
Avenir Hôtel, **10**
Camping Le Catalan, **1**
Hôtel Le Berry, **7**

FOOD
Casa Sansa, **5**
Peace 'n' Love, **8**
Spaghetteri'Aldo, **3**

NIGHTLIFE
Canet-Plage, **2**
Trois Soeurs, **6**
L'Ubu, **9**

Tourist Office: Palais des Congrès, pl. Armand Lanoux (☎04 68 66 30 30; www.perpignantourisme.com). From the train station, follow av. du Général de Gaulle to pl. de Catalogne and take bd. Georges Clemenceau to pl. de la Résistance. The *vieille ville* is across the canal. Veer left on cours Pamarole and continue along the promenade des Plantanes until you see a large glass building on the right. Open from mid-June to mid-Sept. M-Sa 9am-7pm, Su 10am-4pm; from mid-Sept. to mid-June M-Sa 9am-6pm, Su 10am-1pm. Annex at pl. Arago (☎04 68 35 46 73) open M-Sa from mid-June to mid-Sept. 10am-7pm; from mid-Sept. to mid-June 10am-6pm.

Tours: The tourist office offers comprehensive 1-2hr. tours in French. New schedule at the beginning of each summer. €5, under 12 free. **English tours** offered from mid-July to mid-Sept; 1 per week. **Night tours** feature music and dance shows (☎04 68 62 38 84). July-Aug. Tu 9pm; €8.

Budget Travel: Cars Verts Voyages, 10 rue Jeanne d'Arc (☎04 68 51 19 47; www.carsverts-voyages.com). Open May-Sept. M-Sa 8:15am-noon and 2-6:30pm; Oct.-Apr. M-F 8:15am-noon and 2-6:30pm. Organizes daytrips June-Sept. to **Andorra** (€32), **Barcelona** (€38), and **Mt. Canigou** (€44).

Laundromat: Laverie Foch, 23 rue du Maréchal Foch. Wash €2.90-6.50, dry €0.50 per 6min. Open daily 7am-8:30pm.

Police: Av. de Grande Bretagne (☎04 68 35 70 00).

Hospital: Hôpital St-Jean, av. du Languedoc (☎04 68 61 66 33).

Internet Access: Cyber Espace, 45 bis av. du Général Leclerc (☎04 68 35 36 29), facing the bus station. €2 per 30min., €3 per hr.; 8-10am ½-price. Open July-Aug. M-Sa noon-1am, Su 1-8pm; Sept.-June M-F 8am-1am, Sa noon-1am, Su 1-8pm. Cheap (€2.10-3 per hr.) Internet cafes also line av. du Général de Gaulle.

Post Office: Quai de Barcelone (☎04 68 51 99 12). **Currency exchange** and **Western Union** available. Open M-F 8:30am-7pm, Sa 8am-noon. **Postal Code:** 66000.

ACCOMMODATIONS AND CAMPING

Cheap hotels are on **avenue du Général de Gaulle,** 10min. from the *centre-ville.*

Avenir Hôtel, 11 rue de l'Avenir (☎04 68 34 20 30; www.avenirhotel.com), off av. du Général de Gaulle. Colorful if stuffy rooms with terraces and decorations painted by the owner. Breakfast €4.50. Beware of the communal shower's high price (€3.20 per day). Reception M-Sa 8am-11pm, Su 8am-noon and 6-11pm. Reservations recommended. Singles €18-24, with toilet €27, with shower €30, with bath €36; doubles €21-24/27/30/36; triples €39; quads €42. Extra bed €6. AmEx/MC/V. ❶

Auberge de Jeunesse La Pépinière (HI), allée Marc-Pierre (☎04 68 34 63 32), on the edge of town. From the train station, go down av. du Général de Gaulle and turn left on rue Valette. Turn right on av. de Grande Bretagne, left on rue Claude Marty before the police station, and right on allée Marc-Pierre. Recently renovated rooms with bright lockers. Outdoor terrace. Breakfast €3.50. Internet €1 per 30min. Free Wi-Fi. Reception 7:30-11am and 5-11pm. Check-out 11am; strictly enforced. Lockout 11am-5pm. Open from Mar. to mid-Nov. Dorms €15. Cash only. ❶

Hôtel le Berry, 6 av. du Général de Gaulle (☎04 68 34 59 02). Family run. Each clean room has A/C, TV, shower, and toilet. Reception 9am-10pm. Singles €30-40; doubles €35-45; triples €45-50; quads €50-55. Prices higher July-Aug. MC/V. ❷

Camping Le Catalan, route de Bompas (☎04 68 63 16 92). Take bus #15 (dir.: Bompas) to Lidl, which is in view of the campground (15min.; every 15min.-1hr. until 7pm but irregular schedule, check with tourist office or CTPM for exact times; €1.10). 94 sites with access to playground, laundry, and hot showers. Snack bar and pool open July-Aug. Wheelchair-accessible. July-Aug. 2 people with car €18, extra person €5; Sept.-Oct. and Mar.-June €14/4. Electricity €3.50. MC/V. ❶

FOOD

Local *charcuterie,* Catalan *pâté,* and *escargots* with garlic are Perpignan's specialties as well as nougat in flavors like caramel or almond. **Place de la Loge, place Arago, place de la République,** and **place de Verdun** in the *vieille ville* stay lively at night, as restaurants dish out French and Spanish fare. Pricier options and candlelit tables line **quai Vauban,** while **avenue du Général de Gaulle,** leading into town from the train station, has as many kebab shops and cheap *boulangeries* as it does Internet cafes. Fresh produce can be found at the open-air markets on **place Cassanyes** (open daily 7:30am-1:30pm) and **place de la République** (open Tu-Su 7:30am-1:30pm). A huge **Casino** supermarket is on bd. Félix Mercader. (☎04 68 51 56 00. Open M-Sa 8:30am-8pm, Su 8:30am-12:30pm.)

Peace 'n' Love, 40 rue de la Fusterie (☎06 08 33 67 84). Vegetarian restaurant that will also satisfy carnivores. Funky blue lighting. Everything costs €6.50, and most dishes are enough for a full meal. Try the cumin-spiced vegetable curry with bread. Desserts €3-5. Open M-W noon-2:30pm, Th-Sa noon-2:30pm and 7-10:30pm. Cash only. ❷

Casa Sansa, rue des Fabriques Couvertes (☎04 68 34 21 84), near Le Castillet. Outstanding Catalan food. Worth a trip for the crusty country bread and garlic aioli. Order

THE END OF THE WORLD

Salvador Dalí, whose artistic works are among the most recognizable in 20th-century European painting, never drifted far from his native Catalonia during the course of his long career. Nevertheless, he attributed a special significance to Perpignan; in fact, Dalí considered Perpignan to be the center of the universe. From Dalí's own account, this revelation came to him in the form of a vision of "cosmogonic ecstasy" while quietly sitting in the Perpignan train station on September 19, 1963. He claimed to have viewed the universe in its entirety—and Perpignan was the navel, the place from which the dying universe would one day begin to contract.

The event has its origins in a period in Dalí's work after the bombing of Hiroshima, when he became obsessed with the concept of the dissolution of time, the breakdown of matter, and the extinction of the universe. The vision is the inspiration for Dalí's *The Station of Perpignan*, in which figures of prayer-bent men and women are sucked into the light of a train, pulled by the mysterious gravity Dalí must have felt. Though the experience was certainly unique to the painter—no one else reported enlightening visions of the universe that day—the people of Perpignan don't mind the suggestion that the universe is centered in their local *gare*—after all, wouldn't you like to think the universe revolves around you?

from the illustrated tapas menu (€3-7) to create a €10-15 feast. *Plats* €13-20. *Menu* €19. Open daily 11:30am-3pm and 6-11pm. AmEx/MC/V. ❸

Spaghetteri'Aldo, rue des Variétés (☎04 68 61 11 47). Filling pasta with fresh sauces (€8.50-12). Spaghetti bolognese (€8.50) or gnocchi gorgonzola (€9) won't disappoint. Salads €8.50-9.50. Open Tu-Sa noon-3pm and 7-11pm. MC/V. ❷

👁 SIGHTS

Along La Basse, flower-lined *quais* beg for afternoon strolls; it's also worth setting aside time to wander the incredibly charming *vieille ville*.

PALAIS DES ROIS DE MAJORQUE. An uphill walk across the *vieille ville* brings you to the red-rock walls of Perpignan's 15th-century Spanish citadel. Concealed inside is the Palais des Rois de Majorque, where the kings of the Majorcan dynasty settled. The **Sainte-Croix chapel's** marble facade reveals French, Italian, and Moorish architectural influences. The palace's courtyard serves as a concert hall in July, hosting plays and musical (mostly jazz) performances. *(Av. Gilbert Brutus. Open daily June-Sept. 10am-6pm; Oct.-May 9am-5pm. Ticket sales end 30min. before closing. 1hr. French tours available July-Aug. every 30min.; Sept.-June 2 per day or by reservation. €4, students €2, under 12 free. Concert tickets €5-25; available at FNAC.)*

LE CASTILLET. Guarding the entrance to the *centre-ville*, Le Castillet, originally built by the Spanish in 1368, was intended to repel French invaders. After the Treaty of the Pyrenees in 1659, the castle was transformed into a prison and torture chamber for those who refused to acknowledge the victorious French crown. No longer a frontier pillar, Le Castillet holds the Casa Pairal, a museum of Catalan domestic ware, religious relics, and farm equipment. Visit the reconstructions of Catalan houses as well as the giant statues of the king and queen of Majorca guarding the museum entrance. *(☎04 68 35 42 05. Open M and W-Su May-Sept. 10am-6:30pm; Oct.-Apr. 11am-5:30pm. Guided tours in French twice a month in summer; call for exact dates. €4, students and under 15 €2.)*

MUSÉE HYACINTHE RIGAUD. Back in the *vieille ville*, this museum contains a collection of Gothic paintings by 13th-century Spanish and Catalan masters as well as canvases by Ingres, Miró, Picasso, and Rigaud. The bottom floor houses temporary exhibits. *(16 rue de l'Ange. ☎04 68 35 43 40. Wheelchair-accessible. Open M and W-Su May-Sept. noon-7pm; Oct.-Apr. 11am-5:30pm. €4, students €2, under 18 free.)*

CATHÉDRALE SAINT-JEAN. Partly supported by a macabre pillar depicting the severed head of John the Baptist, this cathedral is a paragon of Gothic architecture. Begun in 1324 and consecrated in 1509, the grandiose cathedral sports an 80m long nave—the third largest in the world. Stunning oil paintings, colorful stained glass, and crystal chandeliers designed in Renaissance, Baroque, and 19th-century religious styles compose the decor. (☎04 68 51 33 72. Open M 7:30am-noon and 3-7pm, Tu-Su 7:30am-7pm. Mass Su 8, 10:30am, 6:30pm.)

NIGHTLIFE

Perpignan is not known for its nightlife, but a few bars scattered on the tiny streets around Le Castillet keep a small crowd entertained until the morning. The clubs lining the beaches at nearby **Canet-Plage** (bus #1 from the train station, irregularly every 30min.-1hr. 6:30am-7:30pm) provide the wildest nightlife. However, getting back to Perpignan means paying €20-25 for a taxi, except on Saturday nights, when a bus service runs between Perpignan and the Canet clubs. (Buses leave from the Castillet at 11:45pm, 12:45, 2:10am; buses return from Canet-Plage 12:10, 1, 4, 5am. Check www.route-66.fr or call ☎06 09 49 89 27 for up-to-date schedules. €1.)

L'Ubu, 40 pl. Rigaud (☎04 68 38 63 30; www.ubujazz.com). Literary cafe with live jazz most nights. Free Internet. Beer €2.30. Open M-Sa 10am-2am. AmEx/MC/V.

Trois Soeurs, 2 rue Fontfroide (☎04 68 51 22 33). The chic, the stylish, and the well-to-do frequent the plush seats of this club. Beer €3-5. Mixed drinks €7-8. Live jazz Sept.-June W 7pm. Open Tu-Sa 10am-2am. AmEx/MC/V.

FESTIVALS

Procession de la Sanche, on Good Friday (Apr. 10, 2009). A cross is paraded through the *vieille ville* to the Église St-Jacques.

Fête de St-Jean, June 23. A sacred fire is brought from Mont Canigou to Le Castillet.

Festa Major (☎04 68 66 30 30), 2 weeks surrounding the Fête de St-Jean. A vast celebration of Catalan culture, filled with traditional dancing, music concerts, and food tasting, culminating in a *son et lumière* (light show).

La Fête des Vins (☎04 68 51 59 99), 2 nights at the end of June. Be prepared to make merry—stands hand out wine samples between bd. Wilson and the cours Palmarole. Cheese, *foie gras,* and Catalan lamb. Empty glass at entrance €3.

Estivales de Perpignan (☎04 68 86 08 51; www.estivales.com), in July. Brings world-renowned theater and dance to town. Buy tickets online or at the Palmarium, next to the tourist office annex. Open daily from mid-June to mid-Sept. 10am-6:30pm; Oct.-May 10am-5:30pm. Prices vary; student discounts available.

Jeudis de Perpignan, July-Aug. every Th 7:30-11:30pm. Free musical performances and traditional Catalan dancing from the 1st Th after Bastille Day.

Visa Pour l'Image (☎04 68 62 38 00; www.visapourlimage.com), 1st 2 weeks in Sept. Photojournalism festival highlights current events. Draws an international crowd.

DAYTRIPS FROM PERPIGNAN

VILLEFRANCHE-DE-CONFLENT

Trains (☎04 68 96 63 62) *run from Perpignan to the Villefranche train station (1hr., 6-7 per day, €7.50). Couriers Catalans Buses* (☎04 68 35 29 02) *run from Perpignan directly to the gates of the ramparts around Villefranche (1hr.; M-F 5 per day, Sa 6 per day; €9.60, free with tourist pass). From the train station, located 200m before the town gates, cross the bridge and bear right along the highway to reach the centre-ville. The walls that surround the city have 2 gates that lead to the parallel main streets. The left gate leads to rue St-Jacques; the right gate opens onto rue St-Jean.*

Don't pass up a trip to the spectacular village-in-a-fortress Villefranche-de-Conflent (veel-frahnsh-duh-kahn-fluh), which lies deep in the Conflent mountains but is only a 1hr. (free) bus ride from Perpignan. The impenetrable Fort Liberia, a mere 734 underground steps above Villefranche, offers a stunning view of Mt. Canigou, and nearby stalagmite caves take visitors deep inside the mountains. Nature lovers will find canyons, valleys, and hiking trails only a short trip away on the *petit train jaune*, which goes into the heart of the Pyrenees.

Built into the mountainside high above the town, **Fort Liberia** takes the form of two overlapping hexagons, meant to prevent attacks from the building's front and back. The stronghold was constructed in 1681 by Vauban in order to protect Villefranche and the rest of Catalonia from the Spanish army. The towers and narrow passageways make for an interesting tour, while the view of picturesque Villefranche amid sensational peaks, including Mont Canigou, is breathtaking. The **"Staircase of 1000 Steps"** leads back down to the city; although there are actually 734 steps, they're more than enough to discourage most from walking all the way up. To reach the fort, catch the *navette* (shuttle) from the train station or the parking lot at the town gates (10min.; July-Aug. every 30min., Sept.-June request at the St-Jacques info desk) or take the 30min. hike up along the road that begins on the side of the train station farther from town. Buy tickets at the tourist office or at the fort entrance. (☎04 68 96 34 01. Open daily July-Aug. 9am-8pm; Sept. and May-June 10am-7pm; Nov.-Feb. 10am-5pm; Mar.-Apr. 10am-6pm. €5.80, including *navette* €8; students €5/7; ages 5-11 €2.80/4.10. *Navette* free for visitors who arrive on the *petit train jaune*.)

After a sweaty climb down from Fort Liberia, cool off by going underground. The magnificent **Grandes Canalettes** contain water-carved galleries, stalactite-filled grottoes, underground lakes, and a bottomless pit. In July and August, a *son et lumière* show is held at an auditorium in the heart of the caves. (☎04 68 96 23 11; www.grotte-grandes-canalettes.com. Open from mid-June to mid-Sept. daily 10am-6pm; from mid-Sept. to Oct. and from Apr. to mid-June daily 10am-5:30pm; Nov.-Mar. Su 2-5pm. ☎04 68 05 20 20; www.3grottes.com. Open daily July-Aug. 10am-7:30pm; Sept.-Mar. 10am-5:30pm; Apr.-June 10am-6pm. €8, ages 5-12 €4; 2 caves €12/6. Visit to Les Canalettes next door only by guided tour; reservations required. *Son et lumière* July-Aug. daily 6:30pm. €11, under 18 €6; includes guided tour. AmEx/MC/V.) Accessible through an entrance in the middle of rue St-Jacques, Villefranche's 11th-century **ramparts** include rock passageways in the remarkably well-preserved walls of the city, with occasional peepholes onto city alleys and mountainsides. (☎04 68 96 16 40. Open daily July-Aug. 10am-8pm; Sept. and June 10am-7pm; Oct.-Dec. and Feb.-May 10:30am-12:30pm and 2-5pm. For guided group tours, call ahead. €4, students €3, under 10 free. Audio tour €3.) Running 63km through the Pyrenees, the **petit train jaune** departs from the train station and links Villefranche to Latour-de-Carol (3hr., 3-7 per day, €18). The train runs through mountain valleys on spectacular viaducts, stopping at 20 small towns. The train also carts skiers to the fashionable **Font-Romeu** (2hr., 3-8 per day, €10.30). Equipped with snow machines and chair lifts, this resort offers first-rate skiing. (☎04 68 30 60 61. Day pass €28. €4 student discount outside of *vacances scolaires*.) The *petit train jaune* does not take reservations, so arrive at the station at least 1hr. ahead (2hr. from mid-July to mid-Aug.) or in the early morning.

The tourist office (☎04 68 96 22 96), **post office,** and Mairie (town hall) are all together at 1 pl. de l'Église. The tourist office provides free town maps. (All three open July-Aug. M-Sa 10am-noon and 2-6pm; Sept. and May-June M-F 10am-noon and 2-5pm, Sa 10am-noon; Oct.-Apr. M-Sa 10am-noon.)

CÉRET

Buses run from the train and bus station in Perpignan to the center of Céret (45min., 8-11 per day, €4.40). Pick up a schedule at the gare routière office in Perpignan. Most buses stop outside Perpignan at a stop that, confusingly, is called either pont or rue du 19 Mars. From the bus stop, turn back toward the traffic circle and follow the signs to Céret-Centre. At the next traffic circle, marked by a large fountain, turn right and continue to follow signs onto rue St-Férréol. At its end, turn left and make the 2nd left onto av. Clemenceau; the tourist office is on the corner (20min.). If your bus stops at Céret-Centre, follow av. Clemenceau uphill toward the centre-ville.

Tucked into a valley in the foothills of the Pyrenees, Céret (suh-ray) blossoms in the spring. Each season the president of France receives the first *cérises* (cherries) from the nearby orchards. Known as the "Cubist Mecca," Céret was the beloved stomping ground of Chagall, Picasso, Manolo, and Herbin. As a result, it is home to one of the best modern art museums in France. At the same time, the town is far enough into the hills for spectacular hiking.

The ▓**Musée d'Art Moderne,** 8 bd. du Maréchal Joffre, is located uphill from the tourist office. The collections in this modern building are composed primarily of personal gifts to the museum by artists including Picasso, Matisse, Braque, Chagall, and Miró. Rotating every three months, the temporary exhibits are usually minor outside of the summer but superb from mid-June to mid-September. The year 2009 will feature a retrospective "Centaine de Paysage à Ceret," celebrating the 100-year anniversary of the first artist *séjours* in Ceret with collections from all the major artists who spent time in the village. (☎04 68 87 27 76; www.musee-ceret.com. Wheelchair-accessible. Open from mid-June to mid-Sept. daily 10am-7pm; late Sept. and May-June daily 10am-6pm; Oct.-Apr. M and W-Su 10am-6pm. Guided visits daily July-Aug. 10:30am and 3pm, Sept.-June or in English upon reservation. €5.50, students €3.50, under 12 free. Temporary exhibits €8/6/free. Guided visits €3.50.) In the *centre-ville*, the **marble fountain** of pl. des Neuf-Jets reminds visitors of the town's dual French and Spanish roots. Originally, the fountain's Castilian lion faced Spain. Now it faces France, symbolizing France's 1659 victory over Spain. According to legend, the **Pont du Diable** (Devil's Bridge), which links the town center to its outskirts, couldn't be successfully built until the devil agreed to aid in its construction. Satan demanded the right to the first soul to cross the bridge, but the villagers foiled him by sending a sacrificial black cat across it. However, the devil got the last laugh, taking revenge by loosening one stone from the bridge.

From May 31 to July 1, Céret celebrates the **Grande Fête de la Cérise** and the **Festival de Bandas** with two days of cherry markets and Catalonian music. In late June or early July, the **Querencias—Festival de Musique de Céret**—features musical and dance performances. (☎04 68 87 00 53. Tickets €20 for 1 night, €30 for 2.) The most raucous festival, **Céret de Toros,** occurs every year for three days in mid-July, during which the town hosts three *corridas* (bullfights) and one *novillada* (a bullfight with an uncertified fighter). Music livens the streets well into the night. (☎04 68 87 47 47; www.ceret-de-toros.com. Tickets €35-86 for each *corrida*, €27-56 for the *novillada*.) For a week at the end of July, the **Festival de la Sardane** commemorates traditional Catalan folk dancing with lively concerts and processions. The festival culminates in the concours des Sardanes, where Sardane groups compete against one another in the annual dance tournament and amateurs practice in the streets. (☎04 68 87 00 53. Viewers' fee €10-12.) On September 18, the **Festa Major de Sant Ferriol** (☎04 68 87 00 53) brings runners to town for 6½ and 20km runs.

The **tourist office,** 1 av. Georges Clemenceau, provides a free map with a walking tour of the *vieille ville* and *Les Petits Guides Rando Pyrénées Roussillon* guide with 1-5hr. **hiking** itineraries around Céret. (☎04 68 87 00 53; www.ot-ceret.fr. Open July-Aug. M-Sa 9am-1pm and 2-7pm, Su 10am-1pm; Sept.-June M-F 9am-noon and 2-5pm, Sa 9:30am-12:30pm.)

COLLIOURE ☎04 68

Located where the vineyards and orchards of the Pyrenees meet the blue-green waters of the Mediterranean, Collioure (koh-lee-ohr; pop. 2930) is truly an oasis. Once the prize of Greeks and Phoenicians, the town's rocky harbor became one of Matisse's favorite subjects; artists like Dalí, Dérain, Dufy, and Picasso soon set up their easels as well. Though the artistic avant-garde no longer populates the town, numerous art galleries are housed under its copper roofs. Outside the art world, tourists lie on the pebbly beaches or walk around the harbor to enjoy the evening light play on the stones of the Grand Palais.

▐ TRANSPORTATION

Trains: At the top of av. Aristide Maillol (☎04 68 82 05 89). Ticket office and info desk open daily July-Aug. 6:30am-9pm; Sept.-June 9am-1pm and 2:40-5:45pm. To **Perpignan** (20min., 13 per day, €4.90) and **Barcelona, ESP** (4-5hr., 3 per day, €23) via **Port Bou** (30min., 6 per day, €3.10).

Buses: Leave from carrefour du Christ, at the intersection of av. du Général de Gaulle, route d'Argelès, and rue de la République. Les Courriers Catalans (☎04 68 35 29 02) travels to nearby towns and **Perpignan** (45min.; 5 per day; €6.60, free with regional bus pass).

Taxis: Allo Almaya (☎04 68 82 09 30).

Bike Rental: X-Trem Bike, 5 rue de la Tour d'Auvergne (July-Aug. ☎04 68 82 59 77, Sept.-June 06 23 01 93 01). €10 per ½-day, €18 per day, €85 per week; €200 deposit. Open daily 8:30am-12:30pm, 1:30-2:30pm, 6-7pm. MC/V.

▐ PRACTICAL INFORMATION

Tourist Office: Pl. du 18 Juin (☎04 68 82 15 47; www.collioure.com). From the train station, walk downhill on av. Aristide Maillol to pl. du Maréchal Leclerc. Continue along the canal, then take a left at pl. du 18 Juin. From the Christ bus stop, walk downhill along rue de la République. After crossing the canal, turn right on av. Camille Pelletan and left at pl. du 18 Juin. Free maps and a guide (€5.50) to 1-7hr. regional hikes. Open July-Aug. daily 9am-8pm; Sept. and June M and Sa 9am-noon and 2-6pm, Tu-F 9am-noon and 2-7pm, Sa 9am-noon; Oct.-May M-Sa 9am-noon and 2-6pm.

Tours: Petit train, pl. du 8 Mai 1945 (☎04 68 98 02 06; www.petit-train-touristique. com), across from the post office. 45min. tour of the vineyards up to Fort St-Elme and Port-Vendres. Departures every hr. July-Aug. 10am-8pm; Sept.-Oct. and Apr.-June 10-11am and 2-6pm. €6.50, under 12 €4.50.

Laundromat: 28 rue de la République (☎04 68 98 04 17). Wash €4.20-8, dry €0.50 per 5min. Open daily 8am-9pm.

Police: Rue de la République (☎04 68 82 09 53).

Pharmacy: 7 rue de la République. Open M-F 9am-12:30pm and 3-7:30pm, Sa 9am-12:30pm.

Internet Access: Café Sola, 2 av. de la République (☎04 68 82 55 02). €5 per hr., €7 per 2hr. Free Wi-Fi with purchase of food or drink. Open daily 7am-2am.

Post Office: Pl. du 8 Mai 1945 (☎04 68 98 36 00). **ATM** and **currency exchange** available. Open M-F 9am-noon and 1:30-5pm, Sa 9am-noon. **Postal Code:** 66190.

■ ACCOMMODATIONS

Collioure fills its hotels and beaches to the brim during July and August; the cheapest rooms are €30-40. The best choice is to daytrip from Perpignan.

Hôtel Le St-Pierre, 16 av. du Général de Gaulle (☎04 68 82 19 50; hotel.saint-pierre@wanadoo.fr). From the train station, follow av. Aristide Maillol to pl. du Maréchal Leclerc and turn right onto the bridge. At the rotary, take a left onto av. du Général de Gaulle. Some rooms with balconies and A/C. Breakfast €5.50. Doubles with sink and toilet or shower €40, with toilet and shower €48-56; triples €50; quints €86. AmEx/MC/V. ❸

Chambres, 20 rue Pasteur (☎04 68 82 15 31), in the *centre-ville*. Essentially a *gîte*. Rooms arranged around a staircase; all with double beds and baths. Singles €32; doubles €40, with shower €43, with bath €45; triples and quads €65-72. Cash only. ❷

◪ FOOD

Local produce is sold at a market centered on **place du Maréchal Leclerc** and along the canal toward the Château Royal. (Open W and Su 9am-1pm.) Touristy *crêperies*, pizzerias, and cafes crowd **rue Saint-Vincent** near the port. There's a **Shopi** supermarket at 16 av. de la République. (☎04 68 82 26 04. Open July-Aug. M-Sa 8:15am-8pm; Sept.-June M-Sa 8:15am-1pm and 2:30-7:30pm. MC/V.)

Al Cantou Pizza, 19 rue Pasteur (☎04 68 82 27 79). Delicious takeout wood-oven pizzas €5-10. Open M-W and F-Su 11am-2pm and 6-10pm. Cash only. ❷

La Cuisine Comptoir, 2 rue Colbert (☎04 68 81 14 40). Delicious combinations to go. Cumin-spiced chickpeas and cold basil-chicken salad can contribute to an alfresco meal. Tapas by weight; a selection of 3-4 €15-20. Open daily 11am-6pm. MC/V. ❸

◉ ✾ SIGHTS AND FESTIVALS

In mid-August, the streets of Collioure fill with traditional dance and music for the **Festival de Saint-Vincent.** Midway through the folklore festival, a *corrida* (bullfight) at the arena is followed by a fireworks display over the sea. Every Friday at 9:30pm in July and August, Collioure rocks to the sounds of **Vendredis du Jazz.** Jazz concerts take place in the castle and throughout the streets near the harbor. Contact the tourist office for all festival info.

ÉGLISE NOTRE DAME DES ANGES. This architectural wonder, whose foundations lie deep in the Mediterranean, includes richly decorated side chapels and a monumental Baroque main altar. *(Open daily 9am-noon and 2-6pm. Free.)*

CHÂTEAU ROYAL. Extending from pl. du 8 Mai 1945 to the port, the hulking white stone Château Royal first sheltered the Majorcan kings in the 13th century and was later fortified by both French and Spanish kings during unending border wars. Every architectural element—from the shape of the towers to the design of the ramparts—was designed to guarantee the utmost protection. The château is worth a visit for its spooky underground tunnels and spectacular view of the harbor. In summer, the main courtyard hosts plays and occasional dance performances. *(☎04 68 82 06 43; www.cg66.fr. Open daily July-Aug. 10am-7pm; Sept. and June 10am-6pm; Oct.-May 9am-5pm. 1hr. tours in French available with reservation. €4, students and ages 12-18 €2, under 12 free.)*

CHEMIN DU FAUVISME. This trail retraces the steps of Matisse and Dérain. Masterpiece reproductions are displayed exactly where they were originally painted. The *chemin* begins and ends in front of the tourist office, where the staff distributes free maps and sells a catalogue with detailed descriptions and images of every stop. *(Guided tours available in French July-Aug. Th 3pm. €5.50.)*

LES ANCHOIS ROQUE. Stop by this store for a taste of the harbor. Visitors watch anchovies being prepared and taste a series of the tiny fish preserved in vinegar and flavored with Catalan sauce and Provençal herbs. *(17 route d'Argelès, on the corner of av. du Général de Gaulle. ☎04 68 82 04 99. Store open M-F 8am-7pm, Sa-Su 8am-noon and 2-7pm. Anchovies €8.90 per 350g. Free visit and dégustation for groups.)*

◖ OUTDOOR ACTIVITIES

The **Centre International de Plongée,** 15 rue de la Tour d'Auvergne, offers scuba lessons and rents underwater equipment. *(☎04 68 82 07 16; www.cip-collioure. com. Beginners over age 7 €39 for the 1st dive and lesson; 2nd lesson in ocean €49; 2 lessons €79. 8-session course July-Aug. €295; over 11 only. €25 per dive with scuba card, €35 per dive with scuba card and guide. Snorkeling €23. Open July-Sept. M-Sa 10am-noon and 3-6pm, Su 10:30am-noon and 5:30-7pm; Oct.- Dec. and Apr.-June M-Sa 10am-noon and 3-6pm. MC/V.)*

MILLAU ☎05 65

In a small valley between the Tarn and Dourbie Rivers, Millau (mee-yoh; pop. 25,000) originally put itself on the map as a Roman industrial center acclaimed for its sturdy red pottery. Several centuries later, the town shifted its focus to fine leather production. Today, it continues to export handmade gloves to elegant shops in Paris and New York City. In summer months, the town becomes a vacation haven. Visitors come mainly for hiking trails, mountain sports, spectacular views, and the newly built tallest bridge in the world.

◰ TRANSPORTATION

Trains: In the *centre-ville* (☎05 65 60 34 02). Open M-F 5:30am-8:55pm, Sa 5:45am-8:55pm, Su 6:10am-9:15pm. To **Béziers** (2hr., 3 per day, €17), **Montpellier** (2-3hr., 3 per day, €22-24), and **Paris** (9hr., 1-2 per day, €64). SNCF and La Populaire (☎05 65 61 01 01) connect to **Montpellier** (2hr., 5-8 per day, €16-18). SA Verdie Bel (☎05 62 18 84 54) runs to **Toulouse** (4hr., M-Sa 7am, €26). Info desk (☎05 65 59 89 33) open M-W and F 9am-noon and 2-6:30pm, Th 9am-6:30pm, Sa 9am-noon.

Taxis: Laveissière Roger, 610 rue de Naulas (☎06 85 74 05 07).

Car Rental: Europcar, 3 pl. Frédéric Bompaire (☎05 65 59 19 19; www.europcar.fr). From €274 per week, €727 per month; discount for online booking. 21+. Open M-F 8:30am-noon and 2:30-7pm, Sa 9am-noon. AmEx/MC/V.

✦ ▣ ORIENTATION AND PRACTICAL INFORMATION

To get to the *centre-ville*, take a right out of the train station; after the station parking lot, you will be on rue Georges Pompidou. After one block, turn left on rue du Barry, which becomes rue Droite at the *vieille ville*.

Tourist Office: 1 pl. du Beffroi (☎05 65 60 02 42; www.ot-millau.fr). Provides free city maps, hotel listings, regional maps (€9), and guides with hiking routes and durations (€8). Open July-Aug. M-Sa 9am-7pm, Su 9:30am-4pm; Sept.-June M-F 9am-12:30pm and 2-6:30pm, Sa 9am-6:30pm, Su 9:30am-4pm.

Laundromat: 12 av. Gambetta. Wash €3.20-6.50, dry €0.50 per 5min. Detergent €0.50. Open daily 7am-10pm; last wash 9pm.

Police: 14 rue de la Condamine (☎05 65 61 23 00).

Hospital: 265 bd. Achille Souques (info ☎05 65 59 30 00, emergency 59 31 35.)

Internet Access: Cyber Espace, 2 rue du Barry (☎05 65 59 83 30), en route to the tourist office from the station. €3 per hr. Open M 3-7pm, Tu-Sa 10am-noon and 2-7pm.

Post Office: 12 av. Alfred Merle (☎05 65 59 20 50). **Currency exchange, Western Union,** and **ATMs** available. Open M-F 8:30am-6:30pm, Sa 8:30am-noon. **Postal Code:** 12100.

LANGUEDOC-ROUSSILLON

ACCOMMODATIONS AND CAMPING

Hôtel du Commerce, 8 pl. de Mandarous (☎05 65 60 00 56; fax 60 96 50). From the train station, walk down av. de Alfred Merle and turn right on av. de la République; the hotel is at the end of the street on the 3rd fl. Clean rooms with pearl-white baths, some with mountain views. Breakfast €5. Reception M-F 7am-11pm, Sa-Su 8am-11pm. Reserve at least 1 week in advance. Singles and doubles €27, with toilet €29, with shower €39, with bath €41; triples €52-55; quads €64. Extra bed €10. MC/V. ❷

Hôtel de la Capelle, 7 pl. de la Capelle (☎05 65 60 14 72; www.hotel-millau-capelle. com). From the station, take av. Alfred Merle and turn right onto rue de la République. At pl. du Mandarous, veer left and walk along bd. de Bonald into the parking lot; the hotel is on the far left. A long corridor opens onto plain, sizable rooms with communal bathrooms and mountain views. Breakfast €6. Doubles €30, with bath €39, with bath and toilet €45-48; triples €65-68. AmEx/MC/V. ❷

Gîte de la Maladrerie, rue la Maladerie, with the main office at 25 av. Charles de Gaulle (☎05 65 60 41 84, reservations 61 06 57). If possible, stop at the tourist office for a map; the *gîte* is 30min. from the *centre-ville.* From the station, go down av. Alfred Merle and take the 1st right onto rue d'Alsace-Lorraine. Continue through the traffic circle and through pl. des Martyrs de la Résistance, eventually crossing Pont Lerouge. Follow the road, which turns into av. du Pont Lerouge, to the traffic circle, then turn left onto av. du Languedoc. At the next traffic circle, make a slight left onto av. Louis Balsan. The *gîte* is to the left of the fork. Those willing to make the long trek will be rewarded with homey and clean 2- to 8-bed rooms with valley views. Kitchen. Meals served for groups only. Linen €2. McDonald's around the corner with free Wi-Fi. Reception 6-9pm. Dorms 1st night €14, €13 thereafter. Cash only. ❶

Camping Les Rivages, av. de l'Aigoual (☎05 65 61 01 07; www.campinglesrivages. com), 25min. from the *centre-ville.* Take av. Gambetta to the Pont du Cureplat, then follow the massive billboard signs. The most luxurious of 7 campgrounds across the Tarn River. Amenities include badminton courts, ping-pong tables, 2 pools, tennis courts, squash courts, volleyball net, basketball court, playground, and hot tub. 2-night min. stay for bungalows. Reception July-Aug. 8am-9pm; Sept. and May-June 8am-noon and 2-7pm. Gates closed 11pm-8am. Reserve 2 months ahead for RVs July-Aug. Open from Apr. to mid-Oct. July-Aug. 2 people and tent €27; RV sites or 4-person bungalow €50-70. Sept.-Oct. and Apr.-June 2 people and tent €21; RV sites or 4-person bungalow €39-56. AmEx/MC/V, except for bungalows. ❷

🔋 FOOD

There is a **Super U** on av. du Pont Lerouge, between the train station and the Gîte de la Maladrerie (☎05 65 60 63 69; open July-Aug. M-F 8:30am-8:30pm, Sa 8:30am-8pm, Su 8:30am-1:30pm; Sept-June M-Sa 8:30am-8pm, Su 8:30am-1:30pm; AmEx/MC/V), and the *centre-ville* is dotted with supermarkets. At **place Foche, place Emma Calvé**, and **place des Halles**, markets provide fresh meat and vegetables. (Open W and F 7am-noon.) Selling over 100 types of cheese, **Le Buron**, 18 rue Droite, is a *fromage*-lover's gold mine, specializing in regional Roquefort. (☎05 65 60 39 88. Open M 9am-noon and 3-7pm, Tu-Sa 8am-12:30pm and 3-7:30pm. AmEx/MC/V.) More expensive than those along the coast, Millau's gourmet restaurants offer food produced with fresh local ingredients and an abundance of Roquefort cheese. In the heart of the *vieille ville*, **boulevard** and **rue de la Capelle** have a mixture of sit-down restaurants and cheap pizzerias.

La Casse Croute, pl. Emma Cave (☎05 65 59 45 36), next to the tourist office. Stands out from other sandwich shops for its excellent bread and creative combinations. Try La Campagnarde *tartine* (€3.30), a large piece of country bread toasted and covered with goat cheese, marinated eggplant, honey, and toasted almonds. Sandwiches €3.30-3.70, with a drink and pastry €5.80-6.50. Open daily 9am-7pm. Cash only. ❶

Le Chien à la Fenêtre, 10 rue Peyrollerie (☎05 65 60 49 22). Serves elaborate *galettes* (€3-9) with generous portions of ingredients like salmon, cheese, and duck. Dessert *crêpes* (€2.70-5.90) made with any combination of bananas, chocolate, coconut, or ice cream—and more. The open cooking space keeps you close to the kitchen's matron-in-command, who doles out peppery tips on how to avoid restaurant faux pas. Salads €8.50-9. Open M 7-10pm, Tu-Sa noon-2pm and 7-10pm. MC/V. ❷

Au Bec Fin, 20-22 rue de la Capelle (☎05 65 60 63 04). Nestled in a nook of Millau's *vieille ville*, this restaurant prepares seafood platters on a counter made out of wine barrels. Salads €7.50-13. *Menu* €13-18. Open July-Sept. daily noon-2pm and 7-9:30pm; Oct.-June M-Tu and F-Su noon-2pm and 7-9:30pm. AmEx/MC/V. ❸

🔋 SIGHTS

Millau's most remarkable draw is the outdoor activities (opposite page) it offers—parachuting in the shadow of the world's tallest bridge and among the ancient Gorges of Tarn is a unique experience. Those less inclined to explore the skies can pass the time in Millau's museums.

GRAUFESENQUE. Hard-core history buffs will love the Roman pottery workshops at this archaeological site. In the first century BC, the red ceramic bowls and vases produced here were exported from England to India. Remains of the pots have been uncovered the world over and are used to date the conquests of the Roman army. For those not so in love with clay, this site isn't worth the 45min. trek. *(On route Montpellier, 3km from the city. Follow the directions to the Gîte de la Maladrerie, but instead of veering left toward the gîte, follow the sign to Graufesenque for 15min. Use caution; though traffic is not heavy, the road has no sidewalk. ☎05 65 60 11 37. Open Tu-Su July-Aug. 10am-12:30pm and 2:30-7pm; Sept. and May-June 10am-noon and 2-6pm; Oct.-Apr. 10am-noon and 2-5pm. €4, ages 18-25 €2.70, under 18 free. Combined ticket to the Graufesenque and the Musée de Millau €6.)*

MUSÉE DE MILLAU. This museum displays local prehistoric artifacts and boasts a thorough exhibit on the process of making leather gloves. Animal lovers beware—the film is graphic. *(Pl. Maréchal Foch. ☎05 65 59 01 08. Open daily July-Aug. 10am-6pm; Sept.-June 10am-noon and 2-6pm. €5, under 25 free. Combined ticket to the Graufesenque and the Musée de Millau €6.)*

BELFRY. The ancient tower of the Beffroi rises above the *vieille ville*. Built as a medieval dungeon in the 12th century, the belfry remained an active prison until just after the French Revolution. Today, visitors can wander through the small assortment of ancient jail cells and read the French commentary. *(Rue Droite. ☎ 05 65 59 01 08. Open June-Sept. daily 10am-noon and 2-6pm. €2.70.)*

⚎ ⚏ NIGHTLIFE AND FESTIVALS

Bustling with tourists during the day, Millau does not offer much nightlife. Several cafe-bars sprinkled at the ends of **boulevard de Bonald** serve drinks in a calm, subdued atmosphere and cater to an older crowd.

Millau en Jazz (☎ 05 65 60 82 47; www.millauenjazz.net), 8 days in mid-July. Squares, streets, and concert halls flow with music. Pick up programs and tickets for big names (€17-20, 3 shows for €45) at the tourist office.

Mondial Pétanque (☎ 05 65 61 18 45; http://millau.petanque.mond.free.fr), 6 days in mid-Aug. Thousands of *pétanque* players compete in the annual tournament. International *boule* championship free to viewers.

◣ OUTDOOR ACTIVITIES

The town's greatest asset is the beautiful **Parc Naturel Régional des Grands Causses**, which stretches throughout the region. Primitive humans first discovered this sunbathed region over 200,000 years ago and left behind various carved statues and cave paintings. Today, the 327,070-hectare park offers excellent mountain trails as well as an unlimited number of sporting activities. The tourist office sells **hiking** maps (€9) and guides (€8) as well as **mountain-biking** maps. The **park office,** 71 bd. de l'Ayrolle, can answer questions; it is particularly useful for those setting off on long hikes. (☎ 05 65 61 35 50. Open M-F May-Sept. 9am-noon and 2-6pm; Oct.-Apr. 9am-noon and 2-5pm.) For a fairly easy day hike from Millau (3hr., including walk to trailhead), stop by the tourist office for the *Corniches du Cade Discovery Footpath* guide (€8; in English and French). The guide gives directions for the walk and a catalogue of the flora along the way.

Millau is full of companies advertising every sporting activity imaginable. Most companies don't provide transport; it's best to have access to a car.

Organisation Roc et Canyon, 55 av. Jean Jaurès (☎ 05 65 61 17 77; www.roc-et-canyon.com). Provides transportation (€3-5) to their mountain sites. Paintball €27 per person. Rafting €31, €29 per person in a group. Canoe rental €14-29. Mountain-bike rentals €24 per day. Mountain-biking excursions €31 per day. 50m bungee jump €34. Underground cave climb €33. Rock climbing €29. Reservations recommended. Base near campsites on route de Nant open daily from mid-June to Sept. 9am-7pm. Office at av. Jean Jaurès open from Oct. to mid-June 9am-noon and 2-5pm. Cash only.

Horizon Millau Vol Libre, 6 pl. Lucién Grégoire (☎ 05 65 59 78 60; www.horizon-millau.com), just off pl. Maréchal Foch. Offers the same activities but specializes in hang gliding (€55-130, 5-session initiation course €325). Reserve days ahead. Open daily 10am-noon and 2-6pm. Cash only.

MONTPELLIER   ☎ 04 67

It's hard to find locals who were born in Montpellier (mahn-pehl-yay; pop. 225,000). A college town and cultural center, Languedoc-Roussillon's capital seduces visitors and then compels them to stay. Reputed to be the most light-hearted place in the south, Montpellier prides itself on a diverse population of partygoers and some of the best gay nightlife in France. Amateur theatrical and musical performances sprout up in pl. de la Comédie, academics browse trendy bookstores, and tourists shop for funky flair in hip boutiques.

▶ TRANSPORTATION

Flights: Aéroport Montpellier Méditerranée (MPL; ☎04 67 20 85 00; www.montpel-lier.aeroport.fr), in nearby Mauguio. **Air France** (☎08 20 82 08 20; www.airfrance.fr) has an info office outside the Polygone and flies to **Paris** 10 times per day. La Navette Aéroport **shuttles** between the airport and the tramway stop at pl. de l'Europe (15min., 10 per day 5:45am-8:15pm, €4.90-5.40). Contact Hérault Transport (☎08 25 34 01 34) or visit the airport website for a bus schedule.

Trains: Pl. Auguste Gibert. Office open M 5am-9pm, Tu-Th 6am-9pm, F 6am-9:30pm, Sa 6:15am-9pm, Su 6:30am-9:45pm. To: **Marseille** (2-3½hr., 10 per day, €24-28); **Nice** (4hr., 2 per day, €40-60); **Paris** (3hr., 10 per day, €66-130); **Perpignan** (2hr., 15 per day, €21-26); **Toulouse** (2½hr., 10 per day, €30-34).

Buses: La Populaire, 20 rue du Grand St-Jean (☎04 67 58 75 95; www.cars-la-popu-laire.com). Exit the train station and turn left along the tram tracks; continue until you see the depot on your right. Ticket office open M-Sa 9am-noon and 2:30-6:30pm. To **Millau** (2hr.; M-Sa 6 per day 6:20am-6:30pm, Su 11:05am, 6:30pm; €18).

Public Transportation: TAM, 6 rue Jules Ferry (☎04 67 22 87 87; www.tam-way.com). Open M-Sa 7am-7pm. Runs local **buses** and **trams** connecting the *centre-ville* to the outskirts. Buses run 6:30am-9pm; convenient trams run every 6-7min. 5am-1am. 1hr. tickets for trams and buses €1.30; day pass €3.20; weekly pass €13, students €8.30. Buy bus tickets from the driver and tram tickets from automated dispensers at the train stops. L'Amigo line connects the train station to 12 popular nightclubs on the outskirts of town. Buses leave the station Th-Sa midnight, 1am; return 2:30, 3:30, 5am.

Taxis: TRAM (☎04 67 58 10 10), at the train station. €1.80 base; €1.40 per km during the day, €2.10 at night. €20-25 from station to airport. 24hr.

Car Rental: Ada, pl. Jules Ferry (☎04 67 92 78 77), at the train station. Walk through to platform A and turn right. Continue along the platform until you see a squat white building on the right. From €89 and 100km per day, €229 and 500km per 5 days. Insurance included. 21+; must have had license for 1 year. Open M-Tu and Th-F 8am-1pm and 2-7pm, W and Sa 9am-1pm and 2-7pm. AmEx/MC/V. **Hertz, Avis, Europcar,** and **National** also share this location.

Bike Rental: TAM Vélo, 27 rue Maguelone (☎04 67 22 87 82). €2 per day; €150 and ID deposit. Open M-Sa 9am-7pm, Su 9am-12:30pm and 2-7pm. MC/V.

✦ 🛈 ORIENTATION AND PRACTICAL INFORMATION

Across from the train station, rue Maguelone leads to **place de la Comédie,** the city's lively central square; the tourist office is to the right, at the entrance to esplanade Charles de Gaulle. The *vieille ville* is bounded by bd. Pasteur and bd. Louis Blanc to the north, esplanade Charles de Gaulle and bd. Victor Hugo to the east, and bd. Jeu de Paume to the west. From pl. de la Comédie, rue de la Loge rises to **place Jean Jaurès,** the center of the *vieille ville*.

Tourist Office: 30 allée Jean de Lattre de Tassigny (☎04 67 60 60 60; www.ot-montpel-lier.fr). Free maps and same-night hotel reservation service. Distributes *Sortir à Mont-pellier* and *L'INDIC*, a student guide published in Sept. Wheelchair-accessible. Open July-Sept. M-F 9am-7:30pm, Sa 9:30am-6pm, Su 9:30am-1pm and 2:30-6pm; Oct.-June M-F 9am-6:30pm, Sa 10am-6pm, Su 10am-1pm and 2-5pm.

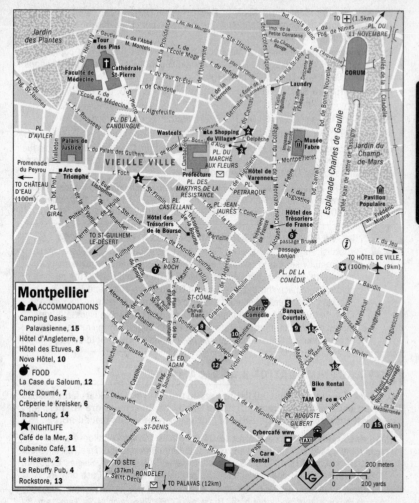

Montpellier

🔺🏠 ACCOMMODATIONS

Camping Oasis
  Palavasienne, **15**
Hôtel d'Angleterre, **9**
Hôtel des Etuves, **8**
Nova Hôtel, **10**

🍎 FOOD

La Case du Saloum, **12**
Chez Doumé, **7**
Crêperie le Kreisker, **6**
Thanh-Long, **14**

⭐ NIGHTLIFE

Café de la Mer, **3**
Cubanito Café, **11**
Le Heaven, **2**
Le Rebuffy Pub, **4**
Rockstore, **13**

Tours: 2hr. city tours in English July-Sept. Sa; times vary, contact tourist office. Tours in French depart daily 5pm; July-Aug. themed tours of the medical school, noted hotels, or Rabelais-related monuments depart at 10am. City tours €6.50, students €5.50; themed tours €6.50-10. A **petit train** (☎06 29 51 27 37) tour of the *vieille ville* leaves from pl. de la Comédie, near the Gaumont movie theater. June-Aug. every 30min. 11am-noon and 2-7pm; Sept. and Apr.-May every 30min. 11am-noon and 2-6pm; Oct.-Mar. W and Sa-Su 11am, 12, 2, 3, 4pm. €6, under 12 €3.

Budget Travel: Wasteels, 1 rue Cambacérès (☎04 67 66 45 79; www.wasteels.fr). Offers good plane, train, and bus ticket prices. Open M-F 9:30am-12:30pm and 2-6pm.

Currency Exchange: Banque Courtois, pl. de la Comédie (☎04 67 06 26 16). €6 commission. 1.2% commission on traveler's checks over €700; €8 commission if less. Open M-F 9:30am-noon and 1:45-5pm.

English-Language Bookstore: Book In Bar, 8 rue du Bras de Fer (☎04 67 66 22 90). Used books downstairs. Open Aug. Tu-Sa 10am-7pm; Sept.-July M 1-7pm, Tu-Sa 10am-7pm. AmEx/MC/V.

GLBT Resources: Le Shopping du Village, 3 rue Fournarié, holds current copies of *IB News* and other regional and national gay magazines with info on restaurants, shops, and clubs. Open M 3-7pm, Tu-Sa noon-7pm.

Laundromat: Lavo Sud, 70 rue de l'Aiguillerie. Wash €3-6.80, dry €0.50 per 5min. Open daily 7am-9pm.

Police: Pl. de la Comédie (☎04 99 74 26 74), next to the tourist office.

Hospital: 371 av. du Doyen Gaston Giraud (☎04 67 33 67 33).

Internet Access: Mostly located on or around rue de Verdun. **Cybercafé www,** 12 bis rue Jules Ferry (☎04 67 06 59 52), across from the train station. €2 per hr. Fax, photocopier, and scanner. Open M-Sa 10am-10pm.

Post Office: Pl. Rondelet (☎04 67 34 50 00). **Currency exchange** and **Western Union** available. Branch at pl. du Marché aux Fleurs (☎04 67 60 03 67). Both open M-F 8:30am-6:30pm, Sa 8:30am-noon. **Poste Restante:** 34035. **Postal Code:** 34000.

RE-FRÊCHE-ING LANGUEDOC-ROUSSILLON. In 2004, the socialist mayor of Montpellier, Georges Frêche, won the regional elections. He promptly set out to revamp Languedoc-Roussillon and its institutions. To begin with, Frêche commissioned a new flag in red and yellow (the region's colors) to replace the old one bearing Languedoc's cross and Roussillon's "Senyera" flag. Frêche also tried to create further unity by reviving the region's ninth-century name, "Septimanie." The name didn't stick, but Frêche's efforts moved Montpellier from the 25th- to the eighth-largest city in France, a huge achievement for Languedoc-Roussillon—or whatever you want to call it.

 ACCOMMODATIONS AND CAMPING

Except for the campground, all listings are in the *centre-ville*. Search **rue Aristide Olivier, rue du Général Campredon** (off cours Gambetta and rue André Michel), and **rue Auguste Broussonnet** (off pl. Albert I) for other reasonably priced hotels.

Hôtel des Étuves, 24 rue des Étuves (☎04 67 60 78 19; www.hoteldesetuves.fr). 13 clean rooms, each with toilet and shower, 7 with bath. Breakfast €5. Free Wi-Fi. Reception M-Sa 6:30am-11pm, Su 6:30am-noon. Reserve 1 week ahead. Singles €23, with TV €25, with bath €45; doubles with TV €37, with TV and bath €45. Cash only. ❷

Nova Hôtel, 8 rue Richelieu (☎04 67 60 79 85; hotelnova@free.fr). Stone staircase leads to large rooms in this family-run hotel. Breakfast €4.60. Reception M-Sa 7am-1am, Su 7am-11am and 7pm-1am. Reservations recommended in summer. Singles €21, with shower €27, with toilet and TV €39-44; doubles €24/27-34/39-44; triples €40-56; quads €63. 5% discount with *Let's Go.* AmEx/MC/V. ❶

Hôtel d'Angleterre, 7 rue Maguelone (☎04 67 58 59 50; www.hotel-d-angleterre.com), off pl. de la Comédie. Large rooms with queen beds, cable TVs, and 24hr. bar. Elevator. Breakfast €5.50. Reception 24hr. Singles and doubles with shower €45, with toilet €50; triples and quads €53-62. 10% discount with *Let's Go.* AmEx/MC/V. ❹

Camping Oasis Palavasienne, route de Palavas (☎04 67 15 11 61; www.oasis-palavasienne.com), in Lattes. From the train station, take tram #2 (dir.: St-Jean de Vedas) to St-Cléophas. Transfer to bus #32 and get off at Oasis Palavasienne. At the traffic circle, turn left and walk under the bridge. The campground is 50m on the right (40min.). 4-star site has sauna, gym, bar, and restaurant overlooking a beautiful swimming pool.

Full of students in summer. Free shuttle to nearby beaches 9:30am, 2:30pm. Reception July-Aug. M-F 8:30am-12:30pm and 2-7:30pm, Sa-Su 8:15am-7:30pm; Sept.-June M-F 8:30am-12:30pm and 2-6pm, Sa-Su 8:15am-7:30pm. From mid-July to mid-Aug 2 people €28; extra person €5. From mid-Aug. to Sept. and from early to mid-July 2 people €22; extra person 4. May-June 2 people €16; extra person €3. AmEx/MC/V. ❷

🗭 FOOD

Montpellier has many reasonably priced restaurants. Standard French cuisine dominates the *vieille ville*. Find great bargains near **rue des Écoles Laïques**, which has Greek, Egyptian, Moroccan, and Lebanese choices. The cheapest sandwich shops cluster on **rue Maguelone** and the streets that radiate into **place de la Comédie.** Morning markets set up daily at **Les Halles Castellane,** on rue de la Loge, and at **Plan Cabanes,** on cours Gambetta. The **INNO** supermarket, in the basement of the Polygone commercial center, past the tourist office from pl. de la Comédie, has some bargains. (Open M-Sa 8:30am-8:30pm. AmEx/MC/V.) If you're looking for something more upscale, wander the streets around the **Église Saint-Roch,** where the offerings are plentiful.

Crêperie le Kreisker, 3 passage Bruyas (☎04 67 60 82 50). Over 50 savory *crêpes* (€2-6.80), topped with ingredients like buttered snails, mushrooms, artichokes, and seafood. Speedy staff also dishes out salads (€6.20-7.10), 30 types of dessert *crêpes* (€1.90-5.70), and a stunning array of ice-cream flavors. Open M-Tu 11:30am-2:30pm and 6:30-11pm, W-Sa 11:30am-3pm and 6:30-11pm. AmEx/MC/V. ❷

La Case du Saloum, 18 rue Diderot (☎04 67 02 88 94). Hip and unassuming. Authentic Senegalese dishes, such as a delicious veal with peanut sauce (€7.80) or *gambas* braised in coconut milk (€8.80). Charming courtyard. Ginger punch €3. *Plats* €8. Open M-F 11am-3pm and 7:30-midnight, Sa 7:30pm-midnight. AmEx/MC/V. ❷

Chez Doumé, 5 rue des Teissiers (☎04 67 60 48 76), near Église St-Roch. Crimson booths, posters, and red-checkered tablecloths. Typical French fare. *Plats* €12-14. *Menus* €12-15. Open M-F noon-2pm and 7:30-11pm, Sa 7:30-11pm. MC/V. ❸

Thanh-Long, 3 rue Durand (☎04 67 58 13 88). Excellent Vietnamese food. Vegetarian options. *Plat* with rice and wine €8. Open daily noon-2pm and 7:30-10pm. Takeout M noon-10pm, Tu-Su 10am-10pm. AmEx/MC/V. ❷

🗭 SIGHTS

🖾**MUSÉE FABRE.** Built on a site where Molière performed from 1654 to 1655, this beautifully renovated museum holds one of the largest collections of fine art outside of Paris. Focusing on 17th- to 19th-century painting, the museum features works by bigwigs like Courbet, Ingres, Poussin, and Delacroix. *(39 bd. des Bonnes Nouvelles.* ☎*04 67 14 83 00. Open Tu, Th-F, Su 10am-6pm, W 1-9pm, Sa 11am-6pm. €6, with temporary exhibition €7; students €4/5.)*

HÔTELS PARTICULIERS. The secret courtyards and intricate staircases of the 17th- and 18th-century *hôtels particuliers* (mansions) hide behind grandiose oak doors. **Hôtel de Varennes,** once Montpellier's treasury, holds two small, free museums. The **Musée du Vieux Montpellier,** on the first floor, traces Montpellier's history through furniture, maps, ceramics, and other artifacts. *(2 pl. Petrarque.* ☎*04 67 66 02 94. Open Tu-Sa 9:30am-noon and 1:30-5pm.)* The adorable second-floor **Musée Fougau** reconstructs 19th-century lifestyles in Montpellier. *(Open W-Th 3-6pm.)* The **Hôtel des Trésoriers de France** houses the **Musée Languedocien,** an archaeological museum that contains everything from medieval artwork to 18th-century perfume bottles. *(7 rue Jacques Coeur.* ☎*04 67 52 93 03. Open M-Sa from mid-June to mid-Sept. 3-6pm; from Sept. to mid-June 2:30-5:30pm. €6, students €3.)* Visit the

Hôtel des Trésoriers de la Bourse, 4 rue des Trésoriers de la Bourse, for its 16th-century architecture. The tourist office has a list of the city's best *hôtels* in its *Montpellier Discovery Guide,* which is available in English.

OTHER SIGHTS. Montpellier's pedestrian streets, bookstores, and sprawling **place de la Comédie** provide some of the city's best entertainment. The **Pavillon Populaire,** near the esplanade Charles de Gaulle, houses free rotating photography exhibitions. (*☎04 67 66 13 46. Open Tu-Su 11am-7pm.)* The **promenade du Peyrou** links the **Arc de Triomphe**—erected in 1691 to honor Louis XIV—to the **Château d'Eau,** the arched terminal of an aqueduct. Though locals claim it dates back to antiquity, it only just turned 500; walk to the top for a view over the western suburbs of Montpellier. **Boulevard Henri IV** leads to the **Jardin des Plantes,** France's first botanical garden. (*☎04 67 63 43 22. Open Tu-Su June-Sept. noon-8pm; Oct.-Mar. noon-6pm. Free.)* Adjacent to the Jardin is Montpellier's **École de Medicine,** one of the oldest facilities of medicine in the Western world; it is housed in a fortress-like complex. Pass by, if only to muse what attending class in a castle is like.

🎵 🎭 ENTERTAINMENT AND FESTIVALS

The **Corum,** on esplanade Charles de Gaulle, and **Opéra Comédie,** 11 bd. Victor Hugo, host theatrical performances and concerts. (*☎04 67 60 19 99;* www.orchestre-montpellier.com and www.opera-montpellier.com. Philharmonic orchestra €17-40, under 27 €14-32. Operas and plays €10-60/8-45. Corum office open M-F 8am-7pm. Opera ticket office open M 2-6pm, Tu-F noon-6pm.)

Printemps des Comédiens (www.printempsdescomediens.com), in June. Open-air theatrical, circus, and dance performances. Contact the Opéra Comédie (above). Tickets €5-28, under 25 and seniors €6-18.

Festival International Montpellier Danse (*☎04 67 60 83 60, reservations 0800 60 07 40;* www.montpellierdanse.com), from late June to early July. Performances, workshops, and films on local stages and screens. Tickets €8-45.

Festival de Radio France et de Montpellier (*☎04 67 02 02 01;* www.festivalradiofrancemontpellier.com), from mid- to late July. Over 100 musical performances. Most free; others €30-50, students and seniors €15-40.

Festival International du Cinéma Méditerranéen (*☎04 99 13 73 73;* www.cinemed.tm.fr). Oct.'s main event for more than 2 decades. Featuring over 250 films and related events, this festival draws close to 100,000 fans.

🎶 NIGHTLIFE

The most animated bars are scattered along **place Jean-Jaurès.** At sundown, **rue de la Loge** fills with vendors, musicians, and stilt-walkers. The best discos, including **La Villa Rouge,** route de Palavas, in Lattes (*☎04 67 06 50 54;* open summer W-Su 11pm-6am; winter Th-Su 11pm-5am), lie on the outskirts of town; take L'Amigo buses (see **Transportation** p. 654) from the train station to their doorsteps. Male-dominated gay nightlife—one of the city's claims to fame—is centered on **place du Marché aux Fleurs** and in the *vieille ville.* There are few lesbian bars, but women are not excluded from any of the bars listed here

Le Rebuffy Pub, 2 pl. Rebuffy (*☎04 67 66 32 76).* Packed with locals and international students. Cheerful pub plastered to the ceiling with posters. Yearly film festival, rotating art exhibits, and board games. Beer €2.60-5.90. Open in summer M-F 9am-2am, Sa 11am-2am, Su 10pm-2am; in winter M-Sa 11am-1am, Su 10pm-1am. MC/V over €8.

Café de la Mer, 5 pl. du Marché aux Fleurs (*☎04 67 60 79 65).* Maritime-themed cafe-bar. The gay hub of Montpellier offers afternoon coffee (€1.50-2.50) as well as pre-party beer (€2.60). Open to all, but a majority of the clientele is male. Open in summer M-Sa 8am-2am, Su 3pm-2am; in winter M-Sa 8am-1am, Su 4pm-1am. MC/V over €10.

Le Heaven, 1 rue Delpech (☎04 67 60 44 18). Techno and glittering disco balls. A perfect dance floor for men to meet men; women are welcome, but few come. Specifically welcomes lesbians every other Tu night. Beer €3-5, €15-24 for a pitcher. Liquor €6. Piano bar M 11pm. Open daily 8pm-2am. Cash only.

Rockstore, 20 rue de Verdun (☎04 67 06 80 00). Model 1950s car sticking out of its facade. Young crowd bounces to pop-rock on the 1st fl. and gyrates to electro above. Grunge bar in the evening and mega-disco by night. Beer €3.80-6.50. Hard liquor €6.50. Live rock concerts (free-€25) Sept.-June 1-5 times per week. Bar open M-Sa July-Sept. 6:30pm-5am; Oct.-June 6pm-5am. Disco opens 11:30pm. AmEx/MC/V.

Cubanito Café, 13 rue de Verdun (☎04 67 92 65 82), near pl. de la Comédie. After 10pm, this revolution-themed bar overflows with 20-somethings who salsa to Latin beats (M and Su) or hip hop (Tu-Sa) while people watch from the terrace. Tapas served noon-9pm. Lunch *menu* with 4 tapas, a drink, and coffee €8.50. Pints €4.50-5.50. Mixed drinks €6.50. Open daily in summer noon-2am; in winter noon-1am. AmEx/MC/V.

◪ DAYTRIPS FROM MONTPELLIER

SAINT-GUILHEM-LE-DÉSERT

Hérault Transport (☎08 25 34 01 34) sends buses from the gare routière in Montpellier to Gignac, where you can switch buses to St-Guilhem (1hr., 2 per day, total €5.40). Stop by the gare routière for a schedule. Buses depart in the early afternoon and return in the late afternoon; exact times vary.

DON'T DESERT YOUR TICKET. If you take the bus from Montpellier to St-Guilhem-le-Désert, you'll have to transfer at Gignac. Keep your receipt for the first leg of the journey—it will save you €1.30 when you switch buses.

With picturesque streets along a dramatic gorge, St-Guilhem-le-Désert (sehn-geel-ehm-luh-day-zayr) has been popular among tourists since the 19th century. Contrary to its name, the village is far from a desert—it suffers from flooding by both water and people. When visitors arrive in summer, local craftsmen open their tiny boutiques, selling anything from pottery to jams, jewelry, and candles. Despite the tourist frenzy, this hamlet, with its hiking trails and lovely river, is a pleasant—and very romantic—daytrip. However, due to limited public transportation from Montpellier, car-less travelers must choose between a short afternoon trip or a longer overnight stay.

St-Guilhem's main attraction is the ninth-century **Abbaye de Gellone.** Founded by Charlemagne's cousin Guillaume, the abbey is a mix of Romanesque, Gothic, Baroque, and Classical architecture as well as a stop for pilgrims on their way to St-Jacques de Compostelle. Unfortunately, part of the abbey looks bare because Gellone's unique eight-gallery vaulted cloister was sold around 1850 for a mere US$4000; it's now on display at the Cloisters in New York City, after a stint as home decoration for American sculptor George Gray Barnard. (☎04 67 57 44 33. Open July-Aug. M-Sa 8am-noon and 2:30-6:10pm, Su 8:30-10:45am and 2:30-6:10pm; Sept.-June M-Sa 7:45-11:50am and 2-5:40pm, Su 8:30-10:45am and 2:30-5:45pm. Free.) Tour the huge chambers of St-Guilhem's caves at **Grottes de Clamouse,** 3km from St-Guilhem on the route de St-Guilhem-le-Désert, overgrown with stalactites and stalagmites. To get there, walk downhill from the tourist office and continue straight ahead; be cautious, as there is no sidewalk or shoulder on the side of the road (40min.). The visit includes a dramatic *son et lumière* (light show). Make sure to stop at the tourist office in the village for a €1.30 discount on the price of entry. The bus that goes from Gignac to St-Guilhem stops at the *grottes* as well. (☎04 67 57 71 05; www.clamouse.com. Open daily July-Aug. 10am-7pm; Sept. and June 10am-6pm; Oct. and Feb.-May 10am-5pm; Nov.-Jan. call ahead, as hours vary. 1hr. guided tour €8.50, students €7.20. Most tour guides speak some English.) For a day of swimming and picnicking, rent a canoe for the 12km descent to **Pont du Diable** (4-6hr.). **Rapido,** 2 route d'Aniane, on the way to the tourist office, rents kayaks and canoes and provides transportation for visitors willing to start at 10am. Call ahead to secure transport. Rental available at other times of the day for those with cars. (☎04 67 55 75 75. 2-person canoe €44. €2 discount with reservation. Open daily July-Aug. 10am-7pm; Sept. and May-June by reservation only. Cash only.)

From the bus stop in the parking lot, walk uphill to the **tourist office.** Staff provides free maps, a guide in English, and advice on hiking, including two 3hr. circuits beginning in town. **Tours** of the village and the abbey are available upon reservation. (☎04 67 57 44 33; www.saint-guilhem-le-desert.com. Tours open mainly to groups, €60 for up to 10 people. Open daily July-Aug. 9:30am-7pm; Sept. and Apr.-June 9:30am-1pm and 2-6pm; Oct.-Mar. 9:30am-1pm and 2-5pm.) There's an **ATM** in the parking lot on the other side of the main road. Make sure to withdraw enough cash; few shops in St-Guilhem take credit cards.

PROVENCE

While Paris has world-class paintings, it's Provence that inspired them. One of France's most diverse regions, Provence boasts ancient Roman ruins, luxurious hilltop castles, endless fields of lavender, and much more. Fierce mistral winds cut through olive groves in the north, while pink flamingoes, black bulls, and white horses gallop freely in the marshy Camargue to the south. With 2600 years of tumultuous history, Marseille is France's second largest city and an energetic melting pot of French, African, and Middle Eastern cultures. The former stomping ground of medieval popes, Avignon combines a fun student vibe with a lively arts scene and world-renowned theater festival. Throughout the Lubéron and the Vaucluse, tiny towns brim with local legends and bold character. The countryside might look familiar, given that masterpieces by Cézanne, Matisse, and Van Gogh—to name a few—have immortalized Provence's beauty. Come summertime, Parisians head to Provence to "escape" the city while foreigners come to see if there's any truth behind all the hype. What they find keeps visitors coming back year after year—a dip in the jewel-green sea, a stroll through earthy vineyards, and a taste of *la vie en rose*.

HIGHLIGHTS OF PROVENCE

PRETEND YOU'RE POPE in the Palais des Papes, the immense Gothic palace built by the French popes in Avignon (p. 681) during their 39-year boycott of Rome.

DO AS THE ROMANS DID and see a show at the Théâtre Antique in Orange (p. 687), home to one of the world's three remaining Roman stage walls.

FIND YOUR INNER VAN GOGH or your new favorite photographer in the artist haven of Arles (p. 683)—but hold on to your ears.

MARSEILLE   ☎ 04 91

Marseille (mahr-say; pop. 821,000) is much like the bouillabaisse soup for which it is famous: an array of ingredients and cultures contribute to the vibrant final product. A blend of color and commotion, the city buzzes with traffic, construction, and endless partying. Although Marseille inherits a typical French legacy—complete with Roman ruins, crumbling forts, and traditional 18th-century art workshops—a walk through its side streets is punctuated by the vibrant colors of West African fabrics hanging in market stalls, the sounds of Arabic music blaring from car stereos, and the smells of North African cuisine wafting out of hole-in-the-wall restaurants. A true immigrant city, Marseille offers a taste of both the ancient and modern cultures of the Mediterranean.

▉ TRANSPORTATION

Flights: Aéroport Marseille-Provence (☎04 42 14 14 14; www.mrsairport.com). **Air France** (☎08 20 82 08 20) flies to **Corsica, Lyon,** and **Paris. Shuttles** (☎08 91 02 40 25, €0.30 per min.) connect the airport to Gare St-Charles (every 20min.; from St-Charles 5:30am-9:50pm, from airport 6:10am-10:50pm; €9).

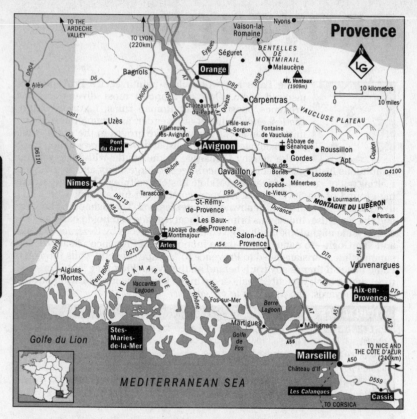

Provence

Trains: Gare Saint-Charles, pl. Victor Hugo (☎08 92 35 35 35). ⓂGare St-Charles. Info and ticket counters open daily 5am-11:15pm. **SOS Voyageurs** (☎04 91 62 12 80) helps visitors find lodgings. Open M-Sa 9am-7pm. Trains to **Lyon** (1hr., 21 per day, €54), **Nice** (2hr., 21 per day, €29), and **Paris** (3hr., 18 per day, €93).

Buses: Pl. Victor Hugo (☎08 91 02 40 25, €0.30 per min.). ⓂGare St-Charles. Ticket counters open M-F 6:15am-7:30pm, Sa 6:30am-6:30pm, Su 7:45am-noon and 12:45-6pm. Buy tickets at the window before boarding the bus. To **Aix-en-Provence** (every 10min. 6:30am-8:30pm, 2 per hr. 9-11:30pm; €4.80), **Cannes** (2-3hr.; 4 per day; €25, students €19), and **Nice** (2hr.; 1 per day; €27, students €19).

Ferries: SNCM, 61 bd. des Dames (☎08 25 88 80 88). ⓂJoliette. Phone line open M-Sa 8:30am-8pm. Office open M-F 8am-6pm, Sa 8:30am-noon and 2-5:30pm. To: **Corsica** (11hr., €39-53); **Algeria** (24hr., €96-258); **Sardinia, ITA** (14hr., €62-70); **Tunisia** (24hr., €146-154). Prices vary according to season, highest June-Sept.

Public Transportation: RTM, 6 rue des Fabres (☎04 91 91 92 10; www.rtm.fr). Runs all **Métro** and **bus** lines. Tickets good for travel 1hr. after validation (€1.70); sold at bus and Métro stations or on board buses. Day pass (€4.50) and 3-day pass (€10) sold at tourist office and bus and Métro stations. Métro lines #1 and 2 stop at train station. Line #1 (blue) goes to the *vieux port* (dir.: Timone). Office open M-F 8:30am-6pm. Métro runs M-Th 5am-9pm, F-Su 5am-12:30am.

Taxis: Marseille Taxi (☎04 91 02 20 20). **Taxi Blanc Bleu** (☎04 94 51 50 00). 24hr. Taxi stands surround the *vieux port* and train station. To hostels from Gare St-Charles €20-30; to the airport from the *centre-ville* €40 during the day, €50 at night.

Car Rental: Avis (☎04 91 64 71 00; www.avis.fr). 21+. Under-25 surcharge €25 per day. Open M-F 6:30am-10:30pm, Sa 7am-8pm. **National/Citer** (☎04 94 05 90 86). Open M-F 8am-10:30pm, Sa-Su 8am-8pm. Both on the left as you exit Gare St-Charles.

⚓ ORIENTATION

Marseille is divided along major streets into 16 arrondissements. **La Canebière** is the main artery of the *centre-ville* funneling into the *vieux port* (old port) to the west and turning into urban sprawl to the east. North of the *vieux port* and west of rue de la République lies **Le Panier**, Marseille's oldest neighborhood. Surrounding La Canebière are several Maghreb (North African and Arabic) communities, including the market-filled **Belsunce** *quartier.* Although travelers should be careful here at night, both Le Panier and Belsunce are great for daytime exploration. Upscale restaurants and chic nightlife cluster around the *vieux port* on **quai de Rive Neuve** and **place Thiers.** Big-name fashion brands and boutiques fill the shops along **rue Saint-Ferreol** and **rue Paradis.** The area around rue Curiol (near rue Sénac) should be avoided late at night. Marseille's two Métro lines are quick but provide limited service. The bus system is more thorough but complex—a map from the tourist office helps enormously. Use buses to access the beach and Les Calanques, a string of islands along the coast.

⓶ PRACTICAL INFORMATION

Tourist Office: 4 La Canebière (☎04 91 13 89 00; www.marseille-tourisme.com) ⓂVieux Port. Free maps and accommodations booking. **Marseille City Pass** includes an RTM day pass, access to tourist office walking tours, a ferry ticket to Île d'If, and admission to 14 museums (1-day €20, 2-day €27). Open M-Sa 9am-7pm, Su 10am-5pm. Annex (☎04 91 50 59 18) at train station. Open M-F 10am-12:30pm and 1-5pm.

Tours: The tourist office offers walking tours in French and English; ask for schedule. **Petit train** (☎04 91 25 24 69) departs on 2 different circuits, to Le Panier and the Basilique, from quai Belges every 30min. Packed with tourists, this ride takes a direct route to the must-see monuments in the city. Runs Apr.-Nov. 10am-12:30pm and 2-6pm. €5, under 18 €3. Hop-on, hop-off bus tours (☎04 91 91 05 82) leave from quai du Port. 1-day pass €18, students €15; 2-day €20/17. Leaves Apr.-Oct. every hr. 10am-1pm and 2:30-5:30pm; Nov.-Mar. 4 per day.

Consulates: UK, 24 av. du Prado (☎04 93 15 72 10). **US,** 12 pl. Varian Fry (☎04 91 54 92 00). Both open M-F 9:30am-noon and 2-4:30pm by appointment only.

Currency Exchange: ID SUD, 3 pl. du Général de Gaulle (☎04 91 13 09 00). Open M-F 9am-6pm, Sa 9am-5pm.

Beyond Tourism: Marseille Volontariat, 14 rue Paul Casimir (☎04 91 79 70 72; www. marseille-volontariat.com). Offers a range of volunteer opportunities by field of civic interest, including prison education, computer training, elderly care, and insurance disputes. Open M-Tu and Th 2:30-5pm, F 10am-noon. See **Beyond Tourism,** p. 81.

Lost Property: 10 bd. Ferdinand de Lesseps (☎04 91 14 68 97). Open M-F 8am-2pm.

Youth Center: Centre Régional Information Jeunesse (CRIJ), 96 La Canebière (☎04 91 24 33 50; www.crijpa.com). ⓂNoailles. Info on short-term employment, recreation, vacation planning, long-term lodging, and services for the disabled. Internet €1 per hr. Open Sept.-June M and W-F 10am-5pm, Tu 1-5pm; July-Aug. hours limited.

GLBT Resources: Lesbian & Gay Pride, 8 bd. de la Libération (☎04 91 85 41 25; www.marseillepride.org).

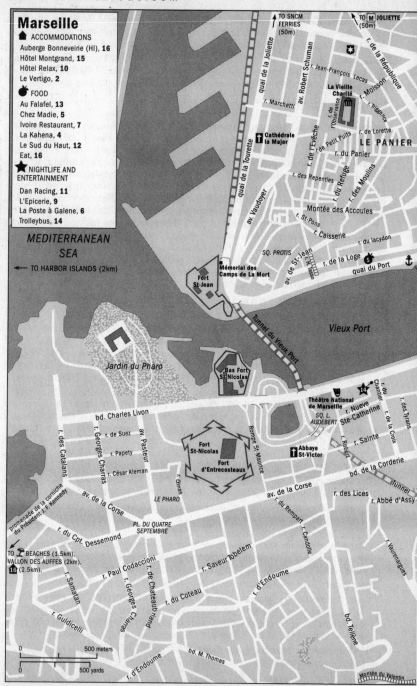

Marseille

ACCOMMODATIONS
Auberge Bonneveine (HI), **16**
Hôtel Montgrand, **15**
Hôtel Relax, **10**
Le Vertigo, **2**

FOOD
Au Falafel, **13**
Chez Madie, **5**
Ivoire Restaurant, **7**
La Kahena, **4**
Le Sud du Haut, **12**
Eat, **16**

NIGHTLIFE AND ENTERTAINMENT
Dan Racing, **11**
L'Epicerie, **9**
La Poste à Galene, **6**
Trolleybus, **14**

MEDITERRANEAN SEA

← TO HARBOR ISLANDS (2km)

TO SNCM FERRIES (50m)

TO Ⓜ JOLIETTE (50m)

r. de la République
quai de la Joliette
av. Robert Schuman
r. Jean-François Lecas
r. Moisson
La Vieille Charité
r. de l'Observance
r. Marchetti
r. Tiggarace
r. de Lorette
r. de l'Evêche
r. de Petit Puits
LE PANIER
Cathédrale la Major
r. du Panier
quai de la Tourette
r. des Repenties
r. du Refuge
r. des Moulins
av. Vaudoyer
Montée des Accoules
r. St-Pons
r. Caisserie
r. du Lacydon
SQ. PROTIS
r. de la Loge
av. de St-Jean
r. H. Tasso
quai du Port
Fort St-Jean
Mémorial des Camps de La Mort
Vieux Port

Jardin du Pharo
Bas Fort St-Nicolas
Tunnel du Vieux Port

Théâtre National de Marseille
r. du Chantier
r. des Tyrans
bd. Charles Livon
SQ. L. AUDEBERT
r. Nueve Ste-Catherine
r. de la Croix
r. des Catalans
r. Georges Charras
r. de Suez
av. Pasteur
Abbaye St-Victor
r. Robert
r. Sainte
r. Papety
r. César Aleman
Fort St-Nicolas
Rompe St-Maurice
bd. de la Corderie
r. des Lices
Tunnel
Fort d'Entrecosteaux
r. Olmas
av. de la Corse
LE PHARO
av. de la Corse
r. Abbé d'Assy
promenade de la corniche du Président J. F. Kennedy
PL. DU QUATRE SEPTEMBRE
r. du Rempart
r. Candolle
r. du Cpt. Dessemond
TO BEACHES (1.5km),
VALLON DES AUFFES (2km),
16 (2.5km)
r. Samatan
r. Paul Codaccioni
r. de Chateaubriand
r. Saveur Tobelem
r. d'Endoume
r. Guidicelli
r. Georges Charras
r. du Coteau
bd. Tellene
r. Vaurenargles
0   500 meters
0   500 yards
r. d'Endoume
bd. M. Thomas
Montée du Valentin

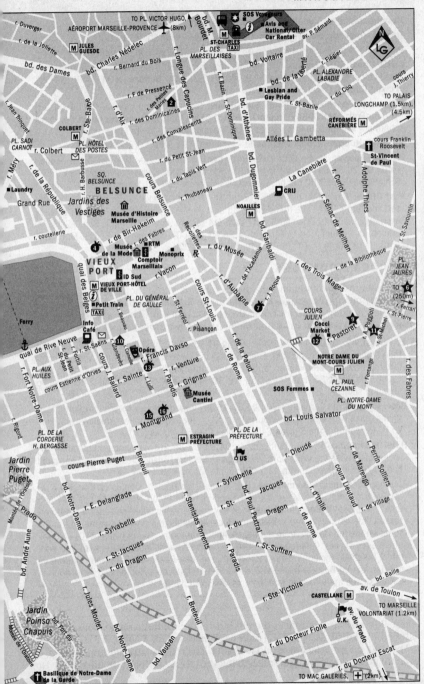

PROVENCE

Laundromat: 8 rue Rudolf Pollack. Open daily 9am-noon and 1-7pm.

Travel Emergency: SOS Voyageurs, Gare St-Charles (☎04 91 62 12 80).

Police: 2 rue du Antoine Becker (☎04 91 39 80 00). Branch in the train station.

Crisis Lines: SOS Femmes, 14 rue Théodore Turner (☎04 91 24 61 50). Rape victim assistance. **SOS Médecins** (☎04 91 52 91 52). **SOS Dentist** (☎04 91 85 39 39). **Poison Control** (☎04 91 75 25 25).

Pharmacy: Pharmacie le Cours Saint-Louis, 5 cours St-Louis (☎04 91 54 04 58) ⓂVieux Port. Open M-Sa 8:30am-7:30pm. 1 of 5 rotating **pharmacies de garde;** check pharmacy windows, the front page of *La Provence,* or with the police.

Hospital: Hôpital Timone, 264 rue St-Pierre (☎04 91 38 00 00). ⓂTimone.

Internet Access: At the **CRIJ** (see **Youth Center,** above). Free Wi-Fi at **Cyber-espace** (☎04 91 24 33 83), located in the CRIJ. **Info Café,** 1 quai Rive Neuve (☎04 91 33 74 98). ⓂNoailles. €3.80 per hr., students €3. Open M-Sa 9am-10pm, Su 2:30-7:30pm.

Post Office: 1 pl. Hôtel des Postes (☎04 91 15 47 00). Take La Canebière toward the sea and turn right on rue Reine Elisabeth as it becomes pl. Hôtel des Postes. **Currency exchange** available. Open M-W and F 8am-6:45pm, Th 9am-6:45pm, Sa 8am-12:15pm. Branch at 1 cours Jean Ballard (☎04 96 11 23 60), off quai des Belges. Open M-F 9:30am-12:30pm and 1:30-6pm. **Postal Code:** 13001.

ACCOMMODATIONS

Pricey establishments cluster in the *vieux port* while the less reputable but temptingly cheap places can be found in the **Belsunce** *quartier.* Exercise caution when picking a budget hotel; the tourist office provides a ▤**list of recommended accommodations.** In summer, reserve at least a week in advance.

▨ **Le Vertigo,** 42 rue des Petites Maries (☎04 91 91 07 11; www.hotelvertigo.fr), near the train station. Young, dedicated, English-speaking owners. Stylish common areas, comfortable beds, a clean kitchen, and spotless bathrooms. Bar open until midnight; beer €2.50. Breakfast €5. Internet €1.50 per 30min. Free Wi-Fi. Reception 24hr. Reserve ahead in summer. 2- to 6-bed dorms €24; doubles €55-65. MC/V over €25. ❷

Hôtel Relax, 4 rue Corneille (☎04 91 33 15 87; www.hotelrelax.fr). ⓂVieux Port. Clean rooms, each with A/C, TV, soundproof windows, shower, and toilet. Breakfast €6. Free Wi-Fi. Reception 24hr. Singles €40; doubles €50-60; triples €70. AmEx/MC/V. ❹

Hôtel Montgrand, 50 rue Montgrand (☎04 91 00 35 20; www.hotel-montgrand-marseille.com), near the *vieux port.* ⓂEstragin-Préfecture. Bright, clean rooms. Renovated hotel. A/C. Singles €52, with bath €59; family rooms €69. MC/V. ❹

Auberge de Jeunesse Bonneveine (HI), impasse du Docteur Bonfils (☎04 91 17 63 30; www.fuaj.org). Take Métro #2 to ⓂRond-Point du Prado. Transfer to bus #44 and take it to pl. Louis Bonnefon. Walk back toward the traffic circle and turn left onto av. Joseph Vidal. Turn left onto impasse du Docteur Bonfils; the hostel is at the end of the street on the left. 10min. from the beach. Adequate rooms. Group hikes (€10) or kayak trips (€40) to Les Calanques in summer. Bar, restaurant, outdoor terrace, and pool table. Breakfast included. Laundry. 3-night max. stay. Reception 6am-1am. Open from mid-Jan. to mid-Dec. Dorms €18. Guests under 18 must be accompanied by an adult or have a signed authorization from parents. AmEx/MC/V. ❶

FOOD

Marseille's restaurants reflect the city's diversity. Options range from African eateries and kebab stands along **cours Saint-Louis** and **rue d'Aubagne** to the *places provençals* on **rue Saint-Saens** and **rue Fortia.** The streets surrounding the *vieux port* are packed with restaurants serving the city's trademark bouillabaisse (a heavy stew made with Mediterranean fish, broth, and a spicy red sauce called *rouille*, or "rust"). Eclectic restaurants line the streets around **cours Julien**. There is a **Monoprix**, 36 La Canebière, a few blocks from the *vieux port*. (☎04 91 54 15 97. Open M-Sa 8:30am-9pm. AmEx/MC/V.) A daily fish market on **quai des Belges** (open 8am-1pm) supplies fresh ingredients for bouillabaisse, while vegetable and fruit markets on **cours Pierre Puget** (open M-F 8am-1pm) and ⓂNoailles on **La Canebière** (open M-Sa 9am-7pm) provide the fixings.

▨ **Ivoire Restaurant,** 57 rue d'Aubagne (☎04 91 33 75 33). ⓂNoailles. Loyal patrons come for excellent authentic West African cuisine and advice from Mama Africa, the exuberant owner. Côte d'Ivoire specialties include *jus de gingembre* (€3.50), a refreshingly spicy ginger drink and natural West African medicine—but be careful whom you drink with, as it's also an aphrodisiac. *Plats* €8.50-12. Open daily noon-5am. Cash only. ❷

Le Sud du Haut, 80 cours Julien (☎04 91 92 66 64). ⓂCours Julien. Inviting decor, spacious outdoor seating, and creative Provençal cuisine. Changing menu includes options like smoked salmon burritos. The ▨ **lunch formule** (€12) is a great deal. *Entrées* €8-11. *Plats* €14-19. Open M-Sa noon-2:30pm and 8-10:30pm. MC/V. ❸

La Kahena, 2 rue de la République (☎04 91 90 61 93). ⓂVieux Port. Tunisian restaurant. Hand-painted plates. Tasty couscous (€9-16) with additions like fresh fish. Speedy service. *Entrées* €5-6. Open daily noon-2:30pm and 7-10:30pm. MC/V. ❸

Chez Madie, 138 quai du Port (☎04 91 90 40 87). The place for a real Marseille splurge. Beautiful port views. Much-praised Provençal cuisine. Sample *émincé de gigot d'agneau* (lamb) with tapénade. Meat *plats* €17-20). Lunch *formule* €17. Free *apéritif* with *Let's Go* (cheers). Open M-Sa noon-2pm and 8-11pm. AmEx/MC/V. ❸

Au Falafel, 5 rue Lulli (☎04 91 54 08 55). ⓂVieux Port. Israeli restaurant with warm pita bread, 1st-class hummus, falafel, and shawarma. Try the surprisingly large *assiette Israelienne falafel* (€7). Falafel sandwich €6.30. *Assiette Israelienne schawarma* €11. Open M-Th and Su noon-midnight, F noon-4pm. AmEx/MC/V. ❷

Eat, 40 rue Montgrand (☎04 91 33 76 88). Wide selection of impressively fresh panini and salads and the array of (very) delicious desserts. Takeout atmosphere, but rustic benches provide seating in the always-crowded space. Sandwich, drink, and dessert combos under €7.50. Create-your-own smoothie €3. Open M-F 8:30am-4:30pm. ❶

◉ ▨ SIGHTS AND BEACHES

Check www.museum-paca.org for more museum info. Unless otherwise noted, all the museums listed below have the same hours (Tu-Su June-Sept. 11am-6pm; Oct.-May 10am-5pm).

▨**BASILIQUE DE NOTRE DAME DE LA GARDE.** A stunning view of the city, surrounding mountains, and island-studded bay make this a must for all travelers. Visit the winding perch in the evening, when crowds are small and the setting sun lends an unforgettable glow to the red roofs below. Climb the stairs to the intimate basilica to see gilded mosaics and touching *ex votos*, symbolic objects presented by the faithful in thanks for protection. The model ships hanging from the ceiling are the work of grateful shipwreck survivors. Towering nearly 230m above the city, the church's statue of the Madonna is regarded by many as the symbol of Marseille. The east face of the church remains pocked with WWII bullet holes and shrapnel scars. *(Take bus #60, dir.: Notre Dame, or from the tourist office, walk up rue Breteuil and turn left onto rue Grignon, which becomes bd. de la Corderie. Turn left onto bd. André Aune to reach the basilica's huge staircase. ☎04 91 13 40 80. Open daily July-Aug. 7am-7pm; Sept.-June 7:30am-5:30pm. Free.)*

HARBOR ISLANDS. A short ride to the islands takes you between the batteries of Fort St-Jean. Resembling a child's sandcastle, the **Château d'If** guards

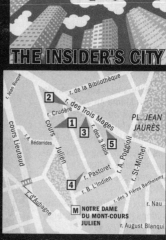

THE INSIDER'S CITY

PL. JEAN JAURÈS

NOTRE DAME DU MONT-COURS JULIEN

COURS JULIEN

An eclectic collection of murals, vintage music and clothing shops, bookstores, theaters, and countless cafes make cours Julien the perfect place to stroll for a bargain. Many shops are closed on Sundays and Mondays.

1. Peruse dusty paperbacks at **Librairie du Cours Julien,** 51 cours Julien.

2. Kaleidoscope, 3 rue des Trois Mages, offers a variety of used records and CDs (€3-15).

3. La Passerelle, 26 rue des Trois Mages, features comic books and a snazzy bookstore cafe—and tiramisu for €3.

4. Street artists have turned **rue Pastoret** and **rue Crudère** into impromptu outdoor galleries with cartoonish spray-paint murals.

5. Rock the bohemian look at **Tola Tola,** 38 rue des Trois Mages, which has a collection of funky clothes, accessories, and souvenirs.

the city from its rocky perch outside the harbor. The tiny island's most famous resident was the fictional count of Monte Cristo. Nearby, Île Frioul housed quarantined plague victims for two centuries, beginning in the 1600s. It was only marginally successful; a 1720 outbreak killed half of the city's 80,000 citizens. In June, crowds enjoy open-air jazz concerts within the crumbling, starlit walls. All events depend on the weather and ferry schedules—check with the tourist office (p. 663) for details. Tiny inlets perfect for swimming make the islands a convenient escape. (*Société des Armateurs Côtiers sends boats from quai des Belges to numerous islands in the bay.* ☎ *08 25 13 68 00. 1½hr. round-trip. Boats leave at 10, 11:30am, 1:30, 3, 4:30pm. €15, students €14. Reserve ahead in high season. Château* ☎ *04 91 46 54 65. Château entry required for visit to Île d'If. €5, ages 18-25 €3.50, under 18 free. Under 18 must be accompanied by an adult.*)

ABBAYE SAINT-VICTOR. Fortified against scurvy pirates and Saracen invaders, this medieval abbey's ◼**crypt** is one of the oldest Christian sites in Europe; its construction in the fifth century brought the first traces of Christianity to the pagan *Marseillais.* The crypt holds the remains of two third-century martyrs, along with photos of their skeletons. Inscriptions and ancient rubble litter the space. The abbey hosts an annual choral concert festival from September to December. (*Rue Sainte, at the end of quai de Rive Neuve. Follow the signs from the quai.* ☎ *04 96 11 22 60, festival info 05 84 48. Open daily 9am-7pm. Crypt €2. Festival tickets €33, students €15.*)

MUSÉE CANTINI. This chic, warehouse-style museum chronicles the region's artistic successes of the last century. Major Fauvist, Cubist, and Surrealist collections—including works by Ernst, Kandinsky, Masson, Matisse, and Miró—are displayed. (*19 rue Grignan.* Ⓜ*Estragin-Préfecture.* ☎ *04 91 54 77 75. €2.50, students €1.50, under 10 and seniors free.*)

PALAIS LONGCHAMP. The sweeping columns, majestic statues, and imposing stone facades of this palace, constructed in 1838, were meant to honor the completion of a canal that brought fresh water to the plague-ridden city. Today, the complex includes a museum, peaceful park, and an observatory. The spacious galleries of the **Musée de l'Histoire Naturelle** are filled with an assortment of stuffed wildlife and fascinating temporary exhibits recounting the history of subjects as diverse as dinosaurs, milk, and human speech. (*Take Métro #1 to* Ⓜ*5 Avenues/Longchamp.* ☎ *04 91 14 59 50. Open Tu-Su 10am-5pm. €3, students €1.50, under 10 and seniors free.*)

PROVENCE

LA VIEILLE CHARITÉ. A formidable example of the famous 17th-century work of local architect Pierre Puget, La Charité was constructed to house the beggars who crowded the entrances of Marseille's churches. Later, the building served as a hospice center for orphans; parents could leave their unwanted children in front of the church, where a wood turnstile near the gate kept the nuns inside from seeing their faces. Now a national historical monument, it contains several of the city's museums. Egyptian, prehistoric, and anthropological collections are held in the **Musée des Arts Africains, Océaniens, et Amérindiens.** Temporary art exhibits are displayed beneath a soaring oval dome in the central **Baroque chapel,** and the **Musée d'Archéologie Méditerranée** houses the city's collection of Egyptian artifacts along with an assortment of ancient Greek pottery. *(2 rue de la Charité. ⓜVieux Port or Joliette. ☎04 91 14 58 80. Temporary exhibits €5, permanent collections €2.50 each; students €2/1.)*

MÉMORIAL DES CAMPS DE LA MORT. This memorial houses sobering exhibits on the death camps of World War II and the deportation of thousands of Jews from the *vieux port* in 1943. Contained in a blockhouse built by the Germans during their occupation of Marseille, the memorial has three levels. Glass panels on the first floor are engraved with poignant quotes by Primo Levi, Elie Wiesel, and Anne Frank; on the second floor, photos display the details of Hitler's control of Marseille. A group of ashes from concentration and death camps provokes reflection on the third floor. *(Quai de la Tourette. ⓜVieux Port. ☎04 91 90 73 15. Open Tu-Su June-Aug. 11am-6pm; Sept.-May 10am-5pm. Free.)*

WATERFRONT. From the Palais du Pharo to the av. du Prado, the promenade de la Corniche du Président John F. Kennedy runs along Marseille's most beautiful stretch of beaches. The picturesque views of the Mediterranean and nearby islands make the typically heavy traffic—human and automotive—bearable. Make a stop at **Vallon des Auffes,** a hidden cove where residents once spun intricate fishing nets by hand from coconut fiber. Today the nets are synthetic, but little else has changed. Rows of brightly painted dories still dip and pull at their moorings as they have for years. Take bus #83 from the *vieux port* (dir.: Rond-Point du Prado) to Vallon des Auffes. The bus continues on to Marseille's public beaches; get off just after it rounds the statue of David and turns away from the coast (20-30min.). Alternatively, take bus #19 (dir.: Madrague) from ⓜRond-Point du Prado. Both the north and south plages du Prado offer sandy stretches, clear water, and stunningly beautiful views of Marseille's surrounding cliffs. *(☎04 91 32 03 90. Open M-Sa 8:30am-8pm.)*

OTHER SIGHTS. The rotating exhibits at the **Musée de la Mode** feature international clothing designers from different periods. *(Espace Mode Méditerranée, 11 La Canebière. ⓜVieux Port. ☎04 96 17 06 00. €3, students €1, seniors free.)* At the nearby **Musée d'Histoire de Marseille,** Greek and Phoenician artifacts reveal Marseille's lively past. Don't miss the massive potter's oven, which dates to the first century BC. The museum ticket also provides access to the adjacent **Jardin des Vestiges,** marked by crumbling medieval foundations. Grab a sandwich in the **Centre Bourse** (above the museum) and picnic among ruins. *(Buy tickets on the 1st fl. and enter through the lowest level of the Centre Bourse mall. ☎04 91 90 42 22. Open Tu-Sa noon-7pm. English text available. €2, students €1, under 10 and seniors free.)* The **MAC, Galeries Contemporaines des Musées de Marseille,** features art from the 1960s to today, including works by César and Wegman. *(69 av. d'Haifa, off av. Hambourg. Bus #23 or 45. ☎04 91 25 01 07; dgac-mac@mairie.marseille.fr. €3, students €1.50.)*

🎵 🎭 ENTERTAINMENT AND NIGHTLIFE

Late-night restaurants and a few nightclubs center on **place Thiers,** near the *vieux port.* On weekends, there's a rush for seats at the bar tables that spill out onto the sidewalk along **quai de Rive Neuve,** but a more eclectic crowd likes to unwind along **cours Julien.** Tourists should exercise caution at night, particularly on the dimly lit streets of the Le Panier and Belsunce *quartiers;* night buses are scarce, taxis are expensive, and the Métro closes early (M-Th and Su 9pm, F-Sa 12:30am). Marseille also has plenty of gay nightlife, and men and women often frequent the same establishments.

BARS AND CLUBS

Dan Racing, 17 rue André Poggioli (☎06 09 17 04 07; www.dan-racing.tk). ⓂCours Julien. Auto-racing decor. Let your inner rock star run wild: 20 guitars, 2 drum sets, and countless other instruments provide the makings for an ear-splitting insta-band. Beer €2.50. Wine €2. Champagne €4.50. Mixed drinks €2.50-3.50. Concerts Th-Sa 9pm; check website for upcoming concerts. Open W-Sa 9pm-2am. Cash only.

Trolleybus, 24 quai de Rive Neuve (☎04 91 54 30 45; www.letrolley.com). ⓂVieux Port. Known as "Le Trolley." Mega-club and Marseille institution. 3 cave-like rooms—each with its own decor—play pop-rock, techno, and soul-funk-salsa. Excellent DJs. Beer from €4.50. Mixed drinks €4-7.50. Cover Sa €10; includes 1 drink; free with *Let's Go.* Open July-Aug. W-Sa 11pm-6am; Sept.-June Th-Sa 11pm-6am. MC/V.

LIVE PERFORMANCES

L'Épicerie, 17 rue Pastoret (☎04 91 42 16 33). ⓂNotre-Dame du Mont. Creative showcase for budding artists. Funky new theater-gallery-cafe features everything from jazz and poetry performances to tango lessons. Open Tu-Sa 2-9pm, Su 3-8pm.

La Poste à Galene, 103 rue Ferrari (☎04 91 47 57 99). ⓂCours Julien. Concert space features popular local groups as well as English and American musicians. Pop, rock, heavy metal, techno, and everything else. Cover free-€25. Open M-Sa from 8:30pm on concert nights, 9:30pm otherwise; shows at 9:30pm.

🎇 FESTIVALS

Ciné Plein-Air (☎04 91 91 07 99; www.cinetilt.org), June-Aug. Free outdoor movies, like in the good ol' days. Don't forget the popcorn!

International Documentary Film Festival (☎04 95 04 44 90; www.fidmarseille.org), June. Embrace your inner docu-nerd. €7.

Lesbian and Gay Pride March, in late June.

Festival Folklore du Château-Gombert, in July. Highlights regional folkloric traditions.

Jazz des Cinq Continents, in late July. Features international jazz artists.

Festival de Musique, Sept.-Dec. A jubilee of jazz, classical, and pop music at l'Abbaye de St-Victor. Pick up a *Festival Guide* from the tourist office (p. 663) for info.

🏛 DAYTRIPS FROM MARSEILLE

LES CALANQUES

GACM, 1 quai des Belges (☎04 91 55 50 09), operates 3-4hr. boat trips along Les Calanques to Cassis and back (from mid-June to Sept. daily 9:30am, with a stop in Friou 2, 2:30pm; from Sept. to mid-June W 9:30am, 2pm, Sa-Su 2pm; €25, ages 6-15 €20, ages 3-5 €13). Tickets are available at the tourist office. Raskas Kayak organizes kayak expedi-

*tions leaving from Auberge de Jeunesse Marseille Bonneveine, at the end of bus line #20.
(☎04 94 73 27 16; www.raskas-kayak.com. 3hr.; 9am, 1, 5pm; €30.)*

Centuries ago, glacial erosion, sea-level fluctuations, and climatic change shaped the southern coasts of Les Calanques (kah-lahnk) into a string of magnificent rock formations. This region, stretching from Marseille to Toulon, provides spectacular natural scenery. Plunging limestone cliffs shelter a fragile balance of terrestrial and marine animals and plants, including foxes and peregrine falcons. They also serve as Marseille's largest outdoor playground for **scuba divers, mountain climbers,** and **cliff jumpers.** If heights and depths aren't your cup of tea, get your thrills by going *au naturel* at one of the **nude beaches** along the coast. Les Calanques are very windy, so check the weather forecast before making plans; boat trips are sometimes canceled.

Hiking is possible, though most of the 28km national trail between Marseille and Cassis (the **GR98**) is only recommended for those with considerable experience and proper supplies and gear. Others can pick a *calanque* (fjord), admire the view, and get their feet wet. Before planning to go on foot, call ☎08 11 20 13 13, a multilingual automated system that provides info on fire risks and opening times for Les Calanques the following day; black means closed, red means open 6-11am, and green or orange means open all day. (Call after 7pm for the most up-to-date information.) Forget about camping and abandon any fire-producing objects (lighters, cigarettes, etc.), all of which are forbidden. In summer, the *massif* is also closed to cars. The most spectacular and most visited *calanques* are those of **Sormiou** (bus #23), **Morgiou** (bus #22), and **Luminy** (bus #21). All buses leave from Ⓜ Rond-Point du Prado and cost €1.70; for each, a ¾-1hr. walk from the bus stop leads to stunning views of the coast, distant Marseille, and the turquoise waters down below. The directionally challenged can join a small group led by a professional guide (Jan.-June and from mid-Sept. to Dec. F 2-5pm, Sa 9am-noon; €15; sign up at the tourist office).

CASSIS

23km from Marseille, Cassis is accessible by bus and train. Buses leave from rue du Prado, past Ⓜ Castellane (40-60min., 10 per day 9:15am-7:30pm, €2.70). Trains run later (15-20min.; from Marseille 24 per day 6am-11:06pm, from Cassis 26 per day 5:17am-10:04pm; €5.10, students €3.70). NAP Tourism runs a ferry twice per day from Cassis port to Marseille's vieux port and then sends a bus back to Cassis (☎04 91 31 90 46). 11:30am, 4pm from Cassis; 5:15, 7:30pm from Marseille. €25. For a taxi from the train station to town (€8-10), call ☎04 42 01 78 96. By bus, take the free #2 shuttle (dir.: Gendarmerie). From the stop, walk 5min. toward the beach and find the tourist office to the right on quai des Moulins. Open July-Aug. M-F 9am-7pm, Sa-Su 9:30am-12:30pm and 3-6pm; Sept.-Oct. and Mar.-June M-F 9am-12:30pm and 2-6pm, Sa 9:30am-12:30pm and 2-5:30pm, Su 10am-12:30pm; Nov.-Feb. M-F 9:30am-12:30pm and 2-5:30pm, Sa 10am-12:30pm and 2-5pm, Su 10am-12:30pm.

With slopes above and an emerald-green port below, Cassis (kah-seess) is a network of staircases, alleyways, and gardens. Wine enthusiasts will enjoy sampling delicate *rosés* from the 14 vineyards that surround the town.

To explore the renowned *calanques* of Cassis, pick up a map from the tourist office and follow the signs to **Port Miou** (30min., following the GR98-51 marked in red and white). The trail continues to the **Calanque de Port-Pin** (30min.). From there, scramble up the green-marked rocky trail and down toward the beach of the stunning **Calanque En Vau** (45min.). The steep trail offers rewarding views but is best for experienced hikers. Avoid getting too close to the cliff on days with strong winds. Bring water, since there are no sources in the *massif*. Grab picnic supplies from the **Petit Casino**, 2 rue Victor Hugo. (☎04 42 01 70 56. Open M-Sa 8am-12:30pm and 3-7:30pm, Su 8am-12:30pm and 4-7pm. MC/V.)

PROVENCE

Boats leaving from the Cassis port can take you to three to eight *calanques*. (½-1½hr., every 30min. for 3 *calanques*, less frequently for more; departures Feb.-Oct. 9:30am-5pm or 6pm; €13-19. Buy tickets at the yellow stands in the port or on board. Cash only.) Explore the crystalline water with a **kayak** at **Club Sports Loisirs Nautiques,** plage de la Grande Mer. (☎04 42 01 80 01; culturel.cassis@wanadoo.fr. Single kayak €40 per day, double €65.) The *calanques* are known for great **diving;** for information, contact **Narval Plongée,** 11 av. de la Viguerie. (☎04 42 01 87 59; www.narval-plongee.com. Dives €27-59. Equipment rental €15. MC/V.) Food and wine connoisseurs will enjoy Cassis's festivals. In early September, dances and a parade, complete with costumes and horses, animate the **Fête du Vin.** On the last weekend of June, the **Fête des Pêcheurs et de la Mer** celebrates Cassis's original source of income: ▢**fish.**

AIX-EN-PROVENCE   ☎04 42

In Aix-en-Provence (ecks-ahn-proh-vahnss; pop. 141,000)—the city of Paul Cézanne, Victor Vasarely, and Émile Zola—nearly every golden facade or dusty cafe has had a brush with greatness. Though lacking a symbol like the arena of Nîmes or the papal palace of Avignon, Aix is an attraction in itself. The best time to visit is outside of July and August; fewer tourists crowd the streets, and a student population of more than 40,000 fuels hip, diverse nightlife.

▐ TRANSPORTATION

Trains: Av. Victor Hugo, off impasse Gustave Desplace. Ticket window open daily 6am-7:55pm. Reservations and info offices open M-Sa 9am-6pm. To **Cannes** (3½hr., 25 per day, €30-32), **Marseille** (1hr., 27 per day, €6.70), and **Nice** (3-4hr., 25 per day, €35-38). The **Gare d'Aix-en-Provence TGV,** 20min. outside of the city, connects travelers to major cities throughout France via the TGV. To **Paris Charles de Gaulle** (3hr., 5 per day, €79-90). Trains also serve Paris Gare de Lyon. The Gare TGV can be reached by shuttles from the bus station (20min., every 15min., €3.70).

TIP   **"TRAIN" WRECK.** Don't take the "train" from Aix to Marseille or vice-versa; you'll end up on an SNCF bus that takes twice as long as the *navette* from the *gare routière,* which runs every 10min., costs €2 less than the SNCF bus, and makes no stops.

Buses: At the train station, routes marked "car" on SNCF's schedule are served by buses. Av. de l'Europe. Info desk open M-F 7:30am-7:30pm, Sa 7:30am-6:30pm. Ticket desk open M-F 6:15am-7:30pm, Sa 6:30am-6:30pm, Su 7:30am-12:30pm and 1:30-6pm. Heavy commuter traffic to **Marseille,** with buses every 10min. (€4.60). Phocéens Cars (☎04 42 27 82 54) goes to **Nice** (2hr.; 5 per day; €27, students €19).

Public Transportation: Aix-en-Bus (☎04 42 26 37 28) runs **buses.** M-Sa 8:30am-5pm. Ticket €1.10, carnet of 10 €7.70; day pass €3.50; all available at the tourist office.

Taxis: Radio Aixois (☎04 42 27 71 11). Base €1.90; €1.40 per km during the day, €1.80 at night and on holidays. 24hr.

Bike Rental: La Rotonde, 2 av. des Belges (☎04 42 26 78 92), at the back of the furniture exchange store. €20 per day, €30 per weekend, €60 per week; students and under 12 €18/26/56; €160 deposit. Includes helmet, pump, and repair kit. Open M-Sa 9:30am-1pm and 2:30-6:30pm. MC/V.

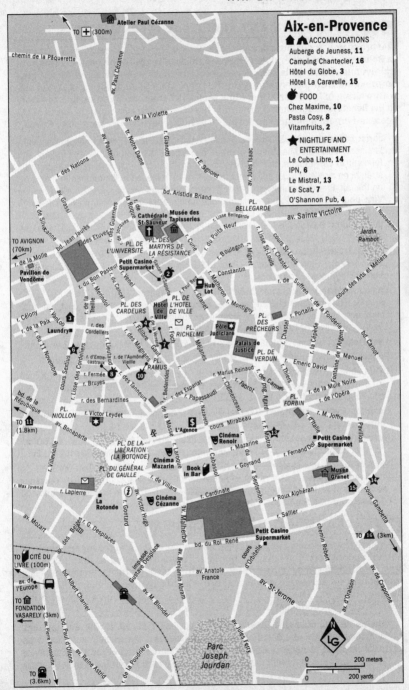

Aix-en-Provence

ACCOMMODATIONS
Auberge de Jeuness, 11
Camping Chantecler, 16
Hôtel du Globe, 3
Hôtel La Caravelle, 15

FOOD
Chez Maxime, 10
Pasta Cosy, 8
Vitamfruits, 2

NIGHTLIFE AND ENTERTAINMENT
Le Cuba Libre, 14
IPN, 6
Le Mistral, 13
Le Scat, 7
O'Shannon Pub, 4

PROVENCE

◼ ⏁ ORIENTATION AND PRACTICAL INFORMATION

The broad and appealing **cours Mirabeau** sweeps through the *centre-ville*, linking **La Rotonde** (pl. du Général de Gaulle) with **place Forbin** to the east. On this central avenue, traffic rolls past decorated fountains, separating countless cafes on one side from classy shops on the other. The pedestrian *vieille ville* sits within a ring of boulevards including **boulevard Carnot, cours Sextius,** and **boulevard du Roi René.** Boutiques and restaurants line the side streets north of cours Mirabeau and create a magical atmosphere at night, particularly near **place Ramus.**

Tourist Office: 2 pl. du Général de Gaulle (☎04 42 16 11 61; www.aixenprovencetourism.com). From the bus station, go up av. de l'Europe, turn left onto av. des Belges, and follow it to La Rotonde; the tourist office is on the right. From the train station, walk straight on av. Victor Hugo and continue as it veers to the left to La Rotonde; the office is on the left. Provides multilingual guides, maps, city **tours** (some in English; €8), and the **Visa pour Aix** card (€2; not available to students or seniors), which provides reduced rates to museums. Organizes excursions to Provence's rural towns, a good option for those without a car (€28-56). Office open July-Aug. M-Sa 8:30am-9pm, Su 10am-1pm and 2-8pm; Sept.-June M-Sa 8:30am-8pm, Su 10am-1pm and 2-6pm.

Currency Exchange: L'Agence, 15 cours Mirabeau (☎04 42 26 93 93 or 26 84 77). Accepts traveler's checks. Open M-F 9am-12:30pm and 1:30-6:30pm, Sa 9am-12:30pm and 1:30-5pm.

English-Language Bookstore: Book in Bar, 1 rue Cabassol (☎04 42 26 60 07). Also a cafe. Hosts monthly English-language readings and book signings, a bilingual book club, and musical performances. Monthly exhibitions feature local artists. Open M-Sa 9am-7pm. Also visit the **Cité du Livre** (see **Sights,** p. 676).

Laundromat: 36 cours Sextius. Wash €3-6, dry €0.50 per 5min. Open daily 7am-8pm.

Police: 10 av. de l'Europe (☎04 42 93 97 00). Call for the **pharmacie de garde.**

Crisis Lines: SOS Médecins (☎04 42 26 24 00) or **Médecins de Garde** (☎04 42 26 40 40). 24hr. medical advice. **Service des Étrangers** (☎04 42 96 89 00) aids foreigners. **Poison Control** (☎04 91 75 25 25).

Hospital: Centre Hospitalier Général du Pays d'Aix, av. Tamaris (☎04 42 33 50 00, urgent care 33 90 28). **Ambulance** (☎04 42 21 37 37 or 21 14 15).

Internet Access: Hub Lot Cybercafé, 17 rue Paul Bert (☎04 42 21 37 31). €3.60 per hr. Wi-Fi at the same rates. 50% discount with *Let's Go.* Open M-Sa 9:30am-9:30pm.

Post Office: 2 rue Lapierre (☎04 42 16 01 65). Open M-F 8:30am-6:45pm, Sa 8:30am-noon. Annex at 1 pl. de l'Hôtel de Ville (☎04 42 17 10 40). **Currency exchange** available at both. Both open M and W-F 8am-6:30pm, Tu 8am-12:15pm and 1:30-6:30pm, Sa 8am-noon. **Postal Code:** 13100.

◼ ◼ ACCOMMODATIONS AND CAMPING

There are few inexpensive hotels near the *centre-ville*, and during festival season all accommodations may be booked. Travelers hoping to find lodging in July should reserve as early as March or April or hope for cancellations. The tourist office can reserve rooms and provide information on guesthouses and nearby châteaux. The tourist office's website can also help with your hotel search. Campgrounds and basic chain hotels lie on the outskirts of Aix.

Auberge de Jeunesse (HI), 3 av. Marcel Pagnol (☎04 42 20 15 99; www.fauj.org). From the *gare routière*, take bus #4 (dir.: La Mayanelle) to the Vasarely and follow signs to the hostel. Alternatively, walk away from the *centre-ville* down av. de l'Europe for 20min. Pass through 3 traffic circles and follow posted signs. 140 bunks in neat rooms.

Breakfast included. Luggage storage €1.50. Linen included. Reception 7am-1pm and 5pm-midnight. Curfew 1am. Dorms €17 with HI card. MC/V. ❶

Hôtel du Globe, 74 cours Sextius (☎04 42 26 03 58; www.hotelduglobe.com). Spacious, well-lit rooms, each with colorful decor, pristine bath, and TV; some with balconies. Terrace on 5th fl. has cathedral view. May-Sept. A/C €4-6. Breakfast buffet €8.80. Parking €9.80. Reception 24hr. Singles €39, with shower €42; doubles with shower and toilet €71-75; triples €92; quads €95. Extra bed €9. AmEx/MC/V. ❸

Hôtel La Caravelle, 29 bd. du Roi René (☎04 42 21 53 05; www.lacaravelle-hotel.com). Cheery, recently renovated, and moderately sized rooms overlook a small garden. Large windows let in plenty of light. Some rooms with A/C; those without have fans. Breakfast €7. Wheelchair-accessible. Reception 24hr. Singles with shared toilet €46; doubles €65, with garden view €70; quads €90. AmEx/MC/V. ❹

Camping Chantecler, Val St-André (☎04 42 26 12 98; www.campingchantecler.com), 3km from the *centre-ville*. Take bus #3 (dir.: Val St-André) from La Rotonde to Val St-André. On a quiet, wooded hill. Views of Mont Ste-Victoire. Pool, restaurant, and bar. Reception 2-6pm. Sites June-Aug €14 per person; Sept.-May €13 per person. ❶

🍴 FOOD

Aix boasts a comprehensive selection of international and Provençal cuisines. The food may be good, but the candy is better. The city's staple *bonbon* is the *calisson d'Aix*, an iced almond-and-candied-melon treat. Other specialties include *merveilles de Provence* (pralines with kirsch and chocolate) and nougat candies. Stop by **Pâtisserie Riederer,** 67 cours Mirabeau (☎04 42 38 19 69), to sample *merveilles*. At dinnertime, tables crowd **rue de la Verrerie, place de L'Hôtel de Ville,** and **place Richelme.** For a place to see and be seen, nothing is better than one of the cafes lining **cours Mirabeau.** Markets with fruits, vegetables, and regional products are on **place de la Mairie** (open Tu, Th, Sa 7am-1pm), **place de l'Hôtel de Ville,** and **place Richelme** (open daily 7am-1pm). Three **Petit Casinos** serve all your supermarket needs: 3 cours d'Orbitelle (open M-F 8am-1pm and 4-8pm, Sa 8am-1pm and 4-7:30pm); 16 rue d'Italie (open Tu-Su 8am-9pm); and 5 rue Gaston de Saporta (open M-F 8:30am-1pm and 3-7:30pm, Sa 8:30am-7:30pm).

▨ **Pasta Cosy,** 5 rue d'Entrecasteaux (☎04 42 38 02 28). With the subtitle "Noodles of the World," this restaurant does not discriminate in its love affair with pasta. Pasta-filled banisters, cheese graters turned lampshades, and a rolling-pin coat rack. Go for the wonderful *fiochetti* (€16) with caramelized pears and a gorgonzola cream sauce. Noodles €13-27. Open M-Sa 7pm-midnight. AmEx/MC/V. ❸

Vitamfruits, 2 rue Bedarride (☎06 03 08 17 33). For an afternoon snack, nothing beats a cheap Nutella *crêpe* (€2.50) or fresh fruit drink (€3) from this small concession stand. Try the peach-raspberry-lemon juice, blended before your eyes. Open July-Aug. M-Sa 8am-1am; Sept.-June M-Sa 8am-midnight, Su 10am-11pm. Cash only. ❶

Chez Maxime, 12 pl. Ramus (☎04 42 26 28 51). Carefully crafted Provençal dishes under a red canopy. Delicious fresh meats, an extensive wine menu, and the lavender *crème brûlée* (€6.70) are highlights. Lunch *menu* with wine €14. *Plats* €13-23. Open Tu-Sa 12:30-2:30pm and 5:30-11pm. AmEx/MC/V. ❸

👁 SIGHTS

Nearly every corner of Aix is marked by a timeworn mansion or elaborate facade, so wandering is the best way to savor the city's charm. The tourist office's maps provide interesting facts on the squares, markets, and fountains.

MUSÉE GRANET. The large and excellent collection here includes nearly 600 works, with an emphasis on the French school from the 17th to 19th centuries. One room contains nine oil paintings by Aix's favorite son, Cézanne. *(Pl. St-Jean de Matte.* ☎*04 42 52 87 97; www.museegranet-aixenprovence.fr. Open Tu-Su June-Sept. 11am-7pm; Oct.-May noon-6pm. €4, students €2, under 18 free.)*

FONDATION VASARELY. This trippy black-and-white museum stands in stark contrast to the rolling green hills of the surrounding countryside. Designed in the 1970s by Hungarian-born artist Victor Vasarely, the father of optical-illusion art, the building resembles a beehive from above. Inside, some of Vasarely's monumental work is on display in eight huge hexagonal spaces. *(Av. Marcel-Pagnol, Jas-de-Bouffan. Take bus #4 from Rotonde Poste, across from the tourist office, to Vasarely.* ☎*04 42 20 01 09; www.fondationvasarely.fr. Open Tu-Sa 10am-1pm and 2-6pm. €7, students and ages 7-18 €4, under 7 free. Audio tours available in English, French, and German; free.)*

CHEMIN DE CÉZANNE. Golden markers trace the footsteps of the artist on a self-guided 2hr. walking tour. Explore Cézanne's haunts, including his birth-place and favorite cafes. Each stop along the *chemin* has a reproduction of the work that he painted there, so you can compare his art to the actual landscapes that inspired him. To visit Cézanne's studio, the **Atelier Paul Cézanne,** where his overcoat and beret still hang in the corner, reserve a day ahead at the tourist office. In summer, music and projected images of Cezanne's art fill the garden at night. *(Atelier at 9 av. Paul Cézanne. Take bus #1 from St-Christophe to Cézanne or walk 10min. uphill on av. Paul Cézanne.* ☎*04 42 21 06 53; www.atelier-cezanne.com. Open daily July-Aug. 10am-6pm; Sept. and Apr.-June 10am-noon and 2-6pm; Oct.-Mar. 10am-noon and 2-5pm. €5.50, ages 13-25 €2, under 13 free. Walking-tour maps available at the tourist office.)*

CATHÉDRALE SAINT-SAUVEUR. A mix of Roman, Romanesque, Gothic, and Baroque styles, this church is pure architectural whimsy. During the Revolution, angry *Aixois* chopped off the heads of the statues. They were re-capitated in the 19th century—albeit *sans* necks. *(34 pl. des Martyrs de la Résistance.* ☎*04 42 23 45 65. Open daily 8am-noon and 2-6pm, except during funerals, Sa weddings, and Su services.)*

CITÉ DU LIVRE. Huge replicas of major French tomes mark the entry to this former match factory, now a cultural center. The **Bibliothèque Méjanes** is the second-largest library in the region and contains ancient volumes from the personal collection of the marquis of Méjanes as well as British and American literature. *(Open Tu and Th-F noon-6pm, W and Sa 10am-6pm.)* World music is available for rent in the "Discothèque" section. Check the info desk for a schedule of films shown at the center's auditorium. *(8-10 rue des Allumettes, southwest of La Rotonde. From the tourist office, go down av. des Belges to a traffic circle, then turn right onto bd. Victor Coq.* ☎*04 42 91 98 88. Borrowing from the Bibliothèque requires a €27 membership.)*

🎵 🎭 ENTERTAINMENT AND NIGHTLIFE

French and foreign films, all in the original language with French subtitles, screen at **Cinémas Mazarin,** 6 rue Laroque, **Cézanne,** 1 rue Marcel Guillaume, and **Renoir,** 24 cours Mirabeau. (☎08 92 68 72 70; www.lescinemasaixois.com. €9, students, under 16, seniors, and the unemployed €7.30. MC/V.) Crowds of students during the year and festival-goers in summer make partying a year-round pastime in Aix. Nightlife picks up on Tuesday and rocks until Saturday. Locals and visitors can be found in pubs until closing at 2am, when the party moves to Aix's clubs. **Rue de la Verrerie** has the highest concentration of bars and clubs, while lanterns sway in the breeze at cafes along the **Forum des Cardeurs.** Gay travelers have few options in Aix; many head to Marseille for nightlife.

IPN, 23 cours Sextius. Head down the stairs and under the small red sign. Cave-like bar is a haven for foreign students—especially Americans, Brits, and Swedes. Soccer on TV during important matches. Beer €3-5. Wine mixed drinks €5. Shots €2, 5 for €8. Live music most nights. Open Tu-Sa 6pm-4am. Cash only.

Le Mistral, 3 rue Frédéric Mistral (☎04 42 38 16 49). Neon-lit dance club has kept Aix's students hopping for 56 years with techno, R&B, and house. Don't arrive in shorts, jeans, or sandals. Cover €15. Open Tu-Sa midnight-5am. MC/V.

Le Cuba Libre, 4 bd. Carnot (☎04 42 63 05 21). Vibrant bar with red accents brings a taste of island life with cigars and tropical mixed drinks. Salsa, hip hop, and rock spun by DJ Xcess. The specialty is its namesake, Le Cuba Libre (€9). Mixed drinks €6-10. Salsa lessons 9-11pm. Happy hour 6-9pm. Open M-Sa 5pm-2am. MC/V over €10.

O'Shannon Pub, 30 rue de la Verrerie (☎04 42 23 31 63). Guinness signs on wood walls and barrels doubling as high tables. Beer €3-5. Mixed drinks €7-9. Shots €2.50. Open M-Sa 10am-2am. AmEx/MC/V.

Le Scat, 11 rue de la Verrerie (☎04 42 23 00 23; http://lescatclub.aix.free.fr). Sophisticated crowd. Free rock concerts in the funky basement. DJ spins in another room. Things heat up at 2am. Beer €4.60. Mixed drinks €13. Open Tu-Sa 10pm-5:30am. Cash only.

▓ FESTIVALS

Aix has festivals, concerts, and special events year-round. **Aix-en-Musique,** 3 pl. John Rewald (☎04 42 21 69 69), sponsors concerts, including "Music on Saturday" programs for children. Check with the tourist office for more info.

Cinestival, 1 week in June. Screenings of hundreds of French and international films cost just €3.50 with the **Billet Scoop,** a free discount card available at the tourist office.

Festival d'Aix-en-Provence, 11 rue Gaston de Saporta (☎04 42 17 34 34; www.festival-aix.com), June-July. Famous performers and rising stars descend on Aix for an enchanting series of operas and orchestral concerts. From €8.

Zik Zac Estival (☎04 42 63 10 11), in July. Hip-hop, rap, and reggae groups perform for student crowds at the Théâtre de Verdure. €15.

AVIGNON   ☎04 90

The heart of Avignon (ah-veen-yohn; pop. 89,500) is a medieval maze replete with fashionable boutiques and old mansions. Looming above the Rhône River is Avignon's architectural jewel—the unparalleled Palais des Papes, a sprawling Gothic fortress known in its time as "the biggest and strongest house in the world." Some 700 years ago, political dissent in Italy led the homesick French Pope Clement V to move the papacy to Avignon. During this period, seven popes erected and expanded the palace, making the city a Rome away from Rome. While foreigners visit Avignon year-round, French tourists descend en masse in July for its renowned theater festival. Budget travelers should be prepared for Avignon's tourist-targeted prices.

▐ TRANSPORTATION

Flights: Aéroport Avignon Caumont (AVN; ☎04 90 81 51 51; www.avignon.aeroport.fr/fr), 8km from town. **Air France** flies to **Paris Orly** (4 per day), and **Flybe** goes to **Southampton** and **Exeter, ENG** (4 per week).

Trains: Gare Avignon Centre, bd. St-Roch, Porte de la République. Info and ticket desks open M 6am-9pm, Tu-Su 7am-9pm. To: **Arles** (20min., 25-30 per day, €8.80); **Lyon** (2hr., 7 per day, €31); **Marseille** (1hr., 18-22 per day, €28); **Montpellier** (1hr., 13 per day, €15); **Nice** (3-4hr., 5 per day, €52); **Nîmes** (30min., 13-15 per day, €8.10). **TGV** departs from a 2nd station outside town, in the Quartier de Courtine. A **shuttle** bus

(€1.10) runs every 15-30min. (5:30am-11:20pm) between the 2 stations; it also stops in front of the post office on rue de la République. Fewer buses on Su. TGV ticket counters open M-Sa 5:30am-9:15pm, Su 6am-9:15pm. To: **Dijon** (3-4hr., 9 per day, €60); **Lyon** (1hr., 14 per day, €42); **Nice** (3hr., 7 per day, €49); **Paris** (3hr., 13 per day, €97).

Buses: 5 av. Monclar (☎04 90 27 38 57). Info desk open M-F 8am-7pm, Sa 8am-1pm. Buy tickets on board. CTM goes to **Arles** (1hr., 5 per day, €7.10), **Les Baux** (July-Aug. only; 1hr., 5-6 per day, €7.20), and **Marseille** (2hr., 1 per day, €19).

Public Transportation: TCRA, av. du Maréchal de Lattre de Tassigny (☎04 32 74 18 32; www.tcra.fr) runs **buses.** Office open M-F 8:30am-12:30pm and 1:30-6pm. Buy tickets (€1.10) on the bus, carnets of 10 (€9.40) at the office.

Boat Shuttle: Navette Fluviale. Follow the signs to the right of Pont d'Avignon. Runs a free shuttle across the Rhône, providing great views of the famous *pont.* Every 15min. July-Aug. daily 11am-9pm; Sept. and Apr.-June daily 10am-12:30pm and 2-6:30pm; Oct.-Dec. and from mid-Feb. to Mar. W 2-5:30pm, Sa-Su 10am-noon and 2-6:30pm.

Taxis: Radio Taxi, pl. Pie (☎04 90 82 20 20). 24hr.

Car Rental: Offices in both train stations. **National/Citer** (☎04 90 27 30 07), at the TGV station. From around €300 per 5 days. Open daily 8am-10pm. AmEx/MC/V.

Bike Rental: Provence Bike, 52 bd. St-Roch (☎04 90 27 92 61; www.provence-bike.com). Bikes €9 per day, €39 per week. Mountain bikes €15/75. Scooters €19/125. Open M-Sa 9am-noon and 3-7pm, Su by reservation. AmEx/MC/V. **Holiday Bikes Provence,** 20 bd. St-Roch (☎04 32 76 25 88; www.holiday-bikes.com). Bikes €8 per day. Scooters from €26 per day. Motorcycles from €58 per day. Open M-F 9am-1pm and 3-7pm, Sa 10am-noon and 4-7pm. Cash only.

⚐ 🔢 ORIENTATION AND PRACTICAL INFORMATION

Avignon's 14th-century ramparts enclose a delightful yet tourist-infested labyrinth of alleyways, squares, and tiny streets. Behind the tourist office, cours Jean Jaurès becomes rue de la République and leads directly to **place de l'Horloge,** Avignon's central square, below the Palais des Papes.

Tourist Office: 41 cours Jean Jaurès (☎04 32 74 32 74; www.avignon-tourisme.com). From the train station, walk straight through Porte de la République onto cours Jean Jaurès; the office is 200m ahead on the right. Provides maps and a sights pass. Open July M-Sa 9am-7pm, Su 9:45am-5pm; Aug.-Oct. and Apr.-June M-Sa 9am-6pm, Su 9:45am-5pm; Nov.-Mar. M-F 9am-6pm, Sa 9am-5pm, Su 10am-noon.

Tours: Tourist office offers 2hr. walking tours W and F-Sa 10am. €7. Themed tours Apr.-Oct. €10-15, under 18 €7. Les Trains Touristiques (☎06 11 35 06 66). 45min. train and bus tours of the *vieille ville*, ramparts, and the Rocher des Doms garden. Tours leave from the Palais des Papes daily every 20min. July-Aug. 10am-8pm; Sept.-Oct. and from mid-Mar. to June 10am-7pm. €7, ages 10-18 €4. Les Provençales, 61 rue Grande Fusterie (☎04 90 14 70 00; www.provence-reservation.com), near Pont St-Benezet. ½-day excursions June-Aug. by bus €30; year-round by minibus €55-110. Bus tours leave from the company office; minibuses pick up customers where they choose. Same company also runs Lavender Tours. Tours visit lavender fields and the lavender museum in Coustellet June-Aug. €40 per ½-day, €90 per day. Flight over lavender fields (from mid-June to mid-July) from €240; min. 2 people. Compagnie GBP (☎04 90 85 62 25; www.mireio.net) runs Mireio Croisières and Bâteaux Bus, which offer **boat tours** along the Rhône with a visit to Pont St-Benezet. 45min. July-Aug. 5 per day; Sept. and Apr.-June 2 per day. €8, with bridge entrance €9. 3 themed dinner cruises. Include stops in Arles, Tarascon, and Châteauneuf-du-Pape. From €29, with dinner €47-63.

Lost Property: 13 quai St-Lazare (☎04 32 76 01 73), at Municipal Police Office.

PROVENCE

Avignon

▲ ACCOMMODATIONS
Camping Pont d'Avignon, **1**
Centre de Rencontres
Internationales/YMCA, **4**
Hôtel Boquier, **14**
Hôtel Mignon, **6**

● FOOD
Le Caveau du Théâtre, **11**
Citron Pressé, **5**
Françoise, **8**
O'Sole Mio, **10**
La Tartinerie, **15**

★ NIGHTLIFE
Les Célestins, **13**
The Cubanito Café, **9**
L'Esclave Bar, **3**
Koala Bar, **12**
Red Zone, **7**

0   200 meters
0   200 yards

TO ▲ (1km)

Île de la Barthelasse

VILLENEUVE

Le Rhône

TO ▲ (1.5km),
VILLENEUVE-LÈS-
AVIGNON

Esplanade
St-Bénézet

Pont St-Bénézet
(Pont d'Avignon)

Musée du
Petit Palais
Les Provenç

Rocher
des
Doms

Notre-Dame
des-Doms

Porte St-
Joseph

Porte de
la Ligne

Porte St-
Lazare

bd. St-Lazare

UNIVERSITÉ

Shakespeare Bookshop
and Tearoom

r. Muguet, r. St-Bernard

r. de la Cârfeterie

PL DES
CARMES

Théâtre
du Chêne
Noir

Palais des
Papes

Avignon Palais
Festival des
Compagnies

Trains
Touristiques

PL DU
PALAIS

Opéra
Théâtre

Régine

PL DE
L'HORLOGE

PL DE
CRILLON

Porte de
l'Oulle

Porte St-
Dominique

r. Velouterie
r. du Rempart
St-Dominique

bd. Raspail

TO ✈
GARE TGV,
NATIONAL/CITER (4km)

Pont de l'Europe

Compagnie GBP
Boat Tours

Porte St-
Roch

Collection
Lambert

Musée
Calvet

Cours JFK

Gare Avignon
Centre

Porte de la
République

Holiday
Bikes

Provence

Lost
and
Found

bd. St-Roch

TO ✈ (1.5km)
Mondial

Provence Bike

Porte St-
Michel

bd. St-Ruf

Porte
Magnanen

Porte
Limbert

Porte
Thiers

bd. St-Michel

av. de la Trillade

TO ✈ (8km)

r. Pierre Sémard

rte. de Montfavet

bd. Limbert

Théâtre du
Chien Qui
Fume

Église de la
Visitation

Théâtre du
Balcon

Les
Halles

Palais de
Justice

TAXI

Musée Angladon

Laundry

Shopi

CRA

Porte
St-Roch

English-Language Bookstore and Book Exchange: Shakespeare Bookshop and Tea-room, 155 rue de la Carreterie (☎04 90 27 38 50), down rue Carnot toward the ramparts. Secondhand (€4-6) and new editions (from €4). English cream teas (3 scones and tea; €5). Open Tu-Sa 9:30am-noon and 2-6pm. MC/V.

Youth Information: Espace Info-Jeunes (EIJ), 102 rue de la Carreterie (☎04 90 14 04 05). Info on jobs, festivals, study, and housing. Open M-F 8:30am-noon and 1-5pm.

Laundromat: 66 pl. des Corps Saints. Wash €3 per 5kg. Open daily 7:30am-8pm.

Police: Bd. St-Roch (☎04 90 16 81 00). Call for the **pharmacie de garde.**

Hospital: 305 rue Raoul Follereau (☎04 32 75 33 33). Open 24hr.

Internet Access: TFMT Cyber Cafe, 29 rue Carnot (☎04 32 76 02 41). Some computers with English-language keyboards. €1 per 30min. Open daily 9am-midnight.

Post Office: Cours John F. Kennedy (☎04 90 27 54 10), near Porte de la République. **Currency exchange** and **Western Union** available. Branch on pl. Pie (☎04 32 74 67 40). Both open M-F 8:30am-6:30pm, Sa 8:30am-noon. **Postal Code:** 84000.

🏕 ACCOMMODATIONS AND CAMPING

When the theater troupes hit town, lodging is generally unavailable no matter how many euro you are willing to spend; reserve up to six months in advance for July and August. The tourist office lists organizations that set up cheap housing during the festival; if hotels are full, festival-goers might consider staying in Arles, Nîmes, Orange, or Tarascon and commuting by train (€5.50-8).

Hôtel Mignon, 12 rue Joseph Vernet (☎04 90 82 17 30; www.hotel-mignon.com). Provençal fabrics, phones, TVs, and A/C. Breakfast included. Free Internet access and Wi-Fi. Reception 7am-11pm. Singles €42-52; doubles €60-73; triples €72-83; quads €94. 20% price increases July-Aug., during festival season. AmEx/MC/V. ❸

Centre de Rencontres Internationales/YMCA, 7 bis chemin de la Justice, Villeneuve (☎04 90 25 46 20; www.ymca-avignon.com). Cross Pont Daladier and continue past Île de la Barthelasse, under the train bridge. At the roundabout, veer left onto chemin de la Justice; the foyer is uphill on your left (35min.). From the post office, take bus #10 (dir.: Les Angles-Grand Angles, M-Sa 2-3 per hr. 6:30am-8pm) to Général Leclerc or bus #11 (dir.: Villeneuve-Grand Terme, M-Sa 3 per hr. 6:30am-8pm) to Pont d'Avignon. On Su, take bus #70 (dir.: Villeneuve-Grand Terme, 5 per day) to Pont d'Avignon. Comfortable bunks. Breakfast €5; dinner €13. Internet €3 per hr. Reception 8:30am-6pm; July-Aug. F-Su reception at restaurant. Apr.-Oct. singles €24, with shower and toilet €35; doubles €30/45; triples €36/54; quads €48/54. Nov.-Mar. singles €20, with shower and toilet €28; doubles €25/36; triples €30/45; quads €40/45. MC/V. ❷

Hôtel Boquier, 6 rue du Portail Boquier (☎04 90 82 34 43; www.hotel-boquier.com). Themed rooms, each with bath, phone, and TV. Breakfast €7. Reception 8am-8pm. Reserve ahead. Apr.-Oct. singles €45-50; doubles €48-57; triples €67; quads €75. Nov.-Mar. singles €50-60; doubles €53-66; triples €75; quads €90. Extra bed €10. Expect €5-10 increase during festival season. MC/V. ❹

Camping Pont d'Avignon, 10 chemin de la Barthelasse (☎04 90 80 63 50; www.camping-avignon.com), on the edge of Île de la Barthelasse. Accessible by the Navette Fluviale (p. 679); take the road ahead to the left, a left at the main road, and a left into the campground. 4-star campground that feels like a hotel. 300 quiet, shaded sites. Restaurant, pool, and tennis courts. Showers. Laundry. Internet access. Reception July-Aug. 8am-10pm; Sept. and June 8:30am-8pm; Oct. and Mar.-May 8:30am-6:30pm. Open Mar.-Oct. 2 people and tent €23. Extra person €5.10. Electricity €2.60-3.10. MC/V. ❷

PROVENCE

⊓ FOOD

There's a selection of creative restaurants on the chic **rue des Teinturiers.** The Vietnamese restaurants on side streets throughout the city are great budget options. A walk up **rue Carnot** and **rue de la Carreterie** reveals artisan bakeries, cheap *sandwicheries,* and reasonably priced *brasseries.* The **Parc du Rocher des Doms,** overlooking the Rhône, provides picturesque picnic spots and has an outdoor cafe. **Les Halles,** the large indoor market on pl. Pie, promises endless amounts of regional produce, chèvre (goat cheese), meats, and wines. (Open Tu-Sa 7am-1pm.) For groceries, try the **Shopi** supermarket, 23 rue de la République. (Open M-Sa 7am-9pm, Su 9am-12:30pm. MC/V.)

Françoise, 6 rue du Général Léclerc (☎04 32 76 24 77). Gourmet meals in an upscale cafeteria-like setting. Françoise herself will seat you. Homemade baked delights include a phenomenal apple-raspberry crumble (€3.50). Sandwiches and salads €3-9. Open M-Sa 8:30am-7pm; during festival daily 8am-11:30pm. AmEx/MC/V over €15. ❷

Le Caveau du Théâtre, 16 rue des 3 Faucons (☎04 90 82 60 91; www.caveaudutheatre. com). Gourmet Provençal cuisine. Local ingredients like floral honey and lavender. Menu changes monthly. Lunch *formule* €11. Dinner *menus* €18-22. Open M-F noon-2pm and 7-10pm, Sa 7-10pm; during festival open daily noon-2pm and 7-10pm. MC/V. ❸

La Tartinerie, 19 pl. de la Principale (☎04 90 82 34 19). Filling, appealing *tartines* (€4.70-9.50) in many varieties. Enormous gourmet salads €8-10. Open July daily 11am-midnight; Aug.-June M-Sa 11am-midnight. AmEx/MC/V. ❷

O'Sole Mio, 23 rue de la Croix (☎04 90 27 94 34). Large *plats.* Terrace. Delicious lasagna €10. Pizzas and pastas €9-13. Open July daily 11am-2:30pm and 6:30pm-midnight; Aug.-June Tu-Su 11am-2:30pm and 6:30pm-midnight. AmEx/MC/V. ❷

Citron Pressé, 38 rue Carreterie (☎04 90 86 09 29). Basic French fare with Lebanese and Indian touches. *Plats* €3-7. *Menu* €12. Open M-Th noon-2:30pm, F-Sa noon-2pm and 7:30-11:30pm; during festival daily noon-2am. Cash only. ❷

⊙ SIGHTS

PASS AND SCORE. Most of Avignon's sights operate on a pass system. Pay full admission for any monument or museum, pick up your pass, get it stamped, and then get 20-50% off at sights you visit the next 15 days (also 30% off some guided tours and up to 20% off tourist excursions).

PALAIS DES PAPES. This golden *palais,* the largest Gothic palace in the world and a UNESCO World Heritage Site, dominates Aix-en-Provence. Begun in 1335 by the third pope of Avignon, Benoît XII, it was completed fewer than 20 years later by his successor, Clement VI. The papal palace is neatly divided into two sections marked by the contrasting styles of their builders: the strict, spare grandeur of the Cistercian Benoît and the astonishing ostentation of the aristocratic Clement. Following the political unrest of the late 18th century, the castle was turned into a prison in 1790 and served as a barracks until 1906, when it was restored and opened to the public. Revel in the massive Great Chapel, whose single nave is 52m long, 15m wide, and 20m tall—typical of the palace's enormous rooms. Don't miss the **Cuisine Haute,** which lives up to its name with a massive chimney. Since 2004, the formerly bare rooms have become home to the **Musée de l'Oeuvre,** a permanent display retracing the complex history of the papacy in Avignon. (☎04 90 27 50 00; www.palais-des-papes.com. *Open daily Aug. 9am-9pm; early Sept. and July 9am-8pm; from mid-Sept. to Oct. and Apr.-June 9am-7pm;*

Nov.-Mar. 9:30am-5:45pm. Last entrance 1hr. before close. Palace and exhibition €9.50, with pass €7.50. Palace and bridge €12/€9. Free audio tour in 8 languages.)

PONT SAINT-BÉNÉZET. This 12th-century bridge is known to French children as the "Pont d'Avignon," immortalized internationally by the song "Sur le Pont d'Avignon." In 1171, Bénézet, a shepherd boy, was commanded by angels to build a bridge across the Rhône. Legend has it that, when he announced his mission to the people of Avignon, they called him crazy. The archbishop, also skeptical, pointed to a gigantic boulder and told Bénézet that he would have to place the first stone himself. Miraculously, the shepherd heaved the rock onto his shoulder and tossed it into the river. This holy shotput convinced the townspeople, who responded with shovels and mortar, finishing the bridge in 1185. Despite the divinely ordained location, the bridge has suffered warfare and the once-turbulent Rhône and now extends only partway across the river. Farther down the river, **Pont Daladier** makes it all the way across and offers free views of the broken bridge. *(☎04 90 27 51 16. Open daily Aug. 9am-9pm; early Sept. and July 9am-8pm; from mid-Sept. to Oct. and Apr.-June 9am-7pm; Nov.-Mar. 9:30am-5:45pm. July-Sept. €4, with pass €3.30; Oct.-June €3.50.)*

MUSÉE DU PETIT PALAIS. Housed in a 600-year-old palace next to the Palais des Papes, this prestigious museum displays a large collection of medieval and Renaissance paintings as well as Romanesque and Gothic sculptures. Look for Botticelli's painting, *La Vierge et l'Enfant*, in room XI. *(Palais des Archevêques, pl. du Palais des Papes. ☎04 90 86 44 58; www.petit-palais.org. Open M and W-Su June-Sept. 10am-6pm; Oct.-May 10am-1pm and 2-6pm. €6, with pass or students €3.)*

COLLECTION LAMBERT. This museum presents three art exhibits per year—from artists like Sol LeWitt, Nan Goldin, and Basquiat—in an 18th-century mansion. The museum also permanently displays two modern pieces: a digitized message and a room illuminated entirely by red neon lights. *(5 rue Violette. ☎04 90 16 56 20; www.collectionlambert.com. Open July-Aug. daily 11am-7pm; Sept.-June Tu-Su 11am-6pm. Guided tours July daily 3pm; Aug.-June F-Sa 4pm. €5.50, with pass or students €4.)*

OTHER SIGHTS. On the hill above the Palais, the beautifully sculpted **Parc du Rocher des Doms** has views of Mont Ventoux, St-Bénézet, and the fortifications of Villeneuve well worth the short climb. *(Open from dawn to dusk.)* While you're at the Palais, stop in next door at the 12th-century **Cathédrale Notre Dame-des-Doms,** which contains the Gothic **tomb of Pope John XXII.** Thick columns support the arched ceiling, while intricate sculptures lace its rims. Sneak a peek at the murals in the chapels that sprout from its sides. *(Open daily July-Aug. 7am-7pm; Sept.-June 8am-6pm. Mass M and Sa 8am, Su 10am.)* The small but satisfying **Musée Angladon,** 5 rue Laboureur, houses temporary summer exhibits and an impressive permanent collection that includes works by Degas, Manet, and Picasso. *(☎04 90 82 29 03; www.angladon.com. Open from mid-Mar. to mid-Nov. Tu-Su 1-6pm; from mid-Nov. to mid-Mar. W-Su 1-6pm. €6, with pass €4, students €3.)* **Musée Calvet** harbors everything from Bronze Age tools to 18th-century silverware, though its main focus is French artists from the 15th to 20th centuries. Works by Claudel, David, and Vernet are part of the permanent collection. *(65 rue Joseph Vernet. ☎04 90 86 33 84. Open June-Sept. M and W-Su 10am-6pm; Oct.-May M and W-Su 10am-1pm and 2-6pm. €6, with pass €3.)*

♫ 🎭 ENTERTAINMENT AND NIGHTLIFE

From October to June, opera, drama, and classical music performances take place in the **Opéra Théâtre,** 1 rue Racine (☎04 90 82 42 42). Rue des Teinturiers stays animated during shows in the **Théâtre du Chien qui Fume,** 75 rue des Teinturiers (☎04 90 85 25 87), the **Théâtre du Balcon,** 38 rue Guillaume Puy (☎04 90 85 00 80), and the **Théâtre du Chêne Noir,** 8 bis rue Ste-Catherine (☎04 90 86 58 11).

The independent **Utopia Cinéma,** 4 rue des Escaliers Ste-Anne, screens a variety of movies. (☎04 90 82 65 36; www.cinemas-utopia.org. €5.50, before 1pm €3.50; 10 showings €42.) When the festival rolls into town, Avignon explodes with activity and bars, shops, and restaurants stay open until early morning. Luckily, the rest of the year promises only slightly tamer nightlife.

▨ **Koala Bar,** 2 pl. des Corps Saints. Pink walls and bubble-shaped chairs draw a talkative crowd. Quieter A/C room upstairs. Mixed drinks €3.60-9. Themed nights W-Su. Open M-Sa 7am-1:30am, Su 7pm-1:30am; later during festival. Cash only.

Red Zone, 25 rue Carnot (☎04 90 27 02 44). Student bar and night club. Music ranges from salsa to R&B. Beer €3.50-4.50. Salsa lessons Tu 9:30-11pm. Open July-Aug. daily 9pm-3am; Sept.-Dec. and May-June M-Sa 9pm-3am; Jan.-Apr. Tu-Sa 9pm-3am. MC/V.

L'Esclave Bar, 12 rue du Limas (☎04 90 85 14 91), by the Pont d'Avignon. Techno, house (Th), and 70s remixes keep a diverse—mostly male—gay crowd dancing under neon lights. Beer €5. Mixed drinks €8. "La Madame" drag show W. Cover July-Aug. €5; includes 1 drink. Open July-Aug. daily 11pm-5am; Sept.-June Tu-Su 11pm-5am. MC/V.

Les Célestins, 38 pl. des Corps Saints. Dramatically red cafe. Techno beats animate a fun-loving crowd. Beer from €2.20. Mixed drinks €3-5. Open Aug. daily 7am-1:30am; Sept.-June M-Th 7am-9pm, F-Sa 7am-1am; during festival daily 7am-3am. Cash only.

Cubanito Cafe, 51 rue Carnot (☎04 66 86 98 04; www.cubanito.fr). A favorite among young tourists and locals. Cuban music in a lively atmosphere. Beer €2.30, after 9pm €3.30. Mixed drinks €5-8. Salsa daily 9pm-1am. Open daily 5pm-1am. AmEx/MC/V.

ꙮ FESTIVALS

Avignon Film Festival (☎04 90 25 93 23; www.avignonfilmfecom), in June. At the Cinéma Vox, the Centre Franco-Américain de Provence sponsors showcases of films directed by French and American up-and-comers. Meals, parties, and lectures to schmooze with the next big thing. French and English subtitles provided. Night showings €6, students €5; morning films €2; 1-day VIP badge with breakfast and lunch €50.

▨ **Festival d'Avignon,** in July. The highlight of Avignon's calendar—a wild, crazy, month-long theater binge. Shakespearean actors rub shoulders all night with *Odyssey* readers, African dancers, and Molière troupes. If you're low on cash, don't despair; tickets aren't necessary for getting in on the action—free theater, parades, and extemporaneous performances overflow into the streets throughout the day and night.

Festival IN (☎04 90 14 14 14; www.festival-avignon.com). Official festival. Europe's most prestigious theatrical gathering. At least 20 different venues, from factories to cloisters to palaces. Reservations accepted from mid-June. Free-€36. Under 25 €13 for all tickets over €13.

Festival OFF, pl. du Palais (☎04 90 85 13 08; www.avignonleoff.com). Cheaper and more experimental, though equally established. Over 700 pieces, some in English. Tickets under €20; holders of the Carte OFF (€13 at the OFFice or tourist office) 30% less. Buy tickets at venue or OFFice.

ARLES ☎04 90

Every street in Arles (ahrl; pop. 52,000) seems to run through the great Roman arena, and the alleys of the *vieille ville* have a surprising number of museums and monuments. The capital of Roman Gaul, Arles was nearly destroyed by invasions in the Middle Ages. The town has since been an artist magnet: Van Gogh lost two years and an ear here. Picasso produced over 150 drawings in 35 days while pondering Arles's bullfights. Today, the annual International Photography Festival fills the town's churches with exhibits. For the adventurous, the Alpilles hills and the Camargue marshlands are just a daytrip away.

PROVENCE

PROVENCE

⌐ TRANSPORTATION

Trains: Av. Paulin Talabot. Ticket office open M-F 5:50am-8:45pm, Sa 6:05am-8:45pm, Su 6:50am-9:30pm. To: **Avignon** (20min., 12-20 per day, €6.40); **Marseille** (50min., 18-27 per day, €13-15); **Montpellier** (1hr., 5-8 per day, €13.70-16.10); **Nîmes** (20min., 8-11 per day, €7.30-9.70).

Buses: La Boutique des Transports (☎08 10 00 08 16; www.laboutiquedestransports. com). Leave from the train station and 24 bd. Georges Clemenceau. Consult tourist office inside the train station for schedules. To **Avignon** (1hr., 5-6 per day, €7.10), **Nîmes** (1hr., M-Sa 5 per day, €5.50), and **Tarascon** (20min., 10-15 per day, €2-3).

Public Transportation: LA STAR, 24 bd. Georges Clemenceau (☎08 10 00 08 16; www. star-arles.fr). **Bus** tickets €0.80; day pass €2. Also runs the free Starlette **shuttle,** which loops around town and serves the tourist office (3 per hr. M-Sa 7am-7pm).

Taxis: ☎06 08 94 98 00.

Car Rental: ADA, 22 av. de Stalingrad (☎04 90 52 07 27; www.ada.fr), near the train station. From €59 per day with 100km. 21+. Open M-F 8am-noon and 2-5:30pm, Sa 9am-noon and 3-6pm. AmEx/MC/V.

Bike Rental: Arles VAE, av. Talabot (☎04 90 43 33 14), in front of the train station. €5 per 4hr., €10 per day, €15 per 2 days. Open July-Aug. daily 9am-7pm; Sept.-June Tu-Sa 9am-noon and 2-6pm. MC/V.

◢▟ ⁊ ORIENTATION AND PRACTICAL INFORMATION

The train station and bus hub are on the south bank of the Rhône, north of the *vieille ville*. The tourist office lies south of the old *centre-ville*, between the commercial center and the residential areas farther south.

Tourist Office: Esplanade Charles de Gaulle (☎04 90 18 41 20; www.arlestourisme. com). From the train station, turn left and walk to pl. Lamartine, and left onto bd. Émile Courbes. At the intersection by the southeast old city tower, turn right onto bd. des Lices. Excellent free maps and brochures. Accommodations service (€1 plus down payment). Open daily Apr.-Sept. 9am-6:45pm; Oct.-Mar. 9am-4:45pm.

Tours: Petit train (☎06 15 77 67 47) leaves from the main tourist office and Les Arènes every 35min. to tour the *vieille ville*. Apr.-Oct. daily 10am-7pm. 35min. €6.50.

Currency Exchange: Arène Change, 22 bis rond-point des Arènes (☎04 90 93 34 66). Open Apr.-Oct. M-Sa 9am-6pm. Several 24hr. ATMs surround pl. de la République.

Luggage Storage: Hôtel Acacias, 2 rue de la Cavalerie (☎04 90 96 37 88). €5 per day. Open daily 7:30am-10pm.

Laundromat: Laverie Miele, 12 rue Portagnel. Wash €3.50-7, dry €1 per 10min. Detergent €0.30. Open daily 7am-9:30pm.

Police: On the corner of bd. des Lices and av. des Alyscamps (☎04 90 18 45 00). Call for the **pharmacie de garde.**

Ambulance: SMUR (☎04 90 49 29 22).

Poison Control: ☎04 91 74 66 66.

Hospital: Centre Hospitalier J. Imbert, quartier Fourchon (☎04 90 49 29 29).

Internet Access: Cyber Espace, 10 rue Gambetta (☎04 90 52 51 30). €3 per hr. Open daily 9am-12:30pm and 2-10pm.

Post Office: 5 bd. des Lices (☎04 90 18 41 15), between the tourist office and the police station. **Currency exchange** available. Open M and Th-F 8:30am-6pm, Tu-W 8:30am-7pm, Sa 8:15am-noon. **Postal Code:** 13200.

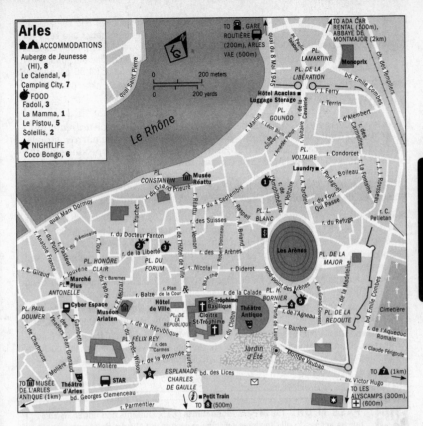

Arles

🏠🏕 ACCOMMODATIONS
Auberge de Jeunesse
  (HI), 8
Le Calendal, 4
Camping City, 7

🍴 FOOD
Fadoli, 3
La Mamma, 1
Le Pistou, 5
Soleilis, 2

⭐ NIGHTLIFE
Coco Bongo, 6

🏠🏕 ACCOMMODATIONS AND CAMPING

Arles has a few inexpensive hotels, especially in the area around **place Voltaire**, but for a little extra it's worthwhile to stay in one of the incredibly charming establishments in the *vieille ville*. The tourist office provides guides to accommodations, *chambres d'hôtes*, and camping options. Reservations are crucial during the photo festival in July and should be made a month ahead.

🏨 **Auberge de Jeunesse (HI)**, 20 av. du Maréchal Foch (☎04 90 96 18 25; www.fuaj. org), 20min. from the station. Take bus #3 to Tourist Office (last bus 7pm). Walk behind the office onto bd. Émile Zola and make a left onto av. du Maréchal Foch. Clean 8-bed dorms. Large, social dining room and garden. Bar open until midnight. Breakfast included. Reception 7-10am and 5-11pm. Lockout 10am-5pm. Curfew July-Aug. midnight; Sept.-June 11pm. Reserve ahead online Apr.-June. Dorms €16. MC/V. ❶

🏨 **Le Calendal**, 5 rue Porte de Laure (☎04 90 96 11 89; www.lecalendal.com) in between Les Arènes and the Théâtre Antique. Provençal decor, amazing views, and beautiful garden. Buffet breakfast €10. Reception 24hr. Reserve 1 month ahead in summer. Singles and doubles €59-119; triples €109-149. AmEx/MC/V. ❹

Camping City, 67 route de Crau (☎04 90 93 08 86; www.camping-city.com). From the tourist office, take the Starlette bus to Clemenceau. Then take bus #2 (dir.: Pont de Crau) to Hermite. To walk, turn right on bd. Georges Clemenceau and continue as it turns into bd. des Lices and av. Victor Hugo. Pass over the train tracks and keep left on route de Crau at the fork (20min.). Closest grounds to town (1.5km). Pool, bar, and restaurant. Well-kept hedges create privacy. Laundry. Bikes €10 per day. Reception daily July-Aug. 8am-1am; Sept. and Apr.-June 8am-9pm. Open Apr.-Sept. €4.50 per person; €16 per car; sites €16. Electricity €4. Cash only. ❶

🍴 FOOD

Arles's cuisine benefits from fresh seafood and hearty Camargue *taureau* (bull) meat. Restaurants with *cuisine régionale* are tucked into the narrow streets, particularly on **place du Forum** and around Les Arènes. Regional produce fills the open-air markets on **boulevard Émile Combes** (open W 7am-1pm) and **boulevard des Lices** (open Sa 7am-1pm). For groceries, try **Monoprix**, 13 pl. Lamartine (☎04 90 93 62 74; open M-Th 8:30am-7:30pm, F-Sa 8:30am-8pm; AmEx/MC/V), or **Marché Plus**, 7 rue de la République (open M-Sa 7am-9pm, Su 9am-1pm; AmEx/MC/V).

▨ **Fadoli**, 46 rue des Arènes (☎04 90 49 70 73), off pl. du Forum. Sandwich bar serves creative panini (€3.50-6; takeout €2.70-5.50) with fresh basil and olive oil. Open July-Aug. daily 10am-midnight; Sept.-June Tu-Sa 11am-7pm. Cash only. ❶

▨ **Soleilis**, 9 rue Docteur Fanton (☎04 90 93 30 76). Don't miss (arguably) the best ice cream in France. Flavors include bitter almond and honey-fennel. Regular cone €1.30. Mountainous sundaes €6.90. Open July-Aug. M 2-6:30pm, Tu-Su 2-6:30pm and 8:30-10:30pm or later; Sept.-Oct. and Mar.-June daily 2-6:30pm. Cash only. ❶

La Mamma, 20 rue de l'Amphithéâtre (☎04 90 96 11 60). Fresh pasta and Italian standards €9-11. Open Tu-Sa noon-2:30pm and 7-10:30pm, Su noon-2:30pm. MC/V. ❷

Le Pistou, 30 bis rond-point des Arènes (☎04 90 43 86 09). View of the Roman amphitheater. Spanish-influenced. Dishes like chicken fricassee in olives match the bullfight-themed decor. *Plats* €11-15. Open Apr.-Sept. M-F and Su 7-9:30pm. MC/V. ❸

👁 SIGHTS

> **TIP**
>
> **PASS IT ON.** The ▨ **Pass Monuments** (€15, students and under 18 €13) gives access to all the sights on this list except the Abbaye de Montmajour. It pays for itself with four uses and is a good idea for anyone staying in Arles for more than a day. You can also purchase a **Circuit Romain** pass, which provides access to the Roman monuments (€10, students and under 18 €8).

LES ARÈNES. Arles is centered on this Roman amphitheater, and while it is somewhat worn—it was built in the AD first century—the overall effect is still impressive. Don't worry about the crowds; the structure was so cleverly designed that it could evacuate the 25,000 spectators who used to congregate here for gladiatorial spectacles in 5min. The small tower offers a view of Arles's rooftops. Bullfights and bull races are staged here from Easter through September. (☎04 90 49 36 86, bullfights 08 91 70 03 70. Open daily May-Sept. 9am-6pm; Oct. and Mar.-Apr. 9am-5:30pm; Nov.-Feb. 10am-4:30pm. Tours in French daily 10am. Weekly bull runs W 5pm. €5.50, students and under 18 €4. Bull runs €7/3.50. Bullfights from €12/6.)

MUSÉE DE L'ARLES ANTIQUE. The best-preserved Roman art and inscriptions are just outside of town. Inside an ultramodern blue building, this awe-inspiring archaeological museum retraces the evolution of the Camargue from prehistoric times through the decline of the Roman empire in the AD sixth century. A 200-year effort has uncovered spectacularly well-preserved sec-

PROVENCE

ond-century mosaics, countless *amphorae* (ancient storage jars), statues, and pieces of jewelry as well as the second-largest collection of antique sarcophagi in the world. *(Presqu'île du Cirque Romain. 10min. from the centre-ville. From the tourist office, turn left, walk on bd. Georges Clemenceau to the end, and follow the signs. Alternatively, take bus #1, dir.: Barriol, from bd. Georges Clemenceau to Salvador Allende. ☎ 04 90 18 88 80; www. arles-antique.cg13.fr. Open daily Apr.-Oct. 9am-7pm; Nov.-Mar. 10am-5pm. Tours July-Sept. daily 3pm in French, 5pm in English; Oct.-June Su 3pm. €5.50, students €4.)*

ABBAYE DE MONTMAJOUR. This medieval abbey, with vast chambers of thick columns and pointed arches, lies 5km outside Arles. A courtyard reveals the magnificent proportions of the abbey's Pons de l'Orme tower. Founded in AD 948 by Benedictine monks, the abbey began as a small commune but slowly amassed a fortune from the gifts monks received for performing spiritual and burial rites. A UNESCO World Heritage Site, the abbey has welcomed visitors ever since Prosper Mérimée opened its doors in the mid-19th century. *(Route de Fontvieille. From the Arles gare routière, take bus #7 or 11. 10min.; M-Sa 18 per day, Su 6 per day; €2-3. ☎ 04 90 54 64 17; www.monuments-nationaux.fr. Open July-Sept. daily 10am-6:30pm; Oct.-Mar. Tu-Su 10am-5pm; Apr.-June daily 9:30am-6pm. Last entry 45min. before close. July-Sept. guided tours in French by reservation. €6.50, ages 18-25 €4.50, under 18 free.)*

THÉÂTRE ANTIQUE. Squeezed between the amphitheater and the gardens, remnants of this ruined theater pale in comparison to the momentous *théâtre antique* in Orange. Only two columns of the stage wall stand among fascinating rubble, but enough remains for modern productions to take advantage of the magnificent acoustics and atmosphere. *(Rue de la Calade. For reservations call Théâtre de la Calade at ☎ 04 90 93 05 23. Open daily May-Sept. 9am-6pm; Oct. and Mar.-Apr. 9-11:30am and 2-5:30pm; Nov.-Feb. 10-11:30am and 2-4:30pm. €3, students and under 18 €2.20.)*

ALYSCAMPS. A twist on "Champs-Élysées" (Elysian Fields), Alyscamps held one of the most famous burial grounds from Roman times until the late Middle Ages. Consecrated by St-Trôphime, Arles's first bishop, it now contains 80 generations of locals. Van Gogh and Gauguin enjoyed strolling through and painting the alleys of unbreakable peace, which were mentioned in Dante's *Inferno*. Sadly, the most elaborate sarcophagi have been either destroyed or removed. *(10min. from town. From the tourist office, head east on bd. des Lices to its intersection with bd. Émile Courbes. Turn right to the roundabout, veer left on av. des Alyscamps, and cross the tracks. ☎ 04 90 49 36 32. Open daily May-Sept. 9am-6pm; Oct. and Mar.-Apr. 9-11:30am and 2-5pm; Nov.-Feb. 10-11:30am and 2-4:30pm. €3.50, students and under 18 €2.60.)*

CLOÎTRE SAINT-TRÔPHIME. Named after Arles's first bishop, this small medieval cloister is a calm and shady oasis. Each carved column is topped by lions in brushwood, saints in stone leaves, and the occasional fluttering bird. The cloister is especially worth visiting from July to September, when the bare chambers of the Episcopal complex showcase an exhibit from the International Photography Festival. *(Pl. de la République. ☎ 04 90 49 36 36. Open daily May-Sept. 9am-6pm; Oct. and Mar.-Apr. 9am-5:30pm; Nov.-Feb. 10am-4:30pm. €3.50, students €2.60.)*

MUSÉE RÉATTU. Once a stronghold of the knights of St-Jean, this museum now houses temporary exhibits as well as a collection of modern art that contrasts with the medieval building's gargoyles and arched ceilings. At the heart of the museum, near exhibits of work by Henri Rousseau and Jacques Réattu, are the nearly 70 drawings with which Picasso honored Arles in 1971. *(10 rue du Grand Prieuré. ☎ 04 90 49 38 34. Open daily July-Sept. 10am-7pm; Oct. and Mar.-June 10am-12:30pm and 2-6:30pm; Nov.-Feb. 1-6pm. €4, students €3; during photography festival €7/5.)*

PROVENCE

🎵 🎭 ENTERTAINMENT AND FESTIVALS

The **Théâtre d'Arles,** bd. Georges Clemenceau, hosts drama, dance, and concerts from October to June. (☎04 90 52 51 51; www.theatre-arles.com/accueil. Tickets €2.40-20.) Arles isn't a town for night owls, but the cafes along **boulevard Georges Clemenceau** attract a crowd with drinks and music. **Coco Bongo,** 14 bd. des Lices, is a large bar with a pleasant terrace. Tropical foliage adds to the atmosphere. (☎04 90 43 55 27. Beer €2.50. Mixed drinks €5.50. Open July-Sept. daily 8am-2am; Oct.-June Tu-Su 8am-midnight. AmEx/MC/V.) Arles is also known for its *ferias*, festivals organized around *corridas*. The two most important ones are the **Feria d'Arles,** held on Easter, and the **Feria du Riz,** during early September, in Les Arènes. (Bureau des Arènes ☎08 91 70 03 70; www.arenes-arles.com. Tickets €17-92.) Those who stop in Arles in summer but outside the festival season can check out the weekly **Courses Camarguaises,** where men race with bulls, Pamplona-style. (July-Aug. W 5pm. €7, under 18 €3.50.)

Fête des Gardians, May 1. Celebrates the brotherhood of herders of the Camargue's wild horses. Every 3 years, the city elects the queen of Arles and her 6 ladies, who then represent the city's customs and history at local events and international exchanges.

Fête d'Arles, 3 weeks from the summer solstice. A tribute to the city's traditional culture. Lighting of a mid-summer fire on the last F in June.

🎭 **Rencontres Internationales de la Photographie,** 10 rond-point des Arènes (☎04 90 96 76 06; www.rencontres-arles.com), 1st week of July. Undiscovered photographers court agents by roaming around town with portfolios under their arms. Established artists hold nightly slide shows (€23-27). Exhibits on display until mid-Sept. Free-€11 per exhibit; all exhibits €35, students €26, under 16 free.

Marché de Noël, mid-Nov. Christmas market draws large crowds in town.

Provence Prestige (www.provence-prestige.tm.fr), 5 days in mid-Nov. Showcases Provençal culture to 25,000 visitors annually.

CAMARGUE

In contrast to Provence's northern hills, the Camargue is a humid delta populated by all manner of wildlife. Pink flamingoes, black bulls, and the famous white horses roam freely across the flat expanse of marshland, protected by the confines of the national park. The Camargue is anchored in the north by Arles and in the south by Stes-Maries-de-la-Mer, the region's official capital and base for expeditions. Bring bug spray: the Camargue breeds mosquitoes.

SAINTES-MARIES-DE-LA-MER ☎04 90

In AD 42, Mary Magdalene, Mary Salomé (mother of the Apostles John and James), and Mary Jacobé (Jesus's aunt) were cast out of Palestine and put to sea to die. According to legend, their ship washed ashore in Stes-Maries-de-la-Mer (sehnt-mah-ree-duh-lah-mehr; pop. 2500, in summer 25,000), where a fortified church now houses their relics. Tourists flock like the resident flamingoes to use Stes-Maries as a base for exploring the surrounding marshland.

◪ ⊉ TRANSPORTATION AND PRACTICAL INFORMATION

The town is wedged between conservation land to the north, sea to the south, and marshes to the east. Everything is less than a 10min. walk away within the town, but a bike, horse, or jeep is useful to explore the landscape around it.

Buses: Pl. Mireille. Autocars Telleschi/Cartreize (☎04 42 28 40 22). To **Arles** (1hr.; M-Sa 5 per day 7:50am-6:10pm, Su 4 per day 7:50am-6:10pm; €5.20).

Taxis: Allô Taxi (☎04 90 97 94 49 or 06 18 63 08 59). 24hr.

Tourist Office: 5 av. Van Gogh (☎04 90 97 82 55; www.saintesmaries.com). Walk toward the ocean on rue de la République and make a right at the roundabout onto av. Van Gogh; the office is on the left. Open daily July-Aug. 9am-8pm; Sept. and Apr.-June 9am-7pm; Oct. and Mar. 9am-6pm; Nov.-Feb. 9am-5pm.

Police: Av. Van Gogh (☎04 90 97 89 50), next to Les Arènes.

Pharmacy: 18 rue Victor Hugo (☎04 90 97 83 02). Call for service when closed. Open M-Sa 9am-12:30pm and 3-7pm, Su 10am-12:30pm.

Post Office: 4 av. Gambetta (☎04 90 97 96 00). **Currency exchange** available. Open M-F 9am-12:30pm and 1:30-5pm, Sa 8:30-11:30am. **Postal Code:** 13732.

▛ ▜ ACCOMMODATIONS AND CAMPING

Rooms fill quickly in the summer, and there are no cheap accommodations. Budget travelers should visit Stes-Maries as a daytrip from Arles.

▨ **Hôtel Méditerranée,** 4 av. Frédéric Mistral (☎04 90 97 82 09; www.mediterraneehotel.com). 14 pastel rooms, rustic furniture, and hand-painted motifs—3 of which have private terraces. Breakfast on terrace €6. Parking €7. Reception 7am-10pm. Reserve 3-4 weeks ahead in summer. Open Feb.-Dec. July-Aug. singles and doubles with full bath €46-55; triples and quads €75-80. Sept.-June singles and doubles with full bath €40-48; triples and quads 62-68. MC/V. ❹

Auberge de Jeunesse Hameau de Pioch Badet HI (☎04 90 97 51 72), 10km north of Stes-Maries. Take bus #20 to Auberge de Jeunesse (10min., 7 per day, €1.70). Camp-style hostel makes a great base for exploring. Owner goes out of his way to help guests. Horse tours €13 per hr., €54 per day. Laundry €3. Bike rental €11 per day; passport deposit. Reception 7:30-10:30am and 5-11pm. Lockout 10:30am-5pm. Curfew midnight, extended during festivals. Reserved primarily for groups Nov.-Jan. Obligatory *demi-pension* with bunk, breakfast, dinner, and linen €32. Cash only. ❷

La Brise, rue Marcel-Carriere (☎04 90 97 84 67; labrise@saintesmaries.com). From the *centre-ville,* face the ocean, walk left, and follow the beachside road until the RV parking lot. Turn left along the fence, then continue around it to the right to reach the entrance of the 3-star campground (15min.). Direct access to the beach. Large pool, supermarket, and snack bar. Organizes water polo, soccer games, karaoke nights, and scuba diving in summer. Laundry. Internet. Reception July-Aug. 8am-9:30pm; Sept.-June 9am-7pm. Lockout midnight. July-Aug. 2 people with car €21; €7.30 per extra person, under 7 €4.20. Apr.-June 2 people with car €19; €6.80 per extra person, under 7 €3.90. Prices drop 30-40% Oct.-Mar. and June. MC/V. ❶

◖ FOOD

The Camargue's main crop is a sweet, fat-grained rice found in *gâteau de riz* (gelatinous rice cakes; €2-3), sold at *pâtisseries,* local restaurants, and on the shelves of supermarkets like **Petit Casino,** 6 rue Victor Hugo. (☎04 90 97 90 60. Open July-Aug. daily 8am-8pm; Sept.-June Tu-Su 8am-12:30pm and 3-7:30pm. MC/V.) A market fills **place des Gitanes** on Mondays and Fridays (open 9am-noon).

A FORGOTTEN SAINT

Stes-Maries-de-la-Mer is burdened with quite an identity complex—the history of the small town is wrapped in the lives and legends of so many saints that it's difficult to keep track. According to medieval legend, St-Lazare—who was resurrected by Christ—built a rickety raft and fled the Holy Land during the first Roman persecutions. On board with him was a virtual zoo of Marys, including the mother of St-Jacques and St-Jean, the sister of St-Joseph, and Mary Magdalene. Their purported landing in Provence brought about the conversion of pagan tribes there. The community, whose name translates to "St. Marys of the Sea," is a distant echo of this ancient legend.

While many still maintain the story of the Marys and their harrowing journey, the Roma invoke a different name when they make their yearly pilgrimage to Stes-Maries-de-la-Mer: Sarah.

For the Roma of Europe, Ste-Sarah—known in Romani as Sara e Kali (Sarah the Black)—is a patron whose image as a wanderer and outsider is of fundamentally Roma heritage. This saint, excluded from the classical Christian narrative, has a history almost as complicated as that of the town where she is now enshrined.

Some say Ste-Sarah was an African servant of the Stes-Maries who crossed the Mediterranean on St-Lazare's raft. In her devotion to her mistresses, she followed the

Restaurants cluster near the waterfront and **rue Victor Hugo,** especially on **place Esprit Pioch,** and serve seafood, paella, *pavé du taureau* (bull)—all generally under €15 and served with refreshing sangria. *Moules-frites* (mussels with fries; €9-12) is a great option for a cheap and filling meal. Restaurants and snack bars with cheaper *menus* line **avenue Frédéric Mistral.** Most *menus* start around €12, but €9 will buy a good lunch. Sadly, restaurants in Stes-Maries are quite similar and not that special; the flip side of this homogeneity is that you can find a decent meal by the ocean almost anywhere.

🗗 SIGHTS

CHURCH. Stes-Maries's focus is its 12th-century church, which has a Romanesque interior and a windowless facade. The subterranean shrine to the Roma St-Sara is quite interesting. Climb the vertigo-inducing staircase for a view of the marshes and orange roofs that color the region. Exercise caution on the roof; it's easy to slip. *(Av. Van Gogh. ☎04 90 97 87 60. Church open daily 8am-12:30pm and 2-7pm. Roof and tower open daily July-Aug. 10am-8pm; Sept.-June 10am-noon and 2-5pm. €2, under 12 €1.50.)*

🌿 FESTIVALS

In July and August, bullfights and horse shows occur regularly at the modern arenas. Throughout the year, **Courses Camarguaises,** which do not end in the death of the bull, take place at Les Arènes. (☎04 90 97 85 86. Tickets €7-8.)

> **Pèlerinage des Gitans,** 2 days in late May. According to legend, the chief of the region's native Roma greeted the Stes-Maries when they arrived and asked that they baptize her people as Christians. Yearly festival unites Roma pilgrims from all over Europe. A costumed procession from the church to the sea bears statues of the saints and reenacts their landing. A pilgrimage on the weekend closest to Oct. 20 hosts the Maries for local residents, with similar ceremonies.

> **Festival du Cheval** (☎04 90 97 85 86), 3 days around July 14. Horses shows, competitions, and rodeos at the Stes-Maries arena. €30-80.

> **Festo Vierginenco,** last Su in July. Celebration of teenage girls' passage into adulthood; girls dress for the 1st time in traditional women's clothing.

🏞 OUTDOOR ACTIVITIES

Most organized visits to the Camargue leave from Stes-Maries; the tourist office has a complete list of tours in the region. Aspiring botanists and zoologists should stop at the **Maison du Parc Naturel Régional de Camargue (PNRC)**, 4km from Stes-Maries, at the Pont de Gau stop on bus #20, which runs between Ste-Maries and Arles. The staff distributes info on the region's unusual flora and fauna, has maps of the Camargue region, and gladly points out all possible walking or biking trails (2-30km). The office also offers panoramic views of the marshes. (☎04 90 97 86 32. Open Apr.-Sept. daily 10am-6pm; Oct.-Mar. M-Th and Sa-Su 9:30am-5pm. Free.) Next door, the **Parc Ornithologique de Pont de Gau** presents visitors with 60 hectares of the *camarguaise* landscape, focusing specifically on regional birds. (☎04 90 97 82 62. Park open daily Apr.-Sept. 9am-sunset; Oct.-Mar. 10am-sunset. Office open daily Apr.-Sept. 9am-7pm; Oct.-Mar. 9am-6pm. €7, under 10 €4. Tours €9, under 10 €5.) Below, *Let's Go* lists the various methods of exploring the Camargue.

HORSEBACK RIDING

The best way to see the Camargue is on horseback. Stables offering tours are scattered throughout the park and in Stes-Maries itself. White Camargue horses can go far into the marshes, wading through deep water to find a range of birds and bulls that you can't see by any other means. Most rides are appropriate for novices. Bring long pants and insect repellent. The **Association Camarguaise de Tourisme Equestre,** at Lieu dit Pont de Rousty, has a list of stables that offer tours. (☎04 90 97 10 40; www.parc-camargue.fr. €13-16 per hr., €35-40 per day; picnic usually included on daytrips.)

BIKING

Although most of the trails are open only to horseback riders and walkers, bicycle touring is yet another great way to see much of the area. Trail maps indicating length, level of difficulty, and dangerous spots are available from the Stes-Maries tourist office and from bike shops. Bring an ample supply of water. A 2hr. ride reveals some of the area, but a whole day is necessary to visit the wide, deserted, white-sand beaches that line the trail. **Le Vélo Santois,** 19 rue de la République, offers free bike delivery within 10km. (☎04 90 97 74 56. €9 per ½-day, €15 per day, €61 per week; passport or ID deposit. Open daily July-Aug. 9am-7pm; Sept.-Nov. and Feb.-June 9am-6:30pm. Cash only.) **Le Vélociste,** 8 pl. Mireille, has similar prices for bikes and also offers daylong packages with **kayaking** for €30. (☎04 90 97 83 26; www.levelociste.fr. Passport or ID deposit. Open from mid-June to Aug. daily 9am-7pm; from Sept. to mid-June M and W-Su 9am-12:30pm and 2-6:30pm. Cash only.)

saints and eventually aided their process of conversion.

Historians and anthropologists, however, point to a connection with the Roma's Indian roots. Ste-Sarah, they say, is a representation of the fierce Hindu goddess Kali, a theory supported by the saint's Romani name.

The Roma's storey is quite different. As they recount, the Roma were a people of the Rhône Valley who, before the spread of Christianity, were polytheistic. Sarah, a local priestess known for the clarity of her foresight, was troubled by a recurring image of three women crying for help on the sea. Responding to their cries, she led her people to the Mediterranean and, seeing the raft of the three Marys in the water, set out in a raft of her own to aid them.

Bucked by the rough seas and in danger of drowning, Sarah nonetheless longed to help the women. She threw off her cloak, which miraculously became a raft on which the women floated to shore. For her kindness, the Marys baptized her, and Sarah became the leader of a new Christian-Roma population.

Every year at the end of May, thousands of Roma travel to Stes-Maries-de-la-Mer to commemorate this image, carrying a statue of their saint to the sea. There, they symbolically await the arrival of the distressed saints. For the Roma, the act is not one of simple devotion; rather, it is symbolic of their choice to live both welcoming of the mainstream and distinct in their identity.

BOATING

Le Camargue, 5 rue des Launes, sends boats from Port Gardian deep into the Petit-Rhône for bird- and bull-watching. (☎04 90 97 84 72; www.bateau-cam-argue.com. 1½hr.; Mar.-Sept. 3 per day, Oct. 2 per day. July-Aug. 1st departure 10:30am, last departure 5:55pm; Sept. and from mid-Mar. to Apr. 1st departure 10:30am, last departure 4:10pm. €10, under 18 €5. MC/V.)

SCENIC DRIVES

For more information about jeep safaris, contact **Le Gitan**, 17 av. de la Républ-ique. Each jeeps hold seven or eight people. (☎04 90 97 89 33; legitansafari@ libertysurf.fr. Open Apr.-Nov. daily 9am-7pm. 2hr. Trips depart May-Sept. 8, 10am, 2, 4, 6pm; Oct.-Mar. 10am, 2pm; Apr. 10am, 2, 4pm. €40.)

NÎMES   ☎04 66

The fabric of Nîmes—or de Nîmes, better known as denim—was first produced here. Now, the distinctly Spanish atmosphere draws foreign and French vaca-tioners in the summer. In June and September, tourists flock to Nîmes (neem; pop. 145,000) for *ferias*—festivals with bull runs, bullfights, and flamenco danc-ing. With affordable accommodations, a gorgeous garden, and a festive weekly market, Nîmes is a comfortable base for short excursions. The region's Roman ruins, especially the Pont du Gard aqueduct, are reasons to stay a night.

█ TRANSPORTATION

Trains: Bd. Talabot. Info office open M-Sa 6am-9pm, Su 6am-10pm. To: **Arles** (25min., 5 per day, €7.30-9.70); **Bordeaux** (6hr., 5 per day, €53-64); **Marseille** (1hr., 9 per day, €19-23); **Montpellier** (30min., 30 per day, €8.40); **Paris** (3hr., 15 per day, €66-104); **Toulouse** (3hr., 15 per day, €38).

Buses: Rue Ste-Félicité (☎04 66 29 52 00), behind the train station. Info office just inside the train station open M-F 7:30am-12:30pm and 2-6:30pm. Lignes du Gard (www.stdgard.com) runs to **Avignon** (1hr.; M-Sa 5 per day, Su 3 per day; €8.30). Cars de Camargue serves **Arles** (M-F 5 per day, Sa 4 per day; €6.30).

Public Transportation: TCN (☎08 20 22 30 30). **Buses** stop running at 9pm; service on most lines is frequent until 8pm. Tickets good for 1hr.; €1, carnet of 5 €4. Buy single tickets on bus, carnets at the kiosks near the station esplanade. Validate on board.

Taxis: TRAN (☎04 66 29 40 11), at the train station. Base €2. 24hr.

Car Rental: Europcar (☎04 66 29 07 94), at the train station. From €129 per day. 21+. Under 25 surcharge €25 per day. Open M 8am-1pm and 2-7pm, Tu-Sa 8:30am-1pm and 2-7pm. AmEx/MC/V.

Bike Rental: Véloland, 54 rue Forez (☎04 66 36 01 80). €9 per ½-day, €15 per day, €60 per week. Open M 2-7pm, Tu-Sa 9:30am-12:30pm and 2:30-7pm. MC/V.

◪ ▮ ORIENTATION AND PRACTICAL INFORMATION

Nîmes's shops, museums, and cafes cluster in the *vieille ville* between **boulevard Victor Hugo** and **boulevard de l'Amiral Courbet.** To get there from the train station, follow av. Feuchères, veer left around the park, then head clockwise around the arena. To reach the tourist office, follow the signs and go straight on bd. Victor Hugo for five blocks until you reach the **Maison Carrée,** a Roman temple in the middle of pl. de la Comédie. The office is a few blocks down.

Tourist Office: 6 rue Auguste (☎04 66 58 38 00; www.ot-nimes.fr). Offers maps, festival info, free accommodations service, and free *Nîmescope*. Info on excursions to Pont du

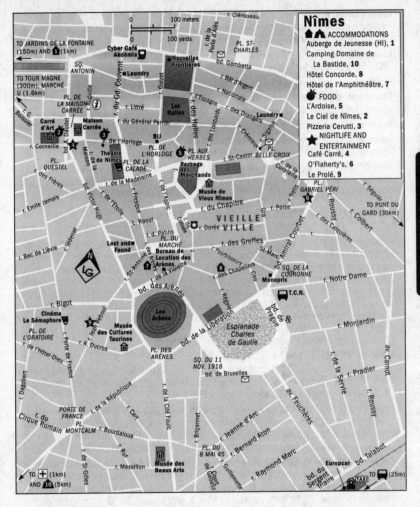

Nîmes

🏠🏠 ACCOMMODATIONS
Auberge de Jeunesse (HI), **1**
Camping Domaine de
  La Bastide, **10**
Hôtel Concorde, **8**
Hôtel de l'Amphithéâtre, **7**

🍎 FOOD
L'Ardoise, **5**
Le Ciel de Nîmes, **2**
Pizzeria Cerutti, **3**

⭐ NIGHTLIFE AND
  ENTERTAINMENT
Café Carré, **4**
O'Flaherty's, **6**
Le Prolé, **9**

PROVENCE

Gard, the Camargue, and nearby towns. Open July-Aug. M-F 8:30am-8pm, Sa 9am-7pm, Su 10am-6pm; Sept. and Easter-June M-F 8:30am-7pm, Sa 9am-7pm, Su 10am-6pm; Oct.-Easter M-F 8:30am-6:30pm, Sa 9am-6:30pm, Su 10am-5pm.

Tours: Tourist office tours of the city July-Sept. Tu, Th, Sa 10am; Oct.-June Sa 2:30pm. €5.50, students €4.50. **Audio tours** €8, 2 for €10. **Petit Train** (☎06 08 63 71 16) gives a tour of Roman monuments and the *vieille ville,* leaving every hr. from esplanade Charles de Gaulle. Tours daily from mid-July to mid-Aug. 10:30am-7:30pm; Sept.-Oct. and Apr.-June 10:30-11:30am and 2:30-5:30pm. €5, ages 2-11 €2.50.

Budget Travel: Nouvelles Frontières, 22 bd. Gambetta (☎04 66 67 38 94; fax 67 38 62), inside the shopping center. Open M-F 9:30am-7pm, Sa 9am-7:30pm.

Lost Property: Rue de la Trésorerie (☎04 66 67 84 29).

Youth Center: BIJ, 8 rue de l'Horloge (☎04 66 27 76 86). Provides info on employment, education, and travel opportunities for students. Free Internet access by reservation; 1 walk-in kiosk is available for checking email. Open M-F 10am-6pm.

Laundromat: 30 rue de Grand Couvent. Wash €3.50-7, dry €0.50 per 5min. Detergent €0.50. Open daily 8am-9pm.

Police: 3 rue du Colisée (☎04 66 02 56 00).

Pharmacy: Grand Pharmacie de L'Esplanade, 9 bd. de Prague (☎04 66 21 31 42). Open M-F 8:30am-8pm, Sa 8:30am-12:30pm and 2-7:30pm.

Hospital: Pl. du Professeur Robert Debré (☎04 66 68 68 68).

Internet Access: Free at the **BIJ** (see **Youth Center,** above). **Cyber Cafe Aèdèmia,** 4 bd. Gambetta (☎04 66 29 78 83). €2.50 per hr. Open daily 10am-midnight.

Post Office: 1 bd. de Bruxelles (☎04 66 76 69 50), at the end of av. Feuchères. **Currency exchange** available. Open M-F 8am-7pm, Sa 8am-12:30pm. Branches at 19 bd. Gambetta and 11 pl. Belle Croix. **Poste Restante:** 30006. **Postal Code:** 30000.

ACCOMMODATIONS AND CAMPING

Auberge de Jeunesse (HI), 257 chemin de l'Auberge de la Jeunesse (☎04 66 68 03 20; fax 68 03 21). Take bus #I (dir.: Alès) to Stade and walk 500m up the hill; helpful signs lead the way from the traffic circle to the Auberge. From the train station, walk straight toward Les Arènes, then around them to the left to arrive at bd. Victor Hugo. From there, follow signs past the canals and *jardin* (40min.). Hostel minibus takes guests to the station (9am, €1.40). Considerate staff. Comfy 4- to 6-bed dorms. Beautiful garden seating area. Fridge, bar, and kitchen. Keycard access. Breakfast €4. Laundry. Internet €1 per 15min. Free Wi-Fi. Reception 7:30am-1am. Reserve ahead Mar.-Sept. Camping €9, with tent rental €11. Dorms €13. MC/V. ❶

Hôtel de l'Amphithéâtre, 4 rue des Arènes (☎04 66 67 28 51; perso.wanadoo.fr/hotel-amphitheatre). 2 17th- and 18th-century upscale hotels. 15 elegant rooms—each with TV and bath, some with A/C—named after French artists. Breakfast €7. Reception 8am-9pm. Singles €41-45; doubles €53-81. MC/V. ❸

Hôtel Concorde, 3 rue des Chapeliers (☎04 66 67 91 03; www.hotel-concorde-nimes.com). Straightforward, clean, and centrally located. An unbeatable deal for groups. Breakfast €5. Reception daily 9am-7pm. Singles €24-34; doubles €26-38; triples with shower and TV €42-44; quads with full bath and TV €49. AmEx/MC/V. ❷

Camping Domaine de La Bastide, route de Générac (☎04 66 62 05 82), 5km south of the train station. Take bus D (dir.: La Bastide, last bus 8pm) to its last stop. By car, drive toward Montpellier and get off at route de Générac. 3-star site with a restaurant and laundry facilities. €9.80 for 1 person, €14 for 2. MC/V over €15. ❶

FOOD

Nîmes specializes in *brandade de morue,* dried cod with olive oil packed in a turnover, pastry, or soufflé. Stock up on picnic food at the markets on **boulevard Jean Jaurès** (open F 7am-1pm) and in **Les Halles** (open daily 6am-12:30pm). There's a **Monoprix,** 3 bd. de l'Amiral Courbet, near esplanade Charles de Gaulle (☎04 66 21 06 36; open M-Sa 8:30am-8:30pm, Su 9am-noon; AmEx/MC/V), and a large **Marché U,** 19 av. Pasteur Paul Brunel, just down the hill from the hostel at the traffic circle (☎04 66 28 80 80; open M-Th 8am-12:45pm and 3-8pm, F-Sa 8am-8pm). *Caladons,* delicious honey cookies with almonds, are Nîmes's favorite sweet. Cafes and bakeries line the squares, while lovely *brasseries* dominate **boulevard Victor Hugo, boulevard de l'Amiral Courbet,** and the **arena.** Terraced **place du Marché,** with a crocodile fountain, reverberates with laughter late into the night, while calmer dinner options line the quiet **rue l'Étoile.**

> **Pizzeria Cerutti,** 25 rue de l'Horloge (☎04 66 21 54 88). Hearty Italian fare. Fresh salads (€5-9.50), pastas (€6.50-8), and pizzas (€7-8.50) with homemade sauces cooked before your eyes. Lunch *formules* €11-13. Open July-Aug. M-Tu and Th-Su noon-2pm and 7pm-midnight; Sept.-June Th-Su noon-2pm and 7pm-midnight. AmEx/MC/V. ❷

> **L'Ardoise,** 5 rue Petits Souliers (☎04 66 21 06 02), off pl. de l'Horloge. Beautifully presented food to a young crowd. *Plats du jour* (€8.50) have included a mouthwatering veal and lemon stir-fry. *Menus* €18-29. Open M-Sa 11am-1am. MC/V. ❷

> **Le Ciel de Nîmes,** pl. de la Maison Carré (☎04 66 36 71 70), in the Carré d'Art. Modern decor and beautiful view. Salads €12. *Plats* €10-17. Reserve ahead. Open Apr.-Sept. Tu-W and Su 10am-8pm, Th-Sa 10am-1am; Oct.-Mar. Tu-Su 10am-8pm. MC/V. ❸

◉ SIGHTS

A combined ticket for all three Roman monuments (€9.80, students €7.50) is available at Les Arènes, Tour Magne, and Maison Carrée. A museum pass (€9.40, students €7.40) allows access to the Musée d'Art Contemporain, Musée des Beaux Arts, and Musée des Cultures Taurines.

LES ARÈNES. France's best-preserved Roman amphitheater still hosts spectacles nearly two millennia after it was built—although these days they involve less blood. Impressive when empty, the amphitheater is awe-inspiring when packed full during concerts and bullfights. (☎04 66 21 82 56. Open daily July-Aug. 9am-7pm; Sept and Apr.-May 9am-6:30pm; Oct. and Mar. 9am-6pm; Nov.-Feb. 9:30am-5pm. Closed on days of ferias or concerts; call in advance or ask at tourist office for a schedule of events. €7.70, students €5.90. Audio tour included with admission.)

JARDINS DE LA FONTAINE. This large and varied hillside park is pleasant—even for those who don't want to stop and smell the roses. Designed in the 18th century, the *jardins* exude French flair with a grand and majestic *place* decorated with water passages, elegant sculptures, and *boules* courts. Steep stairs and meandering alleys lead to colorful gardens with ponds. Full of secret nooks and luxuriant flora, the gardens are among southern France's most beautiful. (Off pl. Foch, to the left along the canals from the Maison Carrée. Garden open daily from mid-Mar. to mid-Oct. 7:30am-10pm; from mid-Oct. to mid-Mar. 7:30am-6:30pm. Free.) Hidden at the top of the large hill and behind deep green foliage is the **Tour Magne.** Built in the Iron Age and modified by Augustus in 15 BC, this massive tower—essentially a blunt stone spike—once represented a corner of the Roman Empire. (☎04 66 21 82 56. Open daily June-Aug. 9:30am-7pm; Sept. and Apr.-May 9:30am-6:30pm; Oct. and Mar. 9:30am-1pm and 2-6pm; Nov.-Feb. 9:30am-1pm and 2-4:30pm. €2.70, students €2.30.)

MAISON CARRÉE AND CARRÉ D'ART. Built with limestone from a local quarry, the imposing temple known as the Maison Carrée served as the center of public life in the first century of Roman rule. Louis XIV liked it so much that he almost ordered it to be brought to Versailles as a lawn ornament. Today, visitors can enjoy a 20min. 3D film inside the ancient monument that traces Nîmes's Roman roots. (☎04 66 21 82 56. Open daily June-Aug. 10am-7:30pm; Sept. and Apr.-May 10am-7pm; Oct. and Mar. 10am-6:30pm; Nov.-Feb. 10am-1pm and 2-5pm. Film shows every 30min. €4.50, students €3.70.) The Maison Carrée faces Norman Foster's ultramodern glass cube, which houses the city's library and the Carré d'Art. The museum displays contemporary works—from monochromatic paintings to pop art—in a fresh, open setting and hosts a variety of temporary exhibitions. (☎04 66 76 35 03; info@carreartmusee.com. Open Tu-Su 10am-6pm. Last entry 5:30pm. Guided tours July-Aug. Tu-Su 4:30pm; Sept.-June Sa-Su 4:30pm. €5, students €3.70.)

MUSÉE DES CULTURES TAURINES. Vivid exhibits examine bullfighting culture, from the types of regional bulls to the role of female *toreras*. Captions are in French, but all visitors will understand the clothing and videos of the fatal *corridas*. *(6 rue Alexandre Ducros. ☎04 66 36 83 77. Open June-Oct. Tu-Su 10am-6pm, until 9pm on feria days and during the Jeudis de Nîmes. €5, students €3.70.)*

OTHER SIGHTS. The classy **Musée des Beaux Arts,** with marble pillars and mosaic floors, features paintings of the Dutch, Flemish, French, and Italian schools from the 15th-18th centuries. *(Rue de la Cité Foulc. ☎04 66 67 38 21. Open Tu-Su 10am-6pm. €5.10, students €3.70.)* Next to the cathedral, the **Musée du Vieux Nîmes,** in a 17th-century Episcopal palace, displays artifacts from the Middle Ages through the 19th century as well as an exhibit on the history of blue jeans that honors Nîmes as the birthplace of denim. *(Pl. aux Herbes. ☎04 66 76 73 70. Open Tu-Su 10am-6pm. Guided tours 1st Sa of the month 3pm. Free.)*

♪ ENTERTAINMENT

Cinéma Le Sémaphore, 25 rue de la Porte de France (☎04 66 67 83 11). Screens films in their original languages. €5.90, under 25 €5, noon shows €4.

Les Arènes, office at 4 rue de la Violette (☎08 91 70 14 01; www.arenesdenimes.com). Concerts, movies, plays, and operas take place at the old Roman arena throughout the year. Open M-F 10am-6pm, Sa 9am-noon.

Théâtre de Nîmes, 1 pl. de la Calade (☎04 66 36 65 00). Over 70 shows per year, from theater to dance to musical performances. Oct.-June only. €15-30, students ½-price.

⬛ NIGHTLIFE

Students in Nîmes head for the makeshift restaurant-bars on the beach in summer. Lignes du Gard (www.stdgard.fr) runs buses to beach hubs **Le Grau du Roi** and **La Grande Motte** (both 1hr., July-Aug. 7-8 per day, round-trip €7-10). Outside festival season, nightlife in Nîmes is slow, and bars are your best bet.

Le Prolé, 20 rue Jean Reboul (☎04 66 21 67 23). Courtyard bar where young and old alike come to enjoy good company and good drinks. Beer €2.50-5.20. Jazz concerts July-Aug. F 8pm. Open M-Th and Sa 9am-10pm, F 9am-midnight. Cash only.

Cafe Carrée, 1 pl. de la Maison Carrée (☎04 66 67 50 05). Locals fill outside tables. Lively bar by night. Beer €2.50-6. Mixed drinks €6-7.50. Open daily 7am-2am. MC/V.

O'Flaherty's, 21 bd. de l'Amiral Courbet (☎04 66 67 22 63). Dart-filled bar popular with Anglophone tourists. Pints €4-5.20. *Menus* €12-18. Live music Sept.-June. Live Irish, country, and rock shows Th. Open M-F 11am-2am, Sa-Su 5pm-2am. AmEx/MC/V.

❋ FESTIVALS

Ferias (☎08 91 70 14 01). To see the city's pride and glory, try to visit during one of these famous bullfights. The **Feria des Vendanges** is in mid-Sept., and the more boisterous **Feria de Pentecôte** will be on May 31 in 2009. For 5 days, the streets resound with the clattering of hooves as bulls are herded to Les Arènes for *corridas*, where they face death at bullfighters' hands. €20-100; reserve at least 1 month ahead.

Courses Camarguaises, in the summer. Fighters strip decorations from the bulls' horns, narrowly avoiding the lethal points, and then vault over barriers to safety. Purchase tickets at 4 rue de la Violette. Cheap seats usually available on event day. Up to €15.

Fête de Nîmes, in the summer. For music lovers, the greatest thrill of visiting Nîmes may be watching some of the hottest acts in contemporary indie, pop, and R&B play in the surreal venue of the crowded amphitheater. The famous *fête* brings the likes of Radiohead, Alicia Keys, and James Blunt. Most events are packed into July, and information is available at the tourist office and the arena box office (☎04 66 58 38 00). €10-30.

Jeudis de Nîmes, July-Aug. Th 6pm-midnight. Craftsmen, painters, artists, and musicians fill every street corner. Ask the tourist office for a schedule of events.

◼ DAYTRIPS FROM NÎMES

◼PONT DU GARD

> STDG (☎04 66 29 52 00) runs buses to the Pont du Gard from Nîmes (45min.; 9 per day; €4.50-7, summer round-trip ticket €11) and Avignon (45min., 8 per day, €4.80-7.20).

The Pont du Gard, a UNESCO World Heritage Site, is the centerpiece of a 50km Roman aqueduct that once supplied Nîmes with water. Its three levels of arches bridge the 275m wide valley of the Gardon River at a height of 48m. Built by Roman engineers in 52-38 BC to transport water from the springs near Uzès to Nîmes, the aqueduct—an architectural coup de grâce—slopes at a crawling 0.34° gradient, with a total descent of 17m. Ninety percent of the aqueduct is underground; it's a nearly perfect feat of Roman construction.

Though a walk across the bridge is free, the **welcome center** (☎08 20 90 33 30; www.pontdugard.fr) houses a sleek multimedia museum (€7), shows a 25min. film in English and French about the construction of the bridge (€4), and has a children's learning center (€5). Guided tours of the bridge are available in several languages (€5). Day passes for all four activities are available for €12 (students €11). Swimming in the river below the Pont du Gard offers a cool view of the bridge; stairs down to the rocky beach are on the sides of the *pont.* Starting from Collias, you can also paddle 6km from the aqueduct toward Uzès. **Kayak Vert** rents canoes, kayaks, and bikes. The pleasant 2-3hr. paddle meanders downstream to the Pont du Gard. Call a day ahead to arrange for pickup from the *pont.* (☎04 66 22 80 76. Canoes and kayaks €20 per day. Bikes €16 per day. 10% discount for students and guests of the Nîmes Auberge de Jeunesse.)

ORANGE   ☎04 90

Known for its massive and remarkably well-preserved Roman theater, Orange (ohr-rahnjh; pop. 29,000) makes a perfect daytrip from Avignon. Though the *vieille ville* is not stunning, it is easily accessible by train, making a visit worthwhile even if you see nothing but the theater. The summer music and opera festival provides a compelling reason to spend the night in July and August.

◼ TRANSPORTATION

Trains: Av. Frédéric Mistral (☎04 90 11 88 03). Ticket windows open M-F 5:35am-8:20pm, Sa-Su 6am-8:20pm. To: **Avignon** (20min., 15 per day, €5.30); **Lyon** (2hr., 10 per day, €27); **Marseille** (1½hr., 7 per day, €21); **Paris** (4½hr., 5 per day, €73-93).

Buses: TransVaucluse (☎04 90 34 15 59). Ticket office in the Arc de Triomphe open M-Tu and Th-F 8am-12:30pm and 3-5pm, W 8am-noon. Run from cours Pourtoules to **Avignon** (45-70min., M-Sa 14 per day, €6).

Taxis: Taxi Monge, 306 av. du Maréchal Foch (☎04 66 51 00 00).

Bike Rental: Bouti Cycle, 745 av. Charles de Gaulle (☎04 66 34 15 60), past the tourist office. €12 per ½-day, €20 per day. Open M-Sa 9am-noon and 2-7pm.

PROVENCE

PRACTICAL INFORMATION

Tourist Office: 5 cours Aristide Briand (☎04 90 34 70 88; fax 34 99 62), 20min. from the train station. Take av. Frédéric Mistral to the *centre-ville* and keep left as the road becomes rue de la République, then rue St-Martin; the office is on the rotunda's opposite side. Multilingual staff. Maps, daytrip ideas, and accommodations booking. Open July-Aug. M-Sa 9:30am-7:30pm, Su 10am-1pm and 2-7pm; Sept. and Apr.-June M-Sa 9am-6:30pm, Su 10am-1pm and 2-6:30pm; Oct.-Mar. M-Sa 10am-1pm and 2-5pm. Branch at pl. des Frères Mounet. Open July-Aug. daily 10am-1pm and 2-6pm.

Laundromat: 5 rue St-Florent, off bd. Édouard Daladier. Wash €4.10 per 7kg, dry €1.50 per 18min. Open daily 7am-9pm.

Police: 427 bd. Édouard Daladier (☎04 90 51 55 55).

Ambulance: ☎04 90 34 02 66.

Pharmacy: 18 rue St-Martin (☎04 90 34 02 82). Open M 2-7:15pm, Tu-Sa 8:45am-12:15pm and 2-7:15pm.

Hospital: 10 chemin Abrian (☎04 90 11 22 22), near av. Henri Fabré.

Internet Access: Atlas Télécom, 21 rue Victor Hugo. (☎04 90 98 84 82). €1 per 15min., €3 per hr. Open M-Th and Sa 10am-10:30pm.

Post Office: 679 bd. Édouard Daladier (☎04 90 11 11 03). **Currency exchange** available. Open M-F 8am-6:30pm, Sa 8am-noon. **Postal Code:** 84100.

ACCOMMODATIONS

Orange's hotels fill and prices jump in July and August for summer festivals.

Hôtel Saint-Florent, 4 rue du Mazeau (☎04 90 34 18 53; www.hotelsaintflorent.com), near the Roman theater. Spotless rooms beautifully furnished in B&B style. Provençal frescoes and paintings made by owner's family. A/C. Breakfast €7. Free Wi-Fi. Reception 7:30am-11pm. Open from Mar. to mid-Jan. July-Aug. singles with shower €40, with full bath €53; triples and quads €80. From Sept. to mid-Jan. and Mar.-June singles with shower €35, with full bath €45; triples and quads €70. AmEx/MC/V. ●

Hôtel l'Herbier d'Orange, 8 pl. aux Herbes (☎04 90 34 09 23; fax 51 61 12). Comfortable, newly renovated, sunlit rooms near the Roman theater. Rooms facing south have A/C. Breakfast €6. Parking €4. Reception 7am-11pm. Mar.-Sept. singles €32; doubles €37, with bath €50; triples with bath €55; quads with bath €67. Oct.-Feb. singles €25; doubles €30, with bath €45; triples €50; quads €62. AmEx/MC/V. ❷

FOOD

The eateries on **place aux Herbes** and **place de la République** serve standard cafe fare, while the *centre-ville*'s streets have cheaper options. There's a **Petit Casino** on 16 rue de la République. (☎04 90 34 10 43. Open M-F 8:30am-12:30pm and 2:30-7:30pm, Sa 8:30am-8:30pm, Su 8:30am-12:30pm. MC/V.) An open-air market fills the *vieille ville* on Thursday mornings. (Open 7am-1pm.)

Côté Jardin, 23 rue Victor Hugo (☎04 90 30 28 36), off rue St-Martin. Tempting *plats du jour* (€8-14) and salads (€7.50) in a beautiful cave-like dining room or adorable courtyard garden. An atmospheric piano bar makes the restaurant the perfect romantic repose every M, F, and Sa night. Open M and Th-Su 11am-10:30pm. Cash only. ❸

Festival Cafe, 5 pl. de la République (☎04 90 34 65 58). Comfortable purple cushions and outdoor seating. *Plats* €11-17. *Mousse au chocolat* €5. Hearty *menus* €16-26. Open daily 7:30am-midnight. Kitchen open noon-3pm and 7-11pm. AmEx/MC/V. ❸

PROVENCE

🔊 SIGHTS

🏛THÉÂTRE ANTIQUE. The best-preserved Roman theater in Europe, built in the AD first century, is in Orange. Louis XIV is said to have called it the most beautiful wall in his kingdom. The theater originally held 10,000 spectators and was connected to a gymnasium complete with running tracks and sauna. Though the stage wall, 103m wide and 37m high, is one of only three remaining in the world, hundreds like it were once erected by the Romans. After the fall of Rome, this locus of pagan entertainment fell into disrepair. In the mid-19th century, engineers rediscovered its great acoustics and used the three remaining rows as a template for reconstructions. A free audio tour informs the visit, as does a film retracing the monument's history. A ticket to the theater provides access to the **Musée d'Art et d'Histoire,** across the street. The small museum traces the history of Orange, which was successively a Roman colony, a princedom linked to the Netherlands, and finally a French town. Fragments of its cadastres, the most complete Roman land register ever found, are displayed on the first floor. *(☎ 04 90 51 17 60. Theater open daily June-Aug. 9am-7pm; Sept. and Apr.-May 9am-6pm; Oct. and Mar. 9:30am-5:30pm; Nov.-Feb. 9:30am-4:30pm. €7.70, students €5.90.)*

COLLINE SAINT-EUTROPE. Above the theater, amid the ragged remnants of the prince of Orange's castle, St-Eutrope Hill offers a view of the yellow and orange city and its surroundings. *(To climb the hill, exit right out of the theater entrance.)*

ARC DE TRIOMPHE. Orange's other great monument stands on the Via Agrippa, which once connected Arles to Lyon. Though only a 5-10min. walk from the center of town, the arch's remarkably well-preserved facade draws fewer tourists than the theater—and the view here is free. Built during Augustus's time, the 19m high stone structure depicts victories over the Gauls and is a tribute to those who founded the colony of Arausio. *(From the tourist office, walk back into town on rue St-Martin, then turn left on rue Victor Hugo, which soon widens into av. de l'Arc de Triomphe.)*

🎭 NIGHTLIFE AND FESTIVALS

Most of Orange goes to bed early. Friday and Saturday nights draw locals looking to drink and dance to the **Café du Théâtre,** 52 rue Caristie at pl. Frères Mounet, across the street from the Roman theater. *(☎ 04 90 34 12 39. Mixed drinks €4-7. Concerts F-Su 9pm-midnight. Open daily 7am-1:30am. Cash only.)* In August, concerts, films, and shows take the stage. Call the **Service Culturel,** in the Mairie on pl. Clemenceau, to reserve free tickets in advance. *(☎ 04 90 51 57 57. Open M-Th 8:30am-noon and 1:30-6pm, F 8:30am-noon.)*

Les Rencontres Théâtrales d'Orange and **Orange se Met au Jazz,** both from late June to July. Small festivals devoted to theater and jazz, respectively.

🎭 **Chorégies** (☎ 04 90 34 24 24; www.choregies.com), from early July to Aug. Le Théâtre Antique regains its original function with grand operas, choral productions, and symphonies. From €14, students from €8. Maison des Chorégies, next to the theater, has info. Open June-Aug. M-Sa 10am-7pm; Feb.-May M-F 10:30am-12:30pm and 2-5pm.

PROVENCE

THE CÔTE D'AZUR

A sunny place for shady people.
—Somerset Maugham

 Between Marseille and the Italian border, sun-drenched beaches and warm Mediterranean waters form the backdrop for this fabled playground of the rich, famous, and glamorous. Now one of the most touristed places in the world, the Côte d'Azur began as a Greco-Roman commercial base. Prosperous villages sprang up around 600 BC only to be razed by barbarian invaders. Since then, the Riviera has been working toward its modern resort status.

When English and Russian aristocrats began the luxurious habit of wintering on the Côte d'Azur to escape their abominable weather, Nice and its surrounding coastlines became the vacation destination of the world's idle rich. When Coco Chanel popularized the Provençal farmer's healthy tan in the 1920s, parasols went down, hemlines went up, and sun worshipping was born. Today, sunbathers bronze *au naturel* on beaches, high rollers drop millions in casinos, sleek yachts crowd lively harbors, and travelers wander ancient fortifications. Nightfall reveals the Riviera's real pastime: nonstop partying. In July and August, Europe's most extravagant—and often most exclusive—nightclubs overflow with the young, beautiful, and debaucherous until the wee hours.

The Riviera has been the inspiration of artists from F. Scott Fitzgerald to Picasso as well as the chosen resort of celebrities from Brigitte Bardot to Bono. Many towns along its eastern stretch boast a chapel, room, or wall decorated by artists like Cocteau, Chagall, or Matisse. Idyllic villas on plunging cliffs are reminders that the Riviera is an international luxury mecca. Hedonism aside, the Riviera boasts an unmatched cultural richness and vibrancy. Each May, high society makes its yearly pilgrimage to the Cannes Film Festival and the Monte-Carlo Grand Prix, while Nice's raucous Carnaval in February and summer jazz festivals—less exclusive and more budget-friendly—draw a diverse crowd. Despite the Côte d'Azur's reputation for glitz and glamor, penny-pinchers can soak up the spectacle and their share of sun, sea, and sand.

HIGHLIGHTS OF THE CÔTE D'AZUR

TAN ALL DAY on the beaches of Menton (p. 725), the Riviera's hidden gem, surrounded by famous gardens, pristine waters, and a delightful *vieille ville*.

DANCE ALL NIGHT with the young and fashionable in Cannes (p. 736), the most accessible of the Riviera's glam towns.

WHILE AWAY THE AFTERNOON in the medieval streets of St-Paul (p. 713), where the ramparts provide a cultured respite from the fast life along the coast.

NICE   ☎04

Sizzling Nice (neess; pop. 340,000), the former vacation haunt of dukes and tsarinas, continues to seduce tourists with outrageous parties, plentiful shopping, beautiful beaches, and first-class museums. No matter the season, the

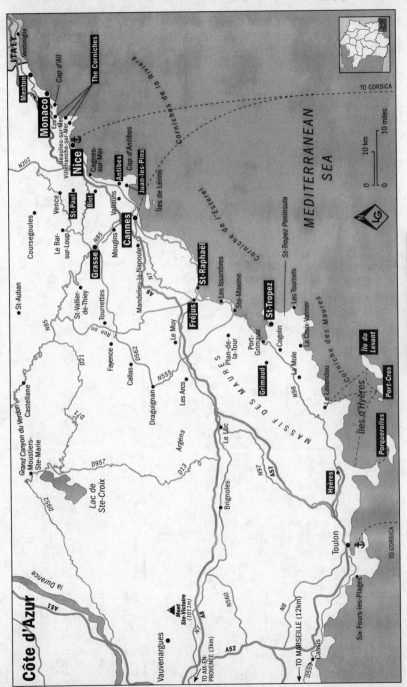

CÔTE D'AZUR

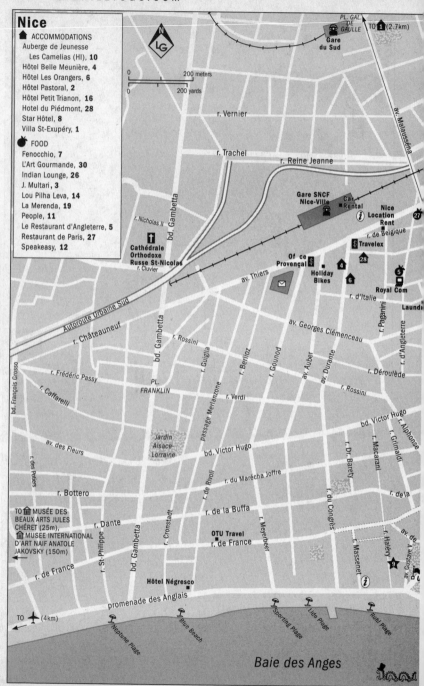

Nice

ACCOMMODATIONS
Auberge de Jeunesse
  Les Camelias (HI), **10**
Hôtel Belle Meunière, **4**
Hôtel Les Orangers, **6**
Hôtel Pastoral, **2**
Hôtel Petit Trianon, **16**
Hotel du Piédmont, **28**
Star Hôtel, **8**
Villa St-Exupéry, **1**

FOOD
Fenocchio, **7**
L'Art Gourmande, **30**
Indian Lounge, **26**
J. Multari, **3**
Lou Pilha Leva, **14**
La Merenda, **19**
People, **11**
Le Restaurant d'Angleterre, **5**
Restaurant de Paris, **27**
Speakeasy, **12**

CÔTE D'AZUR

TO **1** (2.7km)

PL. GAL.
DE
GAULLE
Gare
du Sud

r. Vernier

r. Trachel

r. Reine Jeanne

av. Malausséna

Gare SNCF
Nice-Ville

Car
Rental

Nice
Location
Rent

27

r. de Belgique

Travelex

Of ce
Provençal

28

4

Holiday
Bikes

6

5

Royal Com

r. d'Italie

Laundr

r. Nicholas II

bd. Gambetta

Cathédrale
Orthodoxe
Russe St-Nicolas
r. Cluver

av. Thiers

av. Georges Clémenceau

r. Paganini

r. d'Angleterre

Autoroute Urbaine Sud

r. Châteauneuf

bd. Gambetta

r. Rossini

r. Giuglia

r. Berlioz

r. Gounod

av. Auber

av. Durante

r. Rossini

r. Déroulède

r. Frédéric Passy

r. Caffarelli

PL.
FRANKLIN

r. Verdi

passage Merlanzone

bd. François Grosso

av. des Fleurs

Jardin
Alsace-
Lorraine

bd. Victor Hugo

bd. Victor Hugo

r. Alphonse

r. Grimaldi

r. Macarani

r. de la

r. des Potiers

r. Bottero

r. de Rivoli

r. du Maréchal Joffre

r. de la Buffa

r. Dr. Barety

r. du Congrès

TO **MUSÉE DES
BEAUX ARTS JULES
CHÉRET** (25m),
**MUSEE INTERNATIONAL
D'ART NAIF ANATOLE
JAKOVSKY** (150m)

r. Dante

r. St-Philippe

bd. Gambetta

r. Cronstadt

OTU Travel
r. de France

r. Meyerbeer

r. Massenet

r. Halévy

9

av. Gustave V

av. de

r. de France

Hôtel Négresco

promenade des Anglais

TO ✈ (4km)

Neptune Plage

Blue Beach

Sporting Plage

Lido Plage

Ruhl Plage

Baie des Anges

0   200 meters
0   200 yards

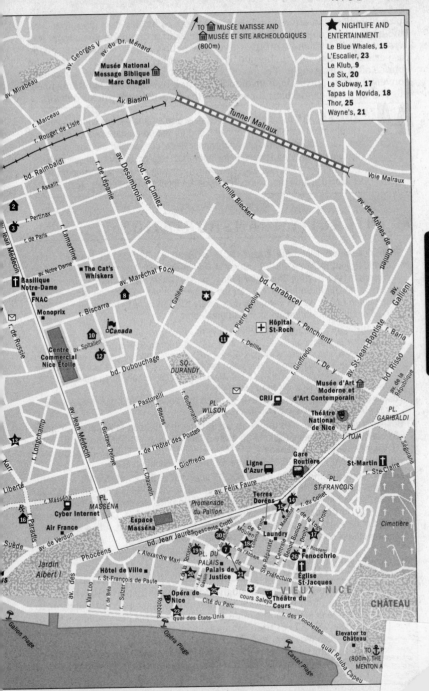

TO 🏛 MUSÉE MATISSE AND
🏛 MUSÉE ET SITE ARCHEOLOGIQUES
(800m)

★ NIGHTLIFE AND
ENTERTAINMENT
Le Blue Whales, 15
L'Escalier, 23
Le Klub, 9
Le Six, 20
Le Subway, 17
Tapas la Movida, 18
Thor, 25
Wayne's, 21

CÔTE D'AZUR

maze of pedestrian streets buzzes with shoppers by day and lively bar- and club-hoppers by night, while an immense seaside promenade gives local joggers an occasion to show off their tans. The pebbly *plages* (beaches) provide the perfect place to relax in the sun by day and gather with friends to watch the sunrise after a long night of clubbing. Nice is also a budget traveler's paradise; convenient transportation, budget lodgings, and reasonable restaurants make this city an inexpensive base for sampling the Côte d'Azur's pricier delights.

> **NOT SO NICE.** Nice's big-city appeal also means big-city crime. Women should avoid walking alone at night, and all should exercise caution around the train station, on av. Jean Médecin, in vieux Nice, around the port, and on the promenade des Anglais. Remember that large groups are still vulnerable to crime. Don't put your bags down when enjoying a meal, buying ice cream, or even trying on shoes—expert thieves are looking to lighten your load.

✈ INTERCITY TRANSPORTATION

Flights: Aéroport Nice-Côte d'Azur (NCE; ☎08 20 42 33 33). **Air France,** 10 av. de Verdun (☎08 20 82 08 20). Open M-F 9am-6pm, Sa 10am-5pm. **EasyJet** flies to **London** (see **Getting There: By Plane,** p. 31). Direct buses on the Ligne d'Azur (every 30min. 8am-9pm, €1) leave for the airport from the train station (#99) and the bus station (#98); before 8am, bus #23 (every 15-25min., €1) makes several stops, including the train station, on its way to the airport.

Trains: There are 2 primary train stations in town.

Gare SNCF Nice-Ville: Av. Thiers (☎04 93 14 82 12). Call M-F 9am-noon or 3-6pm for lost luggage, missed trains, and special assistance. Open daily 5am-midnight. Same-day ticket office open daily 5:20am-11:20pm. Info and reservation center open M-Sa 8:30am-6:30pm, Su 9am-6pm. To: **Cannes** (40min., every 20min., €5.60); **Marseille** (2hr., 16 per day, €27); **Monaco** (15min., every 10-30min., €3.10); **Paris** (5hr., 6 per day, €94).

Gare du Sud: 4 bis rue Alfred Binet (☎04 97 03 80 80), 800m from Nice-Ville. Private outbound trains to **Digne-les-Bains** and **Plan-du-Var.**

Buses: 5 bd. Jean Jaurès (☎04 93 85 61 81). Info booth open M-F 8:30am-5:30pm, Sa 9am-4pm. To **Cannes** (2hr.; M-Sa every 20min. 6:10am-9:45pm, Su every 30min. 8:30am-9:40pm) and **Monaco** (1hr.; M-Sa every 10-15min. 6:30am-8pm, Su every 20min. 6:30am-7:50pm). All bus tickets €1. Buy tickets on board.

Ferries: Corsica Ferries (☎04 92 00 42 93, reservations 08 25 09 50 95; www.corsicaferries.com) and SNCM (☎04 93 13 66 66, reservations 93 13 66 99) send high-speed ferries from the port. Reserve ahead to avoid price increases. Take bus #1 or 2 (dir.: Port). To **Corsica** (€20-40, bikes €10, small cars €40-65). Check your terminal ahead of time, as the 2 terminals are on opposite sides of the port. A free shuttle runs between them. MC/V. See **Corsica** (p. 758) for more info.

▟ ORIENTATION

Gare Nice-Ville is surrounded by a rough-and-tumble neighborhood with cheap restaurants, budget hotels, and X-rated video stores. As you exit the station, to the left is **avenue Jean Médecin,** the main artery toward **vieux Nice,** which is full of shops and *brasseries.* The €1 tram running the length of the road will bring you to the water at **place Masséna,** the site of constant breakdancing, instrumental jam sessions, and impromptu street performances. A left turn onto the pleasant **promenade du Paillon** leads to the bus station and to the large shops around

Nice's main square, **place Garibaldi.** To the right of av. Jean Médecin is **boulevard Gambetta,** the other main water-bound thoroughfare. **Promenade des Anglais,** which becomes **quai des États-Unis** east of av. Jean Médecin, hugs the coast and is a people-watcher's paradise—as are the boutiques and pricey outdoor terraces of the restaurants to the west in the rue Masséna pedestrian zone. Come nightfall, the avenues fill with large crowds of tourists and partygoers. To the left of av. Jean Médecin lie vieux Nice's narrow, pulsating streets and ever-active squares. Continuing along past the old town, you'll find **Port Lympia,** a small harbor on **quai de Lunel** bordered by clubs and bars.

▛ LOCAL TRANSPORTATION

Public Transportation: Ligne d'Azur, 10 av. Félix Faure (☎04 93 13 53 13; www. lignedazur.com). Info booth open M-F 7:15am-7pm, Sa 8am-6pm. **Buses** operate daily 7am-8pm. Tourist office provides Ligne d'Azur bus map and *Guide Infobus.* Purchase individual tickets (€1) and 1-day pass (€4) on board; carnet of 10 (€10) and week-long pass (€15) available only at the office. Noctambus runs 4 routes daily 9:10pm-1:10am. New Nice **tram** runs along av. Jean Médecin and pl. Masséna, connecting the northern reaches of the city to the eastern edge. Stops about every 5min. 6am-2am along its 8.7km route. A/C. Wheelchair-accessible. Prices are same as for buses.

Taxis: Central Taxi Riviera (☎04 93 13 78 78). Be sure to ask for price range before boarding and make sure the meter is turned on. €20-30 from the airport to the *centre-ville.* Night fares (7pm-7am) are more expensive.

Car Rental: Rent-a-Car, 23 rue de Belgique (☎04 93 16 24 16), opposite the station. Open M-F 8am-noon and 2-6:30pm, Sa 9am-noon and 2-5pm. AmEx/MC/V. **Avis, Hertz, National,** and **Europcar** are in the train station to the right. All open M-Sa 8am-noon and 2-5pm. AmEx/MC/V.

Bike Rental: Holiday Bikes, 34 av. Auber (☎04 93 16 01 62; nice@holiday-bikes. com), a few doors down from the train station. Bikes €18 per day, €75 per week; €230 deposit. Scooters €40/175; €500 deposit. Open M-Sa 9am-6:30pm. AmEx/MC/V. **Nicea Location Rent,** 12 rue de Belgique (☎04 93 82 42 71; www.nicealocationrent. com), near the station. Bikes €6 per hr., €18-20 per day; €70-88 per week; €250 deposit. Also rents in-line skates. 5-10% student discount, 10% for reservations by email. Open Feb.-Nov. daily 9am-6pm. AmEx/MC/V.

▛ PRACTICAL INFORMATION

Tourist Office: Av. Thiers (☎08 92 70 74 07; www.nicetourisme.com), next to the train station. Multilingual staff makes hotel reservations and provides *Nice: A Practical Guide* and maps. *Le Pitchoun* (www.pitchoun.com), a free guide published by local students on restaurants, nightlife, and activities, is also sometimes available. Open June-Sept. M-Sa 8am-8pm, Su 9am-7pm; Oct.-May M-Sa 8am-7pm, Su 9am-6pm. Annexes at 5 promenade des Anglais (☎08 92 70 74 07; open June-Sept. M-Sa 8am-8pm, Su 9am-7pm; Oct.-May M-Sa 9am-6pm) and Airport Terminal 1 (☎08 92 70 74 07; open June-Sept. daily 8am-9pm; Oct.-May M-Sa 8am-9pm).

Budget Travel: OTU, 48 rue de France (☎04 97 03 60 90; nice.ville@otu.fr). Books cheap international flights. Arranges tours, language courses, and outdoor excursions within France. Offers discounts on car rentals. Open daily 10am-1pm and 2-6pm.

Consulates: Canada, 10 rue Lamartine (☎04 93 92 93 22; cancons.nce@club-inter-net.fr). Open M-F 9am-noon. The closest **UK** consulate is in Monaco, 33 bd. Princesse

Charlotte (☎+377 93 50 99 54). **US,** 7 av. Gustave V (☎04 93 88 89 55; fax 93 87 07 38). Open M-F 9-11:30am and 1:30-4:30pm.

Currency Exchange: Office Provençal, 17 av. Thiers (☎04 93 88 56 80), across from Gare SNCF. 4% commission on euro-denominated traveler's checks. Open M-F 7:30am-8pm, Sa-Su 7:30am-7:30pm. **Travelex,** 13 av. Thiers (☎04 93 88 59 99), across from Gare SNCF. Open daily 7:30am-6:30pm. No commission on checks issued by some banks; Visa 3%; AmEx 6%. Branch at 2 pl. Magenta (☎04 93 88 49 88). Open June-Sept. daily 9am-7:30pm; Oct.-May M-Sa 10am-5pm.

English-Language Bookstore: The Cat's Whiskers, 30 rue Lamartine (☎04 93 80 02 66). Great selection, from bestsellers to cookbooks. Plenty of regional-interest titles, travel guides, and maps. Small used books section. Open Tu-Th 10am-noon and 2-7pm, Sa 10am-12:30pm and 3-7pm. AmEx/MC/V.

Youth Center: Centre Régional d'Information Jeunesse (CRIJ), 19 rue Gioffredo (☎04 93 80 93 93; www.crijca.fr), near the Museum of Contemporary Art. Posts summer jobs for students and gives info on housing, study, and recreation. Free Internet access with student ID (max. 30min.). Open M-F in summer 9am-6pm; in winter 10am-7pm.

Laundromats: 7 rue d'Italie (☎04 93 85 88 14), near Basilique Notre Dame. Wash €3.50, dry €1 per 18min. Open daily 7am-8pm. 11 rue de Pont Vieux (☎04 93 85 88 14). Wash €2.50, dry €1 per 16min. Open daily 7am-8pm.

Police: 1 av. Maréchal Foch (☎04 92 17 22 22), opposite end from bd. Jean Médecin.

Pharmacie de Garde: 7 rue Masséna (☎04 93 87 78 94). **Médecin à la garde** ☎08 10 85 05 05.

Hospital: Hôpital St-Roch, 5 rue Pierre Dévoluy (☎04 92 03 33 75).

Internet Access: Free at CRIJ (above). **Royal Com,** 23 rue d'Angleterre (☎04 97 20 10 79). €0.50 per 15min. Open daily 7:30am-midnight. **Cyber Internet,** 9 rue Masséna, near the beach. €3.90 per hr. Open daily 10am-11pm.

Post Office: 23 av. Thiers (☎04 93 82 65 22), near the station. Open M-F 8am-7pm, Sa 8am-noon. **Postal Code:** 06033.

ACCOMMODATIONS

This budget-friendly city draws a constant crowd of international visitors, and hostels (in the city and on the outskirts) are often full. For economizing travelers, the city offers two clusters of hotels, near the train station and near the beach. Those by the station are poorly located but generally less expensive than the cluster closer to vieux Nice and the beach. Those traveling alone or planning to indulge in Nice's nightlife would be wise to stay near vieux Nice.

NEAR VIEUX NICE AND THE BEACH

▨ **Auberge de Jeunesse (HI) Les Camelias,** 3 rue Spitalieri (☎04 93 62 15 54; nice-camelias@fuaj.org), near the Centre Commercial Nice Étoile. Ideally located between the train station and vieux Nice. Clean bathrooms and facilities. Kitchen (open 3-10:30pm) and bar (beer €2; open until 11pm). Breakfast included. Small lockers €1. Laundry €3. Internet access €3 per hr. Free Wi-Fi. Reception 24hr. Lockout 11am-3pm. Reserve online only at www.hihostels.com. Dorms €21. AmEx/MC/V. ❶

▨ **Hôtel Petit Trianon,** 11 rue Paradis (☎04 93 87 50 46; hotel.nice.lepetittrianon@wanadoo.fr), left off pl. Masséna. Some of the colorful rooms have balconies; ask when making reservation. Kitchen. Breakfast €5. Laundry €10 per 5kg. Free Internet in lobby. Free Wi-Fi. Reception 8:30am-2:30pm and 6-10:30pm or by request for late arrivals. Reservations required, preferably by email. From mid-June to mid-Sept. singles €30, with bath €35; doubles €40-42/50-53; triples €60-75; quads €76-96. From mid-

Sept. to mid-Oct. and from Apr. to mid-June singles €28-32; doubles €36-38, with bath €44-46; triples €54-66; quads €68-84. From mid-Oct. to Mar. singles €25, with bath €30; doubles €33-35/39-42; triples €50-59; quads €62-74. AmEx/MC/V. ❷

Star Hôtel, 14 rue Biscarra (☎04 93 85 19 03; www.hotel-star.com). Quiet, charming hotel between the train station and vieux Nice. Pastel-colored rooms with comfortable beds have TVs, A/C, clean bathrooms, and soundproof windows. English-speaking owner offers advice on sights and restaurants. Breakfast €6. Wi-Fi. Reception 7am-10pm or by request for late arrivals. Open Dec.-Oct. July-Aug. singles €60; doubles €75; triples €95. Sept. and Apr.-June singles €55; doubles €65; triples €85. Oct. and Dec.-Mar. singles €45; doubles €55; triples €70. AmEx/MC/V. ❹

NEAR THE TRAIN STATION

▓ **Hôtel Belle Meunière,** 21 av. Durante (☎04 93 88 66 15; fax 93 82 51 76), opposite the train station. According to legend, one of Napoleon's generals gave this stunning mansion to his mistress as a gift. Budget favorite now hosts a relaxed crowd in 4- to 5-bed co-ed dorms. Large windows and breakfast included in the social courtyard. Luggage storage available after check-out (€2). Laundry from €5.50. Parking available. Reception 7:30am-midnight; access code after hours. Dorms €17, with shower €22; doubles with shower from €50; triples from €60; quads from €80. MC/V. ❶

▓ **Hôtel Pastoral,** 27 rue Assalit (☎04 93 85 17 22). From the train station, cross av. Jean Médecin and walk down rue Assalit. Well-kept rooms. A private alternative to social hostels. English-speaking owner hands out free maps and advice. Dorms with mini-fridges, A/C, and microwaves. Free beach towel loan or laptop loan within hotel. Breakfast €3. Wi-Fi. Reception 7:30am-midnight or by request for late arrivals. Reservations required. Apr.-Sept. dorms €20; singles with shower €30; doubles €45, with bath €55. Oct.-Mar. dorms €15; singles €25; doubles €35, with bath €40. Extra bed €8. MC/V. ❶

Hôtel Les Orangers, 10 bis av. Durante (☎04 93 87 51 41; fax 93 82 57 82), across from Hôtel Belle Meunière. Basic, clean co-ed dorms with showers and fridges. Free luggage storage. Sheets and blankets provided in dorms. Reception daily 8:30am-2pm and 5:30pm-midnight; key access after hours. Reservations recommended July-Aug. Open Dec.-Oct. Dorms €18; singles €25-35; doubles €42-55; triples €58-65. MC/V. ❶

Hotel du Piemont, 19 rue Alsace Lorraine (☎04 93 88 25 15; hoteldupiemont@ wanadoo.fr). Off the 1st street after the train station, down a small pedestrian street. Absolutely-no-frills hotel has some of Nice's cheapest rooms, especially for groups. Room quality varies greatly; some have full bath, kitchenettes, A/C, TVs, and phones; others have none of the above but are nearly half the price. Reception 24hr. Apr.-Sept. singles and doubles €20-42; triples €45-49; quads €52-58. Oct.-Mar. singles €20-35; doubles €24-41; triples €32-48; quads €48-58. AmEx/MC/V. ❶

OUTSKIRTS

▓ **Villa St-Exupéry,** 22 av. Gravier (toll free ☎0800 30 74 09; www.vsaint.com), 5km from the *centre-ville.* Renowned for great value, social atmosphere, and English-speaking staff. Award-winning hostel attracts young travelers with outstanding amenities, €5.50 pizza, and €1 beer. Most rooms with bath, some with balcony views of Nice. Canyoning and sailing tours led by staff; call or check the website for prices and info. Breakfast included in the common room, which turns into a lively bar at night. Laundry €5. Free Internet (Wi-Fi and desktops). Call for pickup at Comte de Falicon tram stop. Online reservations preferred. Dorms €16-30; doubles €55-80. MC/V. ❶

◘ FOOD

Nice offers the typical big-city repertoire of restaurants, from four-star establishments to basic *brasseries* to holes in the wall. The city's pride and joy is its *niçois* cuisine, cooked in olive oil and flavored with Mediterranean spices. Try the crusty *pan bagnat*, a loaf of bread topped with tuna, sardines, and vegetables, *pissaladière* pizza loaded with onions, anchovies, and olives, and *socca*, or *tourta de blea*, a thin tart with pine nuts. The *salade niçoise* combines tuna, olives, eggs, potatoes, tomatoes, and mustard dressing. Tomato, eggplant, and zucchini are baked to form *ratatouille*. Ask the tourist office for a list of restaurants that serve traditional *niçois* dishes. Load up on groceries from the **Monoprix** supermarket, av. Jean Médecin, near the Centre Commercial Nice Étoile. (☎04 92 47 72 62. Open M-Sa 8:30am-8pm. AmEx/MC/V.) Fresh olives, cheeses, and fruits take over **cours Saleya** during the morning market. (Open Tu-Su 7am-1pm.) Cours Saleya is also home to a flower market; stop by just before it closes for bargain blossoms. (Open Tu-Su 7am-1pm.) A produce market springs up on **avenue Maché de la Libération.** (Open Tu-Su 7am-1pm.) Avoid the unremarkable restaurants on rue Masséna, cours Saleya, and along the promenade des Anglais, which trap tourists nightly. **Avenue Jean Médecin** features reasonably priced *brasseries*, panino vendors, and kebab stands.

▓ **La Merenda,** 4 rue Bosio. Savor the work of a culinary master, Dominique Le Stanc, who turned his back on one of Nice's best-known restaurants to open this 12-table gem. Outstanding *plats* include fried zucchini flowers (€11). Try *ratatouille* (€11) or the *pâtés au pistou* (garlic basil pasta; €11). *Plats* €12-16. Pizza €11. Open M-F noon-1:30pm and 7-9pm. Reserve in person for dinner; seatings at 7 and 9pm. Cash only. ❸

▓ **Lou Pilha Leva,** 10-13 rue du Collet (☎04 93 13 99 08), in vieux Nice. Lively staff dishes out plate after plate of *socca* (€2), *pissaladière* (€2), and *salade niçoise* (€7). The assortment *niçois* (€8) offers a hearty sampling of local cuisine. Enjoy excellent—albeit greasy—grub. Pizza €4.50. Lasagna €9. Open daily 9am-midnight. MC/V. ❷

Le Restaurant d'Angleterre, 25 rue d'Angleterre (☎04 93 88 64 49), near the train station. Local favorite known for traditional French and English favorites. €16 *menu* includes salad, *plat,* side dish, and dessert. Sample 12 Burgundy snails for €18. Open Tu-Sa 11:45am-2pm and 6:45-9:50pm, Su 11:45am-2pm. MC/V. ❸

Speakeasy, 7 rue Lamartine (☎04 93 85 59 50). American expat and longtime vegan prepares every dish in Nice's only completely vegan restaurant. Testimonials from famous vegetarians from Gandhi to Brigitte Bardot line the walls of the cozy interior. Large specials (€9.20) and desserts like banana ice cream—without the cream, of course—satisfy even the staunchest carnivores. 2 courses and dessert €13.50. Open in summer M-F noon-2:15pm and 7-9:15pm, Sa noon-2:15pm; in winter Tu-F noon-2:15pm and 7-9:15pm, Sa noon-2:15pm. Cash only. ❸

Fenocchio, pl. Rosetti (☎04 93 80 72 52), in vieux Nice. Nice's best-loved ice-cream shop. More than 96 flavors, including tomato basil, beer, lavender, black olive, and avocado. 1 scoop in homemade cone €2. Open daily 10:30am-2am. MC/V. ❶

L'Art Gourmand, 21 rue du Marché (☎04 93 62 51 79), in vieux Nice. Chocolatier and *salon de thé.* Beautiful sugared fruits that look more like stained glass can be placed into decorative boxes and saved as souvenirs—if they survive the trip home. Homemade gourmet chocolates €5.20 per 100g. Handmade cookies and tarts €2.90 per 100g. Open Sept.-June 10am-7pm; July-Aug. 10am-midnight. MC/V. ❶

People, 12 rue Pastorelli (☎04 93 85 08 43). A trendy setting for traditional cuisine, with stone walls and a stainless-steel bar. Tasty dishes like beef tartare (€12) and *magret de canard* (duck breast) with *foie gras* (€18) fill enormous chalkboard menus.

CÔTE D'AZUR

Wine €3-6 per glass. *Plats* €8-17. Lunch *menu* €15. Dinner *menus* from €21. Open M noon-2:30pm, Tu-F noon-2:30pm and 5:30-11pm, Sa 5:30-11pm. Cash only. ❸

Indian Lounge, 34 rue Droite (☎04 93 85 38 39; www.indianlounge.fr). Quick, spicy, and cheap Indian fare in a unique setting. Mesmerizing interior full of paper lanterns, Hindu shrines, and enough colors to make a rainbow blush. Projector quietly plays Bollywood films on the wall. Outdoor tables shaded by ornate umbrellas. Try the biryani chicken with rice (€12), vegetable curry (€6), or a variety of Indian breads (€2-4). *Entrées* €2-7.50. Meat *plats* €10-12. Open daily noon-2:30pm and 7pm-1:30am. MC/V. ❸

J. Multari, 26 bd. Gambetta (☎04 93 92 01 99). Excellent, cheap fare served on marble countertops and polished wood tables. Some locations with outdoor terrace. Try a goat-cheese, chicken, or ham sandwich (€3.30), pizza (€1.50), or *crêpe* with Corsican jam (€5). Local favorite also offers a bread selection including whole wheat, organic, and seasoned breads. Branches at: 2 rue Alphonse Karr (☎04 93 87 45 90); 22 rue Gioffredo (☎04 93 80 00 31); 13 cours Saleya (☎04 93 62 31 33); 8 bd. Jean Jaurès (☎04 93 62 10 39; takeout only). All open M-Sa 6am-8:15pm. Cash only. ❶

Restaurant de Paris, 28 rue d'Angleterre (☎04 93 88 99 88). A cheaper sit-down option. Cheap *menu* (lunch €10, dinner €13) includes *entrée, plat,* side dish, and dessert. Salads €7.50. Pizza €7-8.50. Open noon-3pm and 7-11pm. MC/V. ❷

◎ SIGHTS

One look at Nice's waves and you may be tempted to spend your entire stay stretched out on the sand. As the city with the second-most museums in France, Nice also offers history, art, and beautiful architecture. Nice's museums have always been easy on the eyes, but are now easy on the wallet as well; admission to all municipal museums is free as of July 2008. Ask the tourist office or in the museums for a complete listing of the city's offerings.

■**VIEUX NICE.** Hand-painted awnings, beautiful churches, and lively squares await at every turn in vieux Nice. Though filled with the inevitable slew of souvenir shops, vieux Nice remains the heart of the city. *(Tours of the vieille ville start at the tourist office Sa 9:30am. €12.)* Bilingual street signs introduce you to Niçard, a subdialect of the Occitan language still spoken by half a million French. Rue Droite has various handmade furniture stores and mosaic studios. At **Les Trois Étoiles,** you can fill a glass bottle with homemade vinegar, olive oil, or dessert liqueur. *(26 rue Pairoliere. ☎04 93 92 30 83. Open in summer daily 10am-8pm; in winter Tu-Su 10am-8pm. AmEx/MC/V.)* **Terres Dorées** offers fresh-scented handmade soaps and bath products created using regional herbs. *(8 rue du Pont Vieux. ☎04 93 62 63 02. Open M-Sa July-Aug. 10am-7:30pm; Sept.-June 10am-noon and 2:30-7:30pm. MC/V.)*

■**MUSÉE DES BEAUX-ARTS.** Ukrainian Princess Kotschoubey's former villa has been converted into a celebration of French and Italian painting, with works by Dufy, Fragonard, Mossa, Picasso, Rodin, Vuillard, and Van Loo. Dufy captures his city's spontaneity with sensational paintings of the town at rest and at play, while Mossa's sensual, violent work simultaneously intrigues and disturbs viewers. The museum also displays a collection of Chéret's pastel works. The museum, organized by century, can please everyone from hard-core art-history buffs to those who simply like pretty paintings. *(33 av. Baumettes. Take bus #38 to Musée Chéret or #12 to Grosso. ☎04 92 15 28 28; www.musee-beaux-arts-nice.org. Open M and W-Su 10am-6pm. Tours Th and Sa 2:30pm in French, F 2:30pm in English. Free.)*

■**MUSÉE MATISSE.** A 17th-century Genoese villa is the setting for Matisse's three-dimensional works, including dozens of paper-cutting tableaux. The museum contains several of this Nice resident's early masterpieces, such as a painting of Ajaccio, where Matisse felt the first "shock of what became Fauvism." Furniture and other effects, like Matisse's painting table, lend a personal touch, while both early and later works show the artist's progression throughout his long career. *(164 av. des Arènes de Cimiez. Take bus #15, 17, 20, 22, or 25 to Arènes. Free bus tickets between Musée Chagall and Musée Matisse; ask at either ticket counter. ☎ 04 93 81 08 08; www.musee-matisse-nice.org. Open M and W-Su 10am-6pm. Tours in English by reservation. Call for info on lectures. Wheelchair-accessible. Free. Tours €4, students €1.50. MC/V.)*

◾**MUSÉE NATIONAL MESSAGE BIBLIQUE MARC CHAGALL.** This impressive museum was founded by Chagall to showcase an assortment of biblically themed pieces that he gave to the French government in 1966. Twelve canvases illustrating the first two books of the Hebrew Bible are arranged based on color (rather than the temporal development of the Bible), as the artist wished. The museum includes an auditorium with stained-glass panels depicting the creation story. The auditorium hosts concerts; inquire at the entrance. *(Av. du Docteur Ménard. Walk 15min. north from station or take bus #22, dir.: Rimiez, to Musée Chagall. ☎ 04 93 53 87 20; www.musee-chagall.fr. Open M and W-Su 10am-6pm. Last tickets sold 30min. before closing. €8.50, students 18-25 €6.50, under 18 free; 1st and 3rd Su of month free. MC/V.)*

MUSÉE D'ART MODERNE ET D'ART CONTEMPORAIN. A monumental sculpture leaning against an impressive glass facade welcomes visitors to exhibits of French New Realists and American pop artists like ◾Lichtenstein and Warhol. The minimalist galleries pay homage to avant-garde creations, including statues by Niki de St-Phalle and eye-catching color pieces by Yves Klein. Contemporary art temporary exhibits showcase artists from all over. *(Promenade des Arts, near av. St-Jean-Baptiste. Take bus #5, dir.: St-Charles, to Musée Promenade des Arts. ☎ 04 93 62 61 62; www.mamac-nice.org. Open Tu-Su 10am-6pm. Tours in English available July-Aug. by reservation. Free. Tours €3, students €1.50, under 18 free. Cash only.)*

MUSÉE INTERNATIONAL D'ART NAIF ANATOLE JAKOVSKY. This fun and unique museum presents over 200 years' worth of art by the likes of Rousseau and Lakovic. Colorful works from French, American, Spanish, and Croatian artists fill this lesser-known museum. *(Av. Val-Marie, in the Château Ste-Helene. ☎ 04 93 71 78 33. Take bus #38 to the museum's stop. Open M and W-Su 10am-6pm. Free.)*

MUSÉE ET SITE ARCHÉOLOGIQUES DE NICE CEMENELUM. Aspiring archaeologists aren't the only ones who will enjoy these second- and third-century ruins and the museum devoted to them. Thermal baths, streets, and a residential district—the only remains of the Roman town of Cemenelum—can be found just outside the museum's back door. Pottery, figurines, coins, columns, and other artifacts from the town and other ancient civilizations fill every inch of the fascinating museum. Downstairs, interactive displays of ancient Roman games come with directions and an open invitation to try them out. *(160 av. des Arènes de Cimiez, next to Musée Matisse. ☎ 04 93 81 59 57; www.musee-archeologique-nice.org. Open M and W-Su 10am-6pm. Tours Th 3:30pm. Free. Tours €3.)*

LE CHÂTEAU. The remains of an 11th-century fort, Le Château marks the city's birthplace. Celto-Ligurian tribes called the hillside home until they were ousted by the Romans in 154 BC. Centuries later, Provençal counts built a castle and the Cathédrale Ste-Marie on top of the hill as a symbol of their authority over the developing village below. Louis XIV methodically destroyed the château and fortress in 1706; all that remains today is a green park, stone ruins, and Nice's best view at the highest point, ◾Terrace Nietzsche. After the walk to the top, stand in front of the manmade waterfall and cool off in the breeze emanating from its base. In summer, an outdoor theater hosts orchestral and vocal musicians. *(☎ 04 93 85 62 33. Info booth open July-Aug. Tu-F 9:30am-12:30pm and 1:30-6pm.*

Purchase tickets at FNAC in the Nice Étoile center. Park open daily June-Aug. 9am-8pm; Sept. 10am-7pm; Oct.-Mar. 8am-6pm; Apr.-May 8am-7pm. Free walk to the top. Elevator daily June-Aug. 9am-8pm; Sept. and Apr.-May 10am-7pm; Oct.-Mar. 10am-6pm. €0.80 up, round-trip €1.)

CATHÉDRALE ORTHODOXE RUSSE SAINT-NICOLAS. Also known as the Église Russe, this cathedral was commissioned by Empress Marie Feodorovna in memory of her first husband, Tsar Nicholas Alexandrovich. The cathedral stands on the site of the tsar's villa, where he died in 1865. Following its dedication in 1912, the cathedral's ornate gold interior quickly became a haven for exiled Russian nobles. Solemn chants on recording, dim lights, and gold and silver idols now greet modern travelers, exiled or not. *(17 bd. du Tsarevitch, off bd. Gambetta. ☎ 04 93 96 88 02. Open in summer M-Sa 9am-noon and 2:30-6pm, Su 2:30-6pm; in winter M-Sa 9:30am-noon and 2:30-5pm, Su 2:30-5pm. Closed during mass. €3, students €2.)*

JARDIN ALBERT I AND ESPACE MASSÉNA. Jardin Albert I—the city's oldest park—is full of bubbling fountains, hanging flowers, and stoic sculptures. The outdoor **Théâtre de Verdure** presents concerts in summer (contact the tourist office for info). The young—and the young at heart—enjoy a colorful moonbounce in the evenings. Unfortunately, the picturesque park is one of the most dangerous spots in Nice after nightfall. Tourists should avoid crossing the park at night and instead stick to the pedestrian zones on pl. Masséna and av. de Verdun. *(Between av. de Verdun and bd. Jean Jaurès, off promenade des Anglais and quai des États-Unis. Box office open daily 10:30am-noon and 3:30-6:30pm. MC/V.)*

OTHER SIGHTS. Creatively named by the rich English community that commissioned it, the **promenade des Anglais**, a palm-lined seaside boulevard, is filled with children, hand-holding couples, and clusters of backpackers. The stately **Hôtel Négresco** presents the best of Belle Époque luxury with crystal chandeliers and an extensive collection of valuable artwork. The seashore between bd. Gambetta and the Opéra alternates private beaches with crowded public strands, but a large section west of bd. Gambetta is public. The popular **Baie des Anges** is lined with stretches of rock, not sand; bring a beach mat.

🎵 ENTERTAINMENT

Théâtre du Cours, 5 rue Poissonnerie (☎04 93 80 12 67), in vieux Nice. Stages traditional drama and zany French comedies. €15, students €10. MC/V.

Théâtre National de Nice, promenade des Arts (☎04 93 13 90 90; www.tnn.fr). Presents plays and concerts. €10-30, students €7.50-28. Box office open June-July Tu-Sa 1-7pm; Aug.-May Tu-Sa 2-7pm, Su at 1pm for same-day tickets only. MC/V.

Opéra de Nice, 4-6 rue St-François de Paule (☎04 93 13 98 53 or 04 92 17 40 79). Stages productions Sept.-May and hosts visiting orchestras and soloists year-round. €8-40. Ticket window open Tu-Sa 10am-6pm. MC/V.

FNAC, 24 av. Jean Médecin (☎04 92 17 77 77; www.fnac.com), across from the Basilique Notre-Dame. Sells tickets for most musical and theatrical events in Nice. Open M-Sa 10am-7:30pm. AmEx/MC/V.

⬛ NIGHTLIFE

In Nice, lazy days in the sun mean wild nights on the town. Young and lively, the scene in Nice is full of backpackers, young professionals, and students. The bars and nightclubs around **rue Masséna, vieux Nice,** and **Port Lympia** cater to all musical tastes with house, jazz, and rock. As night falls, the **promenade des Anglais** and **place Masséna** fill with street performers and pedestrians.

Exorbitant covers and expensive drinks can make for pricey partying, but discounts are sometimes offered on Thursdays, on Sundays, before midnight, and to well-dressed females. Nice's nightlife is in constant flux, and hot spots shift rapidly; ask around to make sure you're hitting up the latest and greatest *avant-boîtes* (pre-clubs) and *boîtes de nuit* (nightclubs). The dress code is simple: look good, unless you prefer a night in a pub full of foreign backpackers. Almost all clubs and some bars will turn away people in shorts, sandals, sneakers, or baseball caps. Dressing with *classe* (style) is paramount. Still, Nice's dress code is not quite as strict as other places on the Riviera. A good pair of jeans and a nice shirt are often acceptable at even the most happening clubs. For gay nightlife, check out http://aglae.supersonique.net or ask at a local bar for a map listing all of the GLBT-friendly bars and clubs in town.

> **!** **LET'S NOT GO.** Some locals have a reputation for harassing people on the promenade, around the train station, on the beach, and in the Jardin Albert I at night; avoid empty streets and do not walk alone.

CÔTE D'AZUR

■ **Wayne's,** 15 rue de la Préfecture (☎04 93 13 46 99; www.waynes.fr). Huge crowd every night in and around one of vieux Nice's most popular bars. English-speaking bartenders serve travelers while a rowdier crew dances to pop-rock on packed tabletops and benches downstairs. Rock posters and plasma TVs complete the decor. Pints €6. Mixed drinks €7.50. Live music or DJ. Ladies Night Th in low season. Happy hour noon-2pm and 5-9pm; beer €3.90. Open daily noon-2am. AmEx/MC/V.

■ **Thor,** 32 cours Saleya (☎04 93 62 49 90; www.thor-pub.com). Raucous Scandinavian pub is a local favorite. Svelte Anglophone staff pours black shots of fiery *sma gra* (vodka with anise and Turkish pepper; €3) for a playful crowd. Choose between relaxed outdoor seating or jamming with great bands upstairs. Beer €4.50. Shots €3. Live music daily from 10pm. Happy hour 5:30-9pm; beer €3.50. Open daily 5:30pm-2:30am. MC/V.

L'Escalier, 10 rue Bosio (☎04 93 92 64 39; www.pub-lescalier.com). DJs spin R&B, funk, house, and hip hop for a lively mix of locals late into the night. In early evening, a relaxed crowd shoots pool and sips gin fizz (€10), but the real party starts when the expensive cover does. Large selection of beer €4-9. Mixed drinks €10-15. Cover F-Sa after 1am €10; includes 1 drink. Open daily 6pm-5am. MC/V.

Le Klub, 6 rue Halévy (☎04 93 16 87 26). Popular gay club attracts men and women to its sleek lounge, active dance floor, and mirrored stage. Drinks served in plastic cups with lids and straw. Pick up a free Klub Mag, the club's monthly newsletter, at any gay establishment in Nice for up-to-date listings of theme nights like 90's music and karaogay. Mixed drinks €8-10. Cover €11-14. Open W-Su midnight-5am. AmEx/MC/V.

Tapas la Movida, 2 bis rue de l'Abbaye (☎04 93 62 27 46). Hole-in-the-wall bar attracts a young, alternative crowd that enjoys live music and cheap drinks. Figure out how to crawl home before attempting the ■ **bar-o-mètre** (€17), a meter-long box of shots. Live reggae, rock, and ska concerts M-F (€3). Theme parties F-Sa. Happy hour Su; 8 shots €6. Open July-Aug. daily 9pm-12:30am; Sept.-June M-Sa 9pm-12:30am. Cash only.

Le Six, 6 rue Bosio (☎04 93 62 66 64). Between a nightclub and a piano bar. Draws 20- to 40-somethings who dance to Top 40. Original decor, complete with an 18th-century ceiling. Look out for the occasional *soirées tapis* (kissing nights) and "Raining Men" themes. Beer €7. Mixed drinks €5-10. Live music Tu-Su. Open Tu-Su 10pm-4am. MC/V.

Le Blue Whales, 1 rue Mascoïnat (☎04 93 62 90 94). Among the only bars open after 2:30am without a cover charge. Large, relaxed crowd of late-night partygoers. Listen to live music downstairs or play pool upstairs. Beer €4.50. Mixed drinks €8-10. Happy hour 6pm-midnight; mixed drinks €3 off. Open daily 6pm-4:30am. MC/V.

Le Subway, 19 rue Droite (☎04 93 80 56 27), in vieux Nice. Unpretentious, electric atmosphere. Locals and tourists dance to pop-rock in vaulted rooms downstairs while leopard-print stools set the mood in the quieter honeymoon suite of a bar upstairs. Beer €5. Mixed drinks €8. Cover €4. Open daily midnight-5am. Closed M in winter. MC/V.

❊ FESTIVALS

Carnaval (www.nicecarnaval.com), in early spring. Nice gives Rio a run for its money as the promenade des Anglais and the quai des États-Unis host 2 weeks of parades, fireworks, and concerts. Confetti battles, masked balls, and floral processions fill the city with color by day and endless partying by night. Tickets €10-30.

Nice Jazz Festival, Arènes et Jardins de Cimiez (☎08 20 80 04 00 or 08 92 70 75 07; www.nicejazzfest.com), in mid-July. Attracts 55,000 visitors, who listen to 500 musicians in 75 concerts over an 8-day period. The olive trees of the suburb of Cimiez provide an unforgettable backdrop for over 120hr. of fabulous international music. Free shuttle from pl. Masséna during concerts. Concerts 7pm-midnight. Tickets €31-51 per night, students €22-36; 3-day pass €105; 8-day €185. MC/V.

❂ DAYTRIPS FROM NICE

SAINT-PAUL

SAP (☎04 93 58 37 60) sends bus #400 from Nice to St-Paul (1hr., 23 per day, €1). The last buses leave St-Paul for Nice at 7:20pm from the stop just outside the town entrance.

If you visit one medieval village on the Côte d'Azur, make it St-Paul (sehn-pohl). This clifftop hamlet draws more than two million visitors each year to its ivy-covered cobblestone streets. Though touristy, the village remains a pedestrian delight. A walk along the rambling perimeter yields incredible views of the countryside, while an endless variety—both in quality and style—of colorful artwork brightens the doorways of more than 50 tiny galleries. St-Paul attracted a veritable colony of creation when Chagall, Léger, Matisse, Picasso, and several others came to the hilltop for inspiration. Don't miss **La Colombe d'Or** restaurant, once the hangout of artists like Chagall and Folon, who painted the colorful sign himself. The somber 13th-century **Église Collégiale** is a period-appropriate dark, stark church. Its wide, vaulted interior is home to the eerily mounted skull of St-Étienne. (Open daily 9am-8pm.) In a quiet cemetery just outside the southeast end of the village walls is the resting place of Marc Chagall. As you descend the first steps, his gravestone is the third on the right. (Open daily July-Aug. 7:30am-8pm; Sept.-June 8am-5pm.) If so much art leaves you longing for more artistic talent, head to the **Grande Fountain,** built in 1850, to get rid of some loose change and wish for your own inspiration.

Though the village is brimming with galleries, St-Paul's most impressive collection of art is in nearby ▓**Fondation Maeght,** 1km from the *centre-ville.* From the St-Paul bus stop, take chemin de Ste-Claire, to the left of the Chapelle Ste-Claire. Follow this path until it reaches a road, where blue signs will direct you to the foundation. Alternatively, take bus #400 to Fondation Maeght and follow the same signs. The fantastic indoor and outdoor galleries, designed by Joseph Sert to showcase modern and contemporary art, are the perfect backdrop for a stunning collection of works by Arp, Calder, Chagall, Giacometti, Léger, and Miró. Highlights include Miró's whimsical garden labyrinth—which can be viewed from above with a quick climb to the gallery's roof—the Giacometti courtyard, and Chagall's impressive *La Vie.* Temporary exhibits usually change every three to six months. (☎04 93 32 81 63; www.fondation-maeght. com. Open daily July-Oct. 10am-7pm; Nov.-June 10am-12:30pm and 2:30-6pm. €11, students €9, under 10 free. Camera permit €2.50. AmEx/MC/V.)

After your exploring, treat yourself to lentils (€11) or tapas (€4.50) at **Chez Andréas ❸**, rempart Ouest, in the port. This well-designed *salon de thé* is popular with a young local crowd and offers excellent *plats du jour* (€8-12), along with views of the ramparts and the sea. (☎04 93 32 98 32. Open daily noon-midnight. MC/V.) The **tourist office**, 2 rue Grande, is inside the village walls just after the arched entryway. The knowledgeable staff is one of the most helpful around and dispenses free maps, restaurant and hotel listings, and info on galleries. Themed 1hr. tours are available in English by request. (Tours 10am-6pm. €8, under 12 free.) Rent balls for *pétanque* (€5 per person per hr.) or schedule a game with an experienced tourist office liaison. (☎04 93 32 86 95; www.saint-pauldevence.com. Open daily June-Sept. 10am-7pm; Oct.-May 10am-6pm.)

THE CORNICHES

A panorama of rocky shores, beaches, and luxurious villas lines the coast between hectic Nice and high-rolling Monaco. These tiny towns are a break from the bustle of their glamorous neighbors. Though their beaches are small and pebbly—and a few more stops on the train lead to larger, jaw-dropping Menton—short and inexpensive rides still make any town in the Corniches (kohr-neesh) a sweet daytrip from Nice. The train offers an exceptional glimpse of the coast's towns, while cheaper but slower buses maneuvering along the high roads of the Corniches provide views of the cliffs and sea below.

FINDING YOUR NICHE IN THE 'NICHES. Trains and buses between Nice and Monaco serve most of the Corniches. With about two departures per hour, trains from Nice to Monaco stop at Villefranche-sur-Mer (8min., €1.60), Beaulieu-sur-Mer (12min., €1.70), and Eze Bord-de-Mer (20min., €2.40). Several RCA buses (☎04 93 85 64 44; www.rca.tm.fr) travel between Nice and Monaco. Bus #100 leaves Nice every 15min., stopping in: Villefranche-sur-Mer (10min.); Beaulieu-sur-Mer (20min.); Monaco-Ville (40min.); Monte-Carlo (45min.). Eze-le-Village can be reached by bus #82 (20min.; M-Sa 14 per day, Su 6), while bus #81 serves St-Jean-Cap-Ferrat (25min., M-Sa, €1). The last buses to Nice (M-Sa) leave Eze-le-Village at 6:15pm, St-Jean-Cap-Ferrat at 7:50pm, Monte-Carlo at 8:30pm, Monaco-Ville at 8:35pm, and Villefranche-sur-Mer at 8:55pm.

EZE   ☎ 04 93

The medieval village of Eze (ehz; pop. 2500) makes an excellent daytrip for its spectacular views of the coast, historic streets, and scenic hikes. On the top of the Corniches, Eze-le-Village is a tangle of arches and blooming jasmine, bursting with unique—but expensive—souvenir shops and art galleries. These houses, 429m above the sea, have been inhabited for over 25 centuries by everyone from the Moors to the Piedmontese. Now, only a few of Eze's residents live in the medieval village; most people live below in Col d'Eze or even farther down in the seaside town of Eze Bord-de-Mer (also called Eze-sur-Mer). The rocky coast is popular with celebrities; Bono and Princess Antoinette Grimaldi of Monaco frequent nearby villas.

🖭🔂 **TRANSPORTATION AND PRACTICAL INFORMATION.** A taxi (☎06 09 84 17 84) from Eze Bord-de-Mer to Eze-le-Village costs €20. The **tourist office,** pl. du Général de Gaulle, outside the main part of the medieval city, is near the bus stop. (☎04 93 41 26 00; www.eze-riviera.com. Open daily June-Sept. 9am-7pm; Oct. and May 9am-6pm; Nov-Apr. 9am-5pm. Guided 1hr. tours of the medieval village and garden €6; 2-person min.) There is also an annex next to the train station. (☎04 93 01 52 00. Open May-Oct. M-Sa 10am-1pm and 2-6pm.)

🖸 **SIGHTS.** A favorite of photo-snapping tourists, Eze-le-Village recounts the Riviera's tumultuous past with a series of remains. The **Porte des Maures,** a doorway carved into the cliff face, was the Moors' golden ticket into Eze during their 10th-century destruction of Provence. A surprise attack proved highly successful; they maintained control of the village for the following 70 years. Nearby, the **Chapelle de la Saint-Croix** is the oldest building in the village. The austere facade of the **Église Paroissial,** an 18th-century structure, conceals an elaborate Baroque interior adorned with *trompe l'oeil* frescoes, crumbling plaster ironically trimmed in gold, and Phoenician crosses. (☎04 93 41 00 38. Open daily July-Aug. 9:30am-7:30pm; Sept.-June 9:30am-6pm.) The **Jardin Exotique d'Eze** offers fabulous views that stretch all the way from St-Tropez to the Italian coast. Centered on a Savoy fortress that was razed in 1706 by the armies of Louis XIV, the garden displays the earth-goddess sculptures of Jean-Philippe Richard accompanied by the goddess's alluring quotations. Over 400 species of cactuses and exotic plants dot the rocky hillside. (☎04 93 41 10 30. Open daily July-Aug. 9am-8pm; Sept.-June 9am-5pm or 7pm, depending on sunlight. €5.)

Eze-le-Village offers more than narrow streets and pretty vistas. The second-largest factory of the **Parfumerie Fragonard,** built in 1968, clings to the hillside. Free 15min. tours in nine languages explain the elaborate perfume-, cosmetic-, and soap-making processes. (☎04 93 41 05 05; www.fragonard.com. Open daily Apr.-Oct. 8:30am-6:30pm; Nov.-Mar. 8:30am-noon and 2-6pm. AmEx/MC/V.) Another large perfume factory based in Grasse, the **Parfumerie Galimard,** has a small museum in Eze that offers free guided visits. (Across from the tourist office. ☎04 93 41 10 70. Open daily 9am-6:30pm. AmEx/MC/V.)

🖾 **HIKING.** Centuries ago, Théodore de Banville complained that "to reach Eze one has to climb up from the sea or drop down from the sky." Luckily, roads make Eze-le-Village far more accessible these days. For a 75min. hike to the top, follow **chemin de Friedrich Nietzsche** (head down the road toward Monaco, and the trail will be on the left, 100m east of the train station). Wear comfortable shoes and stop by one of the snack stands across from the train station to pick up water before taking off. This path is grueling but rewards hikers with increasingly spectacular and secluded vistas of the Corniches. Nietzsche certainly derived plenty of inspiration from the trail: it was here that he composed the third part of *Thus Spoke Zarathustra.* If you aren't in need of inspiration or sweat stains, bus #112 connects Nice to Eze-le-Village (7 per day). From May through October, daily municipal shuttle #83 also connects Eze-le-Village and Eze Bord-de-Mer (8 per day 9:30am-6:40pm, €1).

A total of 30 trails crisscrosses the landscape and take hikers to the seaside, the **Moyenne Corniche,** and the **Grand Corniche.** Routes range in length and difficulty; most take 1hr. and require sturdy shoes, water, and a map. One leads to the **Oppidum of Mont Bastide** (560m,1 hr., marked in yellow), which offers superior vistas of Eze. The tourist office has maps and info, and **Eze Rando** (☎04 93 01 51 52) offers more details. Some paths have fallen into disuse; check with the office or Eze Rando before you go.

CÔTE D'AZUR

BEAULIEU-SUR-MER ☎ 04 93

Napoleon was known as a man of great action, but apparently not of words—creativity failed him when he named this seaside resort "beautiful place." In the late 19th century, elite English and French visitors who shared Napoleon's sentiment flooded the town, building Belle Époque villas, four-star hotels, and a classy casino. Today, the money has moved on to quieter mansions in nearby St-Jean-Cap-Ferrat, but Beaulieu (boh-lyuh; pop. 3675) still attracts a few stars who dock their yachts in its 800-boat marina. A spectacular Greek villa makes the town a good starting point for the seaside walk to St-Jean-Cap-Ferrat.

▰▱ ORIENTATION AND PRACTICAL INFORMATION. A promenade along the waterfront passes by the major hotels and the large **port de Plaisance,** home to an impressive collection of private sailboats and yachts. Farther along the waterfront is **plage des Fourmis,** a perfect crescent of sand that draws a crowd of bathers. On the other side of the coast toward Eze and Monaco, a longer stretch of beach, the public **plage Petite Afrique,** offers more sand and more families. The **tourist office,** pl. Georges Clemenceau, next to the train station, provides free maps of the village and a schedule of summer festivals. (☎04 93 01 02 21; www.ot-beaulieu-sur-mer.fr. Open July-Aug. M-Sa 9am-12:30pm and 2-7pm, Su 9am-12:30pm; Sept.-June M-Sa 9am-12:15pm and 2-6pm.)

▰▱ ACCOMMODATIONS AND FOOD. Those on a small budget should visit Beaulieu as a daytrip from Nice. If you're set on sleeping here, your best option is **La Riviera ❹,** 6 rue Paul Doumer. Its 11 attractively decorated rooms have spotless bathrooms and striking views of the surrounding cliffs. Each has private shower, toilet, air conditioning, and phone. (☎04 93 01 04 92; www.hotel-riviera.fr. Breakfast €8.50. Wi-Fi. Reception 7am-8pm. July-Sept. doubles €61; triples €85. Oct. and Apr.-June doubles €59; triples €80. Nov.-Mar. doubles €54; triples €75. MC/V.) To pack a picnic for the beach, stop by the pleasant and shady **place du Général du Gaulle** and pick up fresh produce at the open-air market (daily 7am-1pm). There is also a **Petit Casino** at 28 bd. Marini. (☎04 93 01 18 25. Open M-Sa 7:30am-12:30pm and 3:30-7:30pm. V.) Waterfront cafes and restaurants are expensive, while *brasseries* are unremarkable. For the best lunch deal, head to **La Pignatelle ❸,** 10 rue de Quincenet. Try the tasty *niçoise* lunch *menu* with Provençal accents (€15) by the fountain. (☎04 93 01 63 37. *Plats* €17-23. Open M-Tu and Th-Su noon-1:30pm and 7-9:45pm. AmEx/MC/V.)

▨ SIGHTS. On a plateau overlooking the sparkling **Baie des Fourmis,** Renaissance man Théodore Reinach built his dream villa, **▰Kérylos,** which stands as a monument to the eccentricity of wealth and the sophistication of ancient Greece. Completed in 1905, the mansion strives to imitate a second-century BC Greek dwelling. Though modern comforts are hidden throughout, Reinach added artificially aged mosaics, gold-leaf cedar wood ceilings, and an enormous sundial to make the house seem plucked straight out of Athens. The millionaire and his wife ate on reclining woven Greek-style beds, took baths in enormous tubs made of Carrara marble, and showered in an open-air space that catches rainwater, just as the showers of ancient Greece did. A 1hr. audio tour includes stops in the colonnade-filled courtyard, the mosaic bathhouse, and a mysterious antechamber. The gardens, encircled by statues, provide unforgettable views of the Mediterranean while the basement houses imitations of Greek statues and maps of the ancient world's most famous ports. (Open by tour only July-Aug. daily 10am-7pm; from Sept. to early Nov. and from early Feb. to June daily 10am-6pm; from early Nov. to early Feb. M-F 2-6pm,

Sa-Su 10am-6pm. Last entry 30min. before close. Audio tour in English, French, German, or Italian. €8.50, students €6.20, under 7 free. AmEx/MC/V.)

VILLEFRANCHE-SUR-MER ☎04 93

The pastel houses of 700-year-old Villefranche-sur-Mer (veel-frahnsh suhr mehr; pop. 6650) have earned the town a reputation as one of the Riviera's most photogenic areas. The backdrop for dozens of films—including a James Bond installation, *Dirty Rotten Scoundrels*, and multiple Hitchcock movies— the town has lured the likes of Aldous Huxley and Katherine Mansfield to its shores. Today, Villefranche is a vacation spot for families and young people who come to enjoy the closest one gets to a sandy beach in the Corniches.

🔃 PRACTICAL INFORMATION. To reach the **tourist office** from the train station, exit on quai 1 and head inland on av. Georges Clemenceau for about 10min. At pl. Charles II d'Anjou, continue on to the right side of av. Sadi Carnot. The office is at the end of the street, on the edge of Jardin François Binon. Its staff offers a walking tour, plans excursions, and organizes guided tours. (☎04 93 01 73 68; www.villefranche-sur-mer.com. Open July-Aug. daily 9am-7pm; Sept. and June M-Sa 9am-noon and 2-6:30pm; Oct.-May M-Sa 9am-noon and 2-6pm. 1hr. walking tours of the citadel and the *vieille ville* in English July-Aug.W 10am, in French Apr.-Sept. F 9:30am; €8.)

🔃 ACCOMMODATIONS. Though a day in the peaceful Corniches might leave you in no hurry to get back to Nice's wild shore, Villefranche isn't cheap. Fam-ily-owned **La Régence ❹**, 2 av. Maréchal Foch, has nine good-size rooms on top of a *brasserie* along the main drag. Each is well kept and comes with bath, phone, and comfortable bed. (☎/fax 04 93 01 70 91. Breakfast €6. Reception 6am-2am. Singles and doubles from €52; triples €66. Cash only.)

🟦 SIGHTS. As you walk from the station on quai Courbet, a sign for the *vieille ville* directs you along 13th-century **rue Obscure,** the oldest street in Villefranche. The stone arches and shrunken doors served as a backdrop for Jean Cocteau's 1959 film *La Testament d'Orphée*. Along the covered street, yellow lanterns throw long shadows, even at midday. A right at the end of rue Obscure takes you to pl. de l'Église, a tiny square entirely occupied by the **Église Saint-Michel.** In addition to the clock tower, the still-active church contains a wood statue of Christ carved by a slave. At the end of the *quai* stands the pink-and-yellow 14th-century **Chapelle Saint-Pierre,** decorated from floor to ceiling by Jean Cocteau. His trademark style fills the chapel with pastels, which are disrupted by the occasional burst of vivid green and yellow, as seen on exotic ceramic figures by the door. (☎04 93 76 90 70. Open in spring and summer Tu-Su 10am-noon and 3-7pm; in autumn and winter Tu-Su 10am-noon and 2-6pm. Closed from mid-Nov. to mid-Dec. €2.) Above the port is the 16th-century **Citadelle,** which houses four small museums. The most interesting is the **Musée Volti,** dedicated to Antoniucci Volti, who made curvaceous female forms in bronze, clay, can-vas, and copper. (☎04 93 76 33 27; musees@villefranche-sur-mer.fr. Open June-Sept. M-Sa 10am-noon and 3-8:30pm; Oct.-May M-Sa 10am-noon and 2-5:30pm, Su 2-5:30pm. Free.) On weekends, **Jardin François Binon,** between the beach and the museum, provides excellent shopping at the Provençal food market (open Sa 8am-1pm) and the antiques market (open Su 9am-4pm).

MONACO ☎04

In 1297, François Grimaldi of Genoa established his family as rulers of Monaco (mohn-ah-ko; pop. 7100) by overthrowing the town with a few henchmen disguised as monks (*monaco* in Italian). The tiny principality has since jealously guarded its independence and exclusivity. Monaco flaunts its wealth with ubiquitous surveillance cameras, high-speed luxury cars, multi-million-dollar yachts, and the famous casino in the capital, Monte-Carlo. Fashion-conscious residents and visiting celebrities give the impression that the Belle Époque isn't over yet. The sheer spectacle of it all, not to mention the tabloid allure of Monaco's royal family, is worth the trip from Nice.

TO (OR FROM) MONACO, WITH LOVE. Monaco's country code is ☎377. To call Monaco from France, dial ☎00377, then the 8-digit Monaco number. To call France from Monaco, dial ☎0033 and drop the first zero of the French number. French phone cards will not work in Monaco's public phones, but cards purchased in Monaco will work throughout Europe. Cell phones send and receive calls anywhere in Monaco just as in France.

▐ TRANSPORTATION

Trains: The Gare SNCF has 4 points of access: galerie Prince Pierre (behind the old train station), pl. St-Dévote, bd. de Belgique (at the intersection with bd. du Jardin Exotique), and bd. Princesse Charlotte. Open daily 4am-1am. Info desk and ticket window open M-F 5:50am-8:30pm, Sa-Su 5:50am-8:05pm. To: **Antibes** (1hr., every 30min., €6.10); **Cannes** (1hr., every 30min., €7.70); **Menton** (11min., every 30min., €1.70); **Nice** (25min., every 30min., €3.10).

Buses: Buses leave from bd. des Moulins and av. Princesse Alice, near the tourist office. TAM and RCA (☎04 93 85 64 44). To **Nice** (45min.) and **Menton** (25min.). **Cap d'Ail, Eze-sur-Mer, Beaulieu-sur-Mer, Villefranche-sur-Mer,** and **St-Jean-Cap-Ferrat** via Nice route. Buses leave every 15min. Tickets €1.

Public Transportation: ☎04 97 70 22 22; www.cam.mc. 6 **bus** routes serve the principality (M-Sa every 11min. 7am-9pm, Su every 20min. 7:30am-9pm). Bus #4 links the St-Dévote train station to the casino; line #2 connects the *vieille ville* and Jardin Exotique via pl. d'Armes and the casino; lines #5 and 6 connect Fontvielle with the rest of the city. Tickets €1. €4 *carte touristique* offers unlimited travel on day of purchase. Buy tickets on board.

Taxis: ☎04 93 15 01 01. 11 taxi stands, including the casino, pl. des Moulins, and the Ste-Dévote train station. Consult tourist office for complete list. €10 min. charge. 24hr.

Car Rental: Avis, 9 av. d'Ostende (☎04 93 30 17 53). Open M-Sa 8am-noon and 2-7pm, Su 9am-noon. AmEx/MC/V. **Europcar,** 47 av. de Grande-Bretagne (☎04 93 50 74 95; www.europcar.fr). Open M-Sa 8am-noon and 2-7pm. AmEx/MC/V.

Scooter Rental: Auto-Moto Garage, 7 rue de Millo (☎04 93 50 10 80). €37 for 9am-7pm, €45 per day, €260 per week; €150 credit-card or check deposit. Open M-F 8am-noon and 2-7pm, Sa 8am-noon. AmEx/MC/V.

✦ ▐ ORIENTATION AND PRACTICAL INFORMATION

This jam-packed principality can be divided into four neighborhoods (from southwest to northeast): Fontvieille, Monaco-Ville, La Condamine, and Monte-Carlo/Larvotto. **Fontvieille** is home to a small, quiet port. **Monaco-Ville,** the historic and legislative heart of the city, at the top of the enormous *rocher de Monaco* (rock of Monaco), is home to both the Palais Princier and the Cathédrale de

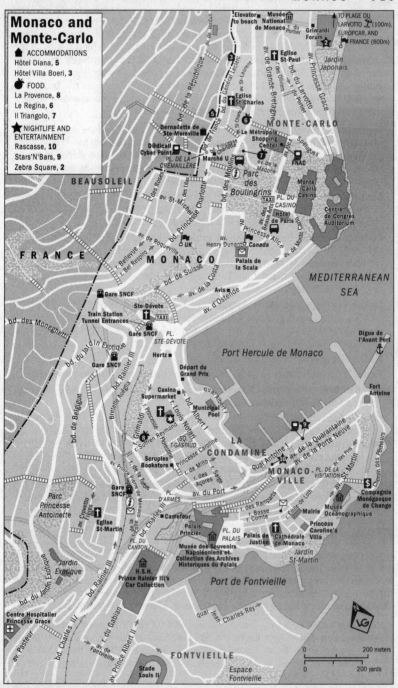

Monaco and Monte-Carlo

ACCOMMODATIONS
Hôtel Diana, 5
Hôtel Villa Boeri, 3

FOOD
La Provence, 8
Le Regina, 6
Il Triangolo, 7

NIGHTLIFE AND ENTERTAINMENT
Rascasse, 10
Stars'N'Bars, 9
Zebra Square, 2

Monaco. **La Condamine**, just below Monaco-Ville, along the main port, is the principality's busiest area—and probably its most affordable. Monaco's glitziest section is concentrated in **Monte-Carlo**, which boasts the fabled tables of the Monte-Carlo Casino and the Carré d'Or, a cluster of thoroughfares lined with luxury boutiques. **Monte-Carlo/Larvotto** contains Monaco's only beach, plage du Larvotto. A 5min. walk uphill from the casino takes you across the border to **Beausoleil**, France, and to reasonably priced hotels and restaurants a stone's throw from the opulence on display at pl. du Casino.

Tourist Office: 2A bd. des Moulins (☎04 92 16 61 16), uphill from the casino. English-speaking staff provides city maps, events brochures, and same-day hotel reservations for free. Open M-Sa 9am-7pm, Su 11am-1pm. Annexes in the train station at the av. Prince Pierre exit, in the chemin des Pêcheurs parking garage, outside the Jardin Exotique, and in the port (open from mid-June to Aug.).

Embassies and Consulates: Canada, 1 av. Henry Dunant (☎04 97 70 62 42); **France,** 1 chemin du Ténao (☎04 92 16 54 60); **UK,** 33 bd. Princesse Charlotte (☎04 93 50 99 54). The nearest **US** consulate is in Nice (☎04 93 88 89 55).

Currency Exchange: Compagnie Monégasque de Change, av. de la Quarantaine (☎04 93 25 02 50), in the chemin des Pêcheurs parking garage; access at the end of the port or from Monaco-Ville near the Musée Océanographique. Offers MC/V cash advances (€50 min., 8% commission). Open M-Sa June-Sept. 10am-5pm; from Oct. to Nov. 4 and from Dec. 26 to May 10am-noon and 2-4pm.

English-Language Bookstore: Scruples, 9 rue Princesse Caroline (☎/fax 04 93 50 43 52). Open June-Aug. M and W-F 10am-7pm, Tu 10am-12:30pm and 2:30-7pm, Sa 10am-12:30pm and 2:30-6:30pm; Sept.-May M-F 9:30am-12:30pm and 2:30-7pm, Sa 9:30am-12:30pm and 2:30-6pm. AmEx/MC/V.

Medical Emergency: ☎04 93 25 33 25.

Police: 3 rue Louis Notari (☎04 93 15 30 15). 5 other stations throughout Monaco.

Hospital: Centre Hospitalier Princesse Grace, av. Pasteur (☎04 97 98 99 00, emergency 97 98 97 69). Accessible by bus #5.

Internet Access: FNAC, 17 av. des Spélugues (☎04 93 10 81 81), in Le Métropole Shopping Center. 20min. free. Be prepared to wait. Open M-Sa 10am-5:30pm. **D@dicall Cyber Point,** 1 impasse Général Leclerc (☎04 93 57 42 14), on the right off bd. du Général Leclerc toward the casino from Beausoleil. €4 per hr. Open 10am-8:30pm. Also at **Stars'N'Bars** (see **Nightlife,** p. 724).

Post Office: Palais de la Scala (☎04 97 97 25 25). Branch across from Hôtel Terminus at the av. Prince Pierre train station exit. 5 additional branches. All open M-F 8am-7pm, Sa 8am-noon. **Postal Code:** MC 98000 Monaco.

ACCOMMODATIONS

If you choose to stay near the casino, chances are you won't have much money left to gamble away. Your best bet is to sleep across the border in Beausoleil, where prices are nearly halved. The hotels aren't far from the casino and boast the best nightlife in the principality. The only other viable options are in **La Condamine** or along **rue de la Turbie, rue Grimaldi,** and **avenue Prince Pierre.**

Hôtel Villa Boeri, 29 bd. du Général Leclerc (☎04 93 78 38 10; www.hotelboeri.com), in Beausoleil, 10min. from the casino. Exit the station at bd. Princesse Charlotte and keep left for 20min. Bd. de France becomes bd. du Général Leclerc. Variety of rooms, from singles with shower to deluxe doubles. A/C, TVs, and phones. Breakfast in bed €9.

Reception 24hr. June-Sept. singles €63; doubles €68; triples €76; quads €105. Oct.-May singles €56; doubles €63; triples €72; quads €90. AmEx/MC/V. ⑤

Hôtel Diana, 17 bd. du Général Leclerc (☎04 93 78 47 58; www.monte-carlo.mc/hotel-diana-beausoleil), in Beausoleil. On the shabby side, this hotel has rooms with firm beds, A/C, TVs, and phones. Cheapest rooms have toilets in hallway. Balconies facing Monaco. Breakfast €6. Private parking €10 per day. Reception 24hr. Reservations recommended. Singles €40-60; doubles €40-70; triples €75. AmEx/MC/V. ❸

🍴 FOOD

Your best bets for budget fare are behind pl. du Palais (**rue Comte Felix, rue Gastaldi,** and **rue Emile de Loth**) or the side streets off **boulevard Albert I** in La Condamine. Fresh food awaits at the fruit and flower market on **place d'Armes** at the end of av. Prince Pierre (open daily 6am-1pm), the **Casino** supermarket at bd. Albert I (☎04 93 30 56 78; open July-Aug. M-Sa 8:30am-midnight, Su 9am-1pm; Sept.-June daily 8:30am-10pm; MC/V), or **Marché U** at 30 bd. Princesse Charlotte (☎04 93 50 68 60; open M-Sa 8:30am-7:15pm; MC/V). **Carrefour,** in Fontvieille's shopping plaza, has anything else you might need. (☎04 92 05 57 00. Open M-Th and Sa 8:30am-9:30pm, F 8:30am-10pm. MC/V.)

La Provence, 22 bis rue Grimaldi (☎04 97 98 37 81). Provençal specialties like beef tartare (€14) and less daring options like pasta (€8-12) and pizza (€9) make this restaurant a worthwhile, if not centrally located, dining option. Come for lunch to escape the heat and enjoy the 3-course lunch *menu* (€16) in the airy interior. Meat *plats* €12-17. *Entrées* €8-15. Open daily noon-3pm and 7-10pm. AmEx/MC/V. ❸

Le Regina, 13-15 bd. des Moulins (☎04 93 50 05 05). English-speaking owner knows regulars by name. Serves delicious pizzas (€10-14), salads (€10-14), pasta (€11-12), and meat and fish dishes (€14-18). Open M-Sa 8am-10pm. MC/V. ❸

Il Triangolo, 1 av. de la Madone (☎04 93 30 67 30). Italian-speaking staff serves enormous pizzas (dinner only; €11-16) and pasta dishes (€12-20) in corner terrace. Desserts €7. Open M-F noon-2:30pm and 7pm-midnight, Sa-Su 7pm-midnight. MC/V. ❸

📷 SIGHTS

🏛**MONTE-CARLO CASINO.** This famous gambling house—where Richard Burton wooed Elizabeth Taylor and Mata Hari shot a Russian spy—shines along the rocky coast. The location is a hotbed for suicide, an end once sought by as many as four high-stakes losers in one week. While optimists tempt fate at slot machines, blackjack, and roulette, the less intrepid can get a drink and check out the lavish Atrium du Casino theater. The gorgeous interior rivals that of Monaco's palace and is well worth the entrance fee. The casino frowns upon shorts, sneakers, sandals, and jeans, but a fancier dress code is not in effect until 8pm. Exclusive *salons privés* (private rooms) require coat and tie and charge an additional €20 cover. The **Café de Paris** next door opens for gambling at 10am with no cover. The 18+ rule is strictly enforced; bring photo ID. (☎04 92 16 20 00; www.casinomontecarlo.com. Slots July-Aug. daily from noon; Sept.-June M-F from 2pm, Sa-Su from noon. Roulette daily from noon. Cover €10. AmEx/MC/V.)

PALAIS PRINCIER. Balanced on *le rocher*, the lavish palace is the occasional home of the tabloid-darling royal family. The stoic palace guard who nominally protects the entrance changes shift with great fanfare daily at 11:55am. When the prince is away, the palace's flag lowers and the doors open to tourists. Audio tours lead visitors by opulent silk walls, gilt furniture, and Venetian crystal chandeliers; for the gossip behind these, you'll have to bring your own tabloid. Memorable stops include the courtyard's grand staircase, the hall of

FRENCH 101

Traveling through France, you will undoubtedly encounter many familiar words on signs and on menus. Though these cognates will seem to help in your struggle to comprehend *le monde francophone*, beware! Some can also lead you astray. Here are some *faux amis* (false cognates; literally, "false friends") to watch out for:

Blesser has nothing to do with spirituality (or sneezing). It means **to hurt,** not to bless.

French *pain* is anything but misery: it's their word for **bread.**

Bras is not a supportive undergarment; it's an **arm.**

Rage is not just any ol' anger; it's **rabies.**

That said, **rabais** is not the disease you can catch from a dog, but rather a **discount.**

A *sale* is not an event with a lot of *rabais*; it means **dirty.**

Draguer means **to hit on,** not to drag—unless you encounter an overly aggressive flirt.

Balancer is **to swing** or to **throw out,** not to steady oneself.

A *peste* is considerably more serious than a bothersome creature. It is a **plague.**

Puéril is not grave danger—recess fights aside—just **childhood.**

Preservatif is not something found in packaged food, but it can be found in other packages—this is the French word for **condom.**

Crayon means **pencil,** not crayon, and *gomme* is not for chewing, unless you like the taste of rubber—it is an **eraser.**

mirrors, the throne room, Princess Grace's official state portrait, and the chamber where the duke of York died. (☎04 93 25 18 31. Open daily May-Sept. 10am-7pm; Oct. 10am-5:30pm; Apr. 10:30am-6pm. Audio tour in 11 languages. €7, students €3.50. Cash only.)

HSH PRINCE RAINIER III'S CAR COLLECTION. If you thought the sweet rides parked in front of the casino were impressive, think again; Prince Rainier III's antique cars put them to shame. You don't have to be a car aficionado to marvel at 100 of the sexiest cars in the world. Gawk at a restored 1924 Model T, the 1956 Rolls Royce Silver Cloud that carried Prince Rainier and Grace Kelly on their wedding day, and the car that captured the first Grand Prix de Monaco in 1929. *(Terrasses de Fontvieille, above the shopping center. ☎04 92 05 28 56. Open daily 10am-6pm. €6, students and ages 8-14 €3. Cash only.)*

MUSÉE OCÉANOGRAPHIQUE. From a distance, it's easy to mistake this majestic building for the royal palace. An educational break from Monaco's excesses, this museum was founded by the prince-cum-marine biologist Albert I. Permanent displays depict the history of marine biology, while more recent exhibits concentrate on modern issues like global climate change. The museum's main attraction is a 90-tank aquarium featuring Mediterranean and tropical sea life. An innovative system pumps 250,000L of seawater directly from the harbor each day to fill the tanks. Visitors gawk at the reconstructed coral reef, shark lagoon, and 1.9m green moray eel—the largest on display in the world. *(Av. St-Martin. ☎04 93 15 36 00. Open daily July-Aug. 9:30am-7:30pm; Sept. and Apr.-June 9:30am-7pm; Oct.-Mar. 10am-6pm. €12.50, students and ages 6-18 €6.)*

JARDIN EXOTIQUE. While Monaco is hardly a desert locale, many species of cactuses imported from America in the 16th century and more recent additions from around the world thrive in this meticulously kept garden. Stone caves and tiny ponds covered with lily pads offer sweeping views. Unless you go early to avoid the heat, you'll be thankful to venture 300 steps down into the cliff side; in addition to housing stalagmites and stalactites, the damp grottoes stay cool at 65°F. *(62 bd. du Jardin Exotique, up the public elevators on bd. de Belgique. Last stop on the #2 bus. ☎04 93 15 29 80; www.montecarlo.mc/jardinexotique. Open daily from mid-May to mid-Sept. 9am-7pm; from mid-Sept. to mid-May 9am-6pm or sundown. Grottoes by tour only; every 30min. 9am-5:30pm. €6.90, students and ages 6-18 €3.60, under 6 free. MC/V.)*

CATHÉDRALE DE MONACO. Thirty-five generations of Grimaldis rest inside this white Neo-

Romanesque Byzantine church, which hosted the 1956 wedding of the late Prince Rainier and Grace Kelly. The somber interior includes an Episcopal throne constructed of white Carrara marble and a quadruple organ. Princess Grace lies in a tomb behind the altar emblazoned with her Latin name, Patritia Gracia. Prince Albert Rainier III's tomb is just to the right of Princess Grace's. Citizens still adorn these two tombs with fresh flowers and handwritten notes. *(Pl. St-Martin, near the Palais.* ☎ *04 93 30 87 70. Open daily Mar.-Oct. 8am-7pm; Nov.-Feb. 8am-6pm. Mass Sa 6pm, Su 10:30am. Free.)*

GARDENS. If a big loss at the casino leaves you raging, practice your Zen meditation at the **Jardin Japonais,** a tranquil seaside spot next to the Grimaldi Forum. Cherry trees, bamboo fountains, and a traditional teahouse invite visitors to relax. *(Open daily 9am-sunset. Free.)* Stroll through the seaside **Jardin Saint-Martin,** between the Musée Océanographique and pl. du Palais. The pleasant grounds offer excellent views of the coast amid flowering trees. *(Open daily 9am-7pm.)* Keep your eyes peeled for **Princess Caroline's villa,** a pink oasis just outside the gardens near the cathedral. It may be difficult to spot between the rows of trees, but the monastic insignia on its gates should tip you off.

OTHER SIGHTS. Though Monaco's beaches can't compare to the rest of the Riviera's stretches of sand, residents and tourists fill the umbrella-speckled **plage du Larvatto.** *(Off av. Princesse Grace. Public elevator from bd. des Moulins drops passengers off to the right of the beach.)* The dolls you played with as a kid were nothing like the fantastic wood-and-porcelain creations at the **Musée National de Monaco.** Housed in a pink villa designed by Charles Garnier, the collection of fragile 18th- and 19th-century dolls features several "automatons" that move and talk; it also displays some of Barbie's best-dressed moments, featuring outfits by Chanel, Dior, and Givenchy. *(17 av. Princesse Grace. Elevator from pl. des Moulins drops pedestrians off next to the entrance.* ☎ *04 93 30 91 26. Open daily 10am-6pm. Automaton demonstrations at 11am and every hr. 2:30-5:30pm. €6, students and ages 8-14 €3.50.)* History buffs will love the crowded cases at the **Musée des Souvenirs Napoléoniens et Collection des Archives Historiques du Palais,** to the left of the palace entrance. The mezzanine level of this jam-packed museum contains Napoleon's legendary cocked hat and a locket with a strand of his hair. The rest of the collection is devoted to the history of Monaco. *(Next to the Palais Princier entrance.* ☎ *04 93 25 18 31. Open daily May-Sept. 10am-6pm; Oct. 10am-5:30pm; Dec.-Mar. 10:30am-12:30pm and 2-5pm; Apr. 10:30am-6pm.*

An *extincteur* is not some sort of bazooka. It is a **fire extinguisher**—much more family-friendly.

Fesses is not a colloquial term for coming clean. Be careful how you use it: it means **buttocks.**

The word *as* is not another way to say *fesses* or even an insult. This is a French compliment, meaning **ace** or champion.

Ranger is neither a woodsman nor your favorite mighty morpher—it's **to tidy up.**

A *smoking* has little to do with tobacco (or any other substance). It is a **tuxedo** or dinner suit.

Raisins are juicy **grapes,** not the dried-up snack food. Try *raisins-secs* instead.

Prunes are **plums.** *Pruneaus* are the dried fruit.

Tampons are **stamps** (for documents), not the feminine care item. If you are looking for those, ask for a *tampon hygiénique* or napkins. To wipe your mouth, you would do better with a *serviette.*

The *patron* is the **boss,** not the customer.

A *glacier* does translate literally to **glacier,** but you're more likely to see it around town on signs for **ice-cream vendors;** *glace* does not mean glass, but rather a frozen treat.

If the French language seems full of deception, think again. *Déception* in French actually means **disappointment.**

€4, students €2. Includes audio tour.) Fashionistas who love big-name labels but not their big-time prices should check out **Second Hand Bernadette de Sainte Moreville** in Beausoleil, where racks stock (nearly) affordable secondhand Chanel, Dior, Armani, and Gucci threads from recent major collections. (9 bd. du Général Leclerc. ☎04 93 78 31 53. Open M-F 10:30am-1:30pm and 4-7:30pm, Sa 10:30am-1:30pm. Jeans €60-100, jackets €85-430, accessories €90-110, blouses €45-75. MC/V.)

NIGHTLIFE

Monaco's nightlife is a little less wild and more sophisticated than that of most locales on the French coast. It has all the signature characteristics of the wealthy Riviera—high fashion, expensive drinks, exclusive clubs—but remains low-key. The real center of attention is the famous high-stakes **casino.** Wherever you go in this glamorous principality, dress in your finest; jeans, sneakers, and flip flops should stay home. Bars are the best bet for most budget travelers, but a lounge by the sea could be worth the pricier drinks. Several can be found near the Monaco sporting complex by the beach, while less formal (and less expensive) bars and pubs are on the other side of **avenue Princesse Grace.** In summer, bars in the *vieux port* stay open until at least 2am.

Rascasse, 1 quai Antoine I (☎04 93 25 56 90; www.larascasse.mc). Cozy bar with portside outdoor seating on the Grand Prix's most famous corner. Stars'N'Bars's (below) young crowd heads here late at night for dancing. Live music and English pop-rock atmosphere downstairs. Upstairs a DJ lights up the party after 11pm with electro music. Pints €9. Mixed drinks €13. Happy hour M-F 6-9pm; drinks ½-price. Open M-F noon-5am, Sa-Su 7pm-5am. Upstairs open Th-Sa 11pm-4am. AmEx/MC/V.

Stars'N'Bars, 6 quai Antoine I (☎04 97 97 95 95; www.starsnbars.com). Portside restaurant by day and lively bar by night. Young crowd of locals and boat workers relaxes over pool and video games out on the port or inside the Grand Prix-themed bar. Creative drinks like "Sex on the Beer" (vodka, peach liqueur, and beer; €8) and bar grub (€7-10). Pints €5.50. Mixed drinks €8-13. DJ spins nightly 10pm-1am. 18+. Happy hour M-F 5:30-7:30pm. Restaurant open July-Aug. daily 9:30am-midnight; Sept.-June Tu-Su 11am-midnight. Bar open 11am until the party moves to Rascasse. AmEx/MC/V.

Zebra Square, 10 av. Princesse Grace (☎04 99 99 25 50; www.zebrasquare.com), on top of the Grimaldi Forum. Patrons in their late 20s and 30s prefer this groovy seaside lounge to the younger club downstairs. Relax on the deck outside, sipping mixed drinks (€15) and stargazing. DJs from 11pm. Open daily M-F noon-2am. AmEx/MC/V.

FESTIVALS

Festival International du Cirque (☎04 92 05 26 00), at the end of Jan. Monaco kicks off the year with a circus exhibition.

Monaco Flower-Arranging Competition (☎04 93 30 02 04), in Mar. Perhaps less of an adrenaline rush than the Grand Prix, but not without its dangers—think thorny stems.

Historical Grand Prix, every other year in May. Antique cars race the Grand Prix circuit. Next on May 15-16, 2010.

Formula 1 Grand Prix, 4 days in May (May 21-24, 2009). The jewel of the World Drivers' Championship. Roads surrounding the *vieux port* are transformed into a harrowing track where the world's best drivers test their skills. If exhaust fumes, snazzy paint jobs, and jumpsuits aren't your thing, think twice about visiting during the race; tourist attractions close, waterfront access is limited, and hotel prices skyrocket.

MENTON   ☎04

Often called the "Secret Riviera," Menton (mohn-tohn; pop. 30,000) is bliss-fully removed from the tourist traps' ice-cream stands and the glare of extreme wealth, yet it still offers the picturesque beaches, lush gardens, and medieval alleys that have made the Riviera famous. With a microclimate that keeps tem-peratures balmy, Menton is beautiful enough to make every visitor wish he could paint, especially when the setting sun turns the water a bright shade of pink. On France's eastern border, the town is flavored with hints of Italy; natives speak French with a decidedly Italian accent, and the local cuisine is spiced with more than the usual amount of zest.

▮ TRANSPORTATION

Trains: Pl. de la Gare. Ticket office open M-F 8:40-11:50am and 2-6:30pm, Sa 9:25-11:50am and 2-6:30pm. Trains run every 30min. (5am-midnight) to: **Cannes** (1hr., €8.30); **Monaco** (11min., €1.70); **Nice** (35min., €4.10); **Genoa, ITA** (2-3hr., 11-14 per day, €15-19); **Ventimiglia, ITA** (10min., €4.40).

Buses: Promenade du Maréchal Leclerc (☎04 93 35 93 60). Walk from the train station and take a left at the 1st major intersection. Open M-F 8:30am-noon and 1:30-6pm, Sa 10am-noon. Rapides Côte d'Azur (☎04 93 85 64 64) runs buses every 15min. (6:30am-7:30pm) to **Monaco** and **Nice**; both €1.

Taxis: ☎04 92 10 47 02. 5 stands in the city. Train station to hostel €8-10. Available daily 5am-11pm; reserve ahead by phone during off hours.

Bike Rental: Holiday Bikes, 4 esplanade Georges Pompidou (☎04 92 10 99 98; www.holiday-bikes.com). Bikes from €15 per day, €60 per week; €230 deposit. Scoot-ers from €35 per day; €500 deposit. Motorcycles and cars also available. Open M-F 9:30am-12:30pm and 3-6:30pm, Sa 9:30am-noon and 5-6:30pm. AmEx/MC/V.

▮▮ ORIENTATION AND PRACTICAL INFORMATION

Menton is divided into the *vieille ville*, the new town, and the beach. **Avenue de Verdun** or **avenue Boyer**—depending on the side of the street—is the main thor-oughfare of the new town. A left turn leads to shops and boutiques on **avenue Felix Faure,** the crowded pedestrian **rue Saint-Michel,** and the *vieille ville*'s heart. The **promenade du Soleil** runs the length of the bay between the old and new towns, funneling into the **quai de Monleon** at the edge of the *vieux port*.

Tourist Office: 8 av. Boyer (☎04 92 41 76 76; www.villedementon.com). From the train station, walk straight out of the station onto av. de la Gare, cross av. de Verdun, and turn right on av. Boyer. An English-speaking staff provides free maps and guidebooks. Open June-Sept. M-Sa 8:30am-7pm, Su 9am-7pm; Oct.-May M-Sa 8:30am-12:30pm and 2-6pm, Su 9am-12:30pm.

Tours: Service du Patrimoine, 24 rue St-Michel. (☎04 93 28 46 85). 24hr. Garden tours in French daily; schedule varies, so call ahead. €5-8.

Police: Rue de la République (☎04 92 10 50 50).

Hospital: La Palmosa, rue Antoine Péglion (☎04 93 28 77 77, emergencies 93 28 72 40).

Internet Access: Le Café des Arts, 16 rue de la République (☎04 93 35 78 67; www.cafedesarts.com). €6 per hr. Open M-Sa 7:30am-8pm; Internet 7:30-11am and 2:30pm-8pm. MC/V over €10.

Post Office: Cours George V (☎04 93 28 64 87). **Currency exchange** available. Open M-W and F 8am-6:30pm, Th 8am-6pm, Sa 8:30am-noon. **Postal Code:** 06500.

ACCOMMODATIONS AND CAMPING

Hôtel de Belgique, 1 av. de la Gare (☎04 93 35 72 66; hoteldebelgique@wanadoo.fr). Great location. 20 rooms with TVs and phones. Breakfast €5.50. Reception 7am-2:30pm and 5:30-10pm. July-Aug. book 3 weeks ahead. Singles with toilet €32; doubles €42, with bath €49; triples €61; quads €82-90. Extra bed €12. AmEx/MC/V. ❷

Hôtel Beauregard, 10 rue Albert I (☎04 93 28 63 63; beauregard.menton@wanadoo.fr). Turn right out of the train station and descend the steps behind Le Chou Chou. Turn right again; the hotel is 80m down the street. Serene breakfast patio and attractive rooms with TV and phone. Breakfast €5.30. Reception 8am-9pm. Reserve ahead July-Aug. July-Aug. singles and doubles €35, with toilet and shower €43; triples with toilet and bath €57. Sept.-June €5-10 less. Extra bed €9. MC/V. ❸

Auberge de Jeunesse (HI), plateau St-Michel (☎04 93 35 93 14; menton@fuaj.org). Take bus #6 (8:40, 11:10am, 2, 5pm; €1); if you walk, beware that the hike is long and abandoned at night. Compensates for remote location with friendly staff, fabulous vistas, and free breakfast (7:30-8:45am). Single-sex rooms are clean, each with 8 sturdy wood bunks. The bar (open daily 5-11pm) serves cheap drinks. Laundry €5. Reception 7am-noon and 5-11pm. Open Feb.-Oct. Dorms €17. Cash only. ❶

Camping Municipal du Plateau St-Michel, route des Ciappes (☎04 93 35 81 23; fax 93 57 12 35), 50 steps shy of the hostel. Amazing views. Olive trees shade rows of tents. On-site restaurant-bar offers affordable pizzas (€8.50), pastas (€9-16), and meat *plats* (€13-19) and features foosball and pool. Laundry July-Sept. Reception M-Sa 8:30am-noon and 3-7pm, Su 8:30am-12:30pm and 5-6:30pm. €8.60 per person; €4 per small tent, €5 per large tent; €13 per car. Electricity €2.80. MC/V. ❶

FOOD

Menton prides itself on quality fruits and vegetables—not surprising for a city whose slogan is "my town is a garden." Sample *mentonnaise* produce at one of the town's three markets: the small **Marché Careï,** av. Sospel (open daily 7am-12:30pm); **Marché Couvert** or **Les Halles,** quai de Monléon, off rue St-Michel (Tu-Su morning); and **Marché du Bastion,** quai Napoléon III (Sa morning). Waterfront restaurants dot the **promenade du Soleil,** but **place du Cap** and **rue Saint-Michel** in the *vieille ville* offer lively alternatives at rock-bottom prices. Street vendors bring an Italian flair, selling panini and *glaces italiennes* (Italian ice cream).

Maison Herbin et Son Arche des Confitures, 2 rue du Vieux College (☎04 93 57 20 29; www.confitures-herbin.com). Jam combinations of Menton's citrus are produced daily in the small kitchen (€3-5). Try the *petales de rose* (rose petal) jam, which tastes like a rose smells. Stop by in the morning to watch the cooks at work. Free guided visits of the kitchen with a *dégustation* M, W, F 10:30am. Open June-Aug. daily 9:15am-12:30pm and 3:15-7pm; Sept.-May M-Sa 9:15am-12:30pm and 3:15-7pm. MC/V. ❶

Le Café des Arts, 16 rue de la République (☎04 93 35 78 67). English-speaking staff serves delicious salads (€8-9), pasta (€9-10), and meat *plats* (€10-13) to diners seated in squishy green booths. Open M-F 7:30am-10pm, Sa 7:30am-3pm. MC/V. ❷

SIGHTS

SERRE DE LA MADONE. Plant lovers will appreciate Menton's gardens—the small town's pride and joy—originally planted in the late 18th century. Among the most exceptional is Serre de la Madone. Designed by the American Lawrence Johnston to be "Heaven on earth," the garden is a designated *monument historique* and the most temperate garden in France. Look out for the enormous ◆**dragon** tree imported from the Canary Islands. *(74 route de Gorbio, at the Serre de la Madone stop on bus #7 (10min., €1). ☎04 93 57 73 90; www.serredelamadone.com. Open Apr.-Oct. Tu-Su 10am-6pm; Dec.-Mar. 10am-5pm. Guided tours Tu-Su at 3pm. €8, students €4, under 12 free.)* Ask the tourist office for a complete list of the town's gardens. June is Menton's official "month of gardens," when private gardens open to the public. Contact the **Service du Patrimoine** (p. 725) for reservations.

MUSÉE JEAN COCTEAU. Locally known as the Bastion, this *musée* is one of Menton's main attractions. The fort was originally constructed by the Prince of Monaco in 1616 to ward off French invasions. Check out the frescoes in the unusual Salle des Mariages. *(Quai Napoléon. ☎04 93 57 72 30. Open M and W-Su 10am-noon and 2-6pm. €3; 1st Su of the month free. Cash only.)*

MONASTÈRE ANNONCIADE. Climb 225m above Menton, where this monastery's small terrace provides spectacular views of the city and sea below. Though the 30min. uphill hike will make your heart race, 15 chapels depicting the Stations of the Cross can help you count your way to the top. The chapels were built by Princess Isabelle of Monaco in gratitude to the Virgin of the Annonciade for curing her leprosy. *(Head toward the bus station; the chemin de Rosaire leads to the top of the monastery. Otherwise, bus #4 leaves from the gare routière (8:30, 11:40am, 2:30, 6:35pm; €1) for the top. ☎04 93 35 76 92. Open daily 8am-noon and 2-6pm. Mass July-Aug. M-Sa 7:30am, Su 10am; Sept.-June M-Sa 11:15am, Su 10am.)*

OTHER SIGHTS. The tower of the **Basilique Saint-Michel** rises majestically above the *vieille ville.* The Baroque facade hides glass-drop chandeliers, a gold crown suspended above a gold-and-marble altar, and a gruesome secret: until 1850, Menton did not have a single cemetery, so paupers were buried in a common grave below the cathedral. *(From rue St-Michel, take a left onto rue des Logettes, then ascend the steps of rue des Écoles Pie. Open M-F and Su June-Aug. 10am-noon and 2-6:15pm; Sept.-May 10am-noon and 3-5:15pm. Mass Su 10:30am.)* Expansive, rocky beaches stretch along the coast from **quai Napoléon III** west to Monaco. If you want sand, head east of quai Napoléon to local favorite **plage des Sablettes.**

❈ FESTIVALS

Fête du Citron, in Jan. Some 250,000 guests come to the Lemon Festival. What began in 1929 as a small flower and citrus exhibition is now a 15-day celebration, featuring a parade of floats covered with 120 tons of citrus—some of which inevitably get mixed up in impromptu lemon fights among rambunctious locals. Themes have included "Astérix in the Land of the Lemon" and "Alice in Wonderland." Missed the festival? Console yourself with a *citronnade mentonnaise* in a local cafe.

ANTIBES   ☎04 93

Antibes (ahn-teeb; pop. 80,000 including Juan-les-Pins) provides a much-needed middle ground on the glitterati-controlled Riviera. Though blessed with beautiful beaches, a truly charming *vieille ville,* and a renowned Picasso museum, the city is less touristed than Nice and more relaxed than St-Tropez. Partygoers and sunbathers prefer neighboring Juan-les-Pins, but you'll need to venture to calmer and more budget-friendly Antibes to find sights other than sand and clubs. In between the twin towns is the unforgettable Cap d'Antibes, a peninsula of rocky beaches and luxurious villas, hidden off winding streets in forests. The area is also a boat lover's paradise, with enormous yachts, sleek sailboats, and smaller fishing vessels rounding the Cap and traversing the white-tipped waves of the Mediterranean.

TRANSPORTATION

Trains: Pl. Pierre Semard. Ticket desk open daily 5:30am-10:45pm. Info desk open daily 9am-8pm. Station open daily 5:25am-12:05am. To: **Avignon** (1hr., 12 per day, €38); **Cannes** (15min., 23 per day, €2.30); **Marseille** (2hr., 12 per day, €25); **Monaco** (1hr., 5 per day, €6.10); **Nice** (15min., 25 per day, €3.60).

Buses: RCA (☎04 93 39 11 39) sends buses from pl. de Gaulle to **Cannes** (20min.), **Nice** (1hr.), and the **Nice airport** (30min.). Schedules at the tourist office. All depart every 20-40min. €1.

Public Transportation: Local **buses** leave from pl. Guynemer (☎04 93 34 37 60). On-site office has maps. Open July-Aug. M-F 8:30am-noon and 2:30-7:20pm, Sa 10am-12:30pm and 2:30-4:30pm; Sept.-June M-Sa 7:30am-9pm. Tickets €1; day pass €4, week pass €10; family ticket €6. Free **minibus** connects travelers to points in the city, including beaches, the train and bus stations, and the *vieille ville* (every 40min. 7:30am-7:30pm). Ask for a map at the tourist office or look for *minibus gratuit* signs.

Taxis: Allô Taxi Antibes (☎04 93 67 67 67). At the train station. €17 from the train station to Juan-les-Pins. 24hr.

Car Rental: Europcar, 26 bd. Foch (☎04 93 34 79 79; www.europcar.fr). From €330 per week; €500 deposit. 21+. Open May-Sept. M-Sa 8am-noon and 2-7pm; Oct.-Apr. M-Sa 8am-noon and 2-6pm. AmEx/MC/V.

ORIENTATION AND PRACTICAL INFORMATION

The city is far from compact, and many sights and accommodations will require taking a bus or renting a bike. From the train station, turn right onto av. Robert Soleau, which connects with **place du Général de Gaulle** and farther down with the tourist office. From here, **rue de la République** (off the far left corner of pl. du Général de Gaulle) passes the bus station and heads into **vieux Antibes,** along the eastern shore, south of the *vieux port.* **Boulevard du Président Wilson** stretches from pl. du Général de Gaulle across the peninsula, funneling into the center of Juan-les-Pins. Follow bd. Albert I from pl. du Général de Gaulle and turn right at the water to reach a long stretch of beach and the beginning of **Cap d'Antibes** (15min.). The tip of the peninsula is 40min. from the base of the Cap.

Tourist Office: 11 pl. du Général de Gaulle (☎04 97 23 11 11; www.antibesjuanlespins. com). Free maps. Info on restaurants, camping, and festivals. Help with same-day hotel reservations. **Tours** of the *vieille ville* M, W, F-Sa 10am-1:45pm (€8, ages 8-16 €3.50, under 8 free). Open July-Aug. daily 9am-7pm; Sept.-June M-F 9am-12:30pm and 1:30-6pm, Sa 9am-noon and 2-6pm. Annex at the train station (☎04 97 21 04 48). Open July-Aug. daily 9am-7pm; Sept.-June M-F 9am-5pm.

Currency Exchange: Delta Change, 17 bd. Albert I (☎04 93 34 12 76). Open M-Sa July-Aug. 9am-12:30pm and 2-6:30pm; Sept.-June 9am-noon and 2-5pm. **Euro-change,** 4 rue Georges Clemenceau (☎04 93 34 48 30). Open M-Sa Apr.-Oct. 9am-7pm; Nov.-Mar. 9am-6pm.

English-Language Bookstore: Heidi's English Bookshop, 24 rue Aubernon (☎04 93 34 74 11). An institution on the Riviera for 16 years and a resource for Anglophones. Experienced staff suggests nightlife hot spots and provides a list of nearby English-speaking doctors. Sells budget-friendly used books perfect for beach reading. Open daily July-Aug. 10am-7pm; Sept.-June 11am-6pm. MC/V.

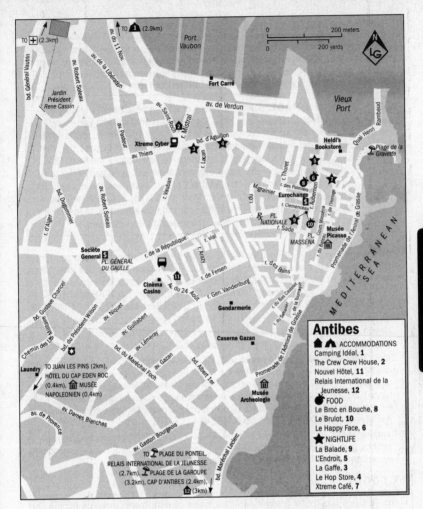

Antibes

🏠🏠 ACCOMMODATIONS
Camping Idéal, 1
The Crew Crew House, 2
Nouvel Hôtel, 11
Relais International de la
  Jeunesse, 12
🍎 FOOD
Le Broc en Bouche, 8
Le Brulot, 10
Le Happy Face, 6
★ NIGHTLIFE
La Balade, 9
L'Endroit, 5
La Gaffe, 3
Le Hop Store, 4
Xtreme Café, 7

Laundromat: Lave Plus, 44 bd. du Président Wilson (☎06 61 86 06 19). Wash €6, dry €0.50 per 5min. Wash, dry, and fold service €10 per 5kg. Open daily 7am-8pm.

Police: 33 bd. du Président Wilson (☎04 92 90 78 00 or 92 90 53 12).

Pharmacy: 63 pl. Nationale (☎04 93 34 01 63). Call the police or consult the local *Nice Matin* newspaper for the **pharmacie de garde.**

Hospital: Chemin des Quatres Chemins (☎04 92 91 77 77).

Internet Access: Xtreme Cyber, 8 bd. d'Aguillon (☎04 89 89 93 88; xtremecyber@club-internet.fr), at the Galérie du Port. €0.12 per min., €5 per hr. Happy hour 2-3pm; double your time for free. Open M-F 10am-8pm, Sa 10am-4pm.

Post Office: Pl. des Martyrs de la Résistance (☎04 92 90 61 00), off rue des Lices. Open M-F 8am-7pm, Sa 8am-noon. **Postal Code:** 06600.

ACCOMMODATIONS AND CAMPING

Antibes has a few affordable options; most lie between the new town and the *vieux port*. Those interested in only a few of Antibes's attractions may want to daytrip from Nice or Cannes. Serious sightseers should stay in the *vieille ville*, while those with a bike or car can stay a bit farther from the *centre-ville*.

> **TIP**
>
> **KEEP IT SHADY.** There are plenty of ways to beat the Riviera heat without an air-conditioned hotel room. Planning is everything—the early morning or late evening are the coolest times to be outside. Look for museums, libraries, or movie theaters—generally air-conditioned places—to pass the afternoon. Even a shady cafe and a cold drink can help battle the heat. Before bed, dampen a pair of thin socks with cold water and put a pair of dry socks on top. The water will draw the heat out of your body, and the dry pair will keep your sheets from getting wet. Most importantly, stay hydrated, watch the booze, limit your bake time in the sun, and take advantage of the easiest escape from impending heatstroke: the majestic Mediterranean.

The Crew House, 1 av. St-Roch (☎04 92 90 49 39; workstation_fr@yahoo.com), near Port Vauban. From the train station, walk down av. de la Libération; after the roundabout, turn right on av. St-Roch. Laid-back Anglophones who congregate here make it a social retreat. Kitchen. Luggage storage. Internet €4.80 per hr. Reception M-F 9am-8pm, Sa-Su 10am-6pm. Lockout 10am-3pm. Dorms Apr.-Oct. €25; Nov.-Mar. €20. AmEx/MC/V. ❷

Nouvel Hôtel, 1 av. du 24 Août (☎04 93 34 44 07; fax 93 34 44 08), next to the bus station. Comfortable beds, individual safes, TVs, and clean bathrooms. Breakfast €5. Reception 7am-8:30pm. Singles €35; doubles €52-62; triples €71-80. MC/V. ❸

Relais International de la Jeunesse, 272 bd. de la Garoupe (☎04 93 61 34 40; www.clajsud.fr), on the Cap. Take bus #4 to the Relais de Jeunesse stop or #2 to the Garoupe stop; walk with the water to your right for 10min. Clean single-sex dormitories close to plage Garoupe. English-speaking staff. Breakfast included. Free luggage storage. Lockers available. Reception daily 8am-10:30pm or by request for late arrivals. Open from mid-Mar. to Sept. Dorms €17. AmEx/MC/V. ❶

Camping Idéal, 991 route de Nice (☎04 93 74 27 07), RN7. For the cheapest deal in Antibes, grab one of 13 spots at this ideally located campground. Family atmosphere. Reception 9am-9:30pm. Sites €11. Cash only. ❶

🍴 FOOD

Vieux Antibes has many budget eateries, most of which serve crispy pizzas and grilled meats. Excellent Provençal restaurants make for a great splurge. **Cours Masséna** hosts budget restaurants and the famous **Marché Provençal,** one of the Côte d'Azur's best. Tempting restaurants, bars, and cafes set up outdoor tables on **boulevard d'Aguillon.** For cheaper prices and great people-watching, head to lively **place Nationale** and **rue Aubernon.** The largest supermarket is **Intermarché,** 2 bd. Albert I. (☎04 93 34 19 10. Open M-Sa 8:15am-7:30pm.)

Le Happy Face, 13 rue Aubernon (☎04 93 34 41 79), across from the market. Recently opened. Modern decor and warm staff. Generous portions. Changing menu of meats, salads, vegetables, rice, and other dishes (each €1-4). Relaxed bar at night. Free Wi-Fi for customers. Open Tu-Su 9am-2am. AmEx/MC/V. ❷

Le Brulot, 3 rue Frédéric Isnard (☎04 93 34 17 76), off av. Georges Clemenceau. Specializes in wood-fired cuisine. Treat yourself to the shrimp *au pastis* (€29) or choose from simple meat (€16-26) and fish (€13-32) *plats*. Lunch *menu* €14. Dinner *menus* €24-42. Open July and Sept. daily 7pm-midnight; Oct.-June M-W 7pm-midnight, Th-Su 1:30-2:30pm and 7pm-midnight. AmEx/MC/V. ❹

Le Broc en Bouche, 8 rue des Palmiers (☎04 93 34 75 60), off rue Aubernon by the Hôtel de Ville. Gourmet food—like artichoke carpaccio (€13)—worthy of the glamorous locale. Fresh, local ingredients. Wine *dégustations* in the *cave* below. Plats €18-27. Open July-Aug. M-Th 7:30-10pm, F-Sa 7:30-11:30pm; Sept.-June M and Th-Su noon-2pm and 7:30-10pm, Tu noon-2pm. AmEx/MC/V. ❹

👁 📷 SIGHTS AND BEACHES

Antibes was once home to Pablo Picasso, Graham Greene, and Max Ernst. The historic village and its highly artistic past left Antibes with a variety of museums that will appeal to art lovers and historians alike.

█MUSÉE PICASSO. This museum displays a large collection of Picasso's paintings, mostly from the 1940s, and photos and video clips of the artist at work. Exhibits change every three months. The museum recently underwent renovations; call for hours and prices. *(Pl. Mariejol, in Château Grimaldi. ☎04 92 90 54 20.)*

FORT CARRÉ. This 16th-century fort guards the entrance to port Vauban, the largest private marina on the Mediterranean. A magnificent view of the city, the port's 2400 yachts, and its new mega-yacht dock—affectionately called "Millionaire's Row"—are worth the uphill hike. Inside the fort, a small exhibit showcases rare 19th-century swords and guns as well as a famous statue of Napoleon on a horse. *(☎06 14 89 17 45. Open Tu-Su from mid-June to mid-Sept. 10am-6pm; from mid-Sept. to mid-June 10am-4:30pm. Fort accessible only by French or English guided tour every 30min. €3, students and seniors €1.50, under 18 free.)*

MUSÉE D'ARCHÉOLOGIE. Antiquity buffs will be thrilled to discover the Greek ceramics and Roman artifacts of ancient Antibes, including 2000-year-old anchors found in the city's harbor. The temporary exhibit sometimes has a more general appeal—past exhibits have included a simulated display in which modern objects were aged 2000 years to look like an archaeological find from the future. The museum's roof offers great views of the Cap and city. *(On the waterfront in Bastion St-André-sur-les-Remparts. ☎04 95 34 00 39. Open July-Aug. Tu and F-Su 10am-noon and 2-6pm, W 10am-noon and 2-8pm; Sept.-June Tu-Su 10am-noon and 2-6pm. French guided tours F 3pm. €3, students €1.50, under 18 free.)*

MUSÉE NAPOLÉONIEN AND HÔTEL DU CAP-EDEN-ROC. This museum is housed in an old battery tower built by Napoleon in 1794 before his coup d'état. Two galleries display a range of Bonapartist paraphernalia, including a bronze casting of the dictator's hand. *(Take bus #2 from pl. Guynemer to Eden Roc. Every M-Sa 40min. 6:50am-7:30pm, €1. ☎04 93 61 45 32. Open Tu-Sa from mid-June to mid-Sept. 10am-6pm; from mid-Sept. to mid-June 10am-4:30pm. €3, students €1.50, under 18 free. Cash only.)*

NOTRE DAME DU BON-PORT. Honoring Jesus's last struggle, the 14 Stations of the Cross decorate the chemin du Calvaire beginning at Port de la Salis. The stations lead up to the church's chapel, which overlooks the Garoupe beaches. Legend has it that the Virgin Mary, drenched in seawater, appeared to an old man visiting the church one stormy night. Antibes locals have dressed up in nautical costumes every year since 1016 on the first Thursday in July to carry the Virgin statue to the shore and commemorate the divine apparition.

OTHER SIGHTS. Antibes has two main public beaches, both sandy but crowded all summer. The larger **plage du Ponteil** features an abundance of snack stands and street vendors, while the smaller **plage de la Salis** is nearly enclosed by rock breakwaters that form a calm, manmade lagoon. *(From the vieille ville, turn right, toward Port Vauban.)* The rocky beach on **Cap d'Antibes** has clear water perfect for snorkeling. *(Take bus #2 from the bus station to Tour Gandolphe (M-Sa every 40min. 6:50am-7:30pm, €1). Follow av. Monseigneurs-Lieutenant Beaumont to the end. Turn left onto the pedestrian road, then right when a small door appears in the surrounding walls; take the dirt path to the isolated beach cove.)* Also on Cap d'Antibes, **plage Garoupe** put itself on the map in the 1920s when celebrities such as Cole Porter, F. Scott Fitzgerald, and Pablo Picasso frequented its sand and surf. **Côte Plongée** provides a great scuba-diving locale. *(On the beach below the Musée Napoléonien, at the corner of bd. Kennedy and bd. du Maréchal Juin. Take bus #2 from pl. Guynemer to Eden Roc (every 40min. 6:50am-7:30pm, €1). Walk along bd. Kennedy to the coast. Descend the stone steps and turn left. ☎06 72 74 34 94; www.coteplongee.com. Open May-Oct. daily 9am-6pm. Intro dive €50; dive from boat €30, at night €45. Snorkel rental €8. MC/V.)*

🎵 🎭 ENTERTAINMENT AND NIGHTLIFE

Cinéma Casino, at 6 and 8 bd. du 24 Août, shows modern films in English. (☎04 93 34 04 37; www.cinefil.com. €7.50, students €6; M-F afternoons €6.) During the annual **Voiles d'Antibes Juan-les-Pins,** held the first week of June, traditional sailing ships from all over the world come to race the 23km of coastline between Antibes and Juan-les-Pins, accompanied by concerts every evening. During the first weeks of July, **Festival d'Art Lyrique** brings world-class soloists and orchestras to the *vieux port.* (☎04 92 90 53 00. Tickets €15-50. MC/V.)

Most clubbers head to **Juan-les-Pins** (p. 734) at night, but the Antibes bars provide an alternative to the club scene. Although they are largely imitation pubs, they can get rowdy late at night. The bars and pubs along **boulevard d'Aguillon** hold happy hours (usually around 6pm) for a fun-loving crowd, while public squares and the Provençal market remain lively late into the night.

▓ **La Balade,** 25B cours Masséna (☎04 93 34 93 00), in the basement of the covered Provençal market. One of the world's few absinthe bars, La Balade serves countless types of the green anise-flavored liquor. A favorite of Baudelaire, Van Gogh, and the 19th-century avant-garde, the toxic drink is now illegal; what you'll find here is its milder cousin, so don't expect to be hit by divine inspiration. Antique absinthe fountains and advertisements from the 1920s add to the allure of the legendary drink. The fainthearted can check out the museum. Open daily 9pm-midnight. AmEx/MC/V.

La Gaffe, 6 bd. d'Aguillon (☎04 93 34 04 06). An energetic staff serves crowds of Anglophones in this unpretentious bar. Squeeze in F-Sa nights to hear local bands play rock hits. Gets livelier after midnight. Wi-Fi. Pints €6. Mixed drinks €7.50. Open-mike night Su 9pm draws some quality—and some hilariously low-quality—musicians. Open June-Aug. M-F 3pm-2am, Sa-Su noon-2am; Sept.-May daily 11am-12:30am. MC/V.

The Hop Store, 38 bd. d'Aguillon (☎04 93 34 15 33). Attracts a sedate pub crowd. Large outdoor seating area. Beer €4-7. Live music Sa-Su. Happy hour 7-8pm. Open daily from May to mid-Sept. 9am-2:30am; from mid-Sept. to Apr. 3pm-12:30am. MC/V.

L'Endroit, 29 rue Aubernon (☎04 97 21 14 10). Plush couches and a chic modern aesthetic provide the perfect spot for locals to gather for a night out. Beer €3. Mixed drinks €10. Drink prices increase by €2 after 10pm. DJs spin house and lounge music nightly 9:30pm. Open Tu-Su June-Sept. 7pm-2am; Oct.-May 8pm-12:30am. MC/V.

Xtreme Café, 6 rue Aubernon (☎04 93 34 03 90). This trendy, centrally located bar packs in revelers of all ages. Wine from €3. Beer €3.50. Mixed drinks €6-8. Open June-Sept. M-Sa 6pm-2am, Su noon-2am; Oct.-May daily noon-12:30am. AmEx/MC/V.

🔳 DAYTRIPS FROM ANTIBES

BIOT

Biot's train station (☎08 92 35 35 35) is 1.5km from the centre-ville; the best way to travel from Antibes is by bus (Sillages ☎04 92 28 58 68). Bus #10 connects Biot Village and the bus station in Antibes (25min.; M-Sa 11 per day, Su 8 per day; €1). To get to the tourist office from the station, head uphill and take a right onto rue St-Sébastien; the tourist office is on the left. The last bus from Biot to Antibes departs at 6pm.

Just 3km from Antibes, the small town of Biot (bee-yoht) hides a host of ceramic, pottery, and *verreries* (glass workshops) behind 15th-century vaults and fortified gates. Once home to the Greeks, Romans, Templars, and Malta knights, Biot is now one of Europe's glass capitals and boasts a rich artistic tradition. Local artists design and sell pottery, woven baskets, and paintings. Beyond their galleries, the narrow streets of vieux Biot are filled with traditional restaurants and refreshingly unique souvenir shops.

The source of much of Biot's modern-day renown, the **Verrerie de Biot,** chemin des Combes, continues to produce its founder's trademark "bubble glass." The *verrerie* was created in 1956 by Eloi Monod, who married the daughter of the founder of the Poterie Provençal (below). After watching his father-in-law create famous Biot pottery, he decided to reproduce it in a new medium: glass. His attempt resulted in the formation of accidental bubbles, for which his glass soon became famous. Visitors can watch master glassblowers form beautiful and unique vases, goblets, and dishes in the workshop. Guided tours of the workshop and the *verrerie's* **Ecomusée** explain the process of glass blowing. (Tours daily June-Aug. 11:30am, 4, 5:30pm; Sept.-May 4:30pm. Free.) Before leaving, be sure to stop by the **Galerie International du Verre,** considered the most prominent glass gallery in Europe. These unique, luminescent glass sculptures, created by 35 international artists, are expensive—as in over €100,000—but a trip through the gallery is free. (☎04 93 65 03 00; www.verreriebiot.com. Open June-Sept. M-Sa 10am-8pm, Su 10:30am-1:30pm and 2:30-6pm; Oct.-May M-Sa 10:30am-1:30pm and 2:30-6pm. AmEx/MC/V.)

The clay found in the fields surrounding Biot permits ceramicists to create enormous jars, several of which are on display at the **Poterie Provençal,** 1689 route de la Mer, 5min. behind the train station. Founded in 1920, the *poterie* (pottery) is the oldest in Provence. (☎04 93 65 63 30; www.poterie-provencale.fr. Open M-Sa July-Aug. 10am-7pm; Sept.-June 9am-noon and 2-6pm.) Follow the signs from the *poterie* to the **Bonsai Arboretum de la Côte d'Azur,** 229 chemin du Val de Pome, a curious addition to Biot's art scene. Two generations of the Okonek family have maintained a collection of the trees in a peaceful Japanese garden. Trees of all ages, from newborns to an elaborate 105-year-old bonsai imported from China, line the arboretum's winding paths. One highlight is the 6m long bonsai forest, the largest in Europe. (☎04 93 65 63 99. Open M and W-Su 10am-noon and 2-6pm. €4, students €2.)

Run by an enthusiastic, English-speaking owner, 🔳**Crêperie du Vieux Village ❸,** 2 rue St-Sébastien, provides a selection of sweet *crêpes* (€3.50-6.50), *omelettes* (€7-11), and pizza *crêpes* (€14-19). The house *cidre* (hard cider) is a local favorite, while the €13.50 *menu* is a delicious bargain. (☎04 93 65 72 73. Open June-Sept. M-W and F-Su 11:30am-2:30pm and 7-9:30pm. Cash only.) Murals of French urban life during the Belle Époque and colorful glass chandeliers create a relaxed atmosphere in the **Café de la Poste ❸,** rue St-Sébastien. (☎04 93 65 19 32. Meat *plats* €18-25. Salads €10-13. Lunch *menu* €19. Open July-Aug. Tu-Su 7am-2am; Sept.-June Tu-Th and Su 7am-2pm, F-Sa 7am-8pm. AmEx/MC/V.)

A free **shuttle** runs in July and August every 10min. from the parking lot at the *verrerie*'s entrance to the village, close to the Musée Fernand-Léger, and to the Poterie Provençal. From October to May, **bus** #10 (€1) stops several times between the village and the train station; ask the driver to let you off at your preferred stop. The **tourist office**, 46 rue St-Sébastien, is in the heart of the village. (☎04 93 65 78 00; www.biot.fr. Open July-Aug. M-F 10am-7pm, Sa-Su 11am-6pm; Sept.-June M-F 9am-noon and 2-6pm, Sa-Su 2-6pm.) There is a free guided tour of the *vieux village* in French (with accompanying translations in English and other languages) that leaves the tourist office Thursday at 3pm; otherwise, ask for the self-guided tour map, available in many languages.

JUAN-LES-PINS ☎04 93

Under the Romans, Antibes was a major port and fishing base. To protect Antibes from the stench of the incoming seafood, Juan-les-Pins (jwahn-lay-pehn; pop. 80,000 including Antibes) was constructed nearby to store and ship the fish. It consisted mainly of sailors' homes and seafood factories until the 1920s, when it was revamped by robber baron Jay Gould. Hundreds of American tourists were drawn to Gould's seaside paradise, and decades later little has changed. Today, the sailors have returned to search for work among the thousands of yachts stationed in Antibes, and Juan-les-Pins is flooded with vacationers seeking sun, sea, and sex—not necessarily in that order. In summer, ice-cream stands and boardwalk shops stay open late, and clubs blast music until the sun summons partygoers back to the beach.

TRANSPORTATION

Trains: Av. de l'Estérel, at the corner of av. du Maréchal Joffre. Open daily 6:40am-9pm. Ticket window open daily 8:50am-noon and 1:40-5pm. To: **Antibes** (5min., 25 per day, €1.20); **Cannes** (10min., 25 per day, €2); **Monaco** (1hr., 9 per day, €6.40); **Nice** (30min., 25 per day, €3.90).

Buses: ☎04 93 34 37 60. Bus #1 (10min., every 30min. 6:55am-7:45pm, €1) runs from Sillages to pl. Guynemer in **Antibes,** where you can transfer to regional buses. #1 Abis Noctantibes shuttles between pl. de Gaulle in Antibes and Juan-les-Pins at night (July-Aug. 8pm-12:20am).

Petit Train: ☎06 03 35 61 35. Runs from rue de la République in Antibes, through the *vieille ville,* to Juan-les-Pins. Although touristy and more expensive, it also provides a guided tour of Antibes. 30min. July-Aug. every hr. 10am-10pm; May-Oct. every hr. 10am-7pm. Round-trip €8, ages 3-10 €3.50. Buy tickets on train. Cash only.

Taxis: ☎04 92 93 07 07 or 08 25 56 07 07. At the Jardin de la Pinède and outside the train station. From the station to Antibes €12-15.

ORIENTATION AND PRACTICAL INFORMATION

To walk from pl. du Général de Gaulle in Antibes, head along bd. Wilson to the beach (25min.). Follow the beach to the right until you see the tourist office.

Tourist Office: 51 bd. Charles Guillaumont (☎04 97 23 11 10; www.antibes-juan-lespins.com). From the train station, walk along av. du Maréchal Joffre and turn right onto av. Guy de Maupassant; the office is 2min. away on the right, at the intersection of av. de l'Amiral Courbet and av. Charles Guillaumont. Open July-Aug. daily 9am-7pm; Sept.-June M-Sa 9am-noon and 2-6pm.

Laundromat: On the corner of av. de l'Estérel and av. du Docteur Fabre (☎04 93 61 52 04). Wash €3.90-9, dry €0.50 per 5min. Detergent €0.40. Open daily 7am-8pm.

Police: ☎04 97 21 75 60.

Pharmacy: 1 av. de l'Amiral Courbet (☎04 93 61 12 96).

Internet Access: Mediterr@net, 3 av. du Docteur Fabre (☎04 93 61 04 03), across from the train station. €2.70 per hr. Open M-Sa 9am-9pm, Su 10am-9pm.

Post Office: Av. du Maréchal Joffre (☎04 92 93 75 50). Open M and W-F 8am-noon and 1:45-6pm, Tu 8am-noon and 2:15-6pm, Sa 8am-noon. **Postal Code:** 06160.

ACCOMMODATIONS AND CAMPING

Animated beaches and incomparable nightlife make Juan-les-Pins a popular vacation spot; it's no wonder luxury hotels and upscale apartments are every-where, while budget lodging is hard to find. The closest campgrounds are two train stops away in Biot (ask the tourist office for more information).

Hôtel de la Gare, 6 rue du Printemps (☎04 93 61 29 96). Small hotel with functional, clean rooms. Breakfast €5. Reserve months ahead. July-Aug. singles and doubles €36; triples €42; quads €62. Sept. and May-June singles and doubles €32; triples €42; quads €52. Oct.-Apr. singles and doubles €29; triples €39; quads €47. MC/V. ❸

Hôtel Parisiana, 16 av. de l'Estérel (☎04 93 61 27 03; hotelparisiana@wanadoo. fr). Bright rooms with A/C, fridges, bath, and TVs. Breakfast €5. Free Wi-Fi. Reception 8am-10pm. Singles €30-45; doubles €42-59; triples €55-71; quads €65-79. Extra bed €11. Prices lower for stays of more than 5 nights. MC/V. ❷

Hôtel Alexandra, rue Pauline (☎04 97 21 76 50; www.hotelalexandra.net). First opened in 1920. Spacious, tastefully decorated rooms, each with A/C, phone, TV, and shower. 1st fl. restaurant serves a Provençal *menu.* Breakfast €7.50. Free Wi-Fi. Reception 8am-8pm. July-Aug. reserve 1 month ahead. Open Mar.-Oct. July-Aug. singles €55; doubles €85; triples €92-98. Sept. and May-June singles €50; doubles €75; triples €82-88. Oct. and Mar.-Apr. singles €45; doubles €65; triples €72-80. AmEx/MC/V. ❹

FOOD

The **Petit Casino** supermarket is on av. de l'Amiral Courbet, across from the tourist office. (☎04 93 61 00 56. Open M-Tu and Th-Sa 8am-12:30pm and 2:30-7:30pm, W 8am-12:30pm, Su 8am-1pm. MC/V.) A **Casino** supermarket is on av. du Docteur Dautheville. (Open M-Sa 8:30am-8pm, Su 9am-1pm.) Meal prices are typically more affordable the farther you walk from the *centre-ville.*

La Bamba, 18 rue du Docteur Dautheville (☎04 93 61 32 64). Serves a large selection of wood-fired meat and fish dishes (€13-24). Pizzas €9-13. *Menu* €23. Open daily July-Aug. 5:30pm-1am; Sept.-June noon-2pm and 7-11pm. AmEx/MC/V. ❸

Ruban Bleu, promenade du Soleil (☎04 93 61 31 02). Beachfront restaurant and boardwalk *brasserie.* At *brasserie:* Pizza €8-14. *Plats* €15-28. *Menus* €18. Restaurant prices €3-5 more. Open daily July-Aug. 7:30am-2am; Sept.-June 7:30am-10pm. V. ❸

La Bretagne, bd. Charles Guillaumont (☎04 93 67 41 54). Eat with an ocean view on the sand. Chair, mattress, and umbrella €12. Pasta €9-14. Open daily 9am-7pm. V. ❸

NIGHTLIFE AND FESTIVALS

In mid-July, Juan-les-Pins temporarily abandons its nightclub obsession for the 10-day **Festival International de Jazz** (Jazz à Juan), which has drawn such perform-ers as BB King. (Jazzajuan@antibes-juanlespins.com. Tickets available at tour-ist office. €25-66, students and under 18 €12-22. MC/V.) Sunset in Juan-les-Pins draws bronzed partygoers to the casino area. Most *discothèques* are open only on weekends in the low season. Fortunately, nearby bars pick up the slack and provide a lively and raucous atmosphere of their own.

BARS

Pam Pam Rhumerie, 137 bd. du Président Wilson (☎04 93 61 11 05; www.pampam. fr). Brazilian-themed. Revelers squeeze in between tikis to sip exotic mixed drinks (€14) served in coconut-, monkey-, and tiki-hut-shaped glasses. Showgirls in bikinis take the stage at 9:30pm. Open daily from mid-Mar. to early Nov. 2pm-5am. MC/V.

Le Crystal, av. Georges Galice (☎04 93 61 62 51), across from Pam Pam. Ice-cream mixed drinks (€10) attract a low-key, relaxed crowd. Open daily 8am-2:30am. MC/V.

Ché Café, carrefour de la Nouvelle Orléans. Pays homage to Mr. Guevara with huge photos and camo-print chairs. Try a tempting lineup of rum shots (€9)—including banana, plantain, coconut, and guava flavors—on the terrace. Beer €6.50. Mixed drinks €8-12. Open daily Aug. 3pm-5am; Sept.-Oct. and Apr.-July 3pm-4am. MC/V.

Zapata's, carrefour de la Nouvelle Orléans. Partygoers pack into the bar and crowd the outside tables to listen to salsa and drink margaritas. Shots €7-9. Mixed drinks €9. Open Apr.-Oct. daily 5:30pm-4am. MC/V.

L'Estérel, 12 av. de l'Estérel (☎04 93 61 31 26), across from rue Jonnard. Escape the overpriced at this laid-back local hangout. Beer €4.40. Mixed drinks €6-7. Shots €2-3; 10 for €18-27. Live music Tu. Happy hour W. Open daily 6pm-2:30am. Cash only.

CLUBS

Le Village, 1 bd. de la Pinède (☎04 92 93 90 00). Brave long lines for the Mexican fiestas. Feisty staff literally sets the bar on fire. Ladies free M-Th before 12:30am. Cover €16. Open July-Aug. daily midnight-5am; Sept.-June F-Sa midnight-5am. MC/V.

Milk, av. Georges Gallice (☎04 93 67 22 74). Swanky crowd. Plush sofas make the entirely white interior relaxing. Drinks €11-17. Cover €16; includes 1 drink. Open July-Aug. daily midnight-6am; Sept.-June F-Sa midnight-6am. AmEx/MC/V.

Whisky à Gogo, 5 rue Jacques Leonetti (☎04 93 61 26 40). Black lights and bubble columns. Young crowd grooves to house. Drinks €11. Ladies free before 12:30am. 18+. Cover €16, students €8; includes 1 drink. Open June-Aug. daily midnight-5am; from Sept. to mid-Oct. Th-Sa midnight-5am; Apr.-May F-Sa midnight-5am. AmEx/MC/V.

BEACHES

The small beaches are crowded by beach clubs, restaurants, and snack stands. Juan-les-Pins's second-biggest playground—after the clubs, of course—is the surf, home to every watersport imaginable. Start at the pontoon dock in front of Hôtel Meridien, where **Water Sports Services,** 15 bd. Baudoin, on Garden Beach, offers water-skiing (€20), wakeboarding (€20), parasailing (€50-60), tubing (€20), and paddle-boat rental by the hour (€20). (☎04 92 93 57 57. Open daily July-Aug. 7am-8pm; Sept.-Oct. and Apr.-June 8am-7pm. Cash only.)

CANNES
☎04 93

The name Cannes (kahn; pop. 67,000) conjures up images of Catherine Deneuve sipping champagne by the pool, Marilyn Monroe posing red-lipped on the beach, and countless other starlets competing for camera time. But when Palmes d'Or turn back into palm trees after the city's renowned film festival, Cannes stashes the red carpet and becomes the most accessible of the Riviera's glam-towns. Cannes draws a wealthy clientele to its palm-lined boardwalk, inviting sandy beaches, and innumerable boutiques—but many fun-loving travelers also come to soak up the sun, play in the waves, and party all night in Cannes's nonstop hot spots at some of the lowest prices on the Côte d'Azur.

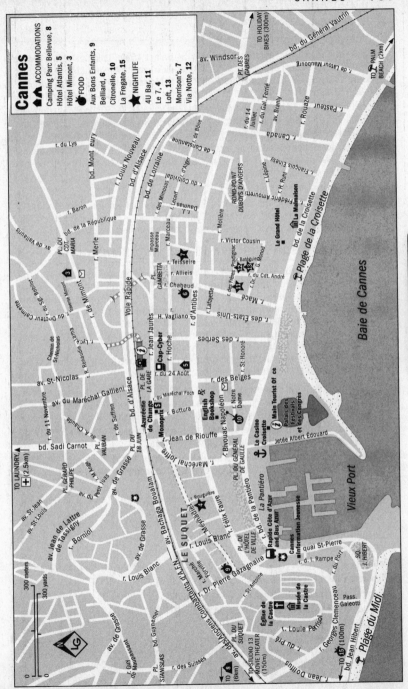

Cannes

ACCOMMODATIONS
Camping Parc Bellevue, **8**
Hôtel Atlantis, **5**
Hôtel Mimont, **3**

FOOD
Aux Bons Enfants, **9**
Belliard, **6**
Citronelle, **10**
La Fregate, **15**

NIGHTLIFE
4U Bar, **11**
Le 7, **4**
Loft, **13**
Morrison's, **7**
Via Notte, **12**

CÔTE D'AZUR

Baie de Cannes

Vieux Port

Plage du Midi

TRANSPORTATION

Trains: 1 rue Jean Jaurès. Station open daily 5:10am-1:15am. Ticket office open daily 5:30am-10:30pm. Info desk open M-Sa 8:30am-5:30pm. To: **Antibes** (15min., €2.50); **Grasse** (35min., €3.70); **Marseille** (2hr., €25); **Monaco** (1hr., €8); **Nice** (40min., €5.80); **St-Raphaël** (25min., €6.10). TGV to **Paris** (5hr., €81-104) via **Marseille.**

Buses: Rapide Côte d'Azur, pl. de l'Hôtel de Ville (☎04 93 48 70 30). To **Nice** (1hr., every 20min., €6) and **Nice airport** (1hr.; every 30min. M-Sa 7am-7pm, Su 8:30am-7pm; €14). Buses to **Grasse** (50min., every 45min., €1) leave from the train station.

Public Transportation: Bus Azur, pl. de l'Hôtel de Ville (☎08 25 82 55 99), runs **buses.** Info and ticket desk open M-F 7am-7pm, Sa 8:30am-noon and 2-6:30pm. €1; weekly pass €11. Buy tickets on board.

Taxis: Allô Taxis Cannes (☎04 92 99 27 27).

Bike and Scooter Rental: Holiday Bikes, 32 av. du Maréchal Juin (☎04 93 94 30 34). Bikes from €14 per day, €65 per week; €230 deposit. Scooters from €32/160; €500 deposit. Open M-Sa 9am-noon and 2-7pm, Su by appointment. AmEx/MC/V.

ORIENTATION AND PRACTICAL INFORMATION

The city's shopping hub is the *centre-ville*, between the train station and the sea; **rue d'Antibes** runs through its center, parallel to the water. From the station, head right on rue Jean Jaurès to reach the *vieille ville*, also known as **le Suquet,** where flea-market-style shopping dominates **rue Meynadier** by day and upscale dining enlivens tiny **rue Saint-Antoine** by night. Stargazers should follow rue des Serbes down to the nocturnal seaside **boulevard de la Croisette.** At the adjacent *vieux port,* Cannes's beautiful beach stretches in both directions along the coast. Two kilometers east, the peninsular stretch of clubs known as **Palm Beach** draws sun-seekers and watersport enthusiasts alike.

Tourist Office: 1 bd. de la Croisette (☎04 92 99 84 22; www.cannes.fr), in the Palais des Festivals. Books tickets for events and provides free maps. Open daily July-Aug. 9am-8pm; Sept.-June 9am-7pm. Branch at the train station (☎04 93 99 19 77). Open M-Sa 9am-7pm.

Currency Exchange: Azuréene de Change, 17 rue du Maréchal Foch (☎04 93 39 34 37), across from the train station. Open daily 8am-7pm.

English-Language Bookstore: Cannes English Bookshop, 11 rue du Bivouac Napoléon (☎04 93 99 40 08; www.cannesenglishbookshop.com). Open M-Sa 10:15am-1pm and 2-7pm. AmEx/MC/V.

Youth Center: Cannes Information Jeunesse, 5 quai St-Pierre (☎04 97 06 46 25; lekiosque625@ville-cannes.fr). Info on jobs and housing. Very helpful staff. Open M-Th 8:30am-12:30pm and 1:30-6pm, F 8:30am-12:30pm and 1:30-5pm.

Laundromat: Point Laverie, 56 bd. Carnot (☎06 09 51 97 91). Wash €6.20, dry €3 per 30min. Detergent €0.50. Open daily 7am-8pm.

Police: 1 av. de Grasse (☎04 93 06 22 22) and 2 quai St-Pierre (☎0800 11 71 18).

Pharmacy: 36 rue d'Antibes (☎04 93 39 01 29).

Hospital: Hôpital des Broussailles, 13 av. des Broussailles (☎04 93 69 70 00).

Internet Access: Cap Cyber, 12 rue du 24 Août (☎04 93 38 85 63). €3 per hr. Discount with student ID. Open daily July-Aug. 10am-11pm; Sept.-June 10am-10pm. MC/V.

Post Office: 22 rue du Bivouac Napoléon (☎04 93 06 26 50), near Palais des Festivals. Open M-F 9am-7pm, Sa 9am-noon. Branch at 34 rue de Mimont (☎04 93 06 27 00). Open M-F 8:30am-noon and 1:30-5pm, Sa 8:30am-noon. **Postal Code:** 06400.

ACCOMMODATIONS AND CAMPING

During most of the year, it's not hard to get a good night's sleep at a reasonable price in Cannes. During the film festival, however, hotel rates triple and rooms need to be reserved at least a year in advance. Book early for summer. Frequent bus service to the campground makes it a wise budget choice.

Hôtel Mimont, 39 rue Mimont (☎04 93 39 51 64; www.canneshotelmimont.com). Exit the train station to the left, then take the underpass next to the tourist office to rue Mimont. Turn right; Cannes's best budget hotel is on the left. Spacious rooms, each with shower, TV, and phone. English-speaking owners eager to help travelers. Ask about *petites chambres* for *Let's Go* readers (€30). Breakfast €6. Free Wi-Fi. Reception 8am-11pm. July-Aug. singles €39, with toilet €46; doubles €46/54; triples €69. Sept.-June singles €34, with toilet €40; doubles €40/47; triples €60. Extra bed €10. MC/V. ❸

Hôtel Atlantis, 4 rue du 24 Août (☎04 93 39 18 72; www.cannes-hotel-atlantis.com), off rue Jean Jaurès. English-speaking owners. Comfortable rooms with showers. Workout room has mini-sauna, massage shower, and hot tub. A/C €5. Breakfast €6. Wi-Fi in lobby. July-Aug. reserve ahead. Singles €50; doubles €56-80; triples and quads €75-130. Prices decrease with longer stay. 5% discount with *Let's Go*. AmEx/MC/V. ❸

Camping Parc Bellevue, 67 av. Maurice Chevalier (☎04 93 47 28 97), in La Bocca. Take bus #2 to Les Aubépines and walk for 500m, following signs for the campground. Large pool and on-site restaurant. Shaded plots. Laundry €3. Reception 8am-8pm. July-Aug. 1 person with tent €15; 2 people with tent €18. Sept. and Apr.-June 1 person with tent €11; 2 people with tent €14. Electricity €3. ❶

FOOD

Though the city is dominated by high-end restaurants, Cannes is also full of quality restaurants with reasonable prices. There are markets on **place Gambetta** and **place du Commandant Maria;** the best is the **Forville market** on rue Meynadier and rue Louis Blanc, as it has a large selection of produce and fish. (All open in summer daily 6am-1pm; in winter Tu-Su 6am-1pm.) The **Monoprix** on the corner of rue Buttura and rue Jean Jaurès carries food, clothing, housewares, and just about everything else. (Open M-Sa 8:30am-8pm.) Good restaurants are in the pedestrian zone, particularly along **rue Meynadier.** The narrow streets of **le Suquet** offer cozy corners for open-air dining, but the ambience adds to the bill.

La Fregate, 26 bd. Jean Hibert (☎04 93 39 45 39). Large bar-*brasserie*-cafe by the beach. Cannes staple since 1947. Extensive menu of Italian-inspired cuisine. Local youths enjoy pizza (€9-14), pasta (€7.50-17), grilled meats (€12-26), and large salads (€4-14) on a bright green-and-yellow terrace. Mixed drinks €9. Open daily June-Sept. 6:30am-2am; Oct.-May 6:30am-1am. AmEx/MC/V. ❸

Aux Bons Enfants, 80 rue Meynadier. 3rd-generation restaurant. Experienced chef constructs a Provençal menu (€22) every day based on what catches his eye at the morning market. Open May-July and Sept. M-Sa noon-2pm and 7:15-9:30pm; Oct.-Apr. M-F noon-2pm and 7-9pm, Sa noon-2pm. Cash only. ❸

Belliard, 1 rue Chabaud (☎04 93 39 42 72). 75-year-old *boulangerie* and *salon de thé* has been treating *Cannois* to scrumptious tarts and baked goods for years. Takeout gourmet plate (€9.50) includes a selection of 3 meat options and 3 *légumes* (vegetables). Try a homemade quiche (€2.50-4.50). Open M-Sa 7am-8pm. V. ❷

Citronelle, 16 rue du Bivouac Napoléon (☎06 63 97 73 08). Market-fresh ingredients. Delicious sandwiches (€3.80-4.50), unique salads (try the Bikini Lime; €4-5), and thirst-quenching natural smoothies (€3.80) to go. Open M-F 10am-6pm. Cash only. ❶

SIGHTS AND ENTERTAINMENT

The fashion-conscious city of Cannes is blessed with countless high-end boutiques, offering some of the coast's best window-shopping. **Boulevard de la Croisette** boasts names like Cartier, Chanel, and Dior. The less pricey **rue d'Antibes** mixes funky shops and chain stores with classy brand names. Head to **rue Meynadier,** a street market, for cheap knockoffs.

L'ÉGLISE DE LA CASTRE. At the top of the Suquet, the church and its courtyard provide an excellent view of the city below. The inhabitants of Cannes had to fundraise for 80 years to complete the costly structure; it was finally finished in the early 17th century. All that work paid off: the *église* houses ornate glass chandeliers and an impressive Neo-Gothic organ. *(Open daily June-Aug. 9am-noon and 3:15-7pm; Sept.-May 9am-noon and 2:15-6pm. Free.)*

MUSÉE DE LA CASTRE. Formerly the private castle of the monks of Lérins, this museum now displays collections of fascinating ancient relics from the Americas, Himalayas, and Pacific. A small exhibit by Provençal artists recalls life in turn-of-the-century Cannes. The museum's real treat is the 12th-century chapel, which houses musical instruments from all over the world. Climb the tower to get a 360° view of Cannes. *(☎04 93 38 55 26. Open Tu-Su July-Aug. 10am-7pm; Sept. and Apr.-June 10am-1pm and 2-6pm; Oct.-Mar. 10am-1pm and 2-5pm. €3.20, students €2.)*

CENTRE D'ART/MALMAISON. Temporary exhibits often address contemporary issues or the latest headlines from around the world. *(47 bd. de la Croisette, to the right of the Grand Hôtel. ☎04 97 06 44 90. Open June-Sept. M-Th and Sa-Su 11am-8pm, F 11am-10pm; Oct.-Nov. Tu-Su 10am-1pm and 2-6pm. €4, under 25 €2. MC/V.)*

CASINOS. Cannes's three casinos provide countless opportunities to break the bank. The least exclusive, **Le Casino Croisette,** has slot machines, blackjack, and roulette. The Greek-inspired interior comes complete with faux-marble statues and an aquarium. *(1 espace Lucien Barrière, next to the Palais des Festivals. ☎04 92 98 78 00. Slots open at 10am; table games daily 8pm-4am. No dress code for slots. No jeans, T-shirts, or sneakers for gambling. 18+. Free entry.)*

NIGHTLIFE

The elite nightspots that make Cannes famous are notoriously exclusive; those looking to get in should dress to kill. Cafes and bars near the waterfront stay open all night for just as much fun at half the price. Park yourself with a cold one and watch the nightly fashion show strut by, headed to private parties in the clubs and casinos. Nightlife thrives around **rue du Docteur Gérard Monod.**

Morrison's, 10 rue Teisseire (☎04 92 98 16 17; www.morrisonspub.com). Casual but lively company. Mahogany bookshelves and quotes by Irish playwrights cover the walls. English-speaking staff. Pints from €5.30. Irish whiskey €8. Live pop and rock W-Th and Su from 9:30pm. Su ladies' night; unlimited wine and beer for women €8. Happy hour 5-8pm. Open daily 5pm-2am. MC/V.

4U Bar, 6 rue des Frères Bradignac (☎04 93 39 71 21; www.bar4u.com). Young, international, unpretentious crowd. Gay-friendly. Live house music. After midnight, exuberant guests transform the bar into a dance floor. Vivacious bartenders. Mixed drinks €9.50. Happy hour daily 6-8pm; beer from €3.50. Open daily 6pm-2am. MC/V.

Le 7, 7 rue Rougières (☎04 93 39 10 36; www.discotheque-le7.com). Even Parisians concede the fame of Le 7, known for outrageous nightly drag shows (2am). Recently refurbished interior. Straight and gay clientele. Mixed drinks €12. Cover F-Sa €16, after 4am €12; includes 1 drink. Open daily 11:30pm-8am. MC/V.

Loft, 13 rue du Docteur Gérard Monod (☎04 93 39 40 39). Dance the night away or simply stand around looking glamorous. Dress your way in or pretend you know someone. Downstairs, the restaurant Tantra morphs into a club F-Sa, and tables serve as dance floors until the party moves upstairs. Live DJ. Mixed drinks €15. Open M-Sa June-Aug. 8pm-2am; Sept.-May 10:30pm-2am. AmEx/MC/V.

Via Notte, 13 rue du Commandant André (☎04 92 98 62 82). Perennial hot spot in the heart of Cannes's late-night scene. Dancing livens up around midnight. Snacks served with drinks until 10pm. Mixed drinks €11. Open daily 6pm-2:30am. AmEx/MC/V.

REEL CANNES. The world-famous Cannes Film Festival only happens once a year, but the city is never quite rid of the influence of the silver screen; even budget travelers can participate in Cannes's connection with film. **Studio 13,** 23 av. du Docteur Picaud (☎04 93 06 29 90; www.mjcpicaud.com), puts together an intelligent, well-crafted program of movies from around the world in its intimate theater. All films, shown in their original languages (with French subtitles), are €6, and only €4 for students. (Showings Sept.-June M-Th and Sa 6 and 8:30pm, F 2:30, 6, and 8:30pm. W €5.) Programs available online, by phone, and from the Cannes Youth Center (p. 738).

FESTIVALS

Festival International du Film, May 13-24, 2009. Stars and star-seekers descend with pomp and circumstance upon Cannes for the world-famous festival. Invite-only—but celebrity-spotting (not stalking!) is always free. Be warned: prices skyrocket.

Fête Américaine and Fête Nationale (☎04 92 98 62 77), July 4 and 14, respectively. American and French independence days celebrated with spectacular fireworks.

Les Nuits Musicales du Suquet, in July. Open-air performances by professional musicians throughout le Suquet. Tickets €30-44.

GRASSE ☎04 93

You'll know you're in Grasse (grahss; pop. 45,000) when the smell of tanning oil turns to jasmine and tea rose. With a unique climate ideal for growing heavily scented flowers, Grasse has been the capital of the world's perfume industry for over 200 years and houses France's three largest, oldest, and most distinguished *parfumeries*. Prepare to be spritzed with a barrage of flowery scents that will leave your nose delightfully overwhelmed. Outside the perfumeries, expansive vistas and tasty restaurants satisfy the other senses. Grasse's proximity to Cannes (15km) makes it a pleasant afternoon excursion.

TRANSPORTATION

Trains: Traverse de la Gare. Ticket window open M-Sa 9am-6pm, Su 9am-noon and 1-6pm—or use the automated machines. Route 4B runs 19 trains to: **Antibes** (€5.30); **Cannes** (€3.40); **Nice** (€7.90); **Ventimiglia, ITA** (€12).

Buses: RCA, pl. Notre Dame des Fleurs (☎04 93 36 08 43). Open M-Th 7:30am-12:15pm and 1-4:45pm, F 7:30am-12:15pm and 1-4pm. To **Cannes** (50min.; M-Sa every 30min. 6am-8:05pm, Su every hr. 7:30am-7:30pm; €1) and **Nice** (1hr.; July-Aug. 14 per day, Sept.-June 23 per day; €1).

Public Transportation: Free **navette** (shuttle) runs around the outskirts of town and connects the train station to the bus station and the rest of the village (M-Sa 7:15am-8pm). **Bus #3** also connects the village with the train station (7:30am-7pm).

Taxis: ☎04 93 36 37 07.

◼◼ ORIENTATION AND PRACTICAL INFORMATION

Most tourist destinations are concentrated in the pedestrian *vieille ville* and on the south-facing hillside. From the train station, take the shuttle or bus #3 to any stop along bd. du Jeu de Ballon to reach the tourist office or its annex. From the bus station, walk a short distance along rue Andre Kalin to av. Thiers and make a left to find the tourist office on your right. Continue past the tourist office along av. Thiers and turn left down a flight of steps when you see signs for **place aux Aires,** a lively square on the edge of the *vieille ville.* Farther downhill, on your left, lies **place du 24 Août,** a large plateau with a valley view within walking distance of the Fragonard perfumery and several museums.

Tourist Office: Cours Honoré Cresp (☎04 93 36 66 66; www.grasse.fr), next to the Palais des Congrès. Hands out maps and restaurant and hotel guides. 1hr. guided **tours** in English July-Aug. Sa at 2pm; €2. Open June-Sept. M-Sa 9am-7pm, Su 9am-1pm and 2-6pm; Oct.-May M-Sa 9am-12:30pm and 2-6pm.

Police: 12 bd. Carnot (☎04 93 40 31 60).

Pharmacy: 26 pl. aux Aires (☎04 93 36 05 35).

Hospital: Chemin de Clavary (☎04 93 09 55 00).

Internet Access: Webphone, 3 rue des Fabreries (☎04 93 77 78 62), just off pl. aux Aires. Laptops can be plugged into modem. €2 per hr. Open daily 10am-9pm.

Post Office: In the garage under the bus station (☎04 92 42 31 11). Open M-F 9am-noon and 2-5pm, Sa 9am-noon. **Postal Code:** 06130.

◼ ACCOMMODATIONS

Grasse has moderately priced hotels but no hostels or good camping options.

L'Oasis Hotel, pl. de la Buanderie (☎04 93 36 02 72), next to the bus station. Grasse's only budget hotel has comfortable, well-kept rooms and accommodating owners. A steal, particularly for those traveling in groups. Breakfast €5. Reception daily 6:30am-10pm. Singles €28-39; doubles €30-39; triples €37-49. AmEx/MC/V. ❷

◼ FOOD

A morning market fills **place du Cours** (open W 7am-1pm). On Saturdays, the flower market on **place aux Aires** usually offers fruit and vegetable stands as well as the blossoms (open 7am-1pm). A **Monoprix** supermarket, rue Paul Goby, is near the bus station. (☎04 93 36 44 36. Open M-Sa 8:45am-8pm. AmEx/MC/V.) *Crêperies* and cafes occupy the *vieille ville.* Centered on cobblestone pl. aux Aires, Grasse's most affordable restaurants also have the best ambience.

Le Rendez-Vous, 35 pl. aux Aires (☎04 93 77 25 54). Dishes on the simple menu are artfully presented. Those hungry enough to eat a horse can try ◼**horse-meat burgers** (with fries; €8.70); those less famished should opt for bacon cheeseburgers (€8.70). Salads €8.50-14. Meat *plats* €12-23. Open daily 9am-midnight. MC/V. ❸

Café des Musées, 1 rue Ossola (☎04 92 60 99 00). Small basement cafe serves creative dishes like *l'assiette St-Marcellin* (roasted St-Marcellin cheese on bread with apples; €12) and homemade desserts (€5.50) in a bright, yellow-tiled interior decorated with fresh flowers. Open M-Sa 8:30am-6:30pm, Su noon-3pm. MC/V. ❸

La Voute, 3 rue du Thournon (☎04 93 36 11 43). Provençal *plats* in a charming 15th-century interior. *Plat du jour* €13. *Menu* €18. Open daily noon-3pm and 7-11pm. AmEx/MC/V. ❸

👁 🎭 SIGHTS AND FESTIVALS

In mid-May, **Expo-Rose** attracts rose growers from around the world for the largest exhibition of its kind. The *Grassois* pay tribute to their flowery source of income again in early August at the **Fête du Jasmin.** This fragrant festival features the election of a Miss Jasmin to preside over the festivities. Even the directionally challenged will have no trouble finding their way to Grasse's three largest *parfumeries*; wafts of *eau de toilette* lead visitors to the factory doorsteps.

■**FRAGONARD.** The most tourist-friendly *parfumerie* gives free tours of its 225-year-old factory, still in use today. An interesting museum on the top floor of the factory displays a large collection of perfume paraphernalia, including bottles ranging from ancient Egyptian to Calvin Klein. Don't miss the creative perfume bottle shapes, which include adorable birds, eggs, and—rather ironically—human feet. *(20 bd. Fragonard. ☎04 93 36 44 65; www.fragonard.com. Open Feb.-Oct. daily 9am-6pm; Nov.-Jan. M-Sa 9am-6pm. Last tour 5:45pm. AmEx/MC/V.)*

MOLINARD. This *parfumerie* is housed in a 19th-century factory designed by Gustave Eiffel—of Parisian tower and Statue of Liberty fame. Free tours take you past scented soap production, enormous perfume vats, and elaborate, aging bottle labels. If you don't find anything to suit your taste, concoct your own personal *eau de parfum* at the 1hr. Tarinologie workshop for €40. *(60 bd. Victor Hugo, 5min. from the centre-ville. ☎04 92 42 33 11; www.molinard.com. Open July-Aug. daily 9am-7pm; Sept. and Apr.-June daily 9am-6:30pm; Oct.-Mar. M-F 9am-12:30pm and 2-6pm, Sa 9am-noon and 2-6pm. Tours July 9:30am-6pm; Aug.-June 9:30am-noon and 2-5:30pm. Reservations required for Tarinologie workshop. AmEx/MC/V.)*

GALIMARD. Louis XIV's perfume and pomade maker founded the Galimard factory in 1747 to keep the Sun King smelling divine. The factory offers 2hr. sessions with a ■**professional nose,** who will help you create a personal fragrance for €45 in the Studio des Fragrances. *(73 route de Cannes. From the bus station, take bus #600 (dir.: Cannes) and make sure the driver knows you want to go to La Blauquière (€1). From the stop, walk downhill for 5min. ☎04 93 09 20 00; www.galimard.com. Open daily June-Sept. 9am-6:30pm; Oct.-May 9am-12:30pm and 2-6pm. Reservations required. AmEx/MC/V.)*

THE LOCAL STORY

FRAGRANT FINDS

While some translate *eau de toilette* as "toilet water," a short walk through any perfume boutique in Grasse proves that the translation is more than misleading. Designer *eau de toilette* flies off the shelves in this perfume capital, but how is it any different from perfume?

All fragrances are a combination of raw materials that give them their specific scents and three other substances: perfume oil, alcohol, and water. Perfume has a higher concentration of perfume oil, around 18-24%, than does *eau de toilette* (8-12%), while *eau de parfum* falls in between (15%). A higher percentage of oil gives a stronger effect—for a real punch in the nose, try solid perfume in the form of a cream or paste, called "concrete," which contains 30-40% perfume oils.

Once you've chosen your scent, the best places to wear it are the insides of wrists and elbows or behind the ears; body heat in these places helps the perfume do its job. Natural fabrics such as silk and wool release scents particularly well. Give perfume about an hour to disseminate and release its various layers of scent. Finally, try to keep perfume bottles away from heat and sunlight and remember that the air in opened bottles causes perfumes to spoil slowly; buying smaller amounts is a good idea for infrequent use. More questions? The experts at Fragonard Parfumerie can offer tips for choosing, wearing, and storing perfume.

A NOSE BY ANY OTHER NAME. The master smellers of the perfume industry—known as "noses"—produce high fashion's most famous fragrances. The best noses train for 15 years, studying scents and chemistry before ever extracting an essence; by the time they're ready to mix a scent, students have memorized more than 3000 smells (the average person can only handle about 200). Noses can even distinguish the difference between jasmine grown in Grasse and that grown elsewhere! All French noses are trained at one of two French olfactory schools—one in Grasse and the other in Versailles. It can take up to two years for a nose to mix a new scent, and even the most prolific noses never produce more than three or four perfumes per year. As there are only 10 in all of France, noses are hot commodities and are required by contract to renounce alcohol, cigarettes, and spicy foods.

MUSÉE INTERNATIONAL DE LA PARFUMERIE. To make sense of all these scents, head to this superb museum, where exhibits showcase perfume production across the globe. Look for the 3000-year-old mummy's hand and foot, apparently preserved by their perfume. *(8 pl. du Cours Honoré Cresp. ☎ 04 97 05 58 00. Open June-Sept. daily 10am-6:30pm; Oct.-May M and W-Su 10am-12:30pm and 2-5:30pm.)*

MUSÉE JEAN-HONORÉ FRAGONARD. This museum features erotic canvases by the libertine painter and Grasse native, whose name was adopted by the perfumery in 1926. *(23 bd. Fragonard. ☎ 04 93 36 01 61. Open June-Sept. daily 10am-6:30pm; Oct.-May M and W-Su 10am-12:30pm and 2-5:30pm.)*

OTHER SIGHTS. The **Musée Provençal du Costume et du Bijou,** next to the Fragonard factory, offers a small collection of 18th- and 19th-century clothing and jewelry, most of which is displayed on faceless mannequins. A less creepy highlight is the collection of intricate, ornamental crosses. *(☎ 04 93 36 91 42. Open daily 10am-1pm and 2-6:30pm. Free.)* At the highest point in the *vieille ville,* the Romanesque **Cathédrale Notre Dame-du-Puy** displays three works by Rubens as well as Fragonard's only religious painting, *Lavement des Pieds,* commissioned especially for the Baroque chapel. *(☎ 04 93 36 11 02. Open M-Tu and Th-F 9:30am-6pm, W 9:30-11:30am and 3-6pm, Sa 9:30-11:30am and 3-7pm, Su 8-11:30am.)*

GRAND CANYON DU VERDON   ☎ 04 92

Sixty kilometers off the coast, Europe's widest and deepest gorge is a world apart from the geographically tame beaches and vineyards that Provence is known for. The gorge is especially worth a visit for its watersports; the nearby town of Castellane is home to a micro-industry of adventure outfits that plan nearly every excursion imaginable. Though the tree-speckled, chalky canyon is appealing, most people come for the Verdon River and the Lac de Ste-Croix.

▰ **TRANSPORTATION.** Castellane, 17km east of the canyon and the largest village in the area, is unfortunately a bit of a pain to reach from the coast. VFD **buses** (☎ 08 20 83 38 33) run from Grasse (70min.; depart from Grasse 8am, return 6:20pm; €6.30). Autocars Sumian (☎ 04 42 54 72 82) runs from Marseille to Castellane once per day (July-Aug. M-Sa), stopping at several smaller villages around the canyon along the way. The canyon itself can be equally difficult to access. In July and August, Transports GUICHARD (☎ 04 92 83 64 47) sends a **shuttle** from Castellane toward Point Sublime, La Palud, and La Maline (30-75min., 2 per day, €6.80). Otherwise, **taxis** run from Castellane to various points throughout the region (☎ 04 92 83 61 62 or 83 60 80; from €30).

◪ **PRACTICAL INFORMATION.** The Castellane **tourist office,** at the end of rue Nationale, has bus schedules, free *Sentier Martel* maps, and brochures on adventure outfitters. (☎04 92 83 61 14; www.castellane.org. Open July-Aug. M-Sa 9am-12:30pm and 2-7pm, Su 10am-1pm; Sept.-Oct. M-Sa 9am-noon and 2-5pm; Nov.-June M-F 9am-noon and 2-5pm.) Get cash for your adventure tour at the **ATM** at 3 pl. Marcel Sauvaire, by the bus stop (☎08 20 06 43 91). Before venturing into the canyon, stock up on **outdoor gear** at **L'Échoppe,** 36 rue Nationale, Castellane's only outdoor outfitter. (☎/fax 04 92 83 60 06. Open July-Aug. M-Sa 8am-12:45pm and 3:30pm-7:30pm, Su 4-7pm; Sept. and June M-Sa 9am-12:30pm and 2:30-7:30pm; Apr.-May M-Sa 9:30am-noon and 3-7pm. MC/V.) Find **Internet** at **Aqua Verdon,** 9 rue Nationale, by the tourist office.

◪◪ **ACCOMMODATIONS AND FOOD.** Because shuttle access is so infrequent, it might be worth spending the night in Castellane and heading for the gorge early the next morning. An endless number of large, excellent campgrounds can be found in the area surrounding the canyon, but one of the closest to Castellane is **Camping Le Frédéric Mistral** ❶, 12 av. Frédéric Mistral, 5min. from the *centre-ville.* Crowded but shady plots are offset by excellent amenities like an on-site *boulangerie,* clean showers and facilities, and laundry (€4). Ping-pong tables, swing sets, and organized *boules* tournaments add to the fun-loving atmosphere. (☎04 92 83 62 27. Reception daily 9am-12:30pm and 2-8:30pm. €7-9 per person. Electricity €3. Cash only.) If you're looking for a comfortable place to put your feet up after a long day of bungee jumping and rafting, walk 15min. out of town along route des Gorges du Verdon, near the bus stop, to **Le Moulin de la Salaou** ❸. This small hotel boasts a restaurant on the first floor, a spacious common area with a pool table, and 11 cozy rooms with showers. On weekends during the low season and every night in July and August, the hotel is also home to the only *discothèque* within 50km. If you're lucky, one of the club's popular foam parties will coincide with your stay in Castellane. (☎04 92 83 78 97; www.moulin-salaou.com. Restaurant *menus* €10-24. *Discothèque* cover €8; includes 1 drink. Open July-Aug. daily 11pm-4am. Breakfast €6. Reception daily 8-10:30am and 4pm-midnight. Open Apr.-Sept. Doubles €39-45; triples €43-50; quads €46-56; quints €50-62. MC/V.) Several budget restaurants are located on **place de la République** and along **rue Nationale.** Pick up groceries at the **Petit Casino** on pl. de l'Église. (☎04 92 83 63 01. Open Tu-F 8:20am-noon and 1:30-5pm, Sa 8:20am-noon. MC/V.)

◪ **HIKING.** The canyon's most traveled trail is **Sentier Martel,** a.k.a. the **GR4** trail. The 6-8hr. hike traces the river for 14km from La Maline east to Point Sublime, passing through tunnels and caves rumored to have once hidden fugitives. To reach the trailhead, drive east from La Palud or Verdon for 8km to La Maline. Red and white markers at the Chalet de la Maline indicate the route. Bring flashlights, sturdy footwear, and plenty of water. Though the trail is easily navigable with a free map and directions from the Castellane tourist office, guides are available upon request. (Contact Daniel Duflot, chemin des Listes; ☎04 92 83 67 24; accueil@rafting-castellane.com. Or Jean-Luc Herry, 12 bd. de la République; ☎04 92 83 75 74; contact@aquavivaest.com.)

◪ **OTHER OUTDOOR ACTIVITIES.** The Verdon River's water flows into **Lac de Sainte-Croix;** at the mouth of the gorge is a perfect spot for canoeing and kayaking. The **GR4** trail past La Palud-sur-Verdon takes you there by foot. By car, take D952 past La Palud to Moustiers and follow signs to Ste-Croix-de-Verdon or take D955 before Moustiers to Comps-Artuby. From there, D71 toward Les Salles-sur-Verdon brings you to the lake. A number of watersport outfits

CÔTE D'AZUR

run trips through the canyon—including **rafting, kayaking, canoeing, canyoning, hydrospeeding, aqua-trekking, tubing,** and **rock-climbing** excursions—and competition keeps prices reasonable. Companies that offer a variety of comparable services and prices include: **Aboard Rafting,** 8 pl. de l'Église (☎04 92 83 76 11; www.aboard-rafting.com); **Acti-Raft,** route des Gorges du Verdon, at the end of rue Nationale near the tourist office (☎04 92 83 76 64; www.actiraft.com); **Aqua Viva Est,** 12 bd. de la République (☎04 92 83 75 74; www.aquavivaest.com); and **Base Sport & Nature,** 10 rue de la Fontaine (☎04 92 83 11 42). Though rafting and kayaking are the most conventional activities, summer water levels are only high enough about twice a week. (Usually Tu and F; for info, call ☎04 92 83 69 07.) Prices are generally about €33 per 2hr. "discovery" trip (rafting, kayaking, canyoning, etc.), €45-55 per half-day, and €65-75 per day. Hydrospeeding tends to be about €10 more. **Verdon Escalade, Les Subis, La Palud/Verdon** offers rock-climbing excursions (contact Fred Devoluet, ☎04 92 83 75 51; www.verdones-calade.com) while **Top Jump,** 42 chemin des Presses in Cagnes-sur-Mer, outfits walk-in bungee jumpers during the summer. (☎04 93 73 50 29; http://topjump. free.fr. €60 per jump. Open from mid-July to Aug. daily 1-5pm, or by reservation.) **La Ferme Équestre du Pesquier,** route de Digne, in Castellane, organizes **horseback-riding** tours of the region (☎04 92 83 63 94; www.chevalverdon.com. €20 per 90min., €39 per ½-day, €58 per day.) Reservations a few days in advance are recommended. Most adventure companies don't accept credit cards, so bring cash. For those planning to spend a lot of time outdoors, bug repellent may also be a good idea, as flies and mosquitoes take up residence around the canyon at the same time that adventure-seekers do.

SAINT-RAPHAËL ☎ 04 94

While St-Tropez limits its streets to the classy and glam, the young and brash St-Raphaël (sehn-rahf-aye-ell; pop. 32,000) welcomes everyone else with open arms. The town's most appealing area surrounds the beach, where one can find inexpensive food and miles of sand. Midway through the summer, the board-walk turns into a carnival in the evenings, packed with gaming booths and flirt-ing teenagers. Get your heart racing with a go-cart ride or get your face sticky with some cotton candy, but come to St-Raphaël—a town that rests boldly on the border of tackiness—and be prepared to feel like a kid again.

▉ TRANSPORTATION

St-Raphaël is a major stop on the coastal rail line shuttling passengers among the Riviera's resort towns.

Trains: Pl. de la Gare. Ticket booths open daily 6:30am-9pm. Info office open daily 6:30am-10pm. To **Cannes** (25min., every 30min., €6.10), **Marseille** (2hr., 6 per day, €25), and **Nice** (1hr., every 30min., €11).

Buses: Leave from behind the train station. Estérel Cars (☎04 94 53 78 46) serves **Fréjus** (25min., every hr. 7:30am-6:40pm, €1.40). Sodetrav (☎04 94 95 24 82) goes to **St-Tropez** (1hr., 10 per day 6:25am-9pm, €9.80). Beltrame (☎04 94 95 95 16) goes to **Cannes** (1hr., 8 per day, €7.20) via **Trayas** and to the airport in **Nice** (1hr., 4 per day, €22). Buses run later July-Aug. but are unreliable year-round.

Ferries: Les Bateaux de St-Raphaël (☎04 94 95 17 46), at the *vieux port.* To **St-Tropez** (1hr.; in summer 5 per day; €13, round-trip €22; July-Aug. W-Th a return ferry from St-Tropez leaves at midnight). Those at the hostel in Fréjus can ask about 10% discounts.

Taxis: ☎04 94 83 24 24.

🔒 PRACTICAL INFORMATION

Tourist Office: 99 quai Albert 1 (☎04 94 19 52 52; www.saint-raphael.com), by the port. Books accommodations. Signs throughout town point in the wrong direction toward the old tourist office; head to the port to find the new office. Internet free for 10min. Open July-Aug. daily 9am-7pm; Sept.-June M-Sa 9am-12:30pm and 2-6:30pm.

Laundromat: Top Pressing, 34 av. du Général Leclerc (☎04 94 82 24 05). Wash €5, dry €2-4. Open M-Tu and Th-F 8am-12:15pm and 1:30-6pm, W and Sa-Su 8am-12:15pm.

Police: Rue de Châteaudun (☎04 94 95 24 24).

Internet Access: Cyber Bureau, 123 rue Waldeck Rousseau (☎04 94 95 29 36), in the shopping center beside the train station. Computers and Wi-Fi. €2 per 15min., €6 per hr. Open M-F 8:30am-7pm, Sa 8:30am-1:30pm.

Post Office: Av. Victor Hugo (☎04 94 19 52 00), behind the station. Open M-F 8am-6:30pm, Sa 8am-noon. **Postal Code:** 83700.

🔒 ACCOMMODATIONS

Package tourism runs rampant in St-Raphaël, making the independent traveler feel like the only person in the world who has not purchased a scuba excursion to go with the traditional room-and-breakfast combo. While accommodations are not cheap here, they are more convenient than those in Fréjus and far more budget-friendly than those in St-Tropez.

🏨 **Hôtel les Pyramides,** 77 av. Paul Doumer (☎04 98 11 10 10; www.hotellespyramides. fr). Exit left from the station, make a right onto av. Henri Vadon, and take the 1st left onto av. Paul Doumer. Well-kept, airy rooms, each with A/C, toilet, shower, and TV. Spacious lounge and outdoor patio. Beach 100m away. Breakfast €7. Free Wi-Fi in lobby. Reception 7am-9pm. Reservations required. Open from mid-Mar. to mid-Nov. From mid-June to mid-Sept. singles €35; doubles €50-68; triples €70; quads €80. From mid-Sept. to mid-Nov. and from mid-Mar. to mid-June prices drop. Extra bed €13. AmEx/MC/V. ❸

Hôtel le Mistral, 80 rue de la Garonne (☎04 94 95 38 82), by the train tracks. Bright rooms and a summery restaurant. Cheapest rooms have a shared hallway toilet; most have showers. Breakfast €5-7. Reception 7am-9pm. Reserve ahead. July-Aug. singles €40-56; doubles €45-65; triples €80; quads €101. Sept. and Apr.-June singles €30-48; doubles €35-58; triples €70; quads €80. MC/V. ❸

🔒 FOOD

It can be hard to come by interesting dining spots in a town where carnival stalls provide the entertainment. The most lively and affordable restaurants are near the *vieux port,* **quai Albert I,** while snack and ice-cream stands stretch down **cours Jean Bart** into Fréjus. The **Monoprix** supermarket is at 14 bd. Félix Martin, by the train station. (☎04 94 19 82 82. Open M-Sa 8am-7:30pm. AmEx/MC/V.) Morning markets color **place Victor Hugo** and **place de la République.** Find fresh fish at the *vieux port.* (All markets open Tu-Su 7am-12:30pm.)

La Romana, 155 bd. de la Libération (☎04 94 51 53 36). Delicious thin-crust pizzas (€9.50-12) and meat and seafood *plats* (€12-24) in a wannabe Italian bistro with Roman columns and bronze statues. *Menus* €17-24. Open July-Aug. daily noon-2:30pm and 7-11pm; Sept.-June M-Tu 7-11pm, W-Su noon-2:30pm and 7-11pm. MC/V. ❸

Le Grillardin, 42 rue Thiers (☎04 94 40 46 14). Try the specialty, *marmite de pêcheur* (€20), a thick soup made from fish, olive oil, and cheese. Grilled meats €13-18. Pizzas €8.50-12. Open July-Sept. M, W, Su 7pm-1am, Tu and Th-Sa noon-2:30pm and 7pm-1am; Oct.-May M-Tu and Th-Su noon-2pm and 7-11pm. MC/V. ❸

CÔTE D'AZUR

🔲 🔳 NIGHTLIFE AND BEACHES

Thirty kilometers of public sand run along the coast from St-Raphaël west through Fréjus; in summer every inch that isn't covered with baking bodies is taken up by snack vendors or mini-carnival rides. Avoid the crowds; take a bus to more remote beaches, like the stunning one in **Dramont** (take bus #8, dir.: Trayas, from the *centre-ville*).

La Réserve, promenade René Coty (☎04 94 95 02 20; www.la-reserve.fr). Choice spot for sunbaked clubbers. Ladies free M-Th. Cover €15; includes 1 drink. Open July-Aug. daily 11:30pm-5am; Sept.-June Th-Sa 11pm-4:30am. AmEx/MC/V.

Marine & Blanc, 1 promenade des Bains (☎04 94 19 22 45; www.marine-et-blanc. com), across from the casino on plage du Veillat. Beach-level restaurant and lounge. Mixed drinks €10. Open daily 11am-midnight. AmEx/MC/V.

FRÉJUS
☎04 94

The main attractions of Fréjus (fray-jooss; pop. 52,000), founded by Julius Caesar, are relics of its Roman role. The town's ruins—situated among cafes, modern shops, and high-rise apartments—have earned it the nickname "Pompeii of Provence." A superb hostel and an eclectic array of sights make Fréjus a welcome change from the beach party next door in St-Raphaël, although the city outside of the historical center and port is spread out and rather ugly.

🔲 TRANSPORTATION

Trains: Rue Martin Bidoure (☎08 92 35 35 35). St-Raphaël receives most trains.

Buses: Pl. Paul Vernet (☎04 94 53 78 46), next to the tourist office. Open M-F 8:30am-noon and 2-5:30pm, Sa 9am-noon. To **St-Raphaël** (M-Sa until 7:10pm, Su 6:05pm; later July-Aug.); ask for schedules at the tourist office.

Local Transportation: Pl. Paul Vernet. Local **buses** (€1.10) connect the *vieille ville* to the beach.

Taxis: ☎04 94 51 51 12.

🔳 🔳 ORIENTATION AND PRACTICAL INFORMATION

Tourist Office: 325 rue Jean Jaurès (☎04 94 51 83 83; www.ville-frejus.fr). From St-Raphaël, take bus #6 to pl. Paul Vernet (€1.10). 2hr. guided **tours** July-Aug. Tu and Th-F; €5, students €3. Open June-Sept. daily 9am-7pm; Oct.-Mar. M-Sa 9:30am-noon and 2-6pm, Su 9:30am-noon; Apr.-May daily 9:30am-6pm.

Laundromat: La Pastorale, 132 rue Grisolle (☎06 08 88 49 70). Wash €4-5, dry €0.60 per 10min.

Police: Rue de Triberg (☎04 94 51 90 00).

Crisis Line: SOS Médecins (☎04 94 62 06 76).

Pharmacy: 62 rue du Général de Gaulle (☎04 94 51 28 98).

Hospital: Centre Hospitalier Intercommunal, 240 av. de St-Lambert (☎04 94 40 21 21), on the corner of av. André Léotard.

Post Office: Av. Aristide Briand (☎04 94 17 60 80), downhill from the tourist office. Open M-F 8am-6:30pm, Sa 8am-12:30pm. **Postal Code:** 83600.

CÔTE D'AZUR

ACCOMMODATIONS

Fréjus's 7km beach, a 20min. walk from the *centre-ville*, is closer to St-Raphaël than to Fréjus—making a stay in Fréjus advisable only to those coming for the *vieille ville* and its surrounding sights.

Auberge de Jeunesse de St-Raphaël-Fréjus (HI), chemin du Counillier (☎04 94 53 18 75; frejus-st-raphael@fuaj.org). From the Fréjus tourist office, take av. du 15ème Corps d'Armée. After passing 2 roundabouts, turn left on chemin de Counillier (30min.). Alternatively, bus #10 (€1.10) leaves from behind the bus station for the hostel at 7:09 and 9:04pm. From St-Raphaël, buses (1 per hr. 7:20am-7pm) head to Les Chênes (or Paul Vernet, a farther but more frequent stop). From Les Chênes, walk up av. Jean Calliès to chemin du Counillier; from Paul Vernet, follow directions from the tourist office. There is a shuttle from the hostel to the beach and to the St-Raphaël train station (M-Sa 8:40am, 11:20am, Su 9:20am), and bus #10 makes the reverse trip at 6:45pm. Among the Côte d'Azur's best hostels. Peaceful 170-acre spread of parkland. Ask the knowledgeable staff about discounts on canoe rentals, sailing lessons, and ferry tickets. Small kitchen open 6-9pm. Beer €1.50. Breakfast included. Laundry €3. Internet €3 per hr. Bike rental €7 per day. Reception 8am-noon and 6:30-11pm; phone during these hours for reservations. Lockout noon-5:30pm. Open Mar.-Oct. Camping €10 per person with tent. Dorms €13; quads with shower and toilet €16. Cash only. ❶

Hôtel La Riviera, 90 rue Grisolle (☎04 94 51 31 46; fax 17 18 34), in the historic center. Functional rooms and a popular *brasserie*. Breakfast €6. Reception Tu-Su 2-6pm. Reservations required in summer. Singles and doubles €35-40, with shower and toilet €45; triples and quads €60. MC/V. ❸

FOOD

The Provençal market fills **rue de Fleury** and **place Formigé** with fruits, vegetables, and handmade trinkets (W and Sa mornings). Bus #10 drops shoppers off directly. There's a **Casino** supermarket on the corner of av. du 15ème Corps de l'Armée and av. André Léotard, at the second roundabout on the way to the hostel. (Open M-Sa 8:30am-8pm, Su 8:30am-12:30pm. MC/V.) Budget restaurants cluster around **place de la Liberté** and **place Paul-Albert Février.**

Chez Bananes, rue St-François de Paul (☎04 94 44 15 71), off rue Juan Jaurès. Unique twists on classic dishes. Innovative owner/chef incorporates fresh fruit into pastas (€7-11) and meat *plats* (€11-15). Open daily 10am-10pm. AmEx/MC/V. ❸

Les Micocouliers, pl. Paul-Albert Février (☎04 94 52 16 52). Classic regional dishes like *daube de boeuf à la provençale* (beef stew with Provençal-style marinade; €14) and *soupe au poissons* (fish soup; €9.20) on shaded, yellow outdoor tables. Pasta €8. *Menu provençal* €17. Open daily noon-2:30pm and 6:30-10pm. MC/V. ❸

SIGHTS

A Fréjus sight pass (€4.60) includes admission to the amphitheater, theater, archaeological museum, and several other sights; inquire at sights.

EPISCOPAL BUILDINGS. Resting on what is presumed to be the site of the ancient Roman town center, the Episcopal Buildings make a good starting point for all things Roman in Fréjus. Today, the **baptistry, cloister,** and **cathedral** retain their position at the heart of the *vieille ville*. Exposed walls and a floor of uneven stone slabs reveal 2000 years of building and rebuilding. The octagonal baptistry, constructed in the AD fifth century and now visible only through a glass wall, is one of France's oldest buildings. The spectacular 12th- to 14th-century cloister contains a wood ceiling decorated with over 1200 miniature paintings of medieval life and fantastical creatures. Next door, Gothic cathedral doors depict devastating 10th-century Saracen raids on Fréjus while the interior displays an impressive church organ, gilded altarpieces, and dramatically lit relief sculptures. *(58 Rue de Fleury. ☎04 94 51 26 30. Cloister open June-Sept. daily 9am-6:30pm; Oct.-May Tu-Su 9am-noon and 2-5pm. Doors and baptistry accessible only by 40min. guided tour in French; English info available. €5, students €3.50, under 18 free.)*

ROMAN AMPHITHEATER. Built in the AD first and second centuries to entertain 10,000 rowdy, homesick soldiers, the Roman amphitheater lacks the embellishments of those in Arles or Nîmes. While those theaters were designed for more discerning patrician eyes, Christians and lions were slaughtered here just as frequently as they were in Rome. Today, stands are built into the ruins to accommodate concerts and bullfights. *(Rue Henri Vadon. ☎04 94 51 34 31. Open May-Oct. daily 9:30am-12:30pm and 2-6pm; Nov.-Apr. Tu-Su 9:30am-12:30pm and 2-5pm. €2. Contact tourist office for concert and bullfight schedule.)*

ROMAN THEATER. The original wall of Fréjus's other ancient forum remains intact; the rest now hosts concerts and plays. In July, the remains of the theater are turned into an outdoor performance space for Les Nuits Auréliennes, a weeklong theater festival. *(From the roundabout at the tourist office, walk 250m on rue Grande Bretagne. ☎04 94 53 58 75. Open May-Oct. daily 9:30am-12:30pm and 2-6pm; Nov.-Apr. Tu-Su 9:30am-12:30pm and 2-5pm. €2. Theater festival tickets from €33.)*

BASE NATURE. Outdoor enthusiasts shouldn't miss this 150-acre former military base, on some of the best beaches in the area, reserved for all things extreme. Areas are designated for basketball, BMX biking, football, rugby, skateboarding, and swimming. In October, the converted airplane hangar houses **Roc d'Azur**, billed as the world's largest all-terrain biking competition. *(From pl. Paul Vernet, take bus #9 (dir.: St-Raphaël, 15min., €1.10) to Base Aeronavale. ☎04 94 51 91 10. Open daily June-Sept. 8am-9pm; Oct.-May 8am-6pm. Call for equipment rental prices.)*

SAINT-TROPEZ ☎04 94

Luxe, calme, et volupté (luxury, calm, and sensuality) are what Matisse saw in St-Tropez (sehn-troh-pay; pop. 5400) and immortalized in his painting of the same name. Sixty-four years after he and other Neo-Impressionists, including Paul Signac, first brought fame to the fishing hamlet, Brigitte Bardot's nude bathing scene in *Et Dieu Créa la Femme (And God Created Woman)* sealed the town's celebrity status. Ever since, the former village has bewitched everyone from Hollywood stars to daytripping backpackers. Less ostentatious than Monaco but classier than larger coastal cities, St-Tropez sees fashionistas, yachtsmen, and ogling tourists rubbing elbows on the *vieux port* and in the narrow, shop-lined streets. Of course, this high-society playground's charm comes with a price: restaurants, bars, the boat ride there, and even campsites are sure to make a significant dent in your wallet.

◣ TRANSPORTATION

Reaching the "Jewel of the Riviera" requires some effort, as it lies well off the rail line. Getting to the small beaches and villages outside of town is also a hassle. The fastest and cheapest way to travel to the town itself is by boat. Beaches require a long walk or bike ride, rides on infrequent buses, or a ◼**black Hummer limo with tinted windows and a bodyguard/driver.**

Buses: Sodetrav, av. du Général Leclerc (☎04 94 97 88 51), across from the ferry dock. Open July-Aug. M-Sa 8:30am-8pm, Su 10:15am-1:30pm; Sept.-June M-F 10am-noon

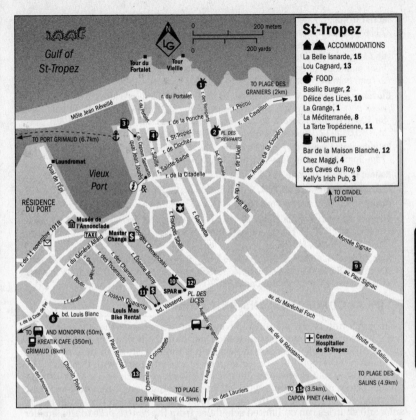

St-Tropez

🏠🏠 ACCOMMODATIONS

La Belle Isnarde, **15**
Lou Cagnard, **13**

🍎 FOOD

Basilic Burger, **2**
Délice des Lices, **10**
La Grange, **1**
La Méditerranée, **8**
La Tarte Tropézienne, **11**

🍷 NIGHTLIFE

Bar de la Maison Blanche, **12**
Chez Maggi, **4**
Les Caves du Roy, **9**
Kelly's Irish Pub, **3**

and 2-4pm, Sa 10am-noon. To **St-Raphaël** (2hr.; July-Aug. 12 per day, Sept.-June 10 per day; €12) and **Toulon** (2hr.; July-Aug. 14 per day, Sept.-June 9 per day; €19).

Ferries: Les Bateaux de St-Raphaël (☎04 94 95 17 46; www.tmr-saintraphael.com), at the *vieux port*. To **St-Raphaël** (1hr.; July-Aug. 5 per day, Sept.-June 4 per day; €13, round-trip same-day return €22).

Taxis: ☎04 94 97 05 27.

Bike Rental: Louis Mas, 3-5 rue Quarenta (☎04 94 97 00 60). Bikes €12 per day, €42 per week; €170 deposit. Scooters €34-37 per day; €205 deposit. Open from mid-June to Aug. M-Sa 9am-7pm, Su 10am-1pm and 5-7pm; from Easter to mid-June M-Sa 9am-12:30pm and 2-6:30pm. AmEx/MC/V.

◼🔢 ORIENTATION AND PRACTICAL INFORMATION

St-Tropez's glamorous lifestyle rises and falls with the seasons, warming up in May and June, sizzling from July to August, and winding down in September. Shops, museums, and nightlife have limited hours from September to June, but in July and August St-Tropez is active all day. The town is condensed and pedestrian-friendly. Much of the action is along the *vieux port*, which is packed with cafes and restaurants that transform into bars and lounges at night.

Tourist Office: On the corner of quai Jean Jaurès and rue Victor Laugier (☎04 94 97 45 21; www.saint-tropez.st). From the bus stop facing the port, go right and walk along the water until the office. Multilingual staff. Municipal shuttle schedules (€1), free maps, and *Manifestations* event guide. Open daily from late June to early Sept. 9:30am-8pm; from mid-Sept. to early Oct. and from late Mar. to mid-June 9:30am-12:30pm and 2-7pm; from mid-Oct. to mid-Mar. 9:30am-12:30pm and 2-6pm.

Currency Exchange: Master Change, 18 rue Général Allard (☎04 94 97 80 17), off the *vieux port.* Open July-Aug. daily 7am-9pm; Sept.-Oct. and Mar.-June M-Sa 9am-8pm, Su 10am-1pm and 3-8pm. **Societé Générale,** pl. des Lices (☎04 94 12 81 40). Open M-F 8:15am-12:15pm and 1:50-5:25pm, Sa 8:15am-12:25pm.

Laundromat: Laverie du Pin, 13 quai de l'Epi. Wash €5.60, dry €2. Open M-Sa July-Aug. 7am-9pm; Sept.-June 9am-1pm and 3-7pm.

Police: Pl. de la Garonne (☎04 93 54 86 65, at night 97 09 22), by the new port.

Pharmacy: Pharmacie du Port, 9 quai Suffren (☎04 94 97 00 06).

Hospital: Av. du Maréchal Foch (☎04 94 79 47 11).

Internet Access: Kreatik Cafe, 19 av. du Général Leclerc (☎04 94 97 40 61; www.kreatik.com). €2 per 10min., €4 per 30min., €7 per hr. Open M-Sa 9:30am-midnight, Su 2-10pm. AmEx/MC/V.

Post Office: Pl. Alphonse Celli (☎04 94 55 96 50), between the new and old ports. Open M-F 8:30am-noon and 2-5pm, Sa 8:30am-noon; opens at 9:30am on 2nd and 4th Th of every month. **Postal Code:** 83990.

🏠🏕 ACCOMMODATIONS AND CAMPING

St-Tropez's hotels are plentiful but incredibly expensive; the cheapest ones require reservations months in advance, particularly during July and August. A stay in St-Raphaël is easier on the wallet but forces visitors to limit their time and miss out on nightlife—or forfeit a night's rest to party with the stars. The closest hostel is in Fréjus. Camping is the cheapest option close to St-Tropez, though prices remain shockingly high and no campgrounds are within walking distance. A ferry connects the campground at Port Grimaud with the peninsula, and shuttles run on limited schedules from the *centre-ville* to the smaller grounds flanking St-Tropez's beaches. These campgrounds are popular and often full; book months in advance. Camping on the beach is prohibited.

La Belle Isnarde, route de Tahiti (☎/fax 04 94 97 13 64 or 97 57 74). Closest entrance on chemin de la Belle Isnarde, 15min. from the bus station. From pl. des Lices, turn right on av. du Maréchal Foch, right again onto rue de la Résistance, and left onto av. de la Résistance, which becomes chemin de la Belle Isnarde. The hotel is on the left. Converted farmhouse. Light pink doors open onto spacious rooms with large windows with thick shutters. Breakfast €9. Reception 7am-10pm. Open from Easter to mid-Oct. Singles and doubles with shower €75, with shower and toilet €85. Cash only. ⑤

Lou Cagnard, 18 av. Paul Roussel (☎04 94 97 04 24; www.hotel-lou-cagnard.com). Impeccably maintained, adorable Provençal-themed rooms, each with shower and phone. Breakfast €9. June-Sept. 1-week min. stay. Reception 8am-8:30pm. Open from late Dec. to early Nov. Apr.-Sept. singles and doubles €64-122; from Oct. to mid-Nov. and from mid-Dec. to Mar. €52-85. MC/V. ⑤

🍴 FOOD

St-Tropez's vibrant restaurant scene stretches along the *vieux port* and behind the waterfront. Save pennies for club covers by grabbing pastries from the *boulangeries* near **place des Lices.** For fruits and vegetables, as well as an array of antiques, books, and clothing, try the *grand marché* on **place des Lices** (Tu and Sa 7:30am-1pm) or the morning market on **place aux Herbes**. There's a **Monoprix** at 9 av. Général Leclerc. (☎04 94 97 07 94. Open July-Aug. daily 8am-10pm; Sept.-June M-Sa 8am-8pm. AmEx/MC/V.) A **SPAR**, 16 bd. Vasserot, is on pl. des Lices. (☎04 94 97 02 20. Open Apr.-Sept. M-Sa 7:30am-7:30pm, Su 8am-7:30pm; Oct.-Mar. M-Sa 7:30am-1pm and 3:30-7:30pm, Su 8am-1pm and 4-7:30pm.)

La Méditerranée, 21 bd. Louis-Blanc (☎04 94 97 00 44), in pl. de la Croix-de-Fer. Surprisingly affordable Mediterranean *entrées* (€11-13), *plats* (€12-18), and desserts (€8-11) in an elegant garden shaded by umbrellas and overhanging trees. Lunch *plat du jour* €15. Open July-Aug. daily noon-2:30pm and 8pm-midnight. AmEx/MC/V. ❸

Basilic Burger, pl. des Remparts (☎04 94 97 29 09), near the citadel. Juicy burgers (with fries; €9-10) with a French fare and sizable salads (€8-9). *Menus* €12-15. Open daily July-Aug. 10am-9:30pm; Sept.-June 10am-7pm. MC/V. ❸

La Grange, 9 rue du Petit St-Jean (☎04 94 97 09 62). Delicious handmade pastas (€16-27) in a farm-inspired setting. Open daily 8pm-12:30am. AmEx/MC/V. ❸

La Tarte Tropézienne, pl. des Lices (☎04 94 97 04 69). St-Tropez pie is 1 of 3 famous local sweets. Pastries from €1.20. Sandwiches and pizzas €2.80-4.30. Open daily July-Aug. 6am-10pm; Sept.-June 6am-8pm. MC/V. ❶

Délice des Lices, pl. des Lices (☎04 94 54 89 84). The place to hit before or after a night out. Panini and sandwiches €3.50-5. Pizza €3.30. Beer €2-3.50. Bottle of wine €6. Open May-Sept. 24hr.; Oct.-Apr. until 2am. Cash only. ❶

👁 ✦ SIGHTS AND BEACHES

St-Tropez's pride and joy is its endless white sandy coastline; most of the "sights" here can be found in or out of bathing suits, as the young and beautiful—and the rest—come to the shore to show off their bronzed bodies. Marathon tanning is practically a sport in itself, but those who prefer a more active approach will find a series of watersport companies along the beach.

A *navette* leaves from pl. des Lices (schedules vary; ask the tourist office) for **Les Salins** (M-Sa 5 per day, last shuttle returns 6:10pm; €1), a rather secluded spot, and for **Capon Pinet** (M-Sa 4 per day, last shuttle returns 5:20pm; €1), the first stretch of the famous **Pampelonne** shoreline. Walking is another option. From the *vieux port*, head to the citadel and follow the path that passes Tour Portalet, Tour Vieille, and the cemetery. You'll reach **plage des Graniers,** another decent swimming spot. Keep going until you wind up in **Baie des Canebiers,** home to Les Salins (2.8km, 50min.). Farther south, the trail leads to Capon Pinet, and the footpath starting there leads to **plage Tahiti,** halfway up a cliff (3.5km, 1hr.). Popular beach clubs are **Coco Beach, Le Club 55,** and **Morea Plage.** Lounge chairs at these clubs cost at least €15 per day; you're better off walking along the coast to find a swimming spot, getting a glimpse of celebrity villas along the way. Sunbathers who miss the shuttle back to town can take a taxi from Pampelonne to the port (€25-30) or walk along route de Tahiti (3km). Many spots allow nude sunbathing; in St-Tropez, only tourists have tan lines.

Travelers generally don't come to St-Tropez for the museums. Nevertheless, **Le Musée de l'Annonclade,** pl. Grammont, is a good break from a day of sun, sand, and shopping. This converted chapel houses Fauvist and Neo-Impressionist paintings by Bonnard, Matisse, and Signac as well as a number of Riviera images. Check out the modest bathing suits in images of St-Tropez from the 1930s and marvel at just how much things have changed in this one-time fishing village. (☎04 94 97 04 01. Open M and W-Su June-Sept. 10am-noon and 2-6pm; Oct.-May 10am-1pm and 4-7pm. €6, students €4.) The **citadel**, a 17th-century fortress above the port, contains rotating artistic and historical exhibits. (☎04 94 97 59 43. Open daily Apr.-Sept. 10am-12:30pm and 1:30-6:30pm; Oct. and Dec.-Mar. 10am-12:30pm and 1:30-5:30pm. €4.50, students €3.)

NIGHTLIFE AND FESTIVALS

St-Tropez celebrates its historic ties to the idle rich with yearly golf tournaments and sailing regattas, including the famed three-day **Giraglia Rolex Cup** in mid-June, which concludes with an open-sea race from St-Tropez all the way to Genoa, Italy. Every May 16-18, during **Les Bravades**, locals pay homage to their military past and patron saint with costumed parades. June 29 brings **Saint-Peter's Day** and a torch-lit procession honoring the saint of fishermen. Pick up a copy of *Manifestations* from the tourist office for monthly festival info. The height of St-Tropez's excess and exclusivity is its wild nightlife. Bars and clubs can be found in the same areas as restaurants around the port and surrounding **place des Lices**. For clubbing, dress to impress the strict bouncers.

Les Caves du Roy, av. Paul Signac (☎04 94 56 68 00; www.lescavesduroy.com), in the Hôtel Byblos. Perfect that high-society swagger and shell out a cool €25,000 for a bottle of Cristal to share with the celebrity next to you at the bar. Vodka and tonic €25. Open July-Aug. daily 11pm-5am; Sept. and June F-Sa 11:30pm-4am. AmEx/MC/V.

Chez Maggi, 7 rue Sibille (☎04 94 97 16 12). Diverse crowd gathers at this popular restaurant and bar. Sophisticated but unpretentious. A great place for backpackers to wear their finest and sample the good life. Mixed drinks €10-11. DJ after 11pm. Theme nights (disco night M, pirates and kama sutra Sa) bring larger crowds. Open Apr.-Oct. daily 7pm-3am; Feb.-Mar. Th-Sa 7pm-3am. AmEx/MC/V.

Bar de la Maison Blanche, pl. des Lices (☎04 94 97 52 66), on the patio of the Maison Blanche hotel. Low-hanging trees create a secluded, tranquil atmosphere for champagne (€16-17) and mixed drinks (€15). Open Mar.-Jan. daily 8pm-2am. AmEx/MC/V.

Kelly's Irish Pub, quai Frédéric Mistral (☎04 94 54 89 11), at the *vieux port*. Low-key Anglophone crowd. Grab a Guinness (€4) to enjoy on the large outdoor patio overlooking the water. Mixed drinks €10. Open daily 10am-3am. AmEx/MC/V.

DAYTRIPS FROM SAINT-TROPEZ

GRIMAUD. Less ritzy but more endearing than the city, the villages of the St-Tropez Peninsula make excellent daytrips. With their stunning hilltop settings and unforgettable views, these gems are becoming prized real estate and major tourist destinations. The best of the peninsula is delightfully peaceful Grimaud (gree-moh), surrounded by the vineyards of 354 wine producers. The **castle** of Grimaud controlled the Gulf of St-Tropez—fittingly known as the "Gulf of Grimaud"—until the late 19th century. From its towers, you can look down on the medieval village itself and also get a choice view of the gulf. Few can resist the charm of Grimaud's cobblestone lanes and fountain-filled *places*. Above the fairy-tale **place Neuve**, signs point to the 12th-century Romanesque **Église Saint-Michel**. *(Open daily 9am-6pm. Sodetrav (☎04 94 97 88 51) sends buses from St-Tropez to Grimaud (30min., M-Sa 13 per day, €2.80). Alternatively, take the ferry to Port Grimaud (20min., every hr.) and catch the hourly petit train at the top of Prairies de la Mer campground. (☎04 94 54 09 09; €3.) The tourist office, 1 bd. des Aliziers,* *is just past the bus stop.* ☎ *04 94 43 26 98; www.grimaud-provence.com. Open July-Aug. M-Sa 9am-12:30pm and 3-7pm, Su 10am-1pm; Sept. and Apr.-June M-Sa 9am-noon and 2:30-6pm; Oct.-Mar. M-Sa 9am-12:30pm and 2:30-5:30pm.)*

HYÈRES   ☎ 04 94

While the *îles* are this area's highlight, you have to sleep somewhere. That's where Hyères (ee-ehr; pop. 51,500) comes in.

TRANSPORTATION AND PRACTICAL INFORMATION. The train station is located at the top of av. Édith Cavell, off av. Gambetta, between the port and *centre-ville*. **Trains** run to Marseille (1-2hr., 6 per day, €14) and Toulon (25min., 7 per day, €3.70). Sodetrav **buses** (☎04 94 12 55 00) run to St-Tropez (1-2hr., 8 per day, €16) and Toulon (1hr., every 20min., €1.70), while Phocéens-Cars (☎04 93 85 66 61) goes to Cannes (1hr., 2 per day, €25) and Nice (2hr., 2 per day, €26). Buses run from rue du Soldat Ferrari, past the Casino des Palmiers.

The **tourist office,** 3 rue Ambroise Thomas, offers maps and ferry schedules. (☎04 94 01 84 50; www.ot-hyeres.fr. Open July-Aug. M-Sa 8:30am-7:30pm, Su 3:30-7:30pm; Sept.-June M-F 9am-6pm, Sa 10am-3pm.) Other services include: **police**, pl. Henri Dunant (☎04 94 65 02 39); a **pharmacy,** 7 bis av. Gambetta (☎04 94 65 01 15); a **hospital,** 597 bd. du Maréchal Juin (☎04 94 00 24 00); **Internet** at **La M@ison de l'Internet,** rue Soldat Bellon, on the third floor of the Centre Olbia (☎04 94 65 92 82; €3 per 30min.; open M-F 9am-12:30pm and 2-5:30pm); and a **post office,** 3 rue Édouard Branly (☎04 94 12 43 60; open M-Tu and Th 8:30am-6:30pm, W 9am-6pm, Sa 8:30am-noon). **Postal Code:** 83400.

ACCOMMODATIONS AND FOOD. Budget accommodations in Hyères are scarce. A good option near the port is **Hôtel Le Calypso ❹,** 36 av. de la Méditerranée, a small, colorful hotel with bright rooms and a pleasant outdoor patio. A few rooms have balconies that overlook the sea. (☎04 94 58 02 09. Breakfast included. June-Sept. singles and doubles €45-55; triples €72; quads €81. Oct.-May about €5 less. MC/V.) Closer to the *centre-ville*, **Hôtel du Parc ❸,** 7 bd. Pasteur, offers some of the area's best prices. All rooms have air-conditioning, TVs, and bathrooms. (☎04 94 65 06 65. Breakfast €7. Wi-Fi. Reception daily 7am-8pm. Aug. singles €70-76; doubles €84-92; triples €102-110; quads €120. Sept.-July singles €41-51; doubles €48-61; triples €57-71; quads €65-73. AmEx/MC/V.) The Giens peninsula, extending 8km south of Hyères toward the islands, has several campgrounds; one of the cheapest is **La Presqu'île de Giens ❶,** 153 route de la Madrague, which has clean facilities and organizes windsurfing, diving, and kayaking expeditions. (☎04 94 58 22 86; www.camping-giens.com. 2 people with tent July-Aug. €15; Apr.-Sept. €9.30. Electricity €4.90.)

Avenue Gambetta is lined with enough cafes, *brasseries*, and *boulangeries* to fulfill all possible cravings. For picnic fare, head to the **Casino** supermarket, 20 av. Gambetta. (Open Tu-Sa 7:30am-12:30pm and 4-7:30pm, Su 8am-noon. MC/V.) **Le Jardin ❸,** 19 av. Joseph Clotis, does indeed have a garden, encircled by orange trees. The chef serves octopus stew (€18) and grilled scallop salad (€17) to loyal customers. (☎04 94 35 24 12. Open daily Mar.-Oct. noon-midnight; Nov.-Feb. noon-4pm. AmEx/MC/V.) Try **La Brasserie ❸,** 2 rue Léon Gautier, within La Coupole, for seafood, pasta, and meat dishes. (☎04 94 12 88 00. Salads €9.50-14. *Menus* €13-25. Open daily noon-2:30pm and 7-11pm. MC/V.)

ÎLES D'HYÈRES

Three exotic, underpopulated islands—Porquerolles, Île du Levant, and Port-Cros—lie off the coast between the chic resort of St-Tropez and the metropolis of Toulon. The coastal town of Hyères and the adjacent Giens peninsula serve as good—if expensive—bases for visiting the islands, which Henri II nicknamed the Îles d'Or (Golden Islands) for the way the shale rocks glow in the sun. Today, things look mostly bronze, thanks to the miles of unspoiled beaches and coves that allow for some of the region's best nude sunbathing.

 IF YOU CAN'T TAKE THE HEAT. In summer, the Îles d'Hyères don't see much rain and become susceptible to wildfires. Because of this constant fire risk, the islands close to visitors frequently in July and August. Call ☎04 98 10 55 41 to find out which trails are open.

Ferries to the three islands depart from the Port d'Hyères or from the *gare maritime* at La Tour Fondue on the Giens peninsula. From the bus or train station in Hyères, catch bus #67 (dir.: Ports; €1.70) to either the port or La Tour Fondue or take the less frequent #63 to the port. TLV and TVM ferries are the cheapest way to get to the islands (☎04 94 57 44 07 or 58 95 14 for service to Porquerolles, 57 44 07 for service to Port-Cros or Île du Levant; www.tlv-tvm.com). Ferries to Port-Cros (1hr.) and Île du Levant (1hr.) leave from Port d'Hyères. (Boats depart July-Aug. 8:15, 9:30, 11am, 2:30pm; Sept.-June usually 8:15, 9:30am. Call ahead or get a schedule from the tourist office. To both islands €27, ages 4-10 €24; to 1 island €24/21.) Ferries to Porquerolles leave from La Tour Fondue. (20min; July-Aug. every ½-hr. 7:30am-7pm; Sept.-June every hr. €16, ages 4-10 €14.) Vedettes Îles d'Or et Le Corsaire offers **shuttles** between the islands as well as connections to nearby ports, including St-Tropez. (☎04 94 71 01 02. Boats depart from Port-Cros for Île du Levant 10:15am, 12:15, 5:15pm. €8.) If you've missed the last ferry and the idea of spending a night in a nudist colony doesn't have you shedding your inhibitions—and clothes—call a **boat taxi** to rescue you (☎06 09 52 31 19).

PORQUEROLLES   ☎04 94

The largest and the most easily accessible of the islands, Porquerolles (pohr-kehr-ohll; pop. 342) has a colorful history. It was home to a religious order until François I granted pardons to convicts who promised to live on the island and defend the mainland against pirates; the criminals promptly transformed the island into the ultimate **pirate hideout.** Today, mainlanders and tourists find respite from the hectic Riviera on shady trails and in sun-drenched coves while windsurfers ride the waves just off the coast. The closest beach to the port is crowded and rocky **plage de la Courtrade**; head left from the ferry to reach the more peaceful **plage de Notre Dame.** Find even more seclusion on the other side of the island at **plage du Langoustier.** Around the port and in the *centre-ville*, **bike** shops rent mountain bikes (usually around €12-14 per day) for exploring. An **info office** at the end of the main dock offers free maps and ferry schedules.

ÎLE DU LEVANT   ☎04 94

Like its neighbor, Île du Levant (eel doo lev-ahn; pop. 100) was originally settled by monks. If they saw the island today, they would be uttering *mea culpas* for the next 50 years. This is the home of Héliopolis, Europe's oldest nudist colony; islanders go *au naturel* on the beaches and wear the legal minimum—not much—in the port and the main square. Bathing *au naturel* is mandatory on **plage des Grottes.** The landscape of Île du Levant also offers eye candy on the winding trails in the **Domaine des Arbousiers,** a substantial natural reserve stretching over the island's northwestern coast. The Héliopolis map includes seven trails, three of which skirt the dramatic coastline for miles. A small **Superette** provides basic snacks and cold drinks. (☎04 94 05 90 05. Open M-Sa 9:30am-1pm and 5:30-7:30pm. MC/V over €15.)

PORT-CROS ☎04 94

The smallest and most rugged of the three islands, Port-Cros (pohr-kroh; pop. 30) is a stunning national park that offers three main trails and over 30km of footpaths. The mountainous terrain is home to 114 bird species and 602 indigenous plants. The well-trodden **sentier des plantes** (plant trail) passes by forts and the crowded **plage de la Palud.** To find a solitary spot, continue on the **sentier de Port Man,** accessible by a 4hr. hike that penetrates the island's unpopulated interior. Other themed paths take hikers past forts, mountains, and traces of early human presence. The national park **Info booth** at the port provides maps for €2-4. (☎04 94 01 40 70; www.portcrosparcnational.fr. Open July-Aug. daily 9:15am-12:30pm and 3:30-5:30pm; Sept.-June whenever boats arrive and depart.) **Snorkel** in the turquoise water to view the fascinating sea life. You can also **scuba-dive,** explore the area's wrecks, and search for the 40 lb. *mérou*—a massive grouper once thought extinct. **Sun Plongée** runs open-water dives. (☎04 94 05 90 16; www.sun-plongee.com. Prices change frequently according to fuel costs; generally from €50 for a 1st-time dive. Equipment rental €40. MC/V.)

CORSICA
(LA CORSE)

Bathed in turquoise waters, Corsica was dubbed "Kallysté" (most beautiful) by the Greeks. Behind the island's sun-drenched beaches, patches of scrubby underbrush give way to an endless, unspoiled landscape—nearly one-third of the island is protected nature reserve. Over 100 summits pierce a sky that refuses to rain 310 days of the year, and the rugged landscape makes the island ideal for hikers. Yet all this beauty comes at a price: budget hotels and restaurants are scarce and camping is often the best—if not the only—option.

Though development along the coast has brought a stream of young bikini-clad sun worshippers to the spectacular beaches and older fanny-packed retirees to the picturesque coastal towns, most of Corsica remains untouched. Despite centuries of invasion, it has managed to guard a unique culture that has its own language, cuisine, and customs. In the tiny mountain towns of this island paradise, life proceeds much as it has for hundreds of years. Goats and sheep wander lonely roads. Crumbling hilltop chapels ring with prayers sung in Corse, Corsica's traditional dialect. Even well-trodden resort towns are marked by Genoese towers and bustling markets filled with fresh local produce.

Fiercely defensive of its independent identity, Corsica has long resisted foreign rule. The Corsicans controlled their island until the Genoese took over in 1284. Almost 500 years later, after the 40-year Corsican War of Independence, General Pasquale Paoli reclaimed the island and created a university, government, currency, and army. He also drafted the island's—and the world's—first modern constitution. Nevertheless, the 1768 Treaty of Versailles gave France's Louis XV control of the island, and Corsica found itself divided between the nationalist Paolistes and the Populaires, who swore allegiance to France.

Today, the **Front de Libération National de la Corse** (FLNC) sporadically tries to bomb its way to independence, but most Corsicans deplore this sort of extremism. When President Nicolas Sarkozy, then interior minister, proposed increasing Corsican autonomy in July 2003, the referendum was defeated by a 2% margin—only 49% of Corsicans wanted increased autonomy from France. The island's love-hate relationship with the mainland lives on.

HIGHLIGHTS OF CORSICA

HIKE among the rock formations of Les Calanches (p. 770) near Porto or along stunning Cap Corse (p. 790) to marvel at the Corsican coast's rugged beauty.

DANCE THE NIGHT AWAY in Calvi's (p. 772) nightclubs and sober up on its beaches the next day—both rank among the best on the island.

GET YOUR FEET WET in Bonifacio (p. 793), which offers spectacular scuba diving, snorkeling, and windsurfing.

TRANSPORTATION

BY PLANE. Air France and its partner **Compagnie Corse Méditerranée (CCM)** fly to Ajaccio, Bastia, and Calvi from Marseille, Nice, and Paris. In Ajaccio, the Air

Corsica

0 — 20 kilometers

0 — 20 miles

CORSICA

France/CCM office is at 3 bd. du Roi Jérôme (☎36 54 or 08 20 82 08 20). Hunting around can yield significant savings; ask at a budget travel agency in France.

BY BOAT. Ferry travel between the mainland and Corsica can be rough, and it's not always cheaper than plane travel. High-speed **ferries** (3hr.) run between Nice and Corsica. Overnight ferries from Toulon and Marseille take over 10hr. The **Société National Maritime Corse Méditerranée (SNCM;** ☎08 91 70 18 01; www.sncm.fr) sends ferries from Marseille (€40-58, under 25 €25-45), Nice (€35-47, under 25 €20-35), and Toulon (€40-58, under 25 €25-45) to Ajaccio, Bastia, Calvi, and Île Rousse. It costs €40-305 to take a car, depending on the day and the type of car. In July and August, nine boats travel between Corsica and the mainland, though only three make the trip the rest of the year. The fastest boats **(Navires à Grande Vitesse)** leave from Nice and head to Ajaccio, Calvi, and Île Rousse, crossing in nearly a third of the time. **Corsica Ferries** (☎08 25 09 50 95; www.corsicaferries.com) has high-speed ferries with similar destinations and prices. **SAREMAR** (☎04 95 73 00 96; fax 04 95 73 13 37) and **Moby Lines** (☎04 95 73 00 29; fax 04 95 73 05 50) run from Santa Teresa on Sardinia to Bonifacio (2-5 per day depending on the season; €14-15 per person, €26-52 per car). **Moby Lines** (€15-28) and **Corsica Ferries** (€16-32) cross from Genoa and Livorno in Italy to Bastia.

BY WHEEL AND RAIL. Rumor has it that the Marquis de Sade and Machiavelli collaborated on the design of Corsica's transportation system. **Train** service is slow, limited to the half of the island north of Ajaccio, and doesn't accept mainland rail passes, though a €48 **Zoom pass** allows for seven consecutive days of travel. Check www.ter-sncf.com for more info. **Buses** serve the island, but be prepared for winding roads. If roller coasters aren't your thing, bring some motion sickness medicine. Call **Eurocorse Voyages** (☎04 95 21 06 30) for info.

ROCKY ROAD. Corsica allegedly has the most dangerous roads in France. Those bold or foolhardy enough to rent a car should expect to pay €60-90 per day or €250-365 per week. The unlimited mileage deals are best. Gas stations are scarce; the police can help drivers who run out. Bicycle, moped, and scooter rental can also be pricey. Winding mountain roads and high winds make cycling difficult and risky; drivers should honk before rounding mountain curves. Many roads are too narrow for two cars to pass at one time. Tourists should always give way to local drivers and especially buses, which *Let's Go* strongly recommends for island transport.

BY FOOT. Hiking is an excellent way to explore Corsica. *Randonnées* (hikes) exist all over the island, with panoramas of everything from the mountainous interior to the rocky coastline. Campsites, refuges, and an active backpacking culture ensure that hikers feel at home in Corsica. The longest marked route, the **GR20**, is a difficult 180km, 12- to 15-day trail that takes hard-core hikers across the island from Calenzana (southeast of Calvi) to Conca (northeast of Porto-Vecchio). The GR20 requires excellent physical fitness but rewards hikers with an unparalleled sampling of Corsica's scenery. Do not tackle this trail alone and be prepared for cold, snowy weather even in early summer. For a shorter, less challenging route, try the popular **Mare e Monti,** a seven- to 10-day trail from Calenzana to Cargèse that passes through the pristine **Aitone Forest** and the breathtaking **Gorges de Spelunca.** The easier **Da Mare a Mare Sud** crosses the southern part of the island between Porto-Vecchio and Propriano (4-6 days), leading hikers through green countryside and past prehistoric remains at **Filitosa.** Its northern equivalent, the **Mare a Mare Nord,** is a 12-day trek from Moriani to Cargèse that passes through the university town of Corte before traversing the Tavignanu and Restonica river valleys. The **Mare a Mare Centre** transects the middle of the island from Ghisonaccia to Porticcio and can be completed in seven days. Though easier than the GR20, this trail requires advance preparation and is best enjoyed in autumn and spring. All major trails are administered by the **Parc Naturel Régional de la Corse,** 2 Sargent Casalonga, Ajaccio (☎04 95 51 79 00; www.parc-naturel-corse.com), whose jurisdiction encompasses most of the Corsican heartland. For any route, a *topo-guide* is essential (€14-15; available for purchase by fax, by email, over the phone, or at a Parc Naturel office). The guide includes trail maps, *gîte* and *refuge* listings, and other important practical info. Prospective GR20 trekkers should consider buying *Le Grand Chemin* (€15), a more complete guide that includes elevations and sources of potable water. For more info, contact the Parc Naturel office.

ACCOMMODATIONS

Agence du Tourisme de la Corse, 17 bd. du Roi Jérôme, Ajaccio (☎04 95 51 00 00; www.visit-corsica.com), publishes free guides to Corsica's accommodations, available at tourist offices. Corsica's few budget hotels fill weeks ahead in summer, and it can be nearly impossible to find a room in August. Camping is a great choice all over the island. Nearly every city, small town, or half-forgotten village offers at least one spot to pitch a tent, although many sites tend to be located away from the *centre-ville.* Don't forget to bring your own toilet paper and other amenities when camping, as most sites do not provide them and may be located far from the local *tabac* or supermarket. Resist the urge to set up camp on that stunning mountain ledge: unofficial camping is not only dangerous but also strictly banned and will be met with severe fines. *Refuges* (mountain huts) provide trail-side shelter and camping.

ÇA VA? Perhaps more than their mainland compatriots, Corsicans appreciate a little chit-chat before getting down to business. If you ask how people are doing and are prepared to spend a few minutes rather than a few seconds talking, then you'll get more helpful answers to your questions. Don't hesitate to attempt a few phrases in Corse, either; many Corsicans, especially older people, genuinely appreciate the interest in their traditional language.

AJACCIO (AIACCIU)   ☎04 95

To pronounce this city's name in Corse goes something like this: say the word "eye" and then sneeze. While most Corsicans do take great pride in their unique heritage, nowhere is this more obvious than in the island's capital city, Ajaccio (ah-jahks-ee-o; pop. 60,000). Museums celebrating various Corsican national heroes tell the island's story from ancient times to the present day. Bakeries, pizzerias, and souvenir shops named in their honor line streets like rue Fesch and bd. Sampiero. This is all not to mention Ajaccio's favorite son, the man who brought the rest of Europe to its knees so that he could make eye contact with them: Napoleon Bonaparte. At first glance, Ajaccio, with its countless boutiques, white sand beaches, and palm-lined boulevards, might feel like a Riviera resort. However, the city's traditional Corsican culinary offerings, warm and welcoming locals, and emphasis on the island's history identify it as proudly and authentically Corsican.

⌐ TRANSPORTATION

Flights: Aéroport Campo dell'Oro (AJA; ☎04 95 23 56 56; www.ajaccio.aeroport.fr), 5km away. TCA bus #8 (€4.50) shuttles from the bus station daily 6am-7:25pm and from the airport M-Sa 9am-11:15pm, Su 8am-11:15pm. Flights to **Lyon, Marseille, Nice,** and **Paris.** For info, call **Air France,** 3 bd. du Roi Jérôme, or **Compagnie Corse Mediterranée** (☎08 20 82 08 20 for both; www.airfrance.com, www.aircorsica.com). Airport office open daily 6am-8pm.

Trains: Pl. de la Gare (☎04 95 23 11 03), off bd. Sampiero, 400m from the *gare maritime,* toward the airport. Info office open daily from mid-June to mid-Sept. 6:30am-9:30pm; from mid-Sept. to mid-June 6am-8:30pm. To **Bastia** (3-4hr.; M-Sa 4 per day, Su 2 per day; €22), **Calvi** via **Ponte Leccia** (5hr., 2 per day, €25), and **Corte** (2hr., M-Sa 4 per day, Su 2 per day; €15).

Buses: Quai l'Herminier (☎04 95 51 55 45), at the *gare maritime.* Info office open June-Aug. daily 6:30am-7:45pm; Sept.-May M-Sa 6:30am-7:45pm. **Eurocorse Voyages** (☎04 95 21 06 30) goes to: **Bastia** (3hr., M-Sa 2 per day, €19) via **Corte** (1hr., €11); **Bonifacio** (3-4hr., M-Sa 2 per day, €22); **Calvi** via **Ponte Leccia** (3hr., July-Aug. M-Sa 1 per day, €15); **Porto-Vecchio** (3-4hr., M-Sa 2 per day, €20). **Autocars SAIB** (☎04 95 22 41 99) runs to **Porto** (2hr., 2 per day, €11).

Ferries: Depart from the *gare maritime* (☎04 95 51 55 45). Open June-Aug. daily 6:30am-7:45pm; Sept.-May M-Sa 6:30am-7:45pm; always open for departures and arrivals. **SNCM,** quai l'Herminier (☎04 95 29 66 99; www.sncm.fr), across from the bus station, goes to **Marseille** (12hr., 1 per day) and **Nice** (4hr., 2-3 per week), both for €59-90, students and ages 12-25 up to 38% discount. Office open M-F 8am-8pm, Sa for departures and arrivals (usually 8am-noon). MC/V. **Corsica Ferries** (☎04 95 50 78 82; www.corsicaferries.com), in the *gare maritime,* runs to **Toulon** (5hr., 4-6 per week) and **Nice** (4hr., 1-5 per week), both for €20-45, ages 12-25 €10-35. MC/V.

Public Transportation: TCA, 75 cours Napoleon (☎04 95 23 29 41). **Buses** run every 20min.-1hr., depending on the line. Tickets €1.20, carnet of 10 €9; available at the TCA office, in *tabacs,* and on the bus; validate on board. Buses #1, 2, and 3 go from pl. de Gaulle to the train station or down cours Napoleon toward public beaches. Bus #5 from av. Dr. Ramaroni and bd. Lantivy stops at **Marinella** and the beaches on the way to **Îles Sanguinaires** (7am-7:30pm). Line #8 heads to the airport from the *gare routière* (6am-7:25pm, €4.50). Office open M-Sa 9am-12:30pm and 3:30-6:30pm.

Taxis: Taxi Station, pl. de Gaulle (☎04 95 21 00 87) or on av. Pascal Paoli (☎04 95 23 25 70). **Ajaccio Voyages** (☎06 61 16 40 40). 24hr. €21 to the airport.

Car Rental: ADA (☎04 95 23 56 57; www.ada-en-corse.com), at the airport. 21+. Open daily 8am-midnight. AmEx/MC/V. **ACL Rent-a-Car,** 51 cours Napoleon (☎04 95 51 61 81; www.rentacar.fr), in Hôtel Kallisté and at the airport (☎04 95 23 56 36). 23+. Open daily 8am-8pm. MC/V.

Motorcycle and Bike Rental: Corsica Moto Rent, 51 cours Napoleon (☎04 95 51 61 81), in the Hôtel Kallisté. Scooters and motorcycles from €41 per day, €189 per week; deposit from €600. Helmet and lock included. 23+. Open daily 8am-8pm. MC/V. **Le Bistro du Cours,** 10 cours Napoleon (☎04 95 21 44 75), offers bike-rental services on an hourly or weekly basis. €4 for 1hr., €6 for 2hr., €10 for 6hr., and €13 for 12hr.; call to negotiate a weekly price. Cash only.

✦🛈 ORIENTATION AND PRACTICAL INFORMATION

Cours Napoleon, the city's main thoroughfare, passes by the train station and ends in the *vieille ville* at **place de Gaulle.** A parallel pedestrian street, **rue Cardinal Fesch,** leads to the livelier **place Foch** and, along with side streets such as **rue**

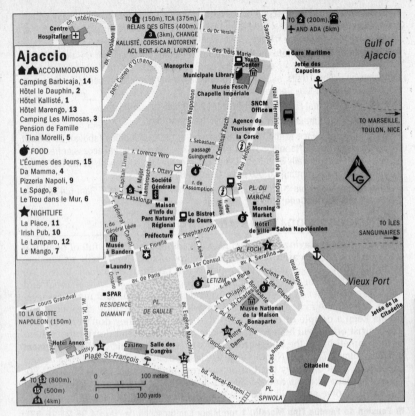

Ajaccio

▲▞ ACCOMMODATIONS
Camping Barbicaja, 14
Hôtel le Dauphin, 2
Hôtel Kallisté, 1
Hôtel Marengo, 13
Camping Les Mimosas, 3
Pension de Famille
Tina Morelli, 5

🍎 FOOD
L'Écumes des Jours, 15
Da Mamma, 4
Pizzeria Napoli, 9
Le Spago, 8
Le Trou dans le Mur, 6

★ NIGHTLIFE
La Place, 11
Irish Pub, 10
Le Lamparo, 12
Le Mango, 7

des Trois Marie, is the perfect place to pick up inexpensive souvenirs. Between pl. de Gaulle and the citadel (an active military base), **boulevard Pascal Rossini** runs above several public beaches, beginning with plage St-François.

Tourist Offices: 3 bd. du Roi Jérôme at pl. du Marché (☎04 95 51 53 03; www.ajaccio-tourisme.com). Distributes maps and city guides with restaurant, hotel, and festival listings. 15min. free Internet access. Same-day hotel assistance. Themed **tours** in French from mid-June to mid-Sept. €5-9. Open July-Aug. M-Sa 8am-8:30pm, Su 9am-1pm and 4-7pm; Sept.-Oct. and Apr.-June M-Sa 8am-7pm, Su 9am-1pm; Nov.-Mar. M-Sa 8am-6pm. **Agence du Tourisme de la Corse,** 17 bd. du Roi Jérôme (☎04 95 51 00 00; www.visit-corsica.com), is a nearby annex. Open M-F 8:30am-12:30pm and 2-6pm.

Currency Exchange: Change Kallisté, 51 cours Napoleon (☎04 95 01 34 45), in Hôtel Kallisté, charges no commission. Open daily 8am-8pm. **Société Génerale,** rue Sergent Casalonga (☎04 95 51 57 06), off cours Napoleon. ATM. High commission on traveler's checks. Open M-F 8:15am-12:15pm and 1:45-5pm.

Youth Center: U Borgu, 52 rue Fesch (☎04 95 50 13 44; centre.u.borgu@wanadoo.fr). Offers information on jobs and housing. Free Internet access (40min. limit; under 25 only). Open from July to mid-Aug. M-F 9am-6pm; Sept.-June M-F 8:30am-9pm, Sa 2-7pm. Closed Aug. 15-Sept. 6.

Laundromat: Hotel Kallisté, 51 cours Napoleon (☎04 95 51 34 45). Open daily 1-8pm. **Lavomatic,** 1 rue Maréchal Ornano (☎06 13 13 64 21), behind the *préfecture,* near pl. de Gaulle. Wash €6, dry €1 per 10min. Open daily 7am-9pm.

Hiking Info: Maison d'Info du Parc Naturel Régional, 2 rue Sergent Casalonga (☎04 95 51 79 00; www.parc-naturel-corse.com), across from the *préfecture.* Free pamphlets on regional trails, wildlife, and lodging in *gîtes* and *refuges.* Open M-Sa June-Aug. 8am-7pm; Sept.-May 9am-noon and 2-6pm.

Police: Rue Général Fiorella (☎04 95 11 17 17), near the *préfecture.*

Hospital: 27 av. Impératrice Eugénie (☎04 95 29 90 90).

Internet Access: Free at the **Youth Center** and at the tourist office (above). **Le Bistrot du Cours,** 10 cours Napoleon (☎04 95 21 44 75). 20min. Internet access or free Wi-Fi with 1 drink. Open daily 8am-2am. **Cyber Espace,** rue Docteur Versini. €2.50 for 30min. or €3.50 for 1hr. Printing €0.50/page. Open M-Sa 9:30-12:30am.

Post Office: 13 cours Napoleon (☎04 95 51 84 75). Open M-F 8am-6:45pm, Sa 8am-noon. **Postal Code:** 20000.

🏠 🏕 ACCOMMODATIONS AND CAMPING

Budget travelers staying in Ajaccio face a trade-off: the city is full of beautiful and conveniently located hotels, but they are almost universally expensive, while its more budget-friendly campsites are far from the *centre-ville.* Call six weeks ahead for stays during June through August—when rates soar and vacancies plummet in most hotels—to find the best deals and make reservations. Ask for their cheapest room, then ask if there's anything cheaper; some hotels keep a couple of old, unrenovated rooms that they don't initially list. The tourist office will help with same-day reservations, but don't expect them to find something in the budget range. If you're really stuck, the **Relais Régional des Gîtes Ruraux,** 77 cours Napoleon, posts last-minute availability in *gîtes* across the island, although they tend to be far from major cities. (☎04 95 10 54 30. Open M-F 8am-12:30pm and 2-5:30pm.) Ajaccio's campsites are well equipped but often involve an uphill hike or a bus ride to the city's periphery.

🏅 **Pension de Famille Tina Morelli,** 1 rue Major Lambroschini (☎/fax 04 95 21 16 97). Welcoming B&B tended by Tina herself. Boasts an authentic French environment and unrivaled low prices. French-speakers will get the most out of the familial atmosphere, but anyone can enjoy 1 of the 4 comfortable rooms and the home-cooked meals. Breakfast included. Reservations recommended far in advance. Singles €50, *demi-pension* €60, *pension complète* €72; doubles €70/100/124. €50 extra bed. Cash only. ❶

Hôtel Kallisté, 51 cours Napoleon (☎04 95 51 34 45; www.hotel-kalliste-ajaccio.com). Follow signs from quai l'Herminier up rue des Trois Marie, then take a right onto cours Napoleon. Each cozy room has a shower or bath, cable TV, and a fan or A/C. Services include currency exchange and vehicle rental. Breakfast €8. Laundry €5, dry €2. Free Wi-Fi. Reception 8am-8pm. Automatic reception machine for arrivals after 8pm; bring a reservation number. June-Sept. singles €69; doubles €79; triples €99. From Oct. to mid-Nov., mid-Dec. to Jan., and Apr.-May singles €59; doubles €69; triples €89. From mid-Nov. to mid-Dec. and Jan.-Apr. singles €56; doubles €64; triples €79. MC/V. ❺

Hôtel Marengo, 2 rue Marengo (☎04 95 21 43 66; www.hotel-marengo.com). From city center, walk along the boardwalk with the sea on your left for about 25min.; turn right on bd. Madame Mère, then left onto rue Marengo. Otherwise, take bus #1, 2, or 5 to Trottel. Close to the beach and some of the city's best nightlife. A/C. Breakfast €7. Reception 8am-8pm. Reservations recommended. Singles with shower June-Sept. €59; Oct. and May €57; Nov. and Apr. €55. Triples with with bath €75-105. MC. ❹

CORSICA

Hôtel le Dauphin, 11 bd. Sampiero (☎04 95 21 12 94; www.ledauphinhotel.com), between the train station and ferry port. Well-kept rooms, each with shower, TV, and Wi-Fi. A/C €8. Breakfast included. Reception 5:30am-midnight. Check-in after 2pm. July-Aug. singles €59; doubles €79; triples €96. Apr.-June singles €54; doubles €69; triples €86. Oct.-Mar. singles €52; doubles €64; triples €79. Extra bed €10. MC/V. ❹

Camping Barbicaja (☎/fax 04 95 52 01 17), 4km away. Take bus #5 from av. Ramaroni, past pl. de Gaulle, to Barbicaja and go straight (last bus July-Aug. 11:05pm; Sept.-June 7:05pm). 150m from a popular beach. Campers enjoy a snack bar, pizzeria, and shaded sites with views of the sparkling bay. Reception 8am-10pm. Open from mid-Apr. to mid-Oct. €6 per person; €2.50 per tent; €2.50 per car. Electricity €2.40. Cash only. ❶

Camping Les Mimosas, rte. d'Alata (☎04 95 20 99 85; www.camping-lesmimosas. com). Follow cours Napoleon away from the *centre-ville.* Turn left on montée St-Jean, which becomes rue Biancamaria and then route d'Alata. Walk straight past the roundabout and take a left onto chemin de la Carrossacia; follow signs 900m inland and uphill to the site (30min.). Alternatively, take bus #4 from cours Napoleon to Brasilia (last bus leaves *centre-ville* 7pm); walk straight to the roundabout and follow the above directions. Walking here involves hills and stray dogs, but a taxi ride from pl. de Gaulle is only €8-10. Clean showers with hot water and large sinks for washing clothes. Reception 8:30am-noon and 2:30-8:30pm. June-Sept. €5.30 per person; €2.50 per tent; €2.50 per car. Electricity €2.50. Oct. and Apr.-May prices 10% lower. Cash only. ❶

▶ FOOD

Though Ajaccio has no shortage of restaurants, the best option is the affordable, extensive ▨**morning market** on **place du Marché.** The endless rows of stalls offer everything for the perfect Corsican picnic: a baguette, a wedge of cheese, and a portion of *charcuterie.* For dessert, pick up Corsican-grown white peaches or chestnut *canistrelli* (cookies) baked that morning. A smaller market opens at **place Abbatucci,** on cours Napoleon. (Both Tu-Su 8am-noon.) The **Monoprix** supermarket is at 31 cours Napoleon. (☎04 95 51 76 50. Open M-Sa July-Sept. 8:30am-8pm; Oct.-June 8:30am-7:20pm. AmEx/MC/V.) A **SPAR** supermarket is at 1 cours Grandval, on the first floor of the Diamant complex. (☎04 95 21 51 77. Open M-Sa 8:30am-8pm, Su 8:30am-12:30pm. MC/V.) In and around **place Foch** are inexpensive pizzerias, panini shops, and *crêperies* as well as many spots serving local dishes. **Rue Maréchal Ornano,** near place de Gaulle, has several international offerings, including Asian, North African, and Creole cuisine. For the freshest seafood, try tiny **rue des Halles,** behind the tourist office.

▨ **L'Ecume des Jours,** bd. Albert Premier (☎06 27 83 16 36), behind Hôtel Imperial. Easily one of Ajaccio's most chic hangouts. Seats range from beanbag chairs to wood blocks. Try the beef tartar or the *charcuterie de Corse* (both €10) or enjoy the buffet (€13). Wine €2.50 per glass. Live music W and Su nights. Open daily 9am-2pm. Cash only. ❸

Da Mamma, passage Guinguetta (☎04 95 21 39 44), off cours Napoleon. Down a small, almost hidden passageway. Packed tables shaded by a eucalyptus tree. €12 soup or salad *menu,* with coffee and dessert, offered until 9:30pm. €11 lunch special includes the *plat du jour, dessert du jour* (hope for the *crème caramel*), and coffee. Meat *plats* €14-22. Open noon-2pm and 7:30-11pm. Reservations recommended. MC/V. ❸

Le Trou dans le Mur, 1 bd. du roi Jérôme (☎04 95 21 49 22). Specialty salads (€7-14) made with fresh seafood and authentic Corsican ingredients like *brocciu* cheese include fresh produce from the market. Vegetarians can enjoy vegetable lasagna or spinach cannelloni (both €11). Open daily Sept.-May 6am-8pm; June-Aug. 6am-10pm. MC/V. ❸

Le Spago, rue Emmanuel Arène (☎04 95 21 15 75), off av. du 1er Consul. A healthy dose of modernity in a sea of old-fashioned restaurants. Metal tables and funky decor. The house specialty, "Le Spago" (BBQ beef with fries and grilled corn on the cob; €16.50), is worthing naming a restaurant after. Meat *plats* (€14-24) go perfectly with a glass of rosé house wine (€2.50). Open daily noon-3pm and 8pm-3am. V. ❸

Pizzeria Napoli, rue Bonaparte (☎04 95 21 32 79). Late-night staple caters to the hungry clubbing crowd after a night of 🎵**Tecktonik dancing.** Get a late snack or grab a seat before 9pm for *menus* like the "Italien" (a trio of pizza, pasta, and dessert; €13). Pasta €7-10. *Menus* €13-17.50. Open M-Th 6pm-3am, F-Su 6pm-6am. Cash only. ❷

👁 SIGHTS

The seven-day €10 **Passmusée** covers entry fees for all five of the sights listed below and is available at the tourist office or any participating museum.

MUSÉE NATIONAL DE LA MAISON BONAPARTE. The boyhood home of France's most famous megalomaniac, the Casa Bonaparte now showcases such memorabilia as a family tree made from locks of hair. Don't miss the trapdoor through which Napoleon fled after his brief return in 1799. *(Rue St-Charles. ☎04 95 21 43 89. Open Apr.-Sept. Tu-Su 9am-noon and 2-6pm; Oct.-Mar. M 2-4:45pm, Tu-Su 10am-noon and 2-4:45pm. Last tickets sold 45min. before closing. €7, ages 18-25 €5, under 18 free. MC/V.)*

SALON NAPOLÉONIEN. The glittering salon was restored in ornate 19th-century style and houses a lavish display of Napoleon's coronation portrait, funerary mask, and personal items. The beautiful main room, with its intricate ceiling and delicate chandeliers, now hosts weddings and official city events. The empty glass display case in the smaller room once held a gold replica of Napoleon's olive-leaf coronation crown, created in 1869 entirely from donations given by the city's inhabitants. To their horror, it was stolen nine years ago during renovations and remains at large. The **Maison Bonaparte,** which originally entrusted the crown to the city's care, now displays a spray-painted model. *(Pl. Foch, in the Hotel de Ville. ☎04 95 51 52 62. Open M-F from mid-June to mid-Sept. 9-11:45am and 2-5:45pm; from mid-Sept. to mid-June 9-11:45am and 2-4:45pm. €5, students €2.30. Written tours in French, English, German, and Italian. Cash only.)*

MUSÉE À BANDERA. This museum chronicles Corsica's past from prehistory to WWII with a collection of maps, models, and elaborate dioramas depicting everything from important naval battles to megalithic stone structures. The galleries are supplemented by rotating exhibits on related subjects, including "Corsican Women." Though the labels require a good command of French, the desk can provide an English, Spanish, Chinese, or German booklet with translations of the museum's placards. Free guided tours are available with a week's notice but are probably unnecessary for this relatively small museum. *(1 rue Général Levie. ☎04 95 51 07 34; histoirecorse@wanadoo.fr. Open daily from July to mid-Sept. 9am-7pm; mid-Sept. to June 9am-noon and 2-6pm. €4, students €2.60. Cash only.)*

OTHER SIGHTS. The **Chapelle Impériale** pays tribute to Napoleon's roots; the chapel's marble interior holds the tombs of many Bonapartes—though Napoleon himself is buried at Les Invalides in Paris. The **Musée Fesch,** home to a large collection of "Virgin and the Child" portraits, will be closed until the end of 2009. Check the website for hours and more information on both museums. *(50-52 rue Cardinal Fesch. ☎04 95 21 48 17; www.musee-fesch.com.)*

🎭 NIGHTLIFE

Ajaccio saves wild nights for July and August, when the summer heat brings well-dressed tourists eager to show off their tans. You might want to trade in your hiking boots and trail-weary T-shirt for some classier duds before going out. In the *centre-ville*, the bar and lounge scene is popular year-round, particularly around **place Foch.** On summer weekends, a strip of bars and clubs around boulevard **Pascal Rossin** draw a younger crowd. A few distant clubs and beaches that require car access provide Ajaccio's hottest summer nightlife, with weekly ragers every Sunday at **l'Ariadne** and **Capo di Fero** (pick up the free *Rendez-Vous* guide from the tourist office for details). Those with cash to spare can head to the **Casino,** bd. Pascal Rossini. (☎04 95 50 40 60. 18+. Open from July to mid-Sept. daily 1pm-4am; Oct.-June M-Th 1pm-3am, F-Su 1pm-4am. MC/V.)

> **La Place,** bd. Lantivy (☎04 95 51 09 10). Downtown Ajaccio's best *discothèque*—at least in the strobe light, eardrum-popping sense of the word. 2 DJs spin the latest tech-tonic hits Th-Sa. Mixed drinks €11. No cover. Open daily 11pm-5am. Cash only.

> **Irish Pub,** 4 rue Notre Dame (☎04 95 21 63 22). More active during the week than most bars in Ajaccio and popular with young locals, this laid-back pub sells over 60 types of beer, including Pietra (a Corsican beer) and, of course, Guinness. Test your skills on the dartboard. Beer €4-7. Mixed drinks €7-12. Open daily 7pm-2am. AmEx/MC/V.

> **Le Lamparo,** résidence Diamant II, bd. Lantivy (☎04 95 51 47 05), off bd. Pascal Rossini. Elegant *avant boîte* (pre-club) keeps regulars coming back with a sophisti-cated ambience and a personable staff. House and lounge open Sept.-Apr. F-Sa. Beer €2.50-5. Wine from €3.50. Mixed drinks €6-8. Open daily 7am-2am. MC/V.

> **Le Mango,** av. Antoine Serafini, corner of pl. Foch. Big-screen TVs, red leather seats, and loud music fill this dark, lively bar. Well-dressed crowd of 20-somethings. House marga-rita €8. Mixed drinks €6. Beer €3-5. Live music on occasion. Open daily 6pm-2am. V.

✳ FESTIVALS

Ajaccio hosts several small film festivals throughout the year. Past festivals have centered on Japanese film, Mediterranean film, and even cartoons. For tickets or more infor on any of these events, visit the tourist office.

> **Festival de Musique d'Ajaccio,** in early July. Ajaccio kicks off a series of small summer festivals with an annual orchestral celebration.

> **Shopping de Nuit,** in July and Aug. Stores stay open until midnight on Fridays.

> **Polyphonies de l'Eté,** in July and Aug. Traditional Corsican music fills Ajaccio's churches.

> **Fêtes Napoleon,** Aug. 15-18. Commemorates the emperor's birth with war reenactments, a parade, ceremonies, and a huge *pyrosymphonie* (fireworks display).

IT'S ALL RELATIVE. Corsica: an island, a region, or what? It's often difficult to discern Corsica's official relation to France. An island it is for sure, but beyond that, things get a bit more complicated. While Corsica is com-monly considered one of France's 26 regions, it is by law a territorial col-lective, which means it has an elected local government—or a certain "free-dom of administration," allowing Corsica to opt for lower taxes on certain goods. The citizens of Corsica have attempted to gain more independence a number of times but have failed. Additionally, though separated from main-land France by the Ligurian Sea, Corsica is considered part of Metropolitan France, as opposed to an overseas department.

PORTO   ☎04 95

Corsica's jagged volcanic mountains, lush pine groves, emerald valleys, and crystalline waters converge at the Gulf of Porto—a hiker's paradise. To the north, a marine reserve conceals grottoes and rare birds and fish. At the center of all the natural wonder lies tiny Porto (pohr-toh; pop. 432), which consists almost entirely of hotels, souvenir shops, and tourist restaurants. Despite the camera-toting sightseers and the inconvenience of getting in and out without a car, Porto is a relatively inexpensive base for the region's hiking trails.

TRANSPORTATION

Buses: Autocars SASAIB (☎04 95 51 42 56) leaves from the top of the main road by the pharmacy for **Ajaccio** (2hr.; from July to mid-Sept. daily 8:15am, 2:15pm, from mid-Sept. to June M-Sa 8:15am, 2:15pm; €11) and **Calvi** (2hr.; July-Aug. daily, from mid-May to June and Sept. M-Sa; €17). Purchase tickets on board. Autocars Mordiconi (☎04 95 48 00 04) leaves from the parking lot at the base of the marina, in front of the minigolf course. From July to mid-Sept., buses run to **Corte** (M-Sa daily 2pm, €20) via **Evisa** (€17). Buy tickets on board. Buses don't run in bad weather.

Taxis: Taxis Ceccaldi-Ange Félix (☎04 95 26 12 92 or 06 85 41 95 89).

Car, Bike, and Scooter Rental: Porto Location (☎04 95 26 10 13), near Haut Porto's supermarkets. If the desk is unattended, ask at **La Cigale.** Cars from €65 per day, €298 per week; €298 deposit. 18+; must have been licensed for at least 2 years. Scooters €50/198; €610 deposit. Bikes €18/68. Open Apr.-Oct. daily 8:30am-7:30pm. MC/V.

ORIENTATION AND PRACTICAL INFORMATION

Porto consists of two clusters of buildings along a main road. The upper town, **Haut Porto** or **Quartier Vaita** (*Guaïta* in Corsican), is 800m up and inland from the coastal area, **Porto Marina,** where some 15 hotels and restaurants vie for waterfront space. A stream runs through town, separating shops and boutiques in the north from boat slips and beaches to the south. A pedestrian bridge at the river's mouth provides access to the opposite shorelines.

Tourist Office: (☎04 95 26 10 55; www.porto-tourisme.com), a short way up the main road from the Tour Génoise and the sea. Distributes topo-guide of 29 regional hikes for all skill levels (€2.50), bus schedules, and info on watersports, boat trips, and lodging. English spoken. Open July-Aug. M-Sa 9am-7pm, Su 9am-5pm; Sept. and June M-Sa 9am-7pm, Su 9am-1pm; Oct.-May M-Sa 9am-5pm.

Laundromat: Lavo 2000 (☎04 95 26 10 33), next to Hôtel Bon Accueil. Wash €8, dry €0.15 per min. Detergent €0.50. Open daily 9am-9pm. Cash only.

Police: Gendarmerie Maritime (☎04 95 51 75 21), on the port.

Pharmacy: (☎04 95 26 11 79), at the entrance to quartier Vaita.

Medical Services: ☎04 95 26 13 13. Open 3-6pm or in an emergency.

Post Office: (☎04 95 26 10 26), between the marina and Haut Porto. Open July-Aug. M-F 9am-12:30pm and 2-5pm, Sa 9-11:30am; Sept.-June M-F 9am-noon and 2-4pm, Sa 9-11am. **Postal Code:** 20150.

ACCOMMODATIONS AND CAMPING

Porto's abundance of indistinguishable hotels makes the town affordable most of the year, but in July and August prices skyrocket for even modest lodgings. Make summer reservations well ahead of time. Some of the cheapest accommodations in Corsica are *gîtes* in the pleasant village of **Ota,** a departure point for many hikes. From Porto Marina, head up the main road and take a hairpin left just before the supermarkets; follow signs to D124 and Ota (1hr.). The bus from Ajaccio to Porto also stops at Ota (20min., M-Sa 2 per day, €3).

Camping Les Oliviers (☎04 95 26 14 49; www.camping-oliviers-porto.com). Walk away from the marina to the end of Haut Porto; the campground is just before the bridge leaving Porto toward Ajaccio on D81. Luxurious site with swimming pool, pizzeria, restaurant, sauna, spa, fitness room, Wi-Fi, and tennis courts. Staff organizes canyoning trips, waterside hiking trips, and climbing excursions, then rejuvenates trekkers with a 1hr. shiatsu massage; prices vary for all services. Showers free. Reception 8:30am-8:30pm. Open Apr.-Oct. €6.80-9.10 per person; €3-6.50 per tent; €2.50-3.50 per car. Electricity €4. 2- to 8-person bungalows €281-1250 per week. AmEx/MC/V. ❶

Bon Accueil (☎04 95 26 12 10 or 06 73 89 55 40; www.bonaccueil.porto.com), on the main road. A cheerful staff manages clean, colorful, and well-located rooms. All with bath, some with balconies. Social bar downstairs. 1 room sleeps up to 6 guests (€111). Breakfast €6.50. Wi-Fi. 24hr. reception. From mid-June to Aug. singles and doubles €41-71; triples €61-81; quads €81-91. Sept.-May prices drop by €5-10. MC/V. ❸

Chez Felix (☎04 95 26 12 92), in Ota. Homey 4- to 8-bed dorms make this hostel feel more like someone's house. Kitchen access. Breakfast €6. Linens €3. Dorms €13, with *demi-pension* €32; doubles with bath and *demi-pension* €45-50. MC/V. ❶

Le Lonca, route de la Marine (☎04 95 26 16 44; hotel.lelonca@wanadoo.fr), next to the post office. Well-kept, modern rooms with large baths, some with balconies overlooking the hills. Each has TV and A/C. Pool. Breakfast €8. Reception 7am-10pm. Open Apr.-Oct. Aug. singles and doubles €85-120; triples €100-135; quads €150. Sept. and July singles and doubles €65-85; triples €80-100; quads €115. Apr.-June singles and doubles €55-75; triples €70-90; quads €105. MC/V. ❺

Hôtel Brise de Mer (☎04 95 26 10 28; www.brise-de-mer.com), across from the tourist office. Bright bedspreads in 20 clean, functional rooms, each with shower or bath, toilet, and balcony. Request a sea view. Includes a bar, TV room, and terrace restaurant. Breakfast €8. Reception daily 9am-9pm. Open Apr.-Oct. Aug. singles and doubles €80-85, with *demi-pension* €125-130; triples €100; quads €125. July and Sept. singles and doubles €60-65/80-110; triples €75; quads €95. May-June singles and doubles €55-60/78-105; triples €70; quads €90. April-Oct. singles and doubles €50-55/75-100; triples €65; quads €85. MC/V. ❺

Camping Le Sole e Vista (☎04 95 26 15 71), on the right before the supermarkets when entering Porto. 1km from the beach. Free daytrips to Scandola Nature Reserve, the Gorges de la Spelunca, and Capu D'Ortu, a local mountain. On-site bar. Breakfast €5. Laundry €4.50. Reception 9am-noon and 1:30-9pm. Open Apr.-Sept. €6 per person; €2.50 per tent; €1.50 per car. Electricity €3.50. Cash only. ❶

🍴 FOOD

There are two adjacent supermarkets in Haut Porto on D81. One is **SPAR.** (☎04 95 26 11 25. Open July-Aug. M-Sa 8am-8pm, Su 8am-noon and 5-8pm; Sept.-June M-Sa 8:30am-noon and 3-7pm. MC/V.) The other is **Supermarché Banco.** (☎04 95 26 10 92. Open July-Aug. M-Sa 8am-8pm, Su 8:30am-12:30pm and 4-8pm; Sept.-Oct. and Apr.-June M-Sa 8am-noon and 3-7pm. MC/V.)

La Marine (☎04 95 26 10 19), on the main road across from the tourist office. One of the better deals in town makes it easy for hikers to carbo-load. Youthful staff serves up tasty pizzas (€5.50-9), pastas (€5.50-7.50), and a series of extensive *menus* (€9-15) on a street-side terrace. Open Apr.-Oct. daily noon-4pm and 6:30-11pm. V. ❷

La Tour Génoise (☎04 95 26 17 11), behind the aquarium. Mouthwatering cuisine served by attentive staff. Spacious terrace at the base is great for people-watching and enjoying fresh seafood. Traditional Corsican *menus* €17-20. Wheelchair-accessible. Open Apr.-Oct. daily noon-2pm and 7-10:30pm. AmEx/MC/V. ❸

⚙ 🏠 SIGHTS AND HIKING

Hiking enthusiasts could spend weeks exploring the trails that radiate from the Gulf of Porto into the countryside. Routes range in difficulty, but each one provides an unforgettable vista of rugged peaks, verdant valleys, or seaside cliffs.

GORGES DE LA SPELUNCA. The old mule track from Ota to Evisa is a good option for hikers of all skill levels. This trail (5-6hr. round-trip) winds through the deep Gorges de la Spelunca, past 15th-century bridges and spots for picnics and swimming. To get to the gorges from Porto, take a left at the fork and walk 5km to **Ota** (see **Accommodations and Camping,** p. 768, for buses). Marked in orange, the trail begins at the top of the stairway to the left of the town hall, but to reduce the walk you can pick it up farther down the main road at the first Genoese bridge, called **Ponto Vecchio** (45min.). Another 15min. walk in the maquis to **Pont de Zaglia** offers incredible vistas of rose-colored cliffs plunging into the sea. The trail continues uphill until it reaches **Evisa** (3hr.). The 1hr. hike back to Porto is relatively easy, leaving you time to stop and smell the cistus (white and pale pink flowers) and lavender. There are no afternoon return buses from Evisa and only one from Ota.

Those with energy to spare can hike on to find chestnut trees and 50m tall pines in the **Forêt d'Aitone** between Evisa and Col de Vergio. This trail leads directly out of the village of Evisa, part of the **Tra Mare e Monti,** and is famous for its *piscines naturelles* (swimming holes formed by pooling waterfalls). Follow the orange markers; the pools are about an hour from town. Beyond the pools, a more difficult and secluded trail to **Col de Vergio** (6-7hr.) takes hikers higher into the **Forêt Domanial,** where a *gîte d'étape* marks its intersection with the GR20; in order to do this hike, you'll have to spend the night in Evisa.

LES CALANCHES DE PIANA. The astounding rock formations of the Calanches resemble, in the words of Guy de Maupassant, a "menagerie of nightmares petrified by the whim of some extravagant god." Hikes in this alien landscape range from easy to extremely steep. Piana, picturesque with its white houses and beautiful church, is a good base for exploring the Calanches, as it is on the Ota-Ajaccio bus line. The **Château Fort,** a mild hike, begins 6km south of Porto on D81 and rewards minimum effort with expansive views of the gulf and the Calanches (25min.). Ask the Ota-Ajaccio bus driver to stop at **Tête de Chien,** a rock formation in the shape of a dog's head, and take the path that runs along the mountain crest. A fortified castle overlooks the sea from a large promontory. A more demanding hike awaits 2km farther south, off D81. The marked trail, which begins near the stadium, climbs 900m to the 1294m **Capo d'Orto** (3hr.). From the summit, another trail leads back to Porto but is much more difficult. Hikers should consult the tourist office before attempting the descent.

The gratifying 🏠**Sentier des Muletiers** leaves directly from Piana and takes hikers on a quick forest ramble before heading into the heart of the looming rocks. Used until the mid-19th century, when Napoleon III opened the Porto-Piana road, this mule track is an excellent introductory hike. To catch the trail, head uphill immediately to the right of the *syndicat d'initiative;* 1km down the road, 100m after the **Mezzanu** bridge, take the trail on the right and then the downhill path on the left. Cross the stadium diagonally and walk over a footbridge to reach the right bank of the brook. Turn left onto chemin de Palani and walk for 10min. until you reach a stone wall, which is where the mule track begins (30min.). Another 30min. up the cliffside path leads to dizzying views of the Calanches between Piana and Porto. The trail continues down the other face and ends at a statue of the Virgin Mary by D81 (15min.), which you can take to return to Porto (30min.). Those wishing for a longer hike (3hr. round-trip from Piana) should instead abandon the mule track after 50m and take a right into a small pine forest. The path reaches a small pass, crosses the Palani chestnut field, and arrives at the gorgeous **Fontaine d'Oliva Bona** (15min.). Continue downhill until the ruins of **Dispensa** and return to Piana via the Route des Calanches (2.5km). As with Capo d'Orto, the return trail is steep and difficult, so retracing your steps might be a wise choice.

Southwest of Piana lies the spectacular ◼**Capo Rosso,** a peninsula that marks the southern boundary of the Gulf of Porto. Perched at the top is the tiny **Tour de Turghiu,** accessible by a demanding 1-2hr. scramble up the sun-drenched outcropping. The path begins easily enough, leading downhill past crumbling sheep pens and shepherds' huts. As you wind around to the base of the summit, the landscape, covered with underbrush, gives way to burnt-red rock. A nearly vertical 1hr. section leads straight to the tower at the apex of the peninsula. The stone structure is still in excellent condition, and, if your calves can carry you up the narrow staircase, you'll find astounding views of the distant Calanches in the Gulf of Porto. To reach the trailhead from Piana, take D824 toward Arone; it is situated on a large bend just next to a tiny snack stand and parking lot (15min. by car, 1hr. by foot). There is little shade on this hike; wear plenty of sunscreen and bring extra water.

SCANDOLA. Off-limits to hikers and divers, the caves and wild terrain of the Réserve Naturelle de Scandola protect many species of Corsican wildlife and can be explored only by boat tour from Porto. In and around both sides of the port is a slew of boat tour companies offering tours of Scandola, Les Calanches, and swimming in **Girolata,** a fishing village just south of Porto accessible only by boat. With such fierce competition, prices are constantly changing—a little shopping before choosing a company should pay off. Arrive before 9am or make reservations in person the day before to find the best deals, which usually hover around €30-50, and don't forget to bring cash. If guided tours aren't your thing, be your own tour guide and rent a boat from **Le Goëland,** on the marina next to the minigolf center, which rents Zodiacs and other small motor craft capable of holding up to 10 passengers. (☎04 95 26 15 88 or 06 81 06 88 08. No permit necessary. €75 per ½-day, €115 per day; ID deposit. Gas €1.70 per L. Cash only.) Again, however, there are several boat-rental options, including companies that rent smaller

IN RECENT NEWS

WHY DID THE CHICKEN CROSS THE ROAD?

For that matter, why did the dog or the goat or the cow cross the road? Well, in Corsica, the answer is becoming pretty clear: the island has a growing problem with unattended and unidentified domestic and farm animals.

It is currently estimated that between 15,000 and 20,000 unclaimed animals roam the relatively small island. This includes the descendents of pets—stray dogs and cats—as well as goats, sheep, cows, and even donkeys. Besides causing ownership disputes in rural areas that depend on such livestock for wool or meat, the unidentified animals have been known to wander onto famously treacherous roads. With twists and turns every few hundred meters in some areas, the likelihood of a car collision with an unattended animal is high in Corsica's mountainous regions. Although instances of severe human injury due to such a collision are rare, it is not uncommon to see a dead chicken or cat on the side of the road.

Efforts are currently being undertaken to relieve the problem, specifically aimed at capturing wild farm animals—which are larger, more dangerous, and certainly more economically valuable. So, if you're driving on the island, be on the lookout for animals in the road. Those not behind the wheel should be on the lookout anyway—you just might bump into the local donkey.

boats like kayaks, so a short walk around the marina to find the most afford-able option is definitely worth the extra 10min.

BEACHES AND OTHER SIGHTS. The raison d'être for Porto's hotels and post-card shops is one of Corsica's oldest Genoese towers, the 1549 **Tour Génoise**. The sturdy lookout was built as part of an effort to improve the coastal defense system. From 1510 to 1620, around 100 towers were built to safeguard Corsica from unrelenting Turkish pirates. Any *torregiano* (tower guard) who deserted his post was immediately put to death. *(Open daily July-Aug. 9am-7pm; Sept. and Apr.-May 11am-7pm. €2.50, under 12 free. Cash only.)* At the foot of the tower, the vaulted ceilings of the powder magazine provide a lofty home for the **Aquarium de la Poudrière.** Worth a stop, the aquarium identifies aquatic creatures from the Gulf of Porto and—in true French fashion—indicates which species are necessary for a good bouillabaisse. Each tank is designed to recreate the aquatic regions found in the Scandola nature reserve; if you don't get to see the local sea crea-tures on a dive or boat tour, the aquarium is worth your euro. *(☎04 95 26 19 24. Open daily Oct.-Mar. and May-Aug. 8am-9pm; Sept. and Apr. 10am-7pm. €5.50. Ticket for aquarium and Tour Génoise €6.50. Cash only.)* In the marina, three diving companies vie to lead tourists on scuba and snorkeling excursions. All three make use of 15 sites in the gulf and takes experienced divers to the edge of the Scandola reserve. *(Mediterranée Porto Sub ☎06 89 03 76 17; www.plongeecorse.fr. École de Plongée Generation Bleue ☎04 95 26 24 88 or 06 85 58 24 14; www.generation-bleue.com. Centre de Plongee du Golfe de Porto ☎04 95 26 10 29 or 06 84 24 49 20; www.plongeeporto.com. All offer 1st-time dive experiences from €40 or up to 10 dives for around €360.)* Once again, arrive early or make reservations in advance. Directly across the channel from the Tour Génoise lies Porto's pebbly public beach. Surrounded by plunging cliffs and pounding surf, the broad crescent is the perfect place to catch some rays.

CALVI ☎04 95

Often called Corsica's Côte d'Azur, Calvi (cal-vee; pop. 5700) has some of the best and worst traits of that better-known coastline. With all the hoopla of any ritzy coastal resort, Calvi abounds with swanky nightspots, local artwork, over-priced knick-knacks, and the tourists to shell out money for it all. However, beyond the souvenir shops and gleaming white yachts, Calvi has elements of the rugged beauty and solitude that make Corsica unique. A star-shaped cita-del above town, endless cliffside beaches, and rocky peaks are an attraction for both high- and low-rolling visitors. Rollicking nightlife—the best on the island—draws party-seekers from all over, and a series of beachfront camp-sites makes Calvi a choice backpacker destination.

🚇 TRANSPORTATION

Flights: Aéroport de Calvi Ste-Catherine (CLY; ☎04 95 65 88 88), 7km southeast of town. **Air France** (☎36 54; www.airfrance.com) and subsidiary **Air Corse Medi-terranée** (☎04 95 65 88 60 or 08 20 82 08 20; www.aircorsica.com) fly to **Lille, Lyon, Marseille, Nice,** and **Paris.**

Trains: Pl. de la Gare (☎04 95 65 00 61), near Port de Plaisance. Open daily from June to mid-Sept. 6:30am-9:30pm; from mid-Sept. to June 7am-9pm. Purchase tickets at station. To **Bastia** (3hr., 2 per day, €19), **Corte** (2hr., 4 per day, €16), and **Île Rousse** (1hr., 2 per day, €4.50). In summer, Tramways de la Balagne also sends trains to **Île Rousse** (1hr., June-Sept. 10 per day, €4.50).

Buses: Autocars Ceccaldi (☎04 95 22 41 99) departs from the Super U for **Porto** (2hr.; July-Aug. daily 3pm, from mid-May to June and Sept. M-Sa 3pm; €18). Les

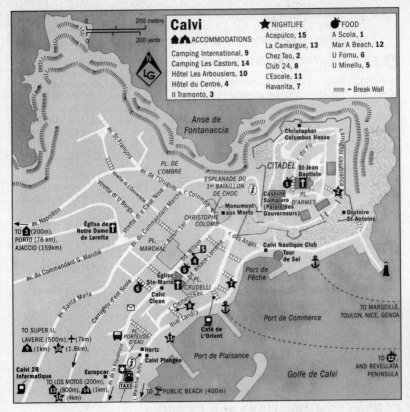

Beaux Voyages, bd. Wilson (☎04 95 65 11 35), leaves from the agency at pl. Porteuse d'Eau, by the tourist office, which sells tickets. Open May-Oct. M-Sa 9am-noon and 2-7pm; Nov.-Apr. M-F 9am-noon and 3-7pm. To **Bastia** (2hr., M-Sa 6:45am, €17) via **Île Rousse** (25min., €3.50). Corse Voyages (☎04 95 21 06 30) runs buses to **Ajaccio** (4hr., M-Sa 1 per day, €26) via **Ponte-Leccia** (€10). Buses depart from pl. Porteuse d'Eau. Buy tickets on board.

Ferries: Agence TRAMAR, quai Landry (☎04 95 65 01 38), in Port de Plaisance. Open July-Sept. M-F 9am-noon and 2-6pm, Sa 9am-noon; Oct.-June M-F 8:30am-noon and 2-5:30pm, Sa 8:30am-noon. MC/V. Both SNCM (☎04 95 65 17 77. 3hr.; 7 per week; €35-50, ages 12-25 €18-27) and Corsica Ferries (☎04 95 65 43 21. 3hr., 5 per week, €20-38) send boats to **Nice** and **Marseille** and have offices near Capitainerie du Port de Commerce. Open 2hr. before boat arrivals. Book early for best prices.

Taxis: ☎04 95 65 03 10 or 04 95 65 30 36. Airport to *centre-ville* €15-25. 24hr.

Car Rental: Europcar, av. de la République (☎04 95 65 10 35, airport 04 95 65 10 19), across from the train station. €74 per day, €291 per week. 21+. Open May-Sept. M-Sa 8am-7pm. AmEx/MC/V. **Hertz,** 2 rue Maréchal Joffre (☎04 95 65 06 64, airport 04 95 65 02 96). €89 per day, €295 per week. 21+. Under-25 surcharge €29 per day. Open July-Aug. daily 8am-8pm; Sept.-June M-Sa 8am-8pm. AmEx/MC/V.

Bike and Scooter Rental: Loc Motos, av. Christophe Colomb (☎04 95 47 31 30; www. calvimoto.com). Bikes July-Aug. €21 per day. Scooters July-Aug. from €40 per day. Both €5-10 less Sept.-June; cheaper for longer rentals. Open daily 9am-9pm. MC/V.

◀▎**7** ORIENTATION AND PRACTICAL INFORMATION

The city is easy to walk, connected by one main road that follows the curve of the coast and changes names several times, from **boulevard Wilson** between the citadel and the post office to **avenue de la République** and **avenue Christophe Colomb** when leaving the city. The pedestrian, souvenir-shop-lined **rue Clemenceau** begins from pl. Porteuse d'Eau, below the post office, and runs up to the citadel, below bd. Wilson, parallel to the port. **Quai Landry,** along the water, connects the ferry port at one end with port de Plaisance at the other.

Tourist Office: Port de Plaisance (☎04 95 65 16 67; www.balagne-corsica.com). From the back of the train station, turn left past the end of the tracks. On the 2nd fl. of the 1st building on the right. Staff offers maps and city guides and arranges private tours of the citadel or the city. Open from June to mid-Sept. daily 9am-noon and 2-6pm; from mid-Sept. to Apr. M-F 9am-noon and 2-5pm; May M-Sa 9am-noon and 2-6pm.

Laundromat: Laverie, av. Christophe Colomb, in Super U Plaza. Wash €6, dry €4. Open daily 7:30am-10:30pm. **Calvi Clean,** bd. Wilson, between the citadel and the post office. Wash €7, dry €5. Open daily 7am-10pm.

Police: Port de Plaisance (☎04 95 65 44 77 or 06 11 60 17 96).

Internet Access: Cyber-Calvi, av. de la République (☎04 95 33 71 35; www.cyber-calvi. com), across from the train station. €1.50 per 15min., €5 per hr. Open daily 10am-noon and 3-7pm. Cash only. **Calvi 2B Informatique,** av. Santa Maria (☎04 95 65 19 25), near Hôtel Regina. €1 per 20min. Open June-Sept. M-F 9:15am-12:30pm and 2-9pm, Sa 9:15am-9pm, Su 3:30-9pm; Oct.-May M-Sa 9:15am-noon and 2-7pm. **Café de L'Orient** (☎04 95 65 00 16), on quai Landry. €4 per 30min., €6 per hr., €10 per 2hr. Wi-Fi at same rates. Open Apr.-Sept. daily 9:30am-10pm. Cafe open until 2am. MC/V.

Post Office: Bd. Wilson (☎04 95 65 90 90). Open July-Aug. M-F 8:30am-6pm, Sa 8:30am-noon; Sept.-June M-F 8:30am-5:30pm, Sa 8:30am-noon. **Postal Code:** 20260.

🏠 📷 ACCOMMODATIONS AND CAMPING

Though compact, Calvi packs in many pricey three- and four-star hotels. A few budget options exist, albeit farther from the *centre-ville*. In the summer, inexpensive options fill up quickly; reserve far in advance. Calvi has one of the only hostels in Corsica—a **Relais International**—but it is tucked far in the hills above the city. Your best bet may be camping; a series of sites lines the coast toward Bastia. In the summer, most are connected to the center by the slow, 50-year-old **Tramways de la Balagne,** which drivers humorously call the TGV—for *trains à grande vibration.* Still, there are a few sites within walking distance of Calvi.

Il Tramonto, route de Porto RN 199 (☎04 95 65 04 17; www.hotel-iltramonto.com). From the citadel, walk 800m with the sea on your right. Prime hilltop location. 18 rooms, 9 with balconies and views of the distant lighthouse and the Girolata peninsula. Each has a bath or shower, phone, and large, comfortable bed; most have TVs. Breakfast €5. Reception 24hr. Open from Apr. to mid-Oct. Singles and doubles July €46-50; Aug. €50-60; Sept. and June €40-55; May €35-40; Apr. €32-35. Studios and apartments available July-Aug. for rental; call for prices. Extra bed €13-16. MC/V. ❹

Hôtel Les Arbousiers, route de Pietramaggiore (☎04 95 65 04 47). Take the 2nd road on the right along av. de la République, after the Super U. 40 rooms await at Calvi's largest budget hotel. Spiraling wood staircase, lounge, elegant 1st fl. restaurant, and 2nd fl. breakfast terrace. Most rooms have TVs, private baths, phones, and balconies. Breakfast

€8. Free parking. Open Apr.-Sept. July-Aug. singles €66; doubles €76. Sept. and June singles €55; doubles €60. Apr.-May singles €46; doubles €50. MC/V. ❺

Hôtel du Centre, 14 rue Alsace-Lorraine (☎04 95 65 02 01), behind rue Clemenceau. Functional white rooms in the heart of Calvi. Accommodating, English-speaking manager keeps a sizable stack of dog-eared English-, French-, and German-language paperbacks. Free luggage storage, even after check-out. Breakfast €5; order the night before. Reception daily 8am-9pm. Open from June to early Nov. June and Oct. singles and doubles €29-36; triples €40. July and Sept. singles and doubles €34-43; triples €50. Aug. singles and doubles €38-50; triples €58. Cash only. ❸

Camping International, RN 197 (☎04 95 65 01 75), 1km from town. From the train station, walk down av. de la République past Super U and Hôtel L'Onda; after the minigolf sign, turn right (15min.). Lively atmosphere, plenty of shade, and a warm reception. Flowering trees surround a bar and pizzeria (pizzas €6-13). Showers free. Reception daily 8am-1pm and 2-10pm. Open May-Sept. July-Aug. €6.50 per person, €3.60 per tent, €1.70 per car. Sept. and May-June €5.20 per person; €3 per tent; €1.50 per car. Electricity July-Aug. €3.50; Sept. and May-June €3. MC/V. ❶

Camping Les Castors, route de Pietramaggiore (☎04 95 65 13 30; www.castors.fr), 700m from the *centre-ville.* Well equipped with a snack bar, large pool, and water slide. Internet €0.10 per min. Wheelchair-accessible. Reception daily 7am-10:30pm. Open Apr.-Oct. June and Sept. €7.60 per person; €2.90 per tent. July-Aug. €9.60 per person; €4.30 per tent. Oct. and Apr.-May €6.50 per person; €2.80 per tent. AmEx/MC/V. ❶

 FOOD

Aside from street-side panini vendors and a smattering of pizzerias, cheap eats are rare in Calvi. For the best deal on sandwiches, try the **Super U,** av. Christophe Colomb. (☎04 95 65 04 32. Open July-Aug. M-Sa 8:30am-8:30pm, Su 8:30am-1pm; early Sept. and June M-Sa 8:30am-7pm; from mid-Sept. to May M-F 8:45am-7pm. AmEx/MC/V.) A handful of restaurants set up tables in the lovely **citadel,** with appropriately sky-high prices. Below, narrow **rue Clemenceau** is filled with specialty food shops and a small covered market beside the Église Ste-Marie. (Open daily 8am-noon.) **Quai Landry** is packed with pricey cafes, *brasseries,* seafood spots, and *glaciers* (ice-cream parlors). Most restaurants on the beach are overpriced except for cheap beach chairs (€7) and drinks. **Le Bout du Monde,** quai Landry, is the best of these eateries and sometimes serves dinner by the water (book 1 day ahead). For moderately expensive but high-quality meals, the pedestrian alleys between **port** and **boulevard Wilson** have the best food and ambience without the hordes of promenading tourists.

> ⭐**TIP** **THE CATCH OF YESTERDAY.** On days following bad weather, beware of restaurants serving *poisson du jour*—it won't be as fresh as they claim, since fishermen stay home on windy mornings.

U Minellu, traverse de l'Église (☎04 95 65 05 52). The terrace offers a break from tourist-filled rue Clemenceau, while the interior is decorated with portrait photographs of Corsicans in traditional dress. Excellent €17.50 *menu* offers the island's best. Begin with the savory *tarte aux blettes* (beet tart) and follow with a traditional *plat* like *sanglier* (wild boar) served with fresh corn polenta. Pasta €12-17. Open July-Sept. daily 6:30-11:30pm; Mar.-June M-Sa 11am-2pm and 7-10:30pm. Cash only. ❸

U Fornu, bd. Wilson (☎04 95 65 27 60). Trees surround quiet tables at this local staple. Elegant pink and gray interior. Seafood specialties include shrimp ravioli (€16) and baked octopus (€16). €17.50 *menu* highlights Corsican cuisine with *soupe corse,* storzapreti (spinach and fresh cheese), and *Fiadone* (€5.50), a traditional Corsican cake. Open daily 10am-2pm and 7-11pm. Cash only. ❸

A Scola (☎04 95 65 07 09), in the citadel. Elegant, cozy *salon de thé* offers delectable homemade pastries (€6-8) to accompany 17 varieties of tea (€3.50), ranging from Orange Pekoe to Russian Rouchka—and, of course, English Earl Grey. Salads, *omelettes*, other light lunch fare (€10-16), and mouthwatering melted chocolate cake (€6.50) served in an antique-filled interior. Open daily 9am-7pm. AmEx/MC/V. ❸

Mar A Beach, plage de la Revellata (☎04 95 65 48 30). A day on the beach at this laid-back restaurant on the spectacular Revellata peninsula is well worth the €10 boat taxi (Colombo line leaves daily from the port; call ☎04 95 65 32 10). Eat by the water on beach chairs (€8 per day). Dishes prepared according to "the mood of Chef Mousse." *Crêpes* €2-5.50. Meat *plats* €12-22. Open Apr.-Oct.; hours vary. MC/V. ❸

👁 📷 SIGHTS AND BEACHES

CITADEL. Calvi's remarkable citadel, looming over port de Plaisance, is both a symbol of the city's tumultuous history and the centerpiece of modern life. The 18th-century inscription—*civitas Calvi semper fidelis* (the city of Calvi is always faithful)—crowning the entrance was a gift for the Genoese in thanks for five centuries of loyalty. Just inside the entry, the tourist office annex distributes audio tours and free maps of the citadel. Round the first corner and climb the stairs to reach the citadel's center, dominated by the austere Palais des Gouverneurs. The original *palais* was the oldest building in the citadel, until lightning struck its powder store and the Genoese had to rebuild it.

Like several other Mediterranean towns, Calvi claims to be the birthplace of Christopher Columbus. The theory is that Calvi expatriate Antonio Calvo returned to his hometown in the 15th century to enlist recruits for the Genoese navy. His nephew Christopher caught his eye, so Calvo brought him to Genoa. A few other tenuous leads support the speculation. Calvi is quick to note that Columbus used Corsican dogs in warfare and preferred to keep company with *calvais* officers instead of the Genoese. A plaque in the northern end of the citadel marks the ruins of the house where Columbus was supposedly born. The citadel's other famous residence, the **Giubega house,** sheltered Napoleon and his family in 1793, when they fled political opponents in Ajaccio. (☎04 95 36 74 14. Open June-Sept. M-Sa 10am-5pm. Last entry 1hr. before closing. 1hr. tours in English, French, German, and Italian. €8. MC/V.)

REVELLATA PENINSULA. The first place to visit with a rented bike or scooter in Calvi is the *presqu'île* of the Girolata, an impressive promontory boasting a lighthouse and sensational beaches hidden behind boulders. Its roads are unbelievably bumpy and only get worse as you go, so it is best to park early and hike around the peninsula. On your way back, a right at the stop sign leads to a chapel with a must-see view of the entire bay of Calvi. *(From the citadel, head uphill and away from the town with the sea on your right; the peninsula is only a few kilometers away.)*

OTHER SIGHTS. Calvi and the surrounding area are full of long stretches of sandy beaches and rocky cliffs, making for some of the best scuba diving on the coast. Calvi boasts two particularly well-known sites: **la Bibliothèque,** where rock formations resemble stocked bookshelves, and **le B-17,** a sunken WWII bomber with wings and propellers still intact. **Calvi Plongée,** near the tourist office, runs dives to both sites. High winds sometimes limit dives. (☎04 95 65 33 67 or 06 79 63 57 93; www.calviplongee.com. Open Apr.-Oct. daily 8am-8pm. Reservations highly recommended July-Aug. July-Aug. dives (20-30min., 2-4 per day) €40, 1st-timers €45-50; night dives by request €55; snorkeling trips €19. Sept-Oct. and Apr.-June €5-10 less. Equipment *included. Cash only.)* Closer to shore, shallow water allows beachgoers to walk many meters from the coast, and strong winds make for great windsurfing. The staff at the **Calvi Nautique Club,** near the port, will have you skimming the waves in no time. *(☎04 95 65 10 65; www.calvinc.org. Open daily July-Aug. 9am-noon and 1-7pm; Sept.-June 9am-noon and 2-5pm. Windsurfing equipment €16 per hr.; sailboats €32, €230 deposit; kayaks €10-15 per hr. A ticket system allows you to exchange boats and try different types. MC/V.)* If the 6km expanse of public beach gets too windy, the rocks surrounding the citadel offer secluded and sun-drenched shelter as well as a number of topless (and bottom-less) sunbathers. **Tramways de la Balagne** (see **Transportation,** p. 772) runs to more remote coves farther from town.

🔋 NIGHTLIFE

Lively bars along **port de Plaisance** are perfect people-watching venues on sultry summer nights. Two open-air nightclubs on the road to Île Rousse give St-Tropez a run for its money in the summer: locals come from all over the island for big-name DJs and wild theme parties. Signs posted around town advertise party nights at different spots along the northern coast.

- **Acapulco,** route de Calenzana (☎04 95 65 08 03), nearly halfway between Calvi and Île Rousse. The hottest club in Calvi, with 5 fl. of dancing and drinking, a restaurant, and enough neon lights to make anyone look good. 2 resident DJs keep this *boîte* pumping. Free *navette* (shuttle) runs in summer (call ahead). Open May and July-Aug. daily 11pm-dawn; *soirées exceptionelles* Oct. 31 and some nights in winter.

- **La Camargue** (☎04 95 65 08 70), 25min. up N197 by foot. Spinning beams of light projected into the night sky announce this decadent club. 2 large dance floors, waterfalls, outdoor pools, projection screens, and a jungle-themed bar. Over-30 crowd relives its glory days—fully dressed—in the adjacent piano bar. Free shuttles depart for La Camargue from the port parking lot near the tourist office. Mixed drinks from €8. Cover €10; big-name events have higher covers. Open May-Sept. daily 10pm-5am. MC/V.

- **L'Escale,** port de Plaisance (☎04 95 65 10 75). A cafe during the day, this vibrant bar comes alive on weekend nights, with a crowded dance floor full of young locals and tourists. Top 40 and French classics can be enjoyed with a *piscine* (champagne with ice) or other drinks (€6-9) on the terrace. Closes at 2am. MC/V.

- **Club 24,** port de Plaisance (☎06 15 03 65 82). A modest dance floor, 2 excellent house DJs, and an exuberant staff keep the party going with an eclectic range of music at this well-known. Mixed drinks €8. Open from mid-Mar. to Dec. daily 7pm-2am. MC/V.

- **Havanita,** port de Plaisance (☎04 95 65 00 37). Swaying palms and sexy salsa will remind you of another island. Young crowd knocks back Cuban mixed drinks (€7). Wine €4.50. Happy hour daily 6-8:30pm. Open Apr.-Oct. daily 6pm-2am. Cash only.

- **Chez Tao** (☎04 95 65 00 73; www.cheztao.com), in the citadel. One of Corsica's oldest nightspots caters to a well-dressed crowd with creative mixed drinks (€10-14), wine (€6), and *apéritifs* (€7) served on a candlelit terrace overlooking the sea. This piano bar reveals its wild side on weekends after 1am, when DJs spin disco, funk, house, and 80s until dawn. Happy hour daily 7-10pm. Open June-Sept. daily 8:30pm-5am. MC/V.

❋ FESTIVALS

With a constant influx of tourists and vacationing Corsicans, Calvi is the perfect location for a variety of exciting festivals, concerts, and other events, particularly throughout the summer. Call the tourist office for up-to-date info.

Festival du Jazz (☎04 95 65 00 50), 2 weeks in June. Calvi draws up-and-coming musicians for 15 concerts. Bars along port de Plaisance host nightly performances and jam sessions, which witness some of the summer's best parties. €10.

Calvi on the Rocks (www.calviontherocks.com), in mid-July. Big-name artists come to the open-air music festival at the base of the citadel. MTV often collaborates, attracting some of Europe's best musicians and DJs and their hordes of fans. Contact the tourist office for more information. Nightly pass €15, 4-night Festival Pass €45.

Rencontres Polyphoniques (☎04 95 65 23 57), in mid-Sept. International artists come together for a festival celebrating the worldwide tradition of chanting music. The festival's individual performances in the citadel end with a spectacular joint concert led by A Fileta, one of Corsica's best-known traditional groups. €13-20, under 13 free.

Festival du Vent (☎04 53 20 93 00 or 01 53 20 93 05; www.lefestivalduvent.com), 3 days in late Oct. or early Nov. 40,000 visitors come for a colorful celebration of Corsican tradition, art, music, and sport, with an emphasis on the environment. €15-20.

ÎLE ROUSSE
☎04 95

In 1765, the clever Pascal Paoli decided to build a French port that would give him access to mainland France and divert trade from Genoese-dominated Calvi. Thus, Île Rousse (eel rooss; pop. 2500) was founded largely out of spite. Though both towns eventually came under French control, their historic rivalry was furthered when Calvi constructed an impressive marina, airport, and other tourist-friendly projects. Today, Île Rousse is a perfect hub for watersport enthusiasts tired of flashy Calvi; it also offers hikers leisurely trails in the countryside of the Balagne. The town itself retains its charm; visitors quickly get the sense that everyone knows everyone else.

TRANSPORTATION. Ferries go to Marseille (5-9hr.; 2 per week; €40-58, students €25-45) and Nice (3-10hr.; 2-7 per week; €35-47, students €20-32); call Agence CCR, av. J. Calizi, for info. (☎04 95 60 09 56. Open June-Aug. M-Tu and Th-F 9am-noon and 2-6pm, W 9am-noon and 2:30-6pm, Sa 9am-noon; Sept.-May M-F 8:30am-noon and 2-5:30pm.) **Trains** go to Ajaccio, Bastia, and Calvi. (☎04 95 60 00 50. Open daily July-Sept. 6am-8:30pm; Oct.-June 8am-9:30pm.) Tramways de la Balagne trains hug the coast en route to Calvi (50min., June-Sept. 9 per day, €5.40; MC/V). The train stops at every beach and campsite on its way.

ORIENTATION AND PRACTICAL INFORMATION. At 2km across, Île Rousse is easy to navigate. To get to the tiny **tourist office** from the train station or ferry depot, walk right for 5min. with the ocean on your left to the far side of pl. Paoli. (☎04 95 60 04 35; www.balagne-corsica.com. Open June-Sept. M-Sa 9am-7pm, Su 10am-1pm and 5-7pm; Oct.-May M-F 9am-noon and 2-6pm. Wi-Fi €5 per hour. Cash only.) Find **Internet** access at **Movie Store**, route de Calvi, across from the Casino supermarket. (☎04 95 65 47 97. €2 per 15min., €3 per 30min., €5 per hr. €2 per hr. when purchased in bulk. Open M-Sa 10am-2am, Su 2pm-2am. Cash only.) The **post office** is on route de Monticello, to the left of the supermarket. (☎04 95 63 05 50. Open July-Aug. M-F 8am-6pm, Sa 8am-noon; Sept.-June M-F 8:30am-5pm, Sa 8:30am-noon.) **Postal Code:** 20220.

ACCOMMODATIONS AND CAMPING. Since Île Rousse tends to attract the financially gifted, there's only one budget hotel in town. To find **Hôtel le Grillon ❸**, 10 av. Paul Doumer, go straight on av. Piccioni with the ocean on your left and take a left at av. Paul Doumer. Some of the 16 pastel rooms of this clean and attractive family-owned hotel have balconies and sea views (request in advance). All are equipped with TVs, phones, Wi-Fi, air conditioning, and modern bathrooms. (☎04 95 60 00 49; fax 04 95 60 43 69. Breakfast €5.60. Reception daily 6:30am-10pm. Reserve far in advance. Open Mar.-Nov. June-July and Sept. singles €44, *demi-pension* €63; doubles €47/86; triples €55/115. Aug. *demi-pension* singles €75; *demi-pension* doubles €98; *demi-pension* triples €126. Mar.-May and Oct.-Nov. singles €35, *demi-pension* €55; doubles €36/75; triples €44/105. MC/V.) Campsites stretch along the Balagne coast; hop off the train when you see an enticing one. For a spot closer to the *centre-ville*, head to **Les Oliviers ❶**, in Île Rousse, 800m from downtown on av. Paul Doumer, the main road to Bastia. A bar and pizzeria provide food for happy campers. (☎04 95 60 19 92; lesolivierskalliste@wanadoo.fr. Laundry €6. Reception open 8am-noon and 2-8pm. Open Apr.-Oct. €6.20 per person; €3.70 per tent; €2.70 per car. Electricity €3.50. July-Aug. closed to cars after 11pm. Chalet doubles €85. Bungalows €330-570 per week. MC/V.) From St-Florent, save yourself the arduous uphill trek from the train station and ask the bus driver to stop at the campground.

▣ FOOD. The city's small, signature covered market off **place Paoli,** now a historical monument, has brought the freshest produce to town since 1850. Its stalls still burst with ripe local fruits, olives, and the catch of the day. (Open daily 7am-1pm.) The **Casino** supermarket on the Palais des Allées picks up where the market leaves off. (☎04 95 60 24 23. Open July-Aug. M-Sa 8:30am-7pm, Su 8:30am-1pm; Sept.-June M-F 8:30am-12:30pm and 3-7pm, Sa 8:30am-7pm. MC/V.) *Brasseries* and *crêperies* around pl. Paoli fill with diners hungry for inexpensive eats. For a quiet sit-down meal, try **U Fucone ❸**, on rue Paoli, down the street from pl. Paoli. This welcoming spot offers seafood salad, shark steak, and flan (€15.50) as well as all-you-can-eat *moules-frites* (mussels and fries; €10) and 10 kinds of pizza (€8-10). In winter, the chef serves Alsatian and Savoyard specialties. (☎04 95 60 16 67. Open May-Sept. daily 11am-2pm and 6:30-11pm; Oct.-June hours vary. MC/V.) Hungry photography enthusiasts should make a left off rue Paoli onto rue d'Agilla for **Saetta ❸**, an art gallery/restaurant run by local photographer Antoine Perigot. Specialties—such as calamari—on the €17 four-course *menu du jour* are served in a gallery featuring Perigot's professional photographs of Corsica and Burkina Faso. Both settings are also the subjects of the photographer's two published books, which are

ON THE MENU

WHEN IN CORSICA

Travelers in Corsica quickly learn that, unlike in much of France, grabbing a cheap, quick, and familiar bite to eat is pretty unlikely. As with their language, Corsicans are extremely proud of their food, a unique hybrid of French and Italian cuisines.

Brocciu, a soft sheep's-milk cheese similar to ricotta, is used in everything from ravioli to pastries. Corsicans love their locally produced *charcuterie*—smoked and flavored pork sausage can be found in every supermarket. Pietra, a pale beer, is available at virtually any bar on the island. Chestnut trees—increasingly rare in some parts of the world—grow in abundance in Corsica and are used in *beignets* (chestnut flour doughnuts coated with sugar and sometimes stuffed with *brocciu*). Wild boar meat, usually found in stews and roasts, is a flavorful alternative to ordinary pork.

A few less common Corsican delicacies can create an unforgettable dining experience in their own right. Start with a little *figatellu* (liver sausage). After whetting your appetite for pig's organs, enjoy a hearty serving of *frommage de tete*, which literally means "head cheese" and is made with seasoned pigs' brains. Cap your authentically Corsican meal off with some *fiadone*, a supple cheese tart soaked in liqueur and flambéed.

available for purchase at the restaurant. (☎06 12 73 83 29; www.miccanomi.fr. Open M-F from 6pm. Closing time varies. MC/V.)

BEACHES AND OUTDOOR ACTIVITIES. Like much of Corsica's western coast, Île Rousse is lined with white-sand beaches that are overrun in July and August. For less crowded spots, take the train toward Calvi and get off when you see an appealing stretch. To take advantage of the town's beaches, stop by the **Club Nautique,** across from the train station, and rent a kayak or catamaran to visit Île Rousse's namesake isles and access some of the region's best snorkeling. (☎04 95 60 22 55; www.cnir.org. Reservations recommended. Kayaks €12 per hr. Catamarans €31-39 per hr. 2hr. kayak tour of coastal islands €30 per person. Open Jan.-Nov. daily 10am-6pm. Cash only.)

CORTE (CORTI) ☎04 95

Dynamic Corte (kohr-tay; pop. 6000, when school is in 10,000) sits near the center of the island between snowcapped peaks. The location is fitting, as Corte is considered the intellectual and political heart of Corsica, despite its relatively small size. Home of the island's university, **Universita di Corsica,** the town gave birth to Pascal Paoli's constitution and remains the center of Corsica's nationalist cause, evidenced by the nationalist slogans graffitied on various public buildings throughout the town. Locals have made a serious effort to keep Corsican traditions alive; most speak **Corse,** a language similar to Italian dialects, in addition to French. It's easy to understand the pride of this inland city— perched above the convergence of three rivers, Corte is an eyeful of plunging cliffs and jagged summits that provide Corsica's best hiking.

TRANSPORTATION

Trains: Station at the roundabout at av. Jean Nicoli and N193 (☎04 95 00 80 17). Open M-Sa 6:30am-9pm, Su 7:45am-9pm. To **Ajaccio** (2hr., 4 per day, €13), **Bastia** (2hr., 5 per day, €12), and **Calvi** (2hr., 2 per day, €14) via **Ponte-Leccia.**

Buses: Eurocorse Voyages (☎04 95 31 73 76) sends buses from **Brasserie Le Majestic,** 19 cours Paoli, to **Ajaccio** (1hr., M-Sa 2 per day, €11) and **Bastia** (1hr., M-Sa 1-2 per day, €10). In July and Sept. Autocars Mordiconi (☎04 95 48 00 04) leaves from the train station for **Porto** (2hr., M-Sa 1 per day, €19).

Taxis: Taxis Salviani (☎04 95 46 04 88 or 06 03 49 15 24).

Car Rental: Europcar (☎04 95 46 06 02), next to the train station. From €91 per day, €365 per week; credit-card deposit. Insurance included. 22+. Open M-F 8am-noon and 2:30-6pm, Sa 8am-noon. MC/V.

ORIENTATION AND PRACTICAL INFORMATION

The train station is inconveniently located among major roads, 15min. away from hotels or campsites. But don't despair: the *centre-ville* is pleasant and easy to navigate. To reach it from the station, turn right onto N193, cross the bridge, and take a left, crossing a second bridge onto av. Jean Nicoli. Follow the road until it ends at **cours Paoli,** Corte's main drag. (It's a good idea to look closely at the train station's map before setting off.) A left turn leads to **place Paoli,** the *centre-ville*. Climb the cobblestones of the ascending rue Scoliscia to reach the citadel, the museum, and the tourist office.

CORSICA

Tourist Office: At the citadel (☎04 95 46 26 70; www.corte-tourisme.com). Provides bus and train schedules and a French-English brochure. Open M-F 9am-noon and 2-5pm. Call ahead; hours are subject to change.

Bank: Societé General, rue Paoli (☎04 95 46 00 81). Open M-F 8:10am-noon and 1:50-4:50pm. There is also an **ATM** on allée du 9 Septembre between the Casino supermarket and Hotel-Residence Porette.

Youth Center: Bureau Information Jeunesse de Corte, rampe Ste-Croix (☎04 95 46 80 35; www.a-rinascita.com). Info on housing and job listings. Open M-Th 8:30am-noon and 1-6pm, F 8:30am-noon and 1:30-5pm.

Laundromat: Speed Laverie, allée du 9 Septembre (☎06 82 56 08 31), in the shopping plaza behind Mr. Bricolage. Wash €5, dry €2. Open daily 8am-9pm.

Police: Southeast of town on N2000 (☎04 95 46 04 81).

Hospital: Allée du 9 Septembre (☎04 95 45 05 00).

Internet Access: Grand Café du Cours, 22 cours Paoli (☎04 95 46 00 33). €0.15 per min., €7 per hr.; free Wi-Fi with a purchase. Open daily 7am-2am. **Le Bar Video-Games,** av. de Président Pierucci (☎04 95 47 32 86). €2.50 per 30min., €4 per hr. Open M-Sa 8am-2am. Free Wi-Fi with a purchase in several cafes, including **Café de France,** pl. Padoue (☎04 95 46 20 49). Open daily 6am-2am.

Post Office: Av. du Baron Mariani (☎04 95 46 81 20). Open M-F 8am-12:30pm and 1:30-5pm, Sa 8am-noon. **Postal Code:** 20250.

ACCOMMODATIONS AND CAMPING

Hôtel-Residence Porette (H-R), 6 allée du 9 Septembre (☎04 95 45 11 11; www.hotel-hr.com). Head left and uphill from the train station. At the roundabout, take a right; the hotel is across from the stadium. Rooms overlooking the garden are generally larger, but expect to pay €10 extra in summer. Breakfast buffet €5. Laundry. Sauna (€4), weight room, and restaurant. Reception 24hr. Reservations recommended. Singles €25-29, with bath €42; doubles €30-32/42; triples and quads €65. Cash only. ❷

Hôtel de la Paix, av. du Général de Gaulle (☎04 95 46 06 72), past Hôtel de la Poste. Pleasant rooms range from narrow to enormous. Breakfast €6. May-Sept. singles and doubles €53; triples €66. Oct. and Apr. singles €38; doubles €53; triples €66. Nov.-Mar. singles €38; doubles €45; triples €57. €10-15 more for TV and bath. Cash only. ❹

Camping U Sognu, on D623 (☎04 95 46 09 07). A 15min. walk from pl. Paoli. Follow rue du Professeur Santiaggi until it ends, then turn left and cross the bridge on your right. At the fork, take a right and follow signs. From the train station, turn left and take a right at the roundabout onto av. du 9 Septembre; walk for 10min. and turn left onto D623 after the 1st bridge. Gracious owners and views of the citadel keep campers happy at this converted farm, which offers homemade wood-fired pizzas (€7) and a lively snack bar. Nab a spot on the tree-lined terraces above for the shade. Closed to cars after 11pm. Reception 8am-noon and 4-8pm. Open from late Mar. to mid-Oct. €6.50 per person; €2.50 per tent; €2.50 per car. Electricity €3. Cash only. ❶

Camping Restonica (☎04 95 46 11 59; vero.camp@worldonline.fr). 15min. from the *centre-ville.* From the train station follow, directions to U Sognu (above) but turn left before the bridge. Tents cluster around a small, peaceful, tree-lined stream perfect for wading. Breakfast €6. Laundry €8. Reception daily 9am-10pm. Open from mid-Apr. to Sept. €6.60 per person; €4.60 per tent; €3.60 per car. Electricity €3.80. Cash only. ❶

FOOD

Inexpensive cafes and *brasseries* center on **place Paoli** and along the adjoining **cours Paoli.** For a selection of cheap local cuisine, try **rue Scoliscia** and the surrounding streets. Most restaurants in Corte offer *menus* for €14-18. **SPAR** supermarket, 5 av. Xavier Luciani, is in the town center. (☎04 95 45 08 59. Open July-Aug. M-Sa 7:30am-8:30pm, Su 8:30am-noon; Sept.-June M-Sa 8:30am-noon and 3-8pm, Su 8:30am-noon. MC/V.) The mammoth **Casino** supermarket—a budget traveler's dream—is uphill from the train station on N193. (☎04 95 45 22 45. Open July-Aug. M-Sa 8:30am-8pm; Sept.-June M-F 8:30am-12:30pm and 3-7:30pm, Sa 8:30am-7:30pm. AmEx/MC/V.)

U Museu, rampe Ribanelle (☎04 95 61 08 36), off pl. d'Armes, at the foot of the citadel. Personable staff and charismatic owner serve outstanding regional cuisine to locals and tourists. *Civet de sanglier* (wild-boar stew) will please carnivores, while vegetarians will appreciate the variety of salads (€8-12). Try the *banane flambée* or chestnut cake (both €5.50). Pizza €7.50-9. Pasta €8-13. Meat *plats* €14-20. *Menus* €13-17. Open from early Apr. to late Oct. daily noon-2:30pm and 7pm-2am. MC/V. ❸

A Scudella, 2 pl. Paoli (☎04 95 46 25 31). This restaurant's outdoor views are pleasant, but the best are inside, where guests watch impeccably clad chefs prepare delectable *plats* (€9.20). *Menus* €10-20. Open M-Sa 9am-3pm and 6pm-midnight. MC/V. ❷

U Passa Tempu, rampe Ste-Croix (☎04 95 46 18 73), off cours Paoli. The inviting, speedy staff serves dishes including *brocciu* (local Corsican cheese) for €11-13 in a comfortable, rustic setting. *Omelettes* and savory *crêpes* €2.50-6.50. Meat *plats* €13-18. *Menus* €11-17. Open daily 11:30am-3pm and 7-11pm. AmEx/MC/V. ❷

◎ SIGHTS

VIELLE VILLE. Corte's *vieille ville*—with steep streets and a stone citadel that peers over the valleys below—has long been a bastion of Corsican patriotism. The route to the town center honors two men who led the Corsican national movement: **Jean Pierre Gaffory** wrested control from French hands in 1745 and governed until his 1753 assassination, and the city's best-loved son—**Pascal Paoli**—took control and proclaimed Corte Corsica's capital in 1755. He instituted a constitution and built the university, which now enrolls over 4000 students. In a simple home across from pl. Gaffory, a plaque honors the apartment where **Charles Bonaparte,** Napoleon's father, lived in the 1760s as a student.

MUSÉE DE LA CORSE. Inside the citadel's walls at the top of rue Scoliscia, this museum transforms a 19th-century military hospital into a delightful exhibition space with a collection of Corsica's ethnographic history. Traditional *brocciu* cheese strainers and hand looms, rulebooks and hooded cloaks from religious brotherhoods, and vintage advertisements for Cap Corse Mattei—the island's best-known *apéritif*—reveal facets of Corsican life and culture from the island's many regions and time periods. Exhibits are in Corse and French; consider the 1hr. audio tour, available in several languages (€1.50). Admission includes a visit to Corsica's only inland **citadel,** constructed in 1419. Visitors can explore the pitch-black **dungeon,** thoughtfully outfitted with a stone mattress and pillow, where Corsican patriots were imprisoned during the Italian occupation of WWII. (☎04 95 45 25 45. Museum open July-Sept. daily 10am-8pm; Oct. and Apr.-June daily 10am-6pm; Jan.-Mar. Tu-Sa 10am-5pm. Citadel closes 1hr. earlier than museum. €5.30, students €3.80, under 10 free, seniors €3.80. MC/V.)

OTHER SIGHTS. From pl. Paoli, walk uphill and turn left at the **Église de l'Annonciation** to find the oldest portion of the city walls and a spectacular panorama from the **Belvedere**—a windswept lookout that affords remarkable views of the citadel, winding rivers, and tree-covered valleys below. For those who miss the superior views from the citadel, this is an almost-as-good substitute. Corte's surroundings offer **hiking** (see **Daytrips** below or call tourist office for

maps and information; call ☎08 92 68 32 50 for weather) and **horseback riding.**
Try the **Ferme Equestre Albadu,** 1.5km from town on N193 toward Ajaccio. *(☎04 95
46 24 55. €20 per 1hr., €24 per 2hr., €35 per 3hr., €40 per ½-day, €65 per day; includes picnic.
Reservations required at least 1 day ahead. Cash only.)*

◼ DAYTRIPS FROM CORTE

GORGES DE LA RESTONICA

*The road following the Restonica River from Corte into the gorges is pleasant, but hikers will not
regret renting a car or scooter to avoid the 15km uphill walk to the base, at parking Grotelle
(€5 for cars and €2 for scooters or motorbikes June-Sept.). Be cautious when walking along
the narrow road to parking Grotelle, as there is usually no shoulder and it can be very difficult
for drivers to see around the many twists and turns of the mountain road. Some choose to
hitchhike, but not every car will stop. For safety reasons, Let's Go does not recommend this
option. In July and Aug., a navette (shuttle) whisks hikers up from the Parc Naturel Régional's
info office, down rue du Professeur Santiaggi at the back of pl. Paoli and then right on D623
for 2km; hikers should follow the same route. Call ☎04 95 46 02 12 for detailed schedules.
July-Aug. daily 8am-1:30pm, return 2:30-5pm. €4, under 18 €2.*

Southwest of Corte, tiny D623 stretches 15km through the Gorges de la Restonica (gohrj duh lah rest-ohn-ee-kah), a high-altitude canyon fed by glacial
lakes. Both the canyon and its surrounding lakes provide fantastic hikes into
some of Corsica's most rugged wilderness. The brave-hearted can even take a
dip in the gorge's icy water. Air temperatures at these high elevations can drop
well below freezing even when it's 25°C (77°F) in town; between October and
May, hikers should bring warm layers. The area attracts a lot of traffic; it's best
to start before 8am to avoid the crowds and, in summer, the extreme heat.

Those with time for only one hike should tour the glacial lakes at the top of
the gorge, where hikers of all skill levels enjoy magnificent scenery. From the
Grotelle parking lot, a trail marked in yellow crosses the river and ascends to
the "most visited lake in Corsica," **Lac de Melo** (1hr.). This snow-fed beauty lies
at 1711m and is surrounded by mountains, including Corsica's highest, **Mont
Cinto** (2710m). The trail is designated *facile* (easy), but the climb is steep, rocky,
and slippery when wet; some parts of the trail require scrambling up ladders
or chains. From Melo, the trail continues on the right, still marked in yellow, to
an even more impressive lake, **Lac de Capitellu** (1930m, 45min.). Another 30min.
up, the trail meets the heavily trafficked red-and-white-marked **GR20**, Corsica's
most famous and demanding hike. Hikers will find that the steep climb to this
point is worth it for the breathtaking view of the valley. For a full-day adventure, well-equipped trekkers can follow the GR20 to the left until it intersects
with a trail leading to the **Refuge de Petra Piana,** where hikers can spend the night
(reservations recommended) or continue on to the **Lac de Rotondo** (4hr.). Less
trodden but equally spectacular is the hike to **Lac de l'Oriente.** In the summer,
take the *navette* (shuttle bus) to **Pont de Tragone** and follow the marked trail,
which, after passing shepherds' houses, arrives at the lake (3hr.).

A less crowded day hike goes to **Lac de Scapuccioli,** the highest lake in Corsica (2338m), which remains partly frozen until mid-June. From the Grotelle
parking lot, begin as if doing the Lac de Capitellu hike, but after crossing the
river follow cairns and climb steeply in the direction of the waterfall. Continue
with the brook on your right to find the best way up to the **Lac de Cavacciole**
(2015m). Vegetation slowly disappears as you continue to Lac de Scapuccioli
(3hr.), which has a perfect lookout onto the glacial lakes below. For more
information on Restonica, consult the French-language hiking guide *Tavig-
nano-Restonica* (€13), available in tourist offices.

CORSICA

GORGES DU TAVIGNANO

Take a right onto rue Colonel Feracci off rue Scoliscia just after pl. Gaffory. From rue Feracci, take the 1st left onto rue St-Joseph. When the road forks, go straight onto chemin de Baliri and follow the signs toward the gorges or follow allée du 9 Septembre away from the train station, cross a bridge, and make a left at the fork in the road at the entrance to the haute-ville. The trail is marked in orange (1hr.).

Less rugged and more easily accessible by foot than Restonica—though equally demanding at certain points—the Tavignano (tahv-een-yahnn-oh) gorges are filled with waterfalls, natural pools, and picturesque hiking trails. With no road access, they are likely to be less crowded than their better-known counterpart. The first 2½hr. of hiking along the Tavignano River lead to the **Passerelle du Russullnu** (902m), a wood bridge surrounded by natural swimming pools and flat, picnic-friendly rocks. Bring sunscreen and wear a hat; there is little shade. Bug repellent is also a good idea, as the valley's many small pools are perfect breeding grounds for pests. Furthermore, if the orange markers seem to disappear at any point on this trail, retracing your steps might be in order; there are several smaller trails that run parallel—though closer to the river—that lead to dead ends. Another 3hr. along the same trail lead to the **Refuge de la Sega** (1166m), where hikers can spend the night. (☎04 95 46 07 90 or 06 10 71 77 26. Reservations strongly recommended.) On the left, where the road diverges, are ancient *bergeries* (sheep pens) and huts where transient shepherds used to stay on their way to Plateau d'Alzo; those based in Corte will need to turn back at this point, as further hiking will necessitate an overnight stay.

FORÊT DE VIZZAVONA

Vizzavona is easily reached via a magnificent train ride (1hr., 4 per day, €5.30). The path from Corte leisurely winds along picturesque stone tunnels and narrow bridges. When planning a daytrip to Vizzavona, note that the train station closes for lunch from around noon to 2 or 3pm, when afternoon trains begin arriving.

Rugged mountains and miles of pine forest surround tiny Vizzavona (veez-ah-vohn-ah), leaving its 50 inhabitants with plenty of room to stretch their legs. Several hiking trails of varying difficulty converge at the town, which make it an excellent base for both serious excursions and ambling daytrips. Several small restaurants and *brasseries* by the train station, including one attached to the station itself, are great places to grab lunch or shelter in the rare instance of bad weather. After reaching Vizzavona, go behind the train station, where a billboard lists hiking routes. The easiest, **Cascade des Anglais,** is a 45min. ramble through the forest that ends at a series of plunging waterfalls. The trail is broad and well marked. Unfortunately, its accessibility draws hordes of hikers in summer. The large, flat rocks and shaded coves make ideal picnic spots, and the lagoons offer opportunities for a dip in the water. Those looking for a more solitary site should continue past the base of the falls.

Hard-core hikers might want to take on the **Monte d'Oro,** an unrelenting 2389m summit whose waters feed the streams and rivers of the entire region. From the top, which is covered in snow even in June, hikers can see all the way to Sardinia on a clear day. The base of the trail, marked by cairns and orange circles, sits right in town, at the path leading to Cascade des Anglais. After the footbridge, follow the red-and-white marks of the GR20 until you reach a second footbridge (1hr.). Just before reaching the crest, leave the GR20 and head right toward the **Col du Porc** (Pork Pass); from here, the crest leading to the summit is clear (4hr.). The descent, marked by cairns and yellow paint, leads back to the tall pines of the superb Vizzavona forest and ends at the Vizzavona train station. Monte d'Oro is not for casual hikers; those who attempt a summit bid should be experienced and well equipped, as there is no water along most of the route. Start early (the entire loop takes about 9hr.) and check with the regional park office for weather conditions and detailed maps.

BASTIA
☎ 04 95

Bastia (bah-styuh; pop. 40,000), Corsica's second largest city, is a well-trodden gateway to both the mainland and the island's more picturesque vacation spots. A crumbling *vieille ville* and giant ferry port mean that most visitors overlook this city, but Baroque churches, a magnificent citadel, and war monuments provide plenty of reasons to visit the city. Although Corsicans from more picturesque cities like Ajaccio—Bastia's longtime rival—often criticize the city because it lacks the Mediterranean charm that keeps them in business, it is precisely this difference that makes the city refreshing after visiting one palm-studded *centre-ville* after another. With large public squares and fountains, shaded streets, and plenty of playgrounds, Bastia feels refreshingly lived-in and authentic. The city is also the perfect base for the must-see Cap Corse.

▛ TRANSPORTATION

Flights: Bastia-Poretta (BIA; ☎04 95 54 54 54), 23km from the *centre-ville*. An airport bus (☎04 95 31 06 65), scheduled to coincide with departing flights, leaves from the *préfecture* across from the train station and stops in front of the tourist office (30min., €8). Purchase tickets on board. **Air France** (☎36 54) flies to **Marseille** (1hr., 3-5 per day), **Nice** (50min., 3-4 per day), and **Paris** (1½hr., 6 per day).

Trains: Pl. de la Gare (☎04 95 32 80 61), to the left of the roundabout at the top of av. Maréchal Sébastiani. Open July-Aug. daily 6am-9:45pm; Sept.-June M-Sa 6:10am-8:45pm, Su 6:30am-8:45pm. To **Ajaccio** (3hr., 3-5 per day, €24) via **Corte, Calvi** (3hr., 2 per day, €19) via **Ponte-Leccia** and a bus to **Île Rousse** (2hr., 4 per day, €17), and **Corte** (45min., 5 per day, €12). Train service is less frequent Oct.-Mar.; check with the tourist office for up-to-date schedules.

Buses: Eurocorse, route du Nouveau Port (☎04 95 21 06 31), runs to **Ajaccio** (3hr., M-Sa 2 per day, €21). Autocars Cortenais (☎04 95 46 02 12), go to **Corte** (1hr.; M, W, F 1 per day; €11). Buy tickets on board. Ask the tourist office for a bus schedule.

Ferries: Quai de Fango, next to pl. St-Nicolas; turn left from av. Maréchal Sébastiani, past pl. St-Nicolas. SNCM (☎04 95 54 66 90; fax 54 66 44), by quai de Fango, sails to **Marseille**. Corsica Ferries, 5 bis rue du Chanoine Leschi (☎04 95 32 95 95), chugs to **Nice, Toulon,** as well as **Livorno** and **Savona, ITA.** Moby Lines, 4 rue Commandant Luce de Casabianca (☎04 95 34 84 94; www.moby-colonna-corse.com), serves **Genoa** and **Livorno, ITA.** For details on ferry connections to mainland France, see p. 760.

Taxis: ☎04 95 32 24 24, 34 07 00, or 32 70 70. €35 to airport. 24hr.

Car Rental: ADA, 35 rue César Campinchi (☎04 95 31 48 95; www.ada-encorse.com), with branch at the airport. 21+. Open M-F 8am-noon and 2-6:30pm, Sa 8am-noon. AmEx/MC/V. **Avis, Budget, Europcar,** and **Hertz** share the same locations.

Bike Rental: Objectif Nature, rue Notre Dame de Lourdes (☎04 95 32 54 34; www.objectif-nature-corse.com), 1 block beyond the tourist office. Offers excursions and rents bikes. Mountain and city bikes €12 per ½-day, €19 per day, €40 per 3 days. Canyoning €40-50. Paragliding €60. Open M-Sa 9am-noon and 2-7pm. MC/V.

Scooter Rental: Toga Location Nautique, port de Plaisance de Toga (☎04 95 34 14 14; www.plaisance-location.com), on the right as you enter the port complex. Scooters €65 per day, €300 per week; €1220 deposit. Open M-Sa 8am-noon and 2-6:30pm. MC/V.

Bastia

🏠🏕 **ACCOMMODATIONS**

Camping San Damiano, **11**
Camping Les Orangers, **4**
Hôtel Posta Vecchia, **6**
Hôtel Univers, **3**

🍴 **FOOD**

Café Albert 1er, **5**
Chez Vincent, **12**
A Mandria, **8**
Le Pub Assunta, **9**
U Tianu, **10**

⭐ **NIGHTLIFE**

O'Connor's, **7**
Pub la Pinta, **1**
Maracana, **2**

🔋 ORIENTATION AND PRACTICAL INFORMATION

Place Saint-Nicolas sits at the center of the action, dividing the **vieux port,** citadel, and *vieille ville* to the south from the new town to the north. Bastia's main thoroughfare, **boulevard du Général de Gaulle,** runs along the inland length of the place. Just parallel are two other main arteries, **boulevard Paoli** and **rue César Campinchi.** Facing the mountains, the *vieux port* and citadel are to the left, and the ferry docks are to the right. The train station is toward the mountains from the tourist office, up av. Maréchal Sébastiani and left on rue Paul. The main bus stop is just behind the tourist office, toward the new port. When waiting for a bus, be sure to keep one eye on the road in front of the tourist office; some buses stop across the street if the regular stop is crowded.

Tourist Office: Pl. St-Nicolas (☎04 95 54 20 40; www.bastia-tourisme.com), near the ferries. Has bus schedules and maps of the city, Corsica, and Cap Corse. Free accommodations service. Open daily July-Aug. 8am-8pm; Sept.-June 8:30am-noon and 2-6pm.

Currency Exchange: Société Générale, pl. St-Nicolas (☎04 95 55 19 00).

Youth Center: Centre Regional Information Jeunesse (CRIJ), 9 rue César Campinchi (☎04 95 32 12 13; www.crij-corse.com). Info on health, housing, and employment. Free Internet access for research only (40min. limit). Open M-F 8am-noon and 2-6pm.

Laundromat: Lavoir du Port, 25 rue Commandant Luce de Casabianca (☎04 95 32 25 51), toward the new port from the tourist office, past the Esso station. Wash €6-9, dry €1 per 10min. Detergent €0.40. Open daily 7am-9pm.

Police: Rue Commandant Luce de Casabianca (☎04 95 55 22 22).

Hospital: Route Impériale (☎04 95 59 11 11). The #1 bus goes here from morning to early evening, leaving from in front of the tourist office. Ask at tourist office for times.

Internet Access: Free for research at the **CRIJ** (see **Youth Center**). **Le Cyber,** 6 rue des Jardins (☎04 95 34 30 34), behind the *vieux port.* 12 computers. Open M-F 8am-noon and 2-6pm. **Cyber,** 5 av. Maréchal Sébastiani, down the street from Hôtel Univers. Open daily 9am-2am. **Café Albert 1er,** 11 bd. du Général de Gaulle (☎04 95 31 76 10), on pl. St-Nicolas. Open daily noon-2am. All are €1.50 per 30min.

Post Office: 2 av. Maréchal Sébastiani (☎04 95 32 80 78), at the intersection of bd. du Général Graziani. Open M-F 8am-7pm, Sa 8am-noon. **Postal Code:** 20200.

ACCOMMODATIONS AND CAMPING

Most hotels in Bastia fall outside budget travelers' range. Low season brings lower prices and plenty of vacancies, but hotels fill up quickly come June and stay full as late as mid-October. Camping is a viable option, although all sites are too far from town to walk. Beachgoers can hop off the train a few stops before Bastia or join hikers on local buses (until 7pm) heading into Cap Corse.

Hôtel Posta Vecchia, 8 rue Posta Vecchia (☎04 95 32 32 38; www.hotel-postavecchia. com), just off the quai des Martyrs. Colorful, modern, and centrally located hotel with a few *petites chambres* that remain reasonably priced during the high season—reserve ahead. Each room has private bath, phone, and—except for the *petites chambres*—A/C and TV. Breakfast in bed €6.50. July-Sept. singles and doubles €50-80; triples €90; quads €100. Oct. and Apr.-June singles and doubles €40-63; triples €73; quads €83. Jan.-Mar. singles and doubles €40-55; triples €65; quads €75; weekends often significantly less. Rooms with sea view €10 more. AmEx/MC/V. ❹

Hôtel Univers, 3 av. Maréchal Sébastiani (☎04 95 31 03 38; www.hotelunivers.org), near the train station. Spotless yellow-and-blue rooms. All have soundproof windows, bathrooms, A/C, phones, and TVs. Breakfast €6. Some rooms have Wi-Fi. Reception 24hr. Aug.-Sept. singles €60; doubles €70; triples €99. Jan.-July singles €50; doubles €60; triples €75. Extra bed €10. AmEx/MC/V. ❹

Camping Les Orangers (☎04 95 33 24 09), in Licciola-Miomo. Take bus #4 (15min., €1.30) from the tourist office. Peaceful site with clean showers and bathrooms. Can only accommodate 25 tents and 6 RVs for 4-6 people, so arrive as early as possible. Restaurant and snack bar. Open from May to mid-Oct. Reception 8am-10pm. €5 per person; €3 per tent; €2.60 per car. Electricity €4. Cash only. ❶

Camping San Damiano, Lido de la Marana (☎04 95 33 68 02; www.campingsandamiano.com). Take a bus to La Marana from the *gare routière* (€1.30, 15min.); buses are infrequent—check the tourist office's schedule. Camp under pine trees literally 1 step from the beach. 250 sites. Snack bar and small grocery store. Impeccable showers and bathrooms. Check-out noon. Open Mar.-Oct. €5-7.50 per person; €5-7 per tent; €5-7 per car. Electricity €3.40. Bungalow rental €315-630 per week. Cash only. ❶

◘ FOOD

Bastia's relatively low number of tourists make it much less gastronomically overwhelming than more crowded Corsican cities, but affordable and quality dining options still exist. The city's nonstop sunshine, pleasant squares, and panoramic viewpoints mean plenty of dining alfresco. Nearly every cafe on crowded **place Saint-Nicolas** sets up tables around the perimeter. For better food and a view to match, try restaurants near the citadel or along the *vieux port*. The **quai des Martyrs de la Libération's** broad terraces offer a subdued but touristy atmosphere; come before sunset to enjoy an uninterrupted view of the sweeping horizon. Early birds hit the market on **place de l'Hôtel de Ville,** full of fresh produce, local meats and cheeses, and homemade tarts and pastries. (Open Sa-Su 8:15am-12:30pm.) There's a **SPAR** supermarket at 14 rue César Campinchi. (☎04 95 32 32 40. Open M-Sa 8am-12:30pm and 4-8pm, Su 8am-noon. MC/V.) For traditional Corsican delicacies, stop by **U Paese,** 4 rue Napoléon. This pungent shop—the oldest of its kind in Bastia—offers the the island's best traditional fare, including *brocciu* (sheep's cheese), *canistrelli* (crumbly cookies), and *gâteaux de châtaignes* (chestnut cake). Ask the owner to vacuum-pack your *lonzu* (sausage, €32 per kg) so the aroma doesn't follow you home. (☎04 95 32 33 18; www.u-paese.com. Open M-Sa 9am-noon and 3-7pm. MC/V.)

▨ **U Tianu,** 4 rue Monseigneur Rigo (☎04 95 31 36 67). Gracious staff has served a local clientele for 25 years in this unpretentious, hidden-away restaurant. Presented in a room plastered with separatist posters and portraits of revolutionaries like Che Guevera, mouthwatering Corsican specialties are well worth the €23 *menu* (with *apéritif, entrée, plat,* cheese, dessert, coffee, and *digestif).* Plate of local *charcuterie* and cheese on request (prices vary). Open Jan.-July and Sept.-Dec. M-Sa 7pm-midnight. Cash only. ❹

▨ **Chez Vincent,** 12 rue St-Michel (☎04 95 31 62 50). Enormous pizzas (€7-10) only taste better with a view of the *vieux port* on a shaded terrace within the citadel. Share the popular specialty plate (€21). Reserve ahead to eat outside. Traditional *plats* €8-16. Desserts €5.50-7. Open M-F noon-2pm and 7-11pm, Sa 6-11pm. MC/V. ❸

Le Pub Assunta, 4 rue Fontaine-Neuve (☎04 95 34 11 40). Claims to be a former secret meeting place of Napoleon III and Benedetti Vincent. The well-hidden, leafy courtyard must have been a prime spot for discussing military strategies; luckily, your only tough move is deciding which tasty burger to choose. Options include the mouthwatering double-decker royal cheese (€5.50-10). Pizzas €6-8. Pasta €7-10. Corsican *plat* €15. Open M-Sa 10am-2am, Su 7pm-2am. MC/V. ❷

A Mandria, 4 pl. du Marché (☎04 95 35 17 11). Offers cheap Corsican specialties in an intimate setting. Old black-and-white pictures decorate the stone-and-wood interior, while busy pl. du Marché and Église St-Jean-Baptiste's towers frame the view. Vegetarians can enjoy *cannelloni* with *brocciu* (€12). Homemade lasagna €17. Open M-Sa 11am-1pm and 7pm-midnight. Closing time may vary. AmEx/MC/V. ❸

Café Albert 1er, 11 bd. du Général de Gaulle (☎04 95 31 76 10), on pl. St-Nicolas. Try creative salads or make your own out of 31 ingredients (€7-14). Exhaustive ice-cream selection with profiteroles (€4.90). Open from mid-May to Sept. daily 8am-11pm. ❷

◎ ◿ SIGHTS AND BEACHES

Bastia does not have beaches; they begin 3km to the north and 1km to the south. The closest ones can get crowded, so head north to **Miomo** or farther on to the beautiful sands of the **Cap Corse** for seclusion. Bus #4 leaves every 30min. from pl. St-Nicolas (6:30am-7pm) and travels up to the Cap's small towns and beaches. The closest sandy beach lies between **Erbalunga** (€2.30) and **Sisco** (€2.40); bus #4 heads there and continues to **Pietracorba** (30min., 9 per day, €2.70), which also has a sandy stretch. **Thalassa Location,** 2 rue St-Jean, just behind the *vieux port,* rents **snorkeling** gear. (☎04 95 31 08 77; http://perso. wanadoo.fr/thalassashop. Fins, mask, and snorkel €14 per day. Open Mar.-Oct. M-Sa 9am-noon and 2-7pm; Nov.-Feb. M-Sa 2-7pm. AmEx/MC/V.) Thalassa's **Base Nautique,** just past port Toga on the route du Cap Corse, offers scuba excursions, including night dives. (☎04 95 31 78 90; thalassa.immersion@ free.fr. €36 per hr.; equipment included. Certification courses €130-400. AmEx/ MC/V.) The much-anticipated **Bastia Museum,** inside the citadel, opens in 2009; call or stop by the tourist office for details.

MIND THE MEDUSAS. Bays on Cap Corse can be filled with jellyfish for an entire week but be *méduse*-free the next. If others are out of the water and crowded onto the shore, consider doing the same. Ask park employees at the **Sentier des Douaniers** whether the waters are clear; they can also help if you get stung.

VIEILLE VILLE. A walk through Bastia's *vieille ville* hints at the town's former glory as the crown jewel of Genoese-ruled Corsica. Many of the buildings in this part of the city are in need of repair, but the imposing 1380 **citadel,** also called Terra Nova, has remained intact. Its ramparts reach down the hill and toward the *vieux port,* dwarfing adjacent shops. Within the walls is a public square, **place du Donjon,** where merchants accused of swindling were once tied to a stone *cul nul* (buck-naked) to be laughed at all day. In **place Saint-Nicolas,** the central monument showcases Corsica's independent streak; a bronze widow who has lost two of her children in the war of independence offers up her third to the cause, saying "he belongs to the country."

ORATOIRE DE L'IMACULÉE CONCEPTION. This 18th-century oratory's entrance is paved with stones in the shape of a large sun. The lavish interior, with glass chandeliers and dark-wood walls and pews, is truly striking. During Corsica's brief 1794-96 stint as an Anglo-Corsican kingdom, the little Italian organ would lead "God Save the King," sung by members of parliament before debates in the church. *(Rue Napoléon, toward the citadel from pl. St-Nicolas. Open daily 8am-7pm.)*

ÉGLISE SAINT-JEAN-BAPTISTE. The lofty Baroque interior of the largest church in all of Corsica has gilded domes, a large organ, *trompe-l'oeil* ceilings, and a relief of a rarely represented scene: the circumcision of the infant Jesus. The windows reveal a more recent episode in the island's history: all except for three stained-glass pieces at the back of the church were destroyed during WWII when members of the resistance blew up an Italian munitions cache 5km away. *(Pl. de l'Hôtel de Ville, just behind the vieux port.)*

ECO-MUSÉE. If the church's soaring ceiling makes you feel tiny, this eccentric museum will leave you feeling positively gargantuan. An extraordinarily detailed miniature replica of a traditional mountaintop scene, it features houses, stables, a bakery, a mill, a flowing river, and tiny people who actually move and do work. Each structure is painstakingly precise, right down to the microscopic dishes, functional church bells, and authentic vegetation, which creator René Mattei changes every two weeks. The entire setup took 20 years to complete and now weighs over 10 tons. *(In the citadel's old powder magazine, in the corner opposite the vieux port. ☎06 10 26 82 08; www.eco-musee.com. Open Apr.-Oct. M-Sa 9am-noon and 2-6pm. €3.50, students €3, ages 8-12 €2.50, under 8 free.)*

NIGHTLIFE

Though a few clubs spice up the city's nightlife between September and June, Bastians spend their nights either in *avant-boîtes* (bars and lounges) or in Calvi. In town, the local youth head to the **port Toga**, a 15min. walk from pl. St-Nicolas along the water, away from the *vieux port* and alongside speeding cars. At the roundabout, go right toward the water and under the arches. Other nightlife options are in the faraway **La Marana** area, home to beachside bars and open-air dance clubs. Unfortunately, public transportation doesn't go there at night, and a taxi ride will cost at least €25.

Maracana, port Toga (☎04 95 31 31 77). A lounge with live DJs or bands, thumping club music, and a tiki bar is Bastia's quickest fix for bored party-seekers. Beer €3-5. Mixed drinks €7.50. Open daily 6pm-2am. AmEx/MC/V.

Pub La Pinta, port Toga (☎04 95 34 23 00). Offers a more relaxed and traditional port-side pub atmosphere, with karaoke music and wood paneling like that of a ship. Beer €2.50-5. Mixed drinks €7.50-9. Open daily 6pm-2am. MC/V.

O'Connor's, 1 rue St-Erasme (☎04 95 32 04 97), in the *vieille ville*. Sociable staff at this lively Irish pub offers plenty of beer to a young crowd. Try the 2.5L beer—"the Giraffe"—for €27. Worth checking out year-round, but cold winter nights bring larger crowds looking to warm up. Pints €6.50. Live music or DJs W-Sa. Open W-Sa 7pm-2am. V.

CAP CORSE

Stretching north from Bastia, the Cap Corse (cap cohrss) peninsula is Corsica's most stunning frontier. A perilous, winding road connects the Cap's numerous former fishing villages and marinas and offers breathtaking views of the rugged coastline. Endangered species flourish in the windswept valleys and atop dizzying cliffs, while peregrine falcons and cormorants soar above the coastal landscape. With its vast natural reserve, the Cap is a hiker's dream. Every other turn reveals a Genoese tower, a hilltop chapel, or an Italian tourist sunbathing in his birthday suit. Unfortunately, there are few budget hotels. Camping is a better option; a handful of sites dot the Cap. Bastia is a good base for those motorists, but hikers going past Pietracorbara will have to stay on the peninsula itself, as buses run infrequently and at times that aren't conducive to daytripping. When returning from the windswept shores, plop down in a cafe and try the region's namesake *apéritif*, the Cap Corse, which is like Campari.

 HOLD ONTO YOUR CAP. Cap Corse and the Balagne region are the windiest areas of Corsica. Check the weather forecast when planning to venture out on the water. Wind also makes forest fires more likely; be cautious when camping and call ☎18 or 112 if you see a fire.

Though expensive, the best way to visit the Cap is to drive around the peninsula. Though you can complete the trip in 3hr. without stopping, plan on taking a full day. One look at the captivating northern coastline and you'll be ready to hop out and explore. There are countless places to pull over, including many secluded swimming spots. Consider renting a car in Bastia (p. 785) or Calvi (p. 773), but be cautious: the madcap coastal highway is made even more treacherous by speed-loving local bus drivers.

THE CORSE LESS TRAVELED. In high season, you can see the Cap by bus tour. Up-to-date schedules are available at the tourist office. The eastern side of Cap Corse—including St-Florent and Sisco—is also served by public bus #4 from pl. St-Nicolas in Bastia (see **Bastia: Sights and Beaches**, p. 788). Less frequently, a bus goes all the way to Macinaggio (☎04 95 31 06 65; 50min.; M-F 2 per day, Sa 1 per day; €6.40). When catching a bus back to Bastia, find the stop or wave your arms wildly to hail one—bus drivers are notorious for ignoring hopeful would-be passengers. Also, keep in mind that most buses serve only coastal towns; to explore the inland villages, you'll have to hike. Driving is easiest during the week, when traffic on D80 thins out. To start on the west side in St-Florent, take bd. Paoli in Bastia, then bd. Auguste Gaudin, past the citadel onto N193. For the east-to-west route, follow signs for the Cap on the coastal boulevard north from pl. St-Nicolas.

SAINT-FLORENT ☎04 95

Across from Bastia at the base of Cap Corse, the resort town of St-Florent (sehn flohr-ahn; pop. 1500) draws a crowd of sun-seekers to its wide beaches—arguably the region's best—and sizable pleasure-boat port. Below the expansive Golfe de St-Florent, the town lies at the intersection of three dramatically different regions: the rugged Cap Corse, the fertile Nebbio, and the unforgiving Desert des Agriates. It is an excellent weekend trip from Bastia; although it is close to the city, bus schedules prevent daytripping.

TRANSPORTATION AND PRACTICAL INFORMATION. Autocars Santini (☎04 95 37 02 98) sends **buses** to Bastia (50min.; M-Sa 6:45am, 2pm; €5) and Île Rousse (1hr.; M-Sa 9am, 4:30pm; €10) from the station below port de Plaisance. Buy tickets on the bus. To get to the **tourist office** from the bus station, walk past pl. des Portes, veer right, and continue uphill; the office is on the left. The staff distributes the St-Florent practical guide, which includes a map. Ask for information about regional festivals, including movie showings in June and July. (☎04 95 37 06 04; fax 35 30 74. Open July-Aug. M-F 8:30am-12:30pm and 2-7pm, Sa 9am-noon and 3-6pm, Su 9am-noon; Sept.-June M-F 9am-12:30pm and 2-6pm, Sa 9am-noon. Hours change weekly.)

ACCOMMODATIONS AND CAMPING. Budget travelers will have to search hard for reasonable accommodations, especially in August. Reserve far in advance. A good bet is the **Hôtel du Centre ❹**, rue du Centre, which has clean, spacious rooms with bold flower-print bedspreads. All rooms have showers and phones, most have TVs, and a few allow glimpses of the sea and port. (☎04 95 37 00 68; fax 37 41 01. Breakfast €5. Reception daily 6am-midnight. June-July singles and doubles €50; triples €65; quads €80. Aug. €10 more. Extra bed €8. MC/V.) By far the cheapest option is camping, and a few sites are located south of town along plage de la Roya. To reach **U Pezzo ❶**, head south on CD 81 from the bus station and cross the pedestrian bridge. Walk down the beach until the sign for the Base Nautique; the campground is across the road on your left (15min.). Eucalyptus trees provide plenty of shade for 145 sites near a popular beach. Amenities include a snack bar, pizzeria, and mini-market. Kids will enjoy the tiny on-site animal farm, which features goats and sheep. (☎/fax 04 95 37 01 65. Showers free. Reception 8-11:30am and 3-6:30pm. Open from Apr. to mid-Oct. €14 per 2 people, tent, and car. Electricity €3.50. Cash only.)

CORSICA

◻ FOOD. Create your own meal at **SPAR** supermarket, near the bus stop. (☎04 95 37 00 56. Open June-Aug. M-Sa 8am-7pm, Su 8am-1pm and 5-7pm; Sept.-May M-Sa 8am-noon and 3:30-7pm, Su 8am-noon. MC/V.) The *quai* along port de Plaisance is home to several very similar restaurants. An exception is **Chez Toinu ❸**, the last restaurant on the pier, which offers large portions for moderate prices. The €15 *menu* includes eggplant parmesan or another *entrée*, a *plat*, a cheese course, and the *dessert du jour*. For a lighter meal, try the *moules Pietra* (€8), mussels made with the popular Corsican beer. (☎04 95 37 05 25. Meat *plats* €12-20. Pizza €6-10. Open daily 11am-11pm. AmEx.)

◪ ⚑ BEACHES AND OUTDOOR ACTIVITIES. St-Florent offers several sunbathing options. The town's two principal beaches meet at the port and host crowds of umbrellas in August. North of the citadel lies **plage de l'Ospedale**, a long, pebbly stretch hidden from traffic by a concrete wall. From town, walk uphill on RN 199 (toward Cap Corse); the beach is 10min. past the post office. Boisterous **plage de la Roya**, south of port de Plaisance, tempts a tan crowd with a sandy crescent framed by distant mountains. Plenty of wind makes the area perfect for windsurfing and sailing. **Base Nautique**, at the southern end of the beach, offers one-stop shopping for watersport enthusiasts. (☎06 12 10 23 27; www.corskayak.com. Windsurfing equipment €14 per hr. Kayaks €12-15 per hr. Surf bikes €10 per hr. Catamarans €50. Lessons for novices €50. Kayak expeditions €45. Open June-Sept. daily 8am-8:30pm; Oct. by appointment only. Cash only.) True beach bliss lies farther south at **plage du Lodo** (Lotu in Corse), a tourist-free slice of paradise accessible only by boat. **Le Popeye** makes the 30min. trip from June through September from port de Plaisance. (☎04 95 37 19 07. Round-trip €14, under 18 €6. Purchase tickets 1hr. before departure. Departures at 8:45, 10, 11:15am, 12:30, 1:45, 3:15pm. Return trips noon-7:30pm. Info desk on the port open daily 8am-7:30pm. Cash only.) From plage du Lodo, a 1hr. hike south leads to the pristine **plage de Saleccia**, an isolated spot that will make sun-worshippers think they've found paradise at last.

SISCO VALLEY
☎04 95

Tourist offices hand out a map that lists 21 itineraries on the Cap; **hike #9,** from Sisco (2hr.), is the best. Take bus #4 from pl. St-Nicolas in Bastia to Sisco (30min., every hr., €2.30) and walk with the water on your right until you see signs for **Camping A Casaïola ❶**. The site is a 15min. walk up the road on the left. The English-speaking staff lets sites and offers advice on Sisco's hiking, equestrian, and watersport activities. A restaurant, clean facilities, and shaded plots are welcome comforts after a day's hike. (☎/fax 04 95 35 20 10. Laundry €3. Reception 8am-8pm. July-Aug. €5.50 per person; €4 per tent; €4 per car. Sept.-Oct. and May-June €5 per person, €3.50 per tent; €3.50 per car. Electricity €2.50. Cash only.) From the campground, **trail #9** continues to the left of the campground entrance. Follow the painted orange rectangles along a sun-dappled route that chases a winding streambed before plunging into an expansive valley of wildflowers. The trail splits often and the orange markers are few and far between. Along the way, you'll pass through dense forest and tiny, almost-forgotten villages, where the mountainous backdrop might to convince you to head for the hills permanently—or at least until the next bus to Bastia arrives. You'll see only a few other hikers, but geckos and butterflies provide company throughout, while horses, sheep, and goats help provide one tranquil pastoral scene after another. The path includes lovely footbridges and, after following a paved country road for a short time, leads to Petrapiana, the junction of several other routes. Take a break at Barriggioni, 300m before Petrapiana, to admire the grandiose elegance of **Église Saint-Martin**. From here, you can take a detour

to the 11th-century **Chapelle Saint-Michel,** sitting precariously on a hilltop promontory; follow the signs uphill to the right of the first church. Though entering
the chapel is not allowed, the panoramic view of the bowl-shaped valley below,
sprinkled with Renaissance bell towers, is worth the 1hr. climb. Note that this
demanding hike requires a good pair of hiking boots and long pants to protect
against thorny undergrowth as well as with sunscreen and bug repellent.

BONIFACIO (BONIFAZIU)   ☎04 95

At Corsica's extreme southern tip, the imposing fortress that is the city of Bonifacio (bohn-ih-fass-ee-o; pop. 3000) looms before miles of turquoise sea and
distant Sardinia. Enormous stone ramparts enclose the rambling *haute-ville*,
which sits atop steep, white limestone cliffs. Below the city, waves crash onto
strange rock formations, making grottoes echo with their roar. Its dramatic
landscape, postcard-worthy white sand beaches, and elegant restaurants make
Bonifacio a must-see, but be prepared for high price tags and tourist crowds.

▮ TRANSPORTATION

Buses: Eurocorse Voyages (Ajaccio ☎04 95 21 06 30). Buses depart from the port
parking lot for **Ajaccio** (3hr., M-Sa 2 per day, €22) via **Sartène** (1hr., €12).

Ferries: SAREMAR (☎04 95 73 00 96) and **Moby** lines (☎04 95 73 00 29; www.moby-
lines.de) run to **Santa Teresa** on Sardinia (1hr., 6-7 per day) from the *gare maritime.*
7 rotations per day beginning at 8:30am; last return boat at 7pm. Offices open daily
7:30-9am, 10:30am-noon, 3-7pm, and 9-10pm. Call the day before to reserve. MC/V.

Taxis: At the port (☎04 95 73 19 08).

Car Rental: Europcar, av. Sylvère Bohn (☎04 95 73 10 99). From €95 per day, €294
per week; credit-card deposit. 21+. Open July-Aug. daily 8am-8pm. AmEx/MC/V.

Scooter and Bike Rental: Funscoots (☎06 11 16 35 12, www.funscoots.com) delivers
around Bonifacio for rentals longer than 1 day. Bikes €15 per day; scooters €30-45 per
day; €900 deposit. Call ahead July-Aug. MC/V. **Scoot Rent,** 3 quai Banda del Ferro
(☎06 25 44 22 82), in the Cantina Grill. €50-60 per day; $1700 deposit. MC/V.

▮ ORIENTATION AND PRACTICAL INFORMATION

Bonifacio is divided by a steep climb from the port to the *haute-ville,* which
begins past the pharmacy on the southern side of the port. The main road goes
to Ajaccio in one direction and to nearby campgrounds and beaches in the
other on its way to Porto-Vecchio. Bonifacio is easy to navigate on foot, but the
steep climb to the *haute-ville* could be problematic for older or handicapped
travelers. There is a train-shaped **tram car** service that makes the difficult trip
to the town center (every 15-20 min. 9am-6pm, €5). The blue train just in front
of the port is hard to miss.

Tourist Office: ☎04 95 73 11 88; www.bonifacio.fr. At the corner of av. de Gaulle and
rue F. Scamaroni in the *haute-ville.* Accommodations bookings and free maps. Open
July-Aug. daily 9am-8pm; Sept. and May-June daily 9am-7pm; Oct.-Apr. M-F 9am-noon
and 2-6pm. Annex, at the port, open daily 9am-noon and 2-6pm.

Tours: Many companies offer tours of the grottoes, Bonifacio's claim to fame. While
such tours often last up to half a day, 1hr tours are also available, which take a similar
route and continue to the **Îles Lavezzi.** Relax and explore the idyllic beaches on this
nature reserve before catching a return boat.

CORSICA

Les Vedettes Thalassa (☎06 86 34 00 49). Grottes-Falaises-Calanques tour every hr. 9:15am-4pm, €17.50. Îles Lavezzi-Cavallo tour 7 departures per day, 5 return boats, last return boat 7pm; €32. Cash only.

Marina Croisières (☎04 95 22 91 57), **Rocca Croisières** (☎04 95 73 13 96), **GINA** (☎04 95 23 24 18), and **Corsaire** (☎04 95 06 23 25 14 60) have similar prices and schedules. A short walk from 1 company's stand to the others is the best way to compare prices.

Currency Exchange: Societé Générale, rue St-Erasme (☎04 95 73 02 49), next to the stairs leading to the *haute-ville*. **ATM.** Open M-F 8:15am-noon and 2-6:50pm.

Laundry: 1 quai Comparetti (☎04 95 73 01 03), at the end of the port near the bus stop. Wash €6.20, dry €0.80 per 10min. Open daily 7am-8pm. Coins only.

Police: Rte. de Santa Manza (☎04 95 73 00 17), just off the port.

Hospital: D58 (☎04 95 73 95 73), just before the SPAR supermarket.

Internet Access: The pleasant **Cybercafé Boni Boom**, on the port. Limited number of computers, so be prepared to wait during high season. €0.12 per min., €3 per 30min., €5 per hr.; min. €1. Wi-Fi same rates. Open daily 8am-2am.

Post Office: Pl. Carrega (☎04 95 73 73 73), uphill from pl. Montepagano in the *haute-ville*. Open M-F 8:30am-12:30pm and 2-4pm, Sa 8:30am-noon. **Postal Code: 20169.**

🏠 🏠 ACCOMMODATIONS AND CAMPING

Finding a room in the summer is virtually impossible, and the few available lodgings charge up to twice their normal prices in July and August. Camping is by far the cheapest option—get ready to rough it.

Hôtel des Étrangers, av. Sylvère Bohn (☎04 95 73 01 09), a 10min. walk from the port. Spotless white rooms with tile floors. Warm staff stores guests' luggage for arrivals before check-in time. Relatively low prices make this the best deal in town. A/C and TV in all but the cheapest rooms. Breakfast €5. Reception 24hr. Reservations recommended July-Aug. Open from early Apr. to early Sept. From mid-July to Sept. singles and doubles €48-70; triples €71-76; quads €78-86. From late May to early July singles and doubles €42-54; triples €59-64; quads €66-74. From Apr. to mid-May singles and doubles €35-45; triples €46-52; quads €54-62. MC/V. ❹

Hôtel Le Royal, pl. Bonaparte (☎04 95 73 00 51; www.hotel-leroyal.com), in the *haute-ville*. Spacious rooms above a pizzeria on a lively square, all with A/C, TV, toilet, and shower or bath. Some have sweeping sea views well worth a few extra euro (ask for *côté mer* rather than *côté ville*). Breakfast €6. Reception 24hr. Reserve at least a month in advance in summer. Aug. singles €95; doubles €100-105. July and Sept. singles €70; doubles €75-80. June singles €55; doubles €62-67. Rest of the year singles €40-52; doubles €47-62. Extra bed €15. AmEx/MC/V. ❺

Camping L'Araguina, av. Sylvère Bohn (☎04 95 73 02 96; www.campingaraguina.fr), at the town entrance. Crowded but shady plots ideally located near the port. Plenty of clean showers and sinks, but toilets consist of stalls with a hole leading to a large tank between 2 foot grips; the smell in the bathroom area in summer months is not always fresh. Snack bar. Non-student ID required. Breakfast €5.50. Laundry €5. Limited parking. Reception 8am-8pm. Open from mid-March to mid-Oct. €5.85 per person. July-Oct. €2.40 per tent; €2.40 per car. Mar.-June €2.10 per tent; €2.40 per car. Cash only. ❶

Camping Campo di Liccia, rte. de Porto-Vecchio (☎04 95 73 03 09). The cheapest of a cluster of campgrounds accessible by car or on foot (1hr. from the port). Pool, restaurant, mini-market, and ping-pong. Laundry €5.50. Reception 8am-9pm. Apr.-June €4.50-5 per person; July-Aug. €5-6.20 per person. Apr.-Aug. €1.90-2.70 per tent; €1.90-2.70 per car. Electricity €3-3.60. Cash only. ❶

◘ FOOD

Supermarkets dot the port, including two **SPARs,** one at the beginning of rte. de Santa Manza and another down the street, just inside the port. (☎04 95 73 00 26 or 04 95 73 12 37. Open July-Aug. daily 8am-9pm; Sept. and June M-Sa 8am-8pm; Oct.-May M-Sa 8am-12:30pm and 3:30-7:30pm. MC/V.) The port is mostly lined with mundane tourist traps, but a handful of tiny establishments tucked on streets in the *haute-ville* serve more authentic Corsican cuisine. These charming (but pricey) restaurants are supplemented by a fair number of *crêperies* and pizzerias, allowing diners to enjoy good grub without breaking the bank.

▧ **La Poudrière** (☎04 95 73 01 45). Behind the large cemetery at the southern tip of the peninsula, next to the Église Ste-Mairie-Majeure. Some of the best views on the peninsula. Uses only organic or locally grown products—but adds an international flare with desserts like *délices morocains* (€5). Salmon €8. *Salade du jardin* €7. Shaded terrace features handcrafted wood benches and tables. Open daily 10am-10pm. MC/V. ❷

▧ **U Molinu,** rue Prosper Mérimée (☎04 95 10 34 78), in the *haute-ville,* toward the southern tip of the peninsula. Intimate restaurant with a view of the city's smaller port. Try local specialties like seafood *à la crème Corse* (€12.50) or *aubergines à la Bonifacienne* (Bonifacio eggplant, €12.50). Salads €5.50-11. *Plats* €8-12. *Menus* €15-22. Open daily 9am-10pm; hours may vary in winter months. Cash only. ❸

Kissing Pigs, 15 quai Banda del Ferro (☎04 95 73 56 09), on the port. Annually butchers its own Corsican *charcuterie.* Try the savory selections of club sandwiches (€8-9) and *petits poelons chauds* (hot casseroles; €7-13). Homey interior looks like the inside of a grotto. Open kitchen where diners can watch the English-speaking owners at work. Wine €2-6. Salad €8-12. *Tartines* €8-11. *Menus* €13-20. Extensive dessert menu €5-7. Open daily noon-2pm and 7-10pm. Reservations recommended. MC/V. ❸

L'Archivolto, rue de l'Archivolto (☎04 95 73 17 58), in the *haute-ville.* Tables spill out of the rustic interior onto a tiny terrace. Chef's whim and the market's offerings dictate the ever-changing menu, though dishes are limited to standard Corsican specialties. Owners make diners feel like guests at their home and prefer not to set specific hours; still, the restaurant is generally open around midday for lunch and in the evening for dinner. *Plats* €13-15. Reservations recommended; call 9-11:30am or after 5:30pm. MC/V. ❹

Les Voyageurs, 15 quai Comparetti (☎04 95 73 00 46), serves the cheapest meals in the port. A *plat,* fries, and a drink are only €10-15. Try the bouillabaisse (€10) or treat yourself to fresh mussels (€13). Open daily 9am-3pm and 7pm-10pm. V. ❷

◉ SIGHTS

GROTTOES. A marvel of both constructed and natural architecture, Bonifacio's *haute-ville* boasts 3km long fortifications atop limestone cliffs. Far below the ochre houses, centuries of pounding surf have carved deep, misshapen grottoes into the impressionable white rock. Be sure to take a boat tour of the **bouches de Bonifacio** (the Corsica-Sardinia strait). A small army of shuttle companies has taken over the base of the port and brings tourists to multicolored coves, cliffs, and stalactite-filled grottoes (see **Orientation and Practical Information,** p. 793). For another stunning view, continue along the peninsula, past the cemetery, to Bonifacio's southern tip. Far enough away from the *haute-ville,* this viewpoint lets you enjoy cliffs, sea, and Sardinia peacefully, but hold on to your hat and other valuables: the strong winds here will rob you of them as readily as the local pickpocket. Once there, look for a small sign in the middle of a parking lot for the ▧**Poste du Gouvernail,** where an underground tunnel will lead you—for free—to grottoes carved out by Italians and Germans during

he coastline between Bonifacio
and Porto-Vecchio is one of the
most beautiful in Europe, but
reaching many beaches along
his stretch from Bonifacio is vir-
ually impossible without wheels.
Consider renting a scooter so that
ou can get some quality time on
he sand. Companies in Bonifacio
and Porto-Vecchio offer rentals
or €40-60 per day; deposits are
around €400-1000.

Exercise extreme caution while
driving on the often dangerous
roads of Corsica. Beep when driv-
ng around bends, always wear a
helmet, let other vehicles pass
ou, and be aware of pedestrians
n crowded areas.

Once on your hog—so what
f it can't go over 50kph?—drive
north on N198 from Bonifacio
toward Porto-Vecchio. Turn off at
a sign for Camping Rondinara to
ind the famous plage de Rondinara or continue toward Porto-
Vecchio and take the exit toward
Bonda del Oro to find several
smaller beaches, including plage
de Folaca and plage de Punta
Asciaghju. Pick up free maps of
he area from the tourist offices in
Bonifacio and Porto-Vecchio to go
beach-hopping. At night, check out
Porto-Vecchio's club scene or grab
dinner by the port before heading
safely back to Bonifacio—but don't
orget to turn your lights on!

WWII and to a lookout point only 30 ft. above the sea. *(Poste du Gouvernail open daily 9am-6pm.)*

PORTE DE GÊNES. This arch was constructed with a drawbridge in 1588 as the town's sole entrance. As you pass through, a series of soaring *arc-bou-tants* (flying buttresses) are visible on the build-ings ahead. If they look a little delicate to be brac-ing such massive stone structures, it's because they serve no supporting purpose at all; instead, the narrow arches are used to carry rainwater from one rooftop to the next. *(From the tourist office, head up the steep steps of the montée Rastello, halfway down the port. Turn right to continue up montée St-Roch.)*

BASTION DE L'ENTENDARD. Eager to overthrow colonizing Italians, Corsican nationals joined forces with King Henri II to besiege the town, suc-cessfully razing the Genoese fortress. The trium-phant rebels rebuilt their own stronghold on top of the original. Once a prison, the Bastion's best feature is now the 360° views from its top. While this view is certainly breathtaking, the same—or better—views can be seen from several other points in the area for free. *(Each €2.50 or €6 for all 4.)*

OTHER SIGHTS. There are several ways to enjoy a spectacular—and spectacularly free—panorama. First, rather than turning right at the top of montée Rastello, make a left to find several small hiking trails along the surrounding cliffs and coastline, ranging from a 20min., 1.2km trek with views of the surrounding countryside and sea to an 80min., 5.6km journey to a nearby lighthouse with stun-ning views of more limestone cliffs, waves crash-ing on rocky outcroppings, and Bonifacio itself. Consult the map at the entrance to the hiking area for the various routes available. To get a better look from within the town, make a left at the top of montée St-Roch to place du Marché, at the end of rue Doria. The square looks out onto Bonifacio's steep cliffs, surrounded by sea foam. Immediately ahead is the **Grain de Sable,** a limestone formation that serves as a perch for daring cliff jumpers. The mound just out of reach is Corsica's Italian neigh-bor, the island of **Sardinia,** 12km away. Turn right on rue Cardinal and then left on rue du Sacrement to reach the **Église Sainte Mairie-Majeure,** Bonifacio's oldest building. Home to the **true cross**—or at least a fragment of it from a shipwreck—and the **Loggia,** where the city's important affairs were decided, this small church bears witness to much of Boni-facio's turbulent history. *(Open daily 8am-6pm.)* Just behind the church lies a large cemetery filled with elaborate family tombs and mausoleums.

BEACHES

Bonifacio's beaches are hard to reach and even harder to leave. The ones within walking distance of town are uninspiring by Corsican standards. Otherwise, the peninsula is filled with spectacular beaches, accessible only by car or scooter; a taxi will cost €40-60 round-trip. From the port, take av. Sylvère Bohn back to the entrance of town and then N196 toward Ajaccio or N198 toward Porto-Vecchio. Virtually every exit leads to a beach, including **Cala Longa,** 6km away from Bonifacio, and **plage Maora,** in a natural harbor. On N198, the poorly indicated right turnoff for Camping Rondinara, 20km from town, leads to **plage de Rondinara,** one of Corsica's most famous beaches and possibly one of the best in Europe. Farther down the road, **plage de Folaca** and **plage de Punta Asciaghju** close to Porto-Vecchio connect to form a beautiful strip of coastline.

Even more impressive than the mainland beaches are the pristine sands of the **Îles Lavezzi,** where crumbling rock formations meet turquoise waters. Every ferry company on the port runs boats (every hr.) to this nature reserve, including **Vedettes Thalassa** and **Marina Croisières** (see **Tours,** p. 793, for schedules and prices). Bring water and food; there are usually no supplies available, although some of the tour companies offer lunch as part of the package. Just off the islands, coral reefs teeming with brightly colored fish make for great scuba diving. Check out the companies listed below for your island adventure.

Club Barakouda (☎04 95 73 13 02; www.barakouda.com). A 15min. walk toward the entrance of town. Takes experienced divers on explos at 8:30am (€32-45) and 1st-timers for *baptêmes* (baptisms) at 1:30pm (€50). Call the night before to reserve. Reception July-Aug. 8:30am-6:30pm; June-Sept. less regularly. Cash only.

Bonif Kayak (☎06 27 11 30 73). For those who prefer to stay above water, this company runs kayaking tours of the *bouches de Bonifacio* and other sites. €35. Tours 9am-noon and 3:30-6:30pm. Departs from Piantarella.

CORSICA

APPENDIX

CLIMATE

The French climate varies by region. Though the center of the country generally experiences fairly moderate weather, **Corsica** and the **Côte d'Azur**—like their Mediterranean neighbors—are warmer and drier. Mountainous areas tend to be colder than the rest of France, while the Atlantic and northern coast receive the most precipitation. French summers can be hot and sticky, causing most city-dwellers to flee to the seaside. Winters are snowy in mountainous regions, rainy in Paris and the western and northern coasts, and chilly in the south of France during the weeks when the *mistral*, a fierce wind, blows through.

AVG. TEMP. (LOW/ HIGH), PRECIP.	JANUARY			APRIL			JULY			OCTOBER		
	°C	°F	mm	°C	°F	mm	°C	°F	mm	°C	°F	mm
Cherbourg	4/8	40/47	109	7/12	45/54	49	14/19	57/67	55	10/15	50/60	99
Paris	2/6	36/43	46	7/15	45/60	45	15/24	58/76	57	9/16	48/60	56
Strasbourg	-1/4	30/39	33	4/14	39/57	48	14/24	57/76	39	7/14	45/58	51
Lyon	-1/5	30/41	38	6/16	42/61	57	15/27	59/80	65	7/16	45/61	83
Toulouse	2/10	35/50	51	9/18	48/64	76	13/24	56/78	41	7/17	45/63	43
Bordeaux	2/9	35/49	90	6/17	43/63	48	14/25	57/78	56	8/18	47/65	83
Marseille	2/10	35/50	43	8/18	46/64	42	17/29	63/84	11	10/20	50/68	76
Ajaccio	3/13	38/55	76	7/18	45/64	48	16/27	60/81	10	11/22	52/71	88

To convert from degrees Fahrenheit to degrees Celsius, subtract 32 and multiply by 5/9. To convert from Celsius to Fahrenheit, multiply by 9/5 and add 32.

°CELSIUS	-5	0	5	10	15	20	25	30	35	40
°FAHRENHEIT	23	32	41	50	59	68	77	86	95	104

MEASUREMENTS

France invented—and still uses—the **Système International d'Unités** (metric system). The basic unit of length is the meter (m), which is divided into 100 centimeters (cm) or 1000 millimeters (mm). Fluids are measured in liters (L). A liter of pure water weighs one kilogram (kg), the unit of mass that is divided into 1000 grams (g). One metric ton is 1000kg.

MEASUREMENT CONVERSIONS	
1 inch (in.) = 25.4mm	1 millimeter (mm) = 0.039 in.
1 foot (ft.) = 0.305m	1 meter (m) = 3.28 ft.
1 yard (yd.) = 0.914m	1 meter (m) = 1.094 yd.
1 mile (mi.) = 1.609km	1 kilometer (km) = 0.621 mi.
1 ounce (oz.) = 28.35g	1 gram (g) = 0.035 oz.
1 pound (lb.) = 0.454kg	1 kilogram (kg) = 2.205 lb.
1 fluid ounce (fl. oz.) = 29.57mL	1 milliliter (mL) = 0.034 fl. oz.
1 gallon (gal.) = 3.785L	1 liter (L) = 0.264 gal.

LANGUAGE

French is the official language of France, and the French have always been beyond proud of it. *Par example*, Cardinal Richelieu started *L'Académie française* (the French Academy) in 1635, and the establishment's efforts to preserve language's integrity continue to this day. Nevertheless, choice words like *cool* and *téléphone* have crept in, and most people in larger cities—especially the student population—speak at least some English. Knowing elementary French can't hurt, particularly in smaller towns, but don't be surprised if a native interrupts halfway through your butchered *"Comment ça va?"* to ask if you wouldn't prefer conversing in your own tongue.

PRONUNCIATION AND GRAMMAR

French pronunciation has been duping Anglophones since well before the Hundred Years' War. A few tricks, though, can decode some of the intricacies of this absurdly non-phonetic Romance language.

Final **consonants** are often silent but are always pronounced when followed by an E (e.g., *muet* is mew-AY but *muette* is mew-ET). The S at the end of a plural noun is silent. The letter H is rarely aspirated, the French CH sounds like *SH*, and J is pronounced like the *S* in "pleasure." Rs are perhaps the trickiest phoneme of anyone's French-learning experience, as they originate in the throat, with the tongue arched and blocking the nasal passage. C sounds like *K* if it precedes A, O, or U; it sounds like *S* if it precedes E or I. A Ç always sounds like *S*. QU sounds like *K* if followed by A, E, or I; it sounds like the *QU* in "question" if followed by an O.

Vowels are pronounced precisely: A as the *O* in "mom"; E as in "help" (É becomes the *A* in "hay," È the *AI* in "air"); I as the *EE* in "creep"; O as in "oh." UI sounds like the word "whee." U is a short, clipped *OO* sound; hold your lips as if you were about to say "ooh," but say *EE* instead. OU sounds like *OO*. With few exceptions, all syllables in French words receive equal emphasis.

French is full of nasal sounds, and France is full of foreigners who exagerate them (think Chef Louis from Disney's *The Little Mermaid*—"HEE HEE HEE, HON HON HON.") Lest you start chasing a crab around the kitchen, try not to imitate Louis' accent. Instead, make sure never to make a "chhh" sound when speaking French (that's Hebrew), and practice pronouncing the phrase *"un bon vin blanc,"* which contains five different common French nasal sounds.

Le (pronounced like "look" without the K) is the masculine singular definite article (the); *la* is the feminine. Both are abbreviated to *l'* before a vowel, and *les* (pronounced "lay") is the plural definite article for both genders. *Un* (whose pronunciation has no English approximation) is the masculine indefinite article, *une* its feminine (as in "moon" without the M), and *des* (like "day") its plural. Where a noun or adjective can take masculine and feminine forms, the masculine is listed first and the feminine in parentheses; often the feminine form consists of an additional "e" on the end of the word—e.g., *étudiant(e)*. In general, the plural is formed by adding an "s" to the singular form; this "s," like most final consonants, is silent unless followed by a vowel, in which case it is pronounced as a "z" at the beginning of the next word (e.g., *l'énfant* is lehn-fohn but *les enfants* is lay zohn-fohn). *Tu* is the familiar form of second-person address, and *vous* serves as both the plural and the formal singular forms. *Vous* should always be used to address strangers, authority figures, and older people; *tu* is traditionally used only for close friends and family, although it is now frequently used among those kooky young folk.

PHRASEBOOK

THE BASICS		
Hello/Good day	Bonjour	bohn-jhoor
Good evening	Bon soir	bohn-swah
Hi	Salut	sah-lu
Goodbye	Au revoir	oh ruh-vwah
Have a good day/evening	Bonne journée/soirée	buhn jhoor-nay/swah-ray
Yes/No/Maybe	Oui/Non/Peut-être	wee/nohn/p'tet-ruh
Please	S'il vous plaît	see voo play
Thank you	Merci	mehr-see
You're welcome/My pleasure	De rien/Je vous en prie	duh rhee-ehn/jh'voo-zohn-pree
Pardon me	Excusez-moi/Pardon	ex-ku-zay-mwah/pahr-dohn
Go away!	Allez-vous en!	ah-lay vooz pn
What time do you open/close?	Vous ouvrez/fermez à quelle heure?	vooz oo-vray/ferh-may ah kel uhr
Help!	Au secours!	oh sek-oor
I'm lost.	Je suis perdu(e).	jh'swee pehr-doo
I'm sorry.	Je suis désolé(e).	jh'swee day-zoh-lay
Do you speak English?	Parlez-vous anglais?	par-lay-voo zahn-glay
I don't understand.	Je ne comprends pas.	jh'ne kohm-prahn pas
JUST BEYOND THE BASICS		
Who/What/When/Where	Qui/Quoi/Quand/Où	kee/kwah/kahn/oo
How/Why	Comment/Pourquoi	ko-mahn/pour-kwah
Speak slowly.	Parlez moins vite.	par-lay mwehn veet
I would like...	Je voudrais...	jh'voo-dray
How much does this cost?	Ça coûte combien?	sa coot comb-yen
Leave me alone.	Laissez-moi tranquille.	less-say-mwah trahn-keel
I need help.	J'ai besoin d'assistance.	jhay bezz-wehn dah-see-stahnss
I am (20) years old.	J'ai (vingt) ans.	jhay vehn-tahn
I don't speak French.	Je ne parle pas français.	jh'ne parl pah frahn-say
My name is ( ). What's your name?	Je m'appelle ( ). Comment vous appelez-vous?	JH'ma-pell ( ). kuh-mahn voo-za-pell-ay-voo
What is it?	Qu'est-ce que c'est?	kess-kuh-say
This one/That one	Ceci/Cela	suh-see/suh-lah
Stop!	Arrêtez!	ahr-eh-tay
Please repeat.	Répétez, s'il vous plaît.	reh-peh-tay, see voo play.
How do you say ( ) in French?	Comment dit-on ( ) en français?	kuh-mahn deet-ohn ( ) ohn frahn-say
Do you understand?	Comprenez-vous?	kohm-prehn-ay-voo
I am a student.	Je suis étudiant(e).	jh'swee zeh-too-dee-ahn(t)
Hell is other people.	L'enfer, c'est les autres.	l'ahn-fehr, say lay zoh-truh
EMERGENCY		
Where is the nearest hospital?	Où est l'hôpital le plus proche?	oo ay l'oh-pee-tal luh ploo prohsh
Where is the nearest emergency pharmacy?	Où est la pharmacie de garde la plus proche?	oo ay lah farm-ah-see duh gard lah ploo prohsh
Where is the police station?	Où est la station de police?	oo ay lah stah-si-ohn duh poh-leess
I am ill/hurt.	Je suis malade/blessé(e).	jh'swee mah-lahd/bleh-say
I was attacked.	J'ai été attaqué(e).	jhay ay-tay ah-tah-kay
I was raped.	J'ai été violé(e).	jhay ay-tay vee-oh-lay
I think I broke my arm/my leg/something.	Je pense que je me suis cassé(e) le bras/le jambe/quelque chose.	jh'pohnss kuh jh'me swee kah-say luh bra/luh jhahmb/kel-kuh showz

EMERGENCY		
I need a doctor.	J'ai besoin d'un médecin.	jhay buh-zwahn duhn med-sahn
Help me!	Aidez-moi!	eh-day-mwah
Someone stole...	Quelqu'un m'a volé...	kel-kahn mah voh-lay
... my camera.	... mon appareil photo.	mohn a-par-ray foh-toh
... my purse.	... mon sac.	mohn sahk
... my wallet.	... ma portefeuille.	mah port-foy
... my passport.	... mon passport.	mohn pass-pore
DIRECTIONS		
Please, where is...	S'il vous plaît, où se trouve...	see voo play oo suh troov
... an ATM?	... un distributeur d'argent?	uhn dis-trib-oo-tuhr dar-jahnt
... the bathroom?	... les toilettes/les WC?	lay twah-lets/lay doo-bluh vay say
... the train station?	... la gare?	lah gahr
... the post office?	... la poste?	lah pohst
(to the) right/left	(à) droite/gauche	(ah) dwaht/gohsh
straight	tout droit	too dwah
near to/far from	près de/loin de	pray duh/lwahn duh
north	nord	nord
south	sud	sood
east	est	ehst
west	ouest	west
NUMBERS		
one	un	uhn
two	deux	deuh
three	trois	twah
four	quatre	kah-truh
five	cinq	sank
six	six	seess
seven	sept	set
eight	huit	wheet
nine	neuf	nuhf
ten	dix	deess
fifteen	quinze	kanz
twenty	vingt	vehn
twenty-five	vingt-cinq	vehn-sank
thirty	trente	trahnt
forty	quarante	kah-rahnt
fifty	cinquante	sank-ahnt
hundred	cent	sahn
thousand	mille	meel
TIME		
What time is it?	Quelle heure est-il?	kell uhr eh-teel
It's (11) o'clock.	Il est (onze) heures.	eel eh-(t-ohnze) uhr
open/closed	ouvert/fermé	oo-vehr/fehr-may
until	jusqu'à	jhooss-kah
January	janvier	jhan-vee-eh
February	fevrier	feh-vree-eh
March	mars	marss
April	avril	ah-vreel
May	mai	may
June	juin	jh-wahn
July	juillet	jh-wee-eh

TIME		
September	septembre	sehp-tahm-bruh
October	octobre	ohk-toh-bruh
November	novembre	no-vahm-bruh
December	décembre	day-sahm-bruh
today	aujourd'hui	oh-jhore-dwee
tomorrow	demain	duh-mahn
yesterday	hier	ee-air
noon/midnight	midi/minuit	mee-dee/min-nwee
public holidays	jours fériés	jhoor fehr-ee-ay
the morning	le matin	luh mah-tahn
the afternoon	l'après-midi	lah-pray-mee-dee
the evening	le soir	luh swahr
the day/the night	le jour/la nuit	luh jhoor/lah nwee
Sunday	dimanche	dee-mahnsh
Monday	lundi	luhn-dee
Tuesday	mardi	mahr-dee
Wednesday	mercredi	mehr-kruh-dee
Thursday	jeudi	jhuh-dee
Friday	vendredi	vawn-druh-dee
Saturday	samedi	sahm-dee

SIGHTSEEING			
old town	vieille ville	town center	centre-ville
upper town	haute-ville	guided tour	visite guidée
Could you take our picture?	Pourriez-vous nous prendre une photo?	Is there a guided tour in English?	Y a-t-il une visite guidée en anglais?
Let's go!	Allons-y!	What a shame you only have a Lonely Planet guide.	Quel dommage que tu n'aies qu'un guide Lonely Planet.
TRANSPORTATION			
train station	gare SNCF	bus station	gare routière
taxi stand	arrêt de taxi	transfer	faire la correspondance
one-way ticket	billet aller simple	round-trip ticket	billet aller-retour
PLANES			
flight	vol	check baggage	enregistrer les bagages
window/aisle seat	place côté fenêtre/couloir	Do I have to check this?	Dois-je enregistrer ceci?
customs	la douane	arrival/departure	arrivée/départ
TRAINS			
high-speed train	TGV	ticket window/office	guichet/billetterie
validate a ticket	composter le billet	platform	quai
luggage locker	consigne	track	voie
train car	wagon	What time does the train leave?	À quelle heure part le train?
AUTOMOBILES			
car	voiture	coach bus	(auto)car
speed limit	limite de vitesse	city bus	bus
highway	autoroute	gasoline (unleaded/diesel)	essence (sans plomb/diesel)
automatic/manual transmission	boîte de vitesse automatique/manuelle	gas station	station de service
speeding ticket	citation	spare tire	roue de secours

OUTDOORS			
woods	bois	island	île
farm	ferme	cable car	téléphérique
forest	forêt	hot springs	thermes
chair lift	télésiège	cliff	falaise
slope	piste	hike	randonnée
spring	source	to go camping	faire du camping
to go skiing	faire du ski	to go biking	faire du vélo

AT A HOTEL			
a bedroom with...	une chambre avec...	a single/double room	une chambre simple/double
... a double bed.	... un grand lit.	a room on the street/courtyard	une chambre sur la rue/cour
... two single beds.	... deux lits.	Is breakfast included?	Est-ce que le petit déjeuner est compris?
... a shower.	... une douche.	Where is the youth hostel?	Où est l'auberge de jeunesse?
... a bath tub.	... bains.	May I see the room?	Puis-je voir la chambre?
bed and breakfast	chambre d'hôte	rural hostel-like home	gîte
all meals included/dinner only included	pension/demi-pension	reception	accueil

AT A CAFE OR RESTAURANT			
I would like...	Je voudrais...	Check, please.	L'addition, s'il vous plaît.
What is this?	Qu'est que c'est?	I'm a vegetarian.	Je suis végétarien(ne).
Do you have kosher food?	Avez-vous des plat kashers?	I'm a vegan.	Je suis végétalien(ne).
Is tip included?	Est-ce que le service est compris?	I really need a whiskey right now.	Il me faut un whiskey tout de suite.

AT A BAR			
Can I buy you a beer?	Puis-je t'acheter un demi?	So tell me, what's your number?	Dis donc, quel est ton numéro?
My boyfriend/girlfriend is waiting for me outside.	Mon copain/ma copine m'attend dehors.	He is drunk.	Il a un verre dans le nez.

GLOSSARY

WHERE AND WHAT TO EAT			
bistro	casual restaurant	épicerie	grocery store
boucherie	butcher shop	marché en plein air	open-air market
boulangerie	bakery	pâtisserie	pastry shop
brasserie	bar and restaurant	(super)marché	(super)market
charcuterie	shop selling cooked meats (such as salami) and prepared food	tabac	cigarette shop and news-stand

BOISSONS (DRINKS)			
bière	beer	chocolat chaud	hot chocolate
bouteille de champagne	bottle of champagne	eau platte/gazeuse	flat/sparkling water
café (crème/au lait)	coffee (with cream/milk)	thé	tea
carafe d'eau (du robinet)	pitcher of water (from the tap)	vin rouge/blanc	red/white wine

VIANDE (MEAT)			
agneau	lamb	foie gras d'oie/de canard	goose/duck liver pâté

VIANDE (MEAT)			
andouillette	tripe sausage	jambon	ham
bavette	flank (cut of meat)	lapin	rabbit
boeuf	beef	poulet	chicken
brochette	kebab	rillettes	potted meat
canard	duck	ris de veau	sweetbreads (brains)
cervelles	brains	saucisson	cooked sausage (like salami)
coq au vin	rooster stewed in wine	saucisse	uncooked sausage
côte	chop (cut of meat)	steak	steak
cuisses de grenouilles	frog legs	steak tartare	raw steak mixed with raw eggs
dinde	turkey	veau	veal
entrecôte	side (cut of meat)	à point	medium
escalope	thin slice of meat	bien cuit	well done
faux-filet	sirloin steak	saignant	rare
FRUITS DE MER (SEAFOOD)			
coquilles Saint-Jacques	a scallop dish	huîtres	oysters
crevettes	shrimp	moules	mussels
escargots	snails	poisson	fish
homard	lobster	thon	tuna
FRUITS ET LÉGUMES (FRUITS AND VEGETABLES)			
ananas	pineapple	fraise	strawberry
asperge	asparagus	framboise	raspberry
aubergine	eggplant	haricots verts	green beans
champignons	mushrooms	petits poids	peas
chou-fleur	cauliflower	poire	pear
compote de fruits	stewed fruit	poireaux	leeks
cornichon	pickle	pomme	apple
épinards	spinach	pomme de terre	potato
figue	fig	raisins	grapes
PAIN (BREAD)			
baguette	baguette	galette	savory dinner _crêpe_
brioche	light, buttery roll	gaufre	waffle
pâté feuilletée	puff pastry	pain chocolat	chocolate-filled croissant
OTHER			
ail	garlic	crème fraîche	fresh cream
beurre	butter	froid	cold
chaud	hot	moutarde	mustard
citron	lemon	oeuf	egg
citron vert	lime	poivre	pepper
crème fouettée	whipped cream	sel	salt

INDEX

ABOUT LET'S GO

NOT YOUR PARENTS' TRAVEL GUIDE

At Let's Go, we see every trip as the chance of a lifetime. If your dream is to grab a machete and forge through the jungles of Costa Rica, we can take you there. If you'd rather bask in the Riviera sun at a beachside cafe, we'll set you a table. We write for readers who know that there's more to travel than sharing double deckers with tourists and who believe that travel can change both themselves and the world—whether they plan to spend six days in Bangkok or six months in Europe. We'll show you just how far your money can go, and prove that the greatest limitation on your adventures is not your wallet but your imagination.

BEYOND THE TOURIST EXPERIENCE

To help you gain a deeper connection with the places you travel, our fearless researchers scour the globe to give you the heads-up on both world-renowned and off-the-beaten-track attractions, sights, and destinations. They dive into the local culture only to emerge with the freshest insights on everything from festivals to regional cuisine. We've also opened our pages to respected writers and scholars to hear their takes on the countries and regions we cover, and asked travelers who have worked, studied, or volunteered abroad to contribute first-person accounts of their experiences. In addition, each guide's Beyond Tourism chapter shares ideas about responsible travel, study abroad, and how to give back while on the road.

FORTY-NINE YEARS OF WISDOM

Let's Go got its start in 1960, when a group of creative and well-traveled students compiled their experience and advice into a 20-page mimeographed pamphlet, which they gave to travelers on charter flights to Europe. Almost five decades later, we've expanded to cover six continents and all kinds of travel—while retaining our founders' adventurous attitude. Laced with witty prose and total candor, our guides are still researched and written entirely by students on shoestring budgets, experienced travelers who know that train strikes, stolen luggage, food poisoning, and marriage proposals are all part of a day's work.

THE LET'S GO COMMUNITY

More than just a travel guide company, Let's Go is a community. Our small staff comes together because of our shared passion for travel and our desire to help other travelers see the world the way it was meant to be seen. We love it when our readers become part of the Let's Go community as well—when you travel, drop us a postcard (67 Mt. Auburn St., Cambridge, MA 02138, USA), send us an e-mail (feedback@letsgo.com), or sign up online (http://www.letsgo.com) to tell us about your adventures and discoveries.

For more information, visit us online: www.letsgo.com.

SMART TRAVELERS KNOW:
GET YOUR CARD BEFORE YOU GO

An HI USA membership card gives you access to friendly and affordable accommodations at over 4,000 hostels in more than 85 countries around the world.

HI USA Members receive complementary travel insurance, airline discounts, free stay vouchers, long distance calling card bonus, so its a good idea to get your membership while you're still planning your trip.

Get your card online today:

hiusa.org

MAP INDEX

MAP LEGEND

- ⊞ Hospital
- ℞ Pharmacy
- ✪ Police
- ✉ Post Office
- ⓘ Tourist Office
- $ Bank
- ⚑ Embassy/Consulate
- ▪ Site/Point of Interest
- Library
- TAXI Taxi Stand
- ⌂ Arch/Gate

- ✈ Airport
- 🚌 Bus Station
- 🚂 Train Station
- Ⓜ Metro Station
- 💻 Internet Cafe
- Restrooms
- ✝ Church
- ✡ Synagogue
- ☪ Mosque
- Monastery
- Mountain Range
- Mountain
- 0-999m 1000- >1999m
          1999m

- Theater
- Museum
- Beach
- Hotel/Hostel
- Camping
- Restaurant
- Nightlife/Entertainment
- Shopping
- Funicular
- Ferry Route/Landing
- Pedestrian Zone
- Stairs

- Cave
- Chateau/Fort
- Vineyard
- Lighthouse
- Park
- Beach
- Water
- Building
- City Wall

The Let's Go
compass always
points NORTH.